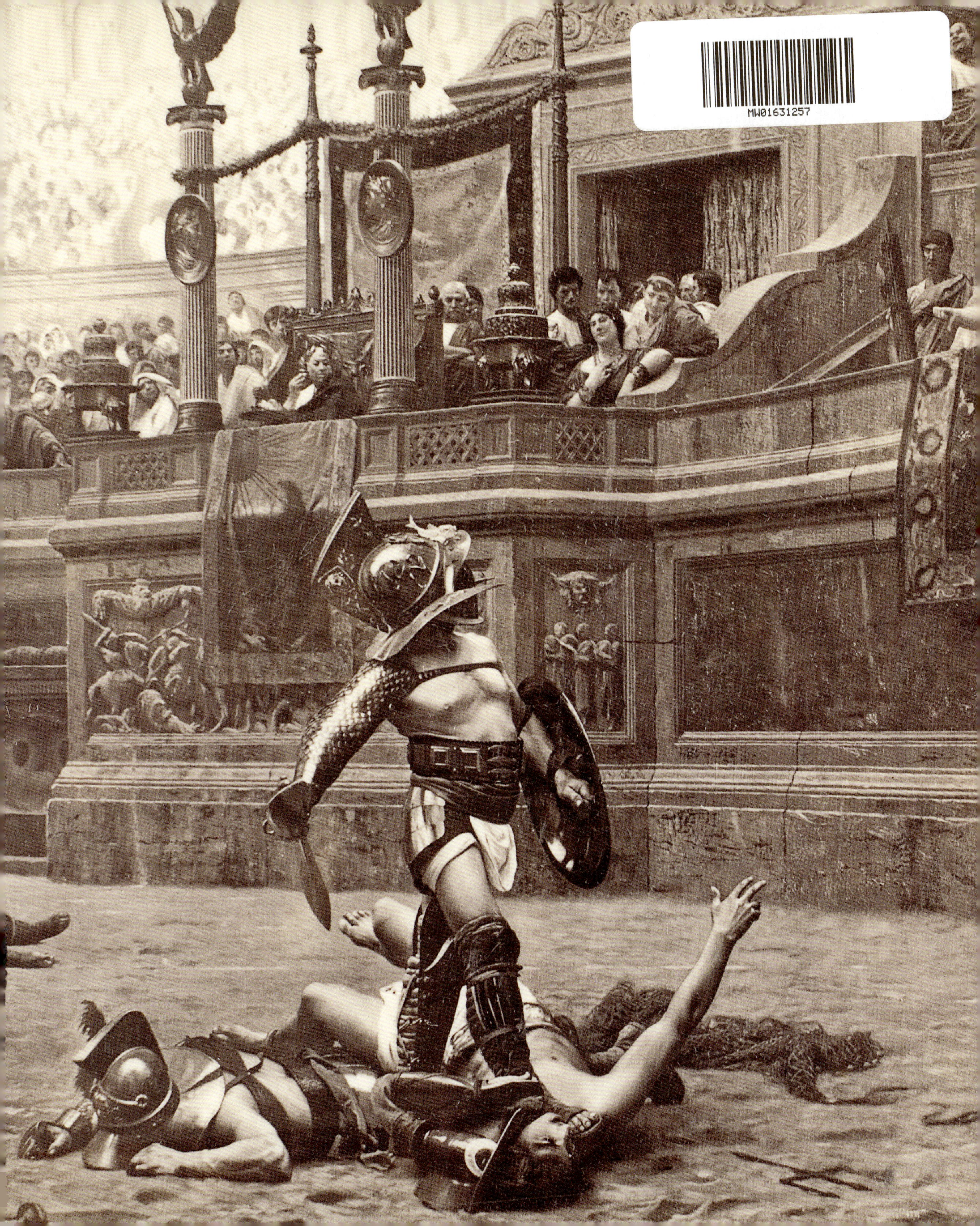

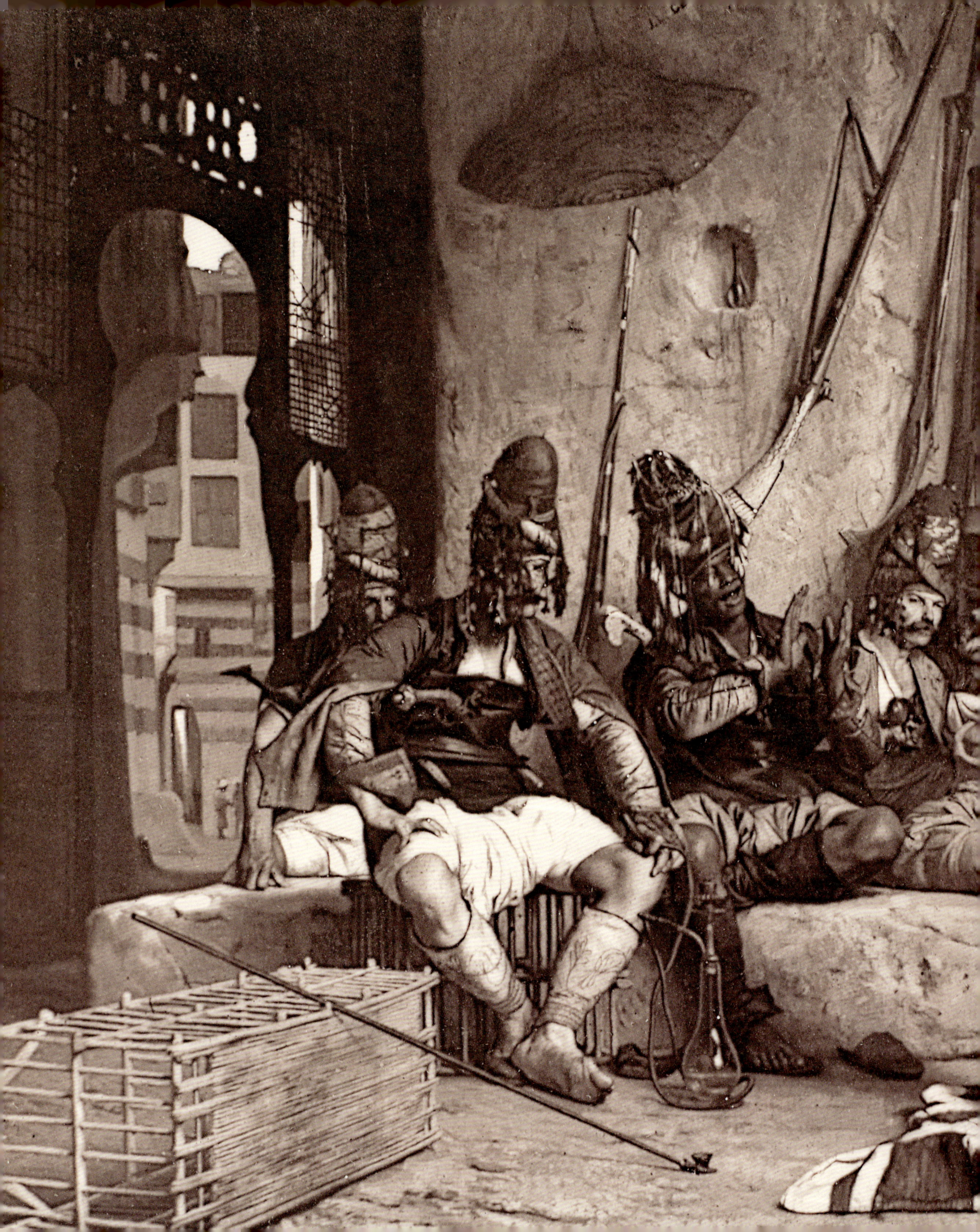

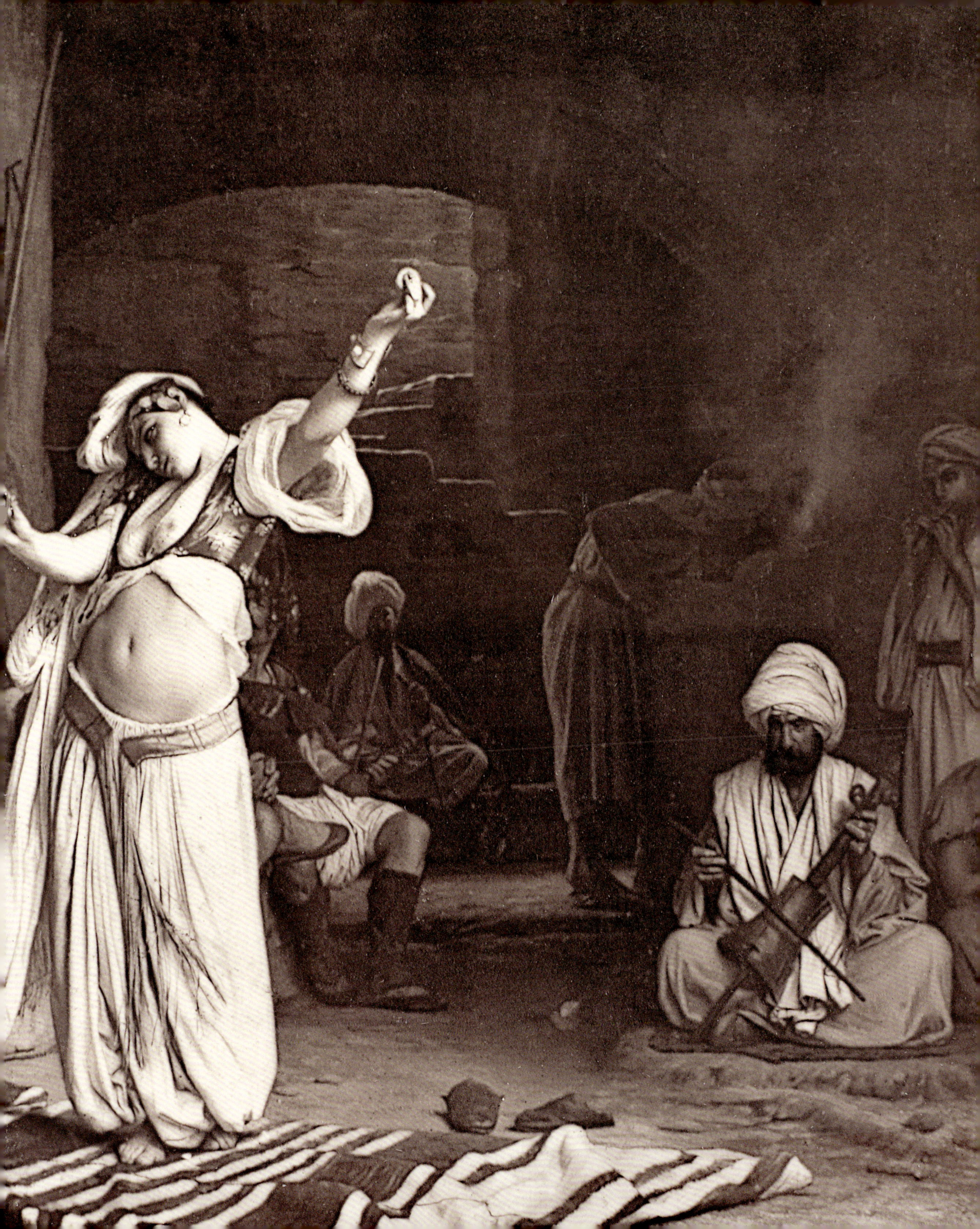

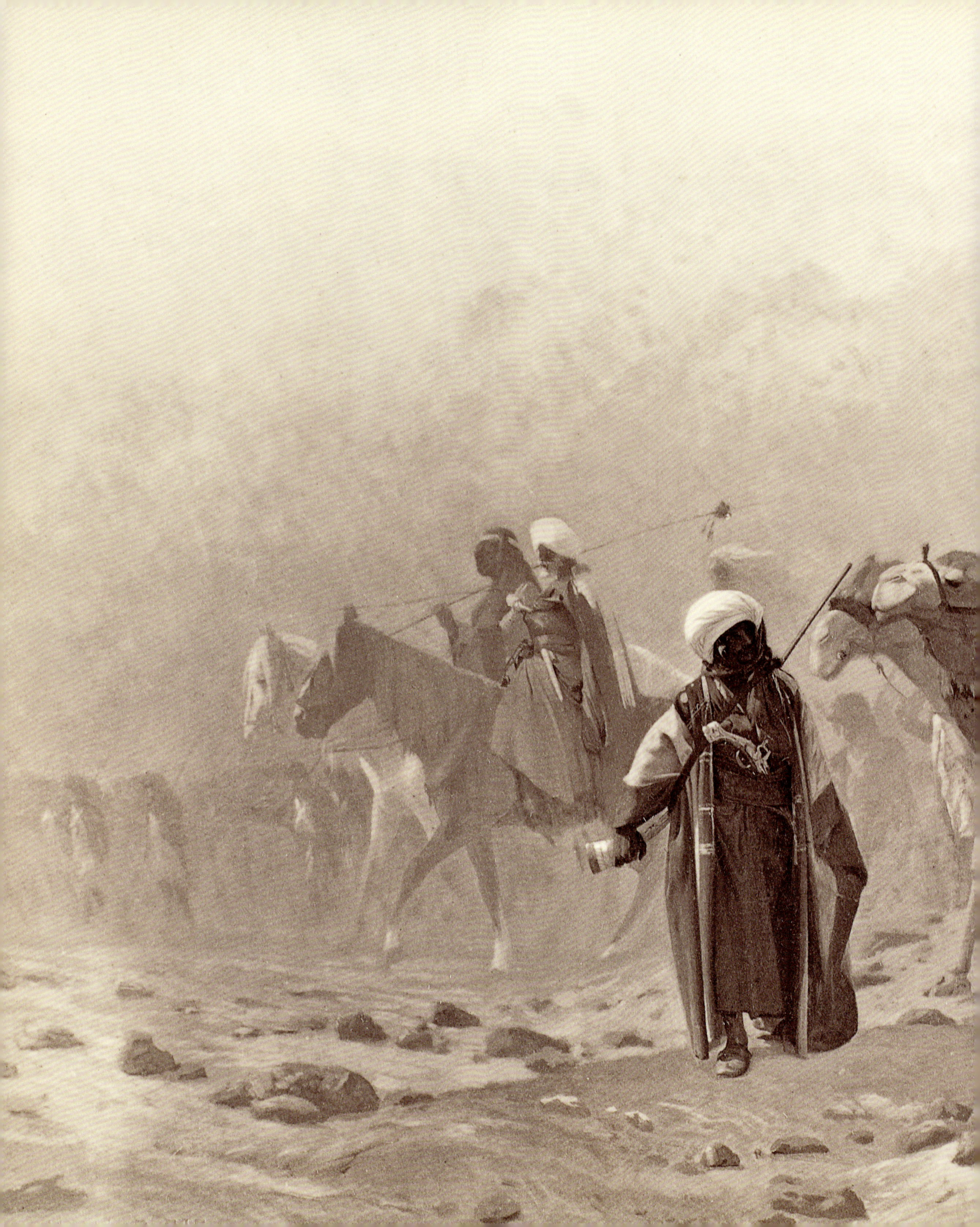

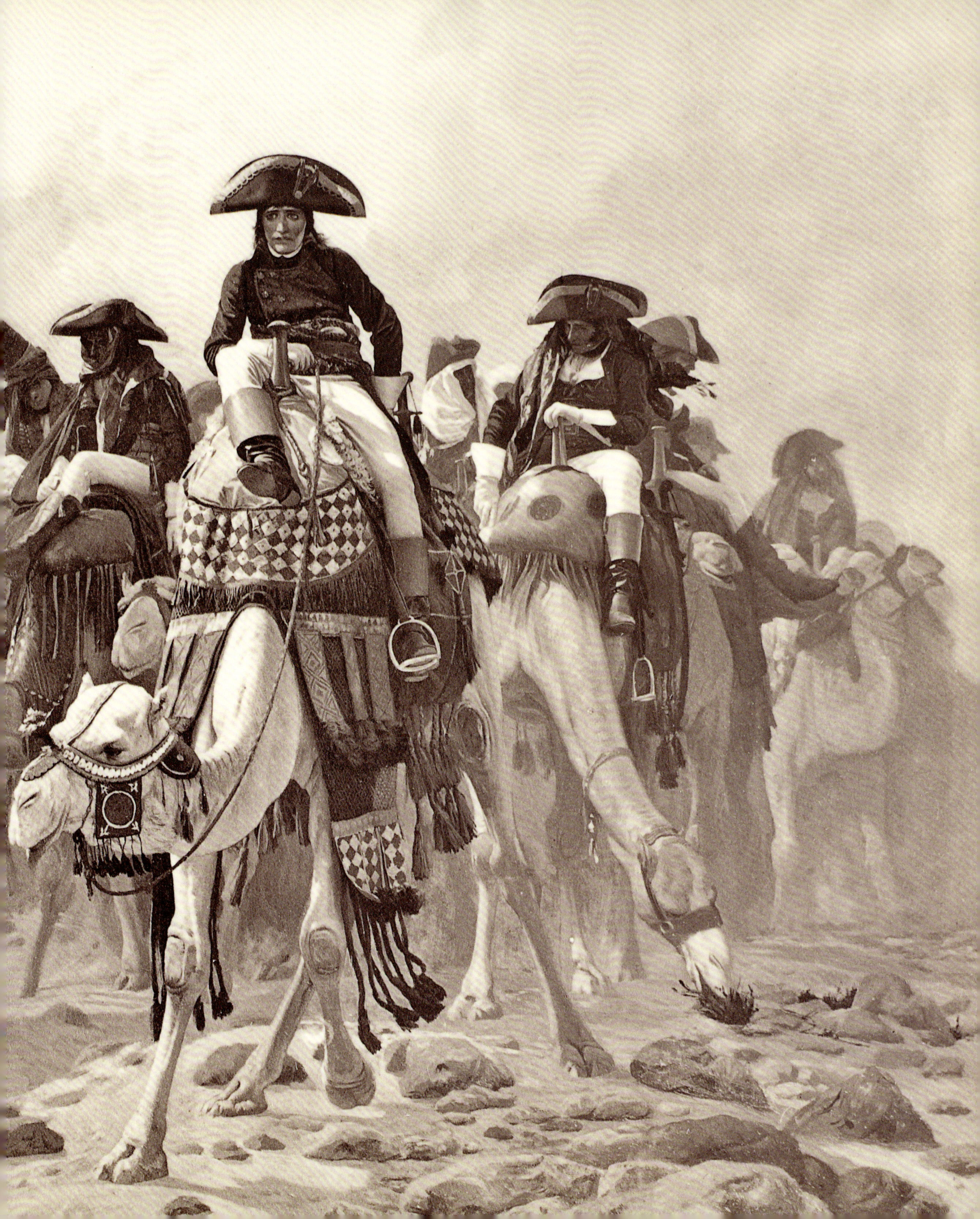

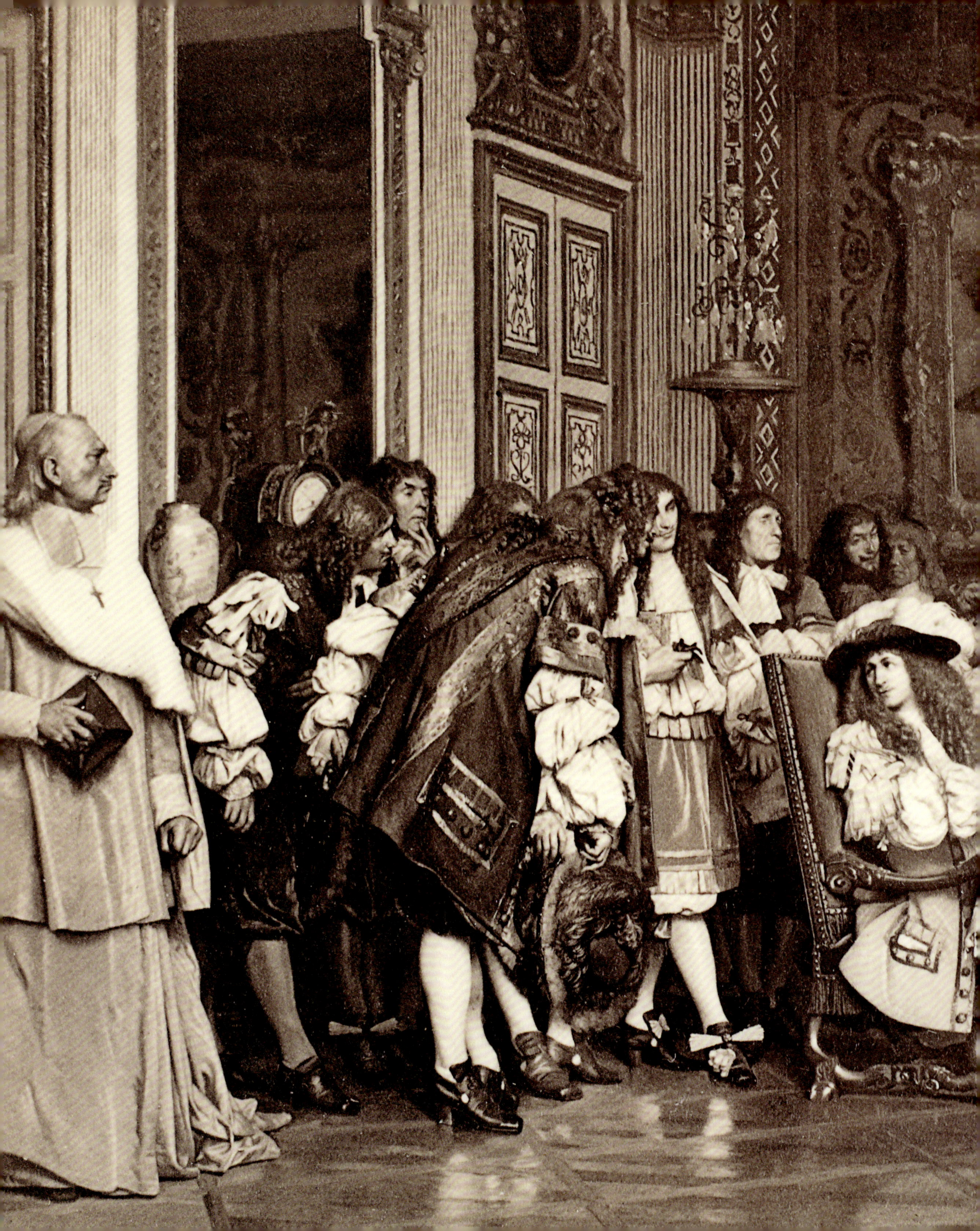

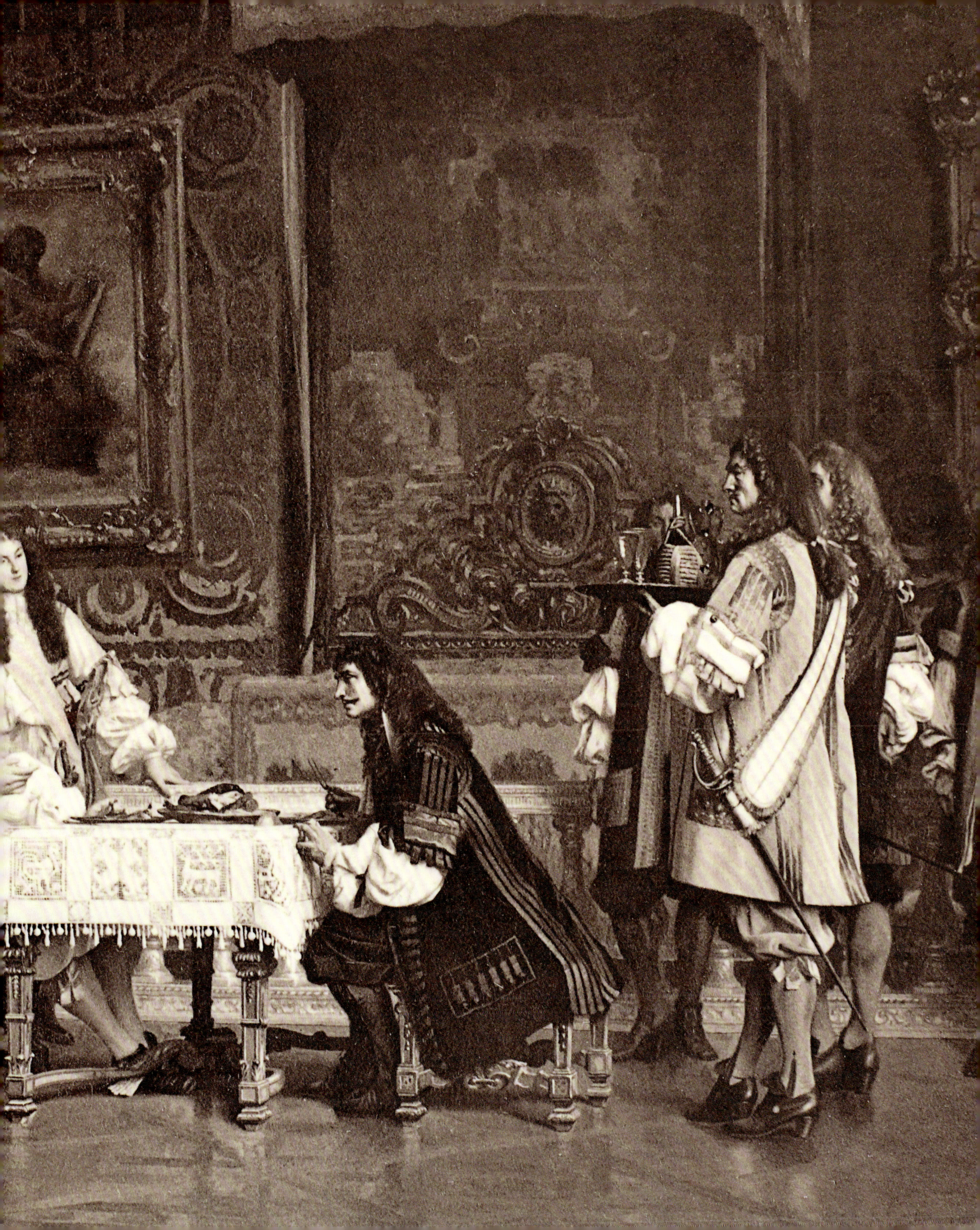

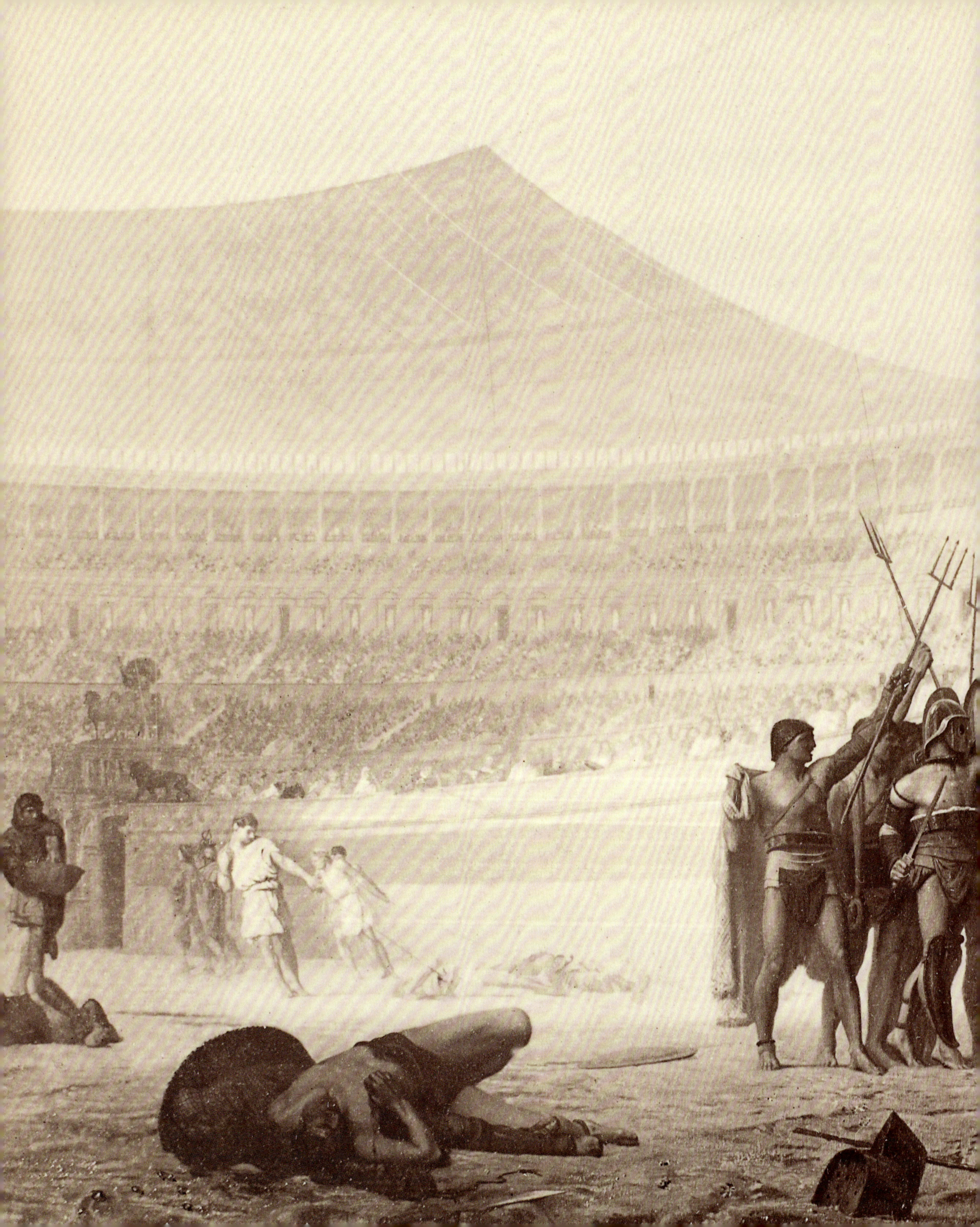

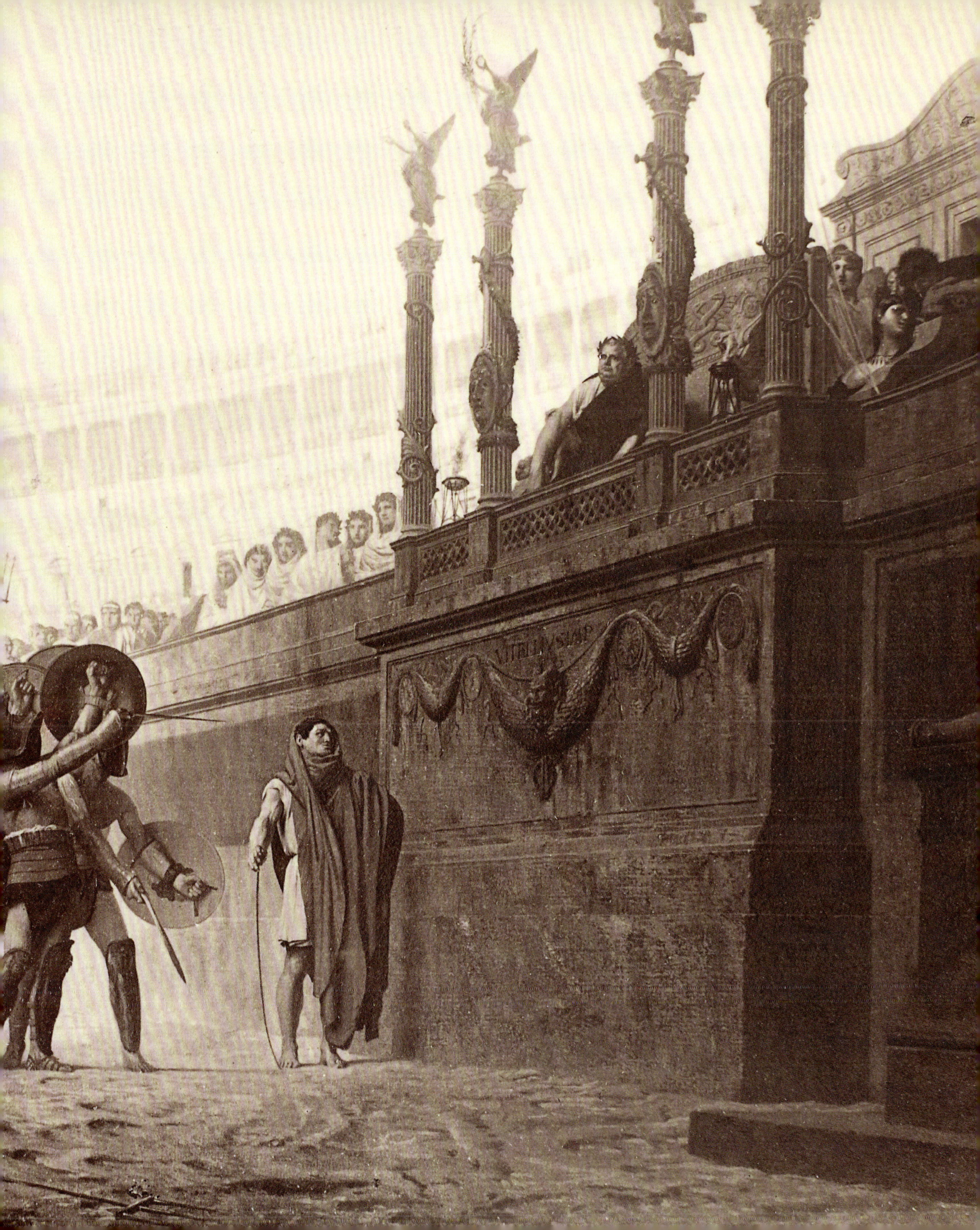

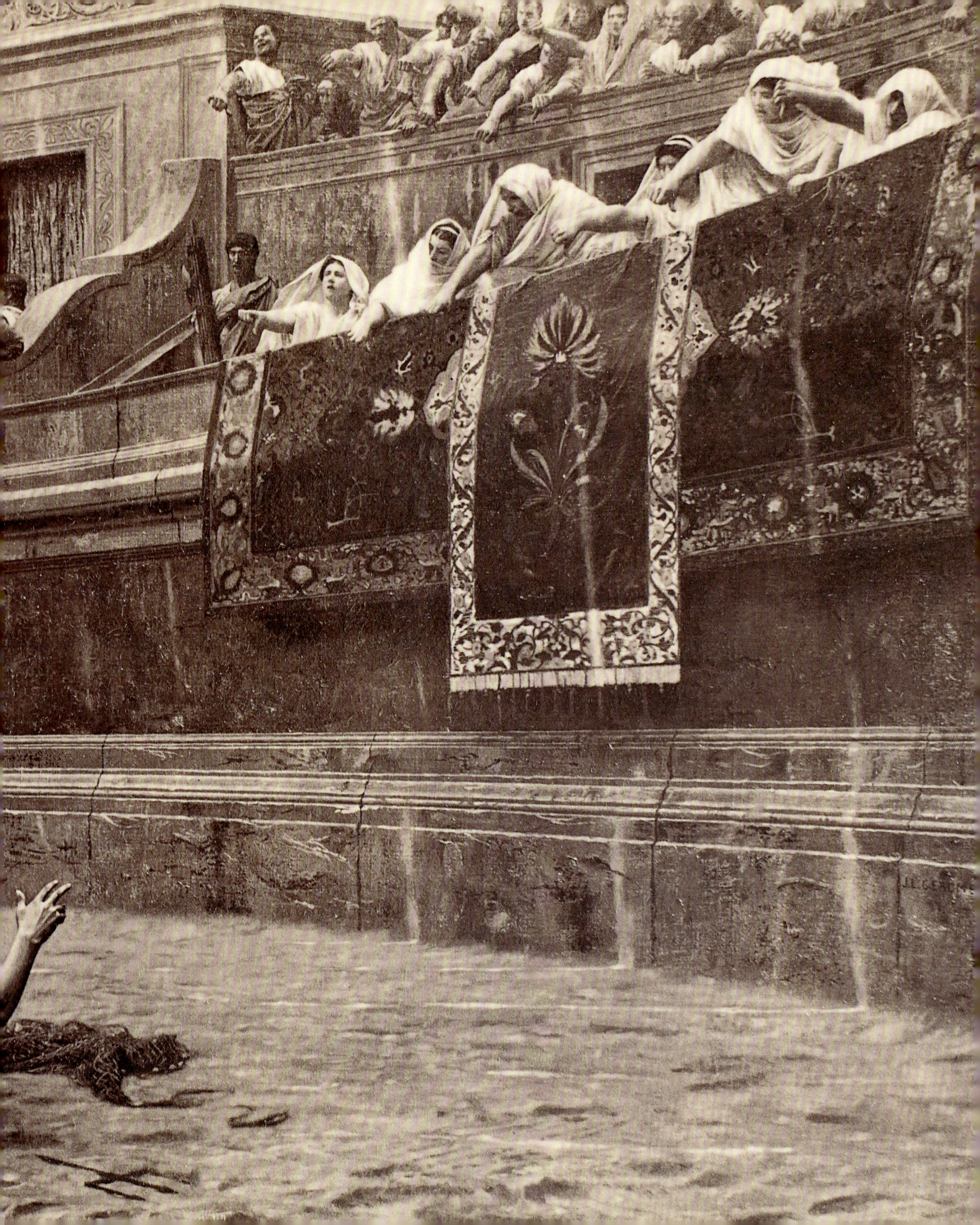

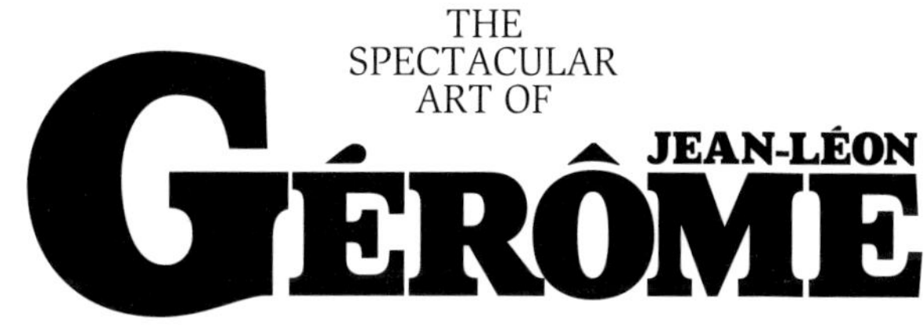

(1824-1904)

SKIRA

This catalogue is published in conjunction with the exhibition
The Spectacular Art of Jean-Léon Gérôme (1824–1904)

The J. Paul Getty Museum, Los Angeles, June 15 – September 12, 2010
Musée d'Orsay, Paris, October 19, 2010 – January 23, 2011
Museo Thyssen-Bornemisza, Madrid, March 1 – May 22, 2011

This exhibition was organized by the J. Paul Getty Museum, Los Angeles, the Musée d'Orsay, Paris, the Réunion des Musées Nationaux, Paris, and the Museo Thyssen-Bornemisza, Madrid.

After Jean-Léon Gérôme, *Pollice Verso* [1872], photograph by Goupil & Cie, "Musée Goupil & Cie" series, no. 1166 (detail), 1872, albumen print, 3 ¼ × 4 ¾ in., Archives, Musée d'Orsay, Paris.

After Jean-Léon Gérôme, *Dance of the Almeh* [1863], photograph by Goupil & Cie, "Musée Goupil & Cie" series, no. 322 (detail), 1864, albumen print, 2 ¾ × 4 ½ in., Archives, Musée d'Orsay, Paris.

After Jean-Léon Gérôme, *Napoleon and his General Staff in Egypt* [1867], photograph by Goupil & Cie, "Musée Goupil & Cie" series, no. 964 (detail), 1870, albumen print, 3 ¼ × 4 ¾ in., Archives, Musée d'Orsay, Paris.

After Jean-Léon Gérôme, *Molière Breakfasting with Louis XIV* [1862], photograph by Goupil & Cie, "Musée Goupil & Cie" series, no. 641 (detail), 1867, albumen print, 2 ¾ × 4 ¾ in., Archives, Musée d'Orsay, Paris.

After Jean-Léon Gérôme, *Ave Caesar, morituri te salutant* [1859], photograph by Goupil & Cie, "Musée Goupil & Cie" series, no. 640 (detail), 1867, albumen print, 3 × 5 in., Archives, Musée d'Orsay, Paris.

After Jean-Léon Gérôme, *Pollice Verso* [1872], photograph by Goupil & Cie, "Musée Goupil & Cie" series, no. 1166 (detail), 1872, albumen print, 3 ¼ × 4 ¾ in., Archives, Musée d'Orsay, Paris.

N° d'édition : L.05EBAN000212
ISBN SKIRA : 9788857207025
ISBN ESFP : 9782081241879

62, rue de Lille 75007 Paris
www.musee-orsay.fr
ISBN : 978-2-35433-058-3

THE J. PAUL GETTY MUSEUM, LOS ANGELES

Acting Director
David Bomford

Associate Director for Collections
Thomas Kren

Associate Director for Exhibitions
Quincy Houghton

Senior Exhibitions Coordinator
Amber Keller

Administrative Assistant for Exhibitions
Kirsten Schaefer

Registration

Chief Registrar
Sally Hibbard

Exhibitions Registrar
Betsy Severance

Exhibition installation

Manager of Preparations
Bruce Metro

Manager of Exhibition Design
Merritt Price

Senior Designer
Nicole Trudeau

Designer
Michael Lira

MUSÉE D'ORSAY, PARIS

President
Guy Cogeval

Director of administration
Thierry Gausseron

Head of fundraising and international exhibitions
Olivier Simmat

Exhibitions director
Hélène Flon

Exhibitions manager
Stéphanie de Brabander

Assistant exhibitions manager
Pascale Desriac

Registration

Chief Registrar
Odile Michel

Registrar
Anne Pouchelon

Exhibition installation

Exhibition design
Loretta Gaïtis

Exhibition graphics
Tania Hagemeister

Exhibition lighting
Stéphanie Daniel

MUSEO THYSSEN-BORNEMISZA, MADRID

Manager Director
Miguel Ángel Recio Crespo

Chief Curator
Guillermo Solana

Exhibition Assistant
Leticia de Cos

Registration
Head Registrar
Lucia Cassol

CURATORS

The J. Paul Getty Museum

Scott C. Allan
Assistant Curator, Paintings Department, J. Paul Getty Museum, Los Angeles

Mary G. Morton
Curator, French Paintings, National Gallery of Art, Washington

Musée d'Orsay

Laurence des Cars
Senior curator, head of the curatorial team, Agence France Muséums, Paris

Dominique de Font-Réaulx
Curator, Musée du Louvre, Paris

Édouard Papet
Senior curator, Musée d'Orsay, Paris

RÉUNION DES MUSÉES NATIONAUX

Director of administration
Thomas Grenon

Head of exhibitions
Marion Mangon

Registrars
Virginie Lagane
Sandra Mazière

We would like to express our deepest gratitude to all the collectors who so willingly and generously loaned works for this exhibition: Mme Lucile Audouy, Lady Micheline Connery, Dr. Jacques Crestinu, M. Alisan Dobra, M. and Mme A. and A. Flamand, Frankel Family Trust, Galerie Elstir (Paris), Mr. and Mrs. Terence and Katrina Garnett, M. David H. Koch, L'Horizon Chimérique (Bordeaux), M. J. Nicholson, His Excellency Sheikh Ghassan I Shaker, Dr. Edward T. Wilson, Dr. P. G. E. Woog, as well as all those who have chosen to remain anonymous.

This exhibition would not have been possible without the close involvement of the following institutions: in France, the Musée Bartholdi, the Musée Georges-Garret, the Département des Estampes et de la Photographie (Department of Prints and Photography) of the Bibliothèque Nationale de France, and the Bibliothèque-Musée de l'Opéra; in the United States of America, the Walters Art Museum, Joslyn Museum of Art, and the Sterling and Francine Clark Art Institute. We would like to express our deepest gratitude to their directors and staff for their support.
We would also like to extend our sincerest thanks to the directors of the following institutions for graciously lending works from their collections:

Germany

Hamburger Kunsthalle, Hamburg

Canada

National Gallery of Canada, Ottawa
Art Gallery of Ontario, Toronto

Denmark

Ny Carlsberg Glyptotek, Copenhagen

United States of America

The Walters Art Museum, Baltimore
Museum of Fine Arts, Boston
The Art Institute of Chicago, Chicago
Cincinnati Art Museum, Cincinnati
The Cleveland Museum of Art, Cleveland
The Dayton Art Institute, Dayton
Detroit Institute of Arts, Detroit
Arnot Art Museum, Elmira
Dahesh Museum of Art, Greenwich
Spencer Art Museum, The University of Kansas, Lawrence
The Getty Research Institute, Los Angeles
The J. Paul Getty Museum, Los Angeles
Malden Public Library, Malden
Minneapolis Institute of Arts, Minneapolis
Yale University Art Gallery, New Haven
New-York Historical Society, New York
The Metropolitan Museum of Art, New York
Chrysler Museum of Art, Norfolk
Joslyn Museum of Art, Omaha
Phoenix Art Museum, Phoenix
Princeton University Art Museum, Princeton
Hearst Castle, California State Parks, San Simeon
Santa Barbara Museum of Art, Santa Barbara
The George Walter Vincent Smith Art Museum, Springfield
Iris and Gerald B. Cantor Center for Visual Arts, Stanford University, Stanford
The Haggin Museum, Stockton
The Sterling and Francine Clark Art Institute, Williamstown

France

Musée des Beaux-Arts, Bordeaux
Musée Goupil, Bordeaux
Musée des Beaux-Arts, Caen
Musée Bartholdi, Colmar
Mairie des Lilas
Musée Anne-de-Beaujeu, Moulins
Musée des Beaux-Arts, Nancy
Musée des Beaux-Arts, Nantes
Bibliothèque Nationale de France, Paris
Comédie-Française, Paris
École Nationale Supérieure des Beaux-Arts, Paris
Musée d'Orsay, Paris
Département des Arts Graphiques, Musée du Louvre, Paris,
Société Française de Photographie, Paris
Musée des Beaux-Arts, Rouen
Musée Massey, Tarbes
Musée des Augustins, Toulouse
Musée National des Châteaux de Versailles et de Trianon, Versailles
Musée Georges-Garret, Vesoul

Great Britain

The National Gallery, London,
Galleries and Museums Trust, Sheffield

Puerto Rico

The Luis A. Ferré Foundation, Museo de Arte de Ponce, Ponce

Qatar

Orientalist Museum, Qatar Museums Authority, Doha

We would like to express our gratitude to the people who generously assisted with our requests for loans, particularly:
Gerald Ackerman, Georges Benhamou, David Breuer-Weil, Stephane Connery, Sebastian Goetz, Barbara Guggenheim, Deborah Hatch, Brian MacDermot, Jean-Claude Mourad, Raffi Portakal, Polly Sartori, Jon Swihart.

The J. Paul Getty Museum

Besides our generous lenders and colleagues at the Musée d'Orsay and Museo Thyssen-Bornemisza, the J. Paul Getty Museum would like to thank the President and CEO of the Getty Trust, James Wood, former Getty director Michael Brand, and acting director David Bomford for their support of this exhibition project. For their efforts in making the exhibition and its attendant programming and events a reality in Los Angeles, particular thanks are due to: in Exhibitions, Quincy Houghton, Amber Keller, and Kirsten Schaefer; in Registration, Sally Hibbard, Betsy Severance, Kathleen Ochmanski, Monique Abadilla, and Cherie Chen; in Exhibition Design, Merritt Price, Nicole Trudeau, Michael Lira, Stephanie DeLancey, and Sabine Kerschbaumer; in Paintings, Sculpture, and Paper Conservation, Yvonne Szafran, Tiarna Doherty, Sue Ann Chui, Brian Considine, Katrina Posner, Ernie Mack, Lynne Kaneshiro, and Stephen Heer; in Preparations, Bruce Metro, Mike Mitchell, Tracy Witt, John Jacoby, Tony Moreno, Peter Shapiro, David Glickman, and Chris Wallace; in Education, Toby Tannenbaum, Clare Kunny, Cathy Carpenter, Peter Tokofsky, Maite Alvarez, Zhenya Gershman, Alice Jackel, Christine Spier, and Ann Steinsapir; in Public Programs, Laurel Kishi, Sarah McCarthy, Mara Gladstone, and contract consultant Andrea Alsberg; in Communications and Public Affairs, John Giurini, Rebecca Taylor, and Amra Schmitz; in Collections Information and Access, Catherine Comeau, Maria Gilbert, and contract editor Chris Keledjian; in the Web department, Susan Edwards; and in Events, Ivy Okamura, Annie Combs-Brookes, and Andrea Bestow.

Curators Scott Allan and Mary Morton would also like to acknowledge the support of their curatorial colleagues at the Getty Museum: in the Paintings Department, Scott Schaefer, Anne Woollett, Peter Kerber, Amanda Herrin, and Jill Hortz; in the Department of Photographs, Judy Keller, Anne Lacoste, Anne Lyden, and Paul Martineau; in the Department of Sculpture and Decorative Arts, Antonia Boström and Anne-Lise Desmas; and in Antiquities, Ken Lapatin. Special thanks are due to Leah Lehmbeck, now assistant curator of the Norton Simon Museum, for her research assistance early on, and most of all to Emily Beeny, graduate intern in the Paintings Department for 2009–10, for her invaluable contributions towards the exhibition's didactic and visual presentation and her excellent editorial work.

Numerous colleagues in the Getty Research Institute should also be mentioned for their expertise, advice, and research assistance, including Director Thomas Gaehtgens; in Collection Development, Marcia Reed and Frances Terpak; in Collections Management, Irene Lotspeich-Phillips, Lora Chin Derrien, and Beth Guynn; in Conservation and Preservation, Stephan Welch and Kevin Young; and in Library Services, for her tireless efforts in obtaining interlibrary loan material, Aimee Lind.

Finally, beyond the auspices of the Getty, the following colleagues are gratefully acknowledged for their key roles in the development of this exhibition: Eik Kahng, chief curator of the Santa Barbara Museum of Art (formerly curator of the Walters Art Museum); Polly Sartori (Sotheby's); and painter and Gérôme enthusiast Jon Swihart. An especially warm thanks is due to pioneering Gérôme scholar Gerald Ackerman, for his passion and guidance.

Musée d'Orsay

For their unwavering support of this exhibition, we extend our deepest thanks to the two successive Presidents of the Musée d'Orsay: Serge Lemoine, under whom this project originated, and Guy Cogeval, who has supported it.

The exhibition would not have been possible without the collaboration and involvement of: Philippe Mariot, head of Archives, Musée d'Orsay, Cédric Carré, and Alexandre Bagnod. We would like to thank them for their active and invaluable support.

We would like to express our particular gratitude to: Joëlle Bolloch, Martine Bozon, Bruno Dapaz, Fabrice Golec, Doris Grunchec, Amélie Hardivillier, Cyrille Lebrun, Nadia Leriche, Dominique Lobstein, Odile Michel, Anne Mény-Horn, Patrick Porcher, Anne Pouchelon, Mathias Raimbaud, Patrice Schmidt, Laurent Stanich, Antoine Tasso and the installation team of at the Musée d'Orsay, Denis Thibaud, Xavier Trémeau.

As well as to the following: Sébastien Allard, Hüma Arslaner, Sylvie Aubenas, Georges Barbier-Ludwig, Hélène Bendejacq, Giovanna Bertazzoni, Régine Bigorne, Philippe Brach, Étienne Bréton, Emmanuelle Brugerolles, Julia Cadic, Jean-Pierre Callu, Jean-Loup Champion, Michael Chkroun, Coralie Coscino, Malcolm Daniel, Caroline Darthiail, Jacques Dauriac, Guillemette Delaporte, Aline Descamps, Sophie Descamps, Michèle Donatien, Blaise Ducos, Marie Dussaussoy, Maximilien Durand, Gwenaëlle Fellinger, Virginia Fienga, Anne-Marie Garcia, Nicole Garnier, Françoise Gauthier, Pascale Gillet, Cécile Giroire, Bruno Girveau, Sebastian Goetz, Sophie Harent, Oualid Hedhibi, Françoise Heilbrun, Charles Janoray, William R. Johnston, Violaine Jeammet, Robert Kashey, Hans Kraus, Chantal Lachkar, Antoinette Le Normand-Romain, Anne Lacoste, Ludovic Laugier, Gérard Lévy, Juliette Lévy, Henri Loyrette, Éva Mangeaud, Géraldine Masson, Catherine Mathon, Clémence Maussion, Rolf Mayer, Jean-Philippe Mesguen, Will Paley, Marie-Astrid Paternotte-Barat, Bruno Perdu, Anne Pingeot, Stuart Pivar, Louis Rivière-Plantegenest, Alain Prévet, François Rambault, Anne Robbins, Pauline Ronet, Marie-Pierre Salé, Sabine Schmidt, Carole Troufléau, Carel van Tuyll van Serooskerken, Isabelle Vaselle, Pierre Vidal, Ariane Villette, David and Constance Yates.

Last but not least, we would like to express our deepest thanks to Gerald Ackerman, without whose advice and enthusiasm the exhibition would not have been possible, and to Eik Kahng, senior curator, Santa Barbara Museum of Art, former curator, Walters Art Museum, Baltimore, for her involvement in the planning of the exhibition.

General editors of the catalogue:
Laurence des Cars,
Dominique de Font-Réaulx
and Édouard Papet

Scott C. Allan,
Assistant Curator, Paintings Department,
J. Paul Getty Museum, Los Angeles

Sylvie Aubenas,
Director, Département des Estampes et de la Photographie,
Bibliothèque Nationale de France, Paris

Laurence des Cars,
Senior curator, head of the curatorial team,
Agence France Muséums, Paris

Dominique de Font-Réaulx,
Curator, Musée du Louvre, Paris

Sophie Makariou,
Senior curator, director, Département des Arts de l'Islam,
Musée du Louvre, Paris

Philippe Mariot,
Head of Archives, Musée d'Orsay, Paris

Charlotte Maury,
Curator, Département des Arts de l'Islam,
in charge of Ottoman collections, Musée du Louvre, Paris

Mary G. Morton,
Curator, French Paintings,
National Gallery of Art, Washington

Dominique Païni,
Critic and film historian

Édouard Papet,
Senior curator, Musée d'Orsay, Paris

Pierre-Lin Renié,
Professor, École des Beaux-Arts, Bordeaux

François de Vergnette,
Associate professor in contemporary art history,
Université Jean Moulin-Lyon 3,
RESEA-LARHRA-UMR 5190

CONTENTS

This reconsideration of the art of Jean-Léon Gérôme, among the most successful artists in the world during the second half of the nineteenth century, was inspired by a surge of interest on the part of art historians, particularly young ones, in recent years. Recipient of numerous official honors, including the highest French national award of distinction, Grand Officer of the Legion of Honor, Gérôme taught thousands of art students who came to his studio at the École des Beaux-Arts from all over Europe, as well as the United States and the Ottoman Empire. His paintings and the mass-marketed reproductions they inspired brought him wealth and international fame, and several of his images have maintained their canonical status in popular visual culture to this day.

Gérôme's reputation and that of the art he was felt to emblematize suffered so profoundly in the twentieth century that there have been few satisfying exhibitions exploring his work. The American scholar Gerald Ackerman has devoted much of his career to the French master, resulting in a monographic exhibition in 1972–73 at the Dayton Art Institute, Minneapolis Institute of Arts and the Walters Art Museum, as well as a catalogue raisonné in 1986, revised in 2000. In 1981, the artist's home town of Vesoul organized an exhibition rich in archival material, and including drawings, sculptures, and photographs, but lacking many of Gérôme's most important paintings. In 2000, the French scholar Hélène Lafont-Couturier organized a brilliant exhibition in Bordeaux, New York, and Pittsburgh on the subject of Gérôme and his dealer Adolphe Goupil, whose global commercial gallery and reproductive print enterprise revolutionized the art world. The present exhibition, *The Spectacular Art of Jean-Léon Gérôme*, gives us an opportunity to look comprehensively at the painter/sculptor for the first time in decades in the United States, and for the first time ever in France and Spain.

Gérôme enjoyed a vibrant American market in the nineteenth century, and he counted numerous Americans among his most important patrons. The Getty Museum is therefore proud and delighted to be the sole American venue of this important international exhibition. Moreover, *The Spectacular Art of Jean-Léon Gérôme* is specifically appropriate to Los Angeles, a city where the production of both highly refined and powerfully popular visual spectacle is the core industry. Since its creation in 1979, the study and presentation of major nineteenth-century artists has been, and remains, the core mission of the Musée d'Orsay. The decision to exhibit the works of Gérôme, for the first time in Paris since his death in 1904, is entirely in line with the museum's duty of displaying the diversity of nineteenth-century creation. Thanks to Gérôme, the Thyssen-Bornemisza Foundation welcomes the first comprehensive exhibition dedicated to a major academic French artist in Spain.

Many people have worked very hard to make this outstanding exhibition a reality. I must, of course, thank Guy Cogeval and his colleagues at the Musée d'Orsay for partnering the Getty Museum in this splendid endeavor. At the Getty itself, I am happy to acknowledge the contributions of our Exhibitions, Design and Registrars departments; but, for planning the exhibition and for their vision, perseverance, and impeccable scholarship, we are indebted to Mary G. Morton, formerly of the Getty Museum and now Curator of French painting at the National Gallery of Art, and to Scott C. Allan, Assistant Curator in the Department of Paintings in the Getty Museum. Working with their curatorial colleagues in Paris, they have produced a timely and essential reassessment of this most brilliant of artists.

David Bomford, Acting Director, J. Paul Getty Museum
Guy Cogeval, President, Musée d'Orsay
Miguel Ángel Recio Crespo, Manager Director, Museo Thyssen-Bornemisza

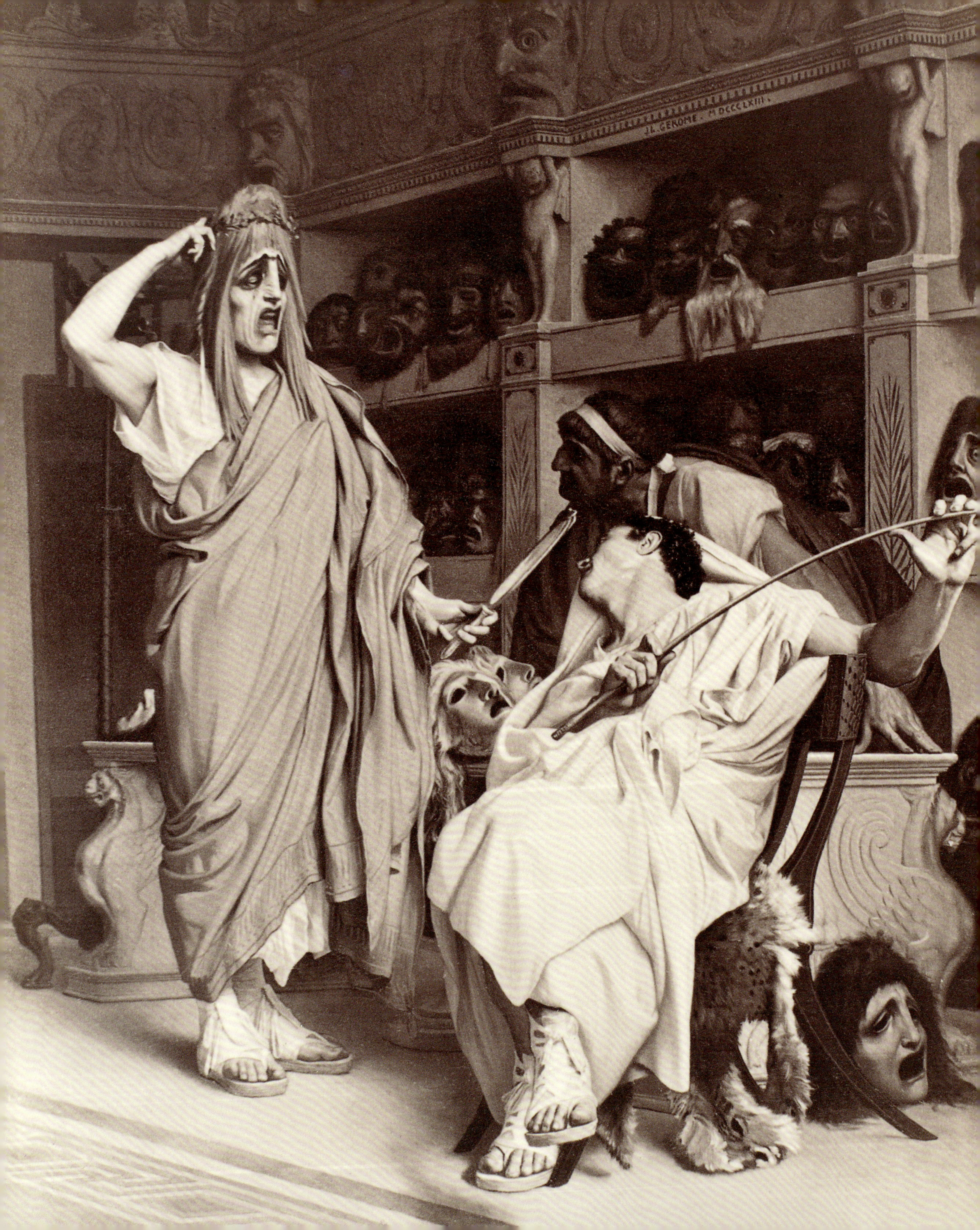
JL. GEROME · MDCCCLXIII ·

A PRECISE, PERVERSE KIND OF BEAUTY

—

Guy Cogeval | Translated from the French by John Lee

CRASH! BANG! WALLOP!

In 1973, at the very height of a pioneering period in the reconsideration of a different nineteenth century, the *Équivoques* show at the Musée des Arts Décoratifs deserved credit for sparking a debate over the status of academic painting and *l'art pompier*. Among other sitting targets, the art historian and critic André Fermigier, writing in *Le Monde*, fired a broadside at Jean-Léon Gérôme's *The Idylle* (cat. 29), a then totally unknown painting depicting the two lovers invented by Longus standing naked at a well, with Daphnis holding a bunch of flowers strategically placed to cover his manhood, while his lady-love harmoniously wiggles her hips in front of an admiring fawn. Stigmatizing the unintentional grotesqueness of it all, Fermigier says of the posy (quoting from memory): "An inch or so further down would have spelt disaster!" And all of a sudden, crash! bang! wallop! an idyllic pastoral scene descends into a farce worthy of the *opera buffa* Offenbach was then busy composing on this same subject. So we have got to admit that Gérôme's painting will often raise a snigger when we feel he is trying too hard to paint some abstruse historical detail in a composition where laborious recomposition is all the more obvious for the moral content handed down from David being no more than a distant memory.

But how can anyone in this day and age be shocked at the humor, unintentional or otherwise, that comes between our conscious perception and the plausibility of the scene he offers his audience, when Pierre et Gilles recreate a flamboyant harpy before our credulous eyes (*Creatures*, 1997), when Luigi Ontani has no compunction in celebrating himself as Dante, and when certain respectable museums are showing paintings, or even monumental sculptures, of that exponent of a never-ending postmodernism, Jeff Koons, engaging in a spot of rumpy-pumpy with his partner, Cicciolina?

Nineteenth-century painting still felt the shockwaves from the mini-scandals that took it forward in leaps and starts. Jean-Léon Gérôme may not look as if he belongs to the famous family of misunderstood daredevils, but appearances can be deceptive! Delacroix was decried for painting pink horses: Gérôme's were orange! Ingres's *Grande Odalisque* was scoffed at for having too many vertebrae, but Gérôme was another one who mangled the female anatomy. Courbet was already renowned for overdoing his backsides, and, like a modern-day Signorelli, our painter does plenty of those too. So, while paying lip service to tradition, reaction, or even regression, Gérôme was really a closet daredevil.

After Jean-Léon Gérôme, *The Greek Comedians* [1863], photograph by Goupil & Cie, "Musée Goupil & Cie" series, no. 474, 1865–66, albumen print, 4 ¾ × 3 ½ in., Archives, Musée d'Orsay, Paris.

THE GRAND MANNER LIQUIDATED

But his is a somewhat paradoxical daring. Did not Gerald Ackerman, the driving force behind the Gérôme revival since the late 1960s, try to show how the paths of Gérôme and Manet, and especially Degas, might have crossed more than once? Such comparisons could be taken further. Already Gérôme was showing something in him that continues to fascinate: an irresistible urge to redraw lines, mix up codes, and very often, never one to understate, to offend good taste. It may sound a little trite, but provocativeness and inner rebellion are likely the operative words here.

The thing is, we are left aghast at his overindulgence in archaeology, his passion for after-the-event reporting, the perverse pleasure he gets out of confining the Orientals to this boundless libido, a combination of fatalism and sadistic voyeurism, and ultimately at his iconoclastic rage in draining this great genre of its abstract purity and outdated morality. This is a man who did a lot of painting on wood, more than Ingres and nearly as much as that other tormentor of antiquity, Böcklin, and here he is giving solid and brilliant form to the worst liberties his depraved imagination can devise. No other Second Empire "academic artist" worked so hard to hasten the end of Davidian rhetoric, whilst reviving the Anacreontic vein, earlier exquisitely explored in the later work of those explorers of the guilty graces of neoclassical Mannerism, Girodet, Gros and Gérard. "Venustas" as against virtue. From this tradition to which he was directly linked through his apprenticeship to Delaroche, Gérôme—the Gérôme we are now adopting as one of our own—abandoned the virtuous for the shameful side. With his insider's knowledge of *The Children of Edward* and *The Execution of Lady Jane Grey*, he also developed a definite taste for the theatricality of the "dramatic moment."

Quite obviously, there is something of a paradox in dismissing the classical ideal like this. Unlike the Realists he cannot abide, Gérôme still claims to offer some form of nobility. But he is a crafty usurper, and his nobility is in form only: literally so. It boils down to extremely accurate drawing, and a mania for careful artistry, to the almost imponderably thin layer of pigment. The authors of this catalogue, especially Laurence des Cars, Dominique de Font-Réaulx, and Dominique Païni, address how this lightweight style ties in with the way Gérôme's paintings can be reproduced in all modes. I would

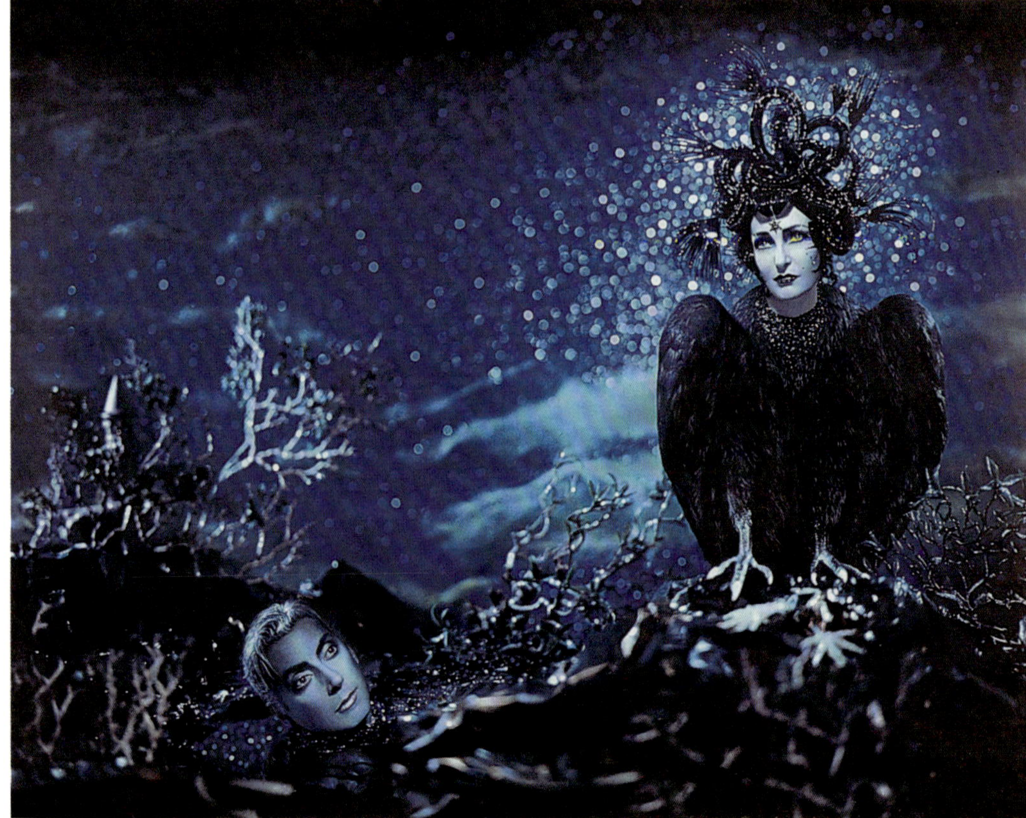

Pierre et Gilles (Pierre Commoy, born 1950, and Gilles Blanchard, born 1953), *Creature*, 1997, model: Siouxie Sioux and Budgie, painted photograph, unique piece, 46 ½ x 58 ¼ in. (framed), private collection.

personally like to highlight if I may how, going beyond its fair description as being "orthodox in its appearance, dissolute in its intent," the painter's *style* lets him get away with murder: the brothels of Pompeii, *almehs* with wayward navels, young boys eyed by ataractic old men, in short an antiquity worthy of Petronius, closer to Aristophanes than to Homer, with his heroes cast down into the mud of history and no longer caught up into the heavens celebrating the common moral order. This was something Gautier understood in 1847, at a time when *The Cock Fight* (cat. 10) was a great success: "[M. Gérôme] displays a certain distinction of style even though he does come from M. Delaroche's studio." We recognize this as a backhanded compliment. Baudelaire went one step further when he pilloried "an artist who substitutes the entertainment provided by a page of erudition for the pleasure of pure painting" (Salon of 1859). With a regular output of some more respectable paintings, Gérôme himself knew fine well what he was doing right. People gradually tired of his philosophical painting, finding it as tedious as the scholarly sonnets in José-Maria de Heredia's *Trophies*.

Stock-still lions at twilight, sphinxes questioning men's destinies, young Napoleon Bonaparte facing the pyramids, or better, priceless allegories of Truth being drawn from the well (he dared!): these were all concessions to the philistinism of the age and the social role of a painter constantly torn between two careers. On the subject of *Molière Breakfasting with Louis XIV* (cat. 84), like something out of Sacha Guitry, Paul Mantz pinpointed his heavily sententious tone: "He feels he has to spell everything out: we do not need this to get the message." So Gérôme would sometimes play the serious pupil or the prig, or claim to have better knowledge of Latin than he actually possessed, while Baudelaire slammed his "meticulousness." Gérôme staged history painting in carpet slippers, where you crept into the private lives of the great through the backdoor, a form that sent the public into raptures, "It must actually have happened like that!"

But this is about saving Private Gérôme! The good news is that he is at his most exciting when he latches onto his avowed taste for adventure and travel. This feeling of an untrammeled existence, his most precious asset, comes to the fore in the rare direct accounts we still have of this diehard wanderlust. To it he owes a whole string of *pifferari* and Italian women. From this deadly dull and repetitive output of pictures, we need to pick out the ones in which the vitality and trace of what was actually seen shows through beneath the commonplace. They convey with real feeling this awareness of time, the frail permanence of the past in the present that fueled the Romantic view of Italy as the final heaven on Earth. The same might be said for the best of Orientalism, which was by no means all cheap and nasty stuff, dripping with ethnocentric implausibility and superciliousness.

Jeff Koons (born 1955), *Dirty Jeff on Top*, 1991, plastic, 55 x 71 x 109 in., Galerie Jérôme de Noirmont, Paris.

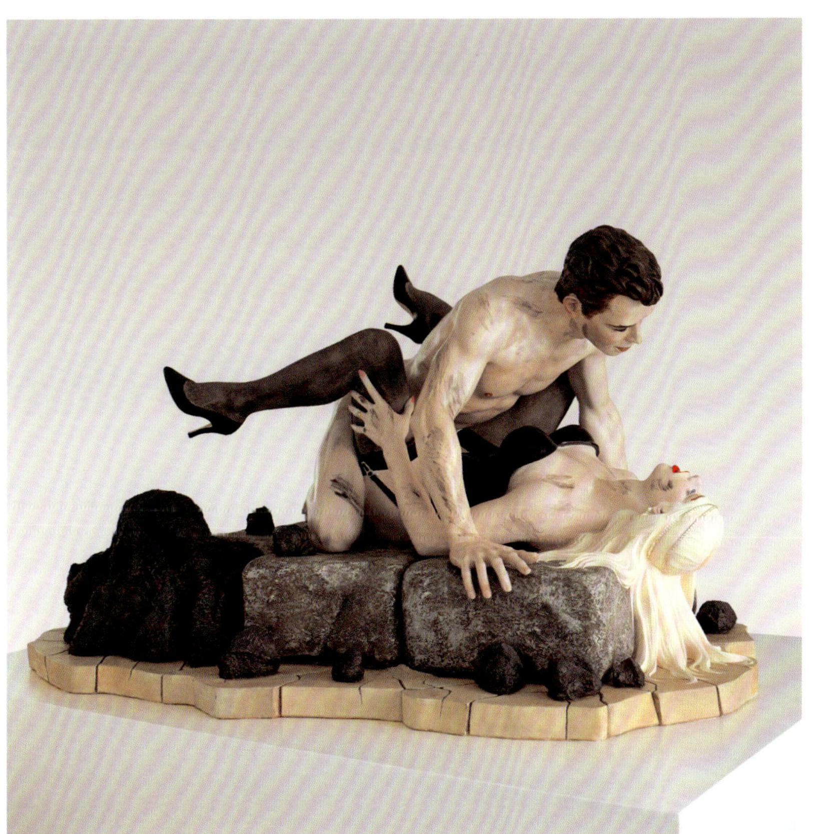

TOWARD CINEMA

There is another area where the chastity of the paintbrush clashes head-on with the liberties of the subject or the *mise en scène*. For Gérôme was not averse to anything risqué, stretching the bounds of the acceptable in Salon painting to the limit. For all that, even the most enthusiastic critics of the day noted his inability to paint living flesh, warm skin, or the weight of bodies. His are all so terribly anemic, and any rapid movement is foreign to them. His *Runners of the Pasha* (cat. 147) are a ton weight. His *Loïe Fuller* (1893, Musée Georges-Garret, Vesoul) expires, cast in concrete. *Pygmalion and Galatea*, dating from 1890, has the very opposite of the desired effect, for the statue is supposed to come to life before our eyes in the sculptor's loving fingers, but in this icy depiction it remains stone cold.

For the painter's women are like marble, and their eroticism is expressed in other ways. Gérôme makes a show of disembodied humanity, marble with no hairs, flesh with no aura. Also he charges it with an ambiguous lasciviousness through his line, with extended curves in voyeuristic scenes. *King Candaules* (cat. 43), which recalls Ingres's *Antiochus and Stratonice* (1840)—only offering the callipygian version of it—is the perfect illustration of this theater of naughty passions, with the viewer as an active accomplice, being roped in as a peeping-tom. Two years later, *Phryné before the Areopagus* (cat. 45) brings us back to tangible temptations. The stupefaction of the judges, mercilessly lampooned, justifies the "hint of ribaldry" (Zola) and the contagious duplicity of a work in which the lechery of some stirs lechery in others. But what makes this major work by Gérôme such an outstanding success is the way the mantle is suddenly whipped away, celebrating the moment and unifying the composition. He was to do it again in *The Grey Cardinal* (cat. 85), the final, perfect image of the sycophancy that was at the core of French culture since before Richelieu.

In conclusion, Gérôme occasionally came up with some quite extraordinary paintings, both important in their own day and having this hauntingly minimalist modernity. Two such are *Golgotha* (cat. 78) and *The Death of Marshal Ney* (cat. 93)—highly inspired paintings, post history paintings, as I said before, and so they come as a clarion call for an archaeology of cinematographic narration. They demand a theatrical development in space. The shadows of the Calvary scene cunningly pointing upwards to a stormy sky literally foreshadow the closing scene in William Wyler's *Ben Hur* (1959). The Roman soldier—who could be the brother of the firing squad commander in the *Ney* picture—turning round to check with the crucified men that indeed "it is consummated," points to a subtle depth marked on the canvas, heralding the shot-countershot technique in modern movies.

Cecil B. De Mille (1881-1959),
The Sign of the Cross, 1932.

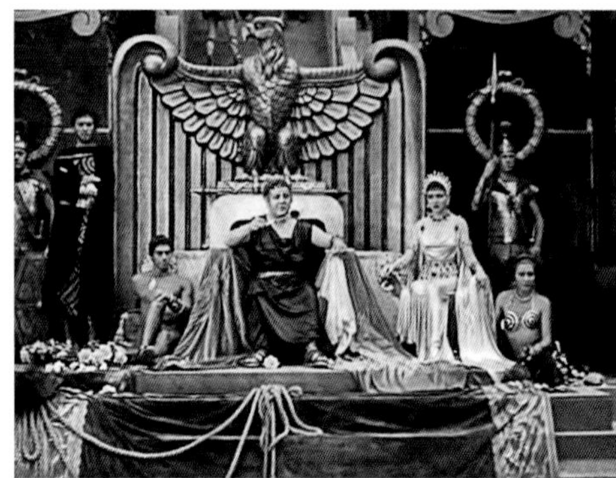

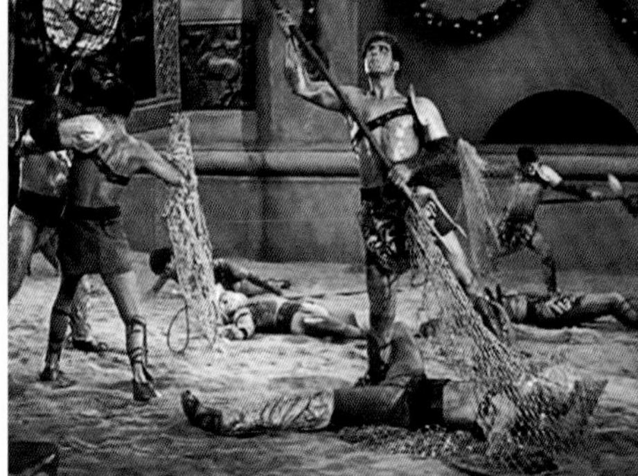

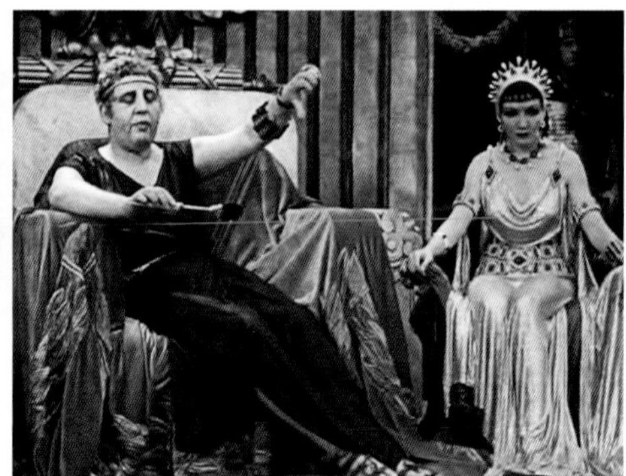

Falling victim to the endless guile of his own virtuosity, Gérôme does seem, especially in his more polished Orientalist paintings, to be falling over himself to please his audience. He seems to be telling his—often American—clientele: "You want to penetrate the secrets of the harem? Come on in! You want a blue *almeh*? Here's one for you! You want to imagine real-life Tanagrans making Tanagra figurines? Here you are. Severed heads at the entrance to the mosque? Just look at these!" Gérôme obligingly panders to your every wish. It is all there to see.

Sometimes Gérôme shows the unshowable, to the point of making you cringe, like a country cousin ruining a posh dinner with a string of crude jokes. You just wish you weren't there. This goes for *The Two Augurs*, illustrating Cicero's famous quip: "Two augurs cannot pass each other in the street without laughing." On the basis of this cruel jibe, he might have painted two ancient figures slyly exchanging a knowing glance. Well, not quite: theirs is side-splitting, red-faced mirth between drinking companions making a night of it. *For Sale* (cat. 157) depicts unwashed, unusable prostitutes wallowing in the incredible filth of a street in the Levant. In his *Saint Jerome* of 1874, a defense and illustration of unashamed kitsch, the lion seems to be there to act as the sleeping saint's bedside rug and to stop his halo from slipping off his head.

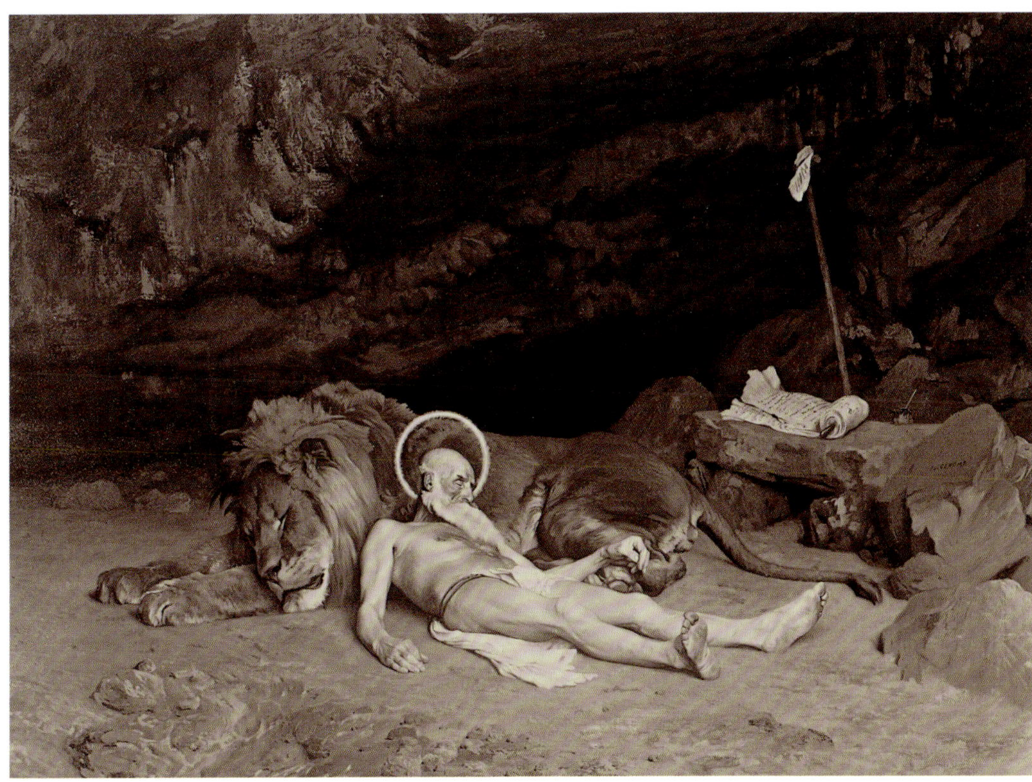

After Jean-Léon Gérôme, *Saint Jérôme* [1874], photograph by Goupil & Cie, *Œuvres de J. L. Gérôme*, Paris, Goupil & Cie, pl. 16, 7 1/3 × 9 3/4 cm, Bibliothèque du musée des Arts Décoratifs, Paris.

As for *Optician's Sign* (cat. 113), which the curators were intent on having in this show, it is literally not something you can look at, even when taken as some pioneer of Duchampism, a pre-echo of the divine Marcel's *Eau de Voilette*.

But is Gérôme alone in making commonness a central feature of his creative art? Did not Courbet himself, in his sublime *The Death of the Stag* (1867), transform a Christmas card snow scene—something like "Hunting Scene in the Forests of Franche-Comté"—into a veritable modern history painting that reinvents Velázquez's *Surrender of Breda*? And what hasn't been written about the cat in Manet's *Olympia*? Or about Ingres's models with their octopus's hands? And doesn't Monet's *Japanese Woman* (1875) also come pretty close to being kitsch?

Falling short of full-blown modernism, Gérôme and his painting thrive on his boundless artfulness. But who would disagree that even his poor taste delights us?

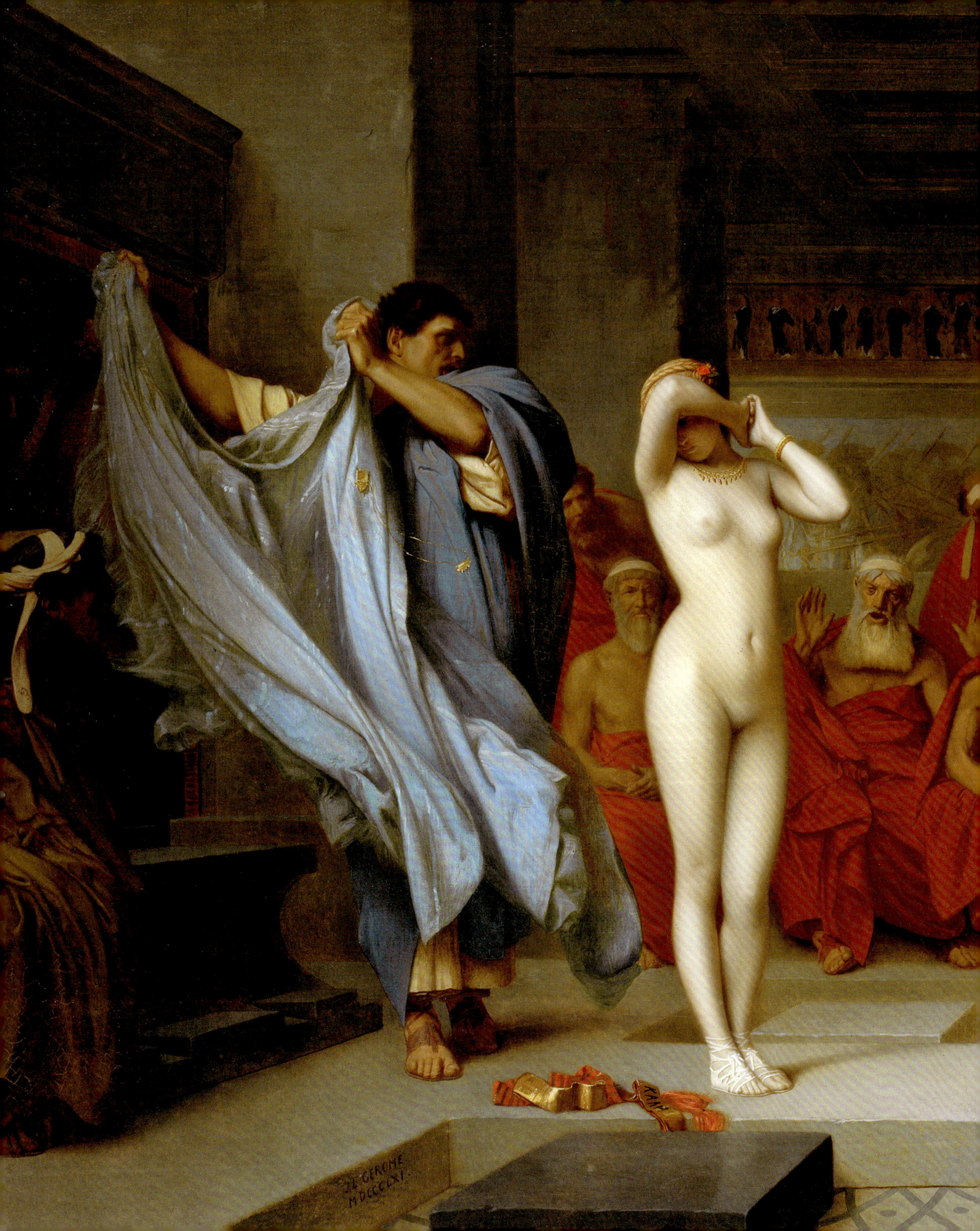
J.L. GEROME
MDCCCLXI

Foreword

PICTURING GÉRÔME

—

Laurence des Cars, Dominique de Font-Réaulx and Édouard Papet | Translated from the French by Deke Dusinberre

The uproar continues, but I couldn't give a..." Gérôme was one of the most famous artists of his day, yet throughout his career he was the object of polemical debate and harsh criticism. Nor did it cease at his death, just when painting totally liberated itself from the codes Gérôme had so staunchly and officially defended. Yet rarely had an artist been admired and collected with such constancy and discernment in America, where many of his paintings headed from the 1870s onward, so it was naturally in the new world that a rehabilitation of his rich, complex oeuvre was first begun in the 1960s (back in his native France, Gérôme's "time in the wilderness" lasted even longer). Without the persistent, pioneering research of Gerald Ackerman, whose work serves as the indispensable foundations of this exhibition, Gérôme would not have recovered the place he merits in the history of art of the latter half of the nineteenth century. We would like to pay tribute here to Ackerman's lifelong commitment, his sincere and unrestrained passion, and the infectious enthusiasm and unfailing generosity of the scholarly welcome that he gave us during the interviews he granted. In 1972, once the bases of the catalogue raisonné of paintings had been established, a groundbreaking exhibition in Dayton, Ohio, finally brought together a significant number of Gérôme's widely scattered works, enabling the essential task of reinterpreting an oeuvre known primarily through black-and-white reproductions of the day. These reproductions were not as good as the fine prints originally marketed by Goupil & Cie, which had played a major role in the phenomenal dissemination of the visual universe proposed by Gérôme, a marvelous creator of pictures.

It would be another ten years before France, in turn, paid a worthy tribute to this son of a goldsmith from the provincial town of Vesoul. Gérôme's exceptional career earned him a renown matched only by his intensely independent spirit. Other, private, shows drew attention to lesser known aspects of Gérôme's work—in 1974, Bob Benamou assembled an initial group of sculptures at the Galerie Tanagra in Paris, including the marble version of *Corinth*, which soon headed for the United States. An exhibition organized by Gérôme's home town of Vesoul was bold and pivotal—the energetic Ackerman found a counterpart in Dr. Gilles Cugnier, who complemented the paintings with major pieces of sculpture and an unpublished set of drawings that confirmed the artist's qualities and strangeness. In his preface to the catalogue, Louvre curator Jacques Foucart stressed the long path traveled from the days of dismissal and distaste for Gérôme's painting, as well as the new avenues that remained to be pursued. One such avenue was the acquisition of Gérôme's work by public institutions in France: the Vesoul museum's acquisition of the set of drawings and the Musée d'Orsay's purchase of *Golgotha* just four years after the museum opened provided strong indications of the quiet yet growing movement to resurrect Gérôme's oeuvre. At the same moment, American museums and collectors were making acquisitions that continued to reconstruct the story of

Cat. 45. *Phryné before the Areopagus* (detail).

Gérôme's fate in his adopted homeland. And at Amsterdam's Van Gogh Museum in 1996, a pioneering show by Andreas Blühm of nineteenth-century polychrome sculpture reestablished the context for Gérôme's own sculpture.

In France, twenty years elapsed after the Vesoul retrospective before another major exhibition was devoted to Gérôme, when Hélène Lafont-Couturier at the Musée Goupil in Bordeaux organized a show that fleshed out the artistic and economic contexts as well as the chronology. Meanwhile, a fine exhibition curated by Sophie Harent at the Musée des Beaux-Arts in Nancy definitively established Gérôme's reputation as a draftsman, just one year prior to the retrospective here—the first to be held in Paris since Gérôme's death in 1904. Initiated at the Musée d'Orsay back in 2006 by its then director Serge Lemoine, this show naturally called for American partnerships; early contacts with the Walters Art Museum in Baltimore laid the foundations for a fruitful collaboration, thanks notably to the commitment of Phillip Johnson and Eik Kahng—without their generous loan of works this exhibition would never have seen the light of day. The first stop for this Gérôme retrospective will be the J. Paul Getty Museum, another valued partnership indebted to the enthusiasm of our American counterparts.

We have decided to picture Gérôme's oeuvre from every angle, showing not just his paintings and sculpture, but also his drawings and his very special relationship to photography. Both exhibition and catalogue feature the man and his work from the start of his career in the 1840s through to his final years. And yet, we obviously had neither the intention or desire to show *everything*—which would have been impossible anyway, given the vast number of canvases. This monographic exhibition therefore reflects specific choices and a point of view. Although it seeks to present Gérôme to a new audience in the early twenty-first century, one that knows his work little or not at all, it does not aim to rehabilitate or plead a special case for him. We want to look at Gérôme through the prism of contemporary visual culture, saturated with all kinds of imagery of multifarious, shifting natures: in a well-deserved twist of fate, Gérôme's eclectic oeuvre, with its simultaneously popular and scholarly appeal, can now be measured by a yardstick on which "high" and "low" art permanently overlap. Gérôme constantly played on an admixture of genres and values, and his technique of collage and displacement, along with his delicate balancing act on the indistinct borderline of good taste and kitsch, look most intriguing to today's eye. Indeed, although Gérôme has often been perceived as a reactionary artist, he displays a modernity based on the originality of his viewpoint and his skill at concocting pictures—a skill simultaneously heightened and masked by his academic training—which create an illusion of reality through artifice and subterfuge. As Dominique Païni stresses in this catalogue, Gérôme's vision inspired the film industry's artistry of illusionistic realism and its artificial creation of accurate scenes.

In fact, Gérôme's oeuvre acknowledged the realm of new imagery at a very early stage. Thanks to contacts he made in the early 1840s in Paul Delaroche's studio, where he met several young painters who would later become talented photographers, Gérôme soon became familiar with the nascent photographic art of his day. Like most artists at that time, by the late 1840s he was using photographs when composing his paintings. Meanwhile, the photographic reproduction of his work, done from 1859 onward at the behest of Adolphe Goupil, who became his father-in-law as well as his dealer and publisher, gave a remarkable boost to the dissemination of Gérôme's oeuvre—thanks to photography, Gérôme's pictures could be seen in many French households. The visual imagination of an entire generation was nourished on his works, in a special yet familiar context, despite the fact that the originals were acquired by private collectors. Furthermore, Gérôme was able to take forthright advantage of photography's reputation for exactitude, which fueled his ambitions of accuracy and verisimilitude. As he wrote in September 1902 in his foreword to Émile Bayard's *Nu esthétique,* "Photography, which has made striking progress in recent years, has forced Artists to abandon old routines and forget old formulas. It has opened our eyes and forced us to look at what we had never seen before, thereby rendering a significant and valuable service to Art. Thanks to photography, Truth has finally come out of her well, to which she will never return."

Thanks to the generosity of lenders—both private collectors and public institutions—we are now able to show all the works we sought, notably the key paintings that made Gérôme such a successful artist during the Second Empire. The only absence, due to reasons of size, is his large canvas for the Exposition Universelle of 1855, *The Age of Augustus*; now in the Musée de Picardie in Amiens, it is the tallest painting in French public collections and would not fit into the Musée d'Orsay's exhibition rooms. But thanks to an oil sketch now in the Getty Museum, Gérôme's sole stab at vast, monumental history painting is fortunately recorded in both the exhibition and catalogue. Furthermore, by organizing the show along thematic lines, we have deliberately taken a few liberties with chronological development. We wanted to avoid the repetitiousness that arises after the 1880s due to Gérôme's reprisal of the same subjects, and we also wanted to show the links between works that deal with apparently different subjects, whether related to antiquity, the Orient, or French history. When discussing the exhibited works in the catalogue, we sought to analyze them in the light of the criticism of the day, which was so prolix with regard to Gérôme. His paintings sparked both praise and damnation, inspiring prose that was often lyrical, rich, and imaginative. Émile Zola himself, although a harsh critic of Gérôme, inevitably gave free rein to his imagination when contemplating a picture devised by Gérôme, which tended to spur the story-telling instincts of the author of the great saga of the Rougon-Macquart family. Such pictures, even when scorned by connoisseurs of art, thus offered highly fertile imagery. Wherever possible, we have tried here to inform readers of critical reactions in Gérôme's own day. Scott Allan devotes a whole essay to the reception of Gérôme's works during the Second Empire, and the end of the catalogue contains a brief anthology of selected texts that have been reprinted in their entirety.

Although he trained in academic institutions and was a favored, faithful disciple of his mentor, Delaroche, Gérôme was not so much a follower as a creator who enjoyed illustrating novel pictorial worlds by employing original, often unique, imagery. He simultaneously embodied the Romantic ambition of exploiting theatrical impact along with a rationalist desire for accurate, precise information as supplied by the scientific research and archaeology of his day. His scrupulous desire for accuracy could take precedence over the intelligibility of a scene, thereby violating academic rules. His relationship to academic arcana was not without contradiction and paradox. Although a model student, he never won the Prix de Rome; it was at the Salons that he found the wellsprings of his public and critical success, just like his reviled fellow Franche-Comté artist, Gustave Courbet. Heir to Jean-Auguste-Dominique Ingres and Delaroche in his attentive concern for handling and finish, he was nevertheless not as successful a portraitist as his predecessors, which he himself recognized. With his respect for line and naturalistic rendering, Gérôme could sometimes be a laborious draftsman, and was obliged to redo certain sketches. In the final canvases he often paid less attention to the accurate rendering of facial expressions than to the skillful overall composition, taking less care with the drawing of a face than with the thrust of a gesture. Gérôme's oeuvre is a paradoxical paragon of academicism. His highly polished work was not totally perfect, and seemed to acknowledge the obsolescence of norms of idealism and naturalism by systematizing them through mechanical repetition. His narrative, subject-driven works were thereby able to escape the constraints of those norms, constantly delighting the eye with fine formal passages where line and color brilliantly orchestrate the pictorial space. Yet these apparent lapses in academic craft did not prevent Gérôme from becoming one of the most respected teachers at the École des Beaux-Arts, where he taught from 1864 onward.

Gérôme apparently acquired a taste for teaching and attentive concern for others at an early stage. In February 1849, aged only twenty-four and without any official teaching job, he wrote letters to the Louvre requesting access to the museum for artists he was already describing as his "pupils." He was a respected and much appreciated mentor, as testimony quoted by Albert Soubies emphasizes: "Gérôme, who always won his students' affection, saw most of them scatter all across Europe every year. They went to Rome, to London, and further afield still, but almost none of them forgot him, and every new year would bring filial greetings from veterans and youths alike. On one of the final days of the year, the great artist received a letter, among others, expressing the heartfelt, amicable devotion of a grateful disciple. After having read this letter with great emotion, Gérôme was about to take up his work again when his valet entered, bursting with pride. 'I, too, sir, have just received a card. Addressed *to me!* Look!' And over the signature of the same letter-writer Gérôme read the message addressed to his servant: 'Take good care of the boss.'"

Studying the diverse talents and styles of Gérôme's students would require another entire exhibition in addition to the monographic one here. In her essay on the favorable reaction to Gérôme's work in the United States, where many of his canvases are still held and are therefore better known than in France, Mary Morton discusses the important contribution made by Gérôme's American students to their master's artistic renown and reputation. The Americans were not only faithful to the letter of his attentive instruction but also to his spirit of curiosity concerning new sciences and recent inventions. This faithfulness, despite the geographical distance and differences in individual talent and style, reveals the affection and respect Gérôme instilled in his American disciples as well as in their French counterparts.

Gérôme was also an elegant man, concerned about his image and appearance until the very end of his life. In a tribute written after Gérôme's death, Soubies described him thus: "[He] died without 'wounds,' succumbing to death suddenly, in full stride and full energy, without a preliminary period of gradual physical decline. Barely one week ago he could be seen, slim and upright like an officer in civilian clothing, at the funeral ceremony for Princess Mathilde." Gérôme was proud of having maintained his youthfully slender figure, neat waist, and lively gaze. His bushy brown hair went gray gracefully, without thinning, becoming a mane that evoked the majestic crown of a lion, that king of animals with whom he liked to identify thanks to the semantic link with his own first name, Léon. Gérôme obviously enjoyed being photographed, as witnessed by the many prints that have survived. This concern for his appearance certainly reflected a refusal to let himself go, a determination to retain control that was also expressed through his fierce loyalty to scrupulous, meticulous artistic craft. As a creator of images, Gérôme was singularly fond of appearances.

The elaboration of Gérôme's identity on the art scene was another polemical affair, as was his future critical fate. Once he got beyond *Néo-Grec* bohemia and the decade of the 1860s when he explored bold visual narratives that provided a revealing context for the appeal of the "new painting," Gérôme rapidly settled into the establishment. He became an official member of the dying academic scene of the last quarter of the nineteenth century, studiously embodying the perfect antimodernist, constantly replaying the same popular role. The issue came to an initial head during the posthumous exhibition of Édouard Manet's works at the École des Beaux-Arts in 1884, a project that Gérôme vehemently opposed. "[Manet] was the apostle of a decadent manner, of a piecemeal art. Here I am, assigned by the Nation to teach young people the grammar of art... I do not think they should be presented with the model of highly willful and lurid work by a man who never developed the rare qualities with which he was endowed." Then, ten years later, when the Caillebotte bequest was offered to the nation, Gérôme went totally overboard, probably being all the more exaggerated and intense due to the silence that had long reigned over the old professor's work. Responding to Henri Bataille's "survey concerning the Caillebotte bequest" in the *Journal des artistes,* Gérôme came across as thoroughly, unpleasantly reactionary. "I repeat, if the State has accepted *such rubbish,* then moral fiber has seriously withered." It might legitimately be assumed that such statements weighed long and heavily on Gérôme's own image in the twentieth century—history's unambiguous verdict on the matter was soon accompanied by indifference and oblivion regarding Gérôme. His art of illusion, always rescued from excess by its rationalist underpinning, never inspired reinterpretations or subversions on the part of the Surrealist generation. Relegated to the status of illustration, it survived primarily, and increasingly anonymously, in the form of pictures that embellished dictionaries, encyclopedias, and history textbooks. Even as the late twentieth century witnessed a veritable revival in the study and knowledge of nineteenth-century art through numerous publications and exhibitions—not to mention the founding of the Musée d'Orsay itself—the exclusively illustrative role assigned to Gérôme's oeuvre was notable. Indeed, his most famous works, all on show here, have rarely been loaned and thus have not been truly seen in recent decades. This mixed picture must nevertheless be significantly nuanced by the precocious American response to Gérôme. Purchased, collected, exhibited, and disseminated as early as the 1870s by American art lovers and museums, Gérôme's paintings infiltrated the new world's historical imagination along with its favorite medium, the movies. As an outstanding creator of imagery, Gérôme has thus become a highly convincing pre-Hollywood artist, his work directly or indirectly finding its surest heritage in an America that appropriates the old continent's history through moving pictures.

Cat. 160. *The Serpent Charmer* (detail).

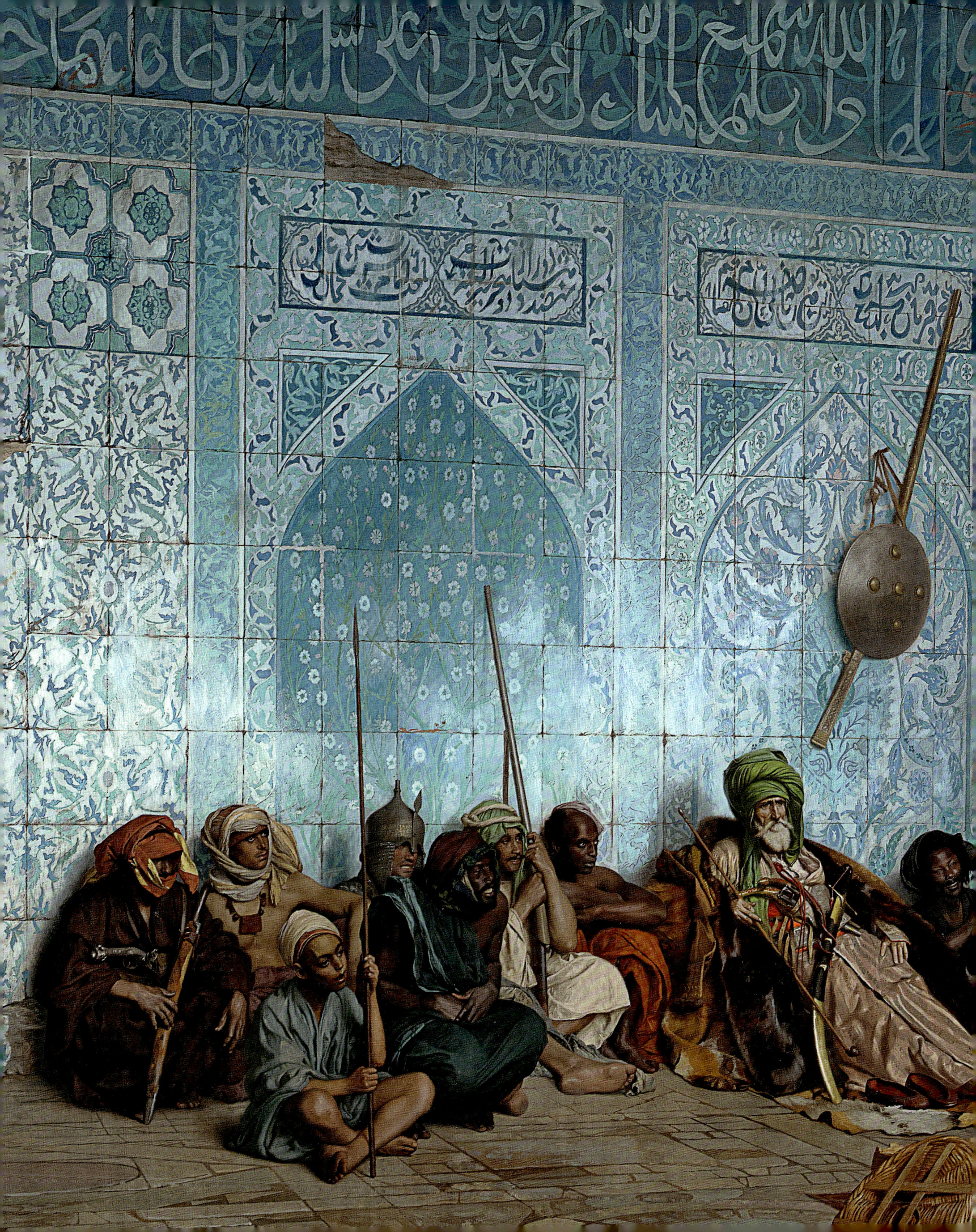

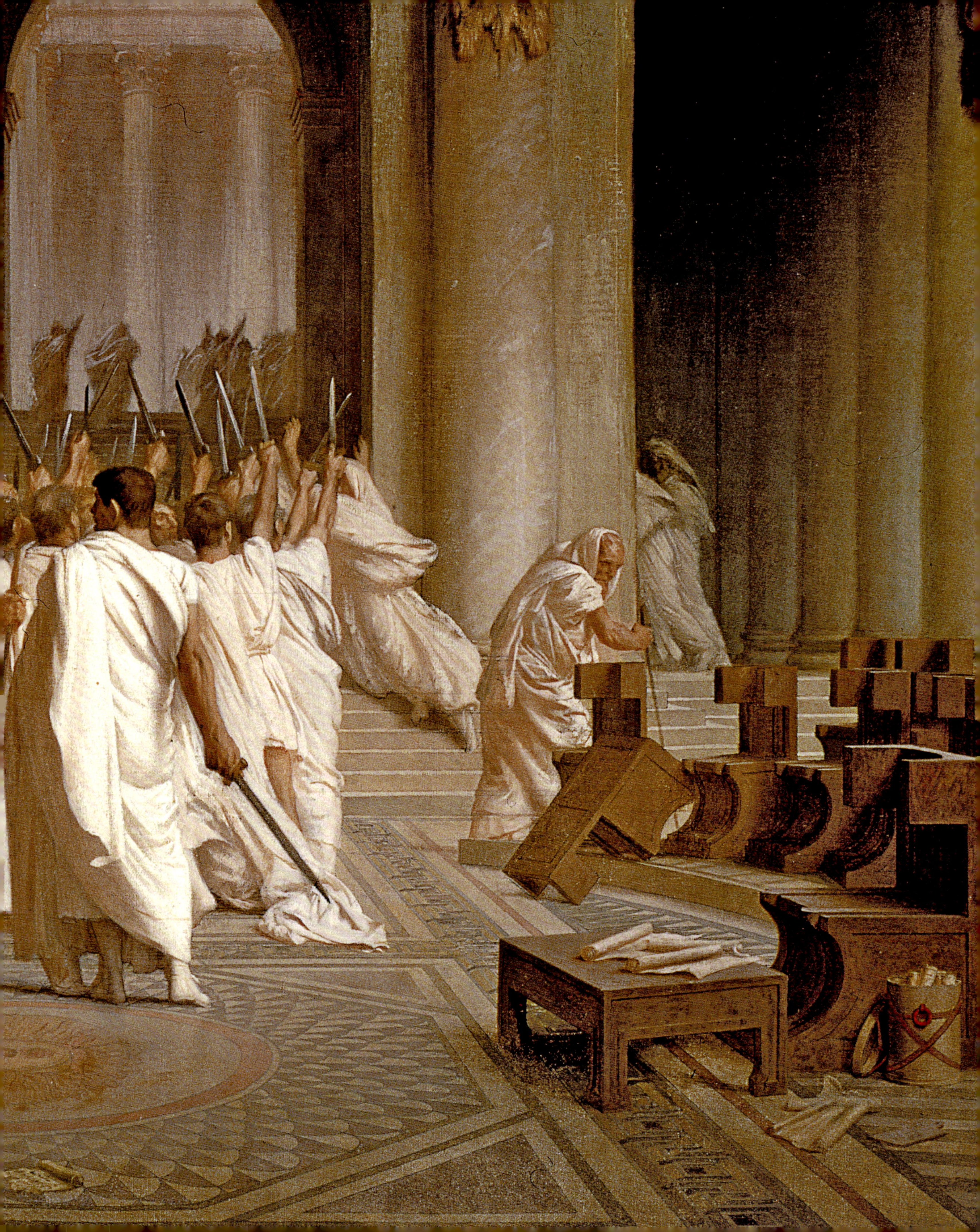

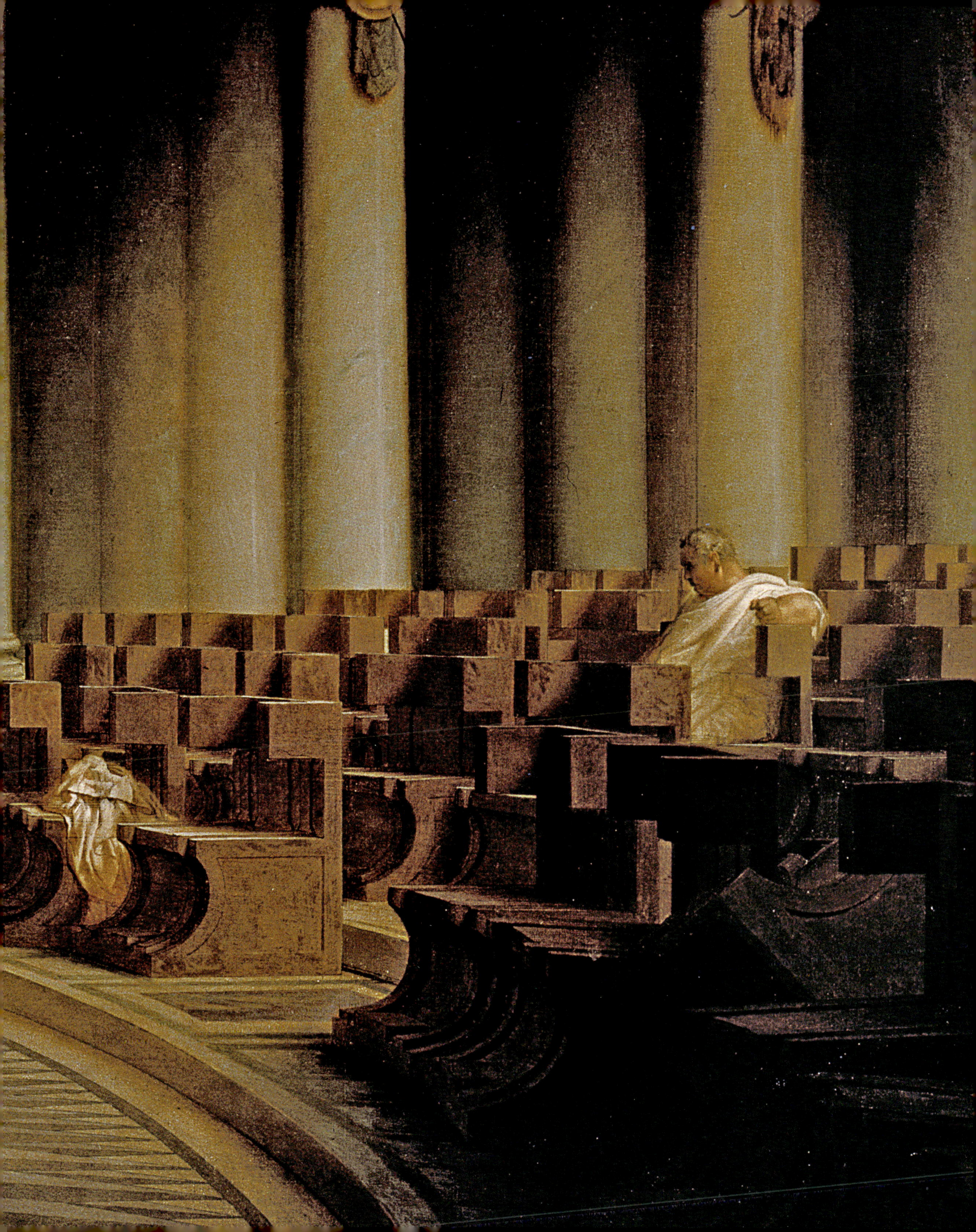

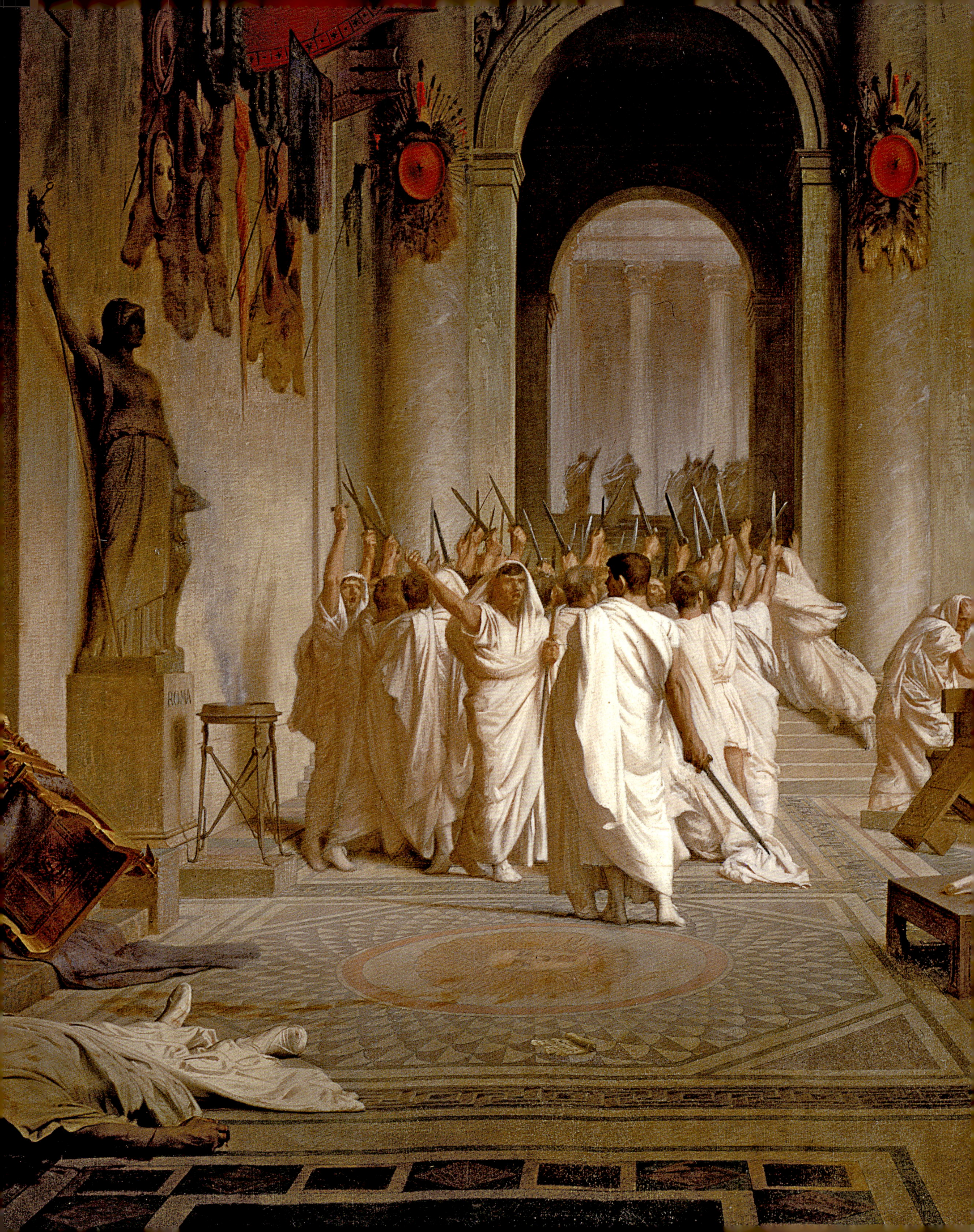
ROMA

GÉRÔME: PAINTER OF HISTORIES

—

Laurence des Cars | Translated from the French by Charles Penwarden

In his "Salon of 1859," having praised Eugène Delacroix, the unrivaled hero of his painterly pantheon, for his unfailing ability to "convey a sensation of novelty," Charles Baudelaire moved on to a diametrically opposed aspect of the painting of the day. Indirectly addressing the thorny question of the new history painting, the poet laid into its most recent iconographic and stylistic incarnation. "French wit, with its epigrammatic bent, combined with an element of pedantry destined to inject a flavor of seriousness into its natural levity, was to engender a school, which the naturally benign Théophile Gautier calls the *Néo-Grec* school and which, with your permission, I shall call the school of the *pointus*. Here erudition serves to disguise the absence of imagination, and for most of the time, therefore, the game consists in transplanting the everyday life into Greek or Roman surroundings."[1] His attack continued, concluding logically with a list of the Salon entries by Gérôme, "the first among the *pointus*," and champion of the *Néo-Grec* school ever since he burst onto the scene in 1847 with *The Cock Fight* (cat. 10).

The three works he presented in 1859 were all in a pronounced antique vein: *King Candaules* (cat. 43), *Ave Caesar, morituri te salutant* (cat. 70), and *Dead Caesar* (ill. 56, p. 122). And yet, where one might have expected Baudelaire's judgment to be pitiless, his writing became more qualified, balancing swipes—Gérôme was reproached for "lacking decisiveness and character" and oscillating between "Ingres and Delaroche"—with compliments, as he acknowledged the "truly powerful" effect of *Dead Caesar*. The parameters of the case called Gérôme were clearly set out: the "noble qualities in M. Gérôme, the main ones being the pursuit of novelty and the liking for great subjects," were constantly threatened or spoiled by "the entertainment provided by a page of erudition" that tended to become a "'catch' and a distraction."[2] Possessor of an ambiguous talent, Gérôme appeared as the most interesting—because the most gifted—player in the shifting values and status of history painting in the mid-nineteenth century. Between the irremediable decline of a system that referred to immutable, absolute values, and its relativist, eclectic reinvention, sliding so easily towards the exponential worlds of the new mass-produced images, Gérôme was an artist of transition.

BETWEEN "INGRES AND DELAROCHE"

Gérôme's dominance during this time of transformation cannot be understood without considering its twin roots in the work of Jean-Auguste-Dominique Ingres and Paul Delaroche. As with any heritage, Gérôme's position involved its share of transgression and deviation. Essentially, he was a painter who invented himself in the fertile context provided by the crisis of the classical ideal and a growing disenchantment with history. The fact is that the "Ingres question" is everywhere in Gérôme's work. It is key to the painter's first significant style, when he revisited his

Previous and opposite pages
Cat. 67. *The Death of Caesar* (detail).

Following pages
Ill. 1. *The Age of Augustus*, 1852–55, oil on canvas, 23 × 33 ft, Musée de Picardie, Amiens, on indefinite loan from the Musée d'Orsay, inv. RF 1983-92.

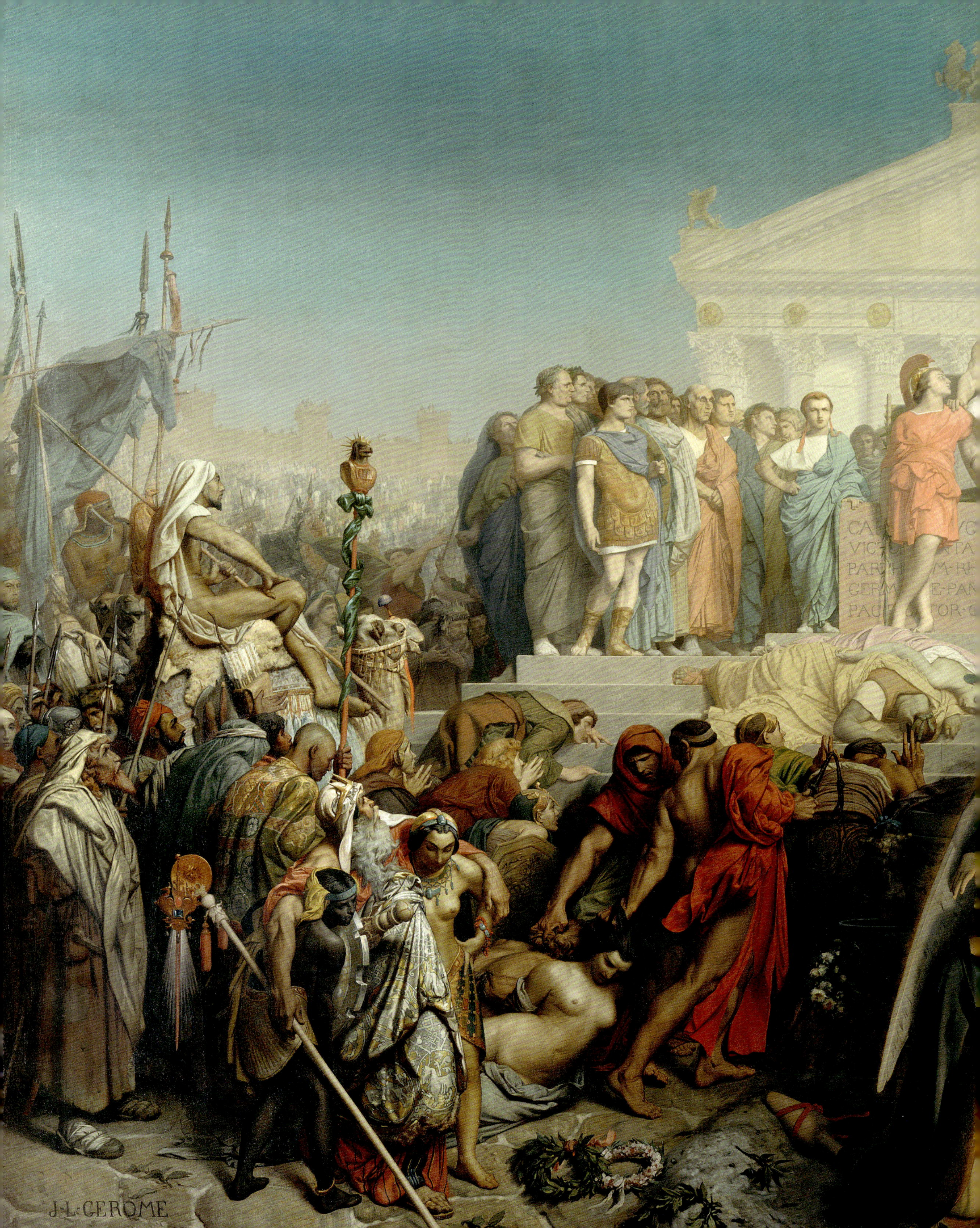
J.L.GEROME

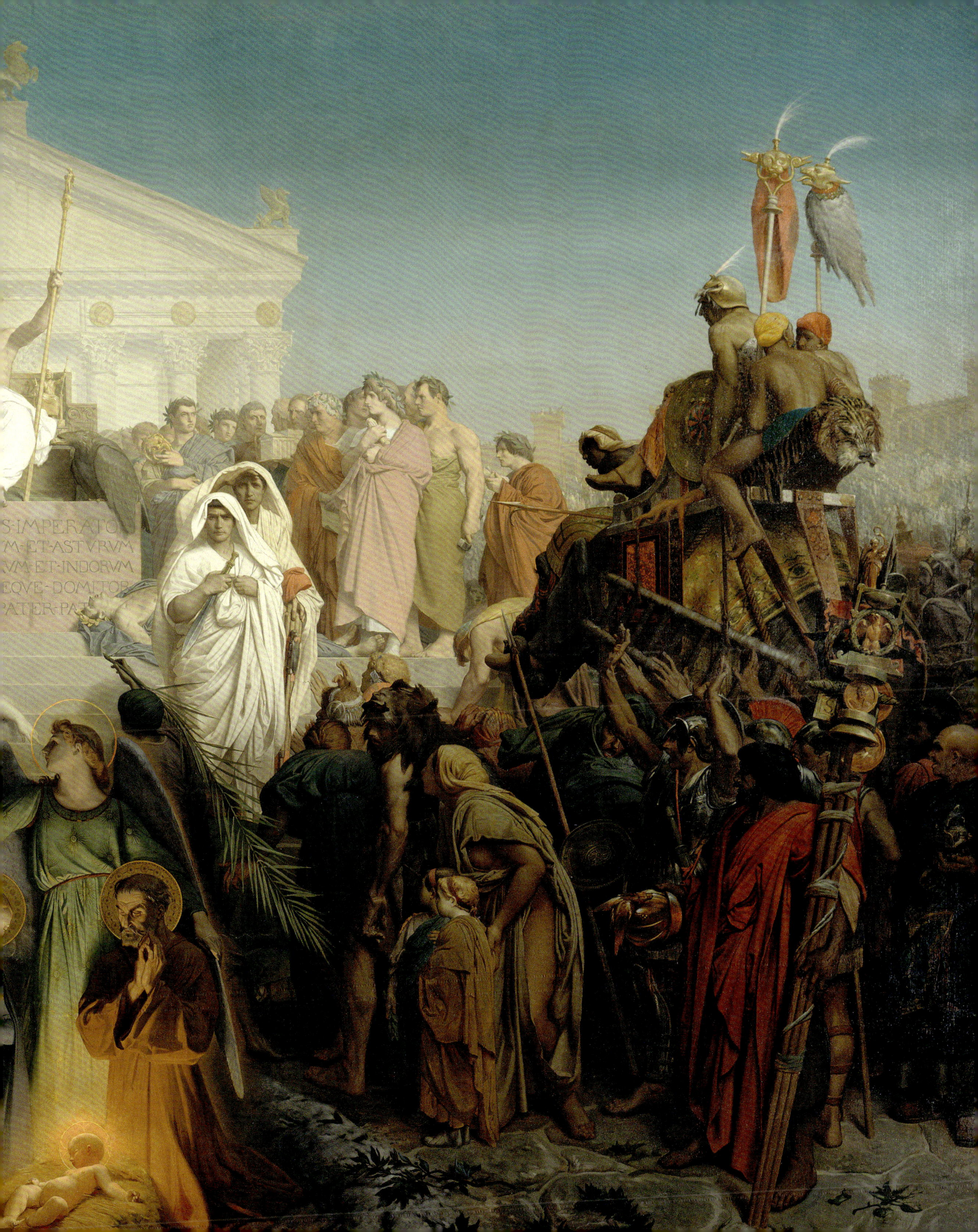
S·IMPERATO
M·ET·ASTVRVM
VM·ET·INDORVM
EQVE·DOMITOR
PATER·PA

Greek sources of inspiration through the prism of the personal and the everyday, or even the perfectly trivial. The small group who shared a communal studio with Gérôme in rue de Fleurus—Jean-Louis Hamon, Gustave Boulanger, and Henri-Pierre Picou—were continuing along the path opened up by Ingres, the heretic from Jacques-Louis David's studio, that "Chinaman lost in the streets of Athens." The lesson of antique-style archaism and of the serpentine line dispensed by *Jupiter and Thetis* (ill. 3), and the more recent variations thereon formulated by followers of the master such as Paul and Hippolyte Flandrin, Amaury-Duval and Henri Lehmann, formed the background to the palace revolution that crystallized around *The Cock Fight*. However, beyond this founding moment which established Gérôme in the role of promising young talent, "who displays a certain distinction of style even though he does come from M. Delaroche's studio,"[3] the reference to Ingres accompanied Gérôme throughout his career. It is patently obvious in his portraits (cat. 34–42), although these represent only a marginal part of the oeuvre. But the claim and the connection became more significant when, for the Exposition Universelle of 1855, Gérôme sought to establish his credentials in the *grand genre*—and in *grand* dimensions (20 33 feet)—with *The Age of Augustus* (cat. 32, ill. 1). Inspired by a passage in the writings of Jacques-Bénigne Bossuet, this huge work was designed to offer all the necessary guarantees of the seriousness and edifying content expected of history painting, and its composition nodded obediently to Ingres's *The Apotheosis of Homer* (1827, Musée du Louvre, Paris). We know that the partial failure of this canvas caused Gérôme to permanently abandon this ideal of painting which was neither his true register nor in line with the aspirations of his generation. However, his increasingly perceptible attraction to a form of realism did not mean that he renounced the most proven Ingresque formulae of seduction. This surprising mixture can be gauged in the painter's complex relation to exoticism and its erotic double, two foundational issues in Ingres's work which Gérôme recomposed with a visual literalness, confident in the effects obtained, foregoing the formal circumvolutions and subjective fragmentations of the elderly master. *King Candaules*, a step away from *Antiochus and Stratonice*, or, later, *The Grand Bath at Bursa* (cat. 167) appropriating *The Turkish Bath*, and *The Moorish Bath* (cat. 166) painted as an echo of *The Valpinçon Bather*, played skillfully on their interpretative distance with regard to Ingres in a cross between archaeological and ethnographic recreation and unabashed painterly fantasy.

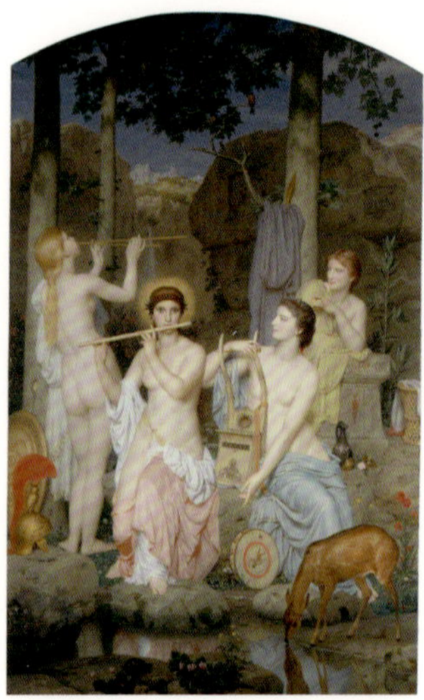

Ill. 2. Charles Gleyre (1806–1874), *Minerva and the Graces*, 1866, oil on canvas, Musée Cantonal des Beaux-Arts, Lausanne.

The second tutelary figure dominating Gérôme's rich system of references was of course Delaroche. The privileged bond between master and pupil laid down a line of force that was central to the development of history painting in the nineteenth century and its substitution of the principle of narration for that of edification. Visiting the Salon of 1831, the German poet Heinrich Heine stressed the importance of Delaroche's role in the emergence of a "historical school," which he described thus: "Delaroche is the leader of such a school. This painter has no great predilection for the past in itself, but for its representation, for the illustration of its spirit, and for writing history in colors."[4] As the child of a post-revolutionary world that witnessed the fall of Napoleon, Delaroche confronted his modern or historical heroes with their human frailty, thus undermining the idealism of David. As the dissemination of reproductions grew increasingly widespread, so the borders between genres became more porous. The undivided reign of the *exemplum virtutis* over history painting was followed by a time when what was expressed was a certain historical disillusionment. The democratization and greater accessibility of historical subjects was part of this process. Contemporaneous with the emergence of the historical novel and Romantic drama, Delaroche's history painting excelled at an unprecedented realism, both in its taste for recreation and in its expression of emotion. The effectiveness of the formal construction of *Cromwell and Charles 1* (Musée des Beaux-Arts, Nîmes), *The Children of Edward* (1831, Musée du Louvre, Paris), and *The Execution of Lady Jane Grey* (1834, National Gallery, London) comes from the perfect narrative legibility of a paradoxically intimate large format. The small number of protagonists enables the gaze to focus on these figures who seem frozen in the moment that precedes or follows the tragedy, just before the curtain comes down. This shifting of representation to its most emotionally expressive moment completed the humanization of history painting. For all its formal nobility, still resonant with the neoclassicism of painters like Pierre-Narcisse Guérin, the world of Delaroche was already a place of historical fatalism. Cromwell's sense of shock on seeing the body of his victim, the fear of the young duke of York as he realizes that the killers will soon be upon him, or the sudden faltering of Lady Jane Grey before she places her head on the block, all signal the fateful moment. The weaknesses of the mighty, or the once mighty, were exposed as the surest indicator of the truth, if not the reality of the scene. In

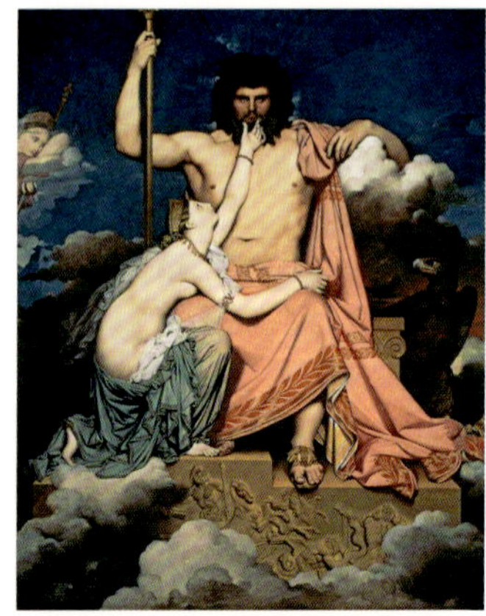

Ill. 3. Jean-Auguste-Dominique Ingres (1780–1867), *Jupiter and Thetis*, 1811, oil on canvas, 128 ¾ × 102 ½ in., Musée Granet, Aix-en-Provence, inv. 803.I.I.

this new visual economy that Delaroche played such an important part in shaping, the audience was at the center of the artist's concerns.

The crowds at the Salon could now extend their appropriation of the work by obtaining its reproduction (Delaroche had been working with Adolphe Goupil since the early 1830s).[5] As popular work that grew from new sources deriving from illustration, and, by a kind of poetic justice, eventually returned to illustration, Delaroche's painting anticipated most of the critical debates that accompanied the changing status of history painting in the second half of the century. When Delaroche tightened his focus to a more modest format and heightened the precision of his reconstitution for *The Assassination of the Duc de Guise*, he took a decisive step towards fusing history and genre painting. In organizing around an empty centre, on one side, the dead body of the leader of the Catholic League, arms outstretched like Christ, and, on the other, the group of assassins vehemently drawing Henri III's attention to the accomplishment of their deed, Delaroche was staging history on a human scale. Anecdote was the best way to gain access to History with a capital H, and one cannot overstate the enduring power of imagery created from such an impure mixture—and not only in painting: as well as other disciplines, the technique was directly adapted by the nascent art of cinema.[6] Gérôme was its direct heir, extending the dynamic of that same tension, without chronological or thematic limits, in order to construct the most convincing examples of his historical vision, from the deaths of Caesar and Marshal Ney to gladiatorial combat and the evocation of Father Joseph.

REALISM AND HISTORIOGRAPHY

As the century advanced, so the rationalist, objective approach stripped history of its philosophical or moral meanings. As the historian Prosper de Barante wrote in 1842: "We are tired of seeing history behave like a docile and well-behaved sophist, lending itself to whatever case people wish to make. What we want from it are facts. Just as we observe in these details, in its movements, that great drama in which we are all actors and witnesses, so we want to know how the peoples and individuals who went before us lived. We demand that they be evoked and brought before us, alive: people will then judge them as they see fit, or indeed will not even think of coming to any precise opinion. For there is nothing as impartial as the imagination: it is enough that a picture of truth be retraced in front of it."[7]

Responding to this call for realism, which was the rallying cry of his generation, in the 1850s Gérôme started developing a singular balance of documentary illusionism and imaginary recomposition. In this respect, there was no fundamental difference between the painter's Orientalist universe and his historical paintings. Both these facets of his work were based on a logic of reconstructing reality in such a way as to retain the image's narrative potential, even when the documentary part of the work's appearance was particularly undiluted or insistent, as was the case in *Golgotha* (cat. 78) and *The Death of Marshal Ney* (cat. 93). This approach eventually generated a self-enclosed world contained in a system of echoes that went from one canvas to another, and from originals to reproductions. In the case of historical scenes, Gérôme's hybrid approach perfectly embodied a vision at once thoroughly verified in relation to the most precise archaeological and historical sources, and offering the kind of colorful evocation of the past that was becoming increasingly widespread at the time.[8] A reader of Louis-Charles Dezobry and Edward Bulwer-Lytton, Gérôme liked to focus on details set off in great ensembles governed by imperious scenographic laws. For example, feeling that the gladiators' weapons in *Ave Caesar* were insufficiently precise, he spent years meticulously preparing the corrective, *Pollice Verso* (cat. 71), having built up an impressive collection of documents on the subject.[9] This was anything but a secondary matter, and indeed Gérôme came to see it as decisive for the success of his painting: "[*Ave Caesar*] falls short in a number of archaeological respects and that, in this case, is a serious flaw, for the gladiators were unique figures who were nothing like the soldiers of the day: strange, enormous helmets, and weapons for attack and defense that were very particular. This is where the truth of the details is important, for it adds to the physiognomy and gives the figures a barbaric, wild, strangeness."[10]

Concerned about detail, but constantly disrupting the context, Gérôme was markedly indifferent to the expression of the passions that had long been a part of historical representations. Differing significantly on this point from Delaroche, in whose work pathos was expressed on faces, Gérôme took a panoramic vision—the panoramic format being his favorite—of history, built on the anonymity of the crowds of Rome or courtiers of Versailles, made up by endlessly interchangeable walk-ons.

By choosing to widen his frame, almost systematically, Gérôme was effectively attenuating the declamatory character of the representation and helping to disrupt the didactic logic of history painting by precluding a legible heroization of the protagonists. When, at the start of the Third Republic, it fell to Jean-Paul Laurens to try to revitalize historical representation, he took up Gérôme's use of the moment before or after the action as a means of suggestion, but adamantly insisted on showing individual reactions in this suspended moment of time.[11] A comparison of Laurens's *The Execution of the Duke of Enghien* (ill. 5) with *The Death of Marshal Ney* is highly revealing in this respect. Instead of the dramatic chiaroscuro of the Laurens painting, which heightens Enghien's stature in the face of death, Gérôme preferred the rawness and the banality of a body left lying in the mud, in the pale light of early morning. In this sense, Laurens's painting was that of a perpetual "fifth act," to use Camille Mauclair's term, whereas in Gérôme the triumph of decor, details, and accessories went hand in hand with a degree of dehumanization. Erasing individual emotion, Gérôme was better able to unfold a continuous vision of historical narrative, anticipating the transition from the global vision of the panorama to the breakdown into sequence-shots.

MIXING GENRES

The inexorable contamination of history painting by genre painting was a critical refrain all through the century. The death knell was sounded many a time, notably by Marius Chaumelin at the end of the Second Empire: "For some twenty years now, at the opening of each Salon, we have heard those lugubrious words ring out: *grande peinture* [classical academic painting] is dying, *grande peinture* is dead! If *grande peinture* is the painting that frequents gods and heroes, that trades in allegories and symbols, that is nourished by the ideal and by style and by all those fine things to which we give the most high-flown names, but which no one has yet been able to clearly define, then it must be admitted that it is indeed very ill. Who will cure it?"[12] In this gradual decline of historical representations, which was constantly being twisted towards accessibility and immediate charm, Gérôme played the leading role, with his ambiguous position reflecting the fundamentally hybrid nature of his painting. On the surface, at least, his smooth, careful painting was in strict conformity with academic norms. Yet this style, which for those who still upheld the Ideal was beyond reproach, did not come directly from the École des Beaux-Arts where—ironically in the light of his longevity as a professor—Gérôme never studied. Its source was Delaroche's revised neoclassicism. Its prime concern was not to respect the norms but to create a pictorial illusion. Gérôme's impersonal manner was chosen for its effectiveness, as a means of convincing and making the beholder an

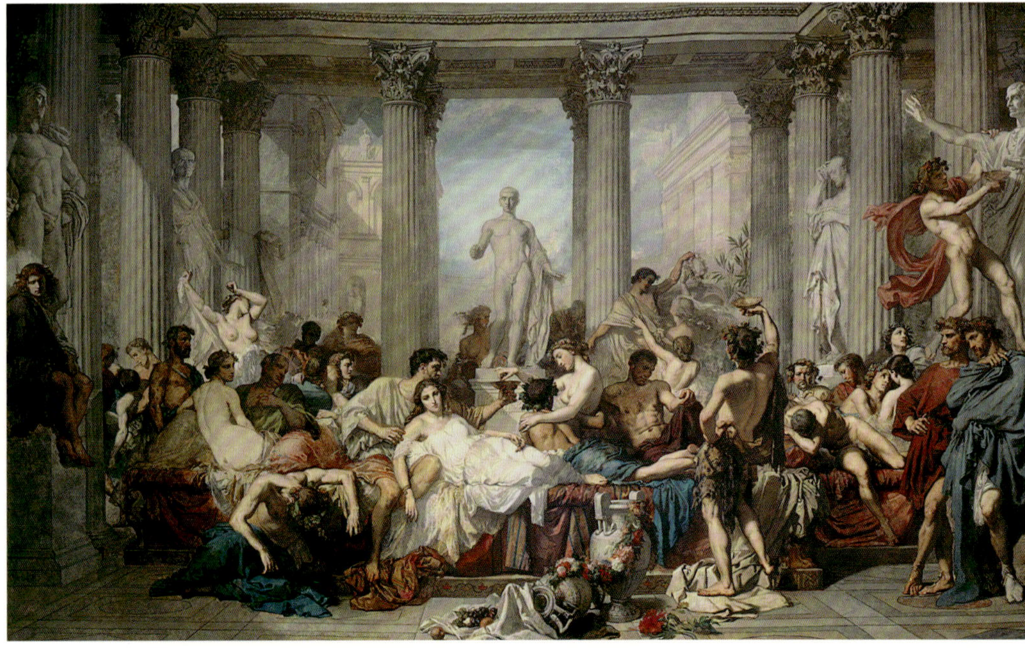

Ill. 4. Thomas Couture (1815–1879), *Romans of the Decadence*, 1847, oil on canvas, 185 ¾ x 303 in., Musée d'Orsay, Paris, RF 3451.

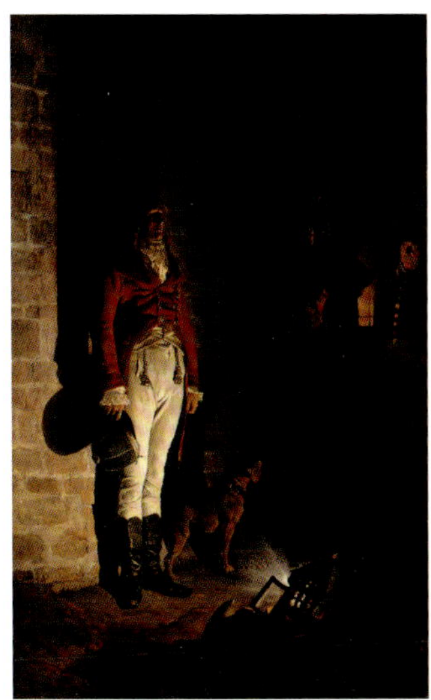

Ill. 5. Jean-Paul Laurens (1838–1921), *The Execution of the Duke of Enghien*, 1872, oil on canvas, 65 × 41 in., Musée des Beaux-Arts, Alençon, inv. D. 874.1.1.

eyewitness of the past. But this visual system based on a very relative neutrality was put in the service of subjects that were themselves considered in terms of minor events and triviality. "Anecdote is the indiscretion of History. It is Clio at her *petit lever*."[13] Thus wrote the Goncourt brothers, recalling the light touch of their beloved eighteenth century, but the meandering path taken by historical narrative in Gérôme's paintings unmistakably conveys the true tone of his work and, no doubt, its true ambition. This could also lead to the delightful and execrable *Molière Breakfasting with Louis XIV* (cat. 84), in which, moving away from Ingres, Gérôme attained the heights of vulgar indulgence in relating the golden legend of the powerful patron and the artist.

This permanent mixing of genres which, decades later, made Hollywood's historical epics and B-movies such a delight, also led Gérôme to some truly original solutions. Thus *Dead Caesar*, *The Death of Marshal Ney* and *Golgotha* were three paintings that opened up new perspectives for the fusion and contraction of chronology and narrative. As we know, they met with a mixed response, especially when they touched on religious subjects, an area where traditional didacticism was harder to avoid. To reduce the death of Christ to a landscape haunted by the shadow of three crosses brought to its conclusion the narrative reform of painted history begun by Delaroche. The old demonstrative structure of the highest genre had not yet disappeared, and was constantly coming to the surface behind Gérôme's "*pointu*" realism, but a shift had definitely occurred. Delaroche's heir went no further than that, locking himself right up to the end of his long career into the often excessive repetition of themes he had already covered.[14] But he, in turn, would be overtaken by his heritage. "Here the subject matter is everything; the painting is nothing: the reproduction is worth more than the work."[15] Émile Zola was right on target, cruelly underlining the subordination of painting to the codes of the reproduced image. A certain kind of history painting was indeed dead, but the coming together of narrative and images, soon to be animated, had only just begun. **L. C.**

1. C. Baudelaire, "Salon de 1859," in *Œuvres complètes* (Paris: Bibliothèque de la Pléiade, Gallimard, 1976), p. 637. "Salon of 1859," translated by P. E. Charvet, *Selected Writings on Art and Literature* (London: Penguin Classics, 1992), p. 315 ff.

2. Ibid., pp. 640–41. English translation, pp. 318–19.

3. T. Thoré, "Salon de 1847," in *Salons de T. Thoré* (Paris: Librairie internationale, 1868), p. 445.

4. H. Heine, *The Salon: or, Letters on Art, Music, Popular Life and Politics* (London: Dutton, 1906), p. 62.

5. On this point see P.-L. Renié, "Delaroche par Goupil: portrait du peintre en artiste populaire," in *Paul Delaroche: un peintre dans l'histoire*, exh. cat. (Nantes: Musée des Beaux-Arts, 1999–2000; also Montpellier: Musée Fabre, 2000), p. 176.

6. *L'Assassinat du Duc de Guise*, a French silent film, 1908 (screenplay by Henri Lavedan, incidental music composed by Camille Saint-Saëns).

7. P. de Barante, preface to *Histoire des ducs de Bourgogne*, 6th ed. (Paris, 1842), vol. 1, pp. xxiv–xxv.

8. On Gérôme's historical references, see the essay by François de Vergnette in this catalogue (p. 113).

9. See catalogue entries 70 and 71.

10. J.-L. Gérôme, *Notes autobiographiques* [1874], ed. G. Ackerman (Vesoul: S.A.L.S.A., 1981), p. 12.

11. See *Jean-Paul Laurens, peintre d'histoire*, exh. cat. (Paris: Musée d'Orsay, 1998; also Toulouse: Musée des Augustins, 1998).

12. M. Chaumelin, "Salon de 1868," *La Presse*, June 29, 1868, p. 1.

13. E. and J. de Goncourt, *Portraits intimes du XVIIIe siècle* [1857–58] (Paris: Flammarion & Fasquelle, 1924), vol. 1, pp. 51–52.

14. See, for example, the development that occurs between *The Christian Martyrs' Last Prayers* (cat. 80) and *Gathering up the Lions in the Circus* (cat. 81).

15. É. Zola, "Nos peintres au Champ de Mars," *La Situation*, July 1, 1867, in É. Zola, *Mon Salon, Manet. Écrits sur l'art* (Paris: Garnier-Flammarion, 1970), p. 127.

Cat. 1

PORTRAIT OF A ROMAN WOMAN

1843–44
Oil on canvas
17 ½ × 15 in.
Signed and dated lower right:
J. L. GEROME, 1844, ROME
The Cleveland Museum of Art, Noah L. Butkin Bequest, inv. CMA 1980.264

Provenance: Commissioned by Joseph Courcelles (Vesoul). Private collection, Belgium. Christie's, London, Feb. 20, 1976, lot 153. Shepperd Gallery, New York. Collection of Mr. and Mrs. Noah Butkin, Cleveland. Noah L. Butkin Bequest, Cleveland Museum of Art, 1980.

Bibliography: H. Lafont-Couturier, *Gérôme* (Paris: Herscher, 1998), p. 11. L. d'Argencourt and R. Diederen, *European Paintings of the 19th Century: The Cleveland Museum of Art, Catalogue of Paintings*, 4 vols. (Cleveland: Cleveland Museum of Art, 1999), vol. 1, pp. 290–93. G. Ackerman, *Jean-Léon Gérôme* (Courbevoie: ACR Édition, 2000), no. 9.

In 1843, when his master Paul Delaroche was forced to close down his Parisian studio and went to Italy, the young Gérôme decided to follow him. What ensued was a stimulating and formative year during which he took his first serious steps as a painter. This is clearly reflected in his *Notes autobiographiques*: "Thus at eighteen I find myself in Italy. I had no illusions about my studio studies, which were in fact very weak... I am now doing studies of buildings, landscapes, figures, and animals... This year is one of the happiest and fullest of my life, and at this time I have certainly made major progress."[1]

The fine and powerful study kept by the Cleveland Museum of Art was one of the young artist's first virtuoso pieces. It belongs to a small series of Roman figures, both male and female, in which Gérôme tried his hand at the iconographic and stylistic vocabulary of the Italian picturesque. However, in the transition from the *Head of a Peasant of the Roman Campagna* (ill. 6), reflecting a mundane reality, to this more ambitious stylized vision, we can already see a whole world of references jostling behind the simple exercise. The model, whose severe features could be those of the famous Anna Rissi, also known as Nana, reappears in another study (Ackerman, no. 9.1) dressed in a more contemporary style. Here, however, she is used for one of the painter's first variations in the antique style.[2]

The glossy, linear manner, clearly attesting to the influence of Jean-Auguste-Dominique Ingres (as inflected by Delaroche), bestows a patrician air on this portrait of a heroine from the Roman street. In this cold vision we can sense the artist moving towards the stylistic concerns and visual borrowings of his later *Néo-Grec* manner. **L. C.**

1. J.-L. Gérôme, *Notes autobiographiques* [1874], ed. G. Ackerman (Vesoul: S.A.L.S.A., 1981), p. 8. 2. On the identity of the model, see A. Luxembourg in L. d'Argencourt and R. Diederen, *European Paintings of the 19th Century: The Cleveland Museum of Art, Catalogue of Paintings*, 4 vols. (Cleveland: Cleveland Museum of Art, 1999), vol. 1, pp. 290–93.

Ill. 6. *Head of a Peasant of the Roman Campagna* (profile), ca. 1843–44, oil on canvas, 18 × 14 ¼ in., Musée Magnin, Dijon, inv. 1938F423.

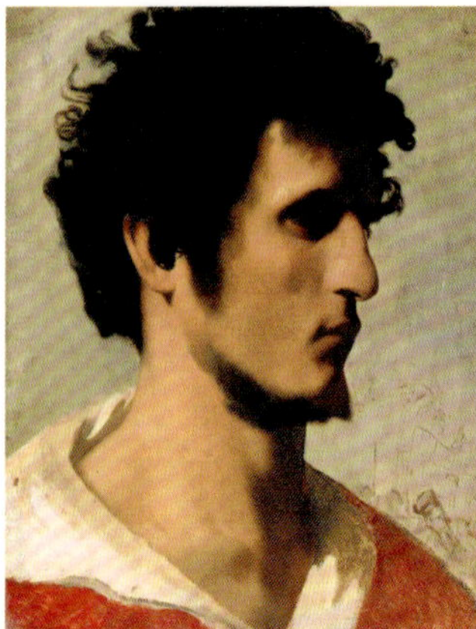

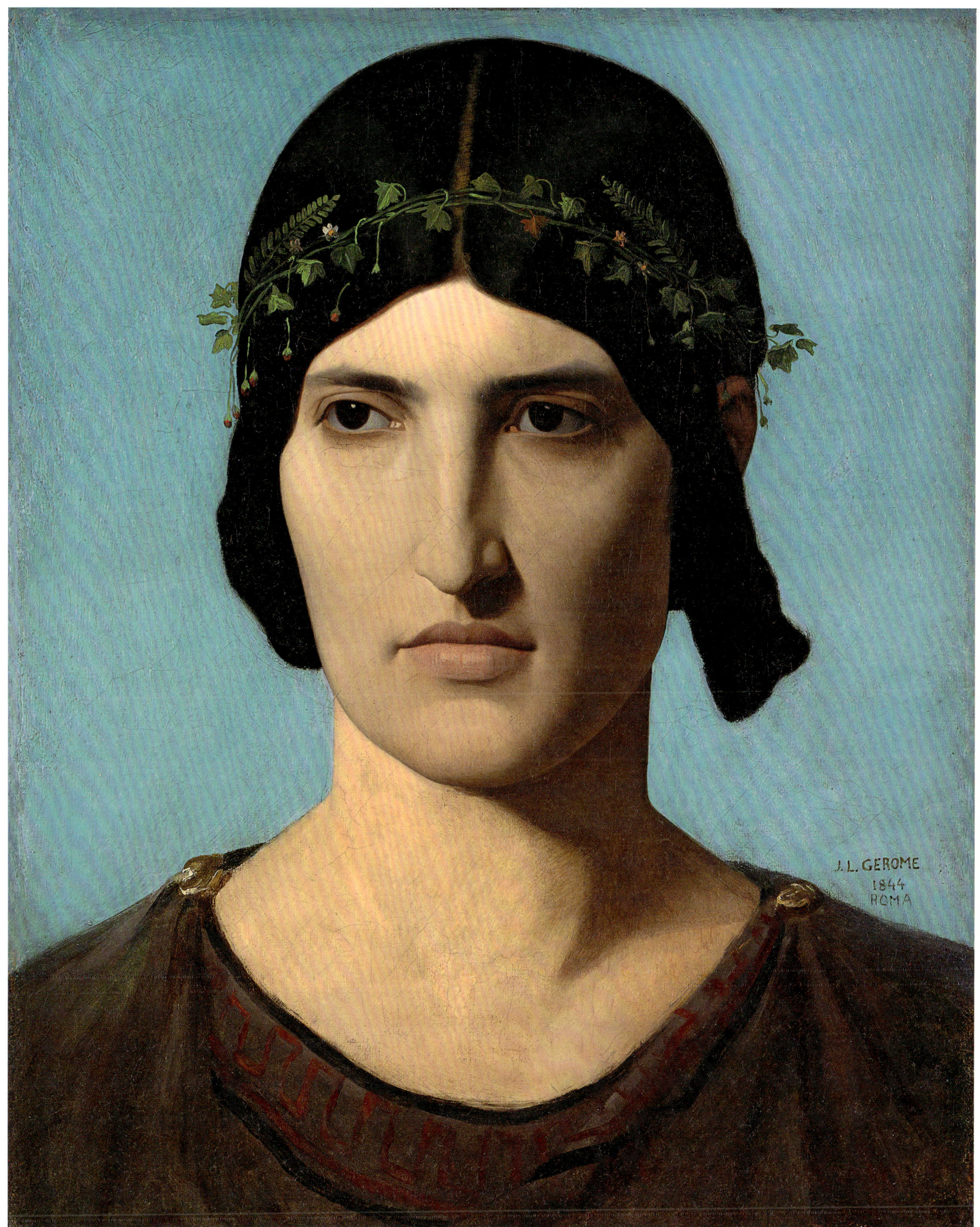
J.L. GEROME
1844
ROMA

Cat. 2

TWO ITALIAN PEASANT WOMEN WITH A CHILD, ALSO KNOWN AS **MEMORIES FROM ITALY**

–

1849
Oil on canvas
34 ¾ × 26 ¾ in.
Signed and dated lower left:
J.L. GEROME 1849
Musée d'Orsay, Paris, inv. RF 2007 14

–

Provenance: Private American collection until 2007. Bought by the Musée d'Orsay, 2007.

–

Bibliography: T. Gautier, *La Presse*, March 1, 1851, p. 2. *Voir l'Italie et mourir: Photographie et peinture dans l'Italie du XIXe siècle*, exh. cat. (Paris: Musée d'Orsay, 2009), cat. 212.

Cat. 3

PIFFERARI

–

1857
Oil on panel
10 × 7 ½ in.
Signed and dated lower left:
J.L. GEROME 1857
Iris and Gerald B. Cantor Center for Visual Arts, Stanford, Estate of Mrs. Frank E. Buck, inv. 1979.67

–

Provenance: Barre sale, 1858. J. H. Meyer, Paris, 1910. Bequeathed to Stanford by Mrs. Frank Buck in 1959.

–

Exhibition History: Salon of 1857.

–

Bibliography: T. Gautier, *L'Artiste*, July 5, 1857, p. 248, reprinted in T. Gautier, *Tableaux à la plume* (Paris, n.d.), p. 195 ff. G. Ackerman, "Gérôme's Pifferari," *The Stanford Museum*, no. 8–9 (1978–79), pp. 9–13. G. Ackerman, *Jean-Léon Gérôme* (Courbevoie: ACR Edition, 2000), pp. 232–233.

Cat. 4

Charles Nègre (1820–1880)

GROUP OF THREE PIFFERARI STANDING IN THE COURTYARD OF 21 QUAI BOURBON

–

1854
Photomechanical reproduction (heliogravure)
6 ½ × 4 ¾ in. [with mount: 20 × 16 in.]
Musée d'Orsay, Paris, inv. PHO 1983 20

Cat. 5

Adrien Tournachon, attributed to (1825–1903)

PIFFERARO

–

ca. 1855
Salt print glued to cardboard
11 ¾ × 8 ¾ in.
Société Française de Photographie, Paris, inv. 308-3

Cat. 6

Adrien Tournachon, attributed to

PIFFERARO

–

ca. 1855
Salt print glued to cardboard
11 ¾ × 8 ¾ in.
Société Française de Photographie, Paris, inv. 308-2

Cat. 7

ITALIAN PLAYING A DOODLESACK

–

1855
Oil on panel
7 ½ × 4 ¾ in.
Signed lower right: *J.L. GEROME*
Private collection

–

Provenance: Goupil & Cie, Paris, 1855. Goupil & Cie, Paris, 1861. London, May 12, 1881, Charles Kurz to Wertheimer (for £168). John Levey Gallery, New York. M. Henry K. Ostrow, Hewlett Harbor, New York. Parke Bernet Galleries, New York, May 4, 1944, lot 15, illustrated with the title "The Street Minstrel." Charles Schier. Michael Lynne Lerner Collection. Sotheby's, New York, Oct. 12, 1994, sale 6603, lot 153.

–

Exhibition History: Exposition Universelle, 1855.

–

Bibliography: Recueil. Œuvres de Jean-Léon Gérôme, BNF Estampes, vol. I, no. 2. G. Ackerman, *Jean-Léon Gérôme* (Courbevoie: ACR Édition, 2000), no. 61.

Cat. 8

PIFFERARO

–

1856
Oil on panel
7 × 5 in.
Signed and dated lower right corner, not in Gérôme's hand; the inscription reads from bottom to top: *J.L. GEROME 1856*
Musée des Beaux-Arts, Nantes, inv. 988

–

Provenance: Bought in 1899 from the Cercle des Beaux-Arts, Nantes.

–

Bibliography: *Mario Fortuny et ses amis*, exh. cat. (Castres: Musée Goya, 1974), no. 122. G. Ackerman, *Jean-Léon Gérôme* (Courbevoie: ACR Édition, 2000), no. 59. *Italiennes modèles: Hébert et les paysans d'Italie*, exh. cat. (Paris: Musée d'Orsay, 2009).

In 1843 the eighteen-year-old Gérôme decided to take a break from his training in order to travel to Italy with his master Paul Delaroche, to whom he was very attached. Gérôme thus enjoyed, several years early, the Italian sojourn that he might have taken had he won the Prix de Rome contest. His trip took him to Rome, Venice, and Naples, resulting in discoveries that he rejoiced over in his *Notes:* "Thus at eighteen I find myself in Italy. I had no illusions about my studio studies, which were in fact very weak... I am now doing studies of buildings, landscapes, figures, and animals... This year is one of the happiest and fullest of my life, and at this time I have certainly made major progress."[1]

Indeed, rather than ancient or Renaissance Italy, it was contemporary Italy that caught Gérôme's attention. He did many pencil studies, as witnessed by a touching little notebook still owned by his heirs. His trip—the first in a long series to Italy, Turkey, and the Orient—thus enabled him, when subsequently elaborating works on canvas, to closely combine accuracy of observation with the influence of contemporary artworks.

The everyday Italy that so appealed to young Gérôme had in fact been fashionable at the annual Salon for several years already. Among others, Léopold Robert, François-Joseph Navez, and Jean-Victor Schnetz had already made a specialty of charming or melancholy genre scenes, sometimes under the cover of religious subjects whose compositions remained faithful to academic tradition, where the dress of traditional young peasant women could offer the double virtue of moderate exoticism and more especially a clear echo of dress worn by figures in old master paintings.

Painted in 1849, *Two Italian Peasant Women with a Child* directly refers to the pictorial trend that grew up alongside early movements toward Italian unification. Gérôme's stylistic debt to Delaroche is very strong here, as it is for most of his canvases of the 1840s—the figure of the child is similar in handling to that of Delaroche's youthful Pico della Mirandola

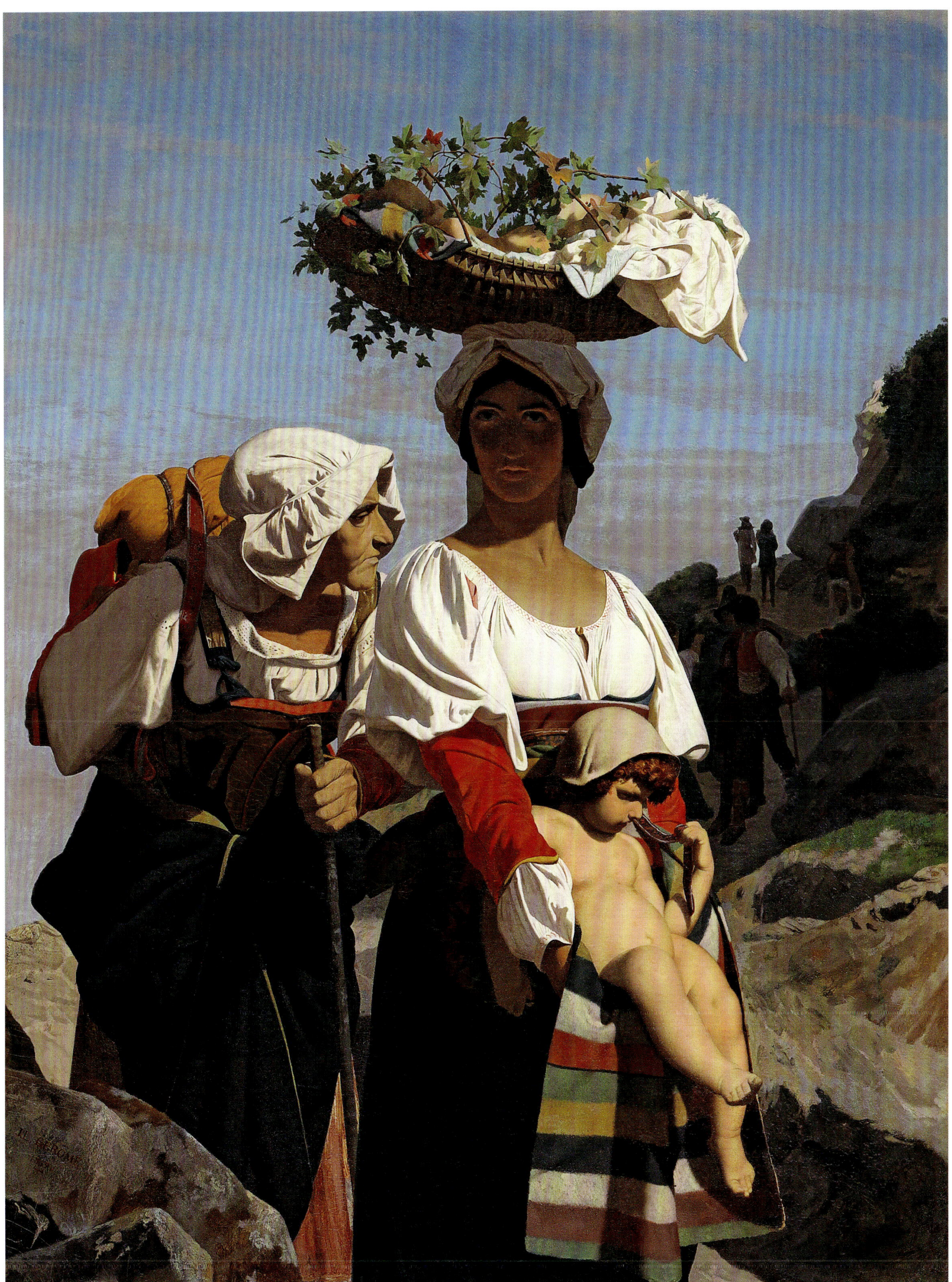

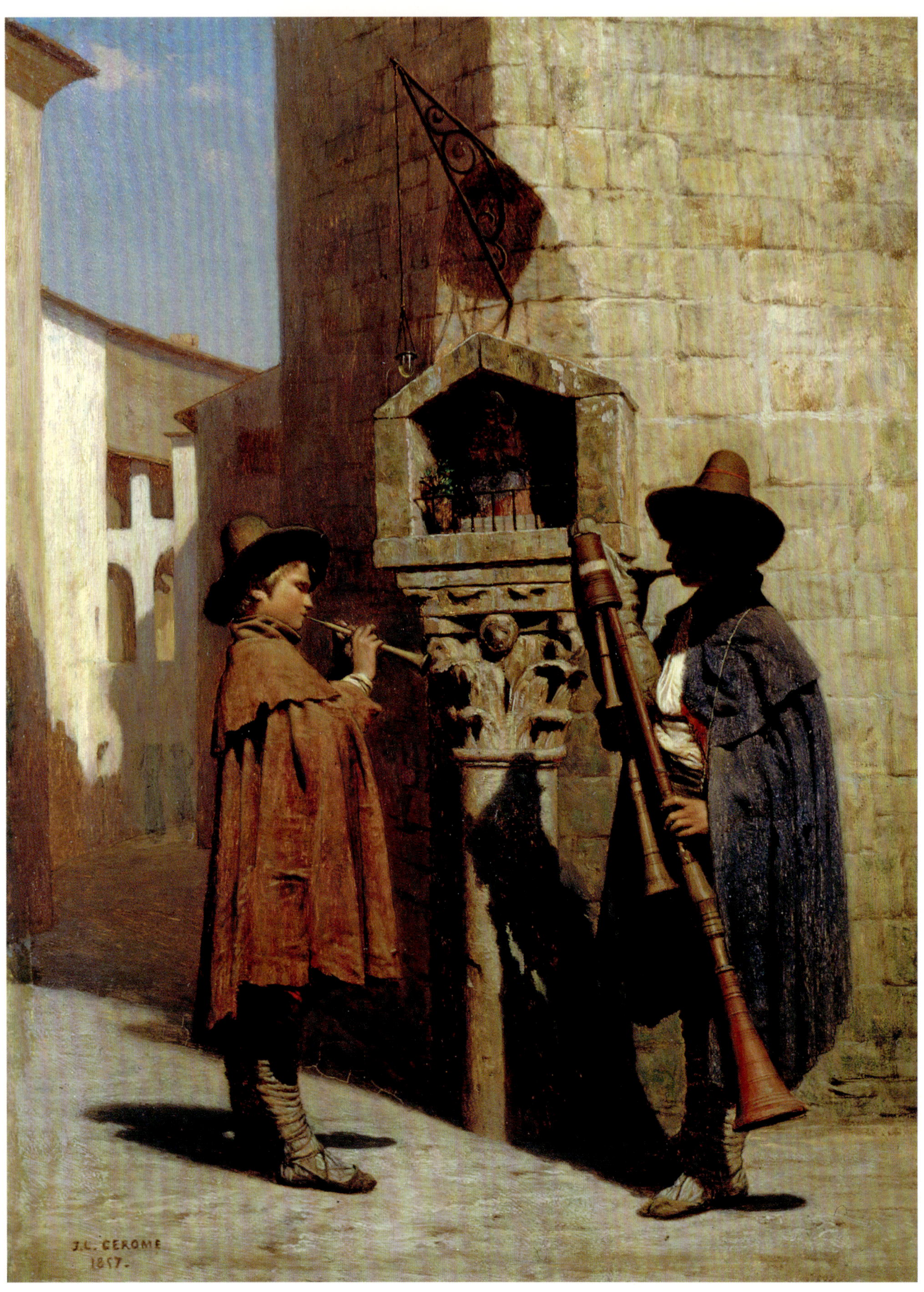
J.L. GEROME
1857.

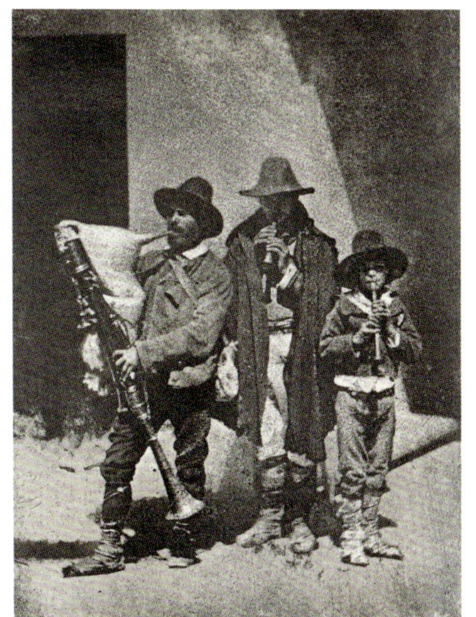

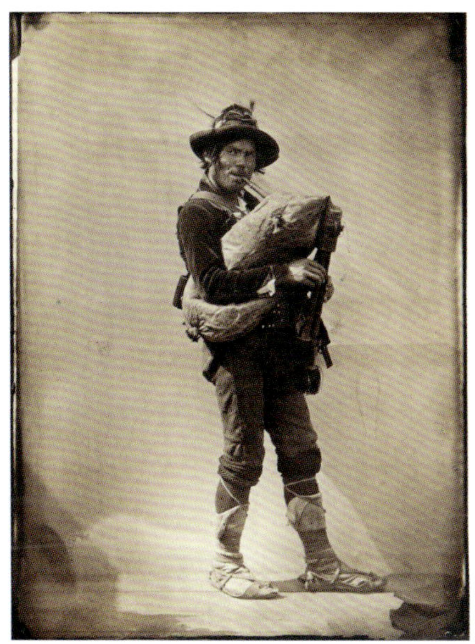

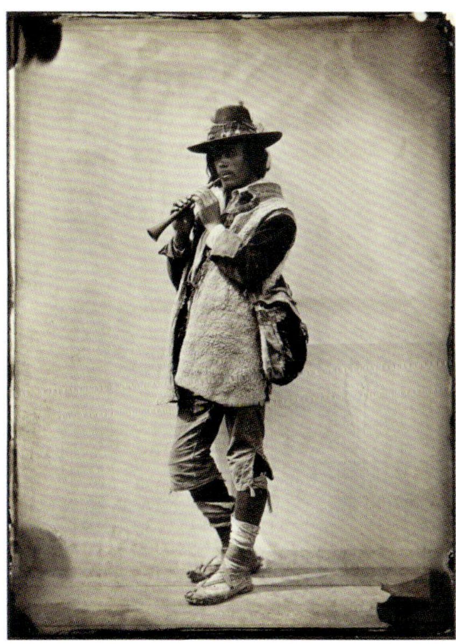

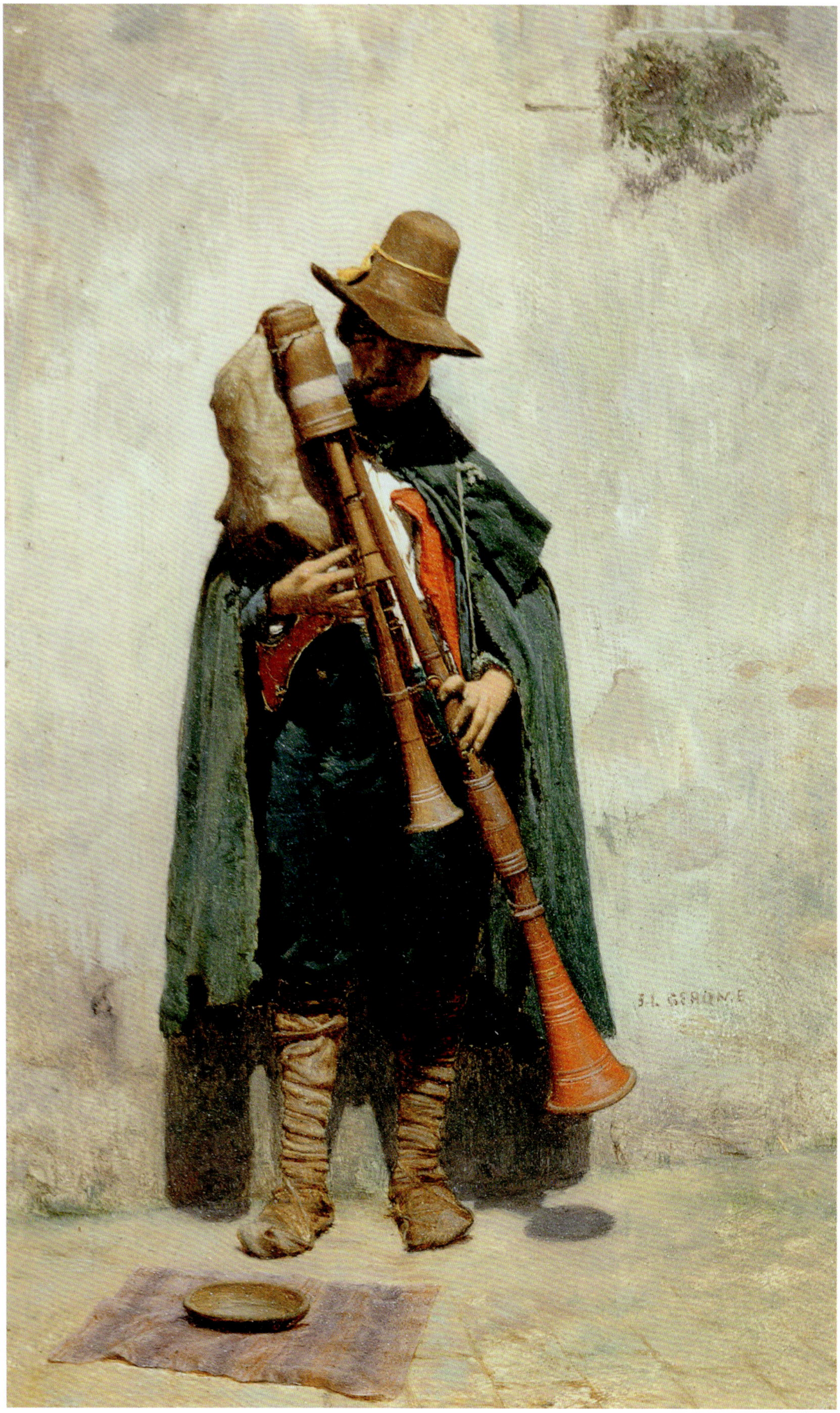

in 1842 (ill. 14, p. 46). The overall composition is fully mastered, with staggered planes that underscore the main scene; the bright colors echo the *Néo-Grec* works exhibited by Gérôme at the Salons in those same years. Although he did not labor over the facial expressions—the young woman's face is even plunged into shadow—the youthful artist's firm brushwork lends the overall work a striking monumentality.

Similarly, Gérôme was able to impart a strong presence to his *Pifferari*, despite the small size of the canvases that he painted several times in the 1850s. He submitted the works on show to the Salon (1855, cat. 7; 1857, cat. 3), which indicates the importance he placed on them.

The motif of a *pifferaro*—or peasant from the Abruzzi region named after his instruments "suonatore di piffero" he played in order to earn a living by performing in villages—represented another evocation of everyday Italy. The young Gérôme probably encountered some of these musicians during his travels through Italy, but a *pifferaro* was also, and above all, already a familiar figure in painting and photographic studios in Paris. Easily recognizable thanks to his instrument, broadcloth breeches, and leather leggings, he became one of the favorite figures of a conventional picturesqueness. His dark, somber presence carried a hint of anxiety even as the wild appearance of his dress might rescue a genre scene from mawkishness. As artist's models, *pifferari* were also the subject of many photographic studies. Charles Nègre, a painter by training who studied alongside Gérôme in Delaroche's studio, became a talented photographer in the late 1840s, and he published several prints that featured these young musicians (or models dressed as such). Meanwhile Adrien Tournachon, brother of Félix Tournachon, the famous photographer called Nadar—both of whom were well known to Gérôme—took the two photographs shown here around 1855 and exhibited them at the Société Française de Photographie in 1857.

When painting his *Pifferari*, Gérôme was inspired not just by his memories but also by these photographic models. He tried to be highly accurate in his rendering of their costumes, an aspiration that might have been fueled by photography. From Tournachon he might also have borrowed the fairly harsh lighting of the figures, which emphasized their silhouetted outlines. Commenting on the *Pifferari* (now in the Cantor Center for Visual Arts, Stanford) when they were exhibited at the Salon of 1857, Théophile Gautier stressed that, "Photography, even if it rendered color as well as shape, could not be any more accurate."[2] Gérôme, as Gautier also pointed out, lent this scene a religious dimension despite the painting's small size, since the musicians turn toward a painted plaster statue of the Madonna. The painting was photographed by Robert Jefferson Bingham in 1859 for Goupil's "Galerie Photographique" series, and marketed by the firm in that form until 1904 or later; this photographic dissemination helped to spread the popularity of the figure of the *pifferaro*.

The Musée Bartholdi in Colmar recently acquired a variant of the Stanford painting, done on cardboard and even smaller than the original yet retaining a certain monumentality thanks to the strong composition. The frame includes a cartouche with the inscription "Offert en mars 1856" (Given in March 1856), which would seem to indicate that it represents an initial conception of the work.[3] **D. F.-R.**

1. Quoted in S. Harent and C. Stoullig, *Dessins de Jean-Léon Gérôme: la collection du musée des Beaux-Arts de Nancy* (Nancy: Musée des Beaux-Arts, 2009), p. 38. **2.** T. Gautier, *L'Artiste*, July 5, 1857, p. 248. **3.** The painting was purchased by the Musée Bartholdi thanks to the generosity of the museum's friends' association (Amis du Musée), inv. 2009-13.

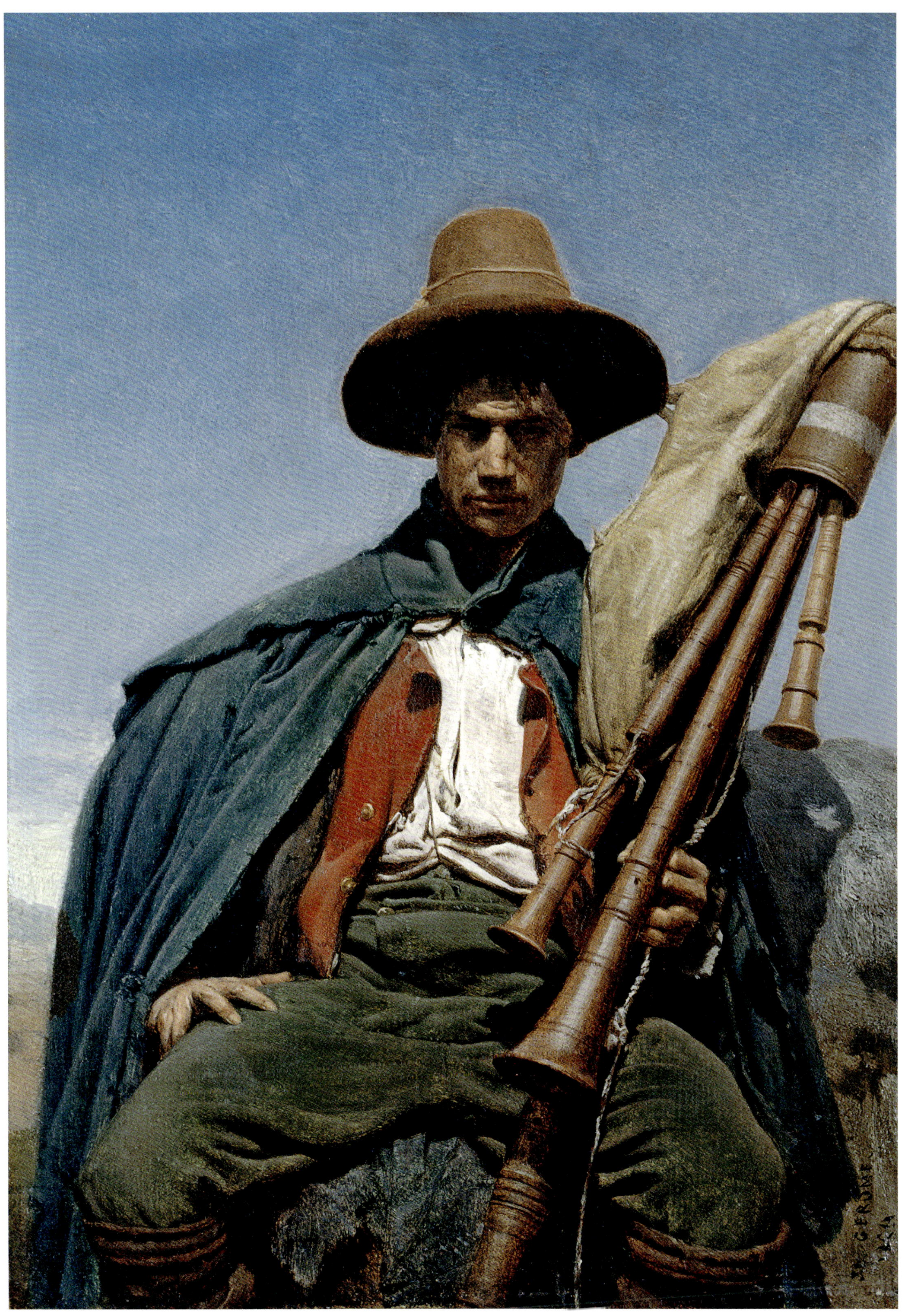
GEROME

Cat. 9

MICHELANGELO (IN HIS STUDIO)

–

1849
Oil on canvas
20 ¼ × 14 ¾ in.
Signed and dated in the center, on the base of the sculpture: *J.L. GEROME 1849*
Dahesh Museum of Art, Greenwich, inv. 1999.8

–

Provenance: Prost's *Catalogue de Paris* includes a "Michelangelo" that was allegedly donated to an artists' association lottery (*Loterie de l'association des artistes*) in April 1850 and to an authors' and playwrights' lottery (*Loterie des gens de lettres et des arts dramatiques*) in April 1851. It is not known whether the same work was donated twice or whether two different works were involved. Hôtel Drouot, Paris, June 3, 1981. PBNY, Oct. 1981, sale no. 4714M, lot 93. Sotheby's, London, June 21, 1983, lot 28. Sotheby's, New York, May 7, 1998, lot 34.

–

Bibliography: G. Ackerman, "The Néo-Grecs," in *The French Academy: Classicism and its Antagonists*, ed. J. Hargrove (Newark: University of Delaware Press, 1990), pp. 168–96. G. Ackerman, *Jean-Léon Gérôme* (Courbevoie: ACR Édition, 2000), no. 26.

This painting was done by the young Gérôme in 1848–49 when he was sharing a joint studio at 27 rue de Fleurus, notably with painters Jean-Louis Hamon and Henri-Pierre Picou.[1]

Gérôme here combined the Romantic infatuation with Michelangelo (as an exemplary artist—a painter, poet, and sculptor who was honored by the high and mighty yet retained his creative liberty and freedom of opinion), with Gérôme's own interest in Greek sculpture and the rejuvenating stimulation such sculpture could impart to artists, as underscored here by the presence of the *Belvedere Torso*, one of the most famous ancient statues ever since it was discovered—and then often copied—in the fifteenth century.

Here Gérôme depicted an aged, blind Michelangelo being guided through his shadowy studio by a young assistant in elegant troubadour dress (a deliberately anachronistic allusion to the medieval revival fashion). The assistant draws the old master toward the powerful forms of the ancient sculpture, here almost twice larger than it actually is. Michelangelo seems to want to grasp its scale and depth in order to reproduce them: in the background is a scarcely roughed-out block of marble, a hammer, and a chisel, apparently suggesting that, despite his age and handicap, Michelangelo is still endowed with all his creative faculties. By placing the *Torso* in Michelangelo's workshop, instead of the Belvedere courtyard where it had been on display since the 1530s, Gérôme was stressing its influence on the Florentine sculptor's art. Gérôme's tribute to this leading Renaissance artist was contemporary with that of Eugène Delacroix (ill. 7). Like Gérôme, Delacroix depicted Michelangelo as a sculptor in the privacy of his own studio. Both artists apparently felt that the status of sculptor rendered Michelangelo's demiurgic power better than that of painter. This decision also reflected nineteenth-century critical appreciation of Michelangelo, whose sculptures inspired numerous artists. Delacroix, however, showed a melancholy artist seated next to his own works, notably the *Medici Madonna*—the Renaissance master's melancholia was certainly designed to reflect Delacroix's own.

The theme of an artist's studio—especially a sculptor's workshop—as a site of creative alchemy became a recurrent motif in Gérôme's work after 1880, as well as of the photographic reproductions of his studios that he had made (cat. 177, 178, 179). *Michelangelo* underscores the precociousness of Gérôme's interest in this theme, of which many nineteenth-century artists were fond. **D. F.-R.**

1. Gustave Le Gray photographed them in this studio in 1848 (cat. 14 and 15).

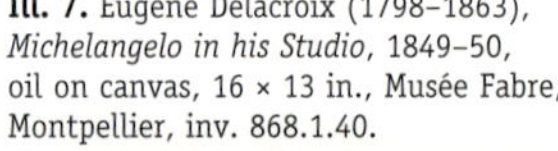

Ill. 7. Eugène Delacroix (1798–1863), *Michelangelo in his Studio*, 1849–50, oil on canvas, 16 × 13 in., Musée Fabre, Montpellier, inv. 868.1.40.

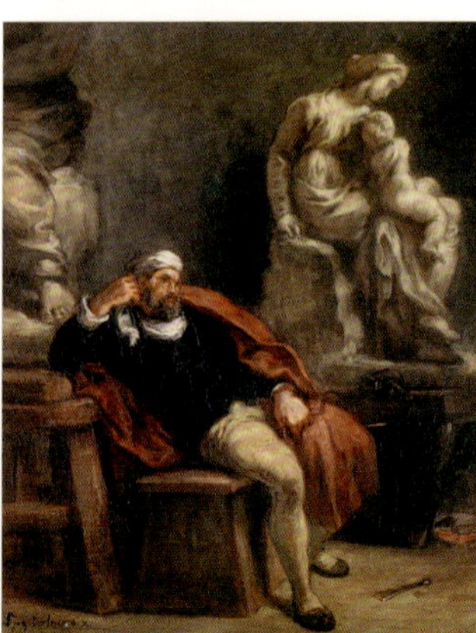

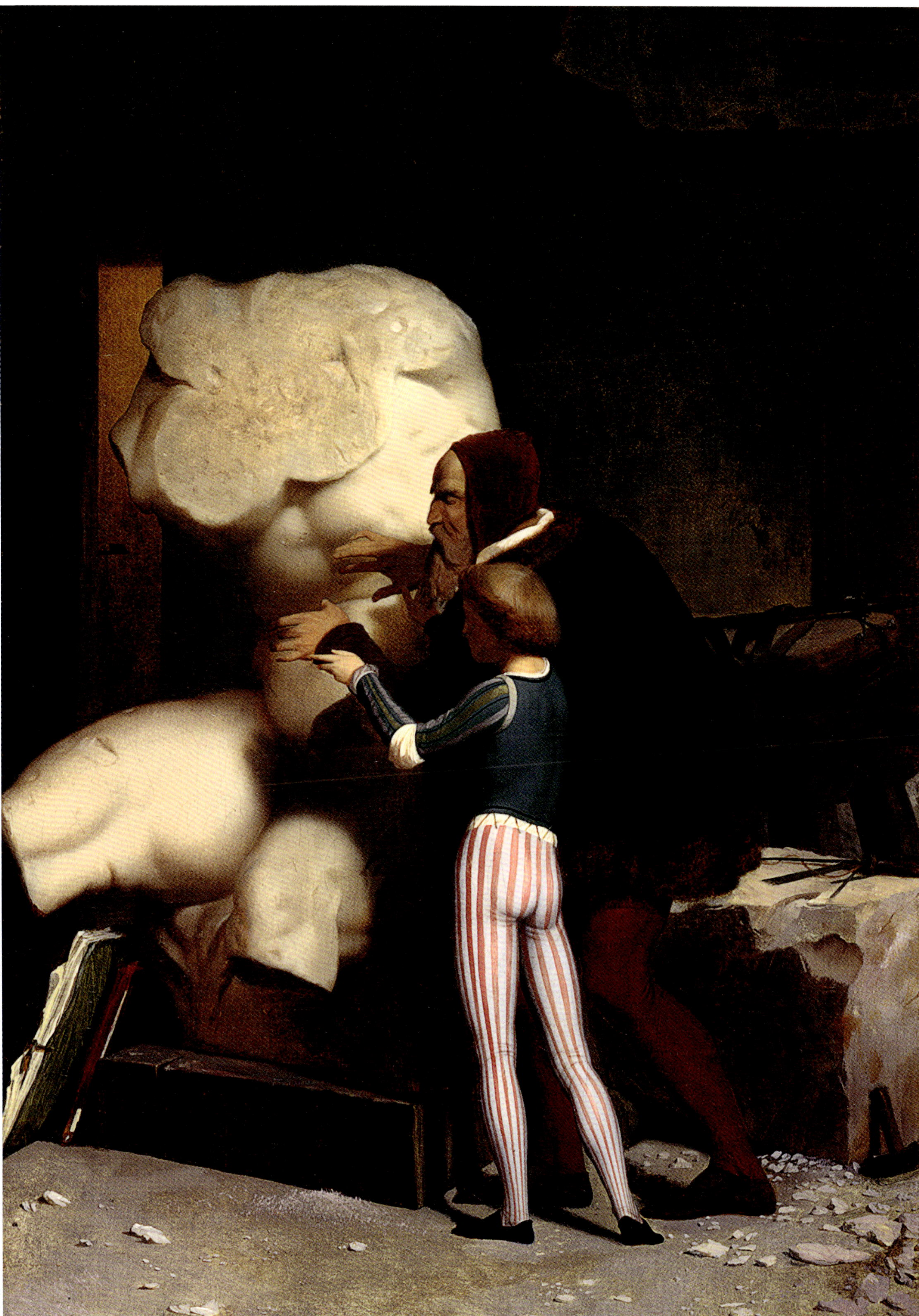

Cat. 10

THE COCK FIGHT

–

1846
Oil on canvas
55 × 80 in.
Signed and dated lower right: *J.L. GEROME 1846*
Musée d'Orsay, Paris, inv. RF 88

–

Provenance: Roux-Laborie collection, purchased from the artist. Up to 1872, the collection of Comtesse H. de Bussat, née Laborie. From 1872 to 1873, A. Goupil collection, Gérôme's father-in-law, purchased from the widowed Comtesse H. de Bussat. Acquired by the State from Goupil in 1873, allocated to the Louvre in 1874. Musée du Luxembourg, Paris. Musée du Louvre, Paris, 1920–86. Allocated to the Musée d'Orsay, 1986.

–

Exhibition History: Salon of 1847, Paris, no. 705.

–

Bibliography: T. Gautier, "Exposition de 1847," *La Presse*, March 31, 1847, p. 1. T. Gautier, *La Presse*, June 2, 1847. T. Gautier, *L'Artiste*, July 4, 1847, p. 14. E. About, *Voyage à travers l'exposition des Beaux-Arts* (Paris: Hachette, 1855), IV, pp. 153–55. T. Thoré, *Salons de T. Thoré* (Paris: Librairie Internationale, 1868), p. 851. E. Montrosier, *Les Chefs-d'oeuvre d'art du Luxembourg* (Paris: Ludovic Baschet Editeur, 1881), pp. 30–32. H. Marcel, *La Peinture française au XIXe siècle* (Paris: H. Laurens, 1905), pp. 190–91. H. Focillon, *La Peinture aux XIXe et XXe siècles* (Paris: A. Picard, 1928), pp. 92–93 and 299. R. Giard, *Le Peintre Victor Mottez d'après sa correspondance (1809–1897)* (Lille: Librairie René Giard, 1934), p. 172. *1869–1958. Aufbruch zur modernen Kunst*, exh. cat. (Munich: Haus der Kunst, 1958), no. 49. C. Sterling and H. Adhémar, *Musée du Louvre. Peintures, École française, XIXe siècle* (Paris: RMN, 1959), vol. II, no. 962. *"Le Salon imaginaire", images des grandes expositions de la seconde moitié du XIXe siècle*, exh. cat. (Berlin: Kunstverein, 1968), no. 54. G. Ackerman et al., *Jean-Léon Gérôme (1824–1904)*, exh. cat. (Dayton: Dayton Art Institute, 1972; also Minneapolis: Minneapolis Institute of Arts, 1973, and Baltimore: The Walters Art Gallery, 1973), no. 1, pp. 30–31. Champfleury, *Le Réalisme*, texts selected and presented by G. and J. Lacambre (Paris: Hermann, 1973), pp. 130–131. H. Hoffmann, "Hahnenkampf in Athen," *Revue archéologique*, 1974, p. 208ff. *Le Musée du Luxembourg en 1874*, exh. cat. (Paris, Grand Palais, 1974), no. 93, p. 81. P. Angrand, "Œdipe enfant et le combat de coqs. J. F. Millet, Léon Gérôme et la critique en 1847," *Gazette des Beaux-Arts*, Nov. 1975, pp. 140–46. J.-L. Gérôme, *Notes autobiographiques* [1874], ed. G. Ackerman (Vesoul: S.A.L.S.A., 1981), p. 8. *J.-L. Gérôme*, exh. cat. (Vesoul: Musée Georges-Garret, 1991), no. 113, p. 101. M. Du Camp, *Souvenirs littéraires* [1892], ed. M. Chaillou (Paris: Balland, 1984), p. 55. H. Lafont-Couturier, *Gérôme* (Paris: Herscher, 1998), p. 17, 80. *Rêve et réalité. Collections du musée d'Orsay* (Kobe: City Museum of Art, 1999; also, Tokyo: National Museum of Western Art, 1999). G. Ackerman, *Jean-Léon Gérôme* (Courbevoie: ACR Édition, 2000), no. 14, pp. 212–13. H. Lafont-Couturier, *Gérôme and Goupil: Art and Enterprise*, exh. cat., trans. I. Ollivier (Bordeaux: Musée Goupil, 2000–1; also New York: Dahesh Museum of Art, 2001, and Pittsburgh: The Frick Art & Historical Center, 2001), p. 16, 21-22, 33-34, 40, 88, 92–94, 158, 166. *Gloria Victis! Victors and Vanquished in French Art*, exh. cat. (Copenhagen: Ny Carlsberg Glyptotek, 2000), no. 32, p. 101. *Le Temps de Degas*, exh. cat. (The Hague: Gemeentemuseum, 2002), pp. 30–31.

Cat. 11

STUDY FOR *THE COCK FIGHT*

–

ca. 1846
Black lead, stump drawing
Circular format, diam. 5 in.
Musée d'Orsay, Paris, conserved in the Département des Arts Graphiques, Musée du Louvre, inv. RF 15704

–

Bibliography: *J.-L. Gérôme*, exh. cat. (Vesoul: Musée Georges-Garret, 1981), p. 101.

Ill. 8. Hippolyte Flandrin (1809–1864), *Polites, Son of Priam, Observes the Movements of the Greeks towards Troy*, 1834, oil on canvas, 80 × 57 in., Musée d'Art Moderne, Saint-Étienne.

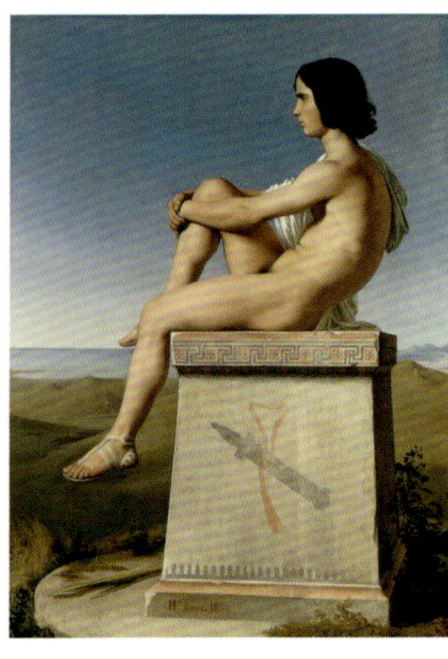

At the age of twenty-three, encouraged by Paul Delaroche, Gérôme made his debut[1] at the Salon with *The Cock Fight*. Although terribly positioned, "hung so high and so badly to hide it from the viewing eye,"[2] the work created a stir and launched the young artist's career, propelling him into the avant-garde of the *Néo-Grecs*.[3] Critics were fairly unanimous in their praise of the work, which made a decisive break with the dissonant diversity of the works exhibited at the last Salon of the July Monarchy, where the other attraction was Thomas Couture's *Romans of the Decadence*, which was intended as an artistic and political manifesto (ill. 4, p. 30). Gérôme skillfully chose a subject where, in a context in which Jacques-Louis David's heroic heritage refused to lie down and die, the novelty lay, above all, in the fact that nobody had "ever before depicted everyday Greece."[4] But the boldness of elevating this trivial genre scene, through its monumental format and dignity, to the lofty level of history painting, paid off. The work's intention was strictly Greek and not antique: "The day M. Gérôme exhibited his *Cock Fight* there was but one cry: Greek! He knows Greek! What gentleness!"[5] Cock fights were much esteemed in antiquity and were the subject of many representations[6] but, as Charles Baudelaire recalled for a nineteenth century audience, they were "naturally reminiscent of Manila or England."[7] It is mainly in the fifth and fourth centuries B.C. that cock fights were especially popular in Athens, where they took place every year in the theater of Dionysos.[8] Gérôme drew inspiration from various sources, brought together by the serious graft of the imagination: mosaics conserved in the national museum of Naples, frescoes from the House of the Vetii in Pompei—which he saw during his trip to Naples in 1843—or a relief published by Frédéric de Clarac.[9] Another source of inspiration was the painting of Attic vases from the collections then available, particularly for the boy's posture (ill. 10), even if the attractive study of the motif in isolation is almost evocative of the Italian Renaissance (cat. 11). The composition is monumental and plays brilliantly on the conventional contrast between the pallor of the girl, placed almost in the center of the composition and wreathed in citrus colors, and the tanned body of her companion. Added to this is the contrast between the dreamy, idealized face of the girl and the verism of the boy goading the cock, who has a whiff of the modern model about him. Against this insouciance of adolescence and these bodies set beneath a radiant sky is opposed the cruelty of the cocks' pitiless battle, depicted in a particularly realistic way—Gérôme comes close here to the sculptor Emmanuel Fremiet, with whom he often went to draw in the Jardin des Plantes. The opposition is reinforced by a workshop "gimmick," which always works: the bright red of the combs is set off against the white drapery behind. Gérôme's debt to Jean-Auguste-Dominique Ingres and to his master Delaroche is indeed particularly

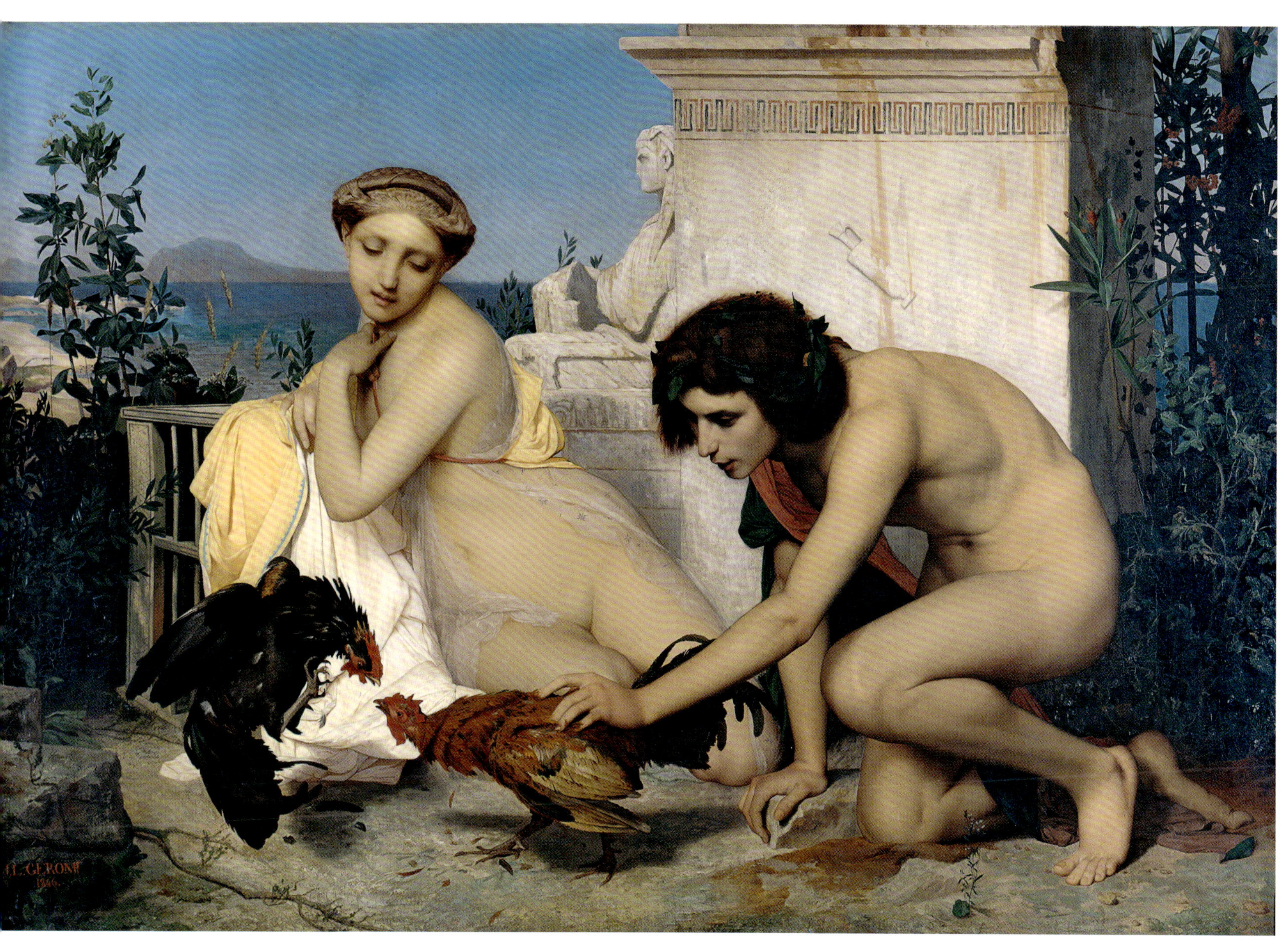
GEROME

Ill. 9. Jules Levasseur (1823–after 1878) after Jean-Louis Hamon (1821–1874), *My Sister is not at Home*, 1856, engraving, 11 ¼ × 16 ¾ in., Musée Goupil, Bordeaux, inv. 93.1.2.1029.

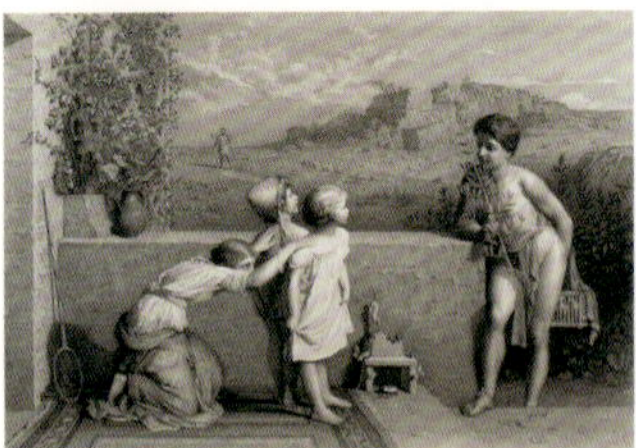

Ill. 10. Anonymous, *Checkers players in front of Troy* (detail), in Eduard Gerhard, *Auserlesene Vasenbilder, Hauptsächlich Etruskischen Fundorts* (Berlin: Reimer, 1847), vol. 3, "Heroenbilder," pl. CXCV–CXCVI, Bibliothèque Centrale des Musées Nationaux, Musée du Louvre, Paris.

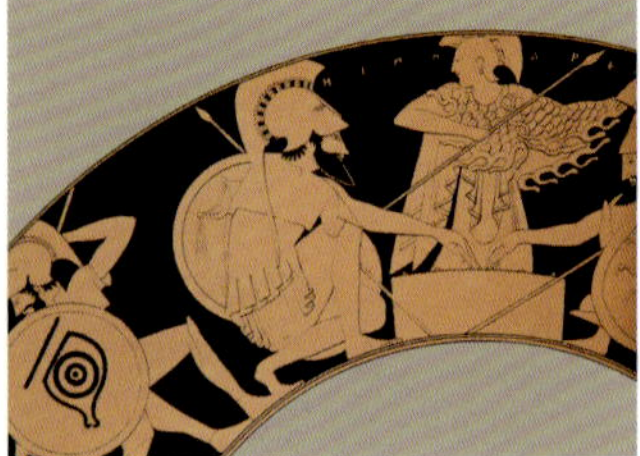

Ill. 11. Alexandre Falguière (1831–1900), *Winner of the Cock Fight*, 1864, bronze, 69 × 43 × 32 in., Musée d'Orsay, Paris, inv. RF 144.

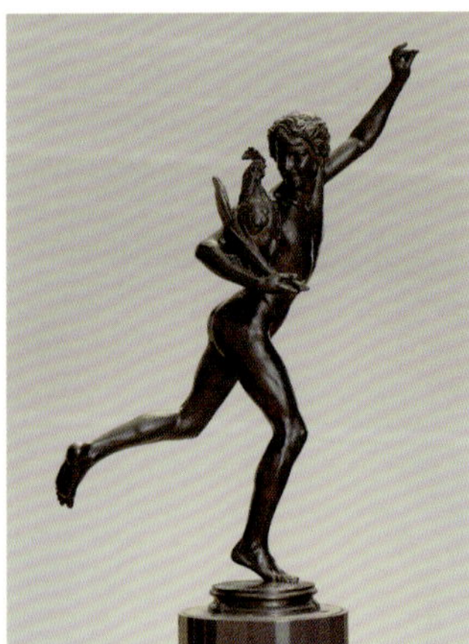

Ill. 12. Maison Christofle, *Cock Fight*, 1873, encrusted and engraved bronze, gold, silver, and red patina, 3 ½ × 17 × 8 in., Musée d'Orsay, Paris, inv. OAO 1693.

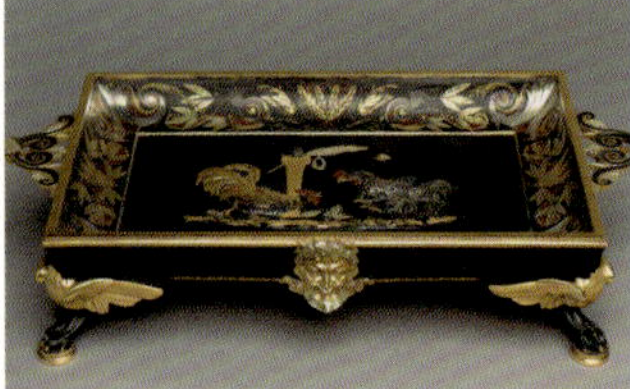

noticeable in this formative work, in which rigorous lines already provide a confident structure for his command of colors, without archaistic rigidity. But the implementation of the setting, scholarly recreated, belongs only to Gérôme, and demonstrates an ease in setting scenes, that he cultivated throughout his career. Another version of *The Cock Fight* is in the Chrysler Museum of Art in Norfolk, Virginia.

The adolescents stand out against the white base of a ruined marble, a hybrid monument that does not really correspond to any antique type—a misinterpretation of a tombstone and a lamp base maybe—decorated with two friezes of carefully tempered polychromy: one figurative, beneath the statue, the other geometric, beneath the ledge of the pedestal. This detail shows that great attention has been paid to contemporary debates about the polychromy of antique sculpture and architecture.[10] The solid section of the base is decorated with an inclined *lekythos*[11] in bas-relief, which seems to be suspended mid-air, a detail that Gérôme probably borrowed from a vase motif rather than a tombstone. An archaic, vandalized sculpture of a feminine figure sitting on a throne—which Théophile Gautier mistook for a sphinx—evokes representations of the oriental goddess Cybele; the almost illegible mass on her knees could thus correspond to the remains of a lion, a traditional accessory in the iconography of this divinity.[12] The learned "accessorization" of an academic nude set in a scene supposed to show a faraway past would become one of Gérôme's hallmarks (cat. 45), and it was for this that Baudelaire reproached the artist ten years later, calling him an "an artist who substitutes the entertainment provided by a page of erudition for the pleasure of pure painting."[13] The whole composition recalls in a more complex manner *Polites, Son of Priam* by Hippolyte Flandrin (ill. 8). But, unlike his elder, Gérôme encloses the scene with Mediterranean vegetation reproduced with great attention to truth and refinement: the oleanders, olive trees, and grass all recall the exoticism of the Mediterranean countryside in the Gulf of Naples; even the mountains slicing the horizon are reminiscent of the silhouette of the island of Capri or the promontory of Sorrento. The young girl is leaning listlessly on the only accessory of the composition, the cocks' cage, decorated with intentionally vernacular geometric figures. The bird cage becomes a recurrent motif, with a cult-like status, which Gérôme placed in a great number of paintings, whatever their inspiration (cat. 167, ill. 150, p. 304), throughout his career. Critics, both conservative and avant-garde, were overwhelmingly favorable. While Étienne-Jean Delécluze considered that the coloring was "hopeless," he still praised the "subtlety of the drawing and the modeling, and a certain aroma of Greek beauty that justifies the choice of subject."[14] Théophile Thoré rejoiced in the emergence of a young talent "who displays a certain distinction of style even though he does come from M. Delaroche's studio."[15] Gustave Planche, after severely discrediting Thomas Couture, pardoned Gérôme for appropriating the history painting format.[16] The world of art was also enthusiastic: if Maxime Du Camp is to be believed, "budding daubers ran from Diaz to Isabey, from Isabey to Delacroix, from Delacroix to Couture, and from Couture to Gérôme shouting: 'David is dead, long live color!',"[17] and the painter Victor Mottez considered Gérôme to be the "pearl of the Salon. Everything else, apart from Corot's landscapes, are not worth mentioning."[18] Gérôme had tried to tempt fate, thanks to Delaroche, by inviting the director of the Louvre to come and see the work before the exhibition.[19] But, indeed Théophile Gautier was the true architect of the painting's success, lauding it in articles in *La Presse* and *L'Artiste*: "Great talent and resources are required to elevate such a minor scene to the rank of a noble composition that no master would disown."[20] Gautier went into raptures over the fowl, "epic, Olympian birds, such as Phidias might have sculpted at the feet of the cruel god Ares."[21] Champfleury saw the work as a materialization of the artist's inconsistency: to him, the figures were simply "children from Etruscan vases, marble children,"[22] while the roguish vitality of the animals was too close to life: he imagined purchasing such birds at the market.[23] To Gautier, strangely, the painting was destined "to ornament the banquet hall of a king,"[24] but it was only purchased by the State in 1873, after belonging to Anatole Laborie, owner of the *Journal des débats*. The work's good fortune was undeniable, and it inspired sculptors[25] and painters, with varying degrees of success, up to the 1880s (ill. 11, 12). As the newly promoted leader of the *Néo-Grecs*—or neo-Pompeians (ill. 9), for he never gave a second thought about mixing his sources—Gérôme here shows the promise of his innovative insight, which would soon go astray, to the great displeasure of some: Edmond About remarked in 1855 that "M. Gérôme was Greek at the first attempt, because he was simple. But it is difficult to stay simple... Success has led M. Gérôme far from the path that he himself laid, and along which his friends behind him followed... Farewell the ephebes crouching on their heels."[26] **É. P.**

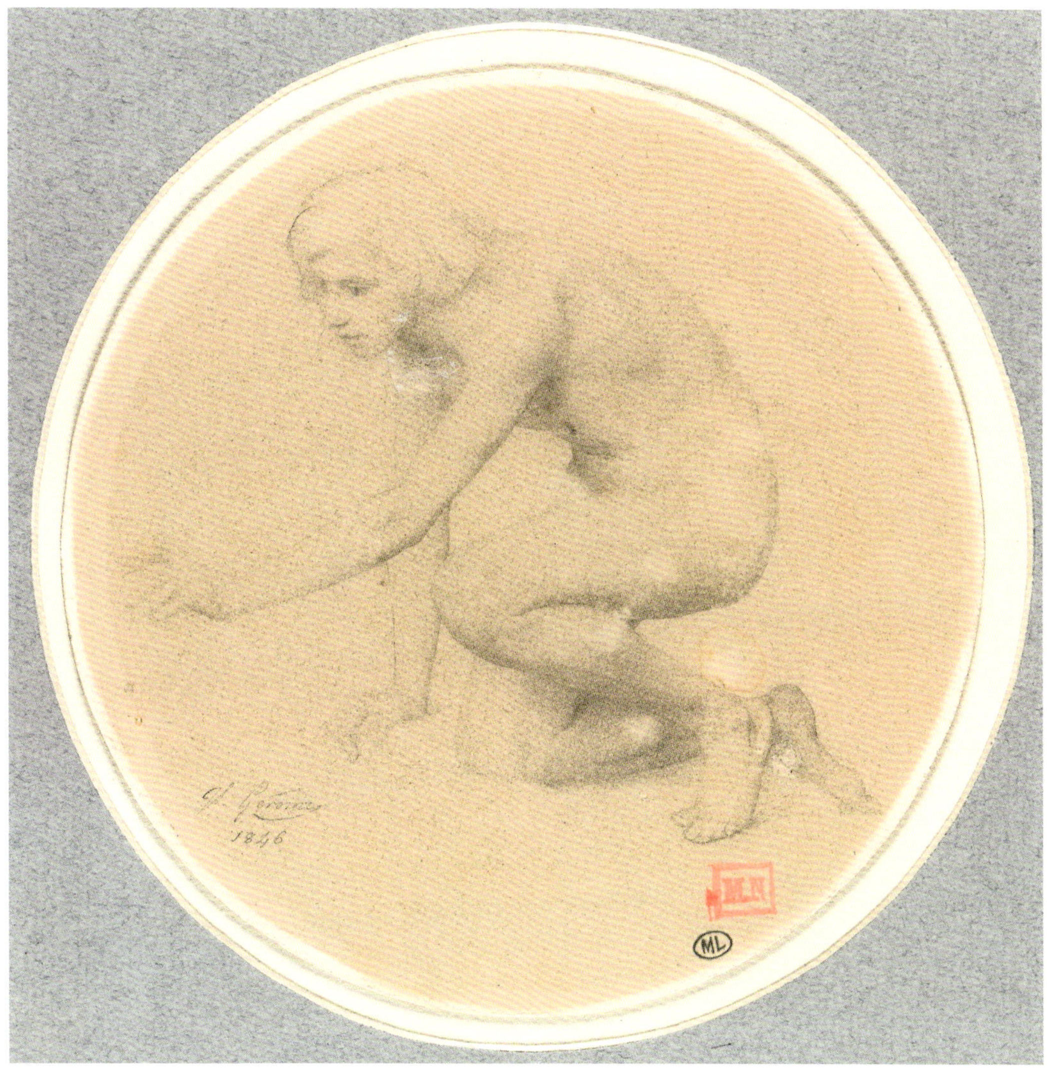

1. J.-L. Gérôme, *Notes autobiographiques* [1874], ed. G. Ackerman (Vesoul: S.A.L.S.A., 1981), p. 8. **2.** M. Du Camp, "En Bretagne," in *Souvenirs littéraires* [1882–83], (Paris: Balland, 1984), p. 55. **3.** Gérôme stated thirty years later: "certainly an overblown success of which no one was more surprised than the author himself" (J.-L. Gérôme [1874] (as in n. 1), p. 8). **4.** Champfleury, "Le combat de coqs," in *Le Réalisme*, texts selected and presented by G. and J. Lacambre (Paris: Hermann, 1973), p. 130. **5.** E. About, *Voyage à travers l'exposition des Beaux-Arts* (Paris: Hachette, 1855), vol. IV, p. 153. **6.** See P. Bruneau, "Le motif des coqs affrontés dans l'imagerie antique," *Bulletin de correspondance hellénique*, vol. 89, no. 1 (1965), pp. 90–121. **7.** C. Baudelaire, "Salon de 1859," in *Écrits esthétiques* (Paris: Union générale d'édition, 1986), p. 314. L. Clément de Ris also remarked that "the two cocks [are] painted and drawn to satisfy the finest of London's connoisseurs" ("Revue de Paris," *L'Artiste*, 1874, p. 123). **8.** The animal held a certain erotic connotation: ephebes would receive both cocks and hares as gifts from their lovers. **9.** "Génies des combats de coqs no. 392," in F. de Clarac, *Musée des sculptures antiques et modernes* (Paris: Imprimerie Royale, 1826–41), pl. 200, no. 225. If he wasn't inspired by a bas-relief of the throne of the priest of Dionysos at the Athens theater, discovered in 1862 in Beulé, Gérôme's intuition for the position of his ephebe is particularly remarkable; see "Trône du prêtre de Dionysos au théâtre d'Athènes: Face extérieure de l'accoudoir gauche, un génie ailé (Agôn) met aux prises deux coqs," in S. Rison, "Le Siège du prêtre de Dionysos…", *Mélanges Holleaux* (Paris: Picard, 1913). **10.** See my essay in this volume (p.291). **11.** Small vase containing perfumed oils, used by athletes or placed on tombs and as funerary offerings. **12.** Thanks to Ludovic Laugier, scientific officer in the Department of Greek, Etruscan and Roman Antiquities at the Musée du Louvre, for his shrewd advice. **13.** C. Baudelaire 1859 (as in n. 7), p. 314. **14.** É.-J. Delécluze, "Salon de 1847 (3e article)," *Le Journal des débats*, Apr. 24, 1847, p. 2. **15.** T. Thoré, "Salon de 1847," in *Salons de T. Thoré* (Paris: Librairie Internationale, 1868), p. 445. **16.** G. Planche, "Le Salon de 1847. La Peinture," *Revue des Deux Mondes*, vol. XVIII (Apr. 1, 1847), p. 363. **17.** M. Du Camp 1984 (as in n. 2), p. 55. **18.** V. Mottez, Apr. 3, 1847, cited by R. Giard, *Le Peintre Victor Mottez* **19.** G. Ackerman et al., *Jean-Léon Gérôme (1824–1904)*, exh. cat. (Dayton: Dayton Art Institute, 1972; also Minneapolis: Minneapolis Institute of Arts, 1973, and Baltimore: The Walters Art Gallery, 1973), p. 30. **20.** T. Gautier, "Exposition de 1847," *La Presse*, March 31, 1847, p. 1. **21.** T. Gautier, "Beaux-Arts. *Jeunes Grecs faisant battre des coqs*," *L'Artiste*, July 4, 1847, p. 221. **22.** Champfleury 1973 (as in n. 4), p. 130. **23.** Ibid. **24.** T. Gautier 1847 (as in n. 21), p. 221. **25.** Charles Lenoir, *Jeune faune faisant battre des coqs*, 1875, marble, place Alzéary-de-Malausséna, Nice. **26.** E. About 1855 (as in n. 5), p. 155.

Cat. 12

SAINT VINCENT DE PAUL

–

1847
Oil on canvas
61 3/8 × 46 1/2 in.
Signed and dated above the arch:
J.L. GEROME MDCCCXLVII
Musée Georges-Garret, Vesoul, inv. 984.6.1

–

Provenance: Painted for the Sisters of Saint Vincent de Paul, Vesoul. Sold during the legal separation of Church and State in 1905. Private collection, 1905. Gift of the association Les Amis du Musée et de la Bibliothèque, 1984 (purchased with the help of the FRAM). Purchased by the Musée Georges-Garret from a Belgian collector in 1983.

–

Bibliography: G. Ackerman, *Jean-Léon Gérôme* (Courbevoie: ACR Edition, 2000), no. 16.

Despite its size and ambitiousness, *Saint Vincent de Paul* is one of the least-known works of Gérôme's youth. Commissioned from him by the congregation of the Sisters of Saint Vincent de Paul in his hometown of Vesoul in 1847, it was sold to a private collector when the French state legally separated from the Catholic Church in 1905, after Gérôme's death. The painting was therefore never reproduced by Goupil in either photographic or engraved form, making its ultimate acquisition by the Musée Georges-Garret in Vesoul all the more important. Paul Delaroche's influence is particularly noticeable here, both in the modeling of the figures and the historical handling of the scene (ill. 13 and 14).

By placing Saint Vincent de Paul, canonized in 1737, in the center of the canvas, Gérôme stressed the saint's work among the poor and destitute; the nuns at his side are an allusion to the ones who commissioned this painting. The artist endowed all the figures with a hieratic power, probably designed to stir admiration among the faithful for this holy man and his disciples. Although the cult of Saint Vincent de Paul was already a venerable one, Louis XIII having promoted it on his deathbed, it saw a revival in the nineteenth century. In 1833 Frédéric Ozanam founded the Conference of Charity to aid the poorest; a few years later it became known as the Society of Saint Vincent de Paul. The church of St.-Vincent-de-Paul in Paris, commissioned toward the end of the Bourbon Restoration from architect Jakob Ignaz Hittorff, was built on the site of the Lazarist mission where the saint had officiated. Completed in 1844, it aimed to reflect the architect's research into Greek polychromy at the time when Gérôme was also taking an interest in this subject. **D. F.-R.**

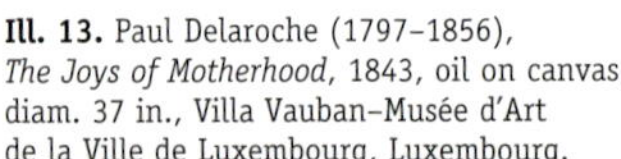

Ill. 13. Paul Delaroche (1797–1856), *The Joys of Motherhood*, 1843, oil on canvas, diam. 37 in., Villa Vauban–Musée d'Art de la Ville de Luxembourg, Luxembourg.

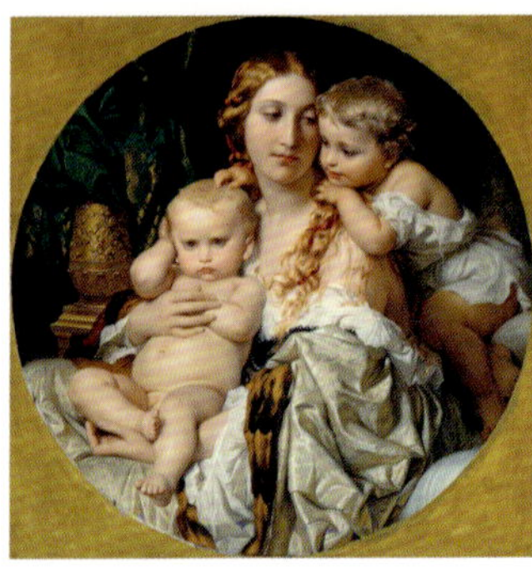

Ill. 14. Paul Delaroche (1797–1856), *The Childhood of Pico della Mirandola*, 1842, oil on canvas, 45 1/2 × 30 in., Musée des Beaux-Arts, Nantes, inv. 902.

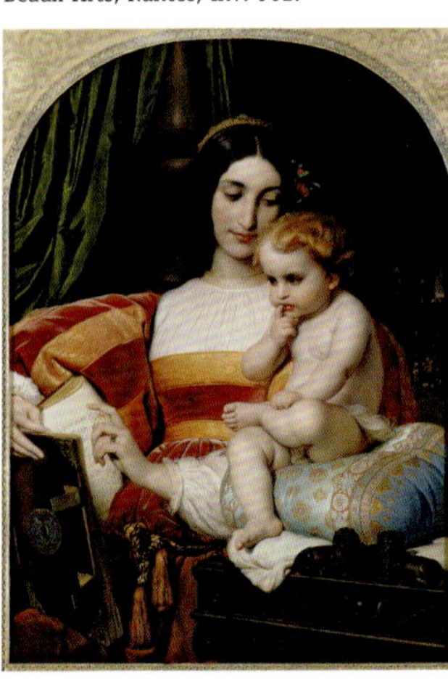

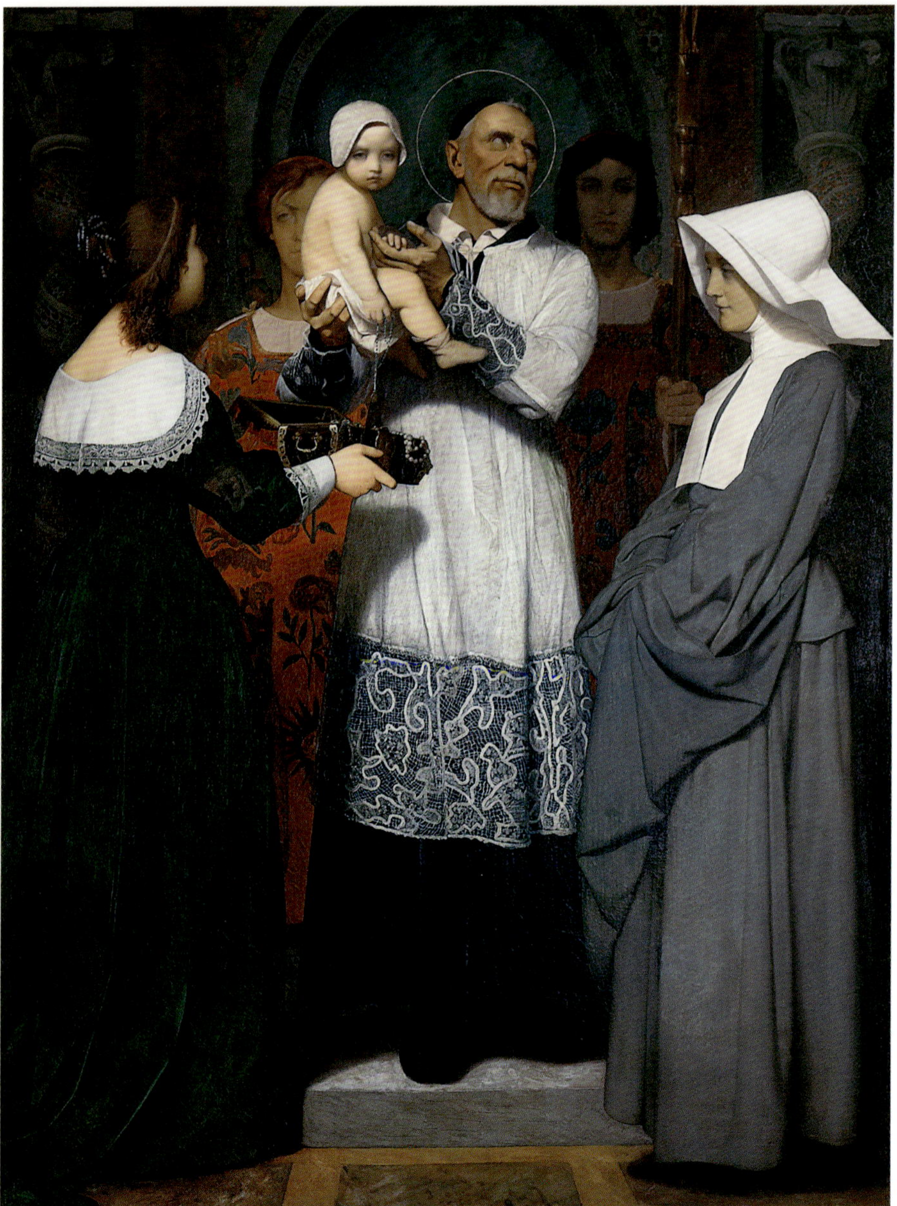

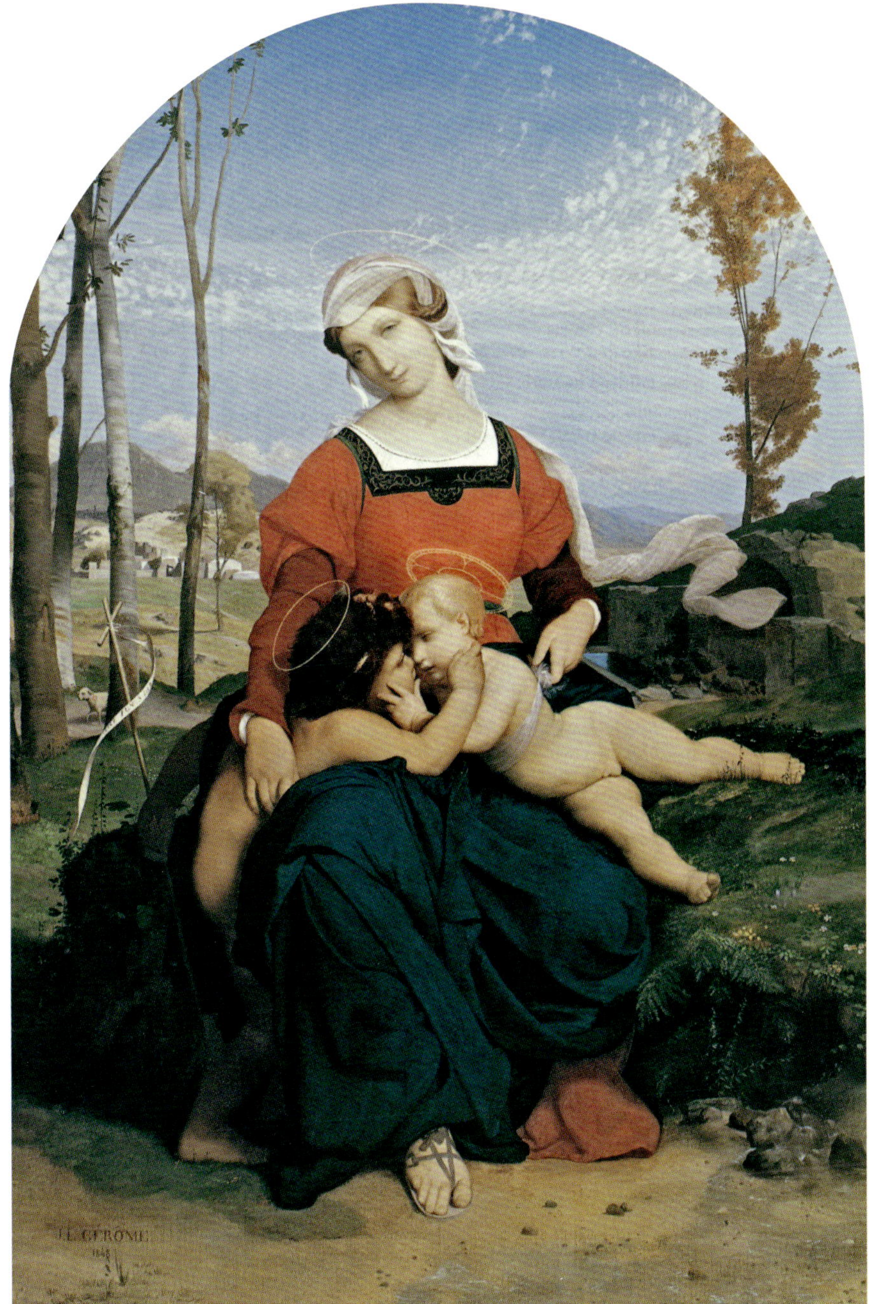

Cat. 13

THE VIRGIN, THE INFANT JESUS, AND SAINT JOHN

1848
Oil on canvas
42 ½ × 29 ½ in.
Signed and dated lower left:
J.L. GEROME/1848
Private collection

Provenance: Tedesco Frères, Paris. John Levy Gallery, American Art Association sale, Apr. 27, 1933, lot 12. Plaza Curiosity Shop. Hammer Galleries, Inc., New York, 1966. Dr. Daniel Ivancho, Pittsburgh. Sotheby's, New York, Oct. 31, 1985, lot 46. Sotheby's, New York, Oct. 12, 1994, sale 6603, lot 81.

Exhibition History: Salon of 1848, no. 1933.

Bibliography: Recueil. Œuvres de Jean-Léon Gérôme, BNF Estampes, vol. XXVII, no. 8. L. Clément de Ris, *L'Artiste*, 5th ser., vol. 1, 1848, pp. 59–60. T. Gautier, *La Presse*, Apr. 27, 1848. F. de Lagenevais, *Revue des Deux Mondes*, 2nd qtr. 1848, pp. 288–89. F. Pillet, *Le Moniteur universel*, Apr. 11, 1848, p. 812. *Gazette des Beaux-Arts*, vol. 5 (1860), pp. 328–30. *Le Moniteur officiel*, Mar. 21, 1860. F. F. Hering, *Gérôme. The Life and Works of Jean-Léon Gérôme* (New York: Cassell, 1892), p. 57. *J.-L. Gérôme*, exh. cat. (Vesoul: Musée Georges-Garret, 1981), p. 111. *Raphaël et l'art français* (Paris: Galeries Nationales du Grand Palais, 1983–84), repr. p. 275. G. Ackerman, *Jean-Léon Gérôme* (Courbevoie: ACR Édition, 2000), no. 20.

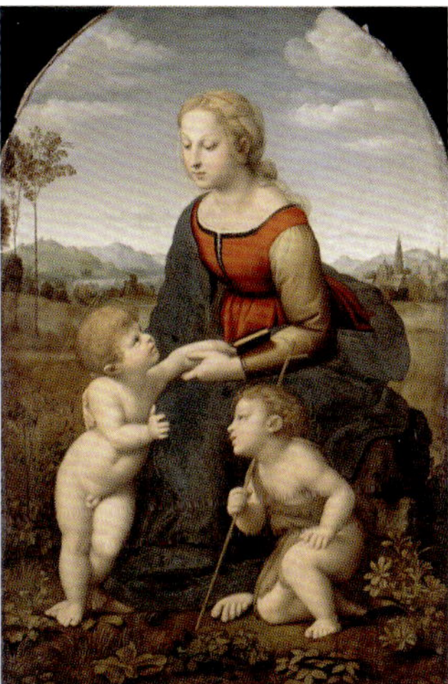

Ill. 15. Raphael (Raffaello Santi, 1483–1520), *Madonna and Child with Saint John the Baptist*, also known as *La Belle Jardinière*, 1507–8, oil on panel, 48 × 31 ½ in., Musée du Louvre, Paris, inv. 602.

This work was one of Gérôme's three entries to the Salon of 1848, together with *Anacreon* (cat. 16) and the *Portrait of Armand Gérôme* (cat. 34). In this eclectic set of works the painter adapted his stylistic approach to each of the genres he was working in: a variation on Jean-Auguste-Dominique Ingres for the portrait, a historically evocative mode inspired by Paul Delaroche for *Saint Vincent de Paul* (cat. 12), and Raphaelism imbued with primitivism for the painting under consideration here. A variant on Raphael's *La Belle Jardinière* (ill. 15), this classically triangular composition was preceded by a very thorough preparatory drawing with softer lines than the painting itself.[1] It is notable that, instead of emphasizing the traditional symbol of redemption, Gérôme chose to focus on Saint John kissing the Infant Jesus. More like cherubs than saviors, these two children will reappear a few years later with the same lively sense of oneness in a work by William Bouguereau (*The Virgin, the Infant Jesus, and Saint John*, 1853, Ponce, Museo de Arte). However, the latter's orthodox academicism is quite unlike the young Gérôme's attempt to combine the classical and the archaic, the strangeness of which was noted by Théophile Gautier: "Although he is a pagan from Pompeii, Gérôme also has an understanding of Christian art. His 'Saint John Kissing the Infant Jesus on the Lap of the Virgin' could have been painted by Overbeck, were it not for the fact that Overbeck does not have that deep understanding of drawing, and that exquisite taste hidden behind the naïvety of the Gothic pastiche. Gérôme is heading for Calvary, but his route takes him via Athens."[2] **L. C.**

1. *Impressionist and 20th Century, Works on Paper*, Londres, Christie's, 29 juin 2000, n° 503. **2.** T. Gautier, « Salon de 1848 », *La Presse*, 27 avril 1848, p. 1.

Cat. 14
Gustave Le Gray (1820–1884)

GROUP OF MEN AND A WOMAN SEATED IN A DOORWAY

–
1848
Salt print
4 ¼ × 5 ½ in.
Signed and dated lower right in black ink: *Gustave Le Gray 1848*
Musée d'Orsay, Paris, inv. PHO 2003 4 40
–
Provenance: Aimé Morot collection. Since 1920 in the family of latest seller. Bought by the Musées Nationaux (committee decision of Apr. 24, 2003, approved by board on Apr. 30, 2003), assigned to the Musée d'Orsay by decision taken on May 12, 2003.

Cat. 15
Gustave Le Gray

SIX MEN STANDING BEHIND A SCREEN IN A COURTYARD

–
1848
Salt print
6 ½ × 8 in.
Musée d'Orsay, Paris, inv. PHO 2003 4 41
–
Provenance: Aimé Morot collection. Since 1920 in the family of latest seller. Bought by the Musées Nationaux (committee decision of Apr. 24, 2003, approved by board on Apr. 30, 2003), assigned to the Musée d'Orsay by decision taken on May 12, 2003.

In 2003 the Musée d'Orsay acquired a collection of manuscripts and photographs that had belonged to Jean-Léon Gérôme and his son-in-law, Aimé Morot. The set of photographs amounts to roughly sixty prints dating from the 1850s to the early twentieth century. These pictures shed light on the rich and complex relationship between Gérôme's art and photography.

Gérôme showed an early interest in the new invention. As a young artist training in Paul Delaroche's studio in the early 1840s, he met several painters who later became talented photographers, notably Henri Le Secq, Charles Nègre, and Gustave Le Gray. Gérôme had a particularly faithful and fruitful friendship with Le Gray. In 1848 Le Gray make a daguerreotype of the painting that Gérôme exhibited at that year's Salon, *Anacreon* (cat. 16 and 19). The photographs acquired by the Musée d'Orsay include two by Le Gray, taken in 1848. He exhibited one of them at the exhibition of the Société Française de Photographie in 1857, thereby indicating its importance in Le Gray's eyes. The catalogue referred to "a positive from a collodion paper negative, made in 1848 and showing M. Gérôme's studio."[1] Both photographs were taken at Le Chalet, the collective studio on rue de Fleurus in the Luxembourg neighborhood of Paris, where Gérôme worked with other young artists who had trained under Paul Delaroche and Charles Gleyre, notably Jean-Louis Hamon. The pictures convey an atmosphere of lively friendship and camaraderie among the young men. Gérôme is seen in the first one (cat. 14), seated at the far right of the doorway. Slim and haughty, he appears here like the determined young man that he was, already enjoying a reputation among critics and academic institutions despite his youth.

These pictures are interesting in more ways than one. They are among Le Gray's earliest paper photographs, made barely one year after Louis-Désiré Blanquart-Évrard adapted the technique invented by William Henry Fox Talbot for obtaining multiple positives from a paper negative. They thereby represent something of a feat: despite the lengthy exposure time, Le Gray managed to produce two group portraits in which the lively, jokey mood of the sitters is fully expressed. These two photographs also underscore Gérôme's close friendship with Le Gray at that time, thereby confirming Gérôme's awareness of photographic methods and uses with respect to his painting. Finally, these tributes to an artist and his peers do not merely embody an artistic tradition dating from the Renaissance but also bring new life to the convention through the casual merriment of the sitters. **D. F.-R.**

1. *Catalogue de la deuxième exposition annuelle des œuvres des artistes et amateurs français et étrangers* (Paris: Société Française de Photographie), 1857, p. 2.

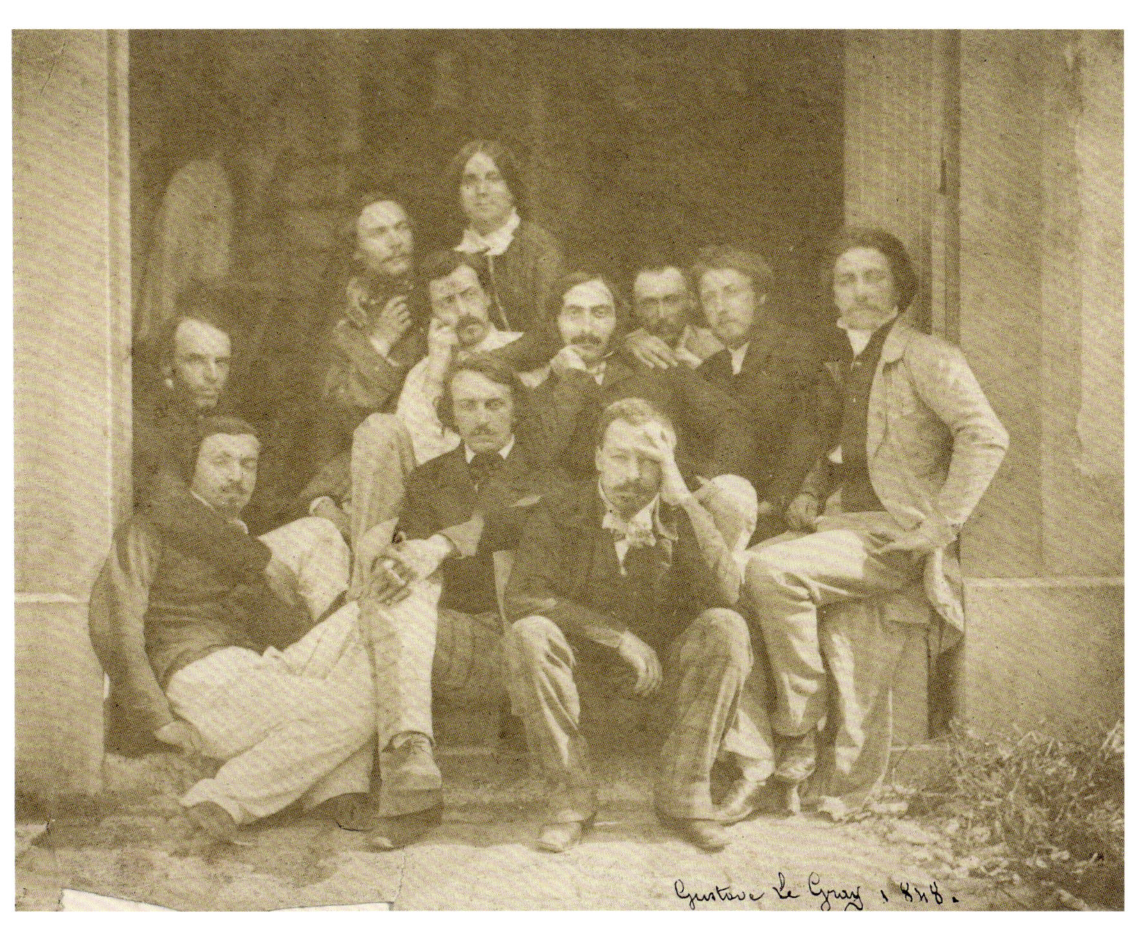
Gustave le Gray, 1848.

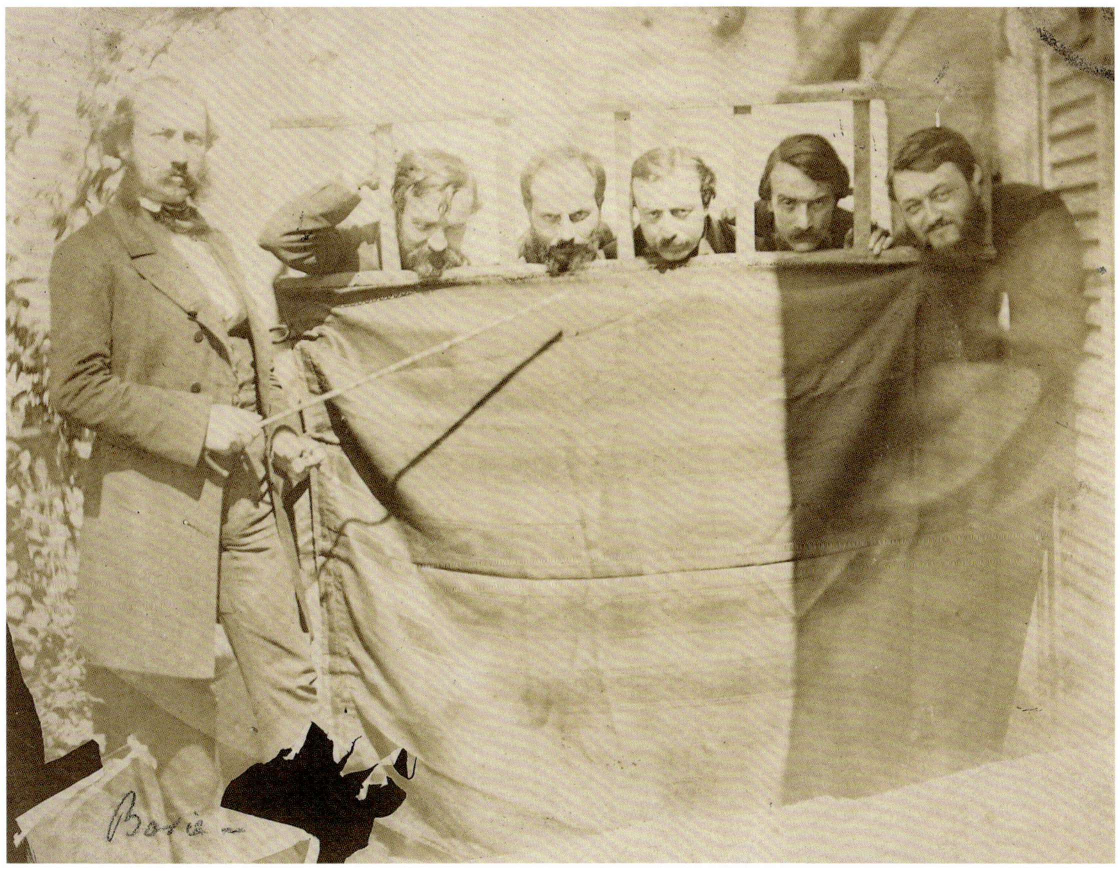

Cat. 16

ANACREON

-

1848
Oil on canvas
53 ½ × 83 ⅛ in.
Signed and dated upper left:
J.L. GEROME 1848
Musée des Augustins, Toulouse,
inv. 2004.1.102

-

Provenance: Purchased by the State in 1848, sent to the Musée de Toulouse.

-

Exhibition History: Salon de 1848, Paris.

-

Bibliography: L. Clément de Ris, "Salon de 1848. Eugène Delacroix, Duveau, Diaz, Gérôme, Lehmann, Fernand Boissard," *L'Artiste*, 5th ser., vol. 1 (1848), pp. 59–60. T. Gautier, "Salon de 1848," *La Presse*, Apr. 27, 1848. F. de Lagenevais, *Revue des Deux Mondes*, vol. XXII, 2nd qtr. 1848, pp. 288–89. F. Pillet, *Le Moniteur officiel*, Apr. 1848, p. 812. T. J. Clark, *The Absolute Bourgeois* (London: Thames & Hudson, 1973), p. 70, also p. 365ff. *J.-L. Gérôme*, exh. cat. (Vesoul: Musée Georges-Garret, 1981), p. 114, no. 114. *La Tradition et l'innovation dans l'art français par les peintres des Salons*, exh. cat. (Fukuoka: Municipal Museum, 1989), no. 85. T. J. Clark, "L'art de la République," in *Le Bourgeois absolu: les artistes et la politique en France de 1848 à 1851* (Paris: Art Édition, 1992), pp. 106–9. S. Boyer, *Les Années romantiques. La peinture française de 1815 à 1850*, exh. cat. (Nantes: Musée des Beaux-Arts, 1995–96; also Paris: Galeries Nationales du Grand Palais, 1996, and Piacenza: Palazzo Gotico, 1996), no. 100, pp. 390–91. G. Ackerman, *Jean-Léon Gérôme* (Courbevoie: ACR Édition, 2000), no. 19. S. Harent and C. Stoullig, *Dessins de Jean-Léon Gérôme: la collection du musée des Beaux-Arts de Nancy*, exh. cat. (Nancy: Musée des Beaux-Arts, 2009), pp. 42-44.

Cat. 17

THREE STUDIES OF FEMALE NUDES, ONE BEING A STUDY FOR *BACCHANTE AND INFANT*

-

ca. 1892
Pencil on beige paper
13 ¾ × 8 ¾ in.
Signed bottom center: *JL. Gérôme*
Private collection, Paris

-

Bibliography: G. Ackerman, *Jean-Léon Gérôme* (Courbevoie: ACR Édition, 2000), no. S 25, p. 391.

Cat. 18

GROUP DANCING IN HONOR OF BACCHUS

-

1848 (?)
Ink and pencil on paper
8 ¾ × 12 ⅝ in.
Monogramm, lower right: *JLG*
Musée Georges-Garret, Vesoul,
inv. 984.7.7

-

Provenance: Purchased from Galerie Lemaire, 1983.

-

Bibliography: *J.-L. Gérôme*, exh. cat. (Vesoul: Musée Georges-Garret, 1981), no. 11, p. 41. S. Harent and C. Stoullig, *Dessins de Jean-Léon Gérôme: la collection du musée des Beaux-Arts de Nancy*, exh. cat. (Nancy: Musée des Beaux-Arts, 2009), p. 16.

Ill. 16. Anonymous, *Group of Bacchic gods* (detail), in Eduard Gerhard, *Auserlesene Vasenbilder, Hauptsächlich Etruskischen Fundorts* (Berlin: Reimer, 1840), vol. 1, "Götterbilder," pl. XXIV, engraving, Bibliothèque Centrale des Musées Nationaux, Musée du Louvre, Paris.

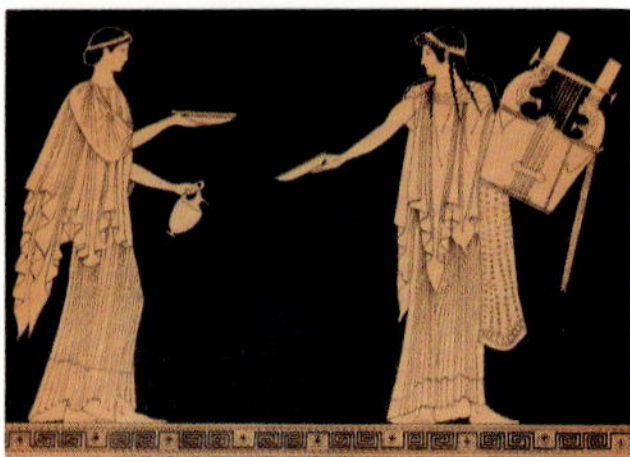

At the age of twenty-four, and following on from the success of *The Cock Fight* (cat. 10), Gérôme exhibited *Anacreon* at the Salon of 1848 alongside *The Virgin, the Infant Jesus, and Saint John* (cat. 13). It was an ambitious work, once more in the history painting format, but this time there could be no suspicion of vulgarity in the subject. The fifth century B.C. Greek poet, Anacreon, from the town of Teos in Ionia, was one of the first famous lyrical poets of Greece, who was invited to the courts of the tyrants, Polycrates of Samos and then Hipparchus of Athens. He invented a special form of versification, the iambic dimeter, and is the famed author of the *Odes*, a eulogy to wine, love, and nature, a Dionysiac work of reverie and melancholy. Anacreontic themes, beyond poetry, had long been popular in Europe, in both the plastic and lyric arts.[1] Having first been translated into French in the sixteenth century,[2] the first half of the nineteenth century in France witnessed a great many versions, including the one published in 1825 by Anne-Louis Girodet himself and illustrated by his own works in an edition revised by Pierre-Alexandre Coupin.[3] Gérôme innovated by choosing a fairly rare theme, illustrated with verve and liberty, but this *Néo-Grec* work, combining different sources of inspiration—antique, "Nazarene," and Venetian, as well as elements of Ingres and even Poussin (ill. 19)—met with mixed reviews. The work however presents a decisive stage in the consolidation of the French *Néo-Grec* aesthetic in its early days, where archaism was posited practically as a manifesto, with bold and refined coloring, deploying rare themes. A pastoral of a distinctly retrospective modernity, *Anacreon* was an eclectic painting, which broke less with tradition than its detractors would have liked to claim. Five years earlier, *Evening* or *Lost Illusions* (ill. 109, p. 231) by Charles Gleyre, Gérôme's second teacher, in a much less melancholy way, had opened up the way to this "reaction of ideas"[4] which, as an alternative to the latest forms of Romanticism, proposed a colder form of antique historicism. In Gérôme's *Anacreon*, as in *The Cock Fight*, the "archaeologically correct" references are more isolated than in *A Greek Interior* (cat. 23), painted two years later, and have been the subject of well-documented reinterpretation: the decoration of the two *lekythoi* at the flautist's feet—the second is hidden by her leg—skillfully introduces Dionysiac iconography from red-figure vases

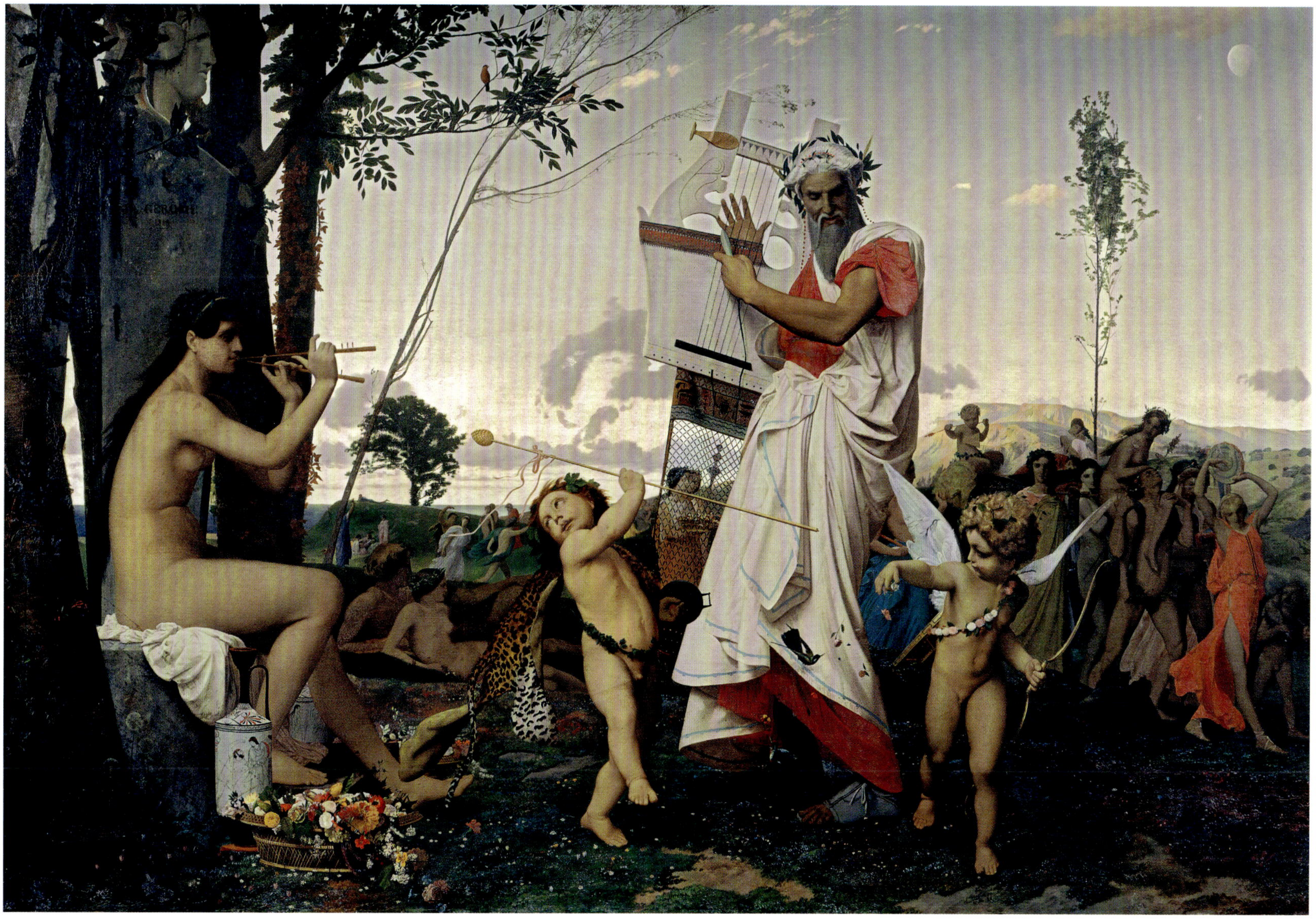

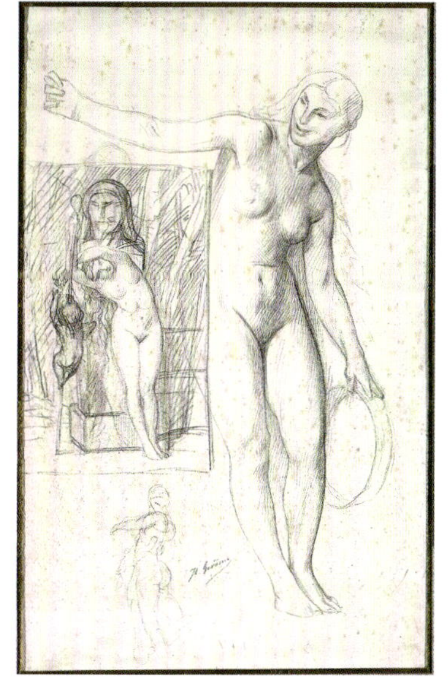

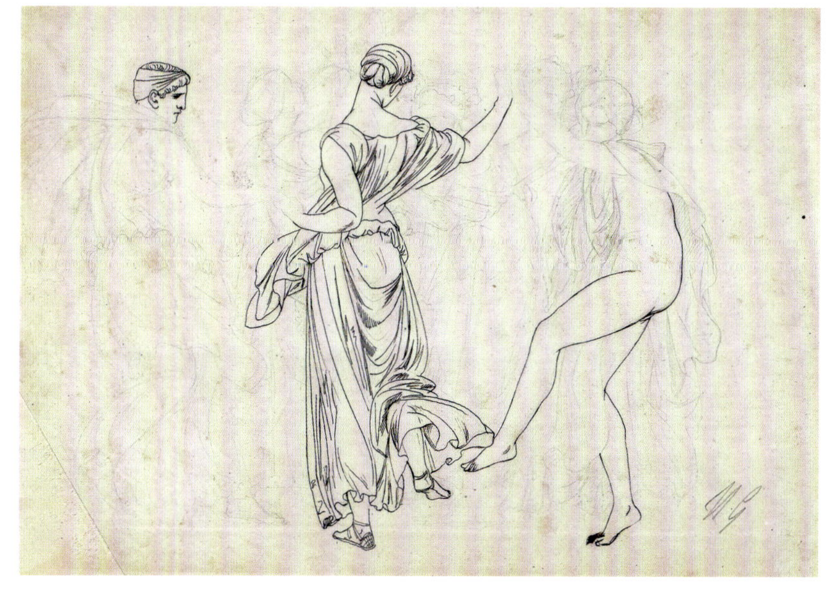

Ill. 17. *Jupiter Trophonius*, in F. de Clarac, *Musée de sculpture antique et moderne*, 1826–41, pl. 1086, engraving, Département des Antiquités grecques, étrusques et romaines, Musée du Louvre, Paris.

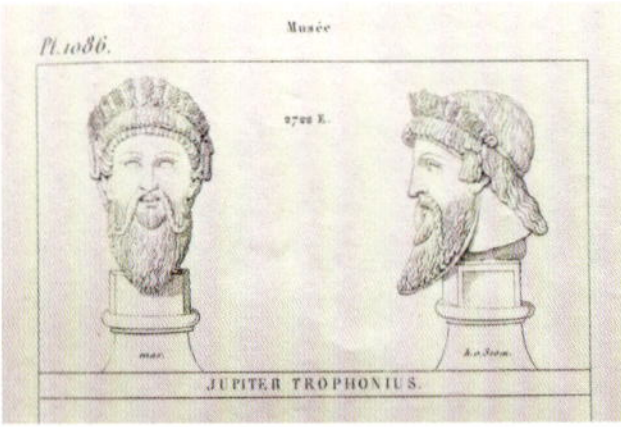

Ill. 18. Émile Hébert (1828–1893), Servant company, Barbedienne foundry, table in Néo-Grec style, 1878, ebony, black-varnished wood, gilt patinated bronze, flowered Saint-Jean marble, 29 × 43 × 26 in., Musée d'Orsay, Paris, inv. OAO 1389.

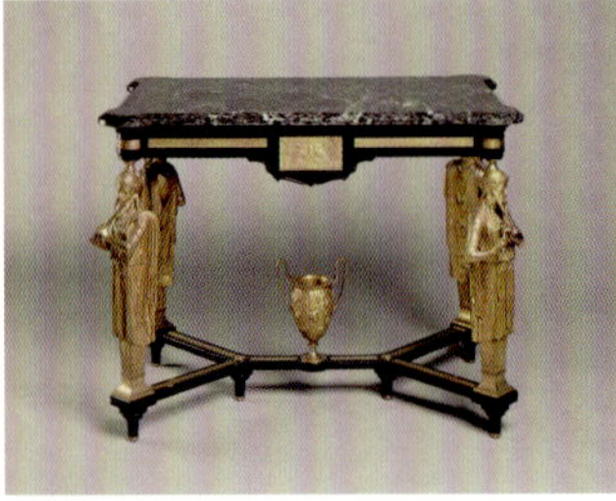

Ill. 19. Nicolas Poussin (1594–1665), *The Triumph of Flora* (detail), 1627, oil on canvas, 55 × 94 in. Musée du Louvre, Paris, inv. 7298.

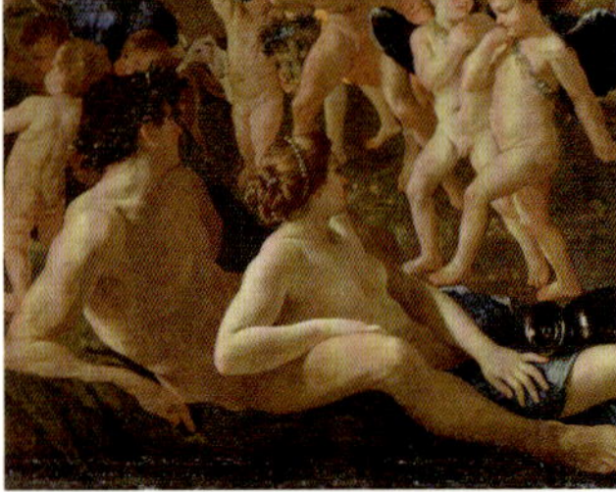

Ill. 20. Léopold Burthe (1823–1860), *Sappho Playing the Lyre*, 1849, oil on canvas, 41 × 27 in., Musée des Beaux-Arts, Carcassonne, inv. D.852.10.27.

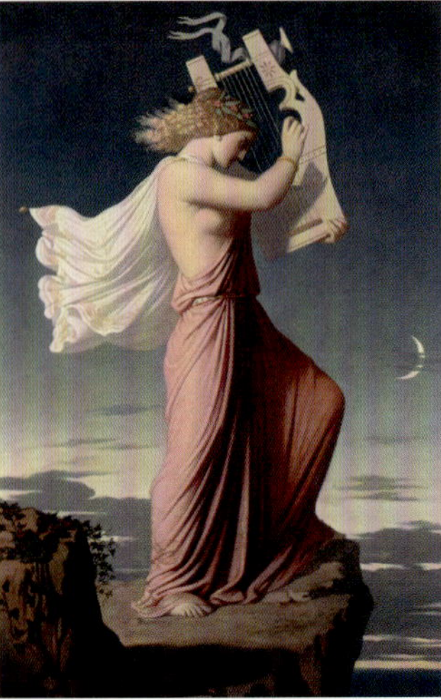

of the classical period onto *lekythoi* with white background, embellishing the palmette motif on the collar.[5] The reconstruction of the lyre is also inspired by vase painting (ill. 16), as are the poet's face and hair, which originate from the painting of vases and archaic Greek sculpture, but also from neo-Attic interpretations of the Roman era (ill. 17)—stylized bearded faces that would meet with a certain success in the decorative arts of the 1850s (ill. 18). Gérôme paid special attention to the study of the face, as seen in one very attractive study, almost a mask, in the collection of the Musée des Beaux-Arts in Nancy.[6] The vespertine scene already reveals all the dramatic qualities developed in Gérôme's painting over the course of the 1850s. The radiant sky of a Mediterranean evening where the moon rises and clouds eddy, the last rays of the sun on the arid mountains in the background contrast with the muffled tones of the dancers—whose isocephalia is skillfully interrupted—and the four protagonists in the foreground: the flautist, the poet—swaying at the hip with monumental serenity—and the rowdy child gods, which left a particularly lasting impression on Luc-Olivier Merson, a pupil of Gérôme. The skinny sapling, straight from Raphael or works of the Quattrocento (ill. 15), the allusion, in the flautist,[7] to the *Concert Champêtre*, then attributed to Giorgione (Titian, *Concert Champêtre*, ca. 1509, oil on canvas, Musée du Louvre, Paris), the almost literal translation of the reclining couple in *The Triumph of Flora* by Nicolas Poussin (ill. 19): all these skillfully composed collages drew attention to the work, even as it was criticized for its exaggerated tendencies toward the style of Ingres.[8] Reviews were mixed in respect of the painting's "archaic" leanings, even though they were far from those of Léopold Burthe a year later in *Sappho Playing the Lyre* (ill. 20), one reviewer criticizing "the puerility of the birds, the spindly trees, the primitive landscapes, creating a disagreeable combination of old German masters and Etruscan painting. Is there really an urgency to turn back the clock?"[9] While Théophile Gautier admits that it was less pleasing to the eye than *The Cock Fight*, he liked its "abstract truth" and defended Gérôme, whose future he said was assured, judging that "it is not his fault if he has the same nature as an adolescent Perugino or Raphael."[10] Gustave Le Gray produced a daguerreotype of the painting of remarkable quality (cat. 19). *Anacreon* was less systematically subjected to the demands of Gérôme's usual penchant for archaeological precision, and is mellowed by its allusions to, or citations from, the masterpieces of classical painting, and rendered unusual by the overall tone of the palette. The work is no doubt more worthy than Gérôme's own subsequent assessment: "A dry, jagged work, the style and intention of which are not bad: if I had already acquired the experience I have since acquired, the work could have been a good thing: instead it is mediocre."[11] Gérôme's loyalty to Anacreontic themes resurfaced, in a totally different aesthetic mode, with a series of four scenes illustrating the *Odes*,[12] which, like many paintings from the 1890s, combine irony and vulgarity without inhibition (ill. 96, p. 206). The work very probably inspired a famous sculpture (Eugène Guillaume, *Anacreon*, 1852, marble, Musée d'Orsay, Paris) and a painting (Goupil & Cie, photograph of J. Mazerolle, *Anacreon*, 1863, Musée Goupil, Bordeaux) that has since disappeared. **É. P.**

1. Raphael (Villa Farnesina), Augustin Pajou and Bertel Thorvaldsen (*Anacreon and Cupid*, 1823, marble, Thorvaldsens Museum, Copenhagen); Jean-Philippe Rameau (*Anacreon*, ballet, 1754); André-Ernest-Modeste Grétry (*Anacréon chez Polycrate*, opera, 1797); Luigi Cherubini (*Anacréon ou l'Amour fugitif*, opera, 1803). **2.** Translation by Philippe II Étienne, Paris, 1574. **3.** *Anacréon, recueil de compositions dessinées par Anne-Louis Girodet et gravées par M. Chatillon, son élève, avec la traduction en prose des odes de ce poète, faite également par A.-L. Girodet, publiée par son héritier et par les soins de MM. Becquerel et P. A. Coupin* (Paris: Chaillou-Potrelle, 1825). *Anacréon et les lyriques grecs, traduits et imités en vers français par Léon Bezout…* (Paris: Marmande-Durebord, 1843), is one of the last published translations to precede the exhibition of the painting. **4.** Louis Dimier, quoted by B. Vouilloux, "1849: une bacchanale méditative," in *Charles Gleyre. Le génie de l'invention*, exh. cat. (Lausanne: Musée Cantonal des Beaux-Arts, 2006–07), p. 155. **5.** We wish warmly to thank Martine Denoyelle, head curator and scientific advisor at the Institut National d'Histoire de l'Art, for her invaluable help. **6.** On the different stages of the elaboration of the composition, see S. Harent, "Études préparatoires," in S. Harent and C. Stoullig, *Dessins de Jean-Léon Gérôme: la collection du musée des Beaux-Arts de Nancy*, exh. cat. (Nancy: Musée des Beaux-Arts, 2009), pp. 42–44. **7.** Which anticipates the posture of *Tanagra* (cat. 168). **8.** F. de Lagenevais, "Salon de 1848," *Revue des Deux Mondes*, vol. XXII, 2nd qtr. 1848, p. 288. **9.** L. Clément de Ris, "Salon de 1848. Eugène Delacroix, Duveau, Diaz, Gérôme, Lehmann, Fernand Boissard," *L'Artiste*, 5th ser., vol. 1 (1848), p. 60. **10.** T. Gautier, "Feuilleton de *La Presse* du 27 avril 1848. Salon de 1848," *La Presse*, April 27, 1848, p. 1. **11.** J.-L. Gérôme, *Notes autobiographiques* [1874], ed. G. Ackerman (Vesoul: S.A.L.S.A., 1981), p. 9. **12.** Probably inspired by Girodet's engravings.

Cat. 19

Gustave Le Gray (1820–1884)

ANACREON,
REPRODUCTION OF THE PAINTING BY JEAN-LÉON GÉRÔME

–

1848

Daguerreotype

6 ½ × 8 ½ in.

Handwritten signature engraved lower left: *Gustave Le Gray d'après Gérôme*

A. and A. Flamand Collection

–

Bibliography: *Gustave Le Gray, 1820–1884*, exh. cat. (Paris: Bibliothèque Nationale de France, 2002), cat. 6, ill. p. 10. *Le Daguerreotype français: un objet photographique*, exh. cat. (Paris: Musée d'Orsay, 2003, also New York: The Metropolitan Museum of Art, 2003–04), cat. 207, ill. p. 288. S. Harent and C. Stoullig, *Dessins de Jean-Léon Gérôme: la collection du musée des Beaux-Arts de Nancy*, exh. cat. (Nancy: Musée des Beaux-Arts, 2009), p. 42.

This daguerreotype reproduces the painting that Gérôme exhibited at the Salon of 1848, and which was shortly afterward bought by the French government for the Musée des Augustins in Toulouse (cat. 16). It is one of the earliest known photographic works by Gustave Le Gray. Indeed, nothing has survived of the work done in Rome by the artist and photographer who was able to combine, according to Sylvie Aubenas, "the two qualities of painter and chemist-photographer, of artist and scientist."[1] This photograph is the only known Le Gray daguerreotype that reproduces an artwork, and it reveals his talent not only through the beauty of the picture but also through its outstanding chemical quality. Le Gray's dexterity in reproducing a canvas without passing through the intermediate stage of engraving would suggest that this was not his first effort. The values of Gérôme's canvas are perfectly rendered, despite the painting's hard-to-reproduce lighter tones.

Gérôme and Le Gray became friendly in the studio of Paul Delaroche, under whom they both trained. At the time the two artists were very close—it was during this period that Le Gray took photographs of Gérôme and his companions in the garden of Delaroche's rue de Fleurus atelier (cat. 14 and 15), those prints being some of the earliest known photographs on paper. The daguerreotype shown here is a kind of mutual tribute between the two artists: it not only shows Le Gray's interest in the photographic reproduction of artworks (in addition to participating in the Mission Héliographique of 1851, Le Gray made numerous paper photographs of artworks between 1850 and 1855, including several views of the Salon of 1852, gathered in an album now held by the Musée d'Orsay), but it also underscores Gérôme's very precocious wish to make a record of his early painterly accomplishments, since the first canvas he showed at the Salon of 1847, *The Cock Fight* (cat. 10), was hailed by the critics. **D. F.-R.**

1. S. Aubenas in *Gustave Le Gray, 1820–1884*, exh. cat. (Paris: Bibliothèque Nationale de France, 2002), p. 23.

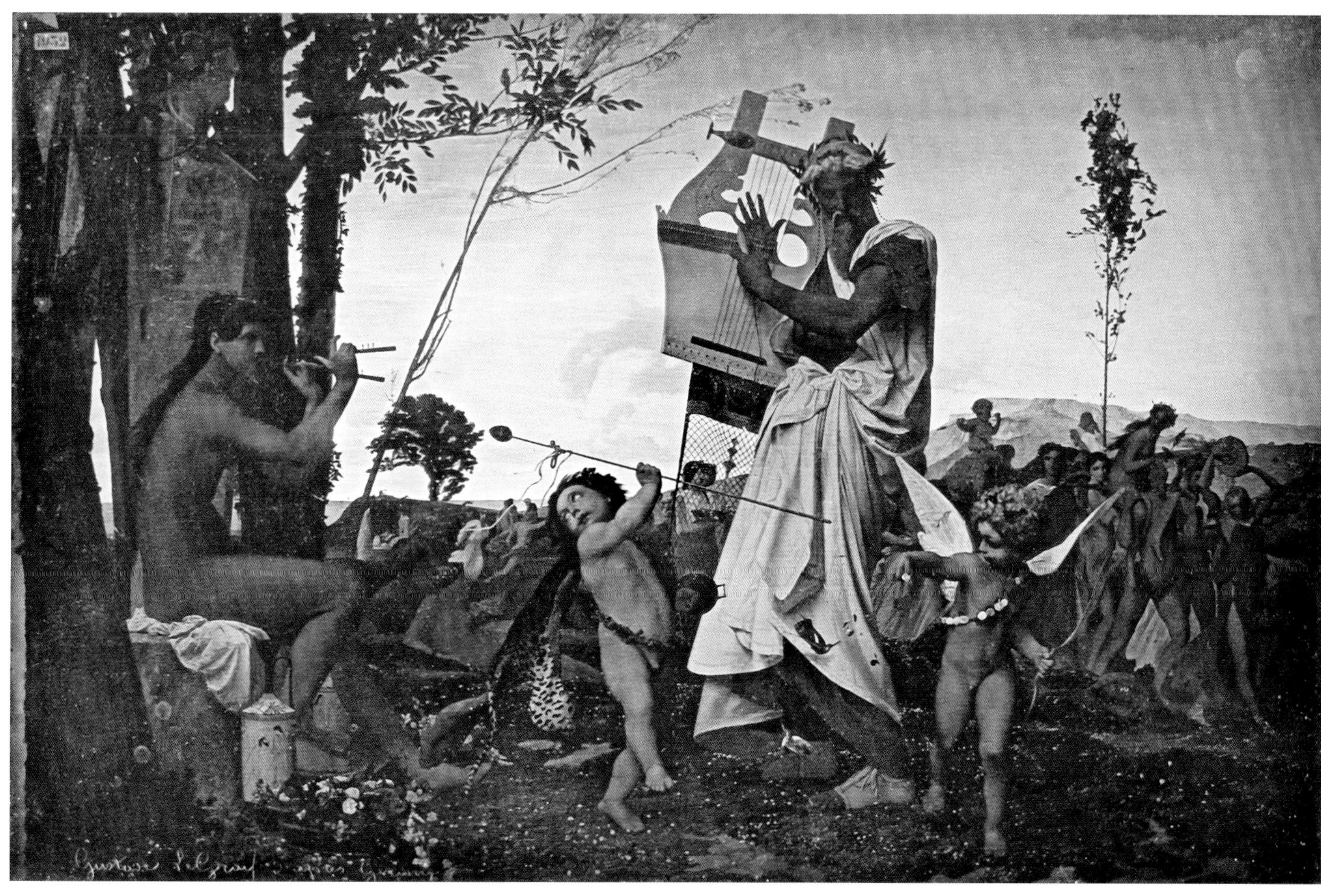

Cat. 20

ANACREON WITH BACCHUS AND AMOR

–

1881
Bronze
28 ¾ × 11 ¼ × 12 ¾ in.
Signed on the left : *JL GEROME*
Inscription: *F. BARBEDIENNE, Fondeur-Paris. RÉDUCTION MÉCANIQUE A. Collas breveté;* on the back of the base, on the rear: *453*
Musée Georges-Garret, Vesoul, inv. 882.7.1

–

Provenance: Gift of the artist to the museum, 1882.

–

Exhibition History: Salon of 1881, Paris.

–

Bibliography: J. Buisson, "Le Salon de 1881. 3e article. La Sculpture," *Gazette des Beaux-Arts*, vol. XXIV, vol. 2, 1881, pp. 214–16. P. Mantz, "Feuilleton du *Temps*, Salon VII," *Le Temps*, June 19, 1881, p. 2. F. Barbedienne and Leblanc-Barbedienne, *Catalogue des bronzes d'art* (Paris: Imp. E. Capiomont & Co., 1894), p. 62. *Exposition universelle des Beaux-Arts. Dix années du Salon de Peinture et de Sculpture 1879–1888* (Paris: Librairie des Bibliophiles, 1889), p. 34. V. Guillemin, "Étude sur le peintre et sculpteur J. L. Gérôme," *Académie des sciences, belles-lettres et arts de Besançon. Procès-verbaux et mémoires. Année 1904* (Besançon, 1905), pp. 134–84. F. Masson, "Notes et fragments de J.-L. Gérôme", *Les Arts*, no. 26 (Feb. 1904), p. 28. H. Roujon, *Notice sur la vie et les peintures de M. Léon Gérôme*, 1904, p. 46. G. Ackerman, in P. Fusco and H. Janson, *The Romantics to Rodin: French Nineteenth Century Sculpture from North American Collections*, exh. cat. (Los Angeles: Los Angeles County Museum of Art, 1980), no. 152, pp. 286–287 concerning the version in the Art Institute of Chicago. *J.-L. Gérôme*, exh. cat. (Vesoul: Musée Georges-Garret, 1981), no. 181, p. 145 on the subject of inv. 890.2.1. G. Ackerman, "Gérôme's Sculpture: The Problems of Realist Sculpture," *Arts Magazine*, Feb. 1986, pp. 83–84. *Cupids, Flights of Fancy, Love and Mischief*, exh. cat. (New York: Dahesh Museum of Art, 1996), no. 11. H. Lafont-Couturier, *Gérôme* (Paris: Herscher, 1998), p. 128. G. Ackerman, *Jean-Léon Gérôme* (Courbevoie: ACR Édition, 2000), no. S. 10.

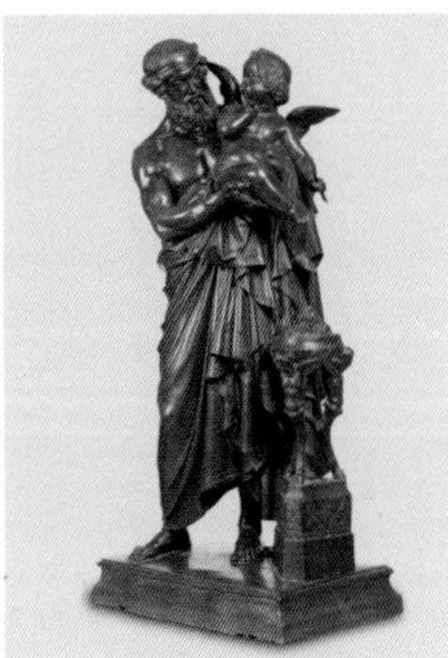

Ill. 21. James Pradier (1790–1852), *Anacreon*, 1845, bronze, 29 ½ in., Musée d'Art et d'Histoire, Geneva, inv. 1954-8.

Cat. 21
Anonymous

ANACREON WITH BACCHUS AND AMOR ON THE SCULPTING TURNTABLE IN GÉRÔME'S STUDIO, FRONTAL VIEW

–

ca. 1881
Albumen print
print: 10 ½ × 8 ¼ in.; mount: 19 × 12 ½ in.
Département des Estampes et de la Photographie, Bibliothèque Nationale de France, Paris, Dc-293 (a+)-Fol., vol. 4

–

Bibliography: F. Masson, "Notes et fragments de J.-L. Gérôme," *Les Arts*, no. 26 (Feb. 1904), p. 28.

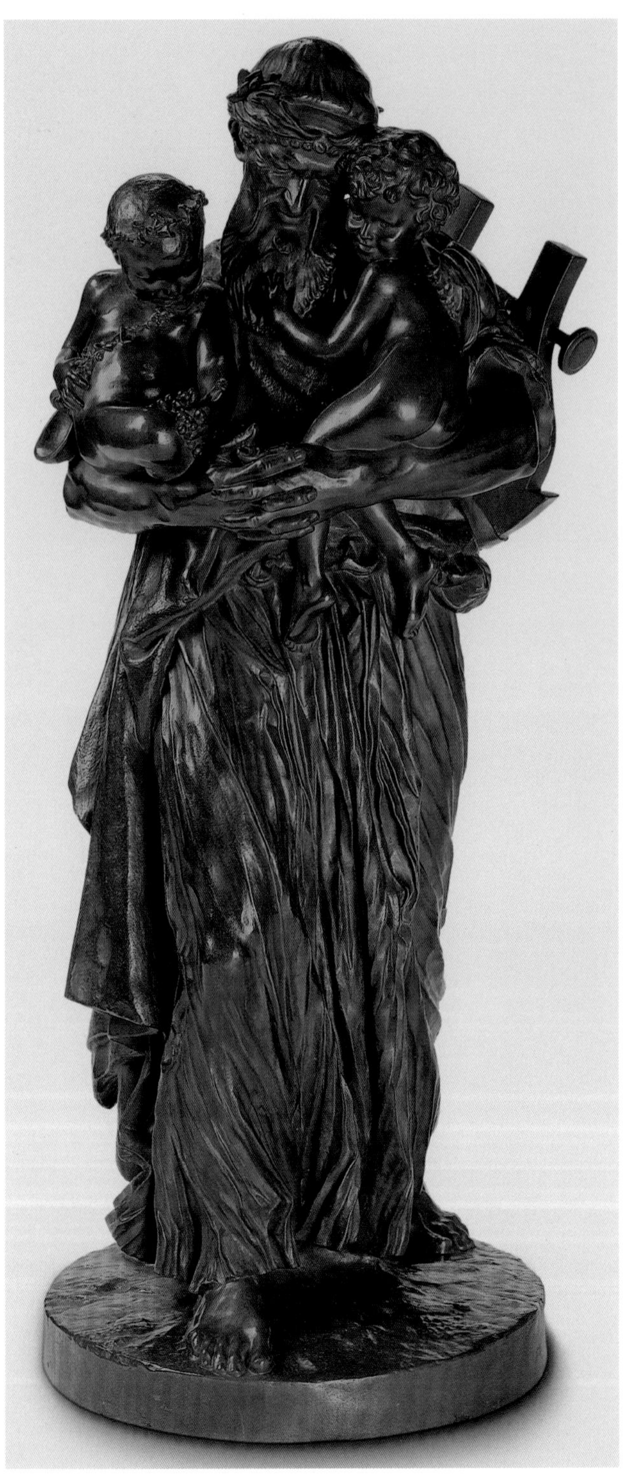

Like many of Gérôme's sculptures, the three-dimensional version of Anacreon is adapted from the painting exhibited in 1848 (cat. 16), but is a considerable departure from it, as though the scene follows on from the moment represented in the painting: in this case, after the dance, the poet is depicted striding along, Amor (or Cupid) and the young Bacchus nestling in his arms, his lyre slung across his back. Created in his early career as a sculptor, there is a sense of a fluid Alexandrine inspiration, which owes much to James Pradier's own *Anacreon* (ill. 21), and also perhaps to a famous classical sculpture in the Louvre, a Roman copy of Lysippus of Sicyon's work *Silenus holding Dionysos.*[1] *Anacreon with Bacchus and Amor* prefigures one of Gérôme's favorite motifs in sculpture: the representation of the creasing of antique drapery in movement (cat. 180). Far from the sensitivity of *Anacreon Plucking a Feather from Cupid's Wings* (ca. 1750, marble, Musée du Louvre, Paris) by Augustin Pajou, Gérôme presents an attractive sculpture, of a classical and naturalist sensuality, the perfect ornament for an elegant library or park. The life-size plaster was exhibited in 1881 at the Paris Salon, and at London's Royal Academy; the marble was purchased by Carl Jacobsen in 1885 (Ny Carlsberg Glyptotek, Copenhagen). The work met with mixed reviews from critics. Paul Mantz felt that "from behind, it looks like an old woman,"[2] and reproached the sculptor for an overall lack of reliability in execution, whereas J. Buisson found it "full of Hellenic good humor"[3] and eulogized Gérôme's promising debut in sculpture. The caster, Barbedienne, distributed a number of copies in five different dimensions,[4] including one three-tenths reduction—a deed of gift by Gérôme to the museum of his home town—which is presented here. **É. P.**

1. G. Ackerman, in P. Fusco and H. Janson, *The Romantics to Rodin: French Nineteenth Century Sculpture from North American Collections*, exh. cat. (Los Angeles: Los Angeles County Museum of Art, 1980), pp. 286–287. **2.** P. Mantz, "Feuilleton du *Temps*, Salon, VII," *Le Temps*, June 19, 1881. **3.** J. Buisson, "Le Salon de 1881. 3e article. La Sculpture," *Gazette des Beaux-Arts*, 1881, vol. 2, p. 216. **4.** F. Barbedienne and Leblanc-Barbedienne, *Catalogue des bronzes d'art* (Paris: Imp. E. Capiomont & Co., 1894), p. 62. Certain copies on the art market exist in gilded bronze.

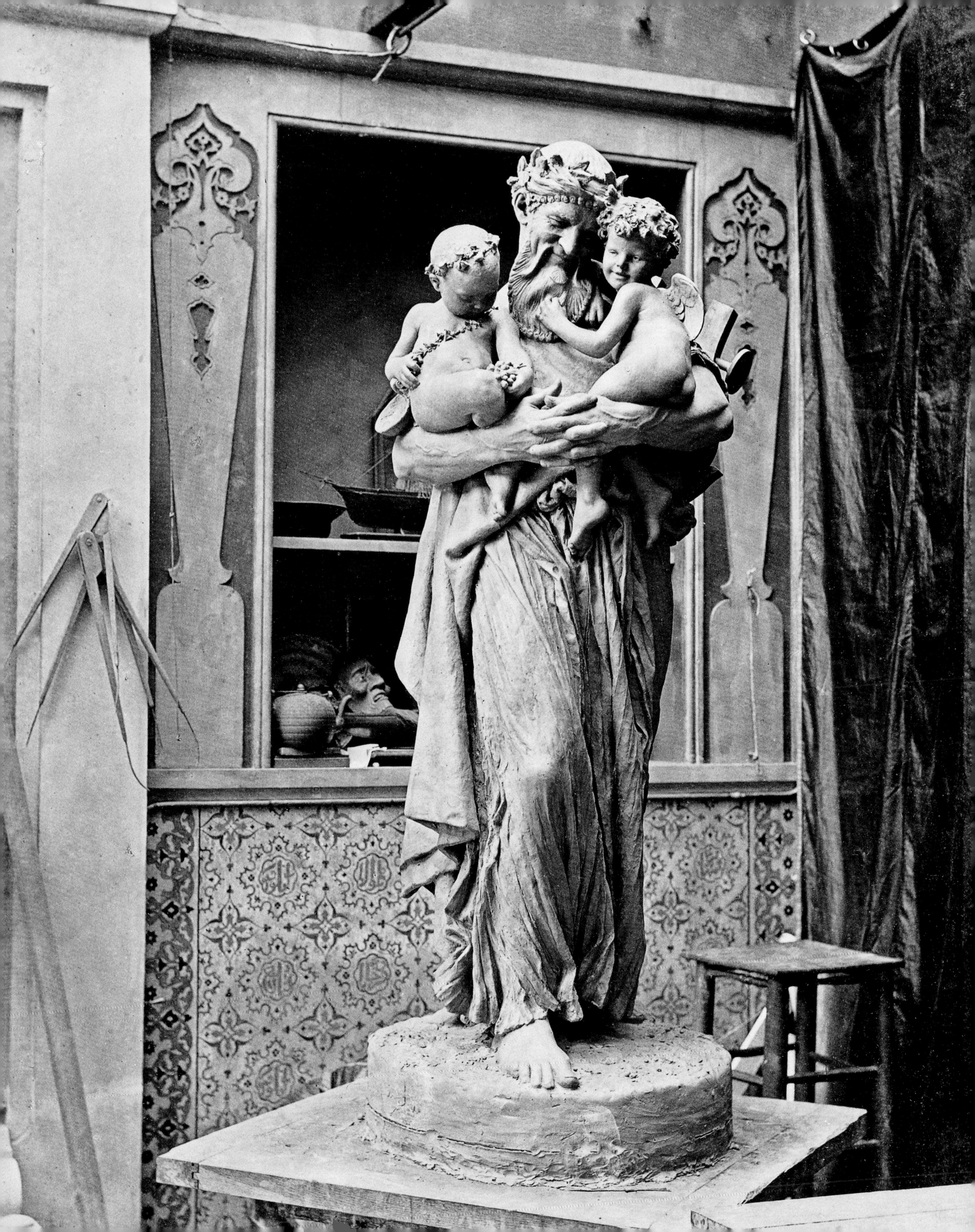

Cat. 22

THE REPUBLIC

1848
Oil on canvas
90 × 76 in.
Mairie des Lilas

Provenance: Competition for a Figure of the Republic, 1848. By an order of June 12, 1848, Gérôme was commissioned to produce a large format sketch. The painting was in Montmartre city hall, 1848–49. Municipal council chamber of the City of Paris, Pavillon de Flore du Louvre, 1879. Mairie des Lilas.

Bibliography: A. J. D., "Concours national: Figure de la République française," *L'Illustration*, May 6, 1848. T. Gautier, "Concours pour la figure de la République," *La Presse*, May 21, 1848. T. Gautier, "École nationale des Beaux-Arts. Exposition des Figures du concours pour la République," *La Presse*, Dec. 5, 1848. P. Haussard, "Concours d'esquisses peintes: Figure symbolique de la République," *Le National*, June 8, 1848. C. Isnard, "Concours des figures symboliques de la République," *L'Artiste*, 5th ser., vol. 1 (June 15, 1848). C. Isnard, "École des Beaux-Arts. Concours. Grands Prix. Envois de Rome. Figures symboliques de la République," *L'Artiste*, 5th ser., vol. 1 (Oct. 15, 1848). P. Mantz, "École des Beaux-Arts. Concours pour la Figure de la République," *La Vraie République*, June 18, 1848. L. Jan, "Portrait de la République (Semaine des esquisses. Détrônement du vieux rire homérique. Revue républicaine. Bonnet rouge et blanc bonnet. Dernier concours)," *Le Siècle*, Nov. 27, 1848. H. Trianon, "École des Beaux-Arts. Concours pour la Figure symbolique de la République française," *L'Illustration*, Oct. 28, 1848. A. Boime, "The Second Republic's Contest for the Figure of the Republic," *Art Bulletin*, vol. 53 (1971), pp. 68–83. T. J. Clark, *The Absolute Bourgeois: Artists and Politics in France 1848–1851* (Greenwich, Conn.: New York Graphic Society, 1973), p. 64ff. M. Agulhon, *Marianne au combat. L'imagerie et la symbolique républicaines de 1789 à 1880* (Paris, 1979), p. 101. *J.-L. Gérôme*, exh. cat. (Vesoul: Musée Georges-Garret, 1981), no. 115, p. 102. M.-C. Chaudonneret, *La Figure de la République. Le concours de 1848* (Paris: RMN, 1987). C. Georgel, *1848, la République et l'art vivant* (Paris: RMN, 1998). G. Ackerman, *Jean-Léon Gérôme*, (Courbevoie: ACR Édition, 2000), no. 24.

Ill. 22. Honoré Daumier (1808–1879), *The Republic*, sketch, 1848, oil on canvas, 28 ¾ × 23 ¼ in., Musée d'Orsay, Paris, inv. RF 1644.

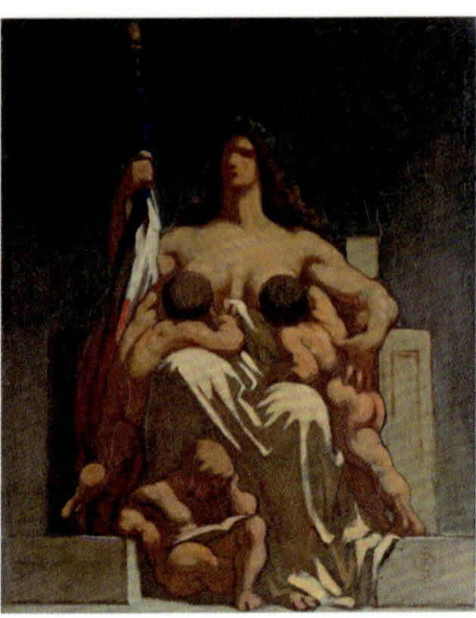

Ill. 23. Menut [Marie-Alexandre Alophe] (1812–1883), *Mademoiselle Rachel Singing The Marseillaise*, 1848, lithography, 13 ¾ × 10 ⅝ in., Comédie-Française, Paris.

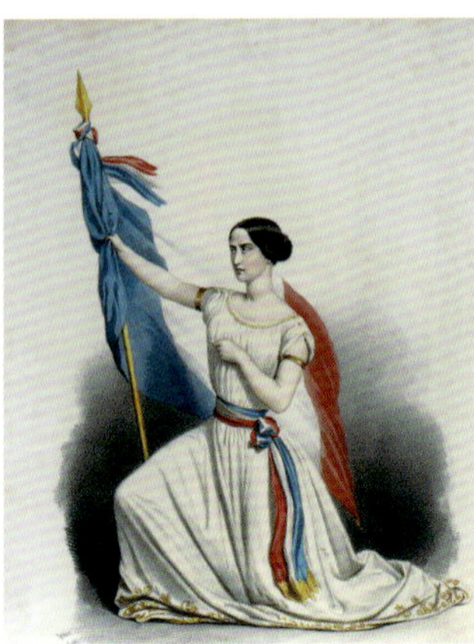

The revolution of February 1848 had ushered in the Second Republic and it was decided that a competition would be held for an allegorical representation of the new regime. In fact, there were three competitions, since the purpose was to obtain not only a painting but also a sculpted figure of the French Republic as well as a medal commemorating its inception. Prepared by the director of the Beaux-Arts, Joseph Garraud, the program was made public by way of the press and posters on March 28. It gave artists less than a month to come up with an oil sketch 25 inches high. The sketches were not to be signed and artists were asked to submit their work with a sealed envelope, a motto, and a sign allowing the work to be identified—all in all, a confusing procedure that few fully understood, much less fully followed. The jury assembled to judge the sketches comprised Jean-Auguste-Dominique Ingres, Léon Cogniet, Paul Delaroche, Eugène Delacroix, Alexandre-Gabriel Decamps, Joseph-Nicolas Robert-Fleury, Jean-Victor Schnetz, and Philippe-Auguste Jeanron. Only Charles Blanc, who represented the interior ministry, was not an artist. It was generally agreed that the results were truly mediocre, and the jury was forced to proceed by successive elimination. When they came together on May 10, only Hippolyte Flandrin was unanimously approved, and after six rounds of voting twenty works out of fifty-eight passed muster, with the most votes going (in descending order) to Hippolyte Flandrin, Henri-Pierre Picou, Charles Landelle, Dominique Papety, Félix Fossey and Gérôme, all of whom, like the lower-ranked Honoré Daumier, were now asked to produce the definitive painting. The second phase of this laborious competition, which dragged on until March 1849, was hardly compelling either for the public or critics. The invention of a new allegory of the Republic was left in suspense. Gérôme's participation in this collective failure (only Daumier stood out thanks to a powerful, original work that marked his debut as a painter (ill. 22)), nevertheless offers an interesting insight into the young artist's ambitions at the time. Still in the first flush of his recent success with *The Cock Fight* (cat. 10), he clearly positioned himself as a champion of the *Néo-Grec* movement in this iconographic exercise.[1] With his classical, hieratic approach making the Republic more of a frozen goddess than a contemporary heroine, Gérôme's approach was quite the opposite of Delacroix's allegory of *Liberty*, which came out of the events of 1830. He may have been inspired by the spectacle of Rachel declaiming *The Marseillaise* (ill. 23), which Théophile Thoré saw as a perfect model: "All the artists competing for the figures of the Republic and Liberty should go and study the perfectly sculptural, majestic poses of Mademoiselle Rachel singing *The Marseillaise*... it is marble by virtue of its nobility, but marble that throbs with life."[2] A sword and laurel in her hands, draped in white, wearing a tricolor belt with a Phrygian cap and crown of laurel, Gérôme's Republic seems to capture the tragedian's patriotic fervor in a sculptural, monumental form on canvas. In going from the sketch[3] (private collection) to the big final version, Gérôme further heightened the statuesque quality of his composition, making the lion sterner (submissive in the sketch, it is seen in severe profile in the final painting), in such a way that this symbol of strength anticipates Auguste Bartholdi's sculpture of the *Lion of Belfort*. Théophile Gautier, however, remained unconvinced by this development: "[I]t is somewhat uncertain, a little round,"[4] was, for the time being, his criticism of Gérôme's composite ideal. **L. C.**

1. Clearly uninterested in complex symbolism, Gérôme reduced the reference to the trinity of the Republic to a simple triangle drawn in at the base of the figure. **2.** T. Thoré, *L'Artiste*, 5th ser., vol. 1 (Apr. 9, 1848), p. 76. **3.** G. Ackerman, *Jean-Léon Gérôme* (Courbevoie: ACR Édition, 2000), no. 23. **4.** T. Gautier, "École nationale des Beaux-Arts. Exposition des Figures du concours pour la République," *La Presse*, Dec. 5, 1848.

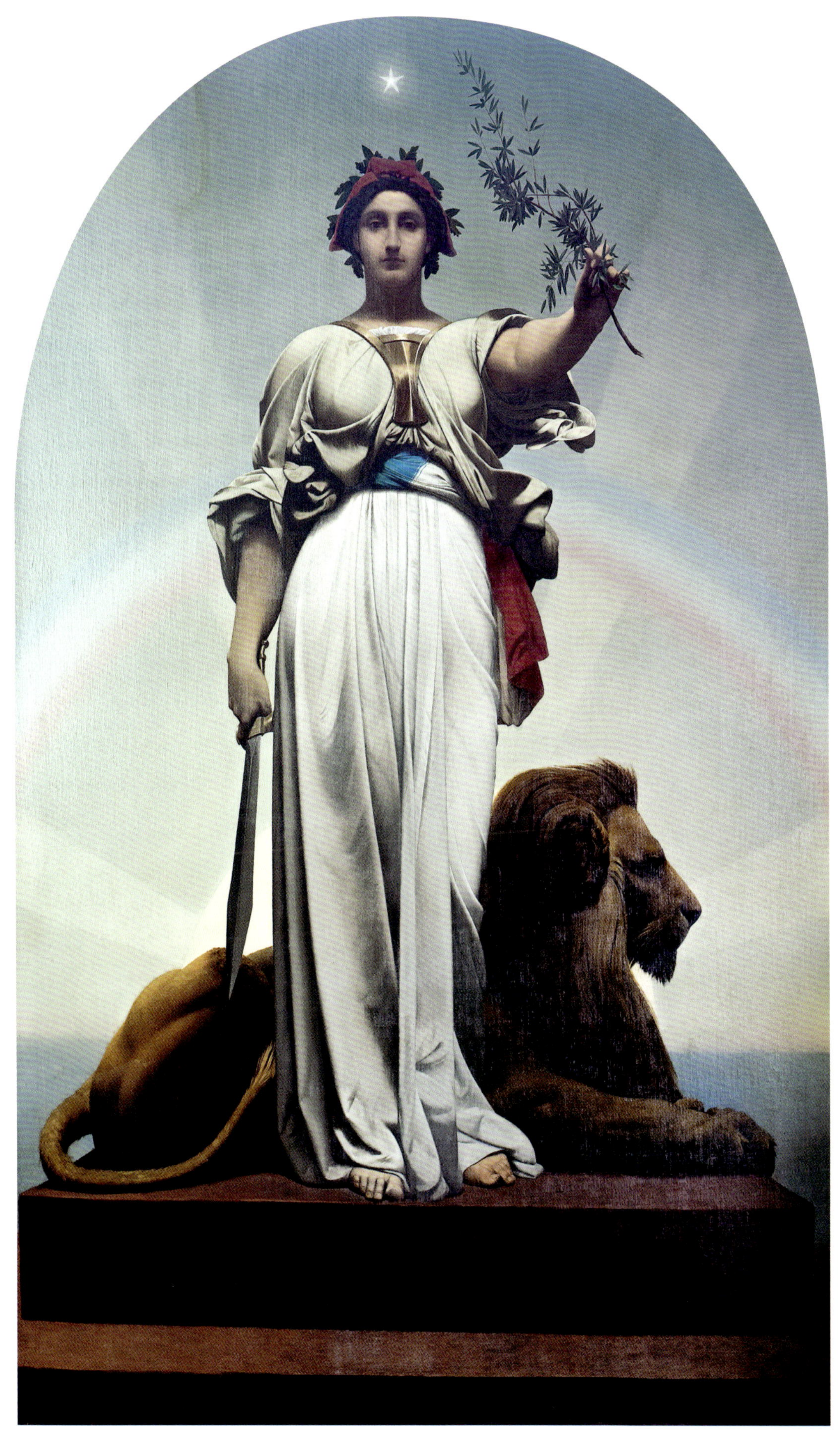

Cat. 23

A GREEK INTERIOR (THE GYNAECEUM)

–

1850
Oil on canvas
25 3/8 × 35 in.
Signed and dated in Roman numerals, bottom right: *J.L. GEROME. MDCCCL.*
Collection of Lady Micheline Connery

–

Provenance: Prince Napoleon sale, Apr. 1868. Purchased by Goupil (for 14,000 francs). Goupil to Binant in 1868 (for 14,400 francs). Straussberg of Berlin sale, Paris, March 31, 1874 (for 18,000 francs). Goupil, Paris, to M. Rafflard, 1875 (for 22,000 francs). Purchased from M. Rafflard, 1875. Sotheby's, London, June 3, 2003, no. 134.

–

Exhibition History: Salon of 1850–1851, Paris, no. 1257.

–

Bibliography: Recueil. Œuvres de Jean-Léon Gérôme, BNF Estampes, vol. VI, no. 4. L. Clément de Ris, *L'Artiste*, 5th ser., vol. 6 (1850), p. 9. P. de Chennevières, *Lettres sur l'art français en 1850* (Argentan: Barbier, 1851). E.-J. Delécluze, *Exposition des artistes vivants* (1850), pp. 116–19. L. de Geoffroy, *Revue des Deux Mondes*, 1850, pp. 947–48. A. de la Fizelière, *Salon de 1850–51*, p. 63. M. Vignon, *Salon de 1850–1851*, pp. 117–19. J. Courtois, *Le Corsaire*, Feb. 15, 1851. G. de Ferry, *L'Ordre*, Jan. 11, 1851. T. Gautier, *La Presse*, Mar 1, 1851. P. Mantz, *L'Événement*, Jan. 30, 1851. L. Peisse, *Le Constitutionnel*, Apr. 1, 1851. P. Petroz, *Le Vote universel*, Jan. 28, 1851. F. Pillet, *Le Moniteur officiel*, Mar. 27, 1851, p. 891. E. Strahan [Earl Shinn], *Gérôme. A Collection of the Works of J.-L. Gérôme in One Hundred Photogravures* (New York: Samuel L. Hall, 1881). *J.-L. Gérôme*, exh. cat. (Vesoul: Musée Georges-Garret, 1981), nos. 12–14 and 42, 45. H. Lafont-Couturier, *Gérôme* (Paris: Herscher, 1998), p. 19. G. Ackerman, *Jean-Léon Gérôme* (Courbevoie: ACR Édition, 2000), no. 29. H. Lafont-Couturier, *Gérôme and Goupil: Art and Enterprise*, exh. cat., trans. I. Ollivier (Bordeaux: Musée Goupil, 2000–1; also New York: Dahesh Museum of Art, 2001, and Pittsburgh: The Frick Art & Historical Center, 2001), pp. 19, 94–96, 156. S. Harent and C. Stoullig, *Dessins de Jean-Léon Gérôme: la collection du musée des Beaux-Arts de Nancy*, exh. cat. (Nancy: Musée des Beaux-Arts, 2009), pp. 45–46.

Cat. 24

CHARACTER STUDY FOR *A GREEK INTERIOR*

–

Ca. 1850
Pencil on paper
8 × 5 in.
Signed bottom right: *À monsieur Diéterle JL Gérôme*
Private collection

–

Bibliography: *J.-L. Gérôme*, exh. cat. (Vesoul: Musée Georges-Garret, 1981), no. 12, p. 41. S. Harent and C. Stoullig, *Dessins de Jean-Léon Gérôme: la collection du musée des Beaux-Arts de Nancy*, exh. cat. (Nancy: Musée des Beaux-Arts, 2009), p. 46, fig. b.

Ill. 24. Brazier tripod, Julia Felix house, Pompeii, First century B.C.– first century A.D., bronze, 36 × 22 3/8 × 18 1/2 in., Museo Archeologico Nazionale, Naples, inv. 27874.

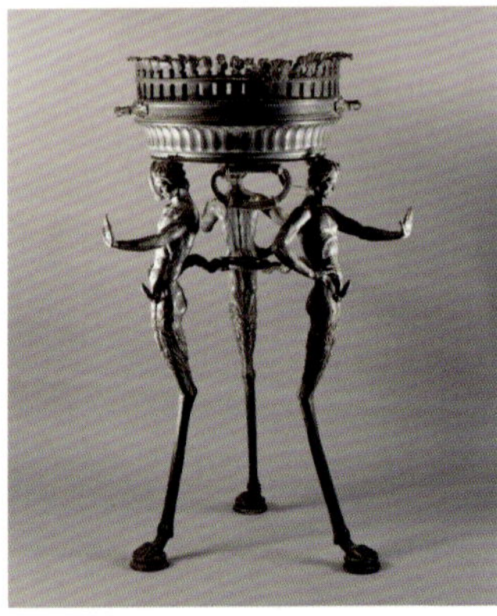

Ill. 25. Auguste Belloc, attributed to (1805–1867), *Woman Lying on a Bed*, ca. 1851-1855, stereoscopic daguerreotype, 3 1/8 × 6 3/8 in., Musée d'Orsay, Paris, inv. PHO 1986-125.

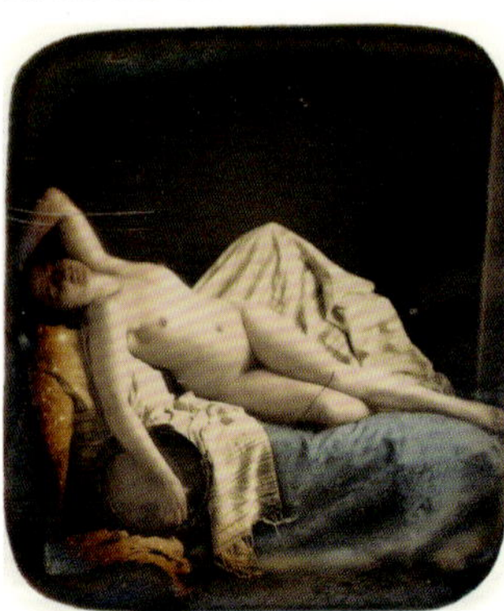

Exhibited at the Salon of 1850–1851, in the company of *Drunken Bacchus and Cupid* (cat. 26), this work, in which it was said that "vulgarity joins forces with distinction,"[1] also drew attention to Gérôme and embroiled him in controversy. Critics reproached him fairly unanimously for the indecency of his subject: a Greco-Roman brothel where an old woman offers women to a young man (who was actually an old man in the first draft conserved at the Musée d'Orsay, oil on canvas, inv. RF 1981 46) while in the background two protagonists, deal concluded, slink away. He was also criticized for an anachronistic mistranslation of the decor (clearly more Pompeian that Greek), the lifelessness of the creation, and the indecency of the composition of the courtesans, "round as spinning tops,"[2] "rubber dolls who by dint of being tugged and pulled are rigid and twisted."[3] The general, fairly cold and linear economy of the composition retains something of Ingres, but only what the leader of the *Néo-Grec* movement had decided to keep: the reference to the painter of the *Odalisque*, who is indeed invoked here, is diluted in the multiplication of bodies, as though subjects of artistic nude photography which flourished in the 1850s,[4] assembled in a living painting (ill. 25). The scene, effectively more Campanian than Attic, was not surprisingly defended by Théophile Gautier, who himself had just returned from Pompeii: "Never has a restoration, a rather a resurrection, been so complete... It is as if this painting has been made by one of the painters who decorated the house of Diomedes."[5] The work evoked Vesuvius's cities and alleged science of "archaism"; whereas Étienne-Jean Delécluze thought that the objects were "screeching in the viewer's eye,"[6] Gautier felt that the juxtaposition of the details was of "perfect taste" and "exquisite choice": such refinement portrayed by the well-informed enthusiast—both archaeologically and sexually—they could only enchant the man who would go on to publish *Arria Marcella*, the following year. *A Greek Interior*, the wickeder version of *Greek Women at the Fountain* by Dominique Papety (ill. 27), was even reminiscent, according to Gautier—in a bold statement reviled by a colleague—of *Stratonice* by Ingres (1840, Musée Condé, Chantilly), and deemed superior to the scrupulous accumulations of "antique bric-a-brac" produced by Ernest Meissonier.[7] Judged by some as a "grimy spot of pagan libertinage under the cover of an Etruscan composition,"[8] this "dumb and ugly"[9] picture is no lewder than Orientalist evocations of cheap seraglios. Thirty-five years later, Gérôme regretted that "The 'Gynaeceum' had had an impact because of the subject (how very sad!) and not the execution."[10] This oriental-style Gynaeceum, an antique harem, set in an elegant Pompeian *domus*, with walls decorated in an approximate "third style,"[11] in the peristyle of which Gérôme arrayed his languorous fixed-price

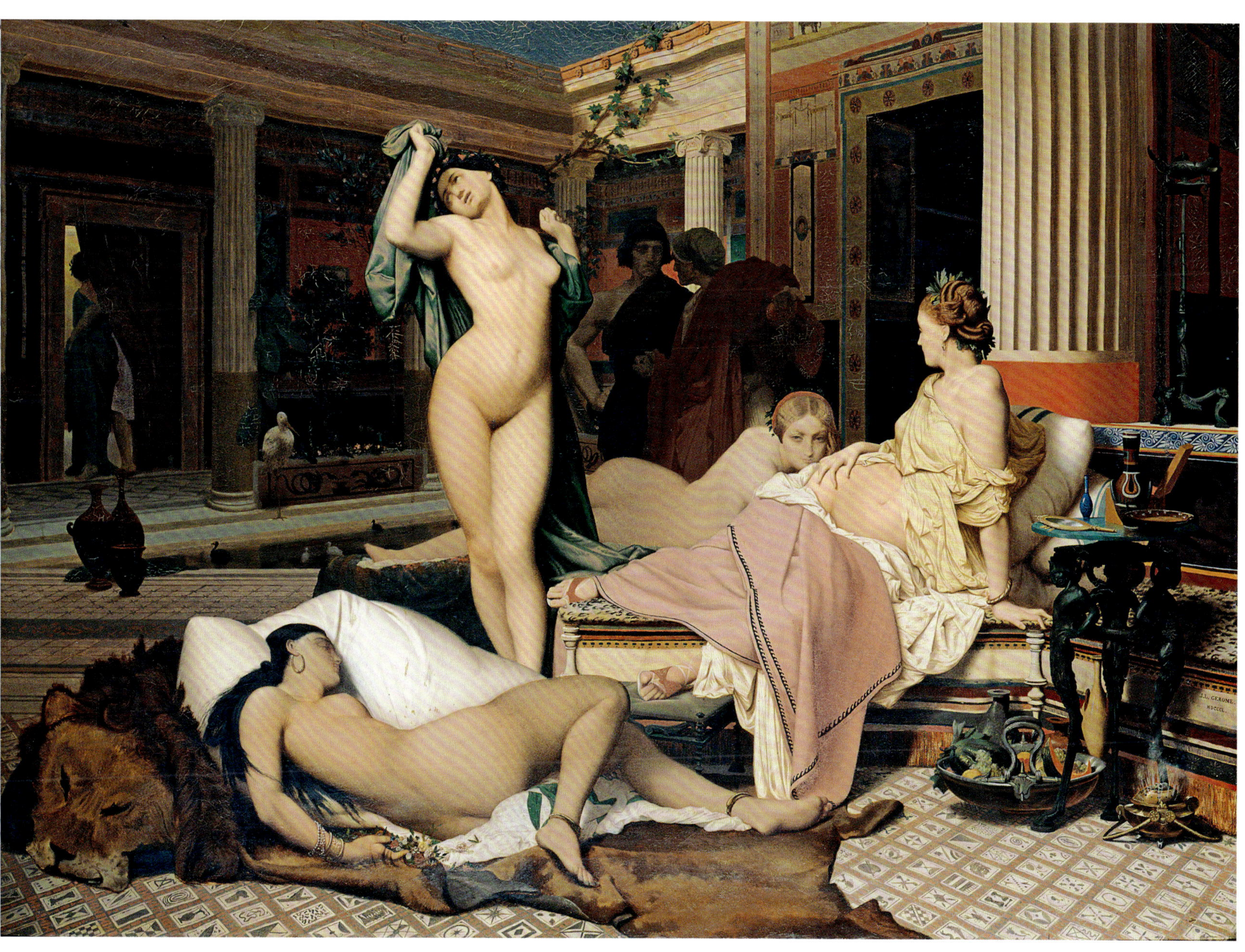
J.L. GEROME
MDCCCL.

Ill. 26. Anonymous, "Differents Vases and Sacrificial Instruments, Pompei," etching published in Raphaël Gargiulo, *Collection of the Most Remarkable Monuments of the National Museum* (Naples, 1869), vol. II, pl. 56 (detail), Département des Antiquités grecques, étrusques et romaines, Musée du Louvre, Paris.

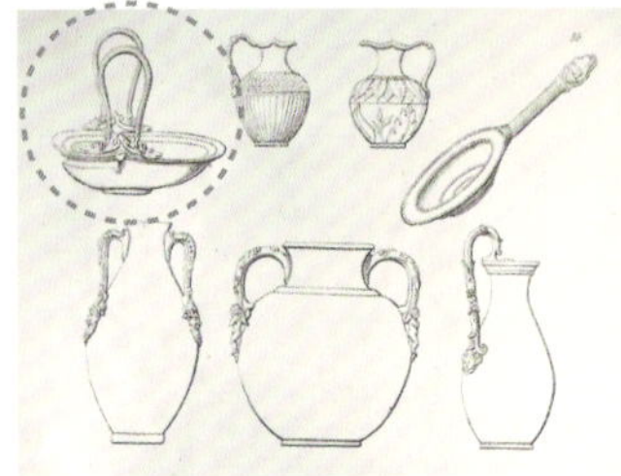

Ill. 27. Dominique Papety (1815–1841), *Greek Women at the Fountain*, 1841, oil on canvas, 22 × 26 in., Musée du Louvre, Paris, inv. RF 1982-27.

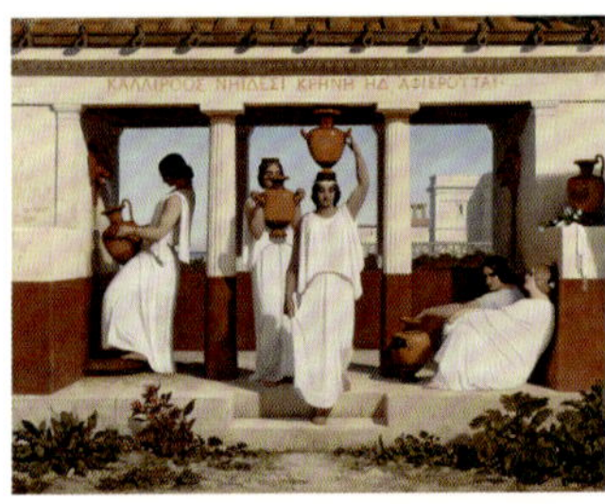

Ill. 28. Théodore Chassériau (1819–1856), *Tepidarium* (detail), 1853, oil on canvas, 67 × 101 in., Musée d'Orsay, Paris, inv. RF 71.

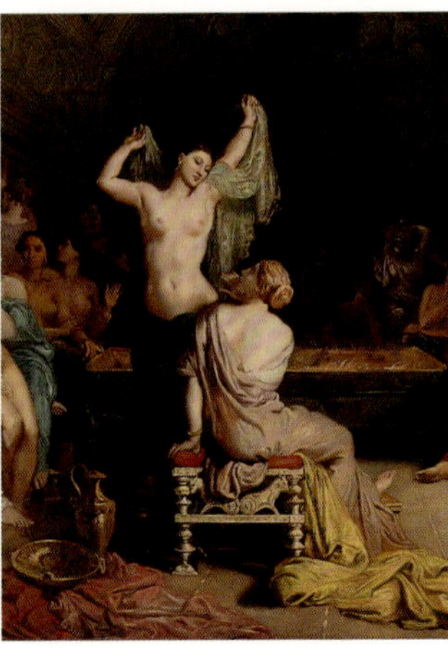

female figures—brunettes, blonds and red-heads—bears no resemblance to the brothel discovered in Pompeii. There are no minimal dark cells adjoining a central corridor; the place seems rather to be devoted to "luxury, calm, and sensual pleasure" in a Baudelairian sense, and the only object that well-informed eyes of 1851 might decipher as pornographic—the tripod—is a censored version of a famous bronze in Pompeii, published at the end of the eighteenth century, and which featured at the time in the "Hell" tableau of the museum at Naples: Gérôme doesn't picture the satyrs ithyphallic, like the copies produced by Neapolitan casters for wealthy tourists (ill. 24). The objects in the scene are more or less precise. The bronze cup with turned-up handles placed on the ground is directly inspired by a "basket-vase" reproduced in a number of collections at the start of the nineteenth century (ill. 26). The lamp, however, is an amalgam of various Pompeian models, and the small blue vase seems rather to be a creation of the Sèvres manufactory. The skin of the lion, Gérôme's cult animal throughout his career (cat. 80, 81, 108, 112, 185), is already present. The evocation of a refined Hellenistic architectural framework through its distant Campanian decadency was ultimately fairly modern and constitutes one of the first tangible signs of the set-designer-like license that Gérôme always took in his reconstructions. The peristyle irresistibly evokes the famous Pompeian house built eight years later on the avenue Montaigne for Prince Napoleon, cousin of the emperor (cat. 33 and ill. 33). The work's fate seems to have been predestined, as it was acquired by the prince and hung beside Ingres's *Turkish Bath* (ill. 136, p. 286). Far from this famous dream of a fantasmatic Orient, *A Greek Interior* is above all a complex scene but also a stereoscopic vision of antique effect, which shows signs of the faithful ways in which Gérôme would create his pictorial compositions throughout his career, once his *Néo-Grec* passion had faded. If the work lacks the sensual nobility and nostalgia of Théodore Chassériau's *Tepidarium*, exhibited two years later (ill. 28), the central figure of which perhaps bears comparison to Gérôme's imaginary courtesan,[12] it nevertheless betrays a desire for radical inspiration, and, once again, for the blurring of genres at the expense of history painting. **É. P.**

1. G. de Ferry, *L'Ordre*, Jan. 11, 1851. **2.** Manuscript copy of an article by A. de Calonne, published in *L'Opinion publique*, 1851, BnF, département des Estampes et de la Photographie, Paris, fund 2-47. **3.** P. Petroz, *Le Vote universel*, Jan. 28, 1851. **4.** See S. Aubenas, "Le nu académique existe-t-il en daguerréotype?," in *L'Art du nu au XIXe siècle: le photographe et son modèle*, exh. cat. (Paris: Bibliothèque Nationale de France, 1998), pp. 24–27. **5.** T. Gautier, "Salon de 1850–1851," 6th article, *La Presse*, Mar. 1, 1851, p. 1. **6.** É.-J. Delécluze, "Exposition de 1850," 5th article, *Le Journal des débats politiques et littéraires*, Feb. 15, 1851, p. 2. **7.** T. Gautier 1851 (as in n. 5). **8.** P. de Chennevières, *Lettres sur l'art français en 1850* (Argentan: Barbier, 1851). **9.** A. de Calonne 1851 (as in n. 2). **10.** J.-L. Gérôme, *Notes autobiographiques* [1874], ed. G. Ackerman (Vesoul: S.A.L.S.A., 1981), p. 9. **11.** Pompeian painting was categorized in 1879–82 by the German archaeologist August Mau into four "styles" spread in an expansive way between the end of the third century B.C. and the destruction of the city in 79 A.D. **12.** S. Guégan, "Derniers Salons," in *Chassériau: un autre romantisme*, exh. cat. (Paris: Galeries Nationales du Grand Palais, 2002; also Strasbourg: Musée des Beaux-Arts, 2002, and New York: The Metropolitan Museum of Art, 2002–3), no. 237, pp. 366, 369.

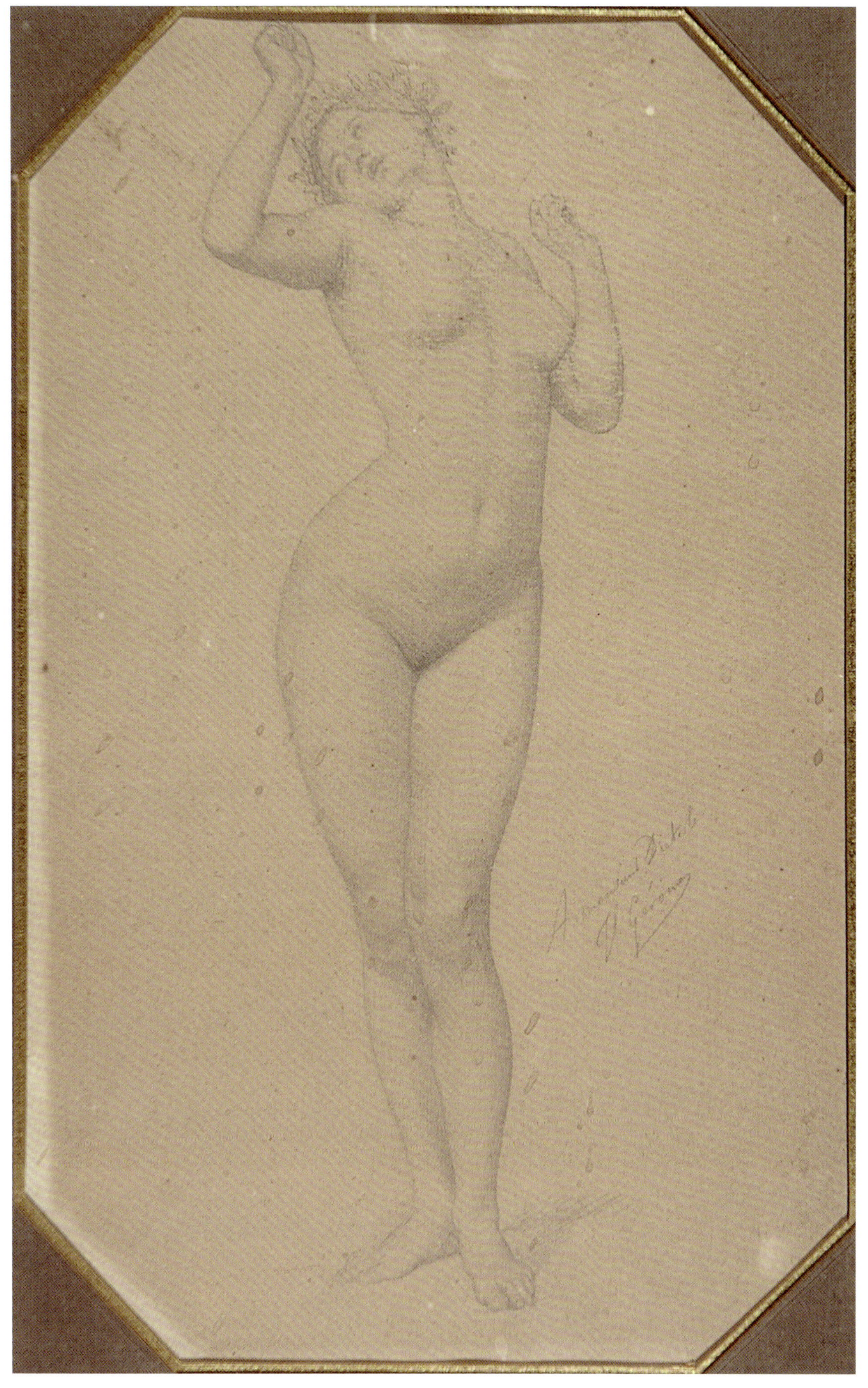

Cat. 25

NIGHT

-

ca. 1850–55
Oil on canvas
30 × 18 in.
Studio stamp, lower left
Musée d'Orsay, Paris, inv. RF 1984-27

-

Provenance: Galerie Joseph Hahn, *Les Peintres français et le grand décor parisien du XIXe siècle* (Paris, 1984), no. 34. Purchased by the Musée d'Orsay, 1984.

-

Bibliography: I. Compin and A. Roquebert, *Catalogue sommaire illustré des peintures du musée du Louvre et du musée d'Orsay* (Paris: RMN, 1986), vol. 3, p. 280. I. Compin, G. Lacambre and A. Roquebert, *Musée d'Orsay. Catalogue sommaire illustré des peintures* (Paris: RMN, 1990), vol. 1, p. 209. *Die Nacht*, exh. cat. (Munich: Haus der Kunst, 1998–99), no. 358. G. Ackerman, *Jean-Léon Gérôme* (Courbevoie: ACR Édition, 2000), no. 35, p. 220. *De Naakte Waarheid: Courbet en het 19e-eeuwse naakt*, exh. cat. (The Hague: Gemeentemuseum, 2006).

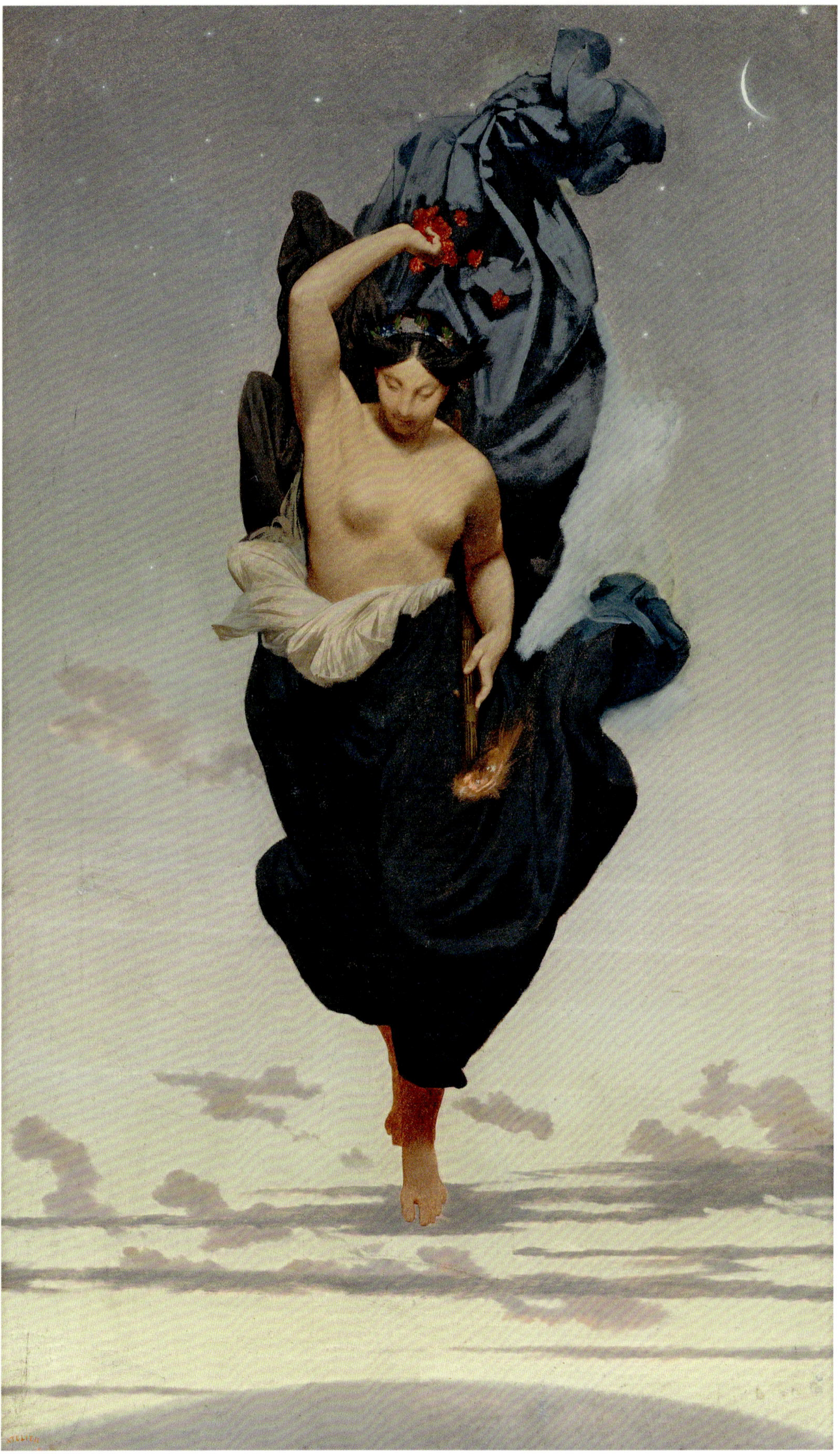

Cat. 26

DRUNKEN BACCHUS AND CUPID

-

1850
Oil on canvas
58 ¾ × 44 ½ in.
Musée des Beaux-Arts, Bordeaux, inv. 6264

-

Provenance: Purchased by the French government for the Bordeaux museum in 1850, dispatched to Bordeaux in 1852.

-

Exhibition history: Salon of 1850-1851, no. 1259.

-

Bibliography: L. Clément de Ris, *L'Artiste,* 5th ser., vol. 6, p. 9. P. de Chennevières, *Lettres sur l'Art français en 1850* (Argentan: Imprimerie de Barbier, 1851), pp. 53–54. L. de Geoffroy, *Revue des Deux Mondes*, vol. 9 (1851), pp. 947–48. A. de la Fizelière, *Salon de 1850–51,* p. 63. C. Vignon, *Salon de 1850-51* (Paris: Garnier frères), pp. 117–19. T. Gautier, "Salon de 1851," *La Presse,* Mar. 1, 1851, no. 131, pp. 1–2. L. Clément de Ris, "Musées de province," *Revue universelle des Arts*, vol. XII (1860), p. 32. P. Galibert, *Chefs-d'oeuvre du musée de Bordeaux* (Bordeaux, 1906), pl. 49. D. Alaux, *Diverses tendances de la peinture française au XIXe siècle et au début du XXe siècle (tableaux du Musée de Bordeaux)*, exh. cat. (Calais: Musée de Calais, 1976), no. 27, p. 00. *J.-L. Gérôme*, exh. cat. (Vesoul: Musée Georges-Garret, 1981), no. 116, p. 103. *Paris autour de 1882. Le développement de la peinture moderne en France et Hôsui Yamamoto*, exh. cat. (Gifu, Japan: Museum of Fine Arts, 1982), no. 20. *D'autres XIXe siècles*, exh. cat. (Bordeaux: Galerie des Beaux-Arts, 1987–88). G. Ackerman, *Jean-Léon Gérôme* (Courbevoie: ACR Édition, 2000), no. 31, pp. 218–19.

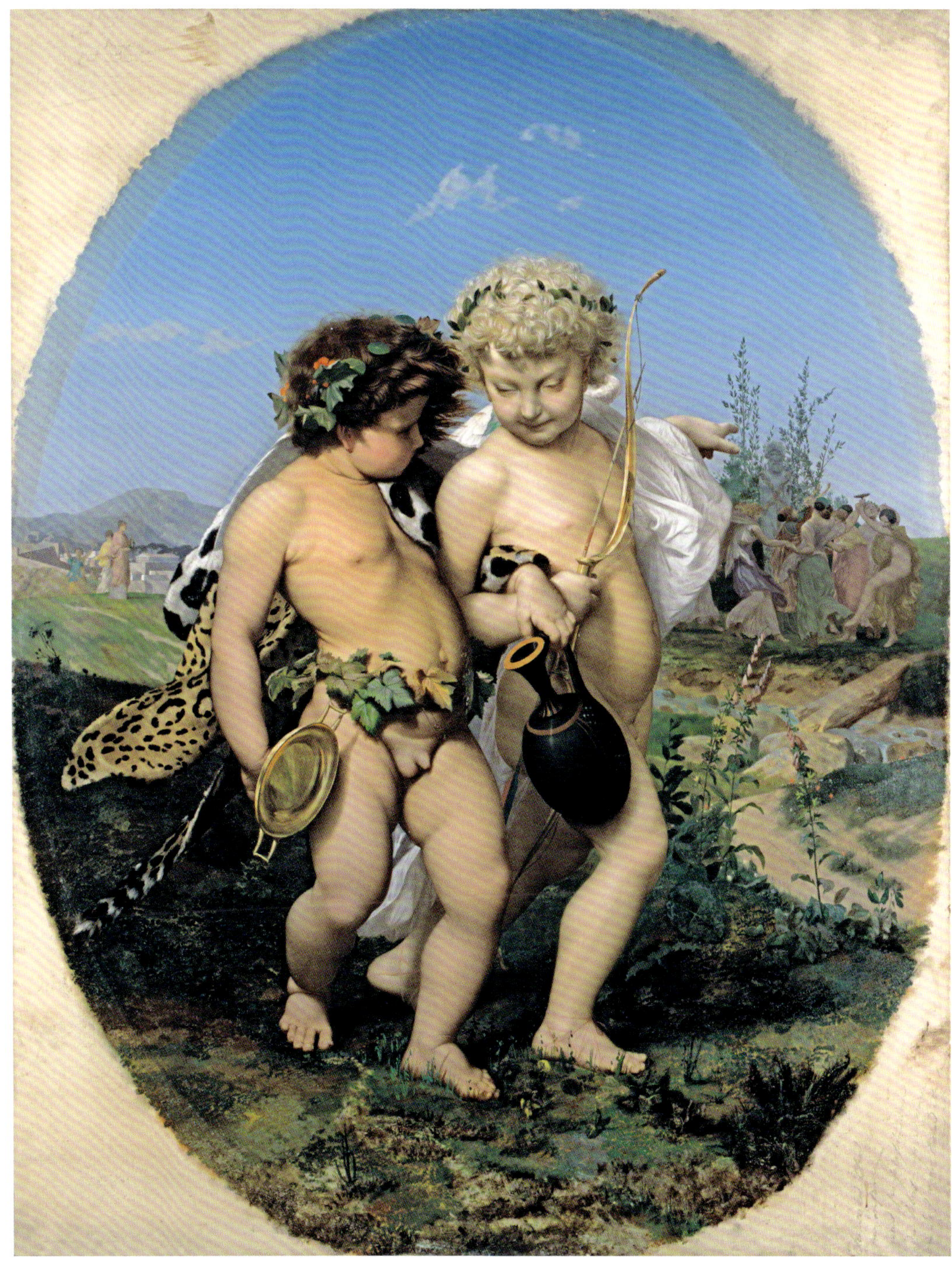

Cat. 27

FRIEZE FOR A SÈVRES VASE, ALSO KNOWN AS **FRIEZE OF THE FOUR PARTS OF THE WORLD PRESENTING THEIR PRODUCTS FOR THE FIRST INTERNATIONAL EXHIBITION IN LONDON, 1851**

1852
Oil on canvas
21 ¾ × 122 in.
Signed and dated on the central plinth: *J.L. GEROME MDCCCLII ANGLETERRE/FRANCE BELGIQUE/AUTRICHE PRUSSE/ ESPAGNE PORTUGAL/TURQUIE/CHINE/ÉTATS-UNIS/ RUSSIE*
Musée d'Orsay, Paris, inv. DO 1980 21

Provenance: Commissioned by the French government for the Sèvres Porcelain Manufactory. Allocated to the Sèvres Manufactory, 1852. On indefinite loan to the Musée d'Orsay, 1980.

Exhibition history: Salon of 1853, Paris, no. 527.

Bibliography: H. Delaborde, "Salon de 1853," *Revue des Deux Mondes*, vol. II (Apr. 1, 1853), p. 1146. T. Gautier, "Salon de 1853," *La Presse*, June 24, 1853, p. 21. L. Clément de Ris, "Salon de 1855," *L'Artiste*, 5th ser., vol. XI, p. 11. *J.-L. Gérôme*, exh. cat. (Vesoul: Musée Georges Garret, 1981), no. 118, p. 104. I. Compin, G. Lacambre, and A. Roquebert, *Musée d'Orsay. Catalogue sommaire illustré des peintures* (Paris: RMN, 1990), vol. 1, p. 210. G. Ackerman, *Jean-Léon Gérôme* (Courbevoie: ACR Édition, 2000), no. 43.

This frieze was commissioned by the government on behalf of the Sèvres Porcelain Manufactory. It was designed to be reproduced on a vase offered to Prince Albert at the Exposition Universelle of 1855 **(cat. 28)**. Since London had organized the first world's fair (the Great Exhibition) in 1851, in an effort to glorify the applied and industrial arts, Paris was determined to respond—and outdo the first event—in 1855. When Gérôme received this commission (the only one of its type in his career), he was perceived as the leader of the *Néo-Grec* school, whose stylistic emphasis on draftsmanship and formal synthesis certainly weighed on the decision of the commissioning body. Gérôme executed this decorative project while he was working on other projects for murals, one for the refectory of St.-Martin-des-Champs (now the Musée des Arts et Métiers) and the other for the chapel of St.-Jérôme in the church of St.-Séverin. In the composition of this frieze Gérôme apparently recalled a painting by his master, Paul Delaroche, the *Hemicycle of the École des Beauxs-Arts*. It was moreover the monumental potential of the frieze work that Gautier chose to stress in his review of the Salon of 1853, where it was exhibited. "The *Frieze for a Sèvres Vase* commemorating the London fair, despite its modest dimensions, represents a major composition that we would like to see executed full scale on the wall of some edifice of public industry, or on the arrival platform of some major railway." Gautier went on to praise Gérôme's allegorical choices. "It is a kind of panathenean procession of industry, aligning all the nations of the globe. In the middle are Plenty, Justice, and Concord in stoically serene poses... Having to execute a decorative frieze upon a purely modern subject, M. Gérôme found himself faced with a serious difficulty, which he felicitously overcame. He symbolized each country as a woman who, despite her antique dress, reflects the national type." The clearly enthusiastic Gautier concluded that this successful exercise promised "a vast future for the young artist, who has just proven with this work that he can be entrusted with the important mural and decorative projects."[1] But the critic's call would go unheeded—Gérôme never pursued a decorative path, although at the dawn of his long career he proved that his changeable, hybrid skills could occasionally be used to purely decorative ends. **L. C.**

1. T. Gautier, "Salon de 1853," *La Presse*, June 24, 1853, p. 21.

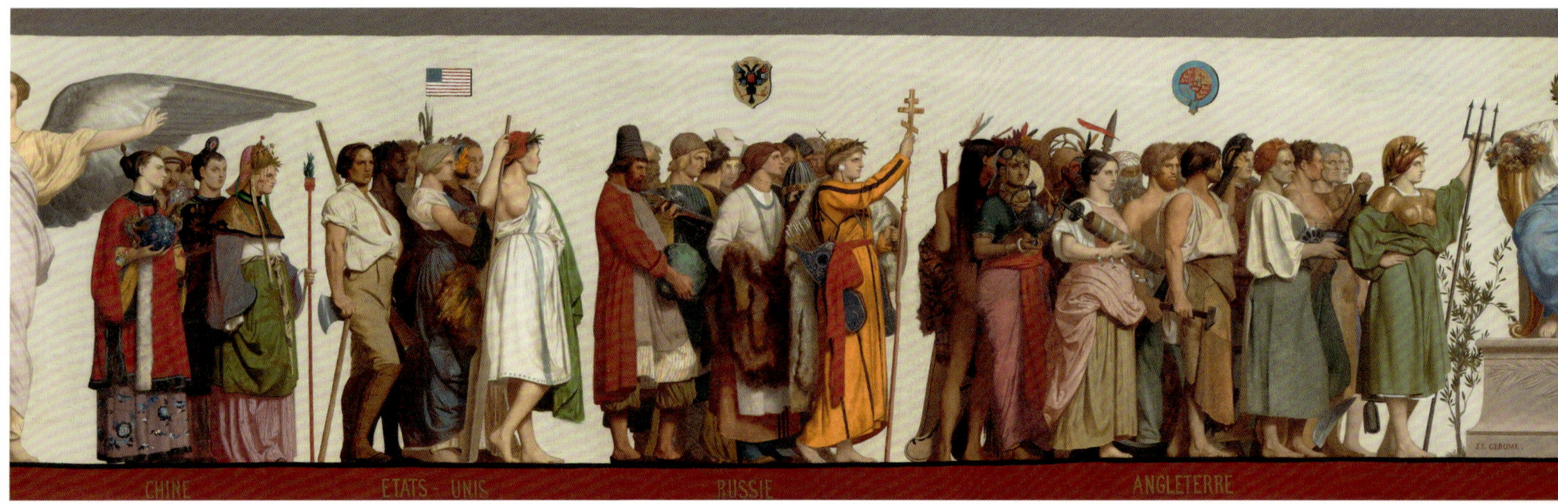

Cat. 28

Sèvres Porcelain Manufactory

Jules-Pierre-Michel Diéterle (1811-1889), draftsman

Antoine-Léon Brunel-Rocque (1822-1883), painter

Antoine Choiselat (active at the Manufactory ca. 1849-1856), modeller

after Jean-Léon Gérôme

COMMEMORATIVE VASE OF THE GREAT EXHIBITION IN LONDON, 1851

-

1855
Porcelain, glaze, gilded bronze
61 × 42 1/4 in.
On the front: *EN COMMEMORATION DE L'EXPOSITION DE LONDRES 1851*; on the back: *EXPOSITION UNIVERSELLE DE 1855 MANUFACTURE IMPÉRIALE SÈVRES*; on the frieze: *Peint par BRUNEL-ROCQUE d'après J.L. Gerome. MDCCCLV ANGLETERRE/ FRANCE BELGIQUE/AUTRICHE PRUSSE/ ESPAGNE PORTUGAL/TURQUIE/CHINE/ÉTATS-UNIS/RUSSIE*; on the neck of the vase: *J. DIETERLE INVENIT 1855/ABONDANCE*.
Buckingham Palace, London, lent by H.M. Queen Elizabeth II, inv. RCIN 90715

-

Provenance: Commissioned by Napoleon III as a gift for Prince Albert, 1853. Presented to Prince Albert by Napoleon III on August 22, 1855, during the British royal couple's state visit to Paris.

-

Bibliography: G. Ackerman et al., *Jean-Léon Gérôme (1824–1904)*, exh. cat. (Dayton: Dayton Art Institute, 1972; also Minneapolis: Minneapolis Institute of Arts, 1973, and Baltimore: The Walters Art Gallery, 1973), p. 10. *J.-L. Gérôme*, exh. cat. (Vesoul: Musée Georges-Garret, 1981), p. 104. H. Lafont-Couturier, *Gérôme and Goupil: Art and Enterprise*, exh. cat., trans. I. Ollivier (Bordeaux: Musée Goupil, 2000–1; also New York: Dahesh Museum of Art, 2001, and Pittsburgh: The Frick Art & Historical Center, 2001), p. 154.

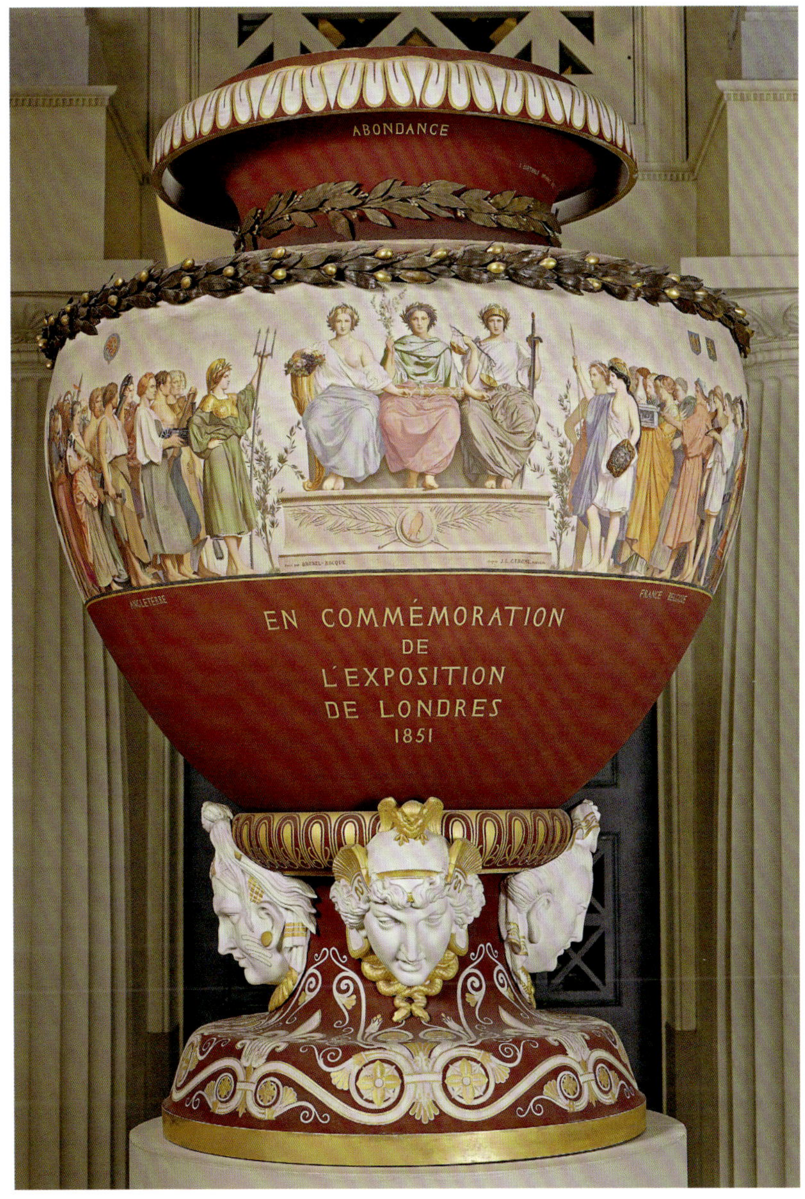

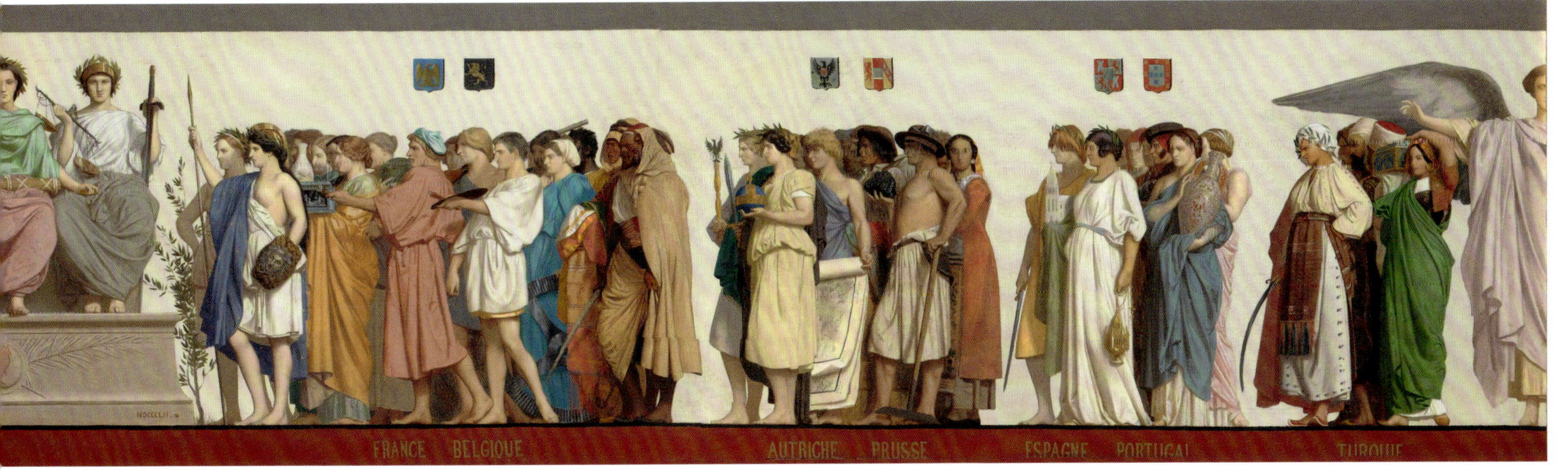

Cat. 29

THE IDYLLE,
ALSO KNOWN AS
DAPHNIS AND CHLOE

–

1852
Oil on canvas
83 ½ × 61 ⅜ in.
Signed and dated bottom right: *J.L. GEROME*
Musée Massey, Tarbes, inv. 872-1-1

–

Provenance: Goupil to M. A. Fould, 1870 (for 4,950 francs). Deed of gift from A. Fould to the Musée de Tarbes; included in all the museum's catalogues (1872, 1883, 1931). Transferred to the Musée de Brest in 1973. Then returned to the Musée de Tarbes.

–

Exhibition History: Salon of 1853, Paris, no. 528. Exposition Universelle, Paris, 1900.

–

Bibliography: L. Boyeldieu d'Auvigny, *Salon de 1853*, p. 56. L. Clément de Ris, *Salon de 1853*, p. 11. T. Gautier, *La Presse*, June 24, 1853, p. 2. P. Mérimée, *Le Moniteur, Salon de 1853*, p. 749. G. Ackerman et al., *Jean-Léon Gérôme (1824–1904)*, exh. cat. (Dayton: Dayton Art Institute, 1972; also Minneapolis: Minneapolis Institute of Arts, 1973, and Baltimore: The Walters Art Gallery, 1973), no. 4, pp. 34–35. *J.-L. Gérôme*, exh. cat. (Vesoul: Musée Georges-Garret, 1981), no. 120, p. 105. A. Fermigier, "Les pompiers et les pointus", *Le Monde*, Sept. 3, 1981, p. 11. *De Courbet à Cézanne*, exh. cat. (Prague, 1982), no. 36, pp. 112–14. *Von Courbet bis Cezanne*, exh. cat. (Berlin: Staatliche Museen zu Berlin Nationalgalerie, 1983), no. 38, pp. 160–62. *Odilon Redon. Rencontres et résonances*, exh. cat. (Gifu: Museum of Fine Art, 1985; also Kunamato: Prefectural Museum of Art, 1985, and Hiroshima: Prefectural Museum of Art, 1986), no. 50, pp. 57–58. G. Ackerman, *Jean-Léon Gérôme* (Courbevoie: ACR Édition, 2000), no. 47. H. Lafont-Couturier, *Gérôme and Goupil: Art and Enterprise*, exh. cat., trans. I. Ollivier (Bordeaux: Musée Goupil, 2000–1; also New York: Dahesh Museum of Art, 2001, and Pittsburgh: The Frick Art & Historical Center, 2001), p. 36, n. 59, 160. S. Harent and C. Stoullig, *Dessins de Jean-Léon Gérôme: la collection du musée des Beaux-Arts de Nancy*, exh. cat. (Nancy: Musée des Beaux-Arts, 2009), p. 47.

Ill. 29. Anonymous, *Apollo and Artemis* (detail), engraving, in Eduard Gerhard (1795–1867), *Auserlesene Vasenbilder, Hauptsächlich Etruskischen Fundorts* (Berlin: Reimer, 1847), vol. 1, "Götterbilder," pl. LXXVIII, Bibliothèque Centrale des Musées Nationaux, Musée du Louvre, Paris.

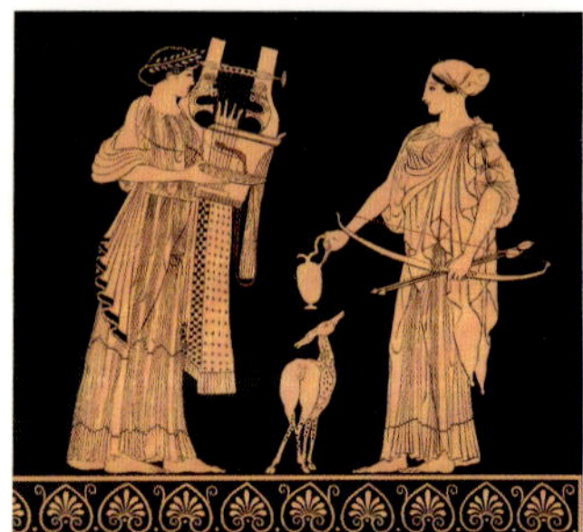

Ill. 30. After Jean-Léon Gérôme, *Return from the Hunt* [1873], photograph by Goupil & Cie reproduced in "Musée Goupil & Cie," no. 1164, albumen print, 7 ¼ × 6 ¼ in., Archives, Musée d'Orsay, Paris.

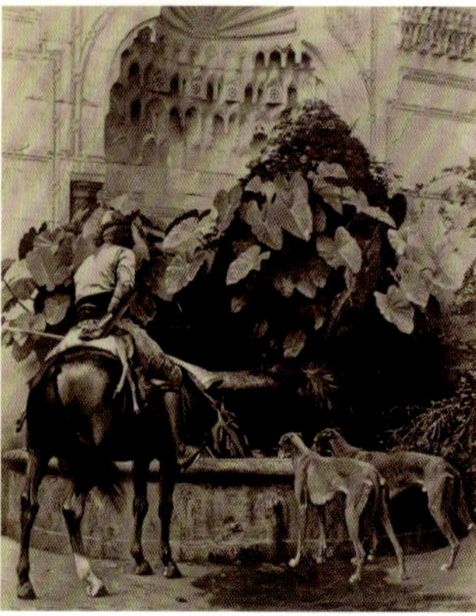

At the Salon of 1853, where Théodore Chassériau was exhibiting *Tepidarium* (ill. 28, p. 60), *The Idylle*, appearing five years after *The Cock Fight* (cat. 10), was an ambitious composition—in a history painting format, it betrayed an "Alexandrine" evolution of the *Néo-Grec* style. The simple composition concentrates on the motif, one of Gérôme's most academic, of two adolescents. The familiar figure of the doe, supposedly the go-between as love awakens, places a graceful animal motif so dear to Gérôme at the heart of the work; with its back to the painter, the doe is inspired by the painting of antique vases (ill. 29). It was likely out of a desire to avoid charges of vulgarity that Gérôme chose here a fairly vague and conventional elegiac theme. The work however was only sold in 1870. It was Théophile Gautier who compared *The Idylle* to an illustration of *Daphnis and Chloe*, the famous Greek novel by Longus, Jacques Amyot's translation of which (1559) had been revised by Paul-Louis Courrier in 1810.[1] Gautier's idea was not without foundation, and the work is possibly evocative of the budding love between the shepherd Daphnis and the goatherd Chloe, but Gérôme does not really seem to have been inspired by the text: "He arrived with Chloe at the nymphs' grotto and gave her his basket and gown to keep, before plunging into the fountain to wash his hair and body. His hair, dark as ebony, clung to his tanned neck... Chloe saw Daphnis and saw how Daphnis was handsome.... She wanted him to not stop bathing, and while she was bathing, she saw him naked, and seeing him this way, she could not help but touch him. When she returned home in the evening, she thought of Daphnis naked and that thought was the start of love."[2] The sculptor Jean-Pierre Cortot (1824–27, marble, Musée du Louvre, Paris) and the painter Baron Gérard (1825, oil on canvas, Musée du Louvre, Paris) had both produced more faithful illustrations of an episode in Longus's novel. Gérôme's pastoral takes place in an antiquity that is more generic than Greek. The wall sheltering the fountain alcove, the flat brickwork and the fountain's motif of a winged Eros seated cross-legged, which is closer to Roman sculpture or the Italian Renaissance, create a timeless setting of an academic style of genuine worth. The vegetation however comes from several continents, and Gérôme combines elephant ear (*Alocasia*) leaves with a vine on which climb nasturtiums and ivy, a kind of reminiscence of a sleepy Roman palace courtyard. Gérôme would revive this motif of a fountain overrun by plants for an Orientalist work, *Return from the Hunt* (ill. 30), in 1873. But blood is thicker than water: the mocking smile of the sculpted Eros, the boy's sidelong glance, Antinous coiffed like a life-class model, the still life of the opportunely placed bouquet—which the caricaturist Cham took the chance to mock[3]—all invite the provocative impertinence of the painter of *A Greek Interior* (cat. 23). Louis Clément de Ris criticized Gérôme "for creating wax figures of a disagreeable tone"[4] and by far preferred another "pastoral" exhibited at the same Salon by another *Néo-Grec* and friend of Gérôme, Jean-Louis Hamon (ill. 9, p. 44), whereas Prosper Mérimée described the figures as "two colored statues with uncertain expressions."[5] Gautier, praising the elegance of the characters, and appreciating that, this time, Gérôme had not aimed for "the Etruscan or primitive Greek of Aegina,"[6] concluded that the painter was "an Athenian born in France two thousand years later, that is all."[7] If he treats anatomies with great care (the legs of the boy were retouched, which is rare in Gérôme's work), this calm image is no doubt the one that most evokes the work of his second master, Charles Gleyre (ill. 2, p. 28).[8] **É. P.**

1. The 1813 edition (Paris: Firmin-Didot) republished, revised, and corrected (Paris: Alexandre Corréard, 1821), then again in 1825 in *Collection des romans grecs* (Paris: Merlin, 1825), leading to the widespread popularity of the text. **2.** Longus, *Daphnis et Chloé* [1810], Amyot's translation, revised and corrected by P.-L. Courrier (Paris: À l'enseigne du pot cassé, 1928), pp. 31–32. **3.** "A young man not daring to offer his bouquet to a young lady out of fear of having nothing else to cover himself with," in *Revue comique du Salon de 1853 par Cham*, for *Le Charivari*, 1853. **4.** L. Clément de Ris, "Salon de 1853," *L'Artiste*, vol. XI, 1853, p. 11. **5.** P. Mérimée, "Salon de 1853," *Le Moniteur*, 1853, p. 617. **6.** T. Gautier, "Salon de 1853," *La Presse*, June 24, 1855, p. 2. **7.** Ibid. **8.** G. Ackerman et al., *Jean-Léon Gérôme (1824–1904)*, exh. cat. (Dayton: Dayton Art Institute, 1972; also Minneapolis: Minneapolis Institute of Arts, 1973, and Baltimore: The Walters Art Gallery, 1973), no. 4, p. 34.

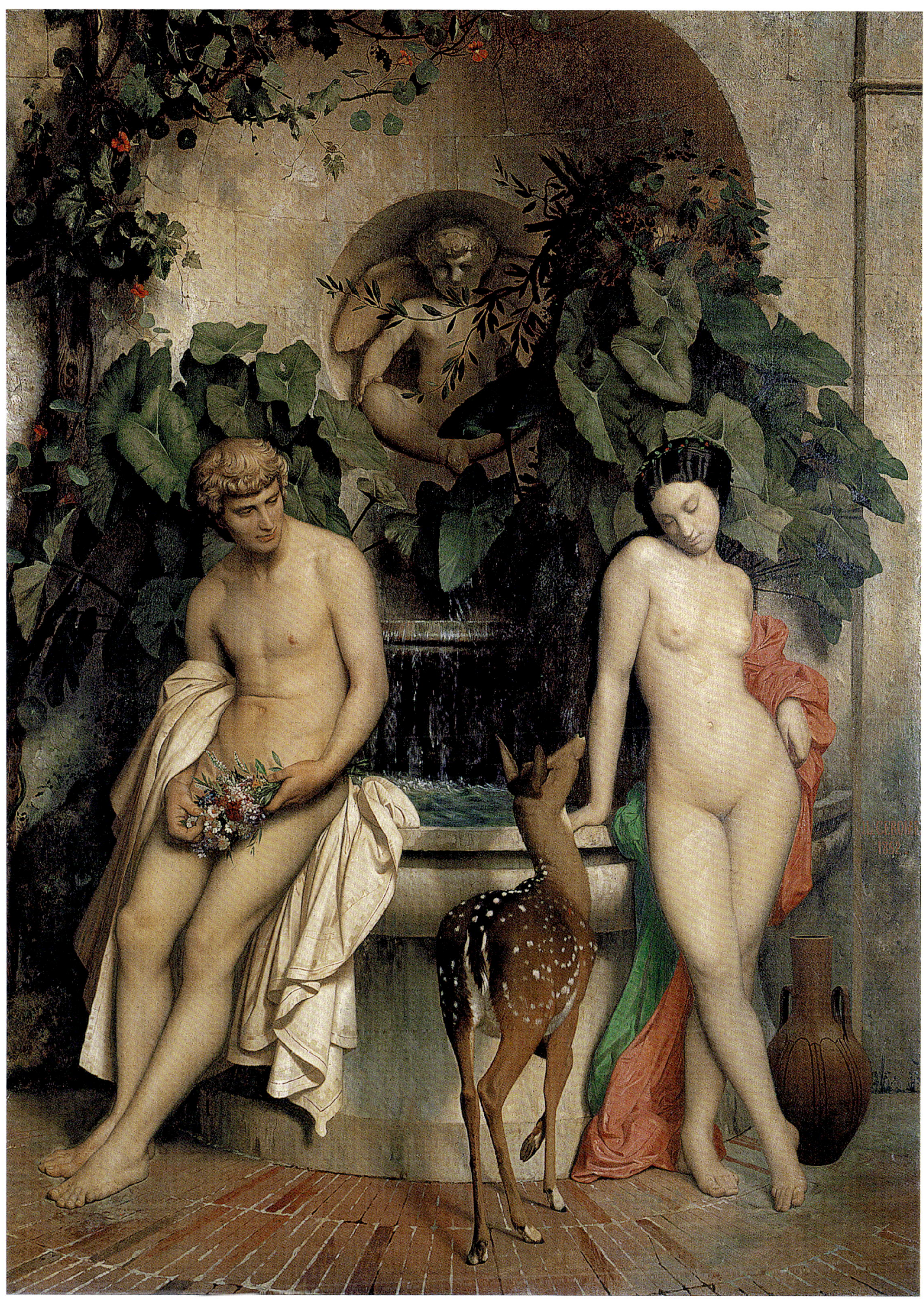
1852

Cat. 30

THE BACCHANTE

–

1853
Oil on canvas
Diam. 18 ¾ in.
Signed and dated lower left:
J.L.GEROME 1853
Musée des Beaux-Arts, Nantes, inv. 987

–

Provenance: Exhibited in Nantes. Purchased by the Musée des Beaux-Arts in 1854.

–

Bibliography: *Catalogue des tableaux et statues du Musée de la ville de Nantes,* 6th edition (Nantes: Imprimerie de Mellinet, 1854), no. 1053. *Catalogue des tableaux et statues du Musée de la ville de Nantes,* 7th edition (Nantes: Imprimerie de Mellinet, 1859), no. 97. *Catalogue des tableaux et statues du Musée de la ville de Nantes,* 8th edition (Nantes: Imprimerie de Mellinet, 1876), no. 754. *Inventaire des richesses d'art de la France: Musée de Nantes* (Paris: Merson, 1883), p. 33. *Catalogue des peintures, sculptures, pastels, aquarelles, dessins et objets d'art du Musée de la ville de Nantes,* 9th edition (Paris: Braun Clément & Cie, 1903), no. 888. M. Nicolle and E. Dacier, *Musée municipal des Beaux-Arts: catalogue* (Nantes: Musée des Beaux-Arts), 1913, no. 987. G. Ackerman, *La Vie et l'oeuvre de Jean-Léon Gérôme* (Courbevoie: ACR Édition, 1986), p. 195, no. 53. C. Ritzenthaler, *L'école des Beaux-Arts du XIXe siècle: les pompiers* (Paris: Mayer, 1987), p. 172. *Figures et paysages: la peinture française du XIXème siècle dans les collections du musée des Beaux-Arts de Nantes,* exh. cat. (Lisbon: Galeria Almada Negreiros, 1992). *Histoires parallèles: la peinture française du XIXème siècle au musée des Beaux-Arts de Nantes,* exh. cat. (Japan: six venues, 1995–96), p. 213 no. 64, p. 137. H. Lafont-Couturier, *Gérôme* (Paris: Herscher, 1998), p. 129, p. 15. G. Ackerman, *Jean-Léon Gérôme* (Courbevoie: ACR Édition, 2000), no. 53. *Kridla slavy: vojtech Hynais, cesti Parizané a Francie* (Prague: Galerie Rudolfinum, 2000–01), p. 434.

Cat. 31

CHILD WITH A MASK

–

1861
Oil on canvas
Diam. 19 ¾ in.
Collection of Terence and Katrina Garnett, San Mateo, California

–

Provenance: Goupil family. Blanche Goupil, inherited by Françoise Bergeret, née De Tarde.

–

Bibliography: G. Ackerman, *Jean-Léon Gérôme* (Courbevoie: ACR Édition, 2000), no. 9.6.

Ill. 31. Silvestre & Cie, *Lysimachos, King of Thracia (323–281 B.C.). Head of Alexander the Great as Zeux Amun,* pl. IX, no. 6, glyptography reproduced in Adrien Blanchet, *Les Monnaies Grecques* (Paris: Ernest Leroux, 1894), départment des Antiquités grecques, étrusques et romaines, Musée du Louvre, Paris.

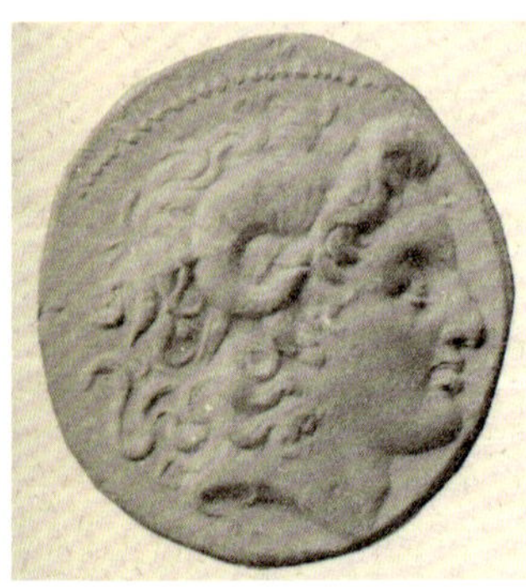

Ill. 32. Anderson for Fratelli Alinari, ca. 1890, photograph of the *Child Removing a Mask,* Rome, second century A.D., marble, Musei Capitolini, Rome.

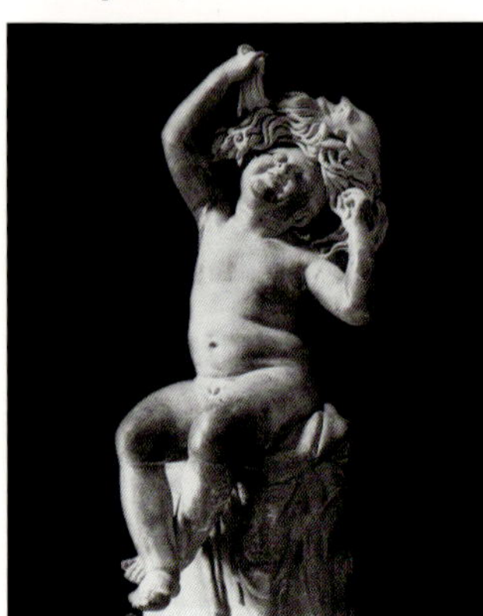

The *Bacchante* is an introspective tondo of a mysterious subject. This hybrid melancholy figure remains one of Gérôme's rare incursions into the domain of the imaginary and presents a very personal interpretation of the supernatural. The iconography of this striking, also physiognomic image, is enhanced by the circular format, which focuses the viewer's eye in a voyeuristic, specular fashion on the violated privacy of the figure; but the work remains enigmatic. In all likelihood Gérôme has transposed a Greco-Roman representation of the Egyptian god Amun, comparable to Zeus or Jupiter; the most admired antique bust during the nineteenth century is that conserved in the museum of Naples;[1] however he would probably also have seen coins, bearing the effigy of Alexander the Great in the dual guise of Zeus and Amun (ill. 31). The young girl with androgynous traits, her eyes lowered, whose bare shoulder sensually emerges from a slashed sleeve and a pelisse, who is more evocative of sixteenth-century Venetian painting, seems lost in a melancholy inner reverie, her head pressed to her shoulder. The naturalistic treatment of the rams' horns emerging from the girl's frizzy hair contrasts with the diffuse animality of her facial features. Could this be a workshop souvenir, a motif discovered by chance while accessorizing a modeling session, or the suggestion of a costume for a masked ball?[2] *Child with a Mask* plays on this iconographic strangeness in a similar way while also providing an allegorical exploration of child portraiture. Masks play an important role in Gérôme's iconographic imagination (*The Greek Comedians,* p. 10) and they feature in a number of scenes featuring the artist's workshop, whether real or imaginary (cat. 174). They are also evocative of certain Pompeian frescoes, or of Hellenistic or Roman statuettes of cherubs, who play games with masks (ill. 32).[3] The costumed child's sidelong gaze, so deep and serious in his or her adult disguise, accentuates the "Ingrisme," pervaded with fantasy, of this beautiful, slightly melancholic portrait demonstrating the possibilities of a genre in which Gérôme seldom worked (cat. 34). This pair of tondi play subtly and powerfully on strangeness; the mastery of Gérôme, an inventor of images and atmospheres, here finds its full measure. **É. P.**

1. K. Blondel, "Ammon," in C. Daremberg and E. Saglio, *Dictionnaire des antiquités grecques, étrusques et romaines d'après les monuments...* (Paris: Hachette, 1877–1919), vol. 1, pp. 230–3. **2.** C. Allemand-Cosneau, in *Histoires parallèles: la peinture française du XIXème siècle au musée des Beaux-Arts de Nantes,* exh. cat. (Japan: six venues, 1995–96), no. 64, p. 213. **3.** See J. Becq, "Masques antiques, études au XIXe siècle," in *Masques, de Carpeaux à Picasso,* exh. cat. (Paris: Musée d'Orsay, 2008–9), pp. 62–67.

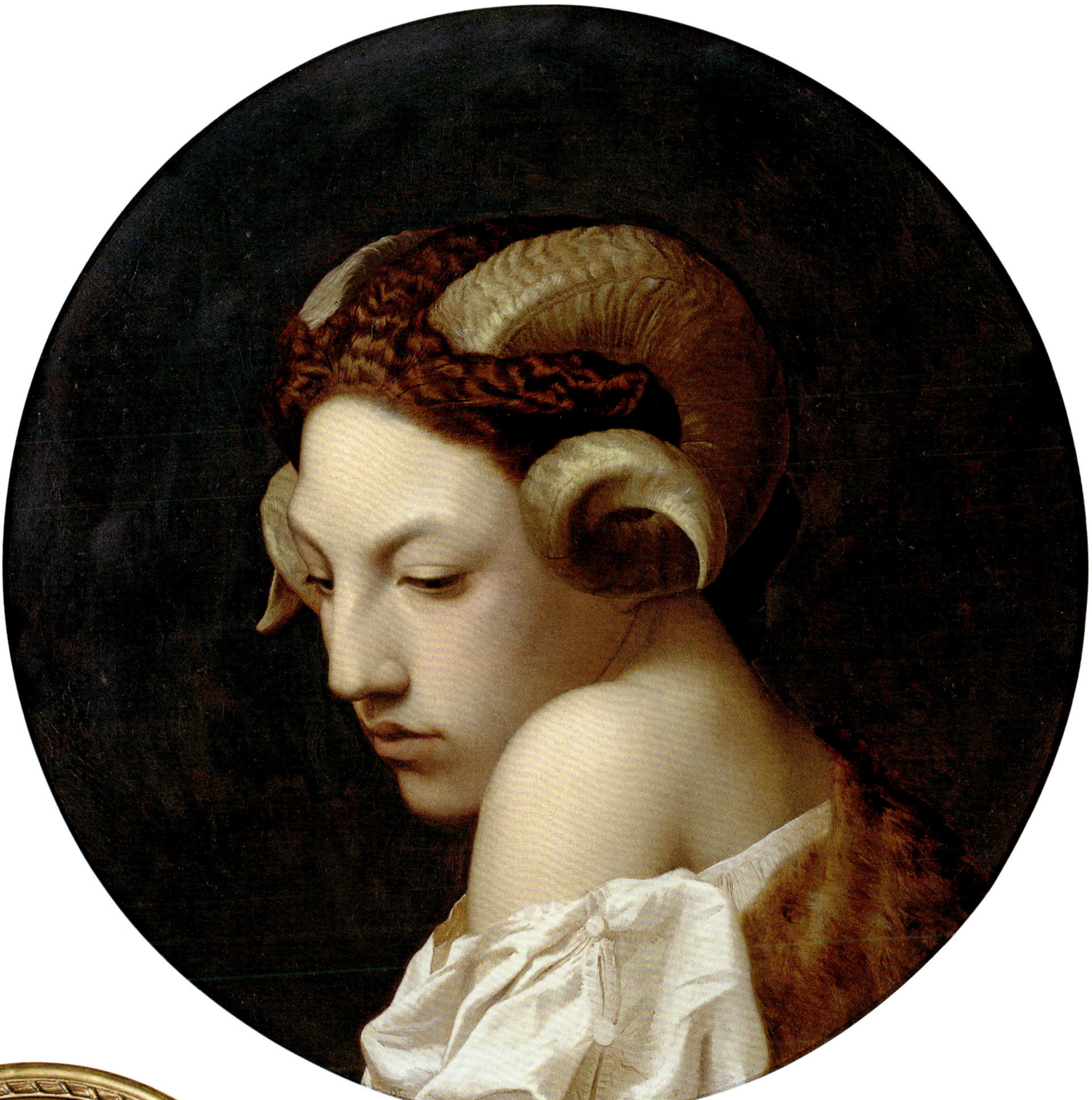

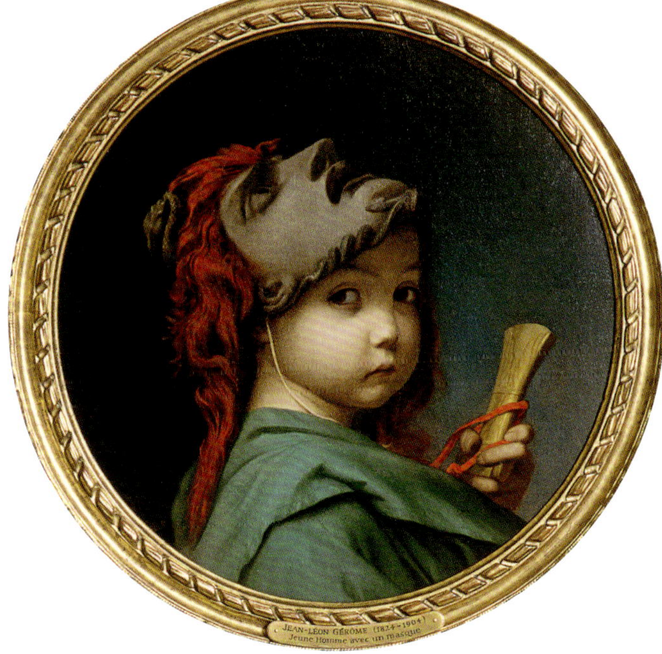
JEAN-LÉON GÉRÔME (1824-1904)
Jeune Homme avec un masque

Cat. 32

THE AGE OF AUGUSTUS (SKETCH)

–

ca. 1853–54
Oil on canvas
14 ½ × 20 in.
J. Paul Getty Museum, Los Angeles

–

Provenance: Gérôme, gift to Victor Borie, Paris, ca. 1862. Borie sale, Guéroult, Paris, Feb. 14, 1881, lot 11. Etienne-François Haro, sale, Galerie Sedelmeyer, Paris, May 30–31, 1892, lot 95 (unsold). Henri Haro, sale, Drouot, Paris, Apr. 2, 1897, lot 152 (unsold). Haro sale, Drouot, Paris, Feb. 9, 1912, lot 13. Private collection, sale, Sotheby's, Monte Carlo, Mar. 5, 1984, lot 1111, to Wheelock Whitney & Co., New York. Sold to the J. Paul Getty Museum, 1985.

–

Bibliography: J.-L. Gérôme, *Notes autobiographiques* [1874], ed. G. Ackerman (Vesoul: S.A.L.S.A., 1981), pp. 9, 11, 21, n. 33. C. Timbal, "Gérôme," *Gazette des Beaux-Arts*, 2nd per., vol. 40, no. 3 (Sept. 1, 1876), pp. 230–31; no. 4 (Oct. 1, 1876), p. 334. C. Blanc, *Les Artistes de mon temps* (Paris: Firmin-Didot, 1876), pp. 431–32. J. Claretie, "J.-L. Gérôme," in *Grands peintres français et étrangers* (Paris: H. Launette; Goupil, 1886), pp. 149–50. C. H. Stranahan, *A History of French Painting from its Earliest to its Latest Practice* (London: Sampson Low, Marston, Searle, and Rivington, 1889), pp. 311, 318, 319. F. F. Hering, *Gérôme: The Life and Works of Jean Léon Gérôme* (New York: Cassell, 1892), pp. 2, 3, 7–12, 61–62, 63. F. Masson, "J.-L. Gérôme, peintre de l'orient," *Figaro illustré*, 2nd ser., no. 136 (July 1901), p. 10. V. Guillemin, "Étude sur le peintre et sculpteur Jean-Léon Gérôme (1824–1904)," *Académie des sciences, belles-lettres et arts de Besançon. Procès-verbaux et mémoires. Année 1904* (Besançon, 1905), pp. 141–43, 180–81. M. H. Spielmann, "Jean-Léon Gérôme: 1824–1904. Recollections," *The Magazine of Art*, vol. 2 (1904), p. 208. C. Moreau-Vauthier, *Gérôme, peintre et sculpteur. L'homme et l'artiste d'après sa correspondance, ses notes, ses souvenirs, les souvenirs de ses élèves et de ses amis* (Paris: Hachette, 1906), pp. 99–108, 112, 288. H. Roujon, *Artistes et amis des arts* (Paris: Hachette, 1912), pp. 76–77. *J.-L. Gérôme*, exh. cat. (Vesoul: Musée Georges-Garret, 1981), pp. 20, 50–51, under nos. 26, 27. A. Boime, "The Second Empire's Official Realism," in *The European Realist Tradition*, ed. Gabriel P. Weisberg (Bloomington: Indiana University Press, 1982), p. 86, fig. 3.8. A. Boime, "Gérôme and the Bourgeois Artist's Burden," *Arts Magazine*, vol. 57, no. 5 (Jan. 1983), pp. 66, 69. G. Ackerman, *The Life and Work of Jean-Léon Gérôme, with a Catalogue Raisonné* (New York and London: Sotheby's, 1986), pp. 37, 42, 58, 198, 199, nos. 64, 64B. B. Foucart, *Le Renouveau de la peinture religieuse en France (1800–1860)* (Paris: Arthena, 1987), p. 268, fig. 246. P. Mainardi, *Art and Politics of the Second Empire: The Universal Expositions of 1855 and 1867* (New Haven: Yale University Press, 1987), p. 80, pl. 51. F. Nicolaus, "Gérôme: Der letzte Ritter der traditionellen Malerei steigt steil auf und geht quälend langsam unter," *Art: Das Kunstmagazin*, no. 2 (1989), p. 75. M. J. Gotlieb, *From Genre to Decoration: Studies in the Theory and Criticism of French Salon Painting, 1850–1900* (Ann Arbor: UMI, 1990), pp. 196–222, fig. 23. G. Ackerman, *Jean-Léon Gérôme: His Life, His Work, 1824–1904* (Courbevoie: ACR Édition, 1997), pp. 35, 39–40, 228, 229, nos. 64, 64.2, ill. p. 35. G. Ackerman, *Jean-Léon Gérôme* (Paris: ACR Édition, 2000), pp. 40, 228, 229, nos. 64, 64.2, ill.. H. Lafont-Couturier, *Gérôme and Goupil: Art and Enterprise*, exh. cat., trans. I. Ollivier (Bordeaux: Musée Goupil, 2000–1; also New York: Dahesh Museum of Art, 2001, and Pittsburgh: The Frick Art & Historical Center, 2001), pp. 33–34, 109, 164. S. Harent and C. Stoullig, *Dessins de Jean-Léon Gérôme: la collection du musée des Beaux-Arts de Nancy*, exh. cat. (Nancy: Musée des Beaux-Arts, 2009), pp. 14–15, fig. 4.

Determined to present the Second Empire in the best possible light at the 1855 Exposition Universelle, the government of Napoleon III allotted the ministry of public education a 300,000-franc budget for artistic commissions. Late in 1852, the young Gérôme received a generous 20,000-franc commission for a monumental canvas on the painter's chosen subject, "The Age of Augustus." On February 1, 1853 he wrote to the comte de Nieuwerkerke, director of fine arts, indicating that he had already "done a large part of the drawings for the picture" and would like a 5,000-franc advance. This was paid on February 15, enabling him to travel to eastern Europe in order to collect ethnographic studies for his composition. By May 8, 1854, Gérôme had finished the cartoon and advanced to the *ébauche* stage of the final work, according to an inspector's report. Several payments were made to Gérôme in the months ahead, and the remaining balance was paid off in July 1855, several months after the painting went on exhibition.[1]

Gérôme based his subject on a passage in Jacques-Bénigne Bossuet's *Histoire universelle* (1681) that evokes the triumphant establishment of the *pax Romana* under Augustus and the coming of Christ: "The remainder of the Republic perished with Brutus and Cassius. Having eliminated Lepidus, Caesar and Antony turned against each other. All the power of Rome clashed on the sea. Caesar won the Battle of Actium. The forces of Egypt and the East, which Antony had on his side, were dispersed. He was forsaken by all his friends, even Cleopatra, for whom he had ruined himself... Everything gave way before Caesar's good luck. Alexandria opened its gates to him, and Egypt became a Roman province. Cleopatra, losing all hope of being able to keep it, killed herself after Antony's suicide. Rome received Caesar with open arms, and, under the name of Augustus and the title of emperor, he established himself permanently as the sole master of the whole empire. In the Pyrenean region, he subjugated the rebellious Cantabri and Astures; Ethiopia sued for peace; terrified, the Parthians sent back the standards that had been taken from Crassus, as well as all the Roman prisoners; India sought an alliance with him; his strength was felt by the Rhaetians or Grisons, whose mountains were no longer a defense; Pannonia recognized

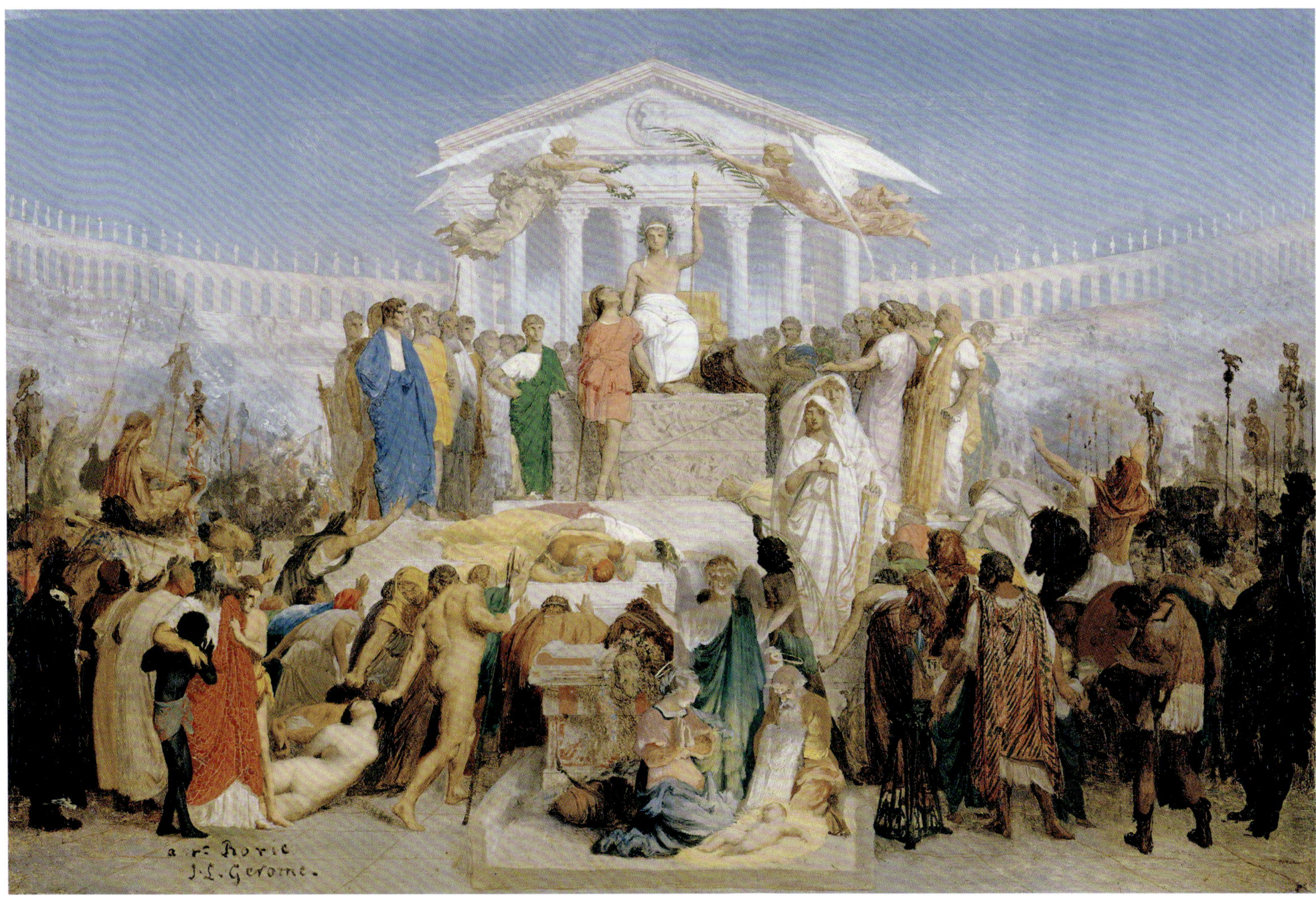

him, Germany feared him, and the Turk received his laws. Victorious on land and sea, he closed the Temple of Janus. The universe lived in peace under his power, and Jesus Christ came into the world."[2]

As Albert Boime observed, the subject resonated directly with the imperialist designs of Napoleon III, who was frequently likened to Augustus. The comparison was a particularly apt one to make at the Exposition Universelle in Paris, where France would play triumphant host to the world.[3]

Synthesizing, as Théophile Gautier wrote, "an entire era and an entire world,"[4] Gérôme's final composition is organized symmetrically around a central, vertical axis (ill. 1, pp. 26-27). At the apex against a cloudless sky stands the temple of Janus. Before it sits the apotheosized Augustus, his scepter-bearing pose echoing that of the Capitoline Jupiter, a statuette of which graces the throne. A Latin inscription on the stone socle below celebrates the emperor's worldly dominion: "Caesar Augustus imperator, victor Canabrorum, Asturum, Parthorum, Rhaetorum et Indorum, Germaniae, Pannoniaeque domitor, pacificator orbis, pater patriae." At Augustus' feet on the right is the imperial eagle, and on the left a personification of Rome in the form of a helmeted woman wearing a red chlamyde and bearing a lance decorated with laurels: a "symbol," Gautier noted, "of peace gained through victory."[5] Gathered further to the left of Caesar are various allied statesmen, while to the right appear various artists: an actor with his mask, the architect Vitruvius with a model, a sculptor with his chisel, and several literary men, the poet Virgil at the forefront. The prominence of Virgil is particularly significant, for not only had he sought in *The Aeneid* to sanction the divinely appointed Roman mission to civilize the world, but he had also written, in his fourth eclogue, of the birth of a child who would restore peace and bring back the golden age. His vision of harmony was understood to have been realized under the reign of Augustus. It would also later be regarded as prophetic of Christ's coming.[6]

On the steps below Augustus, Gérôme alludes to the civil strife that provided the historical context for Virgil's "messianic" eclogue and the emperor's rise to power. At Rome's feet lie the corpses of Marc

Antony and Cleopatra, and to the right, below the eagle, the body of Julius Caesar. Wrapped in white togas, the chief conspirators in his assassination, Cassius and Brutus, descend the steps somberly. Brutus still clutches his traitorous dagger while Cassius, hand on forehead, looks forward as if gazing into the future—one that would bring their final stand for the Roman Republic at Philippi in Greece. While Cassius and Brutus distance themselves from Rome and the Republic fades into memory, the rest of the world surges forth in the bottom half of the composition to pay tribute to Augustus and submit to the new imperial order. In this "phantasmagorical procession," critics saw "men of all races, types and costumes,"[7] in keeping with Bossuet's magisterial evocation as well as Gérôme's nascent ethnographic ambitions. Among those on the right are Indians mounted on an elephant, the Parthians returning the captured Roman standards and jubilant ex-prisoners of war, a northern barbarian sporting animal skins, and a woman dutifully bringing forth her two children, little Roman citizens already. Among those on the left are soldiers and lictors dragging by the hair male and female captives, personifying rebellious provinces brought to heel by force; a richly dressed oriental king ("from some fantastic Transoxianic or Chaldean realm"[8]) supported by a nude woman and shield-bearing slave; and young Arabs and Africans casually perched on their dromedaries. Countless other figures bow, kneel, and otherwise prostrate themselves before the divinized Augustus. Finally, sheltered in the midst of the tumult by an angel's outstretched wings, Mary and Joseph kneel in peaceful adoration of a preternaturally glowing Christ Child. Christ's symbolic placement on a bed of straw in the center of an ashen pit of pagan sacrifice prefigures his own redemptive sacrifice even as it heralds his displacement of the old pagan order.

Besides a number of surviving preparatory drawings for the painting is an advanced compositional oil sketch, shown here. Between the sketch and final work, Gérôme introduced a number of significant changes. For the amphitheatre setting he had initially envisaged, he substituted crenellated ramparts while also downplaying their presence. He adjusted the ornaments on the temple of Janus, adding the quadriga and griffons above the pediment, eliminating the relief medallion of Janus in the center of the pediment, and multiplying smaller Janus medallions along the entablature instead. More crucially, Gérôme eliminated the allegorical figures that had soared above Augustus in the sketch. The symbolic laurel crowns and palm branch they bore have literally materialized in the foreground of the finished picture; the crowns are strewn on the pavement and the palm branch is now offered by an anonymous subject. By eliminating the winged genies, Gérôme was able to reassert Augustus' prominence at the top of the composition and to avoid any confusion that might have arisen from including both pagan genies and a Christian angel.

In the bottom half of the picture, Gérôme made innumerable changes in figure types, poses, costumes, and accoutrements. Generally speaking, these lower ranks are accorded greater prominence in the final composition relative to the Augustus group. Against the classical pyramidal composition of the upper section, the subject peoples form a crescent that rises to swelling peaks in the corners, with the elephant-mounted Indians almost attaining the heights of Augustus himself. Gérôme also increased the scale of the Holy Family, which is less sharply differentiated from the surrounding masses in the sketch. Kneeling more erectly, Mary and Joseph also gain in height, as does the angel, whose protectively outstretched wings have supplanted its earlier pose, hands raised in benediction. The intense yellow-orange glow of the Christ Child, which establishes a competing visual center for the tableau, seems also to have been a relatively late inspiration of Gérôme's.

The critical reaction to *The Age of Augustus* was neither enthusiastic nor dismissive. Some lauded Gérôme for his ambition in tackling *grande peinture*, but many more felt that he had stretched his talent's natural limits.[9] Those who had been charmed by his lighthearted and "naïve" *Néo-Grec* paintings regretted his new intellectualizing ambitions.[10] More generally, Gérôme suffered from a mounting reaction to *art philosophique* and literary tendencies in painting. Bossuet's passage was so sweeping and global in scope, evoking the epochal shift between the pagan and Christian eras, that critics felt that painting—with its visual and spatial limits, as decreed by Lessing—was ill-suited to provide a satisfying translation.[11]

Gérôme's attempt was thus hampered from the start. For dubious critics, the result of his misplaced ambition was anachronistic juxtapositions of noncontemporaneous people and events and an awkward amalgam of historical and allegorical figures. "This large canvas," one frustrated critic asked, "is it a page of religion, history, or philosophy? Neither one nor the other."[12]

Despite Gérôme's attempt at compositional organization, the dominant impression was one of visual confusion. The simple contrast forcefully established in words by Bossuet—between the apogee of the pagan world and advent of Christianity—was apparently lost in Gérôme's teeming cast of characters and multiplication of distracting visual details. And if he attempted to mirror Bossuet's rhetorical opposition by dividing his composition into upper and lower registers, he unfortunately sacrificed the compositional unity of his tableau.[13] Rather than create an integrated visual ensemble, Gérôme seemed to have made two separate pictures: "one tableau added to another tableau."[14] Furthermore, this disjunction was compounded by a lack of stylistic unity. The pyramidal top section, serene, static, and symmetrical, was eminently classical and obviously indebted to the examples of Jean-Auguste-Dominique Ingres's *Apotheosis of Homer* and Paul Delaroche's *Hemicycle* at the École des Beaux-Arts.[15] The Holy Family in the foreground, on the other hand, harkened back in the manner of the German Nazarenes and other archaizing nineteenth-century painters to the religious art of the late Middle Ages and early Renaissance. Again, while this disjunction may have served the purposes of rhetorical contrast, as supporters like Gautier insisted, most critics abhorred the "disjunction of styles" and insisted upon homogeneity.[16]

Some two decades later in his autobiographical notes, prepared for Charles Timbal who was writing an article on the artist for the *Gazette des Beaux-Arts*, Gérôme acknowledged some of the criticism of *The Age of Augustus*, particularly the charge that "it lacked invention and originality" in its reliance on Ingres. At the same time, sensitive about the effort he had invested in the painting, he defended its qualities: "let us say that there are in this composition some well-devised figures, happily arranged groups (like those of Brutus and Cassius, Cleopatra and Antony), arrangements of costumes and draperies in good style, and finally a sum of intentions... for which the public could perhaps have credited me but which it did not. This painting is today in the museum of Amiens, of which it is the most beautiful ornament."[17]

Despite such arguments, Gérôme never repeated the effort. The tremendous success of his *Recreation in a Russian Camp* (cat. 107) at the 1855 Exposition opened up new horizons for the discouraged artist, who would commit himself more than ever to small-scale genre painting. This change of course was immediately apparent at the 1857 Salon where he exhibited various Egyptian travel souvenirs and the sensational *Duel after the Ball* (cat. 51). **S. A.**

1. See Archives Nationales, F/21/83 for the government documents and reports pertaining to Gérôme's commission and payments. He received 3,000-franc installments on May 12, 1854, Jan. 10, 1855, and Feb. 21, 1855. He was paid the final 6,000 francs on July 24, 1855. **2.** *Exposition Universelle de 1855. Explication des ouvrages de peinture, sculpture...* (Paris, 1855), p. 327, no. 3164. English translation from J.-B. Bossuet, *Discourse on Universal History*, trans. E. Forster (Chicago and London: University of Chicago Press, 1976), pp. 68–69. **3.** A. Boime, "Gérôme and the Bourgeois Artist's Burden," *Arts Magazine*, vol. 57, no. 5 (Jan. 1983), p. 69. Patricia Mainardi has additionally suggested that the painting was an Imperial response to Thomas Couture's controversial *Romans of the Decadence*, first exhibited at the Salon of 1847. See P. Mainardi, *Art and Politics of the Second Empire: The Universal Expositions of 1855 and 1867* (New Haven: Yale University Press, 1987), p. 80. **4.** T. Gautier, *Les Beaux-arts en Europe. 1855* (Paris: Michel Lévy frères, 1855), p. 219 ["cette vaste composition, qui renferme tout un siècle et tout un monde sous une forme synthétique"]. **5.** Ibid., p. 220 ["symbole de la paix conquise par la victoire"]. **6.** T. Gautier most notably draws out the link between Virgil's verse and the coming of Christ. See ibid., pp. 224–25. **7.** E. Loudun, *Exposition universelle des beaux-arts. Le salon de 1855* (Paris: Ledoyen, 1855), p. 97 ["une procesion fantasmagorique... hommes de toute race, de tout type et de tout costume"]. **8.** T. Gautier 1855 (as in n. 4), p. 223 ["de quelque fantastique royaume de Transoxiane ou de Chaldée"]. **9.** See, for instance, A. de Calonne, "Exposition universelle des beaux-arts," *Revue contemporaine*, vol. 21 (Aug. 1, 1855), pp. 121–22 ["Aujourd'hui... il a cru l'heure venue pour lui de peindre une de ces grandes allégories qui constatent et imposent un grand talent. M. Gérôme est-il bien sûr que ses forces fussent à la hauteur de son ambition?"]. **10.** See, for instance, E. About, *Voyage à travers l'exposition des beaux-arts* (Paris: L. Hachette, 1855), p. 155 ["M. Gérôme fut grec du premier coup, parce qu'il fut simple. Mais il est bien difficile de rester simple... Le succes a jeté M. Gérôme loin de la route que lui-même avait tracée... Il a accepté la commande d'un énorme tableau d'histoire. Adieu les éphèbes accroupis sur leurs talons et les jeunes filles drapées dans leur *peplus*!... Jamais le talent d'un peintre n'a trouvé plus illustre maître; mais que nous sommes loin de cet admirable petit combat de coqs!"]. **11.** See, for instance, P. Mantz, "Salon de 1855," *Revue française*, vol. 2 (1855), p. 359 ["Il suffit de jeter un coup d'oeil rapide sur cette peinture pour reconnaître quelles difficultés ont empêché M. Gérôme de traduire avec le pinceau le motif indiqué par Bossuet. Il était malaisé, il était presque impossible de faire passer, du livre dans le tableau, une énumération de faits successifs qui, sur la page écrite, s'étalent logiquement dans l'ordre historique, mais qui, transportés sur la toile, frappent l'oeil simultanément, et, quoique séparés par les années, deviennent contemporains pour le regard"]; or E. Loudun 1855 (as in n. 7), p. 98 ["Il a oublié, il ne s'est même pas douté que 'si l'espace est le domaine du peintre, comme le dit Lessing, la succession des temps et le domaine du poète.' Il a embrassé trois ou quatre époques; il a voulu être poète, il n'a pas été peintre"]. **12.** E. Loudun 1855 (as in n. 7), p. 99 ["Cette grande toile, est-elle une page religieuse, historique, philosophique? Ni l'un ni l'autre"]. **13.** See, for instance, A.-J. du Pays, "Exposition universelle des beaux-arts. Les Synthétiques," *L'Illustration*, no. 646 (July 14, 1855), p. 27 ["Mais tandis que le lecteur dégage de la simple phrase de Bossuet un contraste puissant d'idée, le spectateur n'aperçoit ici dans le tableau de M. Gérôme qu'une confusion singulière et embarrassante d'images disparates et qui en rompent l'unité."]; or A. de Calonne 1855 (as in n. 9), pp. 122–23 ["Enfin, ceux qui liront les dix lignes de Bossuet, qui peignent d'un si grand trait le siècle d'Auguste, s'étonneront qu'un artiste intelligent, comme l'est à coup sûr M. Gérôme, ait si mal interpreté un texte si simple dans sa grandeur et se soit égaré dans les détails, lorsque tout lui commandait d'exprimer d'abord la pensée dans son ensemble"]. **14.** P. Petroz, "Exposition universelle des beaux-arts," *La Presse*, July 31, 1855 ["Ces deux parties distinctes... font l'effet d'un tableau ajouté à un autre tableau"]. **15.** See, for instance, A. J. Du Pays 1855 (as in n. 13), p. 27 ["Voici la disposition adoptée par M. Gérôme... Auguste trône dans une sorte d'apothéose qui rappelle... celle d'Homère par M. Ingres, et la partie centrale de l'hémicycle de M. Delaroche."]; and C.-L. Duval, "Beaux-Arts. École française," *Le Globe industriel et artistique*, no. 24 (Oct. 14, 1855), p. 383 ["Après l'Apothéose d'Homère, après l'Hémicycle des Beaux-Arts, tous les jeunes peintres qui font de l'art symbolique se croient obligés de grouper d'une façon toute monumentale le ou les personnages principaux sous prétexte d'unité linéaire..."]. **16.** See, for instance, T. Gautier 1855 (as in n. 4), p. 225 ["Le peintre, afin de mieux faire sentir le contraste entre le monde païen et le monde chrétien... a emprunté à l'art gothique, pour les figures de la sainte Vierge, de saint Joseph et de l'enfant Jésus, sa gracilité naïve..."]; and, by contrast, E. Loudun 1855 (as in n. 11), p. 98 ["l'exécution pèche par le disparate des styles, aussi divers que les sujets accumulés sur la toile"]. **17.** J.-L. Gérôme, *Notes autobiographiques* [1874], ed. G. Ackerman (Vesoul: S.A.L.S.A., 1981), pp. 9–11 ["le tableau a un défaut capital: il manque d'invention et d'originalité. Il rappelle, par son agencement, et malheureusement par ce seul côté, l'Apothéose d'Homère de M. Ingres, dont il est, pour ainsi dire, un paraphrase. Cette faute grave une fois constatée, disons qu'il y a dans cette composition des figures bien trouvées, des motifs de groupe heureusement combinés (tels que Brutus et Cassius, Cléopâtre et Antoine) des arrangements de costumes, des draperies d'un bon style, enfin une somme de volontés parfois couronnée de succès dont le public aurait peut-être dû me tenir compte: ce qu'il n'a pas fait. Cette toile est aujourd'hui au Musée d'Amiens dont elle fait le plus bel ornement"].

Cat. 33

THE ODYSSEY, A WALL DECORATION PROJECT FOR THE DRAWING ROOM OF PRINCE NAPOLEON'S NEO-POMPEIAN RESIDENCE, AVENUE MONTAIGNE

–

1858
Oil on metal
22 × 17 ½ in.
Signed middle right: *J.L. GEROME*
Musée Georges-Garret, Vesoul, inv. 995.1.1

–

Provenance: Purchased with the help of the FRAM, 1995.

–

Bibliography: J.-L. Gérôme, *Notes autobiographiques* [1874], ed. G. Ackerman (Vesoul: S.A.L.S.A., 1981), no. 124, pp. 108–9. *J.-L. Gérôme*, exh. cat. (Vesoul: Musée Georges-Garret, 1981), pp. 108–9. G. Ackerman, *Jean-Léon Gérôme* (Courbevoie: ACR Édition, 2000), no. 84, p. 52. R. Diederen, "From Homer to the Harem: Journeys on the Map and in the Mind," in *From Homer to the Harem. The Art of Jean Lecomte du Nouÿ*, exh. cat. (New York: Dahesh Museum of Art, 2004), pp. 79–85, about another version in a private collection.

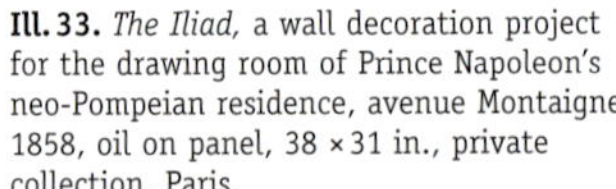

Ill. 33. *The Iliad,* a wall decoration project for the drawing room of Prince Napoleon's neo-Pompeian residence, avenue Montaigne, 1858, oil on panel, 38 × 31 in., private collection, Paris.

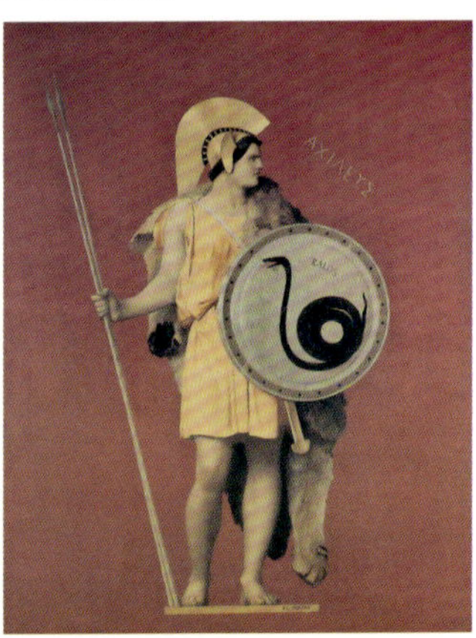

Ill. 34. Gustave Boulanger (1824–1888), *Rehearsal of* The Flute Player *and* The Wife of Diomedes *in the atrium of the house of Prince Napoleon, avenue Montaigne,* 1861, oil on canvas, 32 × 51 in., Musée National du Château, Versailles, inv. MV 5614.

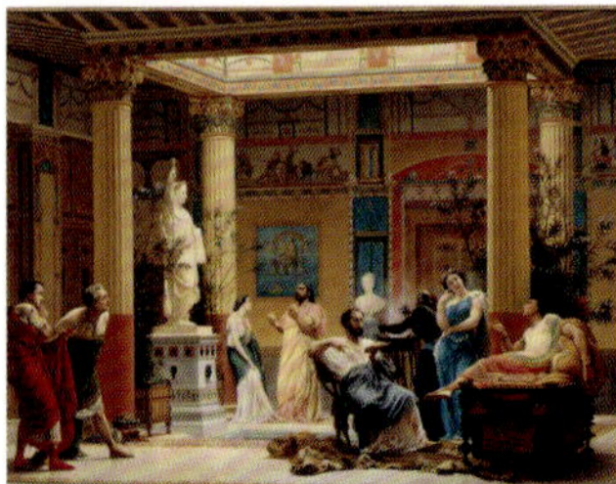

The neo-Pompeian house constructed between 1856 and 1860 in the avenue Montaigne by the architect Alfred-Nicolas Normand for the first cousin of the emperor, Prince Napoleon, was one of the rare neo-antique residences to be constructed in Paris. Despite its brief existence, it lived on in memory: "When you enter the inner vestibule, it seems that the hands of time have been turned back two thousand years on the dial of eternity."[1] The prince had connections with the actress Rachel (cat. 40), Eugène Delacroix, and Théophile Gautier, and six years earlier had purchased *A Greek Interior* (cat. 23), which certainly played a role in the genesis of his luxurious fantasy. He was also in possession of a wealthy collection of Greco-Roman and Egyptian archaeological objects, as well as old master and modern paintings. Gérôme clearly had a role to play in such an exceptional project, which adapted the house of Diomedes or Pansa in Pompeii for the refined society of the Second Empire, and created an enclave disconnected from the reality of the heart of the capital (ill. 34).[3] The paintings in the atrium were produced by Sébastien Cornu, "who understood that it was an archaic reconstruction,"[4] the furniture was by the architect and designer Charles Rossigneux; Gérôme, meanwhile, "the producer of antiquity *par excellence*, quite naturally took on the drawing room. There are three paintings by him, which, in his opinion, are the most beautiful pieces he has ever produced. The central picture represents Homer blind, led by a young Ionian. The mighty countenance of the poet is relaxed, his brow resplendent in thought. The child leaning on Homer is an adorable creation in the flower of youth. In the two pendants that accompany this masterpiece so attractively, the painter sought to immortalize *The Iliad* and *The Odyssey*."[5] The general color scheme of the drawing room, located at the back of the atrium, was "antique red with a black plinth"[6]; Gérôme's paintings, mounted on the walls,[7] were positioned in the center of the panels imitating the so-called "third style" of Pompeian painting, as shown in a drawing conserved in the Musée des Arts Décoratifs in Paris. *The Iliad* (ill. 33), personified by a heroic Achilles, is a particularly successful *Néo-Grec* interpretation, a combination between the painting of Greek vases and Pompeian frescoes. In profile, standing on a plinth, identified by a lateral inscription, against a single-colored background, Gérôme's helmeted Achilles is reminiscent of the figures of the Berlin Painter or the Achilles Painter, Athenian vase painters of the fifth century B.C., whose iconography was distributed in collections of engravings. Through the processes of Pompeian painting, Gérôme adapted the graphic figures of the vases to turn *The Iliad* into a sculpture, both personified and polychrome, floating in the center of the panel. The later addition of the coat of arms of the city of Nantes is perhaps linked to the allegories of European nations imagined by Gérôme of a model of a lighthouse presented at the Paris Universal Exhibition of 1867.[8] As a counterpart, *The Odyssey* is represented as a young woman leaning on an oar, the folds of her cloak billowing in the wind; she owes more to the dancers of Pompeian painting. In 1827 Ingres had delivered, in *The Apotheosis of Homer*, a more appeased Odyssey, a melancholy figure also leaning on an oar. Gérôme's Homeric project for the neo-Pompeian residence certainly influenced his pupil Jean Lecomte du Nouÿ for his first triptych, *Homer Begging*[9], which maybe gives an idea of the central panel of the drawing room of the avenue Montaigne residence, which today is no more. The Pompeian dream of the emperor's cousin, who was considered too republican, was short-lived. After the death of Rachel and the marriage of the prince to Clotilde de Savoie, the home lost its primary reason for being. Sold in 1866, it underwent various vicissitudes, and, despite some protest, was demolished in 1891. **É. P.**

1. T. Gautier, A. Houssaye, and C. Coligny, *Le Palais pompéien de l'Avenue Montaigne. Études sur la maison gréco-romaine ancienne demeure du prince Napoléon, II: Le Palais* (Paris: Librairie Internationale, n.d. [post-1866]), p. 12. **2.** Returned to Ingres in exchange for the Chantilly *Self-Portrait.* **3.** On the neo-Pompeian residence, avenue Montaigne, see M.-C. Dejean de La Batie, "La maison pompéienne du prince Napoléon avenue Montaigne," *Gazette des Beaux-Arts*, Apr. 1976, pp. 127–34; on the interior photography of the neo-Pompeian residence taken by P. A. Richebourg and J. Laplanche, see S. Aubenas, *Des photographes pour l'empereur. Les albums de Napoléon III*, exh. cat. (Paris: Bibliothèque Nationale de France, 2004), no. 121–23, pp. 172–76; on the Temple of the Muses, see *Rachel* (cat. 40) and P. Picard-Cajan, ed., *L'Illusion grecque. Ingres et l'Antique*, exh. cat. (Montauban: Musée Ingres, 2006), pp. 358–65. **4.** T. Gautier et al. (as in n. 1), p. 18. **5.** Ibid., p. 21. **6.** Ibid., p. 20. **7.** M.-N. de Gary, *La Maison pompéienne du prince Napoléon 1856. Dessins de l'architecte Alfred Normand* (Paris: Union Centrale des Arts Décoratifs, 1979), p. 7. **8.** BnF, département des Estampes et de la Photographie, fund Z-47. **9.** Not located; see R. Diederen, "From Homer to the Harem: Journeys on the Map and in the Mind," in *From Homer to the Harem. The Art of Jean Lecomte du Nouÿ*, exh. cat. (New York: Dahesh Museum of Art, 2004), pp. 79–85.

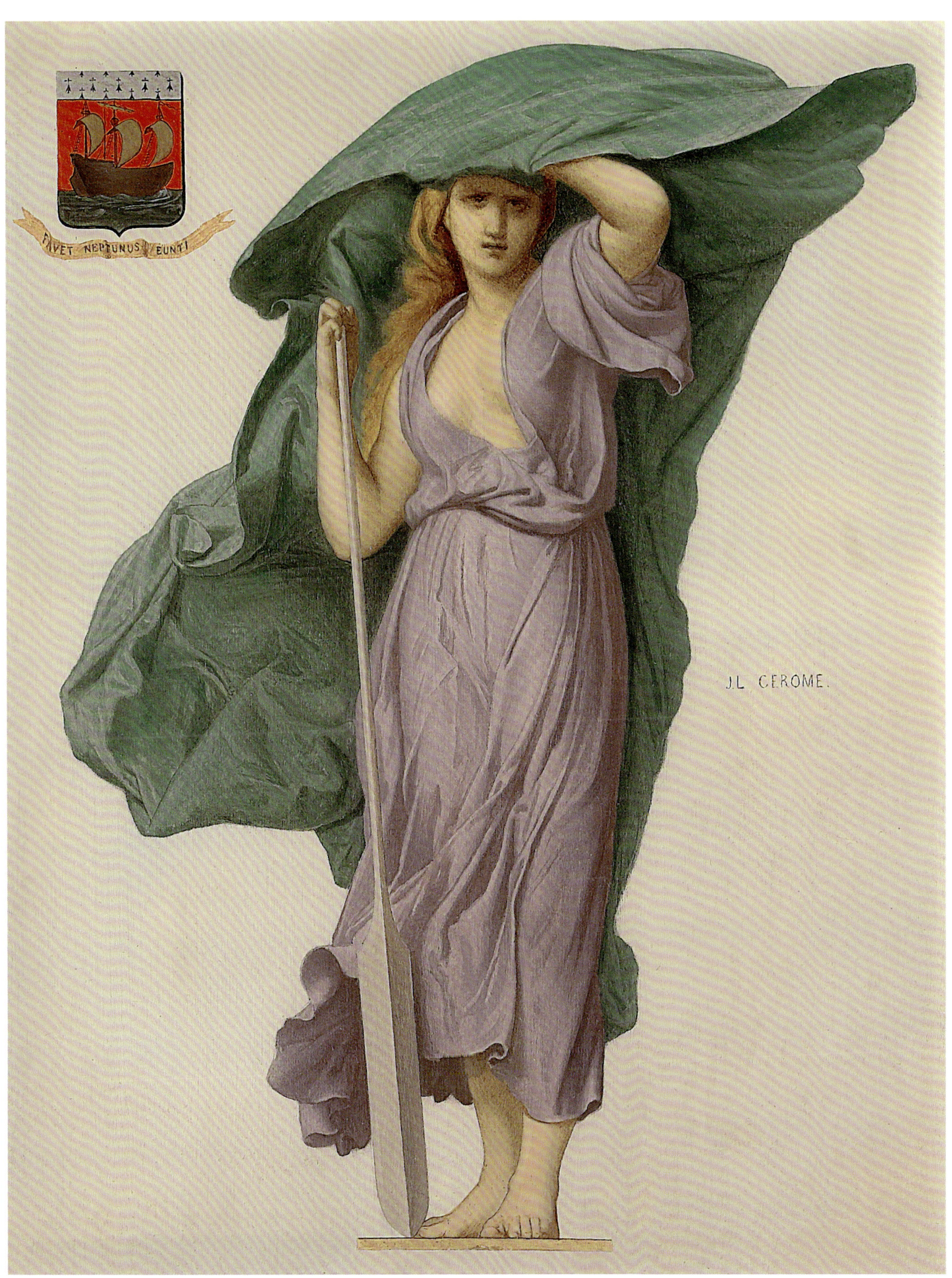
FAVET NEPTUNUS EUNTI
J.L. GEROME.

Cat. 34

PORTRAIT OF ARMAND GÉRÔME

1848
Oil on canvas
19 ¾ × 17 ¼ in.
Signed lower left: *J.L. GEROME*
The National Gallery, London, inv. NG 3251

Provenance: Sir Hugh Lane Bequest, National Gallery, 1917. On loan at the Hugh Lane Municipal Gallery.

Bibliography: M. Davies, *Paintings of the French School* (London: The National Gallery, 1970), p. 69. G. Ackerman, *Jean-Léon Gérôme* (Courbevoie: ACR Édition, 2000), no. 22.

Gérôme painted few portraits and never developed a serious affinity for the genre. Apart from occasional depictions of famous figures from the art world, it is not surprising, therefore, that he tended to limit this kind of work to the personal, family sphere. This portrait of his younger brother Claude-Armand is one of the earliest examples of Gérôme's forays into this domain. A full-length version[1] (whereabouts unknown) was presented at the Salon in 1848, along with *Anacreon* (cat. 16) and *The Virgin, the Infant Jesus, and Saint John* (cat. 13). Compared to the commissions obtained by the young artist at the time in his extremely successful *Néo-Grec* style, this portrait displays a plain, restrained manner that satisfyingly solves the question of the contemporary portrait by its reference to Jean-Auguste-Dominique Ingres. The dark uniform of the École Polytechnique, a perfect equivalent of the modern black clothing evoked by Charles Baudelaire, allows Gérôme to concentrate on the face. With the heavy eyelids and the hint of bags, and the distant, pouting expression, Gérôme's depiction of his brilliant younger sibling—who died of meningitis only two years later—emphasizes not so much his academic prowess as a somewhat chilling melancholy. Formally a remote heir of those Ingres masterpieces *Amédée-David, the Comte de Pastoret* (1826, The Art Institute of Chicago) and *The Duc d'Orléans* (1842, Musée du Louvre, Paris), the *Portrait of Armand Gérôme* establishes Gérôme as a portraitist who refers openly to the unsurpassable models of the preceding generation. **L.C.**

1. See G. Ackerman, *Jean-Léon Gérôme* (Courbevoie: ACR Édition, 2000), no. 21.

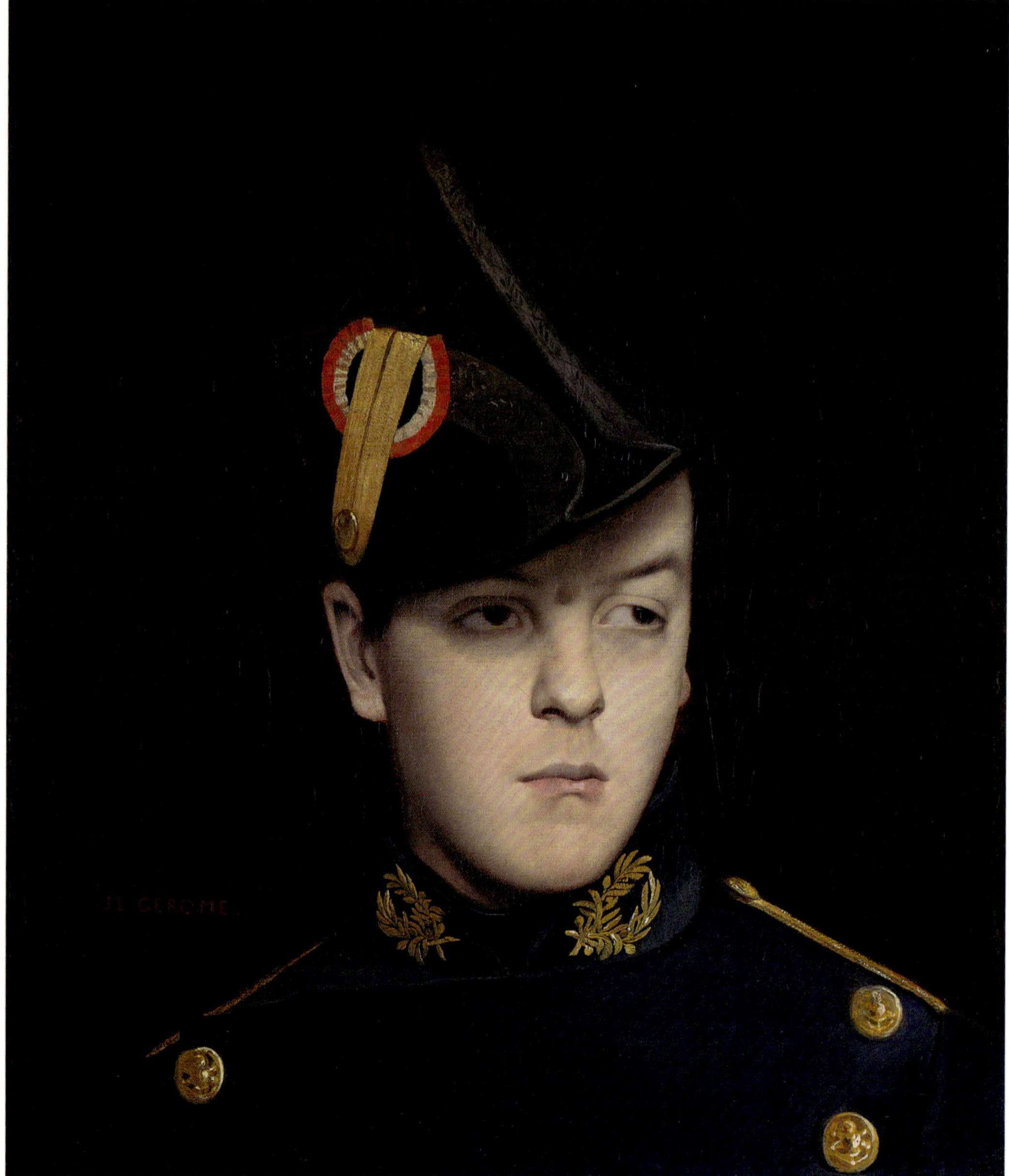

Cat. 35

THE ARTIST'S FATHER AND SON ON THE DOORSTEP OF HIS HOUSE

ca. 1866–67
Oil on panel
10 ½ × 8 ¼ in.
Musée des Beaux-Arts, Rouen, Henri and Suzanne Baderou Bequest, 1975, inv. 975 4 198

Provenance: Hôtel Drouot, Paris, sold under the name *Devant la maison,* June 25, 1951, no. 107.

Bibliography: G. Ackerman, *Jean-Léon Gérôme* (Courbevoie: ACR Edition, 2000), no. 458.6, pp. 350–51.

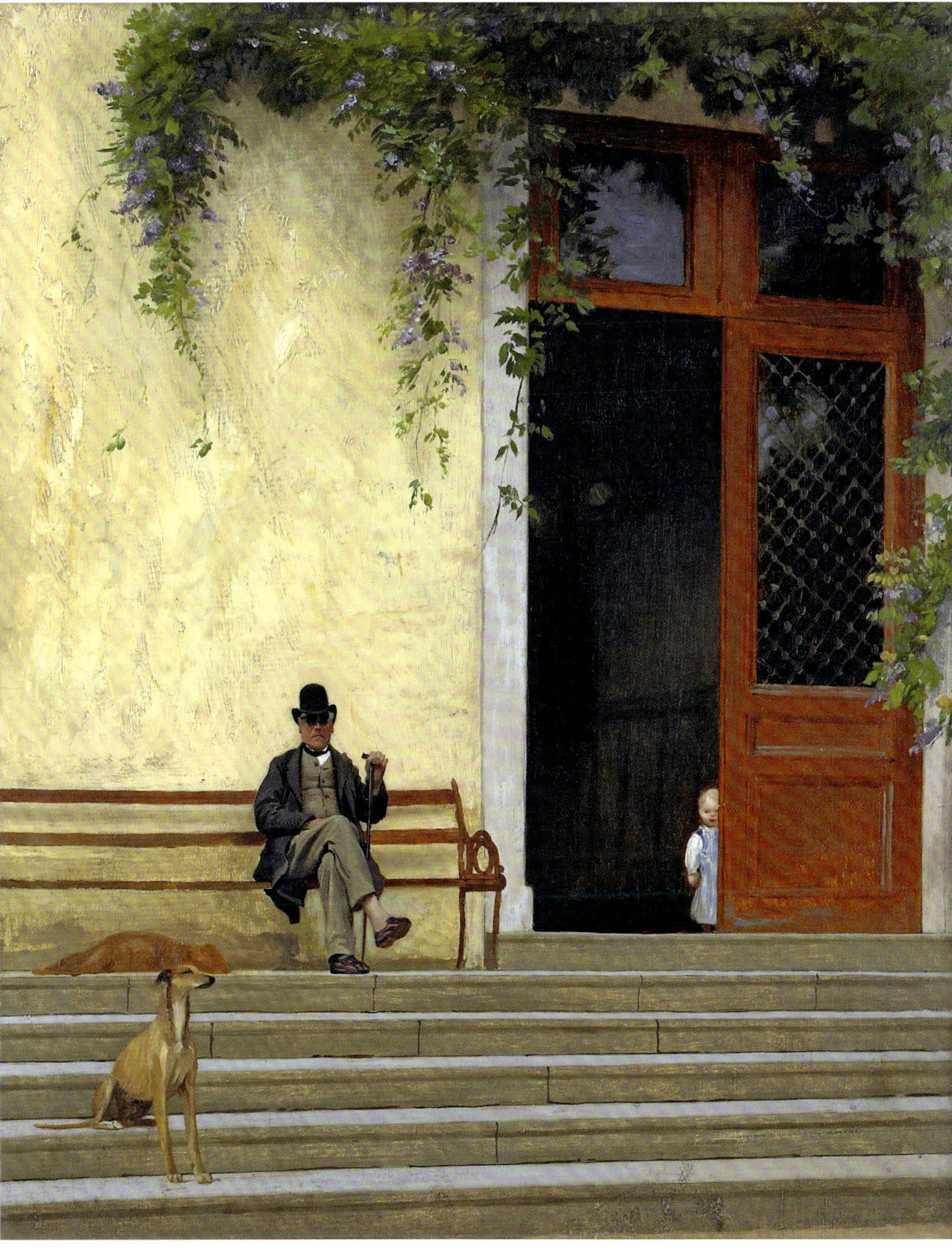

This small panel is one of Gérôme's rare private works. It shows his father Pierre and, in the doorway, his only son Jean (born in 1865), on the porch of the house in Coulevon near Vesoul. Despite the domestic theme, the skillful composition of this work is, like Gérôme's history paintings, inspired by the artist's taste for theatricality. The steps of the porch provide a platform on which the carefully and elegantly dressed old man, wielding a long cane, sits enthroned. The hieratic pose of the dog below reinforces the lordly dignity of the father. The little boy, barely two years old at the time, is only half-painted, being half hidden by the heavy door from which he seems to be watching a scene invisible to the beholder of the painting. The care taken with the large door, including the reflected light on the panes, and the way the foliage forms a kind of large stage curtain, reveal Gérôme's dexterous handling. A truly subtle and elegant homage is being paid by the artist to his father, who came from a modest background yet never opposed his son's desire to become a painter. That painter was able to convey his gratitude here with affectionate skill. **D. F.-R.**

Cat. 36

PORTRAIT OF A LADY

–

1851
Oil on canvas
36 ½ × 29 ⅞ in.
Signed and dated center right:
J.L. GEROME 1851
The Art Institute of Chicago, Restricted Gift of Silvain and Arma Wyler Foundation, 1964, inv. 1964.338

–

Provenance: Paris, Hôtel Drouot, 1964 (sold as anonymous work). Giancarlo Baroni. Hans Calmann, London, 1964. Acquired by the Chicago Art Institute, 1964.

–

Bibliography: R. Rosenblum, *Ingres* (New York: H. N. Abrams, 1967), p. 35, fig. 42. J. Maxon, ed., *The Art Institute of Chicago* (New York: H. N. Abrams, 1971), p. 264 (ill.), p. 281. G. Ackerman et al., *Jean-Léon Gérôme (1824–1904)*, exh. cat. (Dayton: Dayton Art Institute, 1972; also Minneapolis: Minneapolis Institute of Arts, 1973, and Baltimore: The Walters Art Gallery, 1973), no. 2, pp. 32–33. E. Munhall, *Ingres and the Comtesse d'Haussonville* (New York: The Frick Collection, 1985), pp. 120–21, fig. 104. R. R. Brettell, *French Salon Artists, 1800–1900* (Chicago: The Art Institute of Chicago; New York: H. N. Abrams, 1987), p. 28 (ill.), pp. 29, 118. J. Perry Brown, "The Return of the Salon: Jean-Léon Gérôme in the Art Institute," *The Art Institute of Chicago Museum Studies*, vol. 15, no. 2 (1999), p. 158, fig. 3. G. Ackerman, *Jean-Léon Gérôme* (Courbevoie: ACR Édition, 2000), no. 38. J.-P. Cuzin and D. Salmon, *Ingres* (Paris: RMN, 2006), p. 104 (ill.).

Cat. 37

PORTRAIT OF A LADY

–

1850
Oil on canvas
39 ⅛ × 30 in.
Signed and dated center right:
J.L. GEROME. 1850
Ottawa, National Gallery of Canada, inv. 18937

–

Provenance: Acquired by the National Gallery of Canada on the Parisian art market in 1977.

–

Bibliography: G. Ackerman, *Jean-Léon Gérôme* (Courbevoie: ACR Édition, 2000), no. 34.

Cat. 38

PORTRAIT OF MADAME LA BARONNE NATHANIEL DE ROTHSCHILD

–

1866
Oil on panel
19 ⅝ × 14 in.
Signed middle left: *J.L. Gérôme*
Musée d'Orsay, Paris, inv. RF 2004 9

–

Provenance: From 1960 to 2003, in a private collection, Belgium. *Tableaux, dessins, sculptures du XIX*e *siècle*, Hôtel Drouot, Paris, Maître Tajan, Apr. 30, 2003, lot 15. Galerie Elstir, Paris, 2003–4. Acquired by the Musée d'Orsay, 2004.

–

Bibliography: G. Ackerman, *Jean-Léon Gérôme* (Courbevoie: ACR Édition, 2000), no. 166. D. Lobstein, "Acquisitions," *48/14. La Revue du Musée d'Orsay*, no. 20 (spring 2005), pp. 54–55.

Cat. 39

PORTRAIT OF A LADY (MARIE GÉRÔME, NÉE GOUPIL)

–

ca. 1865
Oil on canvas
25 ¼ × 18 ⅛ in.
Musée Goupil, Bordeaux, inv. 97-VI-1-1

–

Provenance: Drouot Montaigne, Paris, De Quay-Lombrail, commissaires-priseurs, Dec. 7, 1995, lot 1. Presented by Mlle Cécile Ritzenthaler. Galerie Pierre Birtshansky, Paris. Purchase by the City of Bordeaux with the support of FRAM Aquitaine.

–

Bibliography: H. Lafont-Couturier, *Gérôme* (Paris: Herscher, 1998), p. 100. G. Ackerman, *Jean-Léon Gérôme* (Courbevoie: ACR Édition, 2000), no. 167.3. H. Lafont-Couturier, *Gérôme & Goupil. Art et entreprise*, exh. cat. (Bordeaux: Musée Goupil; also New York: Dahesh Museum of Art, 2001, and Pittsburgh: The Frick Art & Historical Center, 2001), no. 4, pp. 72–73.

Ill. 35. Hippolyte Flandrin (1809–1864), *Madame Oudiné*, 1840, oil on canvas, 33 × 25 ¼ in., Musée des Beaux-Arts, Lyon.

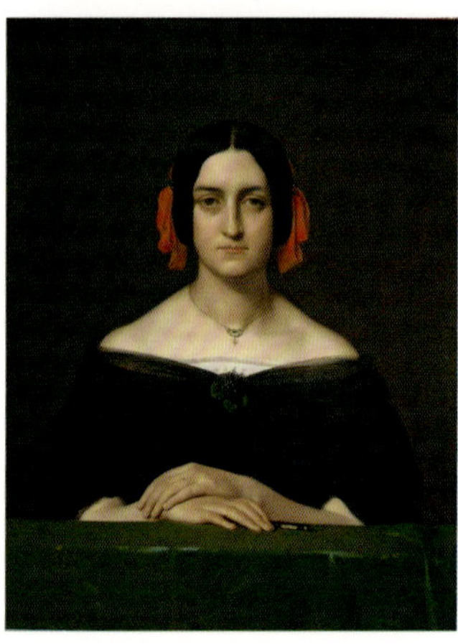

Ill. 36. Jean-Auguste-Dominique Ingres (1780–1867), *Madame Gonse*, 1852, oil on canvas, 29 × 24 in., Musée Ingres, Montauban, inv. MI.28.2.1.

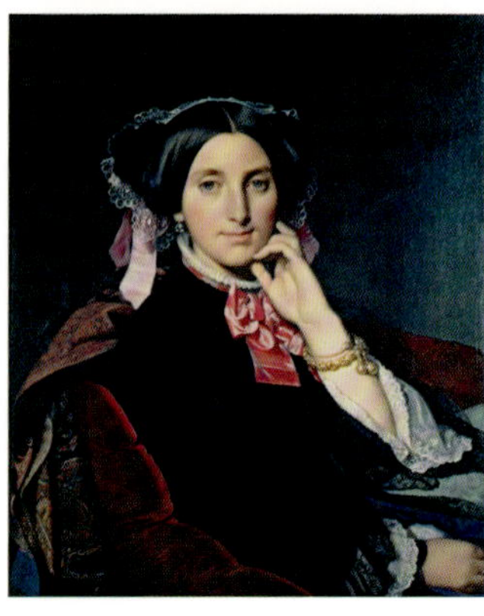

This group of female portraits offers an insight into Gérôme's successive interpretations of the model bequeathed by Jean-Auguste-Dominique Ingres. Representing his first steps in this direction, the portrait in the collection of the National Gallery of Canada (cat. 37) follows closely in the wake of the most radicalized formalist readings by certain students of Ingres. By its archaic-style hieratism and a formal plainness verging on austerity, this work takes up the uncompromising approach adopted by Hippolyte Flandrin in his portrait of Madame Oudiné (ill. 35). Off-center, transposed into the ellipsis of an oval format, the iconic frontality of Flandrin's composition clearly loses its hypnotic power and becomes ordinary. And yet in all his works we still find an almost upsetting insistence on the essential, an enigmatic expressiveness concentrated on the face and hands, which are underscored by the clothes, jewelry, and hair.

A second-generation follower of Ingres who had no links with the official circle of the master's students and followers, Gérôme freely quoted and transposed the reciprocal play of influence that took place between Ingres and his epigones in the 1840s and 50s, especially in matters of female portraiture. A perfect example of this interaction, the portrait at the Art Institute of Chicago (cat. 36) reuses the *punctum* of the hand supporting a face absorbed in silent and pensive reverie. Between the portrait of the *Comtesse d'Haussonville* (1842, The Frick Collection, New York) and that of *Madame Gonse* (ill. 36), Gérôme's canvas can be compared with other works on the same theme, both earlier (Hippolyte Flandrin, *Madame Hippolyte Flandrin*, 1846, Musée du Louvre, Paris) and later (Amaury-Duval, *Madame Loynes*, 1862, Musée d'Orsay, Paris). The neurotically ascetic style of the previous example is followed here by a melancholy opulence in

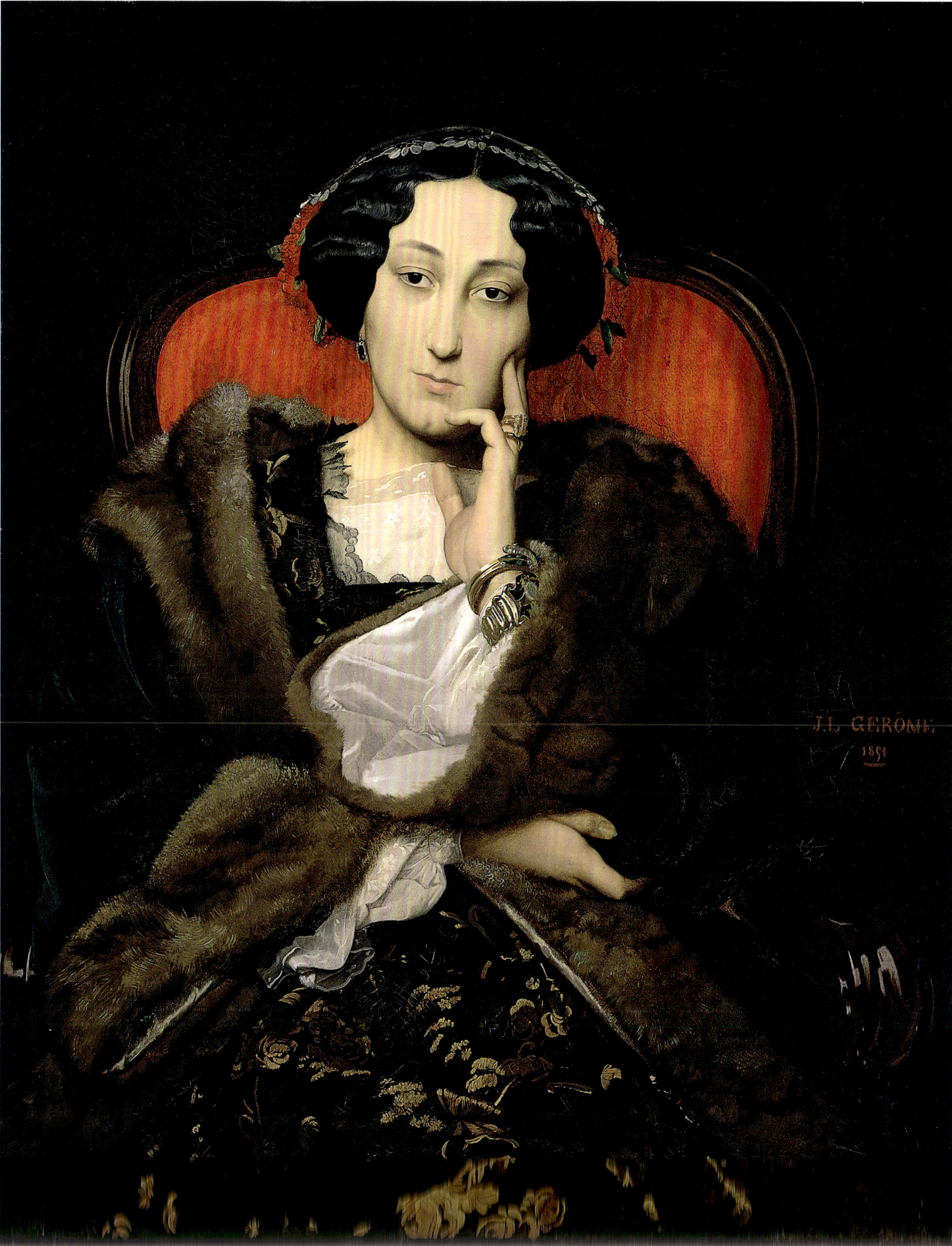
J.L. GERÔME
1851

which Gérôme closely frames and sets a face within the curving forms of an armchair and the orthogonal lines of a fur-trimmed coat. Within this highly characteristic symmetrical setting, the painter loads and overloads his model with fabrics and fur, with jewels and patterns, making this deliberate excess the main subject of his painting. This exercise in contextualization took on a truly dynastic dimension in Gérôme's 1866 *Portrait of Madame la Baronne Nathaniel de Rothschild* (cat. 38). To paint James and Betty de Rothschild's daughter was inevitably to recall the admirable portrait of Betty that Ingres had painted in 1848 (private collection, Paris). And Gérôme certainly quotes—there is that same hand gesture—but he also stands back here to give the full biographical and social dimension of his model. We are in the Faubourg Saint-Honoré and the decor, paintings, and objects reflect the eclecticism of the subject as a collector who bequeathed objects to the Musée de Cluny and Musée des Arts Décoratifs, and Renaissance paintings to the Louvre, among them the *Virgin and Child* by the Master of the Castello Nativity, which can be distinguished on the wall here. In this composite painting saturated with references Gérôme can be seen scrupulously applying himself to the exercise of the commissioned portrait. The situation is very different in the inspired but unfinished *Portrait of a Lady (Marie Gérôme née Goupil)* (cat. 39). As a result of the commercial relations he established in 1859 with the publisher and dealer Adolphe Goupil, Gérôme naturally came to know his daughter Marie, a young woman "of rare beauty" and "charming grace."[1] She married the painter in January 1863 and the couple moved into a townhouse at 6, rue de Bruxelles, near the place de Clichy. Contemporary with their wedding, this portrait reveals the personal side of Gérôme. He

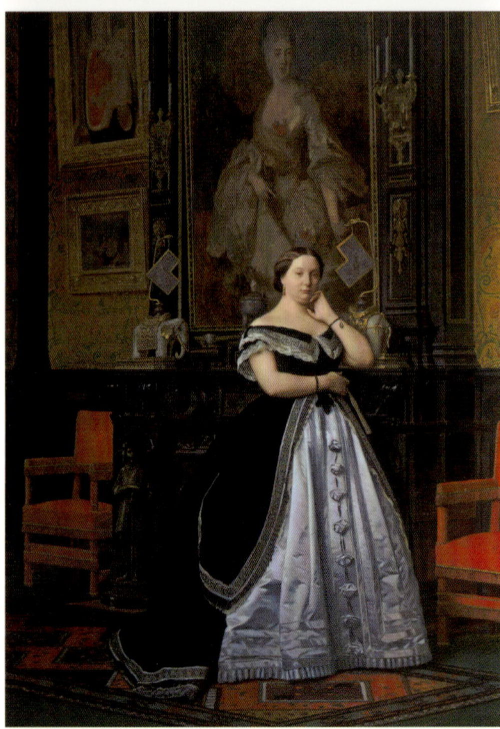

concentrates almost exclusively on the face of his young wife, aged twenty-one at the time, which he treats with a gentleness and a sense of modeling that are rare in his work. This subtle spareness, heightened by the incompleteness of the work, is one of the more sincere expressions of Gérôme the man, who here is more a painter than a portraitist. **L. C.**

1. G. Haller [Wilhelmine Joséphine Fould], *Nos grands peintres* (Paris: J. Boussod, Manzi, Joyant & Cie., 1899), p. 23.

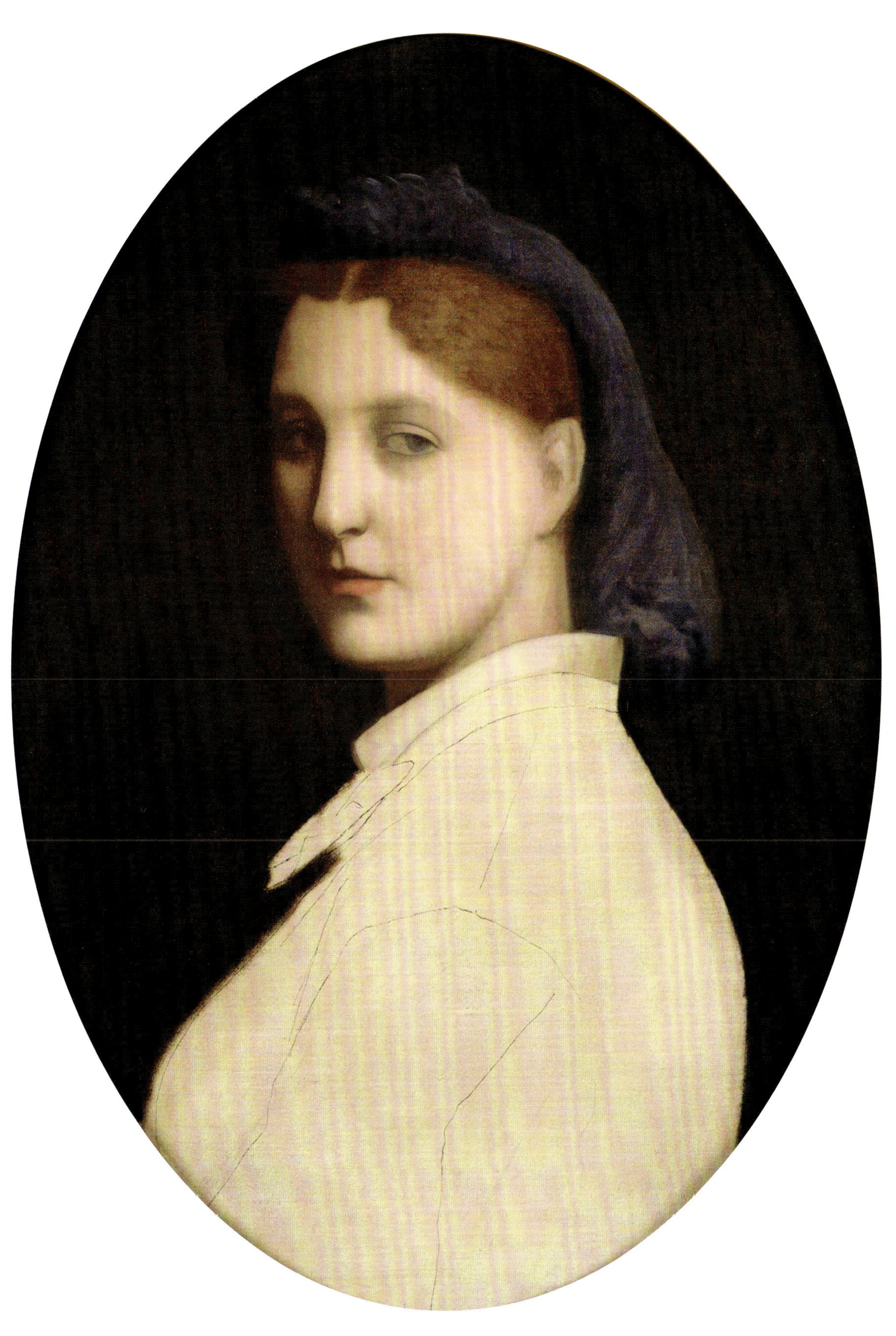

Cat. 40

RACHEL, "TRAGEDY"

–

1859
Oil on canvas
85 7/8 × 59 7/8 in.
Signed and dated at bottom:
J.L. GEROME MDCCMIX
Comédie-Française, Paris, inv. I 73

–

Provenance: Commissioned by the sister of Rachel, Mlle Sarah Félix, after the actress's death. Granted to the Comédie-Française by ministerial order on November 27, 1861

–

Exhibition History: Salon of 1861, Paris, no. 1253.

–

Bibliography: *Catalogue de Paris*, 1883, p. 24. *La Comédie-Française 1680–1962* (Versailles: Château de Versailles, 1962), no. 325. *La Comédie-Française* (Reims: Musée des Beaux-Arts, 1976). *J.-L. Gérôme*, exh. cat. (Vesoul: Musée Georges-Garret, 1981), p. 114. G. Ackerman, *Jean-Léon Gérôme* (Courbevoie: ACR Édition, 2000), no. 114. H. Lafont-Couturier, *Gérôme and Goupil: Art and Enterprise*, exh. cat., trans. I. Ollivier (Bordeaux: Musée Goupil, 2000–1; also New York: Dahesh Museum of Art, 2001, and Pittsburgh: The Frick Art & Historical Center, 2001), pp. 103–104, 151, 165. *Rachel, une vie pour le théâtre, 1821–1858*, exh. cat. (Paris: Musée d'Art et d'Histoire du Judaïsme, 2004), no. 67.

Ill. 37. Amaury-Duval (1808–1885), *Tragedy*, 1854, oil on canvas, 65 × 45 1/4 in., Comédie-Française, Paris.

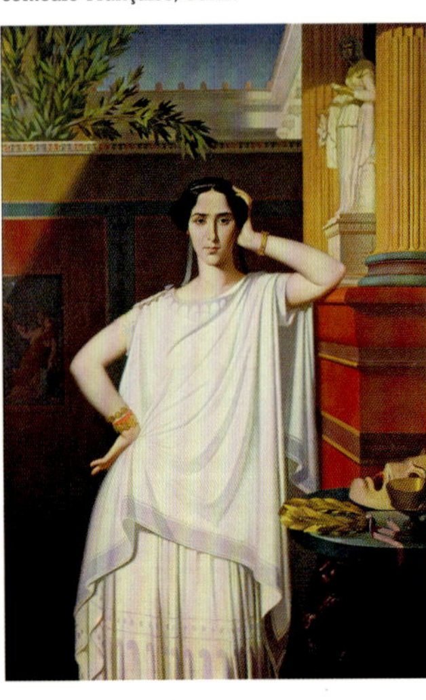

This posthumous portrait was commissioned from Gérôme in 1858 by the tragedian's sister, Sarah Félix. Just after the death of Elisa Félix, known as Mademoiselle Rachel, one of the first *stars* of the modern age, Gérôme celebrated her in an impressive, large-scale canvas in which his purest *Néo-Grec* style aptly enhances his subject. Rachel's short and brilliant career was that of an artist capable of reviving the flame of great classical tragedy in an age when Romantic culture was opening up other perspectives. She was also an independent woman and seducer who chose her lovers from among the most influential circles of Parisian society, just as she controlled her fame by working closely with those in charge of disseminating her image. Between her debut in 1838—when she signed her first contract as a *pensionnaire* (troupe member) of the Comédie-Française—and the 1860s, when, in the years after her death, her star still burned brightly, no less than fifty artists immortalized her in their drawings, paintings, sculptures, lithographs, or photographs.[1] Invariably identified with the roles for which she became famous—Camille in *Horace*, Roxane in *Bajazet*, Phèdre—Rachel took a very literal approach to her portraits, freely modulating for Dubuffe, Devéria, Charles-Louis Müller, Francisque Duret, Auguste Clésinger or Dantan l'Aîné "that modern fever which boils under the coldness of the old tragedy and that always manages to find some escape."[2] In 1854 Amaury-Duval painted her as the muse of Tragedy (ill. 37) by fusing Ingrisme and *Néo-Grec* evocations in a peaceful and somewhat disembodied vision that had a considerable influence on Gérôme's work. Indeed, when he responded to the commission from Sarah Félix, he chose allegory instead of a specific role and, once again, metamorphosed Rachel into Melpomene. The setting and details echo other works but Gérôme is always more accurate in his evocation. For instance, the tripod is inspired by the publication of the duc de Blacas collection. The statuette of the Oracle with snakes will be sculpted by Gérôme years later (Ackerman, S. 51). The whole setting with doric colonnades so much in vogue at that time echoes the Pompeian "folly" commissioned from architect Alfred-Nicolas Normand by Prince Jérôme Napoléon. Construction of this high point of the Parisian Greek style was preceded by the creation of a big model of a temple of the muses, designed by Jacques Hittorff, decorated by Ingres and the sculptor Jean-Auguste Barre, as a gift for Rachel herself. Gérôme also contributed to this project with a series of canvases evoking *The Iliad* and *The Odyssey* (cat. 33). His portrait of Rachel should thus be seen in the context of that particular moment that witnessed the triumph of a historicist yet fantastical *Néo-Grec* style, a style of which Gérôme was the leading champion. For while the paintings by Amaury-Duval and Gérôme are closely connected, the sensibilities behind them are clearly very different. The former closely adheres to the idealist charter drawn up by the Ingriste circle, whereas the latter disrupts that harmony by dramatizing Rachel's presence with a feverish expression and pale-as-death complexion. Seeking the truth of his deceased model, Gérôme based one of his preparatory drawings on a photograph by Nadar. But, a ghost in a world of theater draped in the red of tragedy, Rachel was no more, and Gérôme was depicting only a memory: his strange portrait owes its power to his qualities as a history painter, something he never really ceased to be. **L. C.**

1. See J. Weschler, "Images de Rachel," in *Rachel, une vie pour le théâtre, 1821–58*, exh. cat. (Paris: Musée d'Art et d'Histoire du Judaïsme, 2004), pp. 12–23. 2. T. Gautier, *Portraits contemporains, littérateurs-peintres-sculpteurs-artistes dramatiques, 2e édition avec portrait de Théophile Gautier* (Paris: Charpentier & Cie, 1874).

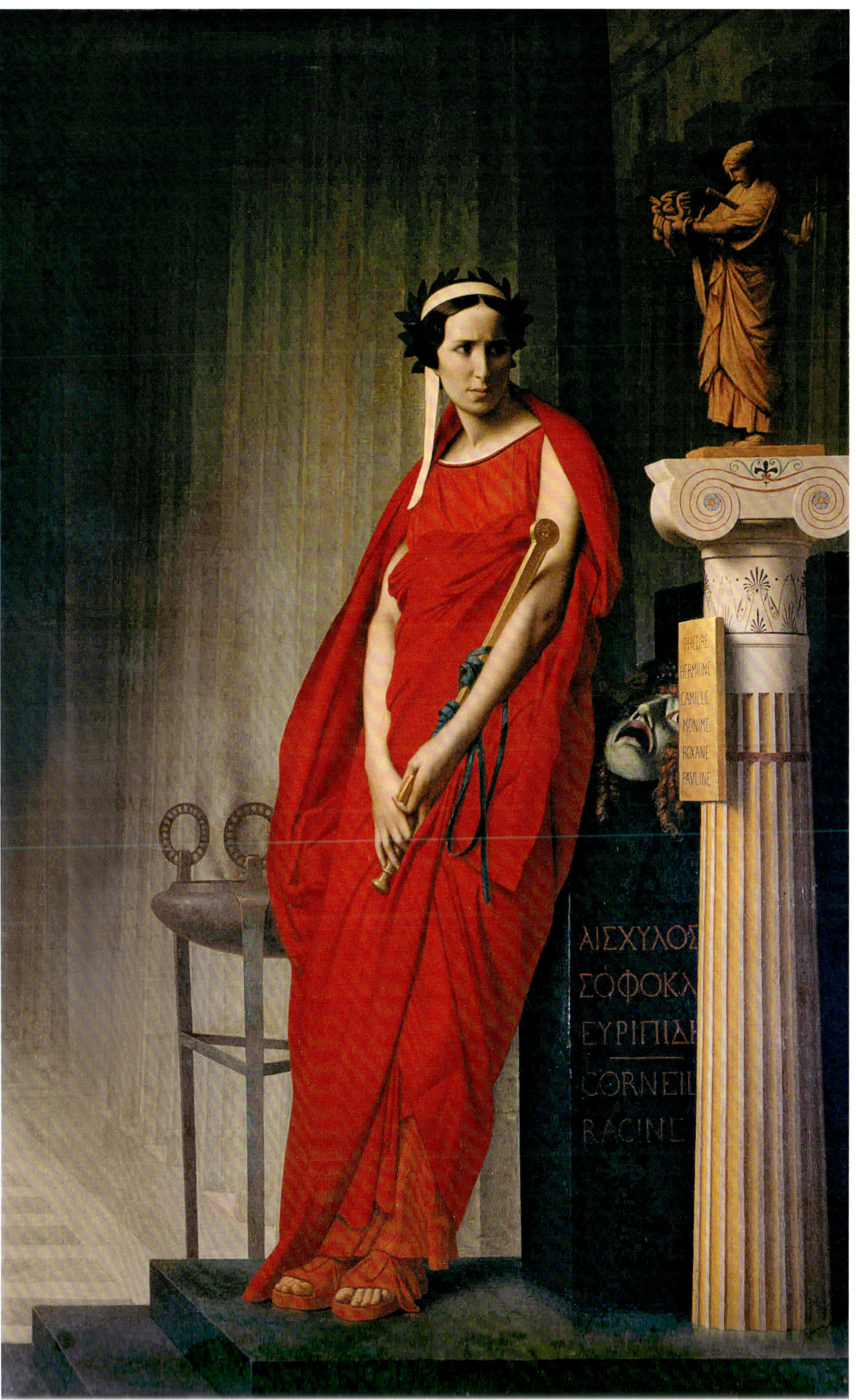
PHEDRE
HERMIONE
CAMILLE
MONIME
ROXANE
PAVLINE
ΑΙΣΧΥΛΟΣ
ΣΟΦΟΚΛ
ΕΥΡΙΠΙΔ
CORNEIL
RACINE

Cat. 41

PORTRAIT OF M. ÉDOUARD DELESSERT

–

1864
Oil on panel
12 × 8 ½ in.
Signed and dated lower right:
J.L. GEROME 1864
Dr. Edward T. Wilson Collection, Bethesda, Maryland

–

Provenance: Édouard Delessert (1828–1898), 1864. Sale, Nouveau Drouot, Paris, Mar. 24, 1986, lot 131. Mackinnon & Strachey, London, 1986. Edward T. Wilson, Bethesda, Maryland, 1986.

–

Bibliography: G. Ackerman, *Jean-Léon Gérôme* (Courbevoie: ACR Édition, 2000), pp. 77, 256–57, no. 149.5.

Delessert hailed from a prominent Swiss banking family that had settled in Lyon and Paris in the eighteenth century. His father Gabriel was a highly notable figure in the July Monarchy, holding various prefectures and rising to the top ranks of the National Guard and Legion of Honour. Gabriel's social prominence was reinforced by the celebrated salons held by his wife, Valentine de Laborde, which included many of the Romantic generation's leading luminaries. For his part, their son Édouard would become active in various aspects of the cultural and intellectual life of the Second Empire. Having originally embarked on a career in law, he turned his energy and attention to travel and photography in the 1850s. A disciple of Prosper Merimée (who had been romantically tied to his mother), Delessert also entertained considerable literary ambitions, founding the critical journal *L'Athenaeum français*, collaborating on the *Revue de Paris*, and publishing various travel accounts.[1]

How Gérôme came to know the multi-talented Delessert is unknown, but the artist's inclusion of himself in the background of this sympathetic hunting portrait suggests that they were close friends or at least moved in the same social circles[2]; their shared interests in travel and photography would certainly have strengthened their ties. Portraying Delessert in fashionable shooting attire with a favorite dog, Gérôme here exhibits his considerable talents as a miniaturist, particularly in his handling of the texture of the sitter's velvet coat and pants and the detailed rendering of his blue argyle socks, which provide a striking color note in an otherwise subdued picture. Belying many critics' negative comparisons of his paintings to enamel, ivory, or porcelain, Gérôme treated the wooded autumnal landscape with an atmospheric softness and freedom of the brush that is beautifully evocative of a cold, misty morning. One is reminded of the landscape background in the much more dramatic *Duel after the Ball* (cat. 51).

A rare male portrait and modern costume study in Gérôme's oeuvre, his depiction of Delessert inserts itself in a long tradition of patrician huntsman portraits and pays particular homage to an 1821 portrait of the sitter's father, Gabriel, painted by Horace Vernet, whose popular stature at that time was not dissimilar to Gérôme's forty years later (ill. 38).[3] **S. A.**

1. See *Voyage aux villes maudites* (Paris, 1853), *Une nuit dans la cité de Londres* (Paris, 1854), and *Six semaines dans l'île de Sardaigne* (Paris, 1855). The Sardinian expedition also yielded a pioneering body of photographic work. Also in the travel vein, Delessert went on to translate Paul Kane's *Wanderings of an Artist among the Indians of North America: From Canada to Vancouver's Island and Oregon through the Hudson's Bay Company's Territory and Back Again* (Toronto, 1858), as *Les Indiens de la baie d'Hudson: promenades d'un artiste parmi les Indiens de l'Amérique du Nord* (Paris, 1861). **2.** There is a good chance, for example, that the two men knew each other through the salon of Adèle Caussin (alias "Mme. Cassin," later la Marquise Landolfo Carcano, 1831–1922), a well-known beauty and art collector whose gatherings included, in addition to prominent politicians and financiers, leading art world figures like Alexandre Dumas fils, Georges Petit, Gustave Doré, and Léon Bonnat. On Caussin's salon and her relationship with Delessert, see A. Maurois, *Les Trois Dumas* (Paris: Hachette, 1957), p. 424. I am very grateful to Edward Wilson for this information. **3.** On Vernet's portrait, see Christie's, London, *West – East: The Niall Hobhouse Collection*, May 22, 2008, lot 99.

Ill. 38. Horace Vernet (1789–1863), *Portrait of Gabriel Delessert in Hunting Costume*, 1821, oil on canvas, 25 × 21 ½ in., private collection.

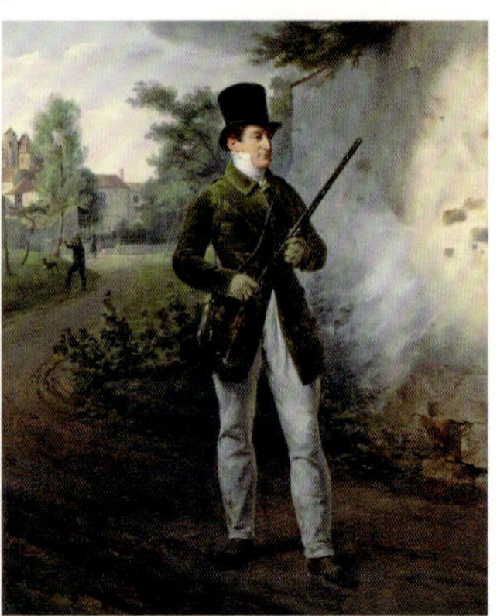

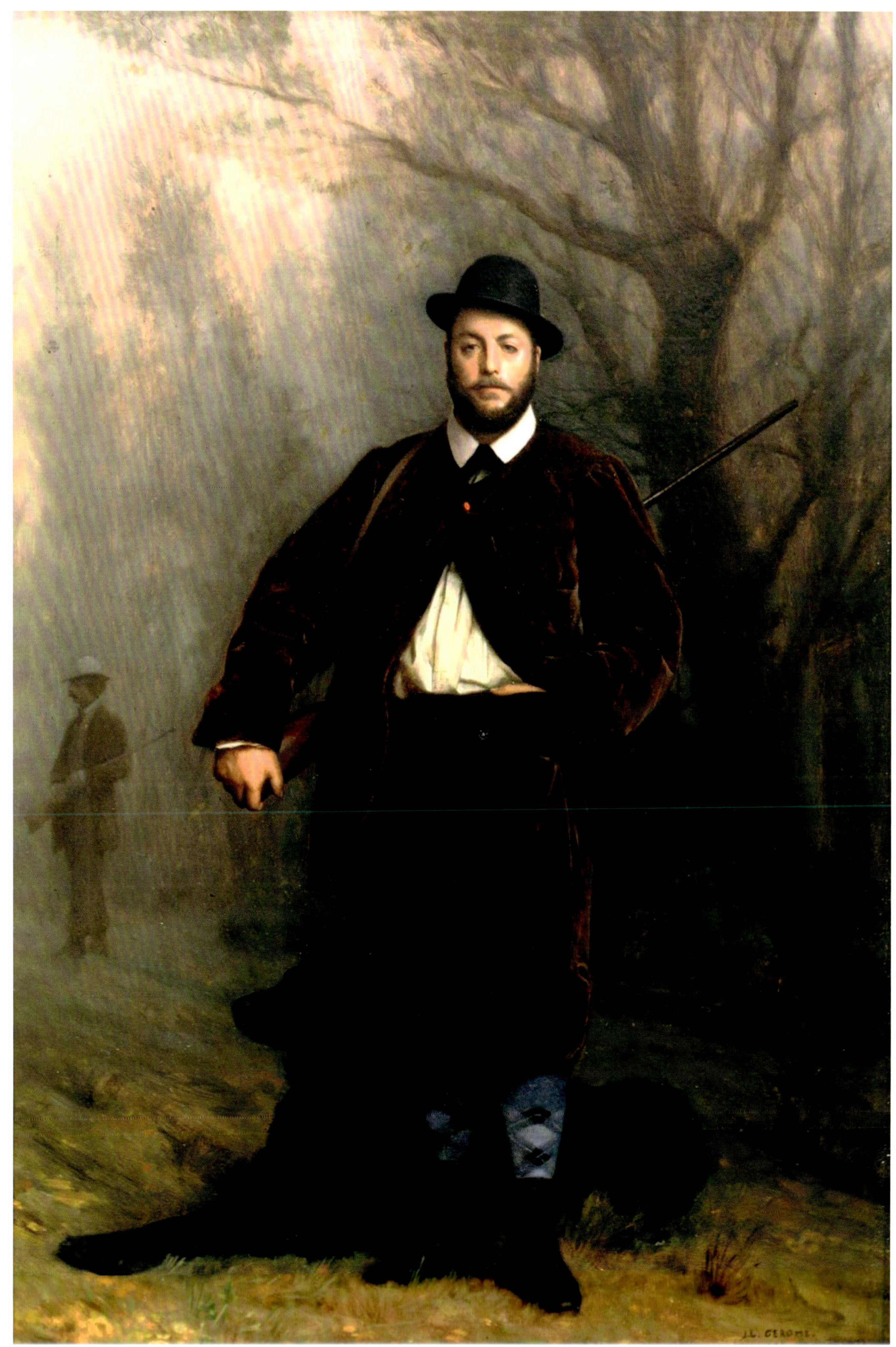
J.L. GEROME.

Cat. 42

PORTRAIT OF CHARLES GARNIER

–
1877
Oil on panel
9 ¾ × 8 ¾ in.
Inscribed upper left: *A MON AMI CH. GARNIER/ J.L. GEROME/ 1877*
Bibliothèque de l'Opéra, Bibliothèque Nationale de France, Paris, inv. MUS 1163
–
Provenance: Charles Garnier. Gift of Mrs. Charles Garnier to the Paris Opéra.
–
Exhibition History: Cercle de l'Union Artistique, Paris, 1877.
–
Bibliography: J. Foucart and L.-A. Prat, *Les Peintures de l'Opéra de Paris, de Baudry à Chagall*, (new edition of *Le Nouvel Opéra de Paris*, by Charles Garnier; Paris: Arthena, 1980), no. 222. *Gérôme* (Vesoul: Musée Georges Garret, 1981), no. 147, p. 124, not exhibited. G. Ackerman, *Jean-Léon Gérôme* (Courbevoie: ACR Édition, 2000), no. 263.

Gérôme was very close to Charles Garnier, sealing his friendship with a portrait painted two years after the opening of the opera house that made Garnier's reputation as an architect.[1] The construction of this major example of nineteenth-century architecture took fifteen years of Garnier's life, leaving him exhausted and—strangely, for a winner of the Prix de Rome—with no other official commission. The latter part of Garnier's career, which was just beginning when Gérôme painted this portrait, was based on private, wealthy clients: Georges Hachette (for Le Cercle de la Librarie), the Monaco theater, Raphaël Bischoffsheim, several villas in Bordighera, the observatory in Nice, the spa at Vittel, etc.

The two men had met in the 1850s, introduced by Théophile Gautier. In 1854 Garnier, who had just returned from a trip to Greece and Turkey with Gautier, published *Île d'Égine: Temple de Jupiter Panhellénien*, a major study on restoring the original polychromy to an ancient edifice, which inevitably appealed to Gérôme's *Néo-Grec* interests.[2] For that matter, Garnier allegedly considered asking Gérôme to decorate the interior of the Opéra, but the idea never bore fruit.[3] Compared to the portrait done by Garnier's close collaborator Paul Baudry, Gérôme's work seeks to be more intimate, capturing the sitter's unique and appealing personality rather than showing the great architect *in situ* (ill. 39). Gérôme's portrait inevitably evokes Frantz Jourdain's description of Garnier: "He had an underlying sense of fun and foolery that put him among the Romantic artists, and his timeless tunic with its turned-down collar, his string tie, and his shaggy hat made no pretensions to supreme social elegance... His tanned trapper's complexion, his large Condé-like nose, his long and undisciplined locks, his twitchy mouth, strong chin, pale eyes and strong features... were impossible to forget after having once laid eyes on him."[4] As a friend, then, Gérôme produced a frank, straight portrait of a fellow master of eclecticism. **L. C.**

1. Part of Garnier's correspondence with Gérôme is held at the École Nationale des Beaux-Arts in Paris (gift of Mme. Charles Garnier): Garnier folder, shelfmark 741, sixty-eight items. 2. C. Garnier, *Île d'Égine: Temple de Jupiter Panhellénien* (Paris: C. Lahure, 1854). 3. G. Ackerman, *Jean-Léon Gérôme* (Courbevoie: ACR Édition, 2000), no. 263, p. 292. 4. F. Jourdain, "Charles Garnier," *Musica*, Oct. 1904, reprinted in *Au pays du souvenir* (Paris: G. Grès & Cie, 1922), quoted by B. Marrey, "Pourquoi un nouvel opéra?," in C. Garnier, *Le Nouvel Opéra* (Paris: Éditions du Linteau, 2001), pp. 17–18.

Ill. 39. Paul Baudry (1828–1886), *Portrait of Charles Garnier*, 1868, oil on canvas, 40 ½ × 32 in., Musée d'Orsay, Paris, inv. RF 2363.

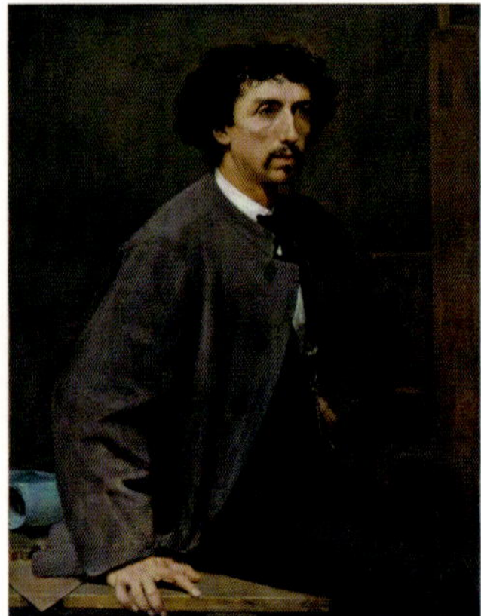

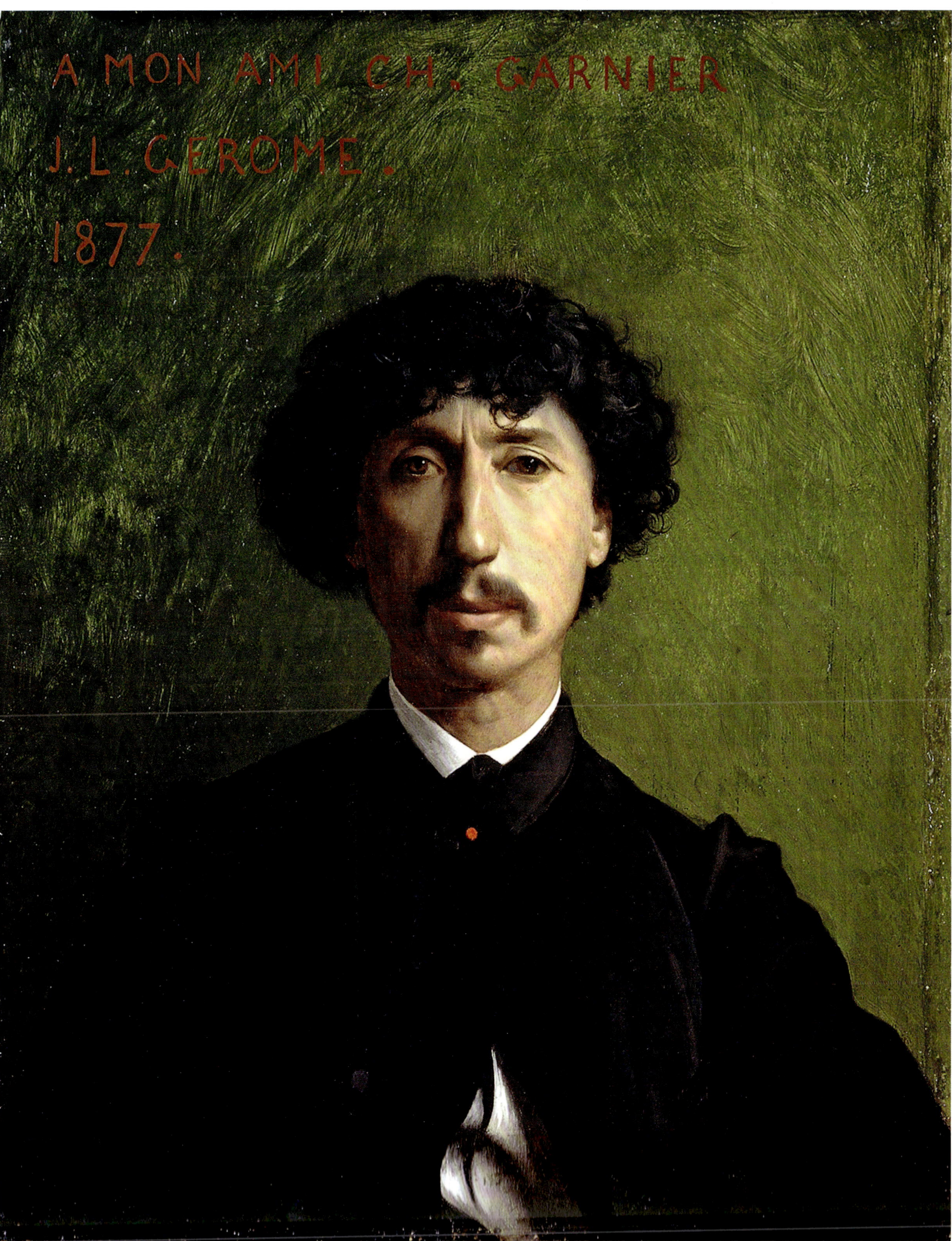
A MON AMI CH. GARNIER
J.L. GEROME.
1877.

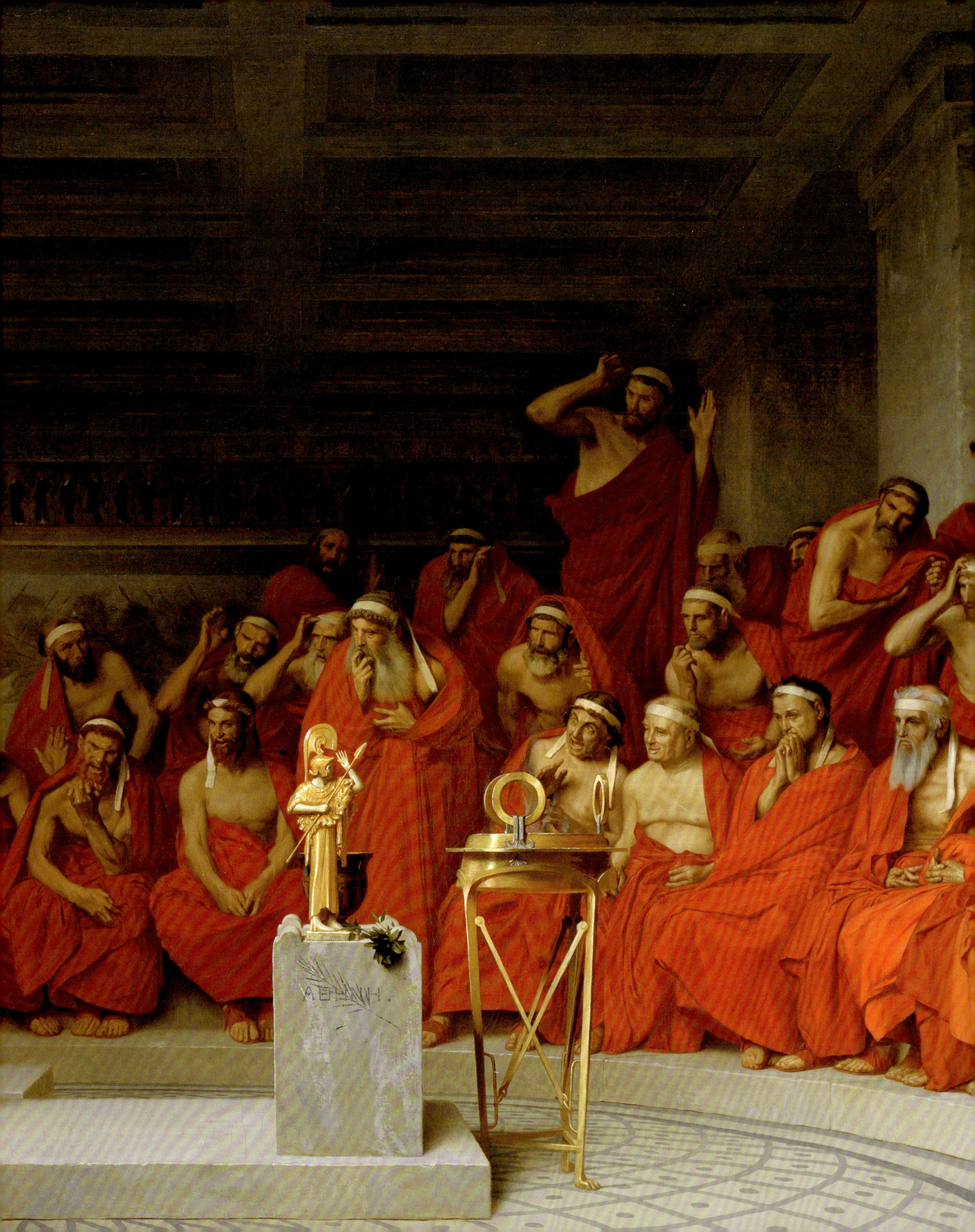

GÉRÔME BEFORE THE TRIBUNAL: THE PAINTER'S EARLY RECEPTION

—

Scott C. Allan

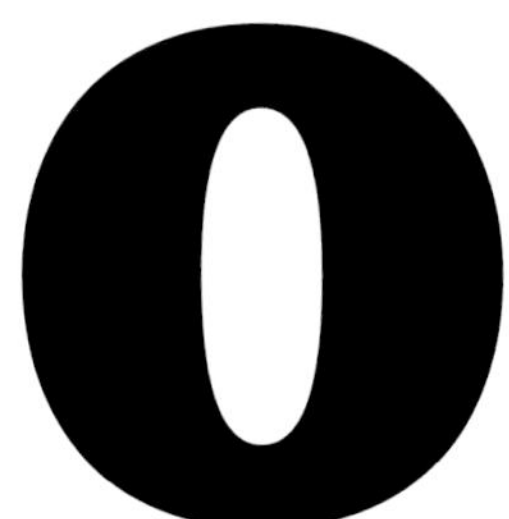

n account of Gérôme's official distinctions, commercial success, and opposition to Impressionism, historians of modern art have routinely dismissed him as the quintessential artist of the Académie, Salon, and bourgeois establishment in the second half of the nineteenth century. The negative tone was indelibly set by Émile Zola, who lambasted Gérôme on the occasion of the 1867 Exposition Universelle in Paris.[1] Zola dismissed him as a cynical manufacturer of anecdotal images for mass reproduction and popular consumption, thereby opposing him to Édouard Manet and the future Impressionists whom he championed for their sincere and original artistic temperaments.[2] Modernist criticism along these lines would persist well into the twentieth century.[3] Gérôme's proponents on the other hand, from Fanny Field Hering to Gerald Ackerman, have consistently privileged the writings of Théophile Gautier.[4] The man of letters launched Gérôme's career in 1847 with an enthusiastic passage on the artist's first Salon submission, *The Cock Fight* (cat. 10), and he found in Gérôme's following works rich material for the literary *transpositions d'art* that often edged out critical analysis in his reviews. Leaning heavily on Gautier, Gérôme's biographers have occasionally admitted more negative voices, but usually only in order to reject them as unfounded, or to diminish them by arguing that Gérôme was his own strongest critic.[5]

The resulting picture of Gérôme's reception is a distorted one. Few were quite as harsh as Zola, fewer still as uncritically positive as Gautier. This essay seeks to provide a more nuanced overview of the criticism attending Gérôme's work as he established his career in the Salons of the 1840s, 50s, and 60s—crucial years of transition for French painting, when traditional academic paradigms were recognized as outmoded but the criteria for a legitimately new art were radically uncertain. Contrary to the modernist caricature of Gérôme as a conservative "academic," he was in fact an extremely controversial figure during this early period—provoking tremendous ire for undermining the values of academic history painting on the one hand while simultaneously being hailed for his popular genre paintings on the other. "No artist," Victor Guillemin observed in 1904, "has been judged so contradictorily by the critics."[6]

The most basic problem was categorizing Gérôme. Patricia Mainardi has argued that his triumph at the 1867 Exposition symbolically ratified the triumph of genre over history painting, whose demise had become an increasingly common refrain throughout the Second Empire.[7] Identifying Gérôme with genre painting, however, had not always been automatic. From the outset, his Salon paintings confused critics on account of their variety. Besides his famous *Néo-Grec* work, with its lighthearted take on classical antiquity, his submissions included religious painting, portraiture, animal painting, and view painting. In 1855, the colossal *Age of Augustus* (ill. 1, pp. 26–27; cat. 32) announced Gérôme's ambitions in the arena of *grande peinture*, but then he made an about-face in 1857,

Cat. 45. *Phryné before the Areopagus* (detail).

turning his attention to easel painting. From that year onward, his production was dominated by Orientalist and historical genre pictures. These easel pictures themselves comprised a wide variety of formats, from preciously small cabinet pieces like *A Turkish Butcher Boy in Jerusalem* (cat. 143), to comparatively large-scale works like *Cleopatra before Caesar* (72 51 in.). Their tone also oscillated—between the tragic and comic, dramatic and familiar, grave and irreverent—and they were inconsistent stylistically. His *Néo-Grec* work suggested an ideal, classicizing manner, but it also hinted at a matter-of-fact realism—in the portrayal of the cocks in *The Cock Fight* for instance—that would come to the fore in his subsequent work.

Such diversity across Gérôme's oeuvre was further complicated by individual works that defied classification. He could treat a non-literary genre subject with the ambitious scale of academic history painting, as in *The Cock Fight*, or he could present elevated historical subjects with the small scale and close attention to detail associated with genre painting, as in *The Death of Caesar* (cat. 67). He could redirect popular comedic characters to grim, tragic ends, as in the *Duel after the Ball* (cat. 51), and he could apparently profane the most sacred dramas, as in *Golgotha* (cat. 78). Here he broke from consecrated type by pushing the drama of Christ's crucifixion off-stage through the device of cast shadows and focusing instead on the panoramic view of Jerusalem with soldiers and bystanders retreating into the distance. Unacceptable to many as a *bona fide* religious picture, it also could not be clearly typed a history or landscape painting on account of the figure scale.[8] Less contentious works similarly befuddled critics. "Is it a landscape?" Charles Clément asked of *Excursion of the Harem* (cat. 129), "is it a figure painting? If it's a landscape, it doesn't have enough interest; if it's a figure painting ... the subject isn't prominent enough."[9] *Paestum* (ill. 40) likewise seemed to involve elements of a landscape, an architectural study, and a pastoral animal scene, "without anything settling the question."[10]

What were critics to make of all these diverse and contradictory cues? For supporters like Edmond About, Gérôme was ever the *chercheur*, willing to take risks rather than repeat earlier successes. "Continual progress" was the law of his art, dictated by his abundant imagination and insatiable curiosity.[11] Detractors, however, only saw a lack of principled direction and were quick to suggest his servility to the dictates of popular fashion and the market.[12]

Behind this last criticism lay the traditional dictum that "high art" be above commerce—an ethical principle that was out of step with modern social, economic, and institutional realities.[13] Gérôme was the product of an academic system geared toward the production of elevated history painting, a genre for which there was inadequate government support and little market. Like most artists, Gérôme had to learn to adapt his academic skills to more popular genres and devise novel pictorial strategies to win over potential buyers and the public. In the process, however, he ran afoul of a critical discourse that was still structured according to the academic theory of the hierarchy of the genres, which dictated the supremacy of history painting and the subaltern status of genre, despite the continual breakdown of the boundaries between the two in practice throughout the nineteenth century.

Decisive in determining Gérôme's critical fortunes was *The Age of Augustus*, the government commission he exhibited at the 1855 Exposition Universelle. A departure from his more frivolous Néo-Grec work, the monumental canvas suddenly raised the question of whether he was capable of history painting on an epic scale. Numerous critics welcomed his audacity. For A. J. du Pays, "M. Gérôme has yielded to a noble desire, that of elevating the level of art, which tends more generally to lower itself, and of interesting the public in artistic ideas of a more severe order."[14] In general, however, the responses were negative. Accentuating its failure was the surprise success in the same exhibition of Gérôme's *Recreation in a Russian Camp* (cat. 107), a small painting he had haphazardly conceived while traveling in eastern Europe with a view to collecting figure studies for *The Age of Augustus*. This curious picture announced Gérôme's talents as an *artiste-ethnographe* and, encouraged by its success, he would subsequently devote himself to genre painting. The works he exhibited in 1857—*Duel after the Ball* and several Egyptian scenes—announced this shift, upsetting conservative critics who accused Gérôme of forsaking the cause of *grande peinture*.[15] Over the next few years, a few held out hope for large-format history paintings from him, but by the early 1860s, the switch to more marketable easel pictures seemed irrevocable. As Maxime Du Camp ruefully recalled in 1863: "M. Gérôme had just offered proof of a very respectable strength ... he had produced an example of *grande peinture*. What was done for him? Nothing ... He was not forced to become what he was supposed to be, a master." Instead of being supported by the State in the cause of history painting, "to which he had raised himself," Gérôme "fell back down to genre, which ... seeks and enjoys facile success."[16]

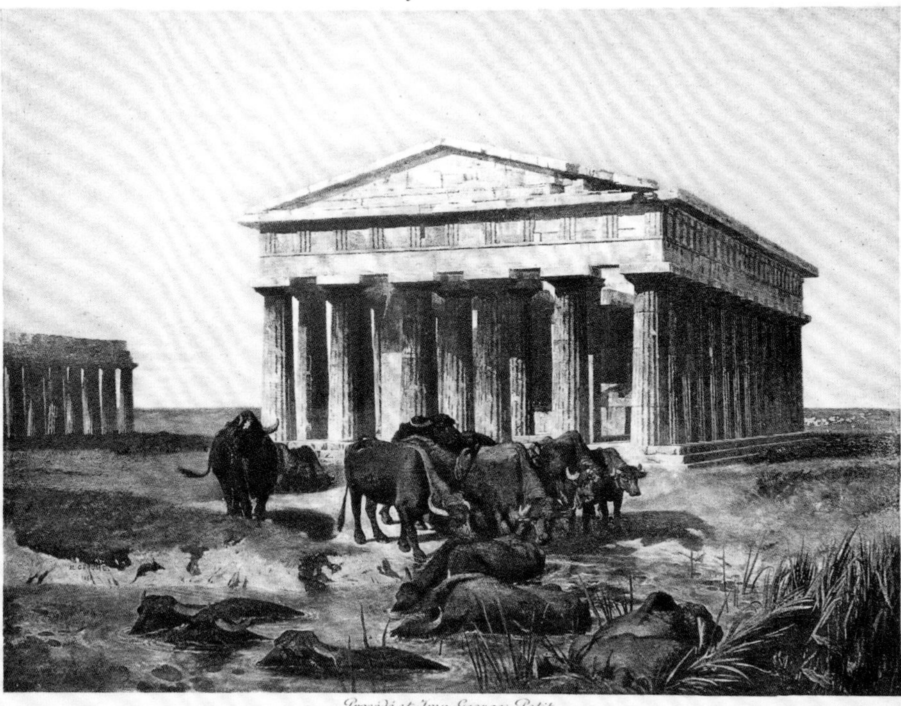

Ill. 40. *Paestum*, from *Catalogue des tableaux modernes, aquarelles, pastels, dessins... provenant de la collection Moreau-Nélaton*, Galerie Georges Petit, Paris, May 11–12 and 14–15, 1900, lot 42, painting lost.

Unlike Du Camp, most commentators saw *The Age of Augustus* as the aberration. It seemed evident that Gérôme lacked the "poetic sentiment," "pictorial intelligence," and idealizing "beauty of forms" necessary to such grand work.[17] His skills were instead of the more straightforwardly descriptive, mimetic kind which critics aligned with genre painting. As the consensus stood in the 1860s: "in descending, he has found his natural level. His innate qualities—a most remarkable spirit of observation, an extreme manual dexterity, a delicate sentiment of the picturesque—have taken the upper hand. His poetic faculties by contrast—imagination, the power to create, transform, [and] idealize—have increasingly diminished. Gérôme was born a genre painter and it is on this modest terrain that he has produced his best works."[18]

Genre painting was respectable in itself, but critics had difficulty countenancing those who did not recognize the limits of their talent within the overarching hierarchy, and Gérôme appeared incorrigible in this regard. Having turned to genre but still showing an interest in serious historical subjects, he proved a mercurial figure in the late 1850s and 1860s, giving conflicting signals about his direction. A case could be made for his elevation of genre painting. The *Duel after the Ball*, for instance, conveyed for some an expressive force and tragic pathos worthy of Shakespeare.[19] *The Prisoner* (cat. 127) was similarly praised for rising above mere observation and anecdote to the level of general moral truths: it offered a universalizing statement about the Orient.[20] Such elevation, worthy of a history painter, was matched by qualities of "drawing and style that are ordinarily employed ... only in *grande peinture*."[21]

But if Gérôme was credited with bringing a history painter's talents to the humbler precincts of genre, he was more widely condemned for approaching history painting with the supposedly trivial mindset of a genre painter.[22] Gérôme's art was taken to be symptomatic of the erosion of boundaries between history and genre painting in the nineteenth century, a state of affairs that can be traced at least as far back as the romantic generation of his master Paul Delaroche, which saw the emergence of the hybrid category of the *genre historique* —applied to paintings that took a more familiar and anecdotal approach to history and emphasized local color and accessory details. What distinguished Gérôme, and made him so threatening, however, was that he seemingly went out of his way to debase history painting, draining it of aesthetic and ethical value, as John House has emphasized.[23]

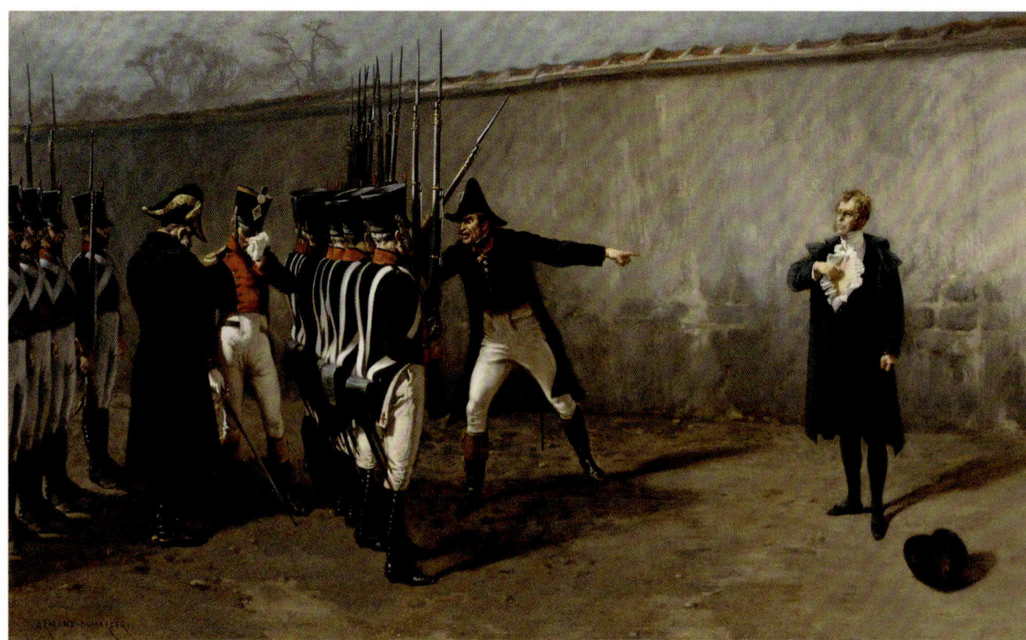

Ill. 41. Charles Édouard Armand-Dumaresq (1826–1895), *The Unwilling Executioners*, oil on canvas, 30 ½ × 50 ½ in., private collection.

Convinced that momentous historical drama lay above Gérôme's abilities, many critics accused him of failing to penetrate the heart of his subjects or, worse, shirking it in bad faith. *The Death of Marshal Ney* (cat. 93), exhibited in 1868, is the most notorious example. The painting treated the political execution of Marshal Ney at the dawn of the Restoration with a striking frankness and immediacy. Through a bold composition that establishes a charged void between the abandoned corpse of Ney and the retreating soldiers, Gérôme focused dispassionately on the physical fact of death and its precise material circumstances—the graffitied wall, muddy road, and dismal weather. While a few sympathetic critics found a chilling dramatic *frisson* in Gérôme's descriptive deadpan,[24] most accused him of perversely avoiding all that was potentially grand, heroic, and pathetic in the subject. By highlighting the drama's ignoble aftermath rather than its emotional climax, Gérôme's painting constituted an evasion. Jules-Antoine Castagnary thus dismissed him: "The drama frightened you, so you show us the end of it. The action was too vehement for your petty means, so you make us look upon its denouement. You call us to the spectacle only after the curtain has fallen ... I tell you ... that is not great art, it is not even minor art."[25] A true history painter, Castagnary insisted, would have given us the affective human drama. He would have depicted Ney upright, heroically facing the firing squad, and he would have evoked the conflicting emotions of the unfortunate officers and soldiers charged with the task of executing a marshal of France.[26] He would have painted, one surmises, something like Édouard Armand-Dumaresq's *The Unwilling Executioners* (ill. 41).

Seeing only travesty, critics were unable to appreciate the dramatic strategies of paintings like *The Death of Marshal Ney* in historical perspective. It might be argued that however vivid and compelling they had originally appeared, the pictures of Delaroche—which often focused on the suspense-filled moments *prior* to the execution of historical figures—may have begun to appear overly theatrical or sentimental by the 1850s. Might Gérôme's focus on denouements, on the moments after Ney's execution or Caesar's assassination, constitute not a facile evasion, but a deliberate strategy to differentiate his works from his master's and to secure, for his time, desired effects of truth and immediacy that eschewed theatricality? Might he not also have been after a kind of history painting as "document" that spoke to the positivist ethos of his time and responded to the radical modes of realism, like that of Courbet, that were making inroads across the lower genres? Might not he have been intent upon modernizing history painting, or even conferring academic legitimacy upon realism? These were not questions entertained at the time; indeed, the charge that Gérôme sought to trivialize history painting had already become rote.

Besides signaling his weaknesses in dramatic conception, critics also persistently cited his ignoble characterizations of historical figures. The philosopher in *Socrates seeking Alcibiades at the House of Aspasia* (ill. 53, p. 110) was "an inept and gauche old prig."[27] Julius Caesar came across in *Cleo-*

patra before Caesar as a "Senate clerk" or "auctioneer," his attitude of "stupid impatience" like that of "a bailiff interrupted in his work by an indiscreet client."[28] In *Molière Breakfasting with Louis XIV* (cat. 84), the king likewise appeared too ordinary in type, having "nothing of the dignity that history lends him"[29]; he appeared to exude the nonchalance of a musketeer or the voluptuousness of an *ancien régime* sophisticate.[30] In certain cases, critics pretended not even to recognize Gérôme's figures. In the *Dead Caesar* (ill. 56, p. 122), the emperor's extremely foreshortened attitude, which presented his head upside down to the viewer; the shadow cast over his face, which gave his skin an inappropriately dark color; and the abundant fabric of his toga, which concealed his body—all contributed to obscure and diminish his heroic identity.[31] As for the fallen Marshal Ney, he might just as easily be taken for a passed-out drunk.[32]

Gérôme fared even worse with his female figures. In a string of paintings beginning with the 1859 *King Candaules* (cat. 43), he staged legendary subjects that hinged upon the sudden revelation of a perfect beauty. "The first exigency of the subject [of *King Candaules*]," Jean Rousseau wrote, "was that [the king's wife] Nyssia be beautiful. It was an opportunity to find the ideal form, to recover the heroic style of antiquity."[33] She had to be so beautiful as to justify the king's prideful exposure of her to Gyges as well as Gyges' subsequent regicide. In the case of *Phryné before the Areopagus* (cat. 45), shown in 1861, Gérôme's challenge lay in representing not only the Praxitelean ideal (Phryné being the renowned model of the famous sculptor) but also the religious respect and chaste admiration that such beauty supposedly inspired in classical antiquity. At stake in the representation of such a figure—pardoned by the Athenian tribunal on the basis of her beauty—was nothing less, Gautier emphasized, than the "moral philosophy of ... Hellenic civilization."[34]

Predictably, Gérôme's nudes were inadequate to such a charge. The contemporary lower-class model seemed all too present in his figures.[35] They manifested shocking errors of anatomical *dessin*.[36] And because of their high polish and monotonous coloration, they also failed to convey the *carnation* of living flesh, assuming instead the look of ivory or wax statuettes.[37] By most accounts, the *beau idéal* eluded Gérôme, making his scenarios seem wholly implausible and ridiculous. As Paul Mantz wrote of *King Candaules*, "how can we believe that Gyges will ever be able to love this poor little puppet and that the imprudent Candaules will lose his crown and life on her account?"[38] Du Camp similarly dismissed Gérôme's Phryné as "a bawdy *lorette* ... whom the Greeks, knowledgeable in beauty, would have immediately condemned if she had no other argument than her nudity."[39]

More objectionable to critics than Gérôme's apparent inability to create beautiful types, however, was the manner in which he treated the male spectators whom he included in his dramatic staging of the nude, particularly in the case of *Phryné*. Here critics were appalled by the Areopagites in whose reactions "all the phases of desire" were all too legible.[40] It seemed inconceivable that these "lubricious and grimacing apes"[41] were supposed to represent "the august magistrates for whom laughter itself was forbidden and whose gravity had become proverbial!"[42] Patiently describing their ignoble expressions constituted a violation not only of moral decorum and good taste, but also of historical truth. By sexualizing the Greek *beau idéal*, Gérôme seemed to betray a "radical ignorance of antiquity" and an all-too-petty modern sensibility.[43] The scene was little different than that produced by "a woman ... stripping in a public place, a café, for example, or a theater."[44] Phryné's attitude of shame was also anachronistic. She should have been depicted as "proud in her triumphant beauty. The painter has produced an ashamed little girl ... hiding her face in a childish movement of modesty. That is not Phryné."[45] It was hard to believe that an artist steeped in the classical tradition like Gérôme did not know better. Critics concluded that he was evidently willing to admit of a glaring *contre-sens* in the interests of sensational appeal, sacrificing truth and tradition for saucy anecdotes that played to the crowd. History painting thus prostituted had become a joke.

What critics did not recognize or articulate was just how deeply aware Gérôme was of the conditions under which paintings like *Phryné* were displayed and viewed. One could argue that *Phryné* wittily drew attention to the spectacularization of art in the popular context of the Salon. The painting appeared to be a vulgarly pandering or iconoclastic gesture, but it honestly avowed what many Salon nudes did not: that such paintings were already subject to indecent, clamorous attention at the massively attended exhibition, and that the fiction of aesthetic autonomy and detached contemplation had already been destroyed. Existing as it did in such a provocative relationship to the typical nude, *Phryné* might even be said to find a strange bedfellow in Manet's *Olympia*. For better or for worse, Gérôme's was an art that was hyper-aware of its conditions of existence and possibility in the public arena.

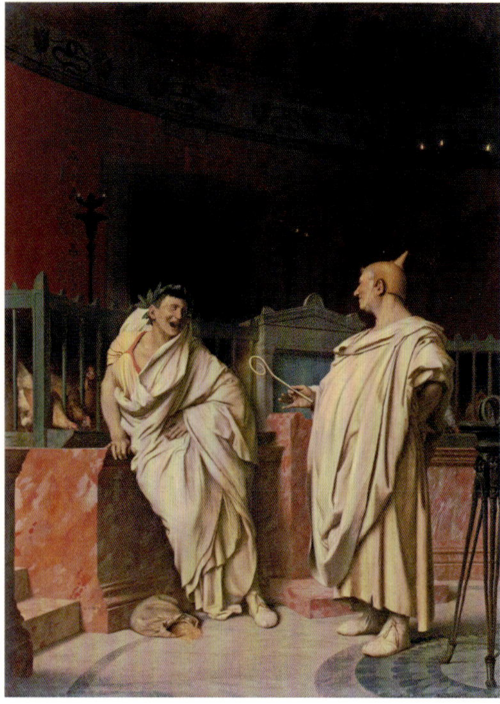

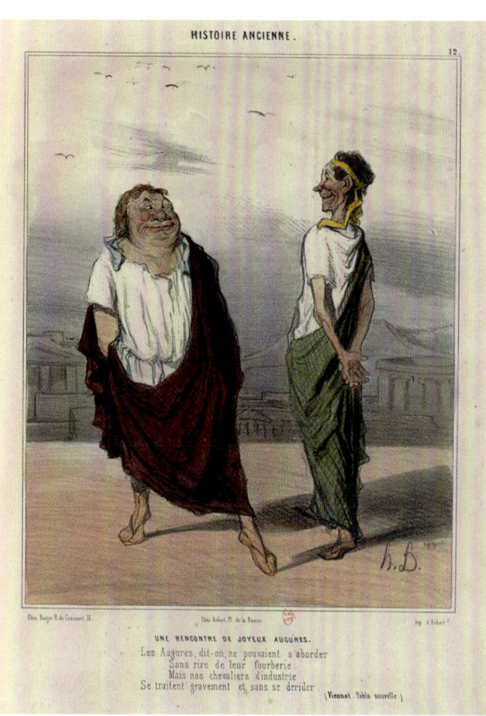

Ill. 42. *The Two Augurs*, 1861, oil on canvas, 25 ¾ × 19 in., private collection.

Ill. 43. Honoré Daumier (1808–1879), "Une rencontre de joyeux augures," in *Histoire ancienne* (Paris: Bauger-Aubert, ca. 1843), pl. 12, Bibliothèque Nationale de France, Paris, inv. DC-180 (P)-4.

The caricatural tendency that *Phryné* announced so brashly was all too readily confirmed by Gérôme's *Two Augurs* (ill. 42), also exhibited in 1861. Here again critics found an inadmissible *contre-sens*. The literary source for the painting, a biting remark by Cicero about the charlatanism of augurs, should have prompted Gérôme to show the augurs exchanging a knowing smile or wink, not splitting their sides with laughter.[46] Critics damningly remarked that Honoré Daumier, who had also treated the subject, could offer the would-be history painter a lesson here (ill. 43).[47] And why had Gérôme lavished so much detailed attention on such a trivial scene?[48] Critics suggested that his irreverent sensibility was better suited to the rapidity of a sketch rather than to a finished painting, where comic laughter resulted all too easily in frozen grimaces.[49]

More to the point, most critics were simply unable to stomach Gérôme's penchant for the "burlesque" when it touched upon antiquity. But here it must be noted that he was responding to widespread challenges to the academic orthodoxies of nineteenth-century classicism. Gérôme's attraction to the erotic, frivolous, or satiric spirit of relatively minor Greek authors like Anacreon and Aristophanes fed directly off a resurgence of interest in these same authors in the literary world.[50] In his more caricatural tendencies, Gérôme simultaneously shared a basic affinity with innumerable comic assaults—in music, theater, and print—upon those who insisted upon making antiquity the object of "a chaste and virginal Stoic reverie," in one satirist's words.[51] Gérôme's irreverent take on antiquity should not simply be attributed to a vulgar imagination, but rather to the de-sacralization of the antique in modern popular culture and to the growing appreciation of the variety of ancient Greco-Roman culture in all its manifestations, high and low.

Whatever the contemporary comic echoes of *The Two Augurs*, Gérôme never exhibited such an uproarious scene in the Salon again. Lasting damage had been done, however, and critics of his subsequent historical pictures were predisposed to dismiss them as caricatures of high art. Of *Molière Breakfasting with Louis XIV* in 1863, for example, Mantz wrote impatiently: "[This] will be, we hope, his last error ... I do not see what is so risible in the episode. M. Gérôme has turned Greek history into vaudeville; if only he would leave ours its gravity."[52] This painting would not, however, be Gérôme's last "error," and by the late 1860s, the lingering perception was that his dominant tendency was toward "the saucy, the comic ... the burlesque."[53] Gérôme may have sought to counter this view with two gravely serious pictures in 1868, *Golgotha* and *The Death of Marshal Ney*, but they too were treated as irreverent affronts in keeping with his prior "parodies" of history painting.[54]

The proverbial triviality of Gérôme's conceptions was unfortunately matched by the perceived *petitesse* of his stylistic means. In historical works like *Ave, Caesar, morituri te salutant* (cat. 70) and *King Candaules*, which pretended to an archaeological reconstruction of the past, Gérôme was criticized, like many practitioners of the *genre historique*, for focusing on accessory details at the expense of the principal human figures. In allegedly treating his historical subjects as pretexts for antiquarian displays, Gérôme reduced the grandeur of the past to microscopic proportions, and history painting to still life.[55] He turned it into a "curiosity shop" or an "exhibition of archaeological gewgaws" of interest only to "amateurs of bric-a-brac."[56]

Gérôme's attention to archaeological minutiae also entailed the sacrifice of essential pictorial qualities. Affiliated from his *Néo-Grec* beginnings with the school of Ingres and *dessin*, Gérôme was automatically perceived to be deficient as a colorist.[57] It was not simply that his color often appeared attenuated, dull, and cold,[58] but that he seemed to lack the intelligence of *coloris*, which, according to academic theory, had less to do with the strength of individual colors and more to do with their concerted interaction. By paying too much attention to individual details, he failed to make the sacrifices necessary to produce a harmonious ensemble,[59] and he sometimes introduced strong individual color notes that disrupted the compositional unity.[60]

Closely associated with Gérôme's neglect of *coloris* was a lack of painterly appeal at the level of facture. For many his brushwork appeared too thin and meager.[61] Also too monotonous, it lacked the vigorous accents and nuances of execution that enlivened the paint surface and helped differentiate the textures of the objects depicted.[62] Indeed, Gérôme pushed finish to a point that rendered his brushwork nearly invisible; his paintings' surfaces were so polished that everything in them took on a frozen, petrified aspect. His works were endlessly likened to porcelain, enamel, wood, and metal.[63]

Gérôme's conscientiously finished works could also certainly be praised as tours de force of dexterity, precision, and finesse, and consequently held up as examples in the face of declining pictorial

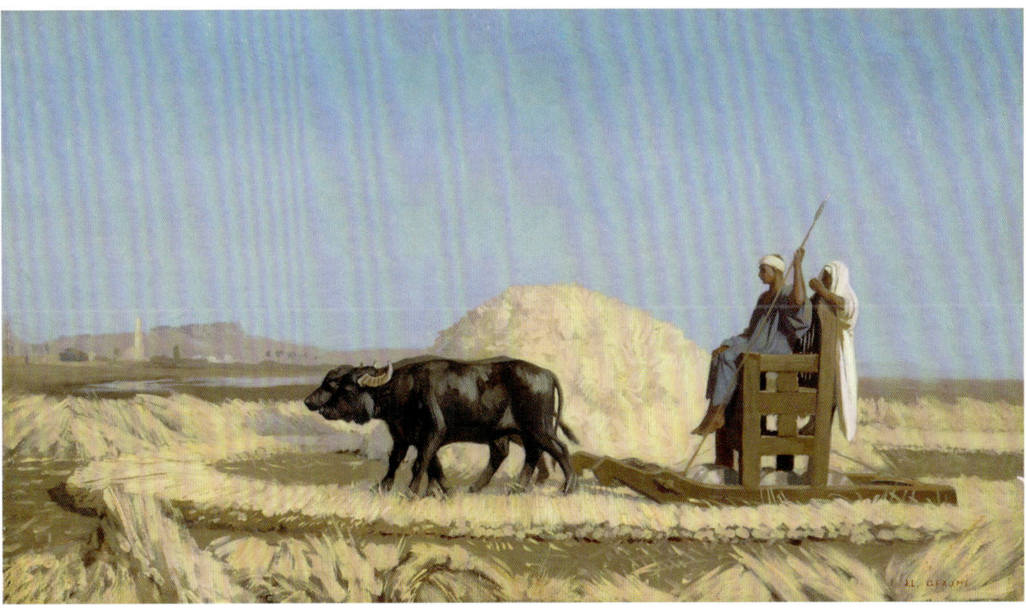

Ill. 44. *The Egyptian Grain-Cutter* (variant), ca. 1859, oil on panel, 8 × 14 in., private collection.

standards.[64] By virtue of such qualities, critics frequently compared Gérôme to seventeenth-century Dutch genre painters like Gerard Dou or Willem van Mieris. In the context of discussions of history painting, which demanded a certain painterly breadth, however, such comparisons were slighting. Critics concerned about the decline of *grande peinture* railed against genre painting for catering to unsophisticated tastes for mimetic illusionism and high finish, and against the philistine bourgeois amateurs who judged such painting *à la loupe*.

Gérôme's perceived deficiencies at the level of execution not only underscored his limitations as a painter. They were also taken as a sign that he had violated the fundamental conditions of painting in the service of extra-pictorial interests. He was accused of effacing his brushwork not only so that his pictures could appeal to the widest possible audience on an exclusively anecdotal or "literary" level,[65] but also so that they could be more easily disseminated through reproduction, whether by engraving or photomechanical means. Zola famously made this accusation in 1867, but he was only repeating what others had been saying for a decade.[66] Early on critics suggested that Gérôme's descriptive precision and polished technique were inspired by or comparable to photography,[67] and after he entered into partnership with Goupil, critics argued that the *raison d'être* of Gérôme's painting was to return to photography through reproduction.[68] Taking this critique to its logical conclusion, commentators claimed that Gérôme's work was in fact better appreciated in reproduction than in the original,[69] so completely had he sacrificed the noble art of painting to the requirements and mechanisms of commercial image production.

It is no exaggeration to conclude, then, that Gérôme's painting represented a profound challenge to, and indeed inversion of, the traditional priorities and values of "high art" and particularly of history painting. The harsh criticism attending Gérôme's historical pictures, however, contrasts sharply with virtually unanimous praise for his ethnographic genre scenes. In 1855, About suggested that the *Recreation in a Russian Camp* might be his masterpiece, affirming: "This is how one responds to criticism."[70] In 1861, the scandal of *Phryné* was partly mitigated by the quiet virtues of *The Egyptian Grain-Cutter* (ill. 44), which some categorically exempted from criticism.[71] In 1863, there was little contest between *Molière Breakfasting with Louis XIV* and *The Prisoner*, which for Louis Enault was "one of the best paintings of the Salon."[72] In 1865, critics found *Prayer on the Housetops* to be incontestably better than the official history painting Gérôme also exhibited that year, *The Reception of the Siamese Ambassadors at Fontainebleau* (cat. 94).[73] And in 1866, if *Cleopatra before Caesar* met with disappointment and ridicule, the *Heads of the Rebel Beys at the Mosque El Assaneyn* (cat. 144) belonged to the "rank of perfect Gérômes."[74]

How are we to account for this split in his reception? Why were critics so uncritical when it came to his ethnographic work? Much can be said for the novelty of his subject matter and the lower stakes of genre painting. In modest works like *The Egyptian Grain-Cutter*, Gérôme was not beholden to textual sources or iconographic tradition as he was in history painting, and so he was afforded greater leeway.[75] Furthermore, he succeeded in making his subjects memorable through a meticulous style that lent them a striking "cachet of local truth"[76] and differentiated his works from the vaguer, more painterly evocations of the East by Romantic predecessors like Delacroix and Decamps. Indeed, the "realist" turn in Orientalist art signaled by Gérôme responded to a growing thirst for detailed information about the world beyond France, particularly the areas in which it had colonial, strategic, or commercial interests. His work addressed the same curious audiences as did contemporary Orientalist photography and popular illustrated periodicals like the *Magasin pittoresque*, which often ran articles of ethnographic interest. Indeed, Gérôme's paintings were enlisted as authoritative documents in such journals,[77] not only because they were reputed to be objective descriptions, but also because their apparent factuality helped perpetuate established cultural stereotypes, about oriental despotism, fatalism, lassitude, sensuality, and so on.[78] Perfectly attuned to contemporary cultural trends, Gérôme's art thus effected, as James Kearns has argued, "the recycling both of romantic Orientalism for a predominantly scientific, positivist culture, and of exoticism in the form of a historic document."[79]

More crucially in the context of Salon criticism, ethnographic genre painting also allowed Gérôme to turn to good account his more egregious "errors" as a history painter. Where, for example, his attention to accessory detail threatened to undermine the priorities of history painting, it served to guarantee the authenticity of his genre paintings, making them, as Elie Roy affirmed, "priceless documents for history."[80] It was precisely through detail that paintings like Gérôme's *Dance of the Almeh* (cat. 154) initiated viewers into an unfamiliar world. "Nobody has penetrated so far into ... [the Orient]," About asserted; "stop for a long time before this painting of the Almeh. Examine in detail the costumes, the decor, the accessories, this *bournous*, these *babouches* ... this *chibouk*, this *narghile* ... and a thousand other details ... You will feel your mind imperceptibly acclimate."[81] As this enumeration of exotic objects suggests, Gérôme's taste for bric-a-brac could be indulged in the realm of ethnographic genre where it supplied necessary local color. Indeed, he seems to have chosen certain subjects as pretexts for the display of oriental souvenirs which he had amassed during his travels. Witness his itinerant merchants, like the ones he exhibited in 1867 and 1869, "hawking their bric-a-brac" and appearing all the more picturesque and typical for doing so.[82]

Gérôme was similarly able to counter his perceived failure in the representation of legendary beauties and noble historical figures with particularized and expressive depictions of contemporary ethnic types. Here his talent as a physiognomist, evident in *Phryné* only at the expense of the subject's dignity, became a positive virtue. Low or ugly types that were potentially indecorous in history painting became objects of curiosity in an ethnographic context. The ugliness of Gérôme's Russian musicians in *Recreation in a Russian Camp* was, for example, "exquisite."[83] His glaring Turkish butcher, surrounded by animal parts, beckoned with "a certain local charm, a savor of a certain rarity."[84] "The poor devils" in *Egyptian Recruits Crossing the Desert* "are not classically beautiful, but it is impossible to doubt the rigorous exactitude of the reproduction. The heads ... truly individual and very diverse, are fine studies."[85] Gérôme thus proved a master of "character."[86]

The project of ethnographic documentation and characterization could also legitimize the more distasteful aspects of Gérôme's art. His penchant for comedy, for example, found an appropriate outlet in scenes like *The Prisoner* (cat. 127). The Arnaut who, in a spirit of ironic raillery, serenades the bound prisoner was entirely of a piece with critics' notions of the Orient: "M. Gérôme has made [viewers] perfectly aware of the state of Egypt, where a ... gentle, submissive race is tortured each day by [Ottoman] conquerors more vulgar, more vicious, and less intelligent than it."[87]

Similarly, Gérôme's taste for erotic titillation found an alibi in pictures like *Dance of the Almeh*, which could be safely viewed, at least by some, as a *scène de moeurs* objectively describing an oriental dance.[88] As such, it could be taken as testimony to the degenerate character of the East rather than the base instincts of the artist or his Western audience. Where Gérôme's Phryné failed to measure up to the Praxitelean ideal of the Greeks, the *almeh*'s lubriciously contorted form accorded with the gross, sensual nature said to typify her "degenerate" race.[89] Where the Areopagites were caricatured through their ignoble reactions to Phryné, the *bashi-bazouks* watching the *almeh*'s dance manifested brutal desires that spoke to their innate characters.[90] One might even suggest that Gérôme turned the negative criticism of *Phryné* into successful Orientalist fare. It had been charged, for example, that he treated *Phyrné* as if it were a slave market scene. The courtesan's gesture was "the gesture more fearful than chaste of a little Circassian girl up for sale in a bazaar in Constantinople."[91] As for the Areopagites, "would it be pure aesthetic contemplation that gives to them the cunning eye of crafty courtiers, suppliers of harems, evaluating in a bazaar the qualities and defects of a slave for sale?"[92] When Gérôme exhibited just such a slave market scene at the 1867 Salon (cat. 156), critics were all too receptive of it as an incisive ethnographic document.[93]

Gérôme's increasing focus on Orientalist work does not simply suggest that he was responding to critics' encouragement and market demand or descending to his "natural level" as a genre painter, but also that he was cannily responding to the critics of his historical work. Equally significant, however, is Gérôme's refusal to abandon historical subjects despite loud calls to do so. He showcased both types of work simultaneously and it seems clear that this was not just a matter of diversifying his market,[94] but that the two genres were somehow complementary, even mutually defining, for him. His ethnographic work had indeed emerged from his concerted preparations as a history painter, as Marc Gotlieb has stressed,[95] and Gérôme would conversely attempt to reinvigorate history painting through means associated with the lower genres, bringing to historical subjects the kind of photographic veracity and attention to local color which he brought to his Orientalist "documents." Such a strategy was certainly in keeping with the Romantic historiographic project, articulated by Jules Michelet and others, of vividly "resurrecting" the past.[96] Nevertheless, a majority of critics still beholden to the hierarchy of genres were unable to welcome Gérôme's efforts, despite the fact that it was commonly understood that the old tradition of *grande peinture* was moribund.

Ultimately, because he was narrowly cast into the role of an apostate or *manqué* history painter who opportunistically threw in his lot with genre, Gérôme became symptomatic of the decline of the French school. As one of the most popular painters in the Salon, he was an obvious target for critics troubled by the rise of an untutored middle-class public for art, and as one of the most financially successful living artists, he became emblematic of the capitalist market forces reshaping the art world. To critics who considered themselves, Claudine Mitchell reminds us, not only the arbiters of taste and moral educators of the public, but also "the upholders of culture and of humanitarian principles," Gérôme's art appeared tainted, the product of moneyed self-interest rather than disinterested aesthetic ideals.[97] From our current perspective, however, the early hostility to Gérôme, which has been eclipsed in histories of nineteenth-century art by the mythologized scandals of the avant-garde, can help us articulate what it was that made his art so novel and indeed modern when it first appeared. Rather than accuse Gérôme of debasing his art, as his earliest critics routinely did, we would do well to revisit his work for what it can tell us more positively about the shifting parameters of both history painting and genre painting, and, more fundamentally, of high art and popular culture, in the late nineteenth century.

1. É. Zola, *Écrits sur l'art* (Paris, 1991), pp. 183–85.

2. Ibid., pp. 137–69, 189–228.

3. For instance, J. Rewald, "Should Hoving Be De-accessioned?", *Art in America* 61, no. 1 (Jan.–Feb. 1973), p. 28.

4. See F. F. Hering, *Gérôme: The Life and Works of Jean Léon Gérôme* (New York: Cassell, 1892), *passim*; G. Ackerman, *The Life and Work of Jean-Léon Gérôme, with a Catalogue Raisonné* (London: Sotheby's, 1986), *passim*.

5. For instance, F. F. Hering 1892 (as in n. 4), pp. 3, 48–49; C. Moreau-Vauthier, *Gérôme, peintre et sculpteur. L'homme et l'artiste d'après sa correspondance, ses notes, les souvenirs de ses élèves et de ses amis* (Paris: Hachette, 1906), pp. 95–96, 97, 99, 151.

6. V. Guillemin, "Étude sur le peintre et sculpteur Jean-Léon Gérôme (1824–1904)," *Académie des sciences, belles-lettres et arts de Besançon. Procès-verbaux et Mémoires. Année 1904* (1905), p. 179 ["Aucun artiste n'a, je crois, été jugé par la critique aussi contradictoirement"].

7. P. Mainardi, *Art and Politics of the Second Empire: The Universal Expositions of 1855 and 1867* (New Haven, 1987), pp. 154–57, 169–72.

8. For instance, T. Gautier, "Salon de 1868," *Le Moniteur universel*, May 2, 1868, p. 585.

9. C. Clément, "Exposition de 1869," *Journal des débats*, June 10, 1869 ["Est-ce un paysage? Est-ce un tableau de figures? Si c'est un paysage, il n'a pas assez d'intérêt; si c'est un tableau de figures ... le sujet ne joue pas un rôle suffisant"].

10. C. Tillot, "Revue du Salon," *Le Siècle*, June 8, 1852 ["sans que rien décide la question"].

11. E. About, "Salon de 1865," *Le Petit Journal*, May 23, 1865, p. 3 ["progrès continu"].

12. For instance, M. Du Camp, "Le Salon de 1863," *Revue des deux mondes*, 2nd per., vol. 45 (June 15, 1863), pp. 890–92.

13. J. House, "History Without Values? Gérôme's History Paintings," *Journal of the Warburg and Courtauld Institutes* 71 (2008), p. 272.

14. A.-J. du Pays, "Exposition universelle des beaux-arts," *L'Illustration* 26 (July 14, 1855), p. 29 ["M. Gérôme a cédé à un noble désir, celui d'élever le niveau de l'art, qui tend plus généralement à s'abaisser, et d'intéresser le public à des idées artistiques d'un ordre plus sévère."].

15. For instance, A. de Calonne, "Exposition des beaux-arts de 1857," *Revue contemporaine* 32 (July 1, 1857), p. 609.

16. M. Du Camp 1863 (as in n. 12), pp. 889–90 ["M. Gérôme venait de faire preuve d'une force très respectable ... il venait de faire acte de grande peinture. Que fit-on pour lui? Rien...on ne le força pas à devenir ce qu'il devait être, un maître ... De la haute peinture historique où il s'était élevé, il est retombé aux tableaux de genre, qui sollicitent et obtiennent les faciles succès"].

17. P. Petroz, "Exposition universelle des beaux-arts," *La Presse*, July 31, 1855 ["la beauté des formes, le sentiment poétique, l'intelligence pittoresque"].

18. C. Clément, "Exposition de 1868," *Journal des débats*, June 3, 1868 ["En s'éloignant de la source et en descendant, il a pris son niveau naturel. Ses qualités natives,—un esprit d'observation des plus remarquables, une extrême habileté de main, un sentiment pittoresque délicat, ont pris le dessus. Les facultés poétiques, au contraire,—l'imagination, la puissance de créer, de transformer, d'idéaliser,—se sont de plus en plus amoindries. M. Gérôme était né peintre de genre, et c'est sur ce terrain modeste, qu'il a fait ses meilleurs ouvrages"].

19. For instance, A. Tardieu, "Salon de 1857 au Palais des Champs-Élysées," *Le Constitutionnel*, June 30, 1857.

20. For instance, C. de Sault, "Salon de 1863," *Le Temps*, June 14, 1863; or A. Nettement, "Salon de 1863," *La Semaine des familles*, Aug. 1, 1863, p. 690.

21. Anon., "Salon de 1863.—Peinture. Boucher Turc, par M. Gérôme," *Le Magasin pittoresque* 31, no. 39 (Sept. 1863), p. 305 ["des qualités de dessin et de style qui ne se déploient ordinairement ... que dans la grande peinture"].

22. For instance, P. Mantz, "Salon de 1859," *Gazette des beaux-arts* 2, no. 4 (May 15, 1859), pp. 198–99; C. Clément 1868 (as in n. 18); or L. Lagrange, "Le Salon de 1866," *Le Correspondant* 32 (May 1866), p. 203.

23. J. House 2008 (as in n. 13), *passim*.

24. For instance, E. About, "Salon de 1868," *Revue des deux mondes*, 2nd per., vol. 75 (June 1, 1868), p. 729.

25. J.-A. Castagnary, *Salons* (Paris: Charpentier, 1892), p. 262 ["Le drame vous a fait peur, vous nous en montrez la fin. L'action était trop véhémente pour vos petits moyens, vous nous en faites voir les suites. C'est quand le rideau est tombé, que vous nous appelez au spectacle. Eh bien! je vous le dis, moi, ce n'est pas là du grand art, ce n'est même pas du petit"].

26. Ibid.

27. T. Pelloquet, "Salon de 1861," *Le Monde Illustré* 8, no. 219 (June 22, 1861), p. 319 ["ce vieux cuistre inepte et gauche"].

28. C. Blanc, "Salon de 1866," *Gazette des beaux-arts* 20, no. 6 (June 1, 1866), p. 516 ["un greffier du Senat"]; C. de Sault, "Salon de 1866," *Le Temps*, May 26, 1866 ["commissaire-priseur"]; L. Lagrange 1866 (as in n. 22), pp. 203–4 ["une sotte impatience"]; and J. Rousseau, "Salon de 1866, " *L'Univers illustré*, no. 547 (June 20, 1866), 391 ["un huissier dérangé, au milieu de son étude, par une cliente indiscrète"].

29. T. Pelloquet, in *L'Exposition: Journal du Salon de 1863*, no. 5 (May 24, 1863), p. 2 ["rien de la dignité que l'histoire lui prête"].

30. For instance, P. de Saint-Victor, "Salon de 1863," *La Presse*, June 14, 1863; or A. Viollet-le-Duc, "Salon de 1863," *Journal des débats*, May 27, 1863.

31. For instance, A.-J. du Pays, "Salon de 1859," *L'Illustration* 33, no. 843 (Apr. 23, 1859), p. 269; J.-A. Castagnary 1892 (as in n. 25), p. 96; or C. Dollfus, "Salon de 1859," *Revue germanique* 6, no. 4 (Apr.–June 1859), p. 242.

32. For instance, B. Bouniol, "L'Amateur au Salon. 1868," *Revue du monde catholique* 21, no. 4 (May 25, 1868), p. 569; C. Clément 1868 (as in n. 18); M. Chaumelin, *L'Art contemporain* (Paris: Renouard, 1873), p. 116; or Anon., "La foire aux peintures de 1868," *La Vie parisienne*, May 30, 1868, p. 387.

33. J. Rousseau, "Salon de 1863," *L'Univers illustré*, June 11, 1863, p. 219 ["Quand il peignit *la Femme du roi Candaule*, la première exigence du sujet était que Nyssia fût belle. C'était le moment de chercher la forme idéale, de retrouver le style héroïque de l'antiquité"].

34. T. Gautier, *Abécédaire du Salon de 1861* (Paris: E. Dentu, 1861), pp. 177–79 ["la morale de cette civilisation hellénique"].

35. For instance, P. Mantz 1859 (as in n. 22), p. 198; or A. de la Fizelière, "L'Art contemporain. Salon de 1861," *Le Siècle*, May 24, 1861.

36. For instance, L. Clément de Ris, "Salon de 1850–51," *L'Artiste* 6, no. 1 (Feb. 1, 1851), p. 9; A.-J. du Pays 1859 (as in n. 31), p. 269 ; or P. de Saint-Victor, "Salon de 1861," *La Presse*, June 2, 1861.

37. For instance, P. de Saint-Victor 1861 (as in n. 36); A. de Calonne, "La Peinture contemporaine à l'exposition," *Revue contemporaine*, 2nd ser., vol. 21 (May 31, 1861), p. 347; or P. Challemel-Lacour, "Le Salon de 1864," *Revue germanique et française* 29, no. 3 (June 1, 1864), p. 540.

38. P. Mantz 1859 (as in n. 22), p. 198 ["comment croire en effet que Gygès pourra jamais aimer cette pauvre petite poupée, et que l'imprudent Candaule perdra à ce jeu la couronne et la vie?"].

39. M. Du Camp, *Le Salon de 1861* (Paris: A. Bourdilliat, 1861), p. 90 ["une lorette égrillarde ... que les Grecs, qui se connaissent en beauté auraient condamnée immédiatement si elle n'avait eu d'autre argument que sa nudité"].

40. Ibid. ["toutes les phases du désir"].

41. J. Rousseau, "Salon de 1861," *Le Figaro*, May 30, 1861, p. 7 ["singes lubriques et grimaçants"].

42. P. de Saint-Victor 1861 (as in n. 36) ["les magistrats augustes auxquels le rire même était interdit, et dont la gravité était passée en proverbe!"].

43. M. Du Camp 1861 (as in n. 39), p. 89 ["ignorance radicale de l'antiquité"].

44. L. Lagrange, "Salon de 1861," *Gazette des beaux-arts* 10, no. 5 (June 1, 1861), p. 264 ["une femme ... se dépouillant toute nue dans un lieu public, un café, par exemple, ou un théâtre"].

45. O. Merson, *La peinture en France: exposition de 1861* (Paris: E. Dentu, 1861), pp. 206–7 ["orgueilleuse de sa beauté triomphante. Le peintre a fait une fillette confuse, interdite et se cachant le visage dans un mouvement enfantin de pudeur.

Ce n'est pas là Phryné"].

46. For instance, P. de Saint-Victor 1861 (as in n. 36).

47. For instance, Jacques [Edmond Bazire ?], "Salon de 1861," *L'Univers illustré*, June 27, 1861, p. 238.

48. See O. Merson 1861 (as in n. 45), p. 210.

49. See T. Gautier 1861 (as in n. 34), p. 183.

50. See R. Canat, *L'Hellénisme des romantiques*, 3 vols. (Paris, 1951–55); and Henri Peyre, *Bibliographie critique de l'hellénisme en France de 1843 à 1870* (New Haven: Yale University Press, 1932), *passim*.

51. E. Pelletan, qtd. in H. Peyre 1932 (as in n. 50), p. 112 ["une chaste et virginale rêverie stoïcienne"].

52. P. Mantz, "Le Salon de 1863," *Gazette des beaux-arts* 14, no. 6 (June 1, 1863), p. 494 ["Son *Molière déjeunant avec Louis XIV* sera, nous l'espérons, sa dernière erreur…je ne vois pas ce qu'il y a de si risible dans l'aventure. M. Gérôme a mis l'histoire grecque en vaudeville; qu'il laisse à la nôtre sa gravité"].

53. M. Chaumelin 1873 (as in n. 32), p. 103 ["le grivois, le comique, le burlesque"].

54. For instance, A. de Belloy, "Promenade à l'exposition des beaux-arts," *Le Correspondant* 38, no. 5 (June 10, 1868), p. 897.

55. For instance, P. Mantz 1859 (as in n. 22), p. 198; and J. Rousseau 1861 (as in n. 41), p. 6.

56. M. du Camp, *Le Salon de 1859* (Paris, 1859), p. 64 ["un magasin de curiosités"]; J.-A. Castagnary 1892 (as in n. 25), p. 95 ["exhibition de brimborions archéologiques"]; and J. Rousseau 1863 (as in n. 33), p. 219 ["les amateurs de bric-à-brac"].

57. For instance, E.-J. Delécluze, "Salon de 1848," *Journal des débats*, Apr. 5, 1848.

58. For instance, P. Mantz, "Le Salon," *L'Evénement*, Jan. 30, 1851.

59. For instance, C. de Moüy, "Le Salon de 1864," *Revue française* 8, no. 44 (June 1, 1864), pp. 243–44.

60. For instance, A. de Calonne 1857 (as in n. 15), p. 611; P. Mantz 1863 (as in n. 52), p. 494; or T. Thoré, *Salons de W. Bürger, 1861 à 1868*, vol. 2/2 (Paris: Renouard, 1870), pp. 173–74.

61. For instance, A. de Calonne 1857 (as in n. 15), p. 611; or Du Camp 1859 (as in n. 56), p. 63.

62. For instance, A.-J. du Pays, "Salon de 1861," *L'Illustration* 38, no. 959 (July 13, 1861), p. 26; or P. de Saint-Victor 1863 (as in n. 30).

63. For instance, B. Bouniol, "Nos impressions au Salon de 1861," *Revue du monde catholique* 1, no. 4 (May 21, 1861), p. 229; A. de la Forge, "L'Art contemporain. Salon de 1861," *Le Siècle*, May 24, 1861; or P. Casimir-Périer, *Propos d'art à l'occasion du Salon de 1869* (Paris, 1869), p. 204.

64. For instance, C. Gueullette, *Les peintres de genre au Salon de 1863* (Paris, 1863), pp. 24–25.

65. For instance, P. de Saint-Victor, "Salon de 1857," *La Presse*, July 11, 1857.

66. For instance, L. Auvray, "Salon de 1863," *Revue artistique et littéraire* 4 (1863), p. 252.

67. For instance, H. de Lacretelle, "Beaux-arts. Salon de 1852." *La Lumière* (Apr. 10, 1852), p. 61; A.-J. du Pays, "Salon de 1857," *L'Illustration* 30, no. 755 (Aug. 15, 1857), p. 107; or A. Cantaloube, "Salon de 1868," *Le Monde illustré* 22, no. 582 (June 6, 1868), p. 366.

68. For instance, J. Graham [Arthur Stevens], "Un Étranger au Salon," *Figaro*, May 31, 1863, p. 3.

69. See G. Lafenestre, "Le Salon de 1869," in *L'Art vivant: la peinture et la sculpture aux Salons de 1868 à 1877* (Paris, 1881), p. 130.

70. E. About, *Voyage à travers l'exposition des beaux-arts* (Paris, 1855), p. 156 ["Voilà comme il faut répondre à la critique"].

71. See J. Rousseau 1861 (as in n. 41), p. 6; and A. de la Forge 1861 (as in n. 63).

72. L. Enault, "Le Salon de 1863," *Revue française* 5 (May–Aug. 1863), p. 310 ["C'est un des meilleurs tableaux du Salon"].

73. For instance, Ch. Wallut, "Le Salon de 1865," *Musée des familles* 32, no. 9 (June 1865), p. 287; and L. Auvray, *Exposition des beaux-arts. Salon de 1865* (Paris, 1865), p. 62.

74. E. About, *Salon de 1866* (Paris, 1866), p. 205 ["rang des Gérômes parfaits"].

75. See J. Rousseau 1861 (as in n. 41), p. 6; and P. Mainardi 1987 (as in n. 7), p. 167.

76. J. Rousseau 1861 (as in n. 41), p. 6 ["cachet de vérité locale"].

77. See Anon. 1863 (as in n. 21), pp. 305–6.

78. See L. Nochlin, "The Imaginary Orient," *Art in America* 71, no. 5 (May 1983), pp. 119–31, 186–90.

79. J. Kearns, "Quelle Histoire? Gautier devant l'œuvre de Gérôme au Salon de 1859," in *Le Champ Littéraire, 1860–1900. Études offertes à Michael Pakenham*, eds. K. Cameron and J. Kearns (Amsterdam: Rodopi, 1996), p. 74 ["c'est le recyclage à la fois de l'orientalisme romantique pour une époque de culture positiviste à dominante scientifique, et de l'exotisme en forme de document historique"].

80. E. Roy, "Salon de 1869," *L'Artiste* (Apr. 1, 1869), p. 89 ["des documents sans prix"].

81. E. About, *Salon de 1864* (Paris: Hachette, 1864), pp. 200–1 ["personne n'a pénétré si loin dans l'intimité de ce monde exotique. Arrêtez-vous longtemps devant ce tableau de *l'Almée*. Examinez en détail les costumes, le décor, les accessoires, ce burnous, ces babouches … ce chibouk, ce narghilé … et mille autres détails … Vous sentirez votre esprit s'acclimater insensiblement"].

82. For instance, M. Du Camp, *Les Beaux-arts à l'Exposition universelle et aux Salons de 1863, 1864, 1865, 1866 et 1867* (Paris: Vve. J. Renouard, 1867), pp. 284–85 ["criant leur bric-à-brac"].

83. E. About 1855 (as in n. 70), p. 156 ["une laideur exquise"].

84. T. Pelloquet 1863 (as in n. 29), p. 2 ["une saveur d'une certaine rareté et d'une bizarrerie étrange"].

85. A. Tardieu 1857 (as in n. 19) ["Les pauvres diables … n'ont pas la beauté classique; mais il est impossible de mettre en doute la rigoureuse exactitude de la reproduction. Les têtes … bien individuelles et très diverses, sont de fines études"].

86. For instance, Anon. 1863 (as in n. 21), pp. 305–6.

87. M. Du Camp 1863 (as in n. 12), p. 891 ["M. Gérôme a parfaitement fait comprendre … l'état de l'Egypte, où une race rêveuse, douce, soumise, est torturée chaque jour par d'anciens vainqueurs plus grossiers, plus vicieux et moins intelligents qu'elle"].

88. For instance, C. de Sault, "Salon de 1864," *Le Temps*, June 8, 1864.

89. For instance, C. de Moüy 1864 (as in n. 59), pp. 242–43.

90. For instance, A. Audeoud, "Exposition de 1864," *Revue indépendante* (July 1, 1864), p. 767; and A.-J. du Pays, "Salon de 1864," *L'Illustration* 41, no. 1115 (July 9, 1864), p. 26.

91. O. Merson 1861 (as in n. 45), p. 207 ["c'est le geste plutôt craintif que chaste d'une petite Circassienne mise en vente dans un bazar de Constantinople"].

92. L. Peisse, "Le Salon de 1861," *Le Constitutionnel*, June 1, 1861 ["serait-ce la pure contemplation esthétique qui donne à ceux-ci l'œil cauteleux de madrés courtiers, pourvoyeurs de harems, expertisant dans un bazar les qualités et les tares d'une esclave mise en vente …?"].

93. For instance, M. Du Camp 1867 (as in n. 82), p. 284.

94. See J. House, review of Ackerman 1986 (as in n. 4), in *The Burlington Magazine* 130, no. 1020 (Mar. 1988), p. 238.

95. M. Gotlieb, *From Genre to Decoration: Studies in the Theory and Criticism of French Salon Painting, 1850–1900* (Ann Arbor: UMI, 1990), pp. 216–18.

96. For useful discussions of nineteenth-century historiography and its impact on art, see S. Bann, *The Clothing of Clio: A Study of the Representation of History in Nineteenth-Century Britain and France* (Cambridge, 1984); B. Wright, *Painting and History During the French Restoration: Abandoned by the Past* (Cambridge, 1997); and G. Gollrad, "Eyewitnessing and the Illustrative Aesthetic: Visualizing History in Eighteenth- and Early Nineteenth-Century France," Ph.D. diss., University of Chicago, 1999.

97. C. Mitchell, "What is to be done with the Salonniers?", *Oxford Art Journal* 10, no. 1 (1987), p. 107.

Cat. 43

KING CANDAULES

–

1859
Oil on canvas
26 ½ × 39 in.
Signed and dated in Roman numerals lower left
The Luis A. Ferré Foundation Inc., Museo de Arte, Ponce, Puerto Rico, inv. 63.0353

–

Provenance: Gérôme to Goupil, 1859. Goupil to Count Le Marois, 1860 (for 8,140 francs). [Péreire sale, Paris, 1891]. J. R. De Lamar to William Randolph Hearst, American Art Association sale, Plaza Hotel, New York, Jan. 29, 1920, lot 30 (illustrated) (for $1,050). Hearst Corporation to Museo de Arte, Ponce, PBNY sale, Mar. 21, 1963.

–

Exhibition History: Salon of 1859, Paris, no. 1239.

–

Bibliography: T. Gautier, "A travers les ateliers," *L'Artiste*, vol. 62, 1858, p. 18. P. Mantz, *Gazette des Beaux-Arts*, 1859, 2, pp. 196–98. E. Strahan [Earl Shinn], *Gérôme: A Collection of the Works of J.-L. Gérôme in One Hundred Photogravures* (New York: Samuel L. Hall), 1881. Engraved by Jules and Alphonse François. *Catalogue de Paris*, 1883, p. 22. F. F. Hering, *Gérôme: The Life and Works of Jean-Léon Gérôme* (New York: Cassell, 1892), p. 87. C. Baudelaire, *Œuvres complètes* (Paris: La Pléiade, 1961), p. 1057ff. J. S. Held, ed., *Museo de Arte de Ponce, Catalogue I, Paintings of the European and American Schools* (Ponce, 1965), no. 73. G. Ackerman et al., *Jean-Léon Gérôme (1824–1904)*, exh. cat. (Dayton: Dayton Art Institute, 1972; also Minneapolis: Minneapolis Institute of Arts, 1973, and Baltimore: The Walters Art Gallery, 1973), no. 8, pp. 42–43. G. Ackerman, "Three Drawings by Gérôme in the Yale Collection," *Yale University Art Gallery Bulletin* 36 (Fall 1976), pp. 8–18. *J.-L. Gérôme*, exh. cat. (Vesoul: Musée Georges-Garret, 1981), p. 110. *French Salon Paintings from Southern Collections* (Atlanta: High Museum of Art, 1983), no. 33, p. 107, ill. *Impressionisme, les origines, 1859–1869*, exh. cat., (Paris: Galeries Nationales du Grand Palais, 1994), cat. 77. H. Lafont-Couturier, *Gérôme* (Paris: Herscher, 1998), p. 106. G. Ackerman, *Jean-Léon Gérôme* (Courbevoie: ACR Édition, 2000), no. 111. H. Lafont-Couturier, *Gérôme & Goupil. Art et entreprise*, exh. cat. (Bordeaux: Musée Goupil, 2000–1; also New York: Dahesh Museum of Art, 2001, and Pittsburgh: The Frick Art & Historical Center, 2001), cat. 10, pp. 13, 19, 21, 25, 27, 36, 76, 77–79, 152–153, 165. S. Harent and C. Stoullig, *Dessins de Jean-Léon Gérôme: la collection du musée des Beaux-Arts de Nancy*, exh. cat. (Nancy: Musée des Beaux-Arts, 2009), p. 50.

Cat. 44

PROPOSAL FOR AN ARCHITECTURAL SETTING

–

ca. 1859
Pen and ink over pencil sketch on tracing paper
8 ⅝ × 10 ¾ in.
Musée des Beaux-Arts, Nancy, inv. TH.99.15,560

–

Provenance: Charavay Frères (rue de Fürstenberg, Paris), bought by the Nancy donor with a letter addressed to architect Gustave Bourgerel. 1999, anonymous gift to the Musée des Beaux-Arts, Nancy.

–

Bibliography: S. Harent and C. Stoullig, *Dessins de Jean-Léon Gérôme. La collection du musée des Beaux-Arts de Nancy*, exh. cat. (Nancy: Musée des Beaux-Arts, 2009), cat. 10, ill. p. 51.

Herodotus recounted the story of King Candaules, a ruler of Sardis in Lydia (Asia Minor) who was killed by Gyges, a man who seized not just the throne but also the king's wife, Nyssia (sometimes known as Rodolphe). Proud of his modest wife's great beauty, Candaules had wanted to share his admiration of her charms with Gyges, one of his guards. But it turned out very badly: outraged by her husband's impudence and overweening pride, the queen urged Gyges to kill the king.

This story inspired one of La Fontaine's fables in 1677: "In life oft ills from self-imprudence spring; /As proof, Candaules' story we will bring./In folly's scenes the king was truly great:/His vassal, Gyges, had from him a bait,/The like in gallantry was rarely known,/And want of prudence never more was shown./My friend, said he, you frequently have seen/the beauteous face and features of the queen;/But these are naught, believe me, to the rest,/Which solely can be viewed when quite undressed... . Fair in person was Gyges to behold; /excuses [by the queen] easy 'twere to mold.../ And on th'exposer all her hatred fell.../What more shall I detail? The facts are plain:/Detested was the king—beloved the swain."[1]

In 1844 Théophile Gautier published in *La Presse* a short story titled *Le roi Candaule*, which earned praise from Victor Hugo. This was the text that inspired Gérôme, just as it had James Pradier before him (ill. 46). Gautier described the shy, modest queen in the following terms. "Nyssia, daughter of the satrap, Megabazes, was endowed with a wonderful purity of features and perfection of forms. That, at least, was the report given abroad by the slaves who waited on her and the ladies who accompanied her to the bath, for no man could claim to know anything of Nyssia other than the color of her veil and the elegant folds that she imparted, despite herself, to the soft fabrics draping her statuesque body."[2] Gautier thus immediately placed the story of King Candaules and his beautiful wife within the register of a hidden sensuality, of a jealously guarded beauty. The story wove the excitement of a mysterious, savage Orient into the scholarly framework of knowledge of the ancient world. The subject could hardly fail to attract Gérôme's attention.

The conception of the painting certainly took a fairly long time—Gautier saw it in Gérôme's studio in the spring of 1858. A preparatory drawing now in Nancy underscores Gérôme's concern for the accuracy of the architectural setting. He sent it to the architect Gustave Bourgerel, who had been a student at the École des Beaux-Arts in the early 1840s, to ask his advice on this point. Like Gérôme, Bourgerel had traveled to Italy in 1843. Continuing on to Greece, Bourgerel made many studies and drawings of buildings at various sites (Naples, Pompeii, Paestum, Syros, Athens, Aegina), thereby becoming one of the finest connoisseurs of ancient architecture. In 1863 Bourgerel published a book with some of his drawings.[3] The setting composed here by Gérôme combined elements from Pompeii with others from Etruria (ill. 45). Influenced by Ionian Greece, these Etruscan works harked back to Asia Minor. The pose of Candaules on the marital bed is not unlike that of the man in the *Sarcophagus of the Spouses* (Musée du Louvre) that Giovanni Pietro Campana unearthed in Cerveteri in 1845.

Despite the lion skin at the foot of the bed, the overall setting seems more Greek than oriental. In his review of the Salon of 1859, Charles Baudelaire complained of the popularity accorded to this painting based on its apparent archaeological accuracy. "*King Candaules* is another pitfall and distraction. Many people grow ecstatic over the furnishings and decoration of the royal bed: this, then, is an Asian bedchamber! A triumph! But is it true that the dreadful queen, so jealous of herself, who felt as sullied by a glance as by a hand, resembled this dull puppet? Furthermore, there is great danger in this kind of subject, located halfway between tragedy and comedy. If an Asian anecdote is not handled in a grim and bloody Asian manner, it will always give rise to comedy."[4]

Beyond the faithful rendering of a setting, the real subject of this canvas—and of Gautier's short story—is the description of Nyssia's sublime body. As Gautier himself wrote, the heart of the plot turned on the refusal of the queen to let herself be seen, to let her husband have her portrait done. "If, instead of Nyssia—daughter of the satrap Megabazes, and steeped in oriental ideas—[Candaules] had married some Greek woman from Athens or Corinth, there can be no doubt that he would have summoned to his court the most skillful of painters and sculptors, and allowed his queen to sit for them, as Alexander the Great later did with his

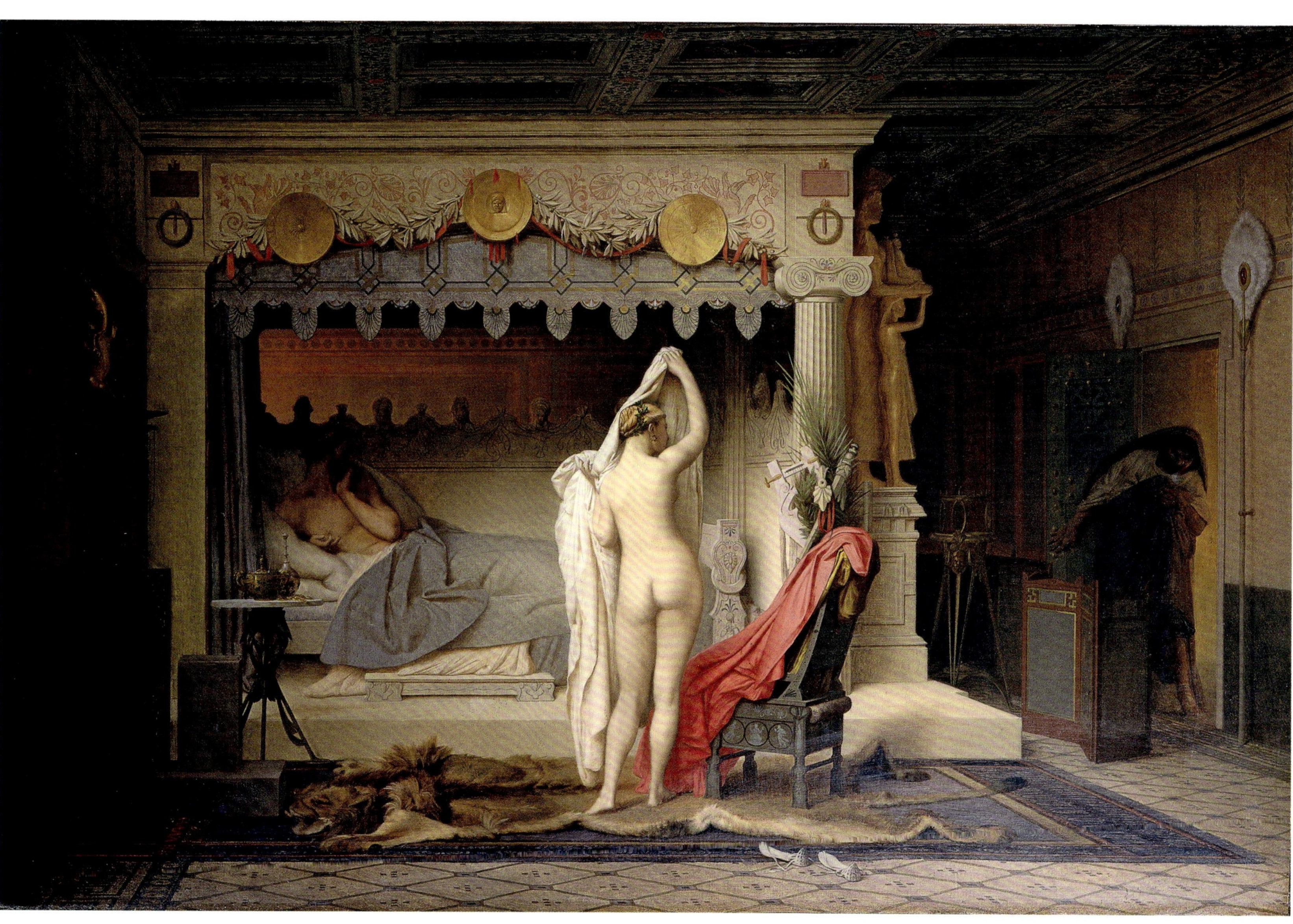

Ill. 45. Gustave Bourgerel (1813-1882), *Fragments d'architecture et de sculpture*, plate LXXII, 1863, print, École Nationale des Beaux-Arts, Paris, inv. 00202A0000 FOL.

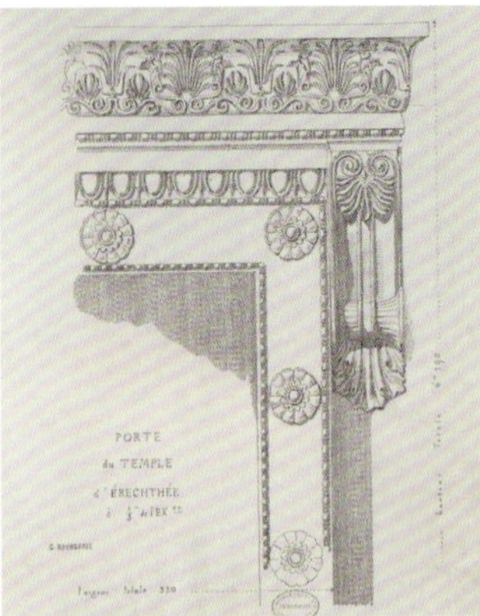

Ill. 46. Jean-Jacques (known as James) Pradier (1790–1852), *Nyssia*, 1848, marble, Musée Fabre, Montpellier, inv. D 848.1.1.

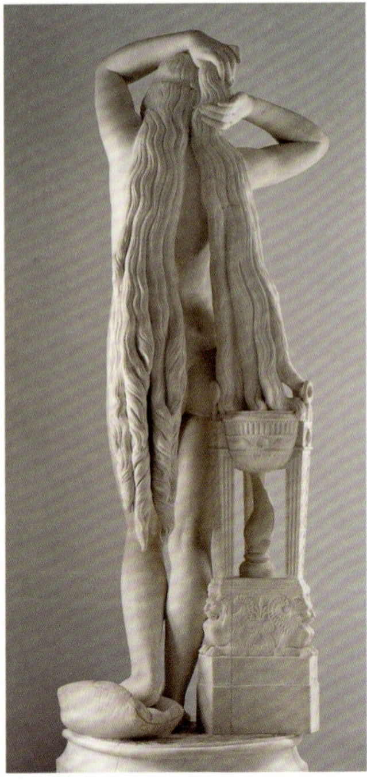

Ill. 47. Pierre-Narcisse Guérin (1774–1833), *Clytemnestra*, 1817, oil on canvas, 135 ¾ × 128 in., Musée du Louvre, Paris, inv. 5185.

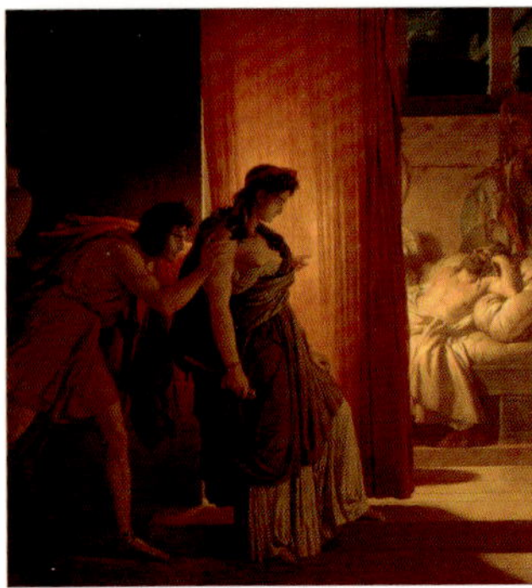

favorite, Campaspe, who posed nude for Apelles. Such a whim would have encountered no resistance from a woman from a land where the chastest of women are proud to have contributed—one her back, another her breast—to the perfection of a famous statue. But shy Nyssia would barely consent to lower her veils in the dark corners of the thalamium."

Choosing this subject for a sculpture or painting, as Pradier and Gérôme did, was a way of deliberately confronting—with the knowing collusion of the public—what was undepictable, of unveiling with voluptuous subtlety what could not be looked at with impunity. Pradier and Gérôme allowed the people of their day to behold freely what cost Candaules his life, as Gautier himself stressed. "What would this shy beauty, who avenged herself so cruelly for the indiscreet revelation of her charms, do to an artist who showed her charmingly naked to all, standing on a lion skin in a half-Greek, half-barbarian apartment at the Herculean's[5] bedside? She would probably forgive him, because the artist made her more beautiful than she had ever been."[6]

Not without subtlety, Gérôme toyed with the interplay of gazes by showing the queen from the back; the beholder of the painting therefore has to imagine the charms that are merely suggested by the curves of her figure. Only Gyges, glimpsed in the shadows near the door, can admire her full beauty, as the story recounts. This painted nude is indebted to Pradier's sculpture, itself inspired, in terms of pose, by the Venus Genetrix. This pose also inspired photographers for the "Studies from Nature" that they produced for artists.

The precise moment depicted here is not clearly established; some people interpret it as the first stage in the plot when Gyges sees the fair queen for the first time, while others, including Gautier, lean toward the concluding moment when the disloyal servant comes to kill Candaules at the queen's invitation. "The moment chosen by the artist is the one when Nyssia drops her garments and signals to Gyges, hidden behind the door, to rush forward and kill Candaules."

This latter option is the crueler and more voluptuous moment, for it suggests that the queen displayed herself naked in front of her husband knowing that it would be for the last time—Candaules' trusting, admiring gaze would soon be belied by the facts. This option is perhaps also more painterly. Indeed, the figure of a lover soon to be the assassin of a reclining husband evokes the murder of Agamemnon by Clytemnestra and Aegisthus as painted by Pierre-Narcisse Guérin in 1817 (ill. 47). Guérin exploited the sense of suspense created by the spatial effect of the door, invoking not just the division between inner and outer, between permitted and forbidden, but also the double physical and moral development implied by the introduction of duration into his transcription of the story. Guérin had been Paul Delaroche's master, and Gérôme was familiar with the neoclassical artist's theatrical inventions, whose heritage he acknowledged.

Gérôme was thus faithful to painterly tradition as embodied not just by Guérin but also David, through his choice of an ancient theme and his attention to archaeological accuracy, not to mention his skillful play on theatrical effects. Gérôme masked his personal penchant for literary and historical subjects that combined sensuality with cruelty beneath his slick finish and thoroughly controlled composition.

Purchased by Goupil in 1859, *King Candaules* marked the start of the fruitful, long-lasting relationship between Gérôme and the dealer-publisher. The line engraving was made from a smaller replica now in the Pushkin Museum in Moscow. In order to dodge censorship of the dissemination of the engraving (although the presence of a female nude would not shock a Salon jury it was likely to offend when seen on shelves in bookstores and print-dealers), Goupil sold this print of Gérôme's painting together with a line engraving of Jean-Louis Hamon's mawkish *My Sister is not at Home* (ill. 9, p. 44). A photographic reproduction of the painting, done from the 1859 Salon version, was nevertheless categorized as licentious by certain commentators.[7] The photographic print thus brought out the sensual realism of Gérôme's painting of the beautiful queen along with the latent eroticism that emanates from many of his canvases, although subtly veiled by the studied recourse to antique models.

D. F.–R.

1. J. de La Fontaine, *Tales and Novels of Jean de La Fontaine* (Paris: Bibliolife, 2007), pp. 283–84. **2.** T. Gautier, "Le roi Candaule," *La Presse*, Oct. 1–5, 1844. **3.** G. Bourgerel, *Fragments d'architecture et de sculpture* (Paris, 1863); based on the colophon, certain plates appear to have been published in 1861. **4.** C. Baudelaire, "Salon de 1859," in *Critique d'art* (Paris: Gallimard, 1972), p. 301. **5.** Candaules was a descendant of Hercules. **6.** T. Gautier, "À travers les ateliers," *L'Artiste*, 1858, new ser., vol. 4, p. 18. **7.** Monsieur le comte d'I. (Henri, comte d'Ideville), *Iconographie des estampes à sujets galants et des portraits des femmes célèbres par leur beauté* (Geneva, 1868), p. 62.

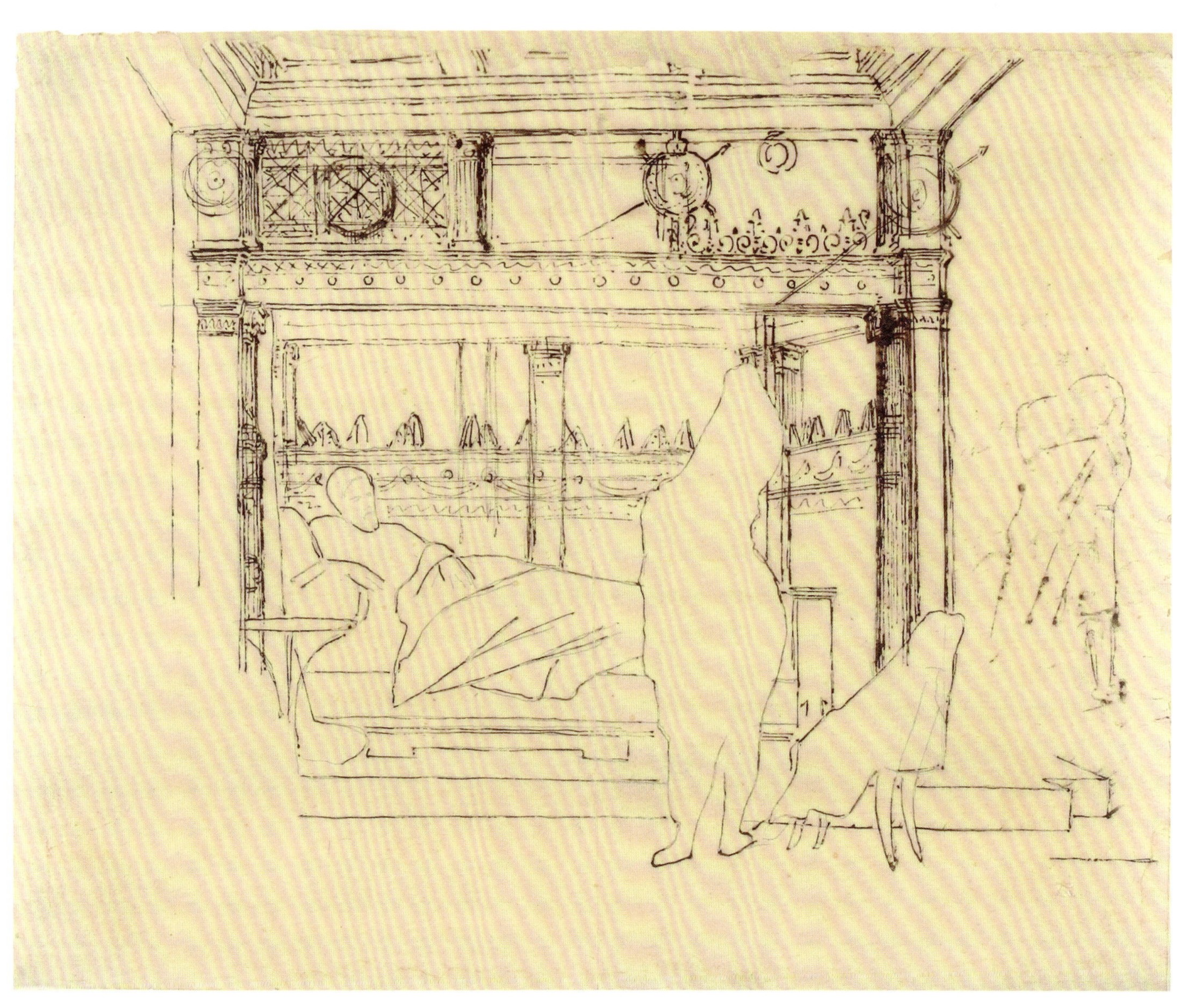

Cat. 45

PHRYNÉ BEFORE THE AREOPAGUS

–

1861
Oil on canvas
31 ¼ × 50 ⅜ in.
Inscription: signed *J.L. Gerome* and dated *MDCCCLXI* lower left, on the step of the dais; on the belt on the ground: *ΚΑΛΗ;* on the altar: *ΑΘΗΝΗ;* on the tapestry behind Hypereides: *ΠΟΣΕΙΔΟΝ ΑΘΗΝΑΙΑ*
Signed and dated lower left, on the step of the platform: *J.L Gerome MDCCCLXI*
Hamburger Kunsthalle, Hamburg, inv. Nr HK-1910

–

Provenance: Mayer auction, Paris, Apr. 1866. Exposition Universelle, Paris, 1867, property of M. H. Schroeder, who made a deed of gift to the Hamburger Kunsthalle in 1910.

–

Exhibition History: Salon of 1861, Paris, no. 1248. Exposition Universelle, Paris, 1867, no. 290.

–

Bibliography: L. Auvray, *Exposition des Beaux-Arts. Salon de 1861* (Paris: Aux bureaux de la *Revue artistique*, 1861), pp. 26–27. H. de Callias, "Salon de 1861," *L'Artiste*, vol. XI, no. 12 (June 15, 1861), pp. 267–68. A. de Calonne, "La Peinture contemporaine à l'exposition de 1861," *Revue contemporaine*, ser. 2, vol. 21 (May 31, 1861), p. 347. A. Cantaloupe, *Lettre sur les expositions et le Salon de 1861* (Paris: E. Dentu, 1861), pp. 68–71. H. Delaborde, "Le Salon de 1861," *Revue des Deux Mondes*, 2nd per., vol. 33 (June 15, 1861), pp. 876–78. É.-J. Delécluze, "Exposition de 1861," *Journal des débats*, May 15, 1861. M. Du Camp, *Le Salon de 1861* (Paris: A. Bourdilliat & Cie, 1861), pp. 86–93. A.-J. Du Pays, "Salon de 1861," *L'Illustration*, vol. 38, no. 959 (July 13, 1861), p. 26. A. de la Fizelière, *A-Z ou le Salon en miniature* (Paris: Poulet-Malassis and de Broise, 1861), pp. 30–31. A. de la Forge, "L'Art Contemporain. Salon de 1861," *Le Siècle*, May 24, 1861. T. Gautier, *Abécédaire du Salon de 1861* (Paris: E. Dentu, 1861), pp. 176–80. L. Lagrange, "Salon de 1861," *Gazette des Beaux-Arts*, vol. 10, no. 5 (June 1, 1861), pp. 263–66. Le Guillois, *Diogène au Salon de 1861. Revue en quatrain* (Paris: Desloges, 1861), p. 9. A. M., "Salon de 1861. Reproduction d'ouvrages exposés," *L'Illustration*, vol. 37, no. 953 (June 1, 1861), p. 343. A. M., "Salon de 1861. Reproduction d'ouvrages exposés, "*L'Illustration*, vol. 38, no. 958 (July 6, 1861), pp. 8–10. A. Nettement, *Poëtes et artistes contemporains* (Paris: Jacques Lecoffre & Cie, libraires, 1862), pp. 399–400, 427. L. Peisse, "Le Salon de 1861," *Le Constitutionnel*, June 1, 1861. T. Pelloquet, "Salon de 1861," *Le Monde illustré*, vol. 8, no. 219 (June 22, 1861), p. 391. É. Perrin, "Salon de 1861," *Revue européenne*, vol. XV (1861), pp. 787–89. J. Rousseau, "Salon de 1861. Les success," *Le Figaro*, no. 656 (May 30, 1861), pp. 6–7. P. de Saint-Victor, "Salon de 1861," *La Presse*, June 2, 1861. C. Vignon, "Une visite au Salon de 1861," *Le Correspondant*, new ser., vol. 17 (May 25, 1861), pp. 157–59. E. M. Kraft and K. W. Schumann, *Katalog der Meister des 19. Jahrhunderts in der Hamburger Kunsthalle*, 1969, p. 96. G. Ackerman et al., *Jean- Léon Gérôme (1824–1904)*, exh. cat. (Dayton: Dayton Art Institute, 1972; also Minneapolis: Minneapolis Institute of Arts, 1973, and Baltimore: The Walters Art Gallery, 1973), p. 10. J. Heusinger von Waldegg, "Jean-Léon Gérôme's Phryné vor den Richtern," *Jahrbuch der Hamburger Kunstsämmlungen*, vol. 17 (1972), pp. 122–42. *J.-L. Gérôme*, exh. cat. (Vesoul: Musée Georges-Garret, 1981), no. 52, pp. 66–68. *Eva und die Zukunft. Das Bild der Frau seit der Französischen Revolution*, exh. cat. (Hamburg: Kunsthalle, 1986, no. 32), p. 109. É. Zola, "Nos peintres au Champ-de-Mars," in *Écrits sur l'art* [1867] (Paris: Gallimard, 1991), pp. 184–85. "*Le Salon imaginaire": images des grandes expositions de la seconde moitié du* XIX*e siècle*, exh. cat. (Berlin, 1968), no. 114. *Degas beyond Impressionism*, exh. cat. (London: National Gallery, 1996; also Chicago: The Art Institute of Chicago, 1996–97), fig. 180. H. Lafont-Couturier, *Gérôme* (Paris: Herscher, 1998), p. 46–47, 49. G. Ackerman, *Jean-Léon Gérôme* (Courbevoie: ACR Édition, 2000), p. 51, no. 135, p. 248–249. H. Lafont-Couturier, *Gérôme & Goupil. Art et entreprise*, exh. cat. (Bordeaux: Musée Goupil, 2000–1; also New York: Dahesh Museum of Art, 2001, and Pittsburgh: The Frick Art & Historical Center, 2001), pp. 23–25, 38, 41, 47, 49–51, 100, 103–104, 117, 152, 165–166. *Exposed: The Victorian Nude*, exh. cat. (London: Tate Britain, 2001–2; also Munich: Haus der Kunst, 2002, New York: Brooklyn Museum of Art, 2002–3, Kobe: Kobe City Museum, 2003, and Tokyo: Geidai Museum, 2003), no. 28, p. 91. É. Papet, "Phryné au XIXe siècle: la plus jolie femme de Paris?," in *Praxitèle*, exh. cat. (Paris: Musée du Louvre, 2007), pp. 362–79 and 384–85, no. 101. S. Harent and C. Stoullig, *Dessins de Jean-Léon Gérôme: la collection du musée des Beaux-Arts de Nancy*, exh. cat. (Nancy: Musée des Beaux-Arts, 2009), pp. 53–59.

Gérôme sent four works to the Salon of 1861 (ill. 100, p. 218): the portrait of Rachel (cat. 40), *Socrates Seeking Alcibiades at the House of Aspasia* (ill. 53), *The Two Augurs*, and *Phryné before the Areopagus*, which was, after *Duel after the Ball* (cat. 51), one of the most famous works produced during the Second Empire, a foil to "modern" painting, and which, more than at the Salon of 1847 (cat. 10), eroded the boundaries between genre painting and history painting. Gérôme had been thinking about the painting for a long time, as testified by the small sketch of 1857 at the Museo de Arte in Ponce.[1] The subject, which at the same time occupied his second master, Charles Gleyre,[2] was not without its advantages: "PHRYNE: famous Greek courtesan, born in Thespies (Boeotia) circa 328 B.C.... Accused of impiety, she was brought before the heliasts and, when the moment came to sentence her, she was saved by the noble gesture of her advocate, Hypereides [who], in one swift, unexpected movement, removed the veil, the *peplos*, in which his client was clothed... When confronted with Phryné's charms, which have served as a model for the greatest artists, the judges were struck with an almost religious fear and refused to let anyone lay a hand on this goddess-like being... Phryné inspired M. Gérôme to produce a very well-known portrait... which met with great success, even if the sentiment behind the composition was much more modern than antique."[3] This entry in the *Dictionnaire universel du* XIX*e siècle* about one of antiquity's most famous hetaera was published nearly fifteen years after *Phryné before the Areopagus* was exhibited at the Salon of 1861 and sums up well the renown and controversy generated by the painting. It was in this work that Gérôme drove furthest his almost obsessional taste for archaeological reconstruction, the result of learned anachronisms, which turned each painting into a highly personal "cabinet of curiosities."

The courtroom, intended to predate the actual episode by a century or two, is an almost literal transcription of an eighteenth century engraving, published in 1823, representing the interior of a famous Etruscan tomb discovered in Tarquinia, the "Cardinal's Tomb," an engraving that met with a degree of success (ill. 48).[4] The frieze of the dancers dressed in black at the back of the room evokes both black-figure vases and the famous murals of the "Tomb of the Dancers" discovered in Ruvo di Puglia, presented in the Naples museum of Archaeology in the nineteenth century and published by the French archaeologist Raoul Rochette.[5] Below, the upper part of a fresco seems to owe much to the very famous *Alexander Mosaic* depicting the Battle of Issus discovered in the House of the Faun in Pompeii (Museo Archeologico Nazionale, Naples). Behind Hypereides, the legendary struggle between Athena and Poseidon for the city of Athens is as evocative of vase painting as of Roman-inspired reconstructions from the Villa Medici.[6] The "most distinguished of the antiquarian painters"[7] went so far as to provide a sophisticated representation of colossal weather-worn pillars. On the altar, the chryselephantine statuette of an archaistic *Athena Promachos* (armed Athena) combines of several sources. Deprived of her shield, she does not respect the canonical figuration of antique

Ill. 48. Franciszek Smuglewicz, *Partie des Catacombes ou souterrains étrusques de l'antique Tarquinia près de Corneto*, 1760, engraving reproduced in Jean-Baptiste-Louis Séroux d'Agincourt, *Histoire de l'Art par les Monumens...*, Paris, 1810–23, pl. X (detail), Bibliothèque de l'INHA, Paris.

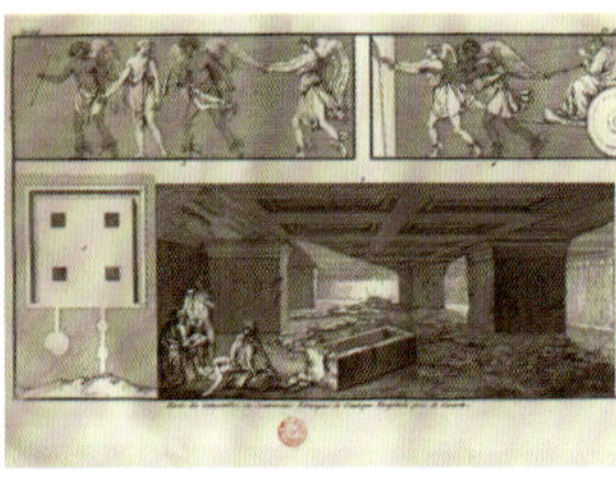

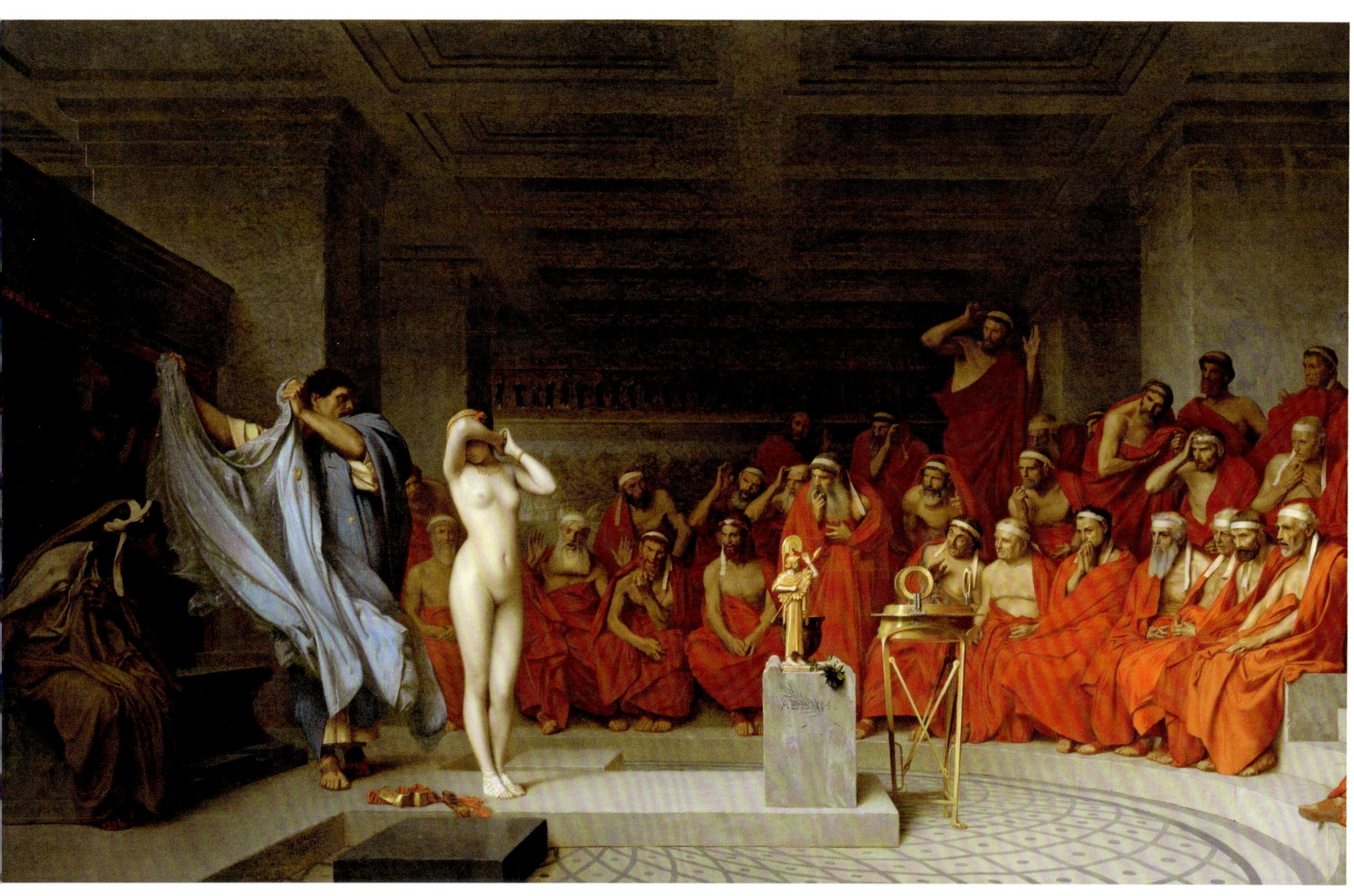

Ill. 49. Anonymous, "Articles in gold. Necklace and other articles," engraving published in Raphaël Gargiulo, *Collection of the Most Remarkable Monuments of the National Museum* (Naples, 1869), vol. III, pl. 12 (detail), Bibliothèque du département des Antiquités grecques, étrusques et romaines, Musée du Louvre, Paris.

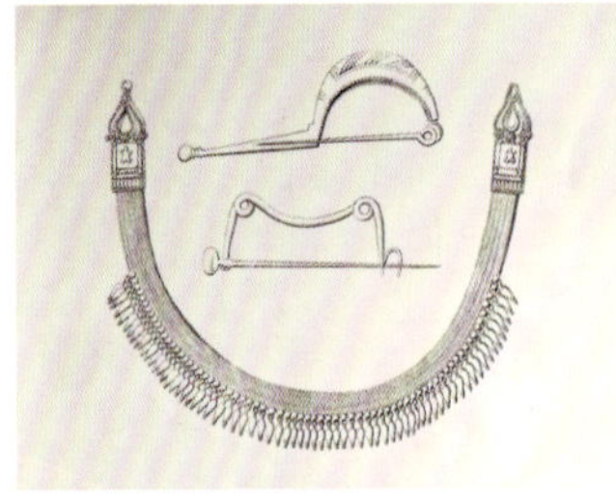

Ill. 50. Jean-Auguste-Dominique Ingres (1780–1867), *Venus Anadyomene*, 1808–48, oil on canvas, 64 ¼ × 36 ¼ in., Musée Condé, Chantilly, inv. PE 433.

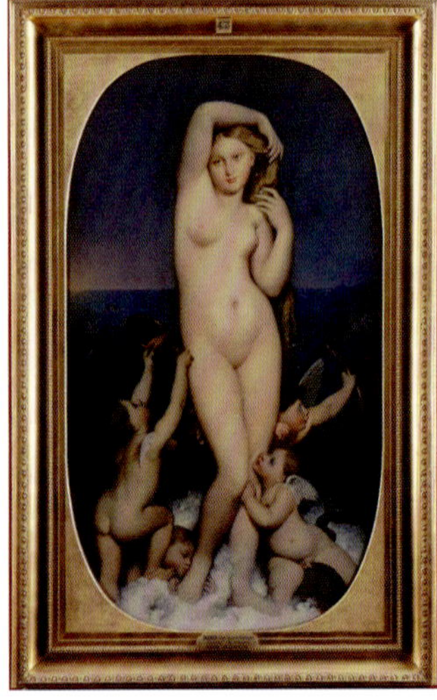

Ill. 51. Attributed to Georges-Daniel de Monfreid (1856–1929), *Tableau vivant after* Phryné before the Areopagus *in the Académie Jullian studio*, ca. 1880-1890, glass negative, 5 × 7 in., Archives, Musée d'Orsay, Paris.

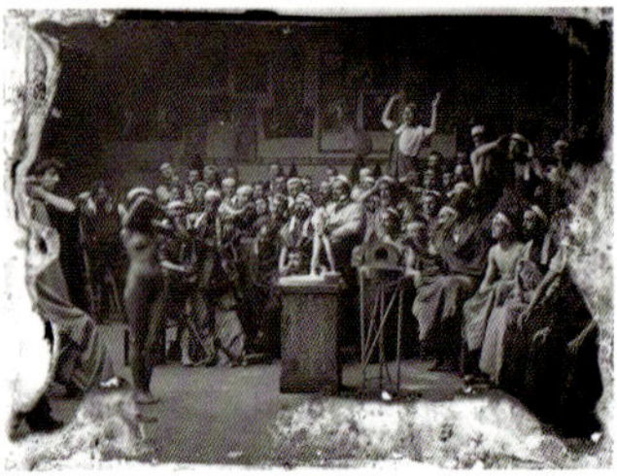

promachoi and appears to be inspired from athletes and their movements visible on some vases, from statuettes of Minerva found in Pompeii or elsewhere, or from a modern statuette produced by James Pradier, *Wisdom spurning Love's darts* (1845, bronze, Musée d'Art et d'Histoire, Geneva), which Gérôme would no doubt have noticed at the Salon of 1846. The tripod placed before the altar of Athena is an attractive hybrid created from a fairly precise reproduction, latches included, of a folding bronze tripod—a very common model in Pompeii—and a tank with fasteners inspired from the Greek studded cauldron tripods of the geometric period.[8] Phryné's necklace[9] is inspired by Etruscan or Hellenistic jewelry (ill. 49) such as that in the Campana collection, reproductions of which Castellani sold to the fashionable of the Second Empire.[10] At the young woman's feet, the gilt belt, which was only used in France to designate the courtesan from the thirteenth century onwards,[11] bears the word "ΚΑΛΗ" (beautiful), evocative of the dedication, "ΚΑΛΟΣ" featuring on a number of vases and Attic cups, a eulogy from ephebe to reputed beauty.[12] It would however have been difficult to remove the clothing of rich Athenians so simply, and they certainly did not venture out naked beneath their gowns. This wealth of archaeological detail assembled in a certainly unorthodox and probably over-clever fashion could not prevent the keen controversy unleashed by the staging of the scene, undermining its basis as a historical painting. Émile Zola was one of its most virulent opponents, denouncing in parallel the instant profitability of this "antiquity through vignettes" sold by Adolphe Goupil, Gérôme's father-in-law: "M. Gérôme works for all tastes. There is something sprightly in him that breathes a bit of life into these dull and dreary pictures. Furthermore, to conceal his total absence of imagination, he has set about producing antique rubbish... In this light, painting becomes a kind of cabinet making."[13] Since *A Greek Interior* (cat. 23), we could reasonably doubt the innocence of Gérôme's intentions: the examination of the mistress of Praxiteles by "twenty satyrs dressed as judges,"[14] the face of each betraying its own perverse "Passions of the Soul," is somewhat reminiscent of a caricature of the Constitution of the Second Republic published in 1850,[15] where the courtesan of Athens is brought back to life as a *Parisienne*. Gérôme finally achieved his goal of pleasing the public, while exasperating the avid devotees of antiquity (Charles Blanc) as well as the defenders of modernist painting (Zola). There was nothing especially revolutionary in the treatment of the nude and its "refrigerated eroticism,"[16] or the use in an artistic environment of photographs of a famous model, Marie-Christine Leroux, known as Roux, commissioned from Nadar[17] (cat. 46); "authorized" female nudes were not scarce at Salons, whether solitary figures or surrounded. The unabashed corruption, in the form of a *tableau vivant*, of one of the greatest monuments of Ingrisme, as *Venus Anadyomene* (ill. 50), which had succeeded in rallying the most recalcitrant three years earlier, was perhaps no less a part of Gérôme's strategy.[18] The body of Phryné, spotlighted in the theatrical setting of his own imagination, contrasts with the red mass of the judges' cloaks and the drab gray of the background. This graphic form, similar to a statuette—which would incidentally be turned out in a number of examples (cat. 47)—perfectly illustrates the old clichés of erotic pallor of the time, but remains much less personified than the "ideal as *trompe l'œil*" of Jean-Auguste-Dominique Ingres, without entirely freeing itself of the master's control. Gérôme, it could be said, therefore missed the chance to rejuvenate the *historical* nude through archaeology, by "undressing in Greek fashion the *grisettes* of the faubourg Saint-Marceau."[19] All Maxime Du Camp saw in the figure was "a bawdy *lorette* whose hips are too high, whose knees turn in, whose hands are too fat, and whose face is sullen,"[20] while Zola saw "a modern mistress caught changing into her nightdress."[21] Edgar Degas summed up the negative response to the work in a similar fashion: "What can be said of a painter who has turned Phryné before the Areopagus into a little girl ashamed, who wants to hide? Phryné did not hide and could not hide, because her nudity was precisely the cause of her glory... I know that it was not Gérôme's intention to create an indecent work, but by failing to understand the realist and logical soul of the Greek race, he nevertheless created an indecent work in the eyes of those who think."[22] The half-opened eye beneath the arm shielding the face of the young woman highlighted the modern vulgarity of the model. For *Phryné before the Areopagus* also constitutes—and the next generation of artists was not wrong when they paid questionable tribute to Gérôme's work (ill. 51)—an implied and transparent reference to the atmosphere of the studio: like a regular life-model, Gérôme's Phryné is standing naked on a dais, amid an exclusively male assembly. What Gérôme therefore unveiled was a fresh, spiced-up version of the *pudicitas* in the age of industrial reproduction: "Why the crowd before this painting? One has to queue to catch a glimpse... Phryné... in her ingenious embarrassment, hides precisely the part of her body that she has the right to show: her face."[23] There is an intense play of gazes here: Phryné only peeks at the judges and at the dominant male viewer of the Second Empire[24]; there is none of the demimonde effrontery of *The Pearl and the Wave* (1863, Prado, Madrid) by Paul Baudry—and the viewer seems to have a stereoscopic view. With its pre-cinematographic qualities, its cleverly orchestrated and corrupted theatricality, the work marked a turning point in the painter's career; this daring *tableau vivant* brought the *Néo-Grec* period of the "Boîte à thé," the studio in the rue Notre-Dame-des-Champs, to a close. Rarely, up to the start of the twentieth century, did a painting give rise, in France and Europe, to so much caricature and parody. The work became a media sensation and turned the tables on the controversy generated by it by being more complex than it actually appeared to be. **É. P.**

1. G. Ackerman, *Jean-Léon Gérôme* (Courbevoie: ACR Édition, 2000), no. 132.2. Preparatory sketches: Musée des Beaux-Arts, Rouen, Musée des Beaux-Arts, Nancy, and private collections. **2.** Ibid., p. 248; É. Papet, "Phryné au XIXe siècle: la plus jolie femme de Paris?," in *Praxitèle*, exh. cat. (Paris: Musée du Louvre, 2007), pp. 362–79 and pp. 384–85. **3.** "Phryné" entry, *Dictionnaire universel du XIXe siècle* (Paris: Larousse, 1875), vol. XII, p. 901. **4.** We would especially like to thank Sophie Descamps, Violaine Jeammet, and Laurent Haumesser, head curators at the Department of Greek, Etruscan and Roman Antiquities at the Musée du Louvre for their precious help in the identification of Gérôme archaeological sources and we are deeply grateful to them. **5.** D. Raoul-Rochette, *Monuments Inédits d'Antiquité. Figures Grecques, Etrusques et Romaines, première partie* (Paris: Imprimerie royale, 1833). **6.** Like that of the architect Louis-Jules André, *Temple de Thésée à Athènes* (Paris: École Nationale Supérieure des Beaux-Arts, 1851). **7.** Cited by A. Soubies, *J.-L. Gérôme (1824–1904). Souvenirs et notes* (Paris: Flammarion, 1904), p. 6. **8.** Eighth century B.C. Gérôme proceeds in the same way, in an even more precise manner, with the tripod visible on the portrait of Rachel (cat. 40), which evokes those found in Delphi or Olympia. **9.** See É. Papet 2007 (as in n. 2), pp. 362–79 and pp. 384–85. **10.** See *Trésors antiques. Bijoux antiques de la collection Campana*, exh. cat. (Paris: Musée du Louvre, 2005–6). **11.** "Ceinture" (belt) entry in the *Dictionnaire universel* (as in n. 3), p. 668. **12.** "*ΚΑΛΟΣ*" figure on the shield of Achilles in *The Iliad* (ill. 33). **13.** É. Zola, "Nos peintres au Champ-de-Mars," in *Écrits sur l'art* [1867] (Paris: Gallimard, 1991), pp. 184–85. See the full citation in the anthology in this catalogue, p. 357. **14.** H. Delaborde, "Le Salon de 1861," *Revue des Deux Mondes*, June 15, 1861, p. 877. **15.** C. Dotal, "Femmes mythiques et légendaires comme allégories modernes au XIXe siècle," in C. Dotal and A. Dratwicki, eds, *L'Artiste et sa muse*, proceedings of the conference at the Académie de France à Rome, Mar. 2-4, 2005 (Paris: Somogy, Éditions d'art and Rome: Académie de France à Rome, 2006), p. 52. **16.** See O. Bonfait, *Maestà di Roma. D'Ingres à Degas. Les artistes français à Rome*, exh. cat. (Rome: Académie de France, Villa Medici, 2003), no. 21, p. 474. **17.** See S. Aubenas, "Modèles de peintres, modèles de photographes," in *L'Art du nu au XIXe siècle. Le photographe et son modèle*, exh. cat. (Paris: Bibliothèque Nationale de France, 1997–98), p. 46. **18.** Gérôme does not mention the painting among his works of 1850–60 on which he commented in his *Notes autobiographiques*, preferring to linger on a more suitable work, *The Age of Augustus* (cat. 32 and ill. 1, pp. 26–27). See J. L. Gérôme, *Notes autobiographiques* [1874], ed. G. Ackerman (Vesoul: S.A.L.S.A., 1981). **19.** A. de la Fizelière, "Salon de 1861," *Revue anecdotique*, new ser., no. 11, 1861, vol. III, p. 246. **20.** "Phryné" entry in the *Dictionnaire universel* (as in n. 3). **21.** É. Zola [1867] (as in n. 12), p. 184. **22.** G. Jeanniot, "Souvenirs sur Degas," *La Revue universelle*, LV (1933), p. 172. **23.** Cited by A. Soubies 1904 (as in n. 7). **24.** P. Serié, "Du modèle à la muse: les peintres de figure sous le patronage de Phryné. Nus au Salon 1861–1901," in *L'Artiste et sa muse* (as in n. 15), p. 21.

Cat. 46
Nadar [Félix Tournachon]
(1820–1910)

STANDING FEMALE NUDE, THE MODEL FOR PHRYNÉ

–
ca. 1860–61
Salt print made from a glass negative
8 × 5 ¼ in.
The Metropolitan Museum of Art, New York, Gift of the Horace W. Goldsmith Foundation, through Joyce and Robert Menschel, 1981, inv. 1991.1174

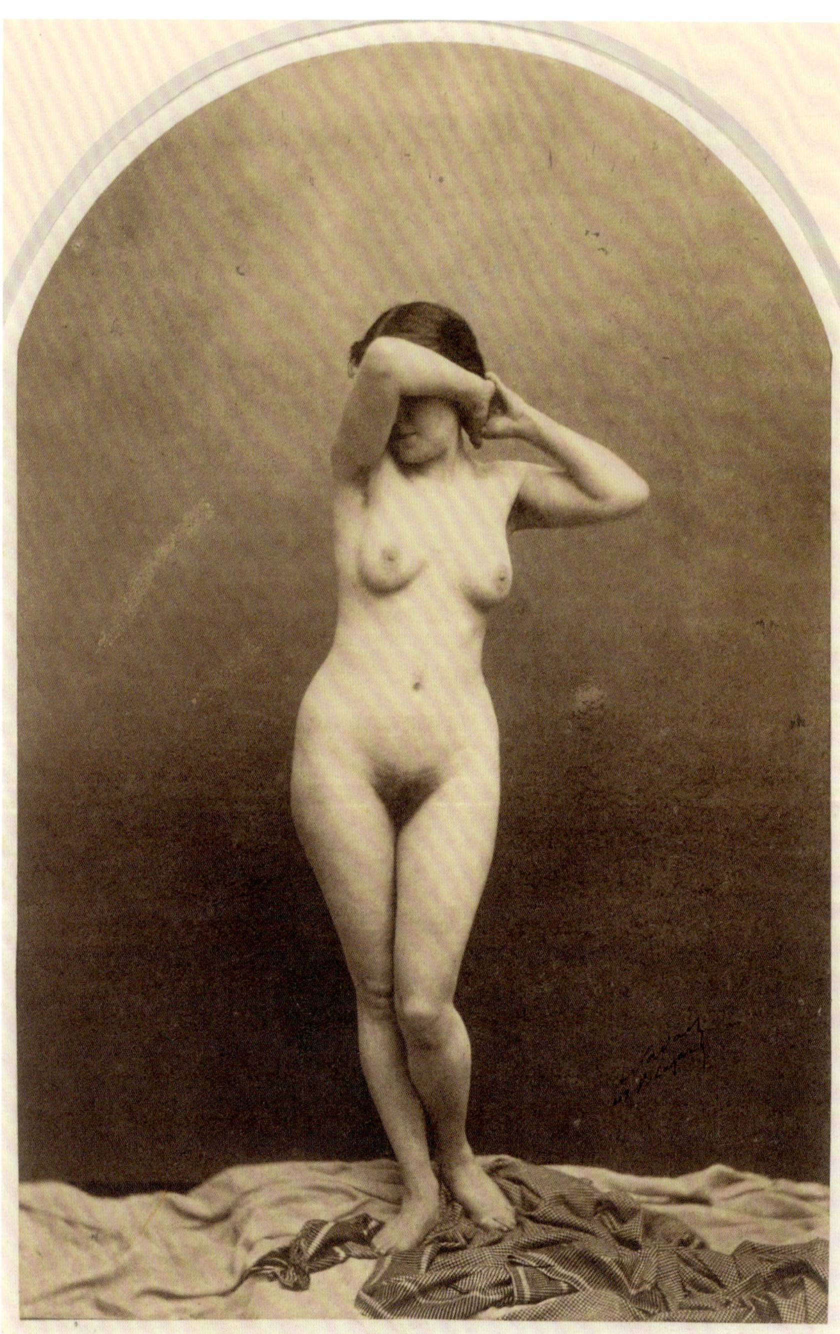

Gérôme commissioned this photograph from Nadar while he was working on *Phryné*, as demonstrated by a letter now in the Département des Manuscrits at the Bibliothèque Nationale de France:
"Dear Monsieur Nadar,
Would you please be so kind as to send me the two photographs of Mme. Leroux? I am unable to get out at the moment—I have two paintings that are not very far along and are not progressing as quickly as I would like. Now that the Salon is approaching I haven't a minute to lose.
Yours faithfully,
J–L. Gérôme
As soon as I finish I'll come by your place one morning to write my name in your album."[1]

This print is one of only three nudes Nadar is known to have made. Gérôme and Nadar maintained a friendly relationship that lasted to the end of the artist's life. The request for the photographs demonstrates the use Gérôme, like many other artists of the day, made of photography : not to replace the model but to help her maintain the chosen pose and gesture, here evoking antiquity.
Thanks to Sylvie Aubenas, we know that the model was Marie-Christine Leroux, whom Henri Murger immortalized as Musette in *Scènes de la vie de Bohème* (*Scenes of Bohemian Life*). She was also known by the name of Marie-Christine Roux. Their relationship is confirmed by the fact that Gérôme used her real name, plus the inclusion in Leroux's post-mortem estate inventory of a drawing by Gérôme. Musette perhaps also posed as the young woman in the 1847 painting, *The Cock Fight* (cat. 10).[2] **D. F.-R.**

1. Département des Manuscrits, Bibliothèque Nationale de France, Paris, Nouvelles acquisitions françaises no. 24 271, feuillet 342 (shelfmark: MF16 610). **2.** S. Aubenas, "Modèles de peintre, modèles de photographe," in *L'Art du nu au XIXe siècle: le photographe et son modèle*, exh. cat. (Paris: Bibliothèque Nationale de France, 1997–98), pp. 46–47.

Cat. 47

Alexandre Falguière (1831–1900), after Gérôme

PHRYNÉ

–

After 1868
Bronze
27 5/8 × 8 1/2 × 8 1/2 in.
Inscription on the rear of the base: *FALGUIÈRE*
George Walter Vincent Smith Art Museum, Springfield, Massachusetts, inv. GWVS-55.23.1

–

Bibliography: G. Ackerman, *Jean-Léon Gérôme* (Courbevoie: ACR Édition, 2000), no. S. 2. H. Lafont-Couturier, *Gérôme and Goupil: Art and Enterprise*, exh. cat., trans. I. Ollivier (Bordeaux: Musée Goupil, 2000–1; also New York: Dahesh Museum of Art, 2001, and Pittsburgh: The Frick Art & Historical Center, 2001), p. 101, for another bronze version.

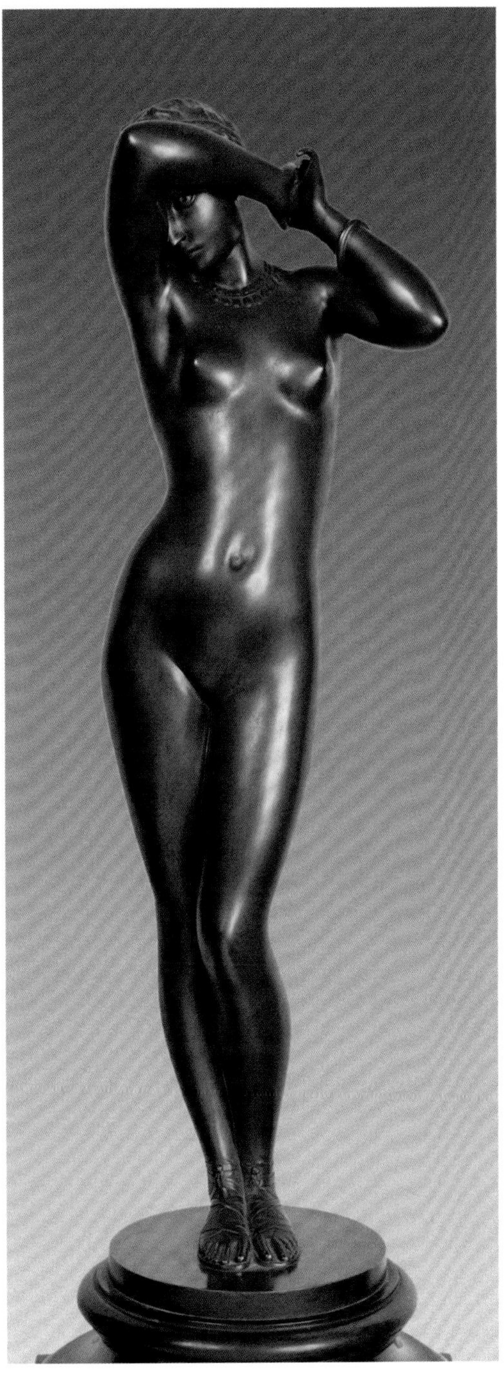

The success of *Phryné before the Areopagus*, which was rapidly distributed through engraving and photography, led Adolphe Goupil and Gérôme to imagine the figure of Phryné in three dimensions. "I didn't reproduce Phryné as a sculpture. It is Falguière who, at the order of the Maison Goupil, modeled this tiny silhouette on the painting and its studies." The Phyrné statuettes were produced in a limited number and sold for 2,500 francs by Goupil; how the first marble versions were created is unknown. It is uncertain whether Falguière cut them himself, but a letter from Goupil to Samuel Putnam Avery dated January 17, 1868 indicates that Gérôme touched up a plaster produced by Falguière.[1] After 1870, however, according to an account by Léonce Bénédite, the marbles were created by Maison Marnyhac, using the photosculpture process perfected by the sculptor Adam Salomon (also known as Antony Samuel).[2] Falguière, the son of a stonecutter from Toulouse, obtained a grant from his home town to study in Paris, where he joined the workshop of François Jouffroy at the École des Beaux-Arts. After winning the Prix de Rome in 1859, definitive recognition came with his *Winner of the Cock Fight* at the Salon of 1864 (ill. 11, p.44) and he became one of the leaders of the neo-Florentine movement aiming to rejuvenate French sculpture at the end of the 1860s. Florence Rionnet recently took stock of Gérôme's bronze works by Goupil.[3] *Phryné* was offered in several dimensions and patinas (brown, gilt, and silver). The statuettes are most frequently signed "Falguière," sometimes with "Gérôme." The bases vary between a simple molded circular pedestal and, occasionally, a square base of more elaborate modeling; rarer still are square bases on circular feet fashioned in the same manner as elements of Roman bedding found in Pompeii or Herculaneum, their edges decorated with antique-style fleurons, and their bands and cartouches bearing the Greek inscription "*ΦΡΙΝΗ*" on a palm. The statuette imitates the pose of Phryné in the painting but the position of the legs has been gently modified. Falguière carried out the commission faithfully however: the supple, perfectly decorative body definitively objectifies the recreation of the hetaera in a suitably academic style, and the various patinas do not at all play on the idea of an archaeological object. An ivory version (The Walters Art Museum, Baltimore) offers a notable variation of the pose of the young woman, in her *contrapposto* as well as in the way she crosses her arms over her face, which is less close to the painting than the statue produced by Élias Robert which has decorated one of the alcoves of the Cour Carrée of the Palais du Louvre since 1855 (ill. 52). **É. P.**

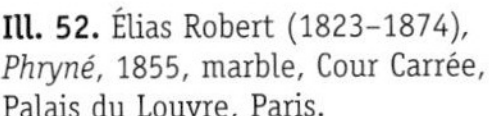

Ill. 52. Élias Robert (1823–1874), *Phryné*, 1855, marble, Cour Carrée, Palais du Louvre, Paris.

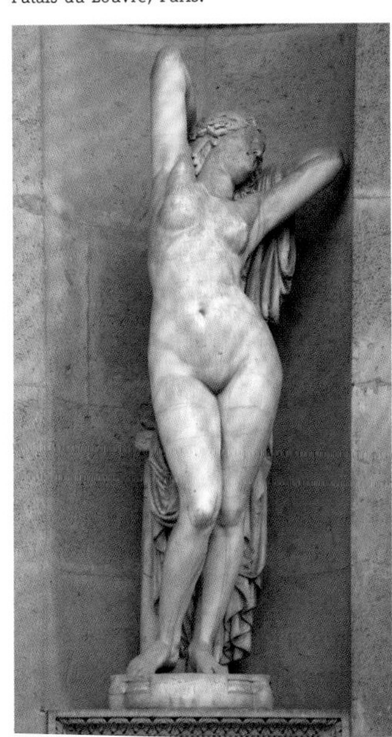

1. G. Ackerman, *Jean-Léon Gérôme* (Courbevoie: ACR Édition, 2000), p. 380. Doubts might even prevail about the paternity of the model: Ackerman reports an account according to which Eugène Delaplanche, another neo-Florentine, and student of Gérôme, was said to have modeled a statuette on Phryné in order to "decorate a table at a reception" in honor of Gérôme. This entry draws on that already published in the *Praxitèle* exhibition catalogue (Paris: Musée du Louvre, 2007).
2. G. Ackerman 2000 (as in n. 1), p. 380.
3. F. Rionnet, "Goupil et Gérôme: regards croisés sur l'édition sculptée," in H. Lafont-Couturier, *Gérôme & Goupil. Art et entreprise*, exh. cat. (Bordeaux: Musée Goupil,2000-1; also New York: Dahesh Museum of Art, 2001, and Pittsburgh: The Frick Art & Historical Center, 2001), pp. 45–53.

Cat. 48

STUDY OF A STANDING NUDE

–

ca. 1861
Pencil on cream paper
14 ¼ × 9 ⅛ in.
Marked in pencil, upper right: *Trelat/Fleury/marré-cheveu* [sic]
Musée des Beaux-Arts, Nancy, inv. TH.99.15.4316

–

Provenance: Bought by the donor at a second-hand market in La Villette, Paris, around 1977. 1999, anonymous gift to the Musée des Beaux-Arts.

–

Exhibition History: S. Harent and C. Stoullig, *Dessins de Jean-Léon Gérôme: la collection du musée des Beaux-Arts de Nancy* (Nancy: Musée des Beaux-Arts, 2009), cat. 15, ill. p. 59.

Cat. 49

STUDY OF A RECLINING NUDE

–

Undated
Red chalk on cream paper
9 × 14 in.
Musée des Beaux-Arts, Nancy, inv. TH. 99. 15. 4302

–

Provenance: Aimé-Nicolas Morot. Bought by the Nancy donor at a second-hand market in La Villette, Paris, in the 1980s. 1999, anonymous gift to the Musée des Beaux-Arts.

–

Exhibition History: S. Harent and C. Stoullig, *Dessins de Jean-Léon Gérôme: la collection du musée des Beaux-Arts de Nancy* (Nancy: Musée des Beaux-Arts, 2009), cat. 25, ill. p. 77.

Cat. 50

RECLINING FEMALE NUDE, STUDY FOR *THE MARABOU*

–

Circa 1889
Pencil on paper glued to vellum paper
Vellum paper: 14 ¾ × 10 ¾ in.; drawing: 12 × 8 in.
On the back, in pencil: *Etude pour une danseuse*
Dr. Edward T. Wilson collection, Bethesda, Maryland

–

Provenance: Separated from cat. 101.

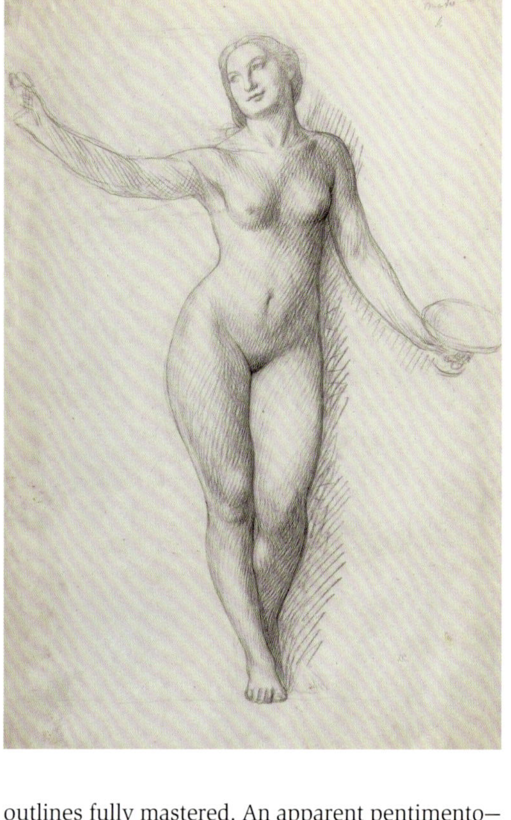

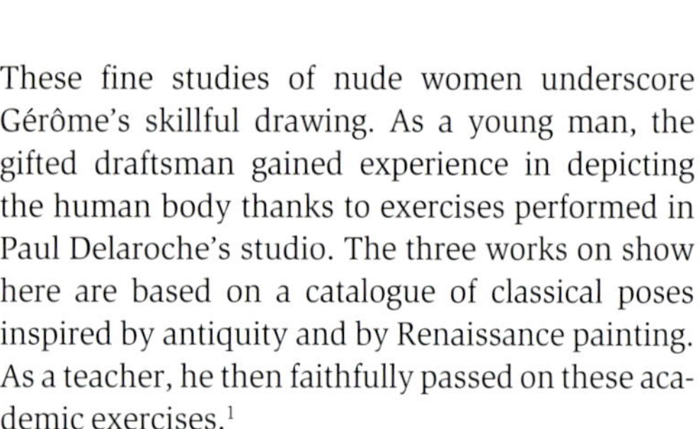

These fine studies of nude women underscore Gérôme's skillful drawing. As a young man, the gifted draftsman gained experience in depicting the human body thanks to exercises performed in Paul Delaroche's studio. The three works on show here are based on a catalogue of classical poses inspired by antiquity and by Renaissance painting. As a teacher, he then faithfully passed on these academic exercises.[1]

The first drawing probably dates from the early 1860s. Sophie Harent rightly compares it to one of the female figures in the painted sketch for *Socrates Seeking Alcibiades at the House of Aspasia* (ill. 53), a work that Gérôme exhibited in the Salon of 1861. The young woman's delicate features and half-smile also evoke, Marie-Christine Leroux, the model whom Gérôme employed for Nadar's photographic study for *Phryné before the Areopagus* (cat. 45), another painting exhibited in 1861. The second drawing shows a reclining nude in the manner of a Venus, a Danaë or—historically closer to Gérôme and certainly the model here—one of Ingres's odalisques. The drawing is not dated; the young woman's face with strong, straight nose and high cheekbones is similar to the one in *Portrait of a Roman Woman* (cat. 1), so it is possible that it dates from the 1840s. The handling is firm, the outlines fully mastered. An apparent pentimento—the woman's left hand having initially rested on a fragmentary column—reinforces the similarity to Ingres's drawings and adds charm to this fine work. **D. F.-R.**

1. At the end of the nineteenth century, in conjunction with Charles Bargue, Gérôme published a drawing manual (*Cours de dessin*) composed of 197 lithographic plates (republished by Gerald Ackerman [Courbevoie: ACR Édition, 2003]). He also wrote a foreword to Émile Bayard's *Nu esthétique*, a series of photographic plates of male and female nude models, both adults and children, in poses inspired by academic tradition (published monthly from 1903 to 1907). Despite this connection, the composition and juxtaposition of models in certain photographs make them look almost like a forerunner to erotic "photo-novels."

Ill. 53. *Socrates Seeking Alcibiades at the House of Aspasia*, 1861, oil on canvas, 7 ⅞ × 12 ⅜ in., private collection.

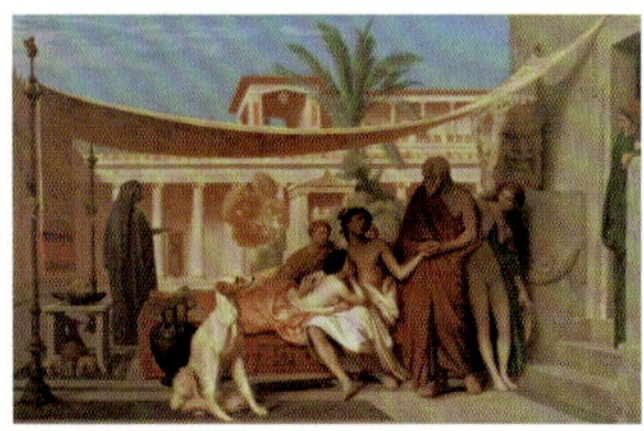

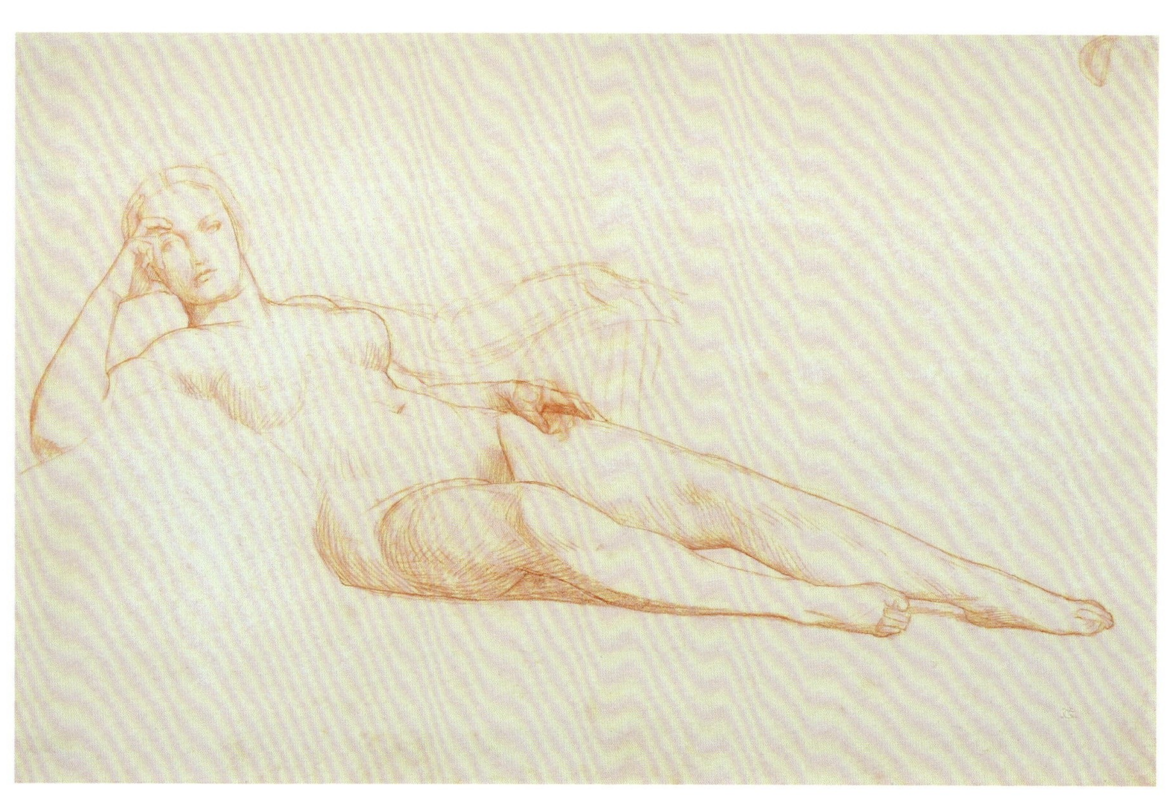

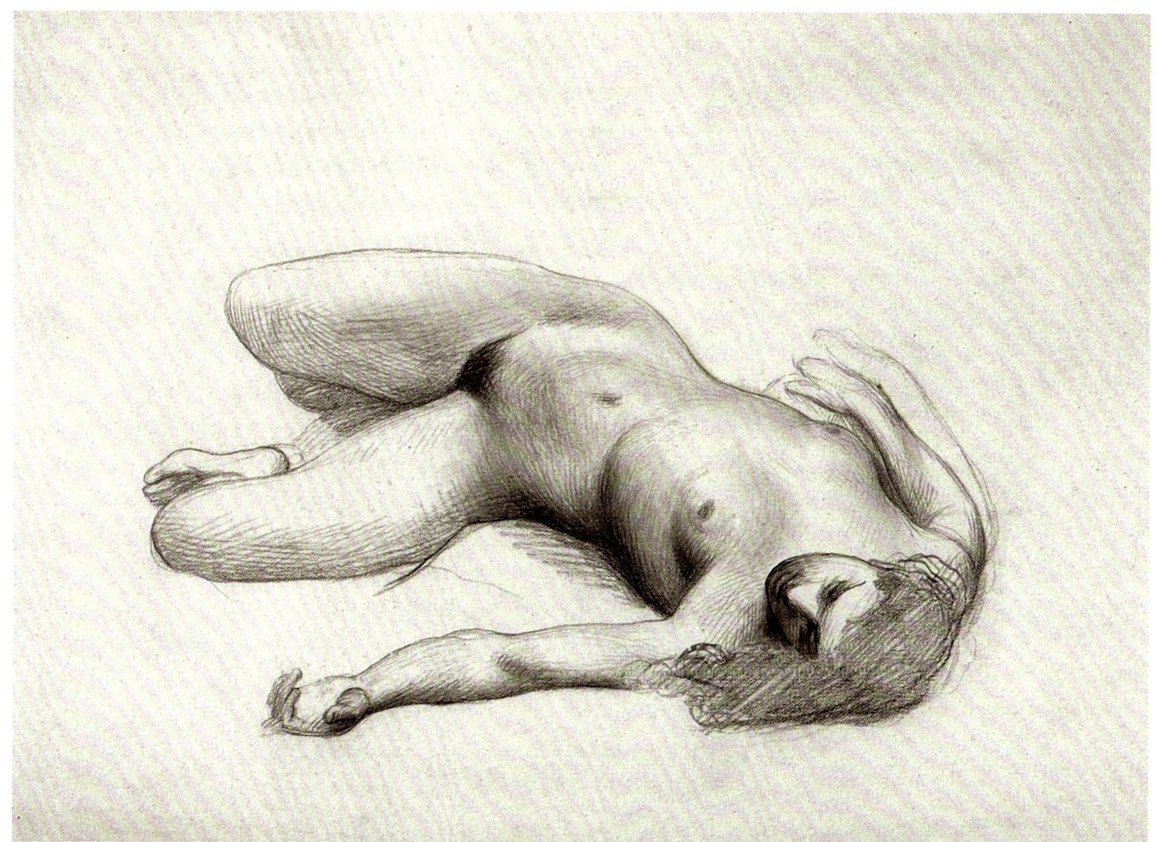

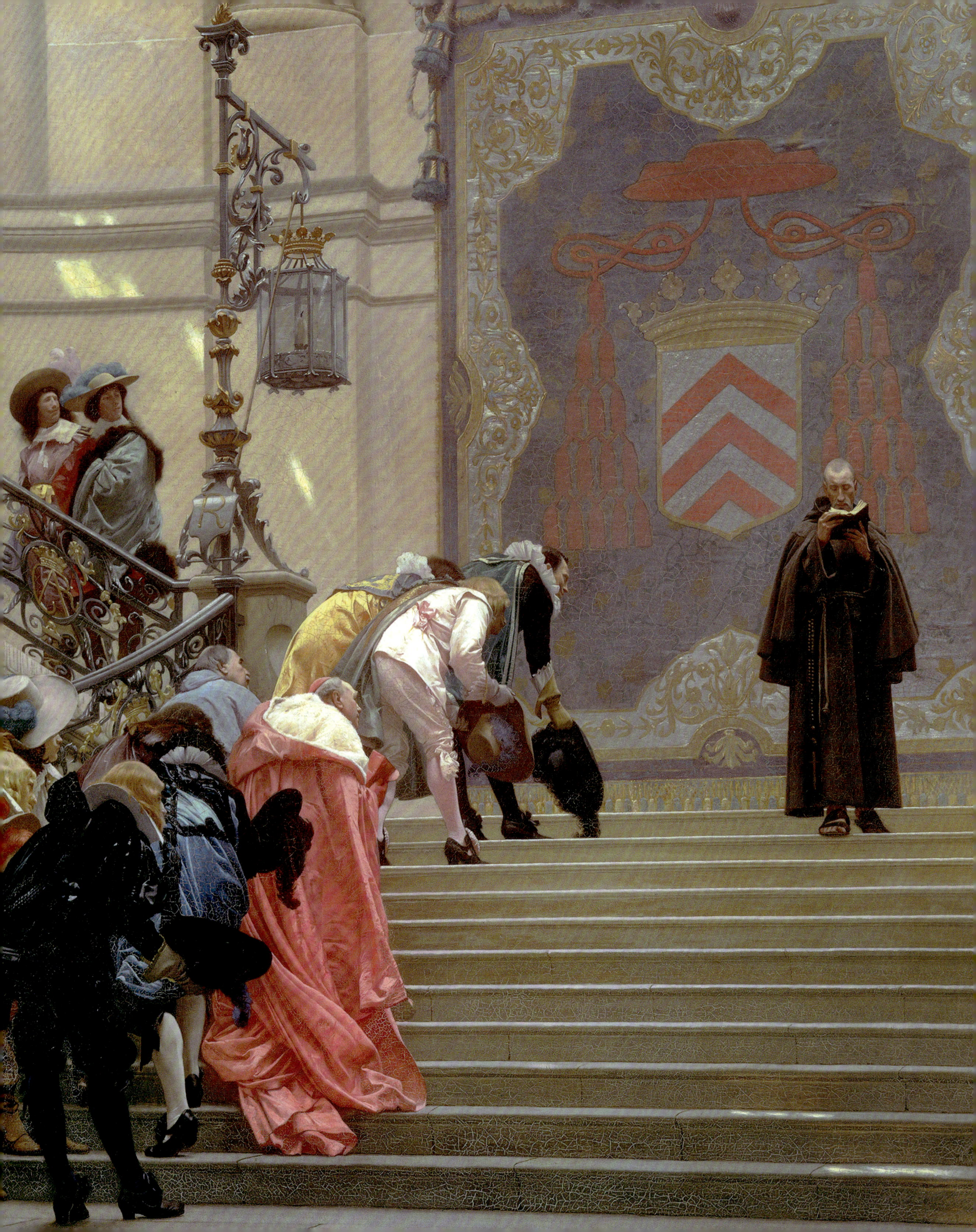

HISTORY ACCORDING TO GÉRÔME

François de Vergnette | Translated from the French by David Radzinowicz

Gérôme's history painting focuses on a handful of periods: antiquity, the seventeenth century, and the Napoleonic age. The taste for the first two of course reveals the artist's concern with the world of classicism, but his scant interest in other periods, almost to the point of neglect, sets him apart from many other painters of his era.

The eighteenth century, especially in vogue during the Second Empire, and in the works of Ernest Meissonier in particular, the Renaissance, a favorite of his master Paul Delaroche and of many painters in the July Monarchy, and the Middle Ages, which had captured the imagination of the Romantics and continued to be referenced by several painters of the Third Republic, such as Jean-Paul Laurens, seldom feature in his oeuvre. In addition, among the host of nineteenth-century artists who treated historical subjects, Gérôme is one of very few to have eschewed scenes from the French Revolution.

This concentration on particular eras is obviously related to the artist's preferred themes. He was fond of depicting violence, especially in subjects from Roman antiquity, tackling circus games and the death of Julius Caesar, as well as the sufferings of Jesus and of the Christian martyrs, but also in contemporary subjects, such as the execution of Marshal Ney and a duel following a fancy-dress ball. Gérôme's other predominant topic was more peaceable: court life in the seventeenth century as an example of the refinement attained by French civilization in the *grand siècle*, with the painter being particularly keen on episodes showing the relaxation of its etiquette, such as *Molière Breakfasting with Louis XIV* (cat. 84), *Jean Bart* (1862, lost), and the *Reception of the Duc de Condé at Versailles* (cat. 86).

This fascination with court life surely has links with the artist's being "familiar with Compiègne and the Tuileries."[1] Gérôme also painted an event at the imperial court in *The Reception of the Siamese Ambassadors at Fontainebleau* (cat. 94) in response to an official commission. Similarly unrelated to themes of violence, Gérôme frequently portrayed literary and artistic creation through depictions of Michelangelo, Raphael, Rembrandt, Dante, Corneille, La Fontaine, and, especially, Molière. In this respect, the painter exemplifies the prevailing Romantic period cult of art and artist.

Gérôme's historical works deal with famous or great men. History as depicted by Gérôme lets little room for the common people, except in scenes from the ancient world set in the arena, and his favorite characters are for the most part sovereigns and conquerors: Julius Caesar, Augustus, Louis XIV, Bonaparte, Frederick II, Tamerlane, etc. Except for the last mentioned, and for Louis XIV, Gérôme not only painted them, he also treated them in sculpture. In addition to the artists and writ-

antiquity. The anecdotal character of his subjects, often minor incidents in history, has, often been remarked upon. Nevertheless Gérôme also tackled more imposing subjects, such as the deaths of Caesar, Jesus, and Ney.

The present essay seeks to explore the reasons for Gérôme's choice of subjects, something about which the artist himself was not especially forthcoming. At first blush, the reasons do not seem ideological in nature—unlike, for instance, with Joseph-Nicolas Robert-Fleury in the July Monarchy, or Jean-Paul Laurens during the Third Republic. Gérôme, however, suggested that his avoidance of subjects with ideological implications was sparked by the problems and arguments occasioned by two canvases exhibited at the Salon of 1868, *The Death of Marshal Ney* (cat. 93) and *Golgotha* (cat. 78). As he put it: "One should definitely touch neither politics nor religion if one wants to be at peace."[2] Later canvases by Gérôme, therefore, deliberately steer clear of these two dangers.

Neither does his iconography appear especially patriotic. There are, for example, no representations of Vercingetorix, Clovis, or Joan of Arc. Moreover, shortly after the defeat of France at the hands of Prussia in 1870, he did not shrink from devoting a picture to Frederick II (*Rex Tibicen*, Salon of 1874, lost), a subject bordering on the ironic that shows the king of Prussia, in the midst of considerable disorder, passionately playing on the flute beneath the mocking smile of a statue of Voltaire.

Many of his themes, though, could never be described as neutral and they echo the political ideas of a man who called himself a reactionary[3] and who remained closely associated with the regime of Napoleon III.

Under the Second Empire he attended the imperial court; his most favorable critics, Théophile Gautier and Edmond About, wrote in newspapers supportive of the emperor. The imperial administration showered him with orders, appointing him professor at the École des Beaux-Arts in 1863. Several of his friends, such as Frédéric Masson and Arsène Houssaye, were still Bonapartists until well after 1870. Gérôme's conservative, Bonapartist political convictions appear in his predilection for great war leaders and for Napoleon Bonaparte, while he also shared Napoleon III's passion for Julius Caesar. Gérôme presents autocrats such as Louis XIV and Frederick II in a good light, and as friends of the arts: the Sun King invites Molière to join him at his table, while Frederick is *Rex Tibicen*. Louis XIV is shown as the epitome of courteousness and wit in the *Reception of the Duc de Condé*. Consolidating this hypothesis of a conservative iconography, Gérôme's explanation of his interest in gladiators—"gladiators played a considerable role in the Roman world: *Panem et circenses*"[4]—may suggest contempt for the populace, while in canvases devoted to the circus games and to Christian martyrdom, the Roman people are portrayed with hideous, cruel expressions. Gérôme's inherent conservatism may also be the reason why no figures from the Revolution or almost any hero of the people appears in his oeuvre save for an amusing scene featuring Jean Bart, where the stress is placed on his nonchalant demeanor.

Gérôme was indeed politically a conservative, but he did not have any great religious convictions, as he suggested in his autobiography when speaking of his journey to the Holy Land.[5] This explains why he dared paint *Golgotha* so untraditionally. Faced with another of his works, *The Grey Cardinal* (cat. 85)—an ironic critique of the influence of the Church on political life—one wonders whether Gérôme might not have been an anticlerical Bonapartist. As the text in the Salon catalogue makes clear,[6] Gérôme's canvas seeks to illustrate the duplicity of Richelieu's Capuchin adviser. Indeed, perhaps the fact that the canvas dates from the year of the institution of the "Ordre Moral" government should not be seen as mere coincidence.

More surely than his political ideas, though, Gérôme's choice of subject is primarily governed by a fondness for the objects and places of the past. His interest in the Roman games, for instance, is supposed to emerge from a visit to the museum in Naples where he saw a gladiator's helmet.[7] The painter had a great love of Versailles, which led him to depict the château or its park in several canvases: *Jean Bart*, *Molière Breakfasting with Louis XIV*, the *Reception of the Duc de Condé*, and *Promenade of the Court in the Garden of Versailles* (Salon of 1896, lost). He recounts how he came to paint this last work as follows: "One day I was invited to dine at Versailles, and, as I arrived late, the host, without waiting for me, went to visit the Trianon with his friends. I started to search for them in the park and returned to town, when, lifting my eyes, I caught sight of the château, its summit glittering in the last rays of the setting sun, with all the rest in shadow and, above, the greenish moon! It was striking, and it gave rise to the *Promenade of the Court*. If I had never been invited to dine at Versailles, if I had not been late, if I had met my comrades, I would never have thought of this subject, though it was well worth the effort required."[8]

After choosing the subject and as work progressed, Gérôme would embark on a program of research for the decor and accessories that occupied such a preeminent place in his finished pictures. The erudition the majority of critics ascribed to Gérôme during his lifetime centers above all on his knowledge of artifacts—an antiquarian's expertise—a characteristic that brings him close to the Troubadour painters and to a contemporary, his friend Meissonier.

Gérôme's selection of subjects from history is often influenced by contemporary paintings. Undeniably on the lookout for new material, such as the execution of Marshal Ney, he was also keen to tackle subjects and themes that had been treated before as a way of displaying his originality. This is inevitably the case with *Golgotha*, as well as for *Molière Breakfasting with Louis XIV*, painted shortly before by Jean-Auguste-Dominique Ingres (1857, Musée de la Comédie-Française, Paris). Gérôme himself stated that the idea of painting the *Reception of the Duc de Condé* entered his mind after seeing a canvas by a painter friend on the same subject but represented in a manner he thought unsuitable.[9] Gérôme had also been motivated to paint a version of Frederick II as music lover in *Rex Tibicen* in the wake of a famous example by the German artist Adolph Menzel: *A Flute Concert of Frederick the Great in Sanssouci* (1852, Nationalgalerie, Berlin).

Furthermore, the choice of some subjects, as well as the development of certain pictures, was also perhaps guided by the plays, novels, or volumes of history Gérôme had read. For example, he was undoubtedly attracted to Father Joseph due to the many references to this figure in novels and plays by Romantic authors, in particular in Alfred de Vigny's *Cinq-Mars*, Victor Hugo's *Marion Delorme*, and Alexandre Dumas's *Three Musketeers*. In the last of the three, the author writes of "the terror the Éminence Grise inspired," and of how "his name... was always uttered in hushed tones."[10]

If reading history books might have encouraged Gérôme to treat such or such a subject, we have already cited other possible origins, and Gérôme should not be seen as one of those traditional history painters whose visual imagination has to be sparked by the written word. Moreover it should be recalled that many of the subjects painted by Gérôme were scarcely abstruse and belonged to the general culture of any educated Frenchman of the nineteenth century, as for example Louis XIV receiving the Grand Condé. It was more often at one remove, when Gérôme needed to fine-tune his settings, that historical documents came into their own. In the notes for the Salon catalogues, Gérôme seeks to justify the period exactitude of certain pictures by referring to historiographical sources, indications which, owing to the paucity of notes or letters by the painter detailing his written sources, are invaluable.

For subjects drawn from Roman history, Gérôme relied on accounts by the major historians of antiquity, such as Suetonius and Plutarch, which he had studied in high school. The idea of showing Caesar's abandoned corpse in *The Death of Caesar* (cat. 67) stems for instance from Suetonius' *The Lives of the Twelve Caesars*. "The painter is on a par with the historian," is how Alexandre Dumas saw it in his account of the picture.[11] And then, as the catalogue remarks, the theme in *Cleopatra before Caesar* (private collection) arises from a passage in Plutarch's *Life of Caesar*.

For the subjects taken from French history, Gérôme had recourse to various historians: Jules Michelet, then a great influence on many painters, but also contemporary historians less well known today. Gérôme's Father Joseph must owe much to the characterization in Michelet, who observes the prelate's "comedy of humility," "with his Capuchin sandals, his rope belt," and his "duplicity."[12] Other, less anticlerical historians, Henri Martin for example, appear less severe on the "Gray Eminence" and the artist did not follow them. It is clear from Gérôme's copy of a passage from the *Histoire des deux Restaurations* by the republican Achille de Vaulabelle—a volume published to great acclaim in 1860—that the painter took inspiration from it for *The Death of Marshal Ney*.[13] Gérôme leant particularly on a phrase by Vaulabelle from the very section he copied out: "In accordance with military regulations, the body was left lying at the place of execution for a quarter of an hour."[14]

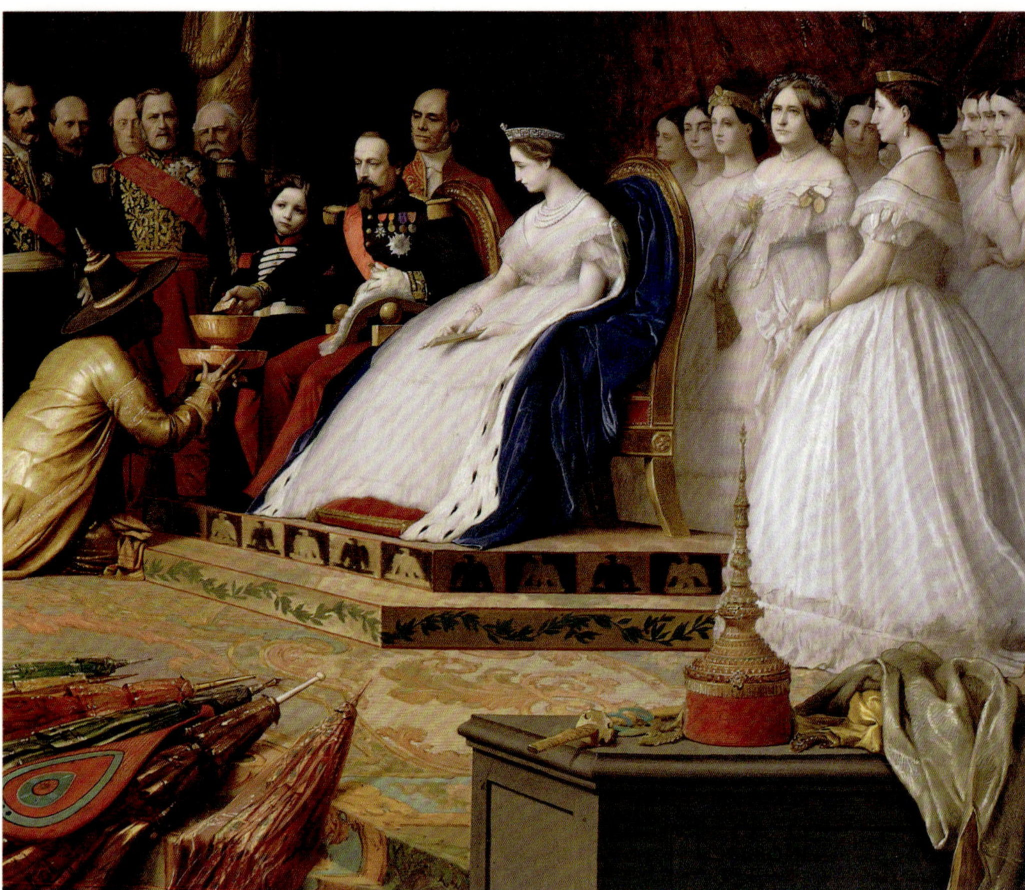

Cat. 94. *Reception of the Siamese Ambassadors at Fontainebleau* (detail).

Opposite page

Cat. 86. *Reception of the duc de Condé at Versailles* (detail).

Not all the events represented by Gérôme are historically verifiable though. The veracity of the episode depicted in *Molière Breakfasting with Louis XIV* was much discussed, its sole source—the *Mémoires* of Madame Campan, quoted by Gérôme in the Salon catalogue—being published only in 1822.

As for the scene shown in *The Grey Cardinal*, it is reported in no historical document. The art critic Philippe Burty brings out the image's paradoxical nature: "What an idea, to have this diplomatic Capuchin, this Father Joseph, who rarely showed his face, puffed up like a peacock in feigned distraction, descend a staircase on which a troop of servants in masquerade are kissing the steps!"[15] But perhaps for Gérôme, a more modern artist than is commonly believed, subject was less significant than motif, an insight suggested in his autobiographical notes, where Gérôme stresses his interest in "the fortuitous discovery of motifs" that "often arises from a handful of elements: an accident, a contrast in color, a stroke of luck."[16]

1. C. Moreau-Vauthier, *Gérôme peintre et sculpteur. L'homme et l'artiste d'après sa correspondance, ses n otes, les souvenirs de ses élèves et de ses amis* (Paris: Hachette, 1906), p. 2.

2. F. Masson, "Notes et fragments de J.-L. Gérôme," *Les Arts*, no. 26 (Feb. 1904), p. 26.

3. H. Roujon, *Artistes et amis des arts* (Paris: Hachette, 1912), p. 88.

4. C. Moreau-Vauthier 1906 (as in n. 1), p. 65.

5. J.-L. Gérôme, "Notes autobiographiques" [1874], *Bulletin de la Société d'Agriculture, Littérature, Sciences et Arts de la Haute-Saône*, no. 14 (1980), p. 15.

6. "And when the courtiers saluted him, he pretended to be reading his breviary and that he hadn't seen them," *Explication des ouvrages de peinture, sculpture... exposés au palais des Champs-Élysées* (Paris: Imprimerie nationale), 1874, p. 115, no. 798.

7. C. Moreau-Vauthier 1906 (as in n. 1), p. 65.

8. F. Masson [1904] (as in n. 2).

9. In our view, this would have been Joseph Caraud's *Retour du Grand Condé* (art market) shown at the Salon of 1863, rather than Charles-Augustin Doerr's canvas on the same subject exhibited at the 1857 Salon (Musée des Château de Versailles et de Trianon, Versailles).

10. A. Dumas, *Les Trois Mousquetaires* (Paris: Librairie générale française, 2006), p. 73.

11. A. Dumas, *L'Art et les artistes contemporains au Salon de 1859* (Paris: Librairie nouvelle, 1859), p. 38.

12. J. Michelet, *Histoire de France* (Paris: Chamerot, 1858), vol. 12, p. 56 and pp. 436–37.

13. DSCN 1908, 1909, 1910, private collection.

14. A. de Vaulabelle, *Histoire des deux Restaurations: jusqu'à l'avènement de Louis-Philippe de janvier 1813 à octobre 1830* (Paris: Perrotin, 1860), vol. 4, p. 121.

15. P. Burty, "Le Salon de 1874," *La République française*, June 9, 1874.

16. F. Masson [1904] (as in n. 2).

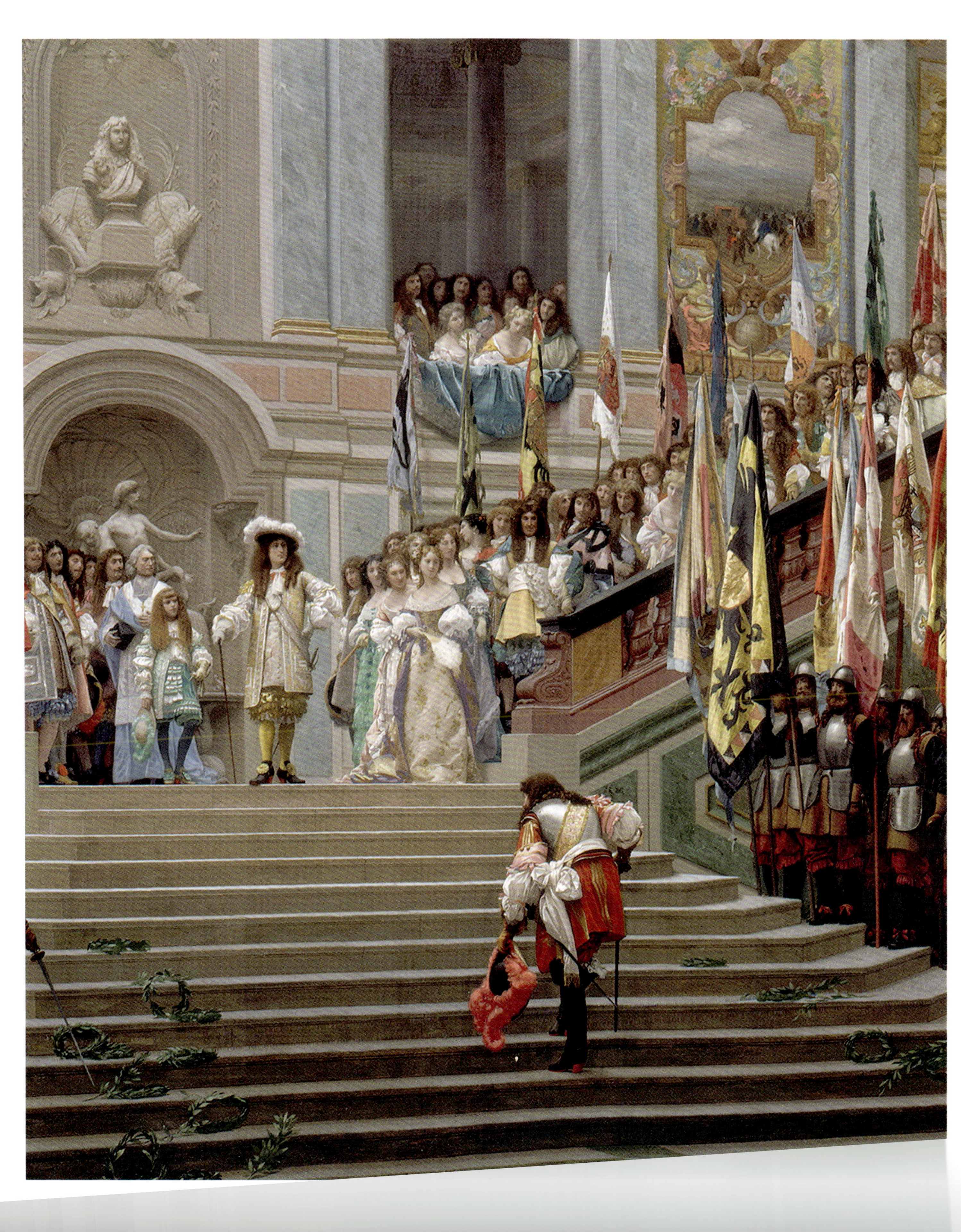

Cat. 51

DUEL AFTER THE BALL

–

1857-1859
15 3/8 × 22 1/4 in.
Signed lower left: *J.L.*
The Walters Art Museum, Baltimore, inv. 37.51

–

Provenance: Replica executed for lithographic reproduction, Shinn-Strahan. National Academy of Design, New York, *Collection of English and French Paintings. Second Annual Exhibition*, 1859, no. 93. Bought from Gambart (organizer of the exhibition) by R. Crofts as agent for the Walters Art Gallery (for $2,500). Cleaned in 1943 and lined in 1957.

–

Bibliography: E. About, *Salon de 1857*. É.-J. Delécluze, *Salon de 1857*. V. Fournel, *Salon de 1857*, p. 744. T. Gautier, *Salon de 1857*. G. Ackerman et al., *Jean-Léon Gérôme (1824–1904)*, exh. cat. (Dayton: Dayton Art Institute, 1972; also Minneapolis: Minneapolis Institute of Arts, 1973; and Baltimore: The Walters Art Gallery, 1973), no. 7, pp. 39-41. *J.-L. Gérôme*, exh. cat. (Vesoul: Musée Georges-Garret, 1981), p. 23, 107, no. 123. W. R. Johnston, *The Nineteenth Century Paintings in the Walters Art Gallery* (Baltimore: Trustees of the Walters Art Gallery, 1982), no. 105. G. Ackerman, *Jean-Léon Gérôme* (Courbevoie: ACR Édition, 2000), no. 78. H. Lafont-Couturier, *Gérôme and Goupil: Art and Enterprise*, exh. cat., trans. I. Ollivier (Bordeaux: Musée Goupil, 2000–1; also New York: Dahesh Museum of Art, 2001, and Pittsburgh: The Frick Art & Historical Center, 2001), pp. 24-27, 34-35, 37, 41, 43, 80-84 (the Ermitage version), p. 105. *The Repeating Image*, exh. cat. (Baltimore/Phœnix: The Walters Art Museum/Phœnix Art Museum, 2007), pp. 43-47.

Cat. 52

DUEL AFTER THE BALL

–

ca. 1857
Oil on canvas
8 3/4 × 13 in.
Private collection

–

Provenance: Gérôme to Ali Pasha. Donald M. Munson Collection. Sotheby's sale, London, May 4, 1995. Private collection.

Cat. 53

DUEL AFTER THE BALL

–

1876
Photogravure published by Goupil & Cie
Brown-toned print
8 1/2 × 12 1/2 in.
Musée Goupil, Bordeaux, inv. 98.I.2.91

Cat. 54

DUEL AFTER THE BALL

–

1890–93
Photograph published by Goupil & Cie, "Carte Album" series on black bristol board, no. 86
Albumen print
3 1/2 × 5 in.
Musée Goupil, Bordeaux, inv. 97.II.2.11 (1)

Cat. 55

DUEL AFTER THE BALL

–

1859
Lithograph by Achille Sirouy
Print with tint stone, before lettering, signed by Gérôme and Sirouy (published in March 1859 by Gambart & Co., London and Paris)
14 3/4 × 21 1/2 in.
Musée Goupil, Bordeaux, inv. 98.I.1.6

Cat. 56

DUEL AFTER THE BALL

–

1869
Etching by Paul-Adolphe Rajon
Printed on loose-leaf chine paper
6 1/2 × 9 in.
Musée Goupil, Bordeaux, inv. 98.I.2.89

Cat. 57

DUEL AFTER THE BALL

–

1867–68
Photograph published by Goupil & Cie, "Galerie Photographique" series, no. 560
Albumen print with gouache and watercolor, gum arabic highlights
8 3/4 × 12 3/4 in.
Musée Goupil, Bordeaux, inv. 99.II.5.1

Cat. 58

DUEL AFTER THE BALL

–

ca. 1867
Photograph published by Goupil & Cie, "Carte de Visite" series, no. 815
Albumen print
2 1/2 × 3 1/2 in.
Musée Goupil, Bordeaux, inv. 90.II.1.255 (1)

Cat. 59

DUEL AFTER THE BALL

–

1876
Photogravure published by Goupil & Cie
Brown-toned print with watercolor and gouache
8 1/2 × 12 1/2 in.
Musée Goupil, Bordeaux, inv. 98.I.2.90

Cat. 60

DUEL AFTER THE BALL

–

1859-1867
Lithograph by Achille Sirouy
Printed with tint stone, colored with gouache and watercolor, gum arabic highlights (an 1867 reissue by Goupil & Cie of the 1859 lithograph published by Gambart & Co.)
14 3/4 × 21 1/2 in.
Musée Goupil, Bordeaux, inv. 94.I.1.8

Cat. 61

DUEL AFTER THE BALL

–

1867–68
Photograph published by Goupil & Cie, "Galerie Photographique" series, no. 560
Albumen print
8 3/4 × 13 in.
Musée Goupil, Bordeaux, inv. 98.II.4.55 (1)

Cat. 62

DUEL AFTER THE BALL

–

1888
Photogravure published by Boussod, Valadon & Cie., "Estampes Miniatures" series, no. 280
3 1/4 × 4 3/4 in.
Musée Goupil, Bordeaux, inv. 91.I.2.277 (1)

Cat. 63

DUEL AFTER THE BALL

–

1859–67
Lithograph by Achille Sirouy
Printed with tint stone on chine appliqué (an 1867 reissue by Goupil & Cie of the 1859 lithograph published by Gambart & Co.)
14 3/4 × 21 1/2 in.
Musée Goupil, Bordeaux, inv. 98.I.1.7

Cat. 64

DUEL AFTER THE BALL

–

1872
Photograph published by Goupil & Cie, "Carte Album" series, no. 86
Photoglyptic print
3 1/4 × 4 3/4 in.
Musée Goupil, Bordeaux, inv. 97.II.2.10 (1)

Cat. 65

DUEL AFTER THE BALL

–

1867
Photograph published by Goupil & Cie , "Musée Goupil & Cie" series, no. 655
Albumen print
3 1/2 × 5 in.
Musée Goupil, Bordeaux, inv. 97.II.3.11 (1)

Cat. 66

DUEL AFTER THE BALL

–

1877
Photogravure published by Goupil & Cie in *Œuvres choisies de J.L. Gérôme*, pl. 6
Printed on chine appliqué
6 3/4 × 10 in.
Musée Goupil, Bordeaux, inv. 95.I.2.110

Ill. 54. Thomas Couture (1815–1879), *The Duel after the Masked Ball*, 1857, oil on canvas, 28 × 35 1/2 in., The Wallace Collection, London, inv. P 370.

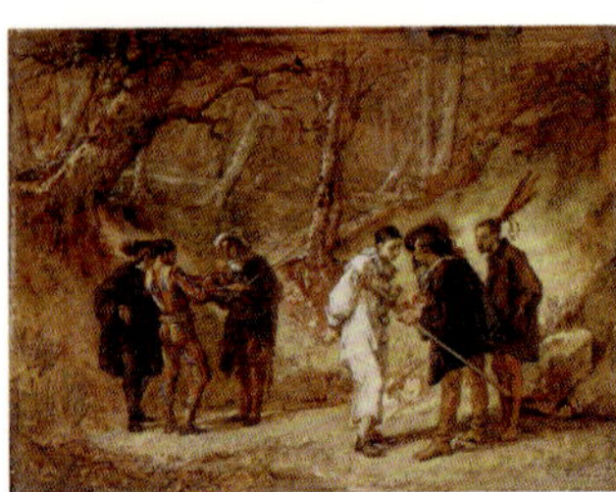

The Château de Chantilly's *Duel after the Ball* was the most highly noticed painting of the Salon of 1857 along with—or rather in counterpoint to—Gustave Courbet's *Young Ladies on the Banks of the Seine*. Although both paintings addressed a subject related to contemporary history, any other similarity of style, subject, and handling obviously ended there. Gérôme's painting was bought by the duc d'Aumale (who was then living in exile in England) when it was exhibited in London by Ernest Gambart in 1858. Aumale and Gérôme did not yet know one another, though they would later meet as fellow members of the Institut de France (Gérôme would execute an equestrian statue of the duke in 1889). The canvas of 1857 is now held by the Château de Chantilly and therefore, like the rest of Aumale's collection, is not available for loan, as stipulated by the duke's will when he bequeathed everything to the Institut de France. The painting on show is a variant done by Gérôme in 1859, after the initial version had been delivered to London, for the production of a commissioned lithograph by Achille

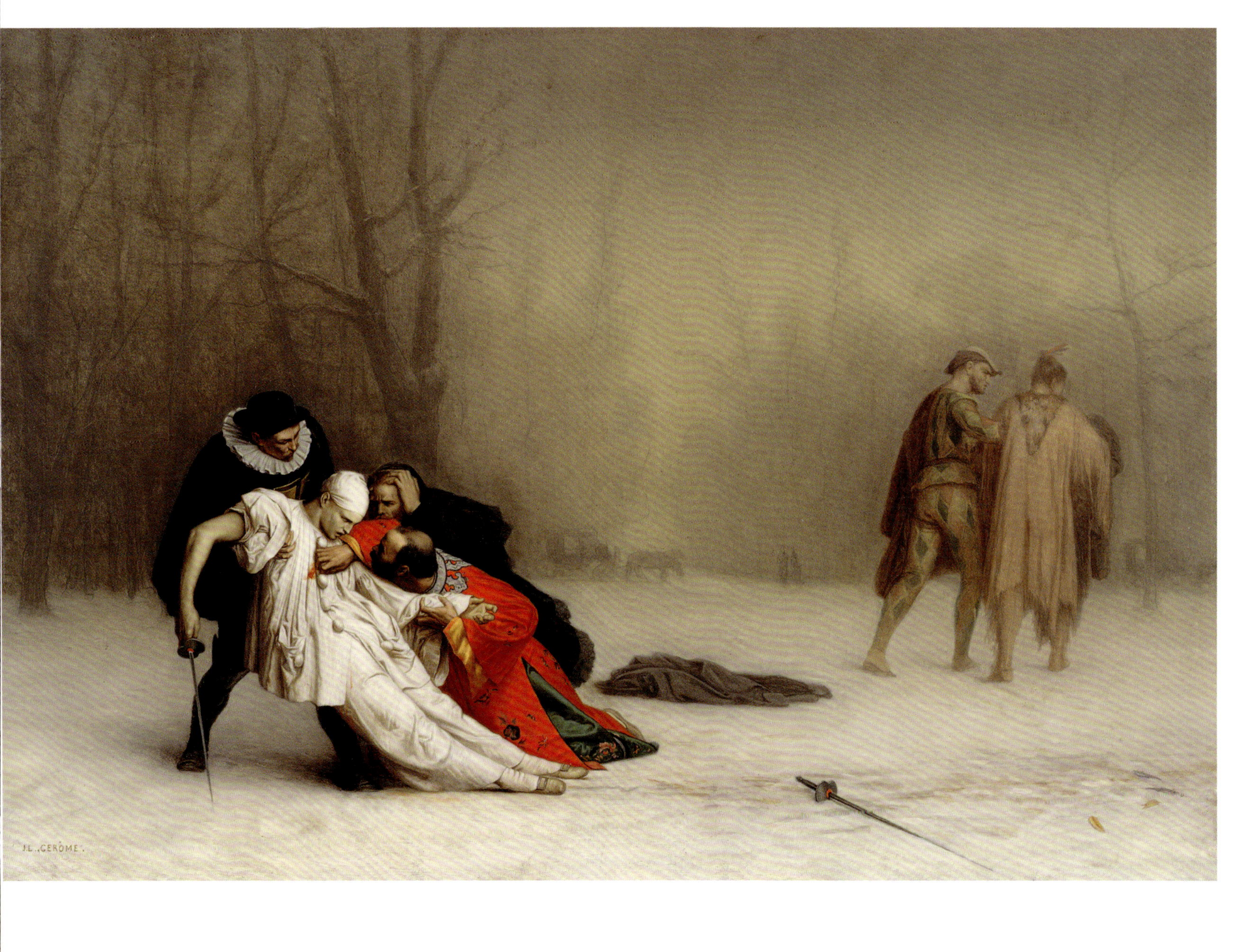
J.L. GERÔME

Sirouy (cat. 55, 60 and 63). A third version, also by Gérôme, was commissioned by Grand Duke Alexander of Russia and is now in the Hermitage Museum in Saint Petersburg.

The painting's subject refers to a real event. On leaving a masked ball in the winter of 1856–57, an elected official named Delus-Montaud fought a duel in the Bois de Boulogne with a former police commissioner named Casimir Boittelle. The incident acquired great notoriety due not just to the personalities of the duelists, but to their costumes, which evoked *Commedia dell'Arte* figures (notably Pierrot, a figure made popular in Paris by Charles Deburau's mime performances at the Funambules theater). The same subject inspired Thomas Couture, who complained of the success encountered by Gérôme's canvas in 1857 given that, he claimed, he had begun his own work beforehand (ill. 54). Couture accurately rendered the site of the tragedy, a copse in the Bois de Boulogne, as well as the adversaries' costumes. But his canvas did not match the dramatic tension of Gérôme's, for he depicted the moment before the duel began, when the duelist's seconds hand the weapon to Pierrot, who becomes a mild creature under Couture's brush.

Gérôme's interpretation is highly skillful, demonstrating the artist's thorough knowledge the dramatic effects and subterfuges painting allowed. He certainly drew his inspiration from the Delaroche's *Murder of Duke of Guise* (Chantilly, musée Condé). Here he managed—despite the fairly small size of the original canvas (19 ¾ 26 ⅜ in.)—to give a simple human-interest story a kind of grandeur not devoid of strangeness. He set the scene on a frosty lawn of the Bois de Boulogne, thereby creating a vast and slightly angled background forming a proscenium. Above all, he shrewdly decided to depict the moment when the wounded Pierrot collapses in the arms of his seconds, while Harlequin accompanies the harsh victor, dressed as an American Indian, toward the carriage awaiting him.

A large gap divides the two groups, permanently separated by the seriousness of events. Although it depicts space, this gap also represents time. Indeed, in *Duel after the Ball* Gérôme first used one of his most efficient painterly techniques, re-employed in *The Death of Caesar* (cat. 67) and the *The Death of Marshal Ney* (cat. 93), juxtaposing victim and assassin on the same canvas, thereby allowing the beholder to reconstruct the narrative thread, hence the elapsed time. He further exploited this theatrical approach by combining great precision in the rendering of costumes with a certain economy of detail, notably a simplified handling of facial features that allows the characters' poses and gestures to convey their expressiveness.

Edmond About was alert to the dramatic wellsprings of Gérôme's painting: "The spectacle of death has sobered everyone; all that remains on the faces of the seconds is terror, fatigue, and signs of stupefaction (from mental exhaustion, carousal, drunkenness). It is cold, the grim cold felt on the morning after a ball. [...] A few parrot feathers that have fallen from the headdress of the Osage Indian indicate that the action lasted for several minutes, and that Pierrot attacked with *coupés.* In the background of the painting you can see one of the weary hackney cabs that has made thirty trips during the night to places such as Bignon's, Vachette's, the Café Anglais, and the Maison d'Or. The setting is as dramatic as the scene played upon it."[1]

Gérôme's painting also inspired Charles Burdin to compose a brief poem, which concludes thus:

Pierrot, alas, slumps from his wound— / inert now is the poor man's head; / we notice that, on icy ground, / his blood, like others', is darkly red.[2]

The caricature published by Gérôme's friend Nadar in his *Salon de 1857* stresses the similarity of the painting's characters with mime and puppet theater. Like About, Nadar appreciated the theatrical aspect of Gérôme's canvas: "The staging is thorough, as you can see, and studied. The painting is solid, delicate yet not dry, while the draftsmanship is meticulous (ill. 55)."[3]

The painting's small size, its theatrical impact, and the sharpness of the dominant thrust of narrative all enabled photographic and engraved reproductions to retain the qualities of the original work. Following its Salon success, it became one of the most widely reproduced paintings of its day. Goupil had it photographed during the exhibition of paintings acquired by Aumale at the Paris Exposition Universelle in 1867. Photographic prints were marketed to the end of the century in all the formats offered by Goupil, from the large and glamorous "Galerie Photographique" pictures to the small *carte-de-visite* size (cat 57, 58, 61). The French title of the work was changed from *Sortie du bal masqué* (Aftermath of the Masked Ball) to *Un duel après le bal* (A Duel after the Ball), probably because the latter was felt to be more expressive, hence more efficient. Thanks to photographic reproductions, this painting, like several other of Gérôme's works, found its way into many middle-class homes, thereby helping to shape painterly tastes of the day. Jules-Émile Saintin thus depicted a photographic reproduction of the painting framed and hanging on the wall of an elegant young woman's apartment (ill. 80, p. 175).

A century later, in 1993, Martin Scorsese recalled the popularity of Gérôme's painting: in his film based on Edith Wharton's novel *Age of Innocence,* the director had Newland Archer, portrayed by Daniel Day-Lewis, take a long look at this picture hanging on the wall of a living room in New York. **D. F.-R.**

1. E. About, *Nos artistes au Salon de 1857 (*Paris: Louis Hachette, 1857), pp. 69–70. **2.** C. Burdin, "Le duel de Pierrot, d'après Gérôme," *Tableaux et paysages*, in *Poésies* (Paris: Librairie des Bibliophiles, 1876). The painting inspired in 1881 a play to Gustave Haller (Mrs. Fould's pseudonyme). **3.** Nadar [Félix Tournachon], *Salon de 1857*, p. 9.

Ill. 55. Nadar [Félix Tournachon] (1820–1910), "Théâtre de Guignol," in *Nadar jury au Salon de 1857*, p. 9, Bibliothèque Nationale de France, Paris, inv. RESAC V-12013.

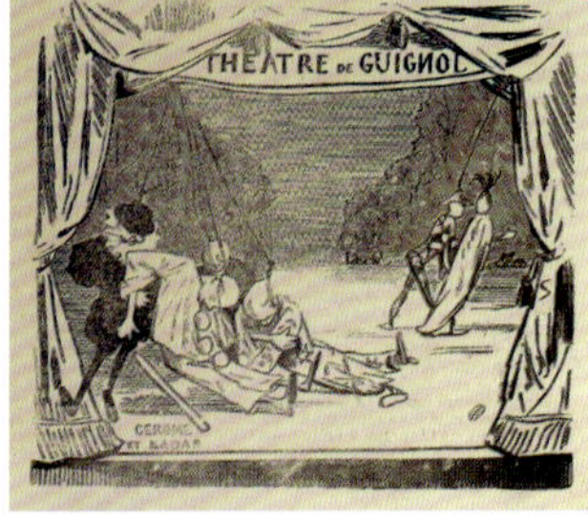

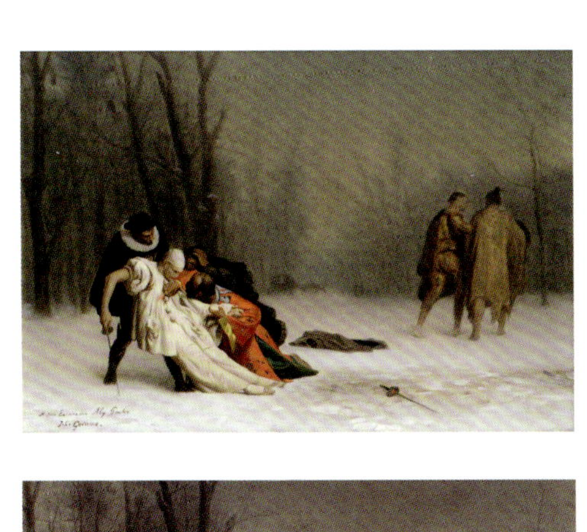
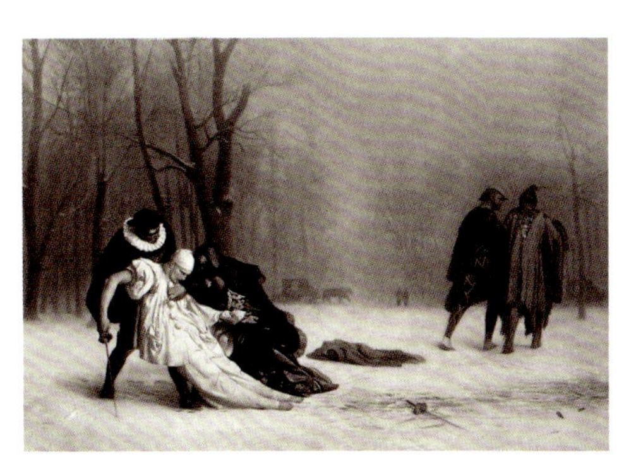
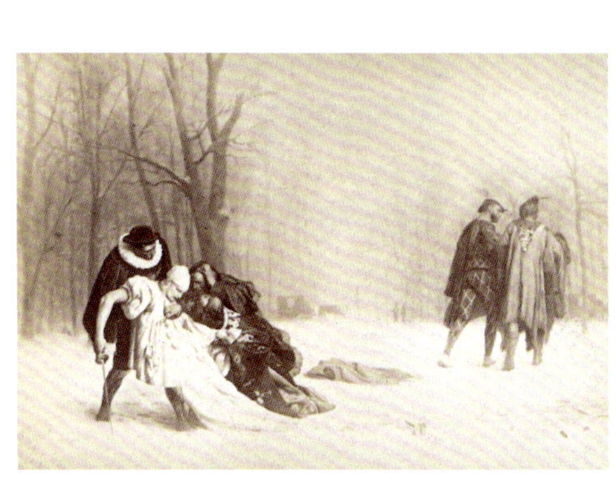
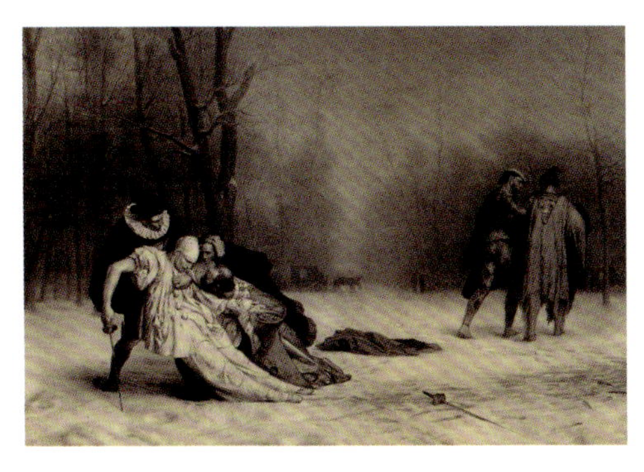
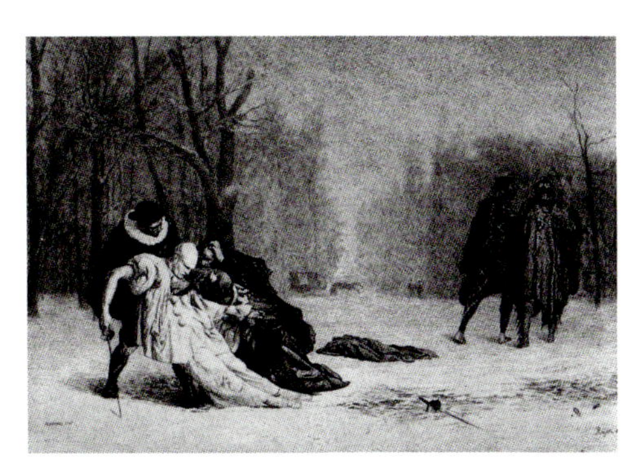
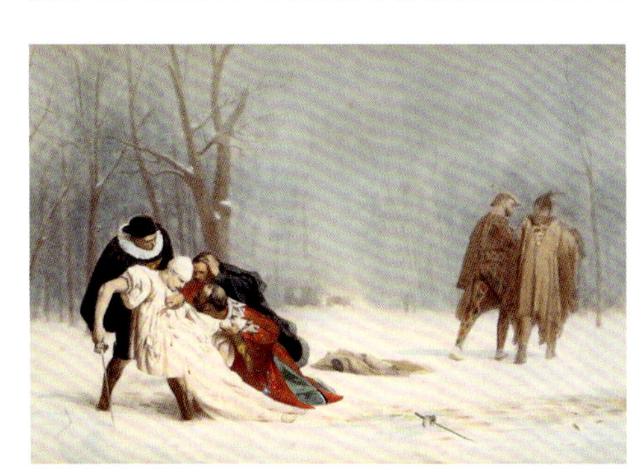
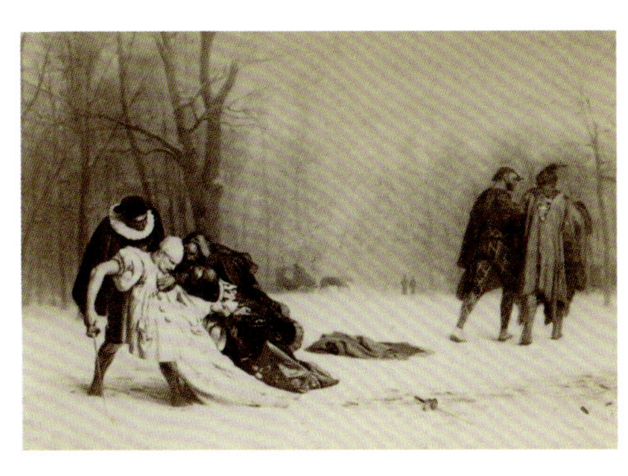
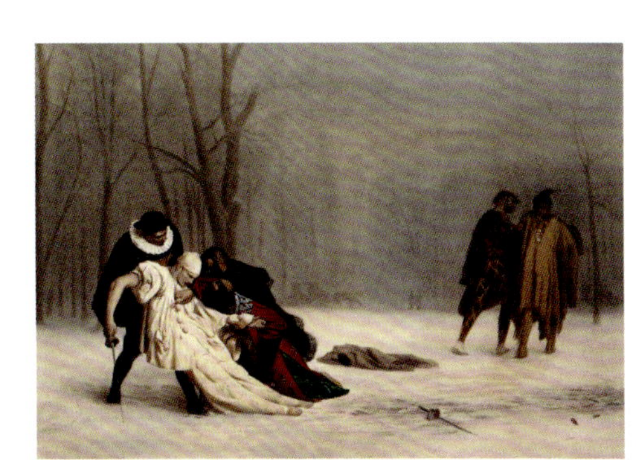
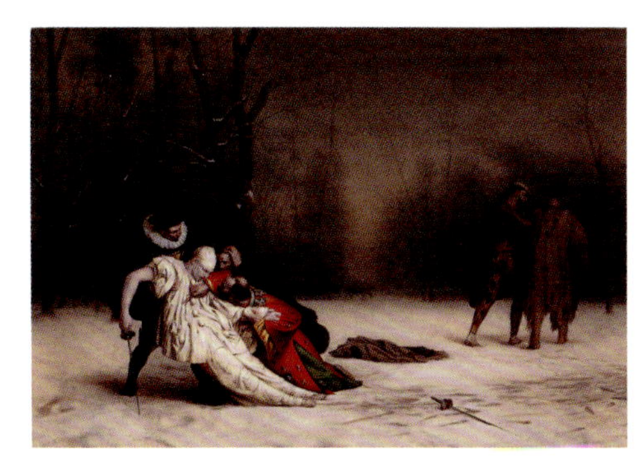
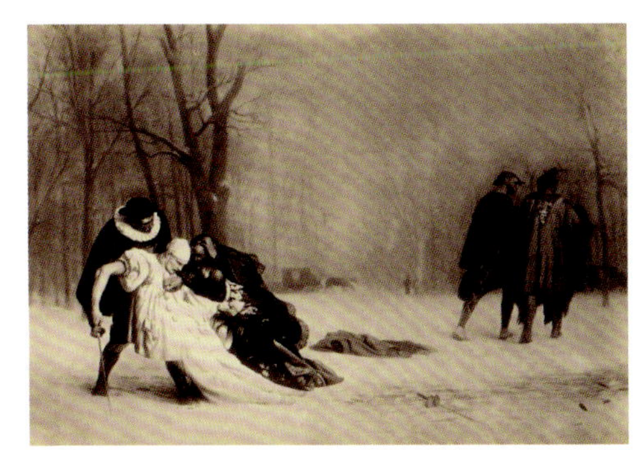
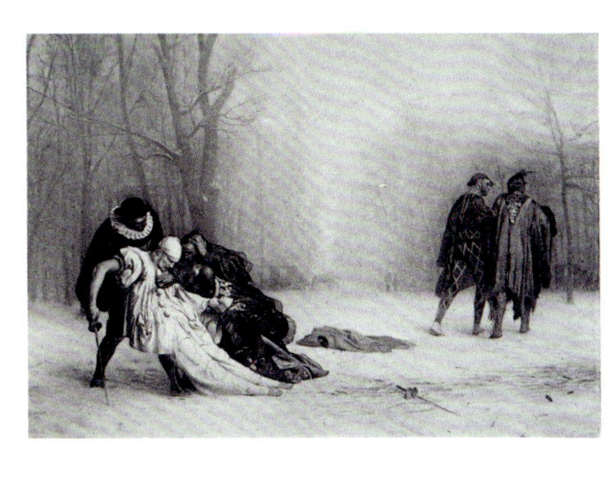
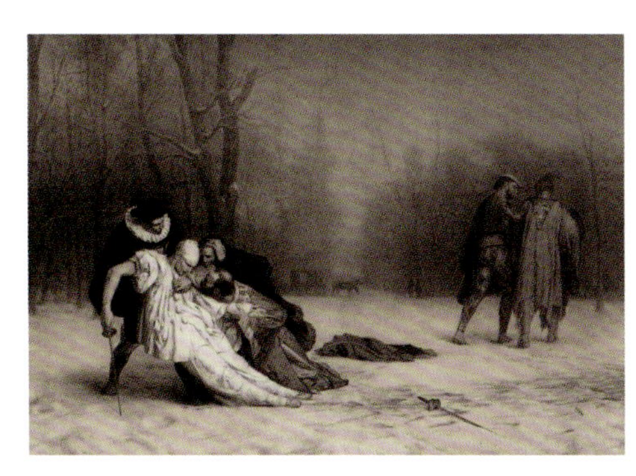
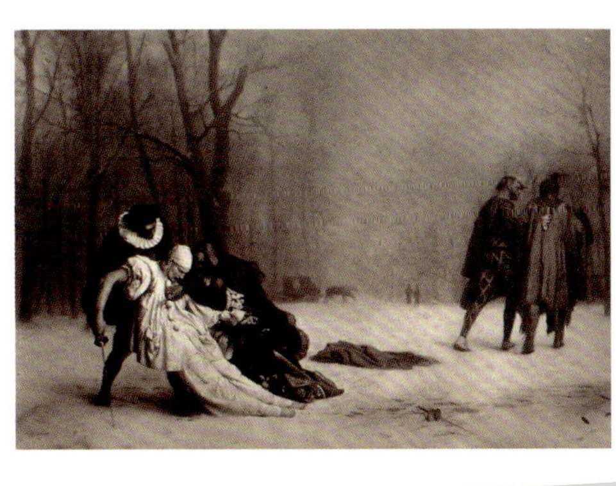
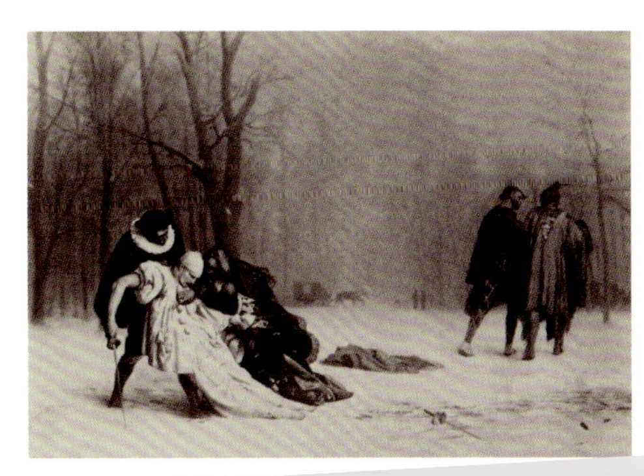
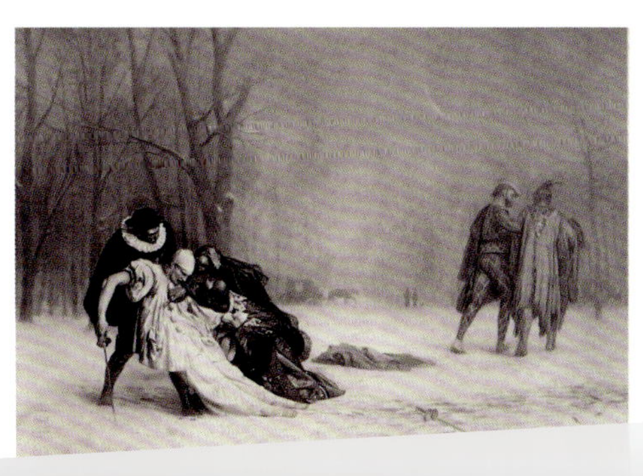

Cat. 67

THE DEATH OF CAESAR

–

1859–67
Oil on canvas
33 ¾ × 57 ¼ in.
Signed and dated lower left:
J.L. GEROME MDCCCLIX
The Walters Art Museum, Baltimore,
inv. 37.884

–

Provenance: Goupil & Cie. M. Caillet, Brussels. M. J. Allard. John Taylor Johnston, 1868–76. John Taylor Johnston sale, New York, Dec. 19–20, 1876, no. 188. John Jacob Astor. Boussod, Valadon & Cie, Paris. Schaus, New York. James B. Haggin. Haggin sale, New York, Apr. 5, 1917, lot. 148. Henry Walters, Baltimore, 1917. Henry Walter Bequest, 1931.

–

Exhibition History: Galerie Goupil, Paris, 1860. Exposition Universelle, Paris, 1867. *New York Centennial Loan Exhibition*, Metropolitan Museum of Art, New York, 1876, no. 94. *Fifth Annual Exhibition of the Yale School of Fine Arts*, New Haven, Connecticut, 1872, no. 172.

–

Bibliography: A. Arago, *Œuvres choisies de J.-L. Gérôme* (Paris: Goupil, n.d.), pl. 14. T. Gautier, "À travers les ateliers," *L'Artiste*, vol. IV (May 16, 1858). T. Gautier, "Exposition de 1859," *Le Moniteur universel*, Apr. 18, 1859. "Bulletin blibliographique, photographies," *Gazette des Beaux-Arts*, no. 8, 1860. F. F. Hering, *Gérôme. The Life and Works of Jean-Léon Gérôme* (New York: Cassell, 1892), p. 116. D. Weir Young, *The Life and Letters of J. Alden* (New Haven: Yale University Press, 1960), p. 45. G. Ackerman, "Gérôme and Manet," *Gazette des Beaux-Arts*, Sept. 1967, pp. 163–76. M. L. Bennett and A. Mongan, *Selections from the Drawing Collection of David Daniels*, exh. cat. (Cambridge, Mass.: Fogg Art Museum, Harvard University, 1968), p. 9, no. 43. A. Boime, "Jean-Léon Gérôme, Henri Rousseau's *Sleeping Gypsy* and the Academic Legacy," *Art Quarterly*, no. 34 (1971), pp. 4, 17, fig. 2. W. Drost, "Kriteria der Kunstkritik Baudelaires," *Beiträge zur Theorie der Kunste im 19. Jahrhundert* (Frankfurt, 1971), vol. 1, pp. 256–85. A. Boime, "Thomas Nast and French Art," *The American Art Journal*, vol. IV, no. 1 (spring 1972), pp. 43–65. G. Ackerman et al., *Jean-Léon Gérôme (1824–1904)*, exh. cat. (Dayton: Dayton Art Institute, 1972; also Minneapolis: Minneapolis Institute of Arts, 1973, and Baltimore: The Walters Art Gallery, 1973), no. 20, p. 62–63. R. K. Meyer, "Jean-Léon Gérôme: The Role of Subject Matter and the Importance of Formalized Composition," *Arts Magazine*, no. 47 (Feb. 1973), p. 33, ill. p. 34. *L'Art en France sous le Second Empire*, exh. cat. (Philadelphia: Museum of Art, 1978; also Detroit: Detroit Institute of Arts, 1979; Paris: Grand Palais, 1979), no. 228. J. Harding, *Artistes Pompiers, French Academic Art in the 19th Century* (New York: Rizzoli, 1979), p. 42. *J.-L. Gérôme*, exh. cat. (Vesoul: Musée Georges-Garret, 1981), p. 65. W. R. Johnston, *The Nineteenth Century Paintings in the Walters Art Gallery* (Baltimore: Trustees of the Walters Art Gallery, 1982), p. 104. J. House, "Manet's Maximilian: History Painting, Censorship and Ambiguity," *Manet, The Execution of Maximilian. Painting, Politics and Censorship*, exh. cat. (London: National Gallery, 1992), pp. 87–111. H. Lafont-Couturier, *Gérôme* (Paris: Herscher, 1998), pp. 40–41. G. Ackerman, *Jean-Léon Gérôme* (Courbevoie: ACR Édition, 2000), no. 168. R. Rosenblum and H. W. Janson, *19th Century Art* (New York: Abrams, 2006), pp. 268–72. H. Lafont-Couturier, *Gérôme and Goupil: Art and Enterprise*, exh. cat., trans. I. Ollivier (Bordeaux: Musée Goupil, 2000–1; also New York: Dahesh Museum of Art, 2001, and Pittsburgh: The Frick Art & Historical Center, 2001), pp. 19–20, 23, 25, 27, 40–41, 43, 51, 96–100, 151, 165. J. Elderfield, *Manet and the Execution of Maximilian* (New York: Museum of Modern Art, 2006), pp. 41–42. R. J. Barrow, *Lawrence Alma-Tadema* (Paris: Phaidon, 2006), pp. 167–69. S. Harent and C. Stoullig, *Dessins de Jean-Léon Gérôme: la collection du musée des Beaux-Arts de Nancy*, exh. cat. (Nancy: Musée des Beaux-Arts, 2009), pp. 48–49.

Ill. 56. *Dead Caesar*, 1859, oil on canvas, 85 ¾ × 125 in., whereabouts unknown.

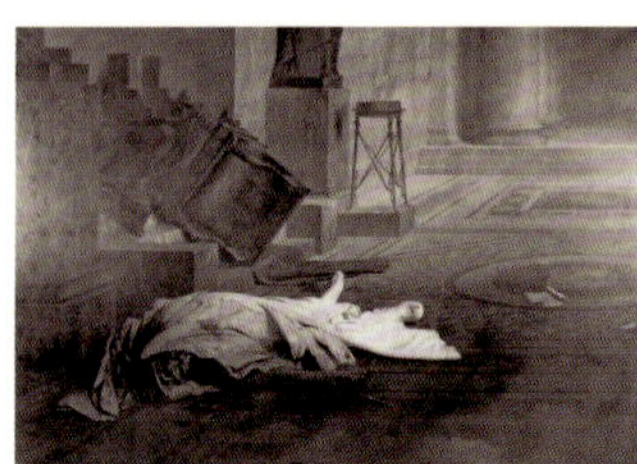

Cat. 68

THE DEATH OF CAESAR

–

1859
Photograph by Goupil & Cie, "Galerie Photographique" series, no. 20
Albumen print
11 ⅝ × 19 ⅞ in.
Musée Goupil, Bordeaux,
inv. 94.III.2.17 (16)

–

Bibliography: H. Lafont-Couturier, *Gérôme & Goupil. Art et entreprise* (Bordeaux: Musée Goupil, 2000–1; also New York: Dahesh Museum of Art, 2001; Pittsburgh: The Frick Art & Historical Center, 2001), no. 41.

Cat. 69

CAESAR CROSSING THE RUBICON

–

ca. 1900
Bronzed plaster
9 ¾ × 9 ¼ × 3 in.
Private collection

–

Provenance: Heirs of the artist.

–

Bibliography: G. Ackerman, *Jean-Léon Gérôme* (Courbevoie: ACR Édition, 2000), no. S 54, p. 398 (for the plaster in the Musée Georges-Garret, Vesoul). *J.-L. Gérôme*, exh. cat. (Vesoul: Musée Georges-Garret, 1981), p. 154 (about a bronze version).

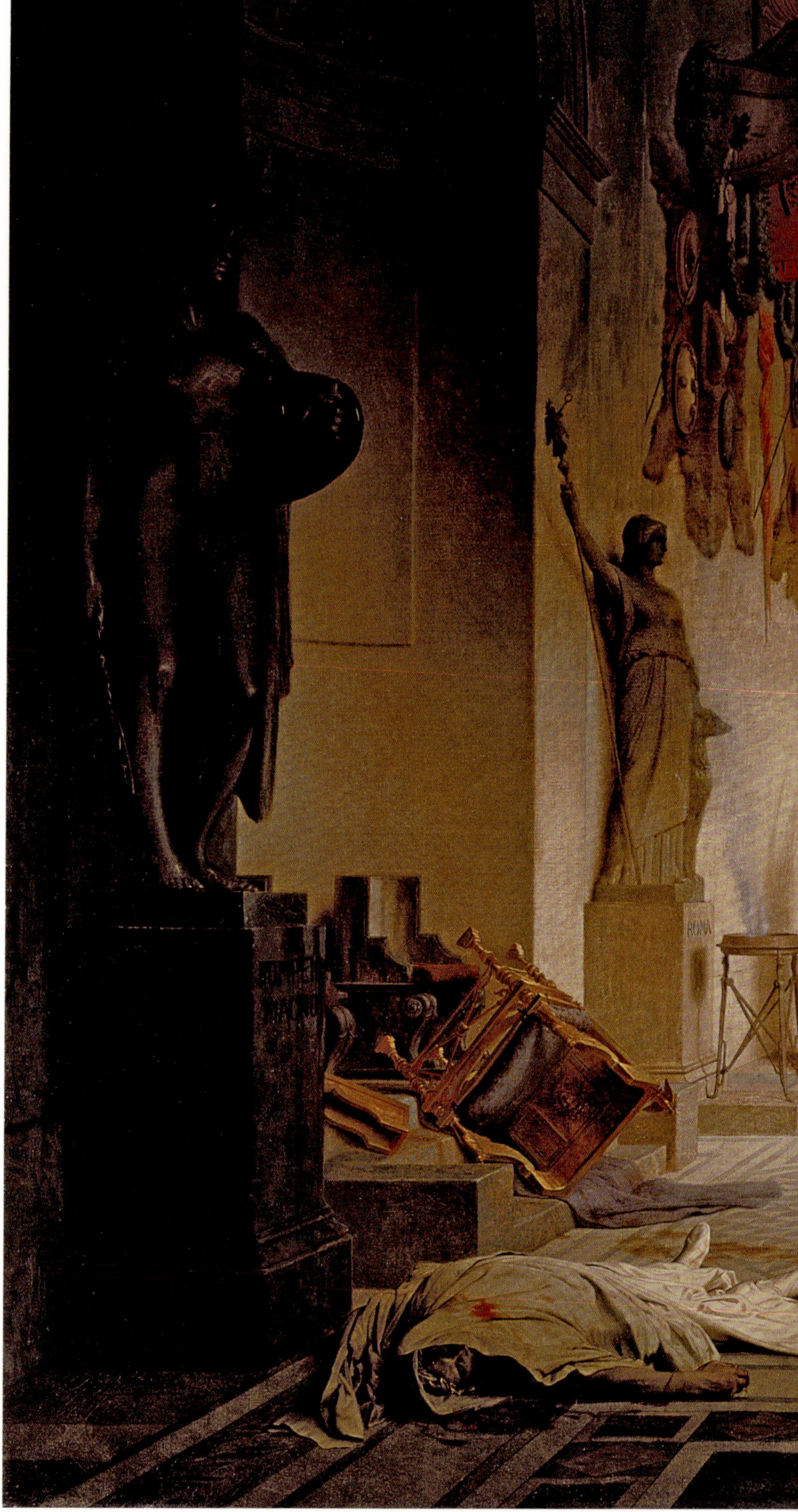

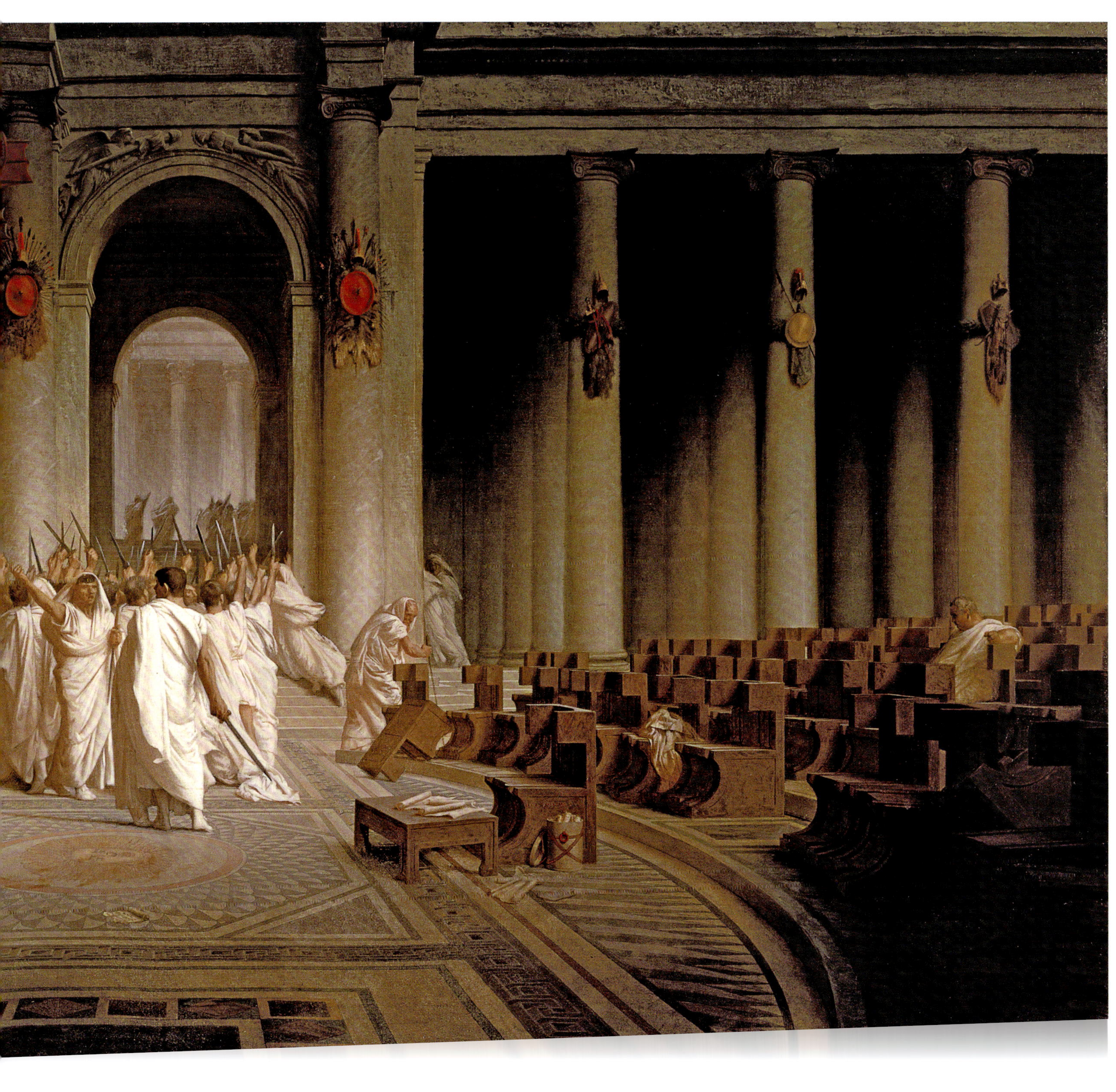

This painting is inseparable from Gérôme's other work on this subject, now lost, which he presented at the Salon of 1859. These two canvases, which he probably worked on simultaneously, share two historical literary sources: Plutarch (*Brutus*, XIV–XVIII), and *The Lives of the Twelve Caesars* by Suetonius, and particularly this famous passage: "Confronted by a ring of drawn daggers, he drew the top of his toga over his face and at the same ungirded the lower part, letting it fall to his feet so that he would die with his lower body decently covered. Twenty-three dagger strokes went home as he stood there ... The entire Senate then dispersed in confusion, and Caesar was left lying dead for some time until three of his household servants carried him home in a litter, with one arm hanging over the side."[1] Working from this reference, Gérôme envisaged two substantially different approaches to the subject. Today, we know the canvas shown at the 1859 Salon only from a poor, old photograph and the engraving of it published in the *Sonnets et eaux-fortes* of Anatole France, published by Philippe Burty in Paris in 1867 preceded by a fine pencil study kept nowadays in Washington.[2] Taking up the procedure of foreshortening already applied to bodies of the plague victims in Marseille for the chapel of St.-Jérôme at the church of St.-Séverin (1854), and anticipating his use of it in *The Death of Marshal Ney* (cat. 93), Gérôme contracted the story around the body of Caesar.[3] The cold, distant vision of the historical account distances the didactic rhetoric of *grand genre*. It was an approach that met with an enthusiastic response from Charles Baudelaire, usually wary of Gérôme's constant tendency to substitute "the entertainment provided by a page of erudition for the pleasure of pure painting."[4] "This time, certainly, M. Gérôme's imagination has been carried away! It was undergoing a moment of fortunate tension when it conceived the idea of his Caesar, alone, stretched out in front of his overturned throne, and of the corpse of this Roman, sometime pontiff, orator, warrior, historian, and master of the world, filling an immense and deserted hall. Criticism has been leveled at this way of presenting the subject; but it deserves the greatest praise. The effect is truly powerful. This dreadful summing up is enough. We all know enough Roman history to picture to ourselves what is left unsaid, the disorder that preceded, and the tumult that followed."[5] Théophile Gautier also approved the results of this felicitous daring, although having seen the other version then in gestation, he sensed the painter's hesitations: "We can remember seeing in his studio an easel painting in which the death of Caesar was given a more anecdotal treatment. The difference between the two Caesars was the same as that between chronicle and history."[6]

Gérôme's second canvas on this theme has a number of features in common with the radical earlier one, but its approach to staging the event places it very much within the illusionistic vision of a recreated Roman world inaugurated at this time by *Ave Caesar, morituri te salutant* (cat. 70). After the tight focus and large format—85 124 ⅞ in. – such dimensions are unusual for him—of the first canvas (ill. 56), in this picture Gérôme returned to the more modestly-sized panoramic format that he favored. Once again, the moment he chose to depict was the one just after the tragedy, but here all the protagonists are present and the setting falls into a three-part composition which carries remote, distanced echoes of Jacques-Louis David's neoclassical rigor in *The Oath of the Horatii*. Iconographically closer, Vincenzo Camuccini's *The Death of Caesar*, a painting that Gérôme could well have seen in Naples, presents the moment of the assassination in keeping with the same principles (ill. 57).[7] The surroundings, one of the most majestically evocative settings in all Gérôme's painting, are formed by the curia in the theater of Pompey in Rome. Onto it the painter grafted all kinds of precise details that contribute to the overall effect of realism. For example, the trophies hanging from the columns are precise copies from plate VIII (*Interior of a Basilica*) of Louis Charles Dezobry's book *Rome au siècle d'Auguste* (Paris, 1846).[8] Going from left to right, the narrative ellipse of the first version is more explicit, from the body of Caesar lying at the feet of the statue of Pompeii, spattered with his blood, to the conspirators moving away like the Roman soldiers in *Golgotha* (cat. 78) or the firing squad of *The Death of Marshal Ney*. The story had thus gained in coherence, but Gérôme's was no longer that of the *exemplum virtutis*; the sense of the anecdotal and the trivial irremediably but deliciously undermined his history painting. This break in the register enabled him to introduce the comical and truly incongruous figure of the corpulent senator, slumping sleepily on his bench, who closes the composition on the right. This supporting role straight out of genre painting here becomes the unconscious spectator of History with a capital H. It is significant that Adolphe Goupil chose this version to publicize and exhibit in his gallery in 1860, instead of the version presented at the Salon the year before, a work that was too harsh and abstract for the visual conventions of the day. The legibility of the first version's staging made it a perfect candidate for reproduction and distribution. In this respect, the albumen print that was part of the dealer and publisher's "Galerie Photographique" series of 1859 perfectly bore out Gautier's observation: "If photography had existed in Caesar's day, we could easily believe that this painting was based on a photograph taken at the time, at the very moment of disaster (cat. 68)."[9] Widely disseminated, and exhibited at a rather early stage in

Ill. 57. Vincenzo Camuccini (1771–1844), *The Death of Caesar*, 1798, oil on canvas, 157 ⅜ × 278 in., Museo di Capodimonte, Naples.

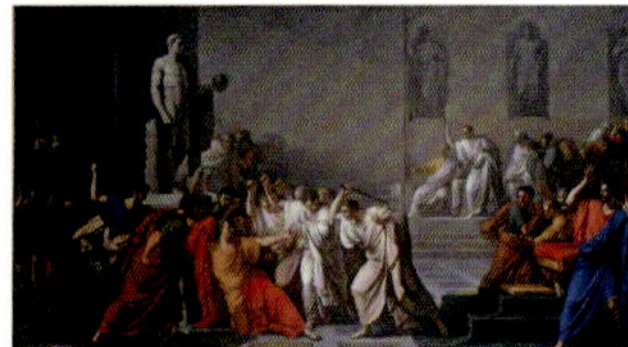

Ill. 58. The death of Caesar in the production of *Julius Caesar* by Herbert Beerbohm Tree, *The Sketch*, Feb. 9, 1898, p. 9.

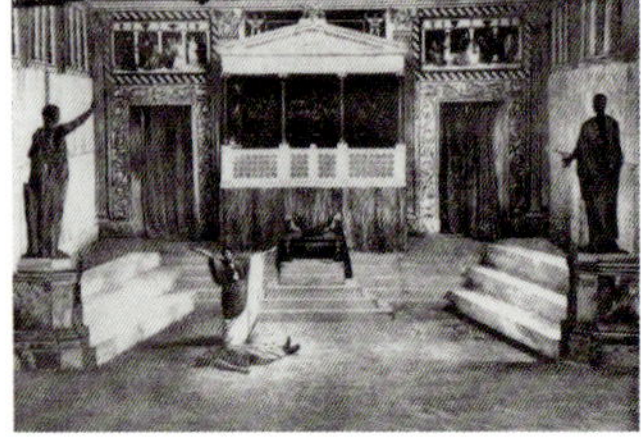

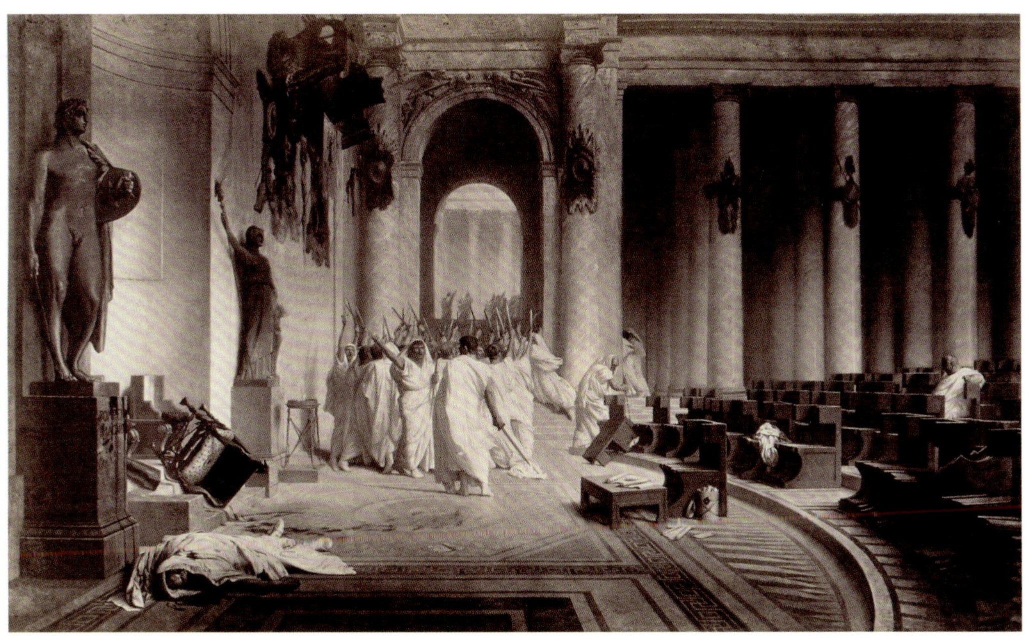

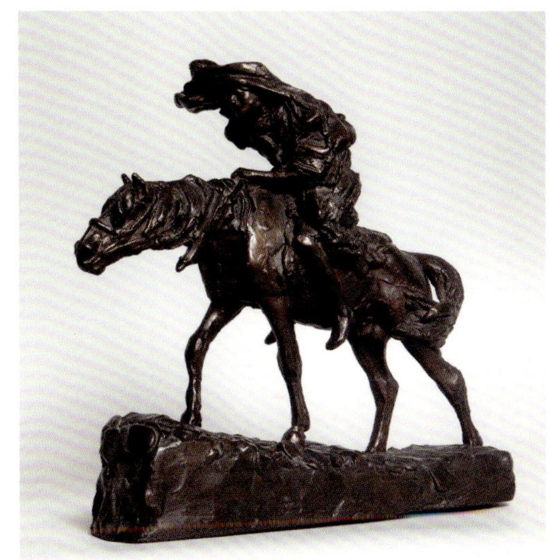

the United States, *The Death of Caesar* became one of Gérôme's most famous paintings, and deservedly so. Its evocative power and its consummate mastery of visual theater, characterized by the favorite device of the central void, was to be a lasting influence on the way other painters depicted and staged drama. From the settings and costumes designed by Lawrence Alma-Tadema for English popular theater towards the end of the century (ill. 58) to the brilliant visual shortcuts of Joseph Manckiewicz's adaptation of Shakespeare's tragedy of *Julius Caesar* (1953), Gérôme long helped find an answer to the question put by Brutus:
"How many times shall Caesar bleed in sport,
That now on Pompey's basis lies along

1. Suetonius, *The Twelve Caesars*, trans. R. Graves (London: Penguin, 1979), p. 41. **2.** See H. Béraldi, *Les Graveurs du XIXe siècle* (Paris: vol. 7, p. 103, no. 3. *The Death of Caesar*, ca. 1859, Washington, The National Gallery of Art, Alisa Mellon Bruce Fund, 1991, inv. 187.1. **3.** Dumesnil compared the work to *Dead Orlando* in the Pourtalès collection, to which Gérôme had access, and which may be another of his references here, alongside Manet's *Dead Toreador*. **4.** C. Baudelaire, "Salon de 1859," in *Œuvres complètes* (Paris: Bibliothèque de la Pléiade, Gallimard, 1976), p. 640. Translated by P. E. Charvet in *Selected Writings on Art and Literature* (London: Penguin Classics, 1993), p. 318. **5.** Ibid., p. 641. **6.** T. Gautier, "Exposition de 1859," *Le Moniteur universel*, Apr. 18, 1859. **7.** Gerald Ackerman was the first to suggest this as a possible source of Gérôme's painting. **8.** W. R. Johnston, *The Nineteenth Century Paintings in the Walters Art Gallery* (Baltimore: Trustees of the Walters Art Gallery, 1982), p. 104. **9.** T. Gautier, "À travers les ateliers," *L'Artiste*, vol. IV (May 16, 1858). **10.** W. Shakespeare, *Julius Caesar*, Act 3 Scene 1, lines 115–17, *The Oxford Shakespeare* (Oxford: The Clarendon Press, 1998), pp. 612–13.

Cat. 70

AVE CAESAR, MORITURI TE SALUTANT

–

1859
Oil on canvas
36 ¾ × 57 ¼ in.
Signed and dated lower left:
J.L. GEROME 1859
Yale University Art Gallery, New Haven, Connecticut, Gift of Ruxton Love, J.R., B.A. 1925, inv. 1969.85

–

Provenance: Goupil & Cie. Gambart, London. Christie's, London, May 3, 1861. Gambart. Petit. Edward Matthews. Christie's, London, June 6, 1891. Graves. PBNY, Apr. 18, 1962. C. Ruxton Love. Gift of Ruxton Love to the Yale University Art Gallery, 1969.

–

Exhibition History: Salon of 1859, Paris. Goupil, New York, 1860, no. 70, as "The Gladiators." Exposition Universelle, Paris, 1867.

–

Bibliography: Z. Astruc, *Les 14 stations du Salon de 1859* (Paris: 1859), pp. 189–90. C. Baudelaire, "Salon de 1859," in *Œuvres complètes* (Paris: Bibliothèque de la Pléiade, Gallimard, 1976), pp. 639–41. A. de Belloy, "Salon de 1859," *L'Artiste*, vol. VI (Apr. 24, 1859), p. 258. H. Delaborde, "L'Art français au Salon de 1859," *Revue des Deux Mondes*, vol. 21 (June 1, 1859) pp. 502–5. É.-J. Delécluze, "Exposition de 1859," *Journal des débats*, Apr. 27, 1859. C. Dollfus, "Salon de 1859," *Revue germanique*, vol. 6, no. 4 (Apr.–June 1859), pp. 242–43. M. Du Camp, *Le Salon de 1859* (Paris, 1859), pp. 63–71. M. H. Dumesnil, *Le Salon de 1859* (Paris, 1859), pp. 88–94. V. Fournel, "Le Salon de 1859," *Le Correspondant*, May 1859, pp. 154–56. J. Rousseau, "Salon de 1859," *Le Figaro*, no. 444 (May 17, 1859), p. 6. T. Gautier, "À travers les ateliers," *L'Artiste*, vol. 4, p. 18. *Le Moniteur universel*, Apr. 23, 1859. A. Houssaye, "3e Salon de 1859," *Le Monde illustré*, vol. 4, no. 107 (Apr. 30, 1859), p. 282. L. Jourdan, *Les Peintres français. Salon de 1859* (Paris, 1859), pp. 34–39, 197–199. P. Mantz, "Salon de 1859," *Gazette des Beaux-Arts*, vol. 2, no. 4 (May 15, 1859), pp. 198–99. A. de Montaiglon, "La peinture au Salon de 1859," *Revue universelle des arts*, vol. 9 (1859), pp. 440, 443–45. A. J. du Pays, "Salon de 1859," *L'Illustration*, vol. 33, no. 843 (Apr. 23, 1859), pp. 268–70. C. Perrier, "Le Salon de 1859," *Revue européenne*, vol. 9 (1859), pp. 296–99. É. Perrin, *Revue européenne*, vol. II, pp. 865–68. P. de Saint-Victor, *La Presse*, Apr. 30, 1859. A. Tardieu, "Salon de 1859," *Le Constitutionnel*, April 22, 1859. G. Vapereau, "Salon de 1859," *Le Figaro*, May 17, 1859, p. 5. J.-A. Castagnary, *Salons* (Paris, 1892), pp. 93–99. A. C. Richie and K. B. Nelson, *Selected Paintings and Sculpture from the Yale University Art Gallery* (New Haven, Conn.: Yale University Press, 1972), no. 77. G. Ackerman et al., *Jean-Léon Gérôme (1824–1904)*, exh. cat. (Dayton: Dayton Art Institute, 1972; also Minneapolis: Minneapolis Institute of Arts, 1973, and Baltimore: The Walters Art Gallery, 1973), no. 9, pp. 44–45. *J.-L. Gérôme*, exh. cat. (Vesoul: Musée Georges-Garret, 1981), no. 49, p. 63. H. Lafont-Couturier, *Gérôme* (Paris: Herscher, 1998), p. 42. G. Ackerman *Jean-Léon Gérôme* (Courbevoie: ACR Édition, 2000), no. 110. H. Lafont-Couturier, *Gérôme and Goupil: Art and Enterprise*, exh. cat., trans. I. Ollivier (Bordeaux: Musée Goupil, 2000–1; also New York: Dahesh Museum of Art, 2001, and Pittsburgh: The Frick Art & Historical Center, 2001), pp. 19, 24–25, 35–36, 41, 51–52, 104, 151, 165. I. Blom, *"Quo Vadis?* From Painting to Cinema and Everything in Between," in *La decima musa. Il cinema e le altri arti*, eds L. Quaresima and L. Vichi (Udine: Forum, 2001), pp. 281–92. C. Bastien, "'L'armure de gladiateur' de la collection Pourtalès conservée au Louvre," *La Revue des musées de France. Revue du Louvre*, vol. 54, no. 4 (Oct. 2004), pp. 44–52. C. Sisi, "Fra Babilonia e Pompei. Teoria e immaginazione dell'antico," in *Alma-Tadema e la nostalgia dell'antico*, exh. cat. (Naples: Museo Archeologico Nazionale, 2007), pp. 139–57.

Cat. 71

POLLICE VERSO

1872
Oil on canvas
38 × 58 ¾ in.
Signed lower right: *J.L. GEROME 1872*
Phoenix Art Museum, Phoenix, inv. 1968.52

–

Provenance: Goupil & Cie as *"La Mort du gladiateur."* M. Fox, Manchester, 1873. A. T. Stewart, New York, 1875–87. A. T. Stewart sale, AAA, New York, March 23–25, 1887, no. 5. Frederick G. Bourne. Mrs. Henry Potter. Alfred Corning Clark, New York. F. Ambrose Clark, New York. Stephen C. Clark, New York. Scriven Foundation, New York, on loan to the Racquet and Tennis Club of New York through 1968. Acquired by the Phoenix Art Museum in 1968.

–

Exhibition History: "Exposition des Mirlitons," Place Vendôme, 1873. World's fair, Vienna, 1873. Centennial Exhibition, New York, 1876, no. 206. Exhibition of the Carnegie paintings, Pittsburgh, 1902, no. 61.

–

Bibliography: F. F. Hering, *Gérôme. The Life and Works of Jean-Léon Gérôme* (New York: Cassell), 1892, p. 88. F. Masson, "Notes et fragments de J.-L. Gérôme," *Les Arts*, no. 26 (Feb. 1904), p. 26. C. Moreau-Vauthier, *Gérôme peintre et sculpteur. L'homme et l'artiste d'après sa correspondance, ses notes, ses souvenirs, les souvenirs de ses élèves et de ses amis* (Paris: Hachette, 1906), pp. 65–66, 150–53. G. Ackerman et al., *Jean-Léon Gérôme (1824–1904)*, exh. cat. (Dayton: Dayton Art Institute, 1972; also Minneapolis: Minneapolis Institute of Arts, 1973, and Baltimore: The Walters Art Gallery, 1973), p. 25, no. 24. *J.-L. Gérôme*, exh. cat. (Vesoul: Musée Georges-Garret, 1981), p. 23. H. Lafont-Couturier, *Gérôme* (Paris: Herscher, 1998), p. 42. G. Ackerman, *Jean-Léon Gérôme* (Courbevoie: ACR Édition, 2000), no. 219. R. Bigorne, "Visions de l'antique," in H. Lafont-Couturier, *Gérôme & Goupil. Art et entreprise*, exh. cat. (Bordeaux: Musée Goupil, 2000–1; also New York: Dahesh Museum of Art, 2001, and Pittsburgh: The Frick Art & Historical Center, 2001), no. 52, pp. 23–25, 38, 40, 43, 52, 104–107, 159, 166. I. Blom, *"Quo Vadis?* From Painting to Cinema and Everything in Between," *Jong Holland*, 2001, pp. 281–92. C. Bastien, "'L'armure de gladiateur' de la collection Pourtalès conservée au Louvre," *La revue des musées de France. Revue du Louvre*, vol. 54, no. 4 (Oct. 2004), pp. 44–52. *The Clark Brothers Collect*, exh. cat. (Williamstown: Sterling and Francine Clark Institute, 2006), figs. 28 and 29, pp. 23–24, 43, 351.

Cat. 72

DEAD GLADIATOR, STUDY FOR *POLLICE VERSO*

–

1872
Pencil on paper glued to vellum
Vellum: 14 ¾ × 10 ¾ in.;
drawing: 8 × 12 ¾ in.
Dr. Edward T. Wilson collection, Bethesda, Maryland

–

Provenance: Separated from cat. 101.

These two paintings, which deservedly rank among Gérôme's most famous works, illustrate his highly original approach to depicting ancient Rome. In fact, representations of gladiatorial combat are extremely rare in his output, as they would be in that of the painters that followed, since the theme went at once from painting to the nascent mythology of the sword-and-sandal film. In his transition, the revealing reference made to the two works in the sets at the first french stage adaptation of *Quo Vadis?*, presented at the Théâtre de la Porte-Saint-Martin in 1901 (ill. 60). Alongside the learned volumes that Gérôme consumed with great gusto when researching the details that went into the highly theatrical realism of these works, it seems reasonable to think that historical novels were another significant source of inspiration. In this particular instance, we should remember the huge success of the novel by Edward Bulwer-Lytton, *The Last Days of Pompeii* (1834), published in France in 1838. Chapter 2 of Book V, in particular, is all about the games held in the arenas, and its opening passage would make a perfect introduction to *Ave Caesar, morituri te salutant*: "There were now on the arena six combatants: Niger and his net, matched against Sporus with his shield and his short broadsword; Lydon and Tetraides, naked save by a cincture round the waist, each armed only with a heavy Greek cestus—and two gladiators from Rome, clad in complete steel, and evenly matched with immense bucklers and pointed swords."[1] In many respects, Gérôme succeeded in turning Bulwer-Lytton's realistic if novelistic evocation into coherent and convincing visual images by exploiting the expressive forms of the bodies and weapons of these unusual warriors. If Gérôme considered *Ave Caesar* and *Pollice Verso* his "two best works," he also acknowledged what, in his eyes, explained the failure of his entry to the 1859 Salon: "Quite a lot of people looked at the first, yet it was not a great success: when executing it I did not have all the documents that I later assembled to make the second."[2] Whereas in another work sent to the same Salon, *Dead Caesar* (cat. 67, ill. 56, p. 122), Gérôme made daring use of narrative and visual contraction, in these first gladiator scenes he showed the first signs of a manic obsession with archaeological detail, which soon took the place of the edifying virtues of *grand genre* painting, and became the chief point of the exercise. As he saw it, *Ave Caesar* "falls short in a number of archaeological respects and that, in this case, is a serious flaw, for the gladiators were unique figures who were nothing like the soldiers of the day: strange, enormous

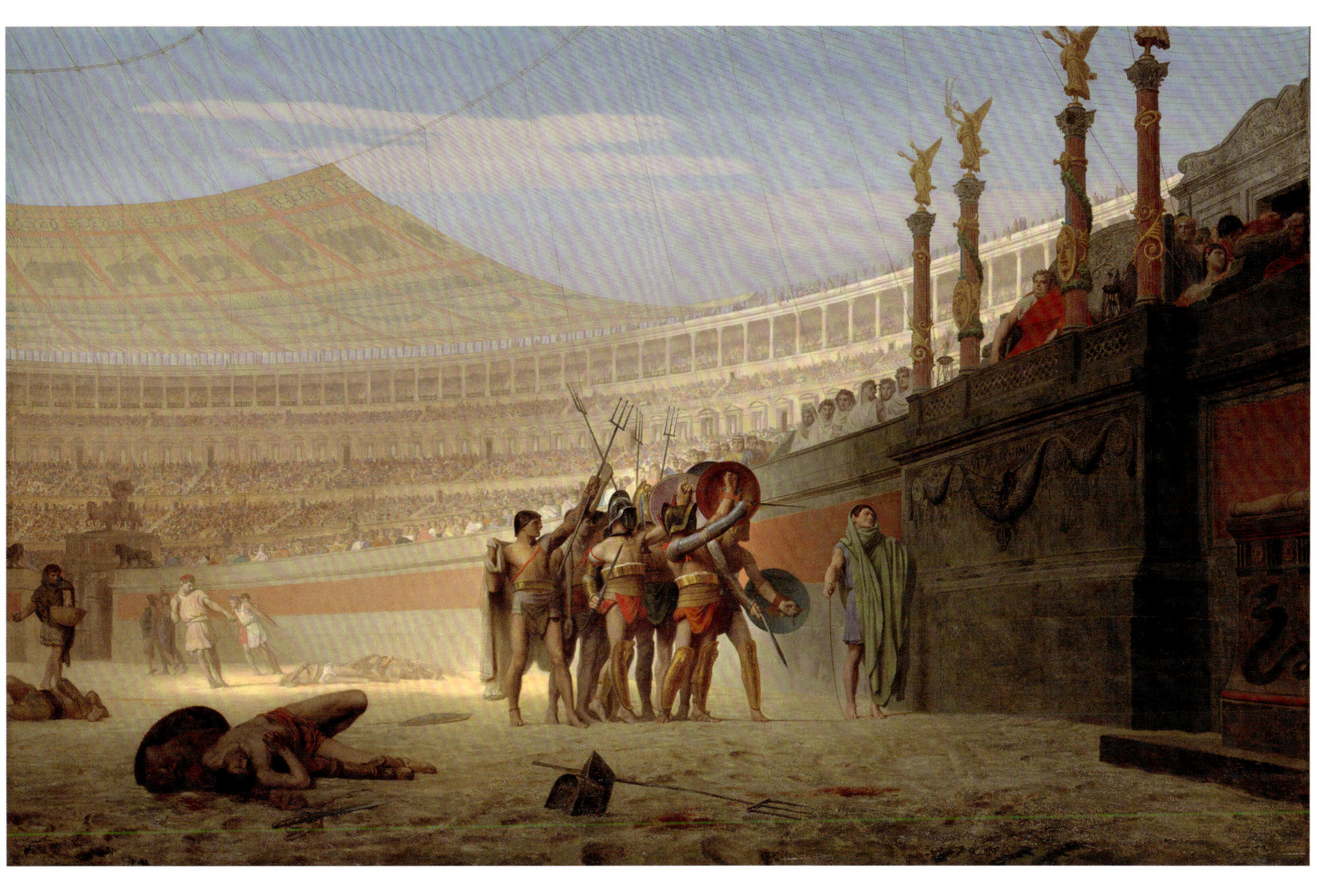

Ill. 59. Gladiator's helmet, Thrace, third quarter of the first century A.D., bronze, Département des Antiquités grecques, étrusques et romaines, Musée du Louvre, Paris, inv. Br 1108.

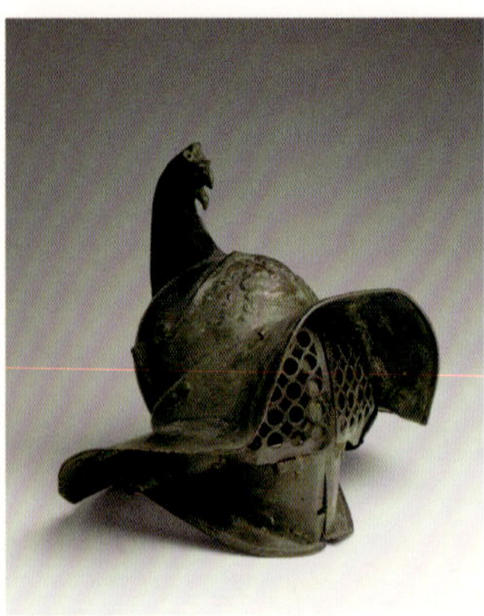

Ill. 60. *The Circus from* Quo Vadis? *at the Porte Saint-Martin Theater*, engraving published in *L'Illustration*, no. 3030 (Mar. 23, 1901), pp. 184–85, Archives, Musée d'Orsay, Paris.

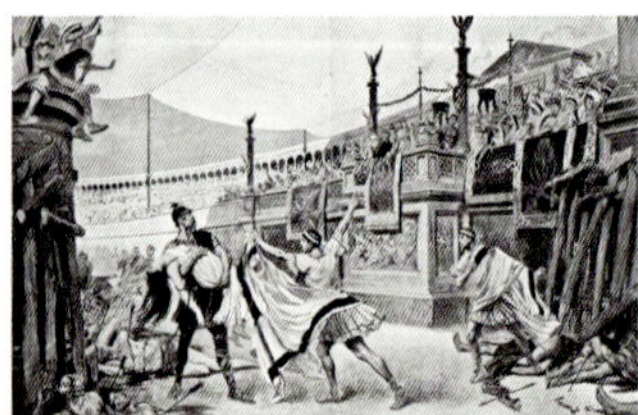

Ill. 61. Jean-Léon Gérôme, drawing reproduced in Édouard de Beaumont, "Armes méconnues," *Gazette des Beaux-Arts*, 2nd per., vol. 17 (1878), p. 502, no. 2.

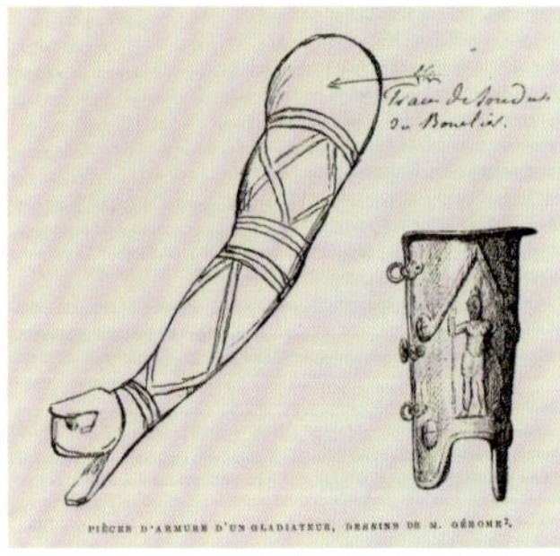

helmets, and weapons for attack and defense that were very particular. This is where the truth of the details is important, for it adds to the physiognomy and gives the figures a barbaric, wild strangeness... and yet the composition was novel, the dramatic aspect well rendered, the effect quite successful and the evocation of the circus under its canopy had been done with a great deal of care."[3] Gérôme had indeed painted the setting of this scene with great care but, as usual, his sources were composite. Thus, while the expression used for the title of the painting, and which it helped to popularize, appears only once in *The Lives of the Twelve Caesars* by Suetonius (during an episode in the life of Emperor Claudius),[4] the arena depicted therein was strongly inspired by the Colosseum, a structure that was not inaugurated until 80 B.C., under Titus. According to Charles Moreau-Vauthier, Gérôme took advice from an architect-cum-archaeologist, but knowledge of the monument had in any case improved considerably since the start of restoration work in 1822. Distorting historical chronology, Gérôme also made highly effective use of his spectacular, panoramic scale. Placing the beholder in the position of eyewitness, as was his wont, he built his composition from the arena floor upwards, thus making the sight of the imperial lodge and the tiers even more overwhelming and grandiose in the vanishing perspective of the architectural ellipsis. In the center, among the corpses, the small group of gladiators, which Gérôme in the end reduced in size compared to his preparatory drawing, bring life with their almost superhuman forms to this new variation on the theme of power and submission.[5] For the *retiarius*, to the left, Gérôme referred directly to a small bronze gladiator figure kept at the Bibliothèque Nationale de France.[6] But in spite of this concern for realism, and the huge success of the painting when exhibited by the Galerie Goupil in 1860, as well as the popularity of its several photographic reproductions, the first of which was made by Robert Jefferson Bingham for Goupil & Cie's 1859 "Galerie Photographique" series, Gérôme would always feel that this first attempt was incomplete.

Thirteen years later, under a title inspired by a poor translation of a passage in Juvenal, the painter returned to this subject, which he dramatized by focusing on a *mirmillo* putting to death a *retiarius*.[7] By now, as for the martyrdom scenes (cat. 80 and cat. 81), the framing and point of view on the combat followed a set formula. The Colosseum was depicted with increased precision, and he made effective use of the light filtered by the canopy, which was only partially evoked in *Ave Caesar*, taking a close-up view of its violent rites. This adjustment enabled the painter to explore the passional tension of the scene, what with the excited crowd and the suspense as the gladiator makes ready to land his death-dealing blow less violently suppressed in the canvas than in a preparatory study kept in Nancy. Between these two paintings, Gérôme steadily built up his documentation on the subject, corresponding with Viollet-le-Duc on the architecture of Roman arenas, and becoming fascinated by the helmets and weapons used by gladiators.[8] The register was that of a faithful rendition of the antique model: "One of my friends, General de Reyffre traveled to Rome and to Naples, where he made good molds of gladiators' helmets, greaves, and bucklers, and it was in these moulds that the galvanoplasty was done, so that I now have in my possession copies that are identical to the originals."[9] It is also thought that in his research Gérôme had access to the pieces of armor kept in the Pourtalès collection in the Louvre, about which Goupil & Cie published an album (ill. 59).[10] Thus, the vanquished *retiarius* in the foreground of *Pollice Verso* is wearing a shoulder plate just like the one in the Pourtalès collection, which can be recognized by the silver crescent moon on the curved part, while a greave from the same collection can be identified in the drawing with which Gérôme illustrated an article by Édouard de Beaumont for the *Gazette des Beaux-Arts* in 1878 (ill. 61). A fine pencil study for the gladiator lying in the background combine this archeological accuracy with a sense of dramatic foreshortening (cat. 72). Although never shown at the Salon, this work was presented at the 1873 world's fair in Vienna and widely disseminated through photographic and photogravure reproduction. No doubt its success was due to the way Gérôme managed to balance the kind of violent and dramatic action that grabs the viewer's attention with a masterful recreation whose vividness bestows credibility on a work that owes as much to archaeology as it does to the imagination. This deftly knowledgeable way with visual imagery was bound to inspire filmmakers, from the earliest sword-and-sandal movies to the most recent productions. When talking to Ridley Scott about *Gladiator* (2000), producer Walter Parkes got him to commit to the project by showing him a reproduction of *Pollice Verso*. "I love to create worlds," responded the director.[11] **L. C.**

1. E. G. Bulwer-Lytton, *The Last Days of Pompeii* (Charlotte, N.C.: IAP, 2009), p. 298. **2.** J.-L. Gérôme, *Notes autobiographiques* [1874], ed. G. Ackerman (Vesoul: S.A.L.S.A., 1981), p. 11. **3.** Ibid., p. 12. **4.** Suetonius, *The Twelve Caesars*, trans. R. Graves (London: Penguin, 1979), p. 192. Graves renders the expression as "Hail Caesar". **5.** *The Gladiators.* Study for *Ave Caesar, morituri te salutant*, black chalk with highlights, Musée Georges-Garret, Vesoul, inv. 984.7.3. **6.** G. Ackerman et al., *Jean-Léon Gérôme (1824–1904)*, exh. cat. (Dayton: Dayton Art Institute, 1972; also Minneapolis: Minneapolis Institute of Arts, 1973, and Baltimore: The Walters Art Gallery, 1973), p. 44. **7.** On the expression *pollice verso*, see E. Teyssier, *La Mort en face. Le dossier gladiateurs* (Arles: Actes Sud, 2009), p. 518. **8.** See *Lettres inédites de Viollet-le-Duc* (Paris: Librairies-Imprimeries Réunies, 1902), pp. 54–55. **9.** F. Masson, "Notes et fragments de J.-L. Gérôme," *Les Arts*, no. 26 (Feb. 1904), p. 26. **10.** C. Bastien, "'L'armure de gladiateur' de la collection Pourtalès conservée au Louvre," *La Revue des musées de France. Revue du Louvre*, vol. 54, no. 4 (Oct. 2004), pp. 44–52. **11.** I. Blom, *"Quo Vadis?* From Painting to Cinema and Everything in Between," in *La decima musa. Il cinema e le altri arti*, eds L. Quaresima and L. Vichi (Udine: Forum, 2001), p. 281.

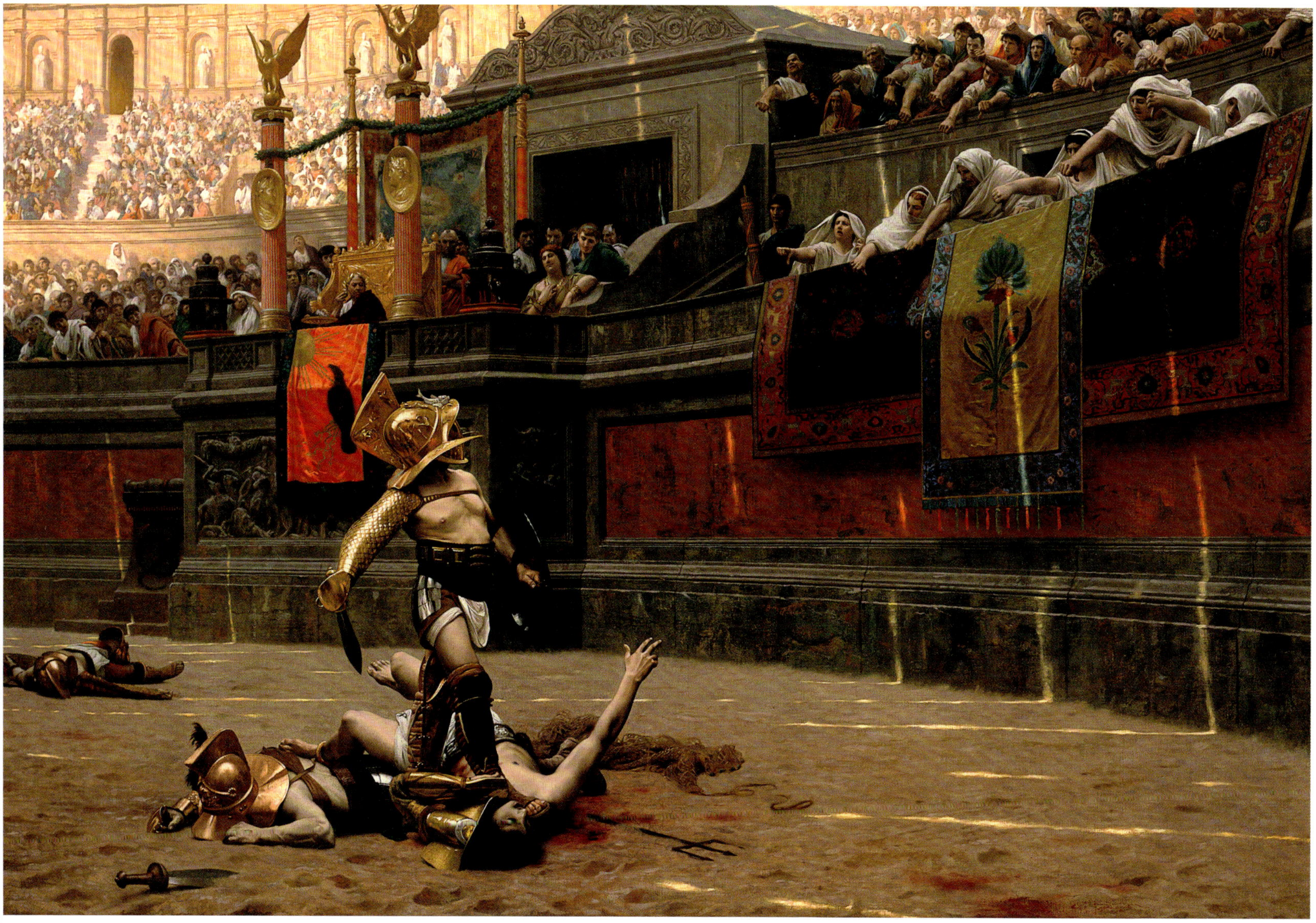

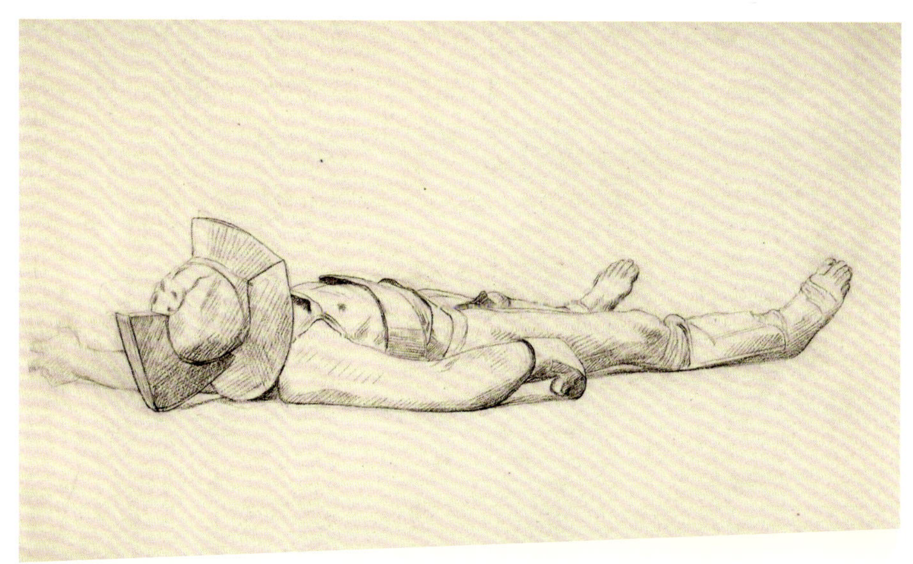

Cat. 73

MIRMILLO

–

ca. 1859–73
Bronze
15 ½ × 5 ¼ × 5 in.
Signed in cursive on the base: *J.L. Gerome*
Phoenix Art Museum, Museum Purchase, Phoenix, Arizona, inv. 1979.47

–

Bibliography: G. Ackerman, *Jean-Léon Gérôme* (Courbevoie: ACR Édition, 2000), no. S. 6 B. *Alma-Tadema e la nostalgia dell'antico*, exh. cat. (Naples: Museo Archeologico Nazionale, 2007-8), n. 34, p. 216. S. Harent and C. Stoullig, *Dessins de Jean-Léon Gérôme: la collection du musée des Beaux-Arts de Nancy*, exh. cat. (Nancy: Musée des Beaux-Arts, 2009), pp. 63–64.

Cat. 74

RETIARIUS

–

1859
Bronze
15 ¾ × 6 × 5 ¾ in.
Signed in cursive on the base: *J.L. Gerome*
Phoenix Art Museum, Museum Purchase, Phoenix, Arizona, inv. 1979.46

–

Bibliography: G. Ackerman, *Jean-Léon Gérôme* (Courbevoie: ACR Édition, 2000), no. S. 5. H. Lafont-Couturier, *Gérôme and Goupil: Art and Enterprise*, exh. cat., trans. I. Ollivier (Bordeaux: Musée Goupil, 2000–1; also New York: Dahesh Museum of Art, 2001, and Pittsburgh: The Frick Art & Historical Center, 2001), p. 52. *Alma-Tadema e la nostalgia dell'antico*, exh. cat. (Naples: Museo Archeologico Nazionale, 2007-8), no. 33, p. 216.

Ill. 62. Pair of gladiator's greaves, third quarter of the first century A.D., bronze, 22 ⅝ × 3 ¾ to 6 ½ × 7 ¼ in., Département des Antiquités grecques, étrusques et romaines, Musée du Louvre, Paris, inv. Br 1169-1170.

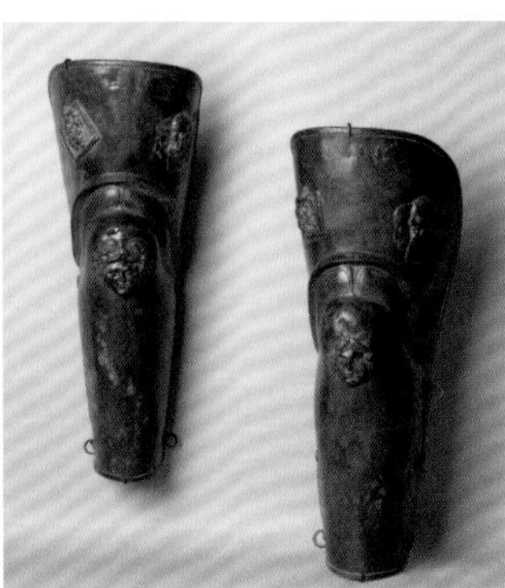

Cat. 75

MODEL FOR *THE GLADIATORS*

–

ca. 1877–78
Wax, gilt traces, wood
7 ½ × 4 ½ × 4 in.
Signed: *J.L. GEROME*; inscription on the base: *à Albert Goupil*
Private collection

–

Provenance: The artist's family.

–

Bibliography: G. Ackerman, *Jean-Léon Gérôme* (Courbevoie: ACR Édition, 2000), no. S. 9.

Cat. 76

THE GLADIATORS

–

1878
Bronze
19 ¾ × 13 ⅜ × 11 ¾ in.
Unsigned, undated
Ny Carlsberg Glyptotek Copenhagen, deed of gift from the artist to Carl Jacobsen, 1885, inv. I. N. 566

–

Bibliography: P. Leroi, "Musées en plein vent," *L'Art*, 1894–1900, p. 1014. L. Ménard, "La sculpture à l'Exposition Universelle de 1878," *L'Art*, vol. XVI (1879), p. 264. A. de Montaiglon, "La Sculpture à l'exposition de 1878," *Gazette des Beaux-Arts*, Sept. 1, 1879, p. 333. "Chronique. France," *Revue des Arts décoratifs*, 1881, vol. II, p. 26. J. Buisson, "Le Salon de 1881. 3e Article. La sculpture," *Gazette des Beaux-Arts*, 1881, pp. 215–16. L. Dubosc de Pesquidoux, *L'Art au dix-neuvième siècle (Première série). L'Art dans les deux mondes. Peinture et Sculpture (1878)*, vol. 1: *France, Belgique, Hollande, Espagne, Italie, Grèce* (Paris: Plon, 1881), pp. 237–39. A. Acker, Vogel, Habert-Dys, Orazi and Fraikin, "J.-L. Gérôme (notes biographiques)," in *Les Contemporains célèbres* (Paris: 1904), n.p. F. Masson, "Notes et fragments de J.-L. Gérôme", *Les Arts*, no. 26 (Feb. 1904), pp. 26–27. G. Bal, "Au jour le jour dans les ateliers," *New York Herald*, Mar. 3, 1905, n.p. "Echos des Arts," *L'Art et les artistes*, Apr. 1, 1905, p. VII. "Growls. The Captain of our Fate: A Monster in Human Shape", *The Sketch*, Mar. 26, 1913, p. 374. C. V. Petersen, *Ny Carlsberg Glyptotek. Fortegnelse over Kunsvaerkerne i den moderne Afdeilng* (Copenhagen, 1927), no. 675. P. Fauré-Fremiet, *Frémiet. Les Maîtres de l'art* (Paris: Plon, 1934), p. 63. G. Ackerman et al., *Jean-Léon Gérôme (1824–1904)*, exh. cat. (Dayton: Dayton Art Institute, 1972; also Minneapolis: Minneapolis Institute of Arts, 1973, and Baltimore: The Walters Art Gallery, 1973), pp. 44, 68–69. G. Ackerman, "Gérôme's Sculpture: The Problems of Realist Sculpture," *Arts Magazine*, Feb. 1986, pp. 82–84. G. Bresc and A. Pingeot, *Sculptures des jardins du Louvre, du Carrousel et des Tuileries* (Paris: RMN, 1986), pp. 143, 188–189, 220–223. A. Le Normand-Romain, "Une politique de regroupement des collections d'Orsay. Retours des dépôts, attributions de l'État et de dépôts consentis au musée," *La Revue du Louvre et des Musées de France*, 1986, no. 6, p. 411. J. Hargrove, *Les Statues de Paris* (Paris: Albin Michel, 1989), pp. 175, 236–237. G. Lacambre, *Les Ateliers d'artistes* (Paris: Hachette/RMN, 1991), p. 23. J. P. Munk and H. Reenberg, *Catalogue. French Sculpture 1* (Copenhagen: Ny Carlsberg Glyptotek, 1993), no. 152, pp. 234–35. G. Bresc-Bautier and X. Dectot, *Art et politique? Arcs, statues et colonnes de Paris* (Paris: Action artistique de la Ville de Paris, 1999). G. Ackerman, *Jean-Léon Gérôme* (Courbevoie: ACR Édition, 2000), no. S. 9 B2. F. Rionnet "Goupil et Gérôme: regards croisés sur l'édition sculptée," in H. Lafont-Couturier, *Gérôme & Goupil. Art et entreprise*, exh. cat. (Bordeaux: Musée Goupil, 2000–1; also New York: Dahesh Museum of Art, 2001, and Pittsburgh: The Frick Art & Historical Center, 2001), pp. 49, 52–53.

Cat. 77

Aimé Morot (1850–1913)
and Jean-Léon Gérôme

GÉRÔME EXECUTING *THE GLADIATORS.* MONUMENT TO GÉRÔME

–

1878–1905
Bronze
141 ¾ × 71 ¾ × 67 in.
Marked on the back of the gladiators: *J.L. Gérôme. Fonte à la cire perdue par E. Gonon 1878*; marked on the back of the lower base: *Aimé Morot. Fonte à la cire perdue A.A. Hébrard*
Musée d'Orsay, Paris, inv. RF 3517

–

Provenance: Monument commissioned in 1905; Aimé Morot, Gérôme's son-in-law, incorporated the original group of *The Gladiators*, which remained in the artist's studio. Jardin de l'Infante, Louvre, 1909. French government, 1967. On loan to Fort du Mont-Valérien, Suresnes, 1969–80. Allocated to the Musée d'Orsay, 1980… entered the Musée d'Orsay, 1986.

–

Exhibition History: Exposition Universelle, Paris, 1878. Salon des Arts Décoratifs, 1882, Paris.

–

Bibliography: *J.-L. Gérôme*, exh. cat. (Vesoul: Musée Georges-Garret, 1981), p. 180. H. Lafont-Couturier, *Gérôme* (Paris: Herscher, 1998), p. 114. G. Ackerman, *Jean-Léon Gérôme* (Courbevoie: ACR Edition, 2000), S. 9 B1.

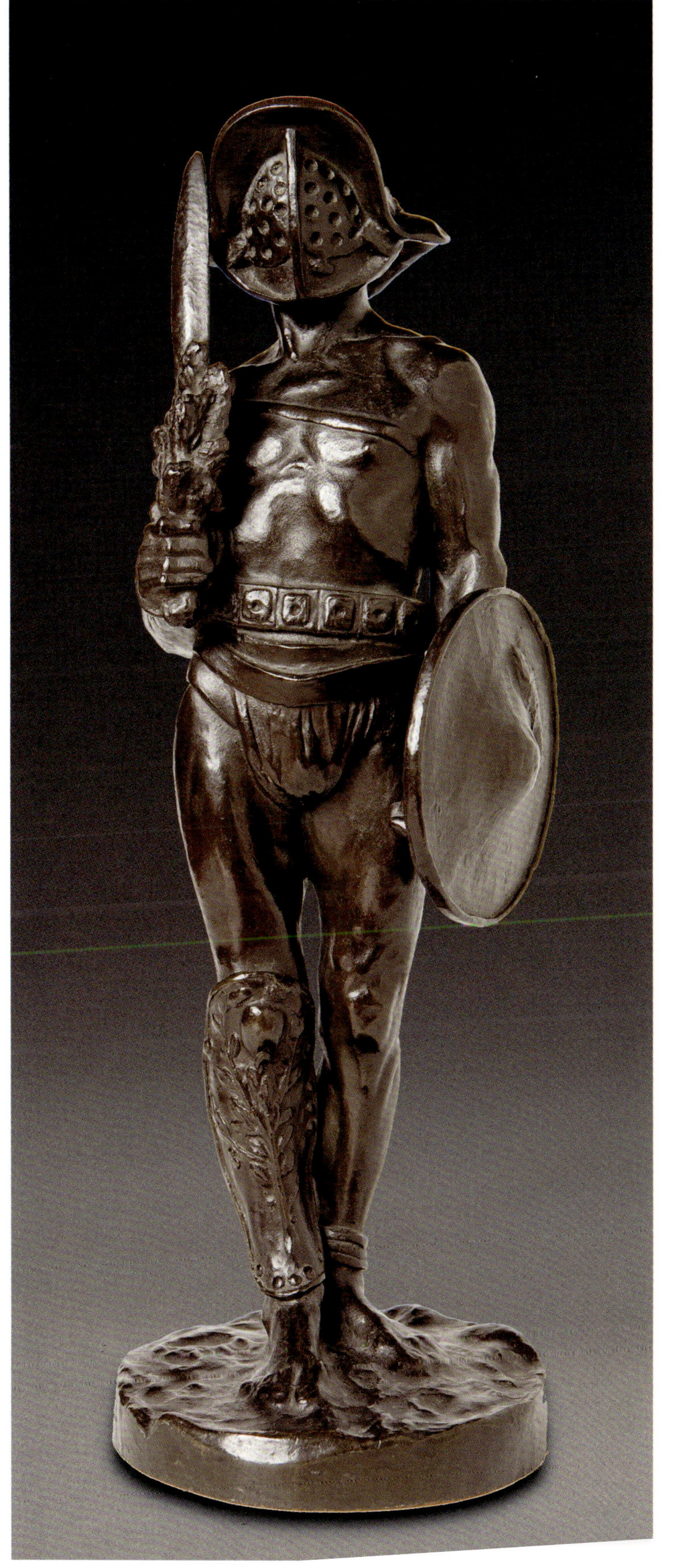

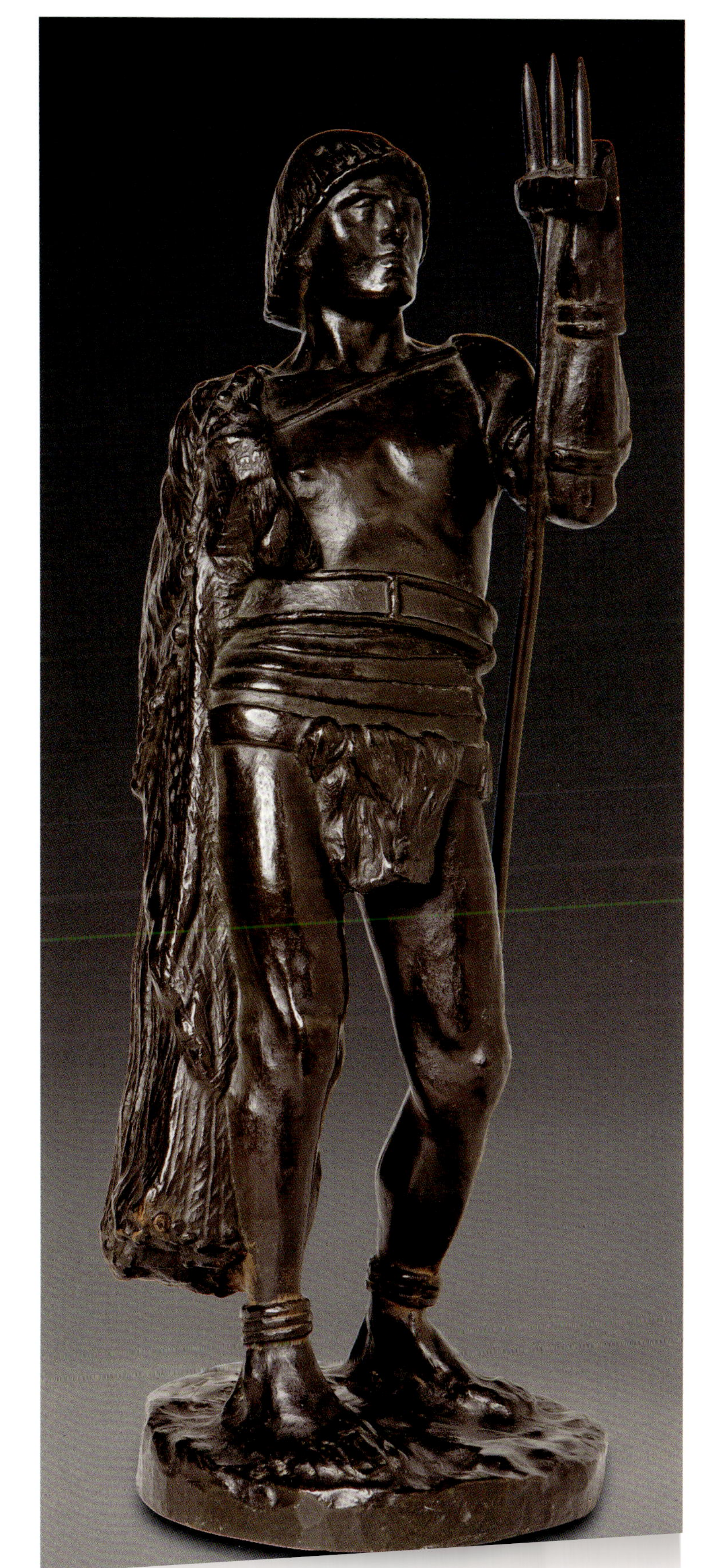

Right from his early visits to the museum in Naples, Gérôme had been fascinated by the armor of gladiators discovered in the seventeenth century in Pompeii, the forms of which were lesser known than the military harnessing, and gave their bearers "a barbarian aspect, savage and strange."[1] He was the first to seek to represent gladiatorial equipment with a concern for exactitude. The *Mirmillo* (cat. 73) and the *Retiarius* (cat. 74) were modeled to create the figures for *Ave Caesar* (cat. 70); the *Retiarius* meanwhile was based on a Roman statuette conserved at the Cabinet des Médailles in the Bibliothèque Nationale de France in Paris. While the representations of these circus warriors of a new inspiration were "remarkable in terms of the harmony established between the subject's strength and sensitivity and of the search for style,"[2] Gérôme expressed his dissatisfaction, several years afterwards, with the archaeological precision of their rendering. Nearly twenty years later, *The Gladiators* group, slightly larger than life, cast by Gonon using the lost-wax process, became the three-dimensional translation of the central motif in *Pollice Verso* (cat. 71). *The Gladiators* was a long-contemplated work, and the first "official" sculpture exhibited by Gérôme. It it was displayed in the entrance vestibule of the Exposition Universelle of 1878: the painter-turned-sculptor had already established his career and did not want to take up space reserved for his younger colleagues.[3] He amusingly recounted some years later, "everyone shook the hand of the vanquished gladiator and the statue was returned with one completely shiny hand; all the patina had disappeared."[4] The work was remarked upon, but met with a mixed reception. For some, the statue was "stranger than it was large" and criticized for its excessive faithfulness in the reconstruction of the costume, which had distorted the proportion of the figures: not only did "archaeology crush art,"[5] but the vanquished gladiator recalled the "dry and awkward painting that the artist had just left behind. His inexperience was revealed especially in the nudes, which lacked mass and breadth"[6]; another speculated that "the small clay or wax model was probably better than the enlargement."[7] Gérôme had carefully studied the accessories, helmets, shoulder plates and greaves (ill.62), thanks to the antique originals in the Pourtalès collection held by the Musée du Louvre, developing his desire for precision to the point of purchasing electroplated copies from other originals from the National Museum of Naples[8]—the *mirmillo* helmet is visible on a shelf in *The End of the Seance* (cat. 176). As faithfully magnified as these accessories were by the slightly oversized scale of the figures (some considered that they "looked like deep-sea divers"[9]), they struggled to convince critics. The eccentricities of the Roman Empire may have also lacked the moral backing of *Néo-Grec* archaism. Few critics acknowledged the novelty of the subject: one, somewhat treacherously, noted "something strange: there is in this unrivaled group more movement, effect, and character than in the artist's painting."[10] Léonce Dubosc de Pesquidoux was alone in admiring *The Gladiators*: "blunter perhaps than the works of experienced sculptors, they are picturesque in their mass; they have a demeanor and an individual style that is worth more than polish and preciosity."[11] Gérôme managed however to create a group of a particularly effective construction, where the most violent visual effect is not the plea for mercy of the vanquished *retiarius*, pinned down by his adversary, his arm shooting out sideward to great effect, so much as the monumental inhumanity of the *mirmillo*, a faceless killing machine. The group had been placed in the garden of Gérôme's residence in Bougival. After his death, as a final episode in the work's eternal game of cross-referencing between painting and sculpture, Aimé Morot, his son-in-law, responsible for the commemorative monument, had the idea of including *The Gladiators* with a figure of Gérôme as he liked to represent himself: at work (cat. 77). The reduced version shown in this exhibition—the only existing copy according to Gerald Ackerman—was given by Gérôme in 1885 to Carl Jacobsen, the founder of the Ny Carlsberg Glyptotek in Copenhagen. **É. P.**

1. J.-L. Gérôme, *Notes autobiographiques* [1874], ed. G. Ackerman, (Vesoul: S.A.L.S.A., 1981), p. 12. **2.** J. Buisson, "Le Salon de 1881. 3e article. La Sculpture," *Gazette des Beaux-Arts*, 1881, 2, p. 215. **3.** F. Masson, "Notes et fragments de J.-L. Gérôme," *Les Arts*, no. 26 (Feb. 1904), p. 31. **4.** Ibid., p. 31. Roughly ten years later, Gérôme produced a *Rétiaire appelant au combat* (plaster, Musée Georges-Garret, Vesoul). **5.** J. Buisson 1881 (as in n. 2). **6.** Ibid., p. 216. **7.** A. de Montaiglon, "La Sculpture à l'exposition de 1878. La Sculpture," *Gazette des Beaux-Arts*, Sept. 1, 1878, p. 333. **8.** See the excellent article by C. Bastien, "'L'armure de gladiateur' de la collection Pourtalès conservée au Louvre," *La Revue des musées de France. Revue du Louvre*, vol. 54, no. 4 (Oct. 2004), pp. 44–52. **9.** P. Leroi, "Musées en plein vent," *L'Art*, 1894–1900, p. 1014. **10.** T. Véron, "Beaux-Arts. Les peintres-sculpteurs et les sculpteurs-peintres," *Revue du Lyonnais*, ser. 4, no. 8 (1879), p. 461. **10.** L. Dubosc de Pesquidoux, *Art au XIXe siècle. Première série. L'Art dans les Deux Mondes. Peinture et sculpture (1878)*, vol. 1: *France, Belgique, Hollande, Espagne, Italie, Grèce* (Paris: Plon, 1881), pp. 238–39.

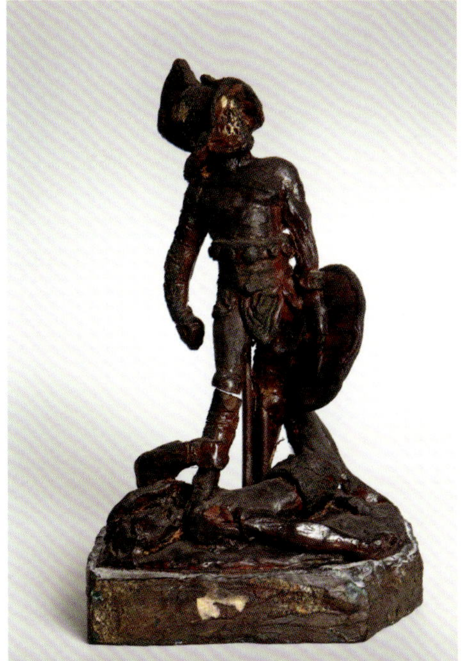

Cat. 75

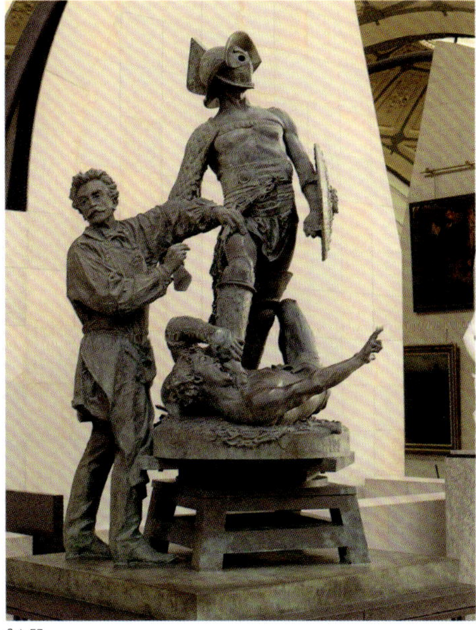

Cat. 77

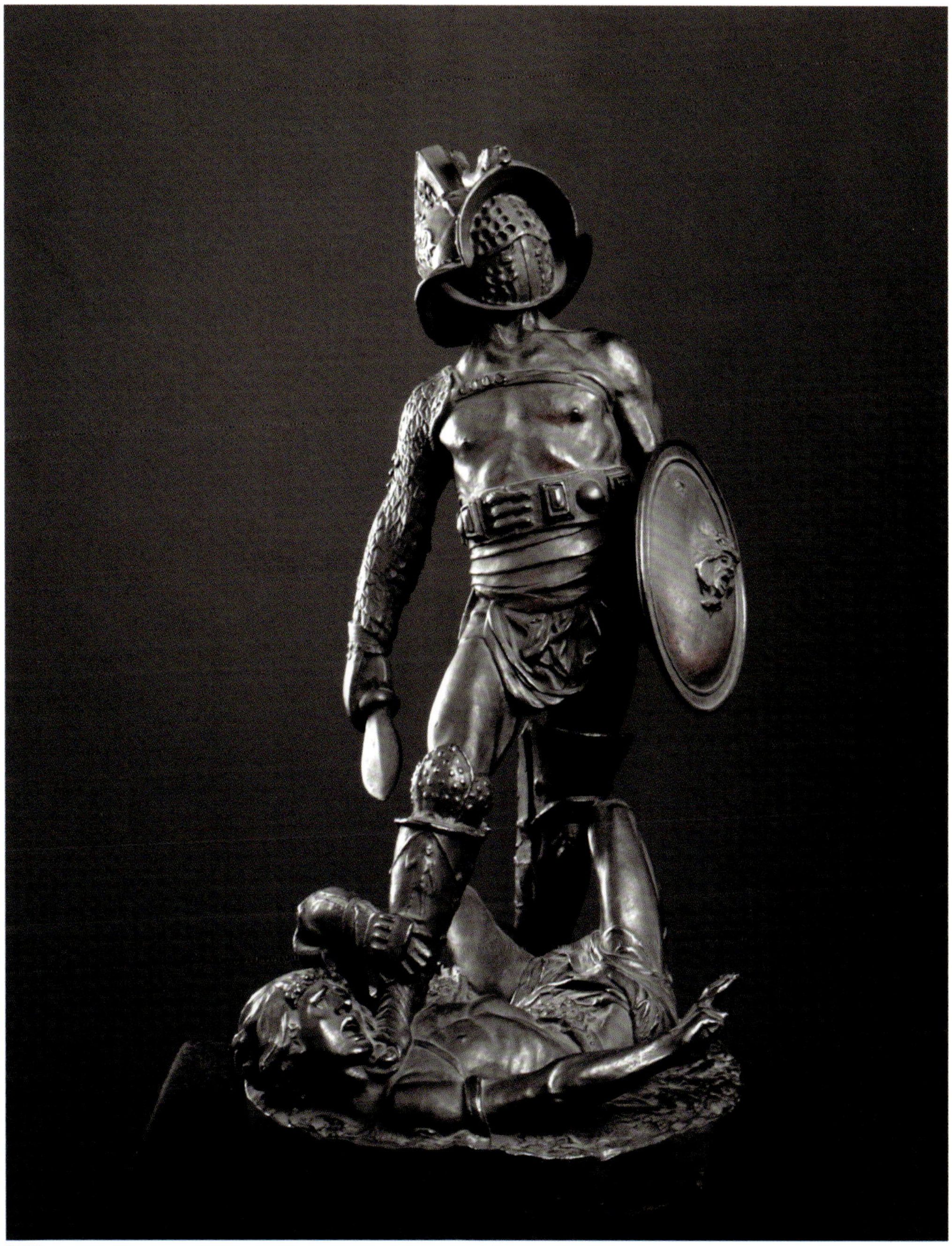

Cat. 76

Cat. 78

GOLGOTHA, ALSO KNOWN AS CONSUMMATUM EST, OR JERUSALEM

–

1867
Oil on canvas
32 × 57 ½ in.
Signed lower left: *J.L. GEROME*
Musée d'Orsay, Paris, inv. RF 1990 7

–

Provenance: Goupil & Cie, Paris, 1871. Goupil to Knoedler, New York, 1871. Henry N. Smith. T. B. Musgrave. James St. Lawrence O'Toole, New York. Private collection, California. Christie's, New York, Mar. 1, 1990, no. 84. Acquired by the Musée d'Orsay, 1990.

–

Exhibition History: Salon of 1868, Paris, no. 1072. Brooklyn Art Association, Mar. 1873, no. 241. Union League Club, New York, Jan. 26, 1875, no. 6. National Academy of Design, New York, 1876, no. 300.

–

Bibliography: E. About, "Le Salon de 1868," *Revue des deux mondes*, vol. LXXV (June 1868), pp. 728–29. L. Auvray, "Expositions des beaux-arts. Salon de 1868," *Revue artistique et littéraire*, vol. 14 (1868), pp. 222–23. A. du Belloy, "Promenade à l'exposition des beaux-arts," *Le Correspondant*, vol. 38, no. 5 (June 10, 1868), pp. 697–98. C. Blanc, *Le Temps*, May 19, 1868. F. Boissin, *Salon de 1868. Études artistiques* (Paris: 1868), pp. 69–70. B. Bouniol, "L'Amateur au Salon. 1868," *Revue du monde catholique*, vol. 21, no. 4 (May 25, 1868), pp. 568–69. A. Cantaloube, "Salon de 1868," *Le Monde illustré*, vol. 22, no. 582 (June 6, 1868). E. Chesneau, *Le Constitutionnel*, no. 126 (May 5, 1868). H. Fouquier, "Salon de 1868," *L'Avenir national*, May 5, 1868. T. Gautier, *Le Moniteur officiel*, May 2, 1868, p. 585. G. Lafenestre, "L'art au Salon de 1868," *Revue contemporaine*, vol. 63 (May–June 1868), pp. 521–25. C. Lavergne [Louis Veuillot], "Beaux-Arts. Exposition de 1868," *L'Univers*, May 21, 1868. L. Leroy, "Session du Salon de 1868," *Le Charivari*, May 14, 1868. P. Mantz, "Salon de 1868. Tableaux reproduits par *L'Illustration*," *L'Illustration*, May 2, 1868. M. de Montifaud, "La peinture d'histoire au Salon de 1868," *L'Artiste*, June 1868, pp. 401–2. A. Nettement, "Salon de 1868," *La Semaine des familles*, no. 34 (May 23, 1868), pp. 542–43. É. Palma, "Salon de 1868," *Revue de Paris*, vol. XI, pp. 414–15. P. Petroz, "Salon de 1868," *Revue moderne*, vol. 46, no. 2 (May 10, 1868), p. 362. H. Rochefort, "Le Salon cette année," *Le Figaro*, May 20, 1868, p. 162. P. de Saint-Victor, *La Liberté*, May 13, 1868. W. Bürger [Théophile Thoré], "Salon de 1868," in *Salons de W. Bürger, 1861 à 1868* (Paris, 1870), vol. 2, pp. 466–69. M. Chaumelin, *L'Art contemporain* (Paris, 1873), pp. 115–18. F. F. Hering, *Gérôme. The Life and Works of Jean-Léon Gérôme* (New York: Cassell, 1892), pp. 204–8. M. Poprzecka, "Le sacré au Salon," in *Saloni, gallerie, musei e loro influenza sullo sviluppo dell'arte dei secoli XIXe e XXe* (Bologna: Clueb, 1979), p. 52. J.-L. Gérôme, *Notes autobiographiques* [1874], ed. G. Ackerman (Vesoul: S.A.L.S.A., 1981), p. 16. B. Foucart, *Le Renouveau de la peinture religieuse en France (1800–1860)* (Paris: Arthéna, 1987), p. 327. *De Manet à Matisse, 7 ans d'enrichissement au Musée d'Orsay*, exh. cat. (Paris, Musée d'Orsay, 1990–91), p. 61. "Album de voyage des artistes en expédition au pays du Levant" (the diary of Willem de Famars Testas), in *Album de voyage des artistes en expédition au pays du Levant*, exh. cat. (Tel Aviv: Tel Aviv Art Museum, also Bayonne: Musée Bonnat, and Paris: Musée Hébert, 1993), no. 38. F. Leeman, "Shadows over Jean-Léon Gérôme's Career," *Van Gogh Museum Journal*, 1998, pp. 88–99. H. Lafont-Couturier, *Gérôme* (Paris: Herscher, 1998), pp. 62–63. *Dream and Reality: Collections of the Musée d'Orsay*, exh. cat. (Kobe: Kobe City Museum of Art, 1999; also Tokyo: National Museum of Western Art, 1999), no. 11. G. Ackerman, *Jean-Léon Gérôme* (Courbevoie: ACR Édition, 2000), no. 169.2. H. Lafont-Couturier, *Gérôme & Goupil. Art et entreprise*, exh. cat. (Bordeaux: Musée Goupil, 2000–1; also New York: Dahesh Museum of Art, 2001; Pittsburgh: The Frick Art & Historical Center, 2001), cat. 31, pp. 21, 25, 37, 40, 88, 90–91, 158, 166. *Pierre Loti, l'Oriental*, exh. cat. (Paris: Musée de la Vie Romantique, 2006).

Ill. 63. *View of Jerusalem*, 1864, oil on canvas, Private collection.

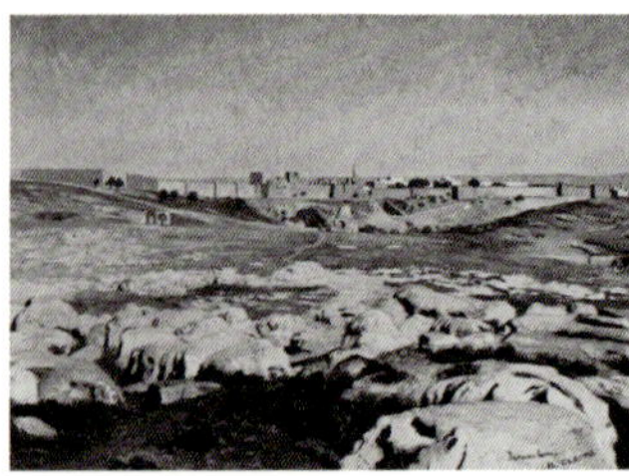

Ill. 64. Auguste Salzmann (1824–1872), *Jerusalem: The Temple Wall, Overall View of the East End*, 1854, salt print from paper negative, 9 × 13 in., Musée d'Orsay, Paris, inv. PHO 1982 113.

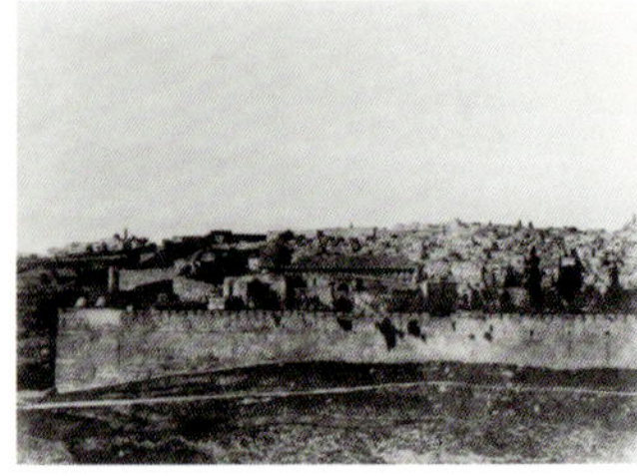

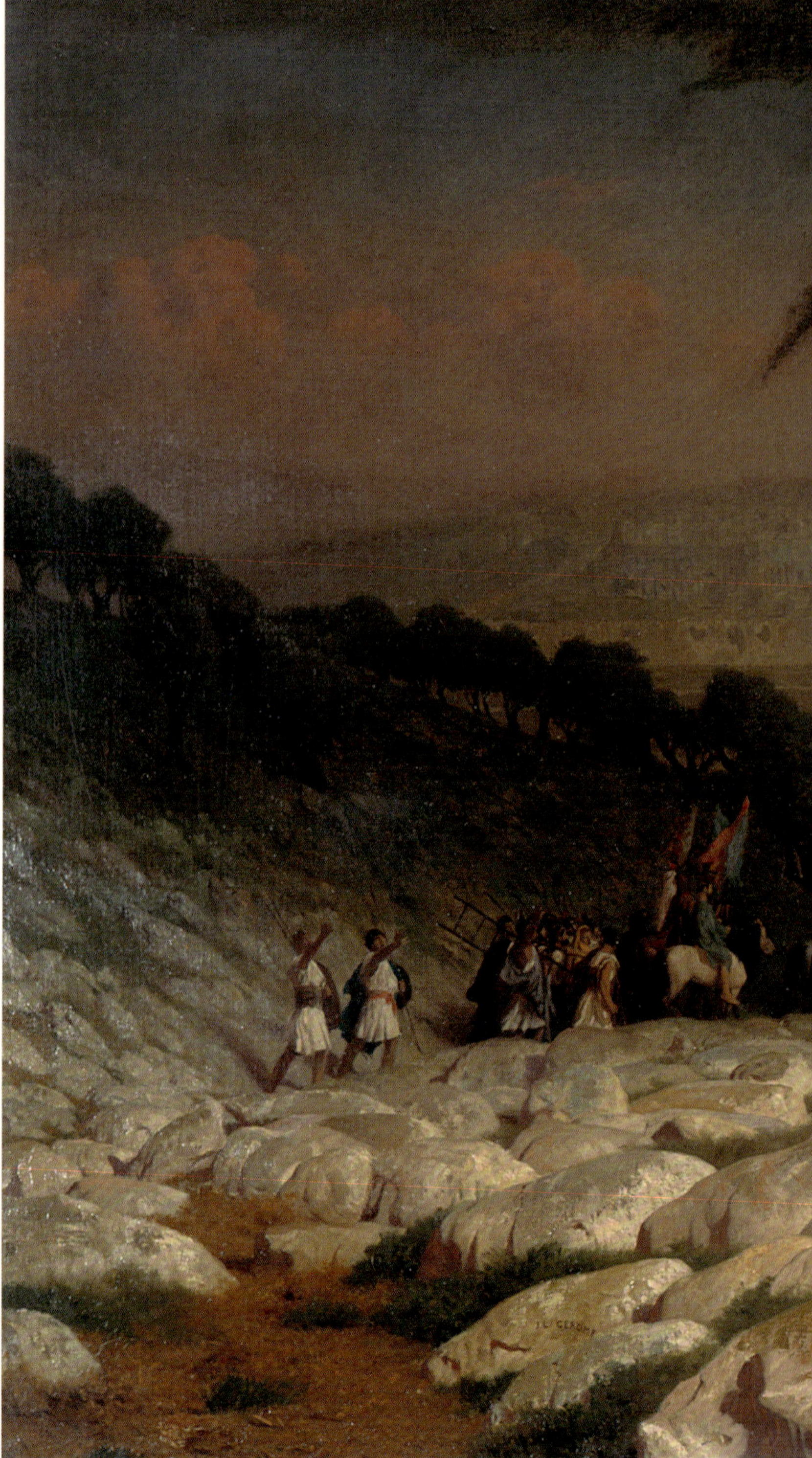

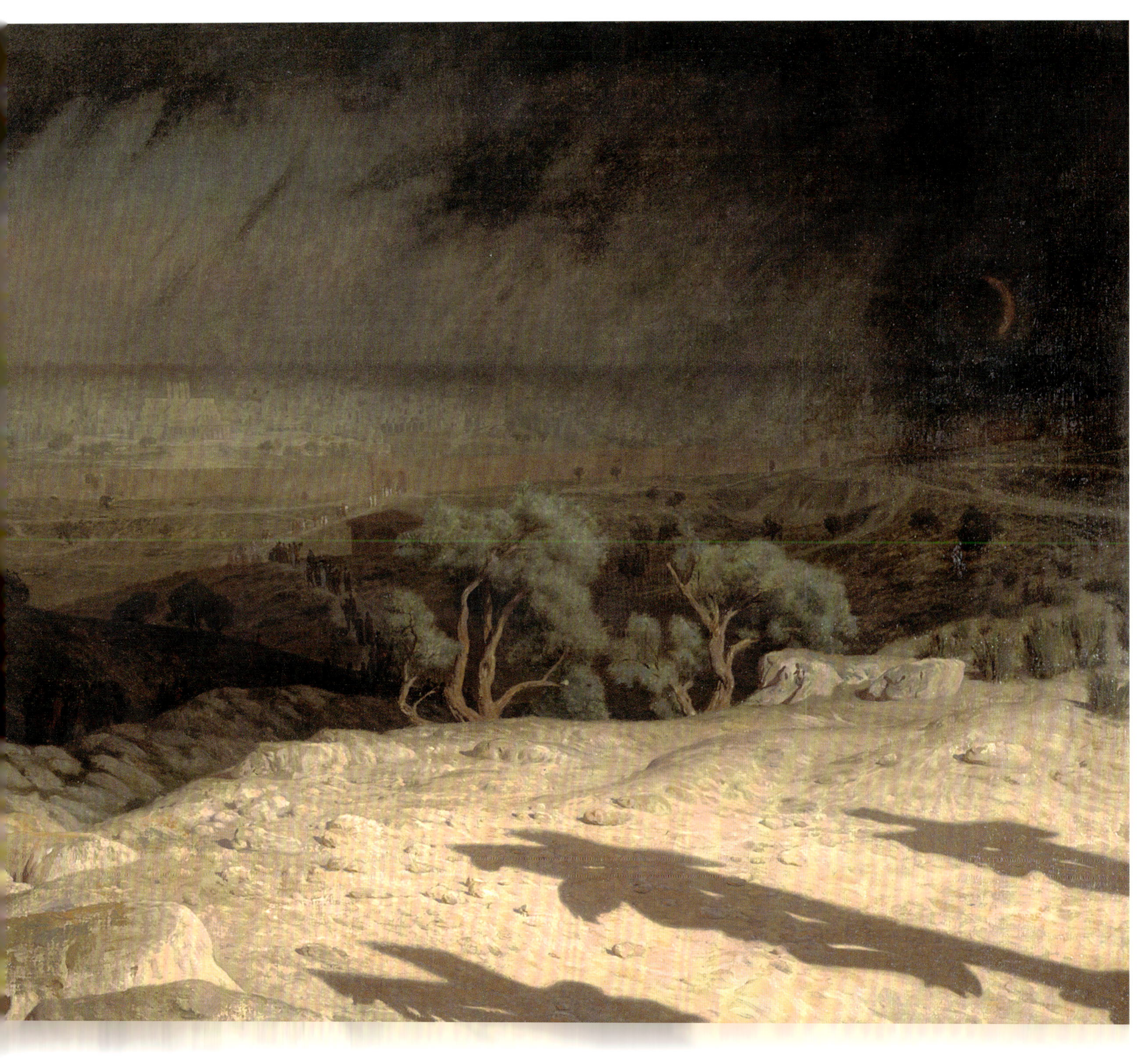

Gérôme's two major entries to the Salon of 1868, *Golgotha* and *The Death of Marshal Ney* (cat. 93) drew some of the most severe criticism of his entire career. In his *Notes autobiographiques*, the painter recalls with a certain bitterness the incomprehension that greeted his attempt to put a fresh slant on religious imagery: "People were amazed that I had turned Christ and the thieves into mere shadows. I had broken with ancient, venerated traditions. And yet I do believe that this Crucifixion scene had a certain poetry, a new way of expressing its subject that belonged very much to the field of painting. But this innovation was not to everyone's taste, as I was indeed made to understand."[1] As for strict history painting, Gérôme's efforts and originality in the religious sphere rested on a highly personal alchemy between a concern for archaeological veracity and an innate theatrical sense that indeed often led him to take liberties with historical reality. Gérôme knew Jerusalem, having traveled there in 1862 and attended the Easter service in the Church of the Holy Sepulcher. In his *Notes*, the painter offers a description of the surrounding landscape that sheds much light on the painting under consideration here: "It is a desolate land, with stones everywhere, scant vegetation, scrawny, tempest-tortured olive trees, but it is not a banal place, and once you have seen it you cannot forget it."[2] His account also describes a "fearsome storm"[3] that broke out over the Holy City, foreshadowing the violent sky here, in these final moments of the Passion. But this did not prevent Gérôme from reconfiguring the topography of the site by transposing in most unlikely fashion a view of Jerusalem executed from the west onto what appears to be an evocation of the Mount of Olives (ill. 63).[4] To help him recreate a plausible general view, Gérôme could have availed himself of photographs such as those of Félix Bonfils or Auguste Salzmann (ill. 64); however, by moving Golgotha to the other side of Jerusalem, he could also stage the Crucifixion in a much more spectacular way. For what "M. Gérôme's photographic eye"[5] gives us here is indeed a drama. The details of the canonical account are certainly in place: the two Roman soldiers, Longinus and Stephaton, who will be the first converts, making their way off; the temple of Venus in the middle distance, and the monumental Temple of Jerusalem in the background. Further, in keeping with the classical tradition, the landscape contributes fully to the action. However, the figure of Christ is seen only as a cast shadow, pushed off to the right of the composition and flanked by the truncated silhouettes of the two thieves. Four years after the publication of Ernest Renan's *La Vie de Jésus* and the debates that it provoked, Gérôme was making his own contribution to a realistic vision of the religious story. And he met with failure: "The original and odd idea of indicating the gibbets that we do not see"[6] disappointed many, and brought down the wrath of Catholic critics: "Veuillot hurled his thunderbolts at me from on high at *L'Univers*."[7] Edmond About and Théophile Gautier, who for once were rather indifferent to Gérôme's efforts, quite failed to grasp the painting's point: "perhaps the idea here is too ingeniously literary for painting ... The effect of this composition is strange and confuses the judgment ... The best title one could give it would be: Picturesque Historical Picture."[8] Albeit in his own ironic vein, André Gill was one of the very few observers who saw *Golgotha* as something other than an exception in Gérôme's oeuvre and understood its fundamental connection with his other large-scale canvases. Gill satirically put his finger on the echoes found throughout the painter's work by turning the shadows of the crosses into decorations and by starting a series entitled *Décès célèbres* (Famous Deaths) which ended with the painter's own death (ill. 65). The off-center composition, the presentation of the victim's racked body, radically foreshortened in the foreground, while his killers move away into smallness and insignificance, are figures of style that link *The Death of Caesar* (cat. 67), *The Death of Marshal Ney*, and *Golgotha* in the gloomy dramaturgy composed at this time by the generally misunderstood champion of the effort to revitalize history painting. **L. C.**

Ill. 65. André Gill [Louis-Alexandre Gosset de Guines] (1840–1885), *Golgotha* by Gérôme, caricature in *Le Salon pour rire* (Paris, 1868), p. 3, Musée d'Orsay, Paris, documentation.

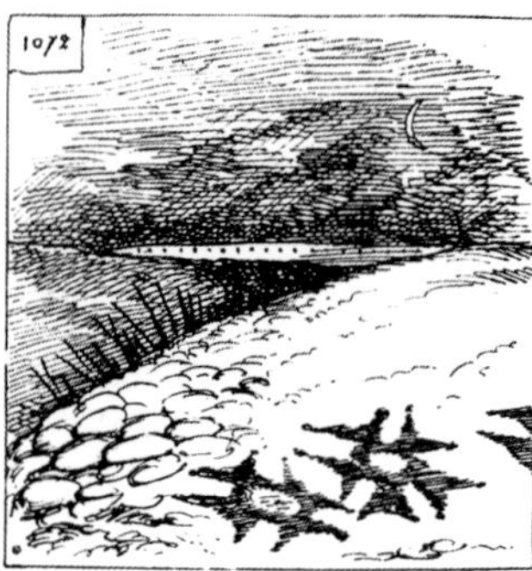

1. J.-L. Gérôme, *Notes autobiographiques* [1874], ed. G. Ackerman (Vesoul: S.A.L.S.A., 1981), pp. 16, 18. **2.** Ibid., p. 15. **3.** Ibid., p. 14. **4.** On this point, see F. Leeman, "Shadows over Jean-Léon Gérôme's Career," *Van Gogh Museum Journal*, 1998, p. 92. **5.** É. Galichon, "M. Gérôme. Peintre ethnographe," *Gazette des Beaux-Arts*, no. 24 (Feb. 1868), p. 151. **6.** T. Gautier, *Le Moniteur officiel*, May 2, 1868, p. 585. **7.** F. Masson, "Notes et fragments de J.-L. Gérôme," *Les Arts*, no. 26 (Feb. 1904), p. 26. **8.** T. Gautier (as in n. 10).

Cat. 79

STUDY FOR *THE CHRISTIAN MARTYRS' LAST PRAYERS*

–

1883
Pencil on green paper
10 × 14 ½ in.
Signed on the left: *J.L.Gérôme*
Musée des Beaux-Arts, Nancy,
inv. TH.99.15.4318

–

Provenance: Galerie Paul Prouté, autumn 1973, cat. 58, p. 118. Anonymous donation to the Musée des Beaux-Arts, 1999.

–

Bibliography: S. Harent and C. Stoullig, *Dessins de Jean-Léon Gérôme: la collection du musée des Beaux-Arts de Nancy*, exh. cat. (Nancy: Musée des Beaux-Arts, 2009), cat. 19, pp. 66–67.

Cat. 80

THE CHRISTIAN MARTYRS' LAST PRAYERS

–

1863-1883
Oil on canvas
34 ⅝ × 59 ⅛ in.
Signed lower left
The Walters Art Museum, Baltimore,
inv. 37.113

–

Provenance: Gérôme to Goupil, 1883. Goupil to Schaus in New York on behalf of William T. Walters of Baltimore, Maryland, 1883 (for 85,000 francs). Lined in 1967.

–

Bibliography: E. Strahan [Earl Shinn], *Gérôme: A Collection of the Works of J. L. Gérôme in One Hundred Photogravures* (New York: Samuel L. Hall, 1881). G. Ackerman et al., *Jean-Léon Gérôme (1824–1904)*, exh. cat. (Dayton: Dayton Art Institute, 1972; also Minneapolis: Minneapolis Institute of Arts, 1973; and Baltimore: The Walters Art Gallery, 1973), no. 36, pp. 86–87. *Romans and Barbarians*, exh. cat. (Boston: Museum of Fine Arts, 1976–77), no. 282. W. R. Johnston, *The Nineteenth Century Paintings in the Walters Art Gallery* (Baltimore: Trustees of the Walters Art Gallery, 1982), no. 108. E. M. Zafran, *French Salon Painting From Southern Collections*, exh. cat. (Atlanta: High Museum of Art, 1983), no. 36. G. Ackerman, *Jean-Léon Gérôme* (Courbevoie: ACR Édition, 2000), no. 313. H. Lafont-Couturier, *Gérôme and Goupil: Art and Enterprise*, exh. cat., trans. I. Ollivier (Bordeaux: Musée Goupil, 2000–1; also New York: Dahesh Museum of Art, 2001, and Pittsburgh: The Frick Art & Historical Center, 2001), pp. 25, 43, 105–107, 161. S. Harent and C. Stoullig, *Dessins de Jean-Léon Gérôme: la collection du musée des Beaux-Arts de Nancy*, exh. cat. (Nancy: Musée des Beaux-Arts, 2009), p. 66.

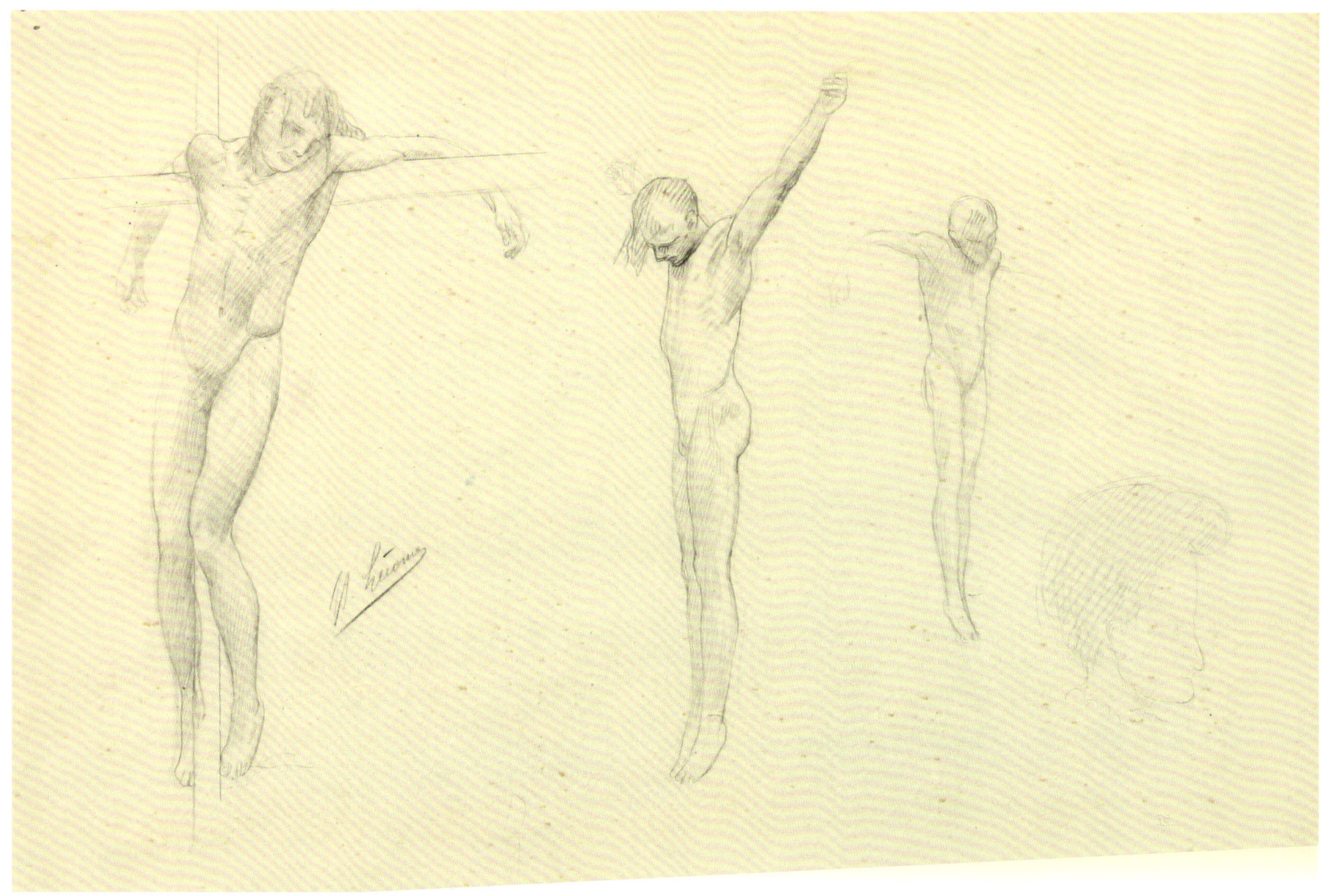

This large painting features a highly dramatic event in Roman history, namely the martyrdom of Christians under the emperor Nero after the burning of Rome in A.D. 64. It was one of a series of paintings and sculptures devoted to Roman games, begun by Gérôme in 1859. The first of the series, exhibited at the Salon of that year, was *Ave Caesar, morituri te salutant* (cat. 70). Work on *The Christian Martyrs' Last Prayers* took a long time, Gérôme having begun it in the early 1860s. In a letter dated July 15, 1883, addressed to the man who commissioned it, William T. Walters, the artist said that he had reworked the composition several times. He also added that, "I feel that this is one of my most thoughtful works, the one over which I have taken the most pains."

Gérôme was probably referring to the research he had done for this canvas. Yet while the artist displayed his usual concern for accuracy, here he also took liberties. Indeed, although the scene is supposedly set in the Circus Maximus—overlooked by the Palatine Hill in the distance—the shape of the amphitheater (distorted to give greater breadth to the scene) suggests the Colosseum. The figures of the martyrs, to be burned because charged with arson, required special attention from the artist, as witnessed by the study now in Nancy. Gérôme wrote, "In the middle ground I placed the figures about to be burned alive. They were usually strapped to crosses and smeared with pitch to fuel the flames."[1] Gérôme's determination to render their wounded poses and gestures, despite their small scale in the final composition, shows how faithful he was to academic practices.

The great success of this painting lies in its highly striking composition. The amphitheater seems to form a panorama with the beholder of the painting at its center. The handling of the spectators, barely sketched on their seats, like the dark outline of the Palatine Hill, also evoke the long, horizontal canvases of the illusionist spectacles known as "panoramas," highly fashionable in the Second Empire period.

The staggered planes in this picture were carefully thought out by Gérôme, allowing him to place in a single picture the various tortures to which the wretches were subjected. In the foreground is a haughty, if not apparently famished, lion who emerges from his cage beneath the amphitheater.[2] Behind it can be seen another lion and a tiger, calmly awaiting their turns to leap forth, as though subject to the artist's desire to control the pacing. In the middle ground, kneeling and mostly dressed in white tunics that signify their innocence (hence unjust deaths), the Christian martyrs are gathered around an elderly man whose handsome philosopher's head evokes Socrates. Face turned heavenward, the man seems to be indicating to his unfortunate companions that a better fate is awaiting them in the afterlife. Further back are the martyrs sentenced to be burned, their crosses lined parallel to the walls of the arena, ringing it. Determined to render time as well as space, Gérôme painted them in different stages of succumbing, so to speak, to the torch. On the left are the poor souls who are already alight, prey to the flames; in the middle the fires have just been lit; on the right the crucified figures wait for the executioner to arrive and do his job.

The overall effect constitutes a truly cruel but efficient depiction. Could it have been inspired by the early chronophotographic experiments of Eadweard Muybridge, who revealed the successive phases of human and animal locomotion? Muybridge's photographs were published in the United States in 1878, then reprinted in a French magazine, *La Nature*. They were noticed by Gérôme, his close friend Ernest Meissonnier, and Edgar Degas. The painter's artifice in introducing a sequential, measurable duration—along with the panoramic illusion—makes this canvas one of Gérôme's most "proto-cinematic" works. He presents the beholder not just with a painting but with a true spectacle, one whose scenic impact justified the liberties taken with archaeological accuracy.

This painting inspired Enrico Guazzoni when he shot *Quo Vadis?* in 1913, not to mention subsequent filmmakers who reprised the story. It is well known that, like Gérôme, many film directors are inspired by events in Roman history. The first ancient subject in the history of the movies was, in fact, a "reconstructed historical scene" based on two *tableaux vivants* showing "Nero testing poisons on slaves" (Georges Hatot, Établissements Frères Lumière, 1896, projected in September 1897).[3] **D. F.-R.**

1. G. Ackerman et al., *Jean-Léon Gérôme (1824-1904)*, exh. cat. (Dayton: Dayton Art Institute, 1972; also Minneapolis: Minneapolis Institute of Arts, 1973; and Baltimore: The Walters Art Gallery, 1973), p. 87. **2.** Apart from historical accuracy, the presence of the lion in the foreground also functions as a kind of self-quotation. Gérôme liked to recall the connection between his middle name, Léon, and the name of the king of beasts. He very often drew lions, as demonstrated by the recent exhibition in Nancy. **3.** On this subject, see Hervé Dumont's recent and valuable study, *L'Antiquité au cinéma* (Paris: Nouveau Monde Editions, 2009), pp. 478–98.

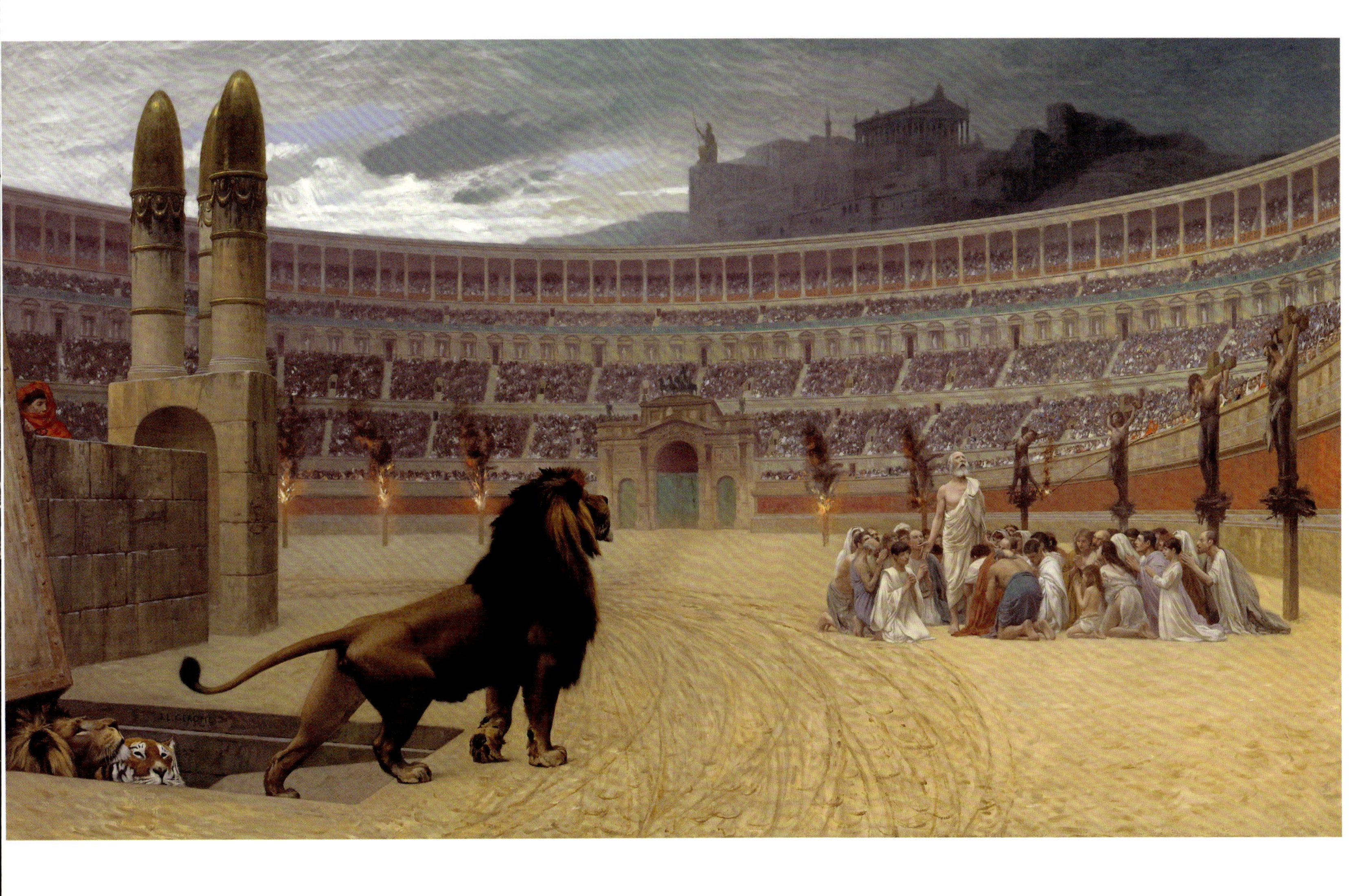

Cat. 81

GATHERING UP THE LIONS IN THE CIRCUS

–

1902
Oil on canvas
32 1/8 1/8 × 51 in.
Signed: *J.L. GEROME*
Private collection

–

Provenance: Schnittjer sale, Parke-Bernet, New York, 1943, sale 421. Charles Gudtradt. Anonymous sale, Christie's, New York, May 22, 1985, lot 167. Anonymous sale, Sotheby's, London, Nov. 22, 1988, lot 29. Donald Munson Esq. sale, Christie's, London, May 4, 1995, lot. 74. Private collection. *19th Century European Art and Orientalist and Spanish Art*, Christie's, London, July 2, 2008, lot 162. Private collection.

–

Exhibition History: Salon des Artistes français, Paris, 1902, no. 706.

–

Bibliography: *J.-L. Gérôme*, exh. cat. (Vesoul: Musée Georges-Garret, 1981), p. 20. G. Ackerman, *Jean-Léon Gérôme* (Courbevoie: ACR Édition, 2000), no. 469. I. Blom, *"Quo Vadis?* From Painting to Cinema and Everything in Between," in *La decima musa. Il cinema e le altri arti*, eds L. Quaresima and L. Vichi (Udine: Forum, 2001), pp. 281–92. R. Bigorne, "Visions de l'antique," in H. Lafont-Couturier, *Gérôme & Goupil. Art et entreprise*, exh. cat. (Bordeaux: Musée Goupil, 2000–1; also New York: Dahesh Museum of Art, 2001, and Pittsburgh: The Frick Art & Historical Center, 2001), pp. 104–7. E. M. Noorman, "Questa rovina viva: Pompei nella letteratura del secondo ottocento," in *Alma-Tadema e la nostalgia dell'antico*, exh. cat. (Naples: Museo Archeologico Nazionale, 2007), pp. 124–37.

In this late painting Gérôme returns to the theme of Christian martyrs nearly twenty years after his *The Christian Martyrs' Last Prayers* (cat. 80). The setting, as before in *Ave Caesar* (cat. 70) and *Pollice Verso* (cat. 71), is that of a composite arena somewhere between the historically accurate Circus Maximus and the dramatically more satisfying Colosseum, which Gérôme preferred to use for his scenes of Roman games (ill. 66). However, while the background is familiar, the tone itself has changed and the sparsely scattered spectators in the almost deserted tiers are observing the last moments of extreme violence. The atrocious spectacle has dragged on, its endless prolongation impelling most of the public to leave. On the blood-spattered sand, the feline horde is shepherded past burned and dismembered bodies to its quarters. Gérôme casts a kindly eye on these strange winners, treating them rather like big, overfed cats. This ultimate sequence, this desolate conclusion to the edifying tale of Christian persecution under Nero, *Gathering up the Lions in the Circus* could well have been inspired by *Quo Vadis?*, a then highly topical book by the Polish writer Henryk Sienkiewicz. Published in Polish in 1896, *Quo Vadis* met immediately with both glory and controversy. In France its translation was published by the Natanson brothers in *La Revue blanche* in 1900, then taken up by Flammarion. Its stage adaptation whose sets owed a lot to *Ave Caesar* (cat. 70) and *Pollice verso* (cat. 71), mounted at the Porte-Saint-Martin theater (ill. 60) between March and September 1901, was also a huge success. The text is full of realistically described scenes pitting barbarism against redemptive faith in the arena: "Blood flowed in streams from the torn bodies. Dogs dragged from each other the bloody limbs of people. The odor of blood and torn entrails was stronger than Arabian perfumes, and filled the whole Circus. At last only here and there were visible single kneeling forms."[1] Thus, while Gérôme no doubt placed his first version under the literary auspices of François-René de Chateaubriand's *Martyrs* (1809), Alexandre Dumas's *Acté* (1838), and Cardinal Wiseman's *Fabiola* (1854), or indeed Ernest Renan's *L'Antéchrist* (1873), at the turn of the century he followed the trend towards an increasingly spectacular illusionism. The connection of Gérôme's painting to cinema is increasingly evident here, and indeed this work was contemporaneous with the first silver screen adaptation of *Quo Vadis?* directed by Ferdinand Zecca and Lucien Nonguet produced by Pathé in 1901. **L. C.**

Ill. 66. Study for *Gathering up the Lions in the Circus*, ca. 1902, soft sketching pencil on vellum paper, 9 × 145 1/4 in., private collection.

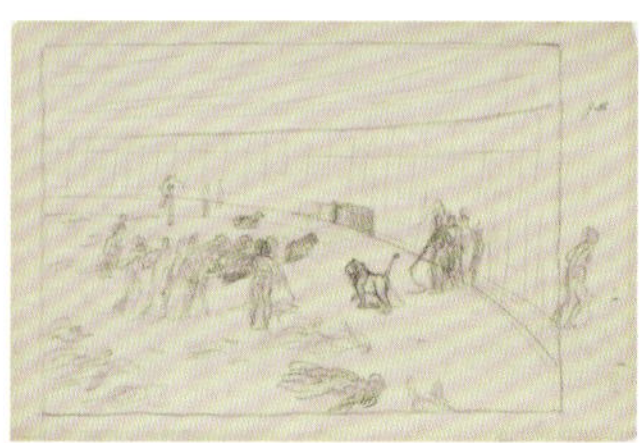

1. Henryk Sienkiewicz, *Quo Vadis?* translated by Jeremiah Curtin in 1896 (Whitefish, Mont.: Kessinger Publishing, 2005), p. 432.

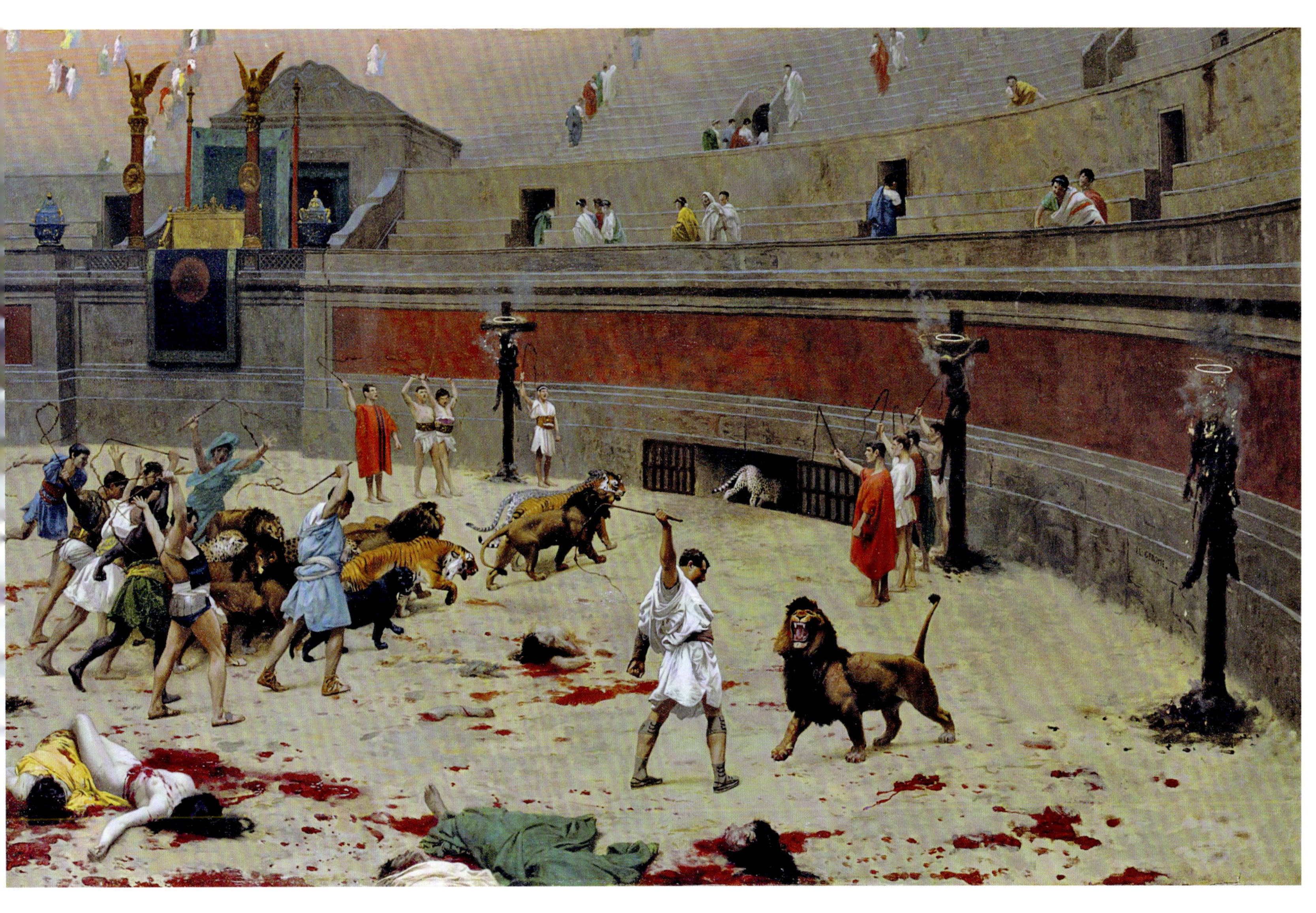

Cat. 82

CAVE CANEM, ALSO KNOWN AS **WAR PRISONER IN ROME**

1880
Oil on canvas
42 ½ × 35 ¾ in.
Signed lower left: *J.L. GEROME*
Musée Georges-Garret, Vesoul. Gift of the artist, 1886, inv. 886.2.1

Provenance: Presented by Gérôme to the city of Vesoul in 1886.

Exhibition History: Besançon, 1880.

Bibliography: *Equivoques*, exh. cat. (Paris: Musée des Arts Décoratifs, 1973), n.p. *J.-L. Gérôme*, exh. cat. (Vesoul: Musée Georges-Garret, 1981), no. 137, p. 119. K. Herding, *Festschrift Max Wyn* (Münster, 1982). G. Ackerman, *Jean-Léon Gérôme* (Courbevoie: ACR Édition, 2000), no. 292.

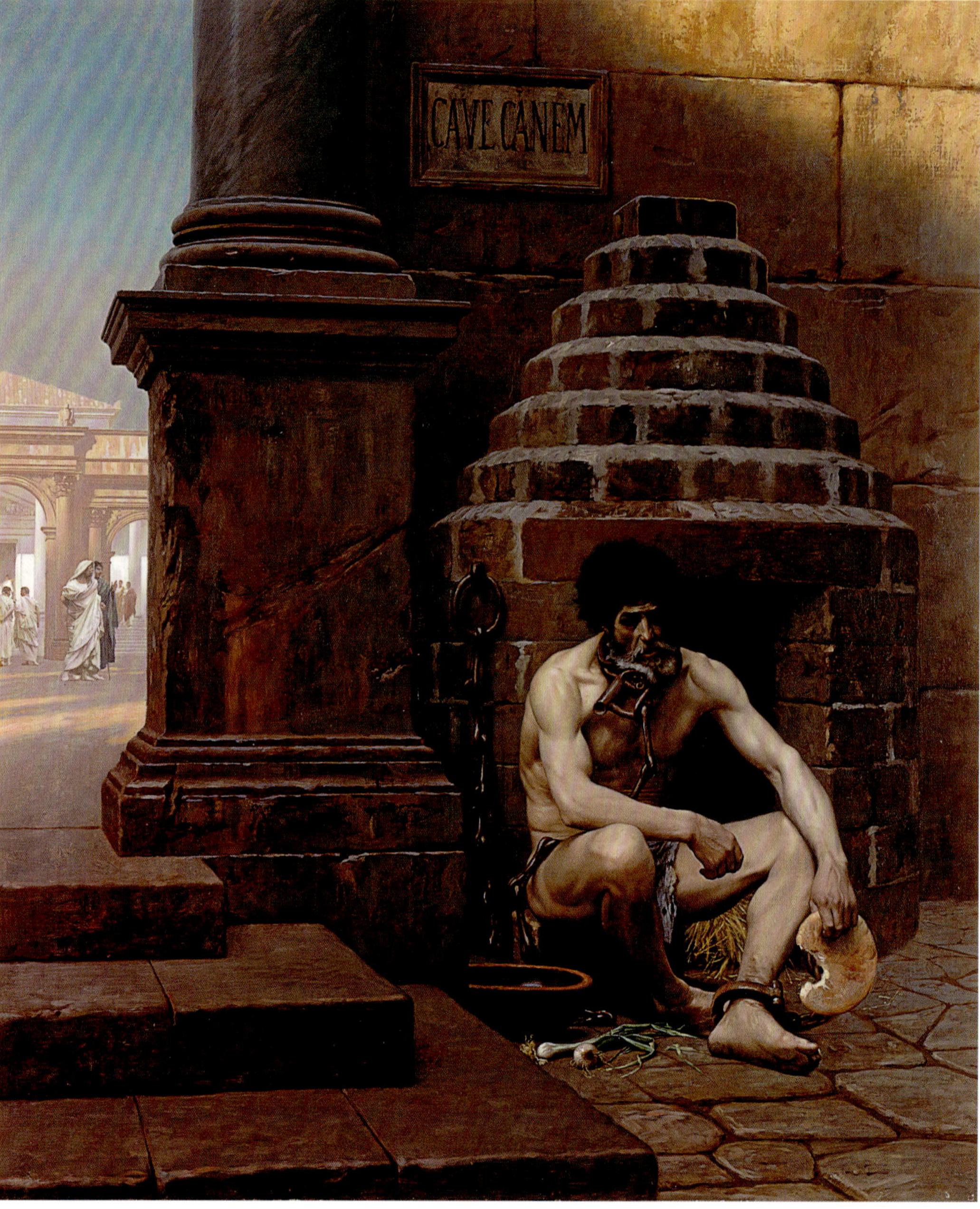

This painting, which Gérôme donated to his home town, is a somewhat nasty pictorial play on words, based on a free interpretation of archaeological sources. The title *Cave Canem* alludes to an inscription found in Pompeii on a mosaic depicting a ferocious dog. Petronius also mentioned a similar inscription in his *Satyricon*.

But here Gérôme has depicted a man chained to the entrance of the Forum in Rome, his sole shelter being a brick doghouse next to the wall. In his hand the wretched man holds a round loaf of bread, from which he has taken a bite; the empty bowl at his side and the gnawed bones on the ground underline the canine analogy.

Despite the misfortune of his situation, the man still flexes powerful muscles, and the artist has given him a philosophical demeanor in spite of his sad expression. Thus, going beyond the literal meaning of the Latin inscription, Gérôme was evoking the famous figure of the Athenian philosopher Diogenes, who lived naked in a barrel in the agora. In Gérôme's painting of Diogenes in the 1860s (cat. 109), he depicted the philosopher surrounded by dogs gathering in deferential curiosity. Thanks to this allusion to his own work, Gérôme thereby reversed the play on words of 1880, lending this wretched figure the aloofness of the philosopher and cynic. **D. F.-R.**

Cat. 83

SAINT SIMEON STYLITES

–

Undated
Black chalk
13 3/8 × 9 3/8 in.
Artist's annotation, bottom: *Rue de l'Odéon, atelier à louer*
Musée Georges-Garret, Vesoul, inv. 984.7.2

–

Provenance: Galerie Paul Prouté, Paris, *Domenico* catalogue, 1980, no. 92. Bought by the Musée Georges-Garret in 1983.

–

Bibliography: *J.-L. Gérôme*, exh. cat. (Vesoul: Musée Georges-Garret, 1981) no. 91, p. 85. *Dessins de Jean-Gérôme. Acquisitions du Musée de Vesoul*, exh. cat. (Vesoul: Musée Georges-Garret, 1991), cat. 26, ill. p. 25.

Saint Simeon was a Syrian ascetic born in Cilicia in the late fourth century; in order to get closer to God, he decided to live on the top of a column, where he is alleged to have spent forty years. The theme of Simeon on his column or pillar (*stylos* in Greek, hence the term Stylites) was depicted as early as the tenth century by Byzantine icon painters.

A subject that combined antique elements with oriental references could not fail to interest Gérôme. The drawing exhibited here thus merges the artist's two favorite sources of inspiration. Simeon, alone on a column with massive shaft and sketchy lotus-shaped capital that evoke ancient Egyptian architecture, stands before a city that forms a hill and an amphitheater whose reliefs suggest Greece or Turkey. The crowd that has gathered to admire the ascetic saint's fervor is dressed in oriental garb. Although directly referring to Simeon's iconography—familiar to Gérôme's contemporaries because made fashionable by inexpensive engravings in the 1830s[1]—the artist indulged in an implausible feature that allowed him to dramatize the theme: the column is so dizzyingly high that it is impossible to see how the holy man could get up it—or down it—since no ladder is visible.

Gérôme's interest may have been stirred by a book by Paul Lacroix, *Histoire de la prostitution chez tous les peuples du monde, depuis l'antiquité la plus reculée jusqu'à nos jours* (A History of Prostitution Among All the Peoples of the World, from Antiquity to the Present Day), which was published in 1851–53. "A passage from the life of Saint Simeon Stylites ... tells us of the eagerness with which courtesans from every land came to feast their eyes on the moving sight of his austerity and their ears on the encouragement of his divine words ... No sooner did the meretrices [i.e. prostitutes], attracted in droves by the saint's fame, see him praying and giving blessings from his column than they renounced their way of life, their lavish garments, their perfumes, their voluptuous pleasures."[2] The saint on his column, attracting courtesans, may perhaps have provided the initial idea behind *Corinth* (cat. 192, 193), Gérôme's last work, which also blended what Édouard Papet elegantly called "a sensual Orient with scholarly Hellenism."

D. F.-R.

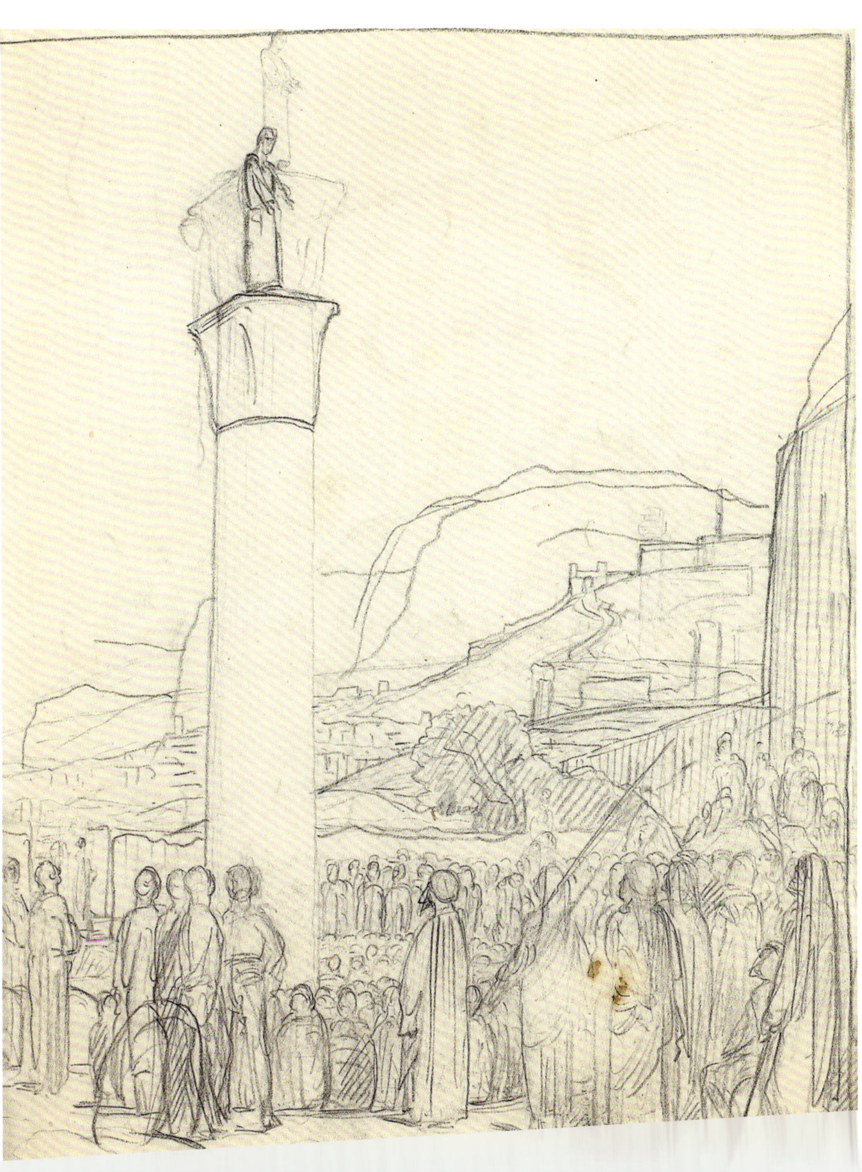

1. J.-M. Papillon, *Planche de saintetés* (Lille: Jean-Baptiste Castiaux, 1807–30). Wood engraving, Musée des Civilisations d'Europe et de la Méditeranée (MUCEM), Marseille, inv. 65.75.586.C. 2. (Paris: Séré), vol. 3, pp. 52–53.

Cat. 84

MOLIÈRE BREAKFASTING WITH LOUIS XIV

–

1862
Oil on panel
18 × 31 in.
Signed above left, on the door: *J.L. GEROME*
Malden Public Library, Malden

–

Provenance: Gérôme to Goupil, Sept. 1862, no. 720 (for 8,000 francs). Goupil to De La Hante, Paris, May 1863 (for 25,000 francs). Repurchased by Goupil, Nov. 1866, no. 2504 (for 25,000 francs). Goupil to Edward Mathews, New York, Nov. 1866 (for 31,775 francs). James H. Stebbins, New York, by 1879. Stebbins sale, American Art Galleries at Chickering Hall, New York, Feb. 12, 1889, lot 68. Collis P. Huntington, New York. P. A. Valentine, New York, by 1923. William Randolph Hearst, 1923. Hearst sale, Parke-Bernet, New York, Jan. 5–7, 1939, lot 14. J. Schmittzer and Sons, New York, 1940. Vose Galleries, Boston, 1940. Sold to Malden Public Library, Dec. 1940.

–

Exhibition History: Salon of 1863, Paris, no. 769. Exposition Universelle, Paris, 1867, no. 294.

–

Bibliography: E. Strahan [Earl Shinn], *The Art Treasures of America: Being the Choicest Works of Art in the Public and Private Collections of North America*, 3 vols. (Philadelphia: G. Barrie, 1880), vol. 1, p. 99. E. Strahan [Earl Shinn], ed., *Gérôme: A Collection of the Works of J. L. Gérôme in One Hundred Photogravures* (New York: Samuel L. Hall, 1881), vol. 1, n.p. F. F. Hering, *Gérôme: The Life and Works of Jean Léon Gérôme* (New York: Cassell, 1892), p. 106. V. Guillemin, "Étude sur le peintre et sculpteur Jean-Léon Gérôme (1824–1904)," *Académie des sciences, belles-lettres et arts de Besançon. Procès-verbaux et mémoires. Année 1904* (Besançon, 1905), p. 150. F. Masson, "Notes et fragments de J.-L. Gérôme," *Les Arts*, no. 26 (Feb. 1904), p. 20. C. Moreau-Vauthier, *Gérôme, peintre et sculpteur. L'homme et l'artiste d'après sa correspondance, ses notes, ses souvenirs, les souvenirs de ses élèves et de ses amis* (Paris: Hachette, 1906), p. 211. R. Rosenblum, "Ingres Inc.," in *Art News Annual*, vol. 33 [issue title: *The Academy: Five Centuries of Grandeur and Misery, from the Carracci to Mao Tse-tung*] (1967), pp. 70–71. G. Ackerman et al., *Jean-Léon Gérôme (1824–1904)*, exh. cat. (Dayton: Dayton Art Institute, 1972; also Minneapolis: Minneapolis Institute of Arts, 1973, and Baltimore: The Walters Art Gallery, 1973), p. 52, no. 13. R. K. Meyer, "Jean-Léon Gérôme: The Role of Subject Matter and the Importance of Formalized Composition," *Arts Magazine*, vol. 47, no. 4 (Feb. 1973), p. 32. R. Anderson, *Thirty Paintings in the Malden Collection* (Malden, Mass.: Public Library, 1975), n.p. *The Second Empire: 1852–1870, Art in France under Napoléon III*, exh. cat. (Philadelphia: Philadelphia Museum of Art, 1978; also Detroit: Detroit Institute of Arts, 1979, and Paris: Grand Palais, 1979), p. 321, under no. VI-72. *J.-L.* Gérôme, exh. cat. (Vesoul: Musée Georges-Garret, 1981), pp. 19, 20. G. Ackerman, *The Life and Work of Jean-Léon Gérôme, with a Catalogue Raisonné* (New York and London: Sotheby's, 1986), pp. 67–68, 72, 212, 213, no. 138. P. Mainardi, *Art and Politics of the Second Empire: The Universal Expositions of 1855 and 1867* (New Haven: Yale University Press, 1987), p. 169. H. B. Weinberg, *The Lure of Paris: Nineteenth-Century American Painters and their French Teachers* (New York: Abbeville Press, 1991), pp. 84–85, pl. 86. E. M. Zafran, *Cavaliers and Cardinals: Nineteenth-Century French Anecdotal Paintings*, exh. cat. (Cincinnati: Taft Museum, 1992; also Washington, D.C.: Corcoran Gallery of Art, 1992, and Elmira: Arnot Art Museum, 1992–93), pp. 44–45, no. 7. G. Ackerman, *Jean-Léon Gérôme: His life, His Work, 1824–1904* (Courbevoie: ACR Édition, 1997), p. 76. H. Lafont-Couturier, *Gérôme* (Paris: Herscher, 1998), p. 53. H. Lafont-Couturier, *Gérôme and Goupil: Art and Enterprise*, exh. cat., trans. I. Ollivier (Bordeaux: Musée Goupil, 2000–1; also New York: Dahesh Museum of Art, 2001, and Pittsburgh: The Frick Art & Historical Center, 2001), pp. 21, 23, 24, 25, 40, 138, 140, 142, 154–55, 165, no. 99. G. Ackerman, *Jean-Léon Gérôme* (Paris: ACR Édition, 2000), pp. 250–51, no. 138.

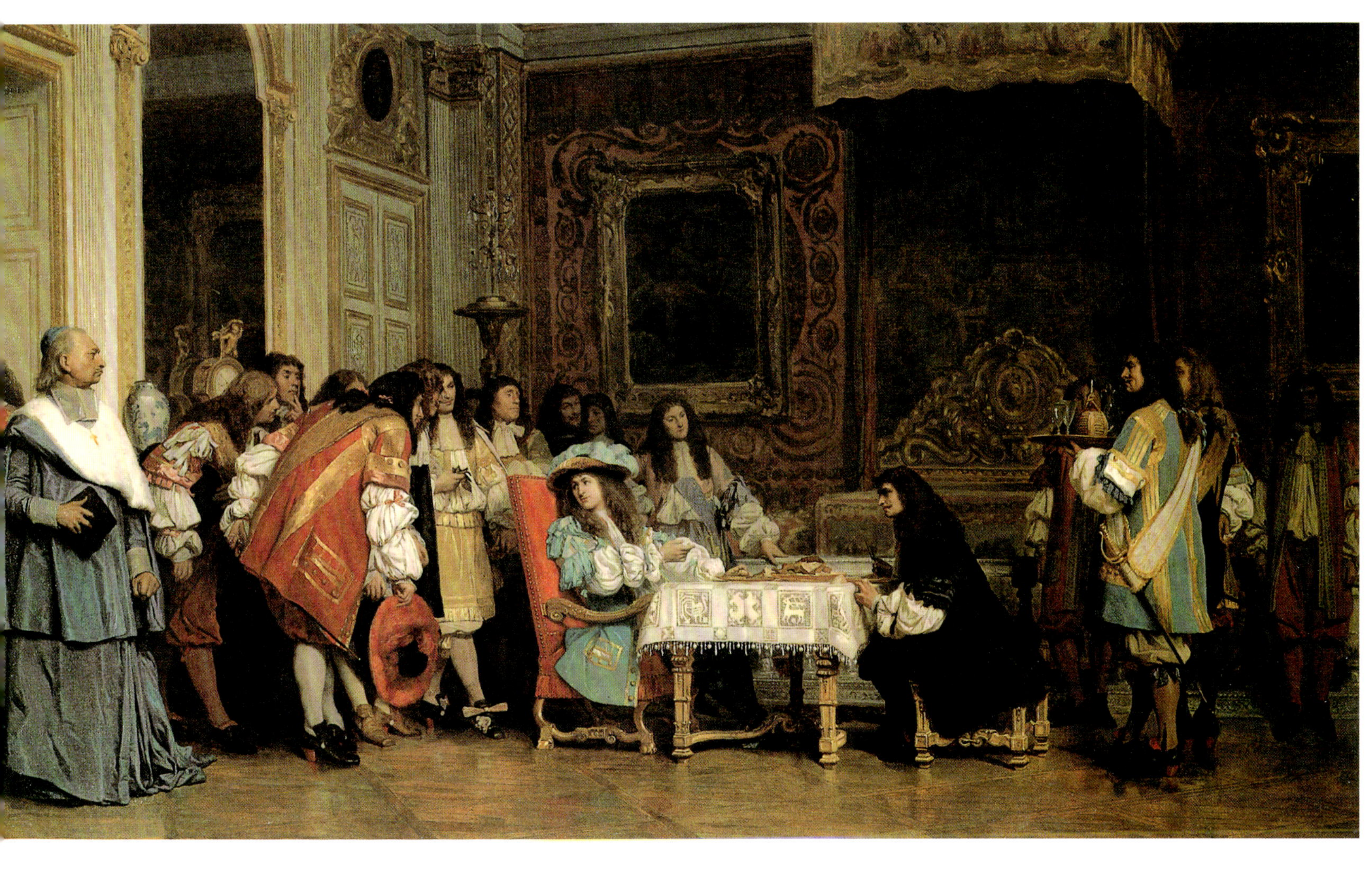

The subject of Louis XIV and Molière derives from an "historical anecdote" based on hearsay and found in the memoirs of Mme. de Campan, first published in 1823. She recounts how Molière, having been made *valet de chambre du roi*, was entitled to sit at table with the other courtiers, a prospect said to have riled them given his lower social status as a *comédien*. To admonish the disdainful *officiers de chambre*, the king made a show of inviting Molière to dine with him, reportedly addressing them thus: "You see me ... dining with Molière, whom my footmen do not consider good enough company for them." After which point, of course, "the entire court pressed Molière with invitations."[1]

The anecdote, which was quickly incorporated into popular histories of France, enjoyed wide currency in the mid-nineteenth century.[2] It was taken as an instance of enlightened royal protection of the arts during the *grand siècle* and, for a post-revolutionary generation, the vindication of distinctions of talent over those of birth.[3] Exhibiting his painting on the theme at the 1863 Salon, Gérôme may likewise have been intent on honoring Napoleon III as a patron of the arts. Having himself been recently received at the imperial chateau of Compiègne, such a gesture would have been a timely one.[4]

Molière Breakfasting with Louis XIV represents Gérôme's first foray into seventeenth-century subject matter, which the Goupil firm had been successfully promoting for several years.[5] In addition to expanding his repertoire of marketable historical subjects, Gérôme evidently sought to rival his contemporary Ernest Meissonier, who specialized in the "cavalier" genre, as well as his former master Paul Delaroche, famous for his lavishly costumed histories.[6] Gérôme found, moreover, a notable precedent in Ingres, who treated the subject of Molière dining with Louis XIV in a painting given to the Comédie-Française in 1857 and subsequently replicated for the market (ill. 67).[7] Gérôme may have had occasion to see Ingres's original when he installed his portrait of the actress Rachel in the Comédie-Française after having shown it at the 1861 Salon (cat. 40).

Ill. 67. Jean-Auguste-Dominique Ingres (1780–1867), *Louis XIV and Molière*, 1857, oil on canvas, 19 ½ × 26 ½ in., Comédie-Française, Paris, inv. I 169.

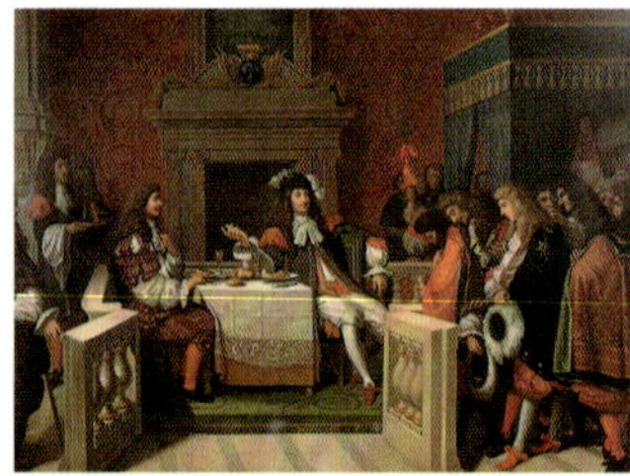

Ill. 68. Jacques-Edmond Leman (1829–1889), *Louis XIV and Molière*, 1863, oil on canvas, 51 ¼ × 94 ½ in., picture destroyed in 1915.

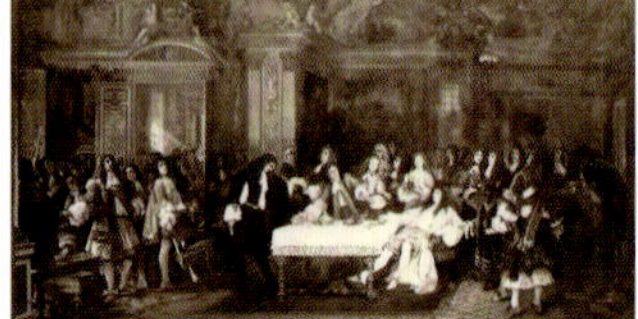

In comparison to Ingres's rather cramped composition, Gérôme's is more openly horizontal, with a larger cast of characters and without any cumbersome architectural details in the foreground. Also more pointed in its telling of the anecdote, Gérôme's painting establishes biting contrasts between, on the right, the modest, soberly clad Molière backed by servants who maintain a dignified, erect bearing, and, on the left, the obsequious huddle of bowing, lavishly dressed courtiers whom the king casually upbraids over his shoulder. The composition is anchored on the left by the bristling archbishop of Paris,[8] whose scarcely contained outrage is met by the hint of a satirical smile on Molière's face.

Around the same time as Gérôme, several of his contemporaries also picked up on the theme. Jacques-Edmond Leman also exhibited a version at the 1863 Salon (ill. 68), and Jean-Hégésippe Vetter presented his own version a year later.[9] Next to Leman's casually jumbled composition, which focuses on the earlier moment of Molière being seated at the king's table, Gérôme's appears positively restrained. Where critics, who often compared the two pictures in their reviews, generally found Leman's treatment of the king's negligent morning *tenue* and nonchalant, slouching pose to be vulgar, they felt that Gérôme's king was comparatively dignified and that Gérôme had a better historical sense of courtly proprieties.[10]

Gérôme did come in for his fair share of criticism, however. Some felt that he could have been more understated in his treatment of the anecdote,[11] and many found his characterizations of Molière and the king to be trivializing. With his "sheepish air," Molière was described as a "prig" or a "procurer's clerk."[12] A prouder expression would have been preferable, as would a more assured pose (a few critics countered that his modest, deferential attitude was entirely fitting for the court context).[13] The king's type was also found to be a little too cavalier, a little too ordinary, the caricaturist Cham taking the liberty of likening him to an Auvergnat peasant. More fundamentally, Gérôme's depictions appeared inadequate as historical portraits, and critics accused him of neglecting to consult the various artistic models available to him.[14] What he certainly had not neglected, however, was the painting's accessory details, which were charged with detracting from the main subject. As Jules-Antoine Castagnary quipped: "Do you know what plays the principal role in his picture?... it's a tablecloth delicately worked by skillful hands; and it's also the parquet, the chimney, the bed, all the furniture."[15] The painting's bright palette was found similarly distracting. The picture presented "an association of crude blues, dull lilacs, [and] immoderate tones of ivory and red capable of irritating the least sensitive eyes," Théodore Pelloquet complained.[16]

The painting nevertheless proved popular. The Goupil firm's various reproductions of it figured prominently in the marketing of Gérôme's work, and the original painting fetched the high price of 31,775 francs when it was sold by Goupil in 1866. An autograph replica would sell for 20,000 francs the following year—the same amount the government had paid Gérôme for his monumental *Age of Augustus* (ill. 1, pp. 26–27) a decade before.[17] **S. A.**

1. Mme. [Jeanne-Louise-Henriette] Campan, *Mémoires sur la vie privée de Marie-Antoinette, reine de France et de Navarre, suivis de souvenirs et anecdotes historiques sur les règnes de Louis XIV, de Louis XV et de Louis XVI*, 2nd ed., 3 vols. (Paris: Baudouin Frères, 1823), vol. 3, pp. 8–9 ["'Vous me voyez, leur dit le roi, occupé de faire manger Molière que mes valets de chambre ne trouvent pas d'assez bonne compagnie pour eux.' De ce moment... toute la cour s'empressa de lui faire des invitations"]. **2.** See, for example, the section devoted to "Louis XIV et Molière" in L. Michelant, *Faits memorables de l'histoire de France... illustrés de 120 tableaux de M. Victor Adam* (Paris: Didier; Aubert & Cie., 1844), n.p. **3.** Ibid. ["... la noblesse ne put guère douter que par son génie il se fut élevé auprès du souverain aussi haut qu'elle par la naissance... C'est cette protection éclairée, ce goût naturel, supérieur à celui de ses courtisans, et qu'il manifestait souvent, qui unissent si intimement Louis XIV aux écrivains célèbres de son temps"]. **4.** H. Lafont-Couturier, *Gérôme and Goupil: Art and Enterprise*, exh. cat., trans. I. Ollivier (Bordeaux: Musée Goupil, 2000–1; also New York: Dahesh Museum of Art, 2001, and Pittsburgh: The Frick Art & Historical Center, 2001), p. 142; see also G. Ackerman, *Jean-Léon Gérôme*, Courbevoie (ACR Édition, 2000), p. 250, no. 138. **5.** H. Lafont-Couturier 2000–1 (as in n. 4), p. 140. At least one critic remarked that the painting had been made specifically to be reproduced by Goupil; see L. Auvray, "Salon de 1863," *Revue artistique et littéraire*, vol. 4 (June 1, 1863), p. 252. **6.** G. Ackerman, *The Life and Work of Jean-Léon Gérôme, with a Catalogue Raisonné* (New York and London: Sotheby's, 1986), p. 67; H. Lafont-Couturier 2000–1 (as in n. 4), pp. 139–40. **7.** Ingres painted the replica in 1859 and sold it for 25,000 francs in 1861. See E. M. Zafran, *Cavaliers and Cardinals: Nineteenth-Century French Anecdotal Paintings*, exh. cat. (Cincinnati: Taft Museum, 1992; also Washington, D.C.: Corcoran Gallery of Art, 1992, and Elmira: Arnot Art Museum, 1992–93), p. 44. **8.** The identity of this figure has been a matter of some uncertainty. One critic in 1863 identified him as Pierre de Marca, who was archbishop of Paris from 1662 to 1663; see A. Paul, "Salon de 1863," *Le Siècle*, June 3, 1863. A usually reliable source, Earl Shinn identified him as De Retz, who was De Marca's immediate predecessor as archbishop; see E. Strahan [Earl Shinn], *The Art Treasures of America: Being the Choicest Works of Art in the Public and Private Collections of North America*, 3 vols. (Philadelphia: G. Barrie, 1880), vol. 1, p. 99. Later Gérôme

Institute, 1972; also Minneapolis: Minneapolis Institute of Arts, 1973, and Baltimore: The Walters Art Gallery, 1973), p. 52, no. 13. **9.** Leman's version entered the collection of the Musée des Beaux-Arts in Arras after the Salon in 1863 and, according to curator M. Jackie Guindet, was destroyed by bombardments during the First World War, in 1915. For Vetter's version, now in the Sénat in Paris, see G. Lacambre, *Le Musée du Luxembourg en 1874*, exh. cat. (Paris: Grand Palais, 1974), pp. 174–76, no. 231. **10.** On Leman's Louis XIV, see A. Paul 1863 (as in n. 8) ["Son Louis XIV, en maillot de soie rose, nonchalamment étendu, manque de tenue et de dignité. Ce n'est pas là le Louis XIV de l'histoire fixé dans l'étiquette la plus scrupuleuse"]; on Gérôme's Louis XIV in comparison, see A. Nettement, "Salon de 1863," *La Semaine des familles*, Aug. 1, 1863, p. 690 ["La figure de Louis XIV est belle est fière; je la préfère à celle d'un autre tableau sur le même sujet exposé au Salon de 1863"]; or O. Merson, "Salon de 1863," *L'Opinion nationale*, June 20, 1863 ["Entre la toile de M. Leman et celle de M. Gérôme, l'hésitation n'est pas permise. Autant la première affiche un goût faux et vulgaire, autant la seconde est d'un caractère calme et plein de réserve. M. Leman a peint un cabaret où tout est bruit et confusion. Je l'entends d'ici ce Louis XIV dégingandé, à peine vêtu, à moitié ivre... il s'écrie: '... les amis, vivent la joie, le bon vin et la bagatelle!' M. Gérôme, mieux avisé, a pensé qu'à la cour du grand roi les choses ne devaient pas se passer tout à fait ainsi, et le maître, avec une majesté naturelle, adresse la parole aux ducs et aux marquis... c'est la dignité vraie et le juste sentiment des convenances"]. **11.** See P. Mantz, "Salon de 1863," *Gazette des Beaux-Arts*, vol. 14, no. 6 (June 1, 1863), pp. 494–95 ["les personnages qui entourent le roi... sont tellement étonnés de voir un comédien prendre part au déjeuner royal, que, pour exprimer leur surprise, ils froncent le sourcil et avancent la lèvre inferieure sans s'apercevoir qu'ils font la grimace. Les intentions sont ici trop soulignées: nous aurions compris à demi-mot"]. **12.** See, for instance, C. De Sault, "Salon de 1863," *Le Temps*, June 14, 1863 ["Le Molière de M. Gérôme a l'air penaud"]; T. Pelloquet, "Salon de 1863," *L'Exposition: Journal du Salon de 1863*, May 24, 1863, p. 2 ["Molière a l'air d'un cuistre"]; and B. Bouniol, "L'Amateur au Salon. Critique et causerie," *Revue du monde catholique*, vol. 6, no. 54 (June 25, 1863), p. 459 ["Le Molière me parait peu flatté, avec sa figure mince et chafouine qui le fait ressembler à un clerc de procureur"]. **13.** See, for instance, J. Claretie, "Lettres familières sur le Salon de 1863," *Jean Diable*, no. 29 (June 13, 1863), p. 461 ["J'aurais voulu ... une expression plus large et plus fière dans le visage de Molière"]; and L. Enault, "Le Salon de 1863," *Revue française*, vol. 5 (July 1, 1863), p. 309 ["Je ne dis rien du Molière, dont la pose manque de l'ampleur et de l'assurance que l'on voudrait voir à un homme tel que lui"]. For the opposing view, see L. Auvray 1863 (as in n. 5), p. 252 ["Quelqu'un nous disait:—Ne trouvez-vous pas que Molière a l'air un peu embarrassée ?— Sans doute, et cela doit-être; on voit que M. Gérôme a eu l'honneur d'être reçu à la Cour, et qu'il a pu y faire ses observations... la modeste attitude de Molière... est ce qu'elle doit être, réservée sans bassesse, sans gaucherie; elle est celle d'un esprit supérieur, qui apprécie l'honneur qui lui est fait"]. **14.** See, for instance, P. Mantz 1863 (as in n. 11), p. 494 ["le Louis XIV n'a pas la moindre ressemblance avec le type consacré, notamment avec le médaillon en cire de Benoît, qui, on le sait, est aussi authentique que le pourrait être un moulage fait sur nature"]; and O. Merson 1863 (as in n. 10) ["ce n'est pas là le visage du poète: pour le faire, l'artiste n'a consulté ni le portrait bien connu du Louvre, ni l'estampe que Boucher a gravée, d'après une effigie du temps"]. **15.** J.-A. Castagnary, "Salon de 1863," in *Salons (1857-1870)* (Paris: Bibliothèque Charpentier, 1892), p. 135 ["Savez-vous qui joue le rôle principal dans sa toile?... c'est une nappe à jour délicatement ouvragée par des mains habiles; et puis, c'est encore le parquet, la cheminée, le lit, le mobilier tout entier"]. **16.** T. Pelloquet 1863 (as in 12), p. 2 ["Il y a là une association de bleus crus, de lilas fades, de tons d'ivoire et de rouges outrecuidants, capables d'agaçer les yeux les moins sensibles"]. **17.** For the replica, G. Ackerman 2000 (as in n. 4), no.

Cat. 85

THE GREY CARDINAL

1873
Oil on canvas
27 × 39 7/8 in.
Signed lower right: *J.L. GEROME*
Museum of Fine Arts, Boston, Susan Cornelia Warren Bequest, inv. 03.605

Provenance: Goupil, Paris, 1873. James H. Stebbins, New York, 1873–89. Stebbins sale, American Art Galleries, Chickering Hall, New York, Feb. 12, 1889, lot 76. H. B. Mason, Boston. Mrs. Samuel Warren, Boston. American Art Artists, sale, New York, Jan. 8–9, 1903, no. 55. Acquired by the Museum of Fine Arts, Boston.

Exhibition History: Salon of 1874, Paris, no. 798. Exposition Universelle, Paris, 1878, no. 357. World's Columbian Exhibition, Chicago, 1893, no. 2924. *Painters of the French School*, Guildhall, London, 1898, no. 38. *Loan Exhibition*, Saint Botolph Club, Boston, Jan. 1901. *Collection of the Late Mrs. S. D. Warren*, Museum of Fine Arts, Boston, 1902, no. 54.

Bibliography: *Le Figaro*, May 6, 1874. *Journal des débats*, June 7, 1874. E. Duvergier de Hauranne, "Le Salon de 1874," *Revue des Deux Mondes*, June 1, 1874, pp. 672–73. L. Gonse, "Salon de 1874," *Gazette des Beaux-Arts*, vol. 10, 1874, pp. 34–36. J. Claretie, *L'Art et les Artistes français contemporains*, 1876, pp. 210–11. S. G. Benjamin, *Contemporary Art in Europe*, 1877, ill. p. 98. "Contemporary Art in France," *Harper's New Monthly Magazine*, Mar. 1877, ill. p. 483. C. Blanc, *Les Beaux-Arts à l'Exposition universelle de 1878*, Paris, 1878, pp. 235–36. É. Zola, "Lettres de Paris," in *Le Sémaphore de Marseille*, May 3–4, 1874, reprinted in *Mon Salon. Manet. Écrits sur l'art* (Paris: Garnier-Flammarion, 1970), p. 207. P. Mantz, "La peinture française," *L'Art moderne à l'Exposition de 1878* (Paris: 1879), p. 48. E. Strahan [Earl Shinn], *The Art Treasures of America: Being the Choicest Works of Art in the Public and Private Collections of North America*, 3 vols. (Philadelphia: G. Barrie, 1880), vol. 1, pp. 99–100. E. Montrosier, *Les Artistes modernes*, Paris, 1881, vol. I, p. 18. E. Strahan [Earl Shinn], ed. *Gérôme: A Collection of the Works of J. L. Gérôme in One Hundred Photogravures* (New York: Samuel L. Hall, 1881), pp. 195–96. J. Claretie, *Les Peintres et sculpteurs contemporains*, Paris, 1884, vol. II, pp. 75–76. F. F. Hering, *Gérôme. The Life and Works of Jean-Léon Gérôme* (New York: Cassell, 1892), p. 216. C. Moreau-Vauthier, *Gérôme peintre et sculpteur. L'homme et l'artiste d'après sa correspondance, ses notes, ses souvenirs, les souvenirs de ses élèves et de ses amis* (Paris: Hachette, 1906), p. 149. *Literature and Poetry since 1850*, exh. cat. (Hartford: Wadsworth Atheneum, 1933), no. 29. *French Painting*, exh. cat. (Pittsburgh: Carnegie Institute, 1936), no. 24. *Fiftieth Anniversary Exhibition*, exh. cat. (Portland: Portland Art Museum, 1942–43), no. 28. *The Two Sides of the Medal: French Painting from Gérôme to Gauguin*, exh. cat. (Detroit: Detroit Institute of Arts, 1954), no. 25. *Clothes Make the Man*, exh. cat. (Denver: Denver Art Museum, 1956). *The Triumph of Realism*, exh. cat. (New York: Brooklyn Museum, 1967–68), no. 8. A. Boime, "Jean-Léon Gérôme, Henri Rousseau's *Sleeping Gypsy* and the Academic Legacy," *The Art Quarterly*, vol. 34, no. 1 (spring 1971), p. 3. G. Ackerman et al., *Jean-Léon Gérôme (1824–1904)*, exh. cat. (Dayton: Dayton Art Institute, 1972; also Minneapolis: Minneapolis Institute of Arts, 1973, and Baltimore: The Walters Art Gallery, 1973), no. 25, pp. 70–71. *French and American Impressionism Crosscurrents*, exh. cat. (Boston: Museum of Fine Arts, 1992). *Cavaliers and Cardinals. Nineteenth Century French Anecdotal Paintings*, exh. cat. (Cincinnati: Taft Museum, 1992), no. 9. H. Lafont-Couturier, *Gérôme* (Paris: Herscher, 1998), pp. 50–51. G. Ackerman, *Jean-Léon Gérôme* (Courbevoie: ACR Édition, 2000), no. 233. H. Lafont-Couturier, *Gérôme and Goupil: Art and Enterprise*, exh. cat., trans. I. Ollivier (Bordeaux: Musée Goupil, 2000–1; also New York: Dahesh Museum of Art, 2001, and Pittsburgh: The Frick Art & Historical Center, 2001), pp. 23–24, 37, 42, 160, 166. *Richelieu. L'Art et le pouvoir*, exh. cat. (Montreal: Musée des Beaux-Arts, 2002–3; also Cologne: Wallraf-Richartz Museum, 2003), no. 176.

Cat. 86

RECEPTION OF THE DUC DE CONDÉ AT VERSAILLES

1878
Oil on canvas
38 × 55 in.
Signed lower right: *J.L. GEROME*
Musée d'Orsay, Paris, inv. RF 2004 15

Provenance: Goupil, 1878. William H. Vanderbilt, New York, via the intermediary of Samuel B. Avery, 1878. Cornelius Vanderbilt. On loan to the Metropolitan Museum of Art, New York, between 1886 and 1903. Vanderbilt sale, PBNY, Apr. 18–19, 1945, no. 138 (for 5,000 dollars). Mr. Hulett C. Merrit, Pasadena, California. George L. Castera, Bel Air, California. Mr. and Mrs. Armand du Vannes, Los Angeles. *19th Century European Paintings, Drawings and Sculpture*, Sotheby's, New York, May 26, 1993, sale 6428, no. 70. Collection of Edmond Safra, Republic National Bank, 1993. Up to 2004, HSBC's Corporate Art Collection. *19th Century European Art including property from HSBC's Corporate Art Collection*, Sotheby's, New York, Oct. 26, 2004, no. 94. Acquired by the Musée d'Orsay, 2004.

Exhibition History: Salon of 1885, Paris.

Bibliography: E. Strahan [Earl Shinn], ed. *Gérôme. A Collection of the Works of J. L. Gérôme in One Hundred Photogravures* (New York: Samuel L. Hall, 1881). *Catalogue of the W. H. Vanderbilt Collection* (New York: 1886), no. 14. F. F. Hering, *Gérôme. The Life and Works of Jean-Léon Gérôme* (New York: Cassell, 1892), p. 239. G. Ackerman et al., *Jean-Léon Gérôme (1824–1904)*, exh. cat. (Dayton: Dayton Art Institute, 1972; also Minneapolis: Minneapolis Institute of Arts, 1973, and Baltimore: The Walters Art Gallery, 1973), no. 28, pp. 74–75. G. Ackerman, *Jean-Léon Gérôme* (Courbevoie: ACR Édition, 2000), no. 265. H. Lafont-Couturier, *Gérôme and Goupil: Art and Enterprise*, exh. cat., trans. I. Ollivier (Bordeaux: Musée Goupil, 2000–1; also New York: Dahesh Museum of Art, 2001, and Pittsburgh: The Frick Art & Historical Center, 2001), pp. 20, 38, 40–41, 148, 161. D. Lobstein, "Acquisitions," *48/14. La Revue du Musée d'Orsay*, no. 20 (spring 2005), pp. 56–57.

After the inaugural *Molière Breakfasting with Louis XIV* (cat. 84), *The Grey Cardinal*, and *Reception of the Duc de Condé* mark the high point of Gérôme's theatrical approach to seventeenth-century French history. The first of the two works was inspired by François Le Clerc du Tremblay, a Capuchin known as Father Joseph who went down in history as the Éminence Grise. In a mixture of history and legend, Father Joseph was, with Mazarin, the most famous of Richelieu's "creatures," as they called the secretaries and counselors of the young Louis XIII's cardinal and minister. In the catalogue of the exhibition *Cavaliers and Cardinals*, Eric Zafran notes that, according to documents kept at the Museum of Fine Arts in Boston, this painting was directly inspired by Edward Bulwer-Lytton's play, *Richelieu or the Conspiracy*, premiered in London in 1839 and put on in Paris in the late 1860s.[1] However, there is no scene in the play that directly matches Gérôme's staging, and indeed the Salon booklet mentions only an anonymous source: "And when the courtiers saluted him, he pretended to be reading his breviary and not to notice them."
As always, Gérôme's inspiration was fundamentally composite, no doubt mixing current theater with more familiar general and literary sources to come up with a disturbing vision of His Eminence's brilliant and feared background operator. The entry from the 1865 edition of Larousse's *Grand dictionnaire universel* is enough to convey the essence of the vision put forward by Gérôme: "a great, reflective intelligence... unscrupulous, too, and capable of combining political cunning with the forms of religious austerity, this monk and statesman, this Éminence Grise, as he was called, was a true minister, with no official title, but with an authority inspiring deference from secretaries of state, ambassadors, and generals."[2] A short passage from *The Three Musketeers* by Alexandre Dumas (1844)—"but *his* name was never mentioned except in an undertone; so great was the terror inspired by his gray eminence, as the familiar of the cardinal was called"[3]—and the description by Jules Michelet in his *History of France* — "With his Capuchin's sandals, his rope belt, the show of humility, he aspired to the cardinal's hat, which would no doubt have given him the means of supplanting his friend"[4]—completed the construction of Father Joseph's legend and accompanying image.
According to Charles Blanc, the composition of this work, whose tremendous effectiveness won it fame and ensured countless reproductions, was inspired by that of *The King's Favorite* by Eduardo Zamacoïs y Zabala (1867, private collection). But to this unlikely model Gérôme added the sweep and dynamism of a scene centered on a staircase—not that of Richelieu's chateau but, as Blanc himself pointed out, that of the Palais-Royal, an architectural setting used frequently by the Romantic generation.[5] (ill. 69). As was his wont, Gérôme distorts the reality of his model, embellishing the staircase with a wrought iron balustrade and lanterns more in keeping with the period, no doubt taken from volumes of decorative styles, and shifting the composition slightly to the side so as to bring in the Tuscan columns of the Palais-Royal arcade, ringing their shafts to add further interest to the dark and dramatic foreground. In front of the tapestry bearing

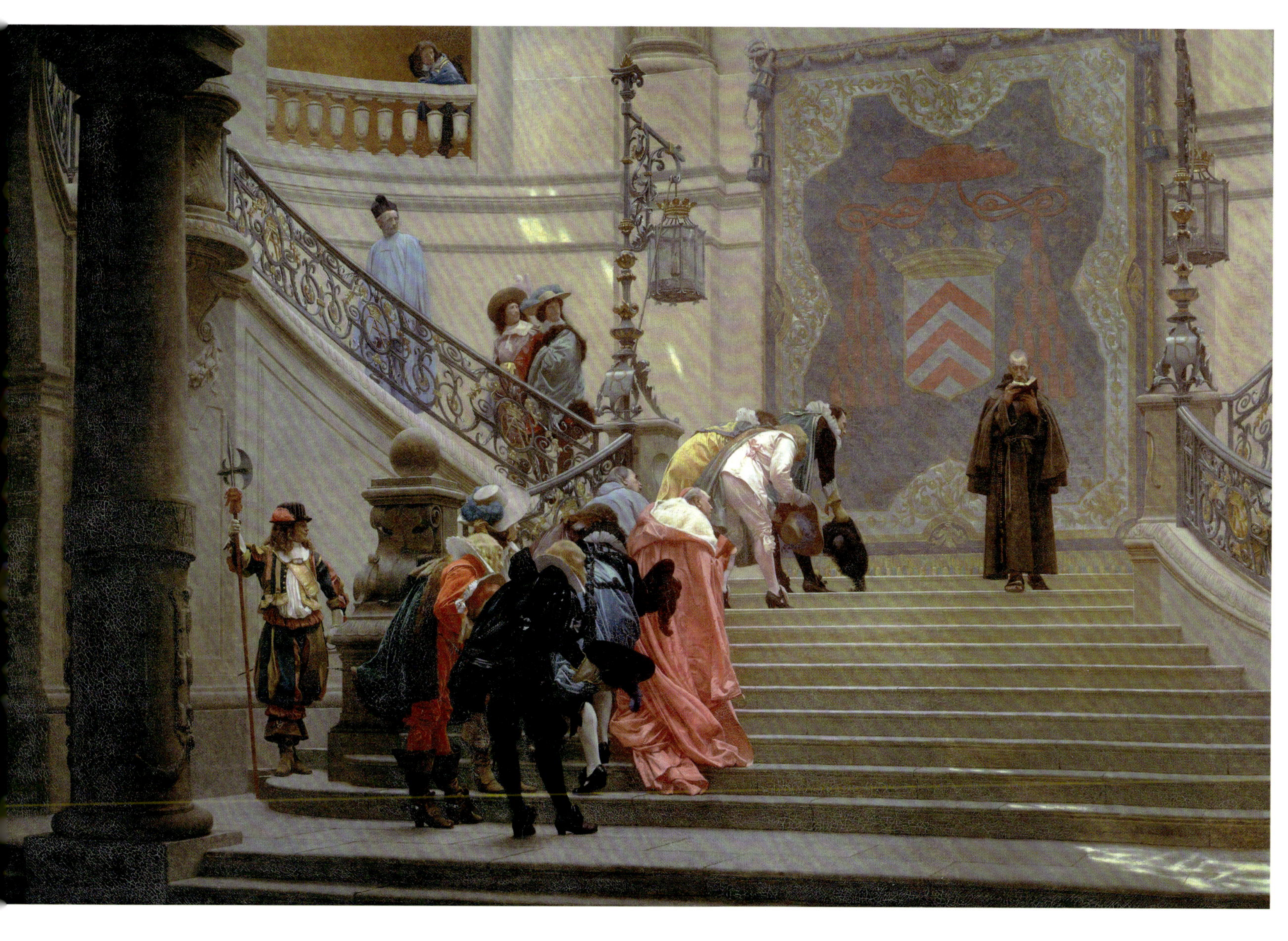

Ill. 69. After Boulot, *The Grand Escalier of the Palais-Royal*, lithograph, Musée Carnavalet, Paris, Topo P.C 33 A.

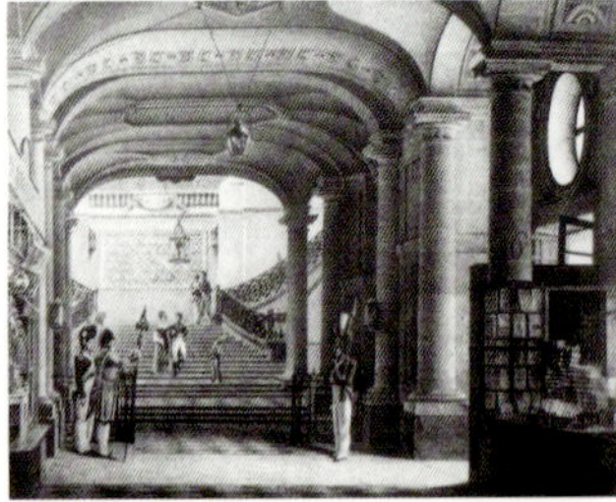

Ill. 70. Blanche Gérôme dressed as the Grand Dauphin for *Reception of the Duc de Condé*, in *Recueil. Œuvres de Jean-Léon Gérôme*, Département des Estampes et de la Photographie, Bibliothèque Nationale de France.

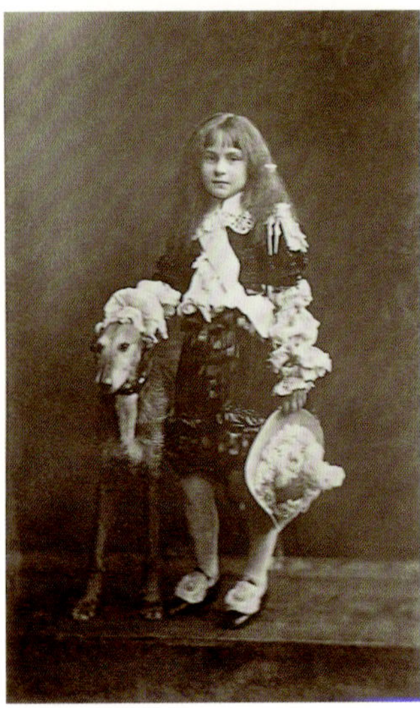

Ill. 71. Hyacinthe Rigaud (1659–1743), *Bossuet*, 1702, oil on canvas, 94 ⅜ × 65 in., Musée du Louvre, Paris, inv. 7506.

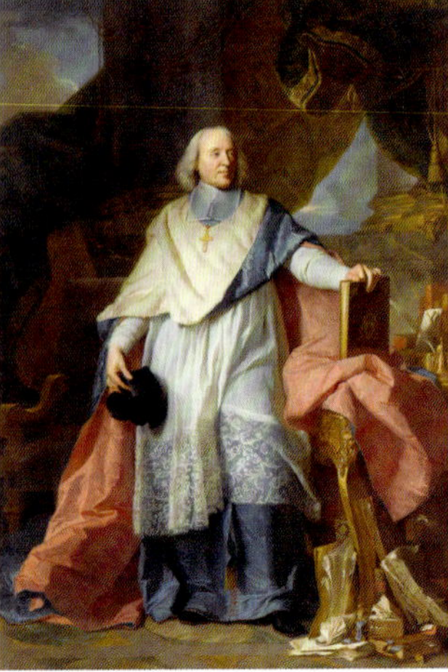

the cardinal's arms, a demonstrative device that Gérôme would repeat in *The Carpet Merchant of Cairo* (cat. 150), he creates an interesting tension between the isolated figure of Father Joseph and the group of courtiers on the left. Using two distinct levels of the stairway, Gérôme carefully separates the moment of official submission and, a few steps higher, that of unofficial commentary.

After the success of *The Grey Cardinal*, in which history painting is founded essentially on the dramatization of anecdote, Gérôme was quick to conceive other canvases on seventeenth-century French subjects. There is a clear architectural and dramatic connection between *The Grey Cardinal* and *Reception of the Duc de Condé*, on which Gérôme sheds some light in his memoirs: "I had long been thinking of Louis XIV receiving the Grand Condé, especially at a time when I had several paintings on my easel representing scenes from those times, for which I had made considerable outlays on costumes. I was well equipped to undertake such a work. But one of my friends had just had the same idea, and was progressing with the picture. It was piteous, albeit executed with a certain amount of talent, for this grandiose scene was set in a small, narrow, wretched staircase, a real servants' staircase."[6] The canvas referred to here by Gérôme could be the one by Joseph Carraud, even if this was executed quite a lot earlier, having been presented at the Salon in 1863 (private collection). In a letter to William Henry Vanderbilt, the first owner of the painting, who installed it in the library of his New York residence,[7] Gérôme described the setting and circumstances of this return to the court by Louis II de Bourbon, prince of Condé, after the long years of disgrace that followed his key role in the revolt of the Fronde. Rehabilitated by his victory over Prince William of Orange at the battle of Senef, the one-time hero of Rocroi, now old and tired, appeared for what was more an emphatic declaration of allegiance than a celebration of his own exploits: "The reception took place on the grand staircase at Versailles. This staircase no longer exists. It was destroyed under Louis XV, but there remains an engraving of it at that time, very well executed, which has enabled me to reconstruct it with truth. In 1674 Condé returned to the court, where he was given a triumphant reception. The king came to meet him on the grand staircase, which he did not usually do. The prince, infirm and suffering from gout, ascended the steps slowly. As soon as he saw the king he said: 'Sire, I beseech your Majesty's pardon for keeping him waiting so long.' 'My cousin,' replied the king, 'do not hurry. When one is loaded down with as many honors as you are, it is difficult to walk fast.' Louis XIV hugged him, kissing him several times. Beside Louis XIV is his son, the duke of Burgundy, called the Grand Dauphin, who was thirteen at the time. He died young, without having reigned, and was the father of Louis XV. Jacques-Bénigne Bossuet, the bishop of Meaux, is behind him. To the left and right stand figures from Court."[8]

Thus the splendid setting of the "ambassadors' staircase," which was well known from the engraving, served as a stage for this new comedy of power.[9] As indicated by the passage from the *Souvenirs* quoted above, Gérôme had acquired period costumes, no doubt when working on *The Grey Cardinal*, so as to make his work more convincing. This research, bringing together the worlds of painting and theater, is bound up with publications and exhibitions that accompanied the creation of the first big private and public historical collections of costumes, and in particular the inception of Auguste Racinet's six-volume *Costume historique*, begun at Firmin Didot in 1872, and the opening in 1874 of an exhibition devoted to "The History of Costume" at the Union Centrale des Arts Décoratifs.[10] In this context, the amusing photograph of Blanche Gérôme dressed as the Grand Dauphin gives a good idea of his painstaking work of representation and recreation (ill. 70). Indeed, in keeping with the traditional iconography of historical figures, as attested by the reference to Hyacinthe Rigaud's portrait of Bossuet (ill. 71), Gérôme deploys his crowd of anonymous extras, who merge with the regimental colors. The X-shaped composition is one with the form of the grand staircase, thus creating a space around the Grand Condé's laborious ascent. Eminently cinematic, the images of *The Grey Cardinal* and *Reception of the Duc de Condé* were for many years powerfully present in filmmakers' imaginations whenever Versailles, musketeers, royal glory, and political machinations were concerned. Sacha Guitry referred directly to this image of Louis XIV and prince of Condé in *Si Versailles m'était conté* (*Affairs in Versailles*, 1954), while the painting's career in America pointed to its rich heritage in Hollywood. **L. C.**

1. E. M. Zafran, *Cavaliers and Cardinals. Nineteenth Century French Anecdotal Paintings*, exh. cat. (Cincinnati: Taft Museum, 1992; also Washington D.C.: Corcoran Gallery of Art, 1992, and Elmira: Arnot Art Museum, 1992-93), p. 48 and notes 2 and 3. **2.** *Grand dictionnaire universel* (Paris: Larousse, 1865), entry on "Père Joseph," pp. 1019–20. **3.** A. Dumas, *Les Trois Mousquetaires* (Paris: Bibliothèque de La Pléiade, Gallimard, 1962), p. 20. Translated by D. Coward, *The Three Musketeers* (New York: Oxford University Press, 2009), p. 14. **4.** J. Michelet, *Histoire de France*, XII, *Richelieu et la Fronde* (Paris: Éditions des Équateurs, 2008), p. 45. **5.** See for example Méry-Joseph Blondel, *Napoléon visitant le Palais-Royal après la dissolution du Tribunal*, 1834, oil on canvas, Musée National du Château de Versailles. **6.** F. Masson, "Notes et fragments de J.-L. Gérôme," *Les Arts*, no. 26 (Feb. 1904), p. 30. **7.** See the photograph published in H. Lafont-Couturier, *Gérôme & Goupil. Art et entreprise*, exh. cat. (Bordeaux: Musée Goupil, 2000–1; also New York: Dahesh Museum of Art, 2001, and Pittsburgh, The Frick Art & Historical Center, 2001), p. 40. **9.** *Catalogue of the W. H. Vanderbilt Collection of Painting* (New York, 1886), p. 112. **10.** On this question see F. Tétart-Vittu, "Le réalisme historique dans le costume de scène. Les liens entre la peinture, l'histoire et la haute couture, à la fin du XIXe siècle. Sources d'inspiration, travail et réalisation," *Art et usages du costume de scène* (Vijon: Lampsaque, 2007), pp. 243–52.

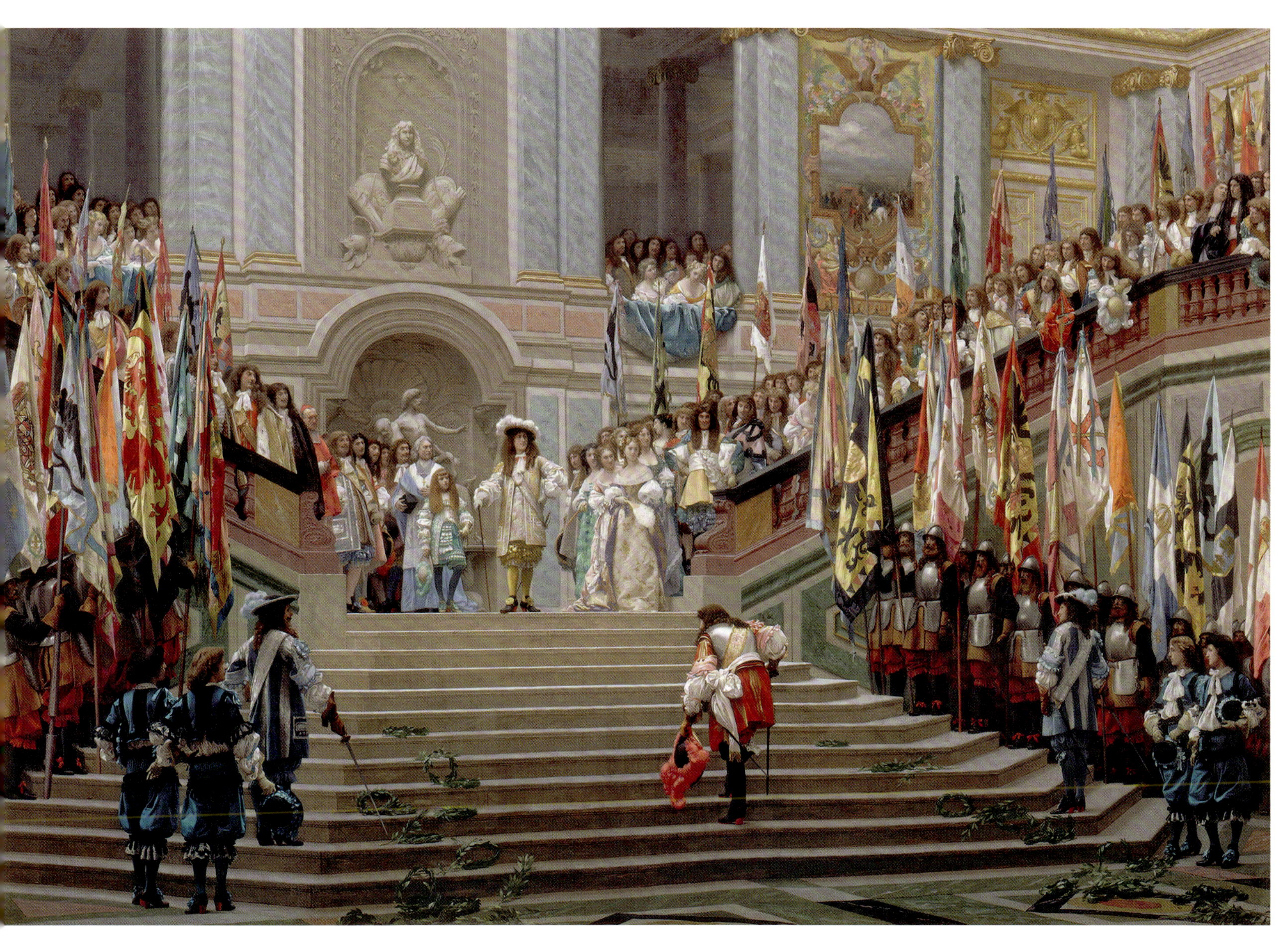

Cat. 87

THE TULIP FOLLY

–

1882
Oil on canvas
25 ¾ × 39 ⅜ in.
Signed lower right: *J.L. GEROME*
The Walters Art Museum, Baltimore, Gift of Mrs. Cyril W. Keene, 1983, inv. 37.2612

–

Provenance:
Gérôme to Goupil, 1882. Goupil to Schaus, New York, Oct. 1882, Goupil stock book 11, no. 16312 (for 50,000 francs). Mary J. Morgan sale, American Art Association, New York, Mar. 8, 1886, no. 156, to J. E. Sutton/ Wysang? (for $6,000). Goupil to William Schaus, New York, June 5, 1908, Goupil stock book 15, no. 29300 (for 25,000 francs). Hermann Schaus sale, New York, Jan. 15–17, 1912, no. 212, to J. C. Evans on behalf of Mr. Thomas Footer (for $1,650). Footer to his daughter Mrs. Cephas H. Glass, 1923. By descent to Mrs. Cyril W. Keene, Baltimore. Donated to the Walters Art Gallery, 1983.

–

Exhibition History:
The Taste of Maryland: Art Collecting in Maryland 1800–1934, The Walters Art Gallery, Baltimore, 1983, no. 49.

–

Bibliography:
F. F. Hering, *Gérôme. The Life and Works of Jean-Léon Gérôme* (New York: Cassell, 1892), p. 242. B. Barryte, "Jean-Léon Gérôme's *The Tulip Folly*," *The Walters Art Gallery Bulletin*, vol. 37, no. 3, 1984. G. Ackerman, *Jean-Léon Gérôme* (Courbevoie: ACR Édition, 2000), no. 310. H. Lafont-Couturier, *Gérôme and Goupil: Art and Enterprise*, exh. cat., trans. I. Ollivier (Bordeaux: Musée Goupil, 2000–1; also New York: Dahesh Museum of Art, 2001, and Pittsburgh: The Frick Art & Historical Center, 2001), pp. 19, 162.

Aside from *Rembrandt Etching a Plate in his Atelier* (1860, lost) and *Wynant Focking* (1883, private collection), this is the only known painting by Gérôme of a Dutch genre scene, the market for which was dominated by Gérôme's rival Ernest Meissonier. In painting *The Tulip Folly*, Gérôme presents an infamous moment in seventeenth-century Dutch history in which market speculation in an exotic luxury good so inflated its value that it threatened national fiscal stability. Gérôme may have had in mind both the economic crash of 1873, the first international recession caused by speculation, as well as the extraordinary market value his own paintings had achieved by 1882.[1]

The exotic Turkish flower became fashionable among the wealthy citizens of Holland in the early seventeenth century. Efficiently transportable as bulbs, tulips were exported from Constantinople to the unlikely climes of northern Europe, where they were carefully cultivated into a variety of colors, petal and leaf patterns. Tulips became an emblem of wealth and worldliness, and within a few decades, they became the rage among the middle class as well. By 1634, values began to run wild, with people trading household items and acres of land for roots of rare species. Investment schemes sprang up, with a corresponding cottage industry of notaries, clerks, lawyers, and dealers. When the bubble inevitably burst, confidence declined, prices descended, and panic set in. Stuck with bulbs that had cost a fortune, people defaulted on loans, leading to a credit crisis.[2]

As historian Simon Schama writes about tulips in seventeenth-century Holland, "It was this transformation from a connoisseur's specimen to a generally accessible commodity that made the mania possible ... The key was reproducibility."[3] Schama could have been writing about reproductive prints after Gérôme paintings when he states, "The tulip simultaneously retained its associations of precious treasure yet was a prize in some form within the reach of the common man."[4]

Gérôme paints an imagined scene inspired by the historic episode in which the Dutch government tried to stabilize the market by driving the flowers' value back up through decreasing supply. Government soldiers are pictured in the back and middle ground destroying beds of flowers, while in the foreground a wealthy Dutchman protects a single potted bloom, one of the rare stripe-patterned species. It is a dramatization of the issues of mass reproduction, market manipulation and luxury-object fetishization pertinent not only to tulipomania, but to the picture-mania surrounding Gérôme's oeuvre of the 1860s and 1870s.

A related painting, a small figure study, hangs in a private collection in California. **M. M.**

1. The market for Gérôme's paintings peaked in 1880 (see graph in H. Lafont-Couturier, "Mr. Gérôme works for Goupil," in H. Lafont-Couturier, *Gérôme and Goupil: Art and Enterprise*, exh. cat., trans. I. Ollivier (Bordeaux: Musée Goupil, 2000–1; also New York: Dahesh Museum of Art, 2001, and Pittsburgh: The Frick Art & Historical Center, 2001), p. 20. See also my essay in this catalogue, "Gérôme in the Gilded Age." **2.** C. Mackay, *Extraordinary Popular Delusions and the Madness of Crowds* (London:, 1852). **3.** S. Schama, *Embarrassment of Riches: An Interpretation of Dutch Culture in the Golden Age* (New York: Knopf, 1987), pp. 350–51. **4.** Ibid., p. 351.

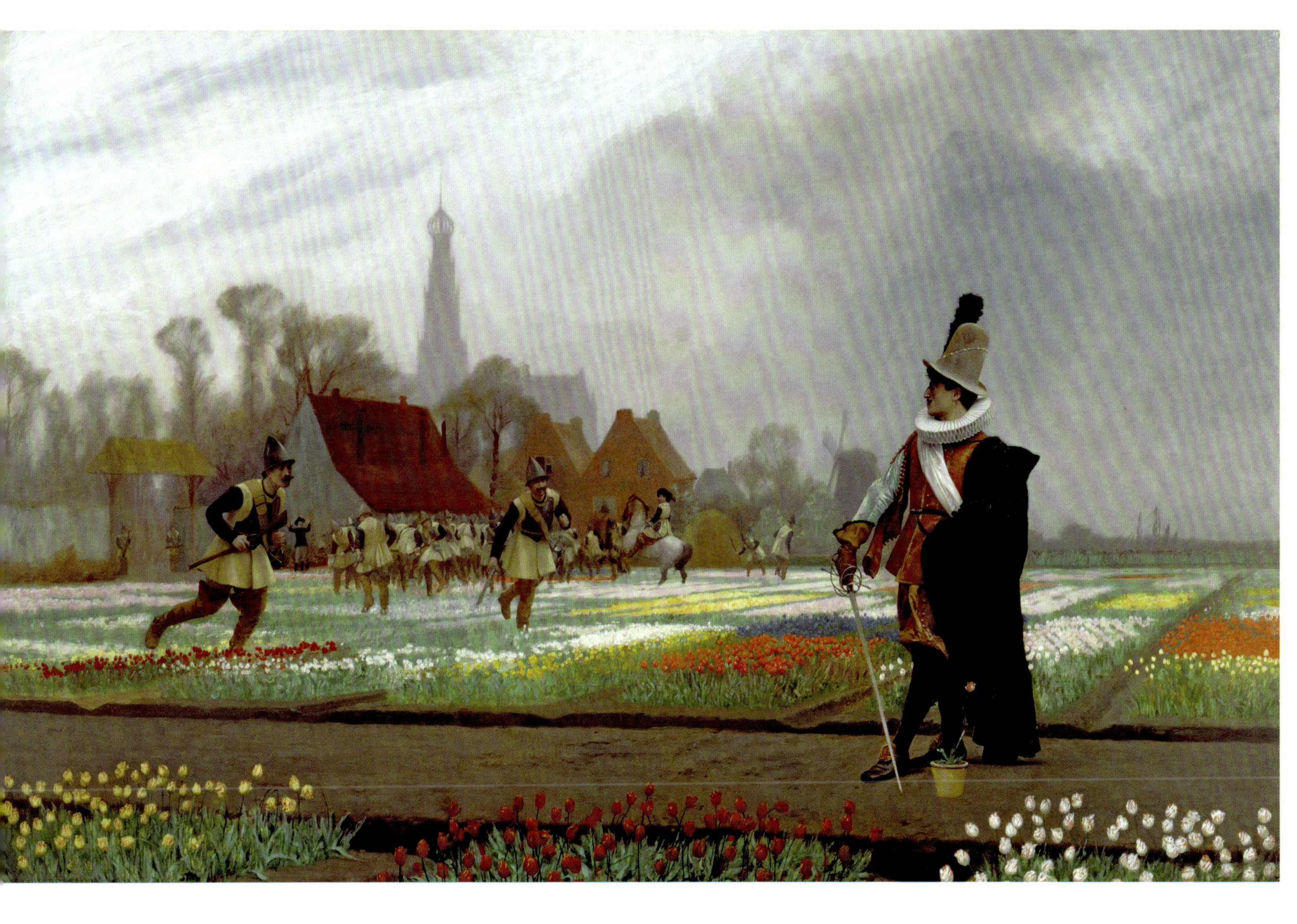

Cat. 88

THE CONSPIRATORS

–

Sketch of the painting exhibited at the Salon of 1892

–

1892
Oil on canvas
24 ¾ × 36 ¼ in.
Musée Georges-Garret, Vesoul (deed of gift from Morot-Dubufe, 1945), inv. 945.2.11

–

Provenance: Gérôme's descendants. Morot-Dubufe deed of gift to the Musée Georges-Garret, 1945

–

Bibliography: G. Ackerman et al., *Jean-Léon Gérôme (1824–1904)*, exh. cat. (Dayton: Dayton Art Institute, 1972; also Minneapolis: Minneapolis Institute of Arts, 1973, and Baltimore: The Walters Art Gallery, 1973), pp. 92–93. *Équivoques*, exh. cat. (Paris: Musée des Arts Décoratifs, 1973), n.p. *J.-L. Gérôme* (Vesoul: Musée Georges-Garret, 1981), no. 143, p. 122. G. Ackerman, *Jean-Léon Gérôme* (Courbevoie: ACR Édition, 2000), no. 407.2.

This work is a sketch or an identically-sized variant of *The Conspirators* (private collection), a late painting exhibited at the Salon of 1892. The generally loose handling and *frottis* technique suggest that it remains somewhat unfinished, while its rather crude aspect underscores the spareness of the composition. Compared to the painting shown at the Salon, here Gérôme avoids the dramatic chiaroscuro effect generated by a lamp on the conspirators' table. Instead, he again exploits spatial void and decentering, two of his favorite stylistic devices for history paintings. This scene, set during the Directory period after the Revolution and shown at the Salon without any other indication, recalls the fine effect produced by *The Death of Caesar* (cat. 67) and *The Death of Marshal Ney* (cat. 93). Nonetheless, the subject could be compared to a scene of Victor Hugo's novel *Quatre-vingt-treize* where Robespierre, Danton and Marat meet in a cabaret, rue du Paon in Paris[1]. Gérôme again plays with his old tricks in what is a light, spirited painting with few pretensions. "*The Conspirators* is above all witty," wrote Émile Bergerat in *Le Figaro*,[2] stressing the entertaining side of this theatrical composition. Faithful to his penchant for the anecdotal fringes of history, Gérôme here produced one of his final renderings of an incidental sidelight. **L. C.**

1. V. Hugo, *Quatre-vingt-treize*, livre deuxième, Le Cabaret de la rue Paon, "Minos, Eaque et Rhadamante," (Paris: Librairie Générale française, 2001), pp. 189–192. **2.** É. Bergerat, "Salon de 1892," *Le Figaro*, Apr. 30, 1892, p. 1

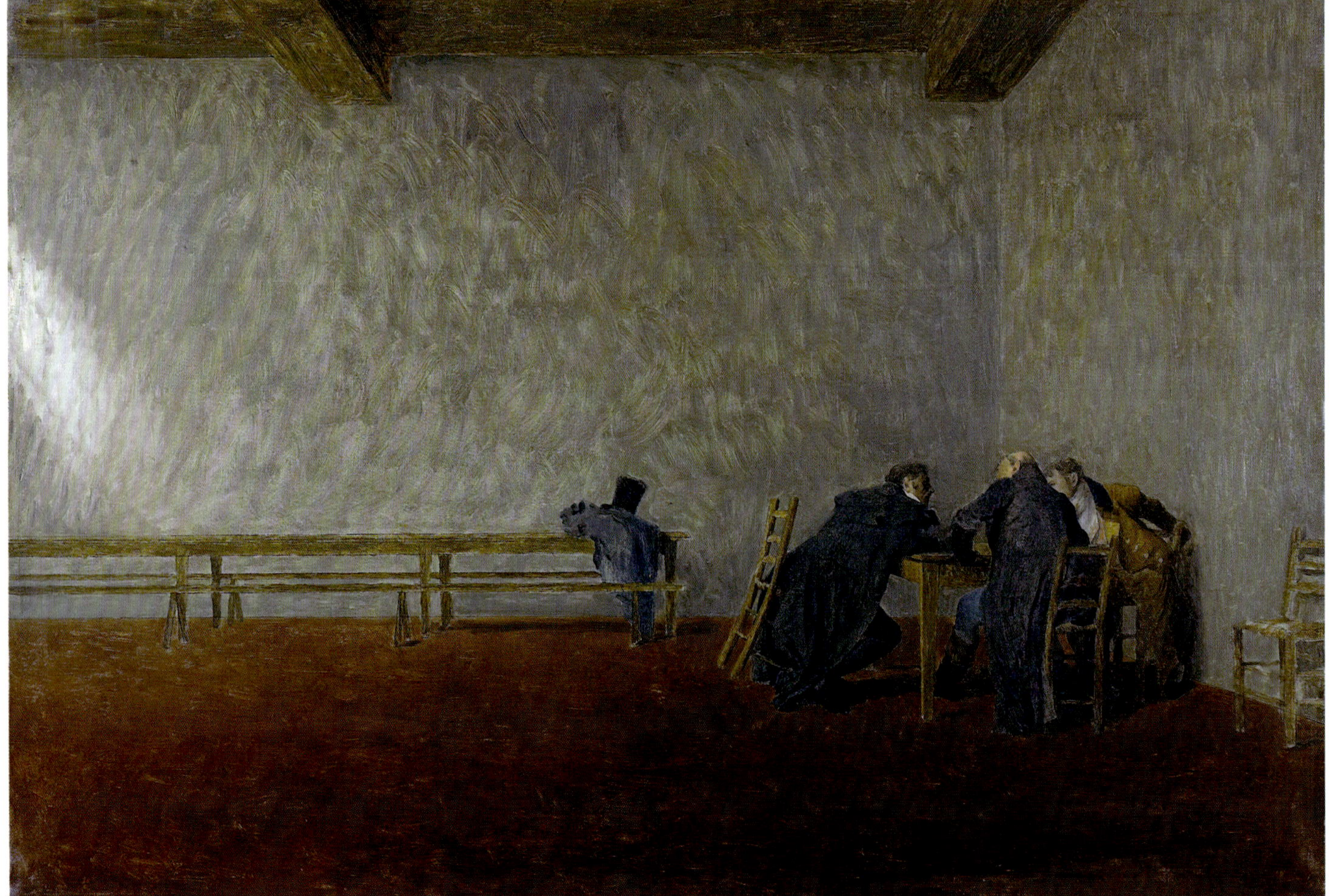

Cat. 89

NAPOLEON AND HIS GENERAL STAFF IN EGYPT, SKETCH

–

1867
Oil on canvas
19 1/8 × 31 5/8 in.
Signed lower left:
à mon ami Frémiet J.L. Gerome
Mohammad Ladjevardian collection

–

Provenance: Gift of Gérôme to Emmanuel Fremiet. Fremiet family. Sotheby's, New York, May 5, 1999, lot 204.

–

Bibliography: G. Ackerman, *Jean-Léon Gérôme* (Courbevoie: ACR Édition, 2000), no. 172.3.

Cat. 90

NAPOLEON IN CAIRO

–

1867–68
Oil on panel
14 1/8 × 9 7/8 in.
Signed lower left: *J.L.GEROME*
Princeton University Art Museum, Princeton (Museum purchase, John Maclean Magie, Class of 1892, and Gertrude Magie Fund), inv. Y1953-78

–

Provenance: F. Schnittjer and Son sale, PBNY, auction 421, July 14–15, 1943, lot 3. Van Doorn Estate sale, 1953. WNG and LRA, 1984, no. 30.

–

Bibliography: G. Ackerman et al., *Jean-Léon Gérôme (1824–1904)*, exh. cat. (Dayton: Dayton Art Institute, 1972; also Minneapolis: Minneapolis Institute of Arts, 1973, and Baltimore: The Walters Art Gallery, 1973), no. 16, pp. 56–57. *Reality, Fantasy and Flesh* (Lexington: University of Kansas Art Gallery, 1973), no. 39. *Orientalism*, exh. cat. (Rochester: Memorial Art Gallery of the University of Rochester, 1982; also New York: Neuberger Museum, 1982), no. 40. G. Ackerman, *Jean-Léon Gérôme* (Courbevoie: ACR Édition, 2000), no. 171. H. Lafont-Couturier, *Gérôme & Goupil. Art et entreprise*, exh. cat. (Bordeaux: Musée Goupil, 2000–1; also New York: Dahesh Museum of Art, 2001, and Pittsburgh: The Frick Art & Historical Center, 2001). *The Lure of the East, British Orientalist Painting* (Yale: Center for British Art, 2008; also London: Tate Britain, 2008; Istanbul: Suna and nan Kiraç Foundation, 2008–9), p. 58, fig. 43.

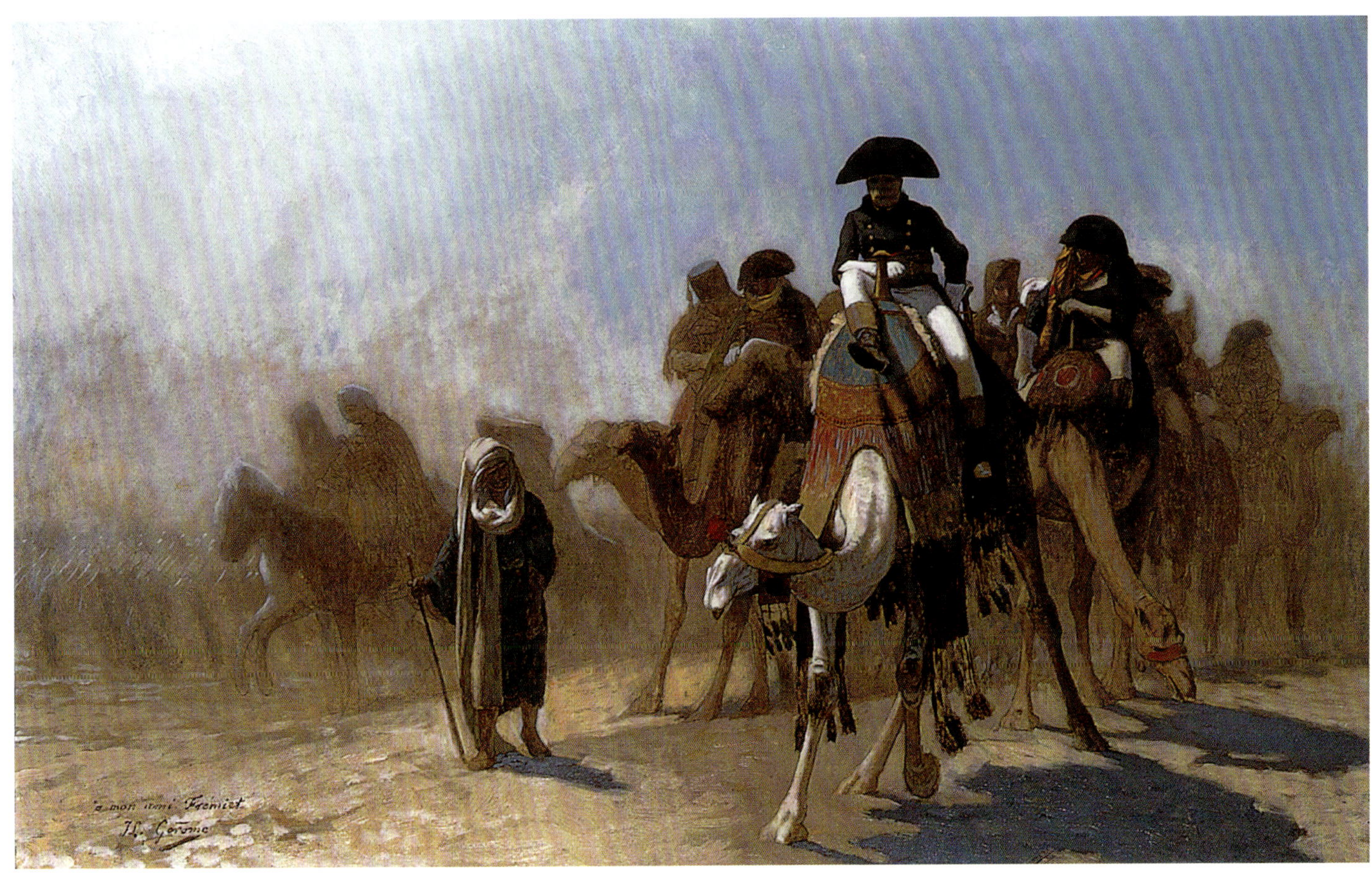

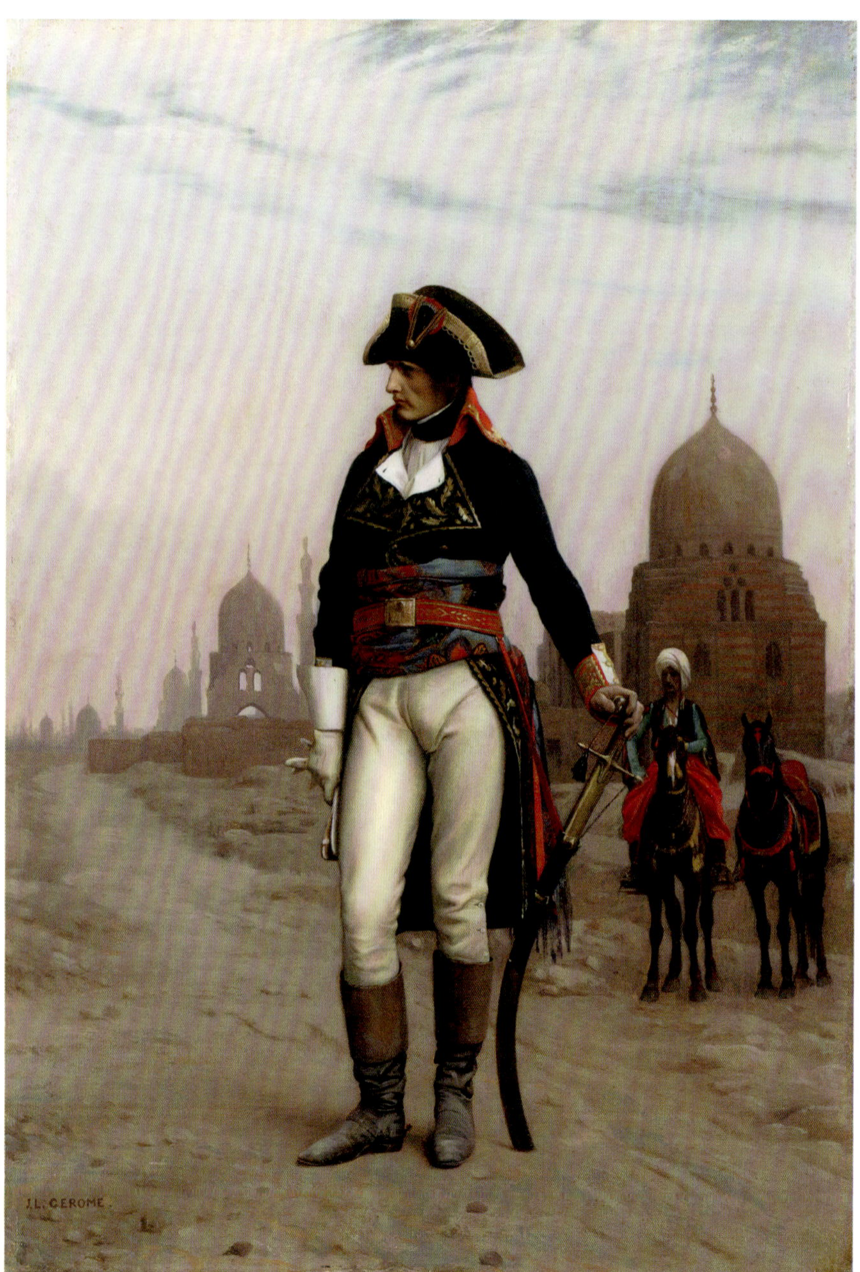

While working on *The Death of Marshal Ney* (cat. 93), Gérôme produced four canvases of Napoleon Bonaparte's military campaign in Egypt. There were certainly ulterior motives to this celebration of Bonaparte, since 1869 represented the centenary of Napoleon's birth. For Gérôme, however, grappling with Napoleonic iconography primarily meant confronting the work of his master, Paul Delaroche. From 1838 onward Delaroche had executed a series of highly original paintings that offered a melancholic, disillusioned image of the emperor. Distinguishing his own work from this personal, generation-specific view, Gérôme revived one of the main foundations of the Napoleonic visual legend by focusing exclusively on the oriental facet of General Bonaparte's rise. Gérôme had done studies of Cairo and its buildings ever since his first stay in Egypt in 1856, studies now used for this set of paintings. Of the four, *Napoleon and his General Staff in Egypt* was closest to the mid-century Orientalist and ethnographic view that allowed Gérôme to devise a new image of the First Consul on campaign. Indeed, it is a more modest version of the majestic camel caravan appearing on the horizon of the endless desert in Léon Belly's *Pilgrims Going to Mecca* (Musée d'Orsay, Paris), exhibited at the Salon of 1861. Clearly distinguished from his general staff (the faces of Kléber, Desaix and Dumas are barely recognizable), Bonaparte advances on his unusual steed into the sharp contrast of the foreground. His figure remains highly recognizable in the light-saturated, sand-heated atmosphere thanks to his famous black felt halt, which Gérôme duly researched.[1] This painting was not exhibited at the Salon, but Adolphe Goupil, whose Bonapartist sympathies were well known, published a photographic reproduction of it in 1868–1869.

Napoleon in Cairo, meanwhile, was more directly based on Gérôme's recorded memories of Cairo. Here the First Consul is shown in front of the Mamluk tombs in Cairo's City of the Dead. The work is based on the same principle of contrast seen in *Bonaparte at Cairo* (Hearst Memorial Castle, San Simeon, California) and *Oedipus* (cat. 92)—the modern conqueror is contrasted with historical symbols of the vanquished country. Gérôme thereby abandoned Delaroche's nostalgia in order to evoke, exploiting his own codes of realistic accuracy, some of the classic depictions of the Egyptian campaign, such as *Bonaparte Visiting Plague Victims in Jaffa* by Antoine-Jean Gros (1804, Musée du Louvre) and *Napoleon Pardoning the Rebels of Cairo* by Pierre-Narcisse Guérin (Musée national du Château, Versailles). More than forty years after Napoleon's death, Gérôme was making his own contribution to imperial legend and propaganda, unabashedly turning Bonaparte into a hero in the eternal landscape of Egypt. **L. C.**

1. Archives, private collection and BNF, département des Estampes et de la Photographie.

Cat. 91

NAPOLEON ENTERING CAIRO

–

1897
Gilded and patinated bronze, wood
Statuette: 15 ¼ × 14 ¼ × 5 ¾ in., with base: 43 in.
Signed on the front of the base: *J.L. GEROME*; marked on the left front of the base: *SIOT FONDEUR PARIS*
Musée Anne-de-Beaujeu, Moulins, inv. 2008.7.1

–

Provenance: Prince Paul Murat collection, 1902. Sale Piasa S.A., Paris, December 10, 2008, lot 94, purchased with the help of the FRAM.

–

Bibliography: *J.-L. Gérôme*, exh. cat. (Vesoul: Musée Georges-Garret, 1981), p. 150. J. M. Humbert, "Confirmations d'une pérennité," *Egyptomania*, exh. cat. (Paris: Musée du Louvre, 1994), no. 310, pp. 464–65. G. Ackerman, *Jean-Léon Gérôme* (Courbevoie: ACR Édition, 2000), S. 38. C. Peltre, *Bonaparte et l'Égypte – Feu et lumières*, exh. cat. (Paris: Institut du Monde Arabe, 2008–9), no. 269, p. 312, for another version. B. H. Papounaud, *La Revue des musées de France. La Revue du Louvre*, no. 2, April 2010, no. 70, pp. 70–71.

Thirty years after his paintings depicting the French military campaign in Egypt, Gérôme again turned to the figure of Napoleon Bonaparte. *Napoleon Entering Cairo*, executed nearly a century after the event itself (July 21, 1798), was exhibited at the Salon of 1897 and immediately purchased by the French government (now in the Sénat, Paris, on loan from the Musée d'Orsay). Critics hailed a statuette that "combined the best qualities of the sculptor and the painter: precise and elegant forms, expressive accuracy of movement, correct historical reconstruction, ingenious selection and skillful execution of attire and props."[1] French sculptor René de Saint-Marceaux also felt that never had Gérôme "so brilliantly displayed, as a sculptor, his usual qualities of skilled, refined taste."[2] Gérôme avoided the exoticism of giving Bonaparte a camel as a mount, which, when it came to a lone figure, might have undermined the heroic tone of this depiction of a future emperor. Particularly appreciated were the extreme delicacy of the modeling and the painstaking attention to details of fabrics, such as the horse "covered with oriental embroideries and a saddle of matchless beauty."[3] Two versions are known of this statuette with its spectacular neo-Egyptian base, a six-columned structure recalling the temples Gérôme had seen during his journey in 1856. It is embellished with a winged Victory flying between the columns and a small scribe recording the future emperor's deeds; these archaeologically dubious additions attest to both the long-lasting popularity of Egyptomania and the importance of the Egyptian campaign in France's collective imagination at the end of the nineteenth century.[4] The names of Bonaparte's companions are inscribed on the low wall between the columns (Menou, Berthollet, Fourier, Lannes, Larrey, Murat, Kléber, Denon, Reynier, Desaix, Monge, Baragauy d'Hilliers) while his victories are listed on the frieze (Gaza, Jaffa, Mount Thabor, Aboukir, Alexandria, Pyramids, Cairo, El-Arish). This declamatory setting reveals the remarkable adaptability of the statuette, which could safely have been transformed into a large public monument. **É. P.**

1. G. Lafenestre, "Les Salons de 1897: II, La sculpture au Salons, La peinture au Champ-de-Mars," *Revue des Deux Mondes*, July 1, 1897, p. 178. **2.** R. de Saint-Marceaux, "La Sculpture aux Salons de 1897," *Gazette des Beaux-Arts*, 1897, vol. I , p. 484. **3.** R. Binet, "Un dernier mot sur les salons," *Art et Décoration*, 1897, vol. I, p. 169. **4.** J. M. Humbert, "Confirmations d'une pérennité," *Egyptomania*, exh. cat. (Paris: Musée du Louvre, 1994), no. 310, pp. 464–65. B. H. Papounaud, *La Revue des musées de France. La Revue du Louvre*, no. 2, April 2010, no. 70, pp. 70–71.

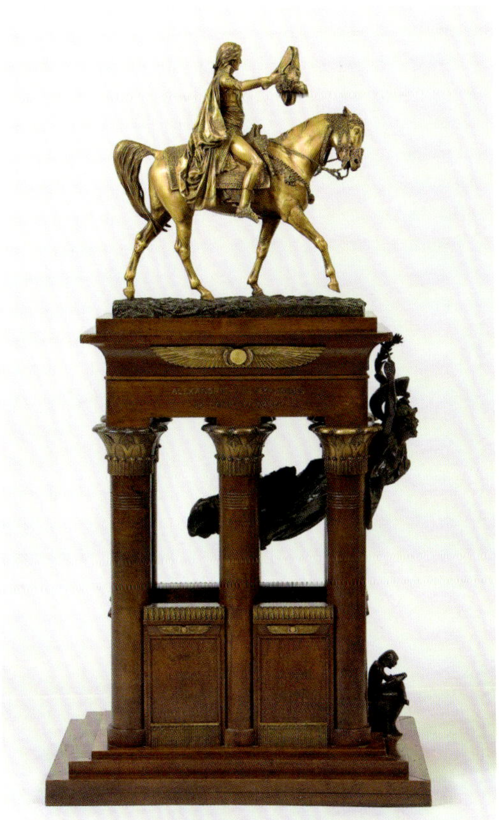

Cat. 92

ŒDIPUS

–

ca. 1863–86
Oil on canvas
23 ¾ × 39 ¾ in.
Hearst Castle, San Simeon, California State Parks, inv. 529-9-5092

–

Provenance:
Gérôme's private collection, 1887. Gérôme to Knoedler, New York, 1892. J. Hayermoert, 1893. Knoedler & Co. to M. C. D. Borden, 1895. Borden sale, American Art Association, New York, Feb. 13–14, 1913, no. 78, as "Bonaparte en Égypte," bought by Knoedler (for $3,500). Knoedler to William Randolph Hearst, Feb. 19, 1913.

–

Exhibition History:
Salon of 1886, no. 1042 as "Oedipe." *The Lure of Egypt: Land of the Pharaohs Revisited*, Museum of Fine Arts, Saint Petersburg, Florida, 1996, no. 18. *Orientalism: Delacroix to Klee*, Art Gallery of New South Wales, Sydney, 1997; also Auckland Art Gallery, 1998, no. 45.

–

Bibliography:
F.-G. Dumas, *Catalogue illustré du Salon* (Paris: Librarie d'art L. Baschet, 1886), p. 10. F. F. Hering, "Gérôme," *Century Magazine* 37, no. 4 (Feb. 1889), pp. 482–85. G. Lafenestre, quoted in "Jean Léon Gérôme," *Académie des sciences, belles-lettres et arts de Besançon. Procès-verbaux et Mémoires. Année 1904* (Besançon, 1905), p. 160. A. Boime, "Jean-Léon Gérôme, Henri Rousseau's Sleeping Gypsy and the Academic Legacy," *The Art Quarterly*, vol. 34, no. 1 (Spring 1971), p. 7. B. B. Frederickson, *Handbook of the Paintings in the Hearst San Simeon State Historical Monument* (1977), no. 5. G. Lacambre, catalogue entry for sketch of *Oedipus*, *Les Oubliés du Caire. Chefs-d'oeuvre des musées du Caire*, exh. cat. (Paris: Musée d'Orsay, 1994–5), pp. 106–7. F. Leeman, "Shadows over Jean-Léon Gérôme's Career," *Van Gogh Museum Journal*, 1997–8, pp. 92–93. H. Lafont-Couturier, *Gérôme* (Paris: Herscher, 1998), pp. 54, 82. G. Ackerman, *Jean-Léon Gérôme* (Courbevoie: ACR Édition, 2000), no. 175. H. Lafont-Couturier, *Gérôme and Goupil: Art and Enterprise*, exh. cat., trans. I. Ollivier (Bordeaux: Musée Goupil, 2000–1; also New York: Dahesh Museum of Art, 2001, and Pittsburgh: The Frick Art & Historical Center, 2001), p. 146. K. Davies, *The Orientalists: Western Artists in Arabia, The Sahara, Persia and India* (New York: Laynfaroh, 2005), pp. 224–25. *Bonaparte et l'Égypte: feu et lumière* (Paris: Institut du Monde Arabe, 2008–9; also Arras: Musée des Beaux-Arts, 2009), no. 273.

Gérôme may have painted this picture in the years leading up to the centenary of Napoleon Bonaparte's birth in 1869. During the 1860s, he painted several images of Bonaparte in Egypt, including a similarly scaled composition of the general on horseback viewing Cairo from a hilltop.[1] Both images are based on Bonaparte's Egyptian expedition, 1798–1801. In this picture, Napoleon admires the magisterial sphinx that guards the famous pyramids of Giza constructed during the reign of King Khafre. Gérôme presents the image from an angle that elides the pyramids, thereby dramatizing the encounter between the two colossi. Napoleon's horse stands still, swishing his tail in the heat, while the general sits tensely in his saddle, his hand and arm perched on his thigh, his face, cast in shade by his hat brim, tilted up to gaze at the Sphinx. The shadow of his entourage, standing at a respectful distance, is perceptible at the left of the picture, while in the distant background the general's troops prepare for battle against the Ottoman Turks.

Napoleon landed in Egypt in June 1798, declaring his intent to free the Egyptians from the Ottoman sultan's oppression. A great French victory took place on the Giza plains, and became known as the Battle of the Pyramids. According to legend, Napoleon rallied his troops on the eve of the battle with the statement, "Soldats! Du haut de ces pyramides quarante siècles vous contemplent!" ("Soldiers, forty centuries look down upon you from these pyramids!") Gérôme pictures the moment when the general himself seems to weigh the immensity of history, diminishing the scale of this solitary figure against the great monster's head.

In 1886 Gérôme exhibited the painting under the title "*Œdipus*," enhancing the purposefulness with which Napoleon contemplates the ancient Sphinx. The story from classical mythology involves Oedipus traveling to Thebes, where he is stopped by the Sphinx and forced to answer a riddle in order to pass or risk gruesome death. Oedipus solves the riddle, kills the Sphinx, and is rewarded by the liberated Thebans with a king's crown. Gérôme casts the soon-to-be crowned general in a similar role of potential liberator.

The American journalist Fanny Field Hering published a reproduction of the painting as the frontispiece to her hagiographic 1889 article on Gérôme. She reports a visit with Gérôme in June 1887 in which she asks after "L'Oedipe," having made a special pilgrimage to see it, and is instantly and graciously accommodated. Gérôme leads her into a private room of his Paris residence and reveals the painting to her. She describes it in rapturous prose, and concludes with a pronouncement from Gérôme, "It is for my children. I would never sell it; I love it too well. We are old friends."[2]

Five years later, Gérôme sold the work to Michel Knoedler in New York. The newspaper magnate William Randolph Hearst acquired this painting's pendant, *General Bonaparte at Cairo* (cat. 90), from Knoedler in 1898, and reunited the two paintings at his castle in San Simeon when *Oedipus* came on the market in 1913. In the Borden sale catalogue, the great American museum director William Valentiner wrote in the introductory notes about this picture, where it was listed as "Bonaparte en Égypte," "It is for us to use these true statements, as any traveler uses the facts before him, as a basis for our musings on the frailty of human life. Gérôme has given us the facts."[3] **M. M.**

1. F. F. Hering, who was much taken with *Oedipus*, suggests that both pictures were executed in 1863 when Gérôme was painting several images of Napoleon. F. F. Hering, *Gérôme. The Life and Works of Jean-Léon Gérôme* (New York: Cassell, 1892), p. 250. Other pictures of Napoleon done around the same time include *Napoleon and his General Staff in Egypt* (cat. 89), and *Napoleon in Cairo* (cat. 90). Later in his career, Gérôme sculpted a composition cast in bronze, *Bonaparte Entering Cairo*, a version of which was exhibited at the Salon of 1897 (cat. 91). **2.** F. F. Hering, "Gérôme," *Century Magazine* 37, no. 4 (Feb. 1889), pp. 484–86. **3.** W. Valentiner, introductory notes, *Notable Paintings by the Great Masters* (New York: American Art Association, 1913).

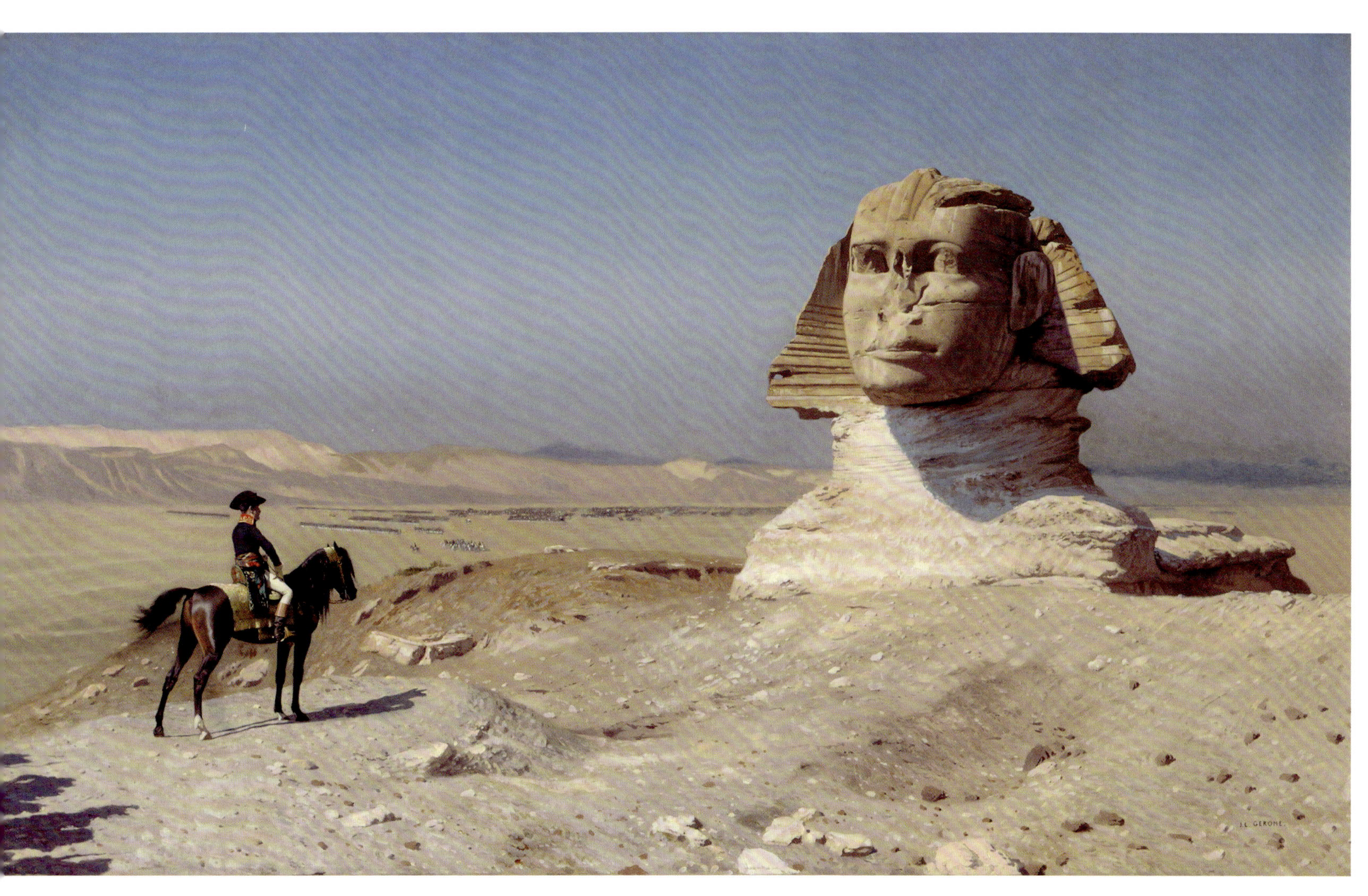
J.L. GEROME.

Cat. 93

THE DEATH OF MARSHAL NEY ALSO KNOWN AS DECEMBER 7, 1815, 9 O'CLOCK IN THE MORNING

1868
Oil on canvas
25 ¾ × 41 in.
Signed lower left: *J.L. GEROME*
Galleries and Museums Trust, Sheffield, inv. VIS.1844

Provenance: Goupil & Cie, 1869. Agnew, 1871. Boussod, Valadon & Cie, 1880. Christie's, London, May 21, 1881. William Leach. Agnew. Sir Alexander Henderson, Bt., M.P. Lord Farringdon, who presented it to the Sheffield City Art Gallery in 1931.

Exhibition History: Salon of 1868, Paris, no. 1071. Royal Academy, London, 1876. Guildhall, London, 1898.

Bibliography: E. About, "Le Salon de 1868," *Revue des Deux Mondes*, vol. LXXV (June 1868), pp. 728–29. L. Auvray, "Expositions des Beaux-Arts. Salon de 1868," *Revue artistique et littéraire*, vol. 14 (1868), pp. 222–23. A. du Belloy, "Promenade à l'exposition des beaux-arts," *Le Correspondant*, vol. 38, no. 5 (June 10, 1868), pp. 697–98. C. Blanc, *Le Temps*, May 19, 1868. F. Boissin, *Salon de 1868. Études artistiques* (Paris, 1868), pp. 69–70. B. Bouniol, "L'Amateur au Salon. 1868," *Revue du monde catholique*, vol. 21, no. 4 (May 25, 1868), pp. 568–69. E. Chesneau, *Le Constitutionnel*, no. 126 (May 5, 1868). H. Fouquier, "Salon de 1868," *L'Avenir national*, May 5, 1868. T. Gautier, *Le Moniteur*, May 2, 1868. G. Lafenestre, "L'art au Salon de 1868," *Revue contemporaine*, vol. 63 (May–June 1868), pp. 521–25. C. Lavergne, *L'Univers*, May 21, 1868. P. Mantz, "Salon de 1868. Tableaux reproduits par L'Illustration," *L'Illustration*, May 2, 1868. M. de Montifaud, "La peinture d'histoire au Salon de 1868," *L'Artiste*, June 1868, pp. 401–2. A. Nettement, "Salon de 1868," *La Semaine des familles*, no. 34 (May 23, 1868), pp. 542–43. É. Palma, "Salon de 1868," *Revue de Paris*, vol. XI, pp. 414–15. P. Petroz, "Salon de 1868," *Revue moderne*, vol. 46, no. 2 (May 10, 1868), p. 362. H. Rochefort, "Le Salon cette année," *Le Figaro*, May 20, 1868, p. 162. P. de Saint-Victor, *La Liberté*, May 13, 1868. W. Bürger [Théophile Thoré], "Salon de 1868," in *Salons de W. Bürger, 1861 à 1868* (Paris, 1870), vol. 2, pp. 466–69. M. Chaumelin, *L'Art contemporain* (Paris, 1873), pp. 115–18. J.-A. Castagnary, *Salons* (Paris, 1892), pp. 253, 261–62. *Exhibition of Naval and Military Work*, exh. cat. (London: Guildhall, 1915). *Art Treasures Exhibition*, exh. cat. (Manchester: Royal Institution, 1960). G. Ackerman, "Gérôme and Manet," *Gazette des Beaux-Arts*, Sept. 1967, pp. 163–176. G. Ackerman et al., *Jean-Léon Gérôme (1824–1904)*, exh. cat. (Dayton: Dayton Art Institute, 1972; also Minneapolis: Minneapolis Institute of Arts, 1973, and Baltimore: The Walters Art Gallery, 1973), no. 21, pp. 64–65. A. Boime, "New Light on Manet's Execution of Maximilian," *Art Quarterly*, fall 1973, p. 189. *J.-L. Gérôme*, exh. cat. (Vesoul: Musée Georges-Garret, 1981), p. 22. W. Kemp, "Verständlichkeit und Spannung: über Leerstellen in der Malerei des 19Jh," in *Der Betrachter ist im Bild* (Cologne: DuMont, 1985), pp. 262–78. *Triomphe et mort du héros: la peinture d'histoire en Europe de Rubens à Manet*, exh. cat. (Lyon: Musée des Beaux-Arts, 1988; also Cologne: Wallraf-Richartz Museum, and Zurich: Kunsthaus), no. 34. *Théophile Gautier, la critique en liberté*, exh. cat. (Paris: Musée d'Orsay, 1997), no. 62. H. Lafont-Couturier, *Gérôme* (Paris: Herscher, 1998), p. 55. G. Ackerman, *Jean-Léon Gérôme* (Courbevoie: ACR Édition, 2000), no. 170. H. Lafont-Couturier, *Gérôme and Goupil: Art and Enterprise*, exh. cat., trans. I. Ollivier (Bordeaux: Musée Goupil, 2000–1; also New York: Dahesh Museum of Art, 2001, and Pittsburgh: The Frick Art & Historical Center, 2001), pp. 146–48, 157, 166. J. Elderfield, *Manet and the Execution of Maximilian* (New York: The Museum of Modern Art, 2006), pp. 113–14. *Painting History: Paul Delaroche and Lady Jane Grey*, exh. cat., (London: The National Gallery, 2010), no. 86.

1868 was a year of controversy for Gérôme. Presented at the Salon, *Golgotha* (cat. 78) and *The Death of Marshal Ney* disconcerted critics and provoked heated debate. In these two canvases which, as he himself said, "gave me so much trouble,"[1] Gérôme was indeed eschewing the traditional codes of heroic treatment. The death of Christ and the execution of a hero of the Napoleonic wars were restored to their archaeological or historical reality. And yet this apparent bareness, underscored by the somewhat austere look of the two paintings, did enable Gérôme to fully explore the workings of a new way of dramatizing the image. The circumstances of the condemnation and execution of Marshal Ney were well known from several accounts, one of the first being *Le Procès du Maréchal Ney*, published by M. Delanoe as early as 1815.[2] However, the most direct source of the painting was no doubt *Histoire des deux Restaurations*, published in 1860 by the republican historian Achille de Vaulabelle, from which Gérôme copied out a passage.[3] Ney, the hero of the armies of the Rhine and Danube, the campaigns in Prussia and Russia, the battles of Eylau and of Friedland, made marshal of France in 1804, duke of Elchingen in 1808, and prince of Moscow in 1812, was involved in all glorious events of the Napoleonic adventure. This did not keep him from going over to the restored monarchy, before he finally rallied to the emperor during the last hurrah of the Hundred Days. Condemned to death for treason by the Chambre des Pairs (House of Lords), he was executed on December 7, 1815, on the avenue de l'Observatoire, and not on the plaine de Grenelle, for "the government, fearing large popular gatherings that might give rise to clashes, took the course of executing him, so to speak, on the sly." The marshal "was in mourning for his father; his clothes were a frock coat in thick blue cloth, breeches and stockings in black silk, and on his head a round hat ... He fell at once ... and in keeping with military regulations, the body was left out for a quarter of

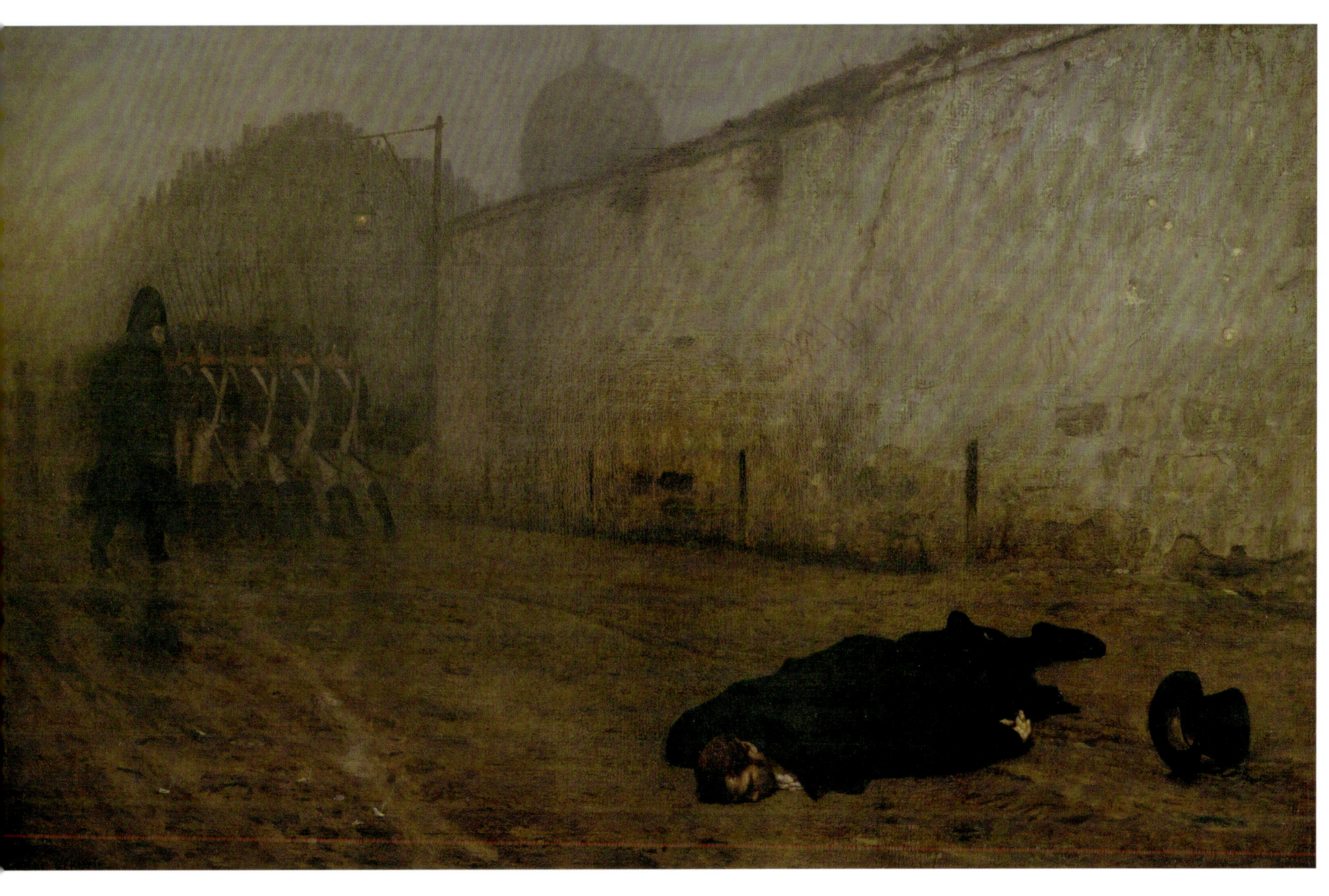

Ill. 72. Édouard Manet (1832–1883), *The Execution of Maximilian*, 1867–68, oil on canvas, 99 1/8 × 118 7/8 in., Kunsthalle, Mannheim.

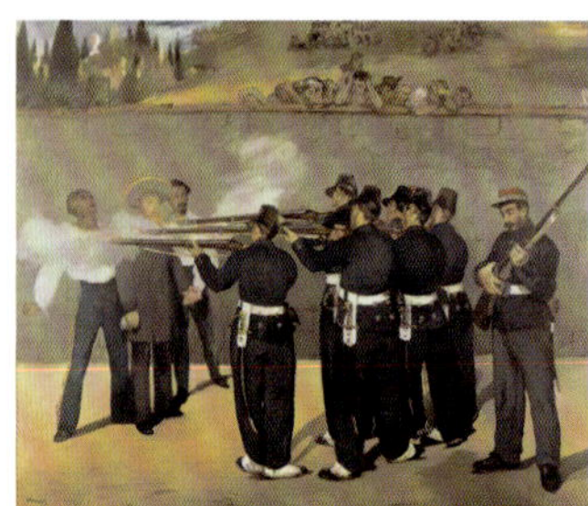

Ill. 73. Jean-Paul Laurens (1838–1921), *The Interdict*, 1875, oil on canvas, 45 5/8 × 71 1/8 in., Musée des Beaux-Arts André Malraux, Le Havre.

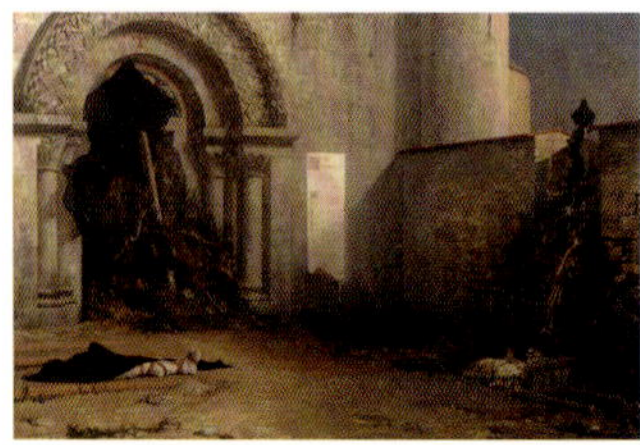

an hour in the place of execution."[4] Gérôme rendered these details with precision, breaking with the emphatic style of popular representation conceived for the illustrations of *L'Histoire de France* by the abbé de Montgaillard.[5] This accuracy stimulated Gérôme's realistic, documentary ambitions, leading here to what is one of the most pared down compositions of his entire career. Like the body of the dead Caesar in the first of his two paintings on this theme, painted in 1859, the corpse of Ney, here emphasized by dramatic foreshortening, is the main subject of the picture (*The Death of Caesar*, cat. 67, ill. 56, p. 122). Studying the echoes found between the work of Gérôme and that of Édouard Manet, Gerald Ackerman has emphasized the visual radicalism that, along with other obvious dramatic and stylistic intentions, Manet's *Dead Toreador* shares with *The Death of Marshal Ney*. Nor can we exclude the possibility that, in placing himself for once on an overtly political terrain, Gérôme was alluding here to Manet's *The Execution of Maximilian* (ill. 72). In his analysis of Manet's work, John House stresses the reasons for the stormy reception of Gérôme's painting, and recalls the explanation given by Edmond About: "Marshal Ney was very nearly expelled from the Salon by those who were most in his debt, for the blood of the bravest of the brave stained the popularity of the Bonapartist party ... The administration considered it a bad thing to evoke such a memory, and politely reminded artists that the exhibition of legal assassination was against the highest propriety."[6] In his memoirs, however, Gérôme reformulated the awkwardness of painting such a sensitive subject in Second Empire France in much more personal terms: "I very nearly became embroiled in a serious affair with the prince of Moscow, the marshal's son. The superintendent of fine arts asked me several times not to exhibit the painting, but I stood my ground and always refused to yield to his demands, telling him that painters are entitled to write history with their brushes just as men of letters are with their pens, which was true."[7] Gérôme's work does not tend towards the radical intensity of *The Execution of Maximilian* with its dramatic composition inherited from Goya's *Third of May*. His vision is as deliberately precise and dry as the statement of the day and time of the execution in the work's French title (*Le 7 décembre 1815, neuf heures du matin*), a mode of realist factuality already manifested by Honoré Daumier in his *Rue Transnonain, April 15, 1834*; the goal is to create the illusion of truth—hence, for example, the half-erased graffiti exclaiming "Vive l'Empereur" on the wall. In his analysis of the painting, Théophile Gautier stressed this quality of detail and the new sense of historical accuracy that, as he saw it, was what made Gérôme's contribution so original: "It is a history painting, but not in the sense in which this word used to be understood. First of all, the frame is very small, as if for a genre scene, and the subject has not yet acquired the distance of the past; it continues, so to speak, to throb and bleed. The artist has handled it with the modern sense of history, going back to the original sources, rejecting vague phraseology and searching instead for the absolute reality of detail. With a searing concision and plainness that are more moving than any dramatic staging, M. Gérôme has represented this lugubrious execution just as it must have happened. It is like a painted statement by an eyewitness."[8] However, this refusal to apply the didacticism expected of history painting, which is why this painting can be seen as the paradoxical companion of Manet's *Execution of Maximilian*, is, in Gérôme's case, simply the foundation of a new dramatization of the narrative, as Wolfgang Kemp makes perfectly clear: "This scene with no apparent action is filled with echoes of the assassination ... the emptiness heightened by the great wall shown at an angle dramatizes the image, becomes filled with pathos and bestows an aura on the dead man: he is the object of the action that the painting suggests but does not show."[9] This false eviction of the story and of pathos enacted behind the meticulous realism of the image was central to the final blossoming of history painting in the last quarter of the nineteenth century. For example, *The Interdict* by Jean-Paul Laurens (ill. 73) whose anticlerical vision of medieval times is typical of this artist from the years of militant republicanism, also focuses on the scene that followed the climax of the action, using a similarly desolate, dramatic space suffused with the sense of death to evoke the events that have just occurred. **L. C.**

1. J.-L. Gérôme, *Notes autobiographiques* [1874], ed. G. Ackerman (Vesoul: S.A.L.S.A., 1981), p. 1. **2.** The publishers were Plancher, Eymery, Delaunay (Paris, 1815). **3.** DSCN 1908, 1909, 1910, private collection. **4.** A. de Vaulabelle, *Histoire des deux Restaurations: jusqu'à l'avènement de Louis-Philippe de janvier 1813 à octobre 1830* (Paris: Perrotin, 1860), vol. 4, pp. 120–21. **5.** Auguste Raffet, *Death of Ney*, in abbé de Montgaillard, *Histoire de France*, 7th edition (Paris: Moutardier, 1834–35), vol. VII, pp. 428–29. **6.** E. About, "Le Salon de 1868," *Revue des Deux Mondes*, vol. LXXV (June 1, 1868), p. 729; J. House, "History painting, Censorship and Ambiguity," *Manet. The Execution of Maximilian. Painting, Politics and Censorship*, exh. cat. (London: National Gallery, 1992), p. 100. **7.** J.-L Gérôme [1874] (as in n. 1), p. 16. **8.** T. Gautier, "Salon de 1868," *Le Moniteur universel*, no. 123 (May 2, 1868), p. 585. **9.** W. Kemp, "Verständlichkeit und Spannung: über Leerstellen in der Malerei des 19Jh," in *Der Betrachter ist im Bild* (Cologne: DuMont, 1985), pp. 262–78.

Cat. 94

THE RECEPTION OF THE SIAMESE AMBASSADORS AT FONTAINEBLEAU

–

1864
Oil on canvas
50 ½ × 102 ¼ in.
Signed and dated in Roman numerals lower right: *J.L. GEROME MDCCCLXIV*
Châteaux de Versailles et de Trianon, Versailles, inv. MV 5004

–

Provenance: Commissioned by the French government.

–

Exhibition History: Salon of 1865 (where it hung in the Salle d'Honneur along with other imperial commissions).

–

Bibliography: L. Auvray, *Salon de 1865*, pp. 21–62. T. Gautier, *Le Moniteur officiel*, June 13, 1865, p. 79. A. Hemmel, "Salon de 1865," *Revue nationale et étrangère*, vol. 21, p. 139. Jahyer, *Salon de 1865*, pp. 81–84. É. Lackroy, "Le Monde des Arts," *L'Artiste*, 1865, vol. I, pp. 83–84. M. de Lescure, "Le Salon de 1865," *Revue contemporaine*, pp. 422–23. P. Mantz, *Gazette des Beaux-Arts*, 1865, vol. 18, p. 12. M. de Montifaud, *L'Artiste*, 1865, vol. I, p. 219. C. de Mouy, "Le Salon de 1865," *Revue française*, pp. 198–99. C. de Sault, *Le Temps*, May 9, 1865. E. Strahan [Earl Shinn], *Gérôme: A Collection of the Works of J. L. Gérôme in One Hundred Photogravures* (New York: Samuel L. Hall, 1881). P. Mérimée, *Correspondance*, ser. 2, vol. 4 (Paris: Le Divan, 1941–1965), pp. 311–13. *The Past Rediscovered, French Painting 1800–1900*, exh. cat. (Minneapolis: Minneapolis Institute of Arts, 1969), no. 41. G. Ackerman et al., *Jean-Léon Gérôme (1824–1904)*, exh. cat. (Dayton: Dayton Art Institute, 1972; also Minneapolis: Minneapolis Institute of Arts, 1973; and Baltimore: The Walters Art Gallery, 1973), no. 15, pp. 54–55. *L'Art en France sous le Second Empire*, exh. cat. (Philadelphia: Philadelphia Museum of Art, 1978; also Detroit: Detroit Institute of Arts, 1879; and Paris: Grand Palais, 1979), no. VI-59. *J.-L. Gérôme*, exh. cat. (Vesoul: Musée Georges-Garret, 1981), no. 132, p. 117 see also nos. 56–57, drawings of figures. A. Boime, "The Second Empire's Official Realism" in G. Weisberg, *The European Realist Tradition* (Bloomington: Indiana University Press, 1982), p. 85ff. A. Boime, "Gérôme and the Bourgeois Artist's Burden," *Arts Magazine* 57, no. 5 (Jan. 1983), p. 68ff. G. Ackerman, *Jean-Léon Gérôme* (Courbevoie: ACR Édition, 2000), no. 148.

Cat. 95

STUDY FOR *THE RECEPTION OF THE SIAMESE AMBASSADORS* (DETAIL)

–

Prior to 1864
Pencil on paper
9 ¼ × 9 to 12 ¾ in.
Musée Georges-Garret, Vesoul, inv. 980.1.8

–

Bibliography: *J.-L. Gérôme*, exh. cat. (Vesoul: Musée Georges-Garret, 1981), no. 66, pp. 69, 71.

Cat. 96

STUDY FOR *THE RECEPTION OF THE SIAMESE AMBASSADORS* (DETAIL)

–

Prior to 1864
Pencil on paper
9 ¼ × 12 ¾ in.
Musée Georges-Garret, Vesoul, inv. 980.1.11

–

Bibliography: *J.-L. Gérôme*, exh. cat. (Vesoul: Musée Georges-Garret, 1981), no. 68, pp. 69, 71. S. Harent and C. Stoullig, *Dessins de Jean-Léon Gérôme: la collection du musée des Beaux-Arts de Nancy*, exh. cat. (Nancy: Musée des Beaux-Arts, 2009), p. 16, fig. 7.

Cat. 97

STUDY FOR *THE RECEPTION OF THE SIAMESE AMBASSADORS* (DETAIL)

–

Prior to 1864
Pencil on paper
9 ¼ × 12 ¾ in.
Musée Georges-Garret, Vesoul, inv. 980.1.10

–

Bibliography: *J.-L. Gérôme*, exh. cat. (Vesoul: Musée Georges-Garret, 1981), no. 65, pp. 69–70.

Cat. 98

STUDY FOR *THE RECEPTION OF THE SIAMESE AMBASSADORS* (DETAIL)

–

Prior to 1864
Pencil on paper
9 ¼ × 12 ¾ in.
Musée Georges-Garret, Vesoul, inv. 980.1.15

–

Bibliography: *J.-L. Gérôme*, exh. cat. (Vesoul: Musée Georges-Garret, 1981), no. 57, p. 69.

Provenance of the forth studies: Morot collection, from the Galerie Huisse, Rouen, 1980.

Ill. 74. Jacques-Louis David (1748–1825), *Coronation of Napoleon I*, 1806–7, oil on canvas, 244 ½ × 385 ½ in., Musée du Louvre, Paris, inv. 3699.

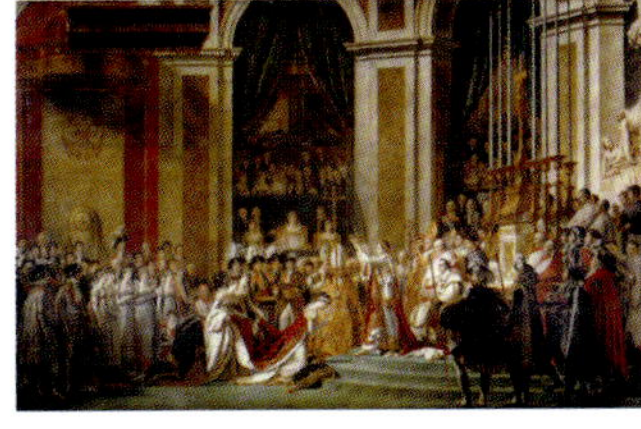

On June 27, 1861, Emperor Napoleon III and Empress Eugénie received the ambassadors of the king of Siam (today's Thailand) with great pomp in the grand Henry II gallery of Fontainebleau chateau. The kingdom of Siam was then opening itself to trade and wished to sign agreements of mutual diplomatic representation with the major Western powers.

A painting to commemorate this reception was commissioned from Gérôme by the Beaux-Arts administration that same year. It was destined for the history museum then housed at Versailles, in order to celebrate the lavish ceremony that represented a symbolic encounter of East and West. Gérôme certainly saw it as a chance to produce a major "contemporary history painting," as well as a possibility to establish closer links to the imperial family—during the 1860s he would be invited several times to evening gatherings at the imperial chateau in Compiègne. Yet the commission also meant a substantial fee: upon its completion in 1864, Gérôme was paid 20,000 francs.

He began the large painting early in 1863, during the first months after his move to a new studio at 6 rue de Bruxelles. The ambitious composition, featuring the slow approach of the Siamese ambassadors toward the imperial French couple enthroned on the dais, is an allusion to Jacques-Louis David's *Coronation of Napoleon I* of 1806–7 (ill. 74). This allusion offered the possibility of a double tribute: the emperor was linked to his august uncle, and the artist also placed himself in the tradition of great nineteenth-century history painters as inaugurated by David. In a somewhat more remote way, obvious iconographic precedents could be found in Antoine Coypel's 1715 painting of *Louis XIV Receiving the Persian Ambassador*.

According to the July 6, 1861 issue of *L'Illustration*, Gérôme remained faithful to the ceremonial pro-

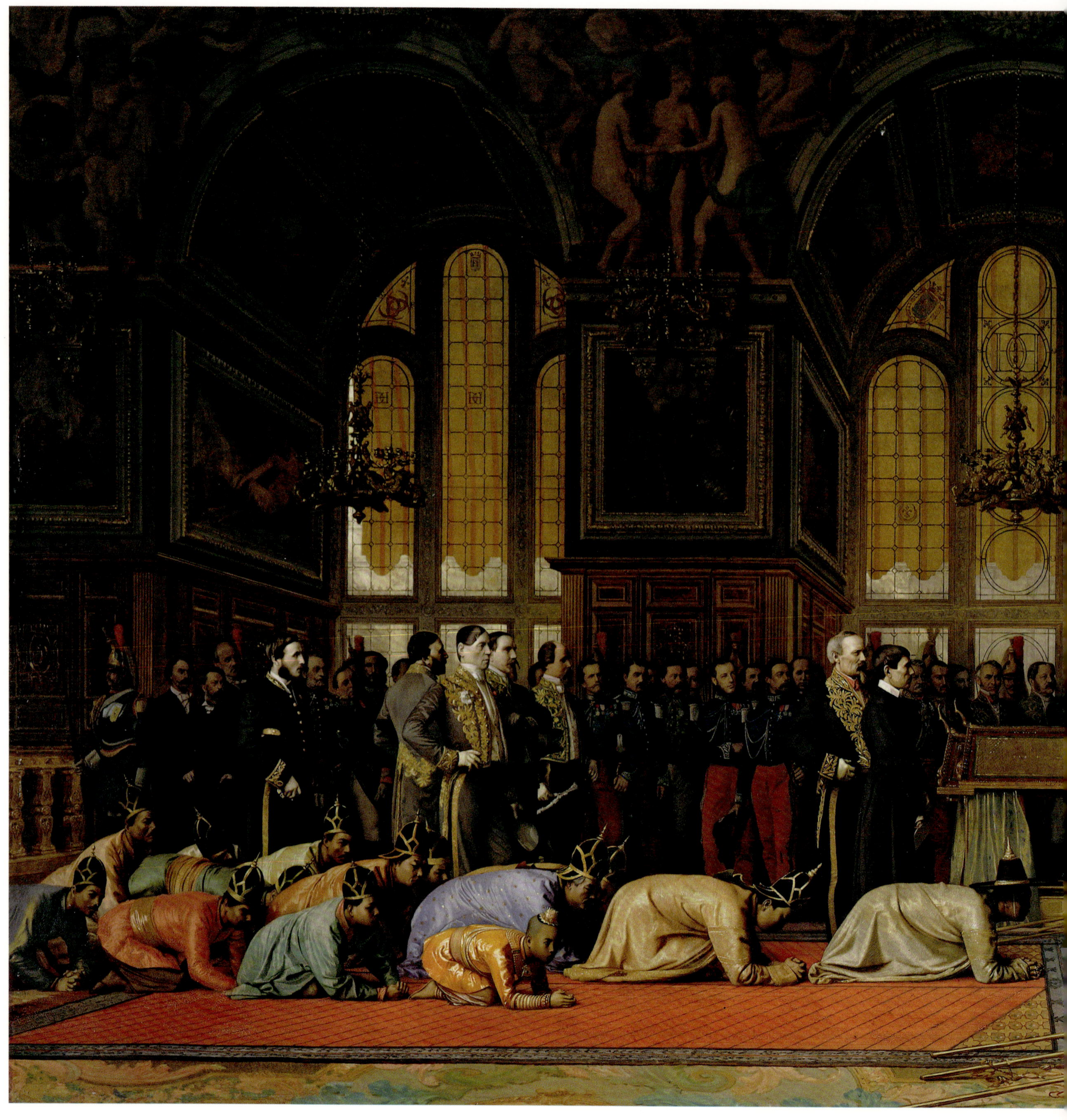

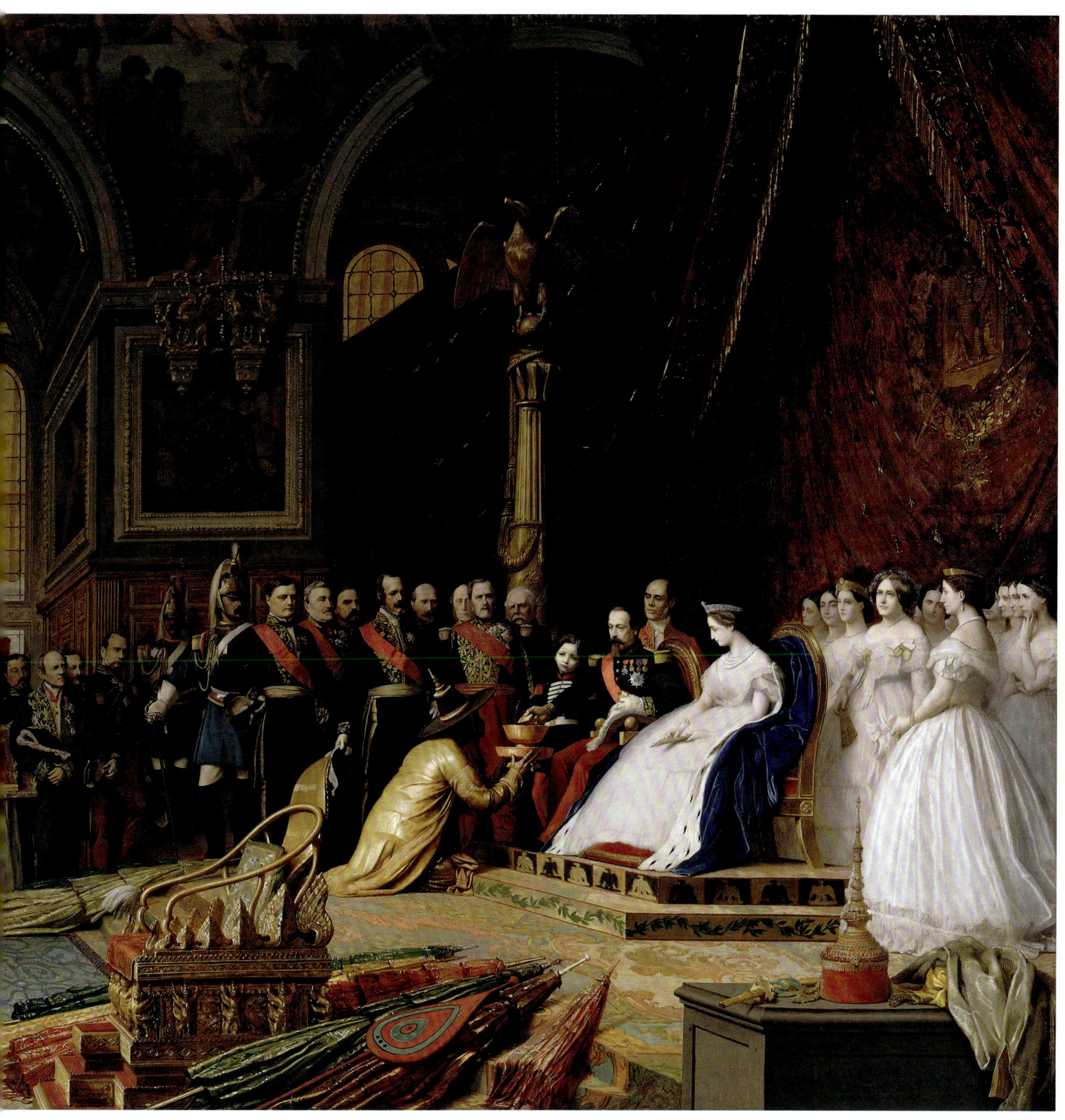

ceedings: "On entering the Henry II gallery, the ambassadors and their retinue fell to their knees and advanced, thus, to the foot of the throne, as they do before their own sovereigns. Once the speech was made and the presents offered, they equally withdrew on their knees, backwards, leaving the audience glumly struck by this posture, which is no longer comprehensible in Europe."[1] (ill. 75).

Prosper Mérimée, who was present at the ceremony, found it terribly boring. Like David, Gérôme was keen to depict the individuals who attended the ambassadorial reception. He therefore painted Mérimée, the author of *Carmen*, beneath the large chandelier in the center of the canvas. Nor did Gérôme overlook himself: the group of three men at the far left of the painting is composed of himself and two artist friends, Ernest Meissonnier and Louis Jadin. Furthermore, Gérôme managed to render the interior decoration of the chateau of Fontainebleau, painted by Primaticcio and Nicolo dell'Abate, with great care and delicacy, as rightly lauded by the critic of *L'Artiste*: "He lightly draws the ornamentation, details the architecture, and enters the darkest shadows to make clear everything they should hide."[2]

From a concern for accurate details, Gérôme wrote a letter to his friend, the photographer Nadar, asking him to take photographs of the Siamese ambassadors.[3] Gérôme then executed approximately eighty drawings, some of which are now part of a fine set held in Vesoul and are exhibited here. They stress the emissaries' prostrate poses; Gérôme delighted in drawing their headgear not only because of its various shapes but also because it was the most visible part of their dress, visually orchestrating the diplomatic procession. Gérôme also did several painted sketches (private collection), the most accomplished being a portrait of the young Pho Xai (*Pho Xai*, oil on canvas, 1861, private collection) in which he depicted the young man's garments and jewelry with great precision. The only relatively relaxed moment in the ceremony—whose etiquette followed the Siamese ambassadors' protocol, unfamiliar to the French imperial court (according to one of the commentators, the empress became impatient with the foreign diplomats' insistence on donning new garments, as was their wont, before appearing in front of the French monarchs)—came when Napoleon and Eugénie took the young Pho Xai in their arms. Gérôme apparently considered depicting this moment but later rejected it as lacking the required solemnity.

Ill. 75. *Reception of the Siamese Ambassadors by the Emperor of the French at Fontainebleau, June 27, 1861*, engraving printed in *L'Illustration*, July 6, 1861, p. 1.

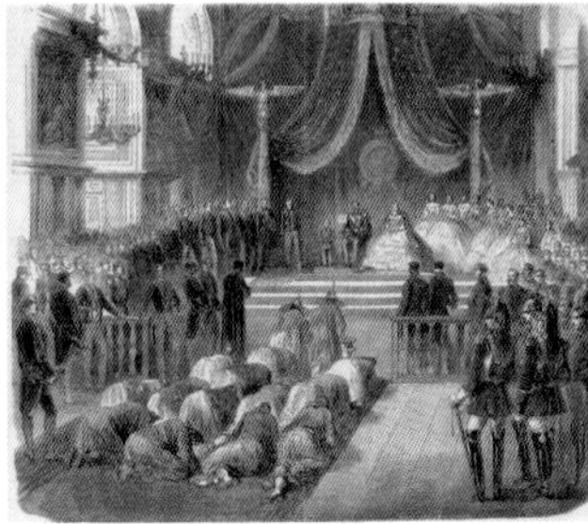

Although Gérôme's composition skillfully conveys the overall chain of events through the long diplomatic procession whose repetition of costumes and poses give an idea of duration, it fails to transcend the event by imbuing it with a life it never had. Paul Mantz felt that the boredom of the ceremony spilled into Gérôme's painting, as he somewhat severely wrote in the *Gazette des Beaux-Arts*. "'How does one become Siamese?' might exclaim an eighteenth-century individual [having read Montesquieu's *Persian Letters*] on seeing M. Gérôme's painting. I will not assume responsibility for answering that question ... This painting, totally devoid of interest, was very boring to paint, and I don't understand why M. Gérôme took on this painstaking task. Skilled at studying and depicting the diverse nature of the races, he has fairly successfully rendered the exotic faces and costumes of the Siamese; but the entire section of the painting that includes the emperor, empress, ladies in waiting, and high court dignitaries is totally vacant, totally wan, totally lifeless."[4] The painting nevertheless appealed to the French and Siamese diplomats. A life-size copy was made by a certain Fouque, painter to the Siamese court in Bangkok, at the expense of the French ministry of foreign affairs.[5]

The Reception of the Siamese Ambassadors occupies an unusual place in Gérôme's oeuvre. Adopting the official tone required by the nature of the commission, the painting combines Gérôme's historical ambitions with his consummate mastery of exoticism. Making a rare foray into contemporary history, he produced a scene of opulent, unyielding imperial pomp whose visual originality remains willfully undermined by the allusions it invokes.

L. C. and D. F.-R.

1. E. Texier, "Revue politique de la semaine," *L'Illustration*, July 6, 1861, p. 2. **2.** É. Lackroy, "Le Monde des Arts," *L'Artiste*, 1865, p. 84. **3.** Département des Manuscrits, Bibliothèque Nationale de France, Nouvelles acquisitions françaises, no. 24271, fols. 345 (MF 16 610). **4.** P. Mantz, *Gazette des Beaux-Arts*, 1865, p. 312. **5.** Archives Centrales, Musées Nationaux, Musée du Louvre, Gérôme file, folder P 17, containing several letters dated May 29 to June 10, 1865, between the king of Siam's consul in Paris (A. Grehan), the French ministry of foreign affairs, and superintendent of arts Nieuwerkerke, concerning a request to copy the *Siamese Ambassadors* in so far as "M. Gérôme's fine painting [is] part of the Exhibition of Living Artists, and shows the reception given at Fontainebleau by Their Majesties the Emperor and Empress for the Siamese ambassadors."

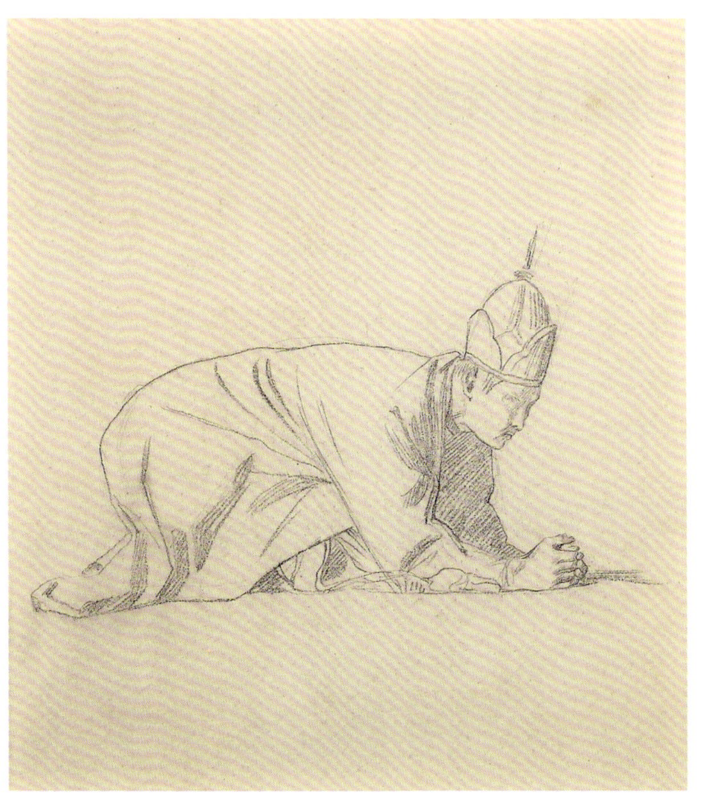
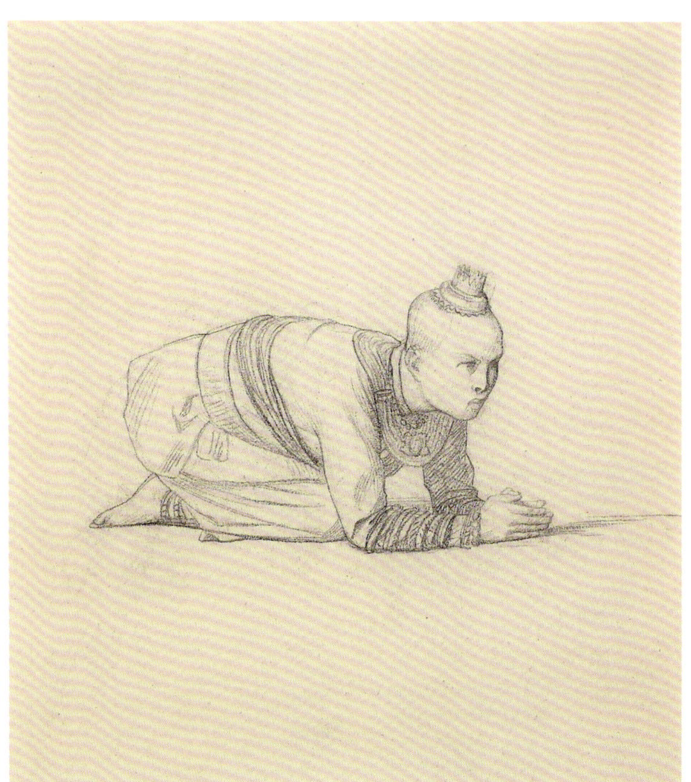
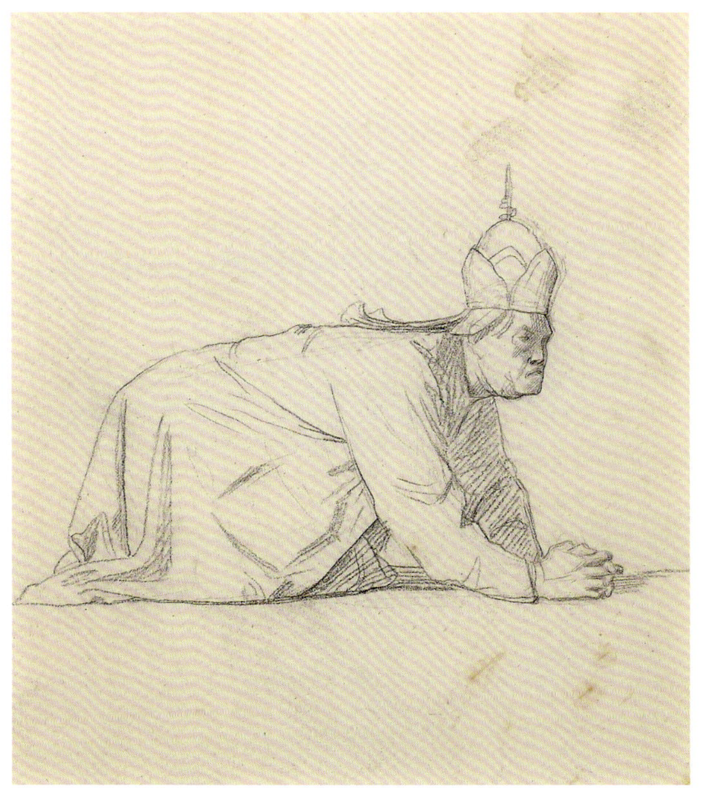
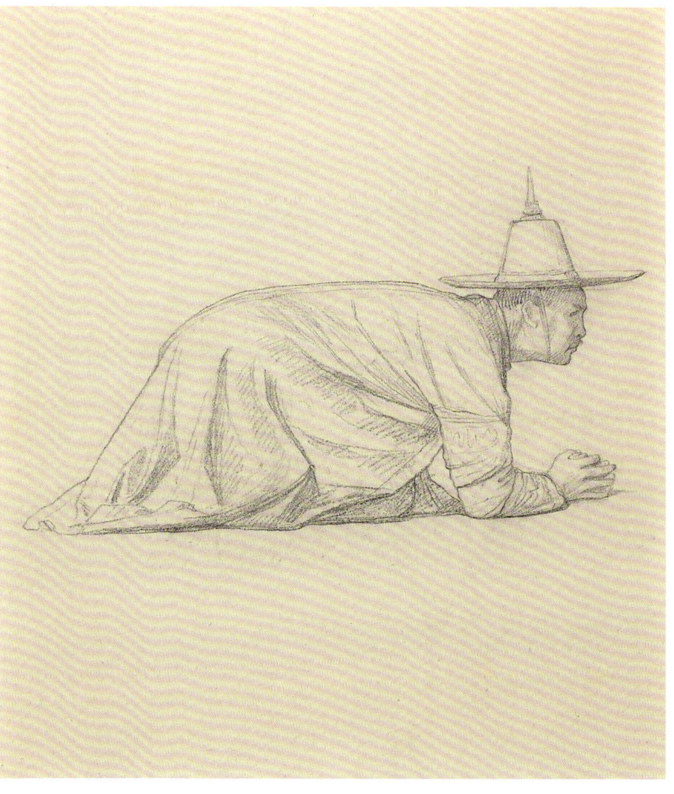

Cat. 99

TRUTH COMING OUT OF HER WELL TO SHAME MANKIND

–

1896
Oil on canvas
35 3/4 × 28 1/4 in.
Signed lower left: *J.L. GEROME*
Musée Anne-de-Beaujeu, Moulins, inv. 78.1.1

–

Provenance: Collection of the artist, 1904 post-mortem estate inventory, no. 60, as "La Vérité au Fouet." Morot family, sold Hôtel Drouot, Paris, Dec. 11, 1972, no. 19. Bought in 1978.

–

Exhibition History: Salon of 1896, Paris.

–

Bibliography: J. Fontsere, "Musée départemental de Moulins," *La Revue du Louvre*, vol. 5–6 (1980), p. 345ff. *J.-L. Gérôme*, exh. cat. (Vesoul: Musée Georges-Garret, 1981), no. 148, p. 125. H. Lafont-Couturier, *Gérôme* (Paris: Herscher, 1998), p. 58. G. Ackerman, *Jean-Léon Gérôme* (Courbevoie: ACR Édition, 2000), no. 424. B. Tillier, *Les Artistes et l'Affaire Dreyfus (1898-1908)* (Seyssel: Champ-Vallon, 2009), pp. 244–246.

Cat. 100

TRUTH COMING OUT OF HER WELL, INITIAL DESIGN FOR *TRUTH COMING OUT OF HER WELL TO SHAME MANKIND*

–

1895
Black chalk
9 3/8 × 8 7/8 in.
Marked on back: stamp of the Morot estate
Musée Georges-Garret, Vesoul, inv. 9847.12

–

Provenance: Morot collection. Galerie Paul Prouté, bought by the museum in 1983.

–

Bibliography: *Dessins de Jean-Gérôme. Acquisitions du Musée de Vesoul*, exh. cat. (Vesoul: Musée Georges-Garret, 1991), cat. 6, p. 14.

Cat. 101

STUDY FOR *TRUTH COMING OUT OF HER WELL*

ca. 1896
Pencil on paper glued to vellum paper
Vellum paper: 14 3/4 × 10 3/4 in.;
drawing: 10 3/4 × 8 in.
Dr. Edward T. Wilson collection, Bethesda, Maryland

–

Provenance: Album probably assembled after Gérôme's death, heirs of the artist. Sale, Sotheby's, Paris, June 27, 2002, lot 187. Dr. Edward T. Wilson collection, 2002. Album bound in brown leather, originally containing 154 folios of Arches vellum paper with cursive *Arches* watermark; red leather label on spine, gold-stamped with title *DESSINS DE GÉRÔME*. Collection of drawings by Gérôme probably assembled after his death, containing various studies, some of which were preparatory drawings for his major paintings: *King Candaules* (cat. 43), *Phryné before the Areopagus* (cat. 45), *Reception of the Duc de Condé at Versailles* (cat. 86), *The Two Augurs* (ill. 42, p. 94), *Pollice Verso* (cat. 71), *Cupid and the Vestal* (cat. 111), *The Carpet Merchant* (cat. 150), *Plaza de Toros*, and *Diana and Actaeon*, plus several sculptures: *Squatting Nude* (cat. 186); cat. nos. 50, 72, 101, 111, 152, 165 were separated from the album after 2002.
After 1904 (?)
Binding: 15 1/4 × 11 1/2 × 2 in.;
folios: 14 3/4 × 10 3/4 in.

–

Bibliography: *J.-L. Gérôme*, exh. cat. (Vesoul: Musée Georges-Garret, 1981), pp. 87, 125.

Ill. 76. *Truth Dead at the Bottom of the Well*, whereabouts unknown, reproduced in *L'Œuvre d'art*, Jan. 20, 1896.

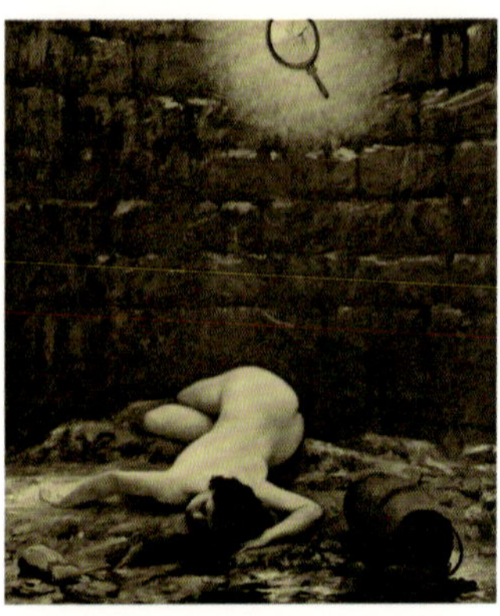

Ill. 77. *Truth at the Bottom of the Well*, 1895, oil on canvas, 39 1/2 × 28 1/4 in., Musée des Beaux-Arts, Lyon, Louis Gille bequest, 1926, inv. B 1395.

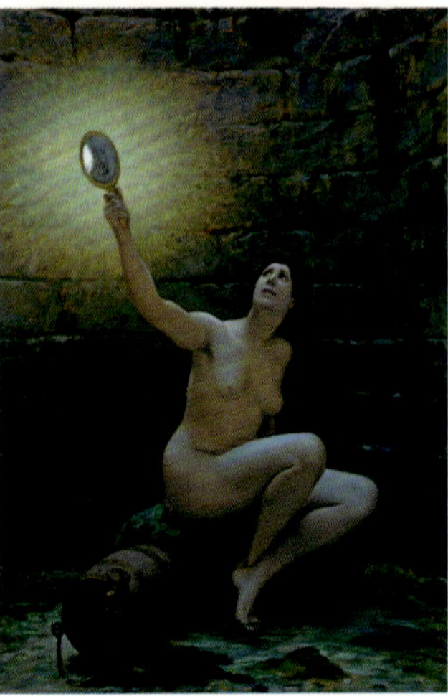

Truth Coming Out of Her Well to Shame Mankind is one of Gérôme's last significant works. It is also one of the strangest, along with two other paintings on the same theme, *Truth at the Bottom of the Well* (ill. 77) and *Truth Dead at the Bottom of the Well* (whereabouts unknown, but fortunately known through its reproduction in the January 20, 1896, issue of *L'Œuvre d'art*, ill. 76). This canvas is a literal illustration of the popular saying attributed to Democritus, "Truth lies at the bottom of a well," as were Édouard Debat-Ponsan's *Truth Coming Out of Her Well* (ill. 79) and Charles Landelle's intriguing *In vino veritas* shown at the Salon of 1885 (ill. 78). In keeping with the allegorical representation of Truth ever since the Renaissance, Gérôme depicts it as a nude woman.

The context of the Dreyfus affair has been advanced as an explanation for Gérôme's three paintings, but that was probably not the case. The painting was conceived almost three years before the famous "J'accuse!" of Émile Zola published in *L'Aurore* on January 13, 1898. More, Bertrand Tillier has recently shown that Gérôme was certainly not *dreyfusard* but as many academic painters, he was against the officer's rehabilitation.[1] It is probable that the conception of these paintings was motivated by something closer to Gérôme's interests and career. Indeed, these depictions of Truth were done by an ageing artist whose manner and style had been severely challenged by a younger generation of artists, notably including the Impressionists, whom he intensely opposed.

The subtitle of the now-lost painting of *Truth Dead at the Bottom of the Well*, "*Mendacibus et histrionibus occisa in putes jacet alma veritas*" (Truth Slain by Liars and Mountebanks), thus probably alluded to artistic rivalries rather than to the injustice of the Dreyfus affair. Gérôme's conceptual attachment to

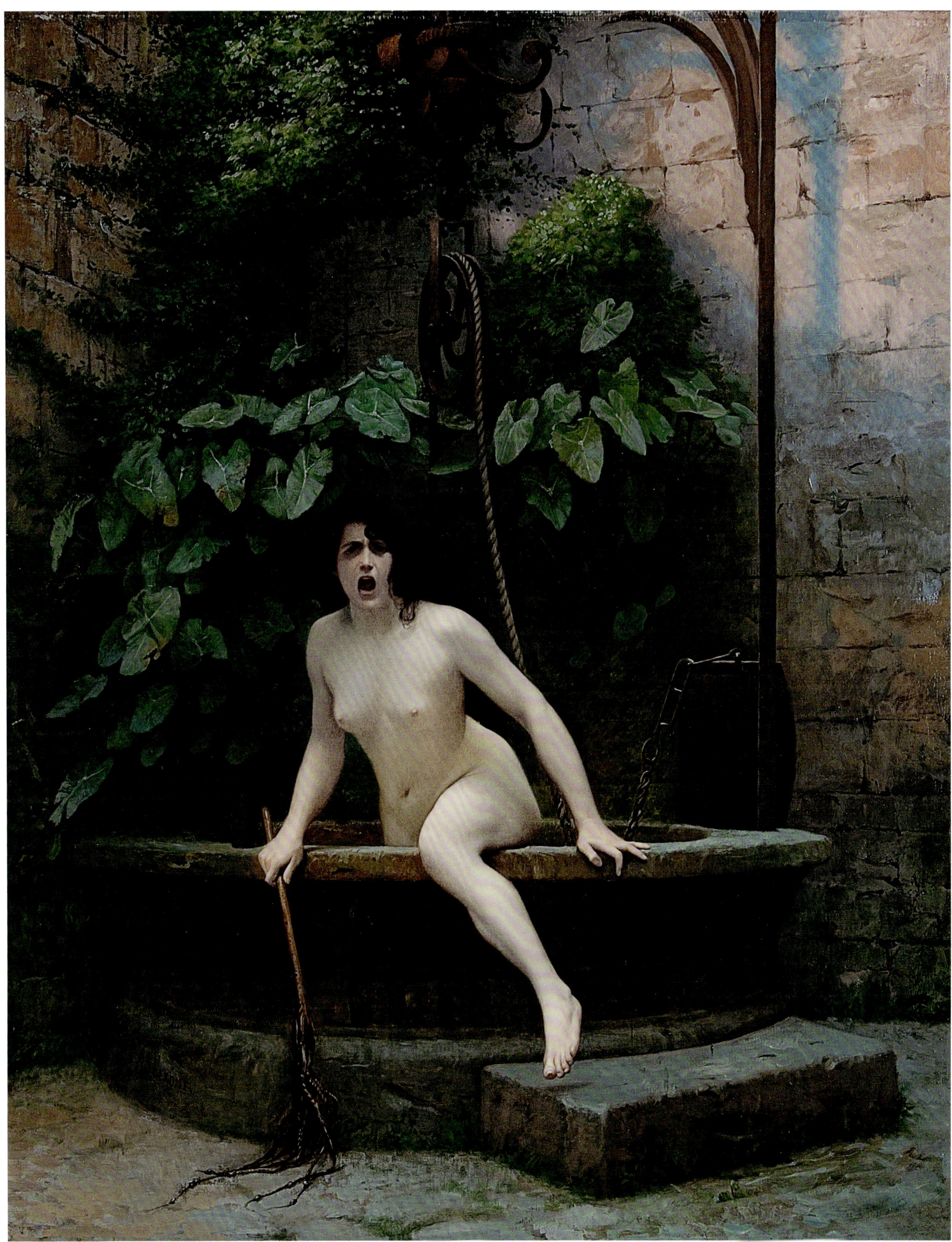

"making it lifelike" and his desire for accuracy and correctness tend to support this explanation—the nude woman thereby symbolizes Truth in Painting. The version of *Truth* on show here, from the Musée Anne-de-Beaujeu in Moulins, shows the nude woman leaving the well not with a mirror to enlighten the world (her most traditional attribute), but holding a whip with which to chastise anyone who contravenes the truth. Whereas the woman in the sketch is raised on a litter by two figures, evoking a statue. Truth here leaves the well with a determination reinforced by the power of her opulent flesh and above all by the expression of violence that distorts her face. Here Truth has the face of Bellona, the goddess of war sculpted by Gérôme (cat. 182). The Edward T. Wilson collection drawing (cat. 99) shows a true sketch of the Moulins painting. The woman's frozen features represent not so much a subtle exercise in character expression as one of the ancient theater masks that had long interested Gérôme, and which he illustrated in a now-lost canvas, *The Greek Comedians*.

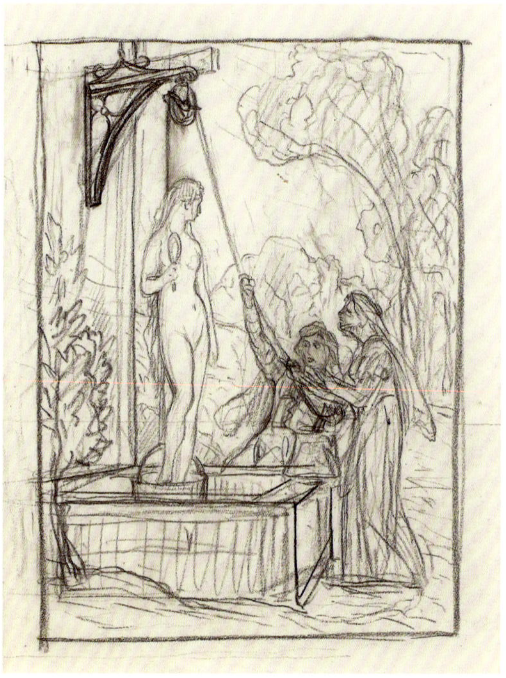

The choice of a subject that not only alluded to a debate contemporary with the painting itself (plus the debates over Realism that had spurred the rivalries of his youth) but also included deliberate quotations of his earlier works, would seem to suggest that this canvas represented Gérôme's way of reaffirming his own choices. He also mentioned the painting without quoting it directly, when he wrote his foreward to Émile Bayard's *Nu esthétique* (see p. 18). Gérôme was perhaps recalling Louis Auvray's crack about the buxom woman in a painting by his scorned rival, Gustave Courbet, namely *The Bathers* (1853, Musée Fabre, Montpellier): "... since Truth lies at the bottom of a well, she should at least be clean."[2] The complex iconography that mixes traditional allusions with Gérôme's own inventions gives this painting a strangeness not devoid of irony and a certain vulgarity that became, after 1885, a mark of the artist's singularity. The reviewer of the Salon of 1896 for *Le Journal des débats* mused over the anger displayed by Gérôme's Truth: "She is leaving her well in great anger, but I could not say whether she is angry at artists, critics, or her dry-cleaner."[3] Whereas Gérôme's paintings during the Second Empire hinged on complicity with a beholder who could follow, along with the artist, the ins-and-outs of the plot, in the last stage of his career Gérôme indulged in the concoction of peculiar scenes that risked sacrificing what had been considered the mark of "great" painting ever since the days of André Félibien: instant comprehensibility. **D. F.-R.**

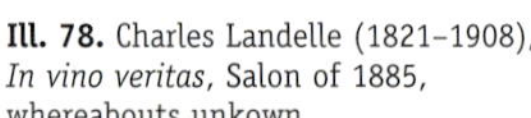

Ill. 78. Charles Landelle (1821–1908), *In vino veritas*, Salon of 1885, whereabouts unkown.

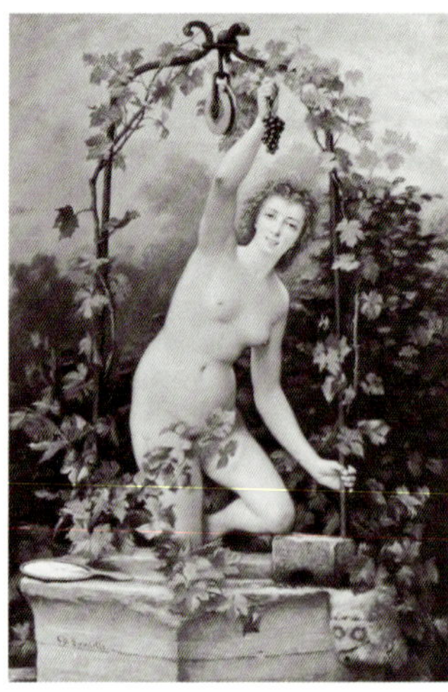

Ill. 79. Édouard Debat-Ponsan (1847–1913), *Truth Coming Out of Her Well*, 1898, oil on canvas, 94 ½ × 59 in., Musée de l'Hôtel de Ville, Amboise.

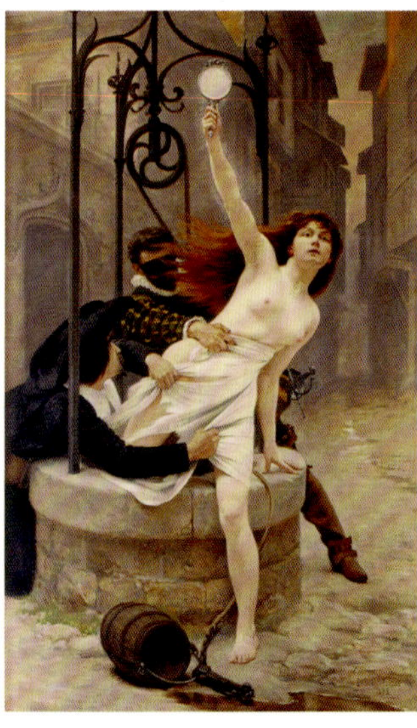

1. Bertrand Tillier, *Les Artistes et l'Affaire Dreyfus (1818-1908)* (Seyssel: Champ Vallon, 2009), p. 244-246. **2.** L. Auvray, *Exposition des beaux-arts, Salon de 1869* (Paris: Veuve Renouard, 1869), p. 56. In 1869 Auvray, a friend of Gérôme, still felt Courbet had gone "astray" along with Édouard Manet, James Tissot, and Gustave Moreau. **3.** "Au Salon," *Le Journal des débats*, Apr. 28, 1896, p. 2.

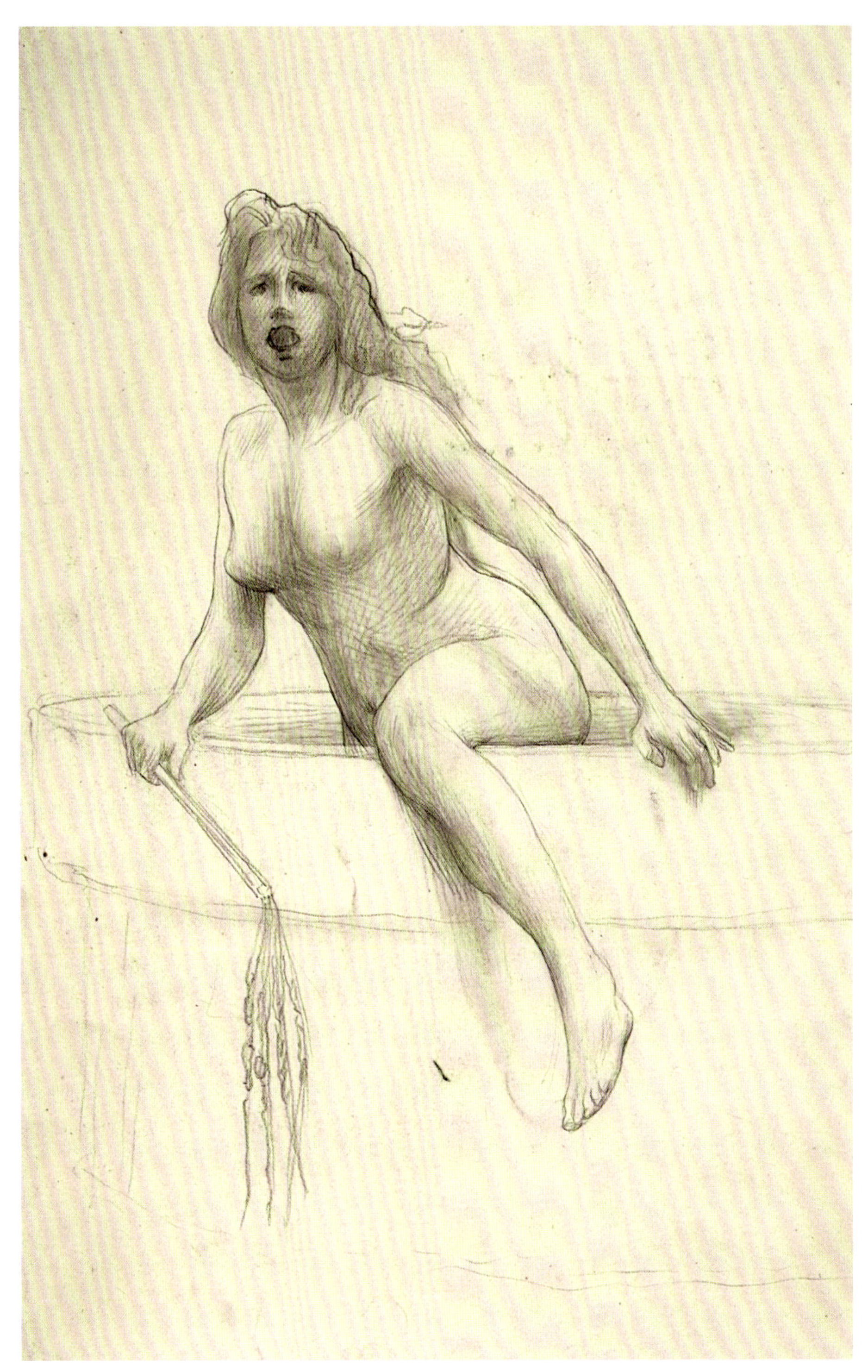

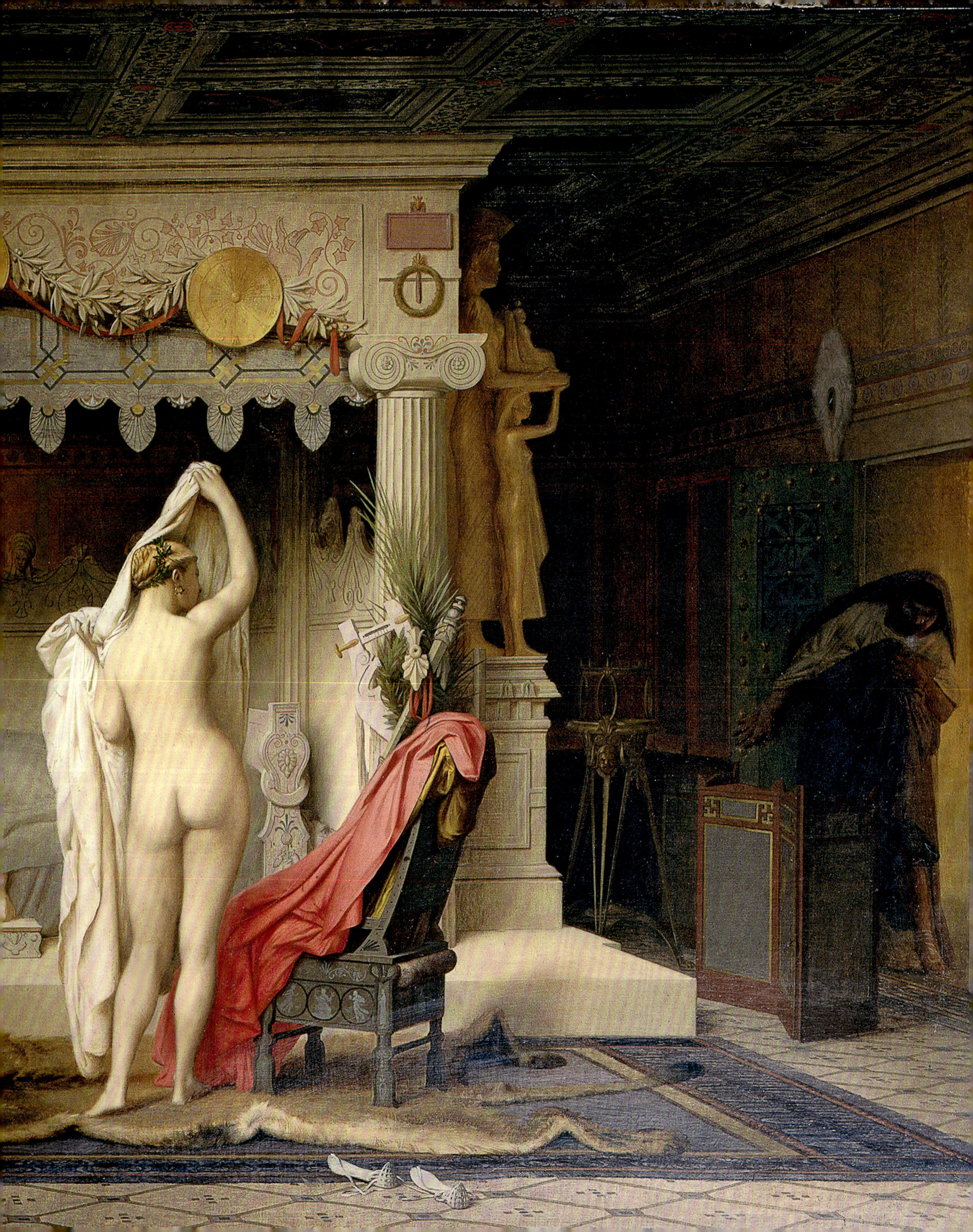

GÉRÔME: WORKING IN THE ERA OF INDUSTRIAL REPRODUCTION

—

Pierre-Lin Renié | Translated from the French by Deke Dusinberre

Gérôme's career coincided with a period of crucial upheavals that affected artistic professions. The waning power of the Académie steadily left greater freedom to the so-called dealer-critic system at the same time that the industrial reproduction of artworks was growing. As early as 1859 Gérôme linked up with one of the largest dealers of the day, Adolphe Goupil, and in 1863 married one of Goupil's daughters, Marie. Goupil was also one of the founders of the publishing house that bears his name. His brilliant initiative, as early as 1846, was to combine trade in reproductions of artworks, then in full boom, with the sale of original paintings. The mobilization of this special synergy was based on a generation of artists whose foremost representative was Paul Delaroche, Gérôme's mentor.[1] Given his special relationship with Goupil and his publicly acknowledged desire to perpetuate his oeuvre through reproductions, Delaroche was one of the artists for whom—and with whom—the system of regular reproduction was developed, a system that was fully operational by the time the next generation came along. Reproductions of works exhibited briefly at the Salon abounded, circulating ever more quickly throughout the world and reaching new audiences. This booming trade increased the fame of artists even as it generated considerable profits. The radical change in the conditions of the appearance of a work of art would have an impact on the production of art itself. Gérôme's career and oeuvre were at the very heart of this revolution.

AN INTERNATIONAL INDUSTRIAL EMPIRE

The firm known as the Maison Goupil arose from Goupil's 1829 partnership with Henry Rittner, who had opened a print gallery on boulevard Montmartre in Paris in 1827.[2] By 1835, the first catalogue of their collection already boasted 845 plates. Although the company's trademark was stylistic eclecticism, the three pillars on which it built its reputation were Delaroche, Horace Vernet, and Ary Scheffer. In 1848 its catalogue listed over 3,000 items. In less than twenty years the Goupil company managed to integrate every stage of production, from the original artwork (which it began selling in 1846) to its final reproduction (printed by the firm itself), which was then marketed throughout the entire world. In the 1860s Goupil had branches in Berlin, London, The Hague, Brussels, and New York.

The growing use of photography and photomechanical printing processes was largely responsible for these developments and for the industrial nature of the Goupil firm. In 1869 it opened a vast plant in Asnières, just outside Paris, to centralize the printing of prints and photographs. Highly modern workshops in this facility functioned as a research center into new photomechanical printing techniques, applied as early as 1872. The diversity of the company's products, its technological innovations, its

Cat. 43. *King Candaules* (detail).

international scope, its long lifespan, and its financial clout set it apart from its many competitors. Yet its failure to update its artistic preferences, combined with the fact that the very form of its products was becoming obsolete at a time when the illustrated press and art books were enjoying great expansion, meant that the Maison Goupil did not survive the First World War.

GÉRÔME AND GOUPIL

Although the contract between Gérôme and Goupil is no longer extant, we know that it required the painter to offer first option on the purchase of his artworks to Goupil, who moreover retained the rights to reproduction.[3] Their first deal went back to 1859 when Goupil bought *King Candaules* (cat. 43) and *Ave Caesar, morituri te salutant* (cat. 70), exhibited at that year's Salon, plus *The Death of Caesar* (cat. 67). These latter two paintings were immediately published in Goupil's "Galerie Photographique" series, launched the year before. An uninterrupted stream of reproductions then followed, the final editions being published in 1901 (namely, *The Gawkers* and *The Poet's Dream*). In total, the gallery handled 337 original paintings by Gérôme, while the publishing branch produced nearly 370 reproductions based on 122 different subjects, that is to say over one-fifth of an oeuvre that itself was marked by numerous repetitions. Some of these autograph copies were directly related to the production of engravings, as was the case with *King Candaules* (also known as *Queen Rodolphe Observed by Gyges*), *Golgotha* (cat. 78) and *Molière Breakfasting with Louis XIV* (cat. 84). Often executed in the dimensions of the planned reproduction, these paintings served as a model for the engraver and made it possible to sell the original canvas before the engraver completed his work.

In distributing his son-in-law's work, Goupil employed the entire arsenal of marketing methods he had developed and perfected year after year. Each new type of publication, each new technological invention, each new series provided an occasion for bringing a successful work by Gérôme back into fashion. Various formats and series followed one another, all priced differently, ranging from small *carte-de-visite* photographs (50 centimes) to large engravings printed in color (120 francs for the engraving of *Golgotha*) and lavish, signed artist's proofs aimed at connoisseurs (100 francs for the François brothers' line engraving of *King Candaules*).

In addition to the mass-produced series of photographic reproductions of Gérôme's oeuvre,[4] a set of eighty-four photogravures was produced in 1877–78, titled *Oeuvres choisies de Jean-Léon Gérôme.*[5] Also issued were no fewer than four portfolios or volumes of photographs that anthologized earlier publications, often enhanced with new pictures. Only the masters of the previous generation—Delaroche, Vernet, and Scheffer—had been accorded such monographs. The space devoted to Gérôme in Goupil's catalogues continued to grow, not only in terms of the number of reproductions available, but also in terms of the importance placed on them. In 1854 and subsequent years, the line-engraving section of the complete catalogue inevitably opened with ones done after the undisputed master, Delaroche; but starting in 1884 only a reproduction of Delaroche's large fresco, the *Hemicycle of the École des Beaux-Arts*, remained in front, followed by three engravings after Gérôme: *Molière Breakfasting with Louis XIV, Dante* and *The Prisoner.* The latter picture violated academic categories, which reserved burin engraving for historical or religious subjects rather than genre scenes. Thus Gérôme's oeuvre, thanks to the space and treatment it was allocated, forged specific new hierarchies at the same time as it participated in the profound changes then underway.

MODERN AUDIENCES AND REPRODUCTIONS

With only a few exceptions, reproductions of paintings by Gérôme were still being listed in the final catalogues issued by Goupil, namely in 1904 for photographs and 1909 for prints. Published in unlimited editions, new runs of these prints and photographs could be reprinted on demand.[6] Tastes still evolved slowly, for the era of the swift turnover of cultural products had not yet dawned. The petty and middling bourgeoisie liked to decorate its walls with pictures of works that had made a splash at the Salon, and Gérôme's eclectic paintings appealed to the expectations of a broad public. The Maison Goupil published every genre executed by Gérôme, from major historical scenes with ancient subjects to the abundant Orientalist compositions via a few religious subjects as The *Entry of Christ into Jerusalem* and even a few portraits (*Mademoiselle Lili*).

Despite wide differences in prices, most reproductions of works by Gérôme sold for the moderate price of five francs or so. This pricing policy targeted the middle classes. Thus, although it may seem

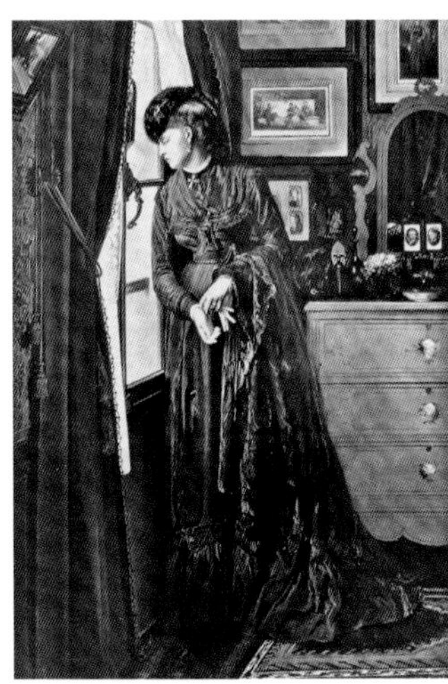

Ill. 80. After Jules-Émile Saintin, *Indecision*, Salon of 1870, photograph by Goupil & Cie, "Galerie Photographique" series, no. 1034, ca. 1871, photoglyptic print, 9 ½ × 6 ¼ in., Musée Goupil, Bordeaux, inv. 97.II.4.155 (1).

surprising that the oeuvre of such a great colorist was the object of so few color reproductions,[7] there is an explanation: the high cost of color (twice that of black-and-white versions) would have excluded this clientele. Similarly, the desire to appeal to the middle class justified the preponderance of photographs and photogravures. Their modernity and mechanical accuracy appealed to the general public, even though these same features were repugnant to print lovers. The latter could turn instead to the five burin-engraved reproductions[8] or to etchings, sold somewhat more cheaply than the photographs. Etchings were not only softer than harsh line engravings, they were also "fashionable."[9] Picking up on this trend, between 1869 and 1874 Goupil published twelve etchings after Gérôme, a significant number given the fact that this technique remained a fringe activity for the firm. It seemed to be an ideal compromise, sufficiently inexpensive to be affordable to the general public yet endowed with the potential artistic quality required by art lovers.

In a matter of decades, the buying public had been transformed. An appetite for pictures was no longer restricted to a few solitary art lovers who stored their collections in portfolios. Pictures were henceforth framed and displayed on the walls of middle-class homes, becoming objects of reverie and the sign of a certain social standing. The commercial success of Goupil and his competitors relied on this new regime, because their output was aimed primarily at the interior decoration of private homes.[10] Émile Zola sharply stigmatized the ubiquitous presence of pictures by Gérôme: "There is no provincial sitting room where an engraving of *Duel after the Ball* or *Molière Breakfasting with Louis XIV* does not hang on the wall, while in bachelors' apartments you will see *Dance of the Almeh* and *Phryné before the Areopagus*, racy subjects that men can enjoy among themselves. More serious folk display *Ave Caesar* or *The Death of Caesar.* Monsieur Gérôme works to satisfy every taste."[11] Testifying to this infatuation, many genre painters included these framed pictures as part of the setting of their interior scenes. Such was the case with Jules-Émile Saintin's *Indecision*, exhibited at the 1870 Salon and published by Goupil (ill. 80). In addition to *Duel after the Ball* it shows *The Florentine Poet* by Alexandre Cabanel and *Heart in Mourning* by Saintin himself. These background images shed narrative light on the scene in which the indecisive young woman—should she stay home or go out? to meet whom?—is caught between memories of old loves, a duel, and a poetic escape into the past.

ICONS AND USES

Today these reproductions provide us with information about the popularity of a given painting by Gérôme. A reproduction targeted a given social class through its retail price. Therefore the number of different editions of a given subject indicates its greater or lesser renown in the Western world, thanks to Goupil's powerful distribution network. Over a period of several decades, the various forms of a given picture, themselves multiplied through availability on different supports (China paper, black bristol board, etc.), in different states (before or after lettering) or in color, penetrated and seeped through the entire society. One of the greatest icons of the second half of the nineteenth century was *Duel after the Ball*, as witnessed by the nine different reproductions of this painting (see p. 118), sold at prices ranging from fifty centimes to twenty-five francs. Gérôme's two other big hits, *Phryné before the Areopagus* and *Molière Breakfasting with Louis XIV*, were produced in nine and eight versions respectively, while the seven basic versions of *King Candaules* made it a notable success (if somewhat more predictable, being a classical nude). In contrast, the single version of *Golgotha*, engraved by Hermann Eichens, turned in a poor performance according to the barometer of popularity. Simultaneously austere and bold—some people would say scandalous, being a Crucifixion without the image of Christ—Gérôme's entirely "off-screen" composition was not addressed to the general public, so there would have been no point in inexpensive editions that were unlikely to sell. Such decisions are the sign of a marketing policy implemented by Adolphe Goupil with his keen sense of the average tastes of the day.

The dissemination of works by artists affiliated with Goupil went beyond the firm's own publications. As the copyright owner, the Maison Goupil could sell reproduction rights to other publishers and makers of manufactured products. The firm's true wealth lay not in the stock of original paintings in its gallery, but in the rights that it held, an immaterial property that could be marketed ad infinitum. The ledger of such transactions for the period 1887–1913, now in the Musée Goupil, records 102 licensing agreements for works by Gérôme. In general the use made of the pictures was fairly standard, such as an illustration in a book or magazine. For instance, the magazine *Historia*, launched in December 1909, published two works by Gérôme, *Ave Caesar* and *The Grey Cardinal*, for which it paid reproduction rights of twenty-five francs each.[12] In a lighter vein, the publishing house Bong & Cie wished to reproduce *Phryné* for its monumental book on "women in nature, legend, society, and manners" (*La Femme dans la nature, dans les moeurs, dans la légende, dans la société*), for which it had to pay one hundred francs.[13] Such variations in the cost of rights were based on the popularity of the image requested, the use to be made of it, and the firm's commercial relationship with the rights-seeker.

During this late period, the earlier popularity rankings seem to have been overturned—the most frequently sought rights concerned *Pollice Verso* and *The Christian Martyrs' Last Prayers*, each with seventeen requests. Goupil's most reproduced work, *Duel after the Ball*, was the object of only six requests, one fewer than its least reproduced, *Golgotha*. Comparisons remain highly relative, however, since the use made of the rights differed substantially, from an engraving to decorate an interior to an illustration in a book or a program for a charity event.[14] The shift nevertheless tends to indicate the creation of new outlets and supports for such images. It also testifies to the increase in religious publications in the late nineteenth century, as well as to the emergence of a new medium especially popular in church circles, namely "lectures with light projections."[15] In 1896 Fanny Field Hering, an ardent promoter of Gérôme's oeuvre, went on a lecture tour of the United States, in which she projected thirty reproductions of works selected by the artist himself, favoring historical and classical subjects in a final gesture of loyalty to the academic system from which he sprang.[16] A parallel market grew up around these popular projection slides, for nothing was easier than to photograph an already published reproduction: the Boston-based company of A. T. Thompson & Co. distributed

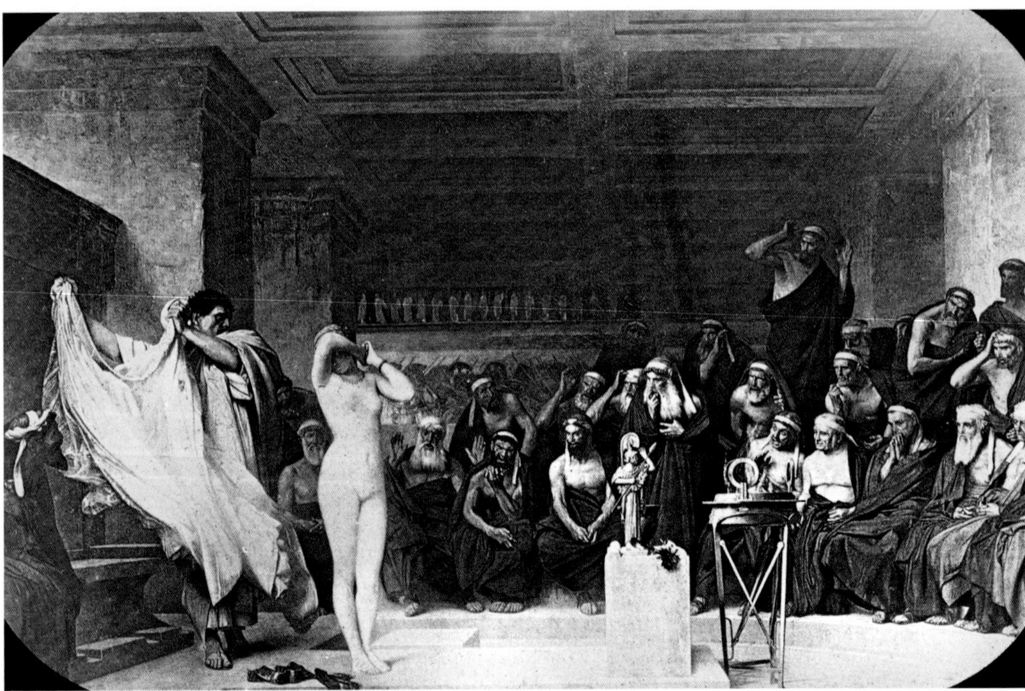

Ill. 81. After Jean-Léon Gérôme, *Phryné before the Areopagus*, 1861, positive glass print for projection, published by A. T. Thompson & Co., 1890s, 3 ¼ × 4 in., George Eastman House, Rochester, inv. 86:1110:0018.

such plates (ill. 81) even though its name does not appear in the surviving ledger of authorizations. The Maison Goupil was nevertheless concerned to preserve its rights and did not hesitate to seize unwarranted copies and to sue for damages.

PAINTINGS, PICTURES, OBJECTS

The most extravagant example of a pirated version of one of Gérôme's works was a huge tapestry based on *Pollice Verso*, produced by the Milan-based company Angioletti and exhibited at the Turin world's fair of 1898 (ill. 82). After the work was seized and a 500-franc fine imposed, the two parties came to an agreement: Goupil authorized Angioletti to manufacture further copies of the tapestry in exchange for a ten percent commission on each sale.[17] But this situation was distinctly different from the frequent seizure of unauthorized reproductions of images on a whole range of manufactured

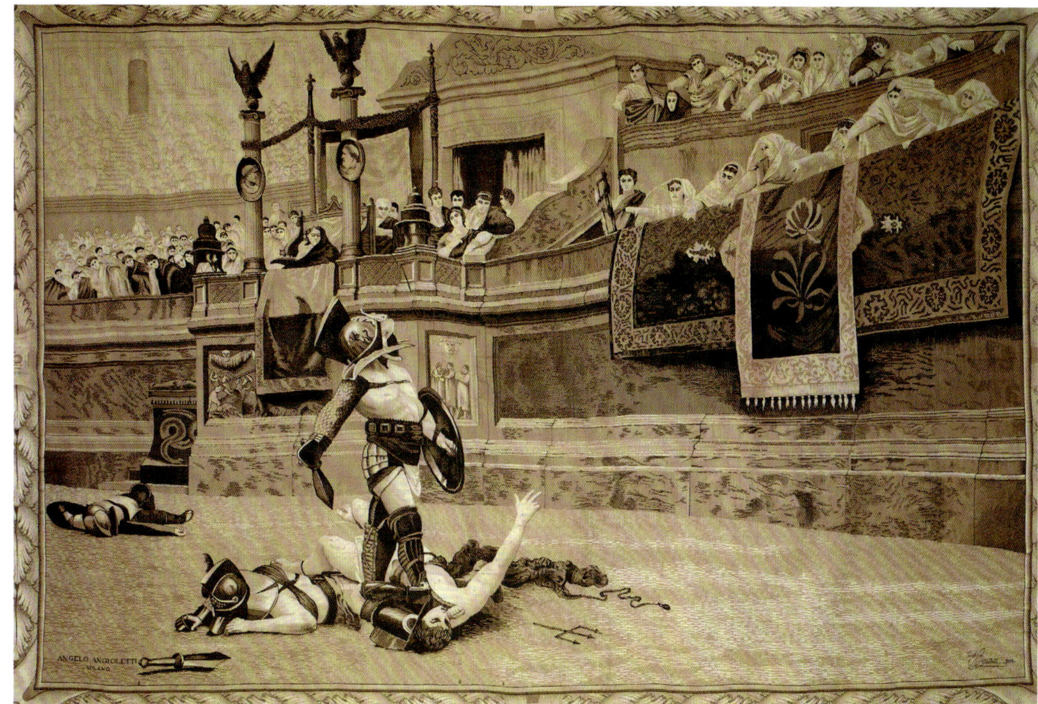

Ill. 82. After Jean-Léon Gérôme, *Pollice Verso*, 1872, tapestry executed by the Angioletti company, Milan, 1898, from a cartoon by Emilio Bestetti, 1897, 106 ¼ × 157 ½ in., Fausta Squatriti & Massimo Angioletti Collection.

supports. The most sought-after—or pirated—images included *A Wedding during the Directoire* and *A Baptism during the Directoire*, painted by Frederik Hendrik Kammerer, a Dutch student of Gérôme who specialized in genre scenes from France's Directory period.[18] These pictures decorated countless objects such as brooches, candy boxes, goblets, place settings, cigarette holders, match boxes, ash trays, wrappers for candy, pocket mirrors, and calendars.[19] Gérôme's oeuvre hardly suited this vast—and highly lucrative—bazaar of imagery. His historic and religious compositions were too strict to be highjacked in this way, and his genre scenes resisted the emphatic anecdotalism required for illustration. Gérôme was trapped in an in-between zone in this era of industrialization: he largely profited from the system of widespread reproduction but still retained an elevated idea of art that was incompatible—in those days—with illustration and the decoration of everyday items. This is one of the reasons his oeuvre appears to play a pivotal role.

Repetitions and standard formulae nevertheless abound in Gérôme's oeuvre. By reducing every painting to a little black-and-white image, reproductions make these repetitions more apparent, stripped of the seductive appeal of large, intensely colored formats. Identically draped over a beam, a carpet moves from The *Chess Players* to *A Street Scene in Cairo* (ill. 83 and 84); figures are repeated

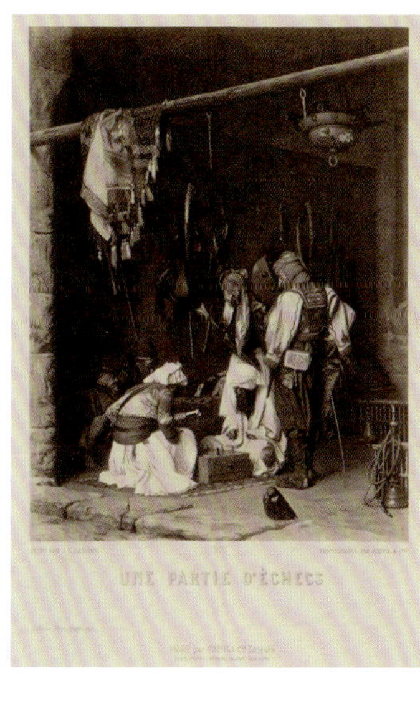

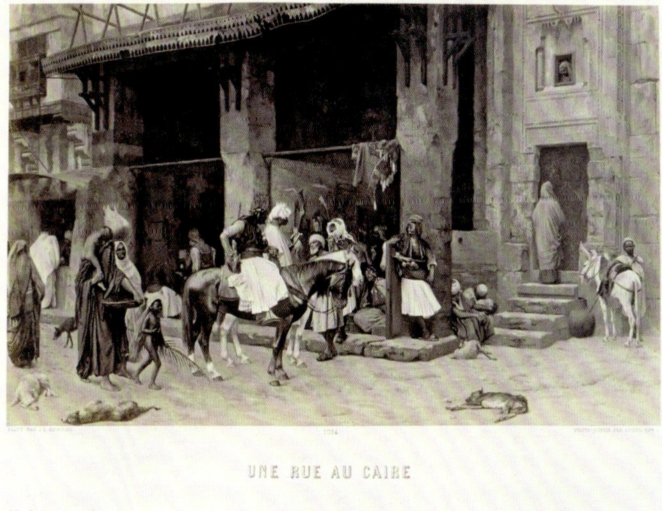

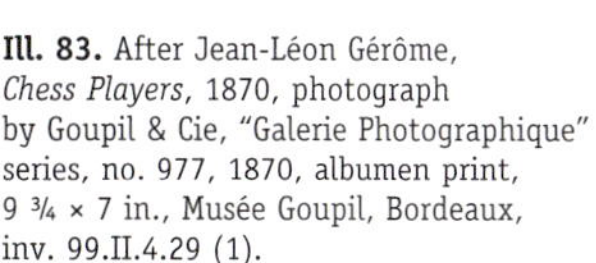

Ill. 83. After Jean-Léon Gérôme, *Chess Players*, 1870, photograph by Goupil & Cie, "Galerie Photographique" series, no. 977, 1870, albumen print, 9 ¾ × 7 in., Musée Goupil, Bordeaux, inv. 99.II.4.29 (1).

Ill. 84. After Jean-Léon Gérôme, *A Street in Cairo*, 1871, photograph by Goupil & Cie, "Galerie Photographique" series, no. 1094, 1872, albumen print, 8 ¾ × 13 ¾ in., Musée Goupil, Bordeaux, inv. 98.II.4.66 (1).

feature for feature in the two versions of *Sabre Dance before a Pasha* and in *The Muezzin* and *The Muezzin's Call to Prayer* ; the same woman hangs her laundry on the terrace roof in *The Muezzin* and *Bonaparte at Cairo*; the same slanting light illuminates *Sabre Dance in a Café* and *The Moorish Bath* ; jagged black lines of birds in flight break the monotony of numerous skies, as in *The Plain of Thebes* and *The Muezzin's Call to Prayer*. These duplicated elements reflect the frantic reproduction and multiplication to which Gérôme's oeuvre was subjected. As a member of the first generation of artists expected to fuel an increasingly diversified and demanding market, Gérôme could scarcely avoid such methods and formulae.[20]

This dominance of imagery and repetitiveness, further devalued by industrial reproduction, constituted an attack on art as far as Zola was concerned. In a vitriolic piece on Gérôme that also spattered Delaroche, Zola asserted that, "As a pupil of M. Paul Delaroche, this artist learned from his master not to paint and bring color to painstakingly researched and invented images. Of course, M. Gérôme works for the Maison Goupil and therefore makes a painting so that the painting can be reproduced by photography and engraving and thus sold in thousands of copies. Here the subject matter is everything, the painting is nothing: the reproduction is worth more than the work."[21]

Critics had already reproached Delaroche for producing nothing other than enlarged historical vignettes that found their true value in reproduction—a scarcely veiled way of saying that Delaroche was no painter.[22] Today, free of dogmatism, we can adopt a new viewpoint and, while not accepting it unreservedly, explore this reproducibility and Gérôme's penchant for reiteration and constant recombination of motifs, establishing the bases of a constituent idiom. His repetitive oeuvre developed a strong element of "image," exaggerated by his slick technique that so exasperated Zola and that was intensified by industrial reproduction. And yet Gérôme did not sink to the level of cheap imagery, as witnessed by his resistance to assimilation by everyday industrial items. From the twentieth century to the present, image and reproducibility have continued to resurface and to haunt modernism, a modernism for which Delaroche and Gérôme might appear to provide early signs.

Ill. 85. After Jean-Léon Gérôme, *King Candaules* [1859], photograph by Goupil & Cie, "Musée Goupil & Cie" series, no. 321, 1864, albumen print, 3 × 4 ¾ in., Archives, Musée d'Orsay, Paris.

1. On this subject, see P.-L. Renié, "Delaroche par Goupil, portrait du peintre en artiste populaire," in *Delaroche. Un peintre dans l'histoire* (Paris and Nantes: RMN and Musée des Beaux-Arts de Nantes, 1998), pp. 173–218.

2. On the Goupil firm, see *État des lieux* nos. 1 (1994) and 2 (1999), the magazine of the Musée Goupil. On the company's early years in particular, see D. E. McIntosh, "The Origins of the Maison Goupil in the Age of Romanticism," *The British Art Journal*, vol. 5, no. 1 (2004), pp. 64–76. The Musée Goupil in Bordeaux today boasts a collection that includes 46,000 prints, 70,000 photographs, and 4,500 engraved copperplates.

3. The relationship between the artist and his dealer/publisher was studied at length in H. Lafont-Couturier, *Gérôme and Goupil: Art and Enterprise*, exh. cat., trans. I. Ollivier (Bordeaux: Musée Goupil, 2000–1; also New York: Dahesh Museum of Art, 2001, and Pittsburgh: The Frick Art & Historical Center, 2001). The catalogue includes this author's list of reproductions of Gérôme's works published by Goupil (pp. 150–63).

4. There were four such series: "Carte de Visite" (1863), "Musée Goupil & Cie" (1860), "Carte Album" (1872), and "Galerie Photographique" (1858), to which should be added the two series of photogravures, "Estampes Miniatures" (1885) and "Estampes Album" (1901).

5. Available as single prints (six francs each) or as a two-volume set with a portrait of Gérôme and a biography by A. Arago (540 francs).

6. The limiting of the number of prints in an edition only began in the 1880s. See P.-L. Renié, "Originaux et reproductions, produits de luxe et imagerie: l'estampe face à l'industrialisation de la production des images," proceedings of the symposium *Histoire de l'art du XIXe siècle (1848-1914). Bilans et perspectives*, Musée d'Orsay / École du Louvre (forthcoming).

7. Five subjects were available in color: *Phryné, Duel after the Ball, Golgotha, Last Prayers*, and *The Two Monarchs*.

8. *King Candaules* (François, 1863), *The Prisoner* (Franck, 1868), *Molière Breakfasting with Louis XIV* (Girardet, 1866), *Dante* (Levasseur, 1870), and *A Collaboration (Molière and Corneille)* (Morse, 1878), to which should be added *Golgotha*, which was a line engraving on an etched ground (Eichens, 1871).

9. C. Baudelaire, "L'eau-forte est à la mode" (1862), in *Curiosités esthétiques: L'art romantique* (Paris: Bordas, 1990), pp. 405–7.

10. See P.-L. Renié, *Une image sur un mur: images et décoration intérieure au XIXe siècle* (Bordeaux: Musée Goupil, 2005). For an abridged English version, see P.-L. Renié "The Image on the Wall: Prints as Decoration in Nineteenth-Century Interiors," *Nineteenth-Century Art Worldwide*, online journal, vol. 5, issue 2, Autumn 2006.

11. É. Zola, "Nos peintres au Champ de Mars" (1867), in *Écrits sur l'art* (Paris: Gallimard, 1991), p. 184.

12. Ledger titled "Autorisations," Musée Goupil, Bordeaux inv. 90.III.1.128 (folio 413, dated May 26, 1911, and folio 418, dated Sept. 24, 1912, respectively).

13. Ibid., folio 402 dated Mar. 12, 1909. The four-volume publication went on sale in 1910.

14. G. W. Clark of London requested authorization to reproduce *Last Prayers* in the program of a charity event. The Maison Goupil granted free use of the picture on condition that this authorization was expressly mentioned. Ledger titled "Autorisations," folio 390 dated Apr. 23, 1907.

15. Although the first photographic plates for magic-lantern presentations appeared as early as 1851, lectures with projected images did not become widespread until later in the century. See L. Manoni and D. P. Compagnoni, *Lanterne magique et film peint* (Paris: Cinémathèque Française, 2009), pp. 207–12.

16. Ledger titled "Autorisations," folio 230 dated Aug. 31, 1896. The thirty works selected by Gérôme were: *Pollice Verso, Ave Caesar, morituri te salutant, Duel after the Ball, The Chariot Race, The Prisoner, Phryné before the Areopagus, The Tulip Folly, The Slave Market, Runners of the Pasha, Socrates Seeking Alcibiades at the House of Aspasia, Molière Breakfasting with Louis XIV, The Death of Caesar, Salomon's Wall, Jerusalem, Reception of the Duc de Condé at Versailles, For Sale, Excursion of the Harem, The Death of Marshal Ney, Reception of the Siamese Ambassadors at Fontainebleau, The Two Augurs, An Arab and his Steed, The Serpent Charmer, The Carpet Merchant, The Conspirators, The End of the Seance, Dance of the Almeh, The Grey Cardinal, Return from the at Hunt, Rembrandt Etching a Plate in his Atelier, Cleopatra before Caesar*, and *King Candaules*.

17. Ledger titled "Autorisations," folios 276 and 278-279, Aug. and Oct. 1898. Only two copies of the tapestry are known to have survived. A book on the subject edited by Fausta Squatriti and Sandro Scarrocchia is scheduled for publication by Nardini in Florence.

18. On the eighteenth-century revival and the Directory revival to which Gérôme contributed, see R. Bigorne, *Mémoires du XVIIIe siècle* (Bordeaux: Musée Goupil, 1998).

19. Ledger titled "Autorisations," folios 156 (1894), 174 (1894), 200 (1895), 222 (1896), 290 (1899), and 348 (1902).

20. On the question of repetition—not just of motifs but of entire compositions—Stephen Bann has demonstrated, in a remarkable analysis of the various versions of *Duel after the Ball*, that while they were the product of commissions they nonetheless constituted variants that culminated in an improvement and in greater clarity. See S. Bann, "Reassessing Repetition in Nineteenth-Century Academic Painting: Delaroche, Gérôme, Ingres," in E. Kahn, ed., *The Repeating Image* (Baltimore: The Walters Art Museum, 2007), pp. 42–43.

21. É. Zola 1991 (as in n. 11), pp. 183–84.

22. See, for example, J. Janin, "Le Salon de 1840," *L'Artiste*, 1840, p. 301; P. Burty, "Publications d'estampes: *Derniers adieux des Girondins*, par M. Édouard Girardet," *Gazette des Beaux-Arts*, Feb. 1, 1859, pp. 189–90; T. Gautier, "Œuvre de Paul Delaroche photographié," *L'Artiste*, Mar. 7, 1858, pp. 153–55.

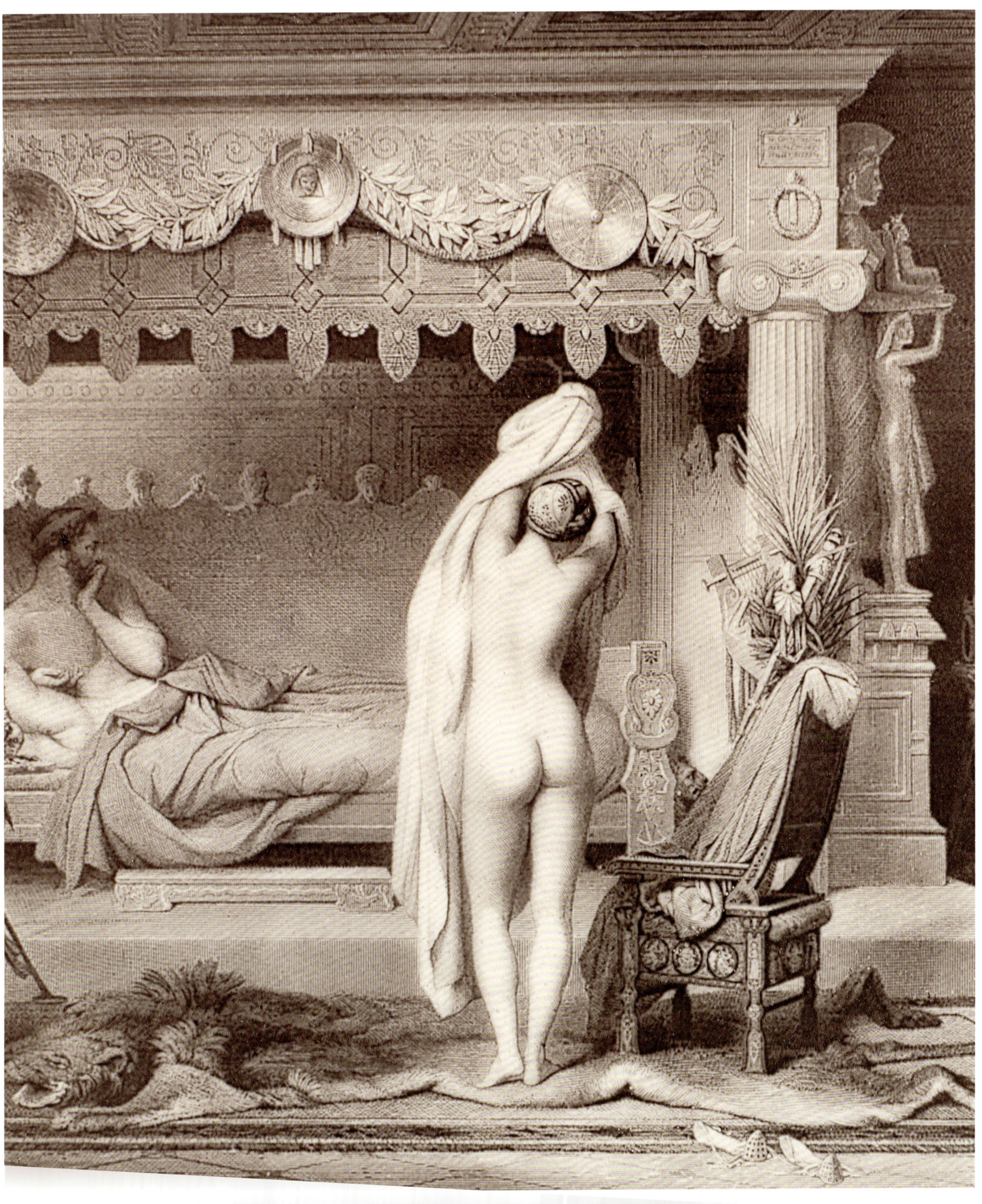

Cat. 102
Robert Jefferson Bingham (1825–1870)

REMBRANDT IN HIS STUDIO

–

After Gérôme's oil-on-panel painting of *Rembrandt Etching a Plate in his Atelier*
1861
Albumen print, "Galerie Photographique" series, no. 93
9 ¼ × 7 ⅞ in.
Musée Goupil, Bordeaux, inv. 99.II.4.34 (1)

Cat. 103
Paul-Adolphe Rajon (1842?–1888)

REMBRANDT IN HIS STUDIO

–

After Gérôme's oil-on-panel painting of *Rembrandt Etching a Plate in his Atelier*
1869
Etching, printed on Holland paper
9 × 7 ½ in.
Musée Goupil, Bordeaux, inv. 93.I.2.1413 (1)

Cat. 104

REMBRANDT IN HIS STUDIO

–

Photograph published by Goupil & Cie
1867
"Musée Goupil & Cie" series, no. 632
Albumen print
4 ½ × 3 ¾ in.
Musée Goupil, Bordeaux, inv. 90.II.3.93 (1)

Cat. 105

REMBRANDT IN HIS STUDIO

–

Photograph published by Goupil & Cie
1872–73
"Carte Album" series, no. 142
Albumen print
4 ½ × 3 ¾ in.
Musée Goupil, Bordeaux, inv. 2000.II.2.32 (1)

Ill. 86. Rembrandt [Harmenszoon van Rijn] (1606–1669), *The Philosopher in Meditation*, 1632, oil on panel, 11 × 13 ½ in., Musée du Louvre, Paris, inv. 1740.

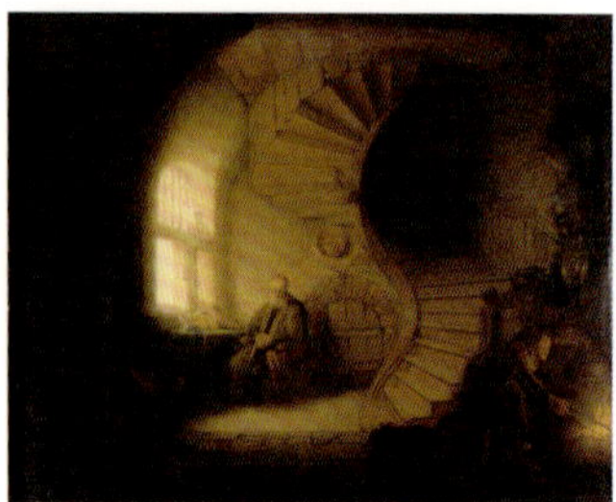

Cat. 106

REMBRANDT

–

Photogravure by Goupil & Cie published in *Œuvres choisies de J.-L. Gérôme*, pl. 23
1877
8 ¾ × 7 ¼ in.
Musée Goupil, Bordeaux, inv. 95.I.2.119 (1)

Provenance of the lost picture: Gérôme to Goupil, 1860, sold to the comte (later duc) de Morny, 1861 (for 6,000 francs). Morny sale, Paris, Mar. 31, 1865, lot 17 (for 20,300 francs). Exposition Universelle, Paris, 1867, property of E. Fould. Fould sale, 1869 (for 15,000 francs). Goupil bought it from Fould and sold it to S. Van Walchren van Wadenoyen, no. 37 (for 19,000 francs). Walchren sale, Paris, Hôtel Drouot, Apr. 24–25, 1876. Serge von Derwies Collection. Sale, Galerie Georges Petit, Paris, November 15, 1906, no. 15.

–

Exhibition History of the lost picture: Salon of 1861, Paris. Exposition Universelle, Paris, 1867

–

Bibliography of the lost picture: *Recueil. Œuvres de Jean-Léon Gérôme,* BNF Estampes, vol. XIV, no. 8. H. Delaborde 1861, *Salon de 1861,* pp. 876–78. T. Gautier, *Salon de 1861,* pp. 176–86. O. Merson, *Expositions de* 1861, pp. 210–12. T. Pelloquet, *Le Monde illustré,* 1861, vol. XIII, p. 391. P. de Saint-Victor, *La Presse,* Jun. 2, 1861. E. Strahan [Earl Shinn], *Gérôme. A Collection of the Works of J.-L. Gérôme in One Hundred Photogravures* (New York: Cassell, 1881). *Catalogue de Paris,* 1883, p. 26. P. Chu, *French Realism and the Dutch Masters* (Utrecht: Haentjens Dekker & Gumbert, 1974), p. 37.

Exhibited at the Salon of 1861, Gérôme's panel painting *Rembrandt Etching a Plate in his Atelier* disappeared in the early twentieth century. On show here are a photograph titled *Rembrandt in his Studio*, taken by Robert Jefferson Bingham after the painting was exhibited at the Salon, and an engraving made by Paul Rajon in the late 1860s. In its day, *Rembrandt* was one of Gérôme's most widely known works due not just to its subject but also to the identity of its first owner, the duc de Morny, half-brother of Emperor Napoleon III. The painting was exhibited again at the Exposition Universelle of 1867, when it belonged to Émile Fould.

Like Gérôme's portrait of Michelangelo (cat. 9), this painting was part of the Romantic tradition of paying tribute to an artist. This tribute is particularly representative of the new reception France was giving to the Dutch artist in the mid-nineteenth century. Indeed, paintings by Rembrandt and other Dutch and Flemish artists of the seventeenth century in general were finally receiving the attention they merited (and have subsequently retained), thanks notably to the writings of Théophile Thoré.[1] Gérôme decided to depict Rembrandt as an etcher, an art in which the latter excelled, his prints being highly valued by art lovers. Paradoxically, even though etching required great precision and therefore as strong a light as possible, Gérôme placed Rembrandt in a dark world lit only by an open window to the left of the painting. In fact, Gérôme was not seeking historical accuracy here, for he wished to honor Rembrandt by evoking one of the painter's most well-known works at that time, *The Philosopher in Meditation* (ill. 86). It had been bought by Louis XVI in 1784 and entered the Louvre when the king's property was confiscated during the Revolution. Gérôme's literal reminders of Rembrandt's work include the overall composition, the dark manner, the technique, and the small size (11×13 ⅜ in. for Rembrandt's painting, 21¾×17 ¾ in. for Gérôme's original panel). The artist underlined furthermore his faithfullness to Rembrandt's paintings. Indeed in his work the Dutch painter wears the white cap and the fur coat Rembrandt chose to wear when he painted himself in his *Artist's Portrait Before the Easel* (1660, Musée du Louvre, Paris).[2] Although doubts had emerged over the authenticity of the *Philosopher* (today dismissed), thanks to its presence in the Louvre and an engraving done in 1771 Rembrandt's painting was very well known at the time.[3] For much of the nineteenth century it was even considered his most important work. Gérôme was therefore evoking a motif thoroughly familiar to his audience. In his review of the Salon of 1861, Théophile Gautier hailed Gérôme's painting as a masterpiece. Immediately stressing the similarities, he wrote, "Here is a veritable subject for painting ... one worth all those intellectual and literary ideas; Rembrandt himself needed no other one for all his paintings and etchings. The plate he is cutting with acid probably expressed an idea of this kind."[4] Gérôme's tribute to Rembrandt was therefore a success. Better, by evoking the figure of a meditating philosopher, Gérôme imbued the image of the painter—meaning both Rembrandt and himself—with a thoughtful, meditative air that elevated his craft to the level of the mind's most noble activity.

There is a certain historical irony—a kind of unintended self-reflexiveness—in Gérôme's celebration of the Dutch painter as a printmaker, in so far as *Rembrandt Etching a Plate in his Atelier* is known today only through an etching, a photograph, and a photogravure, all marketed by Goupil well into the early years of the twentieth century, and all encountering great commercial success, probably due to their close harmony with the original subject of the painting. Their commercial success is indicated by the various formats in which the photographs exhibited here were marketed. **D. F.-R.**

1. W. Bürger [Théophile Thoré], "Rembrandt au Musée d'Amsterdam," excerpted from *L'Artiste,* 1858, vol. IV, pp. 183–88 and W. Bürger [Théophile Thoré], "Les Rembrandt des collections particulières d'Amsterdam" excerpted from *L'Artiste*, Sept. 12, 1858, pp. 17–22. **2.** B. Ducos, "An Icon of Rembrandt Myth," *Rembrandt: three faces of the master* (Cincinnati: Cincinnati Art Museum, 2008), pp. 70–79. **3.** An engraved reproduction of *The Philosopher in Mediation* was published in *Le Musée français, recueil complet des tableaux, statues et bas-relief qui composent les collections nationales* (Paris, 1803), vol. 1. **4.** T. Gautier, *Salon de 1861* (Paris: E. Dentu, 1861), pp. 183–84.

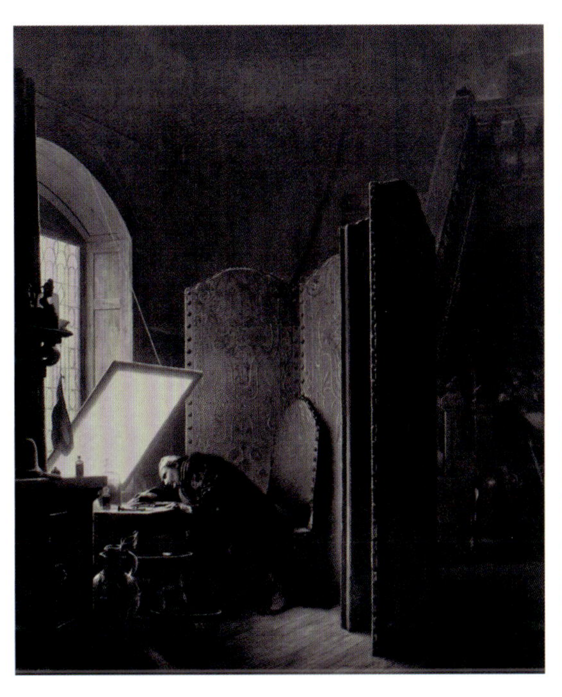

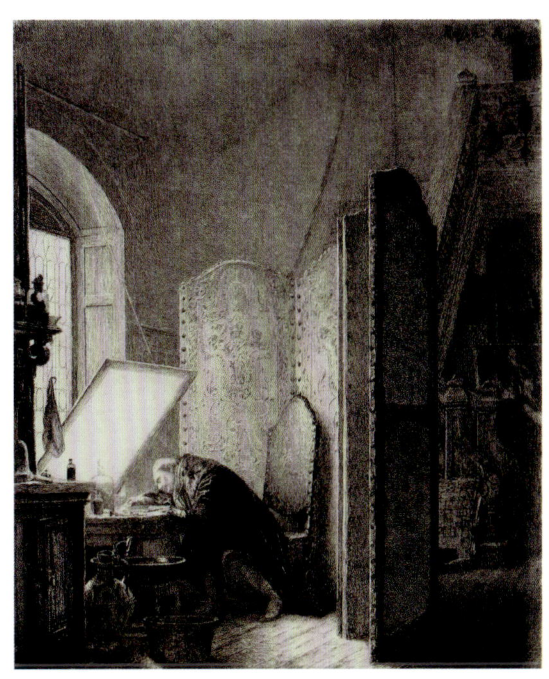

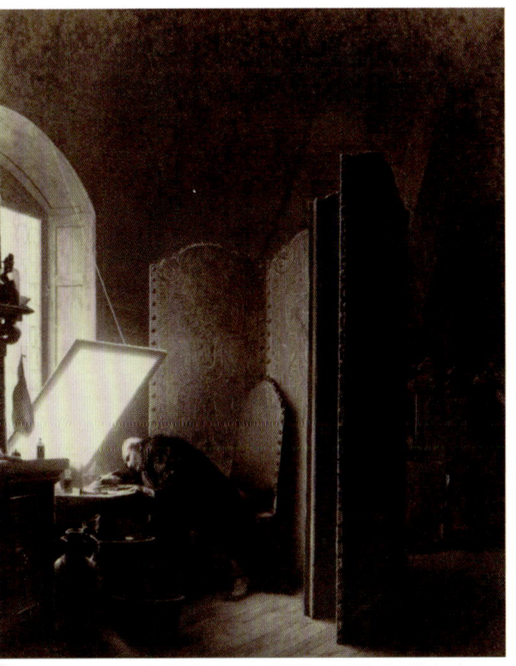

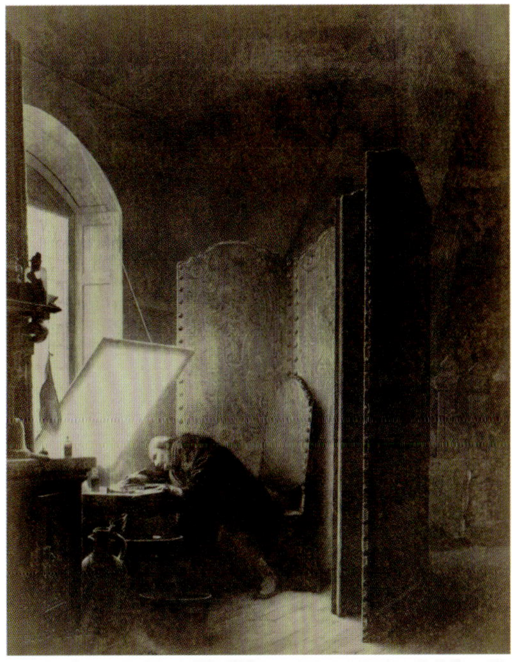

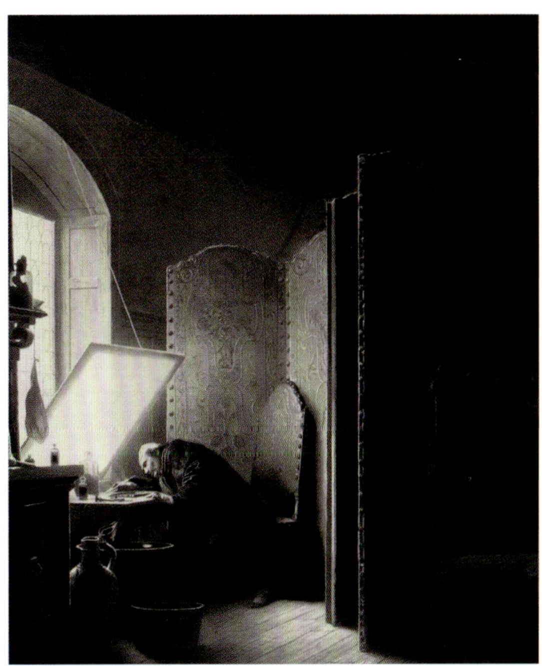

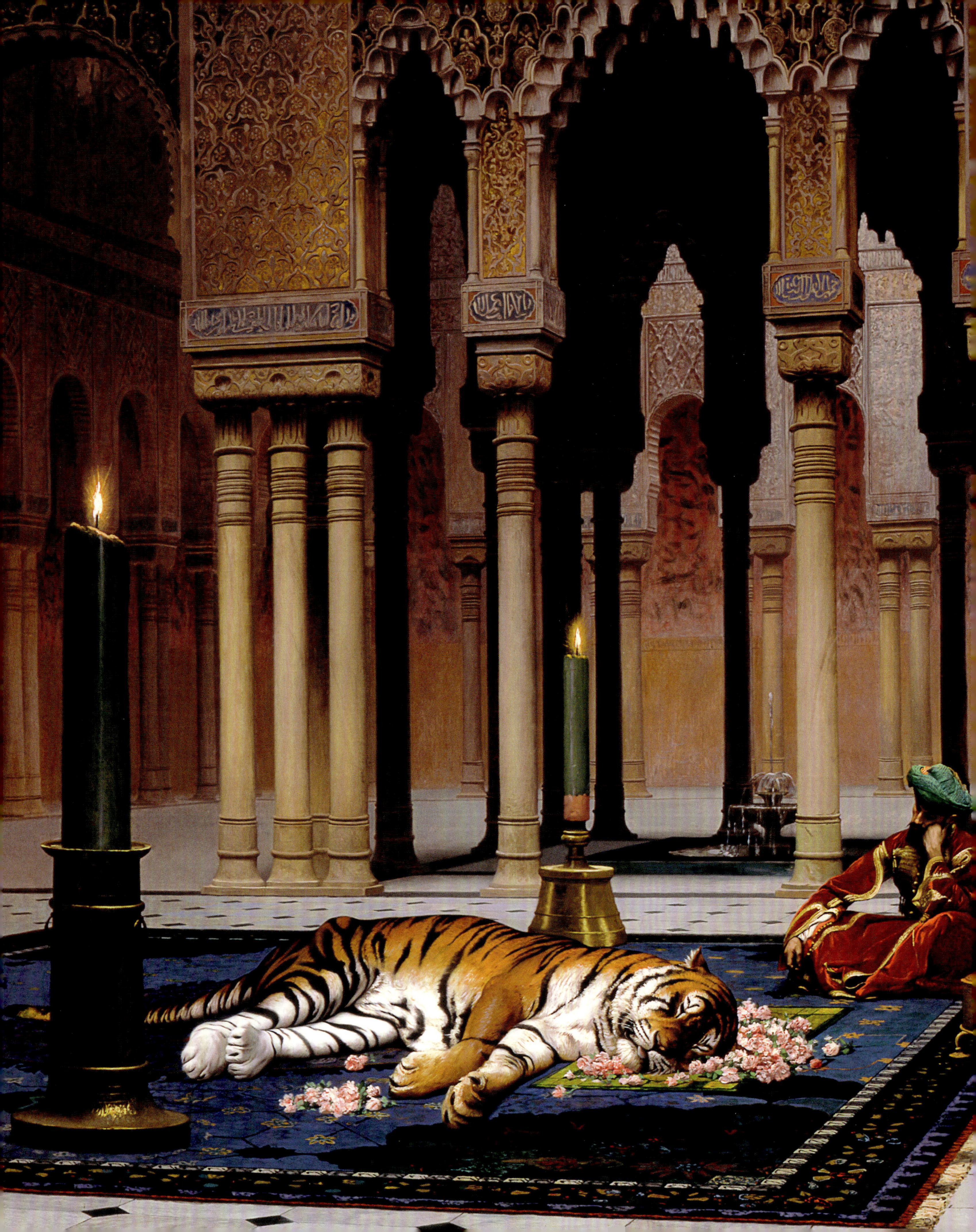

GÉRÔME IN THE GILDED AGE

—

Mary G. Morton

In November 1859, the London-based dealer Ernest Gambart held his second exhibition of French art in a suite of rented galleries at the National Academy of Design, the preeminent art institution in New York. Although it included English paintings, the exhibition of 226 works presented mostly contemporary French pictures, among them two by Jean-Léon Gérôme. *Egyptian Recruits Crossing the Desert* (ill. 103, p. 226) was making its second American appearance, having been included in Gambart's exhibition two years earlier at the International Art Union,[1] and *Duel after the Ball* (cat. 51) was making its American debut. A critic for the *Art Journal* called Gérôme "a rising star of the first magnitude," noting his unique contribution: "Gérôme has a potent idiosyncrasy, a self-willed singularity, which commands more attention than a sounder taste associated with less startling accessories."[2] Another leading art journal of the day, *The Crayon*, was less impressed with the Gérômes, proclaiming them poor investments.[3] Undeterred, Baltimore collector William Thompson Walters acquired *Duel* for $2,500, the first Gérôme to enter an American collection.

By the time of Gambart's 1859 exhibition, *Duel* was already a famous painting in both France and America. The first version of the composition had caused a critical commotion two years earlier at the Paris Salon and was acquired by the duc d'Aumale, one of the great art collectors of the day and a personal friend of the painter. Gérôme completed another version to serve his dealer Adolphe Goupil as a model for reproductive engravings and photographs, and it was then sent to Gambart's exhibition in New York. Its ubiquity in reproduction guaranteed that, by the 1870s, the mention of its title alone could conjure a full image in readers' minds.[4] When it appeared at the Alsace-Lorraine Loan Exhibition in New York in 1874, it was, according to one report, "hailed almost as an old friend by the throngs that pressed around it."[5]

This essay addresses Gérôme's position at the center of a shift in American taste toward contemporary French painting, a concurrent explosion in the art market, and the advent of art speculation. During the first half of the nineteenth century, Americans focused on native, morally instructive art, but the crisis and ensuing loss of national confidence during the Civil War period led to an emphatic turning outward. Collectors, critics and artists sought new sources of inspiration, and looked pointedly toward the Old World.[6] From the late 1850s to the end of the century, Gérôme represented high art in America, and through his paintings and public persona, he served as both a positive and a negative model for Americans seeking to define a new culture. He was idealized for his professionalism, his cosmopolitan Frenchness, his intellectualism, erudition, and refined technical training. But he was also disdained as overly commercial, and suspected of a characteristically French moral degeneracy that some Americans sought to escape in the reconstruction of their national identity. Far from its characterization in twentieth-century scholarly literature as an emblem of stale, rigid

Cat. 110. *The Grief of the Pasha* (detail).

academicism, Gérôme's art was received in America as complex and provocative, at times sharply disturbing and even bewildering in a distinctively modern way. The French master's potent idiosyncrasy elicited a range of impassioned responses from American critics, collectors, and artists. The essay concludes with a brief discussion of Gérôme's legacy in the art of his student Thomas Eakins.

Gérôme's American career coincided with the spectacular fortunes that were made in the United States during and immediately following the Civil War. Millionaires competed with and inspired each other toward ever more extravagant displays of personal wealth, causing "a picture mania," and helping to establish Paris as the center of the international art market.[7] In this highly commercial world of art collecting, successful businessmen such as Alexander Turney Stewart and William Henry Vanderbilt bought as much from discernment as for investment value and the competitive glory of possession. Whereas Gérôme's status in the Parisian art world was determined by powerful journalists and official accolades, in America sale price was the critical barometer.

As the commercial capital of the country, and the point of passage to and from Europe, New York was the undisputed center of the American art world. While old master dealers remained near their carefully cultivated, loyal clientele in Europe, where history, tradition and reputation attracted sales and consignments, picture dealers in New York trafficked mostly in contemporary French and German painting. During the 1860s and early 1870s, the New York art world was highly centralized, with dealers like Gambart playing a "primordial" role in the formation of private collections.[8]

Gambart had no gallery or offices in New York, however, and liaised often with Goupil, the international powerhouse of European contemporary art dealers. Goupil founded an office in New York in 1846, and sent his German protégé, Michel Knoedler, to run it in 1852.[9] Two years later, the office formed the International Art Union to compete with the American Art Union, an organization founded in 1845 to encourage American art. The often defensive American Art Union *Bulletin* accused contemporary French art, defined as the generation of Horace Vernet, Ary Scheffer, and Paul Delaroche, of immorality and lasciviousness.[10] The International Art Union published their mission "to spread through the United States knowledge and taste of superior art," and to present "original productions of the most celebrated artists of the Modern French School" as well as engravings produced in Paris after American artists.[11] An annual subscription of five dollars bought a reproductive engraving and free admission to the Union's exhibitions, which were held in Boston, Philadelphia, and Baltimore in addition to New York. The Union also sponsored American art students in Paris, tempering the commercial base of the operation with an educational mission.[12] This concerted marketing strategy met with significant success. In 1857 Knoedler bought out Goupil & Cie, maintaining the Goupil brand as well as a close business partnership with his mentor.[13] In announcing the gallery's move uptown "following the rest of New York" to 170 Fifth Avenue on the corner of Twenty-second Street, an 1869 article in *Putnam's Monthly* called Goupil's "the first great picture gallery in the US," suggesting that the dealer had done "more to arouse art appreciation in the US than the so-called National Academy."[14]

The infusion of contemporary French art in America, then, was from its inception closely tied to the business of reproductive prints. Sales of original paintings served to promote the sale of Goupil's vast print stock, with print profits far outweighing painting proceeds.[15] Goupil sold a variety of reproductions, from line and mixed-media engravings to lithographs. The firm issued monographic series of lithographs and photographs, an early instance of which was the 1858 monograph of the principal paintings of Gérôme's master Delaroche photographed by Robert Jefferson Bingham. As in the case of Gérôme's *The Death of Caesar* (cat. 67), original paintings were acquired from artists for reproduction, and then sold once their value had been enhanced by the dissemination of their image (ill. 177, p. 345).[16]

Gérôme had been under contract with Goupil since 1859, and by 1863, the year of his marriage to Goupil's daughter, Gérôme had become Goupil's most reproduced painter, with prints of his paintings spreading across France and, through Knoedler, America.[17] That same year, Gérôme sold *Dance of the Almeh* (cat. 154) to Goupil and exhibited it at the Salon. Entered in the Goupil stock book as *Danseuse*, it was sold to Knoedler in 1865 for 20,000 francs ($4,000), alongside *A Turkish Butcher Boy in Jerusalem* (cat. 143), for 6,500 francs ($1,300).[18] Knoedler sold both pictures to New York collector John Hoey in 1867, *Dance of the Almeh* for the extraordinary price of $6,000 and *A Turkish Butcher Boy* for $1,450, the first two Orientalist pictures by Gérôme to enter an American collection.[19] Writing some years later in the *Art Journal*, Lucy Hooper referred to *Dance of the Almeh* as "one of the most frankly indelicate pictures that ever were exposed to public comment."[20] Gérôme's most prolific critic, the Philadelphian-turned New Yorker, Earl Shinn, underlined Gérôme's "disquieting," "provocative" nature in his description of these two paintings. Of *A Turkish Butcher Boy*, he describes the "lad gaping, grimacing, ready to die of ennui," and the "drop of blood in the foreground dwelt on by Gérôme as if a jewel." According to Shinn, the painting received immediate celebrity at the Salon of 1863 because "for the first time the Eternal lassitude of the East was fixed and made striking and because of the frankness with which bleeding and objectionable secrets of the shambles, plucked from the heart of the mystery of a revolting trade, were placed in front and emphasized."[21] For Shinn, the indignant reception of this painting in Paris was warranted by Gérôme's "cynical exposure" of a degraded Eastern society, in which the abasement of the family system, brutal contempt for women, and "the horrors of a carnal religion" result in soulless creatures like the one pictured in *Dance of the Almeh*. Gérôme deserves from the public only the "acrid gratitude of those who convince us of unwelcome truth." Far from a dreamy, erotic, exotic fantasy, then, the painting was, for Shinn, aggressive social realism.[22]

By the mid-1860s, some of Gérôme's most important paintings had made their way to America. Of the thirteen pictures Gérôme exhibited at the Paris Exposition Universelle of 1867, five came from American collections: *Ave Caesar, morituri te salutant* (Edward Mathews) (cat. 70), *Molière Breakfasting with Louis XIV* (Mathews) (cat. 84), *A Turkish Butcher Boy* (Hoey) (cat. 143), *Dance of the Almeh* (Hoey) (cat. 154), and *Heads of the Rebel Beys at the Mosque El Assaneyn* (Stewart) (cat. 144). One of the remaining eight, *The Death of Caesar*, would be bought by an American, John Taylor Johnston, immediately following the Exposition.

It was the art collector and publisher Samuel Putnam Avery, on his first extended visit to Paris, who secured *The Death of Caesar* for Johnston. Avery had been appointed organizer of the American contribution to the 1867 Exposition Universelle, spending six months in Paris meeting artists and dealers and learning the European trade.[23] Avery had entered into partnership with Baltimore financier William Walters in 1864, an enterprise that over the next two decades would result in one of the strongest European art collections in the country as well as the largest private collection of Gérôme paintings. Between 1871 and 1882, Avery made annual summer trips to Europe, mostly London and Paris, gathering inventory. The passage of paintings directly from the living artist's studio to the collectors' hands keenly appealed to Avery's clients, made wary by cautionary tales of fakes and forgeries in the old master market.

In addition to their status as safely authentic, contemporary academic paintings assured conscientious labor and official training in their high level of finish. Subject matter was the most important factor for American collectors in the 1870s, who primarily favored genre paintings that appealed less to intellect, education, or aesthetic refinement than sentiment: social and family life, courtship, weddings, married life, and children. Gérôme's more challenging paintings were too expensive for most of Avery's clients, who bought paintings by his students such as Jean Lecomte du Nouÿ, Pierre-Paul-Léon Glaize, Frederik Hendrik Kammerer, and Ignacio Leon y Escosura.[24]

Relative to the bulk of Avery paintings, then, *The Death of Caesar* was exceptional. It had been known since Goupil's publication of a photographic reproduction in 1859 and received significant critical attention at the Exposition Universelle. Four years after it came to America, Johnston lent it to an annual exhibition at the Yale School of Fine Arts, organized by John Ferguson Weir (the brother of Gérôme's American student Julian Alden Weir). It was included in the Metropolitan Museum's Centennial Exhibition in New York in 1876, and later that year sold to John Jacob Astor for $8,000, having been acquired by Johnston a decade earlier for $1,275, a notable price margin.[25] With its powerful composition, in which "even the lines of architecture conduct the effect," as well as the ghastly thrill of the dead body in the foreground, Shinn considered it not only one of Gérôme's two best paintings (the other being *Ave Caesar*) but a masterpiece of the nineteenth century.[26]

As Gérôme's reputation grew among American collectors, he came to represent French culture generally, and not always in a positive sense. Distinguishing Gérôme as a more sensual realist than his rival Ernest Meissonier, the outspoken critic and collector James Jackson Jarves wrote, "They do not paint ideas, or even emotions, but spectacles. There is a meaning, though, in what Gérôme does; often a lesson of deep import, though, like Macaulay or Thiers in history, he may as an artist be more intent on the picture than the principle."[27] Jarves was disturbed by several aspects of Gérôme's painting, including his carefully crafted surfaces. "Gérôme often finishes to a degree of brush-polish which leaves his figures like porcelain, a vicious practice which mars his great skill in composing." Jarves connects Gérôme's polished surfaces to the demoralizing tendencies characteristic of the French school. According to Jarves, in works such as *King Candaules* (cat. 43), *Phryné before the Areopagus* (cat. 45), and *Dance of the Almeh*, Gérôme does not adhere to the traditional representation of the female nude as divine ideal, but rather paints "to show off the voluptuous attractions of impure women, exhibiting them as prize-animals for amorous men to gloat over. The greater the technical achievement, the more dangerous the painting. Art can dishonor as well as honor a country."

Written in the penultimate year of Napoleon III's Second Empire, Jarves's text connects what he considered to be the general immorality of French art with that of the current French government. Gérôme's "aesthetic immorality" is implicated within a socio-political system that favored power and money over the spiritual or ideal.[28] Jarves equates Gérôme's paintings with the superficially glittering despotism of Second Empire Paris "... holding primarily to strategic and dynastic aims and secondly to diverting the national energies to mercenary considerations and sensual pleasures. Everything is spectacular; a change of fashions in the shop windows being the chief excitement to the passers. Despotism has made of Paris a brilliant bazaar, café and theater; in truth, a well-baited trap for money and morals. Its standard of humanity is low."[29]

Gérôme was felt to represent not only French art but also French political and social culture in part because he was so successfully engaged in Parisian public life. His paintings, however, do not always celebrate the status quo. *Pollice Verso* (cat. 71), which has received surprisingly little scholarly attention despite its fame, is a case in point. Gérôme portrays a scene of mass entertainment during the Roman Empire, the inhumanity, violence, and bloodlust of which were intended to mesmerize and appall. Despite the favor that Gérôme found with the imperial family, the painting reads as a thinly veiled critique of socio-political conditions under imperial rule. *Pollice Verso* was never submitted to the Salon or exhibited publicly during the Second Empire (though it was regularly displayed for his students in his atelier as a source of instruction).[30] Its first exhibition was in 1873 at a private venue, the Cercle de L'Union Artistique (more familiarly known as les "Mirlitons") on the Place Vendôme, and later that year at the world's fair in Vienna. Goupil sold it to an English agent for one of the richest men in America, A. T. Stewart, in 1873 for 80,000 francs ($16,000), securing its celebrity, and completing what Shinn would call "Gérôme's Roman Trilogy" in America: *The Death of Caesar*, and *Pollice Verso*'s "natural pendant," *Ave Caesar*, "that other grand and moody satire on Roman civilization."[31]

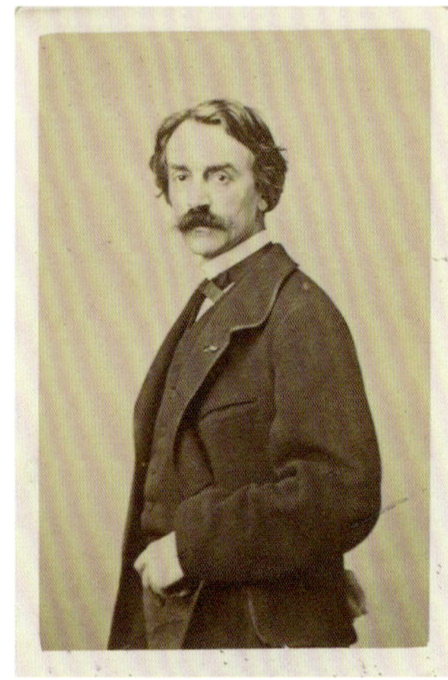

Ill. 87. Neurdein brothers (active 1870–1900), *Gérome*, ca. 1900, albumen print glued to cardboard, 3 ¼ x 2 in., Musée d'Orsay, Paris, inv. PHO 1983 165 529 24.

Stewart was, according to the writer Junius Henri Browne in 1869, "the embodiment of business... emphatically a man of money—thinks money, makes money, lives money."[32] A Scotch-Irish immigrant, he began as a merchant in the dry goods business, established the country's first department store, and by the end of the Civil War was a multi-millionaire. He hung *Pollice Verso* in the specially built art gallery of his private residence constructed in the modern French style on Fifth Avenue at the corner of Thirty-fourth Street (ill. 89). The gallery was dominated by contemporary French academic painters and decorated with a pantheon of painted portrait busts of Rosa Bonheur, Thomas Couture, Delaroche, Vernet, Gérôme and Meissonier, as well as of four American painters.[33] *Pollice Verso* joined other celebrated masterpieces, Bonheur's *Horse Fair* (1853), Bouguereau's *Return from the Harvest*, and Meissonier's *Friedland, 1807* (1868), the latter having been famously acquired for $80,000 at the 1873 Vienna world's fair.[34] The picture gallery was considered the finest in the country, and was maintained by his wife after Stewart's death in 1876 until the sale of his collection in 1887. Stewart's enormous marble pile was embraced as a monument not only to the man's success in business, but also to the burgeoning commercial and cultural power of New York, and of America.

The same year Stewart bought *Pollice Verso*, he also acquired *A Collaboration (Molière and Corneille)*, which had been exhibited at the Salon of 1874. Representing Corneille reading a manuscript to the young Molière, the canvas had reputedly been painted by Gérôme to provoke the interest of French collectors (a likely scenario, given the esoteric French literary source).[35] Gérôme won the gold medal for his contributions to the 1874 Salon, an honor that seems to have inspired American collectors in search of blue chip contemporary art. New York collector James Stebbins acquired the second of Gérôme's three 1874 submissions, *The Grey Cardinal* (cat. 85), paying 60,000 francs ($12,000), double what Stewart had paid for *A Collaboration*.[36] Gérôme was duly priced out of the French market.

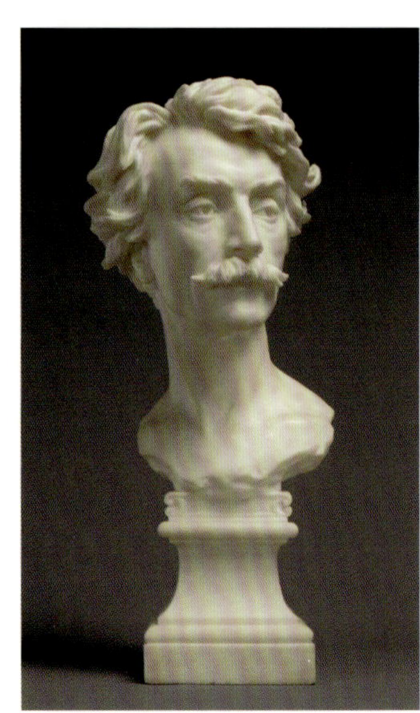

Ill. 88. Jean-Baptiste Carpeaux (1827–1875), *Bust of Jean-Léon Gérôme*, 1872–73, marble, 24 in., J. Paul Getty Museum, Los Angeles, inv. 88.SA.8.

The Grey Cardinal remained in France for some time after its acquisition, installed in Stebbins's

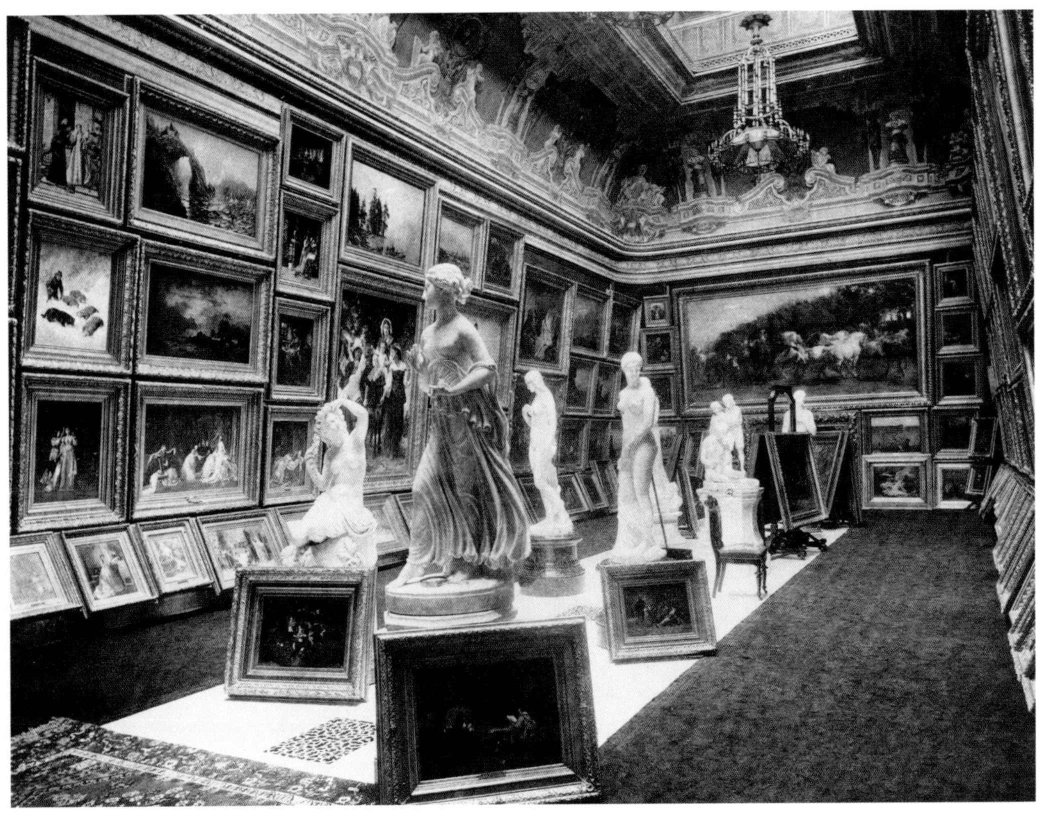

Ill. 89. "A. T. Stewart art gallery in his home on Fifth Avenue at Thirty-fourth Street," in *Artistic Houses, Being a Series of Interior Views of the Number of the Most Beautiful and Celebrated in the United States* (New York: D. Appleton & Co. 1883–84), vol. 1, p. 15, The Metropolitan Museum of Art, New York.

Parisian flat on Avenue Friedland near the Arc de Triomphe. According to Hooper who wrote an article on the Stebbins collection for the *Art Journal*, *The Grey Cardinal* had achieved celebrity status by the time Stebbins acquired it: "Familiar to all Art-Lovers by engraving, description, or photograph, this fine and spirited work needs merely brief mention here."[37] This "piquant glimpse into history," as Shinn put it,[38] portrays the legendary Franciscan cardinal known as Father Joseph, a favorite advisor of Cardinal Richelieu, commanding obsequious greetings from a range of courtiers while immersed, oblivious, in his breviary. This visual meditation on French imperial power was complemented by Stebbins's acquisition of Gérôme's *Molière Breakfasting with Louis XIV*, another painting about the meaningful transgression of aristocratic hierarchy.

By the late 1870s, Gérôme's position among the preeminent representatives of the dominant French school of painting was firmly established for American critics, and estimations of his achievement came into tighter focus. During art exhibitions celebrating the nation's centennial in New York, Gérôme was represented by some of his strongest paintings, including *Pollice Verso, The Chariot Race* (1876, The Art Institute of Chigago, Chigago), *Diogenes* (cat. 109), *The Death of Caesar*, *For Sale* (cat. 157), and *Runners of the Pasha* (cat. 147)[39]. The *Art Journal* published a mixed review of the artist as a kind of retrospective essay, emphasizing his indefatigable industry, his skill as an ethnographic painter, his allegiance to "Nature," his expertly earned and maintained popularity, as well as an undercurrent of scandalous eroticism and brazen provocation.[40]

As the range of his work became more familiar, critics moved well beyond Gérôme's technical mastery to explore further aspects of the painter and his work. Gérôme's intellectual force became a central theme, and descriptions of the painter's working methods foregrounded "the epigrammatic vigor of his conceptions," as one critic put it, "a singularly forcible power of conceiving and placing upon canvas a striking and dramatic incident."[41] Detailed accounts of Gérôme's physical appearance and bearing became more common. Describing his look as "very peculiar," Hooper wrote, "His head, with its deep-set, large eyes, wild masses of grey hair, and pointed grey moustache, is eminently picturesque. He is as thin as a shadow, and is distinguished for extreme industry, excessive irritability, and great dislike to visitors."[42] Gérôme's likeness was extremely well photographed, lithographed, engraved, and sculpted across his career, perhaps more so than any other artist of his time (ill. 87 and 88). He conveyed his intense, lively personality and his social standing in portraits, and journals were happy to reproduce them. Thus he possessed not only the credentials of artistic success, but also the look of a "French master": urbane and cultured, witty, fashionably sharp, and delicately handsome.

Gérôme's stature as a public figure as well as his material success were helpful to Americans trying to establish the importance and respectability of art in the new national culture. Correlating artistic excellence and national pride, many critics and collectors were impressed by the integration of art into French public life, and by the august institutional support that sustained artistic vitality, the École des Beaux-Arts, the Salons, and the art journals.[43] As the most highly decorated artist of his day, Gérôme represented institutional reverence for the arts.

American critics who remained suspicious of the French model, however, included the art critic for *Atlantic Monthly,* Samuel Greene Wheeler Benjamin. Reprising Jarves's criticism of the previous decade, Benjamin blamed the Second Empire for degrading "the character of the nation even below its ordinary standard."[44] Invoking the popular social art theory of the French critic and historian Hippolyte Taine, in which art served as a natural product of its environment, Benjamin disdained French culture as an expression of a corrupt society.[45] Parisians in particular were vilified, their "sensuous love of beauty" overwhelming either moral or political principle.[46] The Tainian connection between art and political culture was made particularly vivid in the case of the "art emporium" that is Paris, as Benjamin described in awesome detail the level of government's fiscal support of the arts.[47] As a natural expression of their Parisian milieu, Gérôme's paintings were portrayed in Benjamin's account as externally beautiful and technically excellent, but overly commercial and lacking in idealism and moral power.[48] Citing *King Candaules, Ave Caesar,* and *The Death of Caesar,* and illustrating *The Grey Cardinal,* Benjamin was unmoved by what he considered emotionally deficient compositions, overly linear and lacking atmosphere.[49] In the final pages of his chapter on French painting, he championed Camille Corot, the artist whose reputation in America would eclipse that of Gérôme within a decade.[50]

Between 1879 and 1884, Earl Shinn published a remarkable account of American private collections in a series of fascicles, which could be bound into three folio volumes. Combined with two volumes on Vanderbilt's collection published concurrently, *Art Treasures of America* is an invaluable historical document of the major art collections of the moment, a geography of taste that measures American collectors' increasing attraction to contemporary European art. Only ten percent of the works listed were by American artists, with contemporary Parisian painters, called the Realist school (Gérôme, Rosa Bonheur, Mariano Fortuny, Mihály Munkácsy, William Bouguereau), and the school of Düsseldorf dominating. By all accounts, the uniformity of taste was striking, with paintings by Gérôme figuring in every major collection.[51]

Shinn, who published under the pen-name Edward Strahan, was perhaps the most engaged and perceptive American writer on Gérôme in the Gilded Age.[52] Having studied in Gérôme's studio as a young man, he was partial to his master's style, but his taste for figural art, draftsmanship, and narrative drama was shared by contemporary collectors. Describing Gérôme's "strange, bold frankness," Shinn had affirmed the painter's preeminence in his review of the 1878 Exposition Universelle, proclaiming "no gallery is complete without him."[53] In his accounts of Gérôme's paintings in *Treasures,* Shinn emphasized the painter's "realism," invoking the ease, instantaneity and faultlessness of photography, as well as a more subversive property associated with the photograph: its ability to strip away false ideals.[54] In his account of William Astor's *Moorish Bath,* for instance, Shinn described Gérôme dismantling the powerful, pervasive ideal of the erotic, exotic woman: "It has been the mission of his career to tear away many and many a veil, and among the most illusory and credulous veils removed by him in his history of revelations is the fixed superstition that the wives of Turks are magnificent and lovely... Disloyal to the divinity of woman in the last degree, Gérôme is eternally telling us the most intimate truths about her, and then asking us with a smile if this is not really the very idol we have worshiped... He reveals and he scoffs secretly deriding his spectator for being strongly and perhaps pruriently attracted to themes he has himself long since found out."[55]

Shinn's conviction in Gérôme's ability to penetrate the truth, even in the exotic Orient, was grounded in his 1874 trip accompanying Gérôme to Egypt, which the critic recorded in an article for *Lippincott's Magazine.*[56] The article assures readers that Gérôme's Middle Eastern forays had little to do with sensual pleasure, but were rather exhaustive cultural explorations. Shinn recounts visits to far-flung, primitive desert towns untrammeled by westerners, led by the indefatigable Gérôme, who was able to converse with the natives in fluent Arabic.

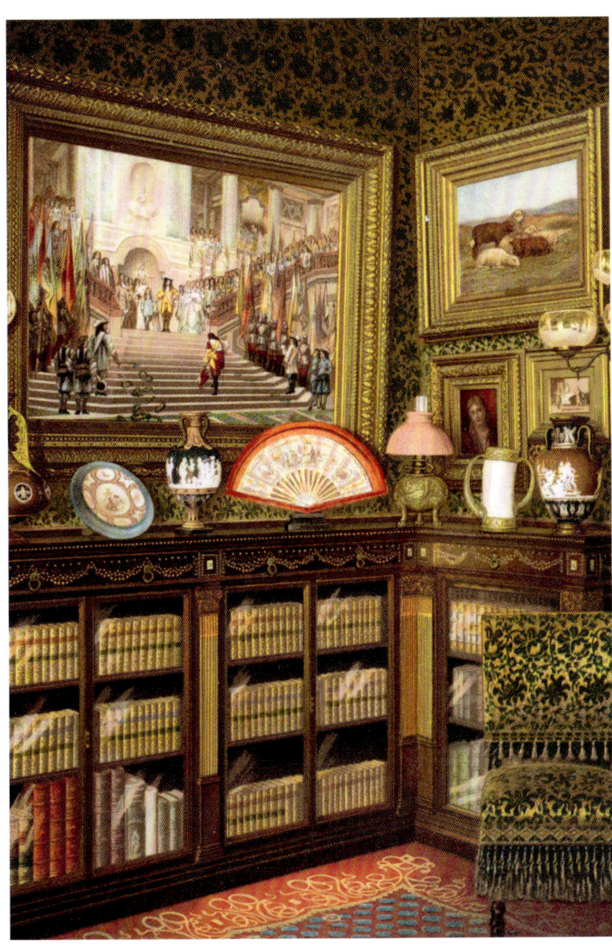

Ill. 90. Mr. Vanderbilt's library with *Reception of the Duc de Condé at Versailles*, reproduced in E. Strahan [Earl Shinn], *Mr. Vanderbilt's House and Collection*, (Philadelphia: G. Barrie, 1883–84).

Shinn was equally impressed by Gérôme's poetical "genius" and what he described as a Poussinian lucidity and inventiveness specific to French intelligence. Despite the volumes devoted by the critic to Gérôme, however, one senses that he could not completely account for the artist's effect: "There is no living painter, and there are very few living writers, whose mind can be called so interesting as the mind of Gérôme."[57]

Shinn's loyal veneration of Gérôme aside, the artist's critical fortune in America began to turn in the 1880s. Gérôme was both positively and negatively associated with the extremely wealthy merchants and industrialists celebrated in Shinn's *Treasures*, his pictures becoming pawns in an escalating game of conspicuous consumption. The most egregious example was the wildly eclectic and voracious Vanderbilt, whose audacious palace, designed as a François I château by Richard Morris Hunt,[58] contained four paintings by Gérôme: *Reception of the Duc de Condé at Versailles* (cat. 86), reproduced *in situ*, in a corner of Vanderbilt's ornate library in Shinn's book, for which Vanderbilt paid 100,000 francs ($20,000) (ill. 90) as well as three Orientalist paintings, the famed *Sabre Dance before a Pasha*, *Bashi-Bazouk Drinking*, and a watercolor, *Asking Alms in a Mosque*.[59]

The editor of *North American Review* listed Gérôme among the corrupting influences commercializing contemporary American art in an article of 1877. He blamed the profusion of wealth and the demand for pictures to decorate ever larger houses for driving the prices of French pictures, the Regnaults, the Meissoniers and Gérômes of Transatlantic fame, to absurd heights, and he accused dealers of surrounding master paintings with substandard knock-offs offered at the same high prices, the "failures of Paris thrown by cargoes upon the American market."[60] The spectacular rise of the picture trade was chronicled in an 1888 book entitled *Art: A Commodity* bemoaning the same phenomenon: dealers selling substandard pictures alongside *chefs d'œuvres*, with news reporters fueling the sensational effect of high prices.[61]

One critic who began to pick up on the increasingly bitter French criticism of Gérôme was George William Sheldon, a writer for the *New York Evening Post*. In an article in 1882, he posited Gérôme as exemplary of the current trend of artists painting purely for popular appeal in order to attain high prices.[62] He included a long citation from the progressive French art critic Philippe Burty, who was piqued by the award of the gold medal at the Salon of 1874 not to his hero Corot but to Gérôme. Sheldon translated and reproduced in full Burty's vilification of Gérôme's art as puerile, inaccurate, and anecdotal, as "weak in conception as the mythology that is danced and sung on the stage of Offenbach." According to Burty, it was Gérôme's official position at the Institut de France and the École des Beaux-Arts, not to mention as son-in-law to Goupil, "the wealthiest of our modern printsellers and picture-dealers," that garnered the medal so deeply deserved by Corot. Registering this as undue abuse, Sheldon defends Gérôme's diligence and work ethic, the courageous audacity of early paintings such as *A Greek Interior* (cat. 23), and the "truth" of his ethnographic paintings, despite their having been conceived for popularity.[63] Despite his flaws as an artist, Sheldon concludes rather meekly, "Gérôme is still very excellent."

By the end of the 1880s, Gérôme's market value no longer occupied the speculative summit. At the Stewart sale in March 1887, Gérôme's *Chariot Race*, for which Stewart had paid $33,000 in 1876, sold for $7,100. *Pollice Verso* cost $20,000 in 1875, and sold for $11,000. *A Collaboration*, acquired in 1875 for $12,000, sold for $8,100.[64] Pictures by other French Salon painters like Meissonier, Alfred Stevens, and Auguste Toulmouche met a similar fate, while work by Barbizon painters such as Constant Troyon appreciated considerably.[65] At the Albert Spencer sale in 1888, Gérôme's famous *Serpent Charmer* (cat. 160) sold for $19,500, a healthy price but less than paintings by both Troyon and Jules Breton.[66]

Barbizon school paintings had been avidly collected in Boston since the 1850s, largely due to the tireless promotion of the American artist William Morris Hunt, and they began to eclipse Salon art in the American market in the 1880s and early 1890s.[67] Collectors and critics championed Corot, Théodore Rousseau, and Jean-François Millet in a concerted shift away from both Gérôme and Meissonier.[68] While the 1876 Centennial Exhibition in Philadelphia included no Barbizon school paintings, they dominated the art pavilion at the 1893 World's Columbia Exposition in Chicago.[69] (The famous 1890 auction battle over Millet's *The Angelus* between a French collector, Alfred Chauchard, and an American collector, in which the French patriot won at a bid of $160,000, donating the painting to the Louvre, trumpeted the market ascendance of Millet.) And with the growing sophistication of the American art world, well-traveled and expertly-advised collectors such as Henry Clay Frick and his contemporary John Pierpont Morgan began confidently acquiring the old masters.

Arriving in the waning years of Gérôme's career in the United States, Fanny Field Hering's elaborate 1892 hagiography, *The Life and Works of Jean-Léon Gérôme*, serves as a detailed demonstration of Gérôme's prestige and success, his fame and authority. Penetrated with "wonder, admiration, and loving reverence" for Gérôme, Hering claims him as "the most eminent representative of high art of the 19th-century."[70] The 288-page folio presented 44 reproductions of Gérôme's art, with text consisting mostly of excerpts from French and American critics and from the master's own notes. Gérôme seems to have actively participated in the publication, accommodating the author during visits to his home and studio and corresponding regularly with her and her publisher in a concerted effort to maintain his hold on American collectors.[71]

By the time Gérôme died in 1904, he was recognized in America as a celebrated lion of the French art world, but also regularly criticized as a second-rate master. Upon his death, one journalist wrote, "A couple of decades ago he doubtless would have been accorded a higher rank. But tastes and ideals change."[72] He was seen as a painter for the masses, employing a premeditated, formal theatricality that was no longer in fashion. His pictures were thought to appeal more to "the sensation-loving than the nature-loving public. They are epic rather than pastoral."[73] Gérôme was deliberate, calculated, precise, and coolly linear when aesthetic fashion had shifted toward passion and color. He excelled in beautifully refined descriptions of detail at a time when synthetic visions were prized. He was a sophisticated player in the official French art world when critics and collectors increasingly celebrated artistic Bohemia.

Alongside his early role in developing the taste for contemporary French painting, Gérôme's greatest legacy in America may in fact be his impact as an art teacher to American painters, particularly during the later 1860s and 1870s. Despite a reputation in later scholarly literature as an overly strict, narrow-minded academician, Gérôme seems to have been a sensitive, passionately committed, and engaged teacher, whose mode of instruction was intense and serious but not personally dogmatic.[74] During his teaching tenure, some one hundred and fifty American students flocked to Gérôme's atelier at the École des Beaux-Arts. Gérôme was one of three painters appointed to head ateliers during the 1863 reform of the École des Beaux-Arts, an event intended to liberate the school from the rigid control of the Académie. Gérôme therefore represented modernity, particularly for the Philadelphia students fleeing the limited confines of the Pennsylvania Academy of Art.[75]

One of those students, Thomas Eakins, wrote a letter home in June 1869, in which he raved about his art teacher in Paris, "who can paint men like my dear master, the living thinking acting men, whose faces tell their life long story? Who has ever done so as him & who will ever do it again like him?"[76] In numerous letters from France during his student years, in his correspondence with Gérôme after his return to Philadelphia, and above all in his paintings, Eakins's embrace of Gérôme as his master and model is clearly evident. In the scholarly literature, however, the impact of Gérôme on his pupil has generally been diminished or simplified. The adoption of Eakins as a hero of American modernism came just as Gérôme was being eclipsed in the art historical canon. As an icon of academicism, Gérôme was hardly helpful in making the case for Eakins's avant-garde innovation and originality.[77]

Scholars tend to overemphasize technique as the primary point of influence of Gérôme on Eakins, although Eakins himself asserted the secondary status of this lesson.[78] Most references to the Eakins-Gérôme relationship involve repudiation of the student by his master, and distinctions of difference from subject matter to painterly touch.[79] There are however elements of Gérôme's oeuvre, articulated by several American critics cited above, that surface in Eakins's work but are acknowledged only indirectly in his letters. Eakins was deeply impressed by the empirical zeal of Gérôme's project, the requirement imposed by the master to look long and hard not only at the human figure, but also at objects first hand. Gérôme's commitment to experiential knowledge was supported by the art history lectures presented by his popular colleague at the École, the positivist critic Taine. Eakins must have been under the spell of both masters when he wrote that one must not simply copy nature, nor create idealized images apart from nature but must, rather, "observe carefully, learn nature's secrets, try to know nature better than anyone else, don't just follow the nature knowledge of the old masters.[80]"

In addition to learning the science of observation from Gérôme, however, Eakins also learned the artifice of creating a heightened sense of realism in his paintings. Both artists used a refined touch, meticulously rendered details, and a cool understated vocabulary of gesture and expression to convey unsettling moments of horror and violence. Their most compelling paintings are superficially inexpressive and impersonal, but they manage to create a deeply disturbing effect. Gérôme and Eakins employed these effects the errant detail or bizarre gesture, the uncanny, off-beat moment, the indirectly uncomfortable unrest to create a quietly subversive, psychological undertow that served their realist agenda. They instilled a sense of tension by combining emotional reserve with searing, sometimes macabre details (what Shinn described as the "almost painful pitch of intensity" of

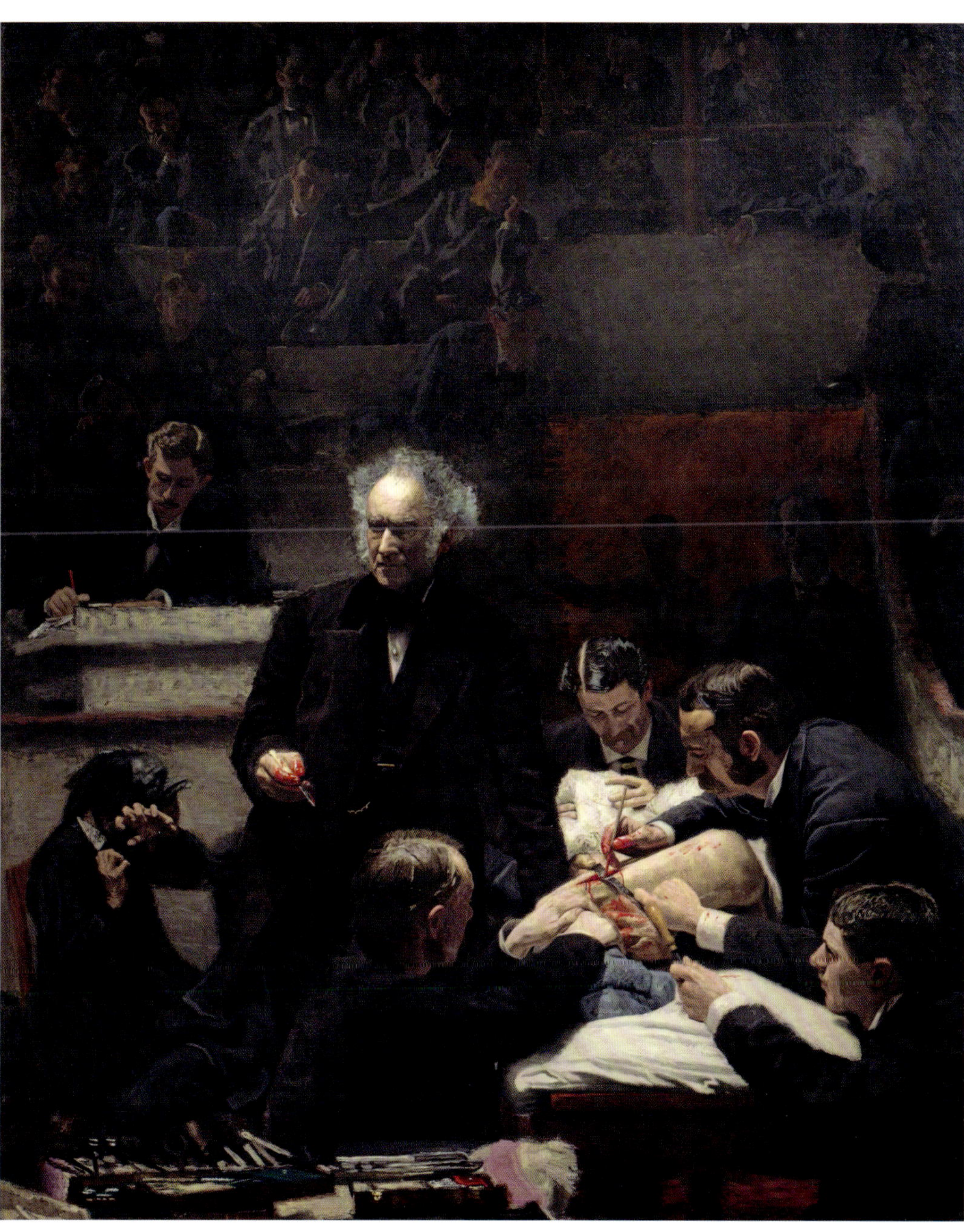

Ill. 91. Thomas Eakins (1844-1916), *The Gross Clinic*, 1875, huile sur toile, 243,8 × 198,2 cm, Philadelphie, Philadelphia Museum of Art and the Pennsylvania Academy of Fine Arts, inv. 2007-1-1.

Gérôme's "scrupulously accurate rendering of accessories").[81] The intent was to enhance the powerful presence, the palpable "realness," of their images.

The scandalous impact of Eakins's famous *The Gross Clinic* (ill. 91) when it was exhibited in 1875 would have certainly been familiar to Gérôme. Reporters discussed the picture in similar terms to those found in Gérôme criticism, praising the painting's technical accomplishments and the power of its realist vision, but deriding its lack of poetry and beauty.[82] Critics were tough on the painting partly because of what they perceived as an overly intense French realism, invoking but not always naming Gérôme.[83] The art critic for the *New York Daily Tribune*, Clarence Cook, wrote that *The Gross Clinic* was "one of the most powerful, horrible and yet fascinating pictures that has been painted anywhere in this century." It is a shame, says Cook, that the work is hung in a public gallery where "men and women of weak nerves must be compelled to look at it. For not to look is impossible."[84]

This effect of attraction–repulsion was noted several years earlier by an English critic in response to Gérôme's *For Sale*, who described "a pervading unpleasantness of tone which, nevertheless, instead of repelling, seems, like the intensity of the realization, to attract us to penetrate its murky depth of meaning."[85] Gérôme thematized this operation in paintings from *The Cock Fight* to *Phryné* and the *Slave Market*, and he created the effect for the viewer in works such as *The Christian Martyrs' Last Prayers* (cat. 80), *The Serpent Charmer*, and *The Death of Caesar*, and of course in *Pollice Verso*, which, according to Eakins, Gérôme used to pull out for students to demonstrate principles of painting in the 1860s.[86] The dramatic space of the arena in *Pollice Verso*, the low point of view alongside the victorious gladiator, the slivers of sunlight breaking through the canopies, the vestals' bloodlust and the indifferent expression of the emperor enhance the terrifying moment of imminent slaughter. There is a cool rationalism in the meticulously composed presentation, a counterpoint to the horror of the scene.

Like *Pollice Verso*, *The Gross Clinic* takes place in a highly organized arena in which the doctor, with the composure of the helmeted gladiator, performs a socially—in this case scientifically—condoned act of violence. Eakins underlines the essential human horror of surgery in the figure of the shrinking woman, and in the glistening blood on Gross's scalpel. Critics questioned the inclusion of these two details, but it is precisely in these off-center, potently dramatic details that Gérôme's influence can be felt.[87]

The year after he painted *The Gross Clinic*, Eakins completed a small, private painting of his father and his friends playing chess in the Eakins home (ill. 92). Hanging on the wall behind the players is an engraved reproduction of Gérôme's *Ave Caesar.* It is a complex though understated homage to the dominant influences in the painter's life.[88] Although Eakins's relationship with his father has received thorough attention in the voluminous literature devoted to the American master, the debt to his artistic "father" may be further illuminated by a deeper understanding of Gérôme's art.

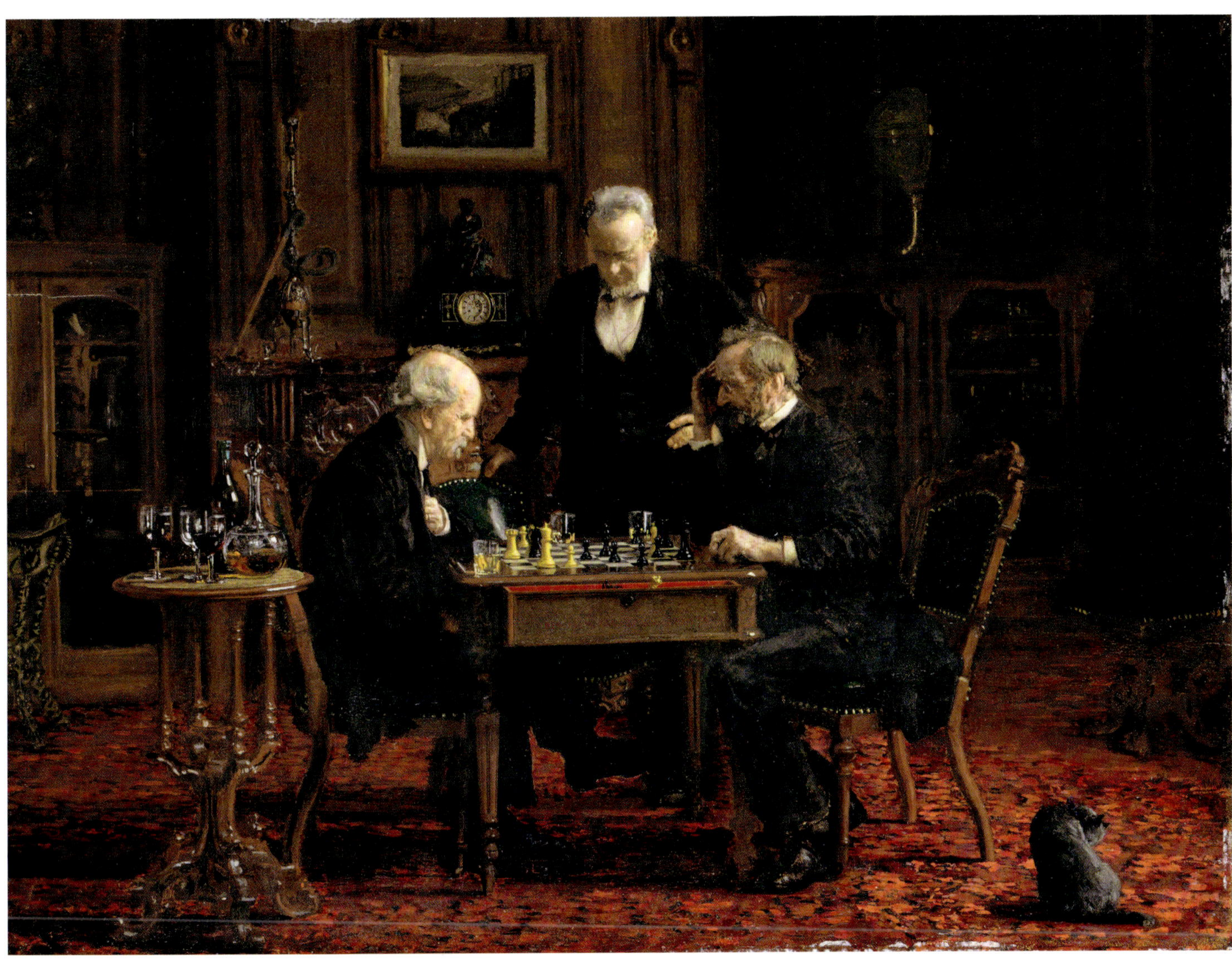

Ill. 92. Thomas Eakins, *The Chess Players*, 1876, oil on panel, 11 ¾ × 16 ¾ in., The Metropolitan Museum of Art, New York, inv. 81.14.

1. In preparing this essay, I am grateful for the research assistance of Sarah Hawley, Joanna Lee, Carol O'Connor, and Ryan Wong, and for editorial suggestions from my kind colleagues Scott Allan, Emily Beeny, Sarah Cash, DeCourcy McIntosh, and Leah Lehmbeck.
Prayer in the House of an Arnaut Chief was also included in the 1857 exhibition. D. McIntosh, Goupil and the American Triumph of Jean-Léon Gérôme, in H. Lafont-Couturier, *Gérôme and Goupil: Art and Enterprise*, exh. cat., trans. I. Ollivier (Bordeaux: Musée Goupil, 2000 1; also New York: Dahesh Museum of Art, 2001, and Pittsburgh: The Frick Art & Historical Center, 2001), p. 34. McIntosh's essay is an excellent account of the market for Gérôme in America, and Knoedler's role in particular.

Prices in this essay are cited in the documented currency, with an approximate conversion in parentheses based on the rate of 5,000 francs per 1,000 U.S. dollar in 1803, as listed on the Global Financial Data website. I thank Julia Armstrong-Totten for guiding me to the GFD website.

2. "The French Exhibition," *Art Journal*, vol. V (1859), p. 188. The critic was reporting on the Paris Salon of 1859, which included *Dead Caesar*, *Ave Caesar*, and *King Candaules*.

3. "Pictures like *The Duel* are poor investments. Posterity will not return first cost for them." *The Crayon*, vol. VI (Dec. 1859), p. 378. See also L. M. Fink, "The Role of France in American Art, 1850–1870.", Ph.D. thesis, University of Chicago, 1970, p. 234.

4. "It is so well known that it would be useless to describe it." *Art Journal*, 2nd ser., vol. 2 (1876), p. 281. For more on reproductions of Gérôme paintings, including *Duel*, see H. Lafont-Couturier 2000–1 (as in n. 1) , and E. Kahng, ed., *The Repeating Image: Multiples in French Painting from David to Matisse*, exh. cat. (Baltimore and New Haven: The Walters Art Museum, 2007 and Yale University Press, 2007).

5. L. Hooper, "Léon Gérôme," *Art Journal*, vol. 54 (Jan. 1877), p. 27.

6. See H. B. Weinberg, *Americans in Paris, 1850–1910: The Academy, the Salon, the Studio and the Artists' Colony* (Oklahoma City: Oklahoma City Museum of Art, 2003); K. Adler et al., *Americans in Paris, 1860–1900*, exh. cat. (London: National Gallery, 2006); H. B. Weinberg, *The Lure of Paris: Nineteenth-Century American Painters and their French Teachers* (New York: Abbeville Press, 1991); and Weinberg's introduction to *The Art Experience in Late Nineteenth-century America* (New York: Garland Publishing, 1976).

7. See A. Boime, "America's Purchasing Power," in *Saloni, gallerie, musei e loro influenza sullo sviluppo dell'arte dei secoli XIX e XX*, ed. F. Haskell (Bologna: CLUEB, [1981]). Between 1866 and 1867, some $300,000 worth of French pictures were sold in the U.S. L. M. Fink 1970 (as in n. 3), p. 403. See also M. Goldstein, *Landscape with Figures: A History of Art Dealing in the United States* (New York and Oxford: Oxford University Press, 2000), p. 27.

8. René Brimo's term. R. Brimo, *L'É volution du goût aux États-Unis d'après l'histoire des collections* (Paris: J. Fortune, 1938), p. 59.

9. My thanks to DeCourcy McIntosh for correcting the record on Knoedler's arrival in New York.

10. L. M. Fink 1970 (as in n. 3), p. 189.

11. R. Brimo 1938 (as in n. 8), p. 57.

12. L. M. Fink 1970 (as in n. 3), p. 187.

13. M. Goldstein 2000 (as in n. 7), p. 34. Vibert died in 1850, and the firm had become known as "Goupil & Cie" by the time Knoedler bought it. Knoedler used the Goupil name until 1875, when the firm became known as "Goupil & Cie: M. Knoedler Successor."

14. "Fine Arts," *Putnam's Monthly*, May 1869, reproduced in S. Burns and J. Davis, *American Art to 1900: A Documentary History* (Berkeley: University of California Press, 2009), p. 644.

15. My thanks to DeCourcy McIntosh for making this point.

16. L. M. Fink 1970 (as in n. 3), pp. 202–3.

17. See H. Lafont-Couturier 2000 1 (as in n. 1). My thanks to DeCourcy McIntosh for clarifying the contractual arrangement: Goupil had the right of first refusal on any image produced by Gérôme; the profit from the resale of the painter's canvases were split 50 50.

18. Goupil Stock Book 2, no. 935, Getty Research Institute (GRI). I am grateful to Agnès Penot-Lejeune, research fellow at the GRI, for creating the database of the Goupil stock books, helping navigate it, and for numerous discussions about Gérôme and Goupil. See Penot-Lejeune's forthcoming article, "The Goupil & Cie Stock Books: A Lesson on Gaining Prosperity through Networking," *Getty Research Journal*, no. 2 (2010).

19. In the Gérôme catalogue raisonné, Gerald Ackerman lists three paintings of Middle Eastern butchers. No. 128 (*Turkish Butcher*) and no. 145 (*A Turkish Butcher Boy in Jerusalem*) are probably the same picture, bought by Hoey from Knoedler in 1867. G Ackerman, *Jean-Léon Gérôme:* (Courbevoie: ACR Édition, 2000).

20. L. Hooper 1877 (as in n. 5), p. 27.

21. E. Strahan [Earl Shinn], *The Art Treasures of America: Being the Choicest Works of Art in the Public and Private Collections of North America* (Philadelphia: G. Barrie, 1880), vol. 3, p. 78. Shinn took the pen-name of Edward Strahan to distinguish his journalistic career from his (Philadelphia Quaker) family name.

22. Shinn's criticism receives further discussion later in the essay.

23. See M. Goldstein 2000 (as in n. 7), pp. 34–49; and M. Fidell Beaufort, H. L. Kleinfield, and J. K. Welcher eds., *The Diaries, 1871–1882, of Samuel P. Avery, Art Dealer* (New York: Arno Press, 1979), as well as L. M. C. Randall, ed., *The Diary of George A. Lucas, an American Art Agent in Paris, 1857–1909* (Princeton, N.J.: Princeton University Press, 1979).

24. M. Fidell Beaufort 1979 (as in n. 23), pp. xxx–xli. Eighty percent of buyers at Avery's auctions were New Yorkers.

25. L. M. Fink 1970 (as in n. 3), p. 448. See also L.M. Fink, "French Art in the United States," *Gazette des Beaux-Arts*, Sept. 1978, p. 94.

26. E. Strahan 1880 (as in n. 21), vol. 1, p. 141.

27. J. J. Jarves, *Art Thoughts: The Experiences and Observations of an American Amateur in Europe* (New York: Hurd and Houghton, 1869), pp. 258–62.

28. Ibid., p. 263.

29. Ibid., pp. 284–85.

30. Letter from Thomas Eakins to Earl Shinn, Jan. 30 1875 (Cadbury Collection, Swarthmore College). Quoted in G. Ackerman, Thomas Eakins and His Parisian Masters Gérôme and Bonnat, *Gazette des Beaux-Arts* 73 (Apr. 1969), p. 242.

31. E. Strahan 1880 (as in n. 21), vol. 1, p. 23. *Pollice Verso* is no. 6837 in Goupil Stock Book 6.

32. J. H. Browne, *The Great Metropolis* (Hartford, Conn.: American Publishing Co., 1869), p. 289. Quoted from J. E. Cantor, "A Monument of Trade: A T Stewart and the Rise of the Millionaire's Mansion in New York," *Winterthur Portfolio*, vol. 10 (1975), pp. 165–97.

33. J. E. Cantor 1975 (as in n. 32), p. 184. The American painters were: Daniel Huntington, Frederick Church, Albert Bierstadt, and Charles Loring Elliot.

34. R. Brimo 1938 (as in n. 8), p. 52.

35. L. Hooper, "Studios of Paris," *Art Journal*, vol. 1 (1875), p. 89. Hooper reports that Gérôme told her that the subject of *A Collaboration* was a "peculiarly French one and calculated to interest Frenchmen especially." An 1875 review in the *Art Journal*, which included an engraving of *A Collaboration*, adds a counterpoint to Jarves's suspicion of Gérôme's finished surfaces. Here the writer is impressed with Gérôme's strategy of mixing controversial content with a highly refined technique: "Mentally his constitution is very peculiar. We cannot accuse him of being immoral because the severity of his style discourages the looseness of mind most favorable to immoral impressions." (p. 48).

36. L. Hooper, "Studios of Paris" (as in n. 35). For *A Collaboration*, see Goupil Stock Book 7, no. 8601, Getty Research Institute.

37. L. Hooper, "American Art – Collections in Paris," *Art Journal*, vol. 1 (1875), p. 153.

38. E. Strahan 1880 (as in n. 21), vol. 1, p. 99.

39. See McIntosh 2000–1 (as in n. 1), p. 38.

40. Gérôme, *Art Journal* (1876), pp. 279–82.

41. L. Hooper 1877 (as in n. 5), pp. 26–27.

42. Ibid., p. 28.

43. See for instance L. W. Havemeyer, *Sixteen to Sixty: Memoirs of a Collector* (New York: privately printed for the family of Mrs. H. O. Havemeyer and the Metropolitan Museum of Art, 1961), pp. 6–7. See also F. F. Hering, *Gérôme. The Life and Works of Jean-Léon Gérôme* (New York: Cassell), 1892. Also Glessner's reference to the sheer volume written on Gérôme's biography, and the general familiarity of his life details. R. W. Glessner, The Passing of Jean Léon Gérôme, *Brush and Pencil* 14 (Apr. 1904), p. 64.

44. S. G. W. Benjamin, *Contemporary Art in Europe* (New York: Harper, 1877), p. 60.

45. Taine's theories, expounded in lectures at the École des Beaux-Arts from 1865 through the 1870s and 1880s, held art as an organic expression of the racial, physical, and historic conditions of a nation. His lectures were widely published and translated. His engraved portrait appears in Benjamin's book early in the chapter on French art. For more on Taine's lectures, see M. G. Morton, Naturalism and Nostalgia: Hippolyte Taine's Lectures on Art History at the École des Beaux-Arts, 1865 1869 , Ph.D. dissertation, Brown University, 1998.

46. S. G . W. Benjamin, "Practice and Patronage of French Art," *Atlantic Monthly* 36 (Sept. 1875), p. 258.

47. Benjamin expresses his astonishment at the total government investment in the arts in 1876, which he quotes at 7,500,000 francs ($1,500,000). S. G. W. Benjamin 1877 (as in n. 44), p. 63; also S. G. W. Benjamin 1875 (as in n. 46), p. 258.

48. S. G. W. Benjamin 1877 (as in n. 44), p. 75.

49. Ibid., p. 95.

50. See for instance Marina Griswold Van Rensselaer review of the Exposition Universelle of 1889, in which she reports, "I heard many tongues say the same thing: It is the apotheosis of Corot." "Impressions of the International Exposition 1889," *Century Magazine*, vol. 39 (Dec. 1889), p. 317.

51. These included the collections of New Yorkers John Jacob Astor, August Belmont, James Stebbins, and John Wolfe, Henry Probasco of Cincinnati, and Henry Gibson of Philadelphia. See also A. Boime 1981 (as in n. 7).

52. Shinn was raised in a Quaker family in Philadelphia, and studied at the Pennsylvania Art Academy. Like fellow academy students Mary Cassatt and Thomas Eakins, he went to Paris to study art, and entered Gérôme's studio in 1866 (with Eakins's help.) On returning to the United States after a year in France, he decided to become an art critic and moved from Philadelphia to New York. He wrote primarily for *The Nation*, publishing his first article on Gérôme in July 1869, a chronicle of his experience studying with the French master. See D. T. Lenehan, "Fashioning Taste: Earl Shinn, Art Criticism and the National Identity in Gilded Age America," Master's thesis, Haverford College, 2005. See also H. B. Weinberg 1991 (as in n. 6), p. 90. In addition to the essays and books cited here, Shinn also published, under the pen-name Edward Strahan, *Gérôme: A Collection of the Works of J. L. Gérôme in One Hundred Photogravures* (New York: Samuel L. Hall, 1881), 4 vols.

53. E. Strahan [Earl Shinn], *The Chefs-d'oeuvre d'art of the International Exhibition, 1878* (Philadelphia: G. Barrie, 1878), p. 22.

54. E. Strahan 1880 (as in n. 21), vol. 3, p. 52.

55. Ibid., p. 5. In 1881 Shinn published a book on modern French art, admitting the continued dominance of the French school. Shinn devotes a whole chapter to Gérôme, describing his highly individual style (not a naturalist or impressionist or idealist.) Shinn defends Gérôme against the Impressionists, disdaining their work as overly fussy in surface texture, while Gérôme penetrates the surface, sculpting the images on the canvas. E. Strahan [Earl Shinn], *Modern French Art* (New York: A. W. Lovering, 1881), pp. 3–4.

56. E. Shinn, "In a Caravan with Gérôme the Painter," *Lippincott's Magazine of Popular Literature and Science*, Mar. 1874, p. 13.

57. E. Strahan 1880 (as in n. 21), vol. 3, p. 6.

58. J. E. Cantor 1975 (as in n. 32), p. 168.

59. While eclectic and voracious, William Henry Vanderbilt had fairly conservative tastes as a collector. He avoided nudes, and preferred pictures "that tell a story," painted in an exacting style. See R. Brimo 1938 (as in n. 8), p. 51. See also the 1886 sales catalogue of Vanderbilt's collection, in which no. 14, "Louis XIV and the Grand Condé," is listed as "painted to order, 1878," and includes a long extract of a "Letter from the Artist" describing the painted scene in detail. The staircase, Gérôme states, was destroyed under Louis XV, "but there remains an engraving of it at that time, very well executed, which has enabled me to reconstruct it with truth." He then goes on to recount the story of Louis XIV receiving the Grand Condé. For the price paid for *Reception of the Duc de Condé at Versailles*, see Goupil Stock Book 9, no. 12784.

60. "American artists either cannot compete, or they alter their style into tasteless copies of the French model." [Allen Thorndike Rice], "The Progress of Painting in America", *North American Review*, no. 124 (May 1877). Quoted from S. Burns and J. Davis 2009 (as in n. 14), pp. 648–49.

61. S. Ford, *Art: A Commodity* (New York: Rogers and Sherwood, 1888). Quoted from S. Burns and J. Davis 2009 (as in n. 14), pp. 649–50.

62. G. W. Sheldon, *Hours with Art and Artists* (New York: D. Appleton, 1882).

63. Sheldon invokes a familiar anecdote about the young Gérôme scraping off his oil sketch from the Roman Campagna with the pronouncement, "That which is so quickly done is sure to be ill done." See L. Hooper 1877 (as in n. 5), p. 26, for another account. About *A Greek Interior*, Sheldon writes, "he had audaciously sneered at the doctrine of common sense which prescribes limits to the public presentation of the nude. The painter, however, was not the man to accept the dictation of the populace or of the connoisseurs; and… his later presentations of the nude have often been extremely obnoxious to the tastes which that picture repelled." He distinguishes Gérôme's realism from that of Meissonier for its imagination, however: "The ability to use his faithful studies of natural objects as material for pictures that glow with imagination is particularly characteristic of this painter, and one of the principal marks that differentiate his work form that of his great rival, Meissonier." G. W. Sheldon 1882 (as in n. 62), pp. 87–88.

64. Prices annotated in Getty Research Institute and Watson Library copies of the A. T. Stewart sale catalogue. *A. T. Stewart Collection of Paintings, Sculptures, and other Objects of Art* (New York, 1887).

65. Comparative prices to those for Gérôme in the annotated Watson Library copy of the A. T. Stewart sales catalogue include: A. Toulmouche, *The Serious Book*, 1874, no. 39, cost $6,000, sold $2,150. Troyon, *Cattle*, 1856, no. 50, cost $2,500, sold $7,150. Alfred Stevens, *After the Ball*, 1874, no. 56, cost $6,000, sold $2,850. Meissonier, *Charity*, 1874, no. 65, cost $24,000, sold $10,500. The two most famous paintings in the Stewart collection, Bonheur's *Horse Fair*, which sold for $53,000, and Meissonier's *Friedland*, which sold for $60,000, achieved high prices but were bought by Stewart at yet higher prices.

66. Jules Breton's *Evening* sold at $20,500, and Troyon's *Drove of Cattle and Sheep* at $26,000. A decade later, *The Serpent Charmer* sold to the dealer Schaus for $10,000–12,000, according to Ackerman 2000. See Getty Research Institute's annotated copy of the *Catalogue of the Albert Spencer Collection of Foreign Paintings* (New York, 1888).

67. A French journalist, Durand-Gréville, noted that Hunt "had a preponderant influence on the emigration of a good part of Millet's oeuvre across the Atlantic." He traveled for six months to visit American private collections, noting, with some alarm, that French paintings numbered not in the hundreds, but in the thousands. É. Durand-Gréville, "La Peinture aux États-Unis: les Galeries privées," *Gazette des Beaux-Arts*, ser. 2, 36 (July 1887), part 1, p. 68. Translation my own. For more on the collecting pattern of Bostonians in French painting, see A. Murphy, "French Paintings in Boston:1800–1900," *Corot to Braque: French Paintings from the Museum of Fine Arts, Boston*, exh. cat. (Boston: Museum of Fine Arts, 1979), pp. xvii–xlvi.

68. See C. Moore, "Modern Art of Painting in France," *Atlantic Monthly*, vol. 68 (Dec. 1891), pp. 805 16; also Durand-Gréville 1887 (as in n. 67).

69. W. G. Constable, *Art Collecting in the United States of America: An Outline of a History* (London and New York: Nelson, 1964), p. 72

70. F. F. Hering, *Gérôme: The Life and Works of Jean-Léon Gérôme* (New York: Cassell, 1892), p. 1. See also Hering, "Gérôme," *Century Magazine*, vol. 37 (Feb. 1889).

71. For more on Hering's publication, see E. Boyer, "Publishing Gérôme," in *Reconsidering Gérôme*, (Los Angeles: Getty Publications, 2010).

72. R. W. Glessner 1904, p. 54. See also R. Gruelle, *Collection of W. T. Walters: Notes: Criticism and Biography* (Indianapolis: Press of Carlon and Hollebeck, 1895), p. 104; and *Academy and Literature*, 66 (Jan.–June 1904), p. 107.

73. Ibid., p. 58.

74. See D. Weir Young, *The Life and Letters of J. Alden Weir* (New Haven: Yale University Press, 1960); and entries by Will Low and Kenyon Cox in J. C. Van Dyke, ed., *Modern French Masters: A Series of Biographical and Critical Reviews by American Artists* (New York: Garland Publishing, 1976, Shinn reported the intense seriousness with which Gérôme approached his teaching responsibilities. According to Shinn, he was never sick, he was "conscientious, implacable, and admirable… His pupils accept him absolutely… Gérôme, whose worldly success has depended upon his never shrinking anything…." Shinn, *Nation*, June 24, 1869, no. IV in series, pp. 352 and 492.

75. D. T. Lenehan 2005 (as in n. 52), p. 15 and H. B. Weinberg 1991 (as in n. 6), pp. 84 and 93. The Pennsylvania Academy was the foremost art school in the United States, and held annual exhibitions of European masters, including paintings by Gérôme. Gérôme's *Egyptian Recruits* was shown at the Pennsylvania Academy in 1860, 1861, and 1862. See A. Cohen-Solal, *Painting American: The Rise of American Artists, Paris 1867 – New York 1948*, trans. L. Hurwitz-Attias (New York: Knopf, 2001), p. 26 and H. B. Weinberg 1991, p. 94.

76. June 24, 1869, Bregler collection, quoted from H. Adams, *Eakins Revealed: The Secret Life of an American Artist* (New York and Oxford: Oxford University Press, 2005), p. 142

77. In their anthology of critical texts on nineteenth-century American art, Sarah Burns and John Davis acknowledge the difficulty for those that celebrate Eakins as an American 'native hero' in accounting for his four years studying with Gérôme. S. Burns and J. Davis 2009 (as in n. 14), p. 589.

78. Gérôme tells us every day that finish is nothing that head work is all & that if we stopped to finish our studies we could not learn to be painters in a hundred life times & he calls finish needle work & embroidery & ladies' work to deride us…. S. Burns and J. Davis 2009 (as in n. 14), p. 591.

79. Adams distinguishes Eakins's paint handling from Gérôme's as less small and fine, more loose and impulsive, in line with Thomas Couture and Léon Bonnat, other French influences on Eakins (Adams 2005 [as in n. 76], p. 154). Barbara Weinberg describes a general reluctance on the part of critics in the late nineteenth century to recognize the American debt to French art as partly an issue of nationalism. Weinberg's book describes the profound relationship between American artists and the Parisian art world, noting remnants of Gérôme's influence in Eakins's carefully observed and recorded anatomical and costume details, his refined surfaces, and some of his light effects. See H. B. Weinberg 1991 (as in n. 6), p. 96 and H. B. Weinberg, *The American Pupils of Jean-Léon Gérôme* (Fort Worth, Tex.: Amon Carter Museum, 1984). Kathleen Foster suggests a profound level of absorption by Eakins of Gérôme's aesthetic. See K. Foster, *Thomas Eakins Rediscovered: Charles Bregler's Thomas Eakins Collection at the Pennsylvania Academy of the Fine Arts* (Philadelphia, New Haven, and London: Pennsylvania Academy of the Fine Arts and Yale University Press, 1997), pp. 32–37. See also G. Ackerman 1969 (as in n. 30); A. C. Braddock, *Thomas Eakins and the Cultures of Modernity* (Berkeley: University of California Press, 2009); L. Goodrich, *Thomas Eakins: Retrospective Exhibition* (New York: Whitney Museum of American Art, 1970).

80. Letter to Benjamin Eakins, Mar. 6, 1868, quoted in S. Burns and J. Davis 2009 (as in n. 14), pp. 589–91.

81. E. Strahan 1880 (as in n. 21), vol. 1, p. 99. Includes a photogravure.

82. A. Cohen-Solal 2001 (as in n. 75), p. 119.

83. Ibid., p. 153. A writer for the *Philadelphia Evening Telegraph* commended Eakins on his unparalleled draftsmanship, and accounted for the "difference in color and subject" not as being French influenced but "because he paints it exactly as it is, not embellish or prettified." W. Clark, "The Fine Arts," *Philadelphia Evening Telegraph*, Apr. 28, 1876. Quoted from S. Burns and J. Davis (as in n. 14), p. 593. A New York critic referred to the power of the picture, and its artlessness. *New York Times*, Mar. 8, 1879.

84. C. Cook, "Society of American Artists," *New York Daily Tribune*, Mar. 8 and 22, 1879. Quoted from S. Burns and J. Davis 2009 (as in n. 14), p. 594.

85. See "Exhibition of the Royal Academy," *Illustrated London News*, May 6, 1871, p. 447.

86. When the painting was sold to Stewart and came to America, Eakins tried to get into the collection to see it. See H. B. Weinberg 1991 (as in n. 6), p. 96.

87. S. Burns and J. Davis 2009 (as in n. 14), p. 593.

88. Adams points out the Gérôme print above Eakins's father's head on the back wall, and discusses it as representing another form of father in this painting about fatherhood. H. Adams 2005 (as in n. 76), pp. 188–89.

Cat. 107

RECREATION IN A RUSSIAN CAMP

–

1855
Oil on canvas
23 × 39 in.
Signed and dated below left:
J.L. GEROME 1855
Collection of Terence and Katrina Garnett, San Mateo, California

–

Provenance: Achille Fould, Paris (d. 1867). Mme. H. Fould to Goupil, May 1873, no. 7946, "La Récréation du camp" (for 34,000 francs). Goupil to Dervis, May 1876 (for 45,000 francs). Henri Marcus, by 1960. By descent to B. Marcus. Private collection, sold, Sotheby's, London, Nov. 25, 1987, lot 19 (for £66,000). Edward T. Wilson, Fund for Fine Arts Inc., Chevy Chase, Maryland. Sold to Terence Garnett, 2004.

–

Exhibition history: Exposition Universelle, Paris, 1855, no. 3164bis.

–

Bibliography: É. Galichon, "M. Gérôme, peintre ethnographe," *Gazette des Beaux-Arts*, vol. 24, no. 2 (Feb. 1, 1868), p. 149. J.-L. Gérôme, *Notes autobiographiques* [1874], ed. G. Ackerman (Vesoul: S.A.L.S.A., 1981), pp. 11, 21, n. 34. C. Timbal, "Gérôme," *Gazette des Beaux-Arts*, 2nd per., vol. 40, no. 3 (Sept. 1, 1876), p. 231. no. 4 (Oct. 1, 1876), p. 334. E. Strahan [Earl Shinn], ed., *Gérôme: A Collection of the Works of J. L. Gérôme in One Hundred Photogravures* (New York: Samuel L. Hall, 1881), vol. 1, n.p. F. F. Hering, *Gérôme: The Life and Works of Jean Léon Gérôme* (New York: Cassell, 1892), pp. 62–63. F. Masson, "J.-L. Gérôme, peintre de l'orient," *Figaro illustré*, 2nd ser., no. 136 (July 1901), pp. 8–10. J.-L. Gérôme, "Notes et fragments de J.-L. Gérôme," *Les Arts*, no. 26 (Feb. 1904), pp. 24, 27. C. Moreau-Vauthier, *Gérôme, peintre et sculpteur. L'homme et l'artiste d'après sa correspondance, ses notes, ses souvenirs, les souvenirs de ses élèves et de ses amis* (Paris: Hachette, 1906), pp. 106–10, 114. G. Ackerman et al., *Jean-Léon Gérôme (1824–1904)*, exh. cat. (Dayton: Dayton Art Institute, 1972; also Minneapolis: Minneapolis Institute of Arts, 1973, and Baltimore: The Walters Art Gallery, 1973), p. 11. *J.-L. Gérôme*, exh. cat. (Vesoul: Musée Georges-Garret, 1981), pp. 20, 48–49, under no. 25. G. Ackerman, *The Life and Work of Jean-Léon Gérôme, with a Catalogue Raisonné* (New York and London: Sotheby's, 1986), pp. 38, 42, 198, 199, no. 66. M. Gotlieb, *From Genre to Decoration: Studies in the Theory and Criticism of French Salon Painting, 1850–1900* (Ann Arbor, Mich.: UMI, 1990), pp. 215–19. G. Ackerman, *Jean-Léon Gérôme: His Life, His Work, 1824–1904* (Courbevoie: ACR Édition, 1997), pp. 41–42. G. Ackerman, *Jean-Léon Gérôme* (Paris: ACR Édition, 2000), pp. 37, 230, no. 66. H. Lafont-Couturier, *Gérôme and Goupil: Art and Enterprise*, exh. cat., trans. I. Ollivier (Bordeaux: Musée Goupil, 2000–1; also New York: Dahesh Museum of Art, 2001, and Pittsburgh: The Frick Art & Historical Center, 2001), pp. 109, 113, 151, 164, no. 55. *19th Century Orientalist Paintings from the Collection of Terence Garnett*, exh. cat. (Washington, D.C.: Royal Embassy of Saudia Arabia, 2007), pp. 30–32, no. 5.

On February 1, 1853, four months after he had received the government commission for *The Age of Augustus* (cat. 32), Gérôme requested an advance payment, which was granted on February 15. That first installment of five thousand francs allowed him, along with his friend Edmond Got, an actor with the Comédie-Française, to set off from Paris for Moscow with the aim of gathering studies for the various subject peoples of the ancient Roman Empire that were to figure in his monumental history painting. Once under way, however, the travelers decided to change course, doubtless on account of the mounting international tensions that would culminate in the Crimean War, which broke out in October 1853. Shifting their sights toward Constantinople, they followed the Danube southeast through the Balkans to the Black Sea—"a tourist trip and not a working trip," Gérôme later remarked.[1] At the inland port of Galatz, in present-day Romania near the southern border of Moldavia, they were stalled while waiting for a boat to ferry them across the Black Sea. Having to spend a week in what he reportedly called a "filthy hole," Gérôme was in a very bad humor, "deaf to the jokes with which the merry Got tried to brighten the situation."[2] To occupy himself, Gérôme studied the soldiers at a nearby Russian camp,[3] and it was thus by chance that he found the subject of his first ethnographic genre painting, signalling a decisive turn away from his preciously classicizing *Néo-Grec* manner. As Charles Timbal wrote: "this is how, having left with the intention of drawing ... the vassals of ... ancient Rome, Gérôme ... found the actors of a small page of contemporary history, whose modest figures, alas, eclipsed those of Virgil and Brutus, but opened up a new vein of success for the one who knew how to see and portray them."[4]

The scene Gérôme exhibited two years later in the 1855 Exposition Universelle is marked by

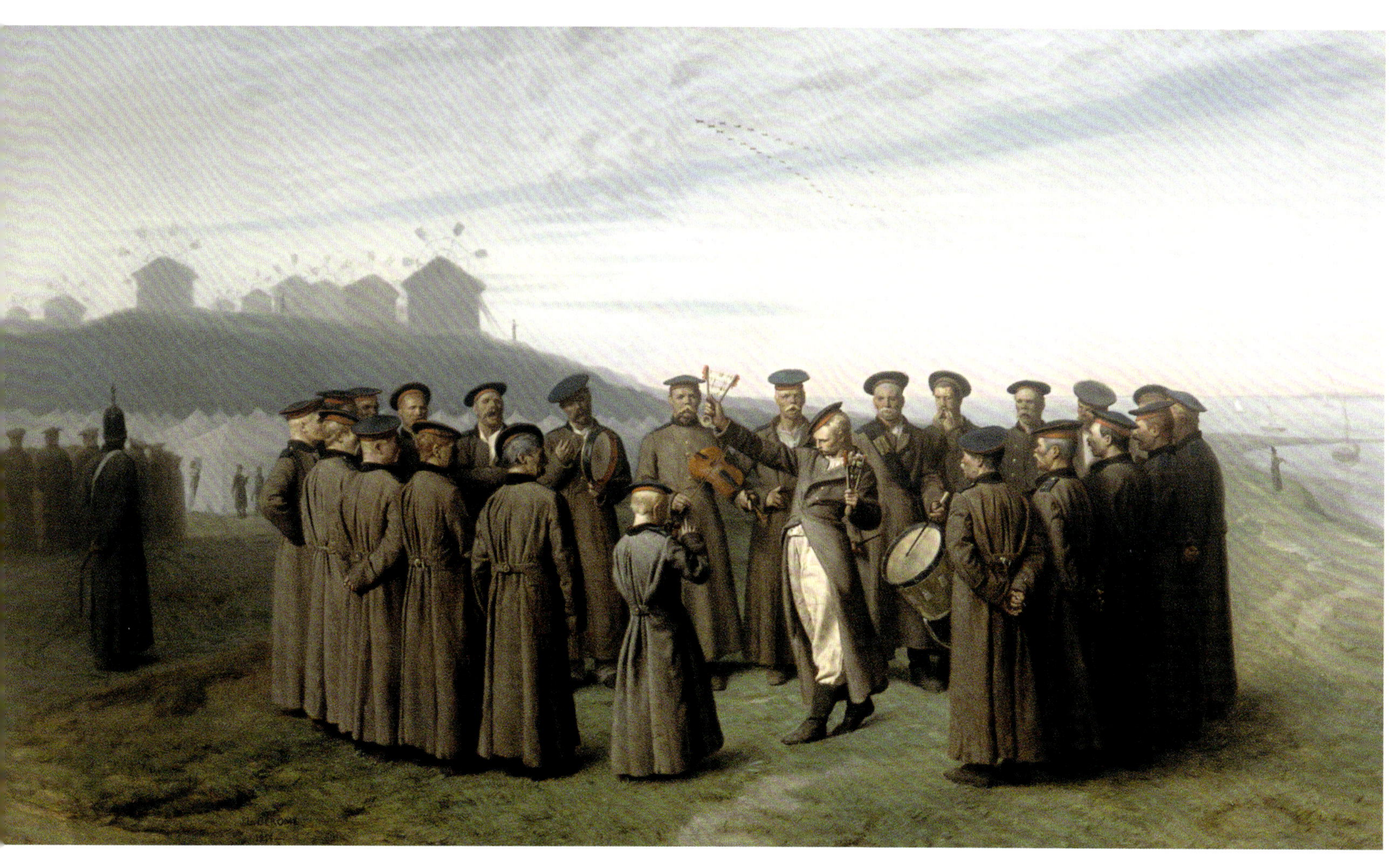

a grim sense of irony that might well have been informed by the artist's dark humor at the time of its inception. The painting shows conscripts singing, whistling, playing instruments, and dancing on command. A guard, menacing whip in hand ("to stimulate joy," Théophile Gautier observed[5]), stands off to the left and directs his attention to a distant circle of conscripts, just as the viewer might imagine himself supervising the circle in the foreground. The scene's joyless tone is reinforced by its "muffled light, as if veiled by ennui,"[6] a leaden sky over the sea of tents and distant range of windmills, the sodden, muddy ground, and the soldiers' gray costume—a greatcoat that for Gautier resembled a "monk's robe" or "hospital gown."[7]

Gérôme did not finish the painting in time for the opening of the Exposition Universelle, having devoted the lion's share of his attention to *The Age of Augustus*. When he had finished his small "souvenir of Moldavia," however, he succeeded in obtaining permission to display it, and space was found in a gallery featuring Portuguese submissions.[8] Although the painting received much less attention in the press than *The Age of Augustus*, a few notable critics singled it out for attention on account of its novelty and curiosity, some going so far as to assert that it was "perhaps his masterpiece."[9] Gérôme was recognized in particular for his incisive characterization of ethnic types. Gautier marveled: "nothing is more curious than these Kalmuk or Tartar types, with flat noses, prominent cheekbones, shaved heads, Albino mustaches, [and] small slit eyes with the lids turned up towards the temples."[10] Others saw in such types a compelling ugliness that was integral to the painting's detached, matter-of-fact appeal. They are "almost frighteningly truthful," E.-J. Delécluze wrote, "because they are not beautiful."[11] Edmond About likewise appreciated their "exquisite ugliness," adding that "their large naïve heads would do honor to an animal painter."[12] Gérôme's talents as a draftsman and his exceedingly precise and refined execution enhanced the picture's status as travel document. "How finely M. Gérôme draws! ... [he] will go far, very far in genre painting," About went on to predict.[13] Later critics would indeed look back on it as inaugurating a matchless suite of genre paintings, mostly Orientalist, that Gérôme submitted to the Paris Salon beginning in 1857.[14]

Recreation in a Russian Camp indeed anticipates elements of these later pictures. It found an immediate sequel in the 1857 Salon with another picture of military conscripts, this time under Ottoman compulsion, in *Egyptian Recruits Crossing the Desert*.[15] The mordant irony of his Russian picture found an echo at that same Salon in *Duel after the Ball* (cat. 51), which capitalized on the contrast between comic masquerade and fateful circumstance. More obviously, the male dancer in the middle of the circle, his hip thrust out and head tilted, curiously anticipates the belly dancer performing for an unruly group of *bashi-bazouks* in *Dance of the Almeh*, shown in 1864 (cat. 154). **S. A.**

1. J.-L. Gérôme, *Notes autobiographiques* [1874], ed. G. Ackerman (Vesoul: S.A.L.S.A., 1981), p. 9 ["voyage de touristes et non de travailleurs"]. **2.** C. Moreau-Vauthier, *Gérôme, peintre et sculpteur. L'homme et l'artiste d'après sa correspondance, ses notes, ses souvenirs, les souvenirs de ses élèves et de ses amis* (Paris: Hachette, 1906), p. 106 ["Il leur fallait attendre une semaine 'dans ce trou infect ...' Tout ceux qui ont connu Gérôme l'imaginent en la circonstance, furieux, arpentant avec impatience la ville—ce trou infect!—sourd aux plaisanteries dont le joyeux Got cherche à égayer la situation"]. **3.** Russia had occupied the Ottoman protectorates of Moldavia and Wallachia (present-day Romania) as part of its bid to extend its southern border in order to gain a port with Mediterranean access, a move that helped precipitate the Crimean War. **4.** C. Timbal, "Gérôme," *Gazette des Beaux-Arts*, 2nd per. vol. 40, no. 3 (Sept. 1, 1876), p. 231 ["Voilà comment, parti pour dessiner dans l'Ukraine les vassaux de la grande Rome antique, Gérôme y rencontre les acteurs d'une petite page d'histoire contemporaine, dont les modestes figures éclipsèrent, hélas! celles de Virgile et de Brutus, mais en ouvrant à celui qui avait su les voir et les pourtraire une nouvelle veine de succès"]. **5.** T. Gautier, *Les Beaux-Arts en Europe*, 2 vols. (Paris: Michel Lévy frères, 1855), vol. 1, p. 228 ["À quelque distance veille un sous-officier, dont le bras replié derrière le dos tient un fouet pour stimuler la joie"]. **6.** Ibid., p. 228 ["On ne saurait imaginer la profonde tristesse de cette toile tenue dans une localité grise, éclairée par une lumière sourde et comme voilée d'ennui"]. **7.** Ibid., p. 227 ["Des soldats russes, vêtus de cette capote de bure grise qui ressemble à un froc de moine ou à une houppelande d'hôpital"]. **8.** Ibid., p. 227. **9.** E. About, *Voyage à travers l'exposition des beaux-arts* (Paris: L. Hachette, 1855), p. 156 ["peut-être son chef-d'œuvre"]. **10.** T. Gautier 1855 (as in n. 5), pp. 227–28 ["rien n'est plus curieux que ces types kalmouks ou tartares, aux nez épatés, aux pommettes saillantes, au crane rasé, aux moustaches d'Albinos, aux petits yeux que brident des paupières retroussées vers les tempes"]. **11.** E.-J. Delécluze, "Exposition universelle. Beaux-Arts," *Journal des débats*, Nov. 24, 1855 ["Des soldats ... sont d'une vérité presque effrayante, car ils ne sont pas beaux"]. **12.** E. About 1855 (as in n. 9), p. 156 ["Ses musiciens sont d'une laideur exquise; leurs grosses têtes naïves feraient honneur à un peintre d'animaux"]. **13.** Ibid. ["Que M. Gérôme dessine finement! ... M. Gérôme ira loin, bien loin dans la peinture de genre"]. **14.** See, for example, O. Merson, "Salon de 1869," *Le monde illustré*, vol. 25, no. 639 (July 10, 1869), p. 27 ["on se souvienne des *Musiciens russes*, des *Chefs arnautes*, du *Hache-paille égyptien* et du *Prisonnier turc* ... cette belle suite ethnographique, où le meilleur du talent du peintre brille dans sa perfection délicate"]. **15.** See G. Ackerman, *Jean-Léon Gérôme* (Courbevoie: ACR Édition, 2000), p. 230, no. 67.

Cat. 108

LION ON THE WATCH

–

ca. 1890
Oil on panel
28 ½ × 39 ⅝ in.
Signed below in the middle: *J.L. GEROME*
The Cleveland Museum of Art, Cleveland, Gift of Mrs. F. W. Gehring in memory of her husband, inv. 1945.25

–

Provenance: Frederick W. Gehring, Cleveland. Gift in his memory from Mrs. Gehring to the Cleveland Museum of Art, 1945.

–

Bibliography: H. S. Francis, "'Lion on the Watch,' by Jean Léon Gérôme," *Bulletin of the Cleveland Museum of Art*, vol. 33 (1946), pp. 47–48. G. Ackerman et al., *Jean-Léon Gérôme (1824–1904)*, exh. cat. (Dayton: Dayton Art Institute, 1972; also Minneapolis: Minneapolis Institute of Arts, 1973, and Baltimore: The Walters Art Gallery, 1973), pp. 84–85, no. 35. G. Ackerman et al., *Jean-Léon Gérôme, 1824–1904: sculpteur et peintre de l'art officiel*, exh. cat. (Paris: Galerie Tanagra, 1974), under no. 25. E. Zafran, *French Salon Paintings from Southern Collections*, exh. cat. (Atlanta: High Museum of Art, 1982–83), p. 110, under no. 35. A. Boime, "Gérôme and the Bourgeois Artist's Burden," *Arts Magazine*, vol. 57, no. 5 (Jan. 1983), p. 70. G. Ackerman, *The Life and Work of Jean-Léon Gérôme, with a Catalogue Raisonné* (New York and London: Sotheby's, 1986), pp. 298, 299, no. 529. S. Monneret, *L'Orient des peintres* (Paris: Nathan, 1989), pp. 150–51. L. d'Argencourt and R. Diederen, et al., *European Paintings of the 19th century*, 2 vols. (Cleveland: Cleveland Museum of Art, 1999), vol. 1, pp. 293–95. G. Ackerman, *Jean-Léon Gérôme* (Paris: ACR Édition, 2000), pp. 372–73, no. 529. Christie's, London, *Orientalist Art*, July 2, 2008, 78, under no. 44.

Gérôme considered the study and representation of animals to be an essential part of the complete artist's training. Spurred by his friendships with noted animal sculptors like Emmanuel Fremiet and Antoine-Louis Barye, he regularly studied animals in the Jardin des Plantes and the menageries of traveling circuses.[1] Beyond artistic studies, Gérôme's passion for animals was evident in the veritable menagerie he kept at home,[2] and in the game-hunting in which he indulged on his various expeditions to northern Africa and the Near East.[3]

Gérôme signaled his abilities as an animal painter from the outset of his public career with *The Cock Fight* (cat. 10) of 1847. Subsequent Salon submissions, which variously featured buffalo, dogs, elephants, camels, and fawns, helped reinforce the general impression of his talents as an *animalier*.[4] It was large cats, and especially lions, however, that would assume signature status in his oeuvre. A powerfully serene lion figured prominently in Gérôme's submission to the 1848 competition for an allegorical image of the French Republic (cat. 22),[5] and lions would reappear in various historical, mythological, religious, and Orientalist scenes over the course of his career. *The Christian Martyrs' Last Prayers* (cat. 80) played a particularly important role in bringing lions to the forefront of his work, his careful studies for that painting providing the impetus for a large number of lion pictures done in the 1880s and 1890s.[6] Typically set in African or Arabian landscapes, these tapped into a ready market for both animal and oriental subjects, allowing Gérôme to capitalize on two areas of recognized strength.

The majority of these pictures focus on solitary male lions. They are variously shown at rest by their caves or the seashore, drinking from puddles or oases in the desert, pursuing their prey or victims themselves of the hunt, or surveying their domain magisterially from above. The Cleveland painting is arguably the most commanding of these works. It features a powerful lion edging stealthily onto a jutting, sun-bleached promontory to survey a desolate expanse of rocky desert below, the object of its predatory attention suspensefully excluded from view. The pyramidal composition, the central position of the lion, the careful rhyming of its forms with the surrounding rock formations, and the sharp silhouetting of its head against the intense blue sky, all contribute to the image's iconic power. As a preparatory oil sketch (ill. 93) suggests, Gérôme sought to amplify this power in the final painting by focusing more closely on the lion, increasing its scale.[7]

For all its topographical detail and anatomical precision, *Lion on the Watch* is an imaginative construction. Gérôme never observed lions in such a desert landscape; by his time, their African habitat was restricted to the sub-Saharan savannah, which he never visited. His experience of big cats, as Louise Lippincott has stressed, was mostly limited to the artificial confines of zoo and circus, which meant that he was usually able to observe only single animals, and those typically at rest.[8] By subsequently depicting lions as solitary creatures, Gérôme obscured the social nature of the pride, and by focusing on the male lion as hunter, he ignored the fact that female lions were the predominant hunters and that they typically operated in groups. When Gérôme did represent female lions, he adhered to nineteenth-century European gender constructs, depicting them in domestic or sexual contexts, maternally tending to their cubs, for instance, or rolling around in heat.[9]

The heroic male lion, on the other hand, fulfilled certain bourgeois male fantasies and was clearly an object of personal identification for Gérôme, one through which the artist may have wished to project a sense of strength, dignity, courage, and mastery, as Albert Boime provocatively argued.[10] The artist's name itself may have encouraged an almost totemic identification with the animal, "Léon" deriving from the Latin for lion, and "Gérôme" recalling Saint Jerome, whose main attribute is the lion.[11] The painter made his identification with the animal explicit in a picture of a lion which he gave to his native city of Vesoul in 1885. Under a device featuring a crown and a rampant lion carrying a painter's palette, the painting is inscribed: "NOMINOR LEO."[12]

Toward the end of his career, Gérôme's identification with lions had become automatic, commentators routinely describing him in flattering leonine terms. Fanny Field Hering wrote, for instance, of a "superb head with mane tossed back, a lion who paints other lions."[13] Caricatures, for their part, lampooned the extravagant, well-documented lengths to which he would go in the painting of lions. One published in *La Revue illustrée*, and captioned "How M.Gérôme paints his lions," shows a dandified Gérôme in military costume painting in a circus cage while simultaneously fending off his unruly models like a would-be lion-tamer (ill. 94), his mahlstick doubling as a defensive weapon. The cartoon inadvertently calls to mind an anecdote about the aged lion Gérôme had perversely acquired from a circus as a pet. As Gerald Ackerman has recounted, the artist was obliged on one occasion to protect himself from the lion by shutting himself in its cage while it paced threateningly around the room. A professional tamer had to be called in to get the lion securely back into confinement and to release the chastened artist.[14] **S. A.**

Ill. 93. *Lion on the Watch*, ca. 1890, oil on canvas, 11 ½ × 16 ½ in., private collection.

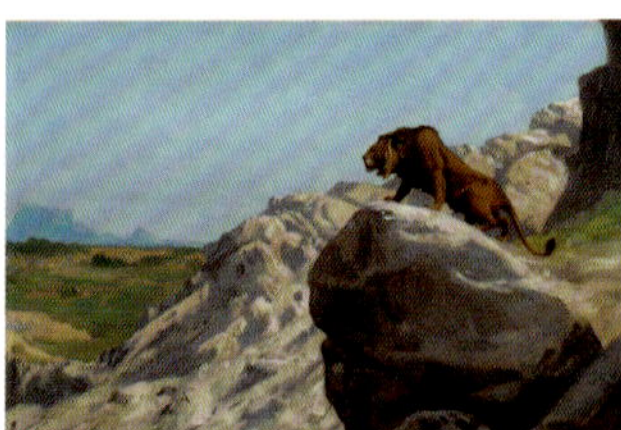

Ill. 94. Anonymous, "Comment M. Gérôme brosse ses lions (How M.Gérôme paints his lions)" *La Revue illustrée*, vol. 15, 1893, p. 353, The Getty Research Institute, Los Angeles, Call # AP1.R48.

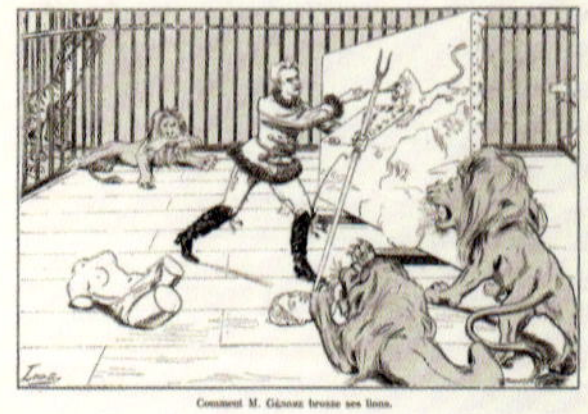

1. See J.-L. Gérôme, "Notes et fragments de J.-L. Gérôme," *Les Arts*, no. 26 (Feb. 1904), p. 28; C. Moreau-Vauthier, *Gérôme, peintre et sculpteur. L'homme et l'artiste d'après sa correspondance, ses notes, ses souvenirs, les souvenirs de ses élèves et de ses amis* (Paris: Hachette, 1906), p. 77; and A. Boime, "Jean-Léon Gérôme, Henri Rousseau's Sleeping Gypsy and the Academic Legacy," *The Art Quarterly*, vol. 34, no. 1 (Spring 1971), pp. 11, 25, n. 68. **2.** C. Moreau-Vauthier 1906 (as in n. 1), pp. 89–90. **3.** See, for example, P. Lenoir, *Le Fayoum, le Sinaï et Pétra: expédition dans la moyenne Égypte et l'Arabie Pétrée sous la direction de J. L. Gérôme* (Paris: Henri Plon, 1872), pp. 90–92; F. F. Hering, *Gérôme: The Life and Works of Jean-Léon Gérôme* (New York: Cassell), 1892, pp. 31, 43, 135–37. G. Ackerman et al., *Jean-Léon Gérôme (1824–1904)*, exh. cat. (Dayton: Dayton Art Institute, 1972; also Minneapolis: Minneapolis Institute of Arts, 1973, and Baltimore: The Walters Art Gallery, 1973), p. 85. **4.** See, for instance, *Paestum* (G. Ackerman, no. 40), *The Idylle* (G. Ackerman, no. 47), *Study of a Dog* (G. Ackerman, no. 48), *The Age of Augustus* (G. Ackerman, no. 64), *Camels at the Fountain (Watering Hole)* (G. Ackerman, no. 72). **5.** See G. Ackerman, nos. 23–24 **6.** See G. Ackerman, nos. 321–22, 353–54, 362–64, 366–70, 422, 432, 469–70, 489, 528, 530–36. On Gérôme's numerous drawings of lions, see S. Harent and C. Stoullig, *Dessins de Jean-Léon Gérôme: la collection du musée des Beaux-Arts de Nancy*, exh. cat. (Nancy: Musée des Beaux-Arts, 2009), nos. 33–35, 37–60. **7.** Regarding this sketch, which recently surfaced at auction, see Christie's, London, *Orientalist Art*, July 2, 2008, lot 44; and Christie's, Paris, *Orientalistes et art moderne arabe et iranien*, Dec. 17, 2008, lot 14. **8.** See L. Lippincott et al., *Fierce Friends: Artists and Animals, 1750–1900*, exh. cat. (Amsterdam: Van Gogh Museum, 2005–6; also Pittsburgh: Carnegie Museum of Art, 2006), p. 124. **9.** See, for instance, G. Ackerman, nos. 367 and 536. **10.** A. Boime 1971 (as in n. 1), pp. 3–30. **11.** Ibid., p. 12; and G. Ackerman 1972–73 (as in n. 3), p. 85. Gérôme would indeed paint the saint with his lion on at least one occasion (G. Ackerman, no. 237). **12.** G. Ackerman, no. 323. **13.** M. de Belina, quoted in F. F. Hering 1892 (as in n. 3), p. 37. **14.** See Christie's, London, 2008 (as in n. 7), p. 78.

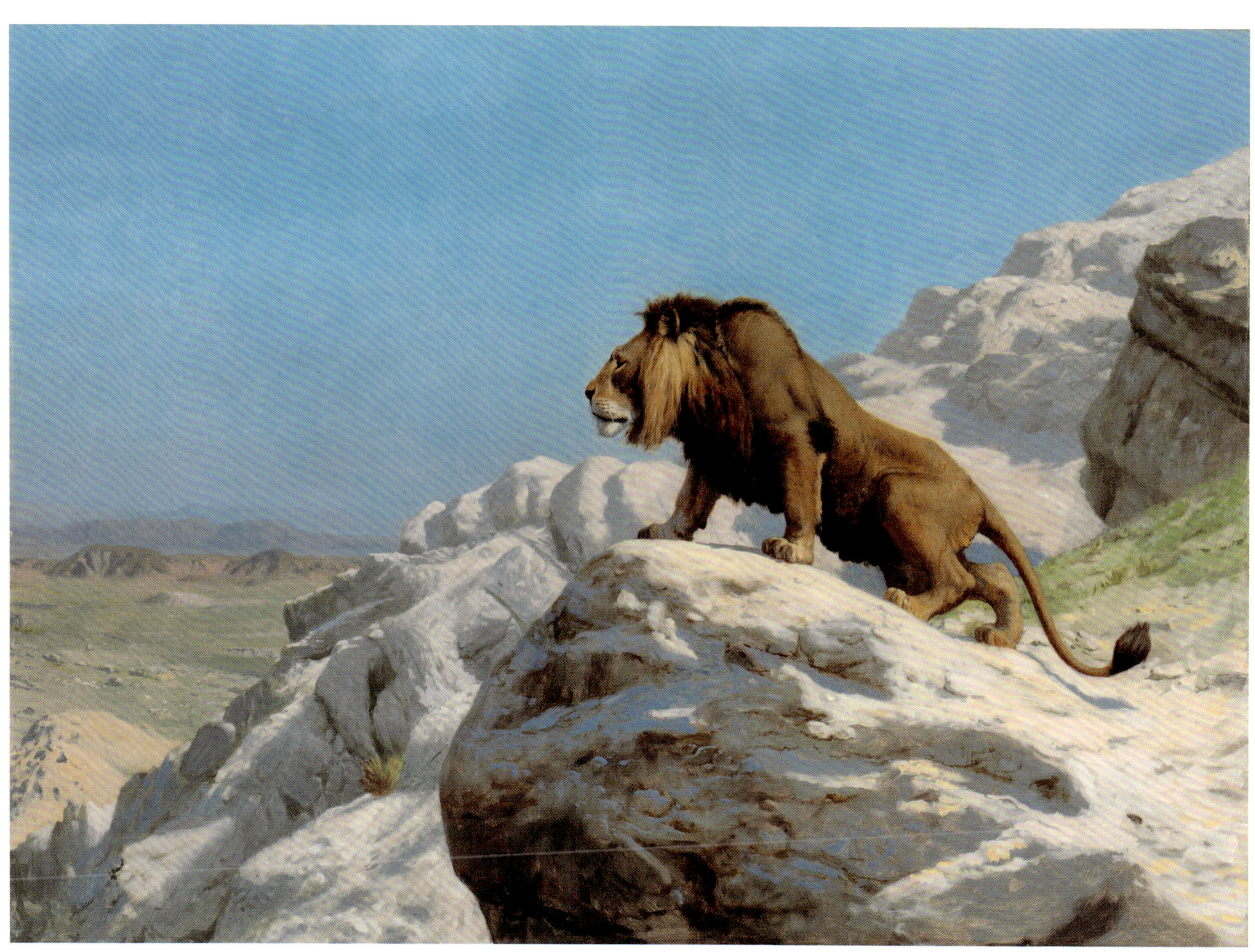

Cat. 109

DIOGENES

1860
Oil on canvas
29 ¼ × 39 ¾ in.
The Walters Art Museum, Baltimore, inv. 37.131

Provenance:
Mar. 1860 to Goupil (for 3,000 francs). Goupil to Gambart, London, Mar. 1861, Goupil stock book 1, no. 1013 (for 4,000 francs). August Belmont, New York, by 1864. Belmont sale, Nov. 12, 1872, Leavitt's, New York, to William T. Walters, Baltimore (for 31,320 francs).

Exhibition History: Besançon, 1860. *The Belmont Gallery, on Exhibition for the Benefit of the U.S. Sanitary commission, Monday, April 4th, to Saturday, April 9th*, New York, 1864, no. 51. *Cincinnati Industrial Exhibition*, 1874, no. 13. *Centennial Exhibition*, New York, 1876, no. 163.

Bibliography: A. de Tanouarn, "Gérôme," *L'Artiste*, vol. X, no. 2 (July 15, 1860), p. 27. Woodcut by H. Linton, *Le Monde illustré*, 1860, p. 353. Photographed by Robert Jefferson Bingham for Goupil's "Galerie Photographique," no. 70, 1860–after 1904. Photogravure by Goupil & Cie, *Œuvres choisies de J.-L. Gérôme*, pl. 18, 7 × 9 ¾ in., 1877– after 1909. E. Strahan [Earl Shinn], *The Art Treasures of America: Being the Choicest Works of Art in the Public and Private Collections of North America*, 3 vols (Philadephie: G. Barrie, 1880), vol. I, p. 86, ill. E. Strahan [Earl Shinn], *Gérôme. A Collection of the Works of J.-L. Gérôme in One Hundred Photogravures* (New York: Samuel L. Hall, 1881). G. Ackerman et al., *Jean-Léon Gérôme (1824–1904)*, exh. cat. (Dayton: Dayton Art Institute, 1972; also Minneapolis: Minneapolis Institute of Arts, 1973, and Baltimore: The Walters Art Gallery, 1973), no. 11, pp. 48–49. R. Meyer, "Jean-Léon Gérôme: The Role of Subject-Matter and the Importance of Formalized Composition," *Arts Magazine* 47 (Feb. 1973), p. 32. W. R. Johnston, *The Nineteenth Century Paintings in the Walters Art Gallery* (Baltimore: Trustees of the Walters Art Gallery, 1982), no. 107. A. Boime, "Gérôme and the Bourgeois Artist's Burden," *Arts Magazine* 57, no. 5 (Jan. 1983), p. 70. G. Ackerman, *Jean-Léon Gérôme* (Courbevoie: ACR Édition, 2000), no. 120. H. Lafont-Couturier, *Gérôme and Goupil: Art and Enterprise*, exh. cat., trans. I. Ollivier (Bordeaux: Musée Goupil, 2000–1; also New York: Dahesh Museum of Art, 2001, and Pittsburgh: The Frick Art & Historical Center, 2001), no. 42, pp. 36, 40, 43, 99–100, 151 (only shown at Pittsburgh).

Diogenes was an ancient Greek philosopher whose canine attributes provided a name for his strain of thought: cynic, or "dog-like" in ancient Greek. Diogenes preferred the company of dogs to that of men, identifying with their frank, direct, shameless approach to life. He lived like a dog himself, engaging in "natural" modes of life that scandalized society, and celebrating the radical idea of freedom.[1]

Diogenes did not lay down a set of philosophical dicta, but rather verbally responded spontaneously to (usually hostile) situations. Cynic philosophy relies mainly on a group of anecdotes about Diogenes in which his words are cited verbatim and often involve some kind of pun or wordplay.[2] Cynicism differs from the other ancient philosophical movements in its rejection of high theory, and in its emphasis on a process of invention. In counterpoint to Platonic abstractions and ideals, Diogenes was "the philosopher of contingency, of life in the barrel, of adapting to the *données* of existence... philosophy not as an escape from but a dialogue with the contingencies that shape the material conditions of existence."[3]

This is the only known instance of Gérôme painting a single philosopher, and one is tempted to see it as an expression of allegiance or inspiration. Within the intensely political/theoretical discourse of 1860s Paris, it is notable that Gérôme would commit to an effigy of the original cynic. Certainly his paintings are distinguished, like *Diogenes*'s quips, by rhetorical cunning, and witty, occasionally shocking expressions. Cynicism for Gérôme, as for Diogenes, was a form of social criticism, of subverting the conventions of society.[4] Painted fairly early in his career, *Diogenes* precedes by a decade Gérôme's position as an outspoken defender of academic ideals against the incursions of the avant-garde Impressionists.

Gérôme deviates in his representation from the traditional portrayal of Diogenes: either searching for an "honest man" with his lantern, or famously answering Alexander the Great's question, "What do you want from life?," with, "For you to get out of my sun."[5] In this painting, Diogenes is pictured as a social outcast, sitting half-naked and cross-legged in his tub, on the margins of the public arena. He is wholly fixated on lighting his lantern, in broad daylight, surrounded by dogs. The dogs are rendered with extraordinary care and skill. Gérôme loved dogs and painted them often. (A critic for the *New York Tribune* suggested that this painting was conceived as an excuse to paint dogs.[6]) Despite Diogenes' reputation for effrontery and impudence, the scene is dignified, even noble.

Gérôme painted a sketch for Diogenes dated 1858 (7 ½ 10 in., private collection, former collection of Pierce Rice, Washington, D.C.). This must be the version of the composition that William Thompson Walters acquired from Goupil in 1865 (stock book 2, no. 1515, 2,150 francs).[7] At some point prior to 1879, Walters sold it and acquired the finished version. **M. M.**

1. *The Cynics: The Cynic Movement in Antiquity and Its Legacy*, eds. R. Bracht Branham and M.-O. Goulet-Cazé (Berkeley, Los Angeles, and London: University of California Press, 1996), pp. 4–5. 2. Ibid., pp. 87–89. Diogenes' philosophy is known primarily through *Diogenes Laertius, Lives and Opinions of Eminent Philosophers* (third century A.D.). 3. Ibid., pp. 88–89. 4. For more on the social subversiveness of cynicism, see D. Krueger, "The Bawdy and Society: The Shamelessness of Diogenes in Roman Imperial Culture," in ibid., pp. 222–39. On the history of Diogenes in French culture in the late eighteenth and nineteenth centuries, see K. Herding, "Diogenes als Bürgerheld," *Boreas. Münstersche Beiträge zur Archäologie*, vol. 5 (1982), pp. 232–54. 5. G. Ackerman et al., *Jean-Léon Gérôme (1824–1904)*, exh. cat. (Dayton: Dayton Art Institute, 1972; also Minneapolis: Minneapolis Institute of Arts, 1973, and Baltimore: The Walters Art Gallery, 1973), p. 48. 6. "The Belmont Collection," *New York Tribune*, Nov. 9, 1872, p. 5. 7. This is probably the 10 × 7.5 in. painting sold as "Diogenes" in the Sherwood-Hart sale in New York in Dec. 1879 for $570 (Ackerman 2000, 120B).

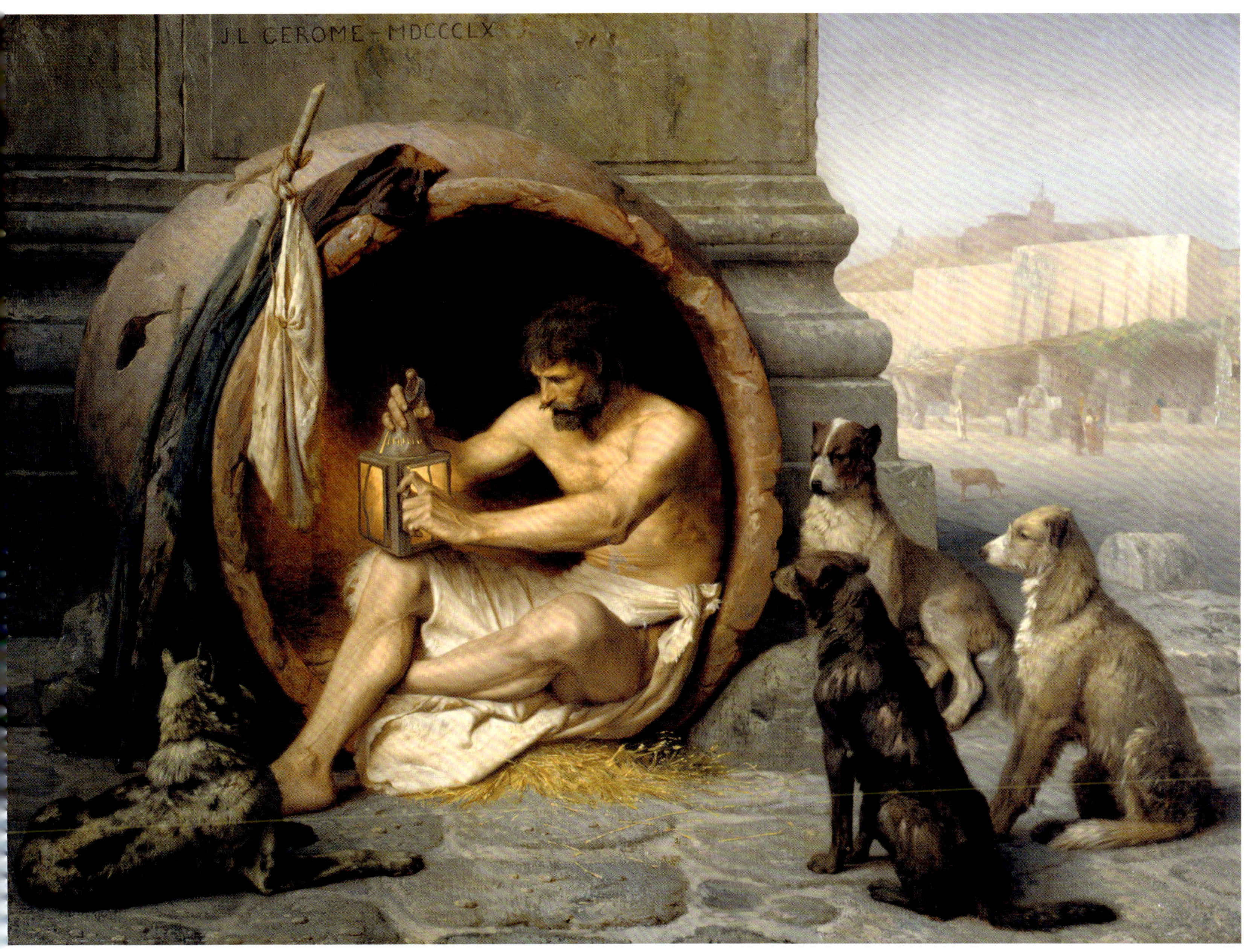
J.L. GEROME - MDCCCLX

Cat. 110

THE GRIEF OF THE PASHA
ALSO KNOWN AS
THE DEAD TIGER

1885
Oil on canvas
36 ½ × 29 in.
Signed on the base of the candle at left
Joslyn Art Museum, Omaha, Nebraska, inv. 1990-I.

Bibliography: G. Ackerman, *Jean-Léon Gérôme* (Courbevoie: ACR Édition, 2000), no. 300.

Ill. 95. Juan Laurent (1816–1892) *North Temple, Lion Courtyard, Alhambra, Grenada*, ca. 1868, albumen print from a glass negative, 13 × 9 ½ in., Musée d'Orsay, Paris inv. PHO 1985 21.

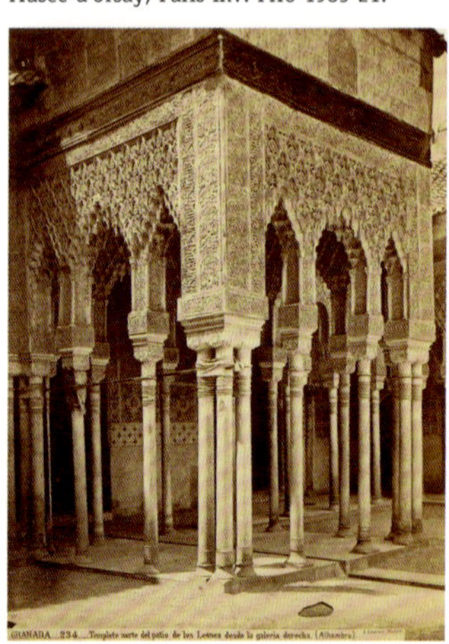

This canvas alludes to a poem by Victor Hugo, "La Douleur du pacha" (The Grief of the Pasha), written in 1827 and published in a collection titled *Les Orientales*. The poem concludes with the lines:
[No, no, 'tis not those dismal figures who /inspire his wretched soul's remorse /through shadowy visions that gleam with blood. /What, then, ails this Pasha, beckoned by war /yet weeping like a woman, vacant and sad? /— his Nubian tiger is dead.][1]

Hugo's poem is faithfully illustrated by Gérôme's painting, inspired by several highly different sources that thereby construct an imaginary, composite Orient (just as Hugo had done half a century earlier). Gérôme invented a singular, highly personal iconography without sacrificing his concern for exactitude or undermining the impression of accuracy that he so often invoked, despite the great liberties he took with reality.
Numerous liberties can be seen here, starting with the magnificent tiger lying dead like a beloved courtesan on a bed of roses, whereas this great beast was known for its ferocity and never allowed itself to be tamed. Here the tiger is mourned—in a scene of grief not unlike a lamentation over the body of Christ after the descent from the cross—by a man dressed in oriental garb. In 1882, Gérôme made several illustrations, along with Benjamin-Constant, for a new publication of *Les Orientales* (Paris: Les Amis des Livres). The frontispice was, already, a sketch for the painting here shown.[2] This pasha evokes an earlier work by Gérôme, being dressed like Marcus Botsaris in a painting of 1874 (cat. 161). The Persian title *pasha*, which meant "lord" in Ottoman Turkey, linked the Middle East (where Gérôme traveled frequently after 1856) not only to Persia but also to Mughal India. Northern India is further evoked by the tiger, being that animal's natural habit, where it was prized as noble game by royal hunting parties, even though Gérôme, following Hugo, feigned belief in a tiger from Nubia. The sultan's great sorrow and his devotion to the tiger perhaps also evoke the Taj Mahal, an architectural wonder erected in memory of a loved one.
The deliberate blending of various "Orients" does not end there, because this Ottoman/Persian/Indian scene is set in the Alhambra palace of Umayyad Spain. This gem of Spanish Islamic architecture was built in the thirteenth and fourteenth centuries, becoming legendary for its grandiose beauty and magnificence as soon as it was completed. Although Gérôme violated chronological and geographical accuracy here, the palace in Grenada presented the beholder with a setting whose lavish beauty perfectly accorded with the universe he was inventing, one worthy of a lord and his beautiful, lifeless tiger. So while this architectural setting was not accurate, it seemed true to life.
Gérôme had been to Spain, yet here he certainly drew inspiration from photographs such as the ones taken and widely disseminated among artists and connoisseurs by Juan Laurent (ill. 95). Gérôme was free in his handling of the floor, in order to give it a precious feel; the two large candle stands, meanwhile, transport the beholder to the Middle East, one being Ottoman in style, the other originating from Safavid Iran.[3]
The Grief of the Pasha allowed Gérôme to combine his penchant for wild beasts—an early interest, given that *Black Panther on the Watch* (Museum of Fine Arts, Boston) was painted in 1851, before he had traveled outside Europe—with his attraction to a distant, sensual Orient. Thanks to his ability to "make it lifelike" by focusing on an *image* of reality rather than its exactness, he made it seem accurate. This subtly colored and skillfully composed painting—a blend of power and emotion, ferocity and fondness—is one of the finest canvases produced by Gérôme during this period. **D. F.-R.**

1. V. Hugo, "La Douleur du pacha," *Les Orientales*, first edition published in January 1829 (Paris: Gallimard), p. 72. *Non, non, ce ne sont pas ces figures funèbres /Qui, d'un rayon sanglant luisant dans les ténèbres, /En passant dans son âme ont laissé le remord. /Qu'a-t-il donc ce pacha, que la guerre réclame, /Et qui, triste et rêveur, pleure comme une femme ?… /– son tigre de Nubie est mort.* The poem was written on December 1, 1827; in an epigraph, Hugo quoted Byron: "Séparé de tout ce qui m'était cher, je me consume solitaire et désolé." [Translator's note: Hugo's quotation was unsourced; it would appear to be a translation of the concluding stanza of Byron's "Fare Thee Well," which includes the lines: "Thus disunited, torn from every nearer tie/Seared in heart, and lone, and blighted."] **2.** A study for the tiger—a squared pencil drawing— is kept at the ENSBA (*Reclining Tiger*, Paris, EBA 7958). **3.** Thanks to Charlotte Maury for pointing out this distinction.

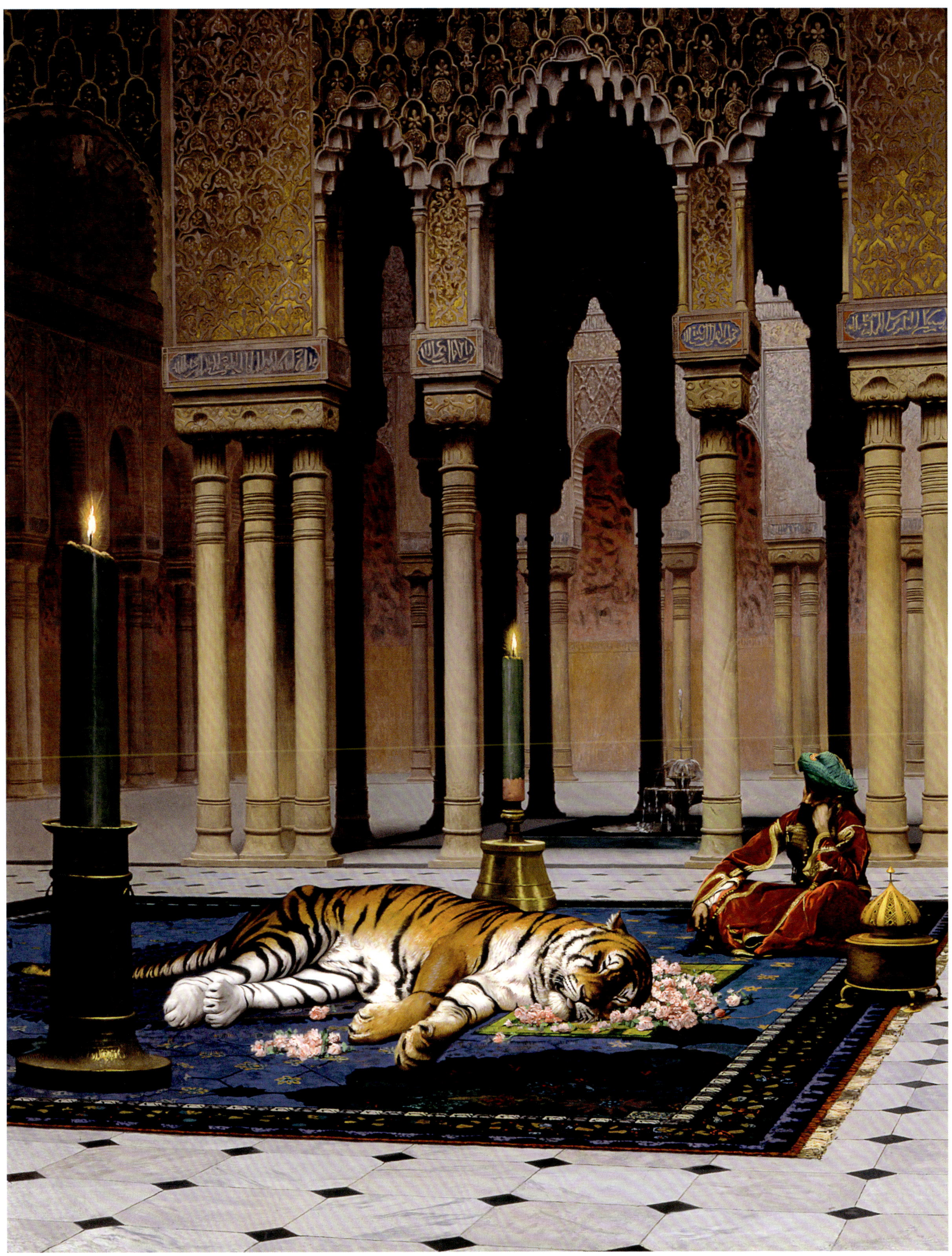

Cat. 111

STUDY FOR *CUPID AND THE VESTAL*

-

ca. 1889 (?)
Pencil on paper glued to vellum paper
12 3/4 × 8 3/4 in.
Dr. Edward T. Wilson collection, Bethesda, Maryland

-

Provenance: Separated from cat. 101.

-

Bibliography: G. Ackerman, *Jean-Léon Gérôme* (Courbevoie: ACR Édition, 2000), no. 356, p. 322. *J.-L. Gérôme*, exh. cat. (Vesoul: Musée Georges-Garret, 1981), p. 87.

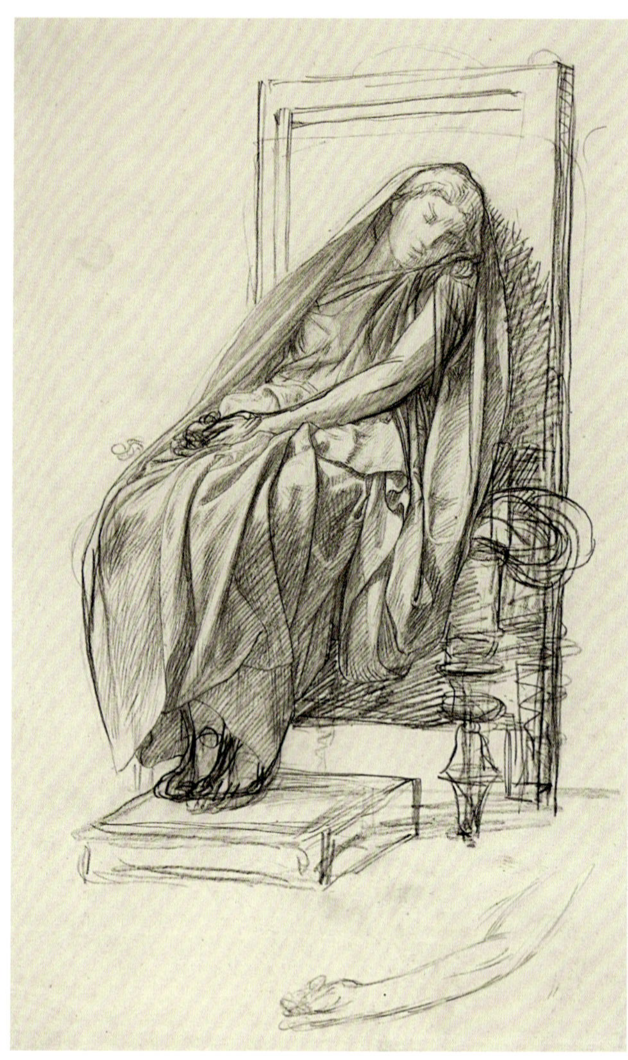

Cat. 112

WHOEVER YOU ARE, HERE IS YOUR MASTER (LOVE, THE CONQUEROR)

–

1889
Oil on canvas
39 1/4 × 63 in.
Private collection

–

Bibliography: G. Ackerman, *Jean-Léon Gérôme* (Courbevoie: ACR Édition, 2000), no. 361.

This large painting with its strange iconography allowed Gérôme to combine two highly different sources that had apparently never been brought together in the same painting. On the one hand we have a figure of Cupid (representing Love) in the traditional form of a winged youth, as already seen in the early 1880s in Gérôme's paintings of the odes of Anacreon, preparatory drawings for which are now held by the Musée Georges-Garret in Vesoul (ill. 96); on the other hand there are wild beasts, the lions and tigers that Gérôme so liked to paint both for their savage strength and for the link he could make between his middle name, Léon, and the name of the king of beasts (several drawings in the Musée des Beaux-Arts in Nancy thus combine lion with tiger).

Gérôme certainly enjoyed inventing this subject, merging allusions to classical antiquity with the Romantic interest in wild beasts. He did so with a distinct sensuality—the tiger in the foreground seems to submit to the imperious gesture of the young, blond tamer with lasciviousness, as the placid lion in the center of the composition looks on; meanwhile, the black panther rolls at Cupid's feet with delightful abandon. This cage of wild beasts thereby alludes, indirectly, to the sensual universe of the seraglio. In the same register, the painting evokes a more ambitious work known as *The Grief of the Pasha* (cat. 110).

In such works Gérôme demonstrates how his rich imagination—marked by a taste for the bizarre, approaching the limits of a certain transgressive vulgarity—was so well served by his painterly skills: the work exhibits a total mastery of draftsmanship, the fur of the beasts is rendered with perfect accuracy, and a rigorous composition underpins the anecdotal subject matter. **D. F.-R.**

Ill. 96. *Anacreon Greeting Cupid*, 1881, black chalk, 9 × 13 1/2 in., Musée Georges-Garret, Vesoul, inv. 986.3.2.

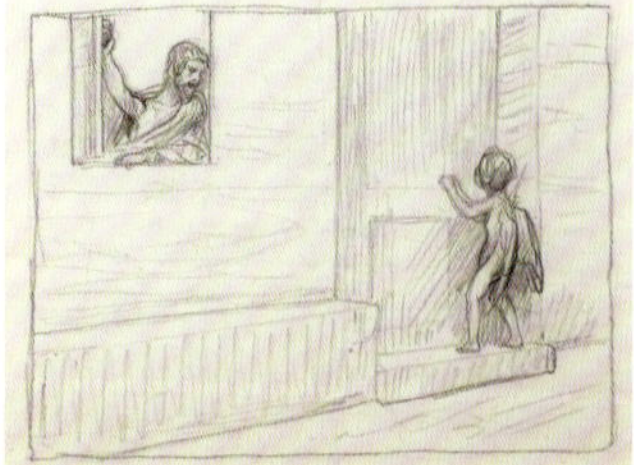

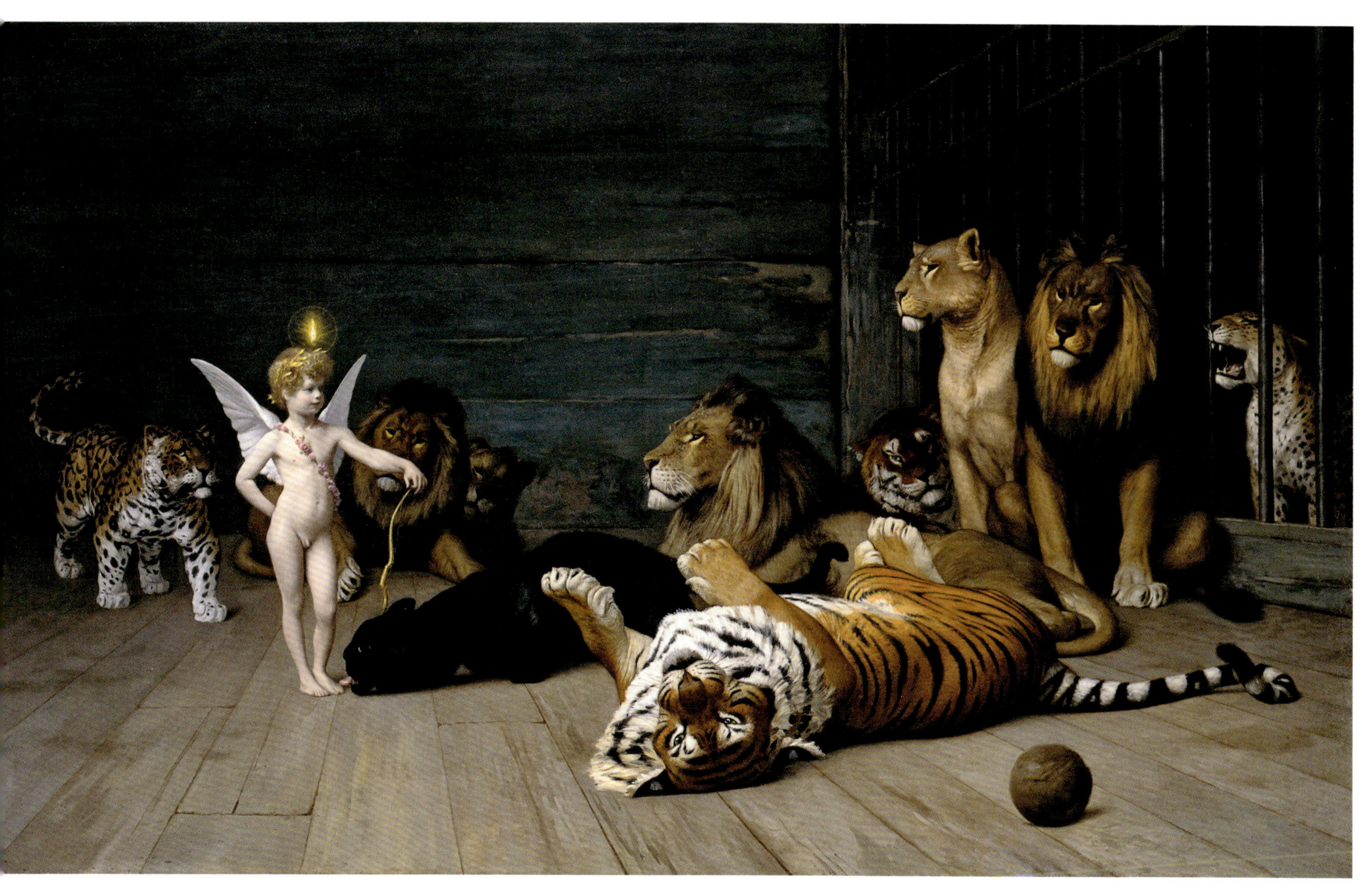

Cat. 113

OPTICIAN'S SIGN

1902
Oil on canvas
34 × 26 in.
Private collection
Signed and dated: *J. L. GEROME BARBOUILLAVIT/ANNO DOMINI/1902;* below: *O PTI CIEN*

Provenance:
Hôtel Drouot, Paris, Ader-Picard-Tajan Auctioneers, June 14, 1985, no. 11. Manoukian, New York. Masco Corporation sale, Sotheby's, New York, Nov. 10, 1998, no. 217 (for $233,500).

Exhibition History:
1900: Art at the Crossroads, Royal Academy of Arts, London, 2000; also Solomon R. Guggenheim Museum, New York, 2000. *Best in Show: The Dog in Art from the Renaissance to Today*, Bruce Museum of Arts and Science, Greenwich, Connecticut, 2006; also Museum of Fine Arts, Houston, Texas, 2006–7.

Bibliography:
C. Moreau-Vauthier, *Gérôme peintre et sculpteur. L'homme et l'artiste d'après sa correspondance, ses notes, ses souvenirs, les souvenirs de ses élèves et de ses amis* (Paris: Hachette, 1906), pp. 47–48. A. Keim, *Gérôme* (New York: Frederick A. Stokes Co., 1912), p. 42. S. Dalí, "The Incendiary Firemen," *Art News Annual*, XXXIII (1967), p. 110. *J.-L. Gérôme*, exh. cat. (Vesoul: Musée Georges-Garret, 1981), p. 136. R. Rosenblum, *The Dog in Art from Rococo to Post-modernism* (New York: Harry N. Abrams, 1988), pp. 69, 70, 86. H. Lafont-Couturier, *Gérôme* (Paris: Herscher, 1998), p. 78. G. Ackerman, *Jean-Léon Gérôme* (Courbevoie: ACR Édition, 2000), no. 476, ill., with signed photograph of the painting.

Gérôme submitted this charming visual rebus to an exhibition of advertising signs made by artists, sponsored by the City of Paris. The painting offers a pun on the French word for optician, *opticien*: "O, petit chien," meaning "oh, little dog" or "au petit chien" meaning "at the [sign of the] little dog." Against a vivid, azure blue, Gérôme paints a small, pert dog sitting up on his hind legs, his head tilted, one ear pricked, wearing a monocle as he gazes intently at the viewer. Gérôme playfully manipulates every element of this object, signing it with mock austerity, "*J.L. GEROME BARBOUILLAVIT/ ANNO DOMINI/1902*" (J.L. Gérôme daubed this picture in A.D. 1902).

The floating pince-nez with its disembodied eyes give the image a strange but pointed character. The painting's frame continues the jest, with embedded opera glasses in the upper corners, and a magnifying glass bulging with a cyclopean eye. Robert Rosenblum refers to the "whimsical, yet disquieting undercurrents" of these elements.[1] The macabre, proto-Dada, Surrealist character of this object was recognized by Salvador Dalí himself, who registered Gérôme's painting as a precursor to Marcel Duchamp's LHOOQ.[2]

There was apparently a precedent in Gérôme's career for this kind of visual joke. For the 1900 Paris Exposition Universelle, in the exhibit of Vieux-Paris, Gérôme made a sign for a toy shop out of sheet metal cut in the shape of a heart, on which he represented Venus emerging from a wave dressed only in a quiver.[3] It was called "Aux armes de Vénus," a pun on the arms of love, weapons of war, and heraldry. **M. M.**

1. R. Rosenblum, in *1900: Art at the Crossroads*, exh. cat. (London, Royal Academy of Arts, 2000; also New York: Solomon R. Guggenheim Museum, 2000); R. Rosenblum and P. Bowron, *Best in Show: The Dog in Art from the Renaissance to Today*, exh. cat. (Greenwich, Conn.: Bruce Museum of Arts and Science, 2006; also Houston, Tex.: Museum of Fine Arts, 2006–7) **2.** S. Dalí, "The Incendiary Firemen," *Art News Annual*, XXXIII (1967), p. 110, where he reproduces the Duchamp picture next to Optician. **3.** É. Charles, "J-L Gérôme, anecdotes et souvenirs," *Liberté*, July 8, 1909.

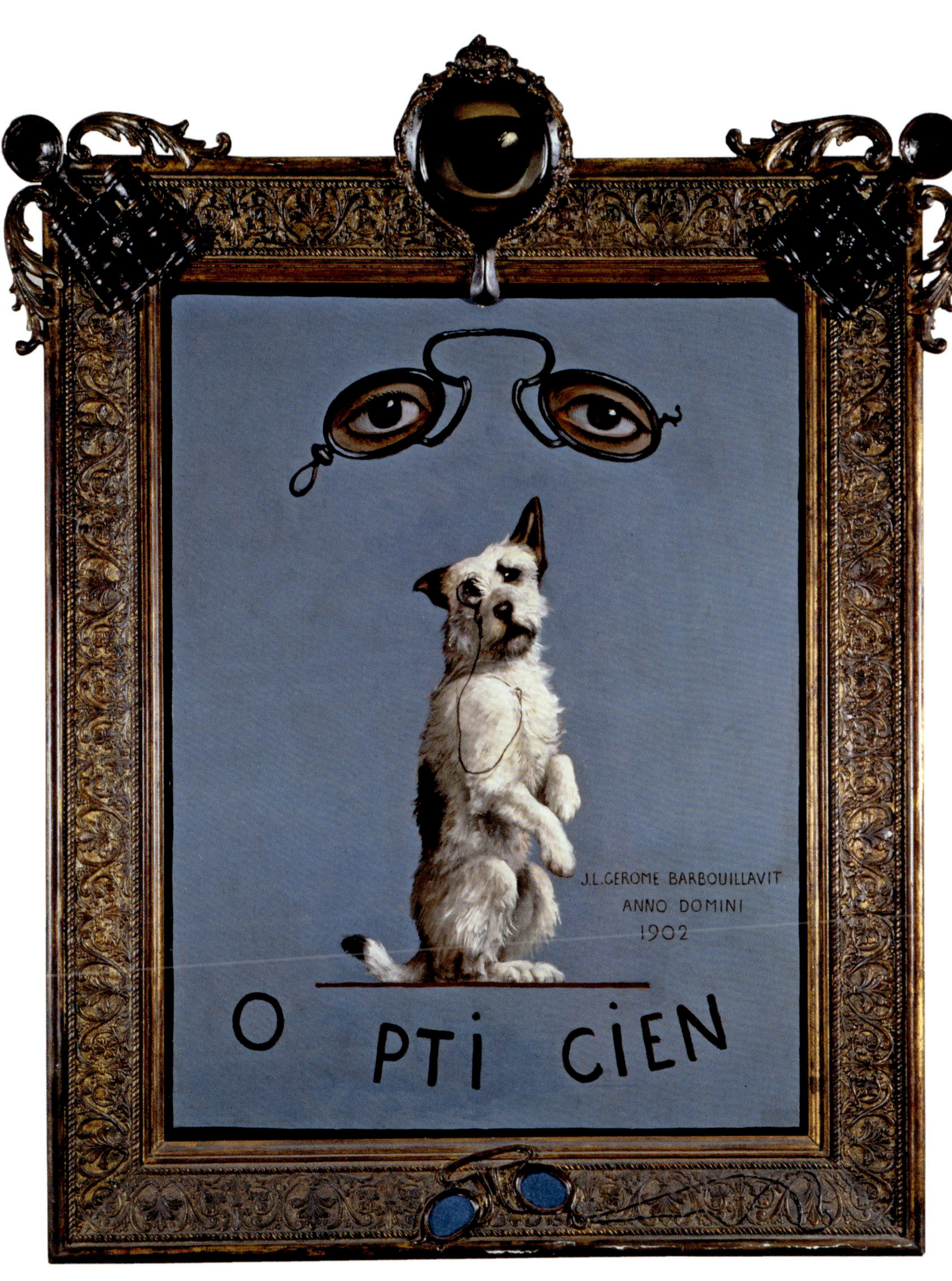
J.L.GEROME BARBOUILLAVIT
ANNO DOMINI
1902
O PTi CiEN

Cat. 114

A CHAT BY THE FIRESIDE

–

1881
Oil on canvas
18 × 15 in.
Signed lower left
Spencer Museum of Art, The University of Kansas, Lawrence, Kansas, inv. 1970.0008

–

Provenance: James Graham and Sons, New York. H. Shickman Gallery, New York, sold to the Spencer Museum of Art, 1970.[1]

–

Bibliography: E. Strahan [Earl Shinn], ed., *Gérôme: A Collection of the Works of J. L. Gérôme in One Hundred Photogravures*, 4 vols. (New York: Samuel L. Hall, 1881), vol. 4, unpaginated. F. F. Hering, *Gérôme: The Life and Works of Jean Léon Gérôme* (New York: Cassell, 1892), p. 242. *Jean-Léon Gérôme and his Pupils*, exh. cat. (Poughkeepsie, N.Y.: Vassar College Art Gallery, 1967), no. 6. G. Ackerman, "A Gérôme Exhibition at Vassar," *The Burlington Magazine*, vol. 109, no. 771 (June 1967), pp. 375–76. *The Neglected Nineteenth Century*, exh. cat. (New York: Shickman Gallery, 1970), no. 18. A. Boime, "À la Mode and Haute Couture," *The Burlington Magazine*, vol. 112, no. 810 (Sept. 1970), p. 646, fig. 126. G. Ackerman, "A Chat by the Fireside," *The Register of the Museum of Art, University of Kansas* 4 (1971), pp. 21–33. G. Ackerman et al., *Jean-Léon Gérôme (1824–1904)*, exh. cat. (Dayton: Dayton Art Institute, 1972; also Minneapolis: Minneapolis Institute of Arts, 1973, and Baltimore: The Walters Art Gallery, 1973), p. 81, no. 32. A. Boime, "Gérôme and the Bourgeois Artist's Burden," *Arts Magazine*, vol. 57, no. 5 (Jan. 1983), p. 70. G. Ackerman, *The Life and Work of Jean-Léon Gérôme, with a Catalogue Raisonné* (New York and London: Sotheby's, 1986), pp. 105, 120, 123, 248, 249, no. 295. C. Juler, *Najd Collection of Orientalist Paintings* (London, 1991), p. 134. G. Ackerman, *Jean-Léon Gérôme: His Life, His Work, 1824–1904* (Courbevoie: ACR Édition, 1997), pp. 126–27. G. Ackerman, *Jean-Léon Gérôme* (Courbevoie: ACR Édition, 2000), pp. 115, 302–3, no. 295.

Gérôme made repeated trips to Istanbul in the 1870s,[2] prompting numerous Turkish-themed genre paintings and signaling a shift in the direction of his Orientalist work, which had been previously dominated by Egyptian scenes. The exotic backdrop of this casually anecdotal yet highly refined picture is a tile-covered fireplace topped with a conical hood, of a type Gérôme would have known from visiting the old Topkapi palace, former residence of the sultanate in Istanbul.[3] It is likely that photographs also aided the artist; the firm of Abdullah frères, for example, is known to have supplied Gérôme with documentary photos of various Turkish sites.[4] A specific source for the Iznik tiles Gérôme depicted here has not yet been identified, but one likely exists, as he had ample opportunity to study the famous Ottoman ceramics in various sites in Turkey, in museums in France, and in his own collection.[5]

Eloquent as ever in orchestrating his composition, Gérôme has used the scalloped rim of the fireplace to link his two protagonists in their idle repartee. The uniformed guard at left has apparently just propped up his rifle against the limestone niche and taken a seat on a cage-like stool (a ubiquitous prop in Gérôme's Orientalist paintings). Warming his hands before taking up his smoking paraphernalia, the guard exchanges an affable word with a gruff, tattered fellow pausing in the act of lighting his pipe. Undisturbed by their pleasantries and melding into the shadows of the hearth, a contented black cat sits quietly before the little fire.

Gérôme's exquisitely polished technique routinely earned him comparisons to Dutch seventeenth-century painters such as Gerard Dou and Willem van Mieris. That presumed level of technical refinement is nowhere more apparent than in Gérôme's treatment of the convex array of tiles decorating the fireplace. He describes a full range of tonal gradations, from the tiles gleaming with reflected light to the dingy, soot-blackened ones shrouded in shadow. The light–dark contrast subtly reinforces, with Gérôme's characteristic visual wit, the social and sartorial contrasts between the immaculate guard and his picturesquely derelict companion. More humorously pointed is the visual pun pairing the latter's two bare feet with the two missing pavement stones in the right foreground. **S. A.**

1. Ackerman identifies this picture with the one Goupil sold to Alberti in 1881 (no. 15776, "Causerie au coin du poële") (see G. Ackerman, *Jean-Léon Gérôme* (Courbevoie: ACR Édition, 2000), p. 302, no. 295). The Alberti sale catalogue of April 13, 1888, however, provides a detailed description of that painting as well as its dimensions, which clearly identify it with a picture now in the Najd collection (Ackerman, no. 296). **2.** In 1871, 1875, and 1879. See G. Ackerman 2000 (as in n. 1), pp. 94, 106. **3.** See G. Ackerman, "A Chat by the Fireside," *The Register of the Museum of Art, University of Kansas*, vol. 4, (1971), p. 26; and G. Ackerman et al., *Jean-Léon Gérôme (1824–1904)*, exh. cat. (Dayton: Dayton Art Institute, 1972; also Minneapolis: Minneapolis Institute of Arts, 1973, and Baltimore: The Walters Art Gallery, 1973), p. 81, n. 32. **4.** See G. Ackerman 2000 (as in n. 1), p. 113. **5.** On Gérôme's use of Islamic tiles more generally, see W. B. Denny, "Quotations in and out of Context: Ottoman Turkish Art and European Orientalist Painting," *Muqarnas*, vol. 10 (1993), pp. 220–21.

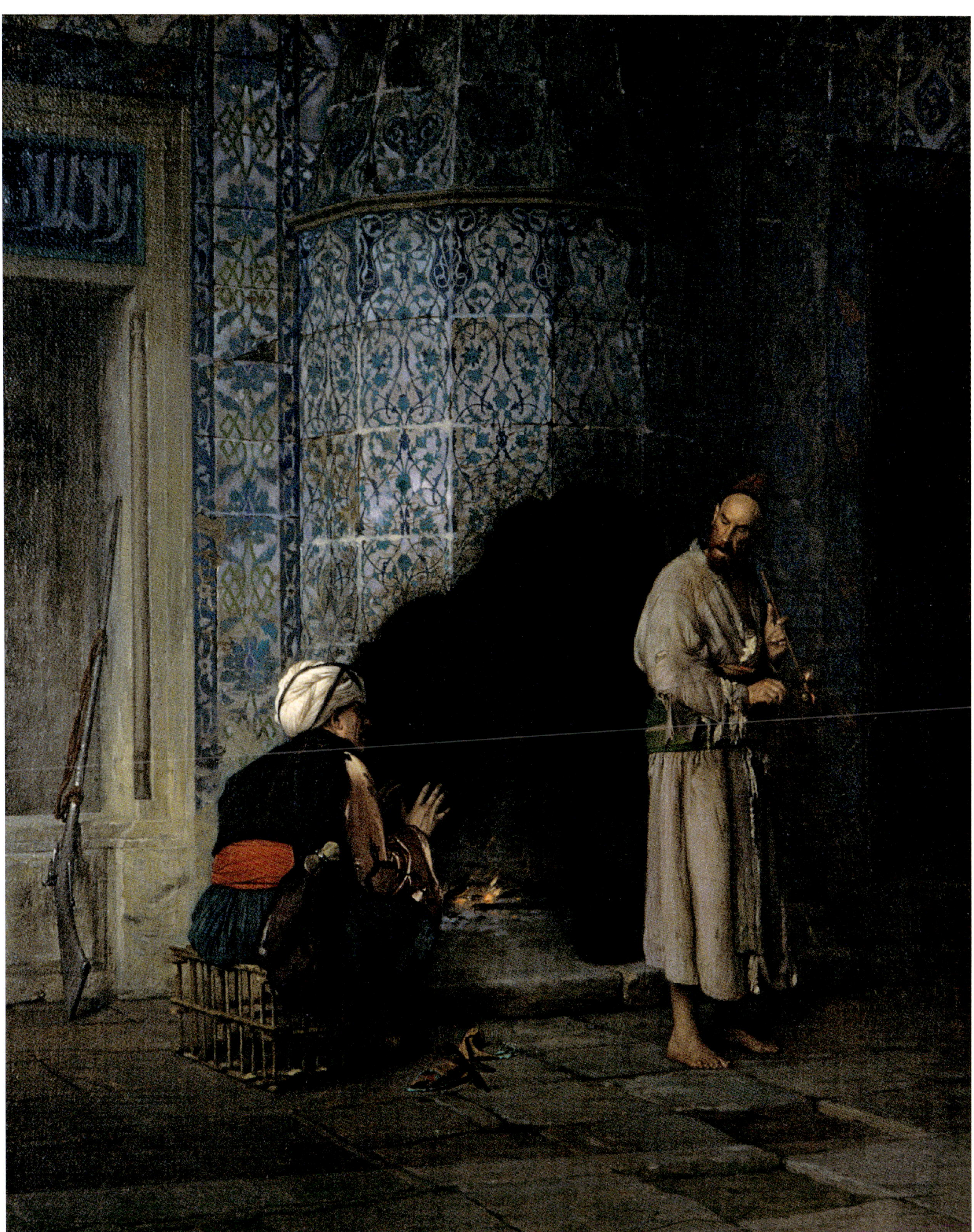

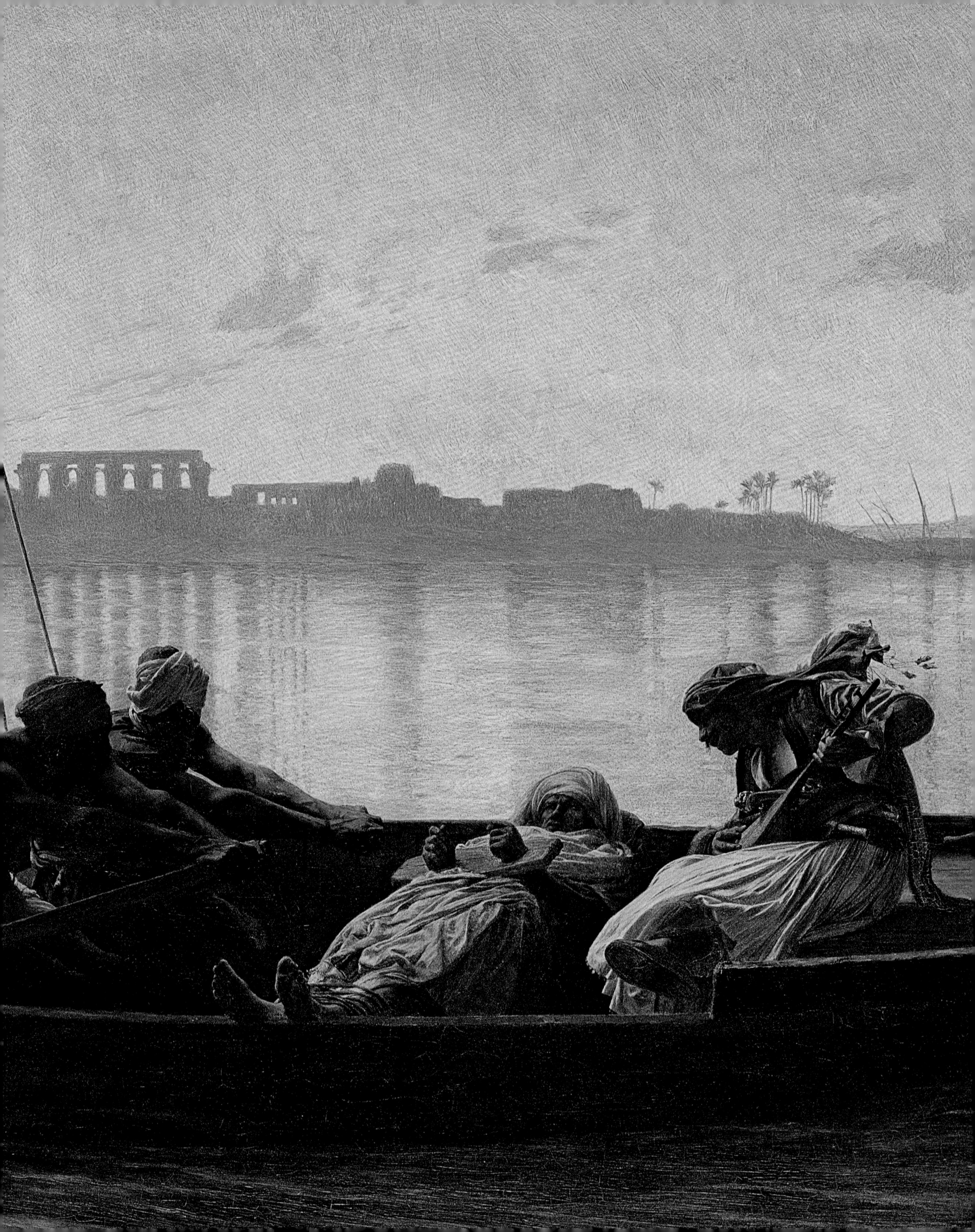

GÉRÔME AND PHOTOGRAPHY: ACCURATE DEPICTIONS OF AN IMAGINED WORLD

—

Dominique de Font-Réaulx | Translated from the French by Deke Dusinberre

The links between Gérôme's oeuvre and photographic works of his day were simultaneously complex and unique. Beyond his specific use of photographic prints in the conception of certain canvases, Gérôme employed photography as a justification for his pictorial subterfuges by exploiting the real proximity between the aesthetics of photography and his own painterly aesthetics, based on precision draftsmanship and clear composition. The comparisons made at an early date between the art of photography and Gérôme's art, rather than doing the artist a disservice, reinforced his obsessive drive for verisimilitude by invoking the new invention's postulate of accuracy and faithfulness to reality.[1]

A FAITHFUL RECORD OF EVERY BUILDING AND LANDSCAPE IN THE WORLD

As soon as its invention was announced, photography—that is, daguerreotypy, the first technique to be unveiled—was hailed for its faultless fidelity to the reality it depicted. In 1839 François Arago, a fervent supporter of Louis-Jacques Mandé Daguerre, gave the first report on daguerreotype technology to France's legislature, and he praised the quality of accuracy that Daguerre's invention took to what Arago felt was its point of culmination. Quoting Paul Delaroche, Gérôme's venerated mentor, Arago claimed that Daguerre's methods "took the perfection of certain requirements of art so far that these methods will become, even for the most skillful artists, a subject of observation and study... What is striking about photographic drawing is that its unimaginably delicate finish in no way upsets the balance of masses, in no way detracts from the overall effect."[2] Jules Janin, when presenting the invention to readers of *L'Artiste*, also praised the daguerreotype's unfailing submission to the reality it depicted. "[I]t is an obedient pencil, like an idea; it is a mirror that retains every impression; it is a faithful record of every building and every landscape in the world."[3]

Daguerre's pictures revealed and displayed details invisible to the naked eye. It lent those details an importance that, in 1839, appealed to their first beholders. The precision of detail further reinforced the postulate of accuracy. Alexander von Humboldt wrote a letter to his friend, the painter Carl Gustave Carus, after having seen Daguerre's first plates in the company of Arago. "In a [photographic] drawing, commented Arago, a five-story house took up roughly three-quarters of an inch of space, yet in the picture you could see that one pane of a window—what a trifle!—had been broken and replaced by paper... The picture also revealed a very thin lightning rod that Arago had not seen with the naked eye... What a boon for architects, to be able to take away, in ten minutes, a picture of the

Cat. 127. *The Prisoner* (detail).

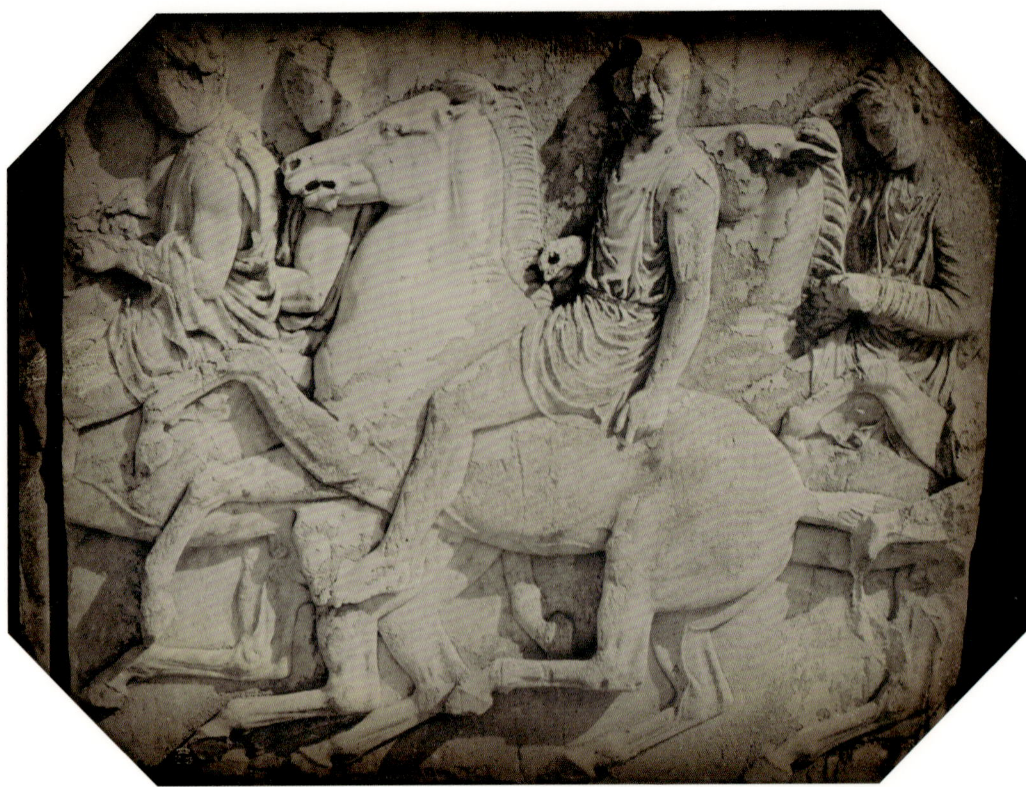

Ill. 97. Jean-Baptiste Louis Gros, called Baron Gros (1793–1870), *Panathenaic Frieze on the Parthenon, Athens*, 1850, daguerreotype, 4 ¼ × 5 ¾ in., Musée d'Orsay, Paris, inv. PHO 1985 77.

entire colonnade at Baalbek or the bric-a-brac of a Gothic church."[4] Humboldt added, concerning a picture of the Louvre, that, "The surface of damp stone, of the stonework of the wall, has a reality (*Wahrheit*) that no copper engraving can match."

The aesthetics of daguerrotypy, a process that produced a unique image on metal, bore many similarities to academic painting. The obligation to compose the scene in advance due to the drawbacks of a long exposure time, the perfect mastery of light required by the laws of optics, and the use of a polished metal plate resulted in pictures whose precise lines and slick surface were not unlike works painted by students of Jean-Auguste-Dominique Ingres and Delaroche.[5] The daguerreotypes that Baron Gros made in Athens in 1850 took these qualities of clarity and fine line to their height. A look at his plates of the Parthenon, which magnificently reproduce the details of the ancient architecture and sculpture, explain the admiration and amazement expressed by his contemporaries, who dubbed him "the Napoleon of the plate" (ill. 97).

PHOTOGRAPHY'S GUARANTEE OF ACCURACY

The invention of photography had a decisive impact—whose scope has not yet been fully analyzed—on pictorial creativity. In a lecture delivered in 1860 to the *Photographic Society of Scotland*, Antoine Claudet, a French photographer living in London, made a resounding case for the artistic nature of photography. He stressed the extent to which the aesthetic appreciation of art would become indebted to photography. "When, in future ages, our descendants stroll through painting galleries and compare the different styles of the various schools, they will certainly be struck by an overall quality of draftsmanship and method in the manner of handling subjects that will indicate the exact period when photography emerged and exercised its influence on the fine arts... Photography is a vocabulary that can guide artists in their translation of nature, an album in which they can find fresh ideas and new inspiration."[6] Claudet welcomed what Charles Baudelaire feared in 1859, notably with regard to the development of academic painting, which Baudelaire felt was becoming too dry from scrupulous attention to details. In the name of craft technique and faithful representation, it overlooked the creative spirit of the artist as expressed in Romantic painting, notably that of Delacroix. "An avenging God has answered the prayers of the multitude," sneered Baudelaire. "His messiah was Daguerre. And so the multitude says, 'Since photography has given us a guarantee of accuracy (that's what they think, the fools!), then art means photography.'"[7] Claudet, in 1860, seemed to be rebutting Baudelaire's scorn.

The link between the aesthetics of Gérôme's paintings and the aesthetics of photography as it emerged with daguerreotypes included verisimilitude as well as accuracy. In 1852 Henri de Lacretelle noted that in Gérôme's *Paestum*, on show at the Salon, "the architectural lines of the temples are rendered with the sharpness of photography."[8] Théophile Gautier, writing about *The Death of Caesar* (cat. 67), quipped with a certain irony, despite his interest in Gérôme's work, that "Never has an historical scene seemed more real. If photography had been known in the days of Caesar, we might think that the painting had been done from a print made on the spot at the very moment of the catastrophe."[9]

ATTENTION TO DETAIL

One of the features of Gérôme's painting, right from the 1847 exhibition of his *Cock Fight* (cat. 10), was his attention to details and the way they signified verisimilitude in an exemplary way.[10] This concern to make details accurate was of course part of the academic tradition epitomized by Jacques-Louis David and, closer to Gérôme, by Delaroche. But the young artist added a new dimension by seeking to base his paintings on the most recent archaeological, ethnographic, and historical research. As Victor Guillemin wrote just after the death of Gérôme in 1904, "his early works [prior to 1854], notable not so much for their historical accuracy as for their literary and archaeological research combined with skilled composition and accurate draftsmanship, attracted much critical attention."[11] Gautier stressed in the late 1850s that Gérôme had inspired followers in the matter. "He was followed by a flock of imitators, known as the Pompeians, of whom Louis Hamon was the most striking. They were notable above all for reproducing little-known archaeological details."[12]

As this catalogue shows, Gérôme's painting has to be deciphered with regard to the knowledge of his day. It was contemporary with a scientific approach to archaeology, with the founding of French archaeological institutes in Athens (1847), Rome (1873), and Cairo (1880), and with the birth of the new field of ethnology (or ethnography, as it was also known).[13] In the mid-nineteenth century, the rationalist desire to organize and categorize knowledge, to explain causes and effects, merged with the pleasure of studying and the discovery of the world as vaunted by the Enlightenment. Gérôme similarly combined his academic skills, grounded in compositional clarity and precise draftsmanship, with a drive for verisimilitude that became a profession, indeed an obsession for the rest of his life. His meticulous research was designed to give the overall scene the true-to-life quality he sought. It was based on an accurate rendering of details, which thereby exaggerated the significance of such details.[14] Gérôme's attention to detail was noted and discussed by all critics, some of whom expressed annoyance, such as Émile Zola at the Salon of 1876. "[Gérôme] has reduced history paintings to the scale of small boudoir pictures, drawing each detail with striking accuracy."[15] Others praised him for it, such as Edmond About at the Salon of 1868. "There is perhaps no artist as complete as Monsieur Gérôme. History painting, portraiture, genre studies, landscape—he encompasses all with the same skill. The ancient and modern, the sacred and the profane, the Orient and the Occident are all equally familiar to him... His talent is based on lengthy study... He has never exhibited a painting that failed to attest to both his original nature and his solid education."[16]

THE "ETHNOGRAPHIC PAINTER'S" IMAGINATIVE FACULTY

Gérôme skillfully played on his reputation for accuracy. Reactions to his depictions of the Orient—one of his favorite subjects after 1855—were based on this alleged quality. Gérôme's travels to that region lent his oriental visions the impact of eye-witness statements, all the more real for being inevitably accurate. In the eyes of his contemporaries, the young painter became an "ethnographer." As Émile Galichon wrote of *The Prisoner* (cat. 127) in 1868, "simply by rendering what he *saw*, Monsieur Gérôme has produced an eminently moral and philosophical work."[17] And yet the scene, as Sophie Makariou and Charlotte Maury point out in their essay (p. 259), bore the seal of the artist's imagination; it was based on the heady vision of an invented, literary Orient that grew from the early eighteenth-century publication of Antoine Galland's French translation of *The*

Arabian Nights. The Orient that Gérôme went off to seek was the one already imagined by Victor Hugo in 1829: "From the above it follows that the Orient—whether as an image or as an idea—has become a kind of general preoccupation for the intellect as well as for the imagination, to which the author of this book has perhaps unwittingly submitted. Oriental colors came, almost by themselves, to leave their mark on all his thoughts and reveries."[18] Galichon himself remained faithful to the Orientalist vision that combined sensuality with violence; indeed, even as he referred to the verisimilitude of Gérôme's vision, he described the bound prisoner's grim excursion down the Nile as follows: "Here we have the Orient in a nutshell, with its implacable fatalism, its passive submission, its steadfast serenity, its brazen insults, and its remorseless cruelty." Gérôme's "accurate" pictures of the Orient seemed all the more lifelike in so far as they faultlessly recreated an Orient his contemporaries expected to see. His pictures put the stamp of authenticity on their fantasies. He fighted for, as Nochlin underlined, "a strategy of realist mystification" and this is particulary true with *A Bashi-Bazouk Dancing* (ill. 98). Bashi-bazouks were mercenary calvarymen in the Ottoman army. Irregular and undisciplined—their name means "depraved (or corrupt) head" in Turkish—they were relatively free to dress as they pleased. But they could be fearsome warriors. Weapon held aloft, their dance evokes the Pyrrhic dance performed by Greek warriors in armor when celebrating a victory. Once again Gérôme combined his extensive knowledge of Greek antiquity with an oriental fantasy here charged with violence.

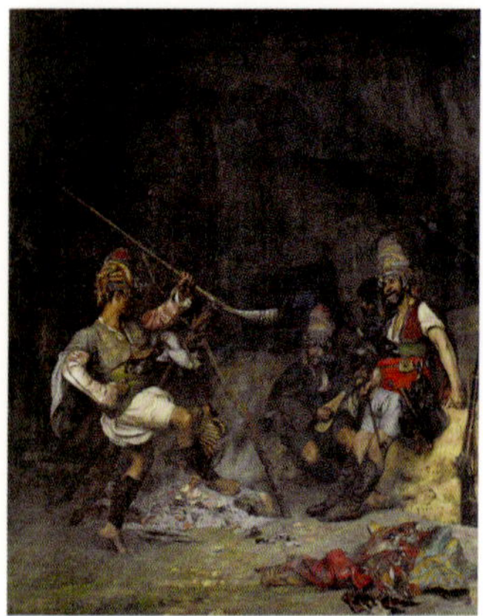

Ill. 98. *A Bashi-Bazouk Dancing* (also known as *The Pyrrhic Dance*), 1878, oil on canvas, 33 × 25 ½ in., National Palace, Ankara.

Although it was never as Western poets and painters imagined it, the Orient that travelers expected to see seemed to be slipping away from them. In 1850 Gustave Flaubert wrote to his mother while staying in Constantinople on his return from Egypt. "For that matter, now is the time to see the Orient because it is fading fast, becoming civilized."[19] This recurring regret for an Orient that was vanishing due to the inroads of the civilization that Westerners were trying to flee, was shared by the archaeologists charged with studying sites and monuments.[20] Thus in 1882, Arthur Rhoné, working at the French archaeological mission in Cairo, complained of the renovations undertaken by Ismail Pasha from the late 1860s onward. "So Cairo will be done for, not only from the standpoint of art, archaeology, and history (for which no one in this nation cares a fig), but also in terms of the charm and pleasantness of life. The capital will become astonishingly ugly and boring, scorching and wind-swept."[21] Underscoring the extent to which the "scholarly" view held by Gérôme's contemporaries was mingled with a fantasy one, Rhoné went on to write, "The great Al Azhar mosque ... alone remains intact like a virgin isle in the midst of the torment of destruction raging all around. It is above all here that artists and historians find the Orient as it was six hundred years go: the Middle Ages with its savage grandeur, its robust faith in the Koran as the source of all knowledge, its hint of fanaticism, its poverty, and all its vermin."[22] As Linda Nochlin has pointed out, "Time stands still in Gérôme's painting... [He] suggests that this Oriental world is a world without change..."[23] Thanks to Gérôme, the Orient seemed to be an immutable scene that Western beholders could contemplate eternally.

PICTORIAL SUBTERFUGE

The postulate of the accuracy of Gérôme's oriental works was reinforced by his acknowledged use of photographic prints. Unlike many of his contemporaries, who disguised their potential recourse to the new invention, Gérôme made no secret of his use of such pictures. He even helped to promote them. The mission he carried out in Egypt with Auguste Bartholdi in 1855-1856 was well known to critics, probably thanks to Gérôme himself; in 1894 Ary Renan recalled as much when he wrote that "Monsieur Gérôme scrupulously gathered documentation on Arabic architecture, on the miraculous river, and on the surrounding retreats while he was [in Egypt]."[24] As official documents made clear, the goal of the 1855-1856 trip was "the study of antiquities from these various lands [Egypt, Nubia, and Palestine], and the photographic reproduction of the main buildings and the most remarkable examples of the various races."[25] We know that Bartholdi took very few photographs of major monuments compared to Maxime Du Camp in 1849 and 1850, except for the *Colossi of Memnon* (cat. 118). Nor did any natives pose for his camera, apparently, the portraits he took being of Gérôme and himself—dressed in the oriental style (ill. 99).[26]

The way Gérôme subsequently employed Bartholdi's prints is particularly interesting. Although he let people believe that these photographic "documents" were used to devise an accurate depiction of the Orient, he did not copy them—for that matter, the calotype process subtly enhanced tonal

Ill. 99. Auguste Bartholdi (1834-1904), *Bartholdi and Gérôme* (?), 1856, salt print, 10 ¼ × 8 in., Musée Bartholdi, Colmar, inv. 1P3/2.

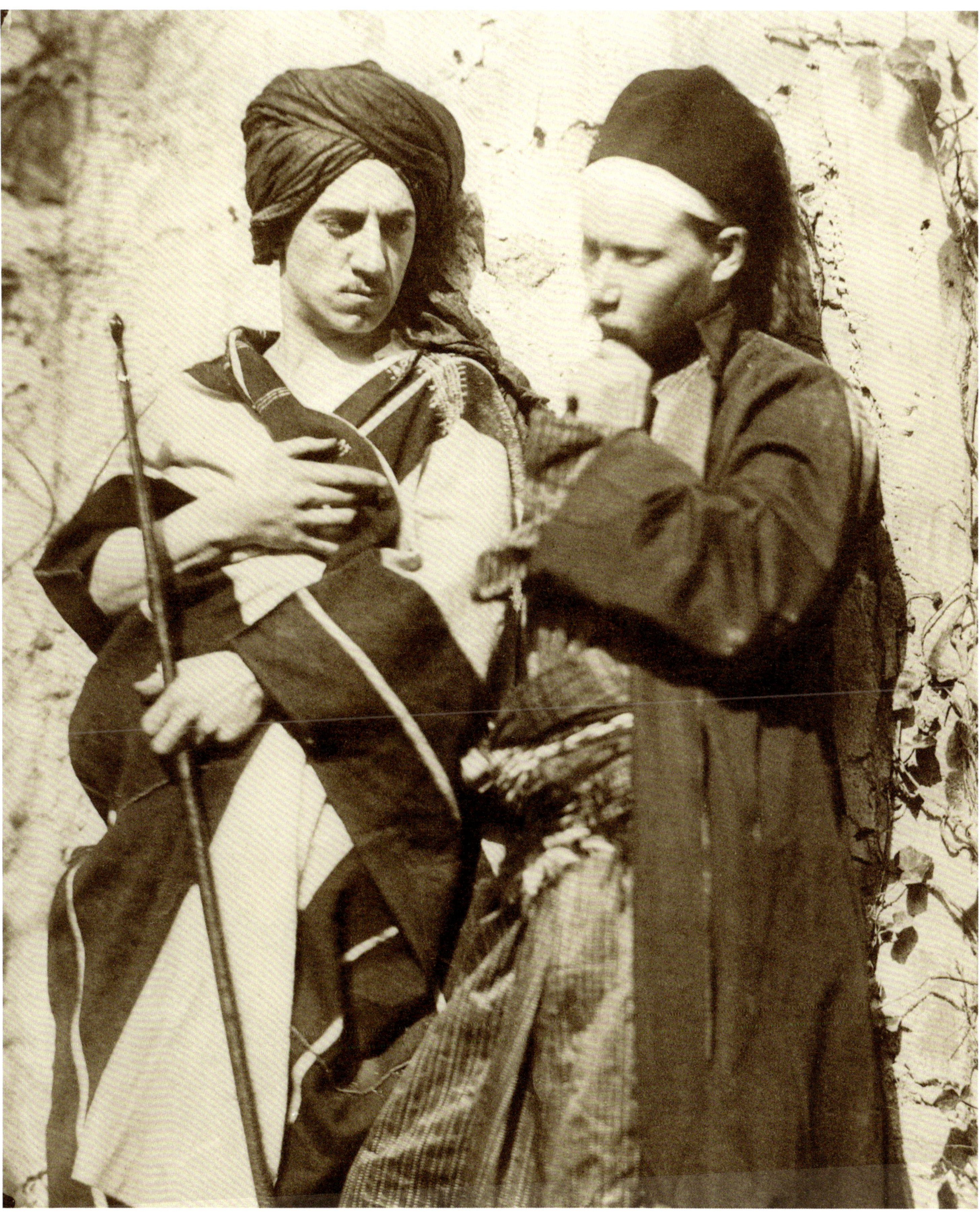

qualities but did not offer the exaggerated precision of detail typical of daguerreotypes. Instead, Gérôme made subversive use of such prints. For instance, in the *Cairene Horse Dealer* (cat. 124) Gérôme used a photo taken by Bartholdi in Yemen, where Gérôme himself never set foot. Using photography's faithfulness to reality—a common belief at the time—as a cover, he concocted skillful subterfuges without sacrificing his ambition to "make it lifelike." His contemporaries fell for the ploy. Thus Galichon could write in 1863 that Gérôme "should be seen as an anecdotal painter, a pleasant, cultivated story-teller rather than a profound historian or a lyrical or imaginative poet. His slick, enameled execution is of a sharpness and accuracy that exclude any *subterfuge* or any reservations, combining skillful staging with ingenious details that earns him the favor of the public, if not the admiration of far-seeing critics."[27]

Similarly, the fierce Arnauts who commonly populated his oriental canvases were not photographed in Egypt but upon his return to Paris, probably on the roof of his studio (by an unknown photographer). Gérôme dictated their poses and gestures, which he later used in various paintings; he paid particular attention to their dress, which made it possible to identify them as Arnauts in his works. Orientalist painting then served as inspiration for photographers—in 1858 Roger Fenton composed a remarkable series of scenes inspired by painting.[28] Exhibited in London in 1859, they skillfully recreated an Orient based on paintings—Fenton produced magnificent photographic genre scenes influenced by his training as a painter. In contrast, the Arnauts photographed in Paris for Gérôme were deliberately used by the artist to lend a sense of eye-witness veracity to his oriental visions.

THE THEATRICAL AESTHETICS OF PHOTOGRAPHY

Gérôme's skillful use of photography went beyond these artifices. He shrewdly took advantage of the new invention's theatrical qualities. No doubt the fact that Delaroche's studio was frequented by young painters who would become talented photographers—notably Gustave Le Gray, Charles Nègre, and Henri Le Secq—allowed Gérôme to appreciate, at an early date, the stagy nature of photography in terms of composition and the use and control of lighting.[29] Thus he took the background of his painting of *The Prisoner* from Bartholdi's photographic view of the Nile at Luxor. Gérôme was probably behind the panoramic format of the print, which rendered the landscape in all its scope, with a linear succession of copses, ruins, and dunes that seemed to accompany the gentle flow of the long river. This borrowed element subtly lent the painted scene a setting that underscored its theatrical composition even as it retained—through the photographic origin of the depicted landscape—a testimonial fidelity to reality. The scenic underpinnings of the play of shadow and light seen in photographic prints were particularly well grasped by Gérôme. It was probably from Félix Bonfils's photographs that he took the contrast of light and shadow that further dramatizes the cruel picture of the *Heads of the Rebel Beys at the Mosque El Assaneyn* (cat. 144), as hailed by critics: "The half-open door offers a glimpse of the sun-lit interior of the mosque, where the columns are posted all too conspicuously. Herein lies the [painting's] picturesque quality: an effect of distant light is enclosed in a shadowy frame."[30] Similarly, the light that illumines every detail of the stones in *Solomon's Wall, Jerusalem (The Wailing Wall)* (cat. 149) might have been inspired by a Bonfils photograph, along with the striking composition that imparts a dizzying height to the wall, reducing the pilgrims to their human dimension in the face of the huge, sacred building.

The theatrical effect of Gérôme's paintings—inspired not only by photographic prints but also, obviously, by a painterly tradition with which he was very familiar[31]—helped him to develop his own style, one that set him apart from his contemporaries and allowed him to refine his obsessive attention to detail. Following Gérôme's death, François Thiébault-Sisson described his oeuvre in the following terms: "[It] incarnates one of the aspects of nineteenth-century French art, a standpoint that viewed the artist as an inventor, creating his own formula himself. From which he then drew the maximum number of effects it offered."[32] Thus Gérôme's staging of "real scenes," developed in the Orient and playing on the eye-witness view of an experienced traveler as apparently nurtured and reinforced by the accuracy of the photographic medium, also underpinned Gérôme's paintings of antique and historic subjects. Although he was scrupulously attentive to the details of costumes and settings, Gérôme often took liberties with the depiction of sites and buildings, sometimes drawn with the help of photography. This approach might lead to partial transformations, such as *The*

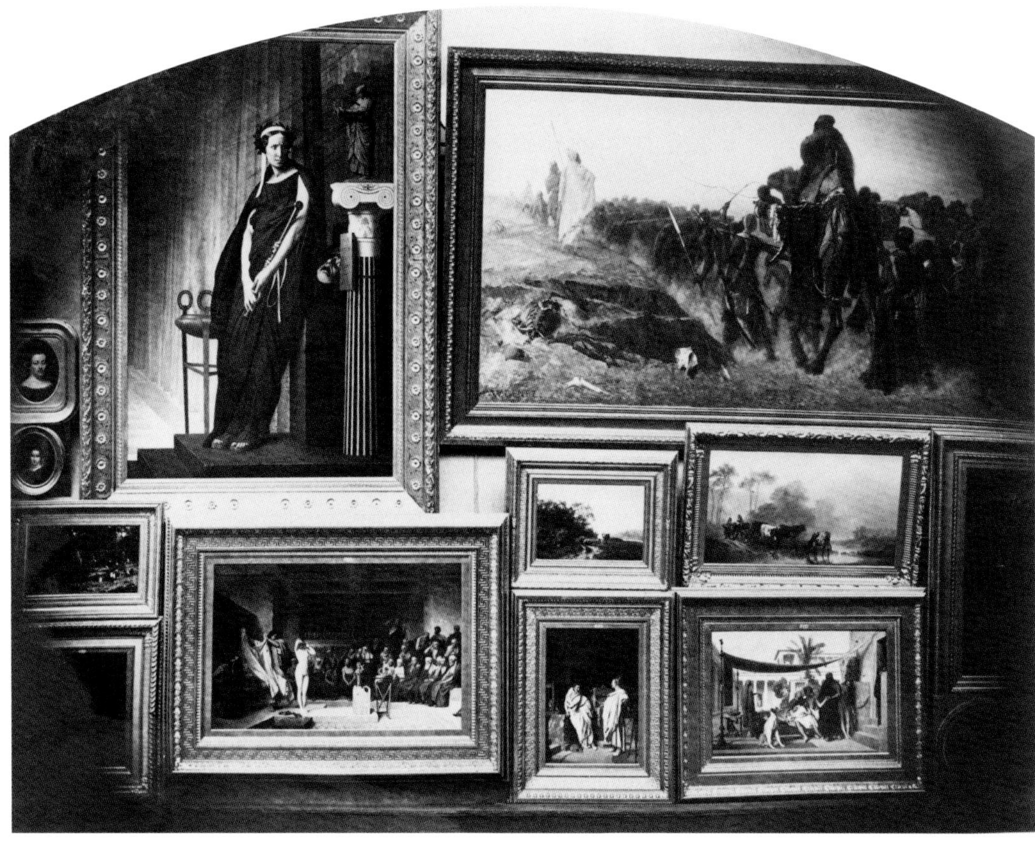

Ill. 100. Albums Richebourg, "Salon de 1861", pl. 18, detail, documentation, Musée d'Orsay, Paris. At the top, from left to right: *Rachel*, no 1253 (cat. 40); Wilhelm Gentz (1822-1890), *Transport d'esclaves traversant le désert*, no 1245; at the bottom from left to right: *Phryné before the Areopagus*, no 1248 (cat. 45), *The Two Augures*, no 1250, *Socrates seeking Alcibiades at the House of Aspasia*, no 1249 (ill. 53, p. 110).

Grand Bath at Bursa (cat. 167) in which an oriental hammam becomes an antique bathhouse, thereby allowing him to combine his two favorite sources of inspiration.

A SHOW DEEMED AUTHENTIC

The narrative aspect of Gérôme's paintings was also underscored by subterfuges developed notably thanks to photography, either through the use of particular prints or the general pretext of the medium's real or alleged aesthetic qualities, such as its close links to the theater. These subterfuges allowed Gérôme to go further than Delaroche in the conception of scenes that were often anecdotal in subject matter but singularly efficient in impressing the beholder. Thus his canvases displayed a new, special relationship to duration, one that simultaneously combined a notion of suspense already invented by Pierre-Narcisse Guérin and Delaroche—one thinks notably of Delaroche's *Children of Edward* (1831, oil on canvas, Musée du Louvre) where a shaft of light sliding underneath the door announces the arrival of Richard III's henchmen to murder the young king and his brother—with a narrative time-scheme modeled on the very elaboration of the canvas, which, despite the guise of accuracy and verisimilitude, was devised through juxtaposition, invention, artifice and collage, all efficiently staged through a fully controlled composition.

This evocation of duration and of *special effects* raises the possibility of the underlying influence—beyond inherent links with the theater—of Gérôme's painting on the movies.[33] Indeed, whereas the theater was a realm of artifice, a simulacrum in which the audience was complicit, Gérôme's paintings—like the movies to come—presented themselves as authentic, postulating the total replacement of the imaginary universe by a real universe for the duration of the show.[34]

Thanks to these artifices and to his skill in making shrewd invention seem so lifelike, Gérôme was able to compose powerful, often very striking images that played on the beholder's immediate grasp of a highly seductive world whose appeal was based on Gérôme's favorite twin registers of sensuality and violence. He had a sharp sense of drama, probably nourished by his frequent attendance at operas and plays. He was a close friend to Jules Claretie (administrative director of the Comédie Française), Charles Gounod, Georges Bizet, Jules Barbier (Gounod's librettist), and Camille Saint-Saens. Gérôme apparently even contributed a "history of the Opera" to a book by Alphonse Royer, *Le Nouvel Opéra, description*.[35] His paintings also inspired theatrical shows. *Duel after the Ball* (cat. 51) was turned into a play by Gustave Haller (the pen-name of Wilhemine Simonin Fould), titled *Le*

Duel de Pierrot and staged in 1881. Bizet's *Djamileh*, performed at the Opéra Comique in 1872, was partly inspired by the voluptuous dance in *Dance of the Almeh* (cat. 154). The impact of Gérôme's scenes was also indebted to crowd effects in the opera, later taken up by the movies; although he paid scrupulous attention to gestures as well as to composition, Gérôme did not take the same care with facial expression. Thus, for example, the sadness of the senseless death of Pierrot in *Duel after the Ball* comes across not so much from the faces of the witnesses as in their poses and gestures along with, of course, the great void in the middle of the canvas that separates the adversaries forever.

"M. GÉRÔME WORKS FOR THE MAISON GOUPIL"

If photography offered Gérôme the artifice of accuracy, it also allowed his work to become widely known through reproduction.[36] Zola, it will be recalled, mocked the popularity of photographic reproductions of Gérôme's paintings, which he ascribed to the artist's very close links to the art dealer and publisher Adolphe Goupil, whose daughter he had married. "M. Gérôme works for the Maison Goupil and therefore creates a painting so that it may be reproduced by photography and engraving and thus sold in thousands of copies."[37] Zola was exaggerating, although on several occasions Gérôme did paint replicas from which photographs or prints could be made after the originals were sold. But Gérôme's wish to have reproductions of his works predated his encounter with Goupil; as early as 1848 he asked Le Gray to make a daguerreotype of *Anacreon* (cat. 19). The remarkable results suggest that this plate was not a one-off affair. The Daguerre technique, wonderfully mastered by Le Gray, served Gérôme's precise draftsmanship well; the photographic plate perfectly respected the balanced composition of the painting, thanks to shrewd geometric correspondence. At an early date, then, Gérôme realized how efficiently photography could help disseminate his works whose overall handling, based on perfect draftsmanship and the subordination of color to drawing, lost little in reproduction despite photography's inability to render Gérôme's coloring. Several of his paintings were photographed by Pierre-Ambroise Richebourg in the 1850s and early 1860s, notably *Prayer in the House of an Arnaut Chief, Pifferari* (cat. 3), and *Louis XI* (1862).[38] We do not know under what conditions the photographs were taken, nor what the connection was between the two men. Richebourg, who had been among Daguerre's earliest disciples, was at that time one of the most skillful photographers of art reproductions, able to overcome numerous technical hurdles.[39] On at least two occasions he photographed the annual Salon, in 1857 (Musée d'Orsay, Paris) and 1861 (ill. 100, p. 219). It is hard to imagine that Gérôme executed his paintings solely with regard to their photographic reproduction: the man—the artist—was too proud and jealous of his technique for that to be the case. But he was certainly aware of the profit to be gained from photography. Thanks to reproductions, his works were widely seen in middle-class homes of the day, insuring the artist a solid reputation. This dissemination also explains Gérôme's great influence on contemporary arts, whether painting, theater, or movies. It was often through photography that his paintings, frequently purchased by private collectors at very steep prices, became known. His painted oeuvre served, in a way, as the basis for pictures disseminated to the general public in various formats, under the attentive eye of Gérôme himself.[40]

PHOTOGRAPHY WITHIN THE STUDIO

After 1880 Gérôme made highly singular use of photography, in direct relation to his painted and sculpted work. Paintings, sculpture, and photography seemed to be conceived with the same intent (a subject that merits further study). Although the aging artist continued to paint oriental scenes, probably to satisfy a clientele that demanded them, he devoted the most interesting facet of his creativity to his own studio. The studio was not just the locus of creativity but was also a source of inspiration and a subject for depiction: here the relationship between artist and model could be used to stage—henceforth more surely than harem scenes—the sensual tension that Gérôme so liked to paint. Painted, sculpted, and photographic depictions of the studio echo one another. The photographs of *Omphale*, which show Gérôme posing with his model, were apparently not so much reproductions of the sculpture as skillfully arranged studies for the many paintings that showed him sculpting, such as *The Artist's Model* (cat. 173), *The End of the Seance* (cat. 176), and *Pygmalion and Galatea* (cat. 175). At the very end of his life, Gérôme painted himself in a pose borrowed from a photograph of his studio: *My Portrait* (1902, whereabouts unknown). The Musée d'Orsay holds a photograph probably taken at the same time, which shows the painter, palette in hand, standing before *Pygmalion and Galatea,* thereby paying tribute to sculptor and painter simultaneously.[41] Thanks to the props and sets often employed in Gérôme's paintings, the studio also appears as the site where his system was elaborated, where the key to his enigmas and subterfuges can be found.

This is certainly the reason that Gérôme was so keen, right from the late 1890s, to gather the existing photographic prints of his work into albums, and to have one or several unfortunately now-anonymous photographers take pictures of those works that hadn't already been reproduced (cat. 177, 178). These albums, donated to the Bibliothèque Nationale de France by the artist's widow after his death, are precious sources of knowledge about Gérôme's oeuvre, and also constitute tangible proof of the trust he consistently placed in photographic technology, allowing him to forge—in part—his own posterity.

1. On this subject, see Henri de Lacretelle's reviews in *La Lumière*, a magazine launched in collaboration with the Société Héliographique. In particular, H. de Lacretelle, "Salon de 1852," La Lumière 16 (Apr. 10, 1852), pp. 61–62.

2. F. Arago, "Rapport à la Chambre des députés," July 3, 1839, quoted in A. Rouillé, *La Photographie en France, textes et controverses, une anthologie, 1816–1871* (Paris: Macula, 1989), p. 39. On the conditions behind and reactions to the announcement of the invention of photography, see F. Brunet, *La Naissance de l'idée de photographie* (Paris: PUF, 2000).

3. J. Janin, "Le Daguerotype," *L'Artiste,* 1839, ser. 2, vol. 2, p. 147.

4. Humboldt's letter to Carus is reproduced in R. Recht, *La Lettre de Humboldt, du jardin paysager au daguerréotype* (Paris: Christian Bourgois, 1992), pp. 9–12.

5. Academic criticism famously established a pejorative comparison between daguerreotypes and Realist painting (notably Courbet's oeuvre), showering on both the same anathema of a "mindless" reality created by a "mechanical," undiscriminating process. Paradoxically, however, the actual images produced by Daguerre's invention were close to the academic painting that rejected them. It is important to distinguish here what critics of the day attributed to the appearance of the products of daguerreotypy from the process itself, which was indeed mechanical and therefore challenged the academic conception of artistic training, based on a lengthy apprenticeship of eye and mind, and executed through meticulous labor. Thus commentators were troubled not so much by the postulate of photography's reproduction of reality as by the fact that its methods did not require submission to the strict rules that the Académie imposed on young artists—the very same rules that Courbet made a point of ignoring. On this subject, see P.-L. Roubert, *L'Image sans qualités* (Paris: Éditions du Patrimoine, 2007).

6. A. Claudet, "Des rapports de la photographie avec les beaux-arts," *Bulletin de la Société française de photographie,* 1861, pp. 265–67.

7. C. Baudelaire, "Salon de 1859, II. Le Public moderne et la photographie," *Écrits sur l'art* (Paris: Gallimard, 1992), p. 277.

8. H. de Lacretelle 1852 (as in n. 1), pp. 61–62.

9. T. Gautier, "À travers les ateliers," *L'Artiste,* 1858, new ser., vol. 4, p. 18.

10. Linda Nochlin, quoting Roland Barthes, stresses the *hypersignifying* role of details. "Such details, supposedly there to denote the real directly, are actually there simply to signify its presence in the work as a whole. As Barthes points out, the major function of gratuitous, accurate details like these is to announce 'we are the real.'" L. Nochlin, "The Imaginary Orient," in *The Politics of Vision: Essays on Nineteenth-Century Art and Society* (New York, 1989), p. 38.

11. V. Guillemin, "Étude sur le peintre et sculpteur, Jean-Léon Gérôme" *Académie des sciences, belles-letres et arts de Besançon. Procès-verbaux et mémoires. Année 1904* (Besançon, 1905), p. 10.

12. Ibid., p. 10.

13. Adolphe Napoléon Didron founded *Les Annales archéologiques* in 1844, testifying to a growing interest in that field. Meanwhile, the French word *ethnographie* first appeared in 1823, followed in 1835 by *ethnographe.*

14. On this subject, see notably the entries in this catalogue devoted to Gérôme's paintings of antique subjects, especially the circus games. They stress the extent to which Gérôme based the verisimilitude of his canvases on the overemphasis of certain significant details—such as the gladiators' leggings and helmets—which encouraged the beholder of the painting to think, "this is how it must have been."

15. É. Zola, "Le Salon de 1876," *Écrits sur l'art* (Paris: Gallimard, 1991), p. 339.

16. Quoted in V. Guillemin 1905 (as in n. 11), p. 49.

17. Emphasis added. See É. Galichon, "M. Gérôme, peintre et ethnographe," *Gazette des Beaux-Arts,* 1868, no. 1, p. 150.

18. V. Hugo, "Préface à l'édition originale, janvier 1829," *Les Orientales* (Paris: Gallimard), p. 23.

19. G. Flaubert, letter to his mother dated Nov. 14, 1850, *Correspondance* (Paris: Gallimard Pléiade, 1973), vol. 1, p. 704.

20. On this subject see Christine Peltre's publications, notably *L'Atelier du voyage, les peintres en Orient au XIXe siècle* (Paris: Le Promeneur, 1995); *Les Orientalistes* (Paris: Hazan, 2003).

21. A. Rhoné, *Coup d'œil sur l'état du Caire, ancien et moderne* (Paris: Imprimerie de A. Quantin), p. 13.

22. Ibid., p. 35.

23. L. Nochlin 1989 (as in n. 10), p. 35.

24. A. Renan, "La peinture orientaliste," *Gazette des Beaux-Arts,* 1894, no. 1, p. 51.

25. Paris, Archives Nationales, F17 2935 B.

26. If a letter from Gérôme to his father (dated Dec. 27, 1855) is to be believed, the young man with shaved head is certainly the artist. "I had my head shaved and am letting my beard grow; soon I won't be far from looking thoroughly like an Egyptian. I'm dark enough for that." Letter held by the Custodia Foundation, Paris.

27. Emphasis added. Quoted in V. Guillemin 1905 (as in n. 11), p. 49.

28. On this subject see G. Baldwin, *Pasha and Bayadere* (Los Angeles: Getty Museum, 1996).

29. Thanks notably to the personality of one of its inventors—Daguerre, who was a man of the theater and performing arts—photography had links to theatrical artifices and lighting right from its very conception. On this subject, see D. de Font-Réaulx, "Le vrai sous le fantastique, esquisse de liens entre le daguerréotype et le théâtre de son temps," *Études photographiques* 16 (May 2005), pp. 152–65.

30. V. Guillemin 1905 (as in n. 11), p. 23.

31. See Laurence de Cars' essay in this catalogue, (p. 25).

32. Quoted in V. Guillemin 1905 (as in n. 11), p. 5.

33. See Dominique Païni's essay in this catalogue, (p. 333).

34. H. El Nouby, *Théâtre et pré-cinéma, essai sur la problématique du spectacle au XIXe siècle* (Éditions A-G. Ninet, 1978).

35. Paris: Michel Lévy, 1875, pp. 6–10 for Gérôme's essay.

36. See Pierre-Lin Renié's essay in this catalogue, (p. 173).

37. É. Zola 1991 (as in n. 15), p. 184.

38. See Recueil: Œuvres de Jean-Léon Gérôme, Estampes, BNF.

39. On this subject, see D. de Font-Réaulx, *L'Œuvre d'art et sa reproduction photographique* (Paris/Milan: Musée d'Orsay/Cinq Continents, 2006).

40. On this subject see the many excellent publications by Pierre-Lin Renié, published by the Musée Goupil in Bordeaux, as well as E. Khang, ed., *The Repeating Image,* exh. cat. (Baltimore: The Walters Art Museum, 2007).

41. That was certainly the reason why the print had been chosen to illustrate Gérôme's obituary in *L'Illustration,* January 16, 1904.

Cat. 115
Auguste Bartholdi
(1834–1904)

MOSQUE OF GIRGEH

–

Between Dec. 10, 1855 and Mar. 8, 1856
Salt print
print: 8 × 10 ¼ in.;
cardboard backing: 12 ¾ × 19 ¾ in.
Signed and dated in ink lower left:
A. Bartholdi – 1855-56
Musée Bartholdi, Colmar, inv. 1P3/24

–

Bibliography: R. Hueber et al., *D'un album de voyage: Auguste Bartholdi en Égypte (1855–1856)*, exh. cat. (Colmar: Musée Bartholdi, 1990), p. 50, no. 12. R. Hueber, *D'aval en Amon: Un itinéraire photographique à travers l'Égypte (1850–1870)*, exh. cat. (Colmar: Musée Bartholdi, 1997), p. 18, no. 18.

Cat. 116
Auguste Bartholdi

BARBER'S SHOP, MINIEH, EGYPT

–

Between Dec. 10, 1855 and Mar. 8, 1856
Salt print
print: 10 ½ × 8 in.;
cardboard backing: 19 ¾ × 12 ¾ in.
Musée Bartholdi, Colmar, inv. 1P3/55

Cat. 117
Auguste Bartholdi

MASHRABIYA, MOKA (YEMEN)

–

Between April 1 and May 19, 1856
Salt print
print: 10 ½ × 7 ½ in.;
cardboard backing: 19 ¾ × 12 ¾ in.
Musée Bartholdi, Colmar, inv. 1P3/77

–

Bibliography: R. Hueber et al., *Au Yémen en 1856: photographies et dessins d'Auguste Bartholdi*, exh. cat. (Colmar: Musée Bartholdi, 1994), p. 84, no. 11A.

Cat. 118
Auguste Bartholdi

SESOSTRIS, COLOSSI OF MEMNON

Between Dec. 10, 1855 and Mar. 8, 1856
Albumen print
print: 9 ¾ × 7 ½ in.;
cardboard backing: 19 ¾ × 12 ¾ in.
Musée Bartholdi, Colmar, inv. 1P4/66

–

Bibliography: R. Hueber et al., *D'un album de voyage: Auguste Bartholdi en Égypte (1855–1856)*, exh. cat. (Colmar: Musée Bartholdi, 1990), p. 52, no. 23; p. 66, pl. 23.

Cat. 119
Auguste Bartholdi

MACHELEY VILLAGE IN FAYUM

–

Between Dec. 10, 1855 and Mar. 8, 1856
Salt print, highlighted with white watercolor
print: 10 ¼ × 8 in.; cardboard backing:
19 ¾ × 12 ¾ in.
Musée Bartholdi, Colmar, inv. 1P3/46

–

Bibliography: R. Hueber, *D'aval en Amon: un itinéraire photographique à travers l'Égypte (1850–1870)*, exh. cat. (Colmar: Musée Bartholdi, 1997), p. 17, no. 16.

Cat. 120
Auguste Bartholdi

"MY HOUSE," MOKA (YEMEN)

–

Between Apr. 1 and May 19, 1856
Salt print
print: 10 × 7 ½ in.;
cardboard backing: 19 ¾ × 12 ¾ in.
Musée Bartholdi, Colmar, inv. 1P3/79

–

Bibliography: R. Hueber et al., *Au Yémen en 1856: photographies et dessins d'Auguste Bartholdi*, exh. cat. (Colmar: Musée Bartholdi, 1994), p. 86, no. 12.

Cat. 121
Auguste Bartholdi

VIEW OF LUXOR FROM THE NILE

–

Between Dec. 10, 1855 and Mar. 8, 1856
Salt print
print: 2 × 10 ¼ in.; support (print underneath a salt print of *A Guard Watch*):
12 ¾ × 19 ½ in.
Musée Bartholdi, Colmar, inv. 1P3/21 b

–

Bibliography: R. Hueber *et al.*, *D'un album de voyage: Auguste Bartholdi en Égypte (1855–1856)*, exh. cat. (Colmar: Musée Bartholdi, 1990), pp. 50–51, no. 17; p. 63, pl. 17.

Cat. 122
Auguste Bartholdi

ELEPHANTINE ISLAND

–

Between Dec. 10, 1855 and Mar. 8, 1856
Salt print
print: 3 ¼ × 10 in.;
cardboard backing: 12 ¾ × 19 ¾ in.
Musée Bartholdi, Colmar, inv. 1P3/29

–

Bibliography: R. Hueber *et al.*, *D'un album de voyage: Auguste Bartholdi en Égypte (1855–1856)*, exh. cat. (Colmar: Musée Bartholdi, 1990), p. 53, no. 30; p. 70, pl. 30.

Cat. 123
Auguste Bartholdi

HODEIDAH (YEMEN)

–

Between Apr. 1 and May 19, 1856
Salt print
print: 10 ½ × 8 in.;
cardboard backing: 19 ¾ × 12 ¾ in.
Musée Bartholdi, Colmar, inv. 1P3/75

–

Bibliography: R. Hueber et al., *Au Yémen en 1856: photographies et dessins d'Auguste Bartholdi*, exh. cat. (Colmar: Musée Bartholdi, 1994), p. 100, no. 26.

Cat. 124

CAIRENE HORSE DEALER (THE HORSE MARKET)

–

ca. 1867
Oil on panel
22 ½ × 17 ¾ in.
Signed lower center, on corner of door:
J.L GEROME
The Haggin Museum, Stockton, California

–

Provenance: Goupil to Knoedler, New York, 1867 (for 10,000 francs). Knoedler to W. L. Andrews, 1868 (for $2,700). Union League Club of Philadelphia, 1873, no. 68. Property of Mr. James S. Mason. Entered the Haggin Collection after 1930.

–

Bibliography: *Recueil. Œuvres de Jean-Léon Gérôme,* BNF Estampes, vol. XVII, no. 17. E. Strahan, photogravure, 1883. P. A. Sanders, *The Haggin Collection* (Stockton, Calif.: Pioneer Museum and Haggin Collection, 1991), p. 84. G. Ackerman, *Jean-Léon Gérôme* (Courbevoie: ACR Édition, 2000), no. 182. H. Lafont-Couturier, *Gérôme and Goupil: Art and Enterprise*, exh. cat., trans. I. Ollivier (Bordeaux: Musée Goupil, 2000–1; also New York: Dahesh Museum of Art, 2001, and Pittsburgh: The Frick Art & Historical Center, 2001), no. 81, pp. 17, 37, 126–127, 156.

Ill. 101. Auguste Bartholdi, *Egyptian Barque*, 1855–56, salt print, 7 ¾ × 10 ¼ in., Musée Bartholdi, Colmar, inv. 1P3/1.

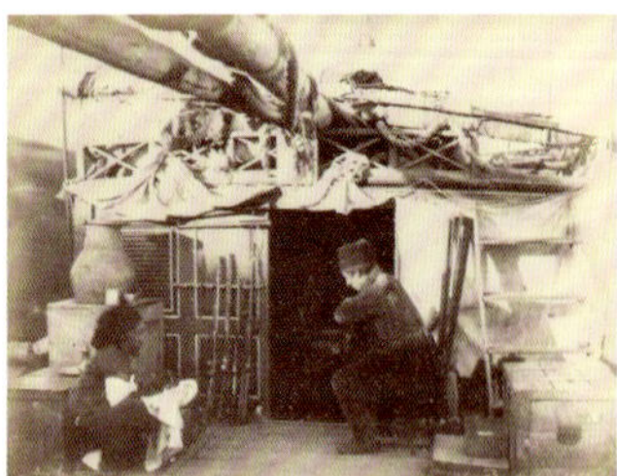

Ill. 102. *The Plain of Thebes*, 1857, oil on canvas, 30 × 51 ½ in., Musée des Beaux-Arts, Nantes, inv. 989.

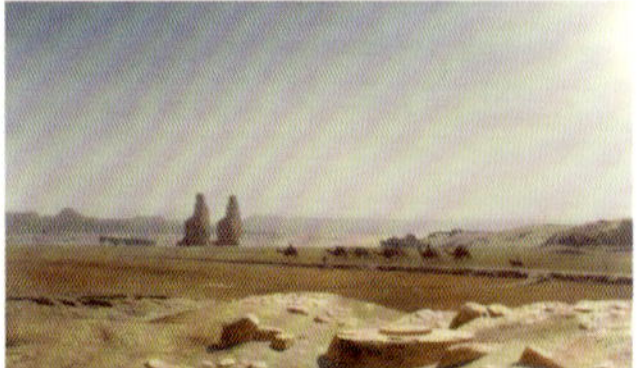

Officially charged by the French ministry of public instruction to gather elements "for the study of antiquities from these various lands [Egypt, Nubia, and Palestine], and the photographic reproduction of the main buildings and the most remarkable examples of the various races,"[1] Jean-Léon Gérôme and the youthful Auguste Bartholdi sailed for Alexandria on November 8, 1855. "[The] Orient was the most frequent of my dreams," Gérôme told his friend Charles Timbal in 1878.[2] They arrived there in early December, and remained together until March 8, 1856, when they returned to Cairo after a long cruise up the Nile in the company of artists Édouard Imer and Eugène Deshayes and a lawyer named Peronnère (ill. 101).[3] In early April 1856 Bartholdi decided to continue his oriental adventure into "Felix Arabia" (Yemen), where he remained until May 19.

It was almost certainly Gérôme who recruited Bartholdi, then a young student at the École des Beaux-Arts, and Gérôme must have exploited his already substantial reputation to convince France's imperial government to charge the pair with a mission that would allow them to travel in pleasant, comfortable conditions. We do not know how Bartholdi learned photography—he was apparently already taking photographs in the summer of 1854. In Egypt and Yemen he took a set of photographs (over one hundred in total) that are now held, along with most of the paper negatives, by the Musée Bateau-Lavoir in Colmar, France.[4] It is also likely that he gave Gérôme a set of his photographs.[5]

The context created by Louis-Désiré Blanquart-Évrard's 1852 publication of photographs taken by Maxime Du Camp during his travels through Egypt, Palestine, and Syria in the company of Gustave Flaubert in 1849 certainly played a major role in the mission assigned to Gérôme and Bartholdi. Thanks to Du Camp, the utopian dream expressed by François Arago when he presented daguerreotypes to French legislators in July 1839 had become a reality—on paper. A few years later, in 1858, photographs taken in 1851 by Félix Teynard were published and marketed by Goupil under the title of *Égypte et Nubie, sites et monuments les plus intéressants pour l'étude de l'art et de l'histoire* (Egypt and Nubia: The Most Interesting Sites and Monuments for the Study of Art and History). Photography generated renewed artistic and historic interest in Egypt with its buildings and landscapes by giving the impression of providing accurate views.

The mission assigned to Gérôme and Bartholdi was probably rather vague in outline; the two artists do not seem to have submitted a report. Based on the photographs taken by Bartholdi, they did not make a point of recording Egypt's key monuments—apart from the Colossi of Memnon—and brought back not a single portrait of the locals they encountered. For both men, it was their first trip to the Orient and the entire journey was marked by the pleasure and excitement of seeing it for the first time.

The influence of Bartholdi's photographs on Gérôme was crucial, although less for their precise details (which they conveyed imperfectly, since the use of paper negatives better rendered overall compositions with effects of light and shade) than for the new theatrical spaces they suggested. The panoramic effect given by Bartholdi's views of Elephantine Island and Luxor (cat. 121 and 122) lent his views of the Egyptian plain a dramatic scope that Gérôme was able to imitate when composing his paintings of *The Prisoner* (cat. 127) and *Excursion of the Harem* (cat. 129). Thus the artist, who drew relatively little during this trip of 1856, relied on Bartholdi's talents as photographer and draftsman; in 1868, during a journey in the company of Albert Goupil, his brother-in-law, Gérôme must have recalled the viewpoints and subjects chosen by Bartholdi and then suggested them to Goupil, to judge by the similarity of certain pictures.

Despite the official description of their mission, which implied objective accuracy, and despite an established reputation as a painter fond of depicting things with great exactness, Gérôme took full liberty when using Bartholdi's pictures. Thus *Cairene Horse Dealer* (cat. 124) was based on two photographs taken in Yemen, where Gérôme had not even accompanied his friend. In order to create a house in Cairo with the expected effect of accuracy, Gérôme combined a *mashrabiya* on a house in Moka (cat. 117) with the outlines of another building in Hodeidah (cat. 123). "Making it lifelike" seemed more important to Gérôme than making it accurate.

This gives the lie to Théophile Gautier who, after having looked at the sketches that Gérôme brought back from Egypt, wrote an article about them. "The young artist, accompanied by a few friends, sailed up the Nile in one of those *cangias* whose picturesque comfort makes a trip to Egypt so pleasurable. Today photography dispenses artists from the need to copy monuments thanks to its now-familiar perfection and its totally faithful prints, which a felicitous choice of viewpoint and timing can endow with great effect."[6]

Bartholdi's photographs were apparently never exhibited; they were probably mounted by Gérôme or the photographer himself. Indeed, in *La Presse*, Paul de Saint-Victor, when lamenting the coolness of Gérôme's Egyptian landscape paintings—notably *The Plain of Thebes* (ill. 102)—penned an indirect tribute to Bartholdi's work: "M. Gérôme apparently forgot to turn on the sun. If the desert shudders only from these pale scumbles, that's just too bad for the desert. It is simply not picturesque... Yet before my eyes I have the calotype photographs so vaguely copied by M. Gérôme, and this mere reflection makes an amazing impression on me."[7]

D. F.-R.

1. Archives Nationales, Paris, inv. F17 2935 B. **2.** J.-L. Gérôme, *Notes autobiographiques* [1874], ed. G. Ackerman (Vesoul: S.A.L.S.A., 1981), p. 11. **3.** On this subject see R. Hueber et al., *D'un album de voyage: Auguste Bartholdi en Égypte (1855-1856)*, exh. cat. (Colmar: Musée Bartholdi, 1990); R. Hueber et al., *Au Yémen en 1856: photographies et dessins d'Auguste Bartholdi*, exh. cat. (Colmar: Musée Bartholdi, 1994); R. Hueber, *D'aval en Amon: un itinéraire photographique à travers l'Égypte (1850-1870)*, exh. cat. (Colmar: Musée Bartholdi, 1997), and C. Bustarret, "Du Nil au Yémen, Bartholdi photographe," *Histoire de l'art* 7 (Oct. 1989), pp. 35–51. **4.** My heartfelt thanks and sincere gratitude go to Régis Hueber, director of the Musée Bartholdi, for his valuable help, constant patience, and unerring knowledge of Bartholdi's sculpted and photographic oeuvre. Most of Bartholdi's negatives were printed on salt or albumen paper, and they are all conserved at Colmar. **5.** Several prints by Bartholdi are held by the Département des Estampes et de la Photographie, Bibliothèque Nationale de France, Paris, shelf-mark Eo95; the Getty Museum holds an albumen print of *Sur la felouque (Egyptian Barque)*, 84.XP.1440.1. **6.** T. Gautier, "Gérôme, tableaux et études, et croquis de voyage," *L'Artiste*, ser. 6, vol. 3 (1856), p. 34. **7.** P. de Saint-Victor, "Salon de 1857," *La Presse*, July 11, 1857, p. 3.

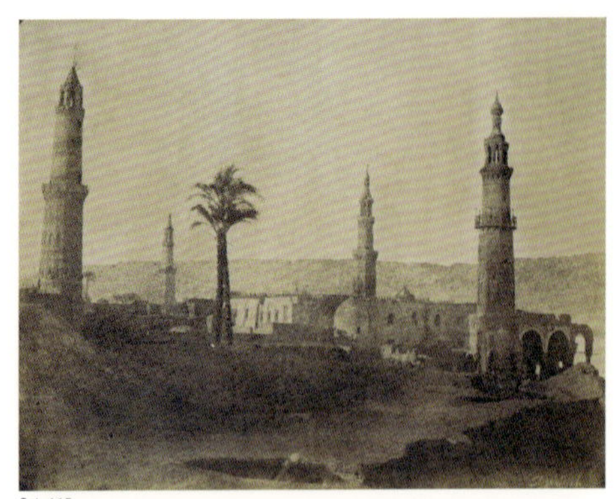
Cat. 115

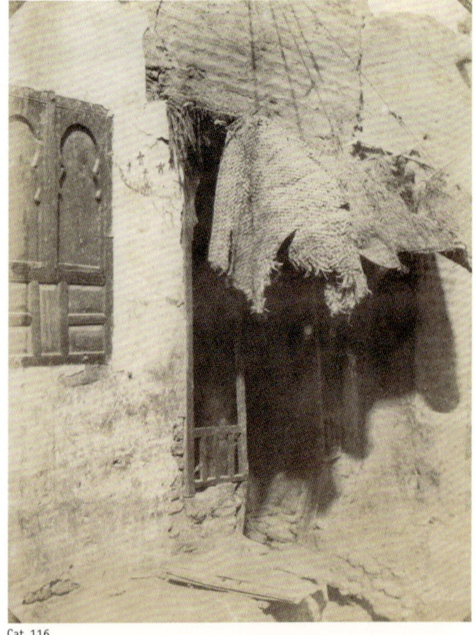
Cat. 116

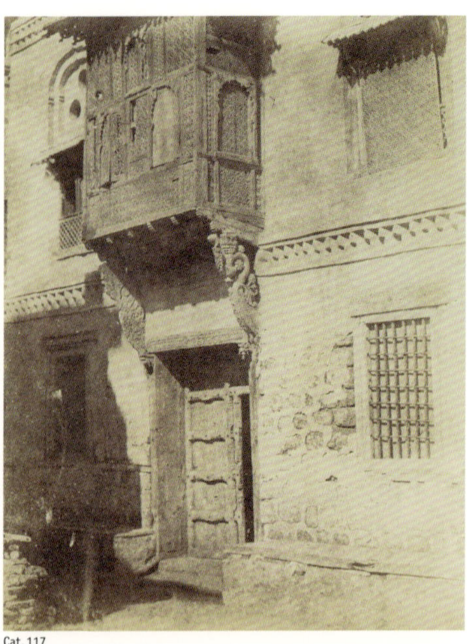
Cat. 117

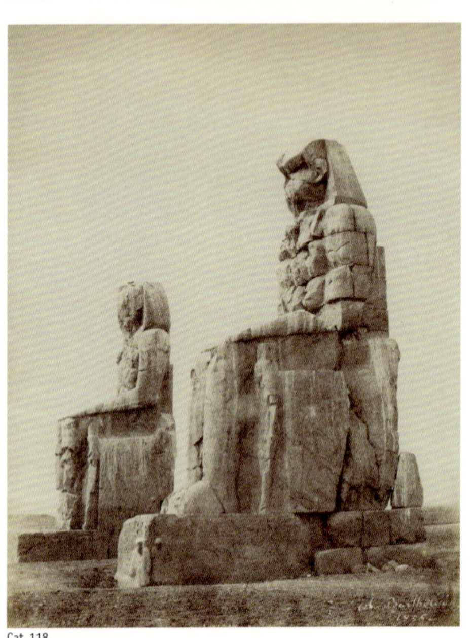
Cat. 118

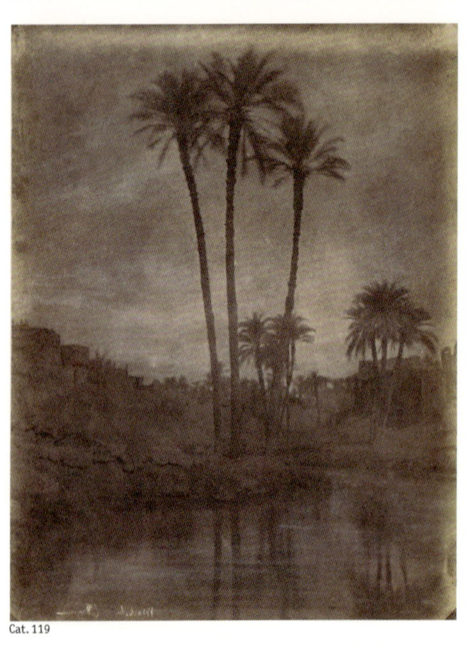
Cat. 119

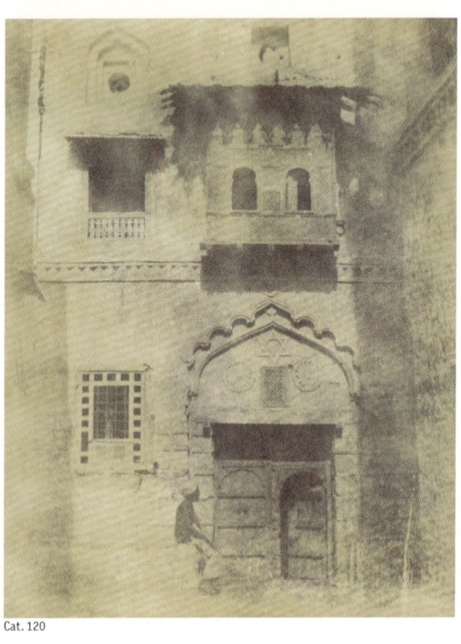
Cat. 120

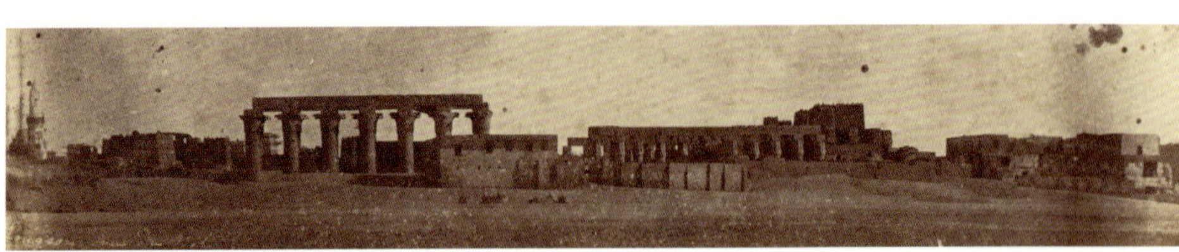
Cat. 121

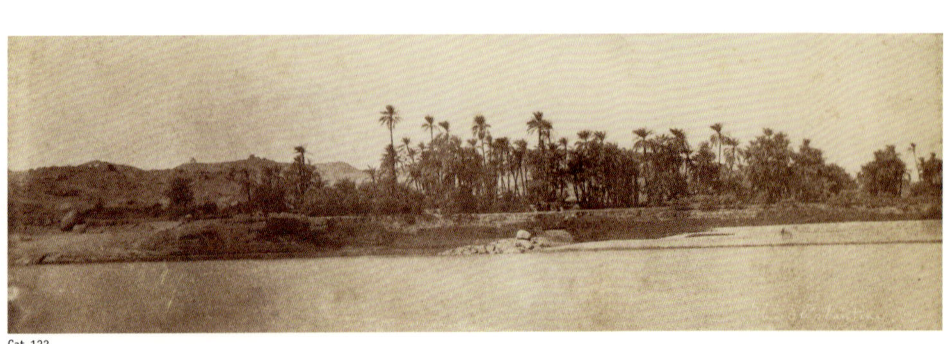
Cat. 122

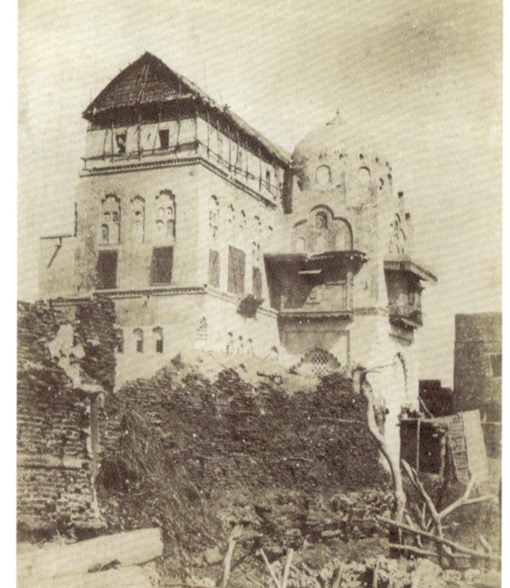
Cat. 123

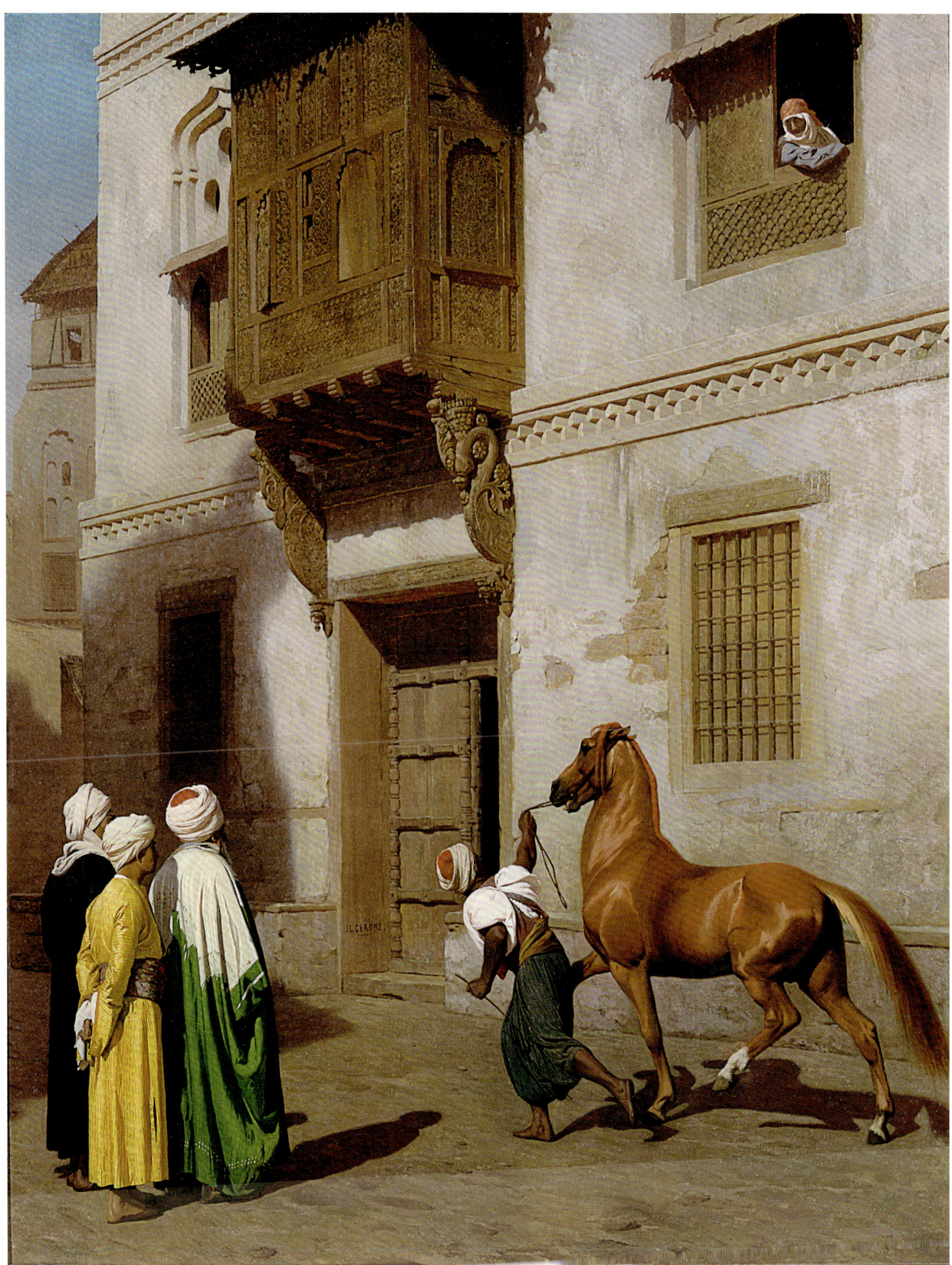
J.L. GEROME

Cat. 125
Anonymous

MALE MODEL IN ORIENTAL DRESS WITH RIFLE ON SHOULDER, ON THE ROOF OF A STUDIO

–

ca. 1856
Salt print made from a paper negative
8 ¼ × 5 ¾ in.
Musée d'Orsay, Paris, inv. PHO 2003 4 21

Cat. 126
Anonymous

FRONTAL VIEW OF MALE MODEL IN ORIENTAL DRESS, ON THE ROOF OF A STUDIO

–

ca. 1856
Salt print made from a paper negative
9 ½ × 6 ¼ in.
Musée d'Orsay, Paris, inv. PHO 2003 4 22

–

Provenance: Gérôme collection, then collection of Aimé Morot, the artist's son-in-law. Until 2003, collection of Jean-François Furieri, inherited from his grandfather, a friend of Aimé Morot. Purchased by the Musée d'Orsay in 2003.

Ill. 103. *Egyptian Recruits Crossing the Desert* (detail), 1857, oil on panel, 25 × 43 ¼ in., private collection.

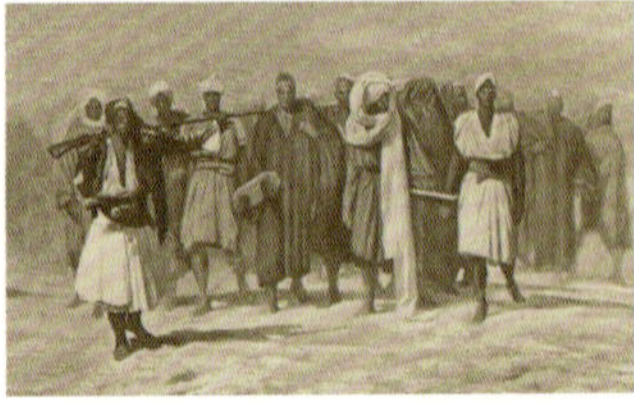

Ill. 104. Alexandre Bida (1813–1895), *An Albanian and a Nubian*, ca. 1851, black chalk, 8 ½ × 8 ½ in., Victoria and Albert Museum, London, inv. SD. 110.

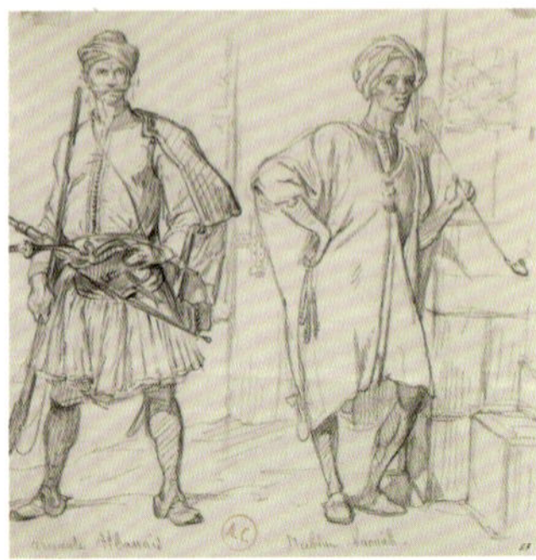

Ill. 105. Adrien Tournachon (1825–1903), *Arab Warrior*, ca. 1857, salt print, 11 ½ × 8 ½ in., Département des Estampes et de la Photographie, Bibliothèque Nationale de France, Paris, inv. EO-99-FOL.

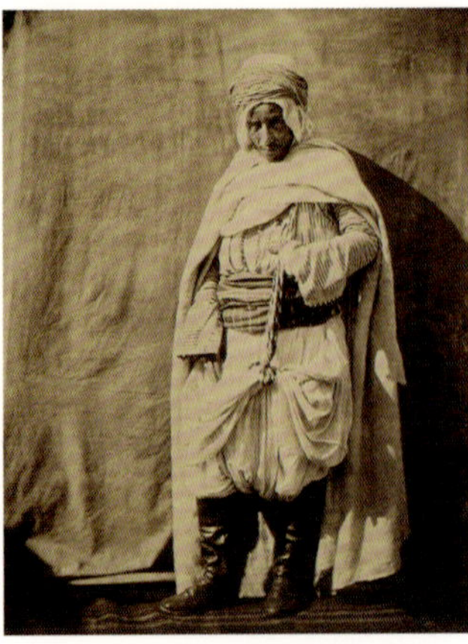

These two photographs are part of a set of four prints from the Gérôme/Morot collection acquired by the Musée d'Orsay in 2003. Along with the two pictures by Gustave Le Gray (cat. 14 and 15), they are the most interesting photographs in this collection.

Two apparently different male models pose in oriental dress on what is probably the roof or terrace of an artist's studio—several props and furnishings can be seen in the background, and a large white reflector is present to augment the lighting. Their garments evoke the Albanian soldiers known as Arnauts, who served in the Ottoman army. Arnauts often crop up in paintings by Gérôme, who liked to paint the way these soldiers dressed. An Arnaut was not just a central figure in a painting of 1857—*Prayer in the House of an Arnaut Chief* (whereabouts unknown)—but also became a common motif in his Orientalist works.[1] The figures in *Egyptian Recruits Crossing the Desert* (ill. 103) are led by an Arnaut whose pose is the same as the "Male model with rifle on shoulder," the rifle being slung across both shoulders. In *The Prisoner* (cat. 127), as José-Maria de Heredia pointed out in a poem dedicated to Gérôme, it is an Arnaut who leans with a certain cruelty over the man lying, bound, in the bottom of the boat. Similarly, an Arnaut can be seen marching in *Arabs Crossing the Desert* (cat. 142).

While Gérôme depicted Arnauts performing military duties, he also included them in various scenes and poses a long way from their soldiers' lives. The most amusing example is the *Arnaut Blowing Smoke at the Nose of his Dog* in which the Arnaut lightly but firmly directs the smoke from his hookah into the nose of his distinguished greyhound.

Arnauts were meant as authentic figures from the Ottoman world, although they became, at Gérôme's turn, a literary conceit. The conceit first appeared in the eighteenth century, but Lord Byron was the first writer to describe an Arnaut's dress and ascribe to him the qualities of physical strength, elegance, and a certain craftiness.[2] The figure of the Arnaut was then taken up by Alexandre Dumas in the early 1850s,[3] and later, after 1870, by many other writers probably influenced by Gérôme. Jules Verne, in *Kéraban-le-têtu* (Karaban the Inflexible), mentioned Arnauts as typical characters that Van Hotten and his valet Bruno expected to see in Constantinople: "Where are they?... These Arnauts with sun-scorched skin showing through the low neckline of their embroidered jackets."[4] Gérôme, like his contemporaries, was undoubtedly attracted to the simultaneously martial and graceful elegance of the Arnauts, who wore a short, square-shouldered jacket over a flowing white skirt—a combination of violence and sensuality. He was also clearly interested in a European people who were Muslims, close to Greece yet in the service of the Ottoman Empire, hence combining East and West in a duality that offered him great theatrical and painterly potential.

For Gérôme, then, the Arnaut was an imaginary figure more than a real one. The motif attracted his attention prior to his first trip to the Orient in 1855-1856, to judge by the photographic approach employed here—it is likely that the photographs taken in Paris were an additional source for the Orientalist canvases exhibited after his trip to Egypt with Bartholdi.

The costume worn by Gérôme's Arnauts was inspired by the one worn by Albanians on plate 64 of *Illustration de l'histoire des Othomans: mœurs, usages, costumes des Othomans et abrégé de leur histoire* (History of the Ottomans: Customs, Habits, and Costumes of the Ottomans with a Brief History) by Antoine Laurent Castellan and Louis Mathieu Langles, published in 1812. Alexandre Bida also did a drawing of one next to a Nubian around 1851 (ill. 104).

It is not known who took these photographs for Gérôme. The poor quality of the prints excludes Le Gray, with whom Gérôme was in close contact at the time. Perhaps they were taken by Adrien Tournachon, whose Arab warrior (ill. 105) is somewhat similar in terms of size of print and oriental motif—Gérôme knew Tournachon through his brother Félix, called Nadar.

Whoever took these pictures, they indicate Gérôme's early interest in photography and emphasize the original way in which he was able to employ photographic models less for their explicit accuracy than as stimuli to his painterly imagination. **D. F.-R.**

1. The 1868 edition of *Le Grand Dictionnaire Larousse* offered the following definition of *Arnautes* or *Arnaoutes*: "a people of the Ottoman Empire who live in Albania and nearby mountain regions, and who supply the Turkish army with its best soldiers. *Arnautes* refer to themselves as *Skypetars*." 2. George Gordon, Lord Byron, *The Giaour*, composed in 1813. 3. In "Récit de deux voyageurs," published in the Dec. 6, 1854 issue of *Le Mousquetaire*, Dumas recounted a tale involving Arnauts who died in Yemen. 4. J. Verne, *Kéraban-le-têtu* (Paris: Librairie Hetzel, 1883), p. 3. Verne's comments on the Salon of 1857—the only one he reviewed—included admiring passages on Gérôme's paintings. See *Revue des Beaux-Arts, tribune des artistes* (Paris, 1857).

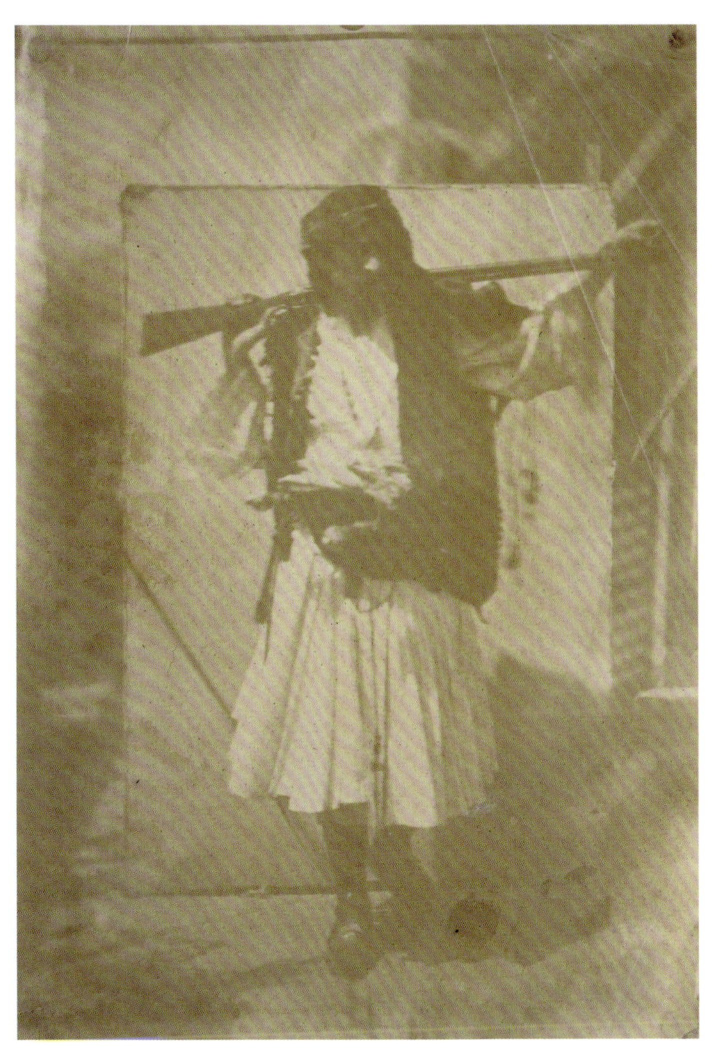

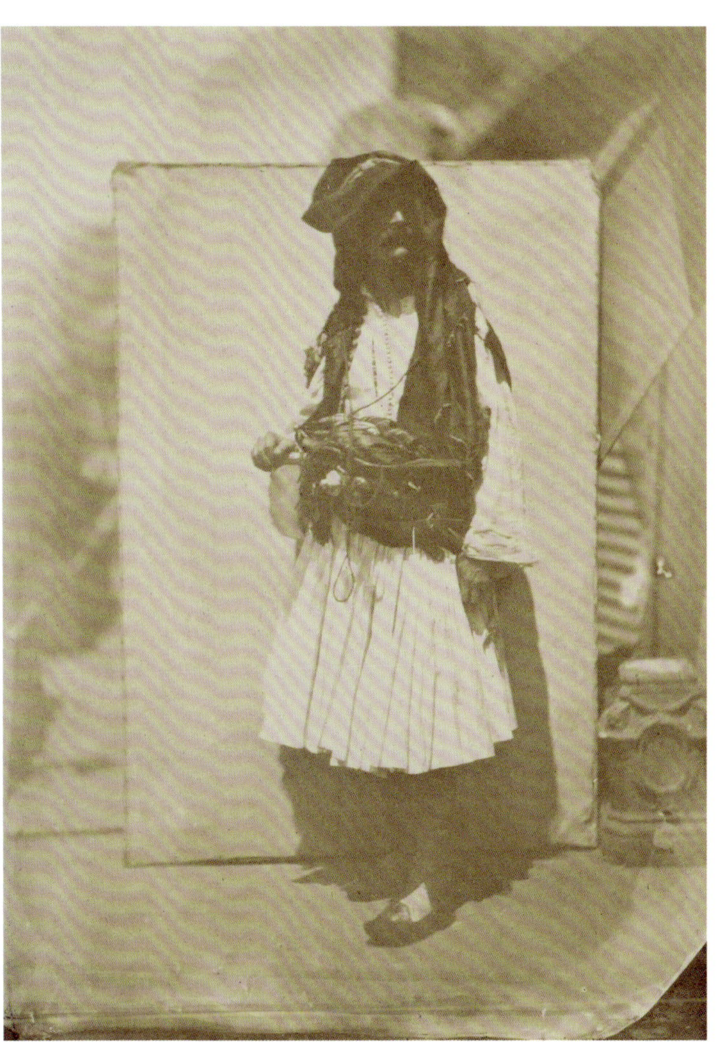

Cat. 127

THE PRISONER

–

1861
Oil on panel
17 ¾ × 30 ¾ in.
Signed and dated on the boat at left
Musée des Beaux-Arts, Nantes

–

Provenance: Sold by Goupil to the Musée des Beaux Arts in 1861 for 10,000 francs.

–

Exhibition History: Salon of 1863, Paris. Exposition Universelle, Paris, 1867.

–

Bibliography: L. Auvray, *Salon de 1863*, pp. 39–40. M. Du Camp, *Salon de 1863*, pp. 889–92. H. Dauban, *Salon de 1863*, p. 39. T. Gautier, *Le Moniteur officiel*, June 18, 1863, p. 878. P. Mantz, *Gazette des Beaux-Arts*, vol. 14, 1863, p. 495. P. de Saint-Victor, *La Presse*, June 14, 1863. C. Vignon, *Le Salon de 1863*, pp. 382–83. C. de Sault, *Le Temps*, June 14, 1865. *Catalogue de Paris*, 1883, p. 30. J. M. de Heredia, "Le Prisonnier", in *Les Trophées* (Paris, 1893), no. 125. M. Nicolle, *Le Musée de Nantes, peintures* (Paris, 1919), no. 57. G. Ackerman et al., *Jean-Léon Gérôme (1824–1904)*, exh. cat. (Dayton: Dayton Art Institute, 1972; also Minneapolis: Minneapolis Institute of Arts, 1973, and Baltimore: The Walters Art Gallery, 1973), no. 12, pp. 50–51. *Équivoques*, exh. cat. (Paris: Musée des Arts Décoratifs, 1973; dimensions given as 19 ⅞ × 31 ⅞ in.). *L'Orient en question 1825–1875*, exh. cat. (Marseille: Musée Cantini, 1975), no. 87. *J.-L. Gérôme*, exh. cat. (Vesoul: Musée Georges-Garret, 1981), no. 131, p. 116. *Orients*, exh. cat. (Nantes: Musée des Beaux-Arts, 1982), no. 19. G. Ackerman, in J. Hargrove (ed.), *The French Academy: Classicism and its Antagonists* (Newark: University of Delaware Press; Cranbury: Associated University Press, 1990), pp. 190–94. *Album de voyage des artistes en expédition au pays du Levant*, exh. cat. (Tel-Aviv: Museum of Art; also Bayonne: Musée Bonnat, and Paris: Musée Hébert, 1993), pp. 30–31. H. Lafont-Couturier, *Gérôme* (Paris: Herscher, 1998), pp. 112–113. G. Ackerman, *Jean-Léon Gérôme* (Courbevoie: ACR Édition, 2000), no. 134. H. Lafont-Couturier, *Gérôme and Goupil: Art and Enterprise*, exh. cat., trans. I. Ollivier (Bordeaux: Musée Goupil, 2000–1; also New York: Dahesh Museum of Art, 2001, and Pittsburgh: The Frick Art & Historical Center, 2001), pp. 19, 25, 59, 115–117, 153, 165.

–

Related works: Replica by Gérôme done in 1863 when the canvas now in Nantes was exhibited at the Salon, oil on panel, 17 ⅝ × 30 ⅝ in., private collection.

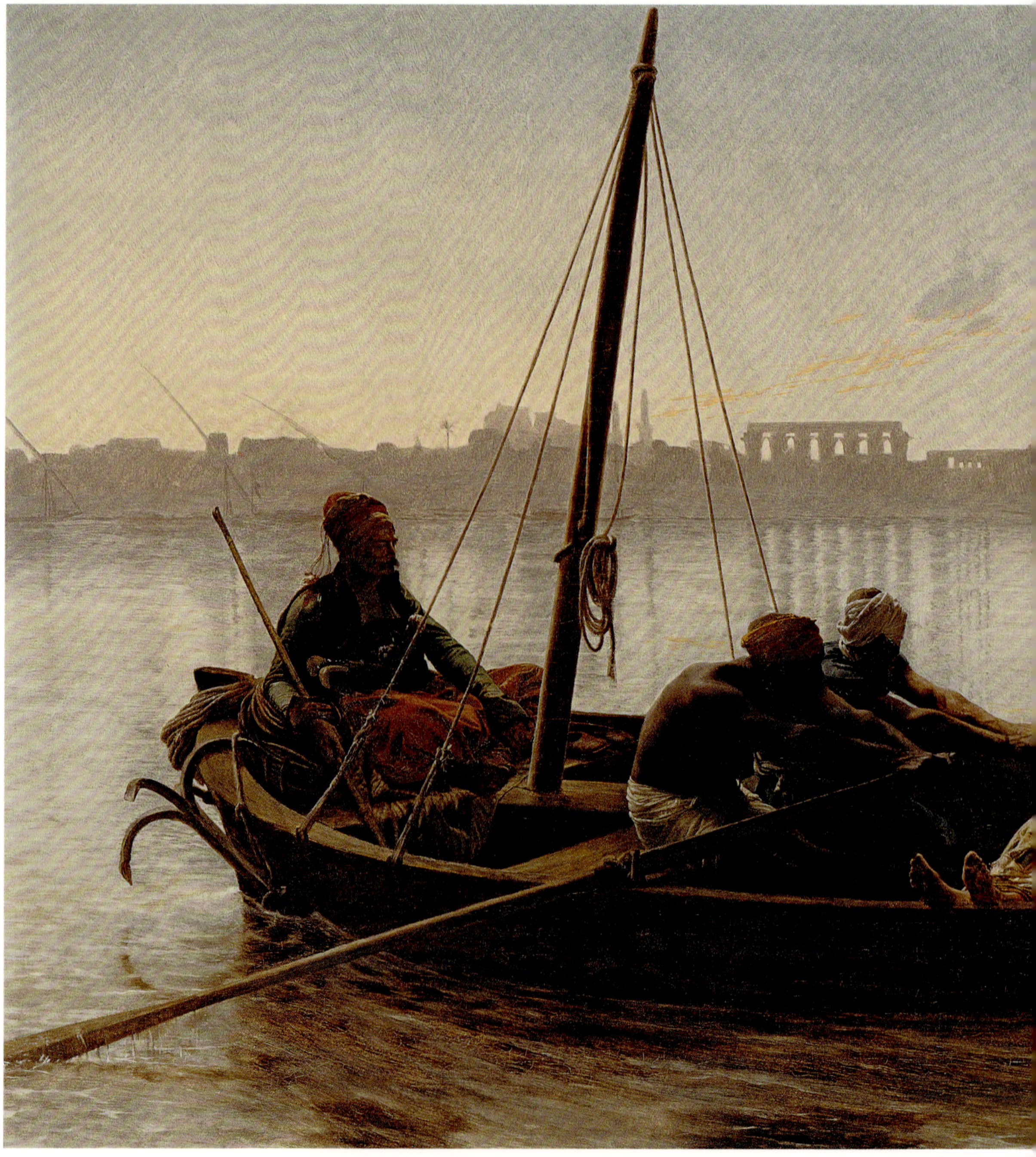

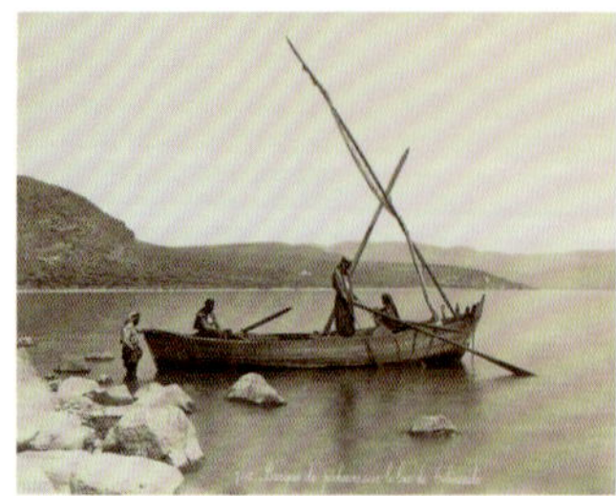

Ill. 106. Félix Bonfils (1831–1885), *Boat of fishermen on the Sea of Galilee* ca. 1870, albumen print, 8 ¾ × 11 in., Département des Estampes et de la Photographie, Bibliothèque Nationale de France, Paris, Eo 128 1.

This painting was bought by the Musée des Beaux-Arts in Nantes before it was exhibited at the Salon. In fact, Gérôme had already shown it at an exhibition in Nantes in 1861. He was well known to Philibert Doré-Graslin, chairman of the museum's supervisory board, who had studied under Paul Delaroche alongside Gérôme, and the two men remained friends. After the show in Nantes, the museum bought the painting for 10,000 francs, a major sum that indicates Gérôme's high reputation and ranking despite his youthful age.

The painting was very well received when exhibited at the Salon of 1863. The year 1863 was a highly symbolic one for the fine arts: given the large number of paintings rejected by that year's jury, Napoleon III decided to authorize the exceptional holding of a Salon des Refusés, where Edouard Manet's *Déjeuner sur l'herbe* was notably hung. The acceptance and popularity of Gérôme's *Prisoner* reveal how appealing his work was to Second Empire audiences, ranging from Salon jury members to various critics.

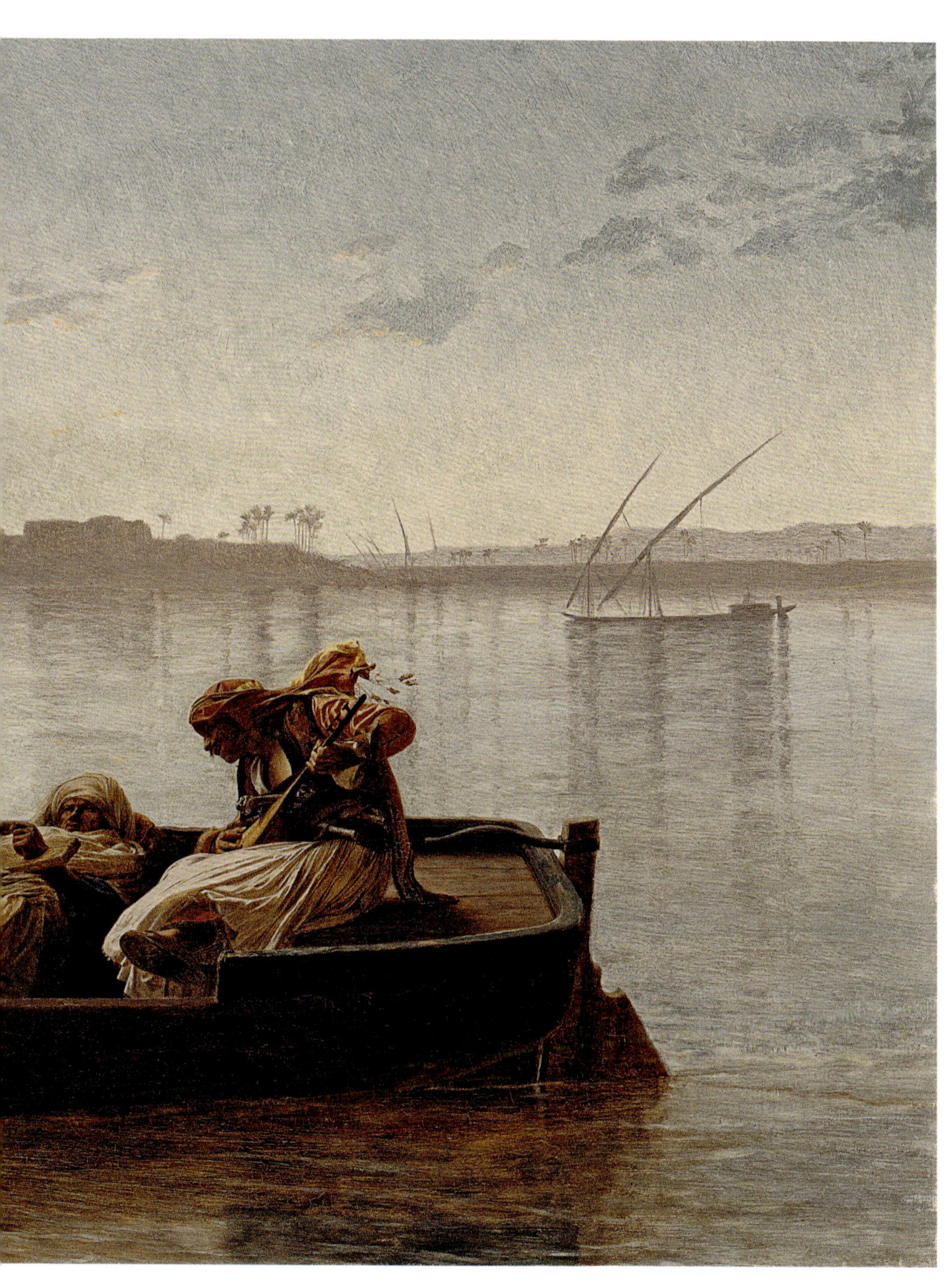

The painting's reception also reveals the ambivalence of France's perception of the Orient, an ambivalence cleverly sustained by Gérôme himself. Ever since his trip to Egypt with Auguste Bartholdi in 1855–56, Gérôme set himself up as an impartial witness of Middle Eastern reality, thanks to his previously acknowledged concern for accurate detail. Thus his poetic fantasy appeared to many commentators as the faithful representation of an authentic reality. Jules Caretie, a close friend of Gérôme, thus claimed that the artist said, "I was out strolling one morning, hunting along the banks of the Nile over by Thebes, when I encountered the boat that is the subject of my painting. The Arnauts are some of the people in the pay of the viceroy, charged with policing the land; the rowers are two fellahs—but who was the prisoner?"[1] Sophie Makariou and Charlotte Maury (p. 260) have pointed out how hard it is to overlook the incongruous nature of this Romanticized scene, with a prisoner being lulled by music along the Nile. Claretie himself, as a man of the theater, stressed the painting's scenic ambitions. "[Gérôme] packs a vast scene into a small frame. A boat flows along the Egyptian river, carrying a prisoner bound hand and foot." The panoramic composition allowed the artist to give the beholder an impression of the duration of the voyage on water, and was certainly based on a photograph that Bartholdi took at Luxor (cat. 121)—the ruins of the archaeological site loom on the horizon, as they do in the photograph. The yearning for a fantasized otherworld—where cruelty and charm merged together, where the gentlest of suns illumined the harshest of scenes—must have been very powerful in order to induce Second Empire critics to accept as true (or at least pretend to) a scene that allows their imagination to run free, as Charles Blanc's did

in 1867. "His *Prisoner* is a little masterpiece. Tightly bound, lying across an Egyptian barque, the captive is taken down the Nile to his final destination, which probably means a beheading by the sword. The boat, propelled by two oarsmen, one of whom is a strong-armed Nubian, glides like an arrow along the quiet waters in the evening glow. The master, stuffed with daggers and pistols, contemplates his vengeance and looks ahead with half-closed eye, in which there appears a flash of ferocious glee beneath the long eyelashes masking it. He reminds me of Richelieu dragging Cinq-Mars to the scaffold on a boat on the Rhone. Meanwhile, a young man with ambivalent expression and languid gaze—an effeminate, lower-class ephebe—sings and strums his mandolin, as though in insult: to the prisoner's sorrow he sings, as instructed, a song of death. The sky is clear, nature serene and happy... Yes, this painting is a little masterpiece. Nothing in it, absolutely nothing, should be changed. *Ne varietur.*"[2]
Like other Frenchmen, Blanc had read Antoine Galland's version of *The Arabian Nights*—Sheherazade, too, delighted in multiplying details and digressions, night after night, to charm the sultan.

Here Gérôme has combined various sources of inspiration: the invention of a legendary Orient was partly fueled by happy memories of his own trip up the Nile with Bartholdi. When he arrived at Luxor, on the Nile, he wrote to his father. "Our trip continues to be as pleasant and delightful as possible, and everything is going according to plan, apart from the wind which does not always blow our way—but that, too, was planned. We are very comfortable on board, we have a good servant and excellent cook and I never dreamed of being so well treated as we are here... The sun shines continuously from dawn to dusk. The weather is superb, neither too hot nor too cold, only one day has been cloudy. Rich people should all spend their winters here, I think it's impossible to find a more magnificent climate."[3] Indeed, Gérôme's painting offers a good rendering of the dusky light and quiet river. The singing Arnaut is a reference to his own art, this costumed character having become a familiar figure in Gérôme's Orientalist paintings since 1857. The scene itself might have been inspired by French history: ever since the publication of Alfred de Vigny's novel *Cinq-Mars* in 1829, the character of Cinq-Mars had become well known. Gérôme certainly knew the Delaroche's painting *The Ceremony boat of the Cardinal of Richelieu* (1829, unknown location). Photography inspired the overall composition; it is also possible that Gérôme referred to, or recalled, pictures and scenes like the one photographed by Félix Bonfils in Palestine, in which the depiction of everyday scenes may include allusions to antiquity (ill. 106).

The Prisoner was one of Gérôme's most famous paintings. The painter told Charles Timbal that it pleased both "connoisseurs and fools."[4] In 1868 José Maria de Heredia published a sonnet, titled "Le Prisonnier," in *L'Artiste.*[5] Both the rhythm and the descriptive passages in the poem, dedicated to Gérôme, are faithful to the painting's poetic fantasy (see Anthology, p. 350). And Thomas Eakins, who studied under Gérôme at the École des Beaux-Arts, was inspired by the figure of the black oarsman when painting his friend John Biglin (ill. 108); having returned to Philadelphia, Eakins used a photograph of *The Prisoner* to copy the pose.[6] It was probably also through photographs and engravings that Vincent Van Gogh (1853–1890) came to know of Gérôme's painting, because he saw and sold them when he worked for Goupil in The Hague. In a letter to his brother Theo, Vincent identified with the wretch painted by Gérôme. "Take Gérôme's *Prisoner*, for example. The man lying on the floor in chains is certainly in a real bind, but to my mind that's preferable to being the other fellow, the little gentleman who is mocking him."[7]

The uniqueness of its subject matter, served by inventive composition and total mastery of the light, makes *The Prisoner* one of Gérôme's masterpieces and one of his most appealing paintings.

D. F.-R.

1. J. Claretie, "Lettres familières sur le Salon de 1863," *Jean Diable*, June 13, 1863, p. 461. **2.** C. Blanc, "À l'exposition," *Le Temps*, June 5, 1867, p. 1. **3.** Letter to his father dated Dec. 27, 1855. Gérôme collection, Custodia Foundation, Paris. **4.** J.-L. Gérôme, *Notes autobiographiques* [1874], ed. G. Ackerman (Vesoul: S.A.L.S.A., 1981), p. 11. **5.** *L'Artiste*, Feb. 1, 1868; later published in *Les Trophées*. **6.** G. Ackerman, "Thomas Eakins and his Parisian Masters, Gérôme and Bonnat," *Gazette des Beaux-Arts* 73 (Apr. 1969), p. 240. **7.** Quoted in *Le Choix de Vincent: le* Musée imaginaire *de Van Gogh* (Amsterdam: Van Gogh Museum; Paris: Éditions de La Martinière, 2003), p. 207.

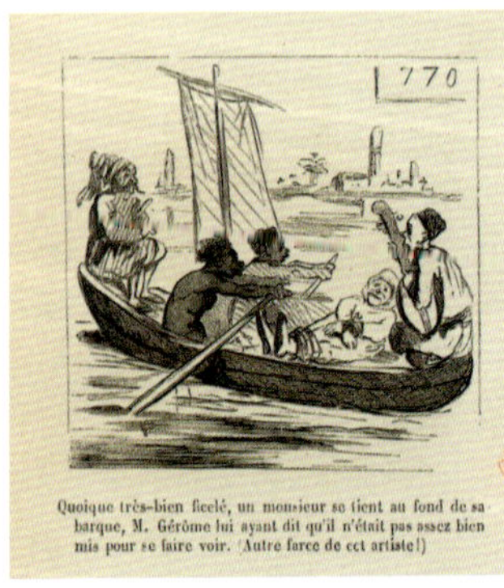

Ill. 107. Cham [Amédée de Noé] (1818–1879), "Although well bound...," caricature of the Salon of 1863, 1863, 2 ⅜ × 2 ⅜ in., Département des Estampes et de la Photographie, Bibliothèque Nationale de France, Paris, inv. YD2-335-8.

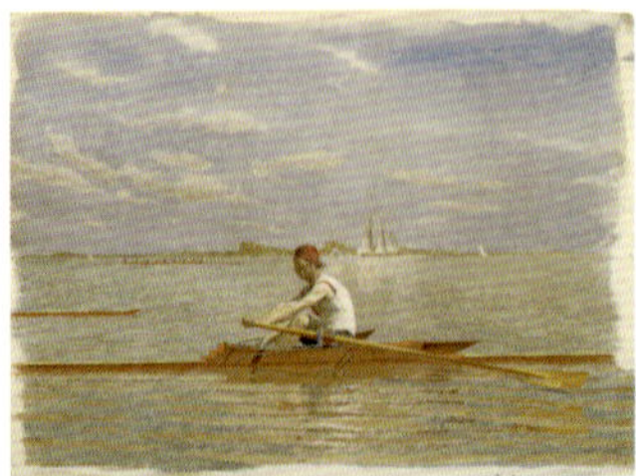

Ill. 108. Thomas Eakins (1844–1916), *John Biglin in a Single Scull*, ca. 1873, watercolor, 19 ¼ × 25 in., The Metropolitan Museum of Art, New York, inv. 24.108.

Cat. 129

EXCURSION OF THE HAREM

1869
Oil on canvas
47 3/4 × 70 in.
Signed on the boat at left: *J.L. Gérôme*
Chrysler Museum of Art, Norfolk, Virginia, Gift of Walter P. Chrysler Junior, inv. 71.511

Provenance: Gérôme to Goupil, then to Blodgeth, 1869 (for 30,000 francs). Entered stock ledgers under the title of "Caïque sur la mer Rouge." According to Ackerman, no painting by Gérôme contains a caique (sailing skiff) as main motif. E. Pinkus, New York. Walter P. Chrysler Junior, who donated it to the Chrysler Museum, 1971.

Exhibition History: Salon of 1869, Paris. World Exhibition, 1873, Vienna.

Bibliography: X. Aubryet, *Journal officiel du soir*, July 2, 1869, p. 718. L. Auvray, *Salon de 1869*, pp. 27–28. Bouniol, "L'Amateur au Salon de 1869," *Revue du monde catholique*, vol. V, p. 534. P. Casimir-Périer, "Salon de 1869: propos d'art," *Revue du Salon*, pp. 203–5. T. Gautier, "Salon de 1869," *Journal officiel*, June 28, 1869. G. Lafenestre, *Le Moniteur universel*, June 27, 1869. E. Roy, "Salon de 1869," *L'Artiste*, vol. III, pp. 88–89. P. de Saint-Victor, *La Liberté*, June 5, 1869. A. Silvestre, "Salon de 1869," *Revue moderne*, vol. 53, p. 153. E. Strahan [Earl Shinn], *Gérôme: A Collection of the Works of J.-L. Gérôme in One Hundred Photogravures* (New York: Samuel L. Hall, 1881). F. F. Hering, *Gérôme: The Life and Works of Jean-Léon Gérôme* (New York: Cassell, 1892), p. 209. Hamstead, 1977, no. 46. *Eastern Encounters: Orientalist Painters of the Nineteenth Century*, exh. cat. (London: The Fine Art Society, 1978), no. 109. *J.-L. Gérôme*, exh. cat. (Vesoul: Musée Georges-Garret, 1981), p. 22. *French Salon Painting From Southern Collections* (Atlanta: High Museum of Art, 1983), no. 34. *Album de voyage des artistes en expédition au pays du Levant*, exh. cat. (Tel-Aviv: Museum of Art; also Bayonne: Musée Bonnat, and Paris: Musée Hébert, 1993), p. 30. *Théo Van Gogh: marchand de tableaux, collectionneur, frère de Vincent (1857–1891)*, exh. cat. (Amsterdam: Van Gogh Museum, 1999; also Paris: Musée d'Orsay, 1999– 2000), fig. 61, pp. 72–73. G. Ackerman, *Jean-Léon Gérôme* (Courbevoie: ACR Édition, 2000), no. 188.

Related work: Sketch, oil on canvas, 31 7/8 × 53 7/8 in., whereabouts unknown

Ill. 109. Charles Gleyre (1806–1874), *Lost Illusions*, 1843, oil on canvas, 61 1/8 × 93 7/8 in., Musée du Louvre, Paris, inv. 10039.

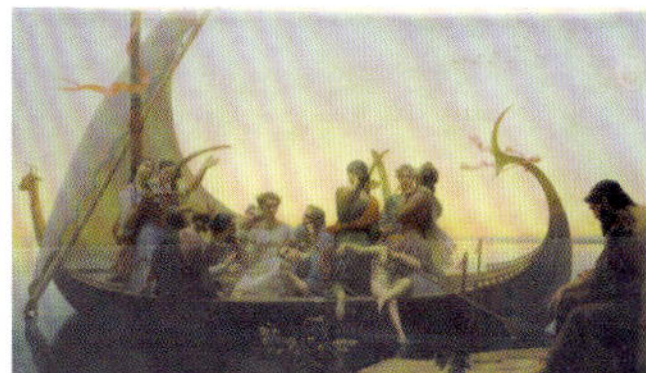

Cat. 128
Félix Teynard (1817-1892)

LUXOR, SMALL BRANCH OF THE NILE, BOAT WITH TRAVELERS

1851–52
Salt print
9 1/8 × 9 1/8 in.
Musée d'Orsay, Paris, inv. PHO 1986 132 28.

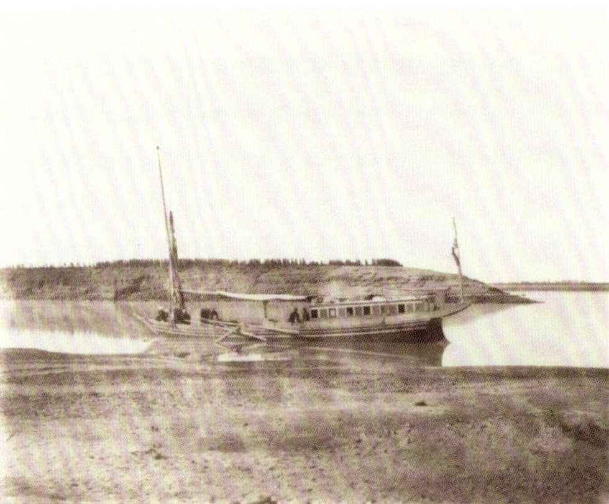

It was certainly the success of *The Prisoner* (cat. 127) that led Gérôme to paint this large canvas, which was exhibited at the Salon of 1869. He re-employed the theme of a boat gliding across the water in an enchanting Egyptian landscape. But here the misfortune of the prisoner and the sadistic violence of his jailers are replaced by the voluptuous sensuality of the harem, a favorite motif in the West's imaginary Orient.

That sensuality is merely suggested here, however. As Théophile Gautier pointed out, far from unveiling the charms of the fair ladies of the harem, Gérôme hides them. "*Excursion of the Harem* shows us a *cangia* sliding down the Nile propelled by ten oarsmen; a cabin on the boat hides the myserious beauties glimpsed behind the curtains, while a musician sings on the prow... The *cangia* glides on the clear, transparent water of the diaphanous river, as though in a kind of luminous haze with magical effect."[1] Thus described, the scene demonstrates Gérôme's skill in playing with temporal effects—the narrative flow evoked by the river, already employed in *The Prisoner*, is here joined by an effect of suspense that obliges the beholder to imagine what can only be glimpsed. Although depicted in a manner that implies accuracy, this scene is implausible. "Harem" originally meant the hidden and forbidden place where the sultan's wives lived. However wealthy the sultan might be and whatever means he allocated to maintaining wives and concubines, taking them on an outing in a boat would go against all custom.

Once again, Gérôme was mingling different sources of inspiration. The overall effect of reverie, of an ideal scene imbued with a certain melancholic restraint, was perhaps suggested to Gérôme by the most famous painting by his own master, Charles Gleyre, *Lost Illusions* (ill. 109). Armand Silvestre seems to allude to Gleyre's painting when praising Gérôme's *Excursion*: "This thoroughly remarkable composition exudes an infinite calm, the calm of warm evenings over quiet waters, before the light wing of night flutteringly disturbs the polished surface of the river and fills the atmosphere with imperceptible vibrations."[2] Edmond About also liked to stress the extent to which Gérôme combined poetic atmosphere with accurate details: "The poetry of the waning day as the landscape on the nearby shore begins to fade, the refinement of tones of gray that veil all while revealing all, this sky and these figures all have the special charm of something exotic very carefully brought back home."[3]

As with *The Prisoner*, when he painted this work Gérôme was recalling his own trips to the Orient. He had just returned from a voyage he took in 1868 with his brother-in-law and a group of friends and artists (cat. 130 to 136). The beauty of the river that reflects the light must be largely the result of his memories and impressions, yet once again photography provided a background for this panoramic composition. Indeed, here Gérôme borrowed the basic composition of a photograph taken several months earlier on the shore of the Red Sea by Albert Goupil (*The Red Sea, Gulf of Aqaba*, cat. 132). In the painting we can see the same mountains and clusters of palm trees photographed by the artist's brother-in-law. And the idea of a scene viewed from a distance, leaving plenty of room for mystery, perhaps came from a photograph by Félix Teynard (cat. 128).[4] Not without irony, Paul Casimir-Périer praised Gérôme's way of skillfully exploiting his painterly qualities: "The artist has again taken the course that best develops the virtues of his painting and mostly eliminates its defects: space, water, small figures, special locations, and recollections or impressions that are personal and characteristic."[5]

Although fantasized and based on poetic and painterly sources, Gérôme's Orient still appears lifelike thanks to his mastery of theatrical composition, his sense of line, and his faithfulness to his own recollections, supported by photography. **D. F.-R.**

1. T. Gautier, "Le Salon de 1869," in *Tableaux à la plume* (Paris: G. Charpentier, 1880), pp. 304–5. **2.** A. Silvestre, "Salon de 1869," *La Revue moderne*, 12th yr., vol. 53, p. 153. **3.** E. About, "Salon de 1869," *Revue des Deux Mondes*, XXXIXth yr., 2nd per., p. 750. **4.** Teynard's photographs were published in 1858 by Goupil in an album titled *Égypte et Nubie, sites et monuments les plus intéressants pour l'étude de l'art et de l'histoire*; given his lively interest in the Orient, Gérôme could hardly have been unaware of these pictures, which constitute a remarkable collection of rare beauty. **6.** P. Casimir-Périer, *Propos d'art à l'occasion du Salon de 1869* (Paris: Michel Lévy, 1869), p. 204.

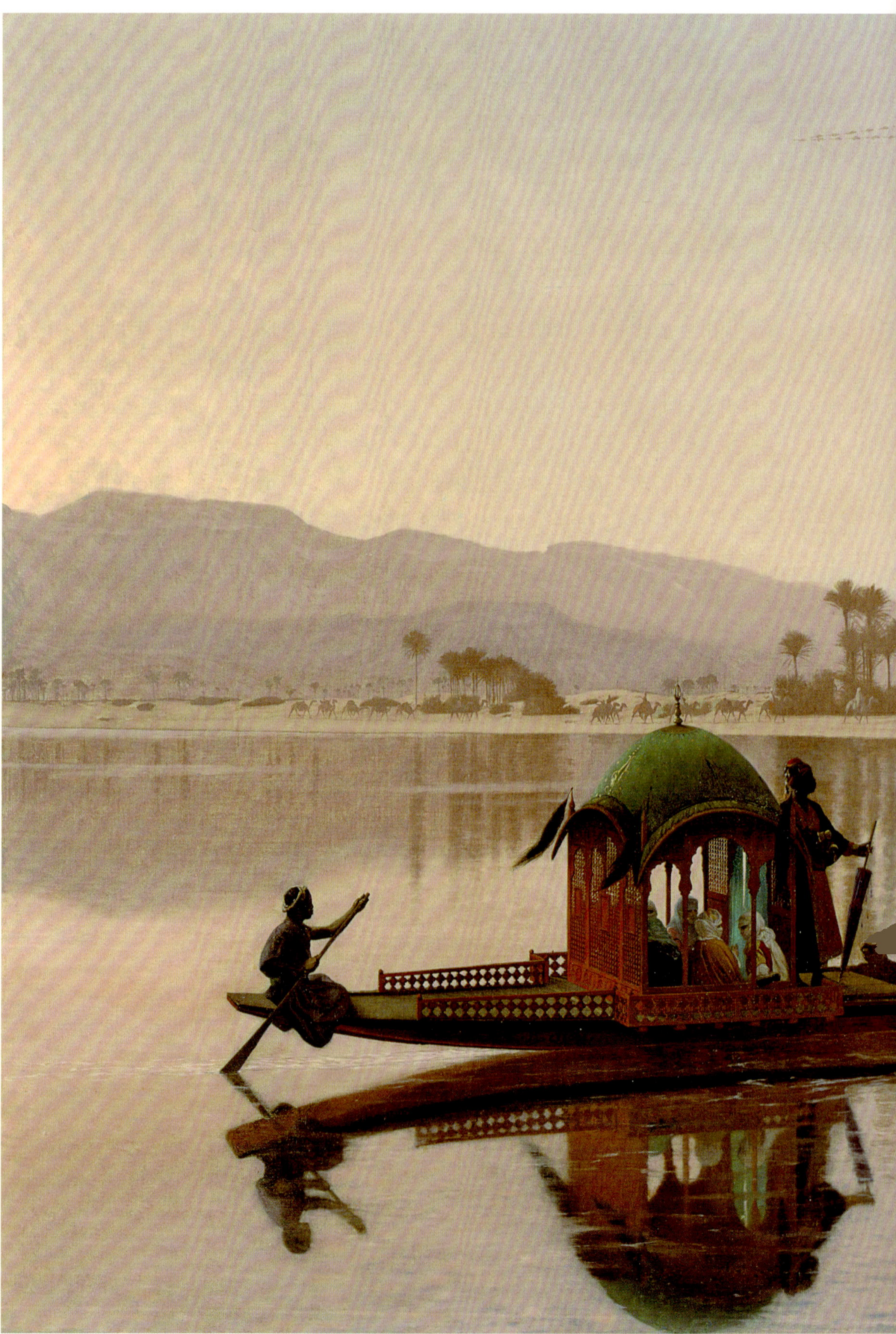

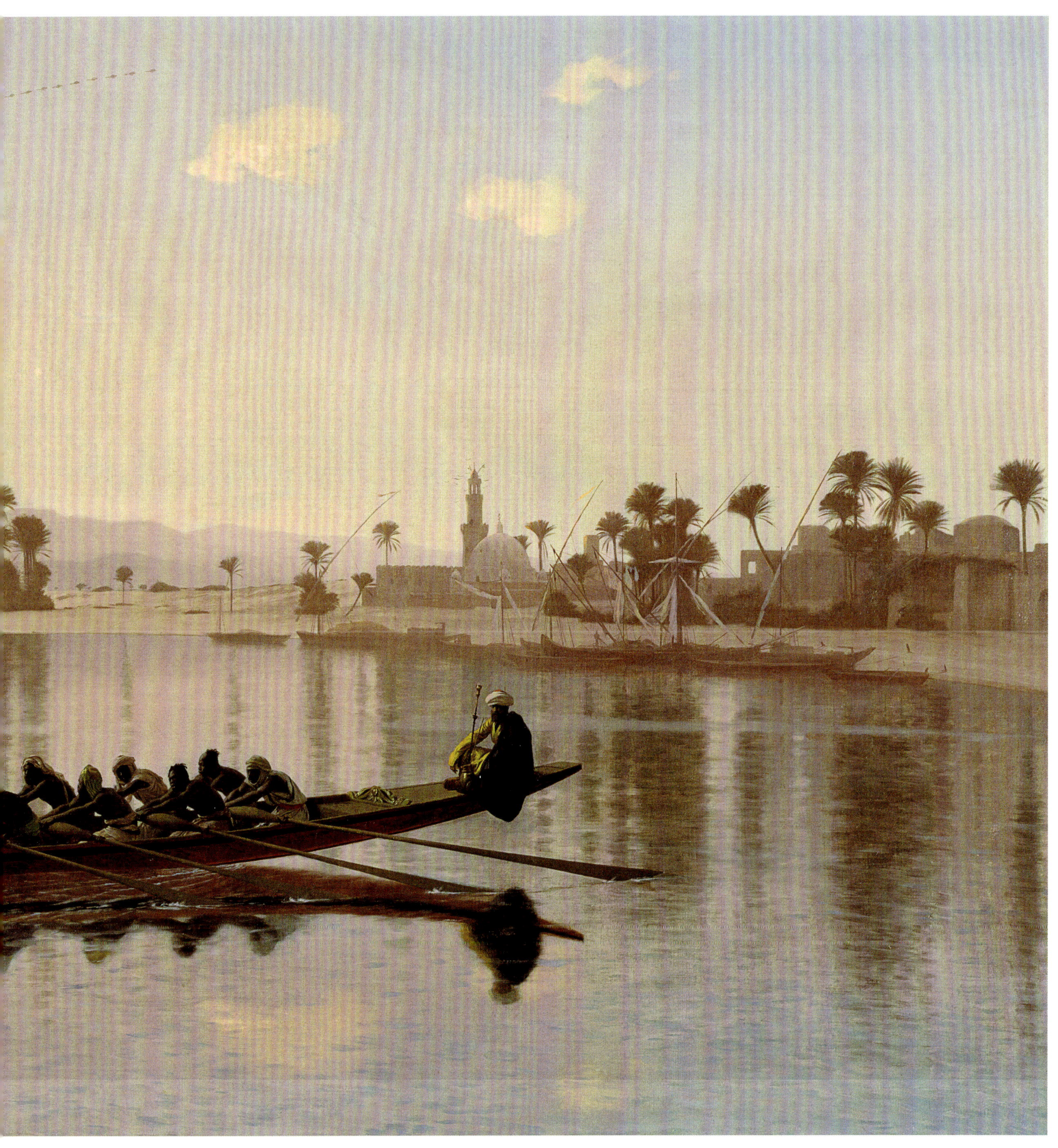

Cat. 130
Albert Goupil (1840–1884)
VIEW OF CAIRO
PLATE 4
–
1868
6 3/8 × 8 1/2 in.

Cat. 131
Albert Goupil
GIZA
PLATE 5
–
1868
6 3/8 × 8 5/8 in.

Cat. 132
Albert Goupil
THE RED SEA AT AQABA
PLATE 41
–
1868
6 1/4 × 8 5/8 in.

Cat. 133
Albert Goupil
SENOURES
PLATE 8
–
1868
6 3/8 × 8 1/2 in.

Cat. 134
Albert Goupil
TWO ARAB ESCORTS
PLATE 55
–
1868
6 1/8 × 8 in.

Cat. 135
Albert Goupil
OUR CAMP IN THE SINAI
PLATE 25
–
1868
6 1/2 × 8 3/4 in.

Cat. 136
Albert Goupil
THE DAMASCUS GATE, JERUSALEM
PLATE 64
–
1868
6 1/2 × 8 1/2 in.

Plates belonging to an album of seventy-seven albumen paper prints taken from wet-collodion glass negatives
Département des Estampes et de la Photographie, Bibliothèque Nationale de France, Paris, UB-331-Petit Folio
–
Provenance: Given by Albert Goupil to Ernest Journault. Purchased by the Département des Estampes et de la Photographie, Bibliothèque Nationale de France, 1996.

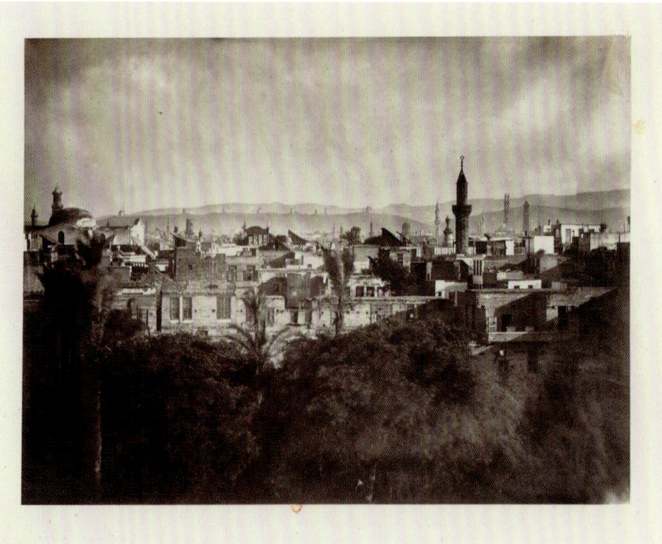

Cat. 130

Gérôme's third trip to the Orient was particularly well documented thanks to Gérôme's own notes, Willem de Famars Testas's diary, Paul Lenoir's book, and to the many studies and sketches done along the way. All that was missing were the photographs taken by the artist's young brother-in-law, Albert Goupil. Famars Testas's diary and a few engraved reproductions in Lenoir's book testified to the existence of these photographs, and their loss was lamented in the catalogue of the exhibition organized by the Musée Hébert in Paris in 1993, devoted precisely to this expedition.

In 1996 the Bibliothèque Nationale de France (BNF) was given the opportunity to fill this gap by purchasing an album that contained photographs. As indicated on the flyleaf, the album belonged to Ernest Journault. The provenance is indirect: the album was bought in the early twentieth century by the family of the person who sold it to the Bibliothèque Nationale. We can only suppose that Albert Goupil gave a copy to each of the seven members of the group. What we do not know, unfortunately, is whether Gérôme himself had a more complete album, that is to say, if the number of prints made over those five months was greater than that contained in this recently resurfaced collection.

The photographs were obviously designed for private use, with no intention of publication or exhibition. Albert Goupil turned out to be a rather poor amateur photographer. Most of his pictures are technical failures: the wet collodion ran and smeared certain images, while other views were darkened by his inexperience with lighting conditions under scorching skies. His composition also left something to be desired—for example, groups were often photographed from too far away. Yet, as often happens with amateur photographs, alongside these failures we find some interesting successes, indeed moments of grace.

Although a few subjects may have been chosen by Goupil alone, it is clear that others resulted from consultation with the painters. The young model Fatma sat for the group in February in Cairo at the request of Famars Testas, appears in photographs by Goupil as well as sketches by Testas and Journault.

Other compositions might have been suggested by Gérôme and his friends with subsequent works in mind; partial reworkings of details from these photographs can be found in paintings done by Gérôme after his return home.

These prints are almost totally devoid of buildings, concentrating on landscapes and figure groups. They closely echo the drawings and watercolors amassed by Léon Bonnat and Gérôme, which suggests that this set of photographs was not an individual work, executed independently of that of the painters, but that Goupil merged his photographic essay with the more ambitious overall project of the trip. **Sylvie Aubenas**

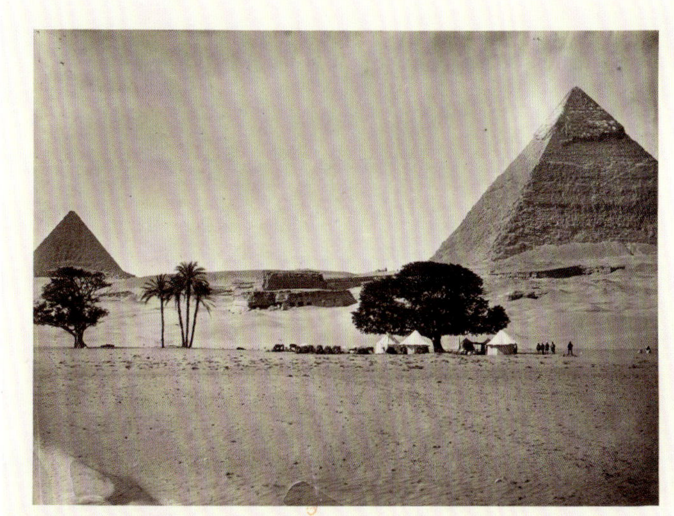
Cat. 131

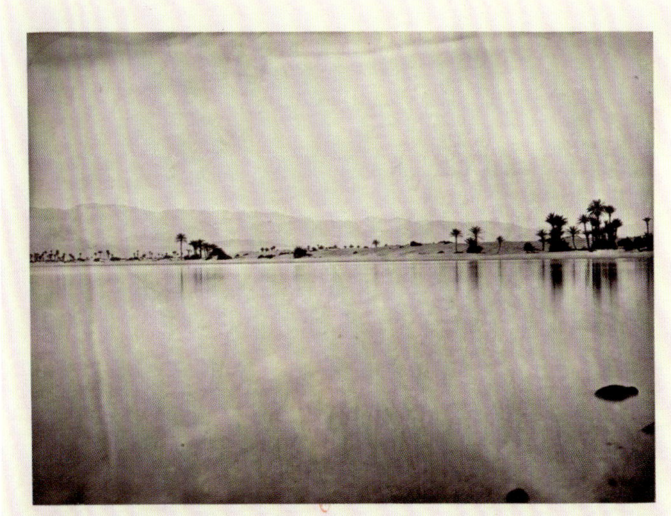
Cat. 132

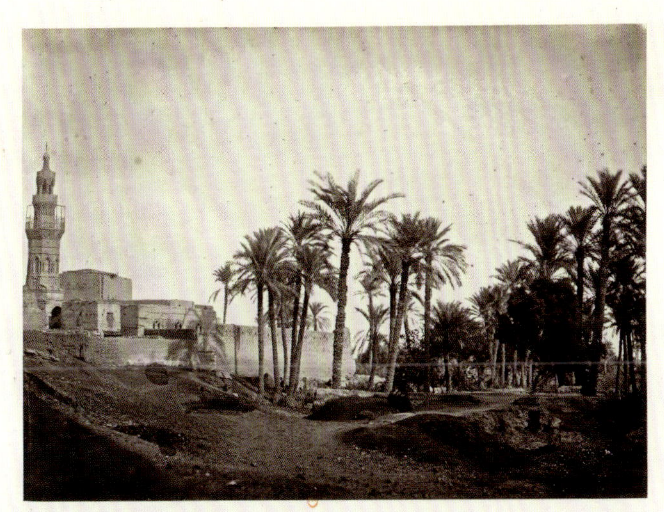
Cat. 133

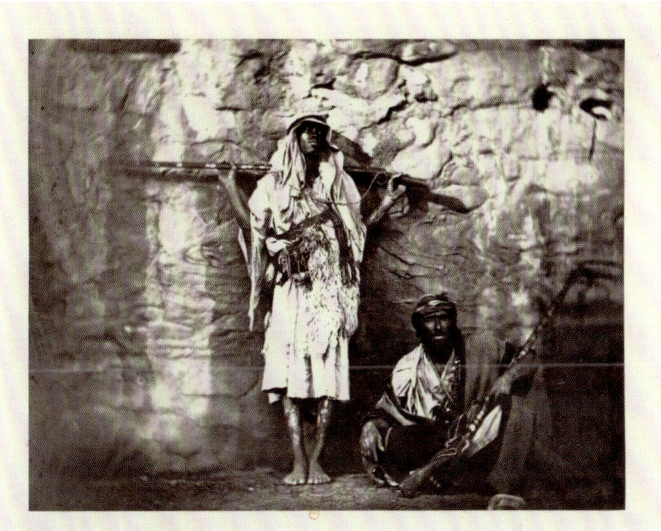
Cat. 134

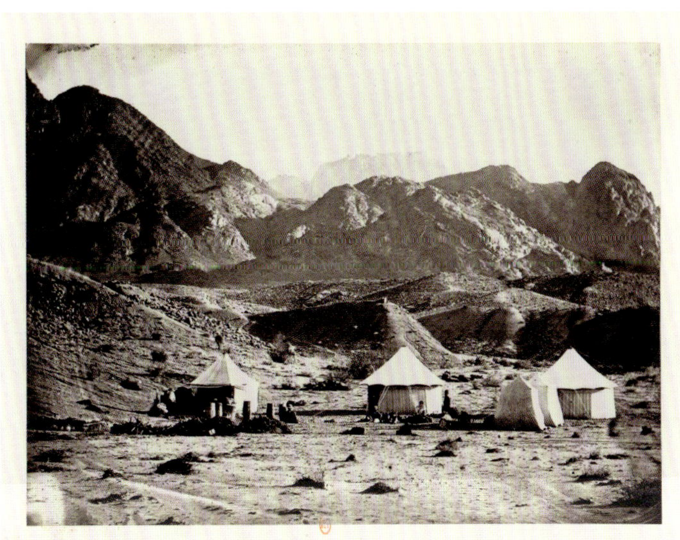
Cat. 135

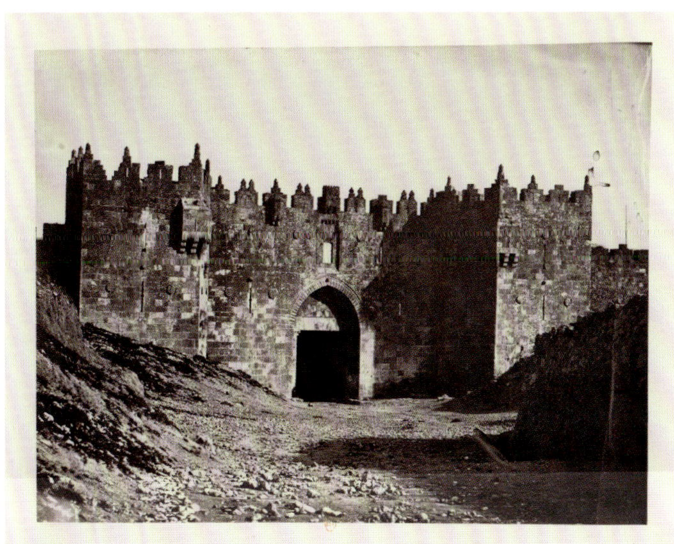
Cat. 136

Cat. 137

ORIENTAL LANDSCAPE, FORTIFIED TOWN (SENOURES?)

–

1868
Oil on paper mounted on canvas
9 ½ × 12 ½ in.
Musée Georges-Garret, Vesoul, inv. 945.2.20.3

–

Provenance: Deed of gift from Morot-Dubufe, 1945.

–

Bibliography: *J.-L. Gérôme*, exh. cat. (Vesoul: Musée Georges-Garret, 1981), no. 172, p. 138.

Cat. 138

ORIENTAL LANDSCAPE, RED SEA

–

1868
Oil on paper mounted on canvas
9 ½ × 12 ½ in.
Annoted lower right : *Mer rouge*
Musée Georges-Garret, Vesoul, inv. 945.2.20.8

–

Provenance: Deed of gift from Morot-Dubufe, 1945.

–

Bibliography: *J.-L. Gérôme*, exh. cat. (Vesoul: Musée Georges-Garret, 1981), no. 169, p. 138.

Cat. 139

ORIENTAL LANDSCAPE, GULF OF AQABA

–

1868
Oil on paper mounted on canvas
9 ⅜ × 12 ⅝ in.
Musée Georges-Garret, Vesoul, inv. 945.2.20.7

–

Provenance: Deed of gift from Morot-Dubufe, 1945.

–

Bibliography: *J.-L. Gérôme*, exh. cat. (Vesoul: Musée Georges-Garret, 1981), no. 173, pp. 138–139.

Cat. 140

MINARETS OF CAIRO

–

1868
Oil on canvas
12 ½ × 9 in.
Musée Georges-Garret, Vesoul, inv. 945.2.21

–

Provenance: Deed of gift from Morot-Dubufe, 1945.

–

Bibliography: *J.-L. Gérôme*, exh. cat. (Vesoul: Musée Georges-Garret, 1981), no. 168, p. 137.

Cat. 141

THE BLUE MOSQUE OR THE AQSUNQUR MOSQUE (BUILT 1341–47, GIVEN DECORATIVE TILING IN 1652–54)

–

1868
Oil on paper mounted on canvas
9 ½ × 12 ½ in.
Musée Georges-Garret, Vesoul, inv. 945.2.20.5

–

Provenance: Deed of gift from Morot-Dubufe, 1945.

–

Bibliography: *J.-L. Gérôme*, exh. cat. (Vesoul: Musée Georges-Garret, 1981), no. 177, pp. 138–139. H. Lafont-Couturier, *Gérôme* (Paris: Herscher, 1998), p. 24.

Gérôme was accompanied on his third trip to the Orient by his brother-in-law, Albert Goupil. As Sylvie Aubenas has pointed out above, the landscape views photographed by Goupil—who was very close to Gérôme and shared his enthusiasm for the Orient—were certainly selected by Gérôme himself. They are not unlike the landscapes photographed by Auguste Bartholdi, who accompanied the artist in 1855 and 1856 (cat. 115 to 123).

The goal of the 1868 expedition was above all artistic. As Paul Lenoir wrote in his diary, "Our goal in leaving for Egypt was to come across subjects for paintings, and to paint them."[1] The small sketches painted by Gérôme (Musée Georges-Garret, Vesoul) underscored this shared intention. Indeed, the artist and his amateur photographer brother-in-law reproduced the same sites from similar viewpoints; Goupil's photograph of the Gulf of Aqaba on the Red Sea presents an image almost identical to Gérôme's painted sketch. Similarly, a painted sketch of Cairo's minarets evokes the photograph.

The fortified town of Senoures was described by Lenoir in the following terms: "We began to leave the sand behind as a village rose in the distance like a vast fortress perched on a high plateau, gracefully crowned by domes and minarets."[2] When comparing the photographs with the sketches made during the trip of 1855-56, it would seem that Gérôme expected photography to provide a faithful overall picture—rather than precise details—that would allow him to provide his future paintings with a background endowed with a certain sense of theater. In 1868, as in 1855-56, he was sensitive to the panoramic effects of photography and to the strong contrast of light and shade, which he recalled in many of his oriental paintings.

Did Goupil make other prints of his photographs that might have subsequently been given to the Egyptian authorities by Gérôme? A letter from the office of the khedive of Egypt, dated November 18, 1868, thanked the artist for "the set of photographs that you kindly sent me, [which] will be a valuable souvenir for me, constantly reminding me of your overly short sojourn in Egypt."[3] Unfortunately, the nature of these photographs was never specified.

D. F.-R.

1. P. Lenoir, *Le Fayoum, le Sinaï et Petra: expédition dans la moyenne Égypte et l'Arabie, sous la direction de Jean-Léon Gérôme* (Paris: Henri Plon, 1872), foreword. 2. Ibid., p. 96. 3. Letter dated Nov. 18, 1868, now in the Gérôme family archives.

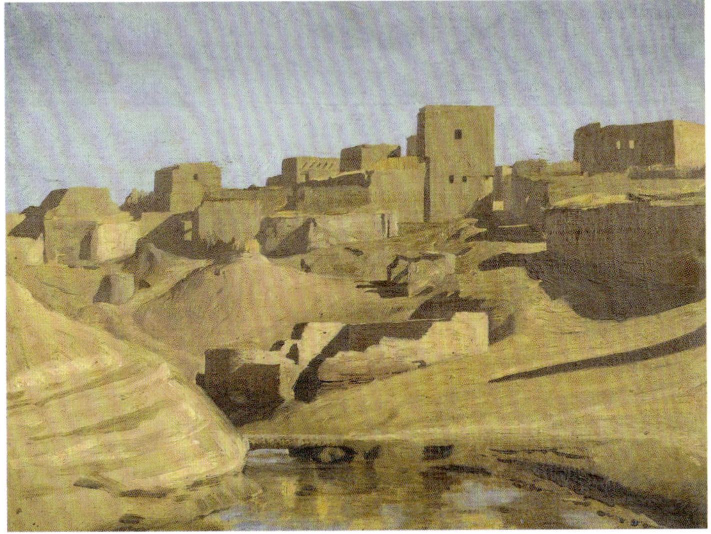
Cat. 137

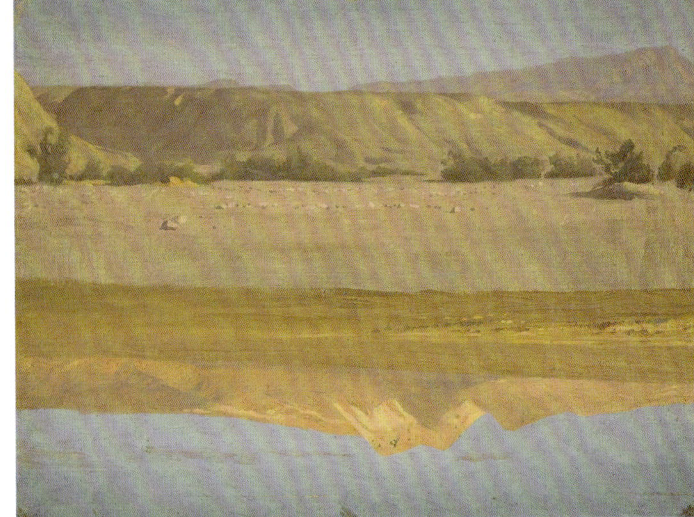
Cat. 139

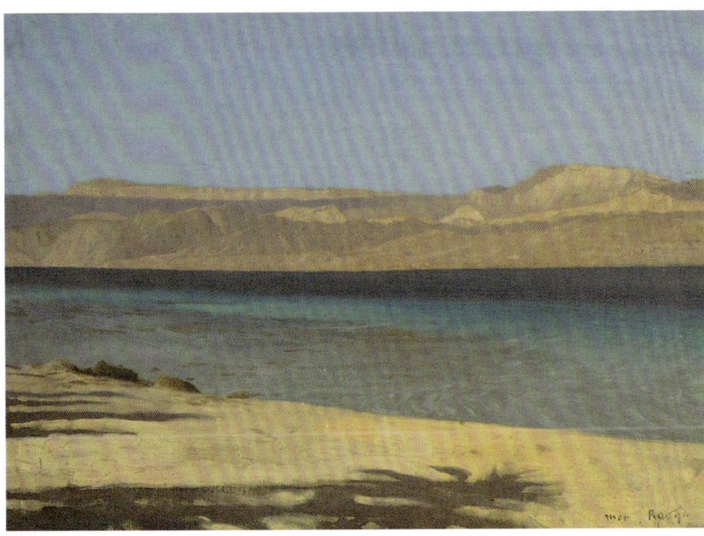

Cat. 138

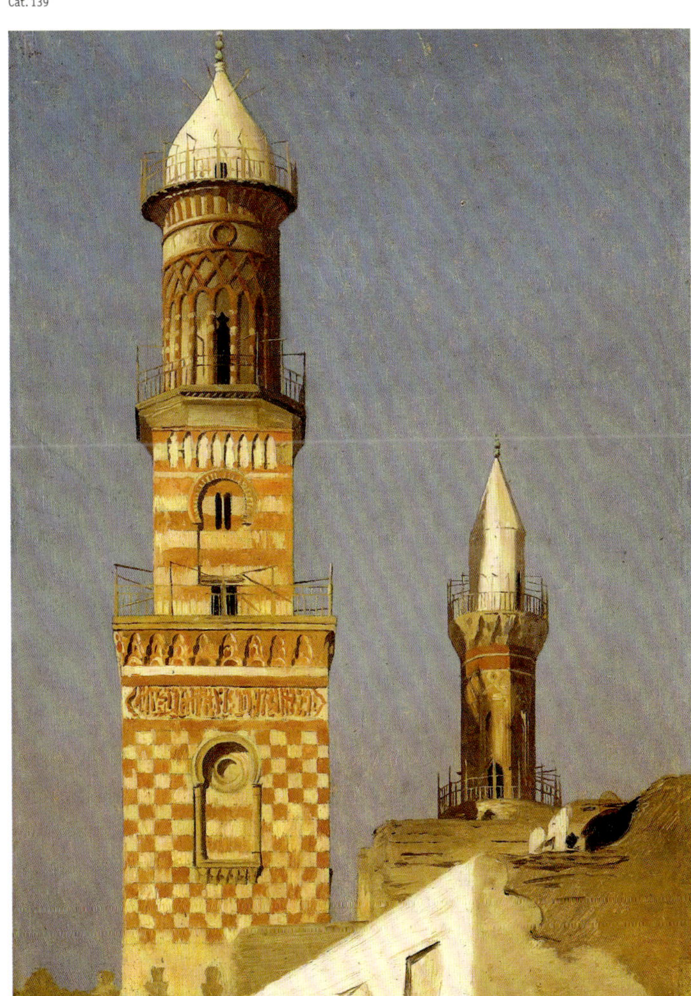
Cat. 140

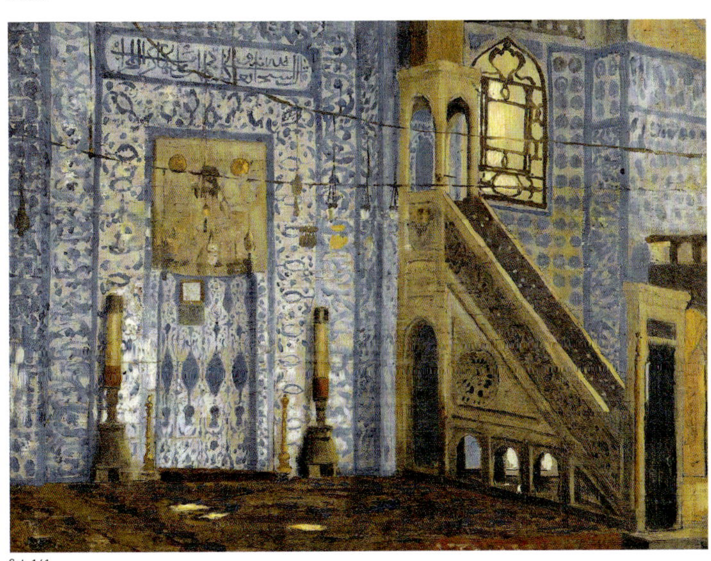
Cat. 141

Cat. 142

ARABS CROSSING THE DESERT

–

1870
Oil on panel
16 ¼ × 22 in.
Signed lower left: *J.L. GEROME*
Najd collection, on loan to the Metropolitan Museum of Art, New York
Not exhibited

–

Provenance: Tuckerman to Goupil, 1880. Goupil to Knoedler, New York, 1880 (for 25,000 francs). Sordoni collection, Wilkes-Barre, Pennsylvania. Mathaf Gallery, London. Najd collection.

–

Bibliography: *Recueil. Œuvres de Jean-Léon Gérôme,* BNF Estampes, vol. VII, no. 7. E. Strahan [Earl Shinn], *Gérôme: A Collection of the Works of J.-L. Gérôme in One Hundred Photogravures* (New York: Samuel L. Hall, 1881). C. Juler, *Najd Collection of Orientalist Paintings* (London: Manara, 1991), p. 132. G. Ackerman, *Jean-Léon Gérôme* (Courbevoie: ACR Édition, 2000), no. 208H. Lafont-Couturier, *Gérôme and Goupil: Art and Enterprise*, exh. cat., trans. I. Ollivier (Bordeaux: Musée Goupil, 2000–1; also New York: Dahesh Museum of Art, 2001, and Pittsburgh: The Frick Art & Historical Center, 2001), no. 64, pp. 114–117, 160.

The setting of this painting is the desert, a popular Romantic motif since the days of Eugène Delacroix and Eugène Fromentin. Gérôme had seen such a landscape during his 1856 trip with Auguste Bartholdi and again in 1868, notably accompanied by Paul Lenoir, Albert Goupil, Léon Bonnat, and Willem de Famars Testas. He was therefore familiar with this harsh, wild, constantly shifting world—Lenoir described a sand storm that hit Gérôme and his companions: "[T]he dune at our backs diminished visibly, lifted as it was by the tempest, invading everything like a cascade... The Arabs, after having lent us a hand in our distress, lay down in the sand, thus avoiding painful contact with the wind, which slashed our faces like the lashes of a whip."[1]

As early as 1856, and despite this experience in 1868, Gérôme depicted the type of figures seen in this canvas as masters of the elements, which they braved with impassive dignity. The frieze-like composition of the painting stresses the riders' determination to confront the elements—they cross the desert with such profound serenity that nothing disturbs the hems of their garments or the harmonious folds of their turbans. The glossy coats of their steeds remain smooth and clean despite the windblown sand. Gérôme thereby modified the Romantic motif: there is nothing here of the swirling power of Delacroix's desert riders. Gérôme's brush lends Arab riders the ancient calm and panache of great viziers straight out of *The Arabian Nights.*

The desert here provides a vast panorama for the unfolding of the scene. This panoramic view of the desert was typical of the photographs taken first by Bartholdi and later by Goupil (ill. 110). Here again, Gérôme turned to photography less for its accuracy of detail than for the rightness of the overall impression it gave. So even though Gérôme's figures resemble the slender young Arabs who accompanied him in 1868, in his canvases they are lent a purely painterly elegance—one of the men on foot in *Arabs Crossing the Desert* is dressed like an Arnaut (cat. 125, 126), whose colorful garments are a long way from the Arabs' fairly simple dress.

D. F.-R.

1. P. Lenoir, *Le Fayoum, le Sinaï et Petra, expédition dans la moyenne Égypte et l'Arabie pétrée, sous la direction de J-L. Gérôme* (Paris: Henri Plon, 1872), p. 84.

Ill. 110. Albert Goupil (1840–1884), *Route Towards Sinaï*, 1868, albumen print from a collodion-on-glass negative, 6 ½ × 8 ½ in., Département des Estampes, Bibliothèque Nationale de France, Paris, Ub331 pt fol., pl. 17.

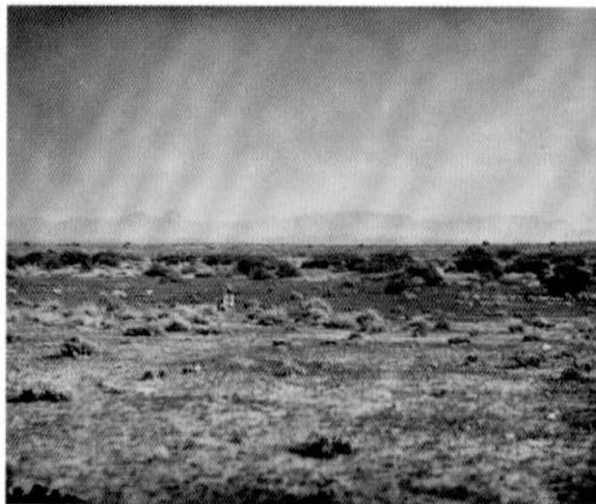

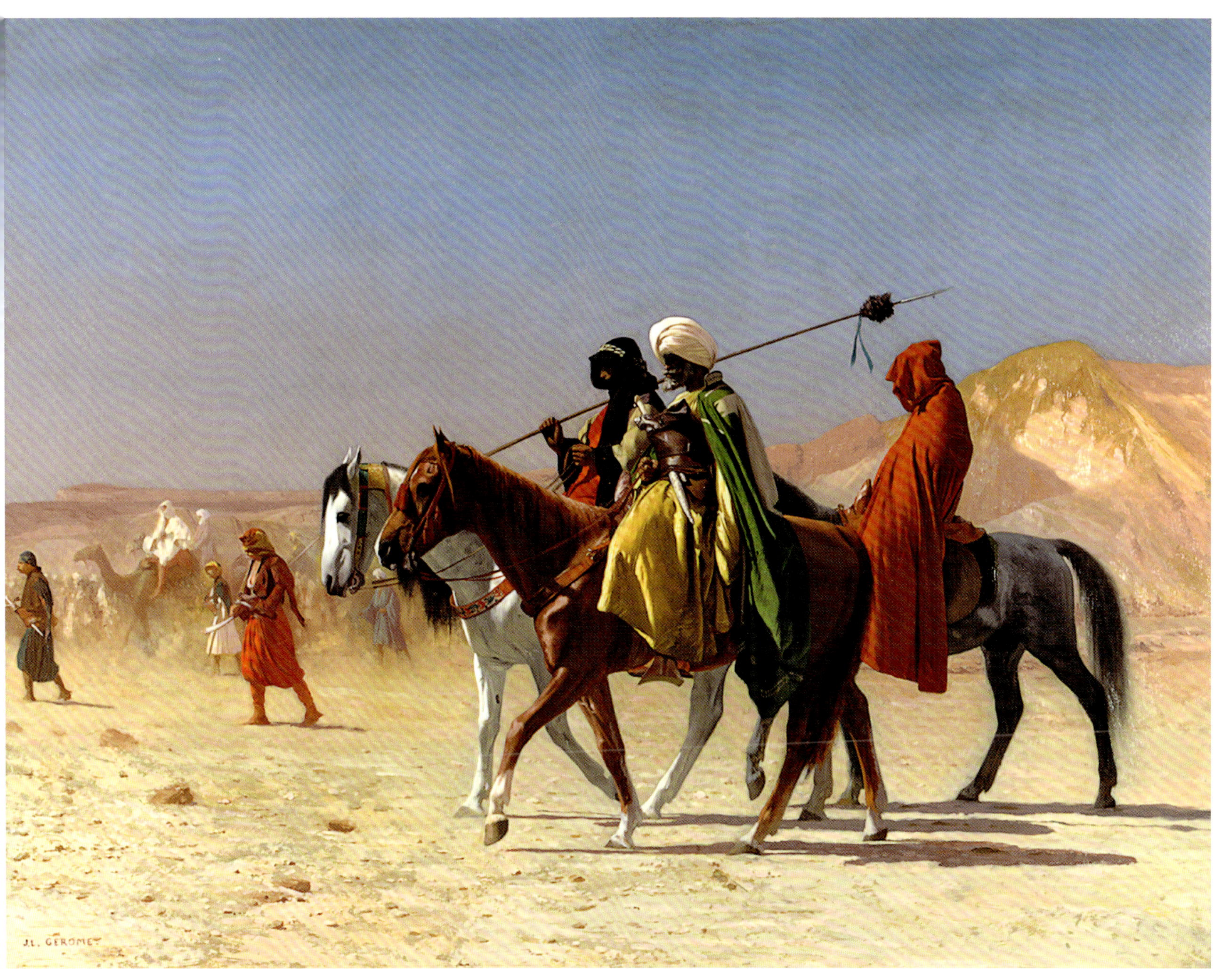
J.L. GEROME

Cat.143

A TURKISH BUTCHER BOY IN JERUSALEM

–

1862
Oil on panel
13 × 10 ½ in.
Signed above right: *J.L. GEROME*
Frankel Family Trust, Santa Ana, California

–

Provenance: Gérôme to Goupil, Sept. 1862, stock book no. 719, "Boucher égyptien" (for 2,000 francs). Goupil to Paul Demidoff, Jan. 1863 (for 6,000 francs). Demidoff sale, Hôtel Drouot, Paris, May 25–26, 1864, lot 4 ("Un Boucher turc. Tableau exposé en 1862 [*sic*]"), to Goupil, stock book no. 1228, "Boucher turc" (for 6,000 francs). Goupil to Knoedler, New York, Jan. 1865 (for 6,500 francs). John Hoey, Jr., New York, by 1867. William B. Dinsmore, New York. Dinsmore sale, Fifth Avenue Art Galleries, New York, Apr. 14–15, 1892, lot 113. H. O'Neill, New York. O'Neill sale, Plaza Hotel, New York, Jan. 20, 1921, lot 61. Mrs. C. F. Darlington, New York. Shepherd Gallery, New York. sold to Mr. & Mrs. Joseph M. Tanenbaum, Toronto, Mar. 1974. Tanenbaum sale, Sotheby's, New York, Oct. 24, 1996, lot 87. Mr. Edward and Mrs. Frances Frankel.

–

Exhibition history: Salon of 1863, no. 771. Exposition Universelle, Paris, 1867, no. 295.

–

Bibliography: E. Strahan [Earl Shinn], *The Art Treasures of America: Being the Choicest Works of Art in the Public and Private Collections of North America*, 3 vols. (Philadelphia: G. Barrie, 1880), vol. 3, p. 78. F. F. Hering, *Gérôme: The Life and Works of Jean Léon Gérôme* (New York: Cassell, 1892), pp. 105, 242. V. Guillemin, "Étude sur le peintre et sculpteur Jean-Léon Gérôme (1824–1904)," *Académie des sciences, belles-lettres et arts de Besançon. Procès-verbaux et mémoires. Année 1904* (Besançon, 1905), p. 150. M. L. H. Reymert et al., *Ingres and Delacroix through Degas and Puvis de Chavannes: The Figure in French Art 1800–1870*, exh. cat. (New York: Shepherd Gallery, 1975), pp. 255–56, no. 106. L. d'Argencourt and D. Druick, eds. *The Other Nineteenth Century: Paintings and Sculpture in the Collection of Mr. and Mrs. Joseph M. Tanenbaum*, exh. cat. (Ottawa: The National Gallery of Canada, 1978), pp. 110–11, no. 34. G. Ackerman, *The Life and Work of Jean-Léon Gérôme, with a Catalogue Raisonné* (New York and London: Sotheby's, 1986), pp. 65, 67, 214–15, no. 145. G. Ackerman, "Gérôme's Oriental Paintings and the Western Genre Tradition," *Arts Magazine*, vol. 60, no. 7 (Mar. 1986), pp. 78, 79, fig. 17. G. Ackerman, *Jean-Léon Gérôme* (Paris: ACR Édition, 2000), pp. 64, 252–53, no. 145. H. Lafont-Couturier, *Gérôme and Goupil: Art and Enterprise*, exh. cat., trans. I. Ollivier (Bordeaux: Musée Goupil, 2000–1; also New York: Dahesh Museum of Art, 2001, and Pittsburgh: The Frick Art & Historical Center, 2001), p. 152.

Ill. 111. Anonymous, *Street Seller (Algeria)*, ca. 1860, albumen print, 10 × 7 ½ in., The Getty Research Institute, Los Angeles, inv. 2008.R.3, box T35, #600/11Unkn.

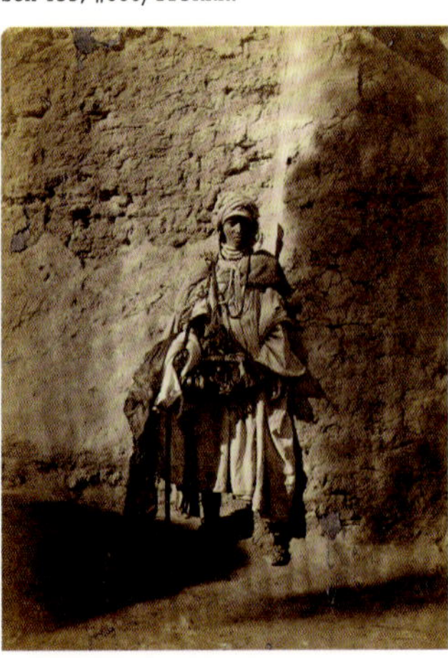

Though sometimes identified as "Boucher égyptien" (Egyptian Butcher),[1] this picture was exhibited at the Salon of 1863 as "Boucher turc à Jerusalem" (Turkish Butcher in Jerusalem) and it is listed as such in the manuscript catalogue of Gérôme's works prior to 1883.[2] The specificity of the title suggests that the picture's subject may have derived from Gérôme's trip to Jerusalem in the spring of 1862.[3] It shows a young butcher leaning up against the buttress of a massive wall. One arm lazily akimbo and the other holding a long pipe, he impassively engages the viewer with a vacant glare and gaping mouth. Immediately adjacent to his head, entrails hang from pegs. Propped up at the base of the buttress below are two sheep's heads, and unceremoniously scattered at the butcher's feet on the stone-paved street are the heads of more sheep and some goats. Above this grisly ordure, the wall reflects the sunlight of an oppressively hot day. The scene could not be farther from the courtly and culinary refinement of seventeenth-century Versailles, where Louis XIV is shown dining with Molière in *Molière Breakfasting with Louis XIV* (cat. 84), also exhibited by Gérôme in the 1863 Salon.

A Turkish Butcher Boy in Jerusalem was among the first of many ethnographic studies of single figures that Gérôme would paint throughout his career. These were evidently easy to produce and they found a ready market, appealing to widespread curiosity about foreign ethnic types, costumes, and characters in a manner similar to mid-nineteenth-century photographs (ill. 111).

The critical reception of the painting in 1863 was generally enthusiastic. Although the more ambitious *Molière Breakfasting with Louis XIV* was severely criticized like many of Gérôme's historical pictures, *A Turkish Butcher Boy* was valued as an ethnographic document and was reproduced as such in popular illustrated journals like *Le Magasin pittoresque*.[4] Critics encouraged Gérôme in his Orientalist vein, pushing him to capitalize on his strengths as a descriptive realist. Gérôme is best, Paul Mantz asserted, when he "puts himself face to face with living reality and copies it naïvely."[5]

Whatever their assumed value as documents, such genre scenes had the added appeal of novelty. Théodore Pelloquet found in *A Turkish Butcher Boy* the "savor of a certain rarity and a strange oddity."[6] That bizarre quality, however, only confirmed common European preconceptions. The butcher, as François Beslay wrote, was depicted "in the lazy attitude so natural to men of the Orient."[7] The animal parts littering the scene similarly conjured up fantasies of Eastern barbarism and brutality. Alfred Nettement likened the butcher to an executioner: "His knife is in his sash; he holds his pipe and his physiognomy exudes a brutal indifference. One divines in his look the soul, without anger and without pity, of a man accustomed to plunging the blade into palpitating entrails. This is only a butcher, but one could easily take him for an executioner."[8] At the 1866 Salon, Gérôme reinforced this association by exhibiting *Heads of the Rebel Beys at the Mosque El Assaneyn* (cat. 144), which featured two guards presiding indifferently over a pile of human heads in a remarkably similar composition. For a few critics, *A Turkish Butcher Boy*'s pretext of ethnographic documentation did not excuse Gérôme's choice of gruesome subject. Claude Vignon did not understand the interest of "this vulgar and repugnant study."[9] Beslay was likewise put off: "it seems that one can hear the flies buzzing around the painting."[10]

Still beholden to the painterly colorism of certain Romantic painters, a few critics also faulted Gérôme for the "cold" polish and precision of his technique. Jean Rousseau thought he had needlessly set himself up for a negative comparison: "Why pick up a theme that Decamps had already treated with all the splendors of color and light, above all when one lacks precisely these qualities? It is to advertise the deficiencies of his talent."[11] Most, however, were able to marvel at Gérôme's technical virtuosity. Théophile Thoré, no friend of the artist, described *A Turkish Butcher Boy* as a "marvel of fine, patient execution."[12] As for Jules Claretie: "I cannot admire enough the freshly cut sheep heads. These miniscule morsels are painted with an exquisite delicacy and astonishing verity."[13] On the occasion of its re-exhibition at the 1867 Exposition Universelle, A. Bonnin classed it among Gérôme's few "perfect works."[14] **S. A.**

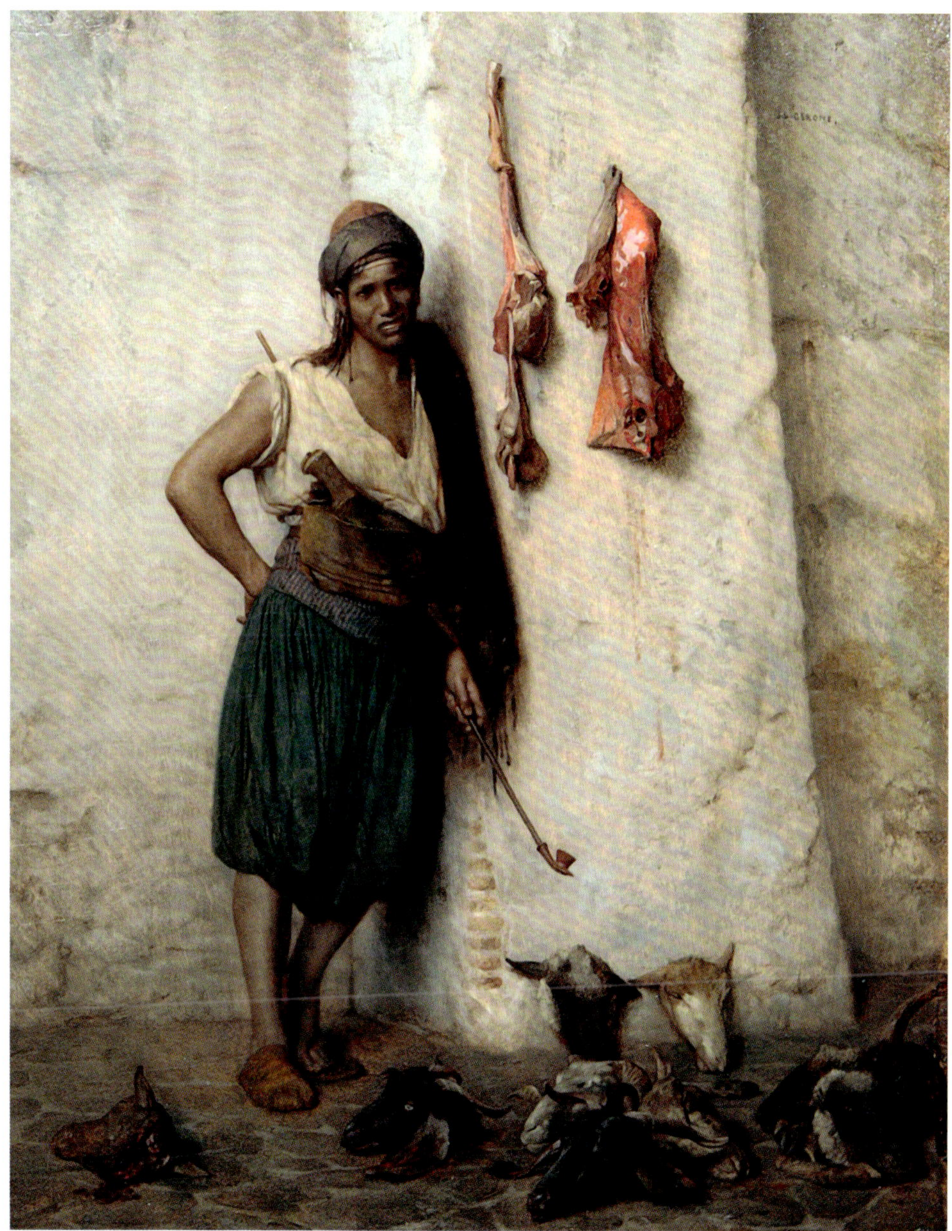

1. In reproductions of the painting published by Goupil, for instance, it was given the title "Boucher égyptien." See H. Lafont-Couturier, *Gérôme and Goupil: Art and Enterprise*, exh. cat., trans. I. Ollivier (Bordeaux: Musée Goupil, 2000–1; also New York: Dahesh Museum of Art, 2001, and Pittsburgh: The Frick Art & Historical Center, 2001), p. 152. There is also some confusion in the Goupil stock books, where the initial 1862 entry is listed as "Boucher égyptien," but the 1864 entry uses the title "Boucher turc," in keeping with the Demidoff sale catalogue of that year. That the pictures are one and the same is confirmed by the fact that Demidoff is listed as the buyer of "Boucher égyptien" in 1863, and that the "Vente Demidoff" is listed as the provenance of the "Boucher turc" in 1864. **2.** See L. d'Argencourt and D. Druick, eds. *The Other Nineteenth Century: Paintings and Sculpture in the Collection of Mr. and Mrs. Joseph M. Tanenbaum*, exh. cat. (Ottawa: The National Gallery of Canada, 1978), p. 110. **3.** See Sotheby's, New York, *19th Century European Paintings, Drawings and Sculpture*, Oct 24, 1996, lot 87, entry by G. Ackerman. **4.** See [Anon.], "Salon de 1863," *Le Magasin pittoresque*, vol. 31, no. 39 (Sept. 1863), pp. 305–6. The painting here provides the author with a pretext for a short discussion of Turkish and Islamic customs and mores. **5.** P. Mantz, "Salon de 1863," *Gazette des Beaux-Arts*, vol. 14, no. 6 (June 1, 1863), p. 495 ["Combien l'habile artiste est mieux inspiré… lorsqu'au lieu de chercher dans le passé des gaietés qui n'y sont pas, il se met face à face avec la réalité vivante et la copie naïvement. Son Boucher turc… est une peinture intéressante"]. **6.** T. Pelloquet, "Salon de 1863," *L'Exposition: Journal du Salon de 1863*, May 24, 1863, p. 2 ["une saveur d'une certaine rareté et d'une bizarrerie étrange"]. **7.** F. Beslay, "L'Art français en 1863," *Revue d'économie chrétienne*, n. s., vol. 4 (May 1863), p. 883 ["dans l'attitude paresseuse si naturelle aux hommes de l'Orient"]. **8.** A. Nettement, "Salon de 1863," *La Semaine des familles*, Aug. 1, 1863, p. 690 ["Son coutelas est à sa ceinture; il tient sa pipe, et sa physionomie respire une indifférence brutale. On devine dans ses regards l'âme sans colère et sans pitié d'un homme habitué à enfoncer le couteau dans des entrailles palpitantes. Ce n'est qu'un boucher, mais on en ferait facilement un bourreau"]. **9.** C. Vignon, "Le Salon de 1863," *Le Correspondant*, vol. 23 (June 1863), p. 383 ["cette vulgaire et répugnante étude de mœurs orientales"]. **10.** F. Beslay 1863 (as in n. 7), p. 883 ["il semble qu'on entende bourdonner les mouches autour du tableau"]. **11.** J. Rousseau, "Salon de 1863," *L'Univers illustré*, June 11, 1863, p. 219 ["A quoi bon ramasser un thème que Decamps avait déjà traité avec toutes les splendeurs de la couleur et de la lumière, alors surtout qu'on pèche précisément par les défauts contraires? C'était afficher les lacunes de son talent"]. Rousseau could have been referring to one of several paintings of Turkish butchers by Decamps, two of which Gérôme may have seen in Paris, one at the 1855 Exposition Universelle and the other in the Decamps sale of 1861. See D. F. Mosby, *Alexandre-Gabriel Decamps, 1803–1860*, 2 vols. (New York: Garland, 1977), vol. 2, p. 419, no. 70, pl. 116B; and pp. 579–80, no. 392, pl. 65A. **12.** T. Thoré, "Exposition de 1867," in *Salons de W. Bürger, 1861 à 1868* (Paris: Vve. Jules Renouard, 1870), p. 351 ["il a une certaine personnalité dans ses représentations de l'Orient moderne, par exemple dans le *Boucher turc*: prodige d'exécution fine, patiente, très-distinguée"]. **13.** J. Claretie, "Lettres familières sur le Salon de 1863," *Jean Diable*, no. 29 (June 13, 1863), p. 461 ["Je ne puis… assez admirer les têtes d'agneaux fraichement coupées. Ces morceaux minuscules sont peints avec une délicatesse exquise et une étonnante vérité"]. **14.** A. Bonnin, *Les Écoles françaises et étrangères en 1867* (Paris: E. Dentu, 1868), p. 99 ["l'Orient lui a inspiré des œuvres parfaits comme le *Boucher turc*"].

Cat. 144

HEADS OF THE REBEL BEYS AT THE MOSQUE EL ASSANEYN

1866
Oil on panel
21 ¼ × 17 ¼ in.
Signed center left: *J.L. GEROME*
Orientalist Museum, Doha, inv. OM.184

Provenance: Property of W. H. Stewart, New York. Exposition Universelle, Paris, 1867, lent by Mr. Stewart. Stewart sale, New York, Feb. 3–5, 1898, lot 39 (for $3,700). Schnittjer and Son, PBNY, 1943 (for $160). Louis Kaplan sale, PBNY, 1944 (for $310). Sugerman, 1945 (for $70). PBNY, Oct. 7, 1977, sale 4026, lot 2290 (for $27,000). Forbes Magazine collection. Christie's, New York, Oct. 14, 1993, lot 260.

Exhibition History: Salon of 1866, Paris. Exposition Universelle, Paris, 1867.

Bibliography: A. Baignères, "Salon de 1866," *Revue contemporaine*, vol. 86 (1866), pp. 350–51. C. Blanc, *Gazette des Beaux-Arts*, 1866, vol. 20, pp. 516–17; vol. 21, pp. 42–44. M. Du Camp, "Salon de 1866," *Revue des Deux Mondes*, vol. 63 (1866), pp. 701–3. T. Gautier, *Le Moniteur officiel*, May 15, 1866, p. 577. M. de Montifaud, "Salon de 1866," *L'Artiste*, 1866, vol. I, p. 200. C. de Sault, *Le Temps*, May 26, 1866. G. Ackerman, *Jean-Léon Gérôme* (Courbevoie: ACR Édition, 2000), no. 161, p. 260-61. H. Lafont-Couturier, *Gérôme and Goupil: Art and Enterprise*, exh. cat., trans. I. Ollivier (Bordeaux: Musée Goupil, 2000–1; also New York: Dahesh Museum of Art, 2001, and Pittsburgh: The Frick Art & Historical Center, 2001), pp. 20, 38, 117, 155, 165.

The mosque of Sheikh El Assaneyn (or El-Hassanein) was built in Cairo in the thirteenth century. It is not known exactly what event Gérôme was referring to in his catalogue entry for the Salon of 1866, which mentioned the public display of the heads of beys executed by Salek-Kachef.

The scene is nevertheless striking: two armed guards on either side of the doorway watch over their sinister booty. Whereas most critics of this abundantly reviewed painting stressed Gérôme's accurate rendering—a commentator even wrote that "the scene is rendered with such horrifying reality that one thinks M. Gérôme seems to have witnessed it"[1]—Maxime Du Camp proudly flaunted his own knowledge of the Orient by pointing out the liberties taken by the artist. "I would take issue with M. Gérôme. In the Orient, severed heads that are exhibited are not hung by the hair, nor are they dumped pell-mell on the steps of a stairway; they are impaled on iron pikes above a doorway or a wall, and remain there until the kites, vultures, and other birds of prey collect the refuse and spirit them away."[2] Du Camp was certainly right—Gérôme never mentioned having witnessed such events. Furthermore, it is often hard to distinguish authentic Western eye-witness accounts from phony ones. Although Du Camp's review of the Salon asserts that he witnessed such executions, a report on Egypt under Muhammad Ali Pasha written by Victor Schoelcher, who was not inclined to be overly subjective, stated that the usual punishments were beating and whipping, which were publicly administered only to men.[3] As to the heads here, they somewhat resemble the ones in Théodore Géricault's *Severed Heads* (prior to 1822, Nationalmuseum, Stockholm). Rather than being hacked off by a sword, Gérôme's heads seem to have been severed by a guillotine.

The subject evokes oriental ferociousness, which was one of the founding pillars—in counterpoint to oriental sensuality—of an Orientalism already strongly present in the Western imagination in Gérôme's time. As Du Camp pointed out, back in 1837 Alexandre-Gabriel Decamps had exhibited a painting titled *The Punishment of the Hooks* (ill. 113), which evoked the alleged savagery of Middle Eastern customs. With Romantic intensity, Decamps's painting depicted the violent mood of the milling crowd that came to witness the dreadful torture.

Gérôme's scene is simpler. The apparent accuracy of the detail economically conveys the whole—while the doorway of the mosque is depicted, as Sophie Makariou and Charlotte Maury discuss in their essay (p. 260), by a stone architrave and heavy, double doors of wood (which Gérôme subsequently used as a studio prop), the artist exploited the effect of shadow and light between the exterior and the interior of the mosque to create a scenic background that reinforces the overall theatricality (ill. 112).

The quest for accuracy makes the apparent horror of the scene seem more remote. As the reviewer for *Le Temps* rightly pointed out, "There is a bizarre contradiction between the artist's neat-and-tidy manner and his pursuit of violently sensual subject matter; using a magnifying glass to paint a mass grave, to paint the horrific, is either over- or underspiced. M. Gérôme seems to be saying to the public, the way one would say to children overly upset at a tragic scene in the theater, 'Don't be afraid, it hasn't really happened.'"[4] A caricature by Cham wittily played on this sense of remoteness (ill. 182, p. 348). Several decades later Gérôme recalled this morbid motif of a pile of heads when he sculpted his *Tamerlane* (cat. 183). **D. F.-R.**

Ill. 112. Pascal Sebah (1823–1886), *Façade of the Al-Azhar mosque*, ca. 1870, albumen print, 9 ¾ × 7 ½ in., Bibliothèque de l'Institut, Paris, Fol Schlumberger 132, f° 43.

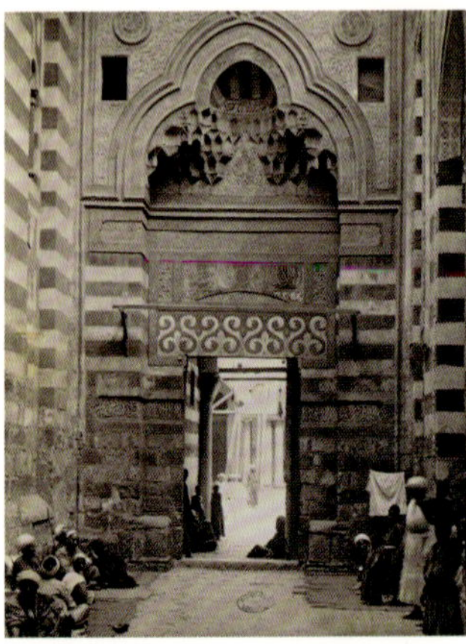

Ill. 113. Alexandre-Gabriel Decamps (1803–1860), *The Punishment of the Hooks*, 1837, oil on canvas, 35 ¾ × 53 ¼ in., The Wallace Collection, London.

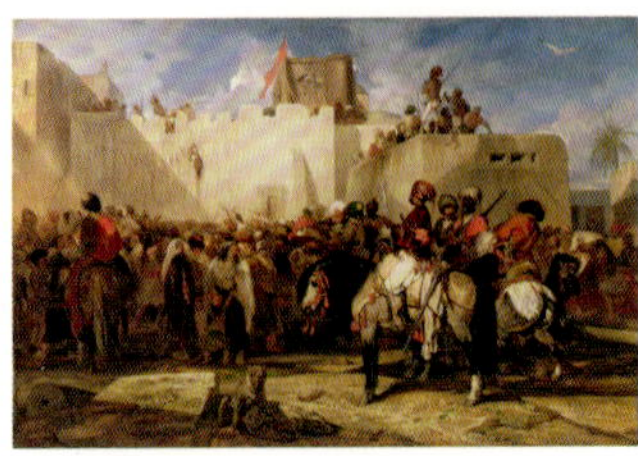

1. "Jean-Léon Gérôme," *Journal des débats*, June 2, 1866, quoted by G. Haller [Wilhelmine Joséphine Fould], in *Nos grands peintres* (Paris: Goupil & Cie, 1892), p. 145. **2.** M. Du Camp, "Le Salon de 1866," *Revue des Deux Mondes*, vol. 63 (1866), p. 703. **3.** V. Schoelcher, *L'Égypte en 1845* (Paris: Pagnerre, 1846), p. 24. Schoelcher mentions that in 1839 a French officer witnessed the beheading of twelve men, but does not however refer to how the heads of the victims were displayed. **4.** C. de Sault, "Salon de 1866, 13e article, 3," *Le Temps*, May 26, 1866, p. 1.

After Jean-Léon Gérôme, *Heads of the Rebel Beys at the Mosque El-Assaneyn* [1866], photograph by Goupil & Cie, "Musée Goupil & Cie" series, no. 571, 1866–67, albumen print, 4 ½ × 3 ½ in., Archives, Musée d'Orsay, Paris.

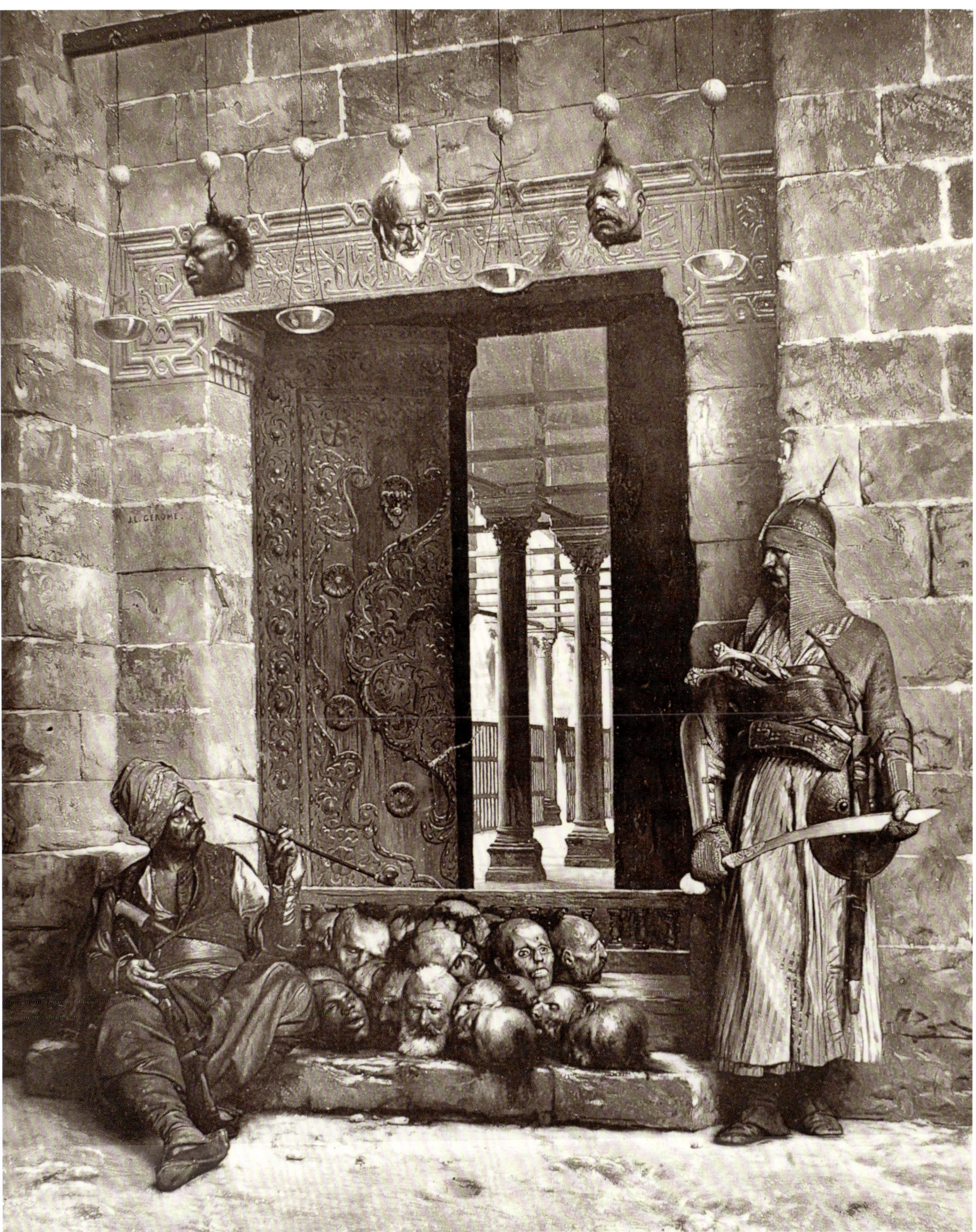
J.L. GEROME.

Cat 145

THE MUEZZIN (THE CALL TO PRAYER)

–

1866
Oil on canvas
39 3/8 × 33 in.
Signed bottom right
Joslyn Art Museum, Omaha, Gift of Francis T. B. Martin (bequest), inv. JAM 1995.3.

–

Provenance: Gérôme to Goupil, March 1865, stock book no. 1612, "Muetzine en prière," (for 5,000 francs). Goupil to Gambart, London, Apr. 1865 (for 10,000 francs). Mr. R. H. Kennedy, New York, 1886. Mrs. H. Van Rensselaer Kennedy, sale, American Art Association, New York, Apr. 26, 1928, lot 77, to J. Laurie Wallace, for Charles W. Martin (for $1,000). Gift to his nephew, Francis T. Martin, 1940. Francis T. Martin bequest to the Joslyn Art Museum, 1992.

–

Bibliography: E. Strahan [Earl Shinn], ed., *Gérome: A Collection of the Works of J. L. Gérome in One Hundred Photogravures* (New York: Samuel L. Hall, 1881), vol. 1, n.p. G. Ackerman et al., *Jean-Léon Gérôme (1824–1904)*, exh. cat. (Dayton: Dayton Art Institute, 1972; also Minneapolis: Minneapolis Institute of Arts, 1973, and Baltimore: The Walters Art Gallery, 1973), p. 24. A. Boime, "Gérôme and the Bourgeois Artist's Burden," *Arts Magazine*, vol. 57, no. 5 (Jan. 1983), p. 71. G. Ackerman, *The Life and Work of Jean-Léon Gérôme, with a Catalogue Raisonné* (New York and London: Sotheby's, 1986), pp. 66, 218–19, no. 163. C. Williams, "Jean-Léon Gérome: A Case Study of an Orientalist Painter," in *Fantasy or Ethnography? Irony and Collusion in Subaltern Representation*, eds. S. J. Webber and M. R. Lynd (Columbus, Ohio: Division of Comparative Studies in the Humanities, Ohio State University, 1996), pp. 121, 123, fig. 3. G. Ackerman, *Jean-Léon Gérôme: His Life, His Work, 1824–1904* (Courbevoie: ACR Édition, 1997), p. 69. G. Ackerman, *Jean-Léon Gérôme: monographie revisée, catalogue raisonné mis à jour* (Courbevoie: ACR Édition, 2000), pp. 67, 260–61, no. 163. H. Lafont-Couturier, *Gérôme and Goupil: Art and Enterprise*, exh. cat., trans. I. Ollivier (Bordeaux: Musée Goupil, 2000–1; also New York: Dahesh Museum of Art, 2001, and Pittsburgh: The Frick Art & Historical Center, 2001), pp. 23, 25, 119, 154. K. Davies, *The Orientalists: Western Artists in Arabia, the Sahara, Persia and India* (New York: Laynfaroh, 2005), p. 271.

Ill. 114. *Prayer on the Housetops*, 1865, oil on canvas, 19 1/2 × 32 in., Kunsthalle, Hamburg.

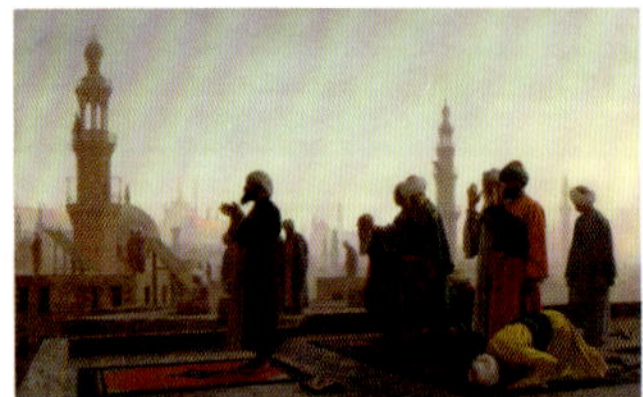

The muezzin's call to prayer from the minarets of Cairo was an evocative element of nineteenth-century travelers' accounts, and the view to be obtained from those structures was likewise appealing to tourists.[1] This painting, raising the viewer to the height of a minaret's upper platform, combines both attractions: a memorable image of Islamic piety and a picturesque cityscape of Cairo. Facing east towards Mecca on a hot afternoon, the muezzin directs his song heavenward, Gérôme giving visual dimension to his voice through a distant flight of birds rising above the dusty horizon. Enlivening the scene below are several picturesque details: a woman hanging laundry and two dogs, one lying asleep in the hot sun and the other sitting at attention, ears perked.[2]

From the outset, respectful depictions of Muslim devotion constituted an important strain of Gérôme's Orientalist production, and they helped promulgate European notions of a devout, traditional Islamic culture—set in romantic contrast to the modern West, characterized by many as skeptical, rational, and scientific.[3] Between the late 1850s and the mid-1860s, Gérôme scored a couple of major Salon successes on the prayer theme: *Prayer in the House of an Arnaut Chief* (1857) and *Prayer on the Housetops* (1865; ill. 114), a scene set upon a Cairo rooftop.[4] The muezzin's call was an important background feature of the latter, anticipating the subject of the present painting and of several later works.[5] The connection between the Omaha picture and *Prayer on the Housetops* is further strengthened by the close similarities between the muezzin in the former and the imam leading devotions in the latter. Gérôme evidently used the same model for both, even depicting him in the same costume of yellow robe, red sash, and dark blue cloak.[6]

The views provided in *The Muezzin* and similar paintings were studio fabrications, even "capriccios,"[7] despite their seemingly photographic veracity. Gérôme's "realist" approach involved an imaginative combination of precisely described details, which individually can often be identified and were probably based on photographic sources or firsthand studies.[8] The most recognizable features of this picture are the principal minaret and the madrasa courtyard immediately below, both of which Caroline Williams has identified with the fourteenth-century Amir Sarghitmish funerary complex in Cairo. Gérôme has excerpted these details from their environs, however, and also altered the relationship of minaret to courtyard.[9] He also seems to have adjusted the scale of the minaret's architecture, shrinking it so as to give prominence to the muezzin and to incorporate as much distinctive architectural detail within the frame as possible. As for the distant view over Cairo, one need only compare the Omaha painting to its smaller replica/variant (Ackerman, no. 164), which shows quite a different array of domes and minarets, to see how freely he altered and recombined details in practice. By the end of the nineteenth century, inevitably through the help of reproductive prints and photographs, Gérôme's artful composition had attained iconic status as an indelible image of the Muslim faith.[10] An etched reproduction of it served, for instance, as an ethnographic document in an 1895 edition of Edward William Lane's *An Account of the Manners and Customs of the Modern Egyptians, Written in Egypt during the Years 1833–1835* (1836), an influential book that had originally served Gérôme himself as a point of reference in his prayer scenes.[11] In the late twentieth century, the image was made to stand, more ominously, for a politically resurgent Islam. Gérôme's reduction of the painting, which had surfaced on the market in 1977,[12] served as the cover image for a 1979 issue of *Time* magazine that was devoted to "Islam: The Militant Revival."[13] **S. A.**

1. See, for instance, P. Lenoir, *Le Fayoum, le Sinaï et Pétra: expédition dans la moyenne Égypte et l'Arabie Pétrée sous la direction de J. L. Gérome* (Paris: Henri Plon, 1872), p. 164; D. Scott, "The Literary Orient," in *The East Imagined, Experienced, Remembered: Orientalist Nineteenth Century Painting*, exh. cat. (Dublin: The National Gallery of Ireland, 1988), pp. 14–15; and M. A. Stevens, ed., *The Orientalists, Delacroix to Matisse: European Painters in North Africa and the Near East*, exh. cat. (London: Royal Academy of Arts, 1984), p. 145, under no. 36. **2.** Lenoir draws attention to such picturesque details in his travel account; see P. Lenoir 1872 (as in n. 1), pp. 88–89. **3.** See A. Boime, "Gérôme and the Bourgeois Artist's Burden," *Arts Magazine*, vol. 57, no. 5 (Jan. 1983), p. 71; K. Davies, *The Orientalists: Western Artists in Arabia, the Sahara, Persia and India* (New York: Laynfaroh, 2005), p. 265. **4.** See G. Ackerman, *Jean-Léon Gérôme* (Courbevoie: ACR Édition, 2000), nos. 71, 152. **5.** Ibid., nos. 70, 201, 273, 280. **6.** C. Williams, "Jean-Léon Gérome: A Case Study of an Orientalist Painter," in *Fantasy or Ethnography? Irony and Collusion in Subaltern Representation*, eds. S. J. Webber and M. R. Lynd (Columbus, Ohio: Division of Comparative Studies in the Humanities, Ohio State University, 1996), p. 121. **7.** M. A. Stevens 1984 (as in n. 1), p. 145. **8.** Gérôme made several oil-sketch studies of minarets, for example. See *J.-L. Gérôme*, exh. cat. (Vesoul: Musée Georges-Garret, 1981), p. 137, no. 168. **9.** C. Williams 1996 (as in. n. 6), p. 121. **10.** The Goupil firm first reproduced the painting through a photograph, which was available from 1865, and then through an etching (from 1869) and photogravure (from 1877). See H. Lafont-Couturier et al., *Gérôme and Goupil: Art and Enterprise*, exh. cat. trans I. Ollivier (Bordeaux: Musée Goupil, 2000-1; also New York: Dahesh Museum of Art, 2001, and Pittsburgh: the Frick Art & Historical Center, 2001), pp. 23,25,119,154. **11.** See E. W. Lane, *An Account of the Manners and Customs of the Modern Egyptians, Written in Egypt during the Years 1833–35* (London and Paisley: Alexander Gardner, 1895), p. 85; and H. Lafont-Couturier, *Gérôme and Goupil: Art and Enterprise*, exh. cat., trans. I. Ollivier (Bordeaux: Musée Goupil, 2000–1; also New York: Dahesh Museum of Art, 2001, and Pittsburgh: The Frick Art & Historical Center, 2001), p. 119. **12.** See Christie's, London, *Important Pictures, Drawings and Prints of Islamic Interest*, Nov. 3, 1977, lot 110. **13.** See A. Boime 1983 (as in n. 3), p. 72, fig. 18. It is the Apr. 16, 1979 issue.

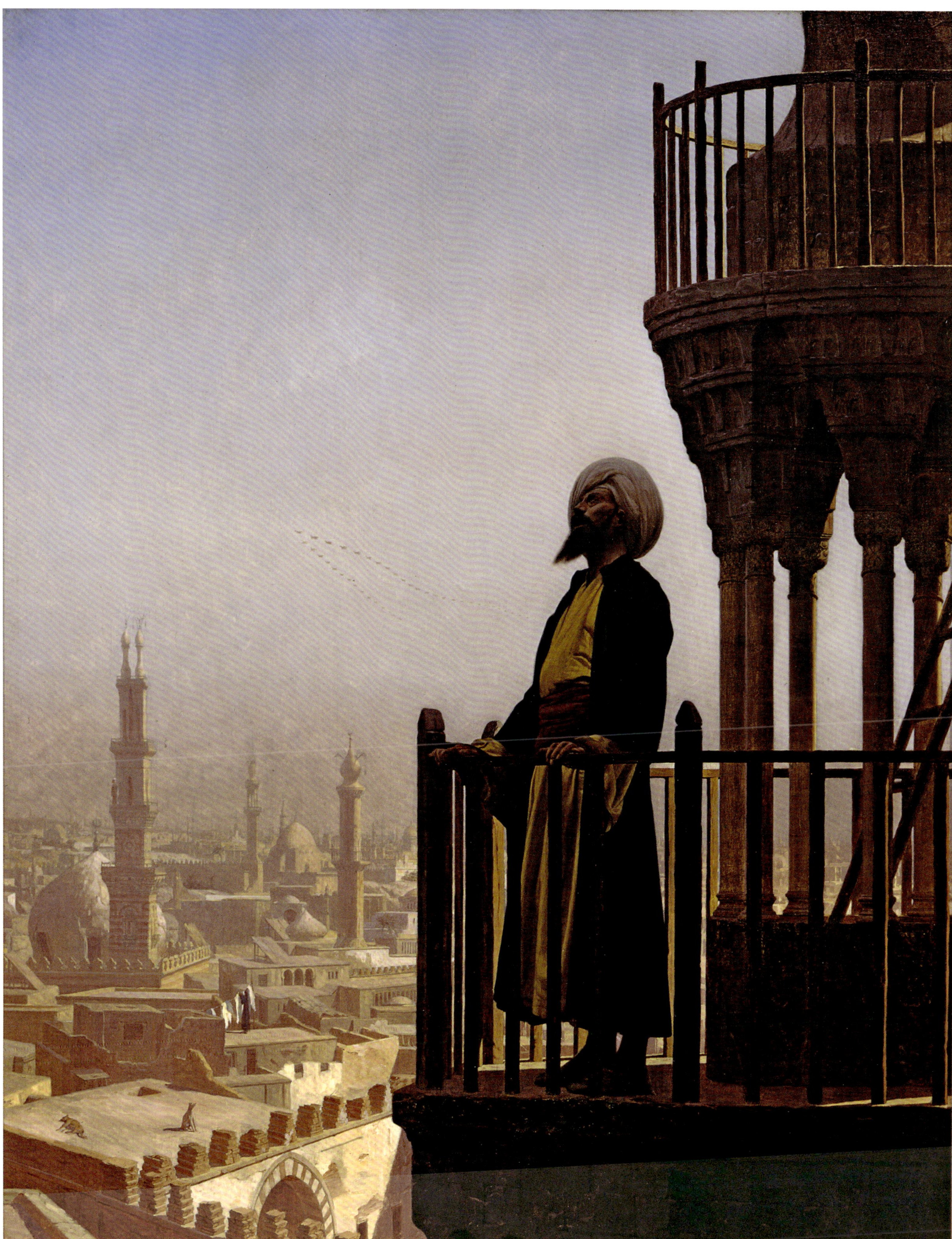

Cat. 146

PUBLIC PRAYER IN THE MOSQUE OF AMR

–

1871 (possibly 1874)
Oil on canvas
35 × 29 ½ in.
Signed above right, on the beam:
J.L. GEROME
The Metropolitan Museum of Art, New York, Bequest of Catherine Lorillard Wolfe Collection, 1887, inv. 87.15.130

–

Provenance: [possibly the picture sold by Gérôme to Goupil, Sept. 1871, stock book no. 5695, "La prière dans une mosquée," (for 6,000 francs). Goupil to Knoedler, New York, Sept. 1871 (for 12,000 francs). Knoedler to Goupil, Mar. 1872, stock book no. 6182, "La prière dans une mosquée - anc. no. 5695" (for 12,000 francs). Goupil to M. Wallis, London, Mar. 1872 (for 15,000 francs)]. Purchased by Goupil, Sept. 1874, stock book no. 9275, "Prière dans une mosquée (style byzantine)" (for 20,000 francs). Goupil to Knoedler, Nov. 1874 (for 40,000 francs). Knoedler to Catherine L. Wolfe, New York, 1874 (for $10,670). Catherine L. Wolfe bequest to The Metropolitan Museum of Art, 1887.

–

Bibliography: E. Strahan [Earl Shinn], *The Art Treasures of America: Being the Choicest Works of Art in the Public and Private Collections of North America*, 3 vols. (Philadelphia: G. Barrie, 1880), vol. 1, pp. 126–27. E. Strahan [Earl Shinn], ed., *Gérome: A Collection of the Works of J. L. Gérome in One Hundred Photogravures* (New York: Samuel L. Hall, 1881), vol. 3, n.p. F. F. Hering, *Gérôme: The Life and Works of Jean Léon Gérôme* (New York: Cassell, 1892), pp. 126–27. A. Hoeber, *The Treasures of the Metropolitan Museum of Art of New York* (New York: R. H. Russell, 1899), pp. 80–81. F. Fowler, "The Field of Art. Modern Foreign Paintings at the Metropolitan Museum. Some Examples of the French School," *Scribner's Magazine*, vol. 44 (Sept. 1908), pp. 381–83. *The Taste of the Seventies: A Special Exhibition Celebrating the Seventy-fifth Anniversary of the Metropolitan Museum of Art*, exh. cat. (New York, 1946), no. 109. R. H. Ives Gammell, *Twilight of Painting: An Analysis of Recent Trends to Serve in a Period of Reconstruction* (New York: G. P. Putnam's Sons, 1946), pl. 23. C. Sterling and M. M. Salinger, *French Paintings: A Catalogue of the Collection of the Metropolitan Museum of Art. II. XIX Century* (New York, 1966), p. 171. G. Ackerman, "A Chat by the Fireside," *The Register of the Museum of Art, University of Kansas*, vol. 4 (1971), pp. 21, 25–26. G. Ackerman et al., *Jean-Léon Gérôme (1824–1904)*, exh. cat. (Dayton: Dayton Art Institute, 1972; also Minneapolis: Minneapolis Institute of Arts, 1973, and Baltimore: The Walters Art Gallery, 1973), pp. 22–23, 72, under no. 26. J. Rewald, "Should Hoving be De-accessioned?" *Art in America* 61, no. 1 (Jan.-Feb. 1973), p. 28. D. A. Rosenthal, *Orientalism: The Near East in French Painting, 1800–1880*, exh. cat. (Rochester, N.Y.: The Memorial Art Gallery of the University of Rochester, 1982), p. 78. A. Boime, "Gérôme and the Bourgeois Artist's Burden," *Arts Magazine*, vol. 57, no. 5 (Jan. 1983), p. 73. M. A. Stevens, ed., *The Orientalists, Delacroix to Matisse: European Painters in North Africa and the Near East*, exh. cat. (London: Royal Academy of Arts, 1984), pp. 65, 142, no. 32. M. A. Stevens, ed., *The Orientalists, Delacroix to Matisse: The Allure of North Africa and the Near East*, exh. cat. (Washington, D.C.: National Gallery of Art, 1984), pp. 65, 144, no. 34. G. Ackerman, "Gérome's Oriental Paintings and the Western Genre Tradition," *Arts Magazine*, vol. 60, no. 7 (Mar. 1986), p. 77, fig. 7. G. Ackerman, *The Life and Work of Jean-Léon Gérôme, with a Catalogue Raisonné* (New York and London: Sotheby's, 1986), pp. 93, 228, no. 200. F. Pouillon, "L'Ombre de l'islam: les figurations de la pratique religieuse dans la peinture orientaliste du 19e siècle," *Actes de la recherche en sciences sociales*, no. 75 (Nov. 1988), p. 30, fig. 9. *Album de voyage: des artistes en expédition au pays du Levant* (Paris: Association Française d'Action Artistique; Réunion des Musées Nationaux, 1993), pp. 31-32. C. Peltre, *L'Atelier de voyage: les peintres en Orient au XIXe siècle* (Paris: Le Promeneur, 1995), pp. 60–61. J. Hardin, *The Lure of Egypt: Land of the Pharaohs Revisited*, exh. cat. (Saint. Petersburg, Fla.: Museum of Fine Arts, 1996), p. 8, no. 19. C. Williams, "Jean-Léon Gérôme: A Case Study of an Orientalist Painter," in *Fantasy or Ethnography? Irony and Collusion in Subaltern Representation*, eds S. J. Webber and M. R. Lynd (Columbus, Ohio: Division of Comparative Studies in the Humanities, The Ohio State University, 1996), pp. 137, 148, n. 78. R. Benjamin, ed. *Orientalism: Delacroix to Klee*, exh. cat. (Sydney: Art Gallery of New South Wales, 1997; also Auckland: Auckland Art Gallery, 1998), p. 198, no. 125. H. Lafont-Couturier, *Gérôme & Goupil. Art et entreprise*, exh. cat. (Bordeaux: Musée Goupil, 2000–1; also New York: Dahesh Museum of Art, 2001, and Pittsburgh: The Frick Art & Historical Center, 2001), pp. 120-121, no. 72. G. Ackerman, *Jean-Léon Gérôme* (Paris: ACR Édition, 2000), pp. 105, 274–75, no. 200. R. Yeomans, *The Art and Architecture of Islamic Cairo* (Reading, UK: Garnet, 2006), p. 23.

Ill. 115. Émile Béchard (active 1870–80), *Interior of the Amr mosque (Old Cairo)*, ca. 1870, albumen print, 10 ½ × 8 in., The Getty Research Institute, Los Angeles, inv. 2008.R.3, box T74, #3447.

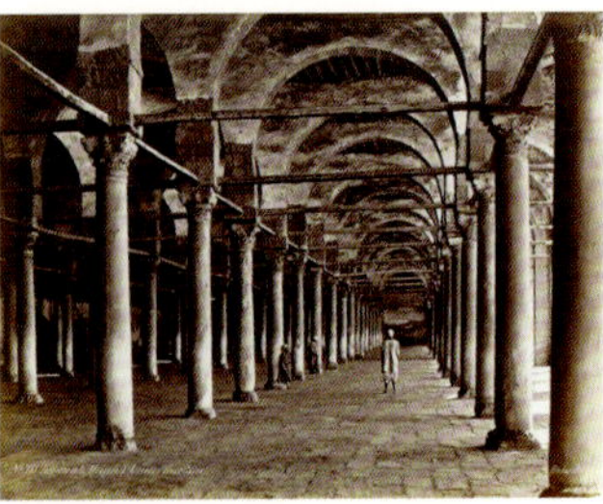

This prayer scene depicts the seventh-century mosque of 'Amr ibn al-'As in Cairo, the city's oldest. Gérôme's dramatic perspective view, which closely accords with contemporaneous photographs (ill. 115), faithfully represents the prayer hall's hypostyle interior, with the rounded arches of its parallel arcades springing from tall impost blocks conjoined by wooden tie beams and set atop columns fitted with recycled antique Corinthian capitals. Gérôme had occasion to study the mosque firsthand during his 1868 trip to Egypt, a visit subsequently recorded by his travel companion, Paul Lenoir. Judging by Lenoir's account, the mosque held touristic interest for the artists as the "cradle of Islam in Egypt" and as a "relic" distinguished by the primitive simplicity of its architecture.[1] Likewise apparent is the fact that in 1868 the mosque was no longer actively used as a place of worship. Indeed, as Pouillon has emphasized, its defunct status was precisely what enabled the non-Muslim westerners both to enter into the mosque and to make artistic studies there.[2] As Gérard de Nerval wrote decades before Gérôme's visit, "nothing defended [it] any more from profanation."[3]

The prayer scene Gérôme ultimately depicted, then, was pure fantasy, despite its quasi-photographic realism. In the interest of pictorial variety, he staged a diversity of male types evoking the social spectrum of Egyptian society. Distinguished in the foreground is an Ottoman dignitary standing on a personal Turkish prayer carpet and wearing a sumptuous, gilt-edged robe and an ornamented weapons belt. Positioned on the bare flagstones at a respectful distance behind him are two Arnaut retainers. This group is contrasted to the rows of Egyptian faithful seen from behind and arrayed on much plainer, collective prayer carpets in the left background. Gérôme has avoided potential monotony here by varying the colors and designs of the worshippers' turbans, their long *gibbehs* or outer coats, and in a few instances, their girdled kaftans.[4] Isolated in turn from these figures is a lone, long-haired and half-clothed mendicant with a begging bowl hanging from his arm, a marginal type that Western artists had frequent opportunity to observe outside of mosques.[5]

Gérôme's famed project of ethnographic documentation did not prevent him, as scholars have recognized, from taking considerable liberties with Islamic custom in what appear to be solemnly respectful descriptions of the prayer ritual. Instead of showing the synchronization of the worshippers' prescribed postures and gestures as one might expect, for example, he shows a variety of attitudes in a single frame to evoke the different moments of prayer and to add pictorial interest. Equally incongruous are the presence of the mendicant, whose state of quasi-nudity would presumably not have been tolerated within the mosque; the flock of pigeons, which recalls the abandoned state of the building as Gérôme in fact encountered it; and the weaponry of the central figure, which would interfere awkwardly with his devotions were he actually to prostrate himself on his carpet.[6] And with a strange irony that has gone unremarked, he wears the exact same costume that Gérôme employed in his fictive portrait of Markos Botsaris (cat. 161), an ethnic Albanian of the Greek Orthodox faith who played a key role in fighting against the Ottomans in the Greek War of Independence. **S. A.**

1. See P. Lenoir, *Le Fayoum, le Sinaï et Pétra: expédition dans la moyenne Égypte et l'Arabie Pétrée sous la direction de J. L. Gérome* (Paris: Henri Plon, 1872), pp. 42–46. **2.** F. Pouillon, "L'Ombre de l'Islam: les figurations de la pratique religieuse dans la peinture orientaliste du XIXe siècle," *Actes de la recherche en sciences sociales*, no. 75 (Nov. 1988), p. 30. It has been reasonably speculated that Gérôme made artistic studies of the mosque *in situ*; see M. A. Stevens, ed., *The Orientalists, Delacroix to Matisse: European Painters in North Africa and the Near East*, exh. cat. (London: Royal Academy of Arts, 1984), p. 142, no. 32. **3.** Cited in F. Pouillon 1988 (as in n. 2), p. 30, n. 13. See G. de Nerval, *Le Voyage en Orient*, 2 vols. (Paris: Garnier-Flammarion, 1980), vol. 1, p. 240 ["... rien ne défend plus contre la profanation"]. **4.** R. Ettinghausen, "Jean-Léon Gérôme as a Painter of Near Eastern Life," in G. Ackerman et al., *Jean-Léon Gérôme (1824–1904)*, exh. cat. (Dayton: Dayton Art Institute, 1972; also Minneapolis: Minneapolis Institute of Arts, 1973, and Baltimore: The Walters Art Gallery, 1973), pp. 22–23. **5.** F. Pouillon 1988 (as in n. 2), p. 26. **6.** Ibid., p. 30.

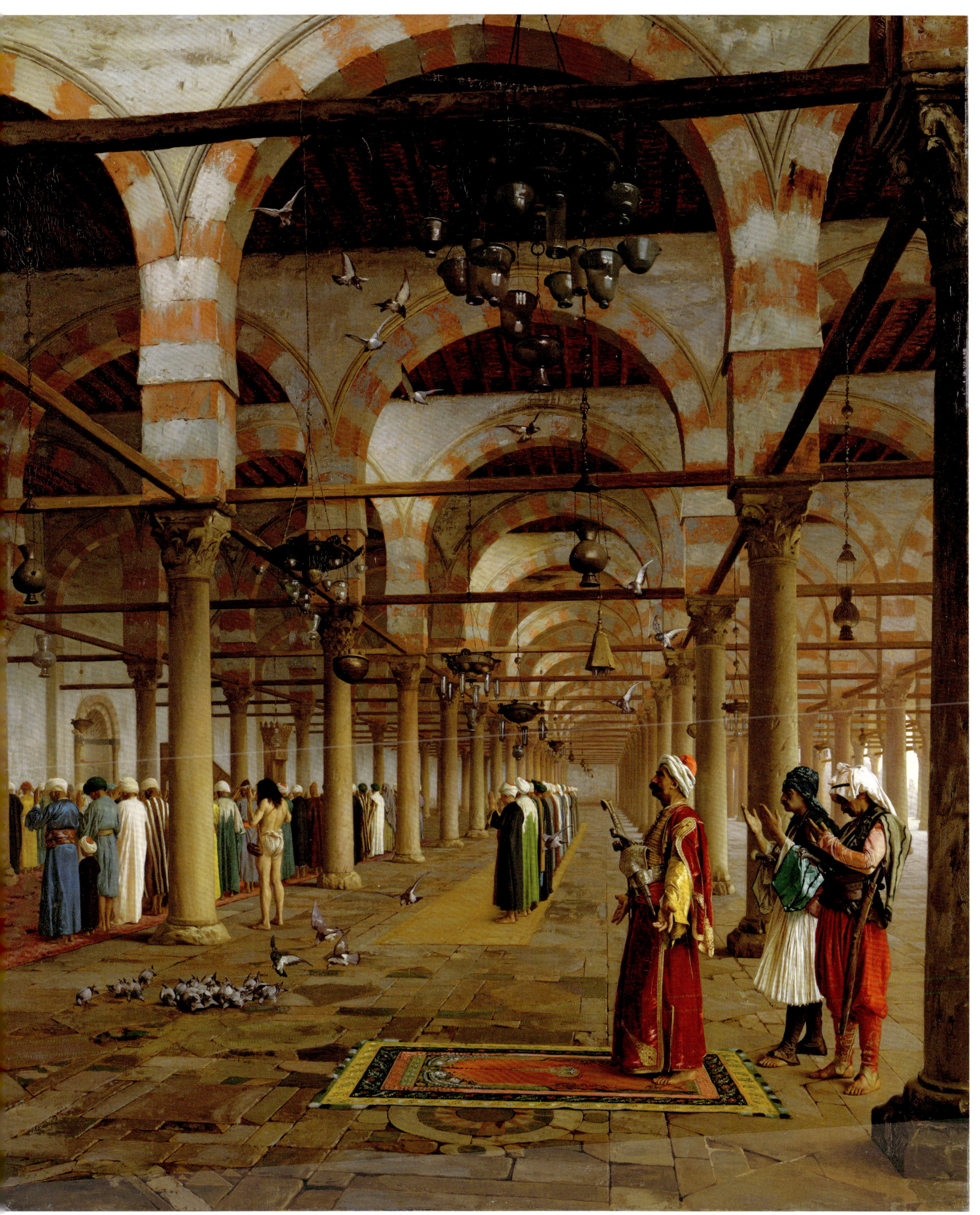

Cat. 147

THE RUNNERS OF THE PASHA

–

1867
Oil on panel
22 × 17 ⅛ × ⅝ in.
The New York Historical Society, New York, The Robert L. Stuart Collection, inv. S-146

–

Exhibition history: Centennal Exhibition, New York, 1876, no. 320.

–

Bibliography: E. Strahan [Earl Shinn], ed. *Gérôme: A Collection of the Works of J.-L. Gérôme in One Hundred Photogravures* (New York: Samuel L. Hall, 1881). *Catalogue de Paris*, 1883, p. 69. Centennial Exhibition, New York, 1876, no. 320. G. Ackerman, *Jean-Léon Gérôme* (Courbevoie: ACR Édition, 2000), no. 180. H. Lafont-Couturier, *Gérôme and Goupil: Art and Enterprise*, exh. cat., trans. I. Ollivier (Bordeaux: Musée Goupil, 2000–1; also New York: Dahesh Museum of Art, 2001, and Pittsburgh: The Frick Art & Historical Center, 2001), pp. 37, 40, 156.

The event depicted here has not been established. It is probable that the two sleek runners precede the procession of the man on horseback—certainly the pasha—to announce his arrival. The moment recalls a passage in Adolphe Joanne's *Voyage en Égypte et en Grèce*: "But what are those clamours? Why do everyone fly? What do they all fear? (...) What's on? There are runners coming, clothed in pale blue and handling long whips."[1] Although the exact iconography remains to be determined, the stylistic sources are clear enough. The scene takes place in front of the gate to the citadel in Cairo, whose two large towers are partly damaged and crumbling. A photograph by Émile Béchard taken around 1870 shows it already restored. The two runners are interesting and revealing for the way Gérôme constantly mixed antique sources with oriental recollections: whereas their figures and dress are similar to men photographed by Félix Bonfils in the late 1860s (ill. 116), their poses recall the runners in the Villa of the Papyri in Herculaneum, excavated from 1750 to 1761 (ill. 117).[2] Gérôme's *Runners*, at first sight so picturesque and lifelike, once again constitute a skillfully mastered subterfuge. **D. F.-R.**

1. A. Joanne, *Voyage en Égypte et en Grèce* (Ixelles-lez-Bruxelles: Delevigne et Callevaert, 1850), p. 64. 2. Although the results of the excavations were not published by Domenico Comparetti and Giulio de Petra until 1883, the excavated objects were already well known.

Ill. 116. Félix Bonfils (1831–1885), *Saïs runners from Cairo*, albumen print, Département des Estampes et de la Photographie, Bibliothèque Nationale de France, Paris, Eo 128 1, no. 665.

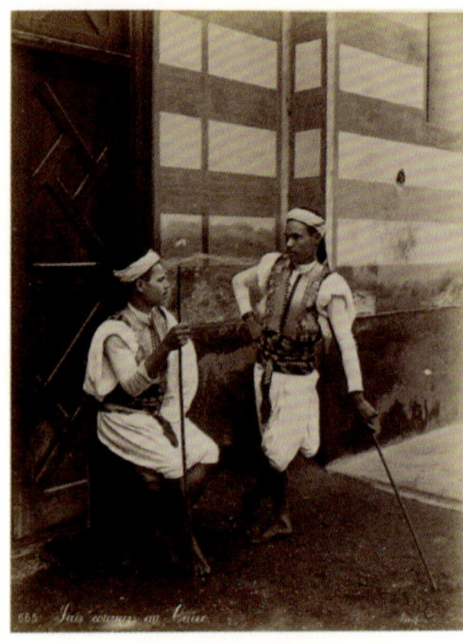

Ill. 117. Anonymous, *Runner* (detail), bronze, Museo Archeologico Nazionale, Naples.

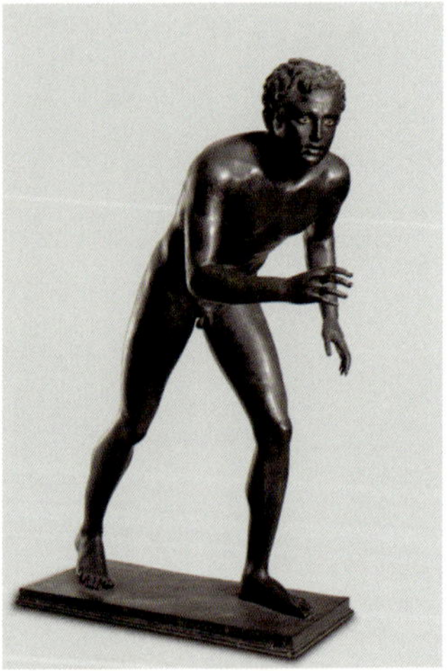

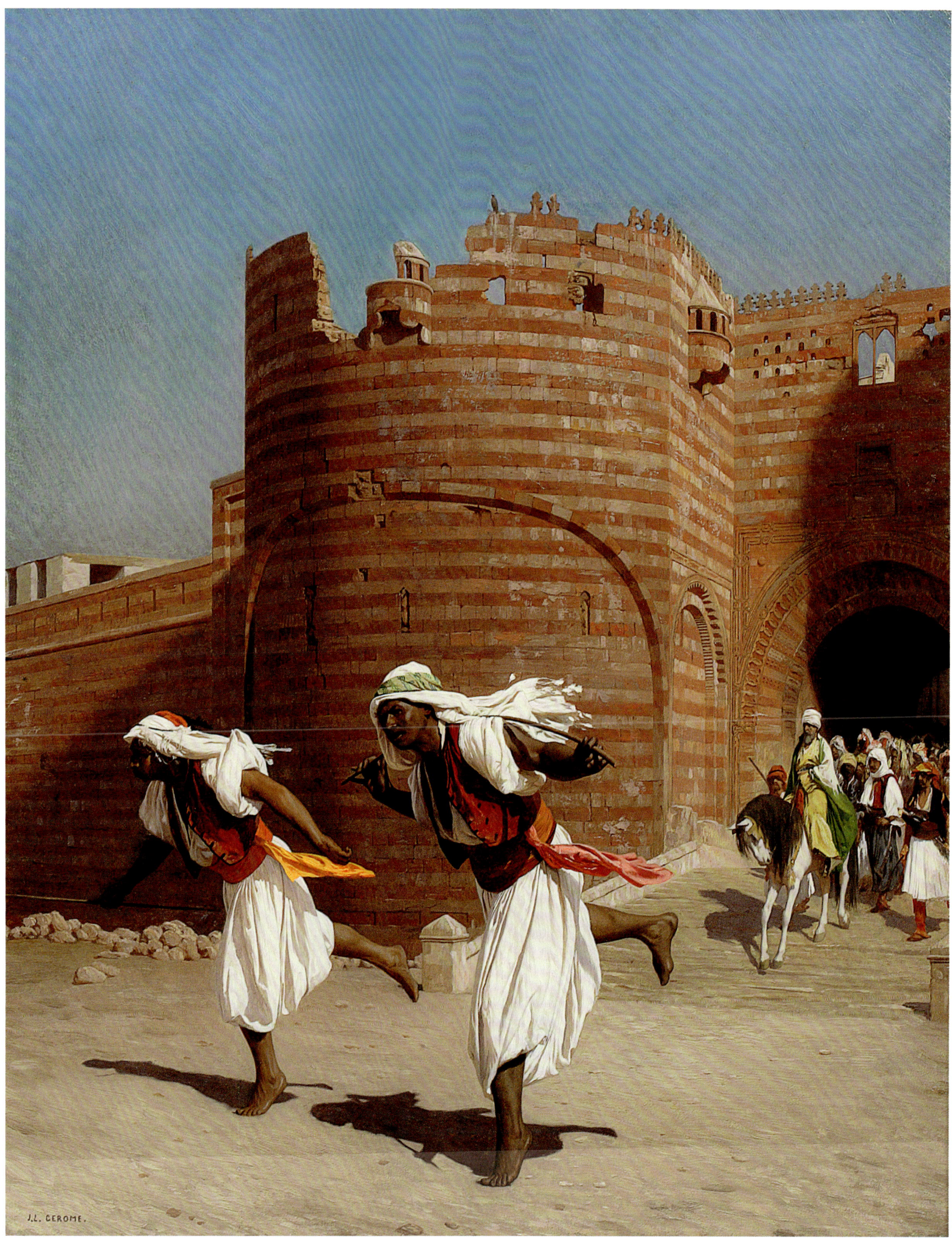
J.L. GEROME.

Cat. 148

THE STANDARD BEARER (UNFOLDING THE FLAG)

1876–78
Oil on canvas
61 5/8 × 19 3/4 in.
The Haggin Museum, The Haggin Collection, Stockton, inv. 1931.391.54

Provenance:
Gérôme to Goupil, June 5, 1878 as "L'Étendard du prophète" (for 6,000 francs). Goupil to Knoedler, July 31, 1878, Goupil stock book 9, no. 12790 (for 12,000 francs). Knoedler to Julius Oehme, New York, 1878. Millard F. Tompkins. Tompkins sale, Mar. 5, 1915, no. 44, to W. H. Richmond (for $575). Haggin Museum, Stockton, California.

Exhibition History:
The Impressionists and the Salon (1874–1886): Honoring the Centennial of the First Impressionist Exhibition. California Collections, Los Angeles County Museum of Art, 1974, no. 27.

Bibliography:
F. F. Hering, "Gérôme," *Century Magazine* 37, no. 4 (Feb. 1889), pp. 482–85. P. Sanders, *The Haggin Collections* (Stockton, Calif.: Haggin Museum, 1991), pp. 86–87. H. Lafont-Couturier, *Gérôme* (Paris: Herscher, 1998), p. 70. G. Ackerman, *Jean-Léon Gérôme* (Courbevoie: ACR Edition, 2000), no. 252. K. Davies, *The Orientalists: Western Artists in Arabia, the Sahara, Persia and India* (New York: Laynfaroh, 2005), p. 236.

The man pictured in this painting wears the costume of the Tuareg people, an ancient nomadic tribe inhabiting the Sahara Desert. For over two millennia, the Tuareg operated the trans-Saharan caravan trade connecting the cities on the southern edge of the great desert to the Mediterranean coast of Africa along five routes. They fought against French colonization, murdering several French explorers and, in 1875, three French missionaries.[1] Gérôme paints this figure in the traditional Tuareg garb, with a fierce gaze made more haunting by knowledge of these recent events. Gérôme might have seen Tuaregs on his Middle Eastern travels, perhaps during his visit to Algeria in 1873. The figure holds a green flag, the traditional color of Islam after the banner color of the tribe of the prophet Muhammad. Green is considered a sacred color in Islam, associated with Paradise.

This picture partakes in the Orientalist stereotype of the armed guard: the fierce warrior sumptuously costumed, draped with weapons, against a massive door or hall. This kind of picture addressed a Western nostalgia for hand-to-hand combat, and the intimate violence erased by the advent of guns.[2] As in the case of *The Standard Bearer*, artists working in this genre often took liberties with the accuracy of costume and weapons. The bow and arrows, for instance, are not typical Tuareg weapons, but were favored studio props belonging to Gérôme. The figure in *Prayer at the Sultan's Tomb* (1878, private collection) bears the same bow and arrows, and they are pictured hanging on the wall in Gérôme's studio in *The Artist's Model* (cat. 173). The green flag of *The Standard Bearer* also appears in this studio painting, leaning against the wall to the left of the sculptor.

Stuffed into the warrior's leather sash, known as the *silahlik*, is a sword that served as a stock weapon for a multitude of paintings by Gérôme of Arnauts, *bashi-bazouks* and Arabs, despite the specificity of traditional weapons pertaining to each of these groups. This sword is a Turkish type known as a *yatagan*, used from the mid-sixteenth to late nineteenth centuries in Turkey and areas under Turkish influence such as the Balkans. Balkan *yatagans* tend to have larger ears and are often of bone or ivory, like the one pictured here. One of the finest and earliest examples is the one made for Suleyman the Magnificent, who ruled over the Ottoman Empire from 1520 to 1566, which is kept in the treasury of the Topkapi palace in Istanbul. Gérôme could have acquired his in Istanbul or Bursa, or in one of the other Turkish cities he visited. Despite the aura of exactitude, then, this picture is not an anthropological record, but rather was done in Gérôme's Paris studio, with the seeming purpose of conjuring a compelling image of menacing Islam. **M. M.**

1. P. Sanders, *The Haggin Collections* (Stockton: Haggin Museum, 1991), p. 86, quoted from H. Lhote, *Les Tuaregs du Hoggar* (Paris: Payot, 1955), pp. 377–80. 2. K. Davies, *The Orientalists: Western Artists in Arabia, the Sahara, Persia and India* (New York: Laynfaroh, 2005), pp. 231–34.

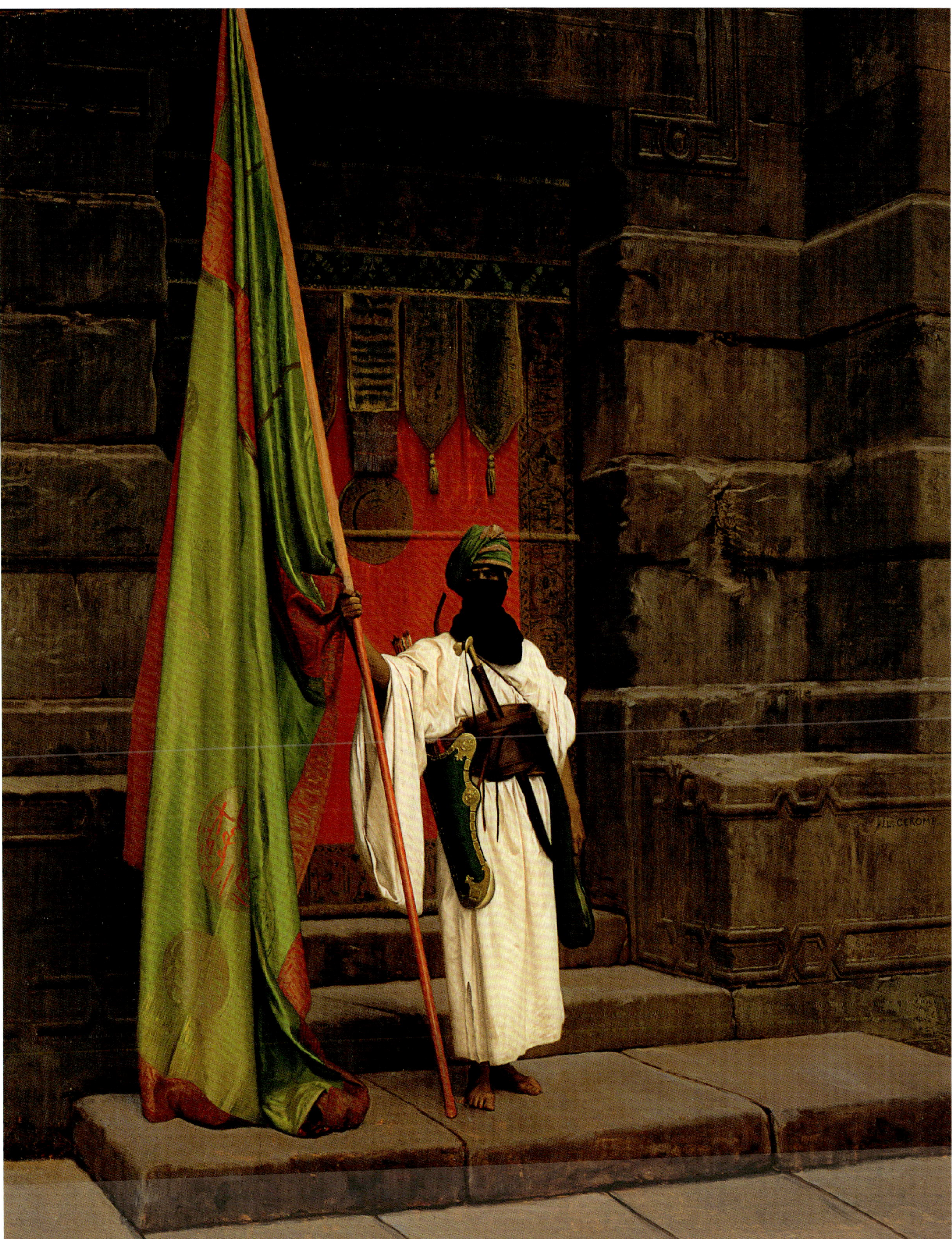
J.L. GEROME

Cat. 149

SOLOMON'S WALL, JERUSALEM (THE WAILING WALL)

1876
Oil on canvas
36 ½ × 29 in.
Private collection

Provenance: Goupil to Lepke, Berlin, 1876 (for 10,000 francs). A Hamburg collector, 1878, M. Donatis. Private collection, Berlin, 1979. Robert Isaacson, New York. Christie's, New York, May 6, 1999, lot 4 (for $2,312,500). French + Company, New York.

Bibliography: *Jean-Léon Gérôme and His Pupils* (Poughkeepsie, N.Y.: Vassar College Art Museum, 1967), no. 8. G. Ackerman, *Jean-Léon Gérôme* (Courbevoie: ACR Édition, 2000), no. 258. H. Lafont-Couturier, *Gérôme and Goupil: Art and Enterprise*, exh. cat., trans. I. Ollivier (Bordeaux: Musée Goupil, 2000–1; also New York: Dahesh Museum of Art, 2001, and Pittsburgh: The Frick Art & Historical Center, 2001), pp. 27, 43, 119, 158.

Gérôme visited Jerusalem in 1868, but it is likely that this painting was based on photographs such as the ones taken in the 1860s and 1870s by Félix Bonfils, which revived Gérôme's memories of his trip. As on other occasions, it would seem that Gérôme used photographs as raw material for his scenic spaces. A striking comparison can be made between this canvas and Bonfils's photograph of the wailing wall (ill. 118). In both, the composition underscores the dizzying height of the wall rising above the faithful; a similar angle of view underscores their human frailty compared to the age-old wall; and an encroaching shadow seems to echo the pilgrims' lamentations.

Gérôme's painting and Bonfils's photograph lend a restrained grandeur to these pious worshippers that does not match a description left in 1876 by Eugène Melchior de Vogüe, then posted in the Middle East. "Back in antiquity Saint Jerome mentioned this custom in one of his letters: 'You will see these people come to weep on the ruins of their Temple,' he wrote. – Which should make the *philosophes* reflect on the persistent vitality of religions... At the foot of the huge wall, a dense crowd presses against the foundation course, their heads barely reaching the top, and smother the venerated stones with kisses, caresses, and tears. Some of them wear local garments, brightly colored silk *gombaz*; but the great majority of them—Jews from Poland, Russia, and Walachia—wear that indescribable dress that so struck us at Saphed, where we saw it for the first time."[1]

By depicting only a few figures, photographer and painter reinforced the contrast between the fragility of the pilgrims and the power of the age-old ruins. **D. F.-R.**

1. E. Melchior de Vogüe, *Syrie, Palestine, Mont Athos, Voyage aux pays du passé* (Paris: Plon, 1876), quoted in *Le Voyage en Orient, anthologie des voyageurs français dans le Levant au XIXe siècle* , ed. J.-C. Berchet (Paris: Robert Laffont, 1985), p. 669.

Ill. 118. Félix Bonfils (1831–1885), *The Wailing Wall in Jerusalem*, ca. 1865–70, albumen print, 11 ½ × 9 ¼ in., no. 141, département des Estampes et de la Photographie, Bibliothèque Nationale de France, Paris, formerly Armand collection, AD-34 (A, 1)-Fol.

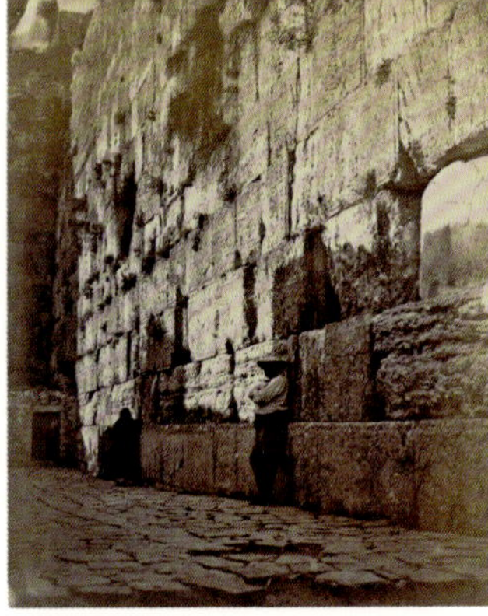

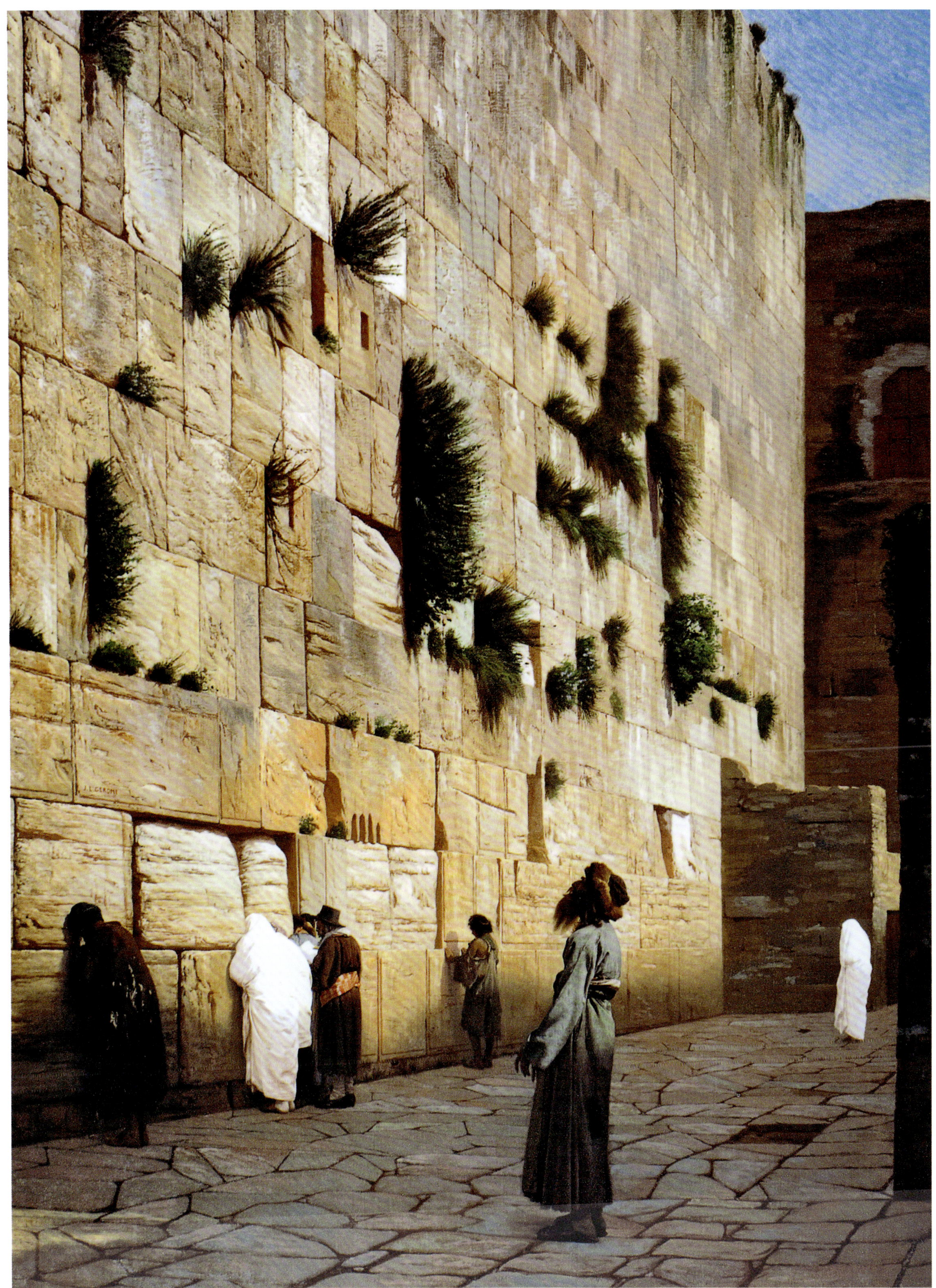
J.L. GEROME

Cat. 150

THE CARPET MERCHANT (THE RUG MARKET IN CAIRO)

–

1887
Oil on canvas
34 × 27 in.
The Minneapolis Institute of Arts, The William Hood Dunwoody Fund, Minneapolis, inv. 70.40

–

Provenance: Gérôme to Boussod, Valadon & Cie., Paris, 1888. Boussod, Valadon & Cie. to Knoedler, New York, 1888 (for 30,000 francs). Edwin Thorne, sold, American Art Association, New York, Jan. 27–28, 1893, lot 63, to William Schaus (Schaus & Co.) (for $15,100). Crocker collection, San Francisco, until 1969. Sloan and Roman, Inc., New York. Sold to the Minneapolis Institute of Arts, 1970.

–

Bibliography: F. F. Hering, *Gérôme: The Life and Works of Jean Léon Gérôme* (New York: Cassell, 1892), p. 255. *Pre-impressionism, 1860–1869*, exh. cat. (Davis, Calif.: Memorial Union Art Gallery, University of California at Davis, 1969), pp. 31, 94, fig. 7. G. Ackerman et al., *Jean-Léon Gérôme (1824–1904)*, exh. cat. (Dayton: Dayton Art Institute, 1972; also Minneapolis: Minneapolis Institute of Arts, 1973, and Baltimore: The Walters Art Gallery, 1973), p. 91, no. 39. R. K. Meyer, "Jean-Léon Gérôme: The Role of Subject Matter and the Importance of Formalized Composition," *Arts Magazine*, vol. 47, no. 4 (Feb. 1973), pp. 32, 34. R. Brettell, "The Diversity of French 19th Century Painting," *Apollo*, vol. 117, no. 253 (Mar. 1983), pp. 242–43, no. 14. A. Boime, "Gérôme and the Bourgeois Artist's Burden," *Arts Magazine*, vol. 57, no. 5 (Jan. 1983), pp. 68, 73. M. A. Stevens, ed., *The Orientalists, Delacroix to Matisse: European Painters in North Africa and the Near East*, exh. cat. (London: Royal Academy of Arts, 1984), pp. 69, 146, no. 37. M. A. Stevens, ed., *The Orientalists, Delacroix to Matisse: The Allure of North Africa and the Near East*, exh. cat. (Washington, D.C.: National Gallery of Art, 1984), pp. 69, 148, no. 39. G. Ackerman, *The Life and Work of Jean-Léon Gérôme, with a Catalogue Raisonné* (New York and London: Sotheby's, 1986), pp. 132, 134, 260, 261, no. 349. S. LaWall Lipshultz, *Selected Works: The Minneapolis Institute of Arts* (Minneapolis: Minneapolis Institute of Arts, 1988), p. 153. W. B. Denny, "Quotations in and out of Context: Ottoman Turkish Art and European Orientalist Painting," *Muqarnas*, vol. 10 (1993), p. 223. G. Ackerman, *Jean-Léon Gérôme* (Paris: ACR Édition, 2000), pp. 142, 145, 318–19, no. 349. S. Day, "The Artist's Eye. Carpet and Textile Collections of the Orientalists," *HALI*, no. 126 (Jan.–Feb. 2003), pp. 99, 101. F. W. Simpson, ed. *European Muses, American Masters, 1870–1950*, exh. cat. (Portland, Maine: Portland Museum of Art, 2004), p. 148. K. Davies, *The Orientalists: Western Artists in Arabia, the Sahara, Persia and India* (New York: Laynfaroh, 2005), pp. 177, 179.

In his 1872 travel account, Paul Lenoir described his 1868 visit in the company of Gérôme to the carpet market in the Cairo bazaar:

"Several of us had a great weakness for those admirable carpets which are made in Persia and which are sold in great quantity in Cairo. While I was making the fortune of several clothing merchants ... [the others] were abandoning themselves to colossal acquisitions in an immense courtyard ... that ... bears the name of the Courtyard of the Carpets. Besides the marvels being sold there in large quantities, this courtyard is very interesting in its own right; it is one of the most picturesque interiors we encountered in Cairo. The displays of the merchants, their cupboards and their reserve chests are veritable masterpieces of sculpture. The verandahs of carved wood protect the stalls from the overly strong action of direct light. The [resulting] half-light, handily managed, worked... to offset the brilliant tones of the admirable carpets passing before our eyes. We were the first to view the most recently arrived stock, and the opportunity was too perfect to miss. It was an orgy... and nothing would have restrained us were it not for the great expense of transporting all these riches. The white-ground carpets were above all the object of our bids."[1]

Painted subsequent to this visit, *The Carpet Merchant* resonates with Lenoir's account. Gérôme has attended to similar aspects as the writer: the brilliance and quantity of the carpets, the picturesque sculptural detailing of the courtyard and merchant stalls, and the carefully controlled lighting. He does not, however, depict European tourists indulging in an "orgy" of buying. Rather, his prospective buyers are a dignified group of men in sumptuous Eastern finery. They manifest the guarded restraint of connoisseurs while two bearded, gesturing merchants make their pitch for a beautiful, large carpet draped over a high balcony. The featured work, like those singled out by Lenoir, is a desirable white-ground carpet—of a medallion type that originated in the sixteenth century and was imitated by nineteenth-century manufacturers.[2] Various onlookers attest to the momentousness of the sale. In the arched passageway off to the right, a boy with a donkey and other servants wait, presumably to assist in the hauling away of purchases. A mysterious figure cloaked in blue emerges from the shadows of a doorway nearby, while turbaned figures observe the scene from the balcony above. An assistant below awaits his cue from the merchants to unroll the few remaining carpets to be shown to the customers. The carpets in a disorderly pile in the foreground have evidently been passed over already.

Carpet-merchant scenes were a part of Orientalist painters' stock-in-trade. Gérôme and many others acquired carpets and assorted curios abroad, lavishly decorated their studios with them, and incorporated them into their work as authenticating local color (ill. 119 and 120).[3] Such paintings inevitably contain a self-referential quality, the collectability of the luxury objects depicted enhancing the collectability of the paintings themselves. Scenes from the oriental bazaar like *The Carpet Merchant* surely reflected Gérôme's own awareness of the luxury-object status of his own high-priced work, as well as his awareness of the well-heeled buyers bidding for a rare example. Not simply a picturesque travel souvenir of the Cairo bazaar then, *The Carpet Merchant* wittily acknowledges its own function as a commodity and simultaneously romanticizes it. **S. A.**

Ill. 119. Ernest-Alexandre Duranton (active in 1886), *The Studio of the Painter Jean-Léon Gérôme*, oil on canvas, 25 × 36 in., whereabouts unknown.

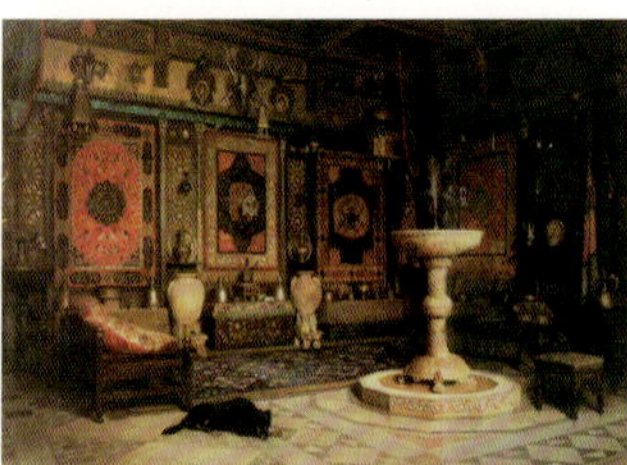

Ill. 120. *Catalogue des objets d'art de l'Orient et de l'Occident. Tableaux, dessins, composant la collection de feu M. Albert Goupil*, sale of Apr. 23–28, 1888 (Paris: Mannheim, 1888), Bibliothèque Nationale de France, Paris.

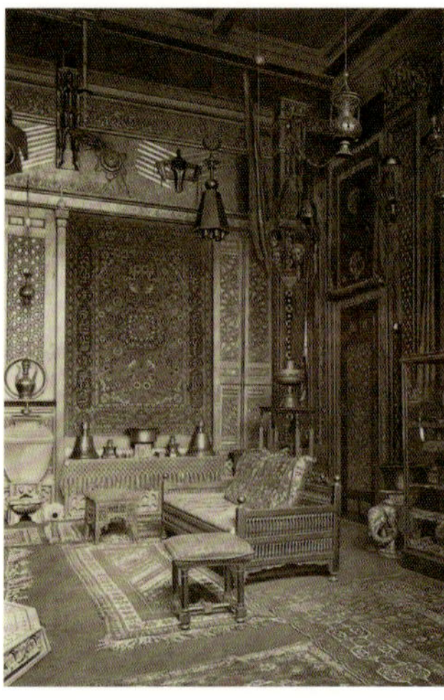

1. P. Lenoir, *Le Fayoum, le Sinaï et Pétra: expédition dans la moyenne Égypte et l'Arabie Pétrée sous la direction de J. L. Gérome* (Paris: Henri Plon, 1872), pp. 160–61. **2.** See W. B. Denny, "Quotations in and out of Context: Ottoman Turkish Art and European Orientalist Painting," *Muqarnas*, vol. 10 (1993), p. 223; S. Day, "The Artist's Eye. Carpet and Textile Collections of the Orientalists," *HALI*, no. 126 (Jan.–Feb. 2003), p. 99. **3.** See S. Day 2003 (as in n. 2), pp. 92–104.

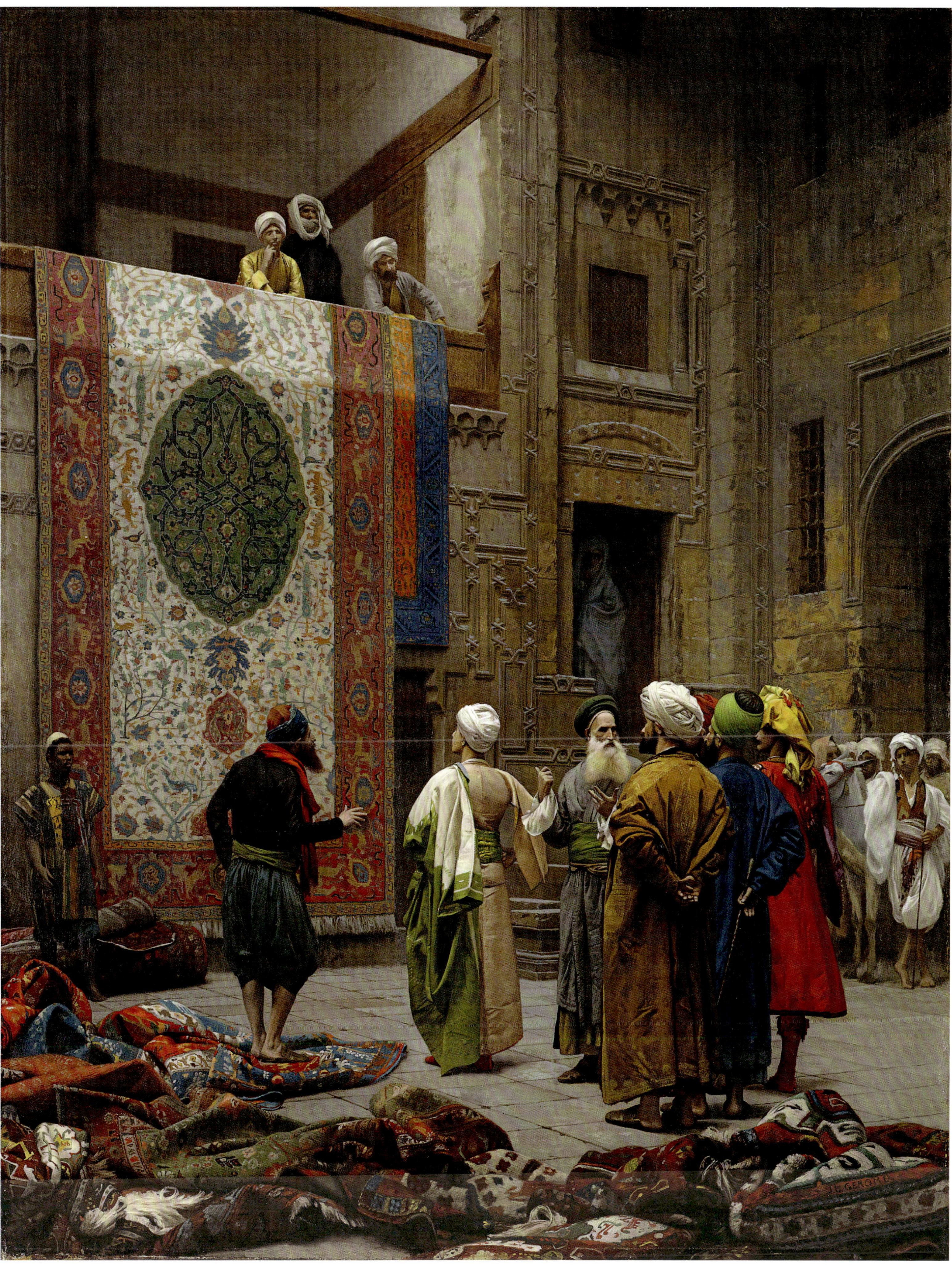

GEROME

Cat. 151

THE COLOR GRINDER

–

1890–91
Oil on canvas
26 × 21 in.
Private Collection, on loan to the Museum of Fine Arts, Boston, inv. L-R-2.1995

–

Provenance: Gérôme to Boussod, Valadon & Cie., 1891. Boussod, Valadon & Cie. to Crist Delmonico, New York, 1891. Mr. E. O. Wolcott, Chicago, by 1892. William H. Dunham, Chicago, 1927–41. By descent to the present owner.

–

Bibliography: G. Ackerman, *The Life and Work of Jean-Léon Gérôme, with a Catalogue Raisonné* (New York and London: Sotheby's, 1986), pp. 272–73, no. 409 (as "lost"). G. Ackerman, "Gérome's Oriental Paintings and the Western Genre Tradition," *Arts Magazine*, vol. 60, no. 7 (Mar. 1986), pp. 78–79, fig. 14. G. Ackerman, *Jean-Léon Gérôme* (Paris: ACR Édition, 2000), pp. 334–35, no. 409.

In an 1891 letter to one of this painting's first owners, Gérôme wrote:

"Sir, I hasten to respond to your letter regarding the picture of the color grinder, of which you are the owner. This work was painted last winter. It is one of those shops that are so numerous in Cairo where they grind all sorts of colors in mortars hollowed out from pieces of granite column. Naturally this powder settles on the sides of the mortar and gives the appearance I have tried to render with its vivid and varied colors. I have made this work with a great deal of care after a study done from nature and I hope I have succeeded in rendering the impression I had."[1]

The study to which Gérôme refers has survived (ill. 121).[2] Anticipating the general aspect of the finished painting, it shows a dilapidated shop with an array of mortars out front as well as a few accessory figures and the obligatory street dogs. In the finished work, Gérôme introduced a more active human element, depicting a man vigorously pounding pigment.[3] He simultaneously made various adjustments to the architectural configuration of the shop-front, reduced the number of animals, limiting himself to a lone dog sleeping in the foreground, and altered the background to include a lively vignette of merchants dealing with veiled and robed women. Finally, Gérôme increased the quantity and brilliance of colors in the mortars, producing a striking sequence of pink, yellow, red, green, and orange.

While of a piece with the picturesque scenes of shops and merchants that were a mainstay of Gérôme's Orientalist production, *The Color Grinder* stands out as a self-reflexive exercise in color and painting, as the artist's description suggests. By identifying the picturesque Orient with a vital artisanal tradition of pigment-grinding, however, Gérôme indirectly draws attention to the fact that modern European painting, including his own, had been effectively severed from its artisanal origins with the introduction of mass-produced, prefabricated paints to workshop practice. **S. A.**

1. "Monsieur / Je m'empresse de répondre à votre lettre au sujet du tableau, le *Pileur de couleurs*, dont vous êtes propriétaire. Cet ouvrage a été fait l'hiver dernier. C'est une de ces boutiques assez nombreuses au Caire, où l'on broie des couleurs de toutes espèces dans des mortiers creusés dans des morceaux de colonne de granit. Naturellement, cette poussière se dépose sur les parois du mortier et donne l'aspect que j'ai taché de rendre avec ses colorations vives et diverses. J'ai fait cet ouvrage avec beaucoup de soin d'après une étude exécutée sur nature et j'espère avoir réussi à rendre l'impression que j'avais ressentie." Letter to an unknown recipient, dated Paris, July 12, 1891. I am grateful to Gerald Ackerman for supplying me with a photocopy of the original letter, which was incorrectly transcribed in G. Ackerman, *Jean-Léon Gérôme* (Courbevoie: ACR Édition 2000), p. 334, no. 409. **2.** See ibid., no. 409.3; and Christie's, London, *19th Century Continental Pictures, Watercolors and Drawings*, Nov 21, 1997, lot 256. **3.** His pose anticipates that of Polyphemus hurling boulders at Ulysses' ship in a painting of ca. 1902 (G. Ackerman, no. 471), as well as that of one of the Romans driving lions from an arena in a gory painting of 1902 (G. Ackerman, no. 469). I am indebted to Gerald Ackerman for this observation.

Ill. 121. Study for *The Color Grinder*, ca. 1890, oil on canvas, 18 × 15 in., private collection.

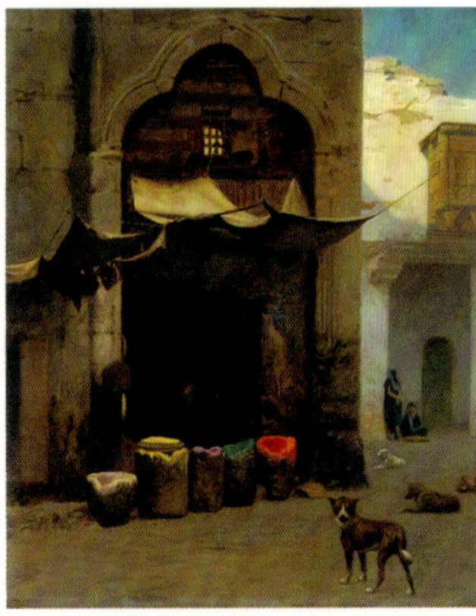

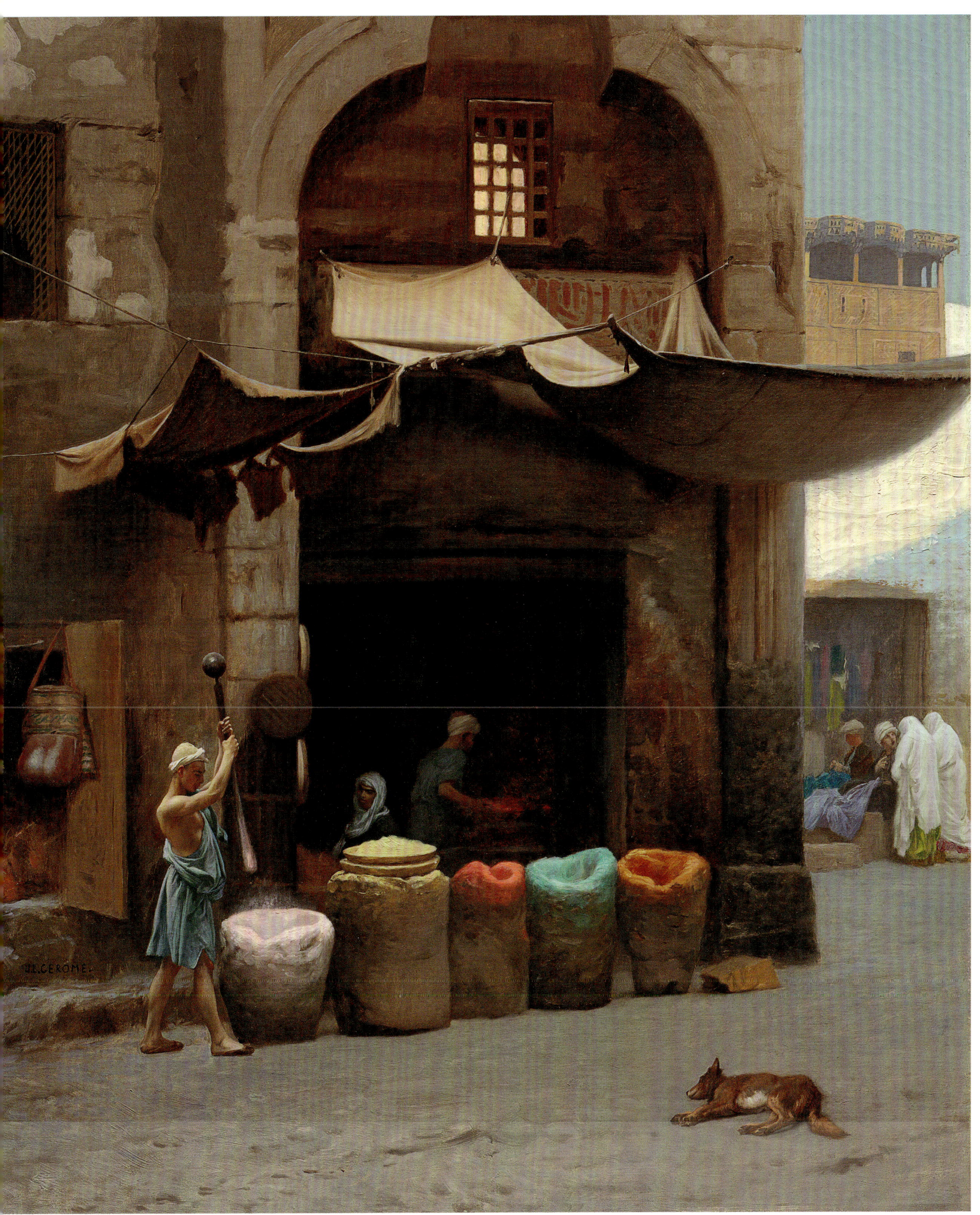
GEROME.

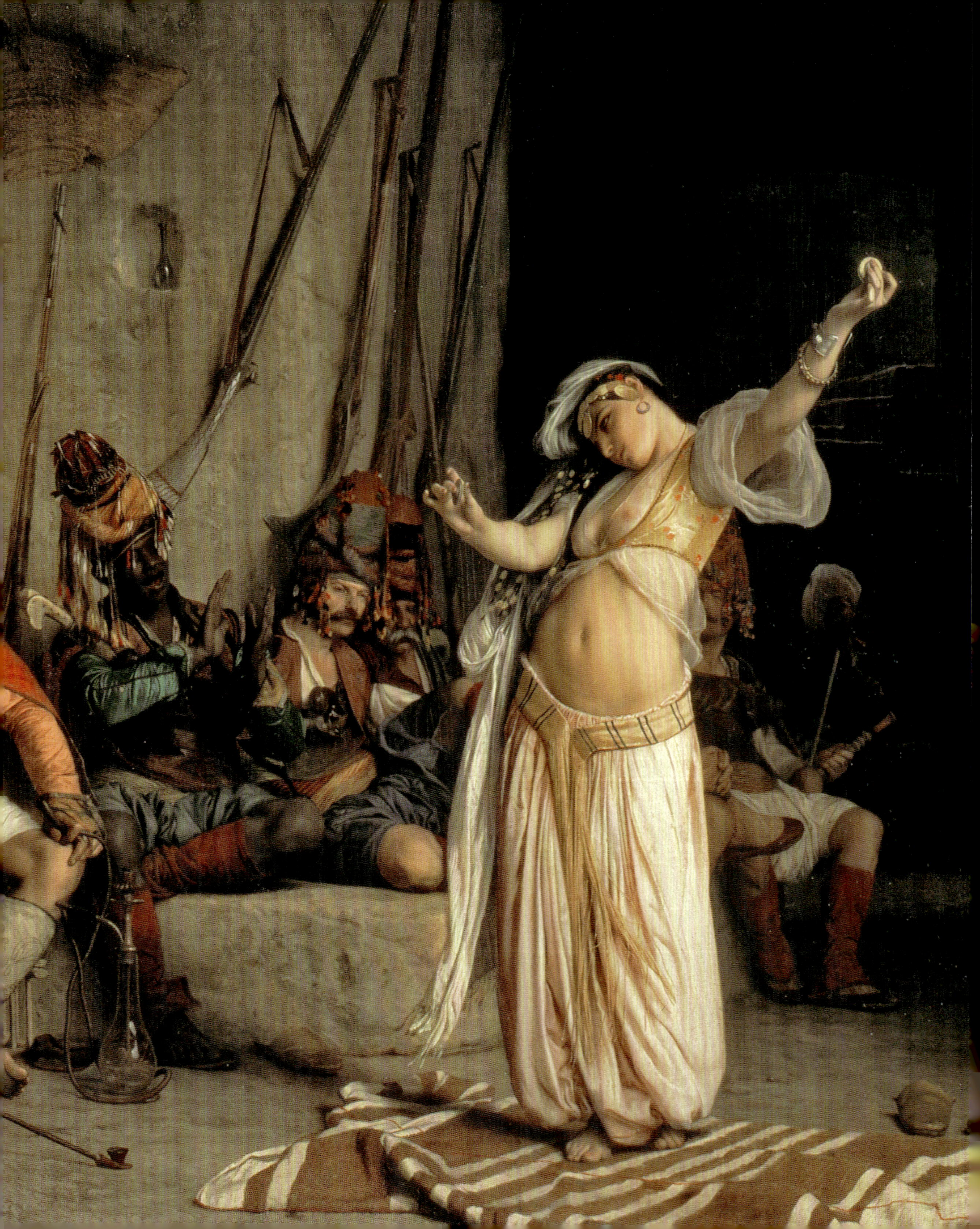

THE PARADOX OF REALISM: GÉRÔME IN THE ORIENT

Sophie Makariou and Charlotte Maury | Translated from the French by Jonathan Sly

GÉRÔME AND THE ENCOUNTER WITH THE ARABIAN ORIENT

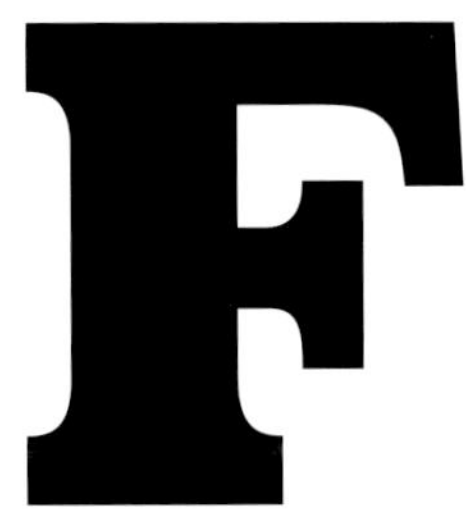

For anybody with a knowledge of the Islamic East who examines Jean-Léon Gérôme's works closely, the experience is fascinating. On discovering the first error, the viewer is intrigued; by the second, third, fourth, and more, astonishment has set in. From 1856 to 1880, Gérôme visited Egypt no less than six times. The first voyage lasted eight months and provided him with enough imagery for a long while. From these eight months, we should naturally subtract journey time; however, from 1850, French ships sailed from Marseille to Alexandria via Malta in seven days. From the 1870s, journeys became faster, and soon Alexandria had a rail connection with Cairo—or you could take a steam boat up the Mahmoudieh Canal. Gérôme was aware how travel had changed.[1]

Gérôme loved the Nile and the river became the protagonist of two unusual works: *The Prisoner* (cat. 127) and *Excursion of the Harem* (cat. 129). *The Prisoner* depicts a temple and papyriform columns, a felucca, and palm trees against the backdrop of Egypt's eternal landscape drenched in watery light. A prisoner is lying stiff and straight, his feet tied and hands in wooden stocks; the *bashi-bazouk* stares sternly into the distance, in a totally different direction to the lute player's mocking gaze. The picture was described as realistic, but how can one not be struck by the incongruity of the *espagnolade* taking place within the boat, where the prisoner is indulged with music as he travels along the Nile? In 1869, *Excursion of the Harem* plays out this same shift in reality in a lighter fashion. The Ottoman ladies, the Nubian oarsmen, the Arab *bashi-bazouks* are all credible actors, a likely group for the scene, and the positioning of each illustrates the hierarchies of Gérôme's contemporaries ("race" versus function) but also the intrinsic perception of an Orient where, according to the convention, command functions are distanced when the skin is darker. The Nile resembles a peaceful inland lake, its banks within close reach. But where has it come from, this Ottoman harem afloat on a boat on the Nile in Upper Egypt? The question must have escaped art lovers at the time, because the artist holds the viewer in thrall with the sunset, the photographic immensity of the sky, the yellow dash of a kaftan, the elegant silhouette of a blue parasol, the sculptural reduction of the oarsmen, and the bright streaks of the women.

In contrast to this experience, Cairo creates quite a shock. Its races, architectural environment, sounds and smells offer a palette of new and different sensations. Gérôme's Egyptian world is inhabited by men and women. But in an Egyptian society undergoing modernization from the top down, the daily reality of the strict segregation between the sexes is revealed, with a certain violence, in *For*

Cat. 154. *Dance of Almeh* (detail).

Sale (cat. 157); the column and magnificent antique-style drapery, at a glimpse, create the connection between the Orient and Rome, a theme dear to the nineteenth century.
Male characters predominate; indeed Gérôme is most likely to have encountered men. There is in his painting a selection of races reminiscent of Edward William Lane's famous work.[2] The *bashi-bazouk* (ill. 122), the muezzin, and the slave or horse sellers are exemplary; and more rarely we find solitary men whose social roles are unclassifiable.

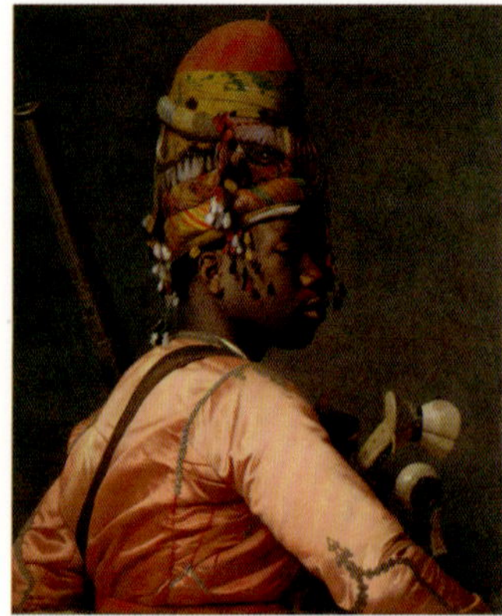

Ill. 122. *Bashi-Bazouk*, oil on canvas, 31 ¾ × 26 in., The Metropolitan Museum of Art, New York.

One of the best examples of the subtle distortions and collages of which Gérôme was fond is *The Muezzin* (cat. 145); a very high minaret with a pepper-pot dome—which is not visible—dominates Old Cairo.[3] In the distance we see a double minaret like that of El-Ghuri at the El-Azhar mosque, a prominent feature of the Cairo cityscape.[4] However, the cubic columns supporting the bulb on its corbelled stalactites (*muqarnas*) are borrowed from Hispano-Maghrebi architecture of the post-Almohad period; the type was made popular by the many Nasrid reproductions of the Alhambra. The plant motifs on the cubic balcony are a clear betrayal of the model. The feature has probably been faithfully copied straight from a book, as Gérôme's first travels to Algeria and Spain only took place in 1873 and 1883.[5] The same year, he painted *Prayer on the Housetops* (1865). The work does not use this artifice and precisely portrays the *malqaf*, the air vents in the roofs to catch the cool prevailing winds. The collective rhythm of the men's prayer—one of the essential principles of public prayer in Islam—has been broken, however[6]; in such an improbable location, this break speaks volumes about the incongruity of the scene.

Gérôme varies his effects; in *Public Prayer in the Mosque of Amr* (cat. 146), a single figure, in the foreground, standing on a prayer rug, is alone in breaking the rhythm. But Gérôme slips in another aberration: in the foreground the *bashi-bazouks* are wearing shoes! How absent-minded does a traveler have to be not to notice that shoes absolutely have to be removed at the threshold of a mosque?
The mosque of Amr, depicted here, evokes Théophile Gautier's image of Cordoba as a "forest of columns." The viewing angle[7] accentuates the jumble of vaults and the linear perspective created by the *saf*, or prayer rug. The floor stones in an *ablaq* style are multicolored while the colors of the arch stones of the vaults alternate,[8] a style that is distinctly Andalusian; the floor and arch stones of the mosque of Amr, however, are actually all of a single color. The theme of color brings picturesqueness and confusion to the site of "public prayer," which can be situated in neither the Orient nor the Occident, in neither Cairo nor Cordoba.
Prayer is a theme depicted on several occasions from all perspectives of Gérôme's imagination. The *bashi-bazouk* also features prominently in his repertoire, followed closely by the sale of slaves and horses. What of these oriental topoi? The scenes are unlikely, or more precisely it is improbable that Gérôme had access to such transactions; however, through this shift, they speak more of what Gérôme perceives of Egyptian and Turkish society, where domestic slavery was prominent and hard to ignore[9]; Gérôme was certainly only too aware of it. There is another category, a female type, that recurs several times in his work, that of the *almeh*.
In the Dayton Art Institute's *Dance of the Almeh* (cat. 154), a *bashi-bazouk* as weary as Velázquez's Mars barely glances at the dancing *almeh*. *Almehs* came into existence in the Islamic Middle Ages and their dissolute morals were condemned by Ibn Sa'id in the twelfth century.[10] In the French language, the word also has its problems; the Arabic "almât"[11] became the French "almée" from 1878, and was used as a pejorative term for wedding dancers. For Frédéric Lagrange, the name was no doubt applied to the famous dancers who played for the khedives, "modestly hidden from male eyes by a curtain," or maybe even, quite conversely, to mistresses made popular in the Egyptian novel of the twentieth century.[12] The significance of the character varies between potential respectability and manifest outrage. Gérôme presents an image of unambiguous sensuality, which confuses practices of gender segregation in Egyptian society of the nineteenth century.
Gérôme is therefore only interested in the women who are actually present in mixed spaces. In this way he is able to stage the female body—as he subsequently depicted women in Ottoman baths—in confrontation with clothed male bodies, as he does here. In so doing he initiates a very productive trend in Orientalist iconography, one which was frequently used in widely distributed forms such as postcards, particularly in North Africa.[13]
When Gérôme pays attention to architectural setting, he is capable of surprises as we have seen. He works not only by the process of *cadavre exquis* but also by lapses in titles. Thus the setting for

Ill. 123. Abdullah frères (Turkey, active 1858–99), *Interior of Topkapi Palace*, ca. 1865, albumen print, private collection.

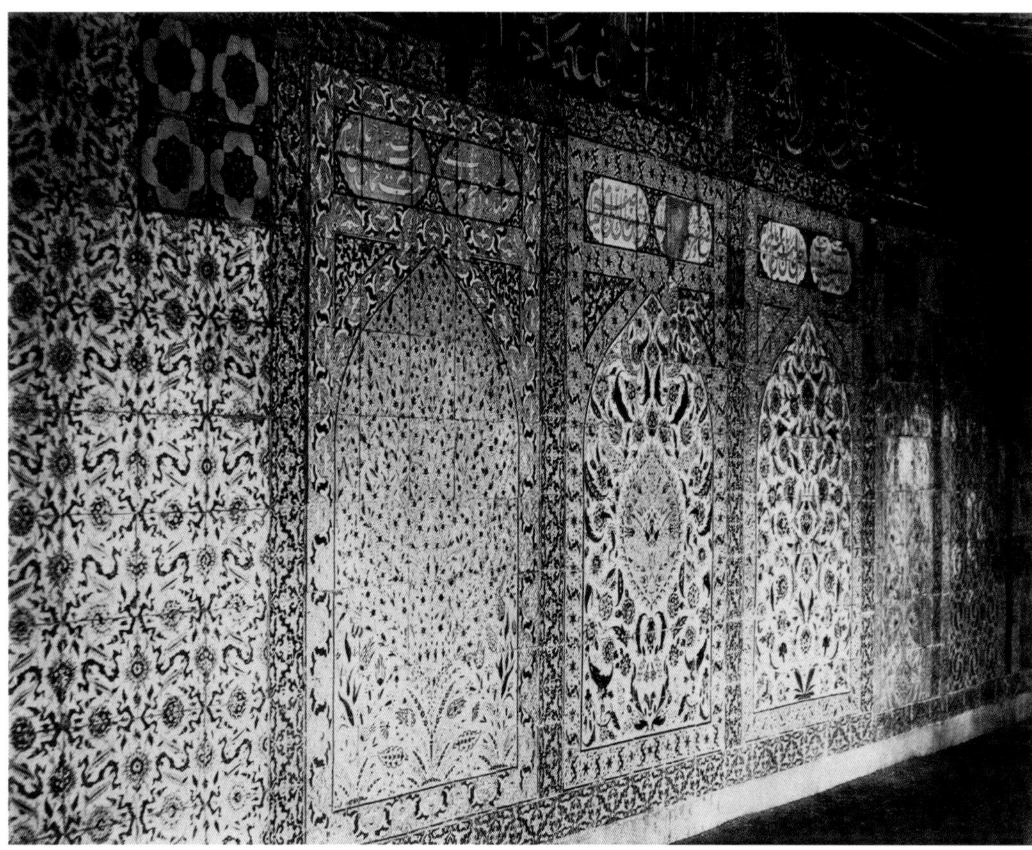

Cairene Horse Dealer (cat. 124) is actually in Yemen, a country he never actually visited. To create settings, though, he uses photographs taken by his 1856 travel companion, the sculptor Frédéric-Auguste Bartholdi. The photo providing Gérôme with the setting here was taken in Moka; the eye of the painter, who seems to have set his easel so firmly in place, actually shifts from place to place: in the background is a Hodeidah residence, also photographed by Bartholdi, which appears to have been realistically depicted right down to the finer details of the façade's beams.[14]

Gérôme sometimes focuses on one feature which then recurs in his work, a studio accessory such as the lightweight wooden cage on which he seats his characters or around which he animates scenes. He does the same with a stone gate with two heavy wooden doors. The theme is used in *Heads of the Rebel Beys at the Mosque El Assaneyn* (cat. 144) in 1866, and returns with variations, such as in *The Standard Bearer* (cat. 148) where it becomes the backdrop for a veiled character, possibly a Tuareg. There are the bands of stone in relief, the rectangular frame; but the *tiraz*, an epigraphical band—the characteristic feature of Mamluk architecture—has disappeared. It seems impossible to identify a precise location: the gate could be that of the mosque of Jawhar Lala, Qayt Bay, Aslam El-Silahdar, or Qijmas al-'Ishaqi—all examples of the second Mamluk period, the artist demonstrating a perfect understanding of the principles of composition involved in fifteenth-century Mamluk architecture without ever succumbing to literal citation. Such immersion in the subject recalls a remark made by Paul Lenoir about his master, who was a constant visitor to mosques.[15] In *The Marabou* (cat. 163), however, he was able to recompose the gate with examples seen during his travels to Algeria (1873) and Spain (1883), drawing inspiration too from the domestic architecture of the Ottoman period in Cairo. Within the painting there is also a possible play on words between the name of the bird and the picturesque figure of North African religion.

A final effect of strangeness and distance in relation to its subject is the recurring presence of the dog, a presence that is barely credible in a world where they are traditionally shunned as impure (*The Color Grinder*, cat. 151). The canine appearance in *Relay of Hounds in the Desert* (1866) is strikingly silent.

Finally, everything comes to life in a similar way in the play of accessories, which are always out of kilter with reality. The *Moorish Bath* (cat. 166) in Boston's Museum of Fine Arts sees the incongruous appearance of a Mamluk basin, which featured in the collection of Albert Goupil,[16] Gérôme's brother-in-law and travel companion in 1868, famous for the oriental lounge in his residence at 9, boulevard Chaptal, in Paris.[17] In *Public Prayer in the Mosque of Amr* (cat. 146), Gérôme enlivens the composition with a historically relevant choice of lighting: polycandelon, *tannur*, and metal lamp based on the Baybars model then in the collection of Charles Schefer, a dragoman in Istanbul before becoming an attaché to the École des Langues Orientales.

MANIPULATIONS AND DISTORTION: GÉRÔME AND OTTOMAN ARCHITECTURE

Gérôme's first contact with the Ottoman Empire can be dated to 1853, at the end of a journey that had taken him to the Balkans and Romania. His return passage to Europe via the banks of the Bosphorus and the Sea of Marmara was simple, but Istanbul, with its teeming life, does not seem to have left a marked impression on him. This first step beyond the oriental threshold had no immediate effect on his artistic production. But the Ottoman capital maybe lacked what Gérôme would soon find in Cairo. At that time, Istanbul claimed to be at the forefront of Eastern modernity, irremediably effacing all sense of elsewhere and foreignness. The many reforms enacted by sultans from the mid-nineteenth century onwards modified costumes, lifestyles, and the urban environment, and many travelers expressed nostalgia for their "dream of the Orient" that they did not want to see disappear. "Reform has ruined all that was poetic in Istanbul and in Muslim habits; if this continues, the country will cease to have anything of curiosity," complained the academician Joseph Michaud in 1830.[18]

Gérôme would not go back to Istanbul before 1871, when he spent longer there, before returning twice in 1875 and 1879. We have scant information about the three voyages—either the artist's movements or the material he brought back—but many of Gérôme's pictures created from the 1870s up to the end of his career reflect an interest in Ottoman architecture. The ceramic facing that adorns both religious and profane edifices initially appealed to his eye as a colorist and enabled him to set his characters against colored backgrounds with a dominance of blue and green. Bathing scenes, conversations by a fireplace, and prayers in a mosque were all subjects where this type of citation appears. The photographic precision with which Gérôme seems to reconstitute facings and other architectural aspects only rarely proceeds from a totally faithful imitation of reality. Behind the illusion of truth are hidden a number of transformations to which he subjects aspects of a reality observed with his own eyes or approached through photography. "There is no law to prevent an author from working *as a painter*; that is to say from bringing together in a creation of the mind a multitude of details drawn from nature and rigorous truth, although they have been selected," writes Edmond About on the subject of Gérôme's work in the dedication of his book *Le Fellah*.[19] Selection, recomposition, and manipulation, are indeed the motivations of Gérôme's art. He is at once the scenographer, costume designer, choreographer, and director; he intelligently selects and positions each element of his compositions. Clothing, objects and backdrops, taken in isolation, may be authentic, but their orchestration is not; the result is often theatrical, surprising, intriguing, and inauthentic.

A picture like *The Serpent Charmer* (cat. 160) lends itself readily to the artist's reconstitution process, and through this work it is possible to trace his stage directions step by step. Beyond the improbable nudity of the snake charmer, shamelessly exposed to an audience of disparate characters selected for the diversity of their physical features and costumes as much as for their age, the eye encounters a solid wall covering two thirds of the painting and rebounds to the main subject of the scene. This broad, entirely ceramic surface, with its bluish tones, cleverly takes its inspiration from the ornamentation of Ottoman monuments. It is crowned by a long inscription in white Arabic script against a blue background; below, it is subdivided into panels alternating between white and blue backgrounds that establish a binary rhythm. The first three panels and the fifth are drawn from the same real building: they form four consecutive sections of the facing of the Topkapi palace, no doubt familiar to Gérôme through the photography of the Abdullah frères (ill. 123).[20] In the narrow corridor of the palace, known as the "Golden Path," space is limited and it can only be photographed tangentially. Gérôme preserves the angle of photography in his work, and continues the perspective line rightwards.[21] In so doing, he has to enlarge the frame of the original image and invent continuity.

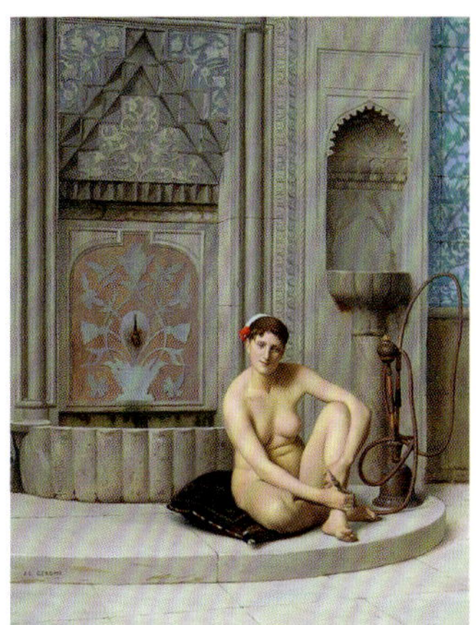

Ill. 124. *Odalisque*, ca. 1902–3, oil on canvas, 16 ¼ × 12 ¾ in., Appleton Museum, Florida State University, Ocala.

In order to do this, he changes the fourth and final panels visible on the photograph, by duplicating the panel with the dark background and shifting a white panel towards the right. This artifice enables him to place the forearm and radiant skin of the snake charmer against a dark background. Further to the right, Gérôme duplicates this panel again, creating a regular alternation of blue and white backgrounds, up to the right edge of the painting. Having created two extra rows, he has to invent the inscriptions above the arcatures. What is more, he elects to make their colors uniform. If Gérôme had stayed faithful to his model, the inscriptions of the blue panels would stand out in white against two blue cartouches, which is not the case. The painter imagined, or desired, a colored harmony dominated by blue and white, simplifying the more extensive palette of the originals, which have notes of red and green. He also had to invent the cap running the breadth of the canvas. The edge of the white calligraphical frieze against the blue background, barely visible in the upper left corner of the Abdullah frères' photograph, could not be used. Spotting this, Gérôme recomposed the inscription by drawing inspiration from a similar frieze in one of the pavilions of the Topkapi palace.[22] Lower down Gérôme even allowed himself a note of false realism. To achieve a "larger than life" effect he created two gaps on the right, one of which nicely completes the original, but very real adaptation that had already disturbed the initial sequencing of the various backdrops. This detail, like so many others, serves to create an illusion and contributes to building precision, which seems at first sight to follow on from a perfect imitation of the real. But as we can see this precision is simply a tool used to recompose an artificial reality.

This form of "detective work" could be applied to a number of other scenes where Gérôme's source of inspiration is both identifiable and modified, reworked and distorted. The fountain before which is seated the *Odalisque* (1903, Appleton Museum, Ocala, Florida), is easily recognizable and relatively faithful to the original monument: the fountain of the library of Ahmet III, in the Topkapi palace (ill. 124). This fountain is located in the third courtyard of the palace, reserved according to protocol for the sultan's male entourage. Placed against the banister of a staircase leading up to the library and below a portico, the fountain looks onto the courtyard and its garden. It is not situated in a hammam of the palace. A raised, round platform creates a higher step on which the young woman can sit. To her right, a small ribbed basin mirrors that of the fountain. However, it does not correspond to the basins we see today, which are bulkier and in the shape of *muqarna* column capitals. Does this mean the fountain, captured in a photograph of the time, was different then? There is room for doubt, but knowing Gérôme, we might suggest another possibility. If the painter had reproduced the capital basin as it was, the pose of the young woman and the movement of her arms, enveloping her left knee and right leg, would have been restricted. Furthermore, there would have been no room for the hookah—an indispensable feature of Gérôme's bathing scenes—the mouthpiece of which the young woman is holding. And towards the right the wall's marble casing has been replaced with blue and white ceramic, another sign of the painter's intervention. Despite these changes, the rendering of the décor has great precision and reflects a thorough knowledge of the model and its tones, such as the red against which the flower bouquet stands out in slight relief (in reality it is gilded).

This surprising combination of photographic "high resolution," aesthetic alterations, and functional distortions characterizes a number of Gérôme's works. Here, a garden fountain or, elsewhere, a public fountain[23] are removed from their original contexts to serve the composition, undergoing revisions and disguises. The *mihrab* of the mosque of Rüstem Pasha, used twice by Gérôme, also undergoes several variations that an inquisitive and expert eye will be constantly entertained at tracking down.[24] The painter also seems to fail to acknowledge or voluntarily ignore the real purposes of the settings he uses. In *Terrace of the Seraglio* (1886), he sets his bathers in the pool of the marble terrace at the Topkapi palace, which he faithfully reproduces (ill. 125).[25] The setting is precise—give or take several details—but the scene is totally improbable. Located between the chamber housing holy relics and the room where princes were circumcised, the Baghdad and Yerevan kiosks, the only frolicking the pool has ever witnessed is that of its attractive fish.[26] It should be added that the women, bathing in the open air and in broad daylight, even in this closed area of the palace, contravene the very strict morality of Ottoman society. Bathing is a purification ritual that is only conceivable in the warmth and confinement of the hammam. Gérôme was probably no fool here; to the distortion of places and the unlikelihood of situations, he likes to oppose the precise imitation of real settings, bringing veracity to his pictorial fiction.

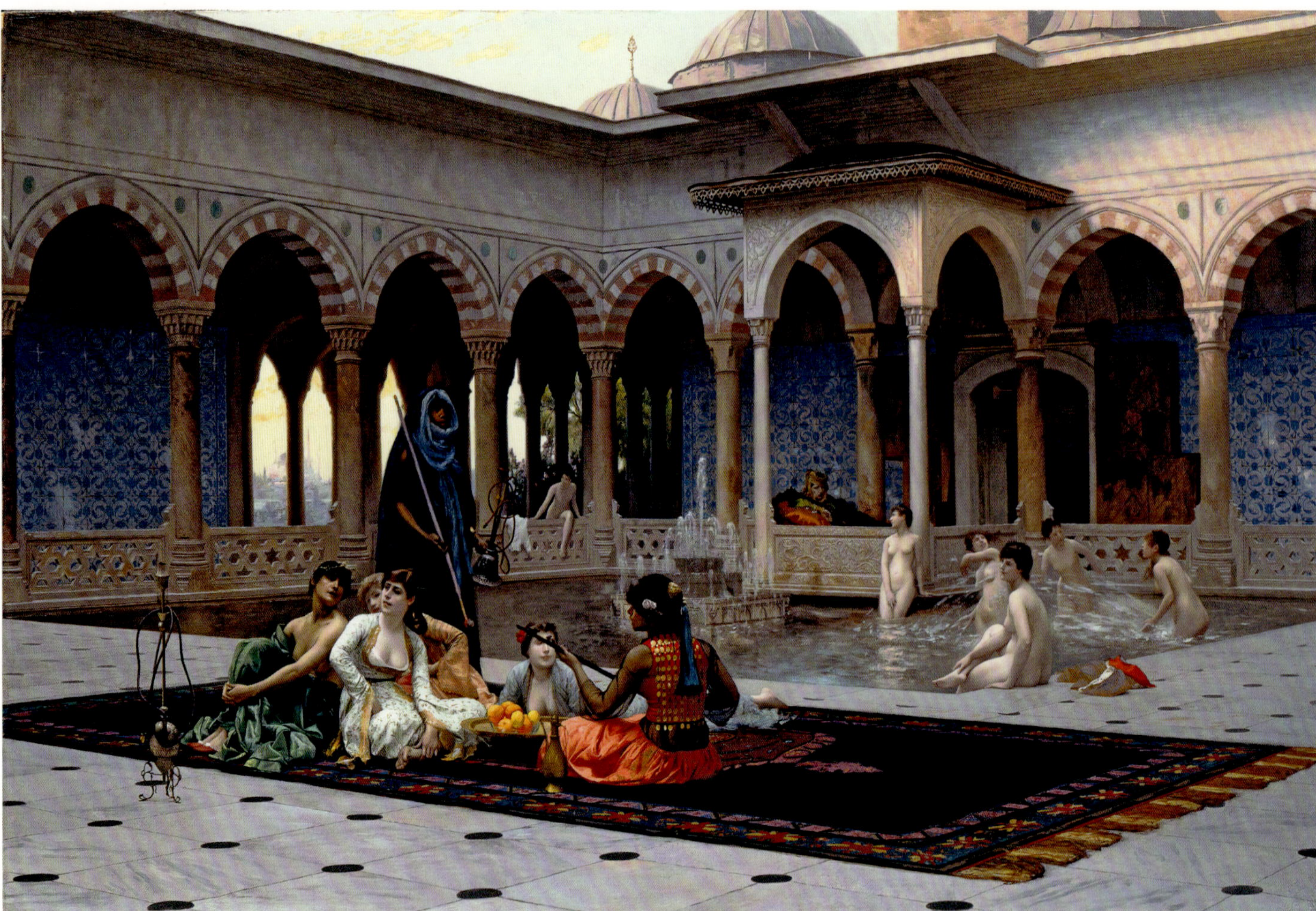

Ill. 125. *The Terrace of the Seraglio*, 1886, oil on canvas, 32 ¼ × 38 in., private collection.

In *Field of Rest* (1876), the infringement of reality is more unexpected. The painter creates a convincing depiction of an Ottoman cemetery, strewn with subsiding tombstones; the tombstones have a stone cap, indicating the deceased's profession in his lifetime. With a slight concession to Romanticism, Gérôme dangerously accentuates the angles of their subsidence, forcing an impression of abandonment and nostalgia. Three women are sitting on a carpet; they are wearing large gowns and fine white veils characteristic of women of the Turkish upper classes in the late nineteenth century. One of them is also holding a parasol, an indispensable modern accessory at the time. The situation is plausible up to this point, as is the perspective over the plain—a vague evocation of the heights of Bursa set on the slopes of the Ulu Dağ mountain range. The anomaly is elsewhere; this time it is not in the situation but in the architecture of the blue building, which is of Iranian inspiration. Its minarets and the form of its dome reveal nothing that is Ottoman but instead evoke Iranian Safavid architecture, such as the domes and minarets of Isfahan. The annex to the monument retains hints of a different monument in Bursa, specifically one side of the famous Green Mausoleum (Yeşil Türbe) of Mehmet I. All Gérôme retains of this hexagonal edifice is the elevation of its facades, which are all identical with the exception of the entrance porch. Cased in turquoise-blue ceramic, punctuated by rectangular windows and broken arches, two facades are here juxtaposed in the same extension. The form is rectangular, as opposed to the original hexagonal form, and crowned by a small dome of no resemblance to the dome and tambour of Yeşil Türbe. The effect is surprising: an edifice of Iranian inspiration dominates the landscape of the Bursa plain, shamelessly juxtaposed by an Ottoman cemetery.

These collages of disparate architectural elements, containing reworked gestures, combined objects, and the blurring of sexual boundaries are commanded by a mimetic hand and eye that gives credence to the claim of Gérôme's "realism." The methodical illusion of Gérôme's work found further emphasis through the means of its reproduction and distribution.[27] We might dare to classify it as an unassuming precursor to the art of the Surrealists. With his informed eye, which constantly fashioned objects and architectural details of great quality, Gérôme, artist and collector, distorted, meaningfully and with verve, the Eastern world that both captivated and no doubt repelled him, deploying his perceptions of what he found aesthetic and censoring heavily in the process.

1. E. Isambert and A. L. Joanne, *Itinéraire descriptif, historique et archéologique de l'Orient* (Paris: Hachette & Cie, Guides Joanne Collection, editions of 1861, 1873, 1878).

2. E. W. Lane, *Manners and Customs of the Modern Egyptians* (London, 1836, 1895; Cairo: American University in Cairo Press, 2003).

3. On the minaret see D. Behrens-Abouseif, *The Minarets of Cairo* (Cairo: American University in Cairo Press, 1985); the pepper-pot form was contemporary with the reign of El-Ghuri (1501–16): Janbalat mosque (1500–1); minaret of the emir Qanibay al-Rammah, built in Nasiriyya in 1506, and beneath the citadel in 1503. Such minarets are characterized by changes in column sections, with the exception of the citadel's which has quadrangular column sections and which probably served as Gérôme's model.

4. Ibid., pp. 149–57.

5. In the 1895 edition of E. W. Lane's book (as in n. 2), p. 77, it is this image that is used to illustrate the call to prayer in a work supposedly containing information verified by the author *in situ*. Crucially, by the time the work was revised, the author had been dead for twenty-two years. The muezzin, sheltered by the same minaret, stands out against the background of a different city, dominated by domes, more evocative of Damascus or Jerusalem; the high silhouette of the Cairo minarets has disappeared.

6. F. Pouillon, "L'ombre de l'Islam. Les figurations de la pratique religieuse dans la peinture orientaliste du 19e siècle," *Actes de la recherche en sciences sociales*, no. 75 (1988), pp. 24–34.

7. Also adopted by Félix Bonfils.

8. The distempering of Cairo monuments in 1869 for the inauguration of the Suez Canal does not seem to have affected the mosque, as the mosque of Amr was disused at the time.

9. O. Pétré-Grenouillot, *Les Traites négrières, essai d'histoire globale* (Paris: Gallimard, 2004).

10. "Drunkenness which is the cause of criminality, the sound of stringed instruments, women of poor repute, their faces uncovered, publicity for places of pleasure," quoted from A. Raymond, *Le Caire* (Paris: Fayard, 1993), p. 101.

11. From *'âlma*, plural *'awâlîm;* M.-N. Bouillet and A. Chassang, eds., *Dictionnaire universel d'histoire et de géographie* (Paris: Librairie Hachette, 1878).

12. F. Lagrange, "L'ad b et l'almée: images de la musicienne professionnelle chez Tawf q al-Hakim et Nag b Mahfuz", *Annales islamologiques de l'IFAO* (online journal), forthcoming.

13. On this subject, consult G. Boëtsch and J.-N. Ferrié, "La Mauresque aux seins nus: l'imaginaire érotique colonial dans la carte postale," in *Images et colonies*, eds. P. Blanchard and A. Chatelier (Paris: Syros, 1993), pp. 93–96, and G. Boëtsch and J.-N. Ferrié, "Du daguerréotype au stéréotype: typification scientifique et typification du sens commun dans la photographie coloniale", *Hermès*, no. 30 (2001), pp. 161–67.

14. R. Hueber et al., *Au Yémen en 1856: photographies et dessins d'Auguste Bartholdi*, exh. cat. (Colmar: Musée Bartholdi, 1994), pp. 84 and 100.

15. Gérôme kept a diary of his 1868 voyage, thirty pages of which were published by C. Moreau-Vauthier, *Gérôme peintre et sculpteur. L'homme et l'artiste d'après sa correspondance, ses notes, ses souvenirs, les souvenirs de ses élèves et de ses amis* (Paris: Hachette, 1906).

16. The basin is today to be found in the collection of the Musée des Beaux-Arts in Lyon.

17. We wish to thank Loreline Simonis for her precious assistance; her excellent work was invaluable to us: L. Simonis, "L'Union centrale des Arts décoratifs et les arts de l'Islam: acquisitions et expositions, 1878–1893," Master's thesis supervised by R. Labrusse, (Université de Picardie Jules-Verne, Amiens, 2007).

18. Quoted from A. Servantie, *Le Voyage à Istanbul. Byzance, Constantinople, Istanbul du Moyen Âge au xxe siècle* (Brussels: Éditions Complexe, 2003), p. 56.

19. Quoted H. Lafont-Couturier, *Gérôme & Goupil. Art et entreprise*, exh. cat. (Bordeaux: Musée Goupil, 2000–1; also New York: Dahesh Museum of Art, 2001, and Pittsburgh: The Frick Art & Historical Center, 2001), p. 121.

20. *Odalisques et arabesques*, p. 68, fig. 8.2. The three panels with alcoves, commissioned by Selim II for the renovation of the baths of the third courtyard, bear the date 1574–75. The date of their reassembly in this corridor is unknown: see G. Necipoğlu, *Architecture, Ceremonial and Power. The Topkapi Palace in the Fifteenth and Sixteenth Centuries* (Cambridge: MIT Press, 1991), p. 132.

21. He also uses this backdrop in *A Bath, Woman Bathing her Feet* (1889) with a darker shade of coloring.

22. The Baghdad kiosk. On this subject, W. B. Denny, "Quotations in and out of Context: Ottoman Turkish Art and European Orientalist Painting," *Muqarnas*, vol. X (1993), p. 220.

23. For example: *Turkish Women at the Bath* (ca. 1876), Hermitage Museum, Saint Petersburg; *After the Bath* (1881), private collection.

24. These two works are conserved in private collections: *The Blue Mosque* (1878, Shafik Gabr collection); *The Mosque of Rüstem Pasha*

25. The same basin would be used again in the *The Pipe Lighter* (ca. 1898), the artist modifying the framing and taking more liberties with the location.

26. G. Necipoğlu 1991 (as in n. 20), pp. 155–58.

27. H. Lafont-Couturier 2000–1 (as in n. 19).

Cat. 152

MUSICIAN, SQUARED-UP STUDY FOR *SABRE DANCE*

–

ca. 1863
Pencil on paper glued to vellum paper
Vellum paper: 14 ¾ × 10 ¾ in.;
drawing: 12 ¾ × 8 in.
Dr. Edward T. Wilson collection, Bethesda, Maryland

–

Provenance: Separated from cat. 101.

Cat. 153

ALMEH OF CAIRO

–

1863
Pencil on beige paper
12 × 8 ¾ in.
Musée des Beaux-Arts, Nancy,
inv. TH.99.15.640

–

Provenance: Anonymous gift.

–

Bibliography: S. Harent and C. Stoullig, *Dessins de Jean-Léon Gérôme: la collection du musée des Beaux-Arts de Nancy*, exh. cat. (Nancy: Musée des Beaux-Arts, 2009), no. 16, p. 61.

Cat 154

DANCE OF THE ALMEH (THE BELLY-DANCER)

–

1863
Oil on panel
19 ¾ × 32 in.
The Dayton Art Institute, Dayton

–

Provenance: Gérôme to Goupil, Oct. 1863, stock book no. 936, as "Danseuse," (for 10,000 francs). Goupil to Knoedler, New York, May 1865 (for 20,000 francs). Knoedler to John Hoey, New York, 1867 (for $6,000). Robert Badenhop, Newark, New Jersey, gift to the Dayton Art Institute, 1951.

–

Exhibition history: Salon of 1864, no. 794. Exposition Universelle, Paris, 1867, no. 297.

–

Bibliography: C. Timbal, "Gérome," *Gazette des Beaux-Arts*, 2nd per., vol. 40, no. 4 (Oct. 1, 1876), pp. 338, 340, 342. E. Strahan [Earl Shinn], *The Art Treasures of America: Being the Choicest Works of Art in the Public and Private Collections of North America*, 3 vols. (Philadelphia: G. Barrie, 1880), vol. 3, pp. 78–79. E. Strahan [Earl Shinn], ed., *Gérome: A Collection of the Works of J. L. Gérome in One Hundred Photogravures* (New York: Samuel L. Hall, 1881), vol. 4, n.p. F. F. Hering, *Gérôme: The Life and Works of Jean Léon Gérôme* (New York: Cassell, 1892), pp. 106–7. F. Masson, "J.-L. Gérome, peintre de l'Orient," *Figaro illustré*, 2nd ser., no. 136 (July 1901), p. 22. V. Guillemin, "Étude sur le peintre et sculpteur Jean-Léon Gérome (1824–1904)," *Académie des sciences, belles-lettres et arts de Besançon. Procès-verbaux et mémoires. Année 1904* (Besançon, 1905), pp. 151–52, 179. *Music and Art*, exh. cat. (Minneapolis: University Gallery, University of Minnesota, 1958; also Grand Rapids: Grand Rapids Art Gallery, 1958), n.p. B. H. Evans, *Fifty Treasures of the Dayton Art Institute* (Dayton: Dayton Art Institute, 1969), pp. 118–19, no. 45. G. Ackerman et al., *Jean-Léon Gérôme (1824–1904)*, exh. cat. (Dayton: Dayton Art Institute, 1972; also Minneapolis: Minneapolis Institute of Arts, 1973, and Baltimore: The Walters Art Gallery, 1973), pp. 53–54, no. 14. D. A. Rosenthal, *Orientalism: The Near East in French Painting, 1800–1880*, exh. cat. (Rochester, N.Y.: Memorial Art Gallery of the University of Rochester, 1982), pp. 76, 80, 164, no. 39, fig. 76. A. Boime, "Gérôme and the Bourgeois Artist's Burden," *Arts Magazine*, vol. 57, no. 5 (Jan. 1983), pp. 66–67, fig. 7. M. A. Stevens, ed., *The Orientalists, Delacroix to Matisse: European Painters in North Africa and the Near East*, exh. cat. (London: Royal Academy of Arts, 1984), pp. 139–40, no. 29. M. A. Stevens, ed., *The Orientalists, Delacroix to Matisse: The Allure of North Africa and the Near East*, exh. cat. (Washington, D.C.: National Gallery of Art, 1984), pp. 141–42, no. 31. G. Ackerman, *The Life and Work of Jean-Léon Gérôme, with a Catalogue Raisonné* (New York and London: Sotheby's, 1986), pp. 63, 68, 110, 214, no. 144. S. Monneret, *L'Orient des peintres* (Paris: Nathan, 1989), 203. Wendy Buonaventura, *Serpent of the Nile: Women and Dance in the Arab World* (1989; New York: Interlink Books, 1998), pp. 86, 88–89. C. Williams, "Jean-Léon Gérome: A Case Study of an Orientalist Painter," in *Fantasy or Ethnography? Irony and Collusion in Subaltern Representation*, eds. S. J. Webber and M. R. Lynd (Columbus, Ohio: Division of Comparative Studies in the Humanities, Ohio State University, 1996), pp. 131, 133, 136, fig. 8. G. Ackerman, *Jean-Léon Gérôme: His Life, His Work, 1824–1904* (Courbevoie: ACR Édition, 1997), pp. 66, 76–77. D. H. Vasseur et al., *Selected Works from the Dayton Art Institute* (Dayton: Dayton Art Institute, 1999), pp. 260–61. G. Ackerman, *Jean-Léon Gérôme: monographie révisée, catalogue raisonné mis à jour* (Paris: ACR Édition, 2000), pp. 65, 252, no. 144. H. Lafont-Couturier, *Gérôme and Goupil: Art and Enterprise*, exh. cat., trans. I. Ollivier (Bordeaux: Musée Goupil, 2000–1; also New York: Dahesh Museum of Art, 2001, and Pittsburgh: The Frick Art & Historical Center, 2001), pp. 24, 25, 27, 36, 40, 50, 51, 129, 130, 133, 152, 165. G. Wohlmann, "Die nackte Lüge. Aktdarstellungen in der französischen Orientmalerei," in *Sprachformen des Körpers in Kunst und Wissenschaft*, ed. G. Genge (Tübingen and Basel: A. Francke, 2000), pp. 238–39, fig. 35. G.-G. Lemaire, *L'Univers des orientalistes* (Paris: Éditions Place des Victoires, 2000), p. 238. S. Harent and C. Stoullig, *Dessins de Jean-Léon Gérôme: la collection du musée des Beaux-Arts de Nancy*, exh. cat. (Nancy: Musée des Beaux-Arts, 2009), pp. 24, 60, under no. 16, fig. a.

Ill. 126. Hippolyte Bellangé (1800–1866), vignette from *Napoléon en Égypte, Waterloo et le fils de l'homme… Édition illustrée par Horace Vernet et Hte. Bellangé* (Paris: E. Bourdin, 1842), between pages 90 and 91, Bibliothèque Nationale de France, Paris, inv. 8-RF-21764.

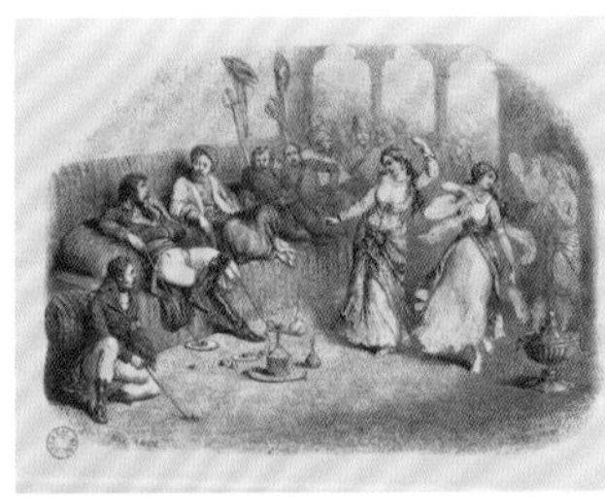

Dance of the Almeh offers an illicit glimpse into a dingy Egyptian café, where a dancing girl performs on a carpet laid down for the occasion. With head dramatically tilted and arms upraised, she plays the finger cymbals while describing a slow, wheeling circle with her hips. Low-hanging pantaloons emphasize her dance's low center of gravity, while a transparent gauze chemisette and yellow silk corselet accentuate and reveal her bosom, leaving bare her ample midsection. Her belly button provides the visual and narrative center of the tableau.[1] Riveting their gazes on her are a group of Ottoman mercenaries or *bashi-bazouks*, armed with pistols and *yatagans* (short daggers) and sporting their distinctive coiled and tasseled headgear. On the opposite side of the *almeh*, a trio of Arab musicians accompanies her dance with the *kamangah* (a string instrument), *darabukkah* (drum), and *zummara* (reed pipe), while a servant in the background quietly goes about preparing the coffee.

A staple of nineteenth-century Orientalist art, the subject of dancing girls, like that of the harem or bath, embodied for would-be travelers the fabled voluptuary pleasures of the East. Before traveling to Egypt, Gérôme would have formed tantalizing notions of such dancers through travel accounts or poetic descriptions like the following, found in Barthélemy and Méry's *Napoléon en Égypte* (1842): "*Les almés de l'Égypte, agiles bayadères, /Aux longs cheveux flottants, aux tuniques légères,/ Secouant les grelots des moresques tambours,/De leurs corps gracieux dessinent les contours./Leur amoureuse voix, féconde en poésie,/Chante la volupté sous le soleil d'Asie;/Leur souffle plus hâté, leurs membres*

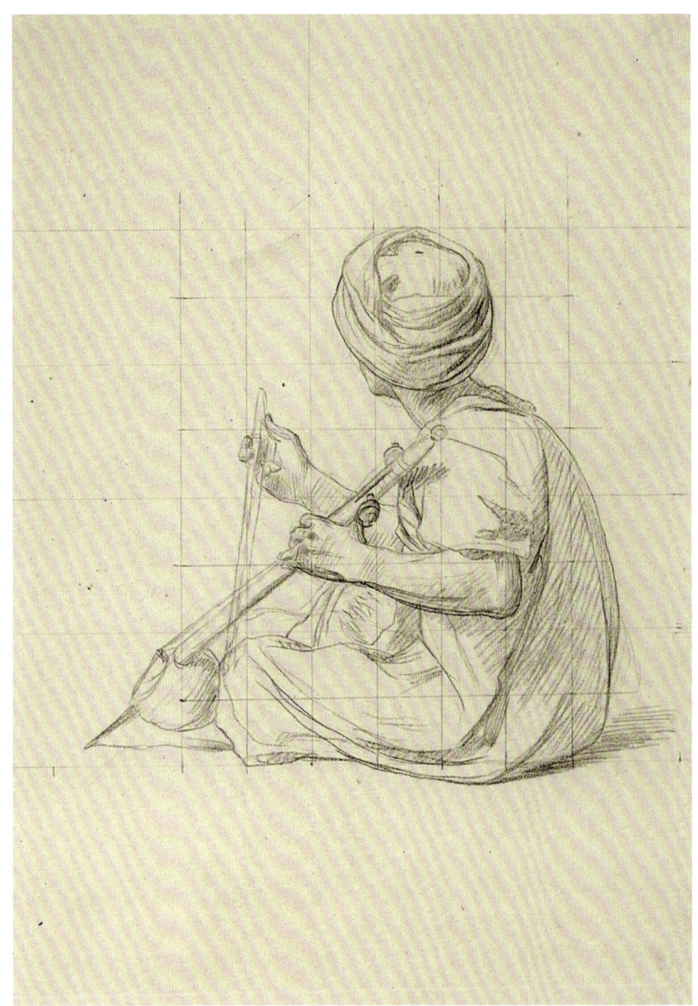

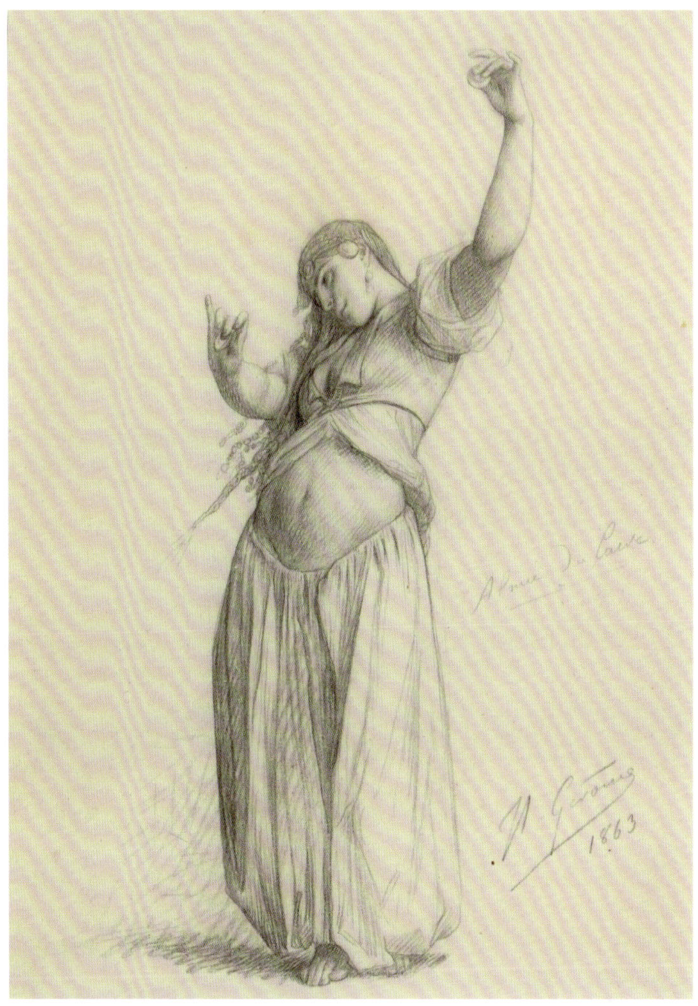

frémissants,/Expriment sans pudeur le délire des sens,/Jusqu'au moment suprême où leur molle attitude/Annonce du plaisir la douce lassitude;/Le châle obéissant, dans leur bras soutenu,/Serre leur taille souple ou presse leur sein nu;/La flamme est sur leur teint, leur regard étincelle,/Une tiède sueur sur la gaze ruisselle,/Et de leur corps lascif, par la danse excité,/S'exhalent des parfums empreints de volupté."[2]

Accompanying this passage was a vignette by Hippolyte Bellangé of *almehs* dancing for French officers (ill. 126), which resonates with Paul Lenoir's description of the dance that he, Gérôme, and their travel companions witnessed during their 1868 expedition to Egypt. Lenoir indeed devoted a whole chapter of his travel account to "Les danseuses" and the opportunities they provided for both flirtatious dalliance and artistic study.[3] Gérôme reportedly obtained some of the girls' costumes, which feature in his numerous representations of *almehs* after 1868.[4] Given the earlier date of the Dayton painting, one might assume that he also witnessed dancers performing on his 1862 voyage to Egypt and the Near East, though he would not have had this chance in Cairo. In an attempt at morality-policing, Muhammad Ali Pasha had issued an edict in 1834 banning the female entertainers from the city, since they had by that point become closely associated with prostitution.[5]

Whatever erotic fantasies belly-dancers fueled in the French imagination, those fantasies seem curiously soured in Gérôme's dispassionately slick, hyper-focused vision. Casting a sinister pall over his scene are the foremost Albanian *bashi-bazouks* who sit with tense, predatory apprehension and glare fixedly at the woman, in sharp contrast to the single black man in their company who claps merrily along (affirming racist stereotypes about the supposedly infantile state of the African mind). Further tension is evident in the closely contained group of Arab musicians, whose grave and scowling miens suggest disdain for the foreign mercenaries at whose arrogant behest they are obliged to perform.

Any such underlying tension went largely unremarked when the painting was first exhibited at the 1864 Salon. Combining voyeuristic appeal and technical virtuosity, *Dance of the Almeh* was a sensational success with the public. "Here's the room of Gérôme, and like everybody else we will go straight to the Almeh," the sympathetic About began his review. From Catholic conservatives to liberal republicans, however, most critics were highly suspicious of Gérôme's popularity. Recognizing the painting's obvious antecedents in *A Greek Interior* (cat. 23), *King Candaules* (cat. 43), and *Phryné Before the Areopagus* (cat. 45)—all of which involved dramatic stagings of the female body—critics suspected Gérôme of cynically speculating "on something completely different from artistic passion,"[6] of pandering to the basest instincts of his audience. Théophile Thoré snidely remarked, "I suppose that the *almeh* and her belly will delight some old millionaire,"[7] while Émile Zola later quipped that one could find reproductions of *Dance of the Almeh* in the quarters of adolescent boys throughout France.[8] For Jules-Antoine Castagnary the painting was a "coldly calculated indecency," and Alfred Nettement likewise reached the conclusion that it had been painted because "that is what sells."[9] Others wondered how such an illicit scene could have been allowed by the authorities to be exhibited "with impunity before the immense Parisian public, before our wives, our mothers, our sons and our daughters," a circumstance particularly galling given the ban on such dances in public in Cairo.[10] These charges of indecency certainly seem to be justified when the picture is compared with contemporary paintings like Léon Belly's *Fantasia*, a relatively tame scene of an Egyptian dancer also exhibited in the 1864 Salon (ill. 127).

Ill. 127. Léon Belly (1827–1877), *Fantasia (Egypt)*, in *Léon Belly*, exh. cat. (Saint-Omer: Musée de l'hôtel Sandelin, 1977), p. 37, no. 63, Archives, Musée d'Orsay, Paris.

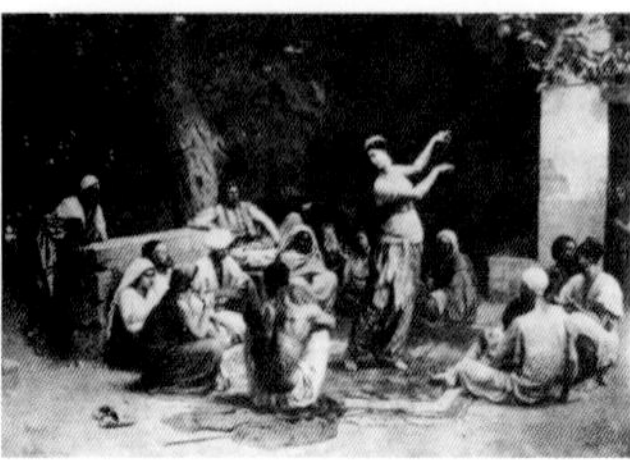

Dance of the Almeh's putative status as an objective "scene of customs,"[11] however, largely spared Gérôme the virulent attacks he had suffered three years before with *Phryné*, which many dismissed as an indecent vulgarization of the classical *beau idéal*. The eroticism of the work could be understood to point less to the prurient interests of Gérôme or his Parisian audience and more to the native characters of the "orientals" depicted in the painting[12]; indeed, several critics claimed that such an earthily voluptuous dance as the *almeh*'s left cold the more refined Europeans who preferred lighter, more ethereal fare.[13] The painting thus found some validation as an ethnographic study that confirmed cultural stereotypes about the degenerate moral character of the East. This, of course, did not prevent some critics from recalling with hypocritical relish their own voyeuristic experiences of belly-dancers in Egypt.[14] **S. A.**

1. As Paul Challemel-Lacour sarcastically wrote: "Tout son tableau tourne autour d'un point culminant, d'un centre à la fois géométrique et idéal, d'un foyer d'où rayonnent sur les personnages du tableau et sur les spectateurs des effluves magnétiques. Voilà pourquoi je suis magnétisé. Ce foyer incendiaire, ce point, ce centre, il faut le nommer, c'est un nombril. C'est là que se croisent tous les regards et que jaillissent les éclairs de toutes les prunelles." P. Challemel-Lacour, "Le Salon de 1864," *Revue germanique et française*, vol. 29, no. 3 (June 1, 1864), pp. 539–40. **2.** [Joseph Pierre Agnès] Méry and [Auguste Marseille] Barthélemy, *Napoléon en Egypte; Waterloo et le fils de l'homme…Édition illustrée par Horace Vernet et Hte. Bellangé* (Paris: E. Bourdin, 1842), pp. 90–91. **3.** P. Lenoir, *Le Fayoum, le Sinaï et Pétra: expédition dans la moyenne Égypte et l'Arabie Pétrée sous la direction de J. L. Gérome* (Paris: Henri Plon, 1872), pp. 96–117. **4.** See, for instance, G. Ackerman, *Jean-Léon Gérôme*, (Courbevoie: ACR Édition, 2000), nos. 202, 227–30, 243, 245, 286, 308–9, 336, and 352. **5.** See M. A. Stevens, in *The Orientalists, Delacroix to Matisse: The Allure of North Africa and the Near East*, exh. cat. (Washington, D.C.: National Gallery of Art, 1984), pp. 129–30, no. 29. **6.** B. Bouniol, "Causeries d'un amateur. Salon de 1864," *Revue du monde catholique*, vol. 9, no. 77 (June 10, 1864), p. 395 ["Il n'est pas possible de se tromper sur la portée de pareilles œuvres, qui trop évidemment spéculent sur toute autre chose que sur la passion artistique"]. **7.** W. Bürger [Théophile Thoré], "Salon de 1864," in *Salons de W. Bürger, 1861–1868*, 2 vols. (Paris: Veuve Jules Renouard, 1870), vol. 2, p. 55. ["Je suppose que l'Almée et son ventre feront les délices de quelque vieillard millionnaire"]. **8.** See "Nos peintres au Champ-de-Mars," in É. Zola, *Écrits sur l'art* (Paris: Gallimard, 1991), p. 184 ["dans les ménages de garçons on rencontre l'*Almée* et *Phryné devant le tribunal*"]. **9.** J.-A. Castagnary, *Salons (1857–1870)* (Paris: Bibliothèque Charpentier, 1892), p. 211 ["indécence froidement calculée"]; and A. Nettement, "Salon de 1864," *La Semaine des familles*, June 25, 1864, p. 612 ["C'est que cela s'achète"]. **10.** L. Lagrange, "Le Salon de 1864," *Gazette des Beaux-Arts*, vol. 16, no. 6 (June 1, 1864), p. 529 ["La police égyptienne interdit les danses d'almées en public. L'Almée de M. Gérôme exécute impunément devant l'immense public parisien, devant nos femmes, devant nos mères, devant nos fils et nos filles cette danse du ventre, le dernier mot de la lubricité"]. **11.** See, for example, C. de Sault, "Salon de 1864," *Le Temps*, June 8, 1864 ["Mais s'il vient de faire un pas de plus dans la voie des Phrynes et des Aspasies, M. Gérôme peut affirmer qu'il peint une scène de mœurs, ce qui n'était certainement pas le fait des tableaux soi-disant grecs dont nous parlons. L'intérêt de couleur locale peut donc atténuer le manque d'élévation de l'*Almée*"]. **12.** See, for example, C. de Moüy, "Le Salon de 1864," *Revue française*, vol. 8, no. 44 (June 1, 1864), p. 243 ["l'Orient aime sa danse peu légère et l'épanouissement sensuel de ses contours sans élégance et sans finesse… elle éveille la sensualité bestiale des brutes caparaçonnées qui l'entourent et l'applaudissent… L'Orient a imaginé ces fêtes des yeux pour plaire aux sens tout en laissant à l'esprit son affaissement énervé. M. Gérôme a bien rendu ces types d'une race dégénérée"]. **13.** See, for example, E. About, *Salon de 1864* (Paris, 1864), pp. 196–97 ["L'esprit tout matériel des Orientaux ne goûterait nullement les exercices aériens d'une Taglioni, d'une Emma Livry, d'une Mourawieff, de ces jolies créatures incorporelles qui nous lancent à coups de pied dans les espaces de l'idéal bleu. Il n'apprécierait pas beaucoup plus la coquetterie frétillante d'une Ferraris ou d'une Petipa, qui babille des jambes et réveille en nous mille fantaisies spirituelles en sautillant devant nos yeux"]. **14.** See M. A. Stevens, in *The Orientalists, Delacroix to Matisse: European Painters in North Africa and the Near East*, exh. cat. (London: Royal Academy of Arts, 1984), pp. 139–40, no. 29.

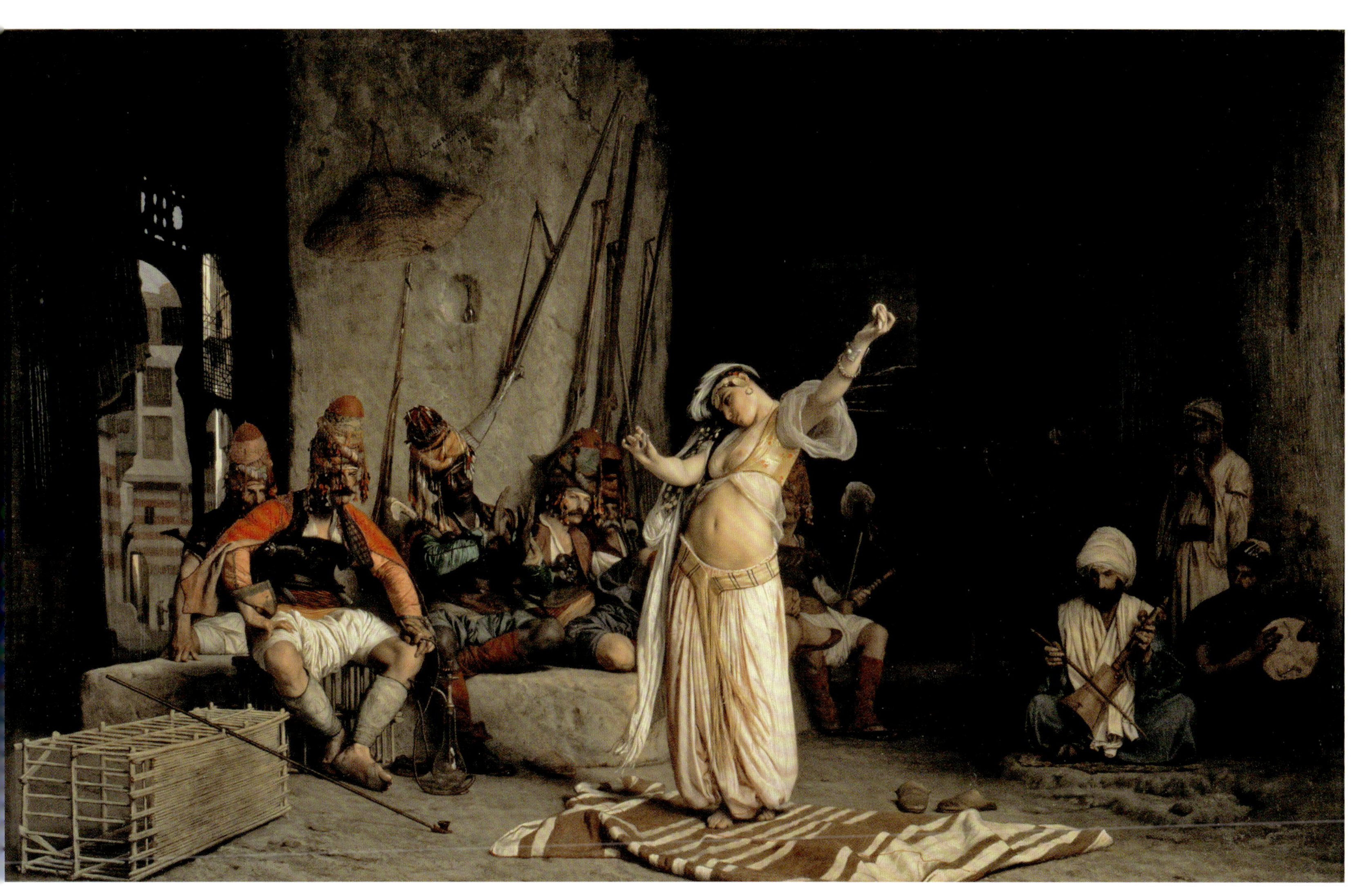

Cat. 155

BASHI-BAZOUK SINGING

–

1868
Oil on canvas
18 × 26 in.
The Walters Art Museum, Baltimore

–

Provenance: James B. Haggin, until 1917. Haggin sale, American Art Association, New York, Apr. 4–5, 1917, lot 40, to R. H. Lorenz, agent for Henry Walters (for $1,400).

–

Bibliography: E. Strahan [Earl Shinn], ed., *Gérome: A Collection of the Works of J. L. Gérome in One Hundred Photogravures* (New York: Samuel L. Hall, 1881), vol. 4, n.p. G. Ackerman, "Thomas Eakins and his Parisian Masters, Gérôme and Bonnat," *Gazette des Beaux-Arts*, 6th per., vol. 73, no. 1203 (Jan. 1969), pp. 243, 255, fig. 24. G. Ackerman et al., *Jean-Léon Gérôme (1824–1904)*, exh. cat. (Dayton: Dayton Art Institute, 1972; also Minneapolis: Minneapolis Institute of Arts, 1973, and Baltimore: The Walters Art Gallery, 1973), pp. 46–47, no. 10. *Americans Abroad: Painters of the Victorian Era*, exh. cat. (San Jose, Calif.: San Jose Museum of Art, 1975–76), n.p. W. R. Johnston, *The Nineteenth Century Paintings in the Walters Art Gallery* (Baltimore: Trustees of the Walters Art Gallery, 1982), p. 105, no. 110. A. Boime, "Gérôme and the Bourgeois Artist's Burden," *Arts Magazine*, vol. 57, no. 5 (Jan. 1983), pp. 64, 70, fig. 1. G. Ackerman, *The Life and Work of Jean-Léon Gérôme, with a Catalogue Raisonné* (New York and London: Sotheby's, 1986), pp. 83, 224, 225, no. 185. G. Ackerman, "Gérome's Oriental Paintings and the Western Genre Tradition," *Arts Magazine*, vol. 60, no. 7 (Mar. 1986), p. 77, fig. 10. J. Perry Brown, "The Return of the Salon: Jean Léon Gérôme in the Art Institute," *Museum Studies*, vol. 15, no. 2 (1989), p. 181, n. 31. G. Ackerman, *Jean-Léon Gérôme: His Life, His Work, 1824–1904* (Courbevoie: ACR Édition, 1997), pp. 83, 87. C. Peltre, *Les Orientalistes* (Paris: Hazan, 1997), p. 145. G. Ackerman, *Jean-Léon Gérôme* (Paris: ACR Édition, 2000), pp. 85, 270–71, no. 185.

This merrymaking scene features Gérôme's favorite *bashi-bazouks* (irregular troops of diverse origin in the service of the Ottoman Empire). The dominant figure, along with two of his companions, wears a pleated white skirt and crimson cloak that identify him as an Arnaut, as Albanian mercenaries were known among Turks and popularized in the West by Romantic writers and artists like Lord Byron and Eugène Delacroix.[1] Perched on a stone furnace, similar to the one Gérôme showed elsewhere being used for casting shot,[2] the Arnaut plays an *oud* while spiritedly singing and tapping his heels, losing a slipper in the process. He marks the culminating point of a comic visual crescendo that begins in the left background with the figure laid out in a narcotic daze. Completing the company opposite the *oud*-player is a raven perched on a wicker cage, cheerfully squawking along.

Bashi-Bazouk Singing is manifestly a studio fabrication. The costumes, props, raven, and model for the principal figure all recur frequently in Gérôme's art. As Ackerman has argued, such paintings constitute an Orientalist reworking of familiar types from Western genre painting.[3] In particular, the *oud*-player is heir to the singing lute-players of Italian and northern European baroque painting (Caravaggio, Terbrugghen, Hals, etc.), and the picture recalls scenes of merry companies and musical parties popular in seventeenth-century Dutch art. Gérôme also capitalized on nineteenth-century tastes for musical themes, reinforcing the association of the lower classes and colorful exotic types with unbridled musical expression.[4] In this respect, Gérôme's Arnaut is a not-too-distant cousin of Édouard Manet's *Spanish Singer* (ill. 128), which had been enthusiastically endorsed with a resounding "*Caramba!*" at the 1861 Salon by Gérôme's loyal defender Gautier.[5]

Of particular interest to Gérôme, Arnauts pervaded his work from the late 1850s onward. They could stand as figures for Ottoman despotism, as in *Egyptian Recruits Crossing the Desert* (1857 Salon; ill. 103, p. 226), in which Arnauts lead forced conscripts on their march, or *The Prisoner* (1863 Salon; cat. 127), in which an Arnaut mockingly serenades the bound captive. They could also represent Muslim piety, as in the *Prayer in the House of an Arnaut Chief* (1857 Salon). In a different vein, the present work—like many others that show Arnauts relaxing, playing chess, or dancing and carousing[6]—emphasizes their jocular *bonhomie* and *jeux d'esprit*, qualities much remarked by contemporaries in Gérôme himself. Fair complexioned and impressively mustached, the mercenaries seem indeed to have functioned as alter egos of sorts for the artist, who was seen to share physiognomic characteristics with them.[7] Perhaps the Arnaut allowed him to project an image of sanguine, domineering masculinity, of insouciant power and freedom, in an Eastern environment over which he himself claimed mastery in his role as intrepid *artiste-voyageur*. **S. A.**

Ill. 128. Édouard Manet (1832-1883), *Spanish Singer*, 1860, oil on canvas, 57 1/4 × 45 in., The Metropolitan Museum of Art, New York, Gift of William Church Osborn, 1949, inv. 49.58.2

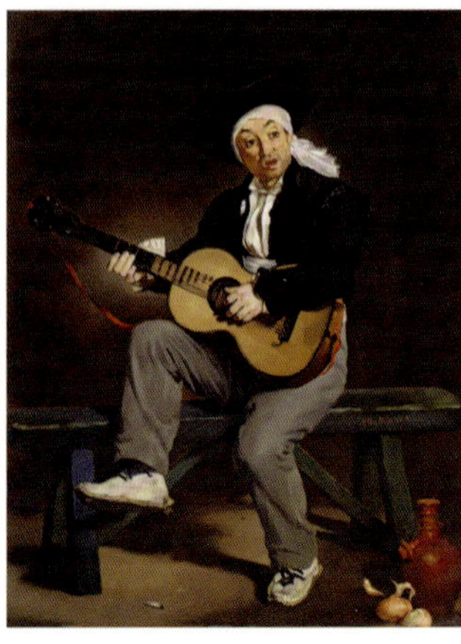

1. See N. Athanassoglou-Kallmyer, "Of Suliots, Arnauts, Albanians and Eugène Delacroix," *The Burlington Magazine* vol. 125, no. 965 (Aug. 1983), pp. 487–91. **2.** See G. Ackerman, *Jean-Léon Gérôme* (Courbevoie: ACR Édition, 2000), no. 317. **3.** See G. Ackerman, "Gérôme's Oriental Paintings and the Western Genre Tradition," *Arts Magazine*, vol. 60, no. 7 (Mar. 1986), pp. 75–80. **4.** Ibid., p. 77. **5.** See *Manet, 1832–1883*, exh. cat. (Paris: Galeries Nationales du Grand Palais, 1983; also New York: The Metropolitan Museum of Art, 1983), p. 63, under no. 10. **6.** See, for instance, G. Ackerman 2000 (as in n. 2), nos. 137, 158, 203–4, 302–7, 316–17, 335–36. **7.** Contemporary critics explicitly identified Gérôme with Arnauts. Jules Claretie thus described the artist: "... un visage osseux, des yeux de lave, un front large, des cheveux noirs, le teint bronzé, quelque chose d'Arnaute, voilà l'homme." *Peintres et sculpteurs contemporains* (Paris: Charpentier, 1873), p. 12.

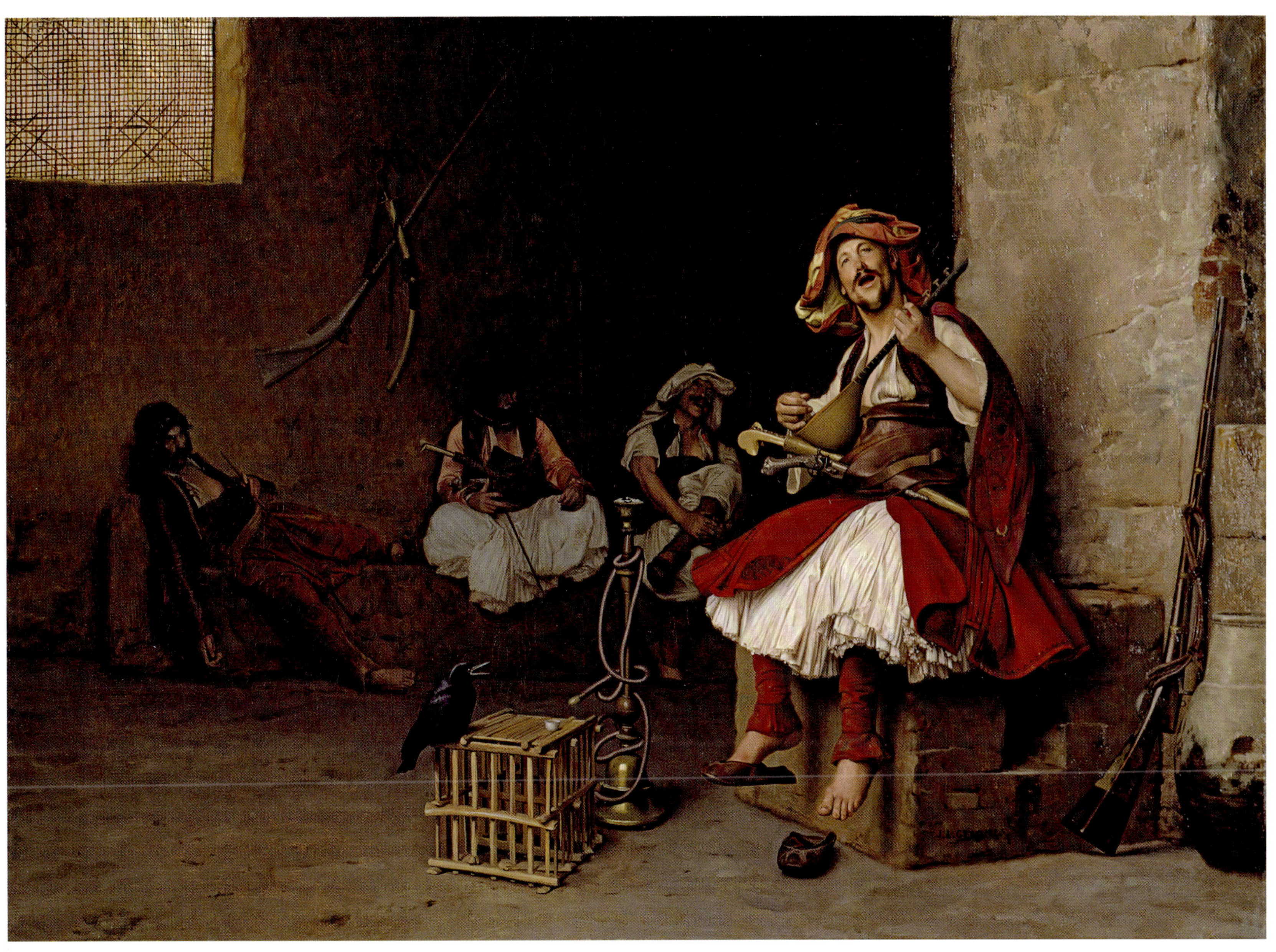

Cat. 156

THE SLAVE MARKET (FOR SALE)

–

1866
Oil on canvas
33 ¼ × 25 in.
Signed lower right: *J.L. GEROME*
Sterling and Francine Clark Art Institute, Williamstown, inv. 1955.53

–

Provenance: Sold by Goupil to Gambart, 1866. Salon of 1867, returned by Gambart. Goupil to M. Mayer, Dresden, 1867. Goupil to August Belmont, New York. August Belmont, New York, 1890. Knoedler, New York, Mr Clark, 1930.

–

Exhibition History: Salon of 1867, Paris. Exhibited in Berlin in 1868.

–

Bibliography: G. Ackerman et al., *Jean-Léon Gérôme (1824–1904)*, exh. cat. (Dayton: Dayton Art Institute, 1972; also Minneapolis: Minneapolis Institute of Arts, 1973, and Baltimore: The Walters Art Gallery, 1973), p. 22, ill. 11. G. Ackerman, *Jean-Léon Gérôme* (Courbevoie: ACR Édition, 2000), no. 162.

Cat. 157

FOR SALE (THE SLAVE MARKET)

–

1871
Oil on canvas
29 ½ × 23 ½ in.
Signed lower right: *J.L. GEROME*
Cincinnati Art Museum, John J. Emery Fund, Cincinnati, inv. 1917.368

–

Provenance: Goupil to J. Lefèvre, 1871 (for 25,000 francs). Knoedler, New York. Auguste Belmont, New York, 1873 (for 45,000 francs). Property of J. Lefèvre.

–

Exhibition History: Royal Academy, London, 1871. "Exposition des Mirlitons," Place Vendôme, Paris, 1873. World's fair, Vienna, 1873.

–

Bibliography: Hering, half-tone illustration. *Recueil. Œuvres de Jean-Léon Gérôme,* BNF Estampes, vol. VII, no. 6. G. Ackerman et al., *Jean- Léon Gérôme (1824–1904)*, exh. cat. (Dayton: Dayton Art Institute, 1972; also Minneapolis: Minneapolis Institute of Arts, 1973, and Baltimore: The Walters Art Gallery, 1973), p. 21, ill. 10. *Orientalism*, exh. cat. (Rochester: Memorial Art Gallery of the University of Rochester, 1982; also New York: Neuberger Museum, 1982), no. 41. G. Ackerman, *Jean-Léon Gérôme* (Courbevoie: ACR Édition, 2000), no. 217.

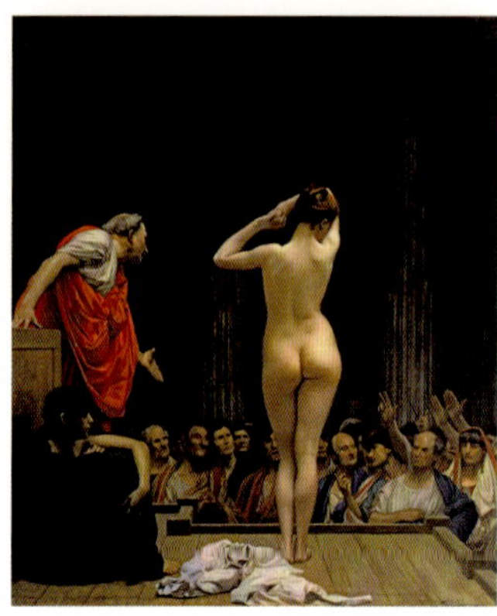

Ill. 129. *Roman Slave Market*, 1884, oil on canvas, 25 ¼ × 22 ½ in., The Walters Art Museum, Baltimore, inv. 37.885.

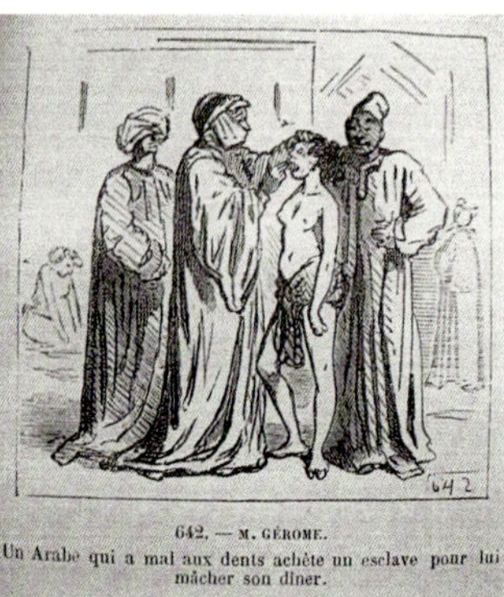

Ill. 130. Cham [Amédée de Noé] (1819–1879), "M. Gérôme. An Arab with toothache buys a slave to chew his dinner for him," in *Cham au Salon de 1867* (Paris: Arnauld de Vresse, 1867), woodcut, Archives, Musée d'Orsay, Paris.

Gérôme indulged in depictions of slave markets several times, a subject that he blithely set either in contemporary Egypt or ancient Rome (ill. 129). This simple observation would suffice to disprove Maxime Du Camp's assertion, when the Clark Institute canvas was exhibited at the Salon of 1867, that he had witnessed such scenes: "*The Slave Market* is a scene drawn from life."[1]

Not that slavery didn't exist in Egypt at the time: in his report on Egypt in 1845, Victor Schoelcher mentioned several times the presence of slaves in houses he had visited in Cairo. The condition of slaves was far from uniform—some of them, stated Schoelcher, were raised like the family's own children, and lacked for nothing.[2] In contrast, he strongly criticized the harsh treatment given to fellahs working the Egyptian plains.

It is hard to know whether open-air slave markets existed, as Gérard de Nerval and Du Camp claimed; Schoelcher doesn't mention them in his report. Knowing Schoelcher's political opinions, it is probable that he would have mentioned them if he had seen them. Whatever the reality, the scene in this painting of 1866—like the Roman market painted in 1884—was not so much a depiction of a real event as a fantasy that was above all sensual and pictorial.

Sensual, indeed overtly erotic, Gérôme's canvases certainly were: why would the merchants—whom Du Camp described as "brigands familiar with every form of abduction and violence"—need to strip naked a woman destined to be a domestic servant? Or, even stranger, why would they check her teeth? This latter gesture evokes horse dealers, and was an unambiguous sign of enslavement. Thus under cover of an observed reality, Gérôme was exhibiting the deepest workings of his imagination to the public in 1867—workings so fully shared by the beholders of his day that they hardly batted an eye. The same public that two years earlier had condemned Édouard Manet's *Olympia* and two years later would splash a bottle of ink over Jean-Baptiste Carpeaux's *Dance* hardly stirred upon seeing a naked woman surrounded by clothed men, a woman who was "subjected, in humble and fatalistic resignation," (Du Camp once again) to the men's deeds and desires.

The scene is set in the Orient, which evoked all kinds of voluptuous liberties, as it had since *The*

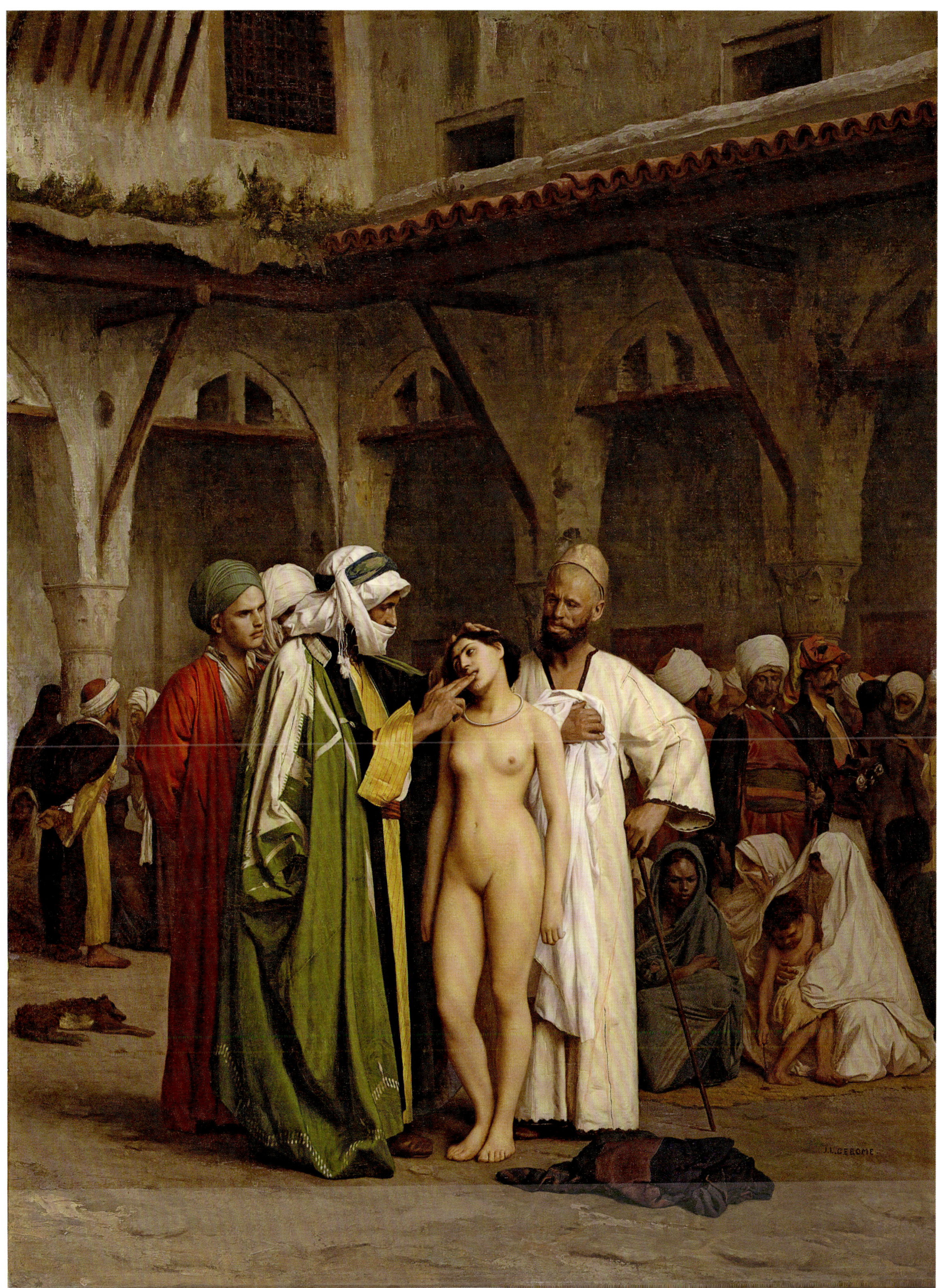
J.L.GEROME

Arabian Nights and especially since the painterly inventions of Jean-Auguste-Dominique Ingres and the poetic inventions of Victor Hugo and Nerval. This feeling was so deeply entrenched that it entertained no doubt. Moreover, Gérôme's manner, so faithful to the draftsmanship and finish of academic art, placed the individual woman at one remove by stressing the antique model behind the flesh-and-blood model, thereby respecting strict artistic precepts even as he created the illusion of some remote reality. This nude woman with her smooth, sleek body exposed to the gaze of ancient or Egyptian slave dealers harked back to Gérôme's own *Phryné before the Areopagus* (cat. 45), which had been a hit at the Salon of 1861. In 1851 already, commenting on Gérôme's *A Greek Interior* (cat. 23), Théophile Gautier stressed the ambivalence of Gérôme's paintings of female nudes; Gérôme wavered between faithfulness to the antique model and the temptations of eroticism, "perhaps because he did not have the jesuitry to call it 'Slave Market' or 'Captives Exhibited for Sale,' believing in an art so chaste, so sober and so pure that his own art would suffice to clothe such an improper subject."[3]

The way in which Gérôme's friend Cham transformed this scene in his caricature of the Salon of 1867 by replacing the woman with a man underscores the difficulty of depicting a woman, henceforth distanced from the ancient model via caricature, in such a pose (ill. 130).

The canvas now in Cincinnati presents a different scene of the same subject matter. Near a stall in which a man with vacant stare is seated—a stall scarcely different from that in *A Turkish Butcher Boy in Jerusalem* (cat. 143) or the one photographed by Auguste Bartholdi in Cairo (cat. 116)—a group of women is gathered. Some are seated, others standing, awaiting the customer who will come to buy them. A nude woman on the far left, with full, sleek figure, once again evokes Gérôme's classical-style nudes. A letter sent by the painter to his wife shows how much he kept on being true to details, despite the overall sensuality of the scene: "I feel now relieved (...), [concerning] what I should finish in the Slaves painting. Yesterday and today, I worked on the parrot which gave me several nervous hesitations, but now I do think it is quite well done...."[4]

The success of Gérôme's paintings, which were disseminated through photography and engravings, underscores the ambivalence of the representation of female nudity in the nineteenth century and the close connection been artistic and moral conceptions. It also reveals the Orientalism behind the sensual perception of the East, which survived in the twentieth-century commentaries that these paintings continued to spark.[5] **D. F.-R.**

1. M. Du Camp, "Salon de 1867," *Revue des Deux Mondes,* XXXVIIIth yr., 2nd per. (May 1, 1867), p. 674. **2.** V. Schoelcher, *L'Égypte en 1845* (Paris: Pagnerre, 1846), pp. 13 and 106. Muhammad Ali Pasha was khedive of Egypt at the time. **3.** T. Gautier, "Salon," *L'Artiste,* 5th ser., vol. 6, p. 117. **4.** Undated, kept at the Custodia Foundation, Paris, fonds Gérôme. **5.** L. Nochlin, "The Imaginary Orient," in *The Politics of Vision: Essays on Nineteenth-Century Art and Society* (New York, 1989), pp. 33–59.

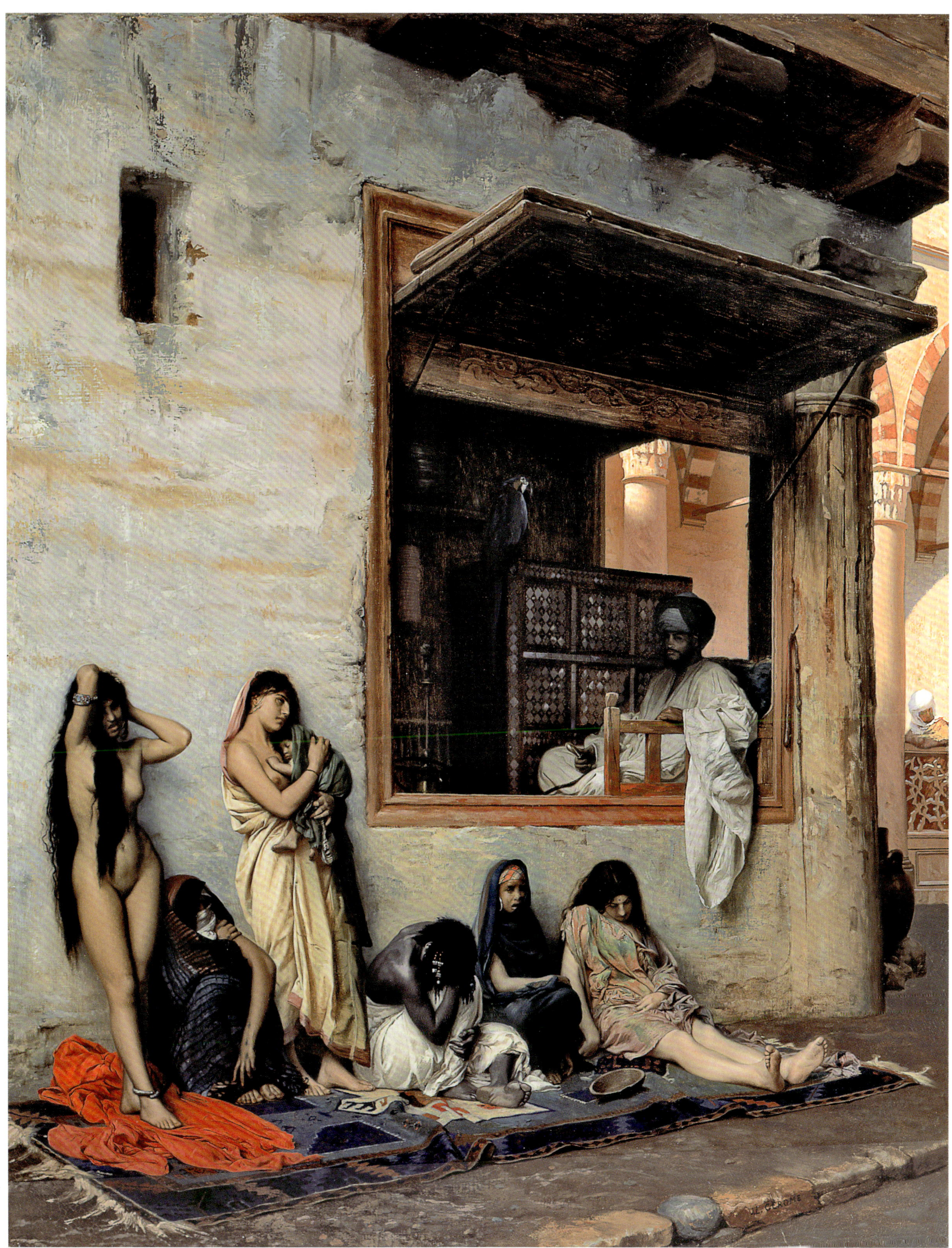
J.L. GEROME

Cat. 158

VEILED CIRCASSIAN LADY

–

1876
Oil on canvas
16 × 12 ¾ in.
Signed top right: *J.L. GEROME*
Orientalist Museum, Doha, inv. OM.696

–

Provenance: No. 11544 in Goupil's stock ledgers. Gérôme to Goupil, Goupil to Knoedler, 1876. John Wolfe collection, sold at Chickering Hall, New York, Apr. 5–6, 1882, to W. F. Whitney, New York (for $3,500). Christie's, New York, Feb. 11, 1997, lot 25.

–

Bibliography: *Recueil. Œuvres de Jean-Léon Gérôme*, BNF Estampes, vol. XI, no. 5.
G. Ackerman, *Jean-Léon Gérôme* (Courbevoie: ACR Édition, 2000), no. 254.

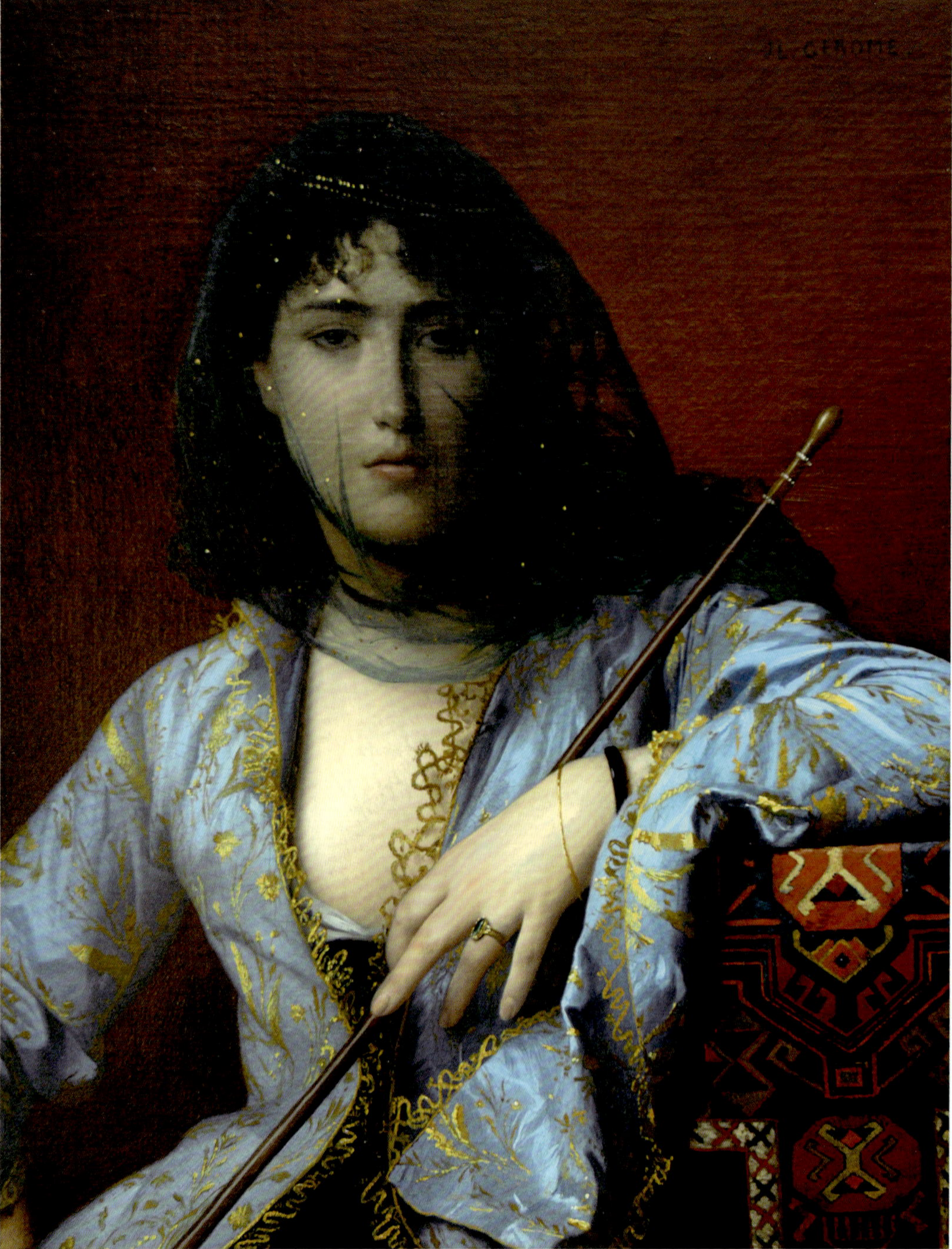

Circassia was a region of the Caucasus; Circassian ladies were known for their great beauty and were highly appreciated as courtesans in the Ottoman empire. In a novel published under the title *La Circassienne* (*The Circassian Lady*, 1881), Louis Énault described a dispute between Abdellah and his female companion after Abdellah bought a beautiful woman in the hope of making a profitable sale to the sultan. "'So be it!' she said to him, 'but don't think you can force me to treat this slave like some princess! Princesses are expensive if you do not manage to sell them.'"[1]

Gérôme was therefore evoking the imaginative realm of oriental sensuality here, as underscored by the gauzy black veil (which emphasizes, rather than masks, the young woman's features) and by the carpet on which she rests her arm. The painting is a tribute to the sitter's beauty, enhanced by the richly embroidered silk kaftan she is wearing. Her hieratic pose, the calm expression on her face, and the strength of her dark, velvety gaze convey her pride and her conviction of her own worth. She knows the value of her beauty.[2]

Whereas the sitter and the props evoke the Orient—an Orient that owed more to the artist's fantasies and imagination than to his actual experience of travel, since he could not have had access to the harem—the half-length composition of the portrait and the brightly lit, uniformly red ground against which the woman is set are reminiscent of Gérôme's early portraits of women, similar to those by Ingres. Gérôme thus remained faithful to painterly tradition even as he demonstrated, thanks to this highly appealing canvas, how well he could rejuvenate it. **D. F.-R.**

1. L. Énault, *La Circassienne* (Paris: C. Blériot, 1881), vol. 2, p. 6. **2.** *A Roman Slave Market* was sold in New York in 1917 under the title of *Sale of Circassian Slave*, thereby alluding to the beauty and sad fate of Circassian women.

Cat. 159

BISHARIN WARRIOR (BOY OF THE BISHARIN TRIBE)

–

1872
Oil on canvas
11 5/8 × 8 5/8 in.
Collection of Terence and Katrina Garnett, San Mateo, California

–

Provenance:
Goupil from the artist Feb. 6, 1872, stock book 6, no. 7565 (for 2,000 francs). Goupil to S. P. Avery, Feb. 1873 (for 4,000 francs). Catherine L. Wolfe to the Metropolitan Museum of Art, 1887. The Fine Art Society, London, 1967. Parke-Bernet, New York, Oct. 24–26, 1956, lot 382. A. Duvannes, Los Angeles. Parke-Bernet, New York, Sept. 24, 1969, lot 143, to the Galt Gallery (for $1,250). The Fine Art Society, Ltd., London, 1967. Mr. and Mrs. Joseph M. Tanenbaum, Toronto. The Fine Art Society, Ltd. Christie's, New York, Oct. 31, 2001, lot 6. Terence Garnett, San Mateo, California.

–

Exhibition History:
Travellers Beyond the Grand Tour, The Fine Art Society, London, 1980, no. 57, as "A Boy of the Bichari Tribe." *19th Century Orientalist Paintings from the Collection of Terence Garnett*, Royal Embassy of Saudi Arabia Washington, D.C., 2007, no. 6.

–

Bibliography:
J. Harding, *Artistes Pompiers: French Academic Art in the 19th Century* (New York: Rizzoli, 1979), p. 18. G. Ackerman, *Jean-Léon Gérôme* (Courbevoie: ACR Édition, 2000), no. 224.

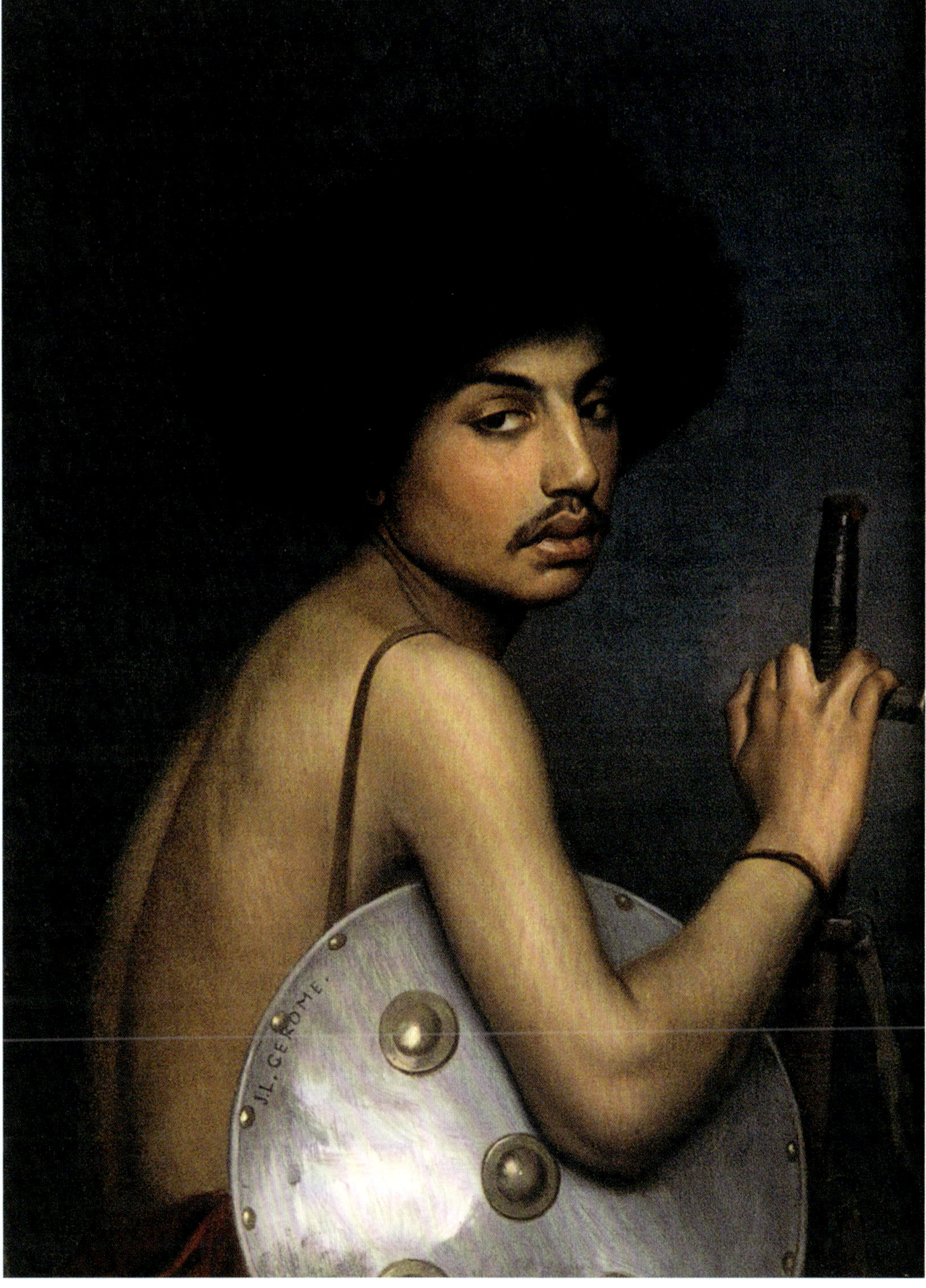

According to Gerald Ackerman, Gérôme discussed this work and a pendant *Arab Warrior* with the American dealer Samuel Putnam Avery in 1871 while the painter was in London during the siege of Paris and the Commune.[1] The title, listed in the Goupil stock book the year it was acquired from Gérôme, identifies the sitter as a member of the Bisharin tribe, a nomadic, pastoral people to be found in the eastern part of the Sudan desert. Gérôme seems to have responded less to the warlike than to the sensual nature of this young man in both pictures. Although he is armed, his relaxed pose, heavy eyelids, full lips, and provocatively splayed fingers on the hilt of the sword create an intimate allure and physical presence. Avery sold the painting to the New York collector and patron of the Metropolitan Museum of Art, Catherine Lorillard Wolfe. It was included in the major bequest she made of nineteenth century pictures to the Metropolitan Museum in 1887, and was deaccessioned in 1956. **M. M.**

1. G. Ackerman, in *Important Orientalist Paintings*, Christie's, New York, Oct. 31, 2001, p. 36, no. 6.

Cat. 160

THE SERPENT CHARMER

1880
Oil on canvas
33 × 48 1/8 in.
Signed lower left: *J.L. GEROME*
The Sterling and Francine Clark Art Institute, Williamstown, inv. 1955.51

Provenance: Gérôme to Goupil, 1880. Goupil to Albert Spencer, 1880 (for 75,000 francs). A. Spencer, sale 1888 (for 95,000 francs) Alfred Corning Clark. Mrs Elizabeth Scriven Clark, New York, to Shaus, 1899 (for $10,000 or $12,000). Virginie Heckster, PBNY sale, January 22, 1942, lot 44 or 86. New York, sold by Durand-Ruel to R. S. Clark, 1942 (for $500).

Bibliography: E. Strahan [Earl Shinn], ed., *Gérôme: A Collection of the Works of J.-L. Gérôme in One Hundred Photogravures* (New York: Samuel L. Hall, 1881). G. Ackerman et al., *Jean- Léon Gérôme (1824–1904)*, exh. cat. (Dayton: Dayton Art Institute, 1972; also Minneapolis: Minneapolis Institute of Arts, 1973, and Baltimore: The Walters Art Gallery, 1973), p. 18, ill. 5. A. Boime, "Gérôme and the Bourgeois Artist's Burden," *Arts Magazine*, vol. 57, no. 5 (Jan. 1983), p. 67. L. Nochlin, "The Imaginary Orient," *Art in America*, vol. 71 (1983), p. 119ff. *J.-L. Gérôme*, exh. cat. (Vesoul: Musée Georges-Garret, 1981), no. 43, p. 59. *Orientalism*, exh. cat. (Rochester: Memorial Art Gallery of the University of Rochester, 1982; also New York: Neuberger Museum, 1982), no. 41. H. Lafont-Couturier, *Gérôme* (Paris: Herscher, 1998), pp. 68–69. H. Lafont-Couturier, *Gérôme and Goupil: Art and Enterprise*, exh. cat., trans. I. Ollivier (Bordeaux: Musée Goupil, 2000–1; also New York: Dahesh Museum of Art, 2001, and Pittsburgh: The Frick Art & Historical Center, 2001), pp. 20, 42, 167. G. Ackerman, *Jean-Léon Gérôme* (Courbevoie: ACR Édition, 2000), no. 282.

Ill. 131. Martial Thabard (1831–1905), *Snake Charmer*, 1875, marble, 55 in., Musée d'Orsay, Paris (plaster, Salon of 1872, Musée de Limoges).

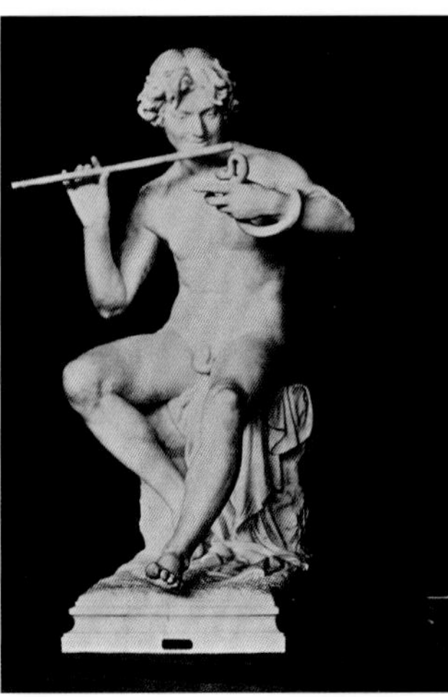

"Above all, Egyptian musicians, Hindou dervishes, and Psylli[1] are patented snake charmers," wrote Alphonse Toussenel in the mid-nineteenth century, as quoted in the entry for *charmeur* in the *Grand dictionnaire universel du XIXe siècle.*[2] Such a dictionary entry reveals the extent to which Gérôme's painting was grounded in widely held ideas about this imaginary Orient. A snake charmer was not so much a reality as a figure likely to instill fascination, terror, delight, and dread in anyone who looked at him. During the 1870s the subject had notably been illustrated in a painting by Charles Landelle (*An Alassaoui Child Snake Charmer*, whereabouts unknown) and a sculpture by Martial Thabard (ill. 131). Like Gérôme, Landelle and Thabard depicted a young lad taming the dangerous creature.

Gérôme offered a highly original interpretation of this subject. Indeed, his knowledge and appreciation of the Orient enabled him, as Charlotte Maury and Sophie Makariou stress in this catalogue (p. 255), to give the painting an apparently accurate, perhaps even authentic, setting. But in fact he showed the young snake charmer in one of the rooms of the Topkapi palace, a highly implausible venue in Gérôme's day for such a performance, far more likely to be seen in the streets and squares of Cairo. For compositional beauty and balance, Gérôme enlarged the decorative wall tiling to achieve the desired effect; and he very certainly referred to photographs distributed by the Abdullah frères, with whom he was in contact (ill. 123, p. 260). Once again, "realistic" did not mean "authentic."[3]

The decision to show a statuesque youth in a pose similar to certain photographs of young models marketed to painters by Louis Igout and Hermann Heid allowed Gérôme to evoke the sensual eroticism—not devoid of a certain violence—of an imaginary Orient. The snake and the young tamer engage in a voluptuous embrace. In one of those cross-genre gestures that Gérôme so liked to make, the motif here obviously alludes to Eve and the serpent of original sin. As Linda Nochlin has pointed out, for beholders of this painting the spectacle is as much about the seated men—attentive and entranced—as it is about the charmer. "Clearly, these black and brown folk are mystified—but then again, so are we. Indeed, the defining mood of the painting is mystery, and it is created by a specific pictorial device. We are permitted only a beguiling rear view of the boy holding the snake. A full frontal view, which would reveal unambiguously both his sex and the fullness of his dangerous performance, is denied us. And the insistent, sexually charged mystery... signifies a more general one: the mystery of the East itself, a standard topos of Orientalist ideology."[4]

It was this oriental mystery that Gérôme sought during his voyages, as did other travelers of his day; as a pictorial subterfuge likely to seduce Western clients, *The Serpent Charmer* was perhaps also influenced by sensual recollections of scenes in Cairo such as the one Gustave Flaubert enjoyed recounting to Louis Bouilhet when describing the lewd dance of male *almehs* (dancing girls) in Cairo. "We have not yet seen any dancing girls. They have all been exiled to upper Egypt... But we have seen dancing boys. Ah! Ah! Ah!... For the dancers, picture two scamps who are passably ugly but charming in the deliberate corruption and depravity of their feminine movements and gaze, being dressed as girls with antimony-painted eyes... When their hips move, the entire rest of their body remains motionless. When, in contrast, their chest moves, nothing else budges. They advance toward you, arms extended and playing copper rattles, while their faces, beneath all the sweat and make-up, remain as inexpressive as statues... The solemnity of the face in contrast to the lewd movements of the body creates quite an effect... It is too beautiful to be arousing, I doubt that the women are as good as the men."[5]

The sensuality of the show of the young snake charmer, although apparently set in the sultan's seraglio in Istanbul, might therefore also reflect "memories of Cairo." **D. F.-R.**

1. The Psylli were a people who lived in what is now northern Lybia and were alleged to be immune to snake venom. Egypt recruited its snake charmers from this tribe. **2.** Paris: Larousse, 1866–77, vol. 3, part 2, p. 1026. **3.** A scene of baths showing a bather, quite similar to the Detroit sculpture, has been painted by Gérôme in the same Topkapi's palace (Paris, private collection). **4.** L. Nochlin, "The Imaginary Orient," in *The Politics of Vision: Essays on Nineteenth-Century Art and Society* (New York, 1989), p. 35. **5.** G. Flaubert, letter to Louis Bouilhet dated Jan. 15, 1850, in *Correspondance* (Paris: Gallimard Pléiade, 1973), vol. I, pp. 571–72.

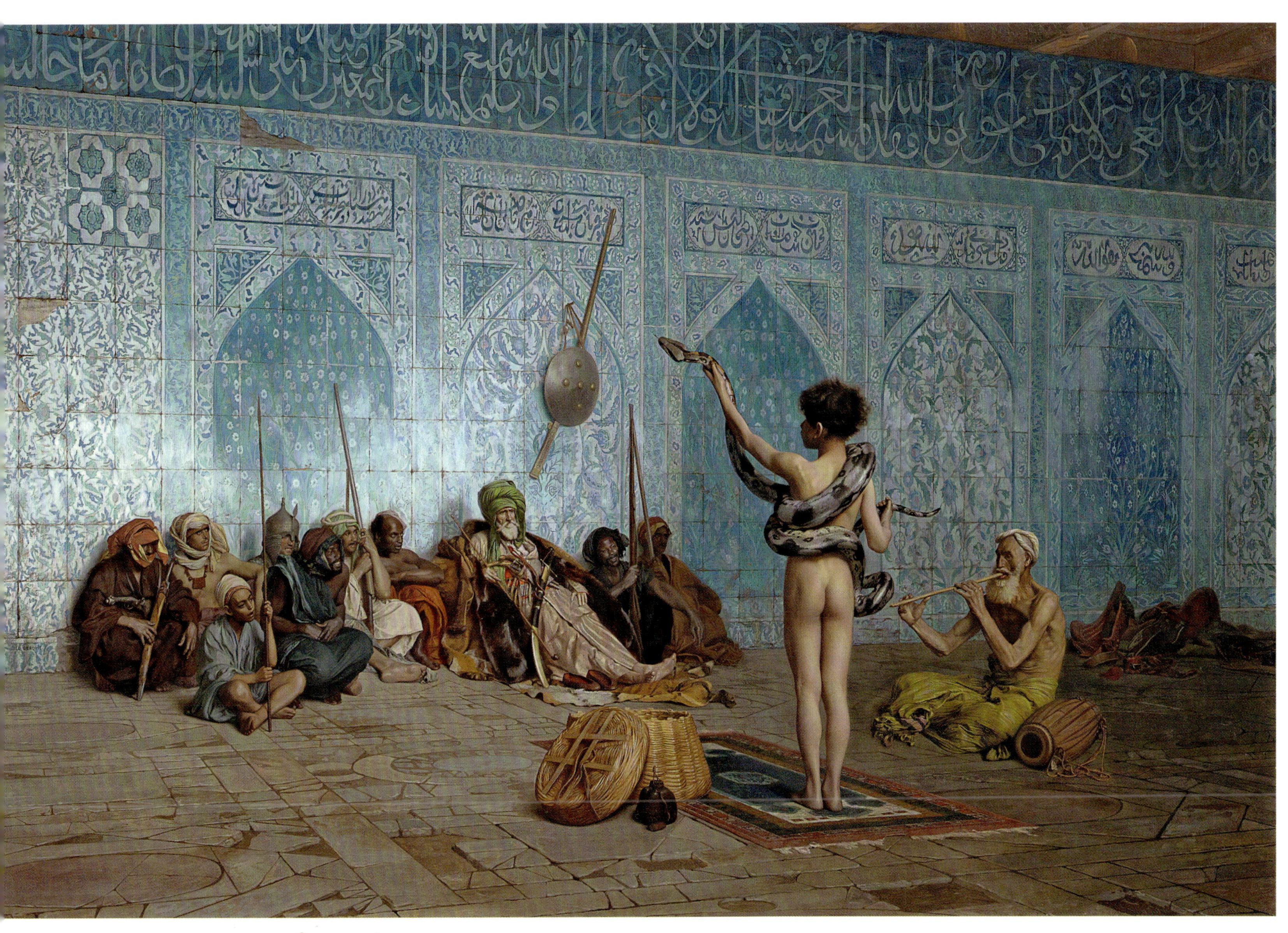

Cat. 161

MARCUS BOTSARIS

1874
Oil on canvas
27 5/8 × 21 1/2 in.
Collection of Terence and Katrina Garnett, San Mateo, California

Provenance:
Goupil to Wallis & Co., London, Mar. 12, 1874, Goupil stock book no. 8798 (for 12,000 francs). Christie's, London, May 23, 1891, no. 54, William Houldsworth to Duncan (for £913), as "Botzaris (Patriot)." M. Knoedler & Co., 1898. H. R. Winthrop, sold Parke-Bernet, New York, Jan. 22, 1942, sale 339, no. 17. Private collection, Chicago. Sold to Maurice Goldblatt, Leslie Hindman Auctioneers, Chicago, May 13, 1990, lot 197 (for $260,000). Sotheby's, New York, Oct. 23, 1990, lot 41. Sotheby's, New York, Feb. 11, 1993, lot 28 (for $266,500). Private collection, Greece, to Garnett, 2005.

Exhibition History:
19th Century Orientalist Paintings from the Collection of Terence Garnett, Royal Embassy of Saudi Arabia, Washington, D.C., 2007, cat. no. 1.

Bibliography:
E. Strahan [Earl Shinn], ed., *Gérôme: A Collection of the Works of J. L. Gérôme in One Hundred Photogravures* (New York: Samuel L. Hall, 1881), vol. 2, pl. LXXV. F. F. Hering, *Gérôme: The Life and Works of Jean-Léon Gérôme* (New York: Cassell, 1892), p. 235; G. Ackerman, *Jean-Léon Gérôme* (Courbevoie: ACR Édition, 2000), no. 239. H. Lafont-Couturier, *Gérôme and Goupil: Art and Enterprise*, exh. cat., trans. I. Ollivier (Bordeaux: Musée Goupil, 2000–1; also New York: Dahesh Museum of Art, 2001, and Pittsburgh: The Frick Art & Historical Center, 2001), pp. 23, 160.

This painting is essentially an historical portrait, the only known painting of the genre in Gérôme's oeuvre. Markos Botsaris was a hero in the Greek War of Independence against the Turks. He fought valiantly during the famous counter-offensive of 1823 in Missalonghi, and led a band of a few hundred Souliot guerillas in a bold attack on four thousand Albanians encamped at Karpenision, where he was fatally wounded. His command passed to his friend and comrade-in-arms, the Romantic hero Lord Byron.

The Greek War of Independence (1821–1830) was a staple of French Romantic art and literature. During the war and for decades after Greece officially achieved independence, the French public was entranced by the exotic, picturesque, heroic details of the distant revolution as they were imagined by journalists, poets, and painters. Both Eugène Delacroix and Ary Scheffer represented famous scenes from the war. Victor Hugo listed Botsaris alongside Washington, Kosciusko, Bolivar, John Brown, and Garibaldi as one of the great freedom-fighters. The most famous representations of Botsaris depict his heroic death in Karpenision, fully exploiting the drama, emotion, violence, and heroism of the story (ill. 132). Delacroix also painted Botsaris as a heroic warrior, and planned a major painting on the scale of *Massacre at Chios* which was never realized.[1]

Politically, however, the legacy of the Greek War of Independence was complicated by the delayed French response to the Turkish incursion. Only in the last two years of the Restoration did France step up military action in defense of Greece, recognizing the imperial benefit of gaining an ally in the Middle East. Paintings were commissioned valorizing the French as liberators of the Greeks against the oppressive Ottoman Empire. Furthermore, the borders of Greece as established in 1830 were highly contested, and contained less than one-third of the Greek population of the region. The first century of Greek statehood was characterized by the constant struggle to expand the country's borders.

Gérôme's portrait seems more responsive to these complications than to a Romantic instinct to celebrate the hero. There are no references in the painting to Botsaris's courageous feat, or visual details specific to him or his heroism. The title alone identifies the figure. The sitter is a model who himself appears in other paintings, and in the same costume (cat. 146). (It is of course unlikely that Botsaris's features were known enough to elicit any sense of likeness from either the artist's brush or contemporary viewers.) Gérôme portrays the man sitting slumped in his outsized chair, sunk deep in thought, aligning the image not only with the complicated legacy of the war, but also with others by Gérôme that explore the isolation and introspection of powerful men.

A smaller version, perhaps a sketch,[2] once owned by William Houldsworth who also owned this painting, is now lost. **M. M.**

1. For images of figures and events of the Greek War of Independence in French art, see N. Athanassoglou-Kallmyer, *French Images from the Greek War of Independence, 1821–1830: Art and Politics under the Restoration* (New Haven: Yale University Press, 1989); R. Huyghe, *Delacroix and Greece* (Athens: Ionian and Popular Bank of Greece, 1971), and O. Mentzafou-Polyzou, *1821: Figures and Themes from the Greek War of Independence in 19th Century Painting* (Athens, 2005). **2.** G. Ackerman, *Jean-Léon Gérôme* (Courbevoie: ACR Édition, 2000), no. 239B.

Ill. 132. Lodovico Lipparini (1800-1856), *Death of Botsaris*, 1841, Museo Civico, Trieste, Civico Museo Sartorio.

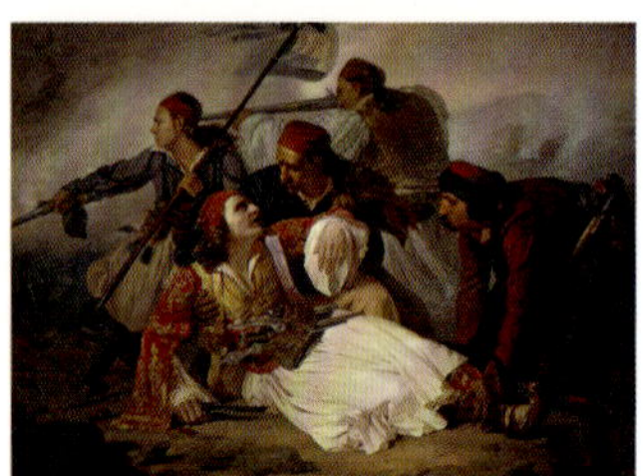

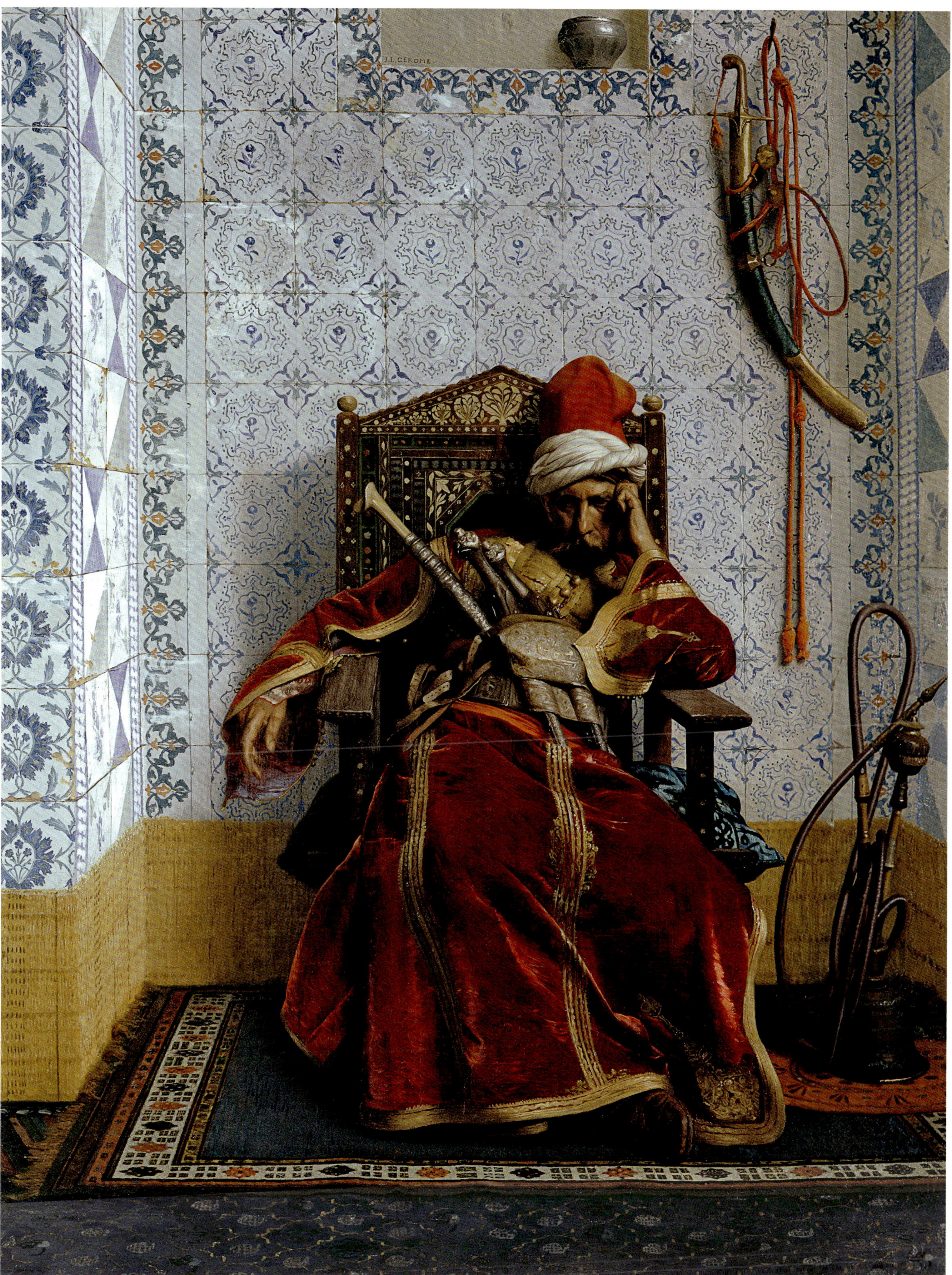
J.L. GEROME

Cat. 162

THE BLACK BARD

1888
Oil on canvas
24 × 20 in.
Orientalist Museum, Doha, inv. OM.706.2008

Provenance: Private collection, New York. Private collection, Connecticut (acquired from the above ca. 1945). Sotheby's, New York, Oct. 23, 2008, lot 168 to Qatar Museums Authority (for $1,172,500).

Exhibition History: Royal Academy, London, 1888, no. 205. Salon of 1892, no. 759.

Bibliography: *Athenaeum*, May 5, 1888, p. 572. *Athenaeum*, June 9, 1888, p. 731. F. F. Hering, *Gérôme. The Life and Works of Jean-Léon Gérôme* (New York: Cassell, 1892), p. 264. G. Ackerman, *Jean-Léon Gérôme* (Courbevoie: ACR Édition, 2000), pp. 316-17, no. 343. E. Weeks, in *19th Century Paintings*, Sotheby's, New York, Oct. 23, 2008, pp. 296–99.

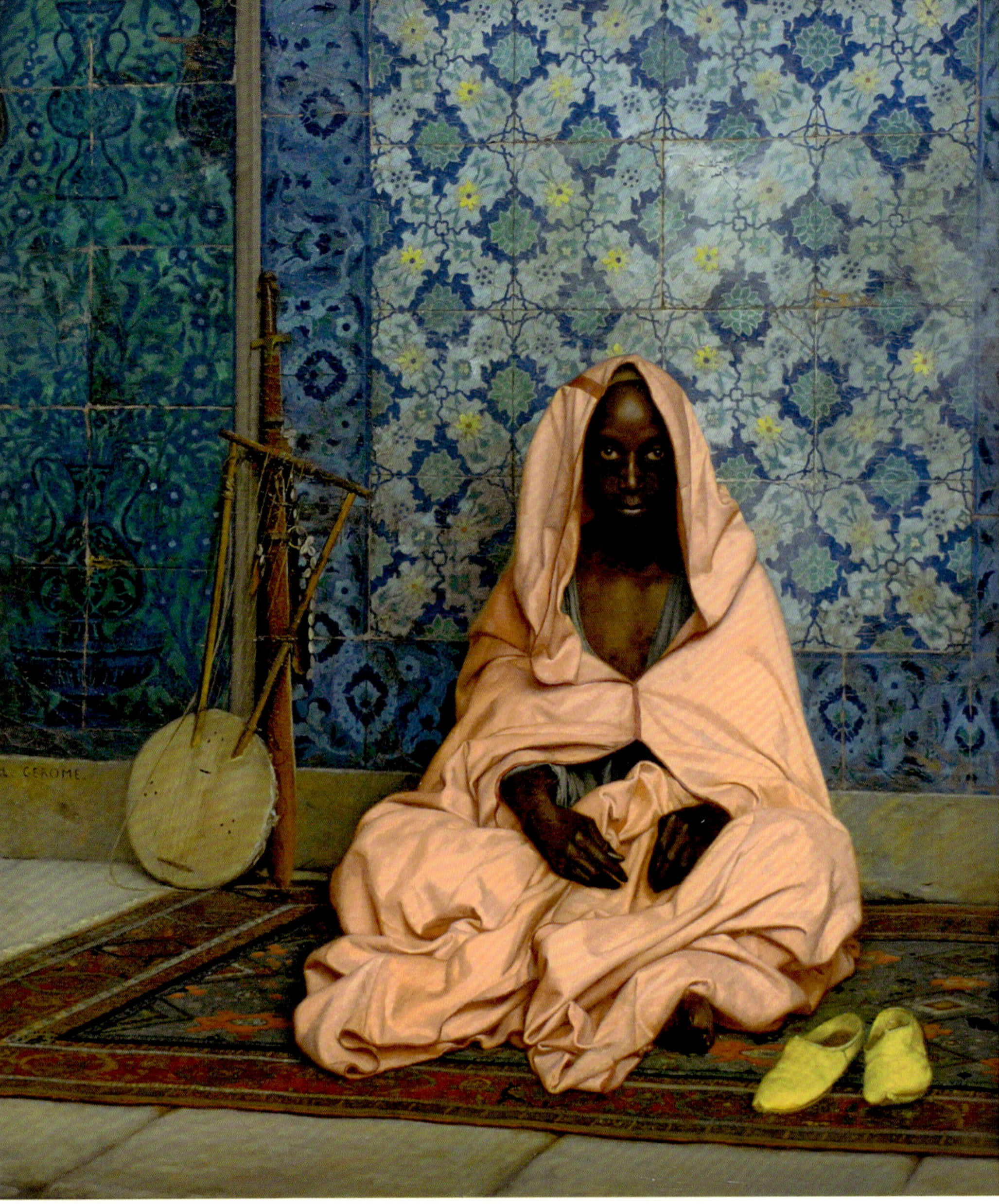

While the sitter in this painting is not identified, he is so individualized and his presence so powerful that the painting qualifies as a portrait. This is the only known depiction by Gérôme of this man. The stringed instrument and long sword leaning against the wall signal his profession as an itinerant musician, and his gnarled hands suggest a man of age and experience. His penetrating gaze is matched by the intensity of color contrasts in the composition, the extraordinary rose robe and the yellow slippers playing off the saturated blues of the tile backdrop. As in *The Serpent Charmer* (cat. 160) and *Marcus Botsaris* (cat. 161), Gérôme may have worked from an Abdullah frères photograph (ill. 123, p. 261) of the tile walls from the Topkapi palace in Istanbul.

Gérôme exhibited this painting alongside five others at the Royal Academy in 1888, marking the first time in many years that Gérôme sent his pictures across the Channel. The pictured was noticed twice in one of London's most popular literary magazines, *The Athenaeum*, where the depicted figure was described as a "Nubian musician" with an East African bowl lyre.[1] Although he had been made Honorary Foreign Royal Academician (H.F.R.A.) in 1869, and enjoyed active market demand in Britain, Gérôme generally focused more on his French and American reception. **M. M.**

1. See E. Weeks, in *19th Century Paintings*, Sotheby's, New York, Oct. 23, 2008, p. 296.

Cat. 163

THE MARABOU (AT THE DOOR OF HIS HOUSE)

–

1888–89
Oil on canvas
29 × 23 ½ in.
Signed lower right
Arnot Art Museum, Elmira, New York

–

Provenance: [Gérôme to Boussod, Valadon & Cie, 1888, then to Wykoop, but 28 ¼ × 23 in.]. Matthias H. Arnot, Elmira, 1900. Bequeathed to the Arnot Art Museum in 1910.

–

Bibliography: *A Collector's Vision: The 1910 Bequest of Matthias Arnot* (Elmira, N.Y.: Elmira Art Gallery, 1989), no. 12. G. Ackerman, *Jean-Léon Gérôme* (Courbevoie: ACR Édition, 2000), no. 371.

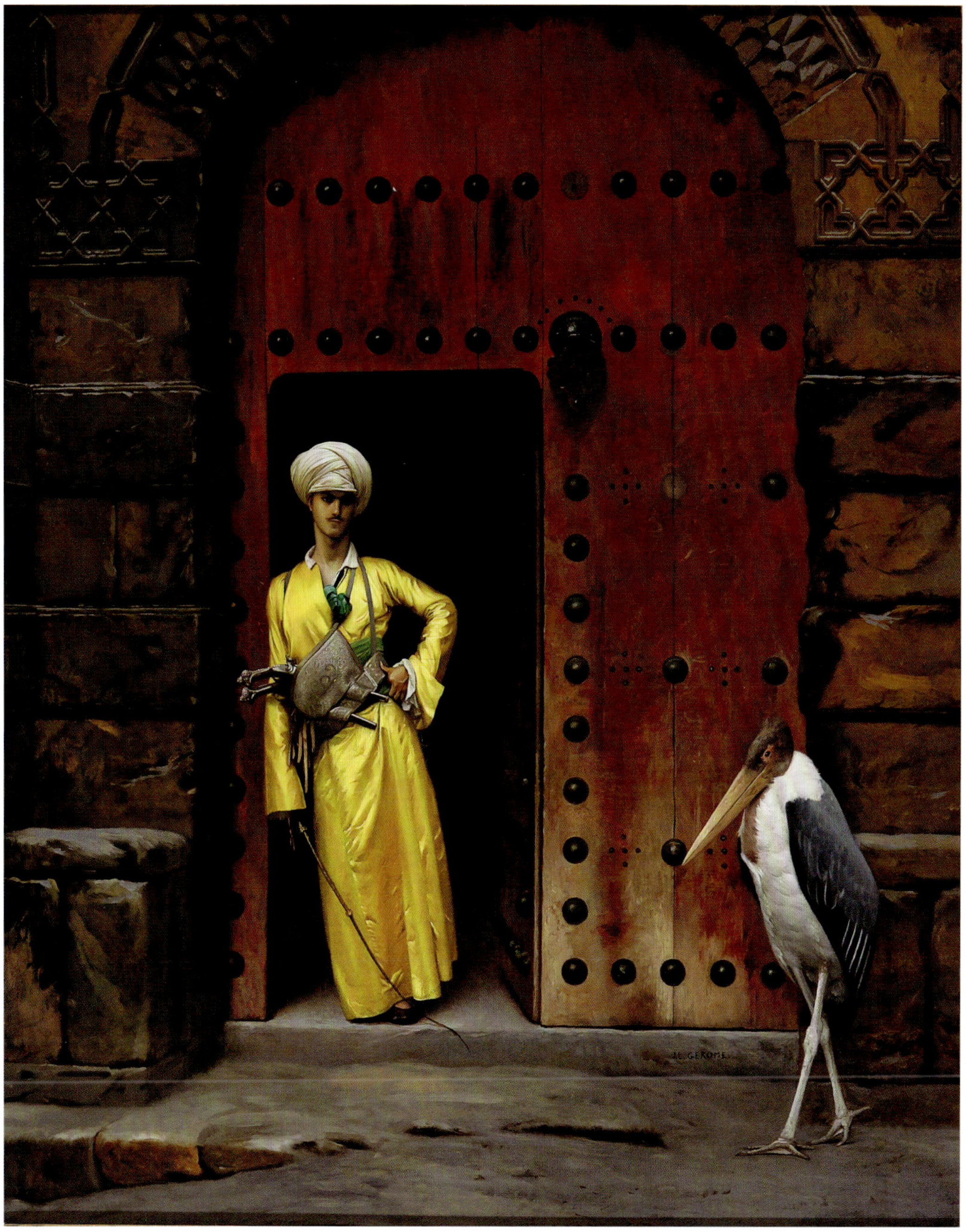

Ill. 133. Emmanuel Fremiet (1824–1910), *Marabou Holding a Caiman Between its Claws*, 1849, bronze, 35 × 11 × 20 ½ in., Musée d'Orsay, Paris.

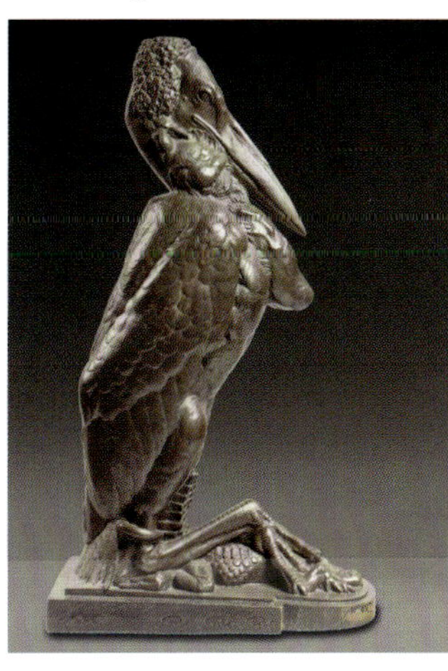

As Sophie Makariou and Charlotte Maury have stressed in their essay here (p. 261), this painting functions on the level of the strange and bizarre. Their analysis also reveals the extent to which Gérôme had fun blending various iconographic, stylistic, and historical sources, especially after 1880. The setting of the scene is not clearly indicated, and yet the style of the doorway, similar to the Ottoman architecture seen in Cairo, evokes Egypt, as does the haughty figure of the gate-keeping soldier. But a marabou—a wading bird from sub-Saharan Africa whose natural habitat was the savannah—was unlikely to be walking the streets of Cairo. By linking it to Egypt, Gérôme was evoking not so much potential memories of his numerous travels but the commission won by his sculptor friend Emmanuel Fremiet for four marabous to support porphyry tables in the Louvre's Egyptian rooms, which were used to that effect at the Louvre's Musée de la Marine, then were moved to the Trocadero museum and on to the naval museum in Rochefort (ill. 133). There can be little doubt that the people who commissioned the works thought that the tall size and thin, sharp beak of a marabou was similar to the ibis, the sacred bird of Egyptian mythology.

Gérôme painted the bird with his usual fidelity to accurate detail—the long legs, pointed beak, and bald head on retracted neck are accurately rendered. But this faithful depiction serves as a pretext for an anthropomorphic analogy between this bird and the holy men in North Africa known as marabouts—in French, the pronunciation and spelling are identical. Indeed, the bird's long folded wings recall a meditating man's arms clasped behind his back while walking along, and the bird's squat head and wide eye lend it a thoroughly human wisdom. As though giving still greater weight to this metaphor, the glances of man and bird seem to intersect, creating a strong diagonal line that underpins the painting's skillful composition. **D. F.-R.**

Cat. 164

THE WHIRLING DERVISH

1889
Oil on canvas
29 × 37 ½ in.
Signed lower left: J.L. GEROME
Private collection, courtesy of Guggenheim, Asher Associates, Inc.

Provenance: Gérôme to Boussod, Valadon & Cie, 1889. Boussod, Valadon & Cie to Bernheim, Paris, 1901 (for 3,500 francs). Bessonneau d'Angers Collection. Hôtel Drouot sale, Paris, July 23, 1954. H. Shickman, Inc., New York. Mr and Mrs. Joseph Tanenbaum, Toronto. Kurt E. Schon, Ltd., New Orleans. LRA & WNG, 1984, no. 41, not exhibited in London. Collection of Coral Petroleum Inc., Houston. Sotheby's, New York, May 22, 1985, sale 5331, lot 34. Jordan Volpe Gallery, *19th and 20th Century Paintings* (New York, 1991), p. 38. Sotheby's, New York, Feb. 12, 1997, sale 6949, lot 43.

Bibliography: *Recueil. Œuvres de J.-L. Gérôme*, BNF Estampes, XXIII, 5. G. Ackerman, *Jean-Léon Gérôme* (Courbevoie: ACR Édition, 2000), no. 459.

Ill. 134. Pascal Sebah (1823–1886), *Group of whirling dervishes*, ca. 1870, albumen print, 5 ⅜ × 3 ⅞ in., Musée d'Orsay, Paris, inv. PHO 1996 5 83.

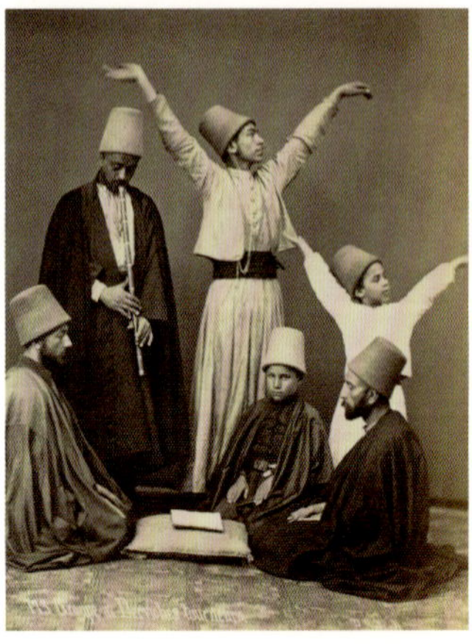

Ill. 135. *Whirling Dervishes*, undated, pencil drawing, 11 × 9 ⅛ in., private collection.

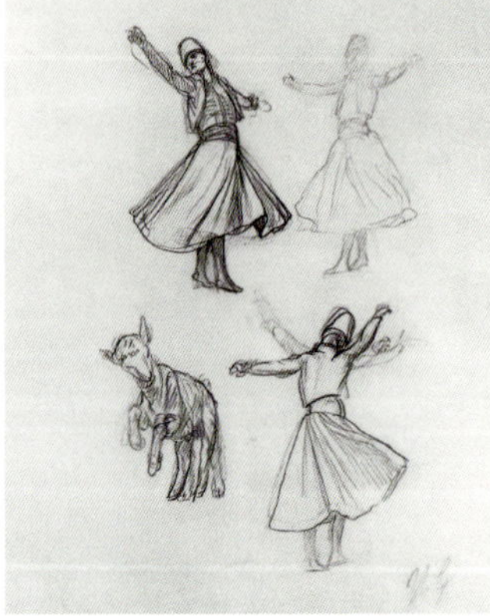

The striking dress and above all the entrancing, spinning grace of their dance turned whirling dervishes into legendary figures of the Orient by the late eighteenth century. Dervishes—from the Persian *derviz*, or "beggar"—belong to a fraternity founded in Konya in the thirteenth century by Jalal ad-Din Muhammad Rumi. The dervishes' ceremonial dance (*sema*) is a manifest expression of their Sufi faith, characterized by great mysticism. Their whirling movement to the rhythm of music, arms raised, induces a meditative trance leading to self-oblivion that brings them nearer to God.

As Théophile Gautier noted, in the nineteenth century dervishes were one of the few Islamic religious groups to allow Western travelers to witness their ceremony. Gérôme thus certainly had an opportunity to see whirling dervishes dance during one of his trips to Turkey.[1] Here he faithfully depicts the dervish's dress, if Gautier's description is to be believed: "The headgear of these Muslim monks is a reddish-brown cap of inch-thick felt, whose shape I can only best compare to an overturned flowerpot stuck on the head; their costume is composed of a waistcoat and jacket of white cloth, a vast pleated skirt of the same color—similar to the Greek fustanella—and narrow trousers, similarly white, that go down to the ankle, all of which has nothing monkish about it to our minds, and even has a certain elegance."[2] This outfit is also the one worn by the models photographed by Pascal Sebah in his studio (ill. 134). No doubt Gérôme, like Gautier, was moved by the throbbing music that accompanied the dance, working its slow enchantment: "The bizarre charm of this melody filled my heart with nostalgia, with unfamiliar landscapes, with inexplicable joys and sadnesses, with a crazy desire to abandon myself to the intoxicating waves of its rhythm."

By painting this dervish with one arm raised, body angled in a rapid twisting movement that flares wide the skirt, Gérôme faithfully illustrated the holy men's dance: "Motionless in the middle of the enclosure, the dervishes become intoxicated on this delicately barbarous and delightfully wild music, whose primitive themes date back to mankind's earliest days; finally, one of them opened wide his arms, spreading them horizontally in the pose of the crucified Christ, then began to spin slowly, slowly shifting his bare feet, which made no sound on the wooden flooring. His skirt, like a bird on the verge of flight, began to flutter and flap. As his speed increased, the soft fabric was lifted by the air that rushed underneath, spreading it into a wheel, hollowing it into a bell in a whirlwind of whiteness, with the dervish at its center."[3]

Once again, despite this apparent accuracy, Gérôme took many liberties with observed reality. Whereas such dances took place within a *tekke*, or dervish monastery, Gérôme here depicts a non-specific locale given an oriental appearance by the dome, by the pointed arches of the niches, and by the colorful yet indistinct calligraphy along the frieze. The wooden floor on which dervishes danced is replaced here by an earthen floor, subtly implying a shift from a religious site to the street. His dervish turns alone, changing a collective religious ceremony into a performance whose mystic import is diminished. And this performance brings its own ambiguity: despite his manly appearance and dark beard, the dervish does not dance flat-footed but on his toes, elegantly evoking the exploits of a prima ballerina at the Opera—his wide skirt thus becomes a graceful tutu (ill. 135). This mixing of genders triggers a sensuality that is reinforced by the ring of onlookers, men whose varied styles and colors of dress seem to constitute a catalogue of oriental types. They have removed their hats and shoes, as though to pray, yet they accompany the dervish's movements with their heads, apparently entranced by the pleasure it gives them.

An attentive look at Gérôme's canvas evokes Flaubert's description, in a letter to his brother, of the "male belly dancers" that he saw in Cairo. "As to the dancing girls of Cairo, they have all been relegated to Upper Egypt. On the other hand, there are male dancers, denizens with a shady profession, dressed as girls who wriggle in fine fashion."[4]

Here again, Gérôme's vision of the Orient was the one his contemporaries expected: sensual, yet with a hint of violence—the men watching the dervish dance are all young, strong, dark, savage. In the hollow of an arch Gérôme has depicted sharp halberds hanging on the wall. Although they reflect the penchant for oriental weapons displayed by Gérôme and his brother-in-law, Albert Goupil, they seem incongruous in a place of worship. Their presence here therefore marks the shift from religious ceremony to sensual show. By combining observed reality with literary and painterly fantasy, Gérôme has once again produced a masterful, pictorial subterfuge. **D. F.-R.**

1. Two sheets of pencil sketches are now in private collections. The larger sheet is apparently a preparatory drawing for the canvas, showing the spectators ringing the dervish, whose feet are placed flat. The other sheet, perhaps done from life, contains three studies of the dervish in poses similar to the one used by Gérôme in the final canvas, along with the depiction of a little calf that also seems to dance (Thanks to Scott Allan for supplying this information). 2. T. Gautier, *Constantinople* (Paris: Michel Lévy, 1853), p. 135. 3. Ibid., p. 138. 4. Gustave Flaubert, letter to his brother dated Dec. 15, 1849, in *Correspondance* (Paris: Gallimard Pléiade, 1973), vol. 1, p. 555.

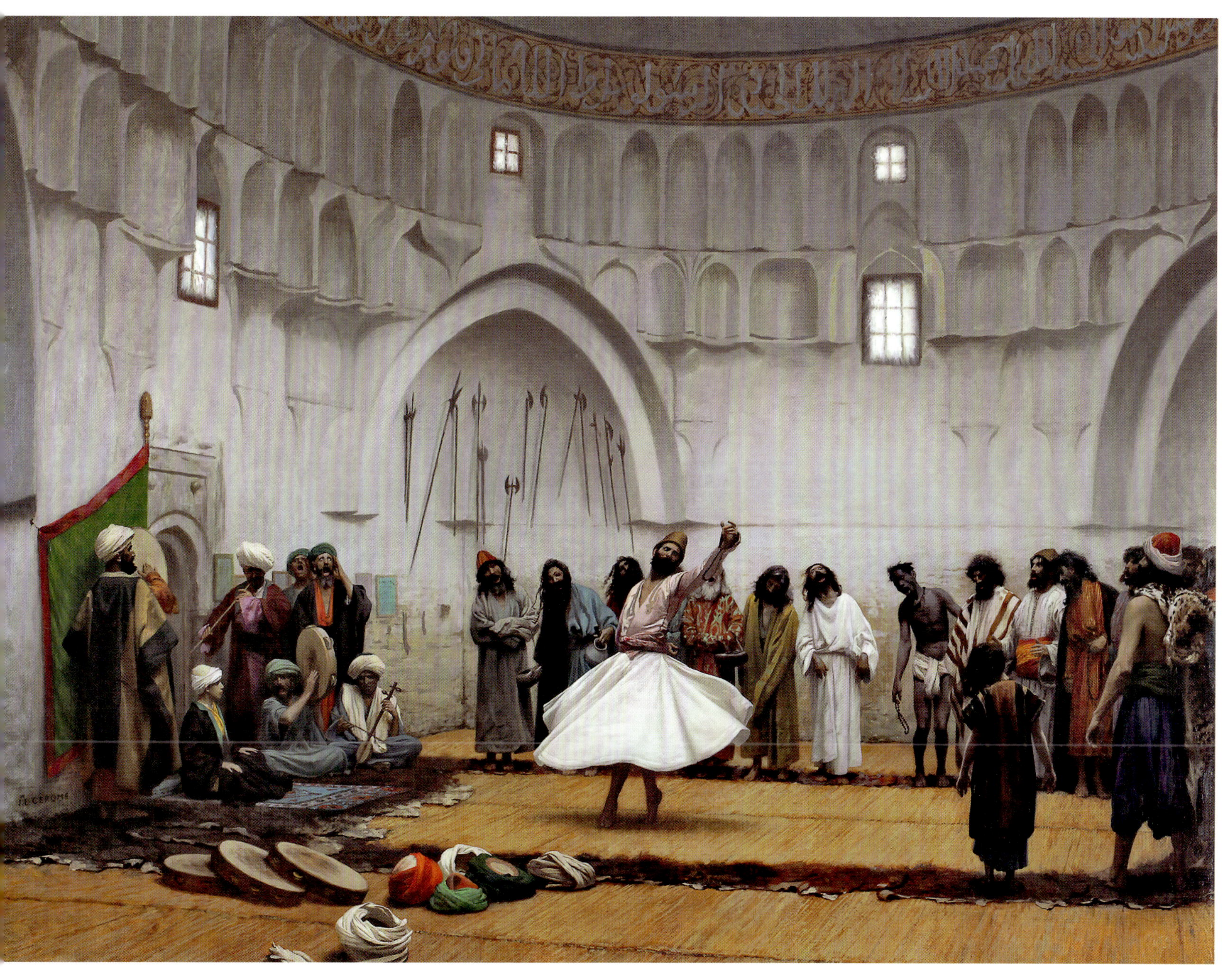

Cat. 165

STUDY FOR *MOORISH BATH*

–

ca. 1872
Pencil on paper glued to vellum
Vellum: 14 ¾ × 10 ¾ in.;
drawing: 12 ¾ × 8 in.
Dr. Edward T. Wilson collection, Bethesda, Maryland

–

Provenance: Separated from cat. 101.

Cat. 166

MOORISH BATH (LADY OF CAIRO BATHING)

–

1872
Oil on canvas
20 × 16 in.
Signed upper right: *J.L. GEROME*
Museum of Fine Arts, Boston, gift of Robert Jordan from the collection of Eben D. Jordan, inv. 24.217

–

Provenance: Gérôme to H. J. Turner, London, 1872 (for 22,000 francs). H. J. Turner, Paris. Turner sale, Christie's, 1903, lot 108. Arthur Tooth and Sons, New York. Eben D. Jordan, Boston. Robert Jordan, Paris, donated to the Museum of Fine Arts, Boston, in 1924. Guildhall, Loan Coll., London, 1898, no. 51. Atlanta, 1983, no. 27. LRA and WNG, 1984, no. 31.

–

Exhibition History: Exposition Universelle, Paris, 1878.

–

Bibliography: G. Ackerman et al., *Jean-Léon Gérôme (1824–1904)*, exh. cat. (Dayton: Dayton Art Institute, 1972; also Minneapolis: Minneapolis Institute of Arts, 1973, and Baltimore: The Walters Art Gallery, 1973), p. 21, ill. 8. *Orientalism*, exh. cat. (Rochester: Memorial Art Gallery of the University of Rochester, 1982; also New York: Neuberger Museum, 1982), no. 43. *Album de voyage des artistes en expédition au pays du Levant*, exh. cat. (Tel-Aviv: Museum of Art; also Bayonne: Musée Bonnat, and Paris: Musée Hébert, 1993), p. 33. H. Lafont-Couturier, *Gérôme* (Paris: Herscher, 1998), p. 76. G. Ackerman, *Jean-Léon Gérôme* (Courbevoie: ACR Édition, 2000), no. 197.

Cat. 167

THE GRAND BATH AT BURSA

–

1885
Oil on canvas
27 ½ × 39 ⅝ in.
Signed lower center: *J.L. GEROME*
Private collection by courtesy of Libby Howie.

–

Provenance: Gérôme to Boussod, Valadon & Cie, 1885. Boussod, Valadon & Cie to "the Emperor of Russia," Oct 1885 (for 34,500 francs). Hermitage Museum, Saint Petersburg, until 1930. Gimbel Brothers, New York, Feb. 19, 1943 (for $1,000). Collection of Judge Paul H. Bucharan, Indianapolis, in 1984. On loan to the Indianapolis Museum of Arts in the 1980s.

–

Exhibition History: Salon of 1885, Paris.

–

Bibliography: E. Strahan [Earl Shinn], *Gérôme: A Collection of the Works of J.-L. Gérôme in One Hundred Photogravures* (New York: Samuel L. Hall, 1881). F. F. Hering, *Gérôme: The Life and Works of Jean-Léon Gérôme* (New York: Cassell, 1892), p. 247. *J.-L. Gérôme*, exh. cat. (Vesoul: Musée Georges-Garret, 1981), p. 25. G. Ackerman, *Jean-Léon Gérôme* (Courbevoie: ACR Édition, 2000), no. 334. H. Lafont-Couturier, *Gérôme and Goupil: Art and Enterprise*, exh. cat., trans. I. Ollivier (Bordeaux: Musée Goupil, 2000–1; also New York: Dahesh Museum of Art, 2001, and Pittsburgh: The Frick Art & Historical Center, 2001), no. 93, pp. 23, 25, 134–36, 159–60, 166.

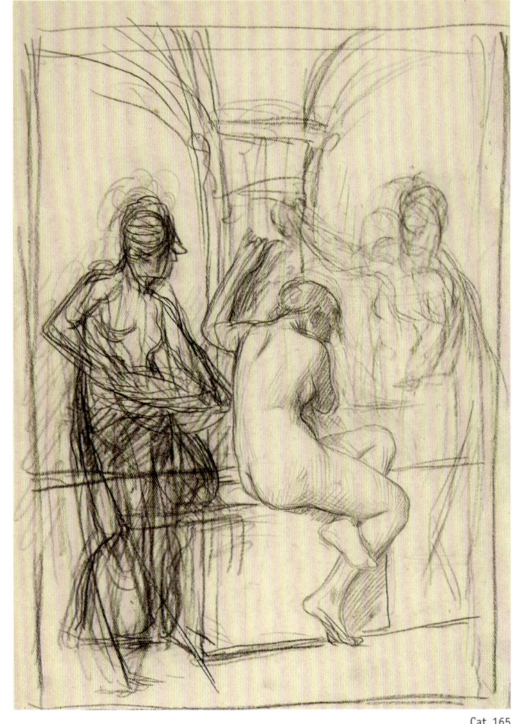

Cat. 165

Ill. 136. Jean-Auguste-Dominique Ingres (1780–1867), *The Turkish Bath*, 1862, oil on canvas, 43 ¼ × 31 ½ in., Musée du Louvre, Paris inv. RF 1934.

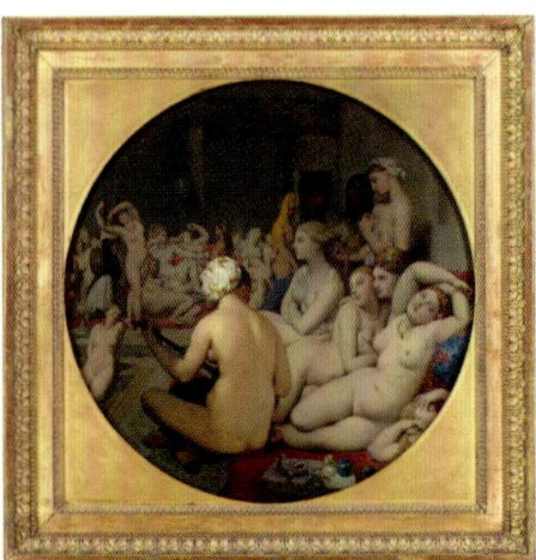

These two works, painted roughly fifteen years apart, evoke one of the favorite motifs of the nineteenth-century Western imagination: the sensuality of oriental baths in which young women lounge indolently. This theme was a recurring one in Gérôme's oeuvre. Both paintings were exhibited during the artist's lifetime, the first at the Exposition Universelle of 1878, the second at the Salon of 1885. Gérôme's source of inspiration was painterly: not only the subject but the French title (*Bain Turc*) of his *Moorish Bath* is indebted to Jean-Auguste-Dominique Ingres (ill. 136). Indeed, although Ingres never traveled to the Orient, he brought a new voluptuousness to a theme that already existed in eighteenth-century painting.

Gérôme, however, was familiar with the Middle East, and his accurate draftsmanship and meticulous handling seem to give his impressions and recollections an exactness based on observation. In both paintings—as in other works that show women bathing (ill. 137)—he plays on the ambivalence triggered by the combination of Western artistic models with accurate details of oriental life, suggesting that he was an eyewitness to such scenes in Cairo, Istanbul, and Bursa. Which was obviously not the case.

The pose and pale skin of the young blond woman in the *Moorish Bath* recall James Pradier's *Odalisque* (ill. 139), itself derived from Antoine Coysevox's *Crouching Venus* (Musée du Louvre, Paris, 1685–86), copied from an antique model from Versailles. However, the baths themselves are premises that Gérôme himself could have visited, notably in Cairo, although containing only men. Gustave Flaubert described such baths to Louis Bouilhet in 1850: "I was alone at the back of the steamroom, watching the light fade through the thick round glass in the domed ceiling; hot water ran everywhere... It was very sensuous, and gently melancholic, to take a bath this way alone."[1] Gérôme could have seen the Ottoman decorative tiling in Cairo or Istanbul. The objects were probably among the things his brother-in-law, Albert Goupil, brought back from the Orient; indeed, the catalogue for the Goupil sale of 1888 included a "hollow basin of the same shape [i.e. flat bottom, vertical sides, flared rim], the exterior and interior of the sides decorated with a band inscribed with Kufic lettering," which sounds

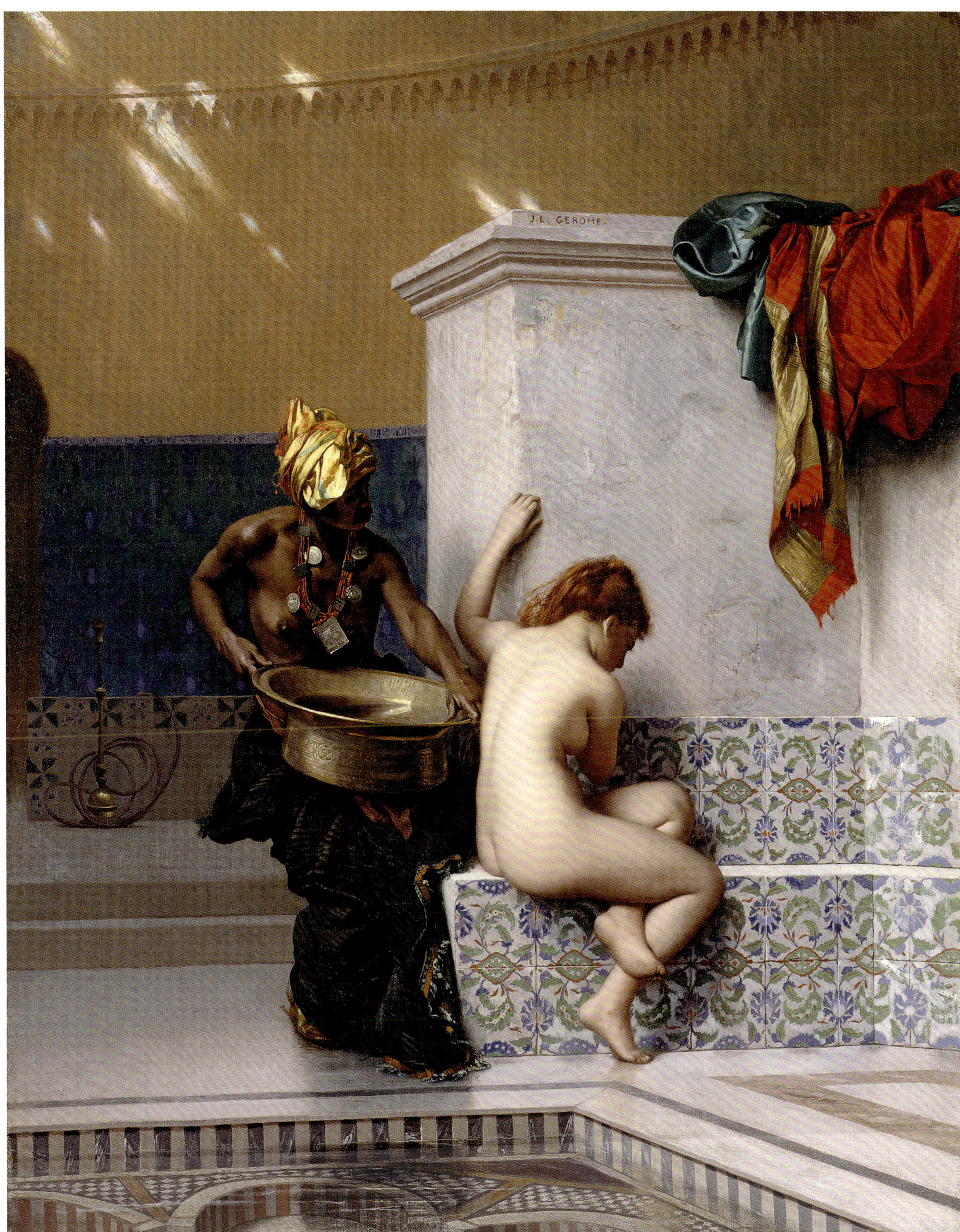

Cat. 166

very similar to the one held firmly by the haughty black slave here.[2] The hookah in the background, meanwhile, resembles one seen in a photograph of Gérôme's studio (Musée d'Orsay, Paris).

Gérôme very certainly based his *Grand Bath at Bursa* on a photograph (ill. 138). As was often the case, it was not exact details that he borrowed from the photographic picture, because we can see the liberties he took with the shape of the arches, transforming the pointed Islamic arch into a rounder one, and placing non-existent medallions on the spandrels. Such modifications and additions allowed him to subtly turn an oriental hammam into Roman baths, and to play on the confusion between an oriental scene and an ancient one, thereby underscoring the extent to which his two favorite sources of inspiration were, to his mind, similar. The breadth of composition of the Pascal Sebah photograph also offered a framework for Gérôme's painting, and he was able to draw on the play of light and shade in the picture. Once again Gérôme was sensitive to photography's theatrical ambitions and stagey quality.

The bodies of the young bathers are as white and sleek as marble—their poses seem to constitute a catalogue of models after the antique, as though anthologizing the photographic studies of academic nudes by Louis Igout. Here again the objects come from the artist's familiar surroundings—the wood-slatted cage on which a young odalisque is seated on the right of the canvas is the very one that Gérôme used when he painted (ill. 150, p. 304).

These two works reveal the talent with which Gérôme produced *lifelike* pictures of his contemporaries' imaginary Orient. The rise of ethnography as a science was also grounded in the exotic charms of a fantasy Orient—indeed, the entry for "harem" in the Larousse dictionary of the French language encouraged readers to turn to *The Arabian Nights* to discover the truth about oriental customs: "[I]f one wishes to have an accurate picture of oriental existence, one need merely open [*The Arabian Nights*]."[3]

Transcending the accuracy of observation that his contemporaries ascribed to him—reducing him to the rank of a faithful but uninventive copier—Gérôme was able to construct a pictorial truth by combining models of Western painting with images drawn from his oriental travels, images still imbued with the voluptuous feelings that he, like Flaubert, experienced there. **D. F.-R.**

1. Gustave Flaubert, letter from Cairo to Louis Bouilhet dated Jan.15, 1850; *Correspondance* (Paris: Gallimard Pléiade, 1973), vol. 1, p. 572. 2. *Catalogue des objets d'art de l'Orient et de l'Occident, tableaux et dessins composant la collection de feu M. Albert Goupil*, Hôtel Drouot, Paris, Apr. 23–27, 1888, lot 67. 3. Volume IX, letter H, p. 74.

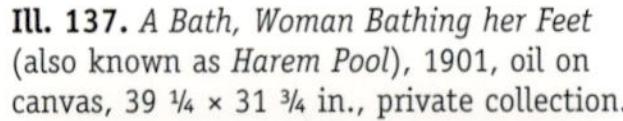

Ill. 137. *A Bath, Woman Bathing her Feet* (also known as *Harem Pool*), 1901, oil on canvas, 39 ¼ × 31 ¾ in., private collection.

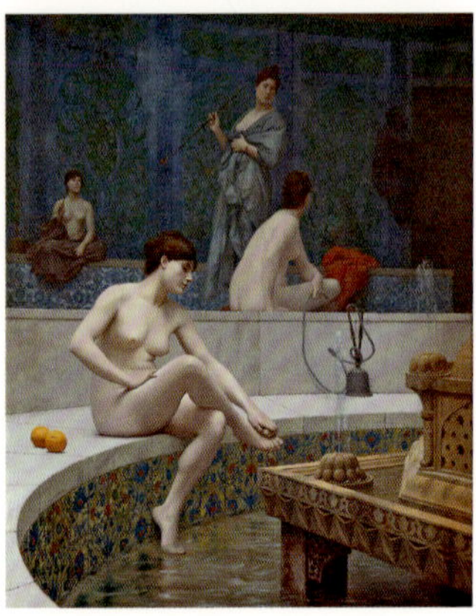

Ill. 138. Pascal Sebah (1823–1886), *The baths of Yénir-Kaplidja, Bursa*, 1894, albumen print, 11 × 10 ½ in., École Nationale Supérieure des Beaux-Arts, Paris, inv. Ph 6656.

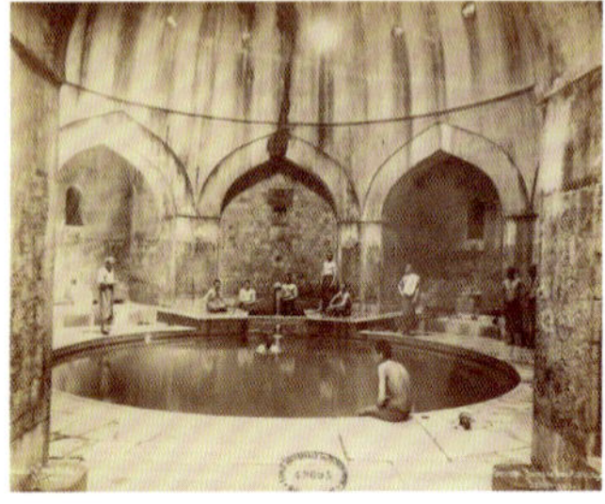

Ill. 139. James Pradier (1790–1852), *Odalisque*, 1841, marble, 2 × 37 × 24 in., Musée des Beaux-Arts, Lyon, inv. H.793.

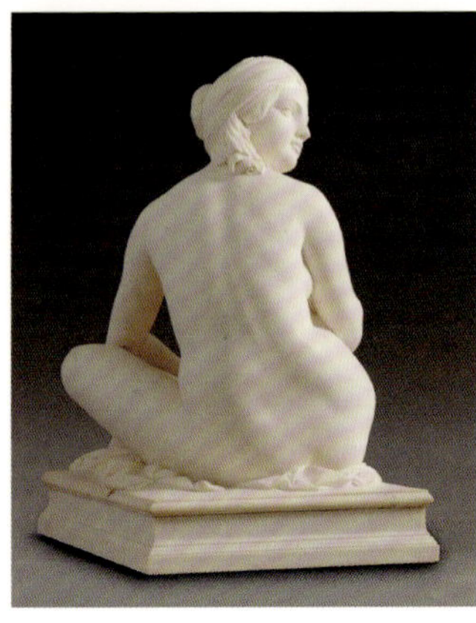

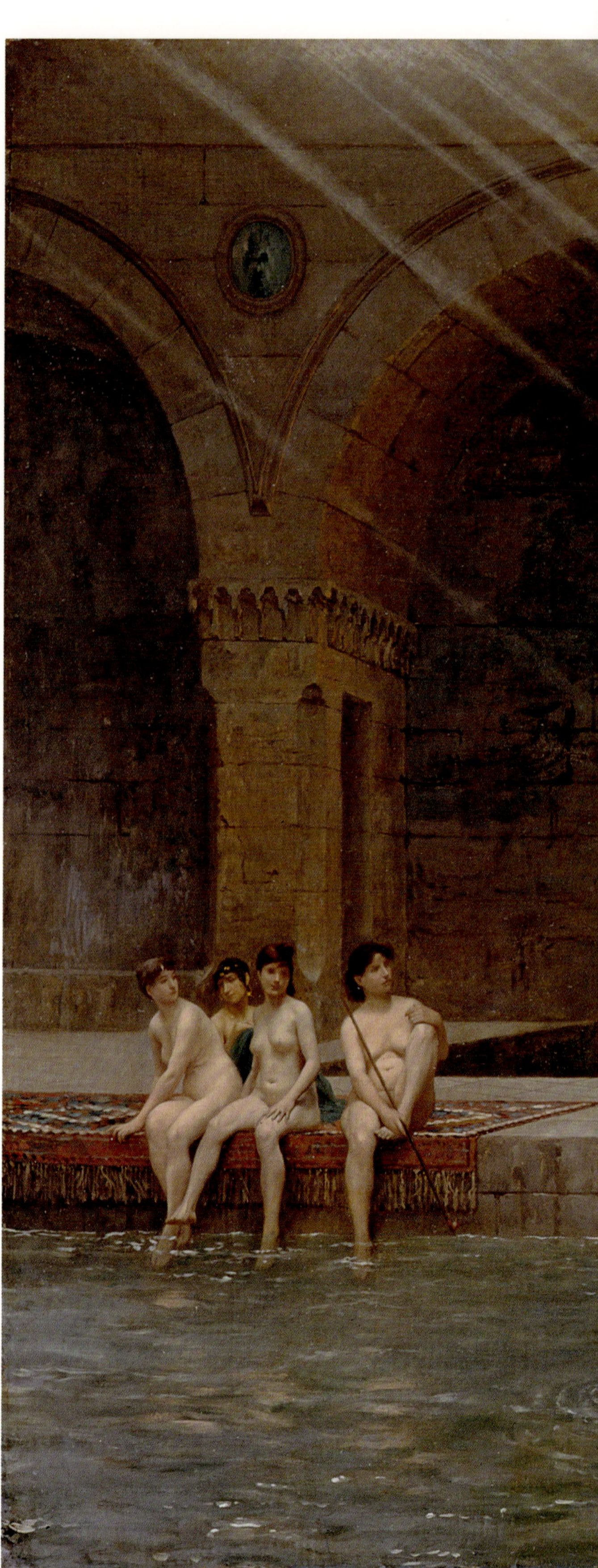

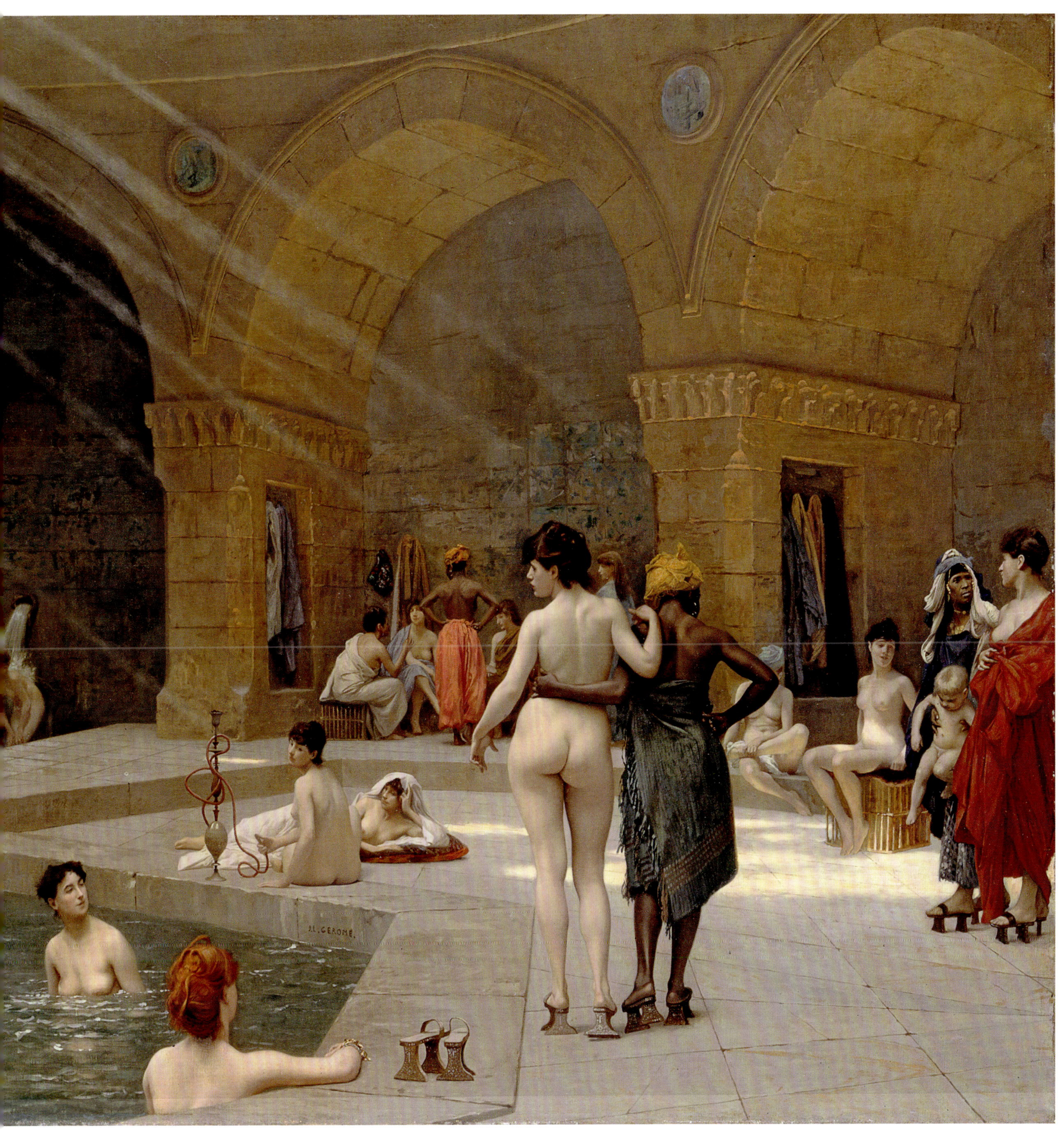
J.L. GEROME.

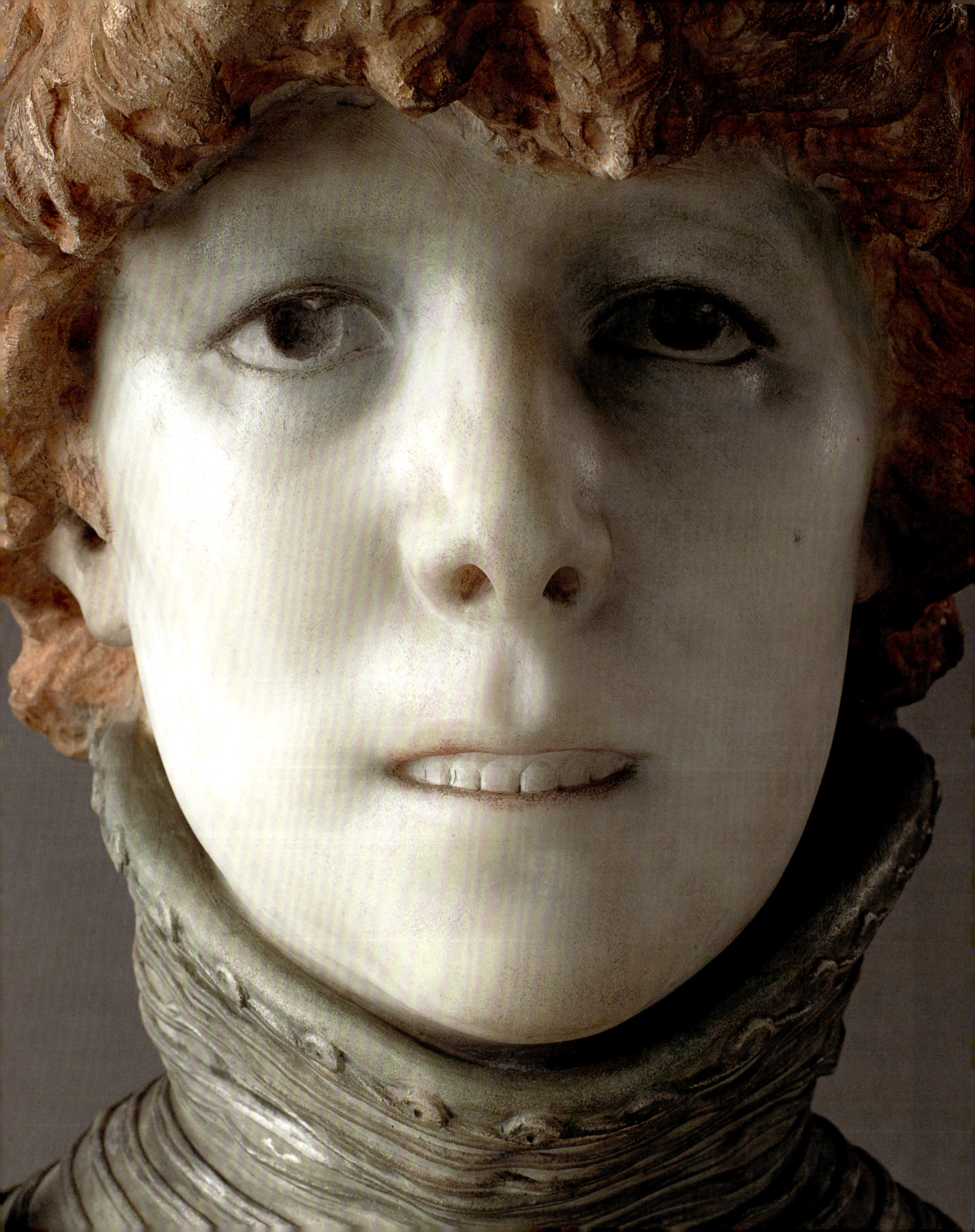

"I have always been surprised that there are some subjects people have never dreamed about tackling."[1]

"FATHER POLYCHROME[2]": THE SCULPTURE OF JEAN-LÉON GÉRÔME

Édouard Papet | Translated from the French by Jonathan Sly

I only came late to sculpture, and it is my great regret"[3]: Gérôme took to sculpture only around 1878, at the age of fifty-five, but he tackled it with all the passion and seriousness of a young artist. His interest in sculpture in the round was nothing new: he had already fashioned figurines as models for his paintings; in 1859, he had created *Mirmillo* and *Retiarius* (cat. 73 and 74) prior to the work *Ave Caesar, morituri te salutant* (cat. 70),[4] before they were included in it, transformed. Ten years later this now recurrent dialogue between painting and sculpture reversed roles under the initiative of his father-in-law, Adolphe Goupil,[5] and statuettes were adapted from figures in his paintings for production in bronze or marble[6]—*Phryné* (cat. 45, 46, 47) or *Dance of the Almeh* (cat. 154), for example modeled by other artists, such as the young sculptors Alexandre Falguière, and Antonin Mercié. The adaptation from one medium to the other was not an isolated phenomenon, and some critics welcomed "a trend that will help art progress, a sure sign of its regeneration."[7] Ernest Meissonier, a close friend of Gérôme, also tried his hand at sculpture, the "instantaneous ecstasy of the creator;"[8] Gustave Moreau was also, at the same time, a gifted sculptor, but did not go beyond the modeling stage, despite his passion for the discipline.[9] Gustave Doré, for his part, remained prisoner to an elegant aesthetic that owed everything to Albert-Ernest Carrier-Belleuse. On the subject of Gérôme, some found this "graft of a young sculptor onto a painter in his fifties"[10] highly successful, and his sculpture left no one indifferent, generating both intrigue and criticism. In the France of the second half of the nineteenth century, such convincing examples of the painter-sculptor—if indeed such a category even existed—were only to be found among aesthetic perspectives diametrically opposed to those of Gérôme, that is to say among the former innovators, who were free from academic shackles: there was for example Honoré Daumier, who felt his commanding way around the form, producing a masterpiece of humanist timelessness and sculptural intelligence; his bas-relief *The Fugitives* (first draft, 1850, plaster, Musée d'Orsay, Paris), was a manifesto of historical sculpture, born in an age of revolution, a work hidden from public view up to the time of its brief exhibition in the Durand-Ruel galleries in 1878, the same year that Gérôme presented his first sculpture *The Gladiators* (cat. 76) at the Exposition Universelle. There were also the modern artists—whom Gérôme steadfastly abhorred: "France is d.....d! Rodin, Pissaro, Monet, Degas are rotten scoundrels"[11]: Edgar Degas, and later Paul Gauguin, not only because these two artists were able to appropriate color in sculpture, each in his own way, but because, as in the case of Gérôme, their separate artistic persuasions soon became complementary. If Gérôme was certainly one of the main artists responsible for the progressive dilution of history painting into genre,[12] this magnificent inventor of images gave the sculpture of his time a chance that it did not take: polychromy as a challenge. Turning to sculpture, for a talent as recognized as he was controversial,

Cat. 187. *Sarah Bernhardt* (detail).

when combined with a renowned, and possibly excessive technical dexterity, an intellectual baggage, and unusual irony, offered a comfortable and stimulating "base."

REALISMS

There exist few studies for Gérôme's sculpture; we have tried to collect as many of them as possible for the exhibition. The small wax model of *The Gladiators* (cat. 75) removes all possible doubt about Gérôme's very real talents in modeling; the model is worthy of Emmanuel Fremiet or Paul Dubois. Equally interesting are the bronzed plaster sketches of *Androcles and the Lion* (cat. 185) and *Caesar Crossing the Rubicon* (cat. 69), and they show Gérôme's interest in a material, fashionable during the 1880s, that combines the freshness of modeling with the appearance of a bronze without the inconvenience of weight or cost.[13] It is not surprising that Gérôme, a fan of new techniques, tried it out, blurring the boundaries, once again, between original modeling and mechanical reproduction. Did he not say about photography—the importance of which for plastic creation he was quickly aware (see Dominique de Font-Réaulx's essay, p. 213)—that it forced "artists to break out of routines and forget formulae[14]"? This obsession with the real, or rather with the plausible recomposition of the real to show, as Gérôme remembered about Meissonier's a stounded reaction in front of a model dressed as a gladiator posing for *Pollice Verso*, "a truth he did not know[15]", is rooted in the work of neo-Florentine sculptors, and their development of an elegant naturalism, beginning in the mid-1860s (Dubois, Falguière), which was naturally followed—politics obliging—by a form of realism that was social, historical, anecdotal, indeed almost neurotic in some genre scenes, and which would go on to become the norm, bringing both extensive possibilities and sterile diversions. With his old friend Fremiet, but with greater distance, he shared the taste for archaeological or historical realism elevated to the heights of the knowledge of the time this "archeologist accuracy" which Gauguin disliked.[16] Although supported by his ability for effective staging firmly developed in his painting, Gérôme's choice may appear tenuous: "archaeology was always his pet hobby... but it went no further when he introduced his obsession to sculpture. The hope that spirit—the spirit of archaeology, worst of all—would be sufficient to breathe life into plaster, marble, or bronze, is one of the most ill-fated aberrations that art has ever produced."[17] He was however one of the rare artists to offer an innovative alternative within the framework of the "academic realism" which absorbed a diverse range of talented artists, sometimes official (ill. 140), and which also authorized Symbolist oddities as much as it flattered the taste of the petite bourgeoisie (ill. 141). If an affinity with Fremiet in terms of youth and archaeological aesthetics enables us to better understand the directions taken, Gérôme managed to escape the rigor that characterized his colleague's production by staging selected and safe "citations" with an element of detachment. So how was he to rediscover, in sculpture, the spirit that, with *Anacreon* (cat. 16) in 1848, had paid off in painting? If we look at the chronological evolution of Gérôme's early sculptures, it is noticeable that his early works, however honorable, also suffer a dual subservience. On the one hand, from his recurrent extraction of motifs from already successful paintings, and the continual reflective interplay between the two media that informs the three-dimensional work, and, on the other, from the monochromy of traditional sculptural materials, marble and bronze. Furthermore, playing the game of reproduction on all fronts entailed certain compromises. Gérôme required little less than ten years "training"—respectable by all accounts—beginning auspiciously with his uncompromising archaeological monument, *The Gladiators*, presented a year after another conspicuous debut, *The Age of Bronze* by Auguste Rodin, and ending with what should properly be thought of as his "first" real sculpture of this second artistic maturity, *Tanagra* (cat. 168), which heralded a new sculptural challenge.

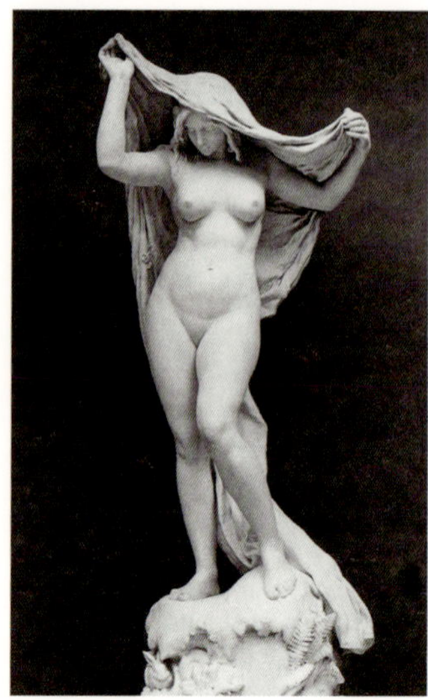

Ill. 140. Louis-Ernest Barrias (1841–1905), *Nature Unveiling herself before Science*, 1893–97, marble, H. 99 ⅝ in., Ny Carlsberg Glyptotek, Copenhagen, inv. I.N. 477.

SCULPTURÆ INSUFFLAT VITAM PICTURA: "THE LIBERTINE SEARCH FOR THE TROMPE-L'OEIL"[18]

Since antiquity, sculpture had almost always been in color, until scholarly and neoclassical art took color away, and established the disembodied white of Greco-Roman marbles, which had been buried for centuries, as an aesthetic norm. Polychromy in antique sculpture and architecture gave rise to lively debates in the early nineteenth century, which only reached a climax

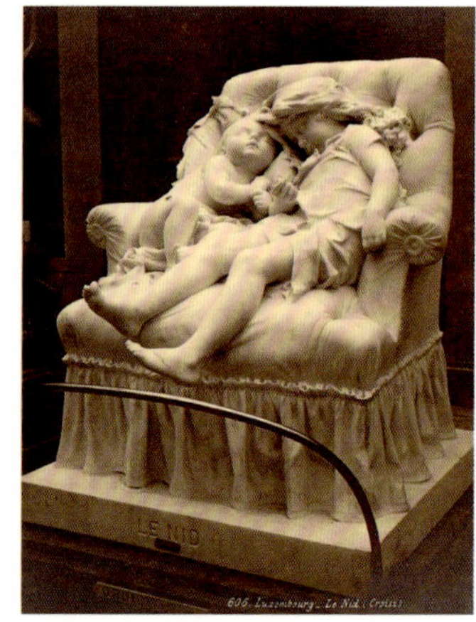

Ill. 141. A. Giraudon, after Onésime Croisy (1840–1899), *The Nest*, 1882, 10 ⅝ × 8 in., silver print, Archives, Musée d'Orsay, Paris.

Ill. 142. Charles Simart (1806–1857), *Reconstruction of Phidias'* Athena Parthenos, 1855, ivory, bronze, silver and gilt, marble, Château de Dampierre, Dampierre.

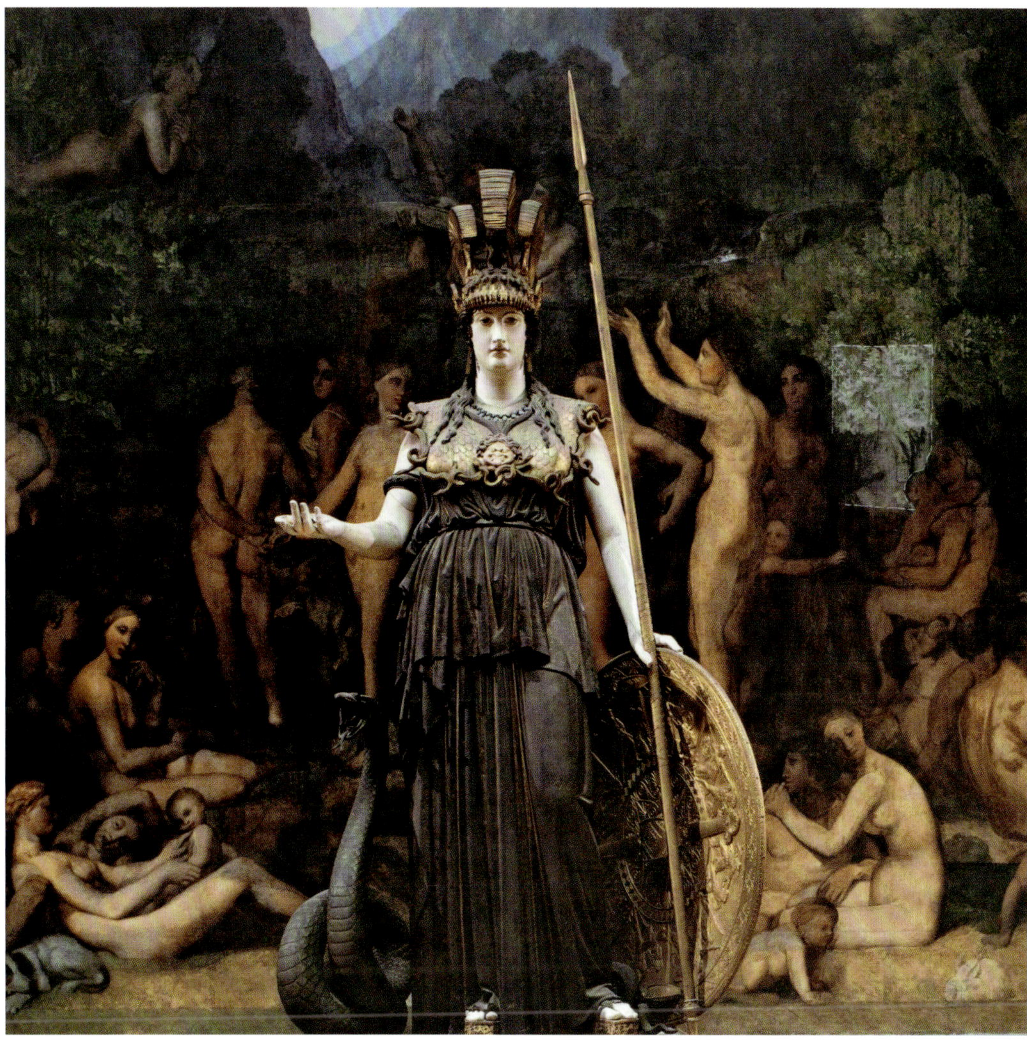

in the 1880s.[19] The theories of the German archaeologist Georg Treu, who excavated the site of Olympia, on the application of the potential revealed in antique polychrome sculpture to modern sculpture, had a considerable impact.[20] Color in contemporary sculpture had few supporters, as Charles Blanc, among many others, summed up perfectly in 1872: "Colorist sculptors will be burned, and it will be a good thing."[21] The choice of polychromy was unambiguous for Gérôme: "I first set about coloring marbles, because I've always been put off by the coldness of a statue if, once the work is finished, it is left in its natural state."[22] Gérôme's works are indeed very far from their "natural state", due to their synthesis, to the point of saturation, of very civilized references. Coloring sculptures was certainly not a new approach in France, having been practised since the 1840s, and gradually color took hold, often on the margins, providing an odd quality of almost inevitable originality. "Natural" polychromy—the assembly of naturally colored materials (marbles and bronzes of different patinas)—had its own virtuoso, Charles Cordier, and its own, much mocked, chryselephantine monument: Charles Simart's reconstruction of Phidias' *Athena Parthenos* (ill. 142). With such credentials, it was ultimately the only form of polychromy genuinely accepted among Gérôme's contemporaries.[23] Gérôme himself was an avid practitioner, and it provided the motivation for some spectacular, technically complex, but slightly dry works, like *Bellona* (cat. 182). The other possibility for color, "artificial polychromy"—wherein marble was painted, most often with a pigmented wax, reviving antique *ganosis* or medieval inspirations with varying degrees of success—was Gérôme's real calling and conquest. He did not adopt the slightly crepuscular tenebrism of its Germanic pioneers whose explorations were contemporaneous to his own, and nothing in his own painted work—apart from rare exceptions, such as the dazzling litotes of *The Death of Marshal Ney* (cat. 93) and *Golgotha* (cat. 78), which were unsuitable for adaptation into sculpture—predisposed him to somber inspiration. Attentive to the archaeological discoveries of his time, Gérôme became interested in a spectacular and precious witness to Hellenistic *ganosis*,[24]

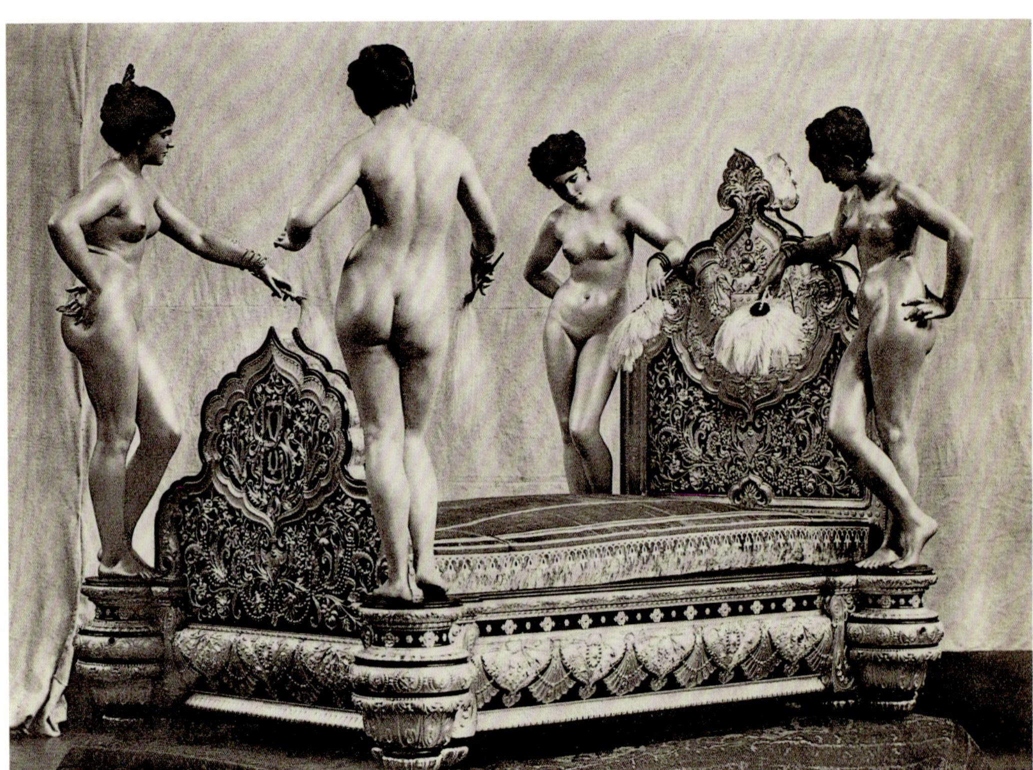

Ill. 143. Bed ordered by the maharadjah of Bahawalpur from Maison Christofle in 1882, photograph reproduced in Luc Lanel, *1839–1939. Centenaire de l'orfèvrerie Christofle* (Paris, 1941), p. XIV.

a major discovery made in 1887 by one of his former pupils, the Turkish painter and archaeologist Osman Hamdi Bey, who was also the founder of the Istanbul Archaeological Museum: "I would like to see the great sarcophagus, said to be Alexander's, with its colors intact, and I am very pleased to learn that the coloring has not altered in contact with the air. Obviously this monument, from what you say, will tell me much about the polychromy of the Greeks, and show what unexpected and considerable effects can be obtained when color and form combine (ill. 144)."[25] Gérôme, faithful to the synthesis of sources that he had long exercised in painting, sought to "revive polychrome sculpture which is essentially decorative."[26] The remark on the decorative aspect of colored sculpture is fundamental, and shows how Gérôme's tastes were pervaded with the spirit of the times. The primary motivation of polychromy for Gérôme was innovation, even if it meant being marginalized, a paradox for one of the most famous artists of his time: "I have suffered many a disappointment in my desire to stand up to our Holy Convention, and my fellow sculptors were filled with loathing and horror at my work, which is all the same to me; I was not expecting such an honor. When my attempts appeared they howled like jackals and must have been heard in Constantinople," he wrote to Hamdi Bey.[27] When polychromy was added to the hyperrealism of representation, the status of the statue became uncertain: to critics, several of Gérôme's sculptures were synonymous with the death of art: "It is simply the antithesis of statuary ... the renunciation of art. The wax figure is close to the painted flesh of corpses; the effect is horrific."[28]

PYGMALION AND ITS SIMULACRA

Gérôme's modern idols, *Tanagra* and *Ball Player*, are disturbing: only in appearance are they imitations of reality under the guise of mimesis. They did not give rise to controversy like Degas's radical *Little Dancer Aged Fourteen* (ill. 145).[29] Gérôme's painted marbles are not socially toxic, and they are no doubt less powerfully sarcastic, but their immersion in the confusion of the aesthetic codes of their time is proof of their paradoxical modernity forged by their difference: they are statues of nudes for "well-informed enthusiasts," leading the imagination towards the extravagant bed ordered by the maharajah of Bahawalpur from the Maison Christofle in 1882 (ill. 143) While the history of taste has deprived us of *Tanagra*'s (cat. 168) original colors and *Pygmalion and Galatea*'s, the individual heads of *Tanagra* (cat. 169, 170), the large version of *The Ball Player* (cat. 189) and the *Squatting Nude* (cat. 186) testify of the excessive sexualization brought about by polychromy. Gérôme created a borderline aesthetics of mystification, "the libertine search for the *trompe-l'oeil*"[30] in three dimensions, formed by a toing and froing with his painting, within the constraints of the tradition. Gérôme's iconographic blundering, however, had been almost constant since *Phryné before the Areopagus*, and, from the 1890s onwards, led to works of *intellectualized* kitsch. This drift was not easy to distinguish, due to Gérôme's sometimes possibly unintentional cunning, except where humorous distance sufficed to curb the unconscious drive of artistic expression in which the inadmissible in scholarly art is laid bare, namely the illustration, free from taboos, of the genre's genuine idiotic vulgarity, and the accessorization of sexuality at the vaguest boundaries of Greco-Roman antiquity and the colonialist Orient epitomizing the *petit* taste. The former Néo-Grec genius of 1840 turned archaeologist stage director under the Second Empire was maybe the best conscientious objector acceptable to a bourgeoisie that provided Gérôme with a very good livelihood. Gérôme, the member of the Institut, the sworn enemy of modernist painting, perfectly orchestrated, both in his own painting and sculpture, the disturbance in codes. The women who haunt Gérôme's sculptural work, always isolated, with the exception of Galatea, are, literally and above all, figures from his studio, in whose solitude Gérôme kept the light of the heliasts' gaze contemplating Phryné's divine forms burning in his own. The studio, whether the communal "Boîte à thé" in the early Néo-Grec days, or the luxurious space of his affluent later years, remained a focus for the creation of series covering Gérôme's full artistic range, especially in sculpture: *Pygmalion and Galatea* (cat. 175), formerly a polychrome marble, a patched-up myth, is the clearest expression of this focus. The studio was an obsessional space, the site for Gérôme's own portraits of himself as sculptor (cat. 173) or painter, where the statues seem to turn their gaze and watch their colorist in action;[31] the crucial later stages of a work are also represented, with all the banalities of the sculptor's studio: stains, sponges, water buckets, and clay-encrusted tools (cat. 176). The studio was also a place where he was photographed, capturing ceremonial images of himself—preferably modeling sculpture—or capturing disturbing portraits of his work (cat. 177 to 179). The studio is a space that permeates all of his work, both in painting and sculpture over time, and is closely connected to the interplay of metaphorical mirrors reflecting and staging the artist's life to the extent of recreating a studio in Pompeii, crowded with Tanagra's own clients (cat. 174); it is also a space where the *Hoop Dancer* series was painted (cat. 172), a series of Tanagras of purest fantasy.

Ill. 144. Franz Winter, *The Alexander Sarcophagus* (Strasbourg: K. J Trübner, 1912), pl. 18, Bibliothèque de l'INHA, Paris.

VIEWS

Until recently, painted statues from the nineteenth century received short shrift. In 1974, the refusal to acquire *Ancient Dancer* (cat. 180) and the irony in which the refusal was couched[32] confirm the enduring prejudice against this illusionism that forces the confrontation with "inferior" circles and the fantasy of the degeneration of art once more. Another significant moment for the history of taste came in 2008, when upon acquisition of the original plaster of *Corinth* (cat. 192, 193) by the Musée d'Orsay, the work was refused classification as a national treasure. Despite his pioneering work in polychrome sculpture in the nineteenth century, Gérôme's own work remains tarnished by suspicion, well analyzed by the artist himself, one hundred years ago: "We are a very conventional people. Praise be to our Holy Routine!"[33] In considering the issue of the gaze, which constituted one of the major motivations of Gérôme's work, what position does his polychrome sculpture have today, as it oscillates between photographic illusionism and our irresistible attraction for the past? Its role no doubt is as an essential link between the aporia of figuration and the return of hyperrealism in the 1960s. "I hope it will largely be forgiven"[34] was Gérôme's expressed wish, not without hindsight, in the twilight of his life, a wish that has clearly been granted. May this exhibition dissipate, from his sculpture even more so than from his painting, the misunderstandings of success.

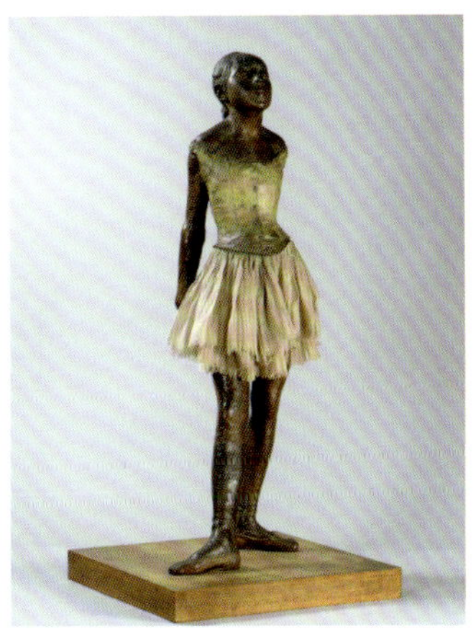

Ill. 145. Edgar Degas (1834–1917), *Little Dancer Aged Fourteen*, 1880, bronze, textile, 38 ⅝ × 13 ⅞ × 9 ⅝ in., Musée d'Orsay, Paris, inv. RF 2137.

Ill. 146. *Self-Portrait Painting The Ball Player*, ca. 1902, oil on canvas, 24 × 19 7/8 in., Musée Georges-Garret, Vesoul, inv. 945.2.16.

1. F. Masson, "Notes et fragments de J.-L. Gérôme," *Les Arts*, n. 26 (Feb. 1904), p. 20, *J.-L. Gérôme*, exh. cat. (Vesoul: Musée Georges-Garret), 1981, pp. 141–57.

2. Marcel Schwob, *Les Œuvres complètes de Marcel Schwob (1867-1905)*, Paris, F. Bernouard, 1927, p. 270.

3. F. Masson, as in n. 2, p. 31. See also G. Ackerman, "Gérôme sculpteur," in *J.-L. Gérôme*, exh. cat. (Vesoul: Musée Georges-Garret), 1981, pp. 141–57.

4. G. Ackerman, *Jean-Léon Gérôme* (Courbevoie: ACR Édition, 2000), no. S.64, p. 402.

5. Florence Rionnet provides a perfect analysis of the issues: "Goupil et Gérôme, regards croisés sur l'édition sculptée," in H. Lafont-Couturier, *Gérôme & Goupil. Art et entreprise* (Bordeaux: Musée Goupil, 2000–1; also New York: Dahesh Museum of Art, 2001, and Pittsburgh: The Frick Art & Historical Center, 2001), pp. 45–53.

6. F. Rionnet 2000–1 (as in n. 3) and É. Papet, "Phryné, la plus jolie femme de Paris," in *Praxitèle*, exh. cat. (Paris: Musée du Louvre, 2007), p. 386.

7. T. Véron, "Beaux-Arts. Les peintres-sculpteurs et les sculpteurs-peintres," *Revue du Lyonnais*, ser. 4, no. 8 (1879), p. 455.

8. *Jean-Louis-Ernest Meissonier – ses souvenirs – ses entretiens*, preceded by a study on his life and his work by O. Gréard (Paris: Hachette, 1897), p. 200.

9. *Gustave Moreau, l'homme aux figures de cire*, exh. cat. (Paris: Musée Gustave-Moreau, 2010).

10. J. Buisson, "Le Salon de 1881. 3e article, la sculpture," *Gazette des Beaux-Arts*, 1881, vol. 2, p. 214.

11. L. Vauxcelles, "Critique humoristique. Gérôme et son oeuvre dépeints par M. Louis Vauxcelles," *New York Herald, Paris*, Jan. 24, 1904, p. 2.

12. H. Loyrette, "La peinture d'histoire," *Impressionnisme. Les origines 1859–1869*, exh. cat. (Paris: Galeries Nationales du Grand Palais, 1994 also New York, The Metropolitan Museum of Art, 1994-95), p. 36.

13. G. Debonliez and François Malepeyre, *Manuels-Roret, Nouveau Manuel complet du bronzage des métaux et du plâtre* [1887] (Paris: Léonce Laget, 1979), pp. 117–42. This material still remains to be studied in greater depth.

14. J.-L. Gérôme, preface to É. Bayard, *Le Nu esthétique. L'Homme, La Femme, L'Enfant. Album de documents artistiques inédits d'après Nature* (Paris: Bernard, 1902), n.p.

15. F. Masson, as in n. 2, p. 27. G. Ackerman,"Gérôme's Sculpture: The Problems of Realist Sculpture," *Arts Magazine*, vol. 60, no. 6 (Feb. 1986), pp. 82–89.

16. *Lettres de Gauguin à sa femme et à ses amis*, ed. M. Malingue (Paris: Grasset, 1946), p. 63. On Fremiet see C. Chevillot, "Emmanuel Fremiet, sculpteur statuaire," in *Emmanuel Fremiet. La main et le multiple*, exh. cat. (Dijon: Musée des Beaux-Arts, 1988–89), pp. 23–65.

17. P. Leroi, "Musées en plein vent," *L'Art*, 1894–1900, p. 1014.

18. "Painting breathes life into sculpture": L. Vauxcelles 1904 (as in n. 11).

19. See A. Blühm, "In Living Color. A Short History of Color and Sculpture in the 19th Century," in *The Colour of Sculpture 1840–1910*, exh. cat. (Amsterdam: Van Gogh Museum, 1996), pp. 11–60.

20. G. Treu, *Sollen wir unseren Statuen bemalen?* (Berlin: Oppenhein, 1884).

21. Letter from Charles Blanc to the sculptor Albert-Ernest Carrier-Belleuse, Jan. 6, 1872, Archives Nationales, Paris, F21 201.

22. Letter from Gérôme to Germain Pabst, Feb. 2, 1892, Bibliothèque Nationale de France, Paris, 4° V 5381.

23. G. Pabst, "La sculpture chryséléphantine. Phidias – Le duc de Luynes – M. Gérôme," *Revue de famille*, 5th yr., vol. II (1892), pp. 334–43.

24. The excavations of the royal necropolis of Saida were published in 1892, with the collaboration of the French archaeologist Théodore Reinach. Istanbul's Imperial Archaeology Museum, known as the "sarcophagus museum," was inaugurated in 1891.

25. Jean-Léon Gérôme to Osman Hamdi Bey, Paris, July 21, 1893, published by H. Metzger, "La correspondance passive d'Osman Hamdi Bey," *Mémoires de l'Académie des inscriptions et des belles-lettres*, new ser., vol. XI (1990), pp. 86–87.

26. Ibid.

27. Ibid.

28. G. Geffroy, "Salons de 1892. Aux Champs-Élysées. VIII Les statues peintes," in *La Vie artistique* (Paris, 1893), p. 289.

29. G. Jeanniot, "Souvenirs sur Degas," *La Revue universelle*, Oct. 15–Nov. 1, 1933, pp. 171–72.

30. L. Vauxcelles 1904 (as in n. 11).

31. F. Chappey, "L'iconographie de Pygmalion et Galatée aux XIXe et XXe siècles: entre introspection et exhibition," in C. Dotal and A. Dratwicki, eds, *L'Artiste et sa muse*, proceedings of the conference at the Académie de France in Rome, March 2–4, 2005 (Paris: Somogy, Éditions d'art and Rome: Académie de France à Rome, 2006), pp. 8–9, and V. I. Stoichita, "The End of the Session: Photography and Sculpture," *The Pygmalion Effect. From Ovid to Hitchcock* (Chicago: University of Chicago Press, 2006), pp. 161–74.

32. Letter from Victor Beyer, head curator in the sculpture department at the Musée du Louvre, to Jacques Dupont, general inspector of historical monuments, June 11, 1974, Documentation, Musée d'Orsay, Paris.

33. F. Masson 1904 (as in n. 2), p. 30.

34. Ibid, p. 32.

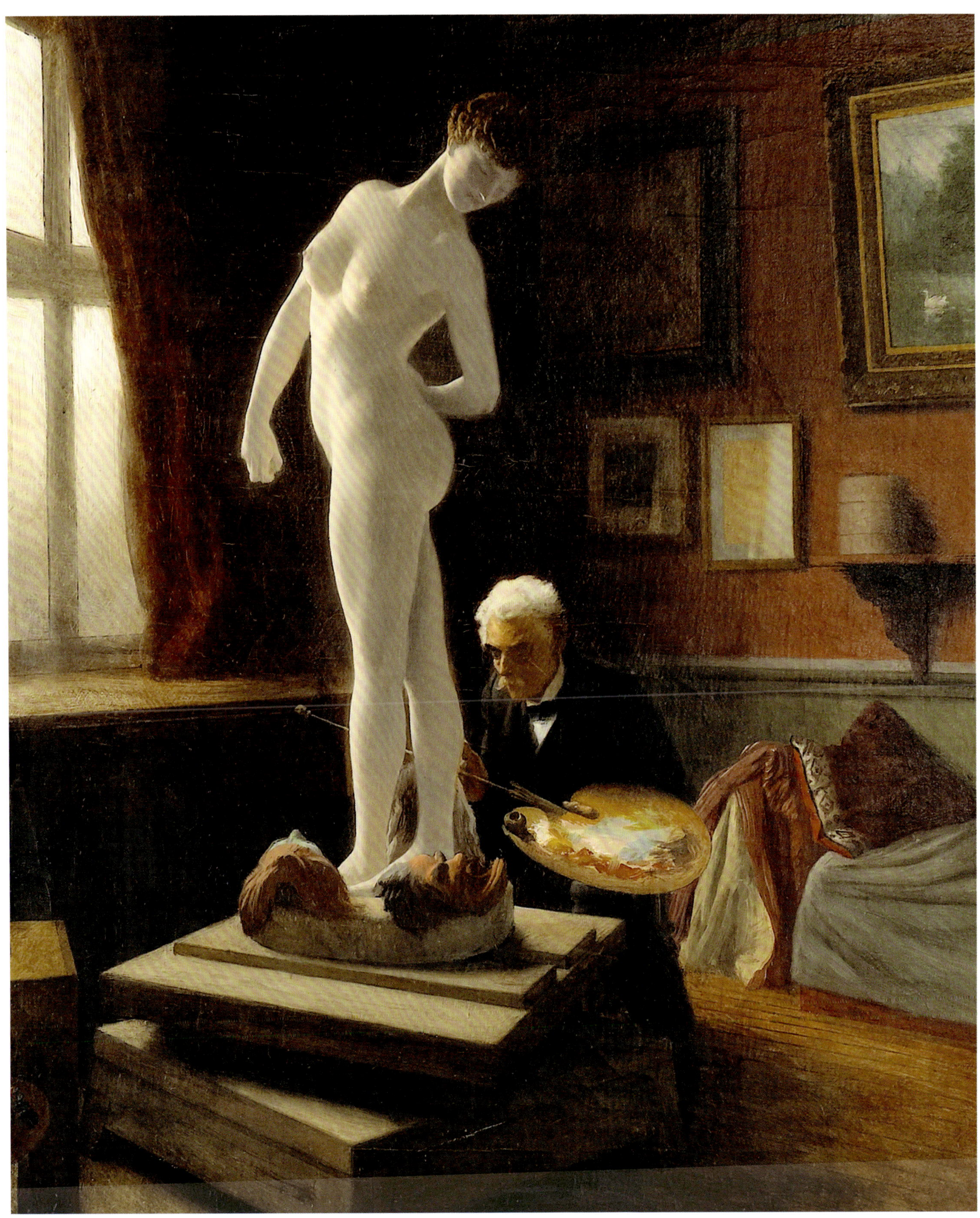

Cat. 168

TANAGRA

–

1890
Marble with polychrome traces
60 5/8 × 41 1/4 × 23 5/8 in.
Inscriptions: *TANAГPA* on a cartouche in front, on the base; on the right rock: *J.L. Gérôme*
Musée d'Orsay, Paris, inv. RF 2514

–

Provenance: Purchased by the State in 1890 (for 10,000 francs). Musée du Luxembourg up to 1929. Musée du Louvre up to 1986. Allocated to the Musée d'Orsay, 1986.

–

Exhibition History: Salon des Artistes français, Paris, 1890, no. 39.

–

Bibliography: C. Mauclair, *Le Musée du Luxemboug* (Paris: Ed. Nilsson, [post 1826], p. 3. M. Albert, "Le Salon des Champs-Elysées," *Gazette des Beaux-Arts*, 1890, vol. II, pp. 62–63. L. de Fourcaud, "L'art décoratif au Salon des Champs-Élysées," *Revue des arts décoratifs*, May–June 1890, p. 343. Le Masque de Velours, "La vie mondaine. Les portraits au Salon," *La Revue illustrée*, 1st qtr 1890, pp. 405–6. J. Antoine, "Critique d'art. Le Salon des Champs-Élysées," *La Plume*, no. 51 (June 1, 1891), p. 191. C. Saunier, "A propos du Luxembourg," *La Plume*, no. 43 (Feb. 1, 1891), p. 62. G. Geffroy, "Salon de 1890 aux Champs-Élysées et au Champ de Mars," *La Vie artistique. 1ère série* (Paris: E. Dentu, 1892), p. 222. E. Pottier, "Les Salons de 1892. La sculpture. Les Arts industriels," *Gazette des Beaux-Arts*, 1892, vol. II, pp. 29–30. H. Bouchot, "Les Salons de 1893. 3e et dernier article," *Gazette des Beaux-Arts*, 1893, vol. II, p. 314. *La Revue de l'art ancien et moderne*, Sept. 1900, p. 122. *The New York Herald*, Jan. 24, 1904. F. Masson, "Notes et fragments de J.-L. Gérôme," *Les Arts*, no. 26 (Feb. 1904), p. 30. H. Jaudon, *Denys Puech et son œuvre* (Rodez: Ed. Carrère, 1908), pp. 201, 248. R. Schneider, *Quatremère de Quincy et son intervention dans les arts (1788–1830)* (Paris: Hachette, 1910), pp. 130–31. L. Daudet, *Souvenirs littéraires* (Paris: Bernard Grasset, Livre de Poche), 1968, p. 361. G. Ackerman et al., *Jean- Léon Gérôme (1824–1904)*, exh. cat. (Dayton: Dayton Art Institute, 1972; also Minneapolis: Minneapolis Institute of Arts, 1973, and Baltimore: The Walters Art Gallery, 1973), p. 95. A. E. Elsen, *Pioneers of Modern Sculpture*, exh. cat. (London: Hayward Gallery, 1973), pp. 16–17, 74–75. *The Impressionists and the Salon (1874–1886): Honoring the Centennial of the First Impressionist Exhibition*, exh. cat. (Los Angeles: Los Angeles County Museum of Art, 1974; also Riverside: Riverside Gallery, University of California, 1974). A. Pingeot, A. Le Normand-Romain, and I. Lemaistre, *Sculpture française XIXe siècle* (École du Louvre, Notices d'histoire de l'art, no. 6) (Paris: RMN, 1982), p. 43. R. Rosenblum et H. W. Janson, *Art of the 19th Century, Painting and Sculpture* (New York: 1984), p. 472. G. Ackerman, "Gérôme's Sculpture: The Problems of Realist Sculpture," *Arts Magazine*, Feb. 1986, pp. 84–85. A. Pingeot, "Le conte sculpté dans la seconde moitié du XIXe siècle," *Romantisme*, no. 78 (1992), p. 16. *The Colour of Sculpture*, exh. cat. (Amsterdam: Van Gogh Museum, 1996, also Leeds: Henry Moore Institute, 1996–97), pp. 11–13, 45, 84, 111 and 128–29. *Jean-Léon Gérôme and the Classical Imagination*, exh. cat. (New York: Dahesh Museum of Art, 1997). H. Lafont-Couturier, *Gérôme* (Paris: Herscher, 1998), p. 90. G. Ackerman, *Jean-Léon Gérôme* (Courbevoie: ACR Edition, 2000), S. 17. H. Lafont-Couturier, *Gérôme and Goupil: Art and Enterprise*, exh. cat., trans. I. Ollivier (Bordeaux: Musée Goupil, 2000–1; also New York: Dahesh Museum of Art, 2001, and Pittsburgh: The Frick Art & Historical Center, 2001), pp. 52–53. É. Papet, "Jean-Léon Gérôme. Tanagra, 1890," *Tanagra. Mythe et archéologie*, exh. cat. (Paris: Musée du Louvre, 2003–4), pp. 43, 45, 48–50. E. Héran, "L'évolution du regard sur la sculpture polychrome," *48/14. La Revue du Musée d'Orsay*, no. 18 (spring 2004), pp. 62–71. A. Caubet, "Les figures antiques de terre-cuite," *Perspective. La Revue de l'INHA*, 2009, no. 1, p. 44.

Cat. 169

TANAGRA HEAD

–

ca. 1890
Polychrome marble
Without base: 17 × 11 × 9 1/2 in.; with base: 21 1/2 × 11 × 9 1/2 in.
Santa Barbara Museum of Art, Santa Barbara, inv. 1993.9

–

Provenance: Marcel Puech, Avignon. Shepherd Gallery, New York. Santa Barbara Museum of Art, California, European Deaccessioning Funds, 1993.

–

Bibliography: G. Ackerman, *Jean-Léon Gérôme* (Courbevoie: ACR Édition, 2000), S. 17.5 (1). D. Saunders, in R. Panzanelli, ed., *The Color of Life. Polychromy in Sculpture from Antiquity to the Present*, exh cat. (Los Angeles: J. Paul Getty Museum, Getty Villa, 2008), no. 35.

Cat. 170

TANAGRA HEAD

–

ca. 1890
Polychrome marble
22 3/8 × 13 3/8 in.
Lucie Audouy collection, Paris

–

Bibliography: *The Colour of Sculpture*, exh. cat. (Amsterdam: Van Gogh Museum, 1996; also Leeds: Henry Moore Institute, 1996–97), no. 11, p. 128. G. Ackerman, *Jean-Léon Gérôme* (Courbevoie: ACR Édition, 2000), no. S. 17.5 (2).

Cat. 171a

TANAGRA

–

1913
Bronze, cast by Siot-Decauville
59 3/4 × 23 5/8 × 26 3/8 in.
Signed under the figure of Athena under the rock: *JL Gérôme*
Musée Georges-Garret, Vesoul, inv. 913.1.1

–

Provenance: Cast in 1913, to be integrated into the monument dedicated to Gérôme, opposite Gérôme's high school in Vesoul (1913). Dismantled around 1938. Moved to a fountain in the park, quai Yves Barbier. Musée Georges-Garret, Vesoul, 1981.

–

Bibliography: *J.-L. Gérôme*, exh. cat. (Vesoul: Musée Georges-Garret, 1981), p. 147, ill. G. Ackerman, *Jean-Léon Gérôme* (Courbevoie: ACR Édition, 2000), no. S. 17 B.1. *Tanagra. Mythe et archéologie*, exh. cat. (Paris: Musée du Louvre, 2003–4), no. 95.

Cat. 171b

HOOP DANCER

–

after 1890
Bronze, onyx
8 7/8 × 3 7/8 × 5 1/8 in.; pedestal: 1 5/8 in.
Musée Georges-Garret, Vesoul, inv. 990.1.1

–

Provenance: Gift of Les Amis du Musée Georges-Garret, 1990.

–

Bibliography: G. Ackerman, *Jean-Léon Gérôme* (Courbevoie: ACR Édition, 2000), no. S 21, p. 388. É. Papet, "Jean-Léon Gérôme: *Tanagra*, 1890," in *Tanagra: Mythe et archéologie*, exh. cat. (Paris: Musée du Louvre, 2003–4), no. 2, p. 50.

Cat. 172

HOOP DANCER

–

after 1891
Polychrome and gilded marble, onyx base
With base: 10 3/4 × diam. 4 in.
Unsigned
Dr. Edward T. Wilson collection, Bethesda, Maryland

–

Provenance: Sotheby's, London, Nov. 11, 1997, lot 103. Schaeffer Collection, Australia, 1997. Christie's, Australia, "At Rona," May 16, 2004, lot 370. Dr. Edward T. Wilson collection, 2004.

–

Bibliography: G. Ackerman, *Jean-Léon Gérôme* (Courbevoie: ACR Édition, 2000), no. S 21, p. 388.

Cat. 173

THE ARTIST'S MODEL

–

1895
Oil on canvas
20 × 15 5/8 in.
Signed and dated lower left, on the portfolio: *J.L. GEROME 1895*
Dahesh Museum of Art, Greenwich, inv. 1995.104

–

Provenance: Estate of Professor Tessier (the artist's stepson). Sold by the Hôtel Drouot, Paris, June 20, 1932, lot 12, to M. R. G. Ledoux-Lebard, Paris. M. Christian Ledoux-Lebard, by inheritance. Auctioned by Sotheby's, New York, Nov. 1, 1995, lot 80 and acquired by the Dahesh Museum of Art, New York.

Exhibition History: *Exposition internationale d'art*, Copenhagen, 1897, no. 247.

–

Bibliography: Recueil. Œuvres de J.-L. Gérôme, BNF Estampes, vol. XII, no. 7. G. Ackerman et al., *Jean- Léon Gérôme (1824–1904)*, exh. cat. (Dayton: Dayton Art Institute, 1972; also Minneapolis: Minneapolis Institute of Arts, 1973, and Baltimore: The Walters Art Gallery, 1973), no. 42, p. 95. "Jean-Léon Gérôme and the Classical Imagination...," *Dahesh Museum Bulletin*, Oct. 1997. H. Lafont-Couturier, *Gérôme* (Paris: Herscher, 1998), pp. 37, 91. G. Ackerman, *Jean-Léon Gérôme* (Courbevoie: ACR Édition, 2000), no. 419.3. *Tanagra. Mythe et archéologie*, exh. cat. (Paris: Musée du Louvre, 2003–4), no. 95, pp. 50–53. V. I. Stoichita, "The End of the Session (Photography and Sculpture)," in *The Pygmalion Effect. From Ovid to Hitchcock* (Chicago: University of Chicago Press, 2008), pp. 168–169.

Cat. 174

SCULPTURAE VITAM INSUFFLAT PICTURA (PAINTING BREATHES LIFE INTO SCULPTURE)

–

1893
Oil on canvas
19 3/4 × 27 1/4 in.
Signed lower left on the box: *J.L. GEROME*
Art Gallery of Ontario, Toronto, Gift of Junior Women's Committee Fund, 1969, inv. 69 / 31

–

Provenance: S. Collins, Pittsburgh, 1893. Sold to Henry Clay Frick, 1895. Frick Collection, Pittsburgh, 1895–99. 1899 to Knoedler, New York. Knoedler to H. Seligman, 1899. Estate of John Mc Vay, PBNY, 1969, auction 2819, purchased by the Junior Women's Committee Fund and given to the Art Gallery of Ontario in 1969.

–

Exhibition History: Cercle de l'Union Artistique, Paris, 1893.

–

Bibliography: G. Ackerman et al., *Jean-Léon Gérôme (1824–1904)*, exh. cat. (Dayton: Dayton Art Institute, 1972; also Minneapolis: Minneapolis Institute of Arts, 1973, and Baltimore: The Walters Art Gallery, 1973), no. 41, pp. 93–94. *Another World Art* (Ontario: Gallery of York University, 1976), no. 10. P. Fusco and H. Janson, *The Romantics to Rodin: French Nineteenth Century Sculpture from North American Collections*, exh. cat. (Los Angeles: Los Angeles County Museum of Art, 1980), no. 154, p. 288. H. Lafont-Couturier, *Gérôme* (Paris: Herscher, 1998), pp. 92–94. G. Ackerman, *Jean-Léon Gérôme* (Courbevoie: ACR Édition, 2000), no. 411. H. Lafont-Couturier, *Gérôme and Goupil: Art and Enterprise*, exh. cat., trans. I. Ollivier (Bordeaux: Musée Goupil, 2000–1; also New York: Dahesh Museum of Art, 2001, and Pittsburgh: The Frick Art & Historical Center, 2001), pp. 42–43, 53. É. Papet, "Tanagra," in *Tanagra. Mythe et archéologie*, exh. cat. (Paris: Musée du Louvre, 2004), no. 5, pp. 50–53.

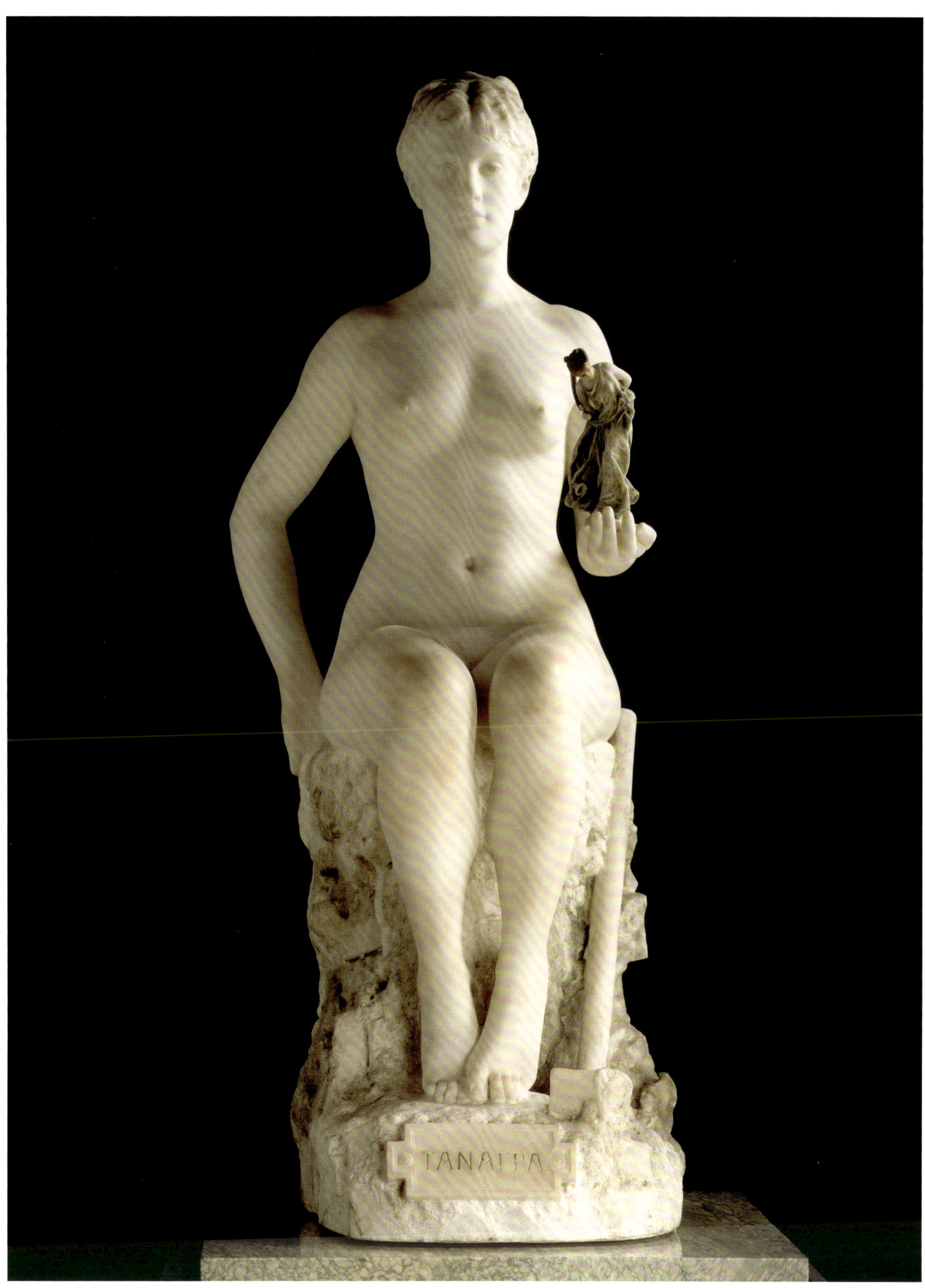
ΤΑΝΑΓΡΑ

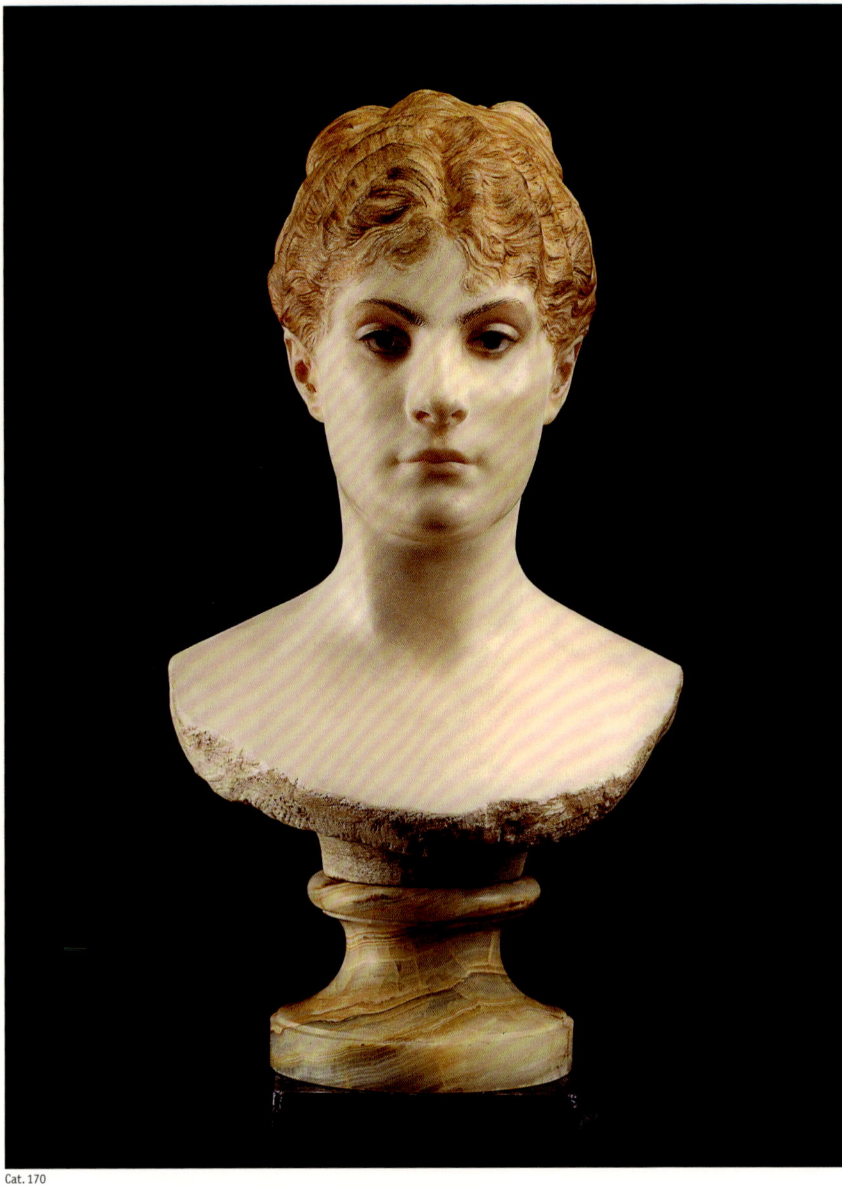
Cat. 170

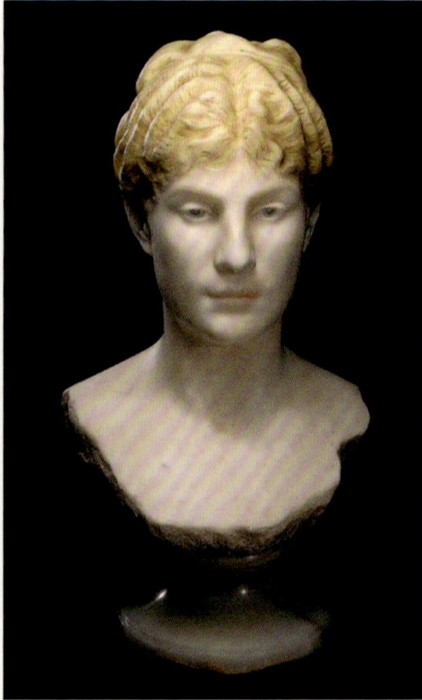
Cat. 169

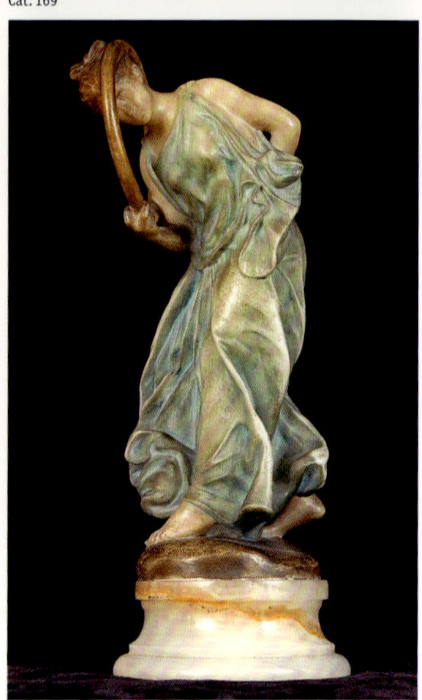
Cat. 172

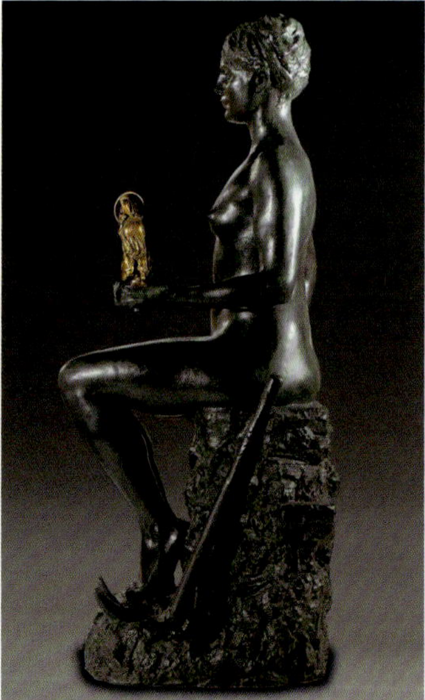
Cat. 171 a and b

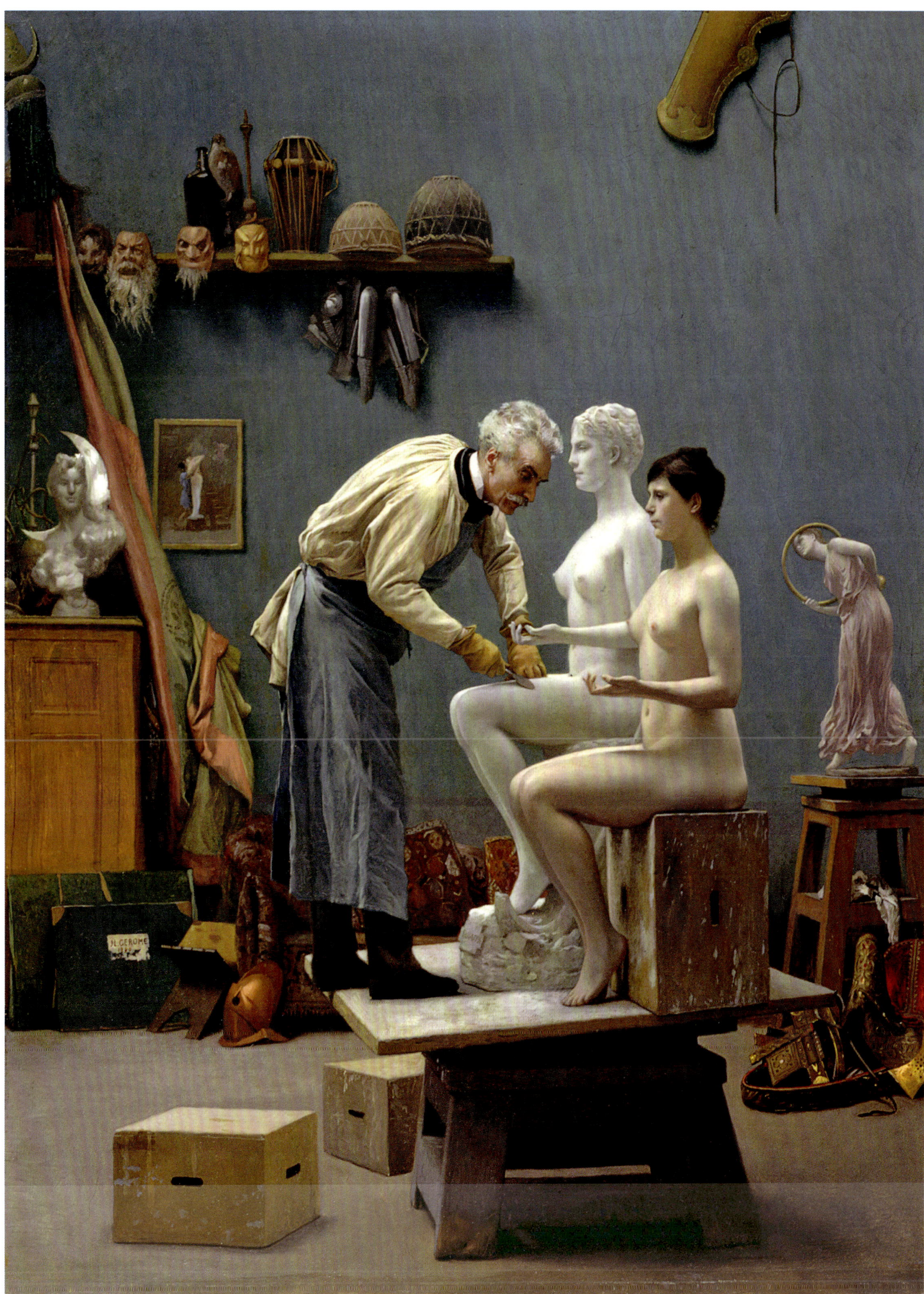

Cat. 173

Ill. 147. G. Taverne, *EMMA. M. Gérôme's usual model, posing for his* Omphale, drawing reproduced in P. Dollfus, *Modèles d'artistes* (Paris: Marpon & Flammarion, 1890), p. 100, Bibliothèque de l'École Nationale Supérieure des Beaux-Arts, Paris.

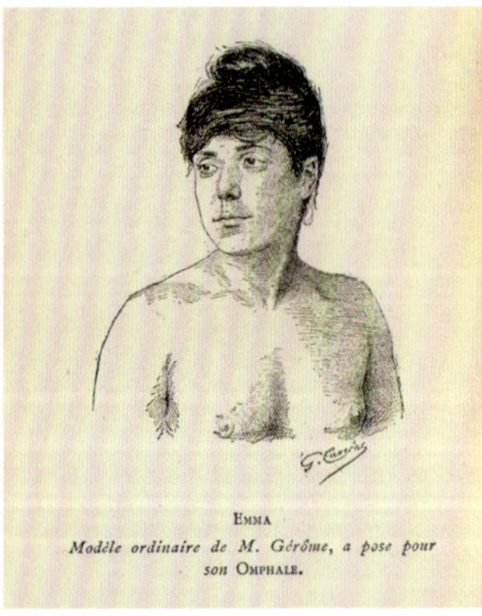

Ill. 148. *Seated woman*, Tanagra, ca. 320–300 B.C., terracotta, polychrome traces, 5 ¾ × 4 ⅛ × 2 ⅜ in., département des Antiquités grecques, étrusques et romaines, Musée du Louvre, Paris, inv. MNB 908.

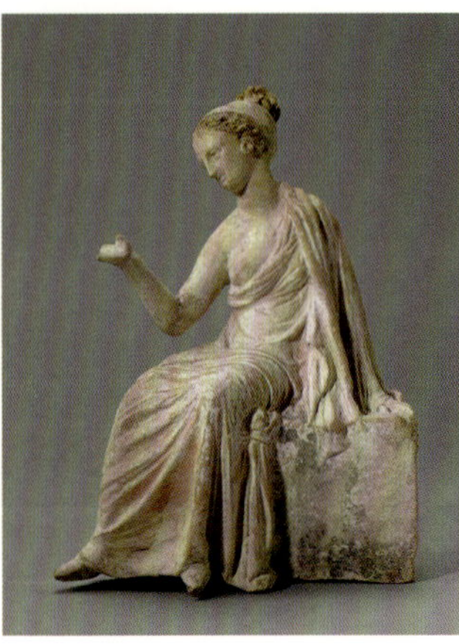

In December 1870, clandestine excavations near Tanagra, a small village in Boeotia, brought to light a set of terracotta funerary figurines (ill. 148). Considered as an echo of Praxitelean sculpture, which some consider to be evidence of the refinement of antique polychromy, they met with instant success among specialists and collectors. Presented for the first time in Paris to a wider public during the Exposition Universelle of 1878, the year that Gérôme exhibited his first sculpture, *The Gladiators* (cat. 76), they became a real craze: the market was suddenly inundated with forgeries and the elegantly draped statuettes were considered as the ancestors of the modern *Parisienne*.[1] Nearly twenty years after the discovery of the site, at the height of the vogue for the Tanagra figures, Gérôme presented his first polychrome sculpture, a *tyche*, an imposing almost Symbolist allegory for the "spirit of the antique city."[2] The effacement, due to zealous cleaning in the 1950s, of the subtle and sensual polychromy of the lips, eyes, and breasts, left only intact the colors of the *Hoop Dancer*, which Tanagra holds in her hand. The pose of the latter evokes a studio atmosphere rather than the seated goddesses of the Greek religion; Tanagra reveals herself as more erotic than heroic. Some critics considered the work to have been created to "stand out in the new era of contemporary sculpture. Artists of the twentieth century will look on it with the same respect that contemporaries of Donatello had for the reliefs of Nicholas of Pisa: it will be looked upon as a 'precursor.'"[3] Others remarked meanwhile that the necessity for such an evocation maybe did not make itself truly felt.[4] Gérôme himself mentions the incomprehension to which his decision to paint the sculpture exposed him: "I remember I had just finished the *Tanagra* marble, and I was preparing colors on my palette; a friend appeared who, seeing me preparing colors before the marble asked: 'What are you going to do?' 'I'm going to paint her.' 'That's impossible.' 'You'll see!,' and just as I was about to apply the first brushstroke, he said: 'I'm leaving. I can't stand here and watch such madness.'"[5] Gérôme's generous nude, with the face of a late nineteenth-century Parisienne, was one of his most famous sculptures: it was widely distributed in the form of reductions, bronzes, colored marbles, and even, like *Bellona* (cat. 182), as a bust or rather a head: two copies of it still exist (cat. 169, 170), their original polychromy intact, the illusionist refinement of which gives a clear, slightly disturbing idea of *Tanagra*'s original appearance. The marble in the Musée d'Orsay further relates to a group of paintings from 1892–93. Gérôme produced two self-portraits in his studio in 1890. *The Artist's Model* shows Gérôme making the final preparations for the sculpture beside his model whom we may recognize as Emma (ill. 147). The artist thus proposes a new version of the myth of Pygmalion and Galatea: a sketch of the picture can indeed be seen hanging under the shelf. The statuette that the Musée d'Orsay's *Tanagra* holds in her left hand is also a creation of Gérôme and derives from antique statues and a famous nineteenth-century forgery. The *Hoop Dancer*, appearing in twelve multicolored versions on the painter's table in *Sculpturae vitam insufflat pictura*, was itself produced in a number of versions by Goupil from 1891 onwards, in two sizes, fashioned in bronze, silver-plated bronze, or gilt. More rarely painted marble copies can be found in bisque or plaster. *Sculpturae vitam insufflat pictura* recreates, with a certain ironic humor, an imaginary studio in Tanagra. The painting offers a delightful synthesis of Gérôme's preoccupations with polychromy, his irresistible taste for learned archaeological details, and his photographic perfectionism. Next to the young painter is a tripod similar to the terracotta tripods found at Tanagra, and on the walls are a whole host of disparate characters[6]: on the upper shelf are forgeries, a *Loïe Fuller*, and a mask of Medusa found in the photographs of Gérôme's studio (cat. 177, 178); on the lower shelf, from left to right, a woman on a cubic seat, the abrupt movement of whom is not Tanagran at all, an archaistic Athena evoking the Athena on the altar of the Areopagus where Phryné is judged (cat. 45), a group playing *ephedrismos*,[7] a *Leda and the Swan* more evocative of the nineteenth century than Boeotia, forgeries; on the window ledge are more forgeries and imaginative forms; against the wall a reduced, polychrome version of *Tanagra*. **É. P.**

1. *Tanagra. Mythe et archéologie*, exh. cat. (Paris: Musée du Louvre, 2003–4). **2.** Gérôme may have been inspired by the *tyche* (τύχη) or rather by the personification of the city of Antioch, an antique marble representing a draped woman sitting on a rock, which was famous in the nineteenth century, a Roman copy of a third century B.C. Greek original attributed to Eutychides (marble, Musei Vaticani, Rome). **3.** E. Pottier, "Les Salons de 1892 (2e et dernier article). La Sculpture. Les arts industriels," *Gazette des Beaux-Arts*, 1892, vol. II, pp. 29–30. **4.** L. de Fourcaud, "L'art décoratif au Salon de 1890," *Revue des arts decoratifs*, May–June 1890, p. 343. See also L. Daudet, *Salons et journaux, Souvenirs des milieux politiques, littéraires, artistiques et médicaux de 1880 à 1908* (Paris: Nouvelle Librairie Nationale, 1917), p. 21. **5.** F. Masson, "Notes et fragments de J.-L. Gérôme," *Les Arts*, no. 26 (Feb. 1904), p. 31. **6.** Many thanks to Violaine Jeammet, head curator at the Department of Greek, Etruscan and Roman Antiquities, for her valuable help in this. **7.** Game from antiquity where a stone is placed on the ground and a ball is thrown at the stone. The player who does not knock the stone over has to carry his rival on his back; see *Tanagra. Mythe et Archéologie* (as in n. 1), no. 181, p. 236.

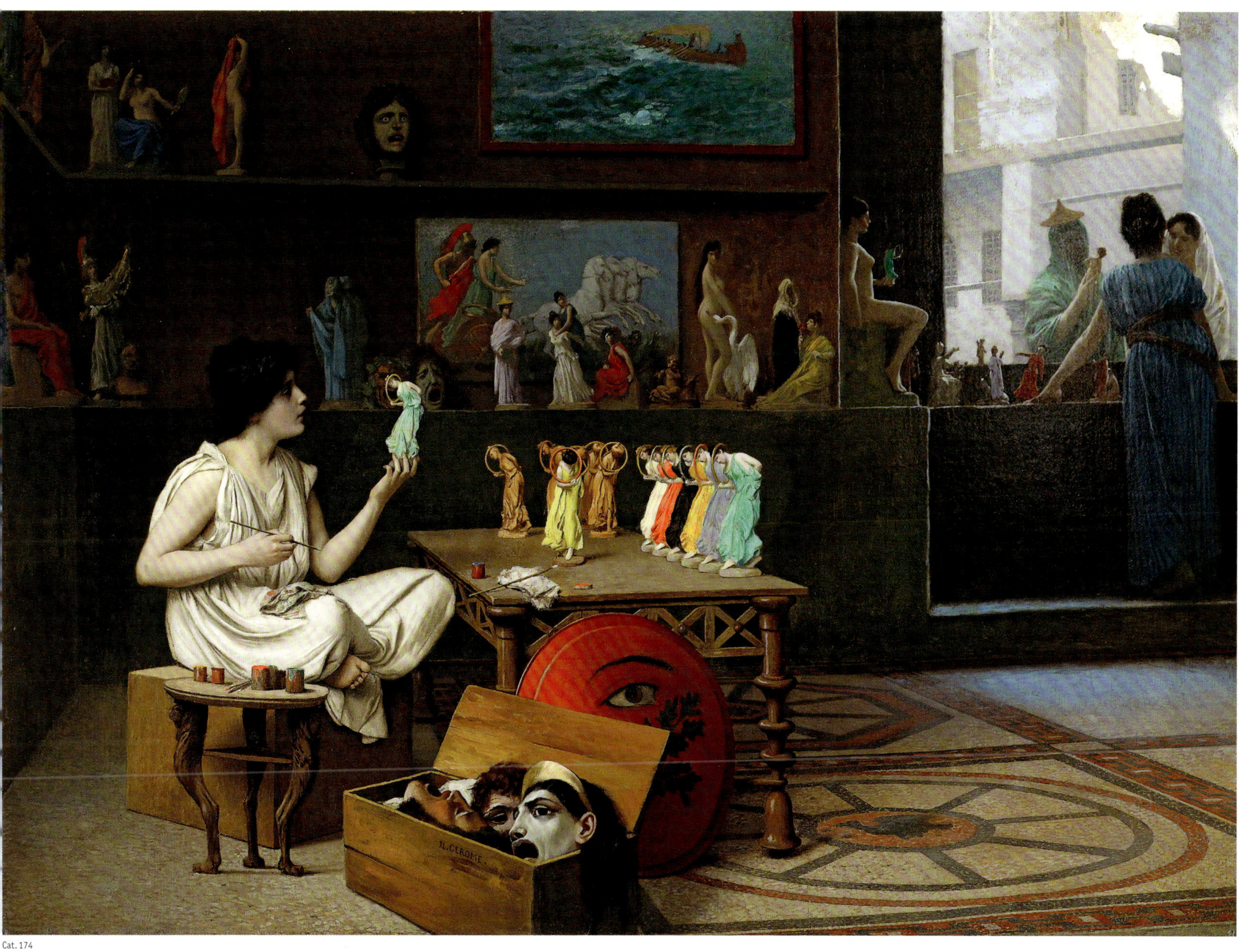

Cat. 174

Cat. 175

PYGMALION AND GALATEA

–

1890
Oil on canvas
35 × 27 in.
Signed on the base of the statue
The Metropolitan Museum of Art, New York, Gift of Louis C. Raegner, 1927, inv. 27.200

–

Provenance: Gérôme to Boussod, Valadon & Cie, 1892. Boussod, Valadon & Cie to C. T. Yerkes, New York, 1892. C. T. Yerkes of Chicago auction, AAA, New York, Apr. 1910, lot 52. P. H. Durgos, New York. Louis C. Raegner, who gifted it to the Metropolitan Museum of Art in 1927.

–

Bibliography: C. Sterling and M. M. Salinger, *French Painting: A Catalogue of the Collection of the Metropolitan Museum of Art*, vol. 2 (Cambridge, Mass.: Harvard University Press, 1966). M. Schneider, "Pygmalion – Mythos des schöpferischen Künstlers (von Falconet zu Rodin)," *Pantheon*, vol. XLV, no. 12 (1987), p. 119. A. Blühm, "In living color," in *The Colour of Sculpture*, exh. cat. (Amsterdam: Van Gogh Museum, 1996; also Leeds: Henry Moore Institute, 1996–7), pp. 46–47. M. E. Shapiro, ed., *Rings: Five Passions in World Art* (exhibition in conjunction with the 1996 Summer Olympic Games), exh. cat. (Atlanta: High Museum of Art, 1996). H. Lafont-Couturier, *Gérôme* (Paris: Herscher, 1998), p. 89. G. Ackerman, *Jean-Léon Gérôme* (Courbevoie: ACR Édition, 2000), no. 385. F. Rionnet, "Goupil et Gérôme: regards croisés sur l'édition sculptée," in H. Lafont-Couturier, *Gérôme & Goupil. Art et entreprise*, exh. cat. (Bordeaux: Musée Goupil, 2000–1; also New York: Dahesh Museum of Art, 2001, and Pittsburgh: The Frick Art & Historical Center, 2001), pp. 21, 42, 52. A. Blühm, "Farbe und Volumen: die Einheit der Künste," in *Wettstreit der Künst: Malerei und Skulptur von Dürer bis Daumier*, exh. cat. (Munich: Haus der Kunst, 2002; also Cologne: Wallraf-Richartz-Museum, 2002), pp. 150–51. *The Nude, Ideal and Reality from Neoclassicism to Today*, exh. cat. (Bologna: Galleria d'Arte Moderna, 2004), no. 32, p. 51. F. Chappey, "L'iconographie de Pygmalion et Galatée aux XIXe et XXe siècles: entre introspection et exhibition," in C. Dotal and A. Dratwicki, eds, *L'Artiste et sa muse*, proceedings of the conference at the Académie de France à Rome, Mar. 2-4, 2005 (Paris: Somogy, éd. d'art and Rome: Académie de France à Rome, 2006), pp. 7–17. V. I. Stoichita, *The Pygmalion Effect. From Ovid to Hitchcock* (Chicago: University of Chicago Press, 2008), pp. 170–73.

Cat. 176

THE END OF THE SEANCE

–

1886
Oil on canvas
17 ¾ × 16 in.
Signed on the box in the foreground: *J.L. GEROME*
Frankel Family Trust, Santa Ana

–

Provenance: Gérôme to Boussod, Valadon & Cie, 1886. Boussod,Valadon & Cie to Henry Graves, Orange, New Jersey, 1886 (for 12,000 francs). Sale to Henry Graves, AAA, New York, Feb 5, 1909, lot 7, to Fowler (for $3,050 dollars). Tennessee collection. Kimbal Sterling, auctioneer, Johnson City, Tennessee, Oct. 21, 1995.

–

Bibliography: Recueil. Œuvres de Jean-Léon Gérôme, BNF Estampes, vol. XXVI, no. 3. F. F. Hering, *Gérôme. The Life and Works of Jean-Léon Gérôme* (New York: Cassell. 1892), photoengraving, p. 168. Reproduced in *J.-L. Gérôme*, exh. cat. (Vesoul: Musée Georges-Garret, 1981), no. 222. G. Ackerman, *Jean-Léon Gérôme* (Courbevoie: ACR Édition, 2000), no. 348. V. I. Stoichita, "The End of the Session (Photography and Sculpture)", *The Pygmalion effect. From Ovid to Hitchcock* (Chicago: The University of Chicago Press, 2008), pp. 172–174.

Ill. 149. Girodet-Trioson [Anne-Louis Girodet de Roussy-Trioson] (1767–1824), *Pygmalion and Galatea*, 1819, oil on canvas, 99 ½ × 79 ½ in., Musée du Louvre, Paris, inv. RF 2002-4.

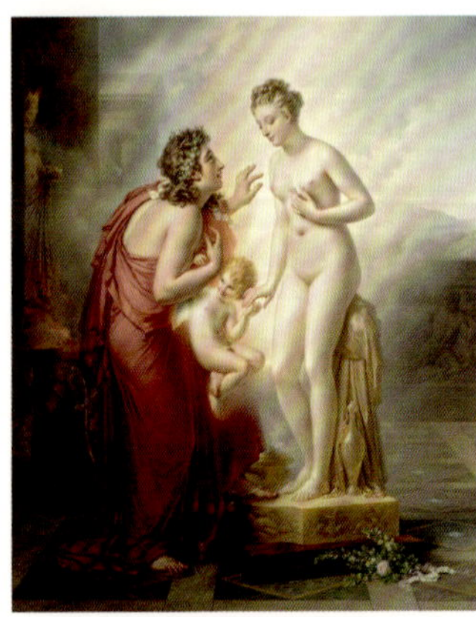

Ill. 150. Anonymous, Jean-Léon Gérôme in front of *Pygmalion and Galatea*, ca. 1892, albumen print, 4 ¾ × 6 ⅝ in., Musée d'Orsay, Paris, inv. PHO 2003 4 15.

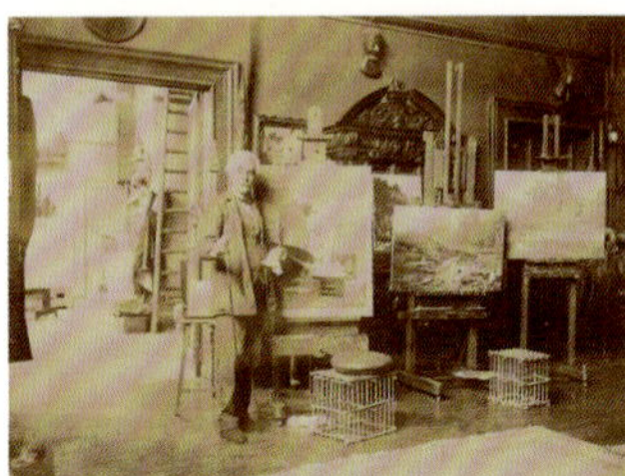

1890 marked a turning point for Gérôme: *Tanagra* (cat. 168), a manifesto for polychrome sculpture, signaled a new direction in his career, and the affirmation of an aesthetic choice he would steadfastly develop. From this moment onwards, many works by Gérôme, who had never been so socially active,[1] maintained an almost permanent interrelationship between painting and sculpture, *The End of the Seance* belongs to this cycle representing the key moment when the clay model is covered by a wet cloth to stop it drying out. Victor Stoichita has recently, and quite rightly, demonstrated that the work echoes a scene from Émile Zola's novel *L'Oeuvre* in which a clay model of the statue of Mahoudeau is destroyed,[2] Gérôme thus crystallizing the theme of the studio: his real studio (cat. 173), imaginary reconstructions of the studio (cat. 174), or metaphorical recreations, as seen in the iconography of *Pygmalion and Galatea*. Drawn from Ovid's *Metamorphoses* (Book X, lines 243–297), the myth had all the necessary ingredients to seduce Gérôme: Pygmalion, a renowned sculptor and grandson of the king of Cyprus makes a vow of celibacy but falls in love with the statue he has created. He implores Venus to let him find a wife as perfect as his work,[3] and his wish comes true when, one day, his statue comes to life. This foundation myth of sculpture, based on the metaphor of the artist as demiurge, much in vogue in the eighteenth century, had already been illustrated in a typically classical form by Anne-Louis Girodet in 1819 (ill. 149). In spectacular fashion, Gérôme undertook two works at the same time, each mirroring the other: the large, unique, polychrome group, which would again give rise to controversy, exhibited at the Salon of 1892, and two paintings that literally revolve around the idea of sculpture. The latter, conserved in Hearst Castle, San Simeon, California, has lost more of its polychromy than *Tanagra* and more than paintings are able to recreate. Where Girodet had treated, with tact and grandeur, the progressive incarnation of Galatea, and Pygmalion's self-control, Gérôme brutally laid bare a scene not meant to be viewed. In the painting housed at the Metropolitan Museum of Art, Galatea—seen from behind

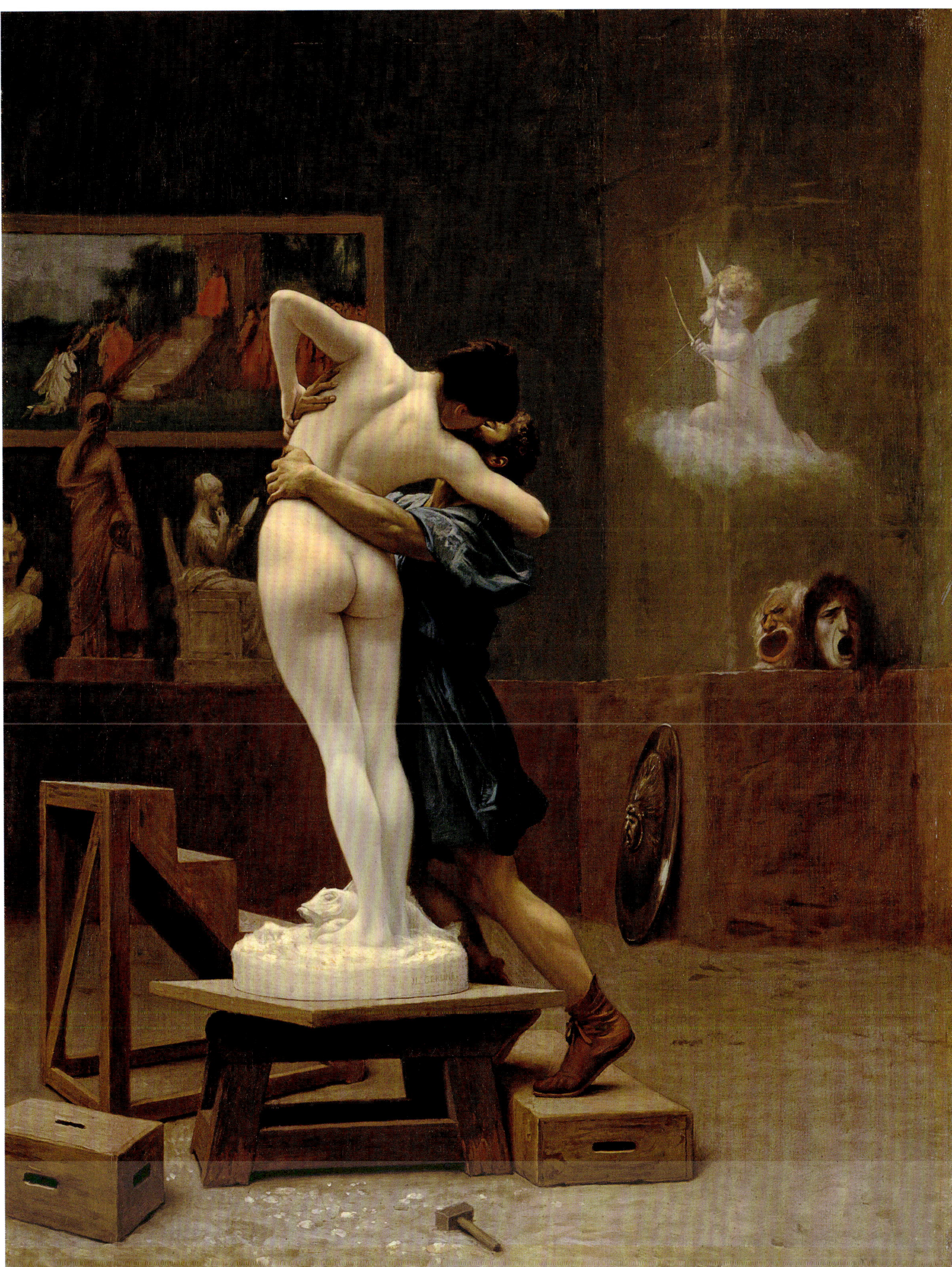

and divided in two by the solid marble still holding her legs prisoner as well as by the eager arm of Pygmalion—embraces Pygmalion openly. No face is really visible—only the lost profile of Pygmalion appears, his closed eyes wrapped up in the emotion of the embrace—apart from the laughing face of Cupid unleashing his arrow from a small incongruous cloud, floating overhead. Here, as for *The Ball Player* (cat. 188)—with which Galatea shares a certain analogy—but also for *Bathsheba*, Gérôme pushes the limits of illusionism, summoning the erotic and dismissing the heroic, clad in the last threads of academic allegory, by playing on several codes: the immediacy of sensualism—and its corollary of petit-bourgeois innuendo about the bohemian artist and his studio; the *risqué* tableau vivant—where flesh-colored costumes allowed liberties to be taken on some Parisian stage; and the codes of the theater. And also through a dual objectification: that of Galatea, obvious and unorthodox, the ideal model who comes to life in the cold light of a Parisian studio, and that of Pygmalion, Gérôme's own personal input, who seems to freeze in the unhoped-for expression of his passion. Studio accessories end up as vaguely sketched silhouettes, a catalogue of recurrent and familiar objects: over-sized Tanagras, theater masks, like fetishes, a shield decorated with the Medusa's head, perhaps a reference to the work of Arnold Böcklin. In the other version (1890, oil on canvas, private collection), Galatea is represented facing the viewer, and Pygmalion seems even more irresistibly caught up in a marble transcription of Prosper Mérimée's *La Vénus d'Ille* (1837).[4] Gérôme had himself photographed while painting the second version, staging the *mise en abyme* of his studio phantasmagorias (ill. 150) and the work appeared on the walls of the studio in *The Artist's Model* (cat. 173). **É. P.**

1. G. Ackerman, *Jean-Léon Gérôme* (Courbevoie: ACR Édition, 2000), p. 156. **2.** V. I. Stoichita, "The End of the Session (Photography and Sculpture)," in *The Pygmalion Effect. From Ovid to Hitchcock* (Chicago: University of Chicago Press, 2008), pp. 172–74. **3.** Frédéric Chappey very pertinently remarks that, in the classical text, the statue is made of ivory: "L'iconographie de Pygmalion et Galatée aux XIXe et XXe siècles: entre introspection et exhibition," in C. Dotal and A. Dratwicki, eds., *L'Artiste et sa muse*, proceedings of the conference at the Académie de France à Rome, Mar. 2-4, 2005 (Paris: Somogy Éditions d'art and Rome: Académie de France à Rome, 2006), p. 7. **4.** P. Mérimée, *La Vénus d'Ille*, 1837. Many thanks to Marie-Pierre Salé, chief curator at the Musée d'Orsay, for her precious help.

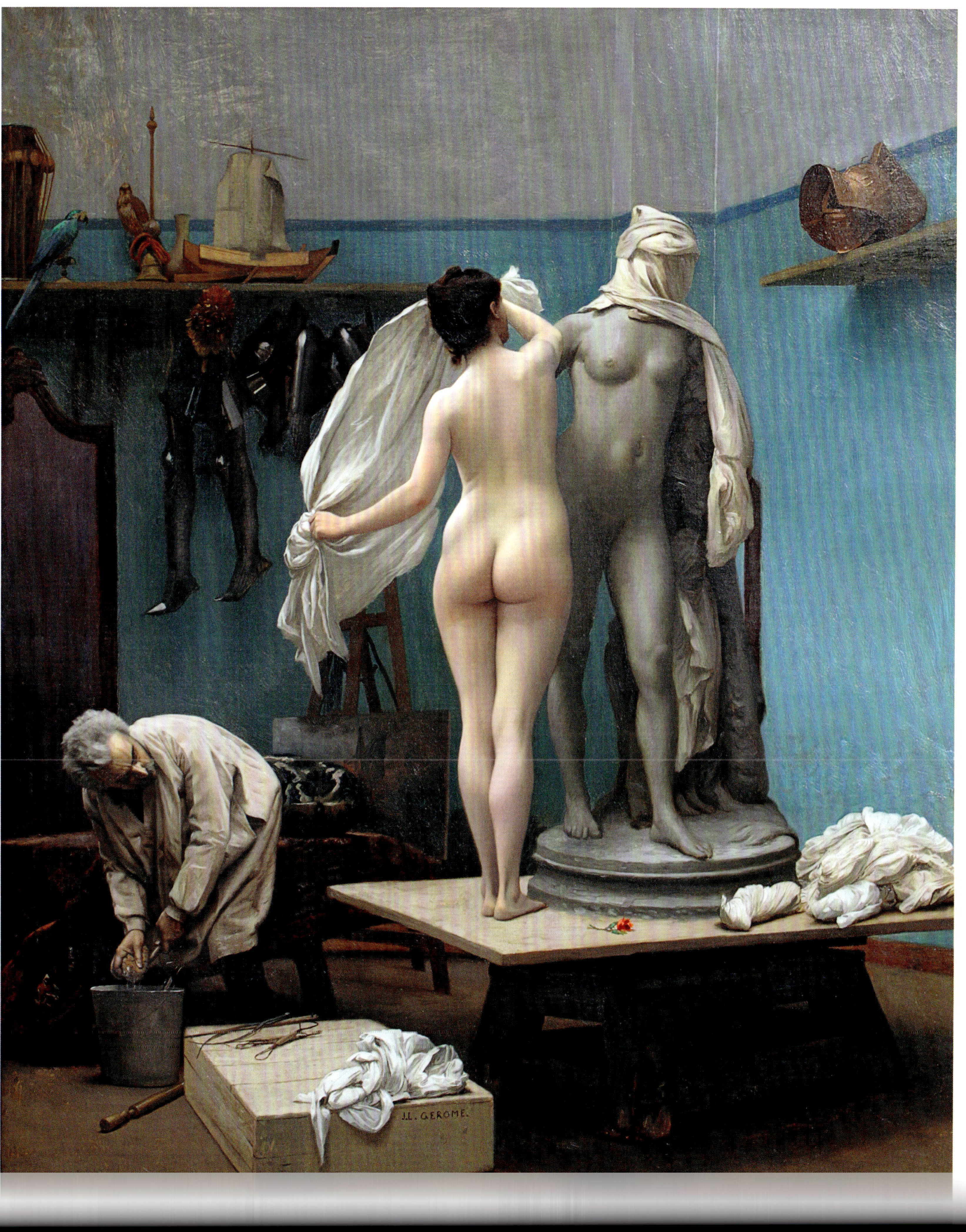
J.L. GEROME

Cat. 177
Anonymous or Louis Bonnard
(active in Paris ca. 1880–90)

JEAN-LÉON GÉRÔME WITH A MODEL IN THREE-QUARTER PROFILE, POSING FOR OMPHALE, PLASTER SEEN FROM BACK

–
ca. 1885
Albumen print
print: 10 ½ × 8 ¼ in.; mount: 19 × 12 ½ in.
Département des Estampes et de la Photographie, Bibliothèque Nationale de France, Paris, Dc-293 (a+)-Fol., tome 27
–
Bibliography: *L'Art du nu au XIXe siècle, le photographe et son modèle*, exh. cat. (Paris: Bibliothèque Nationale de France, 1997–98), p. 142.

Cat. 178
Anonymous or Louis Bonnard

JEAN-LÉON GÉRÔME WITH A MODEL IN FRONTAL VIEW, POSING FOR OMPHALE, PLASTER SEEN IN THREE-QUARTER PROFILE

–
ca. 1885
Albumen print
print: 10 ½ × 8 ¼ in.; mount: 19 × 12 ½ in.
Département des Estampes et de la Photographie, Bibliothèque Nationale de France, Paris, Dc-293 (a+)-Fol., tome 27

Cat. 179
Anonymous

GÉRÔME IN AN APRON, SEATED NEXT TO THE GLADIATORS

–
ca. 1878
Albumen print
print: 10 ½ × 8 ¼ in.; mount: 19 × 12 ½ in.
Département des Estampes et de la Photographie, Bibliothèque Nationale de France, Paris, Dc-293 (a+)-Fol., tome 11
–
Bibliography: *J.-L. Gérôme*, exh. cat. (Vesoul: Musée Georges-Garret, 1981), p. 143.

Ill. 151. Harry C. Ellis (1857–?), Gérôme in his studio with a male model for *The Metallurgist*, albumen print, 7 ½ × 9 ¾ in., Musée d'Orsay, Paris, inv. PHO 2003 4 11.

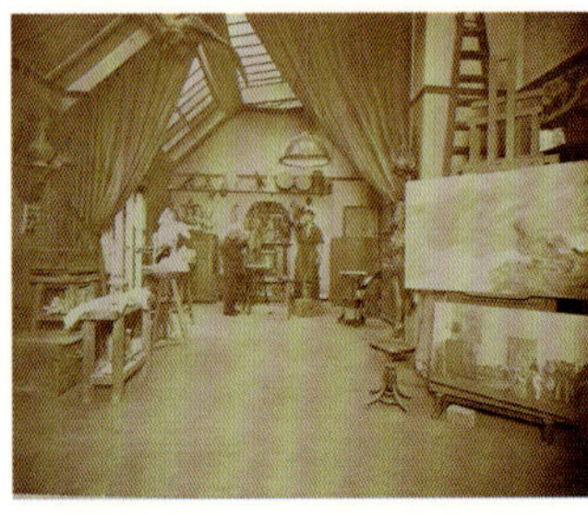

At the end of his life, Gérôme wished to donate photographic reproductions of all his works to the print department (Cabinet des Estampes) of the Bibliothèque Nationale, thereby underscoring not only his concern to valorize his oeuvre as a whole but also his constantly asserted faith in photography to reproduce it. In 1899 he wrote to the dealer Michel Knoedler: "Please be so kind as to photograph the two animal paintings that you own, because I would like to have as complete a collection of my works as possible, given that I have bequeathed it to the Bibliothèque Nationale."[1]

On December 8, 1905, one year after Gérôme died, "twenty-eight albums containing photographic reproductions of the works of J-L Gérôme" were donated to the Cabinet des Estampes.[2]

These photo albums were compiled at the request of the artist himself and basically contain reproductions of paintings commissioned by Goupil. Yet they also contain unpublished photographs of Gérôme's sculptures, which constitute the most interesting part of the bequest. They appear to have been taken in the artist's studio. Most of them go well beyond mere reproductions of the artwork thanks to framing, angle of view, and choice of subject matter. Indeed, they provide original viewpoints on the sculptures (such as the group of *Anacreon with Bacchus and Amor* (cat. 21), photographed on the turntable from various angles) and highlight some striking clusters (such as the series of heads for *Tamerlane* (cat. 184), hanging on the wall like an unusual—if grim—trophy). They even conjure scenes similar to the ones painted by the artist, notably in the case of six photographs, two of which are presented here, showing Gérôme in the studio with his sculpture *Omphale* and the model who posed for it. Through their subject matter and staging—certainly directed by Gérôme himself—these photographs evoked paintings such as *The End of the Seance* (cat. 176), in which the artist composed a highly personal vision of the myth of Pygmalion and Galatea.

Several photos—one of which is included here—show Gérôme next to his most ambitious sculpted group in terms of size, namely *The Gladiators* (cat. 76). They seem to anticipate the monument that Gérôme's son-in-law, Aimé Morot, would sculpt after the artist's death, depicting the sculptor and his work (cat. 77). Morot was certainly aware of these photographs and may have drawn inspiration from them. The J. Paul Getty Museum in Los Angeles holds the negative of one of the prints showing *The Gladiators*, unfortunately with no indication of the name of the photographer.[3]

The size, quality, and careful lighting of these prints emphasize the importance that Gérôme gave to them, as well as his desire to valorize his sculpted oeuvre. What use was made of them? Were they destined solely for posterity, as part of the long-planned bequest to the Bibliothèque Nationale? Did Gérôme consider publishing them? Or did he prefer to keep them within the family? These questions remain unanswered, as does the identity of the person(s) who took the photographs. The photographer(s) was (were) certainly professional, displaying experience and talent. The fact that the compositions were undoubtedly arranged by Gérôme himself suggests that a certainly familiarity existed between artist and photographer(s). The latter may have had a connection with the Goupil firm, but there is no mention of these prints in the Goupil archives in Bordeaux and Los Angeles. However, one photograph of a work by

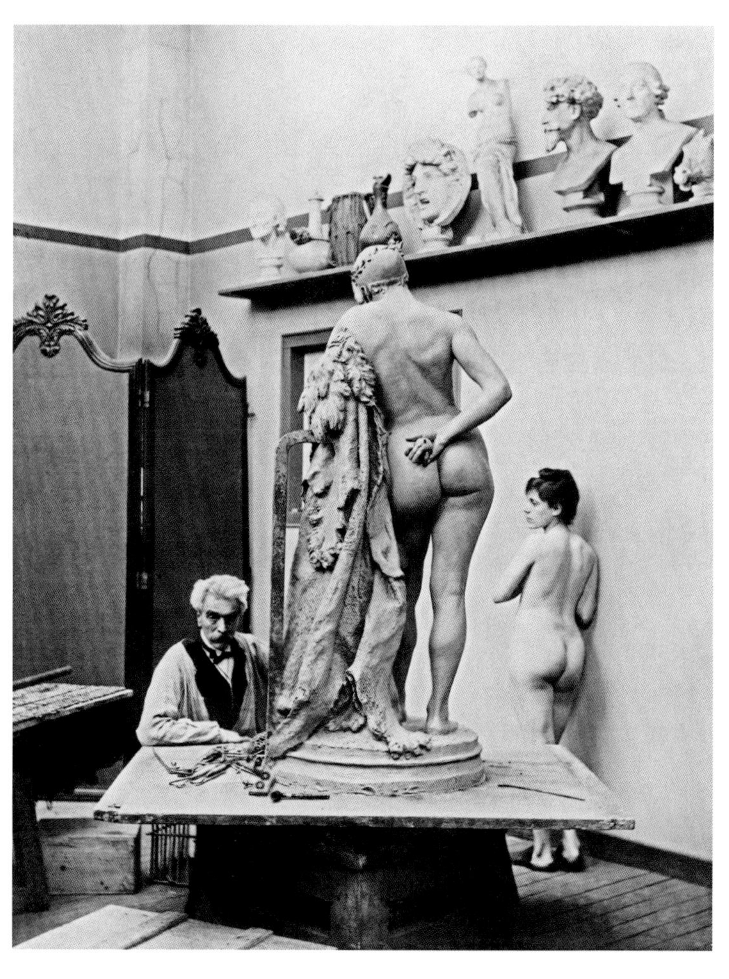

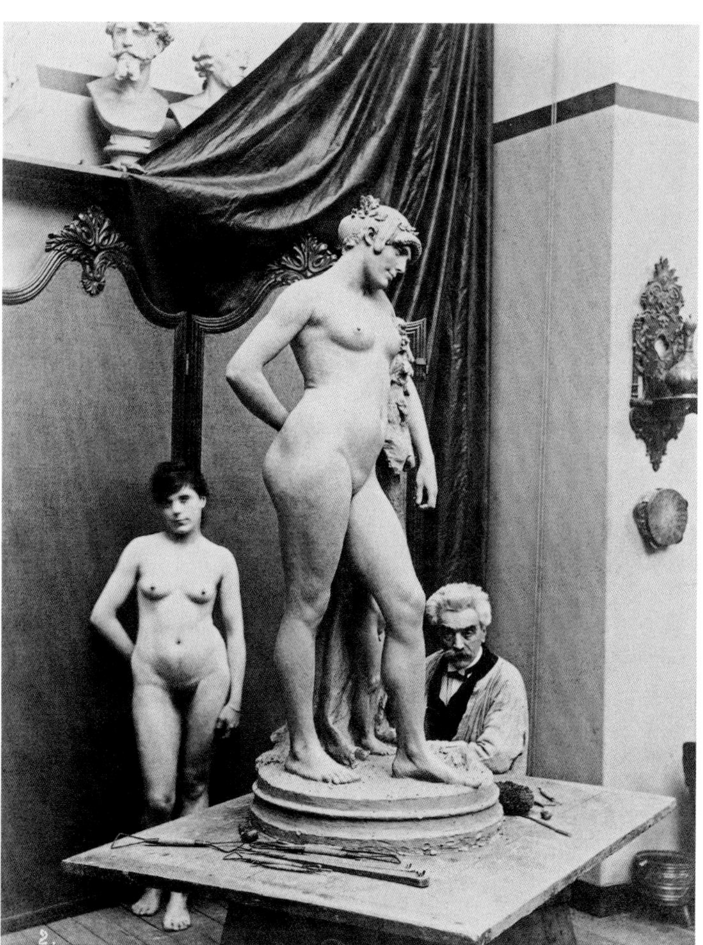

Gérôme, *Pygmalion and Galatea,* was published in the *Gazette des Beaux-Arts* in 1892 with the credit "Boussod and Valadon, heliograph." As far as we know, it is the only one of this set of photographs to have been published.[4] Despite research in the family archives and at the Bibliothèque Nationale de France, no specific reference to the commissioning of these photos has been found.[5]

The name of Louis Bonnard has been mentioned in connection with the photographs showing *Omphale* with sculptor and model; indeed, the young woman had also posed for Bonnard.[6] According to Paul Dollfus, her first name was Emma and she was a "a regular model for M. Gérôme."[7] (ill. 147, p. 302). But little information on Bonnard has come to light, and nothing indicates a link between him and Gérôme.

One photograph published in an exhibition catalogue in the 1930s, having belonged to photography collector Georges Sirot, shows a model whom Dollfus called Marie-Louise posing in a studio for *Tanagra* (cat. 168).[8] This picture, known only through that rather poor quality reproduction, is not included in the albums in the Bibliothèque Nationale de France; nor is any photographer credited. The Musée Georges-Garret in Vesoul keeps a print from one of the photographs showing Gérôme with *Omphale* and the model. It came from Gérôme's house. The following mention is written below the print: "À son élève et ami Courtois, JL Gérôme."

The photographs held in the Gérôme-Morot collection in the Musée d'Orsay also include several photos of Gérôme in the act of painting or sculpting. These most interesting prints are nevertheless not as high in quality as those in the Bibliothèque Nationale's Gérôme albums. One of the Musée d'Orsay photos shows Gérôme beneath the large skylight in his studio (which can also be glimpsed in certain prints showing *The Gladiators*), working on *The Metallurgist*, with a male model posing at its side. This print is signed Harry C. Ellis (ill. 151). It is unlikely, despite the similar subjects—a similarity due more to the artist and model who conceived them than the photographer who took them—that Ellis was responsible for the photographs in the Bibliothèque Nationale de France albums. Indeed, although we do not know at what date Ellis (who was born in the United States in 1857) arrived in Paris, all his signed work—such as his famous photographs of Loïe Fuller dancing in 1914—postdate 1900. **D. F.-R.**

1. Letter dated Sept. 14, 1899. Gérôme collection, Fondation Custodia, Paris. **2.** Archives, Département des Estampes et de la Photographie, 1898–1907, Res. Ye1. "Mme Gérôme, gift 511, December 8, 1905, twenty-eight volumes containing photographic reproductions of the oeuvre of J-L. Gérôme." Unfortunately, no list of the donated prints was included, nor any information on the identity of the authors of certain photographs. **3.** Accession number 84.XP.752.14, bought from Samuel Wagstaff in 1984. **4.** Between p. 242 and 243. Year 31th, 4th period, vol. 8. **5.** I would like to thank Sylvie Aubenas, head of the Département des Estampes et de la Photographie, BNF for her valuable help in carrying out this research. **6.** See *L'Art du nu au XIXe siècle, le photographe et son modèle*, exh. cat. (Paris: Bibliothèque Nationale de France, 1997–98), cat. 74, ill. 161. **7.** P. Dollfus, *Modèles d'artistes* (Paris: E. Marpon & Flammarion, 1906), pp. 100–1. **8.** M. Bovis and F. Saint-Julien, *Nus d'autrefois, 1850–1900* (New York: Georges Wittenborn, n.d.), p. 48. I would like to thank Catherine Mathon, chief curator at the École Nationale des Beaux-Arts, for having brought this catalogue to my attention.

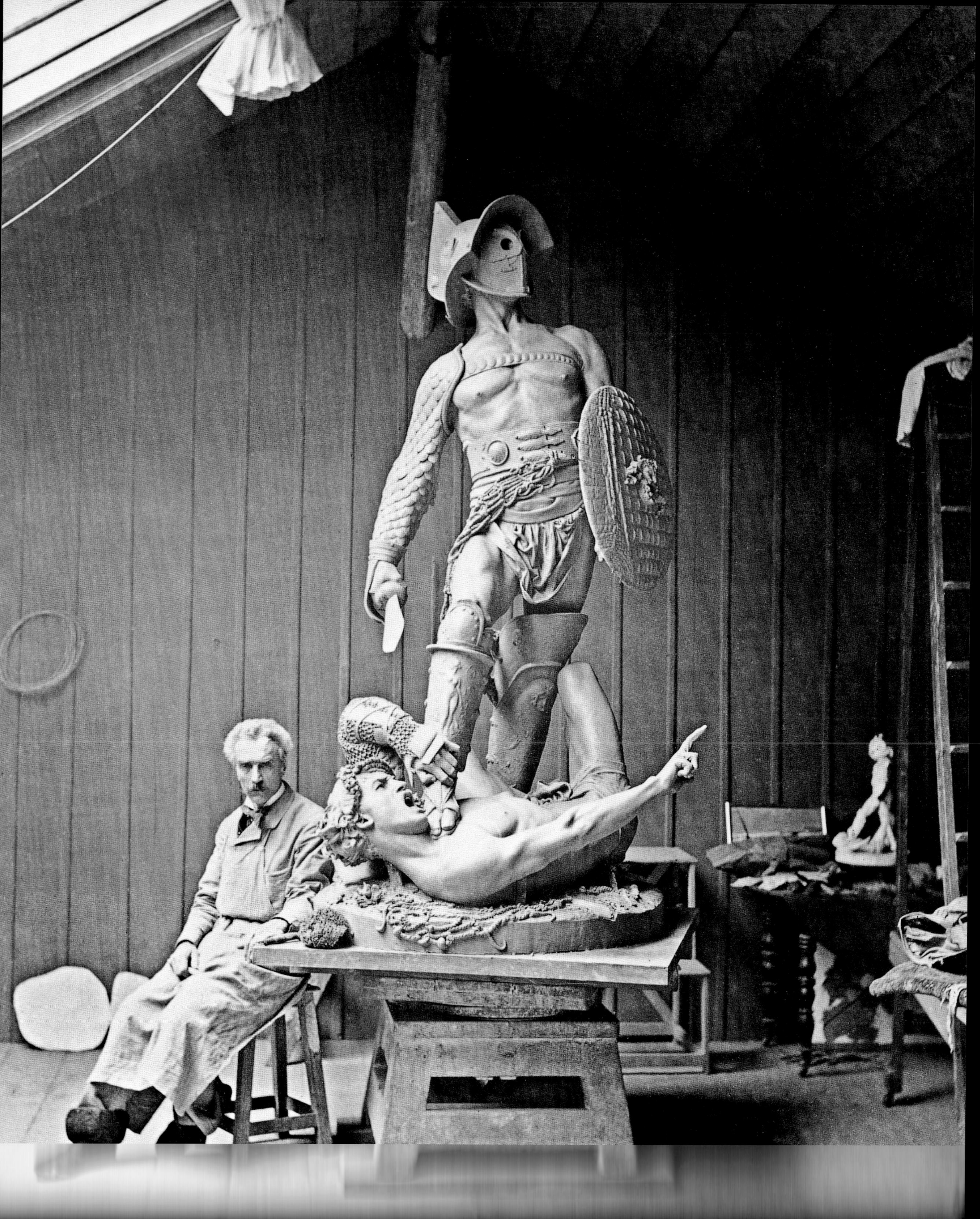

Cat. 180

ANCIENT DANCER

1890
Marble polychrome, ivory, stucco, bronze, and semi-precious stones
37 × 18 in.
Dr. P.G.E. Woog Collection

Exhibitions History: Salon of 1891, Paris, no. 2547 (under the title of *Dancer*).

Provenance: Cercle de l'Union Artistique, Paris, 1893. Decennial Exposition, Paris, 1900. Klaus Preis, Paris, 1973. *Gérôme, sculpteur et peintre de l'art officiel*, Galerie Tanagra, Paris, 1974, no. 8. Dr. P. G. E. Woog Collection.

Bibliography: É. Rod, "Les Salons de 1891 au Champ-de-Mars et aux Champs-Elysées," *Gazette des Beaux-Arts*, 1891, II, p. 30. *Figaro-Salon*, 1900, p. 9. A. Alexandre, "Les joujoux de Detaille & Fremiet," *Le Figaro*, 24 Nov. 1901. G. Ackerman et al., *Jean- Léon Gérôme (1824–1904)*, exh. cat. (Dayton: Dayton Art Institute, 1972; also Minneapolis: Minneapolis Institute of Arts, 1973, and Baltimore: The Walters Art Gallery, 1973), p. 13, ill. 4. *J.-L. Gérôme*, exh. cat. (Vesoul: Musée Georges-Garret, 1981), no. 186 [not exhibited]. G. Ackerman, "Gérôme's Sculpture: The Problems of Realist Sculpture," *Arts Magazine*, Feb. 1986, p. 85. G. Ackerman, *Jean-Léon Gérôme* (Courbevoie: ACR Édition, 2000), S. 20.

Cat. 181

MARY MAGDALENE

1897
Gilded and patinated bronze, marble with traces of polychrome, semi-precious stones, colored glass
19 ¾ × 6 ¾ × 8 ¼ in.
Inscribed on the base, right: *J L GEROME*; on the back: *735I*
Private collection

Bibliography: G. Ackerman, *Jean-Léon Gérôme* (Courbevoie: ACR Édition, 2000), no. S 42.

Ill. 152. *Achelous head pendant*, ca. 480 B.C., filigree, repoussé gold, granulation, H. 1 ½ in., département des Antiquités grecques, étrusques et romaines, Musée du Louvre, Paris, inv. Bj 498.

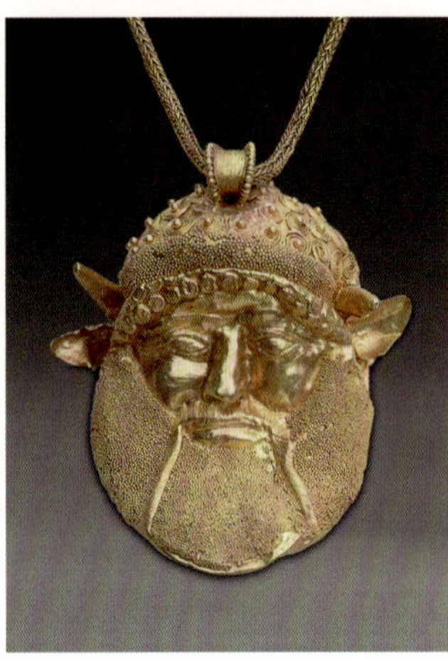

Ill. 153. Victor Ségoffin (1867–1925), *War Dance*, 1905, marble, 98 × 54 × 31 in., Musée d'Orsay, Paris, inv. RF 3686.

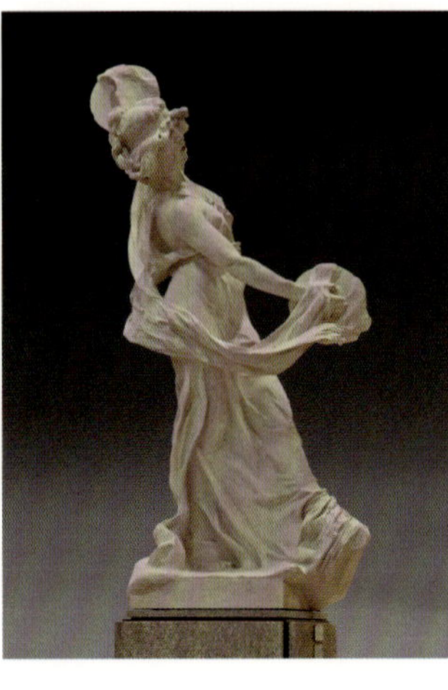

Gérôme was soon tempted by one of the eternal challenges of sculpture: the representation of the movement of fabric: *Anacreon* (cat. 16), *Bellona* (ill. 154, p. 314, cat. 182), *Loïe Fuller* (1893, marble, Musée Georges-Garret, Vesoul), *Moorish Dancer* (1903–4, bronze, marble, lapis-lazuli, private collection). It was possible polychromy would be of valuable help in lending visual interest to the stiffness of the material. *Ancient Dancer* may have been inspired by the famous *Titeux Dancer* (Athens, ca. 375–350 B.C., terracotta, Department of Greek, Etruscan and Roman Antiquities, Musée du Louvre, Paris), the Tanagrian icon of the Musée du Louvre,[1] as well as by the veils of the American dancer Loïe Fuller,[2] from whom Gérôme drew inspiration for a sculpture and painted studies (Musée Georges-Garret, Vesoul). The slightly fixed smile of the ivory face contrasts with the virtuosity of the drapery, produced in marble of different colors. Gérôme, the son of a goldsmith, was particularly interested in the possibilities afforded by ivory for works like this, which were more ambitious than the small statuettes offered by luxury manufacturers. In 1897 he founded the Société de l'Art Précieux, which actively promoted chryselephantine sculpture in order to "open up new avenues in sculpture."[3] The tunic of the dancer evokes a music-hall brand of antiquity, derived from the *chiton* of antiquity, but which left the breasts free beneath a bronze belt decorated with Greek motif, suggestive of First Empire fashions, for which there was a certain craze in Paris around the turn of the twentieth century. The composite necklace, inspired by a disparate range of antiquities, anticipates the necklace created for *Corinth* (cat. 192, 193). It is decorated with an almost exact reproduction of a very famous pendant in the form of the head of Achelous that came to the Louvre in 1861 as part of the Campana collection (ill. 152); the pendant was extremely popular with the public, and reproductions of it were sold by the celebrated jeweler Castellani.[4] Bronze and marble, or gilt bronze versions of the *Ancient Dancer* were distributed by Siot-Decauville.[5] Several years later, Victor Ségoff borrowed the dynamic line of the foot cast in mid-air for his *Danse guerrière* (ill. 153); maybe another borrowing from Gérôme and his *Bellona* (cat. 182) is the head of the screaming figure tossing backwards. Very different is the hieratic *Mary Magdalene* dressed as a Middle-Eastern harlot, sunken in luxurious attire.[6] **É. P.**

1. See V. Jeammet, ed., *Tanagra. Mythe et archéologie*, exh. cat. (Paris: Musée du Louvre, 2003–4; also Montréal: Musée des Beaux-Arts, 2004), no. 95, p. 146. **2.** See *Loïe Fuller, danseuse de l'Art Nouveau*, exh. cat. (Nancy: Musée des Beaux-Arts, 2002). **3.** É. Dacier, "L'art de l'ivoire," *La Revue de l'art ancien et moderne*, vol. XIV, July–Dec 1903, p. 68. See also P. Thiébaut, "Les ivoires de la fin du XIXe siècle au début du XXe siècle," in *Ivoires, de l'Orient ancien aux temps modernes*, exh. cat. (Paris: Musée du Louvre, 2004), p. 179. **4.** See L. Pirzio Biroli Stefanelli, "La collection Campana et le bijou de style archéologique," in *Trésors antiques. Bijoux de la collection Campana*, exh. cat. (Paris: Musée du Louvre, 2006), pp. 94–95 and cat. no. I-9, p. 123. **5.** G. Ackerman, *Jean-Léon Gérôme* (Courbevoie: ACR Édition, 2000), p. 238. **6.** Ibid., p. 934.

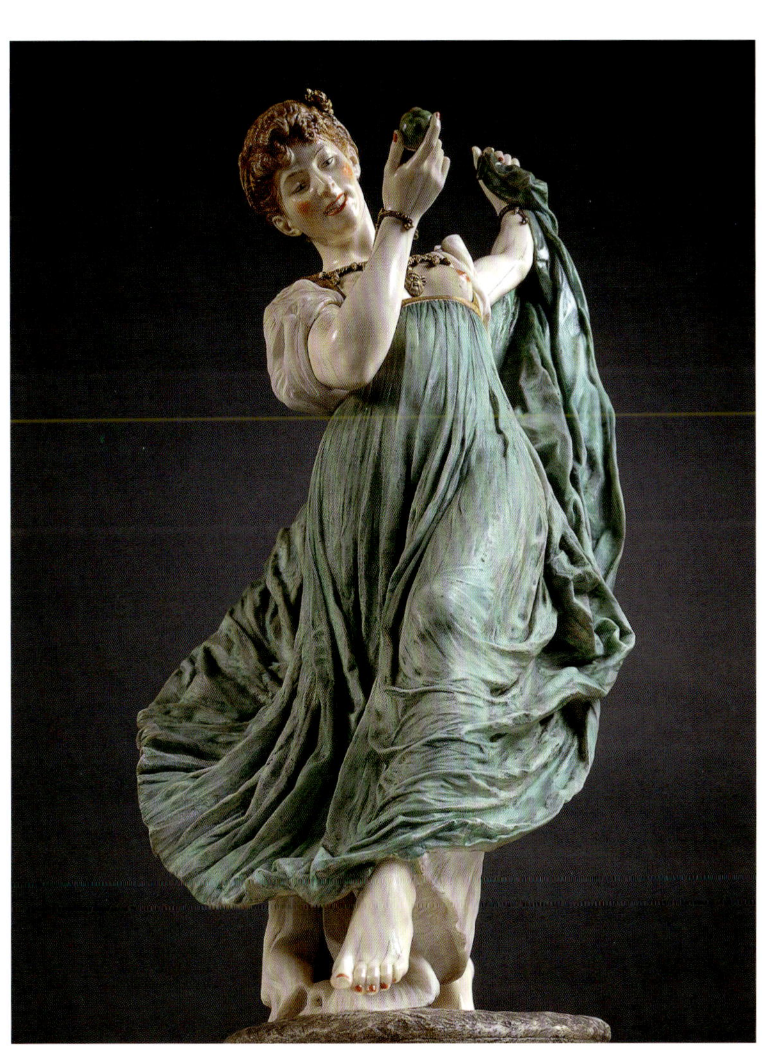

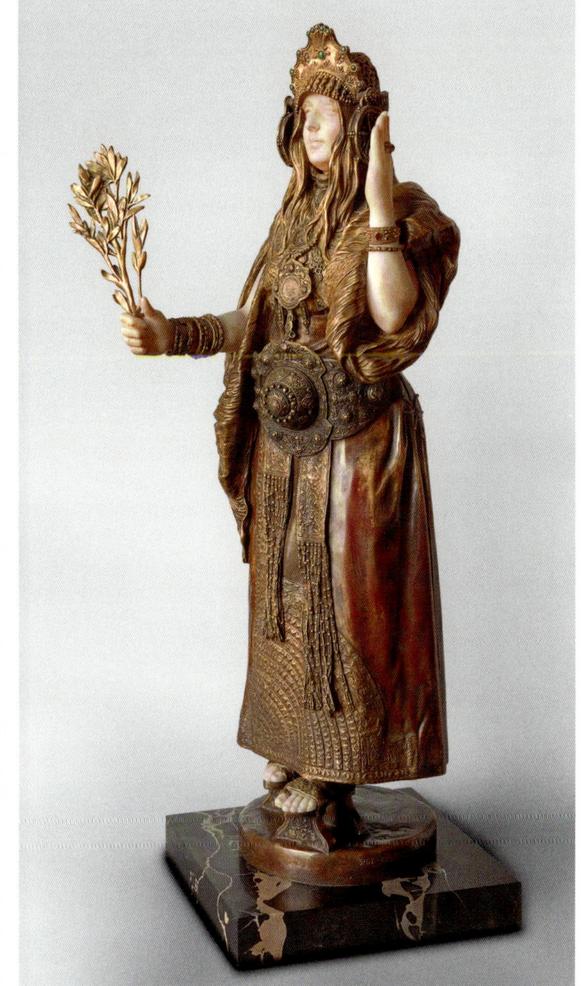

Cat. 182

BELLONA

–

1892
Bronze, patinated plaster, glass
34 × 18 ½ × 11 in.
Signed beneath left arm: *J.L. GEROME;* on the plaque: *BELLONE*
Musée Georges-Garret, Vesoul, deed of gift from Morot-Dubufe, 1945, inv. 945.2.5

–

Provenance: Deed of gift from Morot-Dubufe, 1945.

–

Bibliography: P. Leroi, "Musées en plein vent," *L'Art*, 1892, pp. 1014–15. É. Bergerat, "Salon de 1892," *Le Figaro*, May 4, 1892, p. 3. G. Lafenestre, "Les Salons de 1892," *Revue des Deux Mondes*, vol. 112 (1892), p. 183. G. Pabst, "La sculpture chryséléphantine: Phidias – le duc de Luynes – M. Gérôme," *Revue de famille*, 5th yr., vol. II (1892), pp. 341–43. E. Pottier, "Les Salons de 1892. 2e et dernier article. La sculpture. Les arts industriels," *Gazette des Beaux-Arts*, 1892, vol. II, pp. 30–32. G. Geffroy, "Salon de 1892 aux Champs Elysées," *La Vie artistique* (Paris: E. Dentu, 1893), pp. 287–89. *La Revue de l'art ancien et moderne*, Sept. 1900, p. 122. L. Liard, *Exposition universelle internationale de 1900 à Paris. Rapport du jury international* (Paris: Ministère du commerce, de l'industrie, des postes et des télégraphes, 1904), p. 716. F. Masson, "Notes et fragments de J.-L. Gérôme," *Les Arts*, no. 26 (Feb. 1904), p. 18. *J.-L. Gérôme*, exh. cat. (Vesoul: Musée Georges-Garret, 1981), no. 187. M. Shedd, "Phidias at the Universal Exposition of 1855: The Duc de Luynes and the Athena Parthenos," *Gazette des Beaux-Arts*, Oct. 1986, pp. 123–34. J. van Lennep, ed., *La Sculpture belge au XIXe siècle*, exh. cat (Brussels: 1990), p. 137. A. Blühm, *The Colour of Sculpture, 1840–1910*, exh. cat. (Amsterdam: Van Gogh Museum, 1996; also Leeds: Henry Moore Institute, 1996–97), no. 54, p. 80. G. Ackerman, *Jean-Léon Gérôme* (Courbevoie: ACR Édition, 2000), S. 27.

Ill. 154. *Bellona*, 1892, photoengraving, Archives, Musée d'Orsay, Paris.

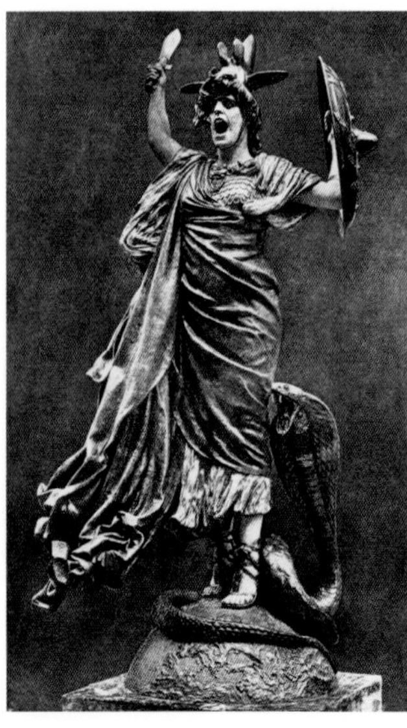

At the Salon of 1893, Gérôme exhibited two polychrome sculptures, a painted marble group, *Pygmalion and Galatea* (Hearst Memorial Castle, San Simeon, California), and a large spectacular bronze chryselephantine, *Bellona* (ill. 154). In creating *Bellona*, a collaborative work, Gérôme had asked Moreau-Vauthier and Delacour to produce the ivory sections, Gautruche the patina, Siot-Decauville the silver plating of the cast bronzes, and Lalique the glass decorative features;[1] the work ultimately cost the tidy sum: 20,000 francs.[2] This freely imaginative representation of the Roman goddess of war, Bellona, is highly ambitious: it was the first time that Gérôme had taken on a larger-than-life chryselephantine mythological figure, and genuine historical sculpture. The work met with mixed reviews: *Bellona* was placed at the exhibition entrance, where all eyes could see it, so it naturally begged comparison with the famous reconstruction of Phidias' *Athena Parthenos* by Charles Simart, the presentation of which had caused a great sensation at the Exposition Universelle of 1855.[3] The historian Germain Pabst considered *Bellona* to be superior and thought that Gérôme had "proved that color could give sculpture a more complete effect and bring out unknown emotions."[4] Others confirmed Gérôme's choice of a "personal creation, in line with tradition, that deployed all the resources of modern technology freely implemented by Hellenic artists."[5] The reference to the famous *Génie de la Patrie* by François Rude barely moved Gustave Geffroy, whose verdict was faithful, almost forty years later, to the criticism suffered by the upright Simart, with an extra turn of the knife when it came to his painting: "With undeniable skill, and craftsmanlike knowledge—better deployed here than in painting—M. Gérôme dresses the ivory statue of *Bellona* in polychrome bronze... which is merely a sampling, and a little excessive with it, because the open mouth is identical in the arrangement of teeth and gums to the restless sets of jaws seen in dentists' windows."[6] The "screaming idol"[7] is intended to be Roman, but her helmet, with its strange ornaments like erect paragnathides (cheek-guards), evokes the headgear of Rude's work, revised with emphasized symbolism. The threatening cobra by the goddess's side is more redolent of Egypt and the pharaohs' uraeus and, whatever Gérôme might have said, of the various proposals for the reconstruction of Phidias' *Athena*, from Simart to the one exhibited by the architect Benoît-Édouard Loviot at the Salon of 1880. A letter from Gérôme to Pabst, discovered by Meredith Shedd, on the subject of the statue's iconography, as it demonstrates Gérôme's resilience: "You speak of the serpent I set beside Bellona, and you fear this is an imitation of Simart's *Minerva* (it is incidentally not my wish to imitate anyone). I have obeyed tradition: the serpent was the animal dedicated to Minerva and Bellona."[8] As usual, Gérôme freely interpreted the iconography of Bellona, the ancient Roman goddess, sometimes as a wife, sometimes as the sister of Mars, god of war, equipped with a shield naturally, but also armed with a lance, torch, and whip.[9] All this is ultimately of little importance, for Gérôme attains his objective: the full singularity of *Bellona*, the antique nature of which is merely the pretext of the subject, is contained in the brutal boldness with which he depicts her open mouth, which runs counter to all the proprieties of art; the image is powerful, worthy of a place in a twentieth-century epic movie, in a scene where a temple is pillaged, or of being placed in the vestibule of the ministry of war, as the armed forces ministry was known in those days. The Vesoul bust gives the full measure of this attempt at *terribilità* that the critic Edmond Pottier little appreciated even if he did correctly analyze its motives, when he wrote of "the hypnotism generated by this excessively open mouth, by these white carnassial teeth, and this magnifying glass gaze."[10] Reproduced in polychrome sandstone by Émile Müller, in bronze, or in tin by Siot-Decauville, the bust loses something of its beauty and, in the pages of the foundry's catalog, more closely resembles a nationalist harridan somewhere between the cajoling smile of *The Laughing Child* by Jean-Antoine Injalbert and the Cléo de Mérode mawkishness of a "Florentine bust by Berstamm."[11] As proof of the decorative success of the work, a polychrome version—this bust perhaps—was placed atop a set of shelves by Charles Plumet.[12] A portrait of Gérôme by Fernand Cormon shows him busily polychroming a small version of the statue, probably the original model (ill. 178, p. 346). **É. P.**

1. *J.-L. Gérôme*, exh. cat. (Vesoul: Musée Georges-Garret, 1981), p. 142. The ivory parts have been restored, after the work was used for several years as a decorative element in a Canadian hotel. **2.** As an indication, sculptures were acquired from the Salon by the State for approximately 8,000 francs. **3.** See M. Shedd, "Phidias at the Universal Exposition of 1855: The Duc de Luynes and the Athena Parthenos," *Gazette des Beaux-Arts*, Oct. 1986, pp. 123–34. **4.** G. Pabst, "La sculpture chryséléphantine: Phidias – le duc de Luynes – M. Gérôme," *Revue de famille*, 1892, pp. 341–43. **5.** G. Lafenestre, "Les Salons de 1892," *Revue des Deux Mondes*, vol. 112 (1892), p. 183. **6.** G. Geffroy, "Salons de 1892 – Aux Champs-Élysées," para. VIII, "Les statues peintes," in *La Vie artistique*, 2nd ser. (Paris: Dentu, 1893), pp. 287–88. **7.** É. Bergerat, *Le Figaro*, May 4, 1892, p. 3. **8.** Gérôme to Pabst, Feb. 2, 1892, Bibliothèque Nationale de France, 4° V. 5381. **9.** "Bellona," in C. Daremberg and E. Saglio, *Dictionnaire des antiquités grecques et romaines d'après les textes et documents...* (Paris, 1877), vol. 1, pp. 685–86. **10.** E. Pottier, "Les Salons de 1892. 2e et dernier article. La sculpture. Les arts industriels," Gazette des Beaux-Arts, 1892, vol. II, p. 32. **11.** "BELLONE de J. L. Gérôme," *Catalogue Siot-Decauville. Fondeur du Ministère des Beaux-Arts et de la ville de Paris. Salons de vente 24, bd des Italiens. Fonderie et Ateliers, 8 et 10 rue Villehardouin Paris*, n. d. [1900], p. 74. **12.** Many thanks to Georges Vigne for pointing this out to me.

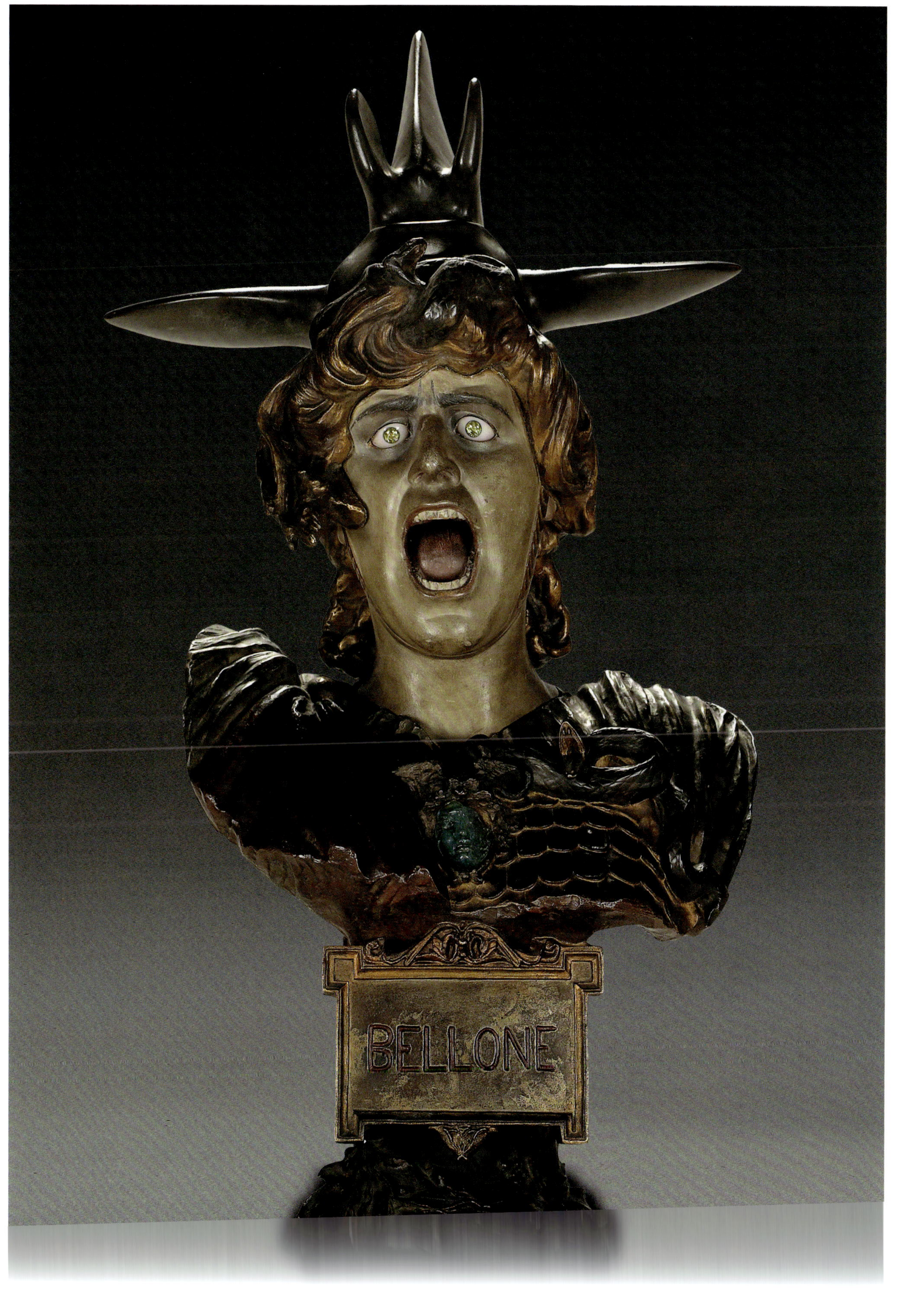
BELLONE

Cat. 183

TAMERLANE

–

1898
Gilt bronze and enamel, damascening, and semi-precious stones
H. 37 in.
Private collection

–

Provenance: Salon of 1898. Portakal Sanat Ve Kültür Evi auction house, Istanbul, Nov. 29, 1998, lot 209. Private collection.

–

Exhibition History: Salon of 1898, Paris, no. 3454.

–

Bibliography: L. Bénédite, "Les Salons de 1898," *Gazette des Beaux-Arts*, 1898, II, pp. 144–45. A. Proust, *Salon de 1898*, Paris, 1898, p. 30. *Revue encyclopédique Larousse*, July 1898, no. 252, p. 591. *Revue encyclopédique Larousse*, no. 322, Nov. 4, 1899, repr. p. 173. V. Champier, "Bronzes statuaires," *Les Industries d'art à l'exposition de 1900*, Paris, 1902, p. 161. L. Bénédite, "Introduction générale. Deuxième partie. Beaux-Arts," in *Exposition universelle internationale de 1900, Rapports du jury international* (Paris: Imprimerie nationale, 1904), p. 572. L. Liard, "Exposition de 1900. - Beaux-Arts", in *Exposition universelle internationale de 1900, Rapports du jury international* (Paris: Imprimerie nationale, 1904), p. 716. *J.-L. Gérôme*, exh. cat. (Vesoul: Musée Georges-Garret, 1981), p. 142. F. Masson, "Notes et fragments de J.-L. Gérôme," *Les Arts*, no. 26 (Feb. 1904), p. 31. G. Ackerman, "Gérôme's Sculpture: The Problems of Realist Sculpture," *Arts Magazine*, Feb. 1986, p. 86. C. Chevillot, *Emmanuel Fremiet. La main et le multiple*, exh. cat. (Dijon: Musée des Beaux-Arts, 1988–89), p. 38. G. Ackerman, *Jean-Léon Gérôme* (Courbevoie: ACR Édition, 2000), no. S. 47.

Ill. 155. Vassili Vassilievitch Verechtchaguine (1842-1904), letter to Jean-Léon Gérôme, Moscow, March 8, 1897, private collection.

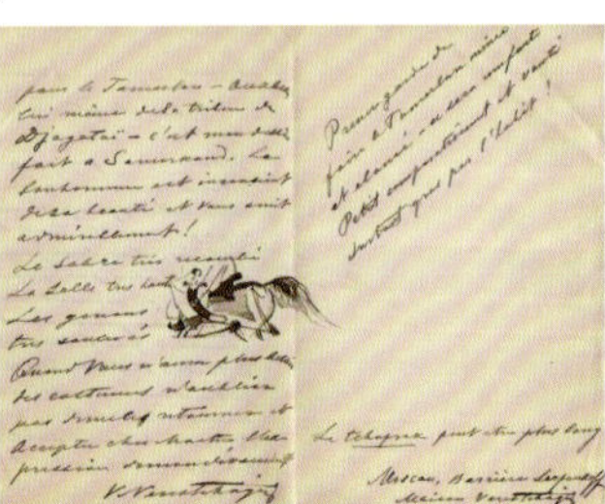

Cat. 184
Anonymous

TERRACOTTA HEADS (*TAMERLANE*) HANGING ON THE STUDIO'S WALL

–

ca. 1898
Gelatin silver print
8 × 6 ½ in. (print), mount: 19 × 12 ½ in.
Département des Estampes et de la Photographie, Bibliothèque Nationale de France, Paris, Dc-293 (a+)-Fol., tome 13

–

Provenance: Gift of Madame Gérôme of twenty-eight albums containing photographs of works by Jean-Léon Gérôme, Dec. 2, 1905.

From the 1890s, Gérôme's reported interest in "reviewing all the great conquerors of the earth"[1] resulted in the representation of the horse in sculpture,[2] started devoting himself to a series of equestrian statues: *Caesar Crossing the Rubicon* (cat. 69), *Napeoleon entering Cairo* (cat. 91), and *Frederick the Great*, among others. Timur Lang was an Uzbekistani warlord known as the "Iron Lord with the limp." Emir of Transoxania from 1370 to 1405, he chased the Mongols from his territories, and in less than twenty-five years formed a vast empire, stretching from Samarkand to the Aral Sea, encompassing Iran, Mesopotamia, Armenia, the Caucasus, eastern Anatolia, and southern Russia. Alongside *Napoleon entering Cairo*, *Tamerlane* is no doubt Gérôme's most ambitious sculpture, for which he carried out particularly detailed research.[3] Always mindful of the need for precision, he also asked one of his former pupils, Vasily Vasilyevich Vereshchagin, to send him from Moscow anything pertaining to military equipment from the time of Tamerlane, as is evident from two delightful letters from the Russian painter. On March 2, 1897, Vereshchagin sent him photographs of "horse breeds in the steppes," and also promised a uniform, which he asked him to send back after use, reminding him in a postscript about Tamerlane: "Don't forget he is the antithesis of the soldier!"[4] On March 8, Vereshchagin confirmed he had dispatched the uniform and explained to Gérôme the shape, use, and names of the different accessories, and recommended that he to "make Tamerlane fine and slender."[5] Several photographs were taken of the work as the clay was being modeled, as well as of the plaster in Gérôme's workshop. It is possible that the pile of severed heads on which Tamerlane's whinnying horse stands is actually a reprise of the morbid mound he depicted before the gate of the mosque of El Assaneyn (cat. 144), and also pays a discreet tribute to Vereshchagin's major early work, *The Apotheosis of War*, dedicated, as an inscription on the frame of the painting indicates, "to all the great conquerors past, present and future."[6] *Tamerlane*, and his "skull with its verdigris complexion,"[7] attracted considerable attention, particularly from the painter Benjamin-Constant, who considered that "nothing has a more savage Orientalism," and he eagerly awaited works depicting Caesar and Alexander.[8] Some found *Tamerlane* "less amusing" than *Napeoleon entering Cairo*; the sculpture seemed to have "come straight from the ring of the Cirque d'Été."[9] Others somewhat pigeonholed the statuette as a luxury curio, stating that "the psychology of this cruel little Mongol is analyzed perhaps a little less rigorously than that of his modern emulators."[10] *Tamerlane* also recalls the *Knight Errant* by Emmanuel Fremiet, created twenty years earlier (ill. 155)[11] and the work of the Russian sculptor Evgeni Alexandrovich Lanceray, who represented a number of heroes of medieval Russia (*Il'ya Muromets*, 1885, bronze, Tretiakov Gallery, Moscow).[12] Borne by an epic spirit barely attained in contemporary Orientalist equestrian statues, *Tamerlane*, a strangely precious object, just manages to transcend the aesthetics of accumulation of which the sculptor was fond. **É. P.**

1. L. Bénédite, "Les Salons de 1898," *Gazette des Beaux-Arts*, 1898, vol. II, p. 144. **2.** F. Masson, "Notes et fragments de J.-L. Gérôme," *Les Arts*, no. 26 (Feb. 1904), pp. 28–29. **3.** Ibid., p. 32. **4.** Vasily Vasilyevich Vereshchagin to Gérôme, Moscow, Mar 2, 1897, private collection. **5.** Vasily Vasilyevich Vereshchagin to Gérôme, Moscow, Mar 8, 1897, private collection. **6.** Moscow, Tretyakov Gallery. See *L'Art russe dans la seconde moitié du XIXe siècle: en quête d'identité*, exh. cat. (Paris: Musée d'Orsay, 2005–6), no. 478, pp. 78, 438. **7.** Quoted by the *Revue encyclopédique Larousse*, July 1898, no. 252, p. 591, from the article, "Promenade de peintre aux Salons de 1898", *Le Figaro*, May 29, 1898. **8.** Ibid. **9.** A. Proust, *Salon de 1898*, Paris, 1898, p. 30. **10.** L. Bénédite, "Les Salons de 1898," *Gazette des Beaux-Arts*, 1898, vol. II, p. 145. **11.** C. Chevillot, "Emmanuel Fremiet sculpteur-statuaire," in *Emmanuel Fremiet. La main et le multiple*, exh. cat. (Dijon: Musée des Beaux-Arts, 1985), p. 38. **12.** See G. W. Sudbury and R. D. Douglas, *Evgueni Alexandrovitch Lanceray. Le sculpteur russe du cheval* (Paris: Favre, 2006).

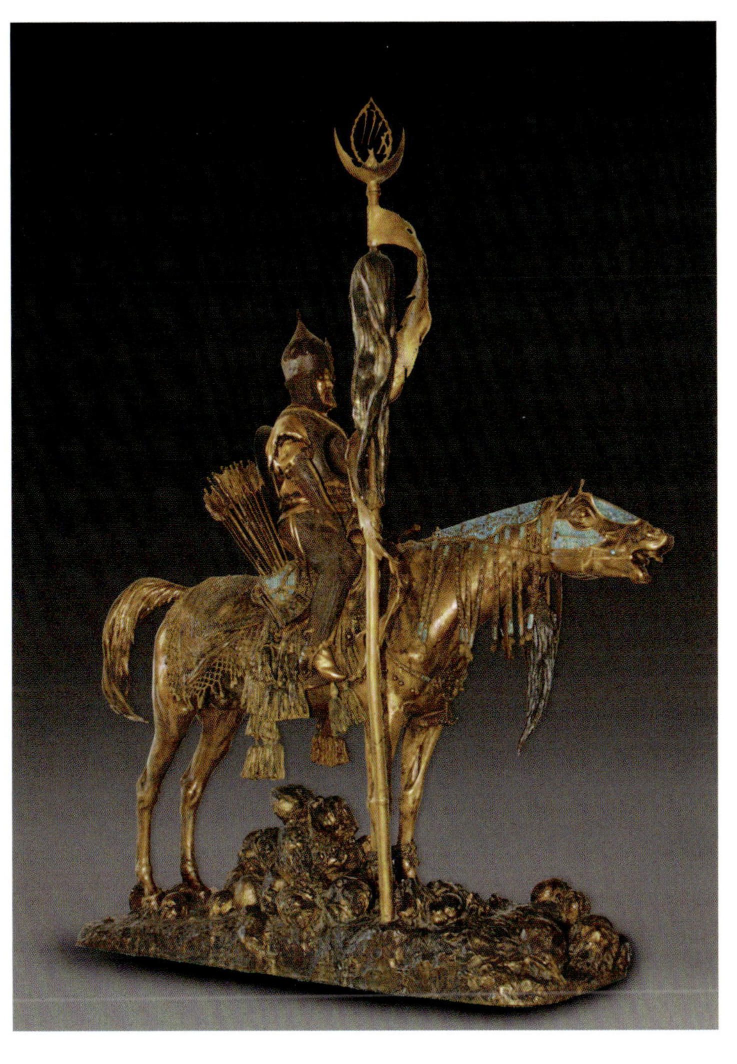

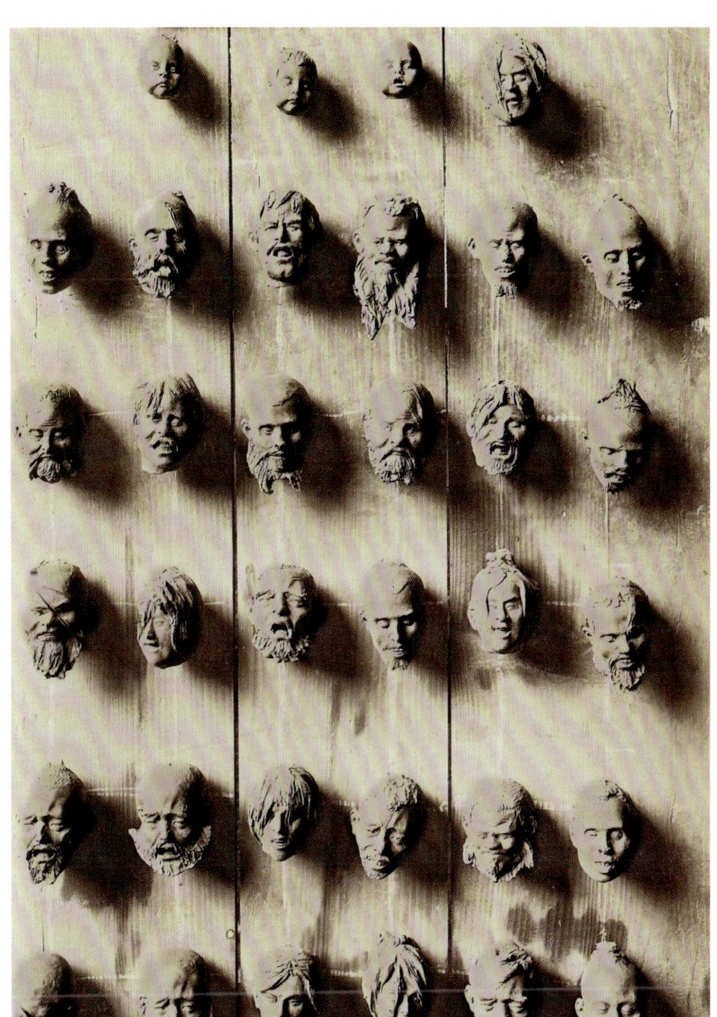

Cat. 185

ANDROCLES AND THE LION

–

ca. 1898?
Bronzed plaster
9 ½ × 4 ¾ × 5 ½ in.
On the base, front, in paint: *ANDROCLES.*
Beneath the base, metal label:
BRONZE PLASTIQUE / E. BEAU & Cie 14 rue Piccini 14 PARIS
L'Horizon chimérique collection, Bordeaux

–

Provenance: *European Sculpture and Works of Art*, Sotheby's, London, July 9, 2002, lot 131. *European Sculpture and Works of Art*, Sotheby's, London, July 8, 2005, lot 118. L'Horizon chimérique collection, Bordeaux.

–

Bibliography: G. Ackerman, *Jean-Léon Gérôme* (Courbevoie: ACR Edition, 2000), S. 46.

Circus scenes long fascinated Gérôme. The moving story of the slave Androcles, from Aulus Gellius' *Attic Nights*, Book V, chap. XIV, in a way provides the optimistic counterpoint to the circus atrocities depicted by Gérôme (cat. 81). At the start of the Christian era, a fugitive slave, Androcles, was captured and thrown to the lions at the circus in Rome. He was spared by a lion of terrifying appearance, which smothered him with affection. The emperor[1] summoned Androcles, who told him that in Africa he had removed a thorn from the foot of a lion, which was causing it great distress, then had lived in the beast's lair for three months. The emperor granted Androcles his freedom and offered him the lion as a gift; the lion accompanied Androcles as he begged on the streets of Rome.[2] Gérôme illustrated two episodes of this edifying anecdote: a painting in which Androcles removes the thorn from the lion's paw (1902, oil on canvas, private collection) and the scene after the miracle, depicting the survivor begging. This study in bronzed plaster, close to the definitive gilt plaster version (ca. 1898, bronze, private collection), bears the inscription "*BRONZE PLASTIQUE / E. BEAU & Cie 14 rue Piccini 14 PARIS*," which could provide rare proof of one of Gérôme's occasional collaborations for the technique of bronzing plaster also used in *Caesar Crossing the Rubicon* (cat. 69). *The Lion Tamer* (ill. 156), representing a gladiator and a defeated lion, belongs to the same approach of staging man's relationship to the lion, Gérôme's totemic animal; the work goes astray in its anecdotalism. **É. P.**

1. Maybe the emperor Caligula. 2. Gérôme very probably knew Victor Hugo's poem, "Au Lion d'Androclès," in *La Légende des siècles*, 1, VIII, "La Décadence de Rome."

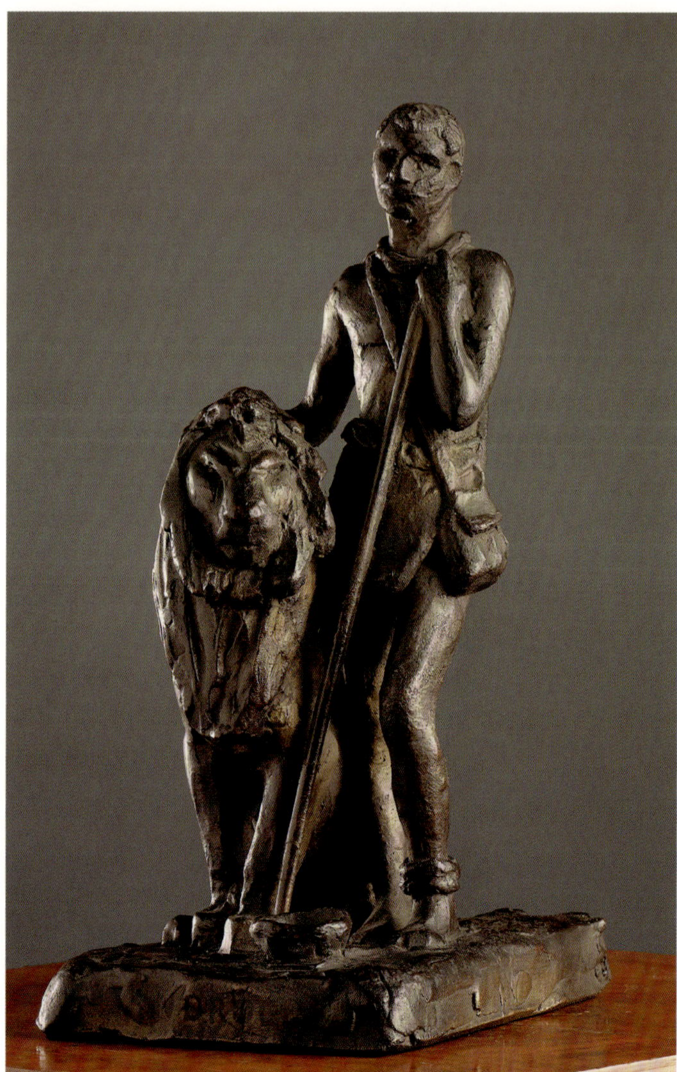

Ill. 156. Anonymous, photograph of a bronze copy of *The Lion Tamer*, ca. 1898, albumen print, 7 ½ × 9 ⅜ in., Archives, Musée d'Orsay, Paris.

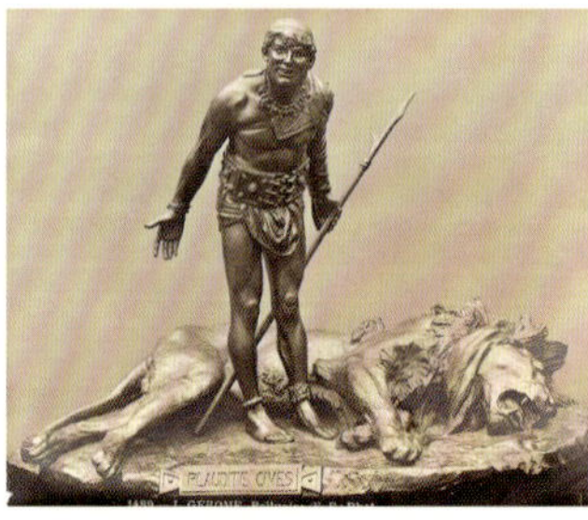

Cat. 186

SEATED NUDE

–

ca. 1898–1902?
Polychromed marble
17 × 13 ¾ × 13 ¾ in.
Detroit Institute of Arts, Founders Society Purchase, Robert H. Tannahill Foundation Fund, inv. 1997.1

–

Provenance: Aimé-Morot collection, Paris. Galerie Elstir, Paris, 1996. Detroit Institute of Arts, 1997.

–

Bibliography: "La chronique des arts. Principales acquisitions des musées en 1997," *Gazette des Beaux-Arts*, Mar. 1998, p. 64. G. Ackerman, *Jean-Léon Gérôme* (Courbevoie: ACR Édition, 2000), S. 70.

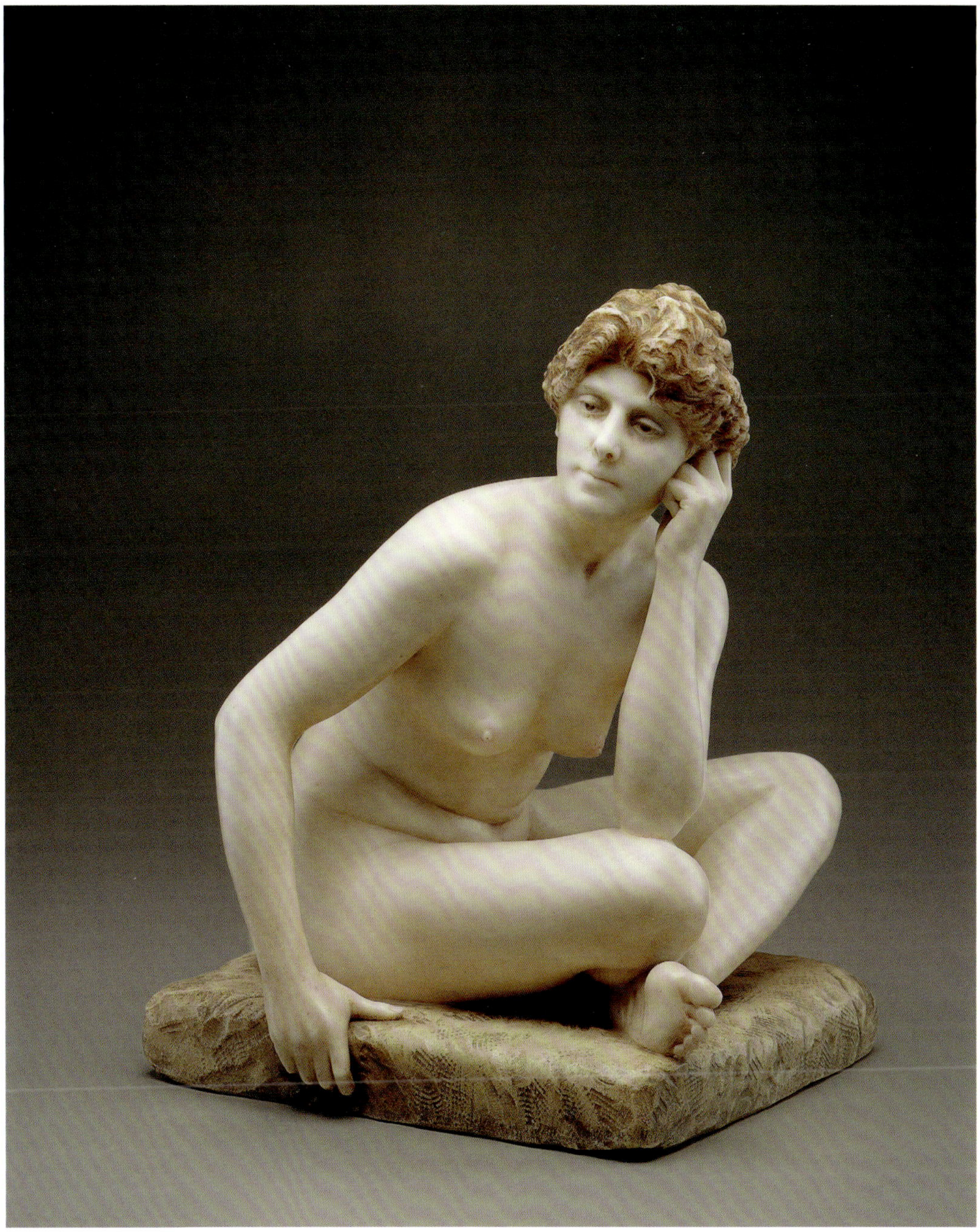

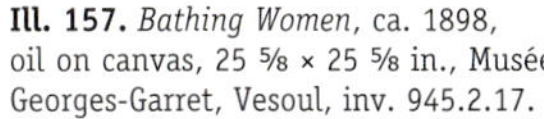

Ill. 157. *Bathing Women*, ca. 1898, oil on canvas, 25 ⅝ × 25 ⅝ in., Musée Georges-Garret, Vesoul, inv. 945.2.17.

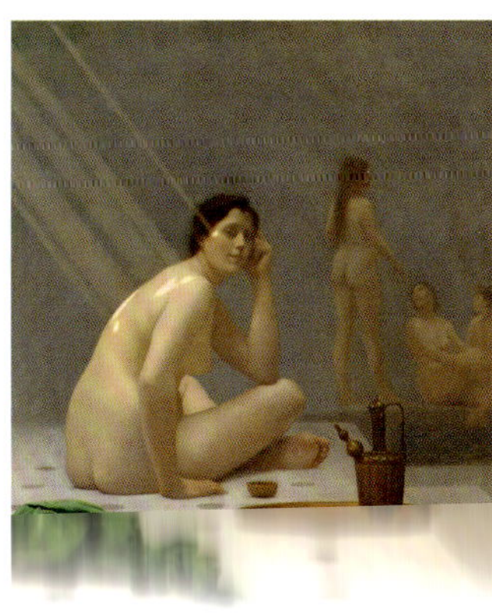

This statuette with its striking presence plays on the distortion between its reduced scale and the illusionism of its polychromy. Nearly identical figures—only the hairstyle and the position of the young woman's right hand are different—are to be found in several hammam scenes painted around 1898, in which the figure stands on a dais (*Bathing Scene*, 1898, whereabouts unknown) or on the precious floor of the bath house (ill. 157). The marble was probably created and painted around 1902, as attested by a photograph of an unlocated painting, *My Portrait* (1902), which represents Gérôme working on the marble, the model offering the viewer a vision of her impressive buttocks. The painting is itself very close to a photograph staging the sculptor in the same conditions (private collection). This nude perfectly illustrates Gérôme's aesthetic perspective at the [illegible] (see p.302) or "Adrienne,"[1]—which contrast with the sensuality of the body and its generous forms. Gérôme reproduces the Orientalist motif of the seated woman on several occasions in his work: it appears in a number of paintings from the early 1880s (*After the Bath*, 1881, private collection) and in his sculptural artistic testament, *Corinth* (cat. 192, 193). The vacant gaze of the slightly turned head recalls that of his *Tanagra* (cat. 168). The realism of the breasts and the folds of the stomach are reinforced by the *morbidezza* of the discrete color applied to the finely grained and polished marble. All of Gérôme's major themes are combined here: the studio, the Orient viewed from a distance through the lens of photography and fading memories, the serial repetition of unclothed beauties, and the artist's erotic obsession, objectifying the female body. É.P.

[illegible]

Cat. 187

SARAH BERNHARDT

–

1895–1901
Polychrome marble
27 ¼ × 16 ⅛ × 11 ⅜ in.
Signed left on the base: *J.L.GEROME*; in front on the base: *SARAH BERNHARDT*
Musée d'Orsay, Paris, inv. RF 1393

–

Provenance: The artist's bequest in her testament of 1896. Musée du Luxembourg, from 1904. Musée du Château de Lunéville, 1924 to 1981. Allocated to the Musée d'Orsay, 1986.

–

Bibliography: *Le Figaro*, Nov. 4th, 1901, p. 1. *The Other Nineteenth Century: Paintings and Scupture in the Collection of Mr. and Mrs. Joseph M. Tanenbaum*, exh. cat. (Ottawa: National Gallery of Canada, 1978), p. 224. P. Fusco and H. Janson, *The Romantics to Rodin: French Nineteenth Century Sculpture from North American Collections*, exh. cat. (Los Angeles: Los Angeles County Museum of Art, 1980), no. 155, pp. 288–90. *J.-L. Gérôme*, exh. cat. (Vesoul: Musée Georges-Garret, 1981), no. 188, p. 150. A. Pingeot and A. Le Normand-Romain, *Histoire d'un art. La sculpture. L'aventure de la sculpture moderne XIXe-XXe siècle* (Geneva: Skira, 1986), p. 85. A. Pingeot, A. Le Normand-Romain, and L. de Margerie, *Musée d'Orsay. Catalogue sommaire illustré des sculptures* (Paris: RMN, 1986), p. 165. *Stars et monstres sacrés*, exh. cat. (Paris: Musée d'Orsay, 1987), no. 105, p. 60. J. Milner, *Ateliers d'artistes. Paris, capitale des arts à la fin du XIXe siècle* (Boulogne-Billancourt: Du May, 1990), p. 136. S. L. Stratton, *Spanish Polychrome. Sculpture 1500-1800 in United States Collections*, exh. cat. (New York: The Spanish Institute, 1993–94; also Dallas: Meadows Museum, Southern Methodist University, 1994, and Los Angeles: Los Angeles County Museum of Art, 1994), p. 19. W. Drost, "L'évolution du concept baudelairien de la sculpture," *Gazette des Beaux-Arts*, Sept. 1994, pp. 42–45. *The Colour of Sculpture 1840-1910*, exh. cat. (Amsterdam: Vincent Van Gogh Museum, 1996; also Leeds: Henry Moore Institute, 1996–7). *Racine: Phèdre, ou le choix de l'absolu*, exh. cat. (Magny-les-Hameaux: Musée National des Granges de Port-Royal 1999), no. 36, p. 154. H. Lafont-Couturier, *Gérôme* (Paris: Herscher, 1998), p. 6. G. Ackerman, *Jean-Léon Gérôme* (Courbevoie: ACR Édition, 2000), no. S. 33M, p. 392. *Portrait(s) de Sarah Bernhardt*, exh. cat. (Paris: Bibliothèque Nationale de France, 2000–1). *Ebenbilder. Kopien von Körpern – Modelle des Menschen*, exh. cat. (Essen: Ruhrlandmuseum, 2002; also Berlin: Martin-Gropius-Bau, 2002), VI/2, pp. 278–79. *Sarah Bernhardt: The Art of High Drama*, exh. cat. (New York: The Jewish Museum, 2005–6, also Amsterdam: Museum of Jewish History, 2007), no. 18, pp. 142, 181.

Ill. 158. Auguste Rodin (1840–1917), *Portrait of Mme Vicuña*, 1888, marble, 22 ⅜ × 19 ⅝ × 14 ⅜ in., Musée d'Orsay, Paris, inv. RF 793.

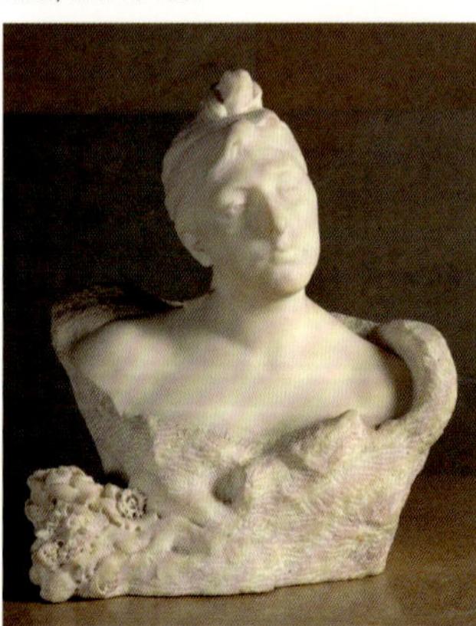

Ill. 159. Jean-Désiré Ringel d'Illzach (1847–1916), *Sarah Bernhardt*, ca. 1890, polychrome wax, 17 ⅜ × 8 ⅜ × 8 ¾ in., Musée d'Art Moderne et Contemporain, Strasbourg, Inv. 55.974. 0. 1077. 55.

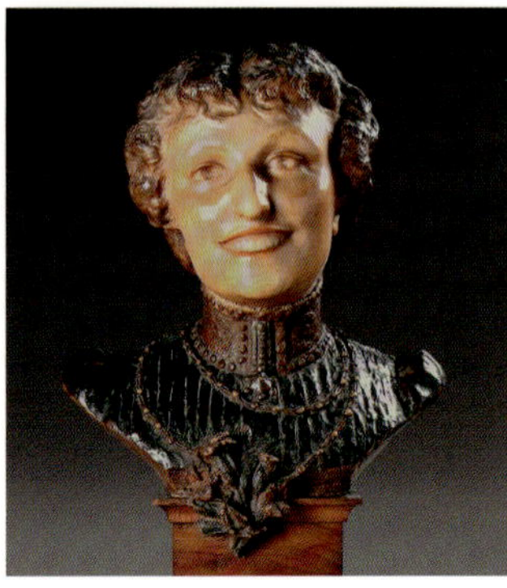

At an interval of forty years and using very different techniques and aesthetics, Gérôme portrayed of two superstars of French society, among the most famous of their age, Rachel (cat. 40) and Sarah Bernhardt. The spectacular polychrome bust of Sarah Bernhardt has a bewitching, immediate presence, and Gérôme's marble remains one of the most striking and direct portraits of the actress, androgynous genius, and *fin-de-siècle* icon, who enduringly marked imaginations for several generations.[1] Photographic illusionism, now reached its high point of technical virtuosity in Gérôme's art, and had a determining impact on his sculpture, without compromising his taste for archaeological detail and humorous illusion. The bust definitively condemns to oblivion the bust producers of official academic realism, however accomplished they may have been (Denys Puech, for example). Furthermore, *Sarah Bernhardt* may also be Gérôme's only possible response to the female portraits produced by Auguste Rodin, whose studio was a necessary port of call for the prominent women of the age (ill. 158). A mature work, created from a great admiration for the model—herself a confirmed sculptor—and a well orchestrated and conscious depiction of himself at work, this bust unashamedly makes connections with neo-baroque allegorical busts, in the facetious positioning of the cupids who are gamely mounting the actress's right shoulder, and with his own study for the portrait of Rachel (cat. 40), from which Gérôme recycles the allegorical figure of tragedy, the Melpomene muse. This muse—who reappears on a small panel with several variations and on the studded cauldron tripod, of which Gérôme was fond (see cat. 40 and 45)—is itself a collection of self-references: the actor trying on his tragic mask—the accessory is practically the same—in *The Greek Comedians* (ill. p. 10), and the drapery of *Bellona* (cat. 182). While it evokes the malignant wax models of his contemporary Jean-Désiré Ringel d'Illzach (ill. 159), this bust is also an imitation *par excellence*: Gérôme would never delve so far into the aesthetics of modern mystification through the reconstruction of antique ganosis (technique of polychromy). Of the woman who inspired "friendship in some, passion in others,"[2] Gérôme reproduced everything up to her coquettishness and beauty worked and staged by the actress herself; it is not hard to imagine her precisely indicating to the sculptor from what direction she should be captured: "It would be difficult to describe her brow, which nobody has probably ever seen, for it was slightly low. As she was ashamed of it, Sarah hid it beneath her magnificent hair. Her coiffure made her look young and accentuated the importance of her eyes which were slightly small... She had a long and harmonious neck, that Sarah liked to wrap up to the chin when she was in society. This was because the signs of age appear earliest on the neck... and no cosmetic or massage can efface them."[3] The cos-

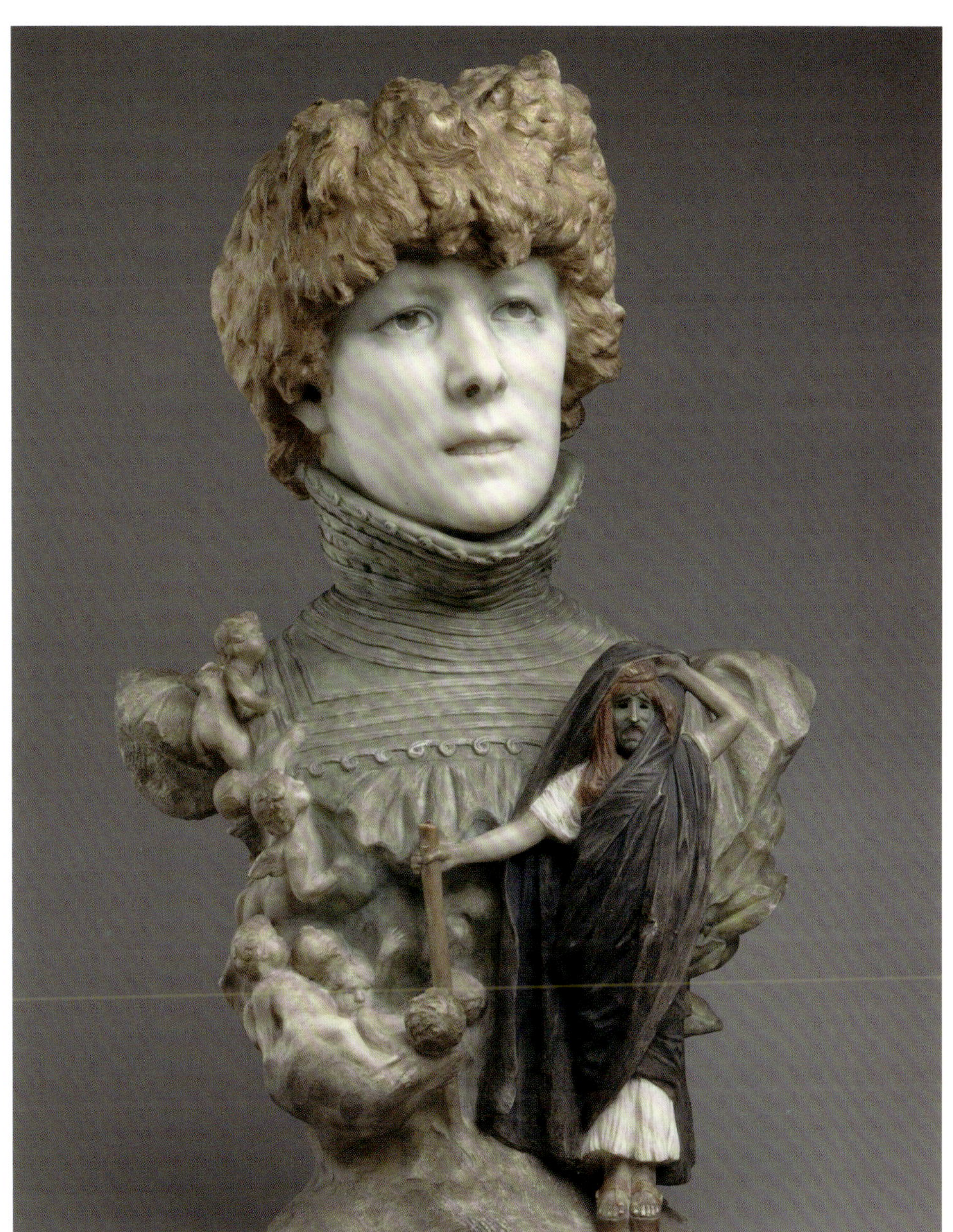

metics of Gérôme's marble polychromy applied to marble by Gérôme were much more effective. The result was a realism that oscillated constantly between the brutality of the representation—the implacable teeth of the *fin-de-siècle* smile—and the refinement of the coloring, which enhances the luxury of the sumptuously decorated mantelet. Gerald Ackerman states that the bust was modeled between 1895 and 1897 and a letter from an assistant of Gérôme, Louis-Émile Décorchemont, sheds new light on the genesis of the work, begun in 1894: "It is ten years since I started work on the bust of Sarah Bernhardt. M. Gérôme was molding it in order to show it to his pupils on the 1st of January."[4] The color was only applied later, in 1901, a date that corresponds with an intense period of activity for "father polychrome"[5] (cat. 188 to 191), as a short piece in *Le Figaro* attests: "MM. Leygue and Roujon have been seen near the Moulin Rouge. So what were the minister and director of the Beaux-Arts doing there? Quite simply visiting the studio of Gérôme. And they chose their moment well. The artist was in the process of finishing the coloring of a bust of Sarah Bernhardt, with its entourage of tiny rosy Cupids; it is a masterpiece of grace and wit, which is destined for the Musée du Luxembourg."[6] A generation later the bust was sent to the Château de Lunéville, where it remained from 1924 to 1981, before becoming a major feature of the Musée d'Orsay in 1986 when it was acknowledged that: "We would not have dared display it earlier in the Louvre."[7] **É. P.**

1. On portraits of Sarah Bernhardt, see *Portrait(s) de Sarah Bernhardt*, exh. cat. (Paris: Bibliothèque Nationale de France, 2000–1). **2.** N. Guibert, "Sarah Bernhardt et son image iconique," in ibid., p. 121. **3.** Ibid., p. 121-122. **4.** G. Ackerman, in P. Fusco and H. Janson, *The Romantics to Rodin: French Nineteenth Century Sculpture from North American Collections*, exh. cat. (Los Angeles: Los Angeles County Museum of Art, 1980), no. 155, p. 288. Letter of Louis-Émile Décorchement to Mme Gérôme, Dec. 23, 1904, private collection. **5.** See my essay in this catalogue, p. 291. **6.** "Échos," *Le Figaro*, Nov. 4, 1901, p. 1. **7.** A. Pingeot and A. Le Normand-Romain, *Histoire d'un art. La Sculpture. L'Aventure de la sculpture moderne, XIXe et XXe siècles*, (Geneva: Skira, 1986), p. 85.

Cat. 188

THE BALL PLAYER

–

1901
Polychromed marble
24 3/8 × 14 1/2 × 10 5/8 in.
Musée des Beaux-Arts, Caen, inv. 309

–

Provenance: Albert Bréaute collection. Deed of gift from Mme Colmont, 1941.

–

Bibliography: G. Ackerman, *Jean-Léon Gérôme* (Courbevoie: ACR Édition, 2000), S. 57.

Cat. 189

THE BALL PLAYER

–

1901
Polychromed marble
65 3/4 × 25 1/2 × 21 1/2 in.
Signed on the base: *J.L. GEROME*
Collection of David H. Koch, New York City

–

Provenance: Princesse de Talleyrand-Périgord, born Anna Gould, Paris. Shepherd Gallery, New York. Gemma Lee of Korea, New York. Shepherd Gallery, New York. Hans Neuffer, Vienna. Shepherd Gallery, New York. Stuart Pivar, New York. Private collection, United States.

–

Exhibition History: Cercle de l'Union Artistique exhibition, 1901. Salon of 1902, no. 2507.

–

Bibliography: A. Alexandre, "La Vie artistique," *Le Figaro*, Feb. 4, 1901, p. 5. Harlor, "Les Salons," *La Grande Revue*, June 1902, p. 685. H. Marcel, "Les Salons de 1902," *Gazette des Beaux-Arts*, 1902, vol. 2, p. 133. "Le Salon de 1902," *Revue de l'Art ancien et moderne*, 6th yr., no. 63, vol. XI (June 10, 1902). *The New York Herald*, Paris, Jan. 24, 1904. G. Ackerman, in P. Fusco and H. Janson, *The Romantics to Rodin: French Nineteenth Century Sculpture from North American Collections*, exh. cat. (Los Angeles: Los Angeles County Museum of Art, 1980), no. 156. *J.-L. Gérôme*, exh. cat. (Vesoul: Musée Georges-Garret, 1981). J. de Caso, "La sculpture française du XIXe siècle dans les collections nord-américaines," *La Revue de l'art*, no. 51 (1981), p. 71. G. Ackerman, "Gérôme's Sculpture: The Problems of Realist Sculpture," *Arts Magazine*, Feb. 1986, pp. 85–88. A. Le Normand-Romain, "La Polychromie," *La Sculpture française au XIXe siècle*, exh. cat. (Paris: Galeries Nationales du Grand Palais, 1986), p. 153. *The Colour of Sculpture*, exh. cat. (Amsterdam: Van Gogh Museum, 1996, also Leeds: Henry Moore Institute, 1996–7), no. 56. G. Ackerman, *Jean-Léon Gérôme* (Courbevoie: ACR Édition, 2000), S. 57, p. 400. E. Héran, "Jean-Léon Gérôme. *La Joueuse de boules*," in *Sculptures de Carpeaux à Rodin*, exh. cat. (Mont-de-Marsan: Musée Despiau-Wlérick, 2000), pp. 99–100. F. Chappey, "L'iconographie de Pygmalion et Galatée aux XIXe et XXe siècles: entre introspection et exhibition," in C. Dotal and A. Dratwicki, eds., *L'Artiste et sa muse*, proceedings of the conference at the Académie de France à Rome, Mar. 2-4, 2005 (Paris: Somogy Éditions d'art and Rome: Académie de France à Rome, 2006), p. 8.

Cat. 190

THE BALL PLAYER

–

1902
Polychrome ivory, gilt bronze, semi-precious stones
H. 10 3/4 in.
Signed on the base: *J.L. GEROME*
Collection of David H. Koch, New York City

–

Provenance: Mr. and Mrs Masson collection, Paris, auction Drouot-Richelieu, Paris, Jean-Louis Picard, January 26, 1994, lot no. 22.

–

Bibliography: G. Ackerman, *Jean-Léon Gérôme* (Courbevoie: ACR Edition, 2000), S. 57 (Ivory). C. Janoray, *the Ball Player* (New York: Charles Janoray, 2008), for another ivory version.

Cat. 191

THE BALL PLAYER

–

After 1902
Gilt bronze
H. 7 1/2 in.
Signed on the base: *J.L. Gérôme*; stamp *SIOT DECAUVILLE FONDEUR PARIS*
Collection of David H. Koch, New York City

–

Bibliography: G. Ackerman, *Jean-Léon Gérôme* (Courbevoie: ACR Édition, 2000), no. S. 57 B3.

Ill. 160. Fratelli Alinari, *Satyr* from the museum of the baths of Diocletian, ca. 1900, silver gelatin print, Archivio Alinari, Florence.

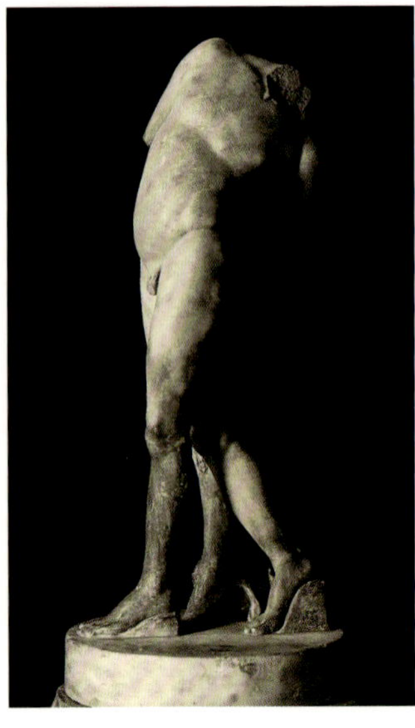

The Ball Player encapsulates the thematic and aesthetic obsessions of Gérôme's late career. The work is a cross-genre reconstruction of an antique marble, the *Satyr*, which Gérôme saw in the museum of the Baths of Diocletian,[1] and which was widely distributed in photographic form (ill. 160), but departs from its model by endowing the figure with the face and hairstyle of a turn-of-the-century *Parisienne*. This disturbing figure with its generous forms, colored with pigmented wax, turns back on herself, smiling, with a provocative tilt of the hip, absorbed in a pseudo-antique game of Gérôme's own invention,[2] where the aim is to cast balls into the open mouths of the three theatrical masks at her feet. This twisting of the female body could already be seen in *Bathsheba*, inspired by the eponymous picture (gilt bronze, Cummer Museum of Art, Jacksonville, Florida). There exist at least two reduced versions of *The Ball Player* in painted marble,[3] including the one at the Musée de Caen (cat. 188) presented here. The work met with decisive success: one of the versions appears in a photograph by François Vizzavona based on *Mon atelier* (1907),[4] a work by Jean-Jacques-Baptiste Brunet, Gérôme's pupil; Siot-Decauville produced a number of gilt bronzes; and Gérôme executed at least three smaller copies, luxury versions in ivory (cat. 190) decorated with the collar of a lioness muzzle exactly the same as in *Corinthe* (cat. 192, 193).[5] It was when he was polychroming *The Ball Player* that Gérôme decided to create his own self-portrait, thrice, in 1902 (ill. 146, p. 297).[6] While it helps us imagine the spectacular effect that the *Pygmalion and Galatea* (cat. 175) group must have offered

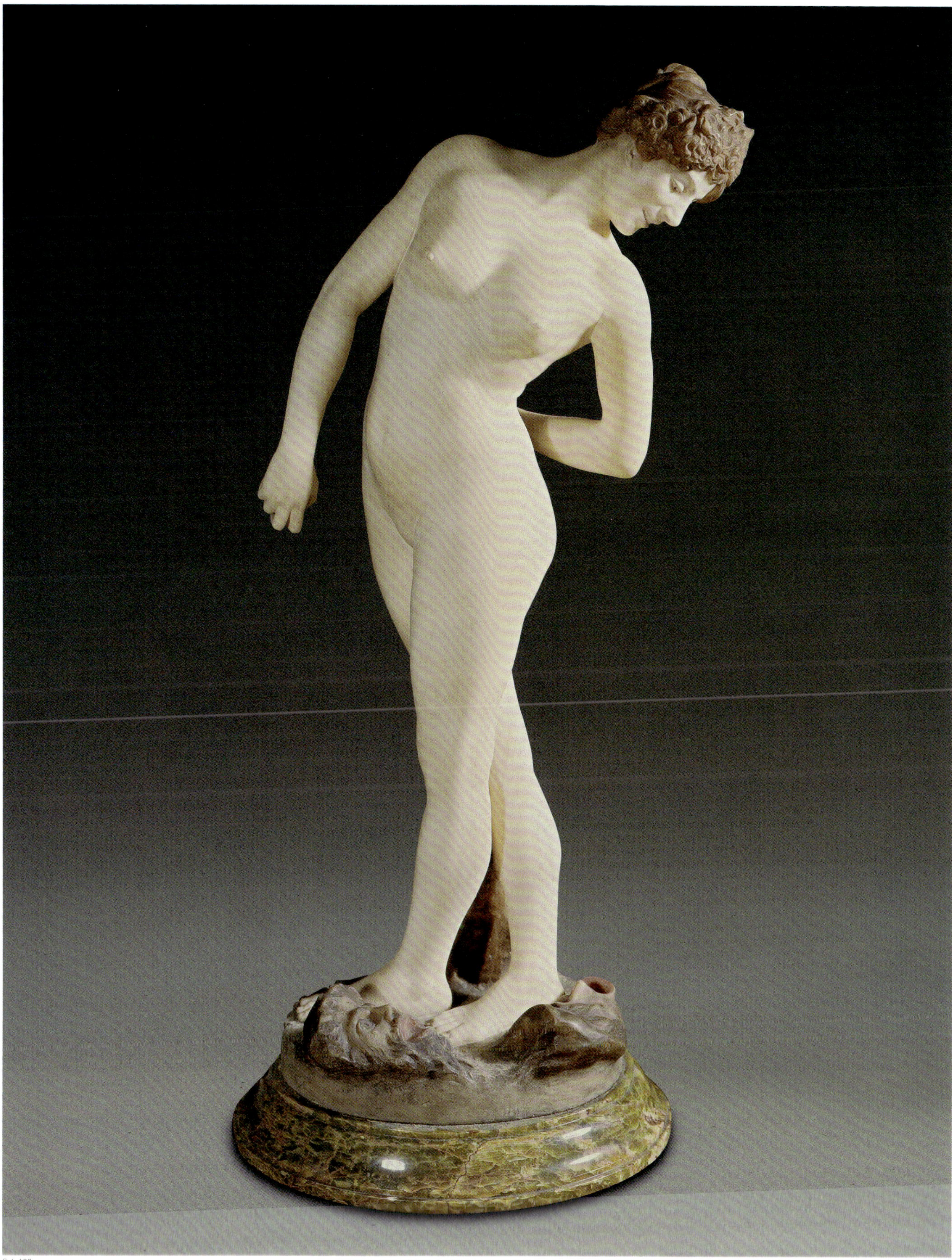

Cat. 188

before the disappearance of its polychromy, *The Ball Player* demonstrates the way Gérôme liked to implement his bold illusion of realism. At the Salon of 1902, where Camille Claudel exhibited *Persée vainqueur de Méduse* (marble, Musée Dubois-Boucher, Nogent-sur-Seine), *The Ball Player* was one of the polychrome sculptures most remarked upon and mocked by critics. *La Pensée sorbonnienne* by Denys Puech, a mawkish neo-baroque assemblage of colored marble was unsurprisingly preferred: it would be difficult to find a better example of the gulf separating Gérôme's experiments from his colleagues' exercises in form. While, to critics, Puech had resolved the aesthetic problems raised by polychrome sculpture "in an ancient Greek fashion," Gérôme was harshly reproached for "the hope of creating the impression of a woman of flesh and blood suddenly transformed into marble... The callipygian lady by M. Gérôme, with her dimples, folds of flesh at the waist, and the pale fatty tones of her skin, at most gives the nagging illusion of dissolute exhibitionism."[7] Arsène Alexandre found the work "highly original, an amusing and learned fancy which is only and overly marred by the excessive darkness of the hair. Polychromy must be perfectly balanced: all color or none at all."[8] However, it is indeed the contrast, attenuated today by time, between the rosy flesh of the body tensed in exercise and the refined colors of the hair and masks that gives Gérôme's sculpture an almost hallucinatory erotic presence when the work first enters the viewer's field of vision (ill. 161). While the balls trapped in the masks—which are far from the "archaeologically correct" masks of *The Greek Comedians*—evoke popular fairground games, the figure of the *Ball Player* might make a perfect brothel sculpture: a rotating base enabling opportune enjoyment of every desired viewing of the body from every desired angle. In managing to stage an isolated figure, Gérôme advances, in all self-awareness, along the razor's edge of the analogy with waxwork museum models, without crossing the "species barrier," which, for the Darwinists of the Salon, would have meant the death of Art[9]: Gérôme's sculpture is above all a manifesto. Without the allegorical pretext of *Tanagra* (cat. 168), the scale of this life-size painted marble directly poses the question of the limits of representation: Jacques de Caso spoke prophetically when, in 1981, he declared "that Gérôme's large nude will have to be taken seriously."[10] **É. P.**

Ill. 161. E.F. Photographer, Paris, *3007. – Gérôme. The Ball Player*, 1902, silver gelatin print, 10 ¾ × 8 ¼ in., Archives, Musée d'Orsay, Paris.

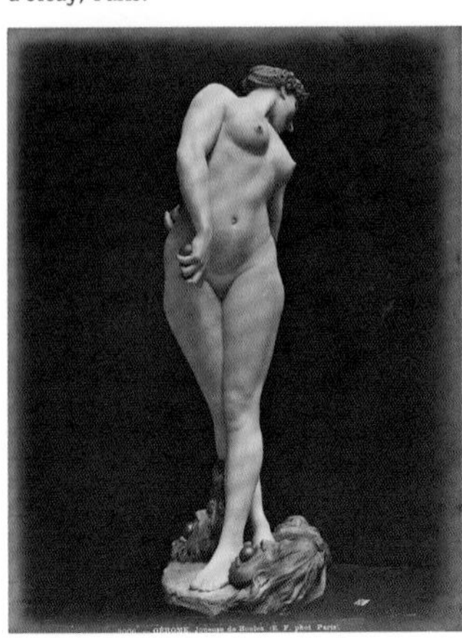

1. Gerald Ackerman was the first to note the similarity of the two works, in P. Fusco and H. Janson, *The Romantics to Rodin: French Nineteenth Century Sculpture from North American Collections*, exh. cat. (Los Angeles: Los Angeles County Museum of Art, 1980), no. 155, p. 289. Furthermore, it also evokes the Bacchante figure in the center of *Jeunesse de Bacchus* (1884) by William Bouguereau (1825–1905). **2.** Ibid. **3.** A polychrome copy, private collection (*Important 19th Century European Painting and Sculpture*, Sotheby's, New York, May 1, 2001, no. 23). **4.** RMN photo agency, Paris, Druet-Vizzavona collection, inv. VZD1286. **5.** See cat. 192, 193, note 1. **6.** He made a gift of the original plaster to the town of Gray, Aug. 12, 1902; see G. Ackerman, *Jean-Léon Gérôme* (Courbevoie: ACR Édition, 2000), no. S. 57. **7.** H. Marcel, "Les Salons de 1902," *Gazette des Beaux-Arts*, 2nd qtr 1902, p. 133. **8.** A. Alexandre, "À l'épatant," *Le Figaro*, Feb. 4, 1901, p. 2. **9.** See my essay in this catalogue, p. 294. On one of the ivory copies, see C. Janoray, *Jean-Léon Gérôme. The Ball Player* (New York: Charles Janoray, 2008). **10.** J. de Caso, "La sculpture française dans les collections nord-américaines,"*Revue de l'art*, no. 51 (1981), p. 71.

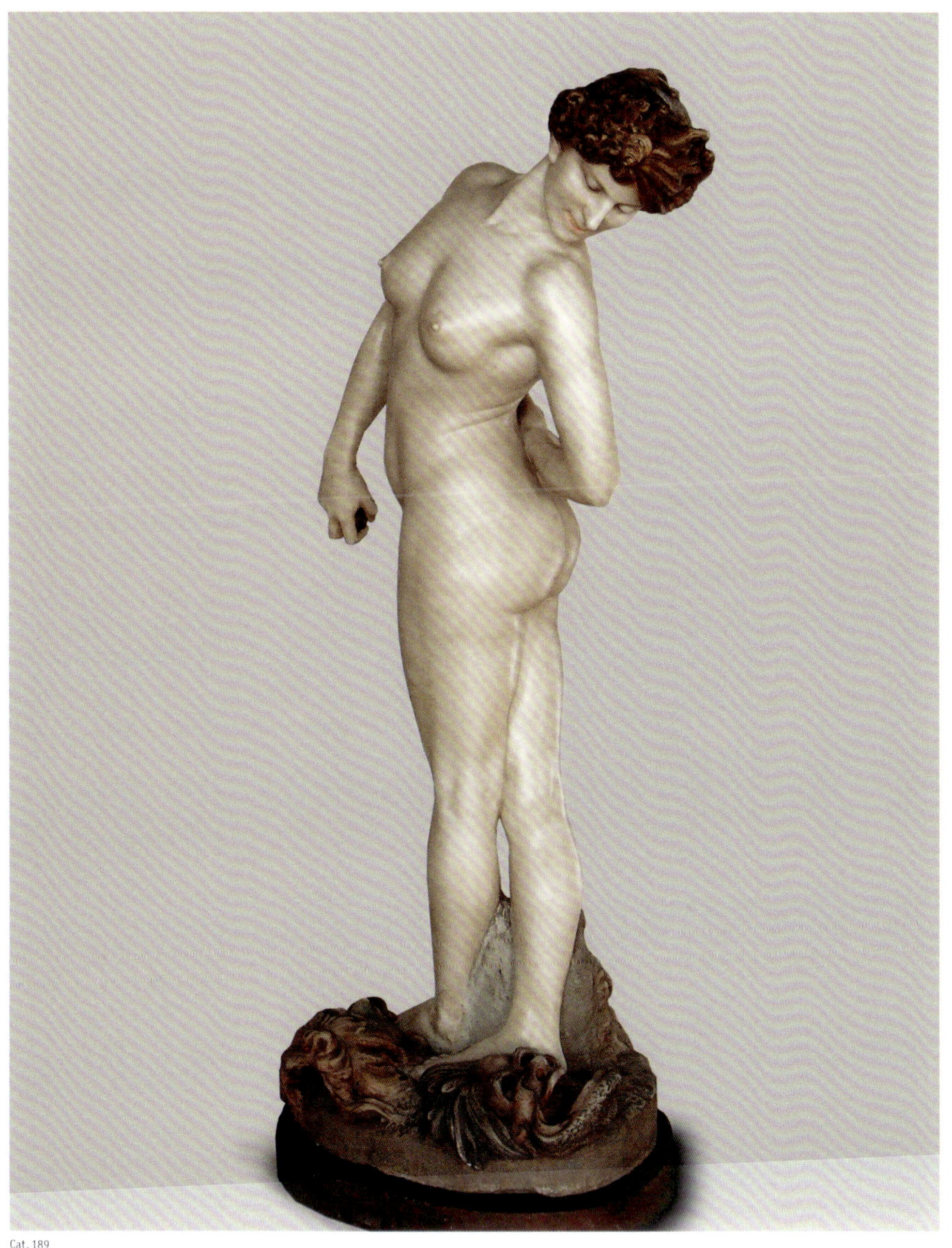
Cat. 189

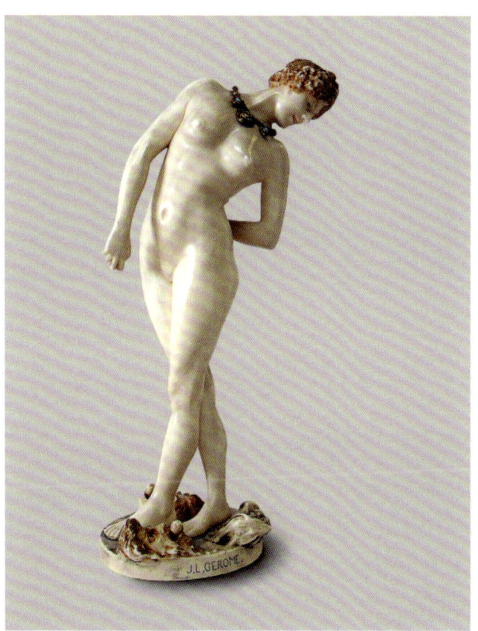

Cat. 190

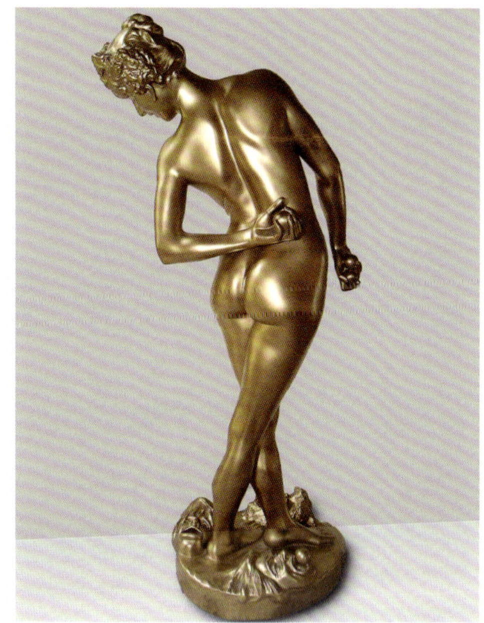
Cat. 191

Cat. 192

CORINTH

–

1903
Painted plaster, wax, metal wires
18 ¾ × 13 × 11 ¾ in.
Musée d'Orsay, Paris, inv. S RF 2008 2

–

Bibliography: *J.-L. Gérôme*, exh. cat. (Vesoul: Musée Georges-Garret, 1981), no. 199, p. 156. G. Ackerman, *Jean-Léon Gérôme* (Courbevoie: ACR Edition, 2000), S. 63. J.-R. Gaborit, "Chapiteau corinthien," *D'après l'Antique*, exh. cat. (Paris: Musée du Louvre, 2000–1), no. 34, p. 180. É. Papet, "Autour de la *Corinthe* de Gérôme," *La Revue des musées de France. Revue du Louvre*, no. 4 (Oct. 2009), pp. 73–84.

Cat. 193

CORINTH

–

1904
Polychromed marble, gilt bronze with enamel, semi precious stones, pâte de verre; column: green marble and gilt bronze
Total height with column: 78 in.
Sculpture alone: H. 21 in.
On the plaque: *NON LICET OMNIBUS/ADIRE CORINTHUM*
J. Nicholson Collection, Beverly Hills, California

–

Provenance: Galerie Tanagra, Paris, 1974, no. 19. Nourhan Manoukian Collection. Auction, Drouot-Montaigne, Paris, Boisgirard, Dec. 17, 1993, lot. 56. J. Nicholson Collection.

–

Exhibition History: Salon des Artistes français, Paris, 1904, no. 2922.

–

Bibliography: J. Dieulafoy, "Les Salons de 1904 – Le Salon des Artistes Français," *Le Correspondant*, Apr. 1904, pp. 481–82. J. de Caso, "La sculpture française du XIXe siècle dans les collections publiques nord-américaines," *La Revue de l'art*, no. 51 (1981), p. 71. P. Fusco and H. Janson, *The Romantics to Rodin: French Nineteenth-Century Sculpture in North American Collections*, exh. cat. (Los Angeles: Los Angeles County Museum of Art, 1980), no. 52, p. 19. *J.-L. Gérôme*, exh. cat. (Vesoul: Musée Georges-Garret, 1981), no. 200, p. 157. L. Relin, "La 'Danseuse de quatorze ans' de Degas, son tutu et sa perruque," *Gazette des Beaux-Arts*, Nov. 1984, p. 174. H. Lafont-Couturier, *Gérôme* (Paris: Herscher, 1998), p. 98. G. Ackerman, *Jean-Léon Gérôme* (Courbevoie: ACR Édition, 2000), no. S. 63. É. Papet, "Autour de la *Corinthe* de Gérôme," *La Revue des musées de France. Revue du Louvre*, no. 4 (Oct. 2009), pp. 73–84.

Corinth is the last object on which Gérôme worked on in the year he died.[1] It sums up his career as a sculptor and constitutes a kind of artistic testament of it. The polychrome plaster model, purchased in 2008 by the Musée d'Orsay, one of Gérôme's rare surviving original plasters, is juxtaposed here for the first time since his death with the marble which was carved after it (cat. 193). The marble sculpture was exhibited posthumously at the Salon des Artistes Français in 1904. Painted and luxuriously decorated with enamel and gilt bronze jewelry created by the caster, Hébrard, and embellished with semi-precious stones, it was completed after Gérôme's death by Louis-Émile Décorchemont, who was then his assistant.[2] The definitive statue shows a naked woman bedecked in jewelry, sitting cross-legged on a gilt bronze Corinthian capital of a green marble fluted column. Hébrard's invoices for the jewelry enable us to date the plaster, in all likelihood, to around 1903, the year in which most of the plasters were fashioned.[3] *Corinth* was subsequently distributed by the firm of Siot-Decauville in the form of slightly smaller gilt bronze versions, enhanced with semi-precious stones, and without the column—the capital alone emerges from the rocky base, producing an "archaeological" effect. Like *Tanagra* (cat. 168), *Corinth* plays, in a much more demonic way, on the Greek idea of the *tyche* but, once more, Gérôme appeals to the Orient to evoke ancient eroticism.[4] To the turn-of-the-century imagination, the main attraction of Corinth, the powerful Peloponnesian city which had a flourishing trade with the Orient, resided in the memory of the *hierodules* (sacred prostitutes) confined within the temple devoted to the goddess Aphrodite.[5] The Latin inscription "*NON LICET OMNIBUS / ADIRE CORINTHUM*" on the cartouche of the definitive version of the work evokes an ancient adage reported by the geographer Strabon: "Rich merchants and military men met their ruin here, their irremediable ruin, which prompted this proverb: 'not every man is made for Corinth.'"[6] The connection with the Orient might be found in Babylon where, according to Herodotus, local *hierodules* would "sit in the ancient enclosure of Aphrodite with a crown of cord upon their heads... Visitors would pass by and make their choice. A woman seated here is not allowed home until a stranger has cast money into her lap and he has lain with her inside."[7] Today, however, it is still difficult to know exactly why Gérôme decided, at the end of his life, to represent an allegory of Corinth, even if this figure seated atop a column is an irreverent evocation of the iconography of the stylite saints of early Christianity, on which Gérôme worked (cat. 83). *Corinth* further evokes a city that was the subject of a number of legends about artistic invention. It was believed to have witnessed the birth of painting, the art of portraiture in sculpture, and its eponymous capital. It is indeed on a Corinthian

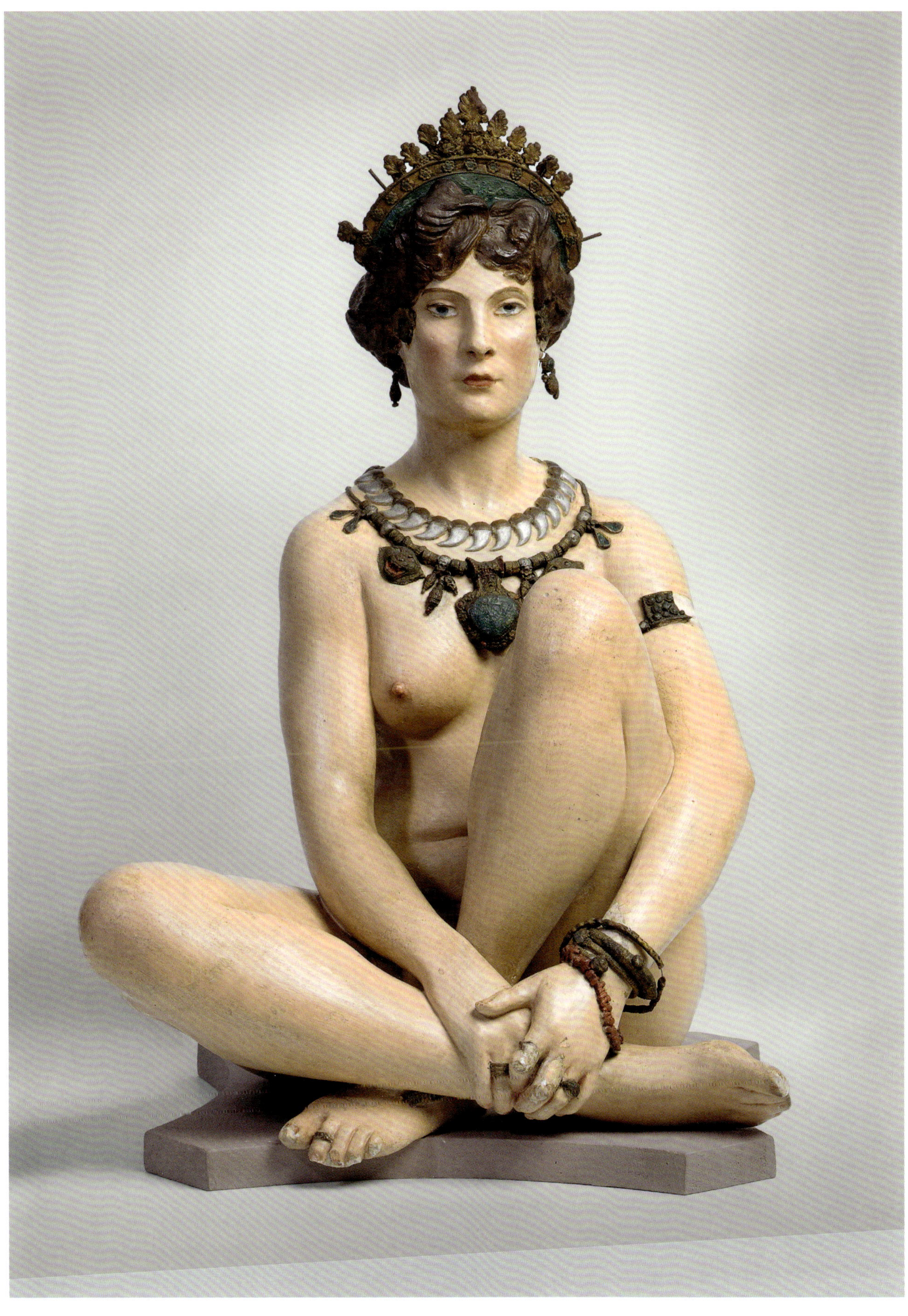

Ill. 163. *Serpentiform ring*, southern Italy, Fourth century B.C., gold, diam. ¾ in., département des Antiquités grecques, étrusques et romaines, Musée du Louvre, Paris, inv. Bj 1140.

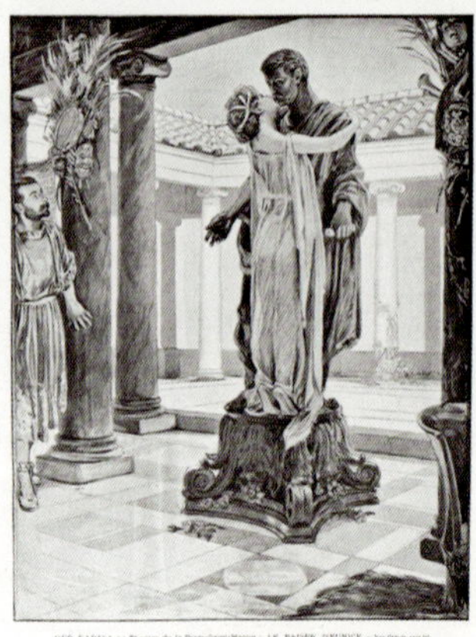

Ill. 164. *Lady of Elche*, photoengraving reproduced in the article by Paul Jamot, "Le Buste d'Elche," *Gazette des Beaux-Arts*, vol. XIX (Mar. 1898), p. 239, Bibliothèque, Musée d'Orsay, Paris.

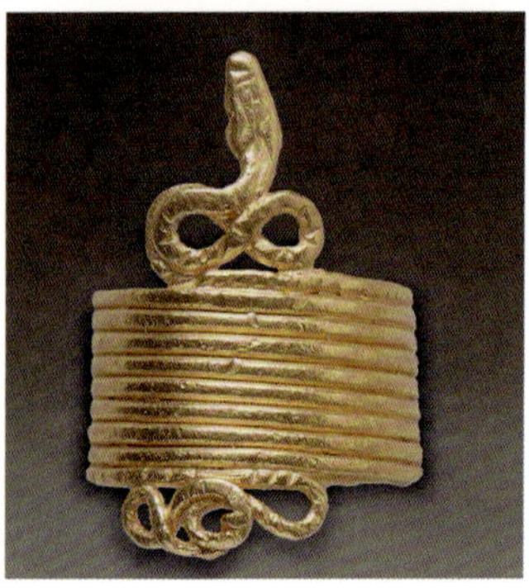

Ill. 165. Frantisek Kupka (1871–1957), "Quo Vadis? au Théâtre de la Porte-Saint-Martin: Le Baiser d'Eunice," cover of *L'Illustration*, no. 3030, Mar. 23, 1901.

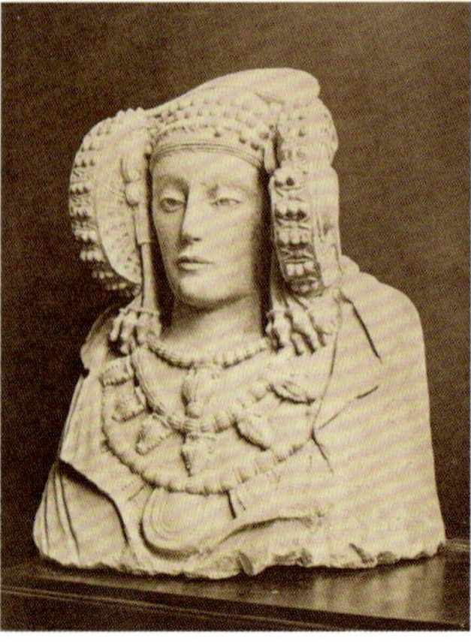

capital, very similar to that discovered in Epidaurus in 1884 and considered as the very prototype of the Corinthian capital, that the courtesan sits, but unorthodox use of Antique architecture was not rare around 1900 (ill. 162). As he had done for *The Gladiators* (cat. 76) twenty-five years earlier, Gérôme researched meticulously to bring authenticity to this figure of fantasy. The jewelry was based on the Greek and Etruscan pieces from the Campana collection, exhibited in the Louvre from 1861, such as the ring visible on the definitive work (ill. 163), as well as on items featuring in a work by Eugène Fontenay, *Les Bijoux anciens et modernes*, published in 1887 and abundantly illustrated. As often with Gérôme, this great concern for precision in his sources went hand in hand with anachronism: just as with *The Ball Player* (cat. 188), the hair of *Corinth* is dressed like that of a twentieth-century *Parisienne*. Gérôme may also have been inspired by a very famous work of the nineteenth century, the *Lady of Elche*, discovered in Spain in 1897 and considered then as the perfect example of the complex synthesis of Mediterranean civilizations. (ill. 164). *Corinth* then is Gérôme's final scholarly demonstration, a hyper-realistic version of the *femme fatale*, and an enigmatic sphinx. It is above all, though, an uncompromising, troubling sculpture, even if Gérôme did not dare depict the courtesan's sex between her spread legs. *Corinth* is a "curiosity study" of a work, governed by a confusion of gender, assembled by Gérôme under the guises of a rigorous historicism. It can also be read as an allegory of the Parisian demimonde and no doubt constitutes one of the most spectacular post-symbolist nudes of the nineteenth century, exuding a morbid sexuality. Gérôme's "Indian idol"[8] met with mixed, generally unfavorable reviews: "Around her press stupefied viewers. Was it Gérôme's desire to forever discredit polychrome statuary of which the Greeks were so fond ... Never would the Greeks have painted flesh as pale as the wax effigies in hairdressers' boutiques."[9] Only the critic Tristan Leclère thought that "three works stood out among the sculpture exhibits of the Salon of 1904; Rodin's *Thinker*, Constantin Meunier's *Miner* and Gérôme's *Corinth*."[10] He offered a highly favorable analysis of Gérôme's exploration of polychrome illusionism, while detecting the aporia: "I don't believe anyone has ever sought to achieve the real like Gérôme... This *Corinth* is a masterpiece, but a masterpiece from the conclusion of an art: it does not open up the way to new attempts; it marks an end; it is the final term in polychrome sculpture. We might of course still find unexpected polychrome combinations, unusual arrangements of different subjects; there is little further left to go; it is a form of art that has reached its limits."[11] **É. P.**

1. This entry draws on my study: É. Papet, "Autour de la Corinthe de Gérôme," *Revue des musées de France. Revue du Louvre*, no. 4 (Oct. 2009), pp. 73–84. **2.** G. Ackerman, "Corinth," in P. Fusco and H. Janson, *The Romantics to Rodin: French Nineteenth Century Sculpture from North American Collections*, exh. cat. (Los Angeles: Los Angeles County Museum of Art, 1980), p. 291. A letter from Louis-Émile Décorchemont to Mme Gérôme, Dec. 23, 1904, suggests the existence of a smaller version in ivory: "The model of the little Corinth which Mme Siot commissioned from you is still at the ivory carver's; he is using it to help him complete the ivory." (private collection). **3.** Invoices for July and October 1903, Gérôme collection, Archives, Musée d'Orsay, Paris. **4.** *The Odalisque* (1902–3, Appleton Museum of Art, Florida State University, Ocala) features exactly the same pose. **5.** The goddess was depicted armed; see Pausanias, *Description de la Grèce*, trans. G. Roux, "En Corinthie", "Corinthe, Quartier Nord, Acrocorinthe", para. 5, (Paris: Les Belles Lettres, 1958), p. 46. **6.** Strabon, *Géographie*, Book XII [vol. IX], 3, 36, trans. F. Lasserre (Paris: Les Belles Lettres, 2003 [1981]), p. 102. **7.** Herodotus, *Histoires*, Book I, "Clio," para. 199, trans. P.-E. Legrand (Paris: Les Belles Lettres, 1993), pp. 197–98. **8.** J. Dieulafoy, "Les Salons de 1904 – Le Salon des Artistes français," *Le Correspondant*, Apr. 1904, pp. 481–82. **9.** Ibid. **10.** T. Leclère, "La Sculpture," in *Salon, Paris, 1904*, preface by G. Geffroy (Paris: E. Sansot, 1904), p. 159. **11.** Ibid., p. 166.

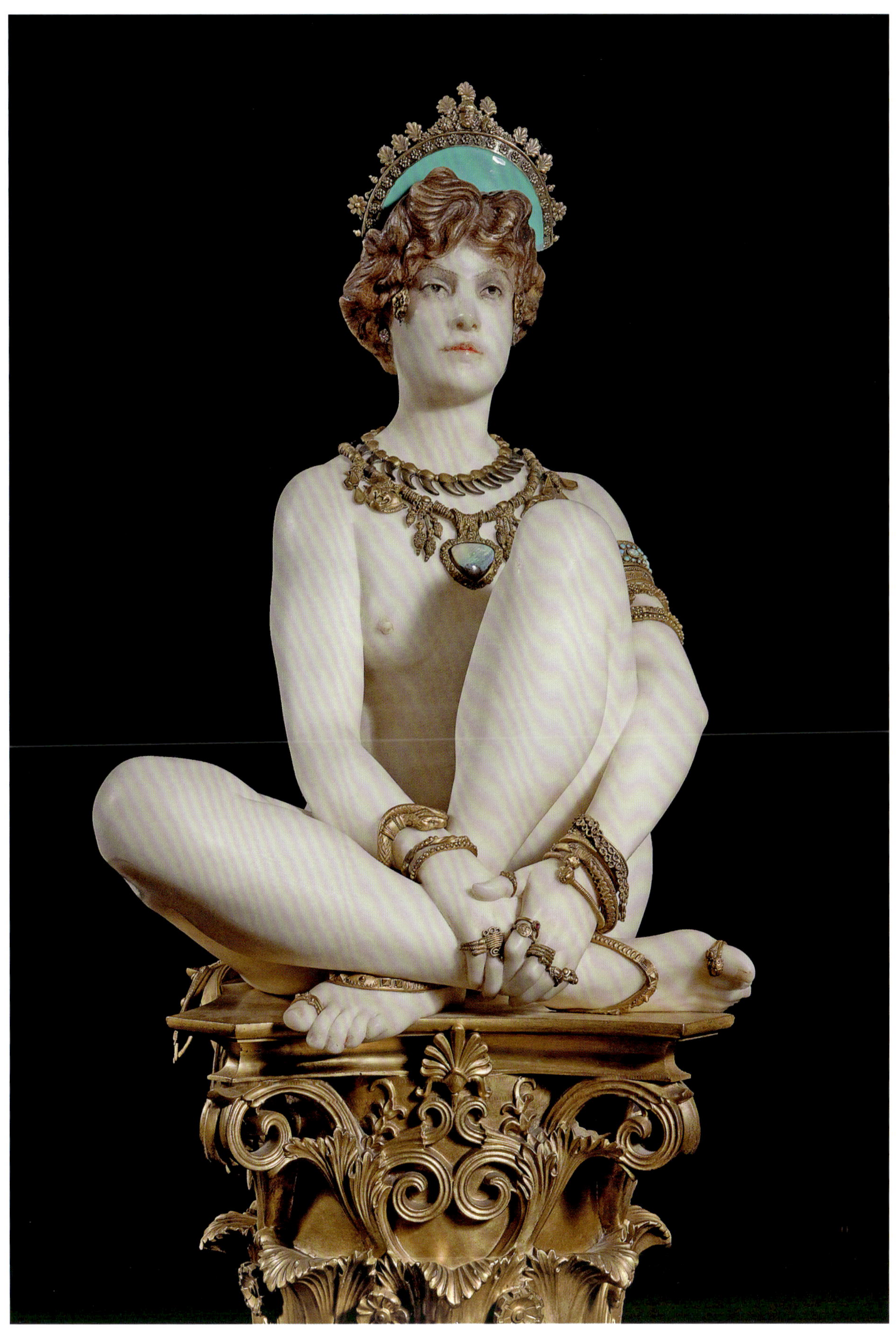

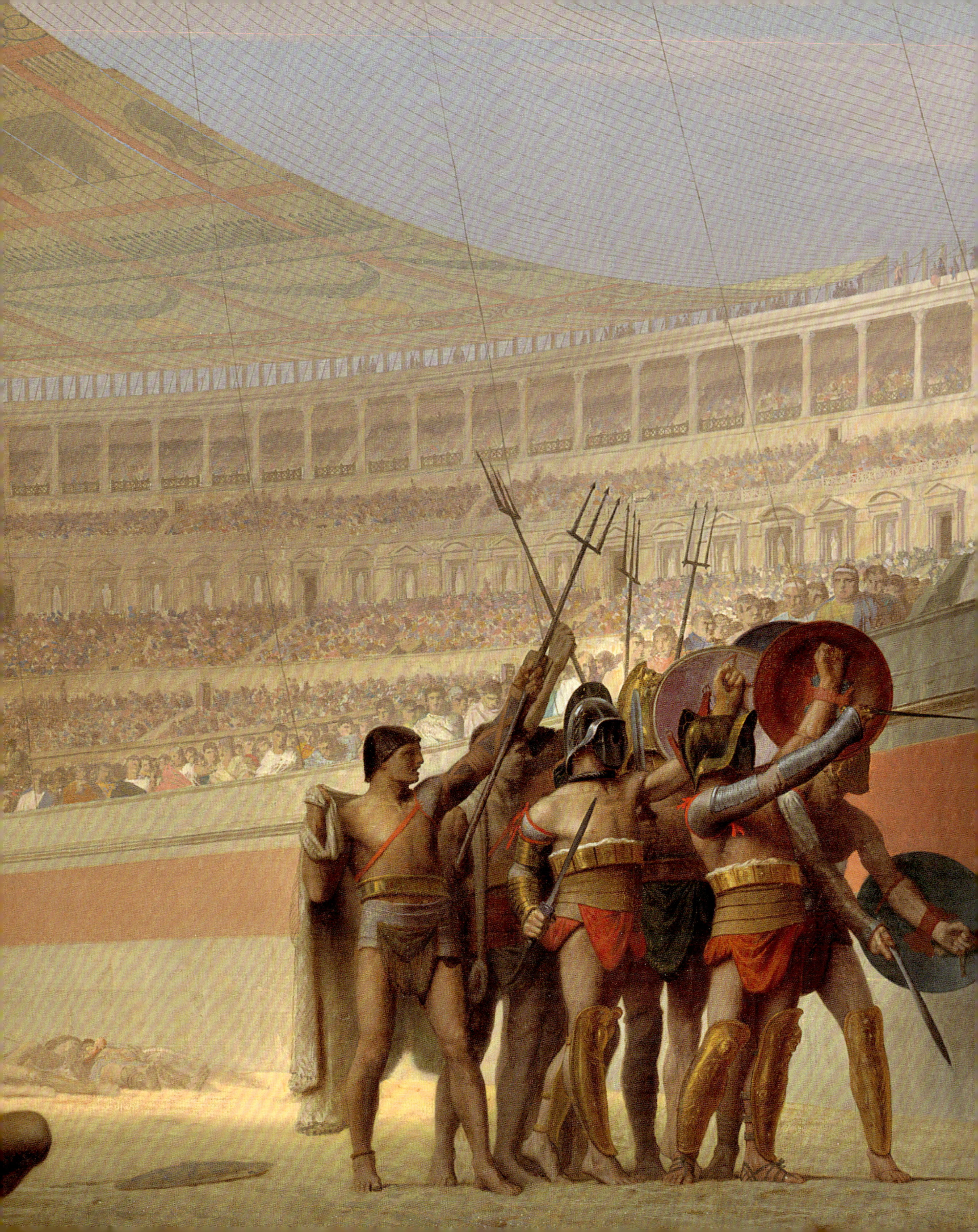

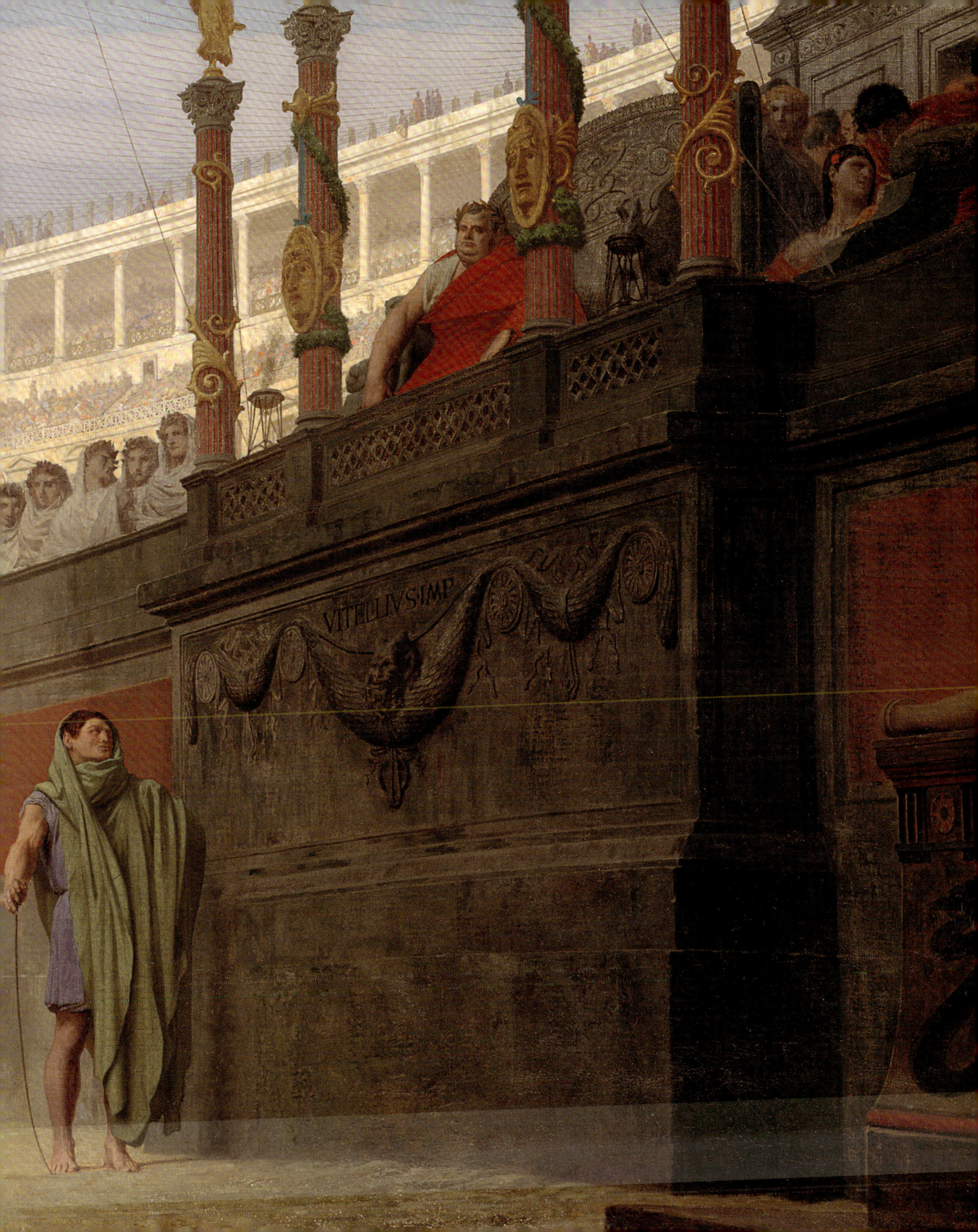
VITELLIVS IMP

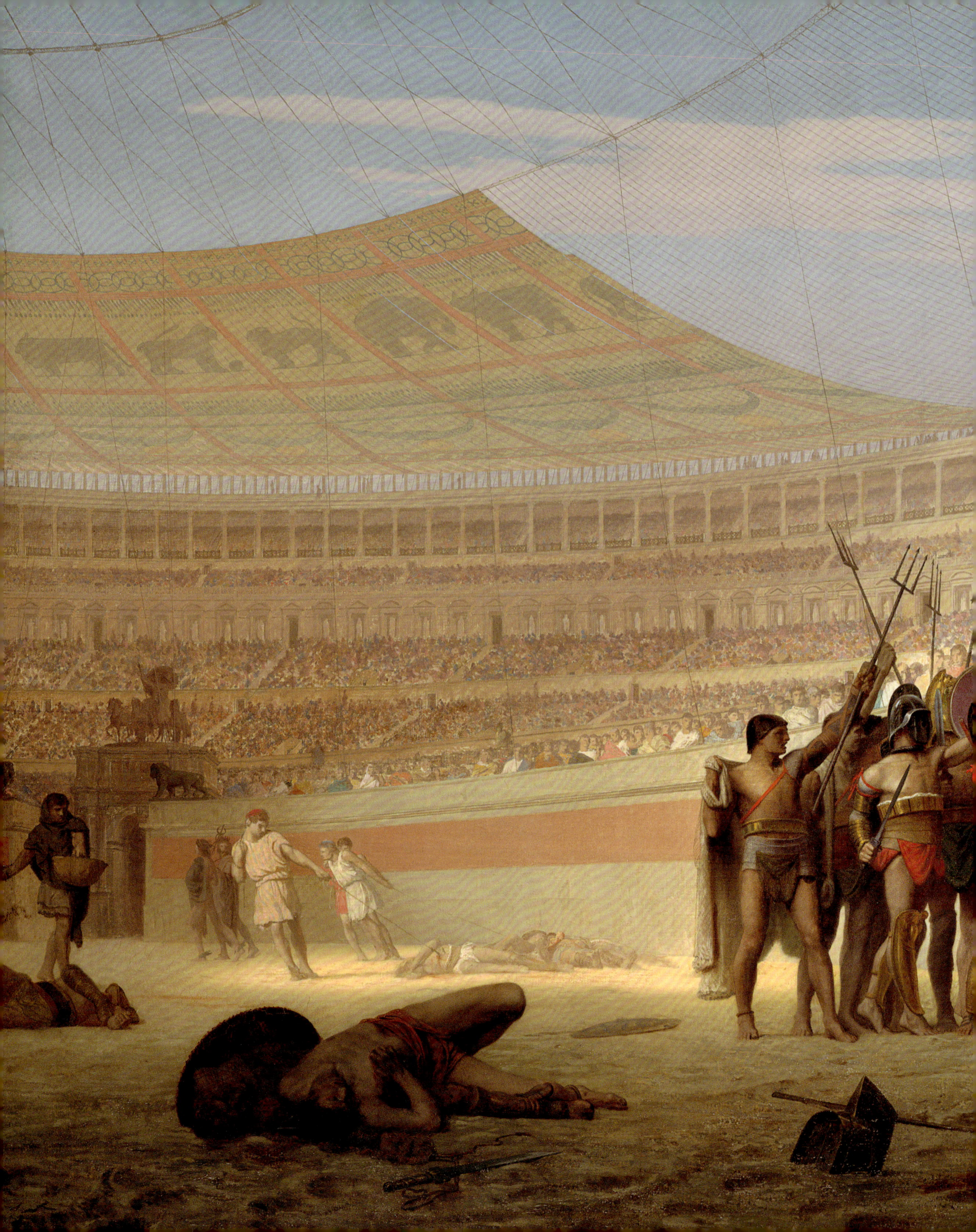

PAINTING THE MOMENT JUST AFTERWARD, OR, GÉRÔME AS FILM-MAKER

—

Dominique Païni

REPRODUCTION

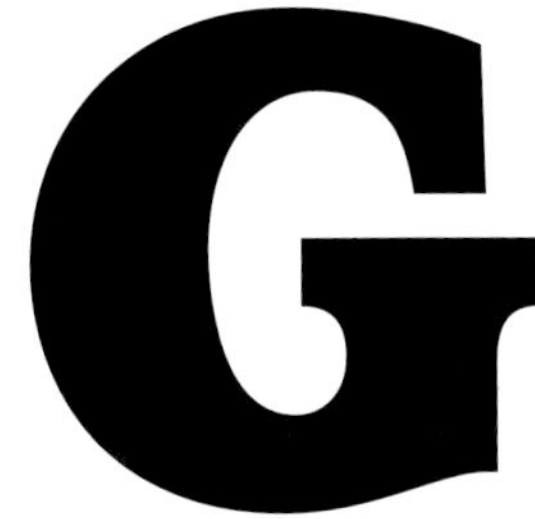

érôme was probably one of the artists of his day most concerned with the *reproduction* of artistic pictures. In the first place, his strong, academically impeccable style was based on scrupulous observation of models; and photography most likely served as the basis for his paintings on various occasions. In the second place, Gérôme was one of the first artists of his century to gain renown through the worldwide distribution of photomechanical reproductions of his art. Photoengraving was invented in 1860 and Gérôme owed some of his instant celebrity to works distributed through this medium on both sides of the Atlantic.[1]

This situation was not to everyone's taste. The most famous complaint came from Émile Zola, who asserted that Gérôme "creates a painting so that it may be reproduced by photography and engraving and thus sold in thousands of copies. Here the subject matter is everything, the painting is nothing: the reproduction is worth more than the work."[2] Other people, such as Théophile Gautier, were stunned by the powerfully real impression made by *The Death of Caesar* as a painting(cat. 67). "If photography had been known in the days of Caesar, we might think that the painting had been done from a print made on the spot at the very moment of the catastrophe."[3]

If we analyze these two points of view, it would be tempting, with hindsight, to compare their divergence to one that arose when the movies were invented: the potential for reproduction further aggravated a lack of esteem for the Lumière brothers' "views" and their rather "ordinary" scenes of everyday life.

When trying to detect an aspect of Gérôme's work that *prefigured* the art of film or left a cinematic heritage, we cannot overlook the virtue of reproduction. Although this virtue does not seem to accord with the art's general virtues, it nevertheless marks the latter half of the nineteenth century's prefiguration of the following century, when the conceptual tandem of "reproduction–dissemination" became a key anthropological phenomenon. And the movies are probably the art whose existence, above all other compositional specificities (framing, editing, etc.), stems from reproduction (photographic fidelity) and dissemination (multiple copies thereof).

The business and family connections that tied Gérôme to the printer and publisher Adolphe Goupil made the artist a *producer–director* of images whose academic style might henceforth be perceived as more complex, given the modernist appeal that paradoxically emerges from his posing as an *industrial painter*. In fact, reproduction played a significant role in the artistic turmoil implied by *The Artist's Model* (cat. 173), an 1895 painting in which Gérôme depicted himself polishing a marble

Previous and opposite pages
Cat. 70. *Ave Caesar, morituri te salutant!* (detail).

statue while the female model is present in the foreground. Apart from the disturbing mimesis between the two figures—rendered distinct by the color of each figure's substance thanks to Gérôme's great illusionist virtuosity—a reproduction on the studio wall of a painting done that same year, *Pygmalion and Galatea* (cat. 175), plunges this turmoil into endless self-reflexiveness—is Gérôme depicting himself as Pygmalion, who brings life to the substance of marble through his labor? And who is the original model here: is the statue a reproduction of the life model or is the latter adopting a pose to imitate the statue? Such questions go round and round, endlessly.

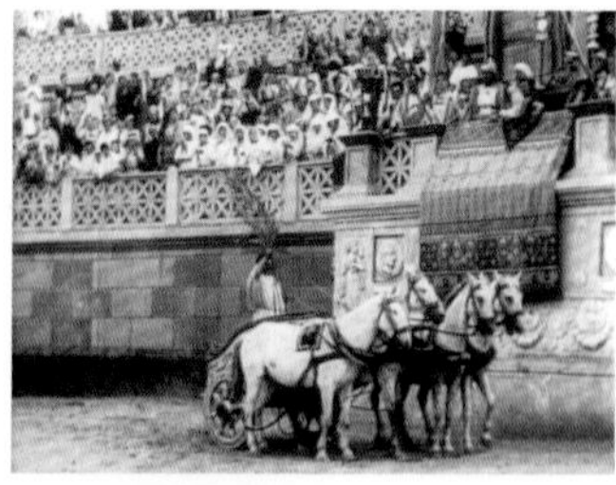

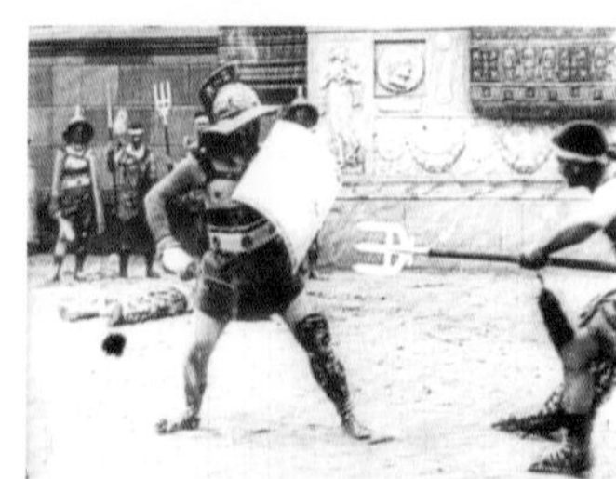

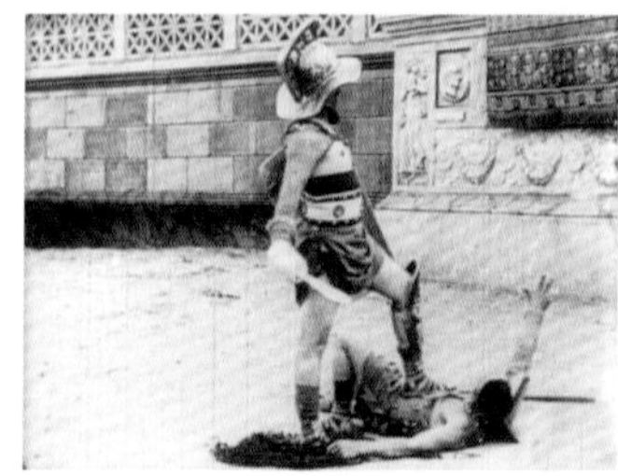

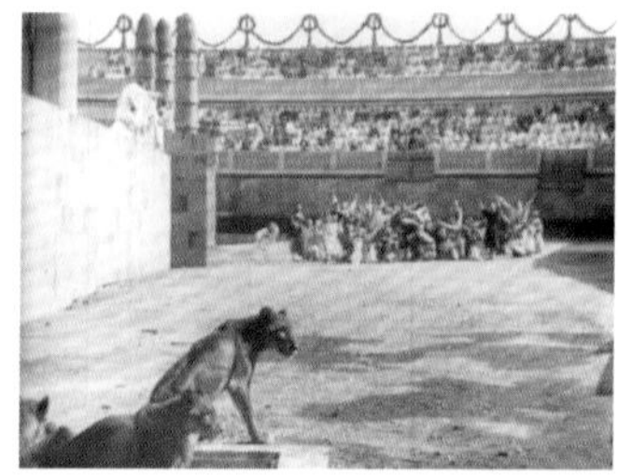

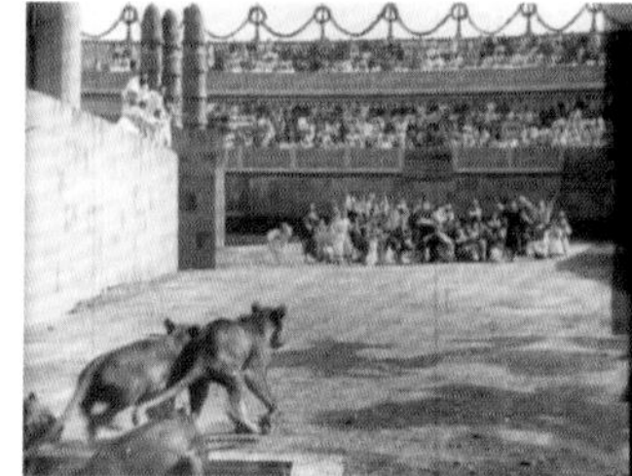

Ill. 165. Enrico Guazzoni (1876-1949), *Quo Vadis?*, 1913.

DEPICTING TIME

A series of five photographs taken in 1885 in Gérôme's studio and ascribed to Louis Bonnard have a *cinematic feel* (cat. 177 and 178). At the very least, the clear adoption of a narrative sequence was obviously conceived by Gérôme, who was the protagonist. What is most fascinating about these snatches of studio life is obviously the motionlessness of the artist, gaze directed straight at the camera, as opposed to the rotations of the sculpture (*Omphale*) and the model, which inscribe movement into the pictures. The fifth in the series—the final "frame" of this strip—recorded Gérôme's exit off-screen. A temporal trace of his "passing beyond" is thus captured on sensitive film. As a true ancestor of Duane Michals's photographic series,[4] it is a kind of pre-cinematic *vanitas* that emerges here: the "shifting lines" of agitation within the picture, blurry figures, a ghostly trace of absence.

Gérôme therefore willingly staged his status as an artist. Like film-makers—particularly modernist ones such as Orson Welles and Philippe Garrel[5]—Gérôme *made a scene of himself* in order to essay his theory of art, even if that theory defended and illustrated academic concepts opposed to innovation. It is nevertheless the case that the physical presence of the artist within his own sphere of creativity would become a typical feature of modern cinema one hundred years later (witness the films of Jean-Luc Godard and Pier Paolo Pasolini).

But do Gérôme's works, properly speaking, hold out the promise of any moving-image legacy?

It is easy to perceive proto-cinematic features in the large painting now in Versailles, *The Reception of the Siamese Ambassadors at Fontainebleau* (cat. 94). Everything about the composition is designed to force the eye to move. This panorama of lavish protocol already prompts a panoramic vision: the eye constantly sweeps from the left of the painting, where the prostrate ambassadors enter, to the far right where the imperial couple is slightly raised, and then back to the left again to repeat the visual sweep. The painting was deliberately composed to produce movement, to make the eye mobile. In the latter half of the nineteenth century it was not unusual to produce monumental, populated scenes that required a certain amount of time to be viewed, yet this *Reception* remains an exemplary panoramic device—one contemporary with the large painted displays known as "panoramas"—which seems to hover between two potential forms of motion. On the one hand, the characters are captured as though in a cinematic freeze-frame; while on the other, the viewing angle does not seem fixed—is the artist's viewpoint advancing or retreating? In both cases, the perspective seems to hover.

Finally, we know that Gérôme, when concocting this scene, ran into difficulties similar to ones encountered much later by the directors of monumental films, notably Cecil B. De Mille and Joseph Mankiewicz. Gérôme struggled to do the portraits of the Siamese ambassadors the way movie directors would struggle to direct extras on their film sets.

COINCIDENCES AND ALLUSIONS

The cinematic appeal of Gérôme's paintings is practically a truism. The epic films shot in Italy and later in Hollywood seemed to borrow their imagery from the painter of *The Christian Martyrs' Last Prayers* (cat. 80). One of the most famous movie incarnations of a model devised by Gérôme was the all-conquering pose of the gladiator in Enrico Guazzoni's *Quo Vadis?* (1913),[6] taken from Gérôme's *Pollice Verso* (cat. 179). The connection is astonishing, and was underscored by the movie director: at the end of the battle, as the victor awaits the emperor's life-or-death decision, the brief, motionless pause is the occasion for this iconographic imitation. The power of Gérôme's image was such that a sculpture largely reproduced its grandiloquence—a photograph now in the Bibliothèque Nationale de France shows a group of gladiators, one of whom is similar to the one seen in *Pollice Verso,* with Gérôme seated at his feet. More reproduction, again and again.

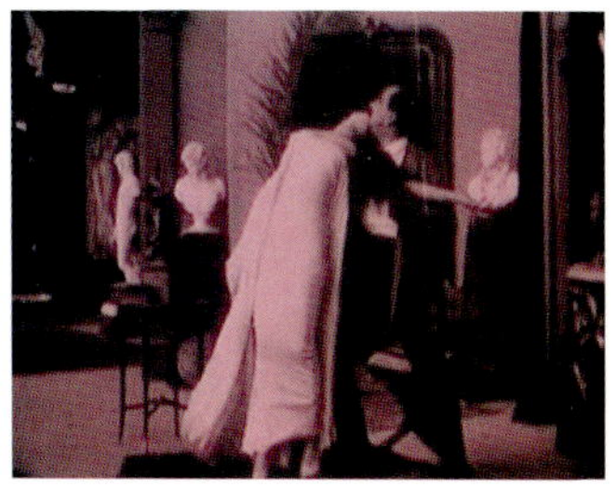
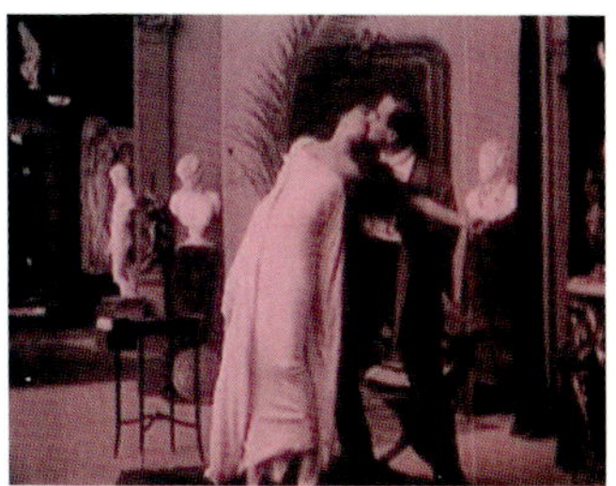
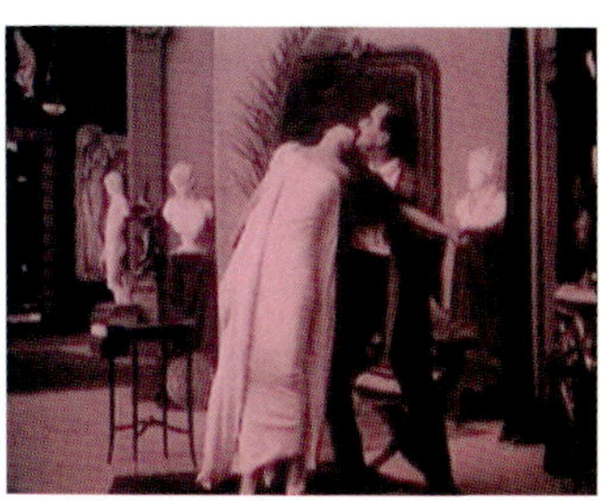
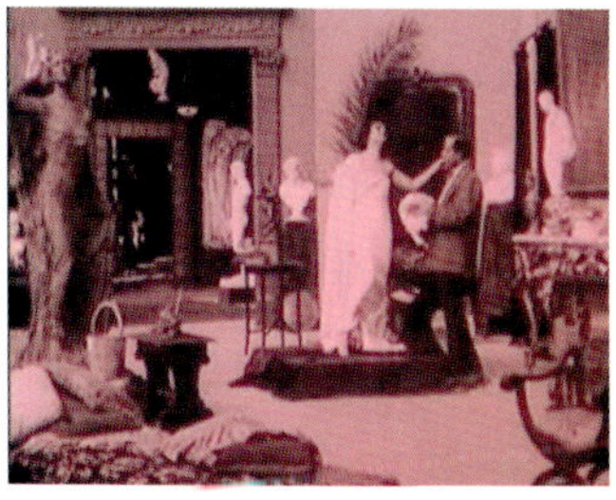
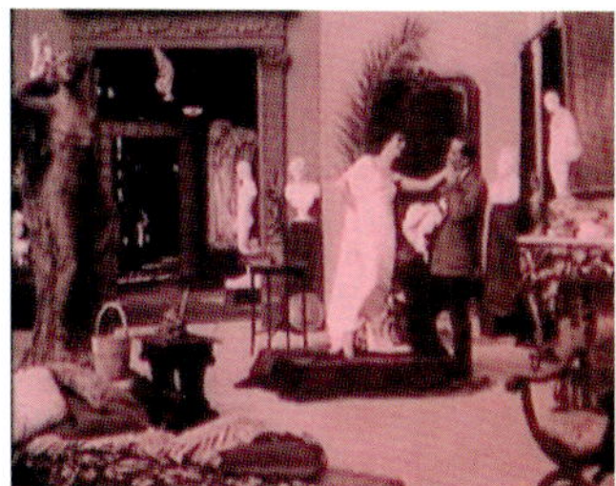

Ill. 166. Alfredo De Antoni (1875–1953), *Il Processo Clemenceau*, 1917.

The Baltimore painting mentioned above, *The Christian Martyrs' Last Prayers,* took over twenty years to gestate, according to several sources confirmed by the artist's own comments. Reproduction of the final work further spurred Gérôme's fame, and Guazzoni probably made another allusion to it in the cruel scene of the movie where the Christians are eaten by lions in the middle of the huge Roman amphitheater. Meanwhile, *The Chariot Race* by Gérôme of 1876 inevitably evokes several Hollywood films of the story of Ben Hur, notably the most famous version directed by William Wyler in 1959 (ill. 167). Gérôme's obvious awkwardness in rendering galloping horses predated his knowledge of the photographic plates made by Eadweard Muybridge, which the artist only saw a few years later.
In 1893, Gérôme sketched the choreographed spins and twirls of Loïe Fuller,[7] barely two years before the first film-makers would record the dancer's arabesques in the temporal dimension of a filmstrip.
The movement of bodies was a particular enthusiasm of Gérôme's, as dazzlingly demonstrated by his *Pygmalion and Galatea,* painted in 1892. Executed the same year as his sketch of Loïe Fuller, this famous work evoked the turn-of-the-century obsession with depicting motion.
Thanks to Georges Méliès, the movies exploited the legend of Pygmalion and Galatea right from the start, unwittingly offering a hermeneutic perspective on the medium's own birth, namely the passage from inanimate to animated, from motionless volumes to changing shapes, from "marble to celluloid."[8]
It might be suggested that the invention of the movies involved a "Pygmalion complex."[9] For a long time—during the first twenty years of its existence, still silent and marked by the symbolism and poetic trends of the nineteenth century—the movies betrayed this origin, for which Gérôme provided a kind of original negative. Thus a scene in a film by Alfredo De Antoni, *Il Processo Clemenceau* (1917), displays an inevitable coincidence with the sculptor's embrace of his model (ill. 166), a motif lyrically established less than thirty years earlier by Gérôme.

SEIZING THE ORDINARY MOMENT

Among Gérôme's most famous works, three other paintings seem to me to interrogate, in similar fashion, the passing of time—that is to say the dimension that became the very *material* of the movies: *The Death of Caesar*, *Golgotha* (cat. 78), and *The Death of Marshal Ney* (cat. 93). From the standpoint of iconography, these works are highly different, yet they all employ the same startling "staging" of an event that has already ended.
The Death of Caesar incorporates a premature cinematic effect, namely movement within depth of field. Théophile Gautier saw an initial sketch of Gérôme's painting in 1858, and his description of the work in his articles on visits to artists' studios of the day corresponds to the one currently held by the Walters Art Museum in Baltimore. But a photograph of it, allegedly taken by the Goupil firm, reportedly singled out Caesar's body *by default,* obscuring the rest of the picture. Gérôme apparently viewed this accident as a potential effect to be used in another version of the same subject.[10] Indeed, that same year Gérôme completed a larger *Death of Caesar*, framed more tightly on the prostrate body, a body that occupied almost all the area of the canvas. Discussed by Charles Baudelaire,[11] this larger, "close-up" shot was included in the "wide-angle" view of the initial version, completed later. It was a kind of experiment in "shot scale" and "tracking out," the better to reveal the architecture and the flight of the conspirators, seen from the back, after the emperor was assassinated.
In 1867 Gérôme painted a most unusual crucifixion that, in certain aspects of composition and drama, boldly prefigures a 1913 painting by Gaetano Previati, *Translation of the Body of Christ.*[12] All that can be seen are the shadows of the three crosses. The city of Jerusalem is depicted in the distance beneath the inevitable storm clouds that accompany the crucifixion story, and the people who attended the event are heading back to the city—they, too, are shown from the back.
Gautier quite rightly wondered about the "anecdotal" nature of this depiction of the climax of the holy story. In fact, Gérôme's approach might be seen as part of a quest for an *ordinary moment,* an attempt to banalize this mythifying murder. This is just what the movies would ultimately do some thirty years later: record and re-present moments made ordinary due to their successiveness, due to the fact that every frame of a film is a photograph of a moment that happens to follow another moment. *Golgotha* depicts just one moment chosen at random from the period that followed an incredible event, an event of the kind that usually calls for history painting, whether religious or not.[13]
The *Death of Marshal Ney* relates, ideally, to history painting. It is one of the last masterpieces of the

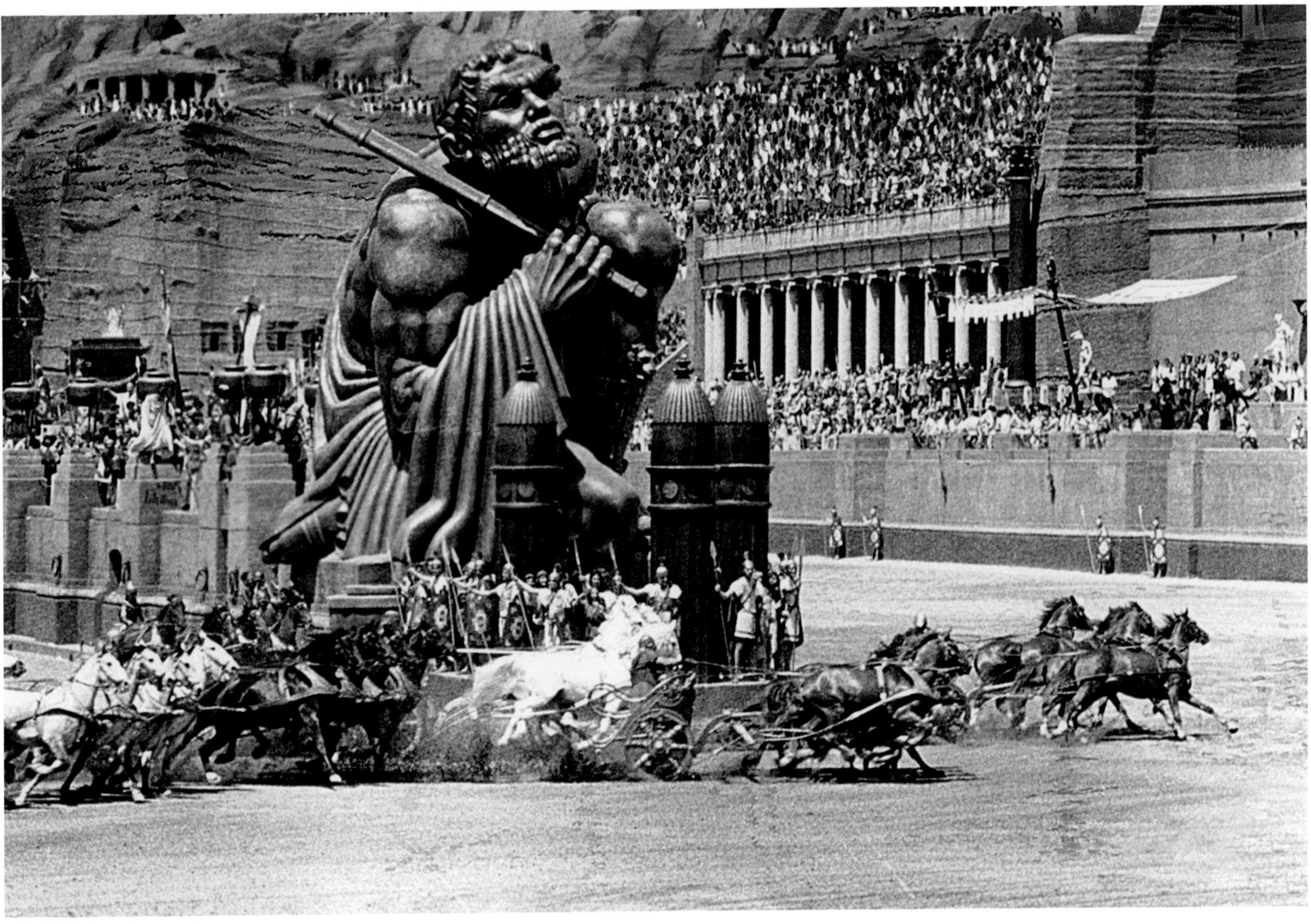

Ill. 167. William Wyler (1902–1981), *Ben Hur*, 1959, film still.

history genre. In the foreground lies Marshal Ney on the ground—like Caesar—face down in the mud. Here a wall, white with dampness, replaces the noble Roman columns. Gautier noted that there was not yet enough historical distance to negate the impression that Ney still bled and breathed. There could be no better way to express the realism that movies would later supply, astonishing the early viewers of the cinematograph.

But what is even more striking is the emphatic staging that entailed painting participants in the event *from the back*.[14] The soldiers are leaving the scene, like the people who crucified Christ and the men who killed Caesar. Gérôme captured this *moment just afterward*, reinforced by an officer's furtive look backward. More than history, the subject painted here is a temporal effect, a crucial moment in history reduced to an ordinary moment of the period that follows what might have been the "decisive," "vivid" or "ideal" moment. The complete title of Gérôme's painting, for that matter, underscores this diffuse, ordinary, thoroughly cinematic temporality: *December 7, 1815, Nine O'clock in the Morning*.[15]

Yes, it was an *ordinary* December day—seen in an anecdotal light—which consigned a sprawling corpse to an indifferent eternity, like so many other bodies that populate a "film noir."

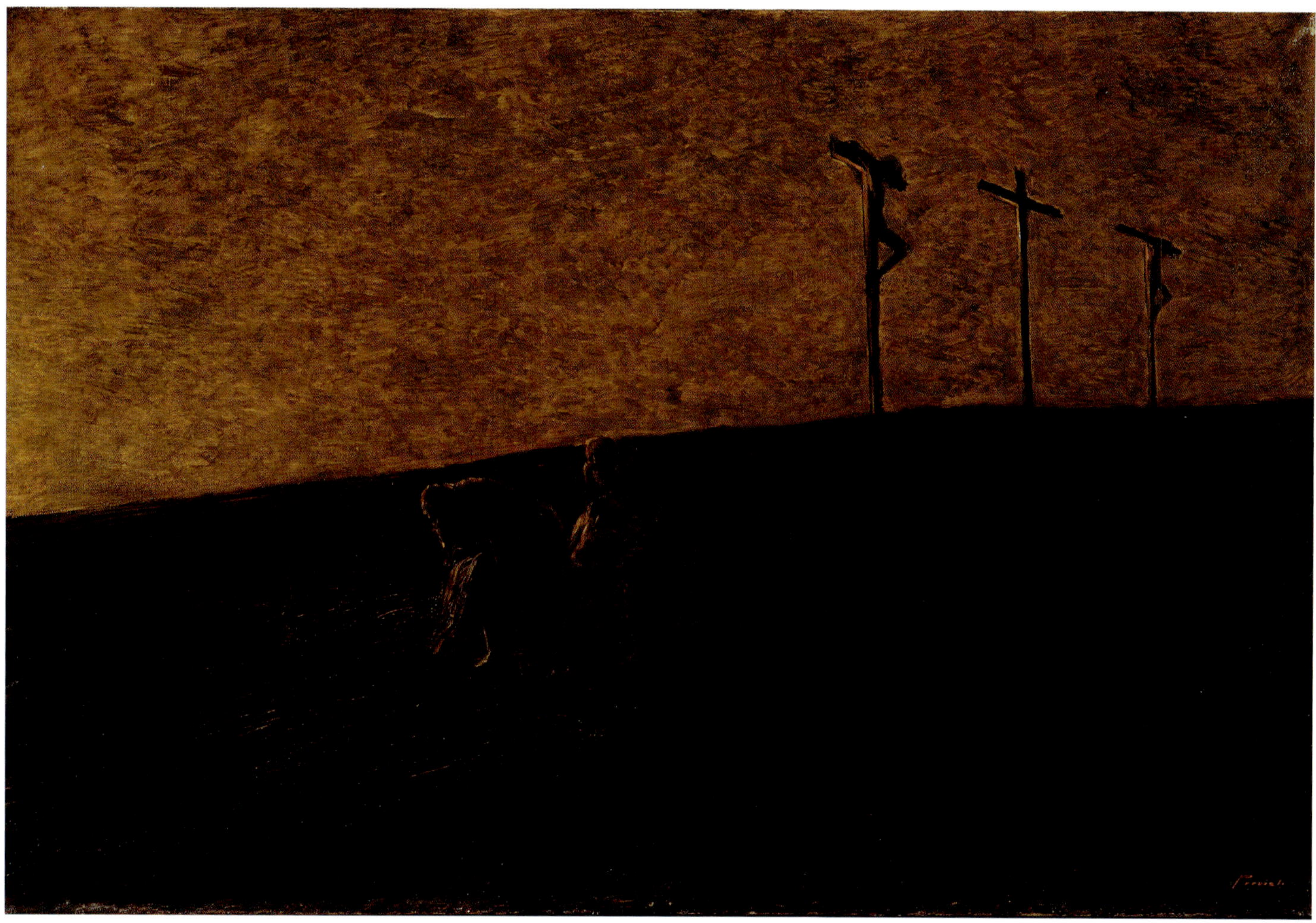

Ill. 168. Gaetano Previati (1852–1920), *Translation of the Body of Christ*, 1914, oil on canvas, 33 × 50 ¾ in., Museo dell'Ottocento, Ferrara.

Following pages

Cat. 112. *Whoever You Are, Here is Your Master* (detail).

1. In 1883 a portfolio of a hundred photogravures was published in the United States. See G. Ackerman, *Jean-Léon Gérôme* (Courbevoie: ACR Édition, 2000).

2. É. Zola, *Écrits sur l'art* (Paris: Gallimard, 1991), p. 372.

3. Quoted by G. Ackerman, 2000 (as in n. 1).

4. See, for example, *The Poet Decorates his Muse with Verse,* a series of six photographs, 2004.

5. I am not citing these names at random but because they evoke a self-centered lyricism, indeed a certain "nineteenth-century grandiloquence."

6. See I. Blom, "Gérôme en *Quo vadis?* Picturale invloeden in de film," *Jong Holland* 4, XVII (2001), pp. 19–28, and "*Quo vadis?* From Painting to Cinema and Everything in Between," in *La decima musa. Il cinema e le altre arti / The Tenth Muse. Cinema and Other Arts,* eds. L. Quaresima and L. Vichi (Udine: Forum, 2001), pp. 281–96.

7. The sketches are now in the museum in Vesoul.

8. This phrase is a deliberately modified version of Eric Rohmer's famous title for a series of articles, "Le Cellulloid et le marbre," *Cahiers du Cinéma* 44 (Feb. 1955) and subsequent issues.

9. D. Païni, "Le complexe de Pygmalion (Sculpter à l'écran)," in M. Frizot and D. Païni, eds., *Sculpter-Photographier,* proceedings of the symposium at the Louvre, Nov. 22–23, 1991 (Paris: Marval, 1993).

10. C. Baudelaire, *Salon de 1859* (Paris: Honoré Champion, 2006), p. 400.

11. C. Baudelaire, *Oeuvres complètes* (Paris: Gallimard Pléiade, 1999), vol. 2, p. 641.

12. Museo dell'Ottocento, Ferrara.

13. This perhaps anticipates, a century in advance, Antonioni's project of filming the *aftermaths* of crises. Michelangelo Antonioni's crises were sparked by marital stories, Gérôme's crises by public history.

14. Jean-Luc Godard once said he could "film landscape from the back."

15. Compare the titles of observations by John Constable, the painter of constantly changing clouds.

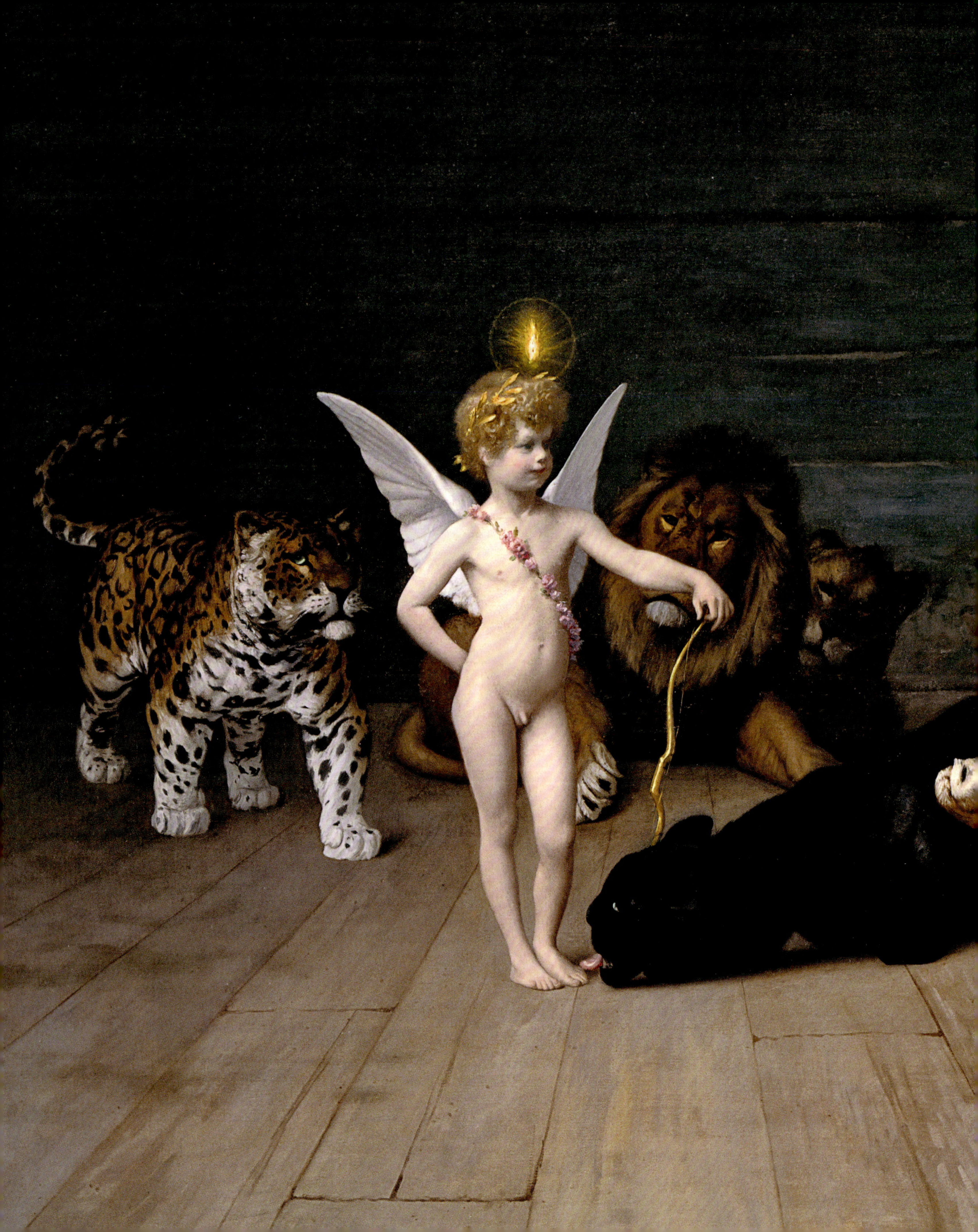

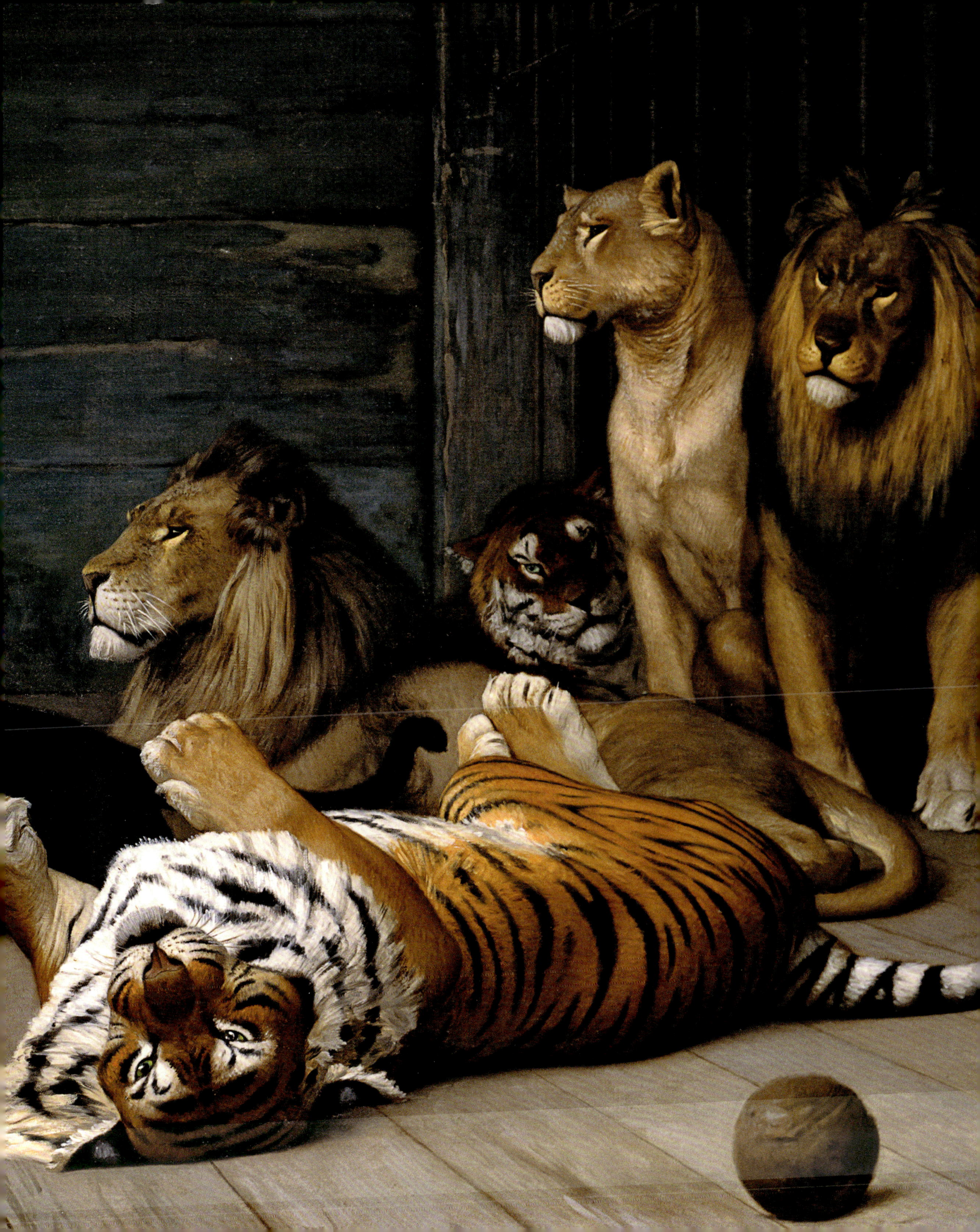

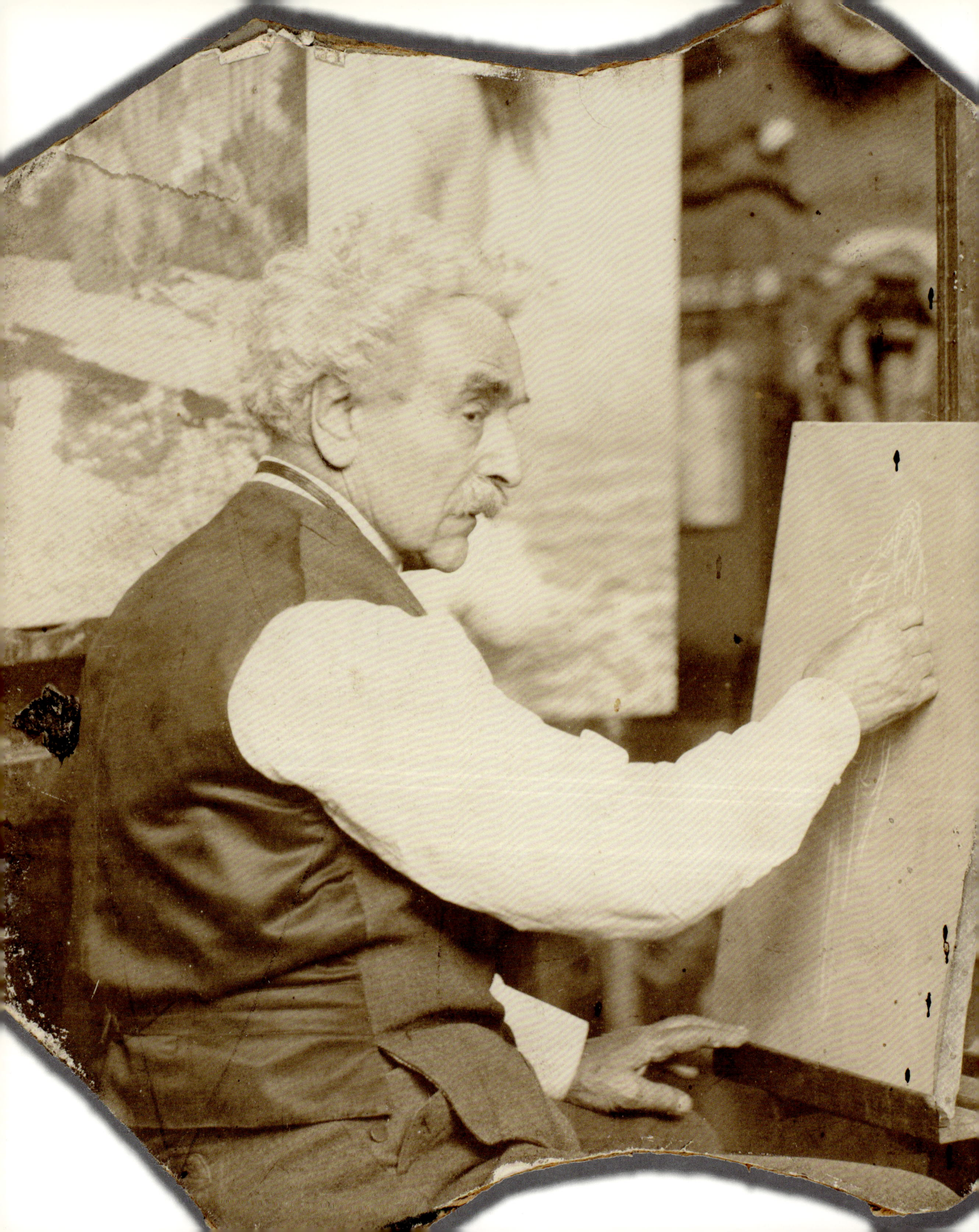

CHRONOLOGY

Philippe Mariot. Translated from the French by David Radzinowicz

.1824

Birth of Jean-Léon Gérôme on May 11 at Vesoul. His father is a goldsmith and jeweler. The same year sees the birth of Alexandre Dumas, Eugène Boudin, Pierre Puvis de Chavannes, Emmanuel Fremiet, and Gustave Boulanger, as well as the death of Anne-Louis Girodet de Roussy-Trioson and Théodore Géricault.

.1825

Charles X of France crowned. Death of Jacques-Louis David and Dominique-Vivant Denon.

.1834

Gérôme begins his secondary education at the high school in Vesoul, learning Latin, Greek, and history, in addition to the subjects usually taught at the time. His drawing teacher is Claude Basile Cariage, a neoclassical painter and onetime student of Jean-Auguste-Dominique Ingres and Baron Jean-Antoine Gros. Showing a precocious talent for drawing, Gérôme attracts the attention of his master who goes on to teach him to copy from plaster casts or models he brings in from Paris.
Every year, pupils show their artworks and, in 1838, Gérôme thus exhibits for the first time, obtaining a prize for drawing.

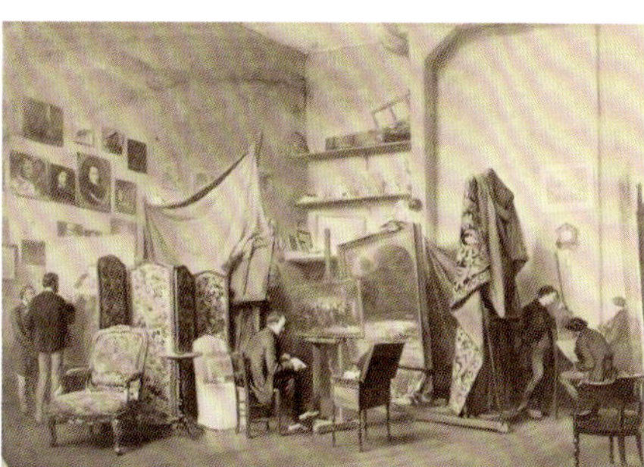

Ill. 170. Robert Jefferson Bingham (1825–1870), photograph of Louis Roux's painting *The Studio of Paul Delaroche*, 1858, albumen print, 5¾ x 8¼ in., Musée d'Orsay, Paris, inv. PHO 1983 165 159 86.

.1838

Gérôme starts painting by copying a picture by Alexandre-Gabriel Decamps, *Learned Monkey and Dogs*. So successful is it that a friend of the painter Paul Delaroche living in Vesoul decides to recommend him to the master.

.1840

Obtaining his baccalaureate in June, by autumn, aged sixteen, Gérôme leaves for the Paris studio of Delaroche (ill. 170). Delaroche was then at the summit of his fame and had just completed the fresco for the hemicycle of the École des Beaux-Arts, the most famous and most accomplished of his works. His studio, a veritable seminary for artists, was by now extremely fashionable and hugely in demand.
For three years Gérôme follows the studio routine: in the morning he draws after casts or the model; in the afternoon the pupils are left to their own devices and sketch in the street or in the countryside; they also copy engravings or old masters in the Louvre and are able to attend lessons in the École des Beaux-Arts, an opportunity of which Gérôme avails himself to improve his mastery of geometry and perspective. A group forms around him in the studio and he is soon acknowledged as its head. Members include: Jean Aubert, Eugène Damery, Henri Pierre Picou, Alfred Gobert, Jean-Louis Hamon, Alfred Arago, Ernest Hébert, Charles Landelle, Charles Jalabert, Adolphe Yvon, and Amédée-Charles-Henri de Noé.

.1841

At the end of the year, his father visits Paris and, satisfied with his son's progress, authorizes him to continue his studies. He also arranges for his son an annual allowance of 1,200 francs, making him an unusually well-off pupil. A generous friend, Gérôme willingly shares his good fortune with others. Eugène Delacroix presents his *Jewish Wedding in Morocco* to the Salon, while Ingres, after six years in Italy as director of the Académie de France at the Villa Medici, returns triumphantly to France.

.1842

Three works by Gérôme, *Monks at the Lectern*, *Chiens savants* and sketch of *A Battle*, presented at an exhibition organized by the Société d'Agriculture in Vesoul, earn Gérôme a bronze medal and a special accolade from the jury. He writes to his father: "My studies are going as well as I could hope for and M. Delaroche continues to be pleased with me" (G. Ackerman, *Jean-Léon Gérôme* [Courbevoie: ACR Édition, 2000], p. 18).

Anonymous, *Jean-Léon Gérôme drawing in his studio*, ca. 1900, albumen print, private collection.
In the background: *Venus. The Star* (1890, oil on canvas).

.1843

Delaroche, forced to close his studio after an accident, leaves for Italy and Gérôme decides to follow him. His traditional training and his interest, fueled by Delaroche, in decorative exactitude meant that he was overwhelmed by enthusiasm for the antiquities of Rome: "So here an immense horizon opens before me," he noted. He is fascinated by everything to do with gladiators (mosaics, paintings, statuettes, etc.) and cannot understand why artists have failed to turn to them for inspiration: "Of all the painters, all the sculptors who have come here and seen this, not one has thought of depicting a gladiator."
His stay in Rome is curtailed by a spell of typhoid fever. Returning at the end of the year, he realizes that, if he wishes to continue living in Rome, he has to go back to Paris and win the Prix de Rome that would entitle him to five years of paid study. Joining the studio of Charles Gleyre for three months, he makes preparations for entering the Prize and moves to the rue de Sèvres.
Gérôme's debt to Gleyre is great: his drawing improves, and he learns how to simplify and purify his forms. Gleyre also influences Gérôme's palette, which remains light in hue and luminous. Gérôme, however, does not opt for historical and mythological set pieces, preferring instead to paint genre scenes from antiquity. His intelligence and the exactitude of his figures earn him the leadership of a coterie of Néo-Grec painters, such as Auguste Toulmouche, J. E. Aubert, Jean-Louis Hamon, and Timoléon Lobrichon. Their works are well executed and often charming but, in Ackerman's words, "sometimes mannered, and their subjects simplistic."

.1844

Delaroche returns from Rome and Gérôme leaves Gleyre to become his assistant for about a year. Gustave Courbet enters the Salon with *Self-Portrait with Black Dog*.

.1845

Gérôme collaborates with Delaroche on a commission for the museum of history at Versailles: *Charlemagne Crossing the Alps and Forcing the Gorges of Mount Cenci, Guarded by the Lombards*. Théophile Gautier publishes *Le Roi Candaule*; and Charles Baudelaire pens his first major work, *Le Salon de 1845*.

.1846

The brotherhood of the "Néo-Grecs," Gérôme, Hamon, Picou and Boulanger, settle together in "Le Chalet," a house divided into several studios on 27 rue de Fleurus, close to the Luxembourg. According to Ackerman, it was probably there, far from the earnest ambience of Gleyre's studio, that these painters would have developed the *style néogrec*. Turning their backs on the seriousness and sobriety of classicism, they opted for lighter, witty themes. They earned the name Néo-Grecs from their predilection for subjects from antiquity, though they were also to some extent regarded as successors to the neoclassical tendency.
As envisaged, Gérôme enters the Prix de Rome and is listed third for his first offering (a sketch after an antique cast). His second entry, however, a composition on the theme of Jacob blessing the children of Joseph, is not ranked at all as the style of the figures, he is told, is "defective."
To "make good" this failure Delaroche advises him to paint a picture with two life-size figures and prepare for the Salon of 1847. In this new composition, Gérôme plans to incorporate both human figures and animals. To pave the way as best as possible for his work, he spends several months going each morning to the Jardin des Plantes to sketch the animals, together with his friends, the sculptors Emmanuel Fremiet and Henri Jacquemart.
In parallel, Queen Marie-Amélie commissions him to produce a copy of Delaroche's *Saint Amélie* and an ornamental panel for a room in the Louvre representing Henri II, after the portrait in the Uffizi ascribed to François Clouet. This constitutes Gérôme's first official order (copies were a frequent means for the State to help young artists).

.1847

Heeding Delaroche's counsel, Gérôme unveils his celebrated *Cock Fight* (cat. 10) at the Salon and wins a third-class medal. He sells the picture to a M. Roux-Labourie for the sum of one thousand francs. Gérôme gains a measure of notoriety, emerging as the figurehead of the Néo-Grec movement. His picture is noticed by Théophile Gautier, who soon becomes a firm supporter of the painter. The poet and art critic writes: "Appearing at first sight to be of the utmost vulgarity, the subject acquires, under Gérôme's fine pencil and delicate brush, rare elegance and exquisite distinction." Gautier's authority was such that the picture became famous. It is a work that belongs to Gérôme's early style when he was under the influence of Gleyre. Thereafter, Gérôme almost completely abandoned compositions presenting life-sized figures.

.1848

At the time of the 1848 revolution, Gérôme becomes a member of the National Guard, being elected captain of the headquarters at the École des Beaux-Arts. The precise nature of Gérôme's duties at the head of this unit is not known. He clearly had the blessing of the republican government, though, like most artists in the second half of the century, he asserted neutrality in political affairs.
Gérôme begins receiving a host of government commissions that mean he will no longer be in financial straits. The City of Paris buys an allegory of the new Republic for 12,000 francs produced by Gérôme in response to a competition.
At the Salon, he unveils a portrait of his brother Armand (cat. 34), *The Virgin, the Infant Jesus, and Saint John* (cat. 13), as well as *Anacreon* (cat. 16), an order from the interior ministry for the museum in Toulouse, costing 1,800 francs and for which he obtains a second-class medal.

.1850

Shows *Drunken Bacchus and Cupid,* as well as *A Greek Interior* at the Salon (cat.26 and cat.23). The first picture will be bought by the State for the museum at Bordeaux, and the second by Prince Napoleon, though the chosen subject created something of a scandal.
In Paris, Gérôme decorates the refectory of the priory of St.-Martin-des-Champs (an interior destroyed in 1965). During the summer, he goes to paint in Barbizon where he is to stay on many occasions between 1850 and 1856.

.1852

Presents a second *Paestum* at the Salon, having shown a painting on the same subject at the Salon of 1849.
For the Exposition Universelle of 1855, the government asks him for a large allegorical picture on a subject of his choice. He decides to tackle the "Age of Augustus."
Gérôme embarks on a journey to central Europe, his final destination being Russia, but he is diverted to Austria by the Crimean War. He follows the course of the Danube, reaching Constantinople. In Romania, he misses the Black Sea boat and has to wait for the next crossing. Gérôme wiles away the time making sketches of a Russian military camp nearby. One morning, he observes a scene full of irony: a Russian officer insists that some of the soldiers forcibly enrolled by the Russians should make music and sing and dance. The result is the picture, *Recreation in a Russian Camp*, 1854 (cat. 107).

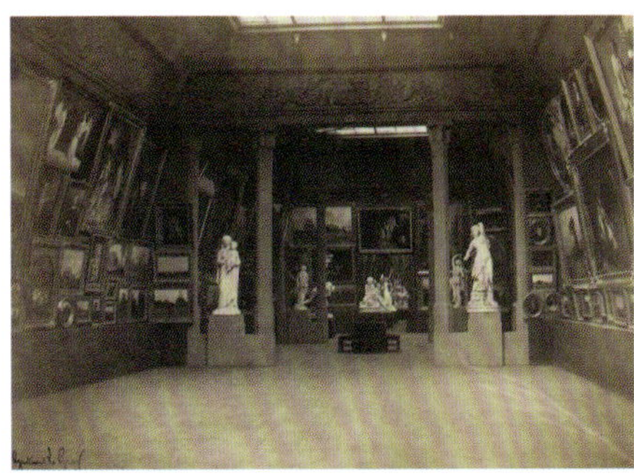

Ill. 171. Gustave Le Gray (1820–1884), *View of the Salon of 1853*, 1853, albumen print, 9¾ x 13¼ in., Musée d'Orsay, Paris, inv. PHO 2000 13 2.

.1853

He sends to the Salon (ill. 171) a *Study of a Dog*, a painted frieze intended for the Sèvres vase to be presented to Prince Albert at the 1855 Exposition Universelle, as well as a large *Idylle* (cat. 29).

.1854

Decorates the St.-Jérôme chapel in the church of St.-Séverin in Paris.

.1855

At the Exposition Universelle he presents *Recreation in a Russian Camp* and *A Flock Tender*, a picture bought by Napoleon III. His painting *The Age of Augustus* receives a mixed reception as it is thought too similar to Ingres's *Apotheosis of Homer*.
He is named Knight of the Legion of Honor and moves into 70 rue Notre-Dame-des-Champs.
Produces seven full-size figures representing the Nations to decorate the transept of the Palais de l'Industrie at the Exposition. He is awarded a second-class medal.
The first personal public exhibition by an artist is held: Courbet's "Pavillon du Réalisme."

.1856

Gérôme leaves Paris and sets out for Egypt, staying there for eight months. This marks the first in a series of regular journeys to the Middle East, especially to Egypt and Asia Minor. As he explains: "My short stay in Constantinople had whetted my appetite and the Orient was my most frequent dream" (G. Ackerman, *Jean-Léon Gérôme* [Courbevoie: ACR Édition, 2000], p.42). He is accompanied by Auguste Bartholdi (who had brought material to take photographs) and the painters Léon Charles Bailly and Narcisse Berchère.
Death of his master Delaroche.

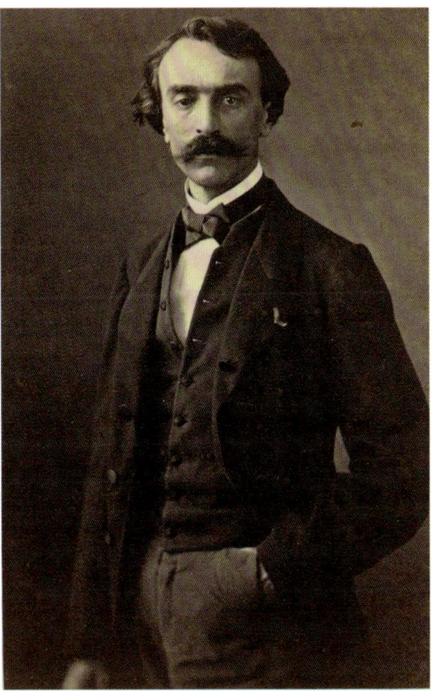

Ill. 172. Félix Nadar (1820–1910), *Gérôme, Painter and Sculptor Born in Vesoul 1824, Died 1904*, ca. 1857–65, albumen print, 3 ¾ x 2½ in., Musée d'Orsay, Paris, inv. PHO 1995 6 285.

.1857

Gérôme (ill. 172) presents at the Salon *Egyptian Recruits Crossing the Desert*, *Memnon and Sesostris*, *Camels at the Watering Place*, and *Duel after the Ball* (cat. 51). This last, a great success at the Salon, is snapped up by the duc d'Aumale.
He moves nearer the Luxembourg, into a series of artists' studios parceled out by the father of Auguste Toulmouche and known as the "Boîte à thé" ("tea caddy"). Toulmouche, Hamon, Picou, Paul Baudry and Lecomte du Nouÿ all have their studio near where Gérôme lives.
Courbet shows *Young Ladies on the Banks of the Seine* at the Salon.

.1858

Gérôme collaborates on the interior of Prince Napoleon's neo-Pompeian house erected on avenue Montaigne in Paris and produces the livery for Pope Pius IX's railway coach for an Italian firm.

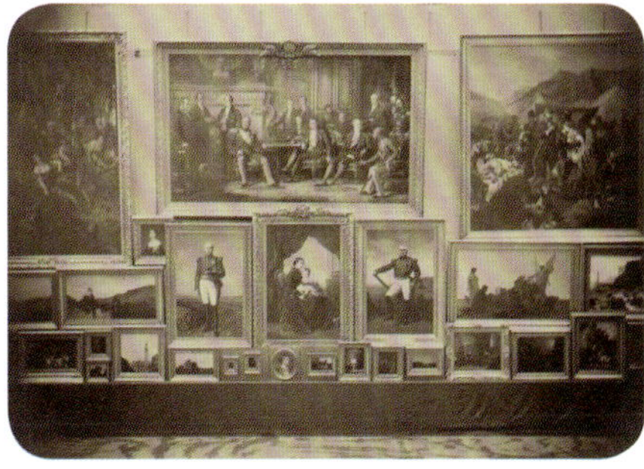

Ill. 173. Pierre-Ambroise Richebourg (1810–1875), *View of one of the rooms of the Salon of 1857, held in the Palais de l'Industrie*, 1857, albumen print, 8 ¾ x 12 ¾ in., Musée d'Orsay, Paris, inv. PHO 2000 13 6.

.1859

Gérôme sends to the Salon *King Candaules* (cat. 43), *Dead Caesar* (ill. 56, p. 122), and *Ave Caesar, morituri te salutant* (cat. 70).
He sets up in business with Adolphe Goupil, his future father-in-law: up to the First World War, 337 pictures by the artist will be sold through the gallery, while the publisher issues some 370 reproductions. With links to many international dealers, Goupil has several branches abroad, enabling him to sell paintings by Gérôme, whose work proves especially attractive to well-heeled American clients. Indeed Gérôme's fame derives, among other things, from the many reproductions of his works produced by Goupil.

.1860

Gérôme buys the château at Coulevon, close to Vesoul, moving in his parents. He opens a private studio.

.1861

At the Salon he presents *Phryné before the Areopagus* (cat. 45), *Socrates Seeking Alcibiades at the House of Aspasia* (ill. 53, p. 110), and *The Two Augurs*, as well as *Rembrandt Etching a Plate in his Atelier*.
He also provides three panels for the *triclinium* in the Prince Napoleon's residence on avenue Montaigne on Homeric themes: *The Iliad* and *The Odyssey* (cat. 33).
Accepting one last government commission, he presents *The Reception of the Siamese Ambassadors at Fontainebleau* (cat. 94).
He lends his picture *The Prisoner* (cat. 127) for an exhibition at the museum in Nantes, which acquires it for 10,000 francs.
Gérôme fights in a duel, probably over a woman. He is struck by a bullet and could easily have lost a hand. The business is hushed up, especially because in 1863 he is to marry the daughter of his dealer, Adolphe Goupil.

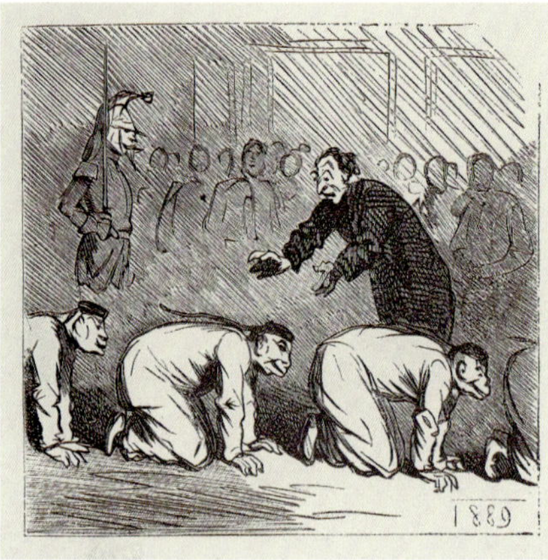

Ill. 174. Cham [Amédée de Noé] (1818–1879), "Gérôme. The interpreter hopelessly trying to make the Siamese ambassadors understand that they are not at court in order to play a game of leapfrog," in *Le Salon de 1865 photographié par Cham* (Paris: Arnauld de Vresse, 1865), Bibliothèque du Musée des Arts Décoratifs, Paris, G 271, vol. 9.

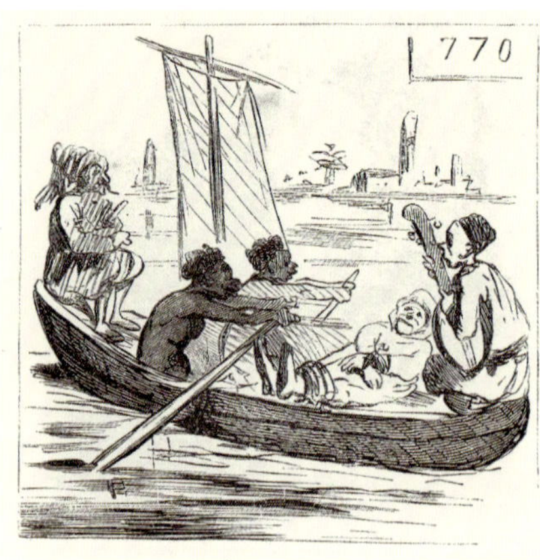

Ill. 175. Cham [Amédée de Noé] (1818–1879), "Though very well tied up, a gentleman lies on the bottom of his small boat, M. Gérôme having told him he was not sufficiently well dressed to be seen (another of this artist's jokes)," in *Cham au Salon de 1863* (Paris: Maison Martinet, 1863), Bibliothèque du Musée des Arts Décoratifs, Paris, G 271, vol. 9.

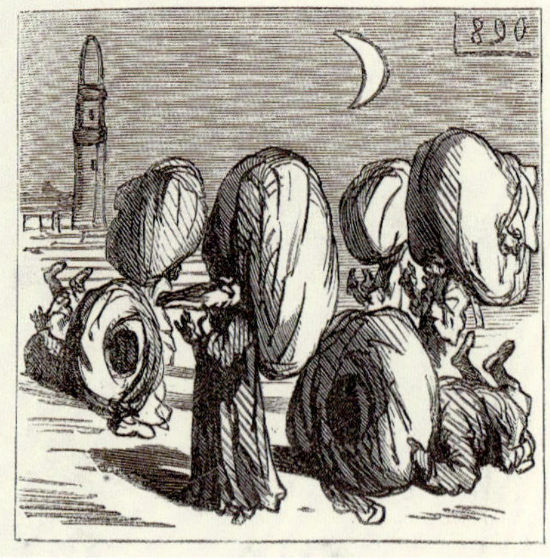

Ill. 176. Cham [Amédée de Noé] (1818–1879), "Gérôme. When one decides to wear a turban, one should not hold back," in *Le Salon de 1865 photographié par Cham* (Paris: Arnauld de Vresse, 1865), Bibliothèque du Musée des Arts Décoratifs, Paris, G 271, vol. 9.

.1862

He leaves on a journey to Egypt and Syria, where he crosses the desert for the first time.

.1863

Gérôme marries Marie Goupil and moves into a mansion at 6 rue de Bruxelles, close to the place de Clichy. They will have five children, including a daughter, Jeanne, born at the end of the year. He sends to the Salon *The Greek Comedians, A Turkish Butcher Boy in Jerusalem* (cat. 143), *The Prisoner* (cat. 127 and ill. 175) and *Molière Breakfasting with Louis XIV* (cat. 84). *The Prisoner* is a triumph at the Salon and remains one of the artist's most celebrated works.
Following the scandal of the Salon des Refusés, an imperial decree suppresses the Académie's control over the Salon and the École des Beaux-Arts. Teaching at the École is also modified. Three painting studios are set up and Gérôme is named head of one of them.

.1864

Gérôme shows *Dance of the Almeh* (cat. 154) and *Portrait of Amédée Thierry* at the Salon.

.1865

He presents *The Reception of the Siamese Ambassadors at Fontainebleau* (cat. 94 and ill. 174) and *Prayer* at the Salon.
He is appointed member of the Institut.
Birth of his son Jean.
Edgar Degas and Claude Monet mark their debut at the Salon with, respectively, *Scene of War in the Middle Ages* and *The Seine Estuary at Honfleur*.

.1866

Gérôme sends to the Salon *Cleopatra before Caesar* and *Heads of the Rebel Beys at the Mosque El Assaneyn* (cat. 144). This second picture creates a stir as many observers think that the severed human heads resemble those of some Parisian critics (ill. 182).
Alfred Sisley and Frédéric Bazille are accepted at the Salon. Paul Cézanne though is rejected.

.1867

Gérôme sends to the Salon *The Slave Market* (cat. 156) and *Old Clothes Merchant of Cairo*.
The Exposition Universelle takes place the same year: Gérôme presents thirteen paintings and obtains a medal of honor with *The Death of Caesar* (cat. 67). He is promoted to the rank of Officer of the Legion of Honor.
Birth of his daughter Suzanne, the future Mme. Aimé Morot.

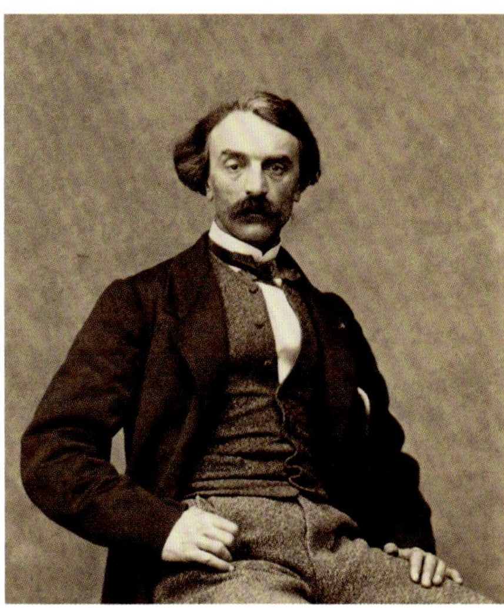

Ill. 177. Goupil & Cie, *J. L. Gérôme*, ca. 1880–90, frontispiece to album, 12 ¼ x 9 ½ in., Getty Research Institute, Los Angeles, inv. 90.R.26.

.1868

Gérôme asks for a sabbatical from the École des Beaux-Arts, leaving the running of his studio in the hands of his friend Gustave Boulanger. He sets out once again for Egypt and Asia Minor, visiting Cairo, Jerusalem, Giza, and crosses the Sinai Desert. His traveling companions are, among others, Albert Goupil (his brother-in-law), his pupil Paul Lenoir, the journalist and novelist Edmond About, the Dutch painter Willem de Farmas Testas, Léon Bonnat, and the journalist Frédéric Masson. Though they hardly venture farther than a hundred kilometers from Cairo, they explore regions rarely visited by travelers and require the assistance of a guide. Gérôme, thanks to the many sketches carried out during his travels, now has a vast range of subjects at his command.
He returns to Paris shortly before the 1868 Salon and exhibits *The Death of Marshal Ney* (cat. 93) and *Golgotha* (cat. 78).
Birth of a fourth child, Blanche.

.1869

Gérôme forms part of the large contingent of French artists and writers dispatched to the inauguration of the Suez Canal. He spends three months traveling about Cairo and Upper Egypt.

.1870

At the outbreak of the Franco-Prussian War, Gérôme moves his more valuable property from his Parisian residence to the home in Bougival. As German troops approach, he leaves for England to guarantee the safety of his wife and children. He returns to France to take part in the defense of Paris but remains only a short time in the capital, which he leaves in extremis in autumn 1870. He thus abandons his house and studio to its fate and moves to London until the end of hostilities. He most probably meets John Abbott McNeill Whistler at this juncture.
Already an honorary member of the Royal Academy since 1869, his reputation precedes him; he exhibits at the institution both in 1870 and 1871.
He paints *Moorish Bath* (cat. 166), the first picture in a series on the hammam, and *Public Prayer in the Mosque of Amr* (cat. 146), the first work to focus on the interior of a mosque.

.1871

As soon as the siege is lifted, he returns to Paris in June.
Gérôme resumes his activities at the Institut and at the École des Beaux-Arts, before setting off for Turkey.

.1873

At an exhibition on the Place Vendôme, he presents *For Sale* (cat. 157) and his famous *Pollice Verso* (cat. 71) These two pictures will also be exhibited at the Vienna world's fair.
Passing through Spain on his way to Algeria and Egypt, he is filled with enthusiasm for the Velázquezes he sees in the Prado. His stay in Algiers is curtailed by an attack of dysentery.
He draws vignettes for La Fontaine's *Fables*, takes sculpture lessons in Fremiet's studio, receiving advice from Bartholdi, Jacquemart, and Degas.

.1874

He sends *The Grey Cardinal* (cat. 85), *Rex Tibicen*, and *A Collaboration* to the Salon, receiving a gold medal for the three pictures. A section of the critical establishment and the public protests: gold medals are not intended for genre painters. Gérôme is in Holland when he hears of these objections and telegraphs at once to refuse the award, but the jury stands firm. In the end, Gérôme donates the medal (valued at 4,000 *francs-or*) to the benefit of students of the École des Beaux-Arts.
The Grey Cardinal quickly joins *Pollice Verso* in an American collection, but both works also become widely known in France through photoengravings.
Writes an autobiography of twenty-seven manuscript pages, entitled *Notes autobiographiques*, addressed to his friend Charles Timbal.
He is raised to the rank of Commander of the Legion of Honor, chairs a committee on the organization of a banquet in honor of Camille Corot, and busies himself collecting funds for the victims of the great Chicago fire.
Returns to Egypt with his pupils Julius L. Stewart and Paul Lenoir. The latter though falls sick on the road and dies in Cairo.

.1875

Birth of Madeleine, his fifth and final child.
He goes to more funerals of fellow artists, in February attending that of Corot. In the course of the funeral oration, the priest launches out on the theme of the immoral life of artists. Finding these remarks intolerable, Gérôme leaves the church in indignation.
He travels to Constantinople for a second time, staying with the sultan's painter, Abdullah Siriez.

.1876

Gérôme is appointed to the higher council for the Beaux-Arts.

.1877

He leaves for Naples.

.1878

During the Exposition Universelle he receives a medal of honor for painting and shows his first large-scale sculpture, *The Gladiators* (cat. 76). Awarded a second-class medal for sculpture and, in spite of its success and the significant investment the piece represents, Gérôme declines to sell it. Less concerned now with the Salon, he increasingly turns to sculpture and away from painting.
His friend Bartholdi unveils *Liberty Enlightening the World* (The Statue of Liberty).

.1879

Gérôme travels through Turkey.

.1880

He undertakes a final journey to Egypt.

.1881

Leaves for Greece.
First Salon des Artistes Français at the Palais de l'Industrie on the Champs-Élysées, independent of the State (replacing the traditional Salon).

.1882

He sends to the Salon *The Tulip Folly* (cat. 87).
With Benjamin-Constant, he produces illustrations for Victor Hugo's poem *Les Orientales*. Gérôme is a member of the jury at the second Salon des Artistes Français. Cézanne is admitted for the first time.

.1883

Gérôme visits Spain.
He paints one of his more significant history paintings: *The Christian Martyrs' Last Prayers* (cat. 80), a painting ordered in 1860 by a Mr. Walters of Baltimore.

.1884

Gérôme is struck by a series of bereavements between 1884 and 1891, losing successively his father, his brother-in-law, his father-in-law, Paul Baudry (a close friend), Gustave Boulanger, and his son.
He opposes the exhibition of pictures by Édouard Manet at the École des Beaux-Arts, explaining that the artist "might have done good pictures. He has been the apostle of the decadent manner." He goes so far as to pen a letter of protest to arts minister Jules Ferry, suggesting that works by the creator of *Olympia* would be better shown at the Folies-Bergère. The scandal arising from this unforgivable insult to Manet forces Gérôme to back down. Finally, after visiting the retrospective, Gérôme concedes: "They're not as bad as I'd feared."

.1886

Gérôme produces illustrations for Victor Hugo's poetry collection, *La Légende des siècles*, and exhibits *Oedipus* (cat. 92).

.1887

He unveils *Omphale* at the Salon, a white marble statue that meets with great success. The State offers to acquire it but Gérôme declines the proposal, explaining that the Beaux-Arts administration has little funding to buy works from artists and that such sums should not be spent on those who, like him, earn a good living.

.1888

Gérôme leaves for London.

.1889

He leaves for Italy.
Exposition Universelle in Paris.

.1890

Gérôme stays in Sicily with his friend the duc d'Aumale. He writes the foreword for a book by Maurice Valette, *Les Révolutions dans l'art*.
He presents *Tanagra* (cat. 168) at the Salon. The piece is bought by the State for ten thousand francs after an agreement made with the artist stipulates that the payment should not come from the sculpture purchasing fund.
In the 1890s, he receives a large number of commissions for painted and carved portraits, in the main from friends: *Bust of Dieterle, Bust of Prévost Paradol, Bust of P. H. Rousseau*…

.1891

He carves *Grief* for his son's tomb in the cemetery at Montmartre.

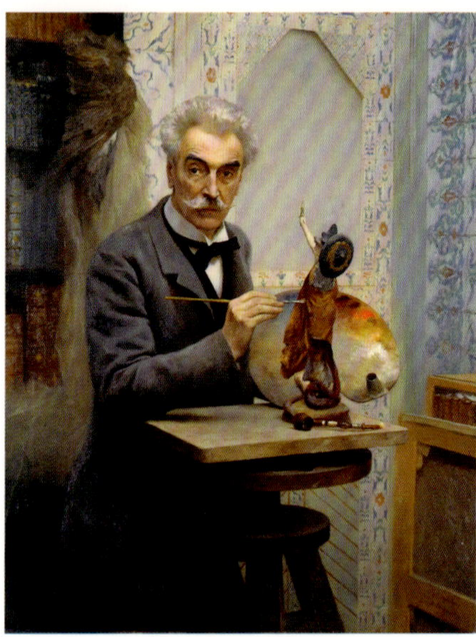

Ill. 178. Fernand Cormon (1845–1924), *Le Sculptor at Work. Jean-Léon Gérôme Painting* Bellona, 1891, oil on canvas, 51 x 39 ½ in., Musée Georges-Garret, Vesoul, inv. 87-602.

.1892

At the Salon he exhibits *Pygmalion and Galatea*, as well as *Bellona* (cat. 175 and 182, ill. 178).

.1893

Gérôme is named honorary president of the Société des Peintres Orientalistes Français.
He presents *The Serpent Charmer* (cat. 160) at the World's Columbian Exhibition in Chicago.
In the picture *Sculpturae vitam insufflat pictura* (cat. 174), the painter comments on his work as a sculptor.

.1894

After Alfred Dreyfus is condemned, Gérôme paints *Truth at the Bottom of the Well*, showing it the following year at the Salon. He endeavors to prevent the Gustave Caillebotte bequest.

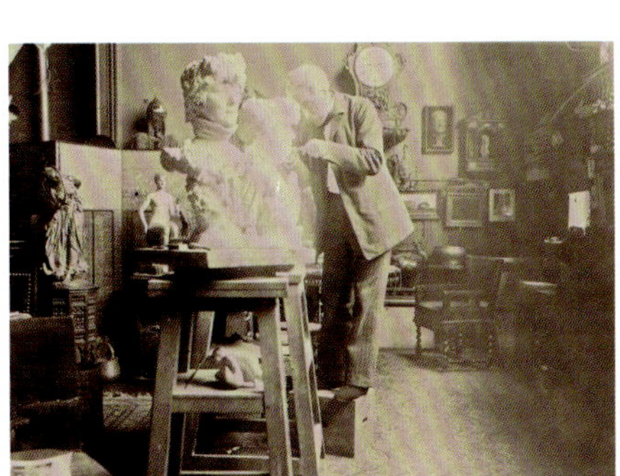

Ill. 179. Anonymous, Jean-Léon Gérôme working on the bust of *Sarah Bernhardt* in his studio, ca. 1895, albumen print, 4 3/4 x 6 1/2 in., Musée d'Orsay, Paris, Gérôme-Morot archives, 2003-647. Visible left to right: on the openwork oriental table a large version (bronze?) of the *Hoop Dancer* (cat. 171b), before the partition a reduced polychrome version of *Tanagra* (cat. 168) and in the alcove of the tabernacle hung on the back wall, right, another reduced version of *Hoop Dancer* (cat. 172).

.1895
Gérôme makes a polychrome bust of *Sarah Bernhardt* (cat. 187).

.1896
Paints *Truth Coming Out of Her Well to Shame Mankind* (cat. 99).

.1897
Towards the end of his life, Gérôme makes a series of small sculptures intended for mass production. He works for almost ten years on a series of historical figures on horseback. The first, *Napoleon Entering Cairo*, much commented on at the Salon of 1897, is bought for ten thousand francs by the State for the Musée du Luxembourg.

.1898
Exhibits *Tamerlane* (cat. 183).

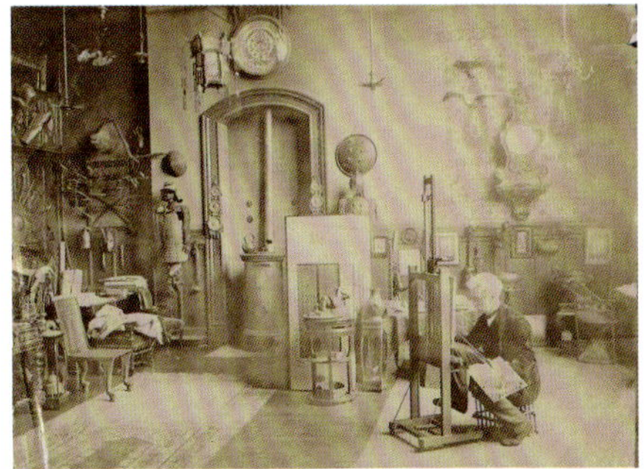

Ill. 180. Anonymous, Gérôme painting in his studio, ca. 1900, albumen print, 8 x 10½ in., Gérôme-Morot archives, Musée d'Orsay, Paris, inv. PHO 2003 4 27.

.1899
Travels to northern Italy with the painters Georges Clairin, Édouard Detaille and François Flameng. They visit Florence, and probably Venice and Padua. On his return, he distances himself from the sculptors he had gone there to admire, referring in a letter to Detaille to "Donatellian jokes in Florence."
The inauguration of his monument to the duc d'Aumale in Chantilly is a success.
He carves *Frederick the Great* and *Caesar Crossing the Rubicon*.

.1900
He is named Grand Officer of the Legion of Honor, the highest rank in the Order. At the inauguration of the Exposition Universelle of 1900, he launches a memorable attack on the school of modern painting. As the president of the Republic is on the point of entering the room devoted to the Impressionists, Gérôme is meant to have buttonholed him with "Stop, Mr. President, we have here a dishonor for France!" In spite of his opposition, the Impressionists carry the day.

.1901
Gérôme shows *The Expiring Eagle of Waterloo*, for a monument in memory of the last combatants of the Grande Armée that will be inaugurated shortly after the death of the artist.

.1902
After forty years as a professor, Gérôme leaves his studio at the École des Beaux-Arts. He presents the life-size polychrome marble version of his *The Ball Player* (cat. 189) at the Salon.

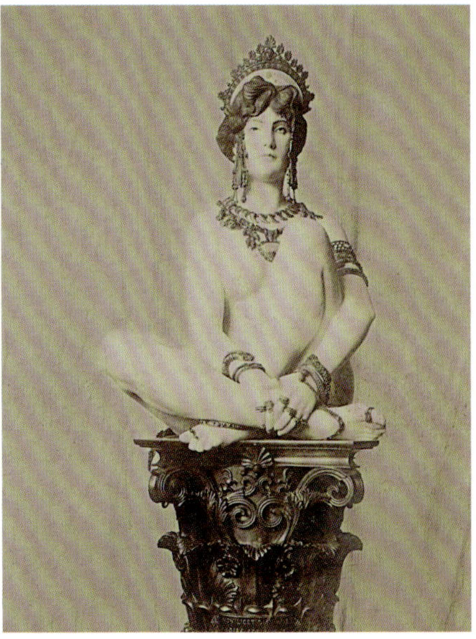

Ill. 181. Anonymous, *Corinth*, ca. 1904, albumen print, 6½ x 4 in., Gérôme-Morot archives, Musée d'Orsay, Paris, inv. PHO 2003 4 17.

.1903
He presents at the Salon his two final canvases: *Sermon in the Mosque* and *View of Medinet El-Fayoum*. He tries to prevent the Amis du Luxembourg from organizing an exhibition of works by Manet, Monet, Camille Pissarro and other Impressionists in two of the museum's rooms.
The Salon d'Automne is set up by the Fauves.

.1904
Jean-Léon Gérôme dies on January 10, 1904, aged eighty. At the time of his death, his studio is still crammed with plaster casts as well as marbles and bronzes. Many of the former, like some of the marbles, are removed to the museum at Vesoul, while others find their way onto the art market.
He wished for a simple funeral, without all the military pageantry to which his rank in the Legion of Honor entitled him. His burial was, however, extremely well attended: the president of the Senate, the director of the Beaux-Arts, a former president of the Republic, Casimir-Périer, the mayor of Vesoul, as well as Bartholdi, Henri Harpignies, Lecomte du Nouÿ, Victor Clairin, and Carolus-Duran.
Gérôme is interred in the Montmartre cemetery.
Although his style was by then outdated, Gérôme had remained in the limelight and his death was noted throughout the Western world, as far as the United States. His output is reckoned to amount to six hundred canvases, the majority sold abroad, sixty sculptures, and hundreds of drawings and studies.
The inventory of his mansion on the boulevard de Clichy is estimated at two hundred thousand francs and the estate valued at a million *francs-or*.

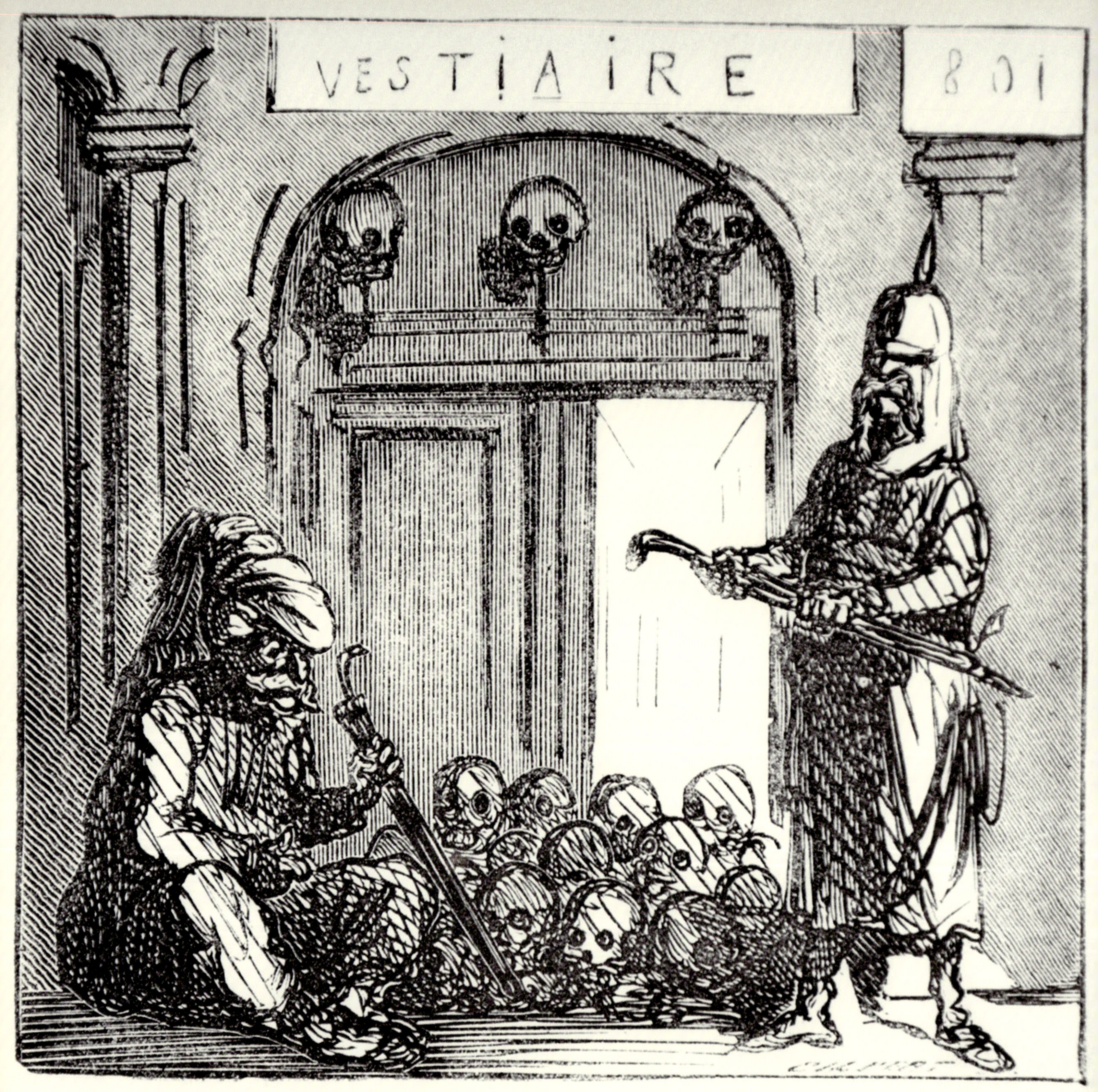

GÉROME.

La Porte d'une mosquée.

— Messieurs, vous êtes priés de déposer vos têtes et vo
parapluies au vestiaire.

ANTHOLOGY OF ARTICLES

Translated from the French by Jonathan Sly

Théophile Gautier,
"Young Greeks at a Cock Fight,"
***L'Artiste*, 4th ser., vol. 9 (1847), p. 221**

Let us rejoice that the seemingly distracted jury at the Salon of 1847 has admitted a charming tableau of great finesse and originality by a previously unheard-of young man, making his debut at the Salon, if we are not mistaken. We are talking of M. Gérôme's *The Cock Fight*.

M. Gérôme's exquisite lines and delicate brush transform this apparently vulgar subject with a rare elegance and refined distinction; the artist's choice of theme may lead one to expect a smaller canvas, as is the wont with such fancies. The figures are however life-size and receive a thoroughly historical treatment. Great talent and resources are required to elevate such a minor scene to the rank of a noble composition that no master would disown.

A chipped-nosed marble sphinx leans against a dry fountain, surrounded by the lush vegetation of warmer climes—arbutus, myrtles, and oleanders, the metallic leaves of which stand out against the calm azure of the sea separated from the azure of the heavens by the violet crest of a promontory. At the foot of the fountain are two adolescents, an ephebe and maiden, who goad the brave birds of Mars into battle.

The young girl leans upon the cage in which the bellicose fowl were contained, in a pose full of grace and elegance. Her pure, slender hands are crossed and delightfully poised; one arm gently presses her budding breast and her bust has that serpentine curve so sought after by the ancients; her foreshortened limbs are skillfully drawn; her head, crowned in exquisite taste with a coronet of ash-blond hair, the delicate tones of which gently contrast with the skin, has a childish sweetness, and a virginal delicacy; her eyes lowered and mouth parting in a smile of triumph—for her cock appears to have the advantage—the maiden casts a distracted eye at the struggle, certain that her wager is won. Nothing could be more delightful than this figure covered only in white and yellow drapery held to her sloping contours by a slender mauve cord; the collection of soft harmonious tones enhances the golden whiteness of the young Greek's body.

The kneeling boy, his hair decked with a wild wreath of leaves plucked from the bushes to hand, leans towards his cock, and strives to kindle its valor. His features, although perhaps too model-like, are drawn with extreme finesse, and we can see that his full attention and soul are focused on the peripeteia of the combat.

The fowls themselves are marvels of drawing, animation and color; Sneyders, Weenix, Oudry, Desportes, Rousseau, or any of the animal painters took twenty years of work to attain the perfection M. Gérôme achieves immediately.

Black and lustrous, with glints of green, neck bent, its triple collar of feathers bristling, eye a-fury, crest bloody, beak open, legs drawn up to its breast, one cock lunges airborne, presenting its adversary two stars of menacing claws and formidable spurs, a marvel of pose, drawing, and color.

The cock with the copper plumage with its russet tones, pinned to the ground, slyly raising its head, and proffering its beak like a glaive on which to skewer his vigilant adversary, is no less worthy of admiration. What is especially remarkable in these cocks is the elegance and singular nobility they bring to their perfect verisimilitude. These are epic, Olympian birds, such as Phidias might have sculpted at the feet of the cruel god Ares, borne by Hera unassisted by Zeus.

These juveniles and cocks make M. Gérôme's picture one of the most charming canvases of the exhibition. What more exquisite way to ornament the banquet hall of a king?

M. Metzmacher's engraving marvelously translates the painter's charming and delicate line; the engraving even manages to render the harmoniously sober color of this painting, justly admired for its style and element of surprise.

Ill. 182. Cham [Amédée de Noé] (1819–1879), "The Doorway of a Mosque," in *Le Salon de 1866 photographié par Cham*, Bibliothèque du Musée des Arts Décoratifs, Paris, cote G 271, vol. 9.

L. Clément de Ris,
***L'Artiste*, 4th. ser., vol. 9 (1847), p. 123**

The success of M. Gérôme, who is exhibiting for the first time in his career, was most outstanding, and let us say outright, most deserved for a debut. One of our finest critics, M. Théophile Gautier, was the first, I believe, to draw attention to *The Cock Fight* (705), and he did so with warmth, color, and an intelligent fellowship for youth in need of a helping hand, which marred nothing of the value of M. Gérôme's work. However, now that this early passion has subsided, and that we can judge the work with a mind less charged and more composed, we must acknowledge that the work is by no means a masterpiece and that many of its parts suffer from an absence of essential qualities. The movement of the young man, leaning over to goad his cock, lacks naturalness and is composed as an academy study; the girl's head is charming and would have considerable grace in any subject, but her movement is not in keeping with the scene taking place before her; her stomach is bereft of form and resembles a dishcloth on a clothes line; the position of the thighs and legs is unjustified; finally, under the pretext no doubt of rendering the bistre tones with which the sun tans the skin of Hellenes, M. Gérôme has given his characters a dull uniform color, like that of old parchment. For us, the painting's merit is to be found in the two cocks painted and drawn to satisfy the finest of London's connoisseurs. The movement of the black cock in particular, tousled by anger, crest aflame, claws fraught, its wings a frenzy of excitement, shows truth in observation and precision of execution which we readily acknowledge and which justifies us in classifying M. Gérôme as an animal artist. More than promise, M. Gérôme has expressed his commitment, and we confidently await his work at the next Salon.

Francis Wey,
***Le Courrier français*, Apr. 13, 1847**

It is our good fortune to report a debut promising great expectations: the source of this satisfaction is M. Gérôme, author of *The Cock Fight*. What naïve, spring-like grace is often expressed in the first paintings of gifted young men, who, dearly in love with their art, bring forth a work embellished with bright exhilaration and all the freshness of first love. M. Gérôme's painting inspires just such thoughts. Surrounded by the hinterlands of the ancient Greek coastline, where the arabesques of the architecture seem to have flowered, among the acanthuses and lotuses, from the very soil beneath them, two adolescents—two lovers perchance, if they have already felt the budding of their youth and the flourish of their mutual beauty—squat nonchalantly at the foot of a cenotaph: the boy takes great pleasure in goading on a cock, somewhat lacking belligerence; his daydreaming, more carefree companion, has launched her champion, crest ablaze, eye agleam, a beast which the weaker hand and marbled skin, the pale rose of adolescence, would have pained to hold.
The storm winds of passion rise from the waves of plumage of the warrior birds cloaked in gold and scarlet. Draping herself on the grass, her hair as golden as Ceres, her pose redolent of the coquettish simplicity of the Athenian women of the temple of Pericles, through two rows of blond lashes, the pale girl casts a marble gaze to her marble breast, while her limpid beauty unites the ideals and graces of poetry at its most chaste with the sensual reality of Ionian statuary. As we contemplate this divine child, caressed but not concealed by her damp diaphanous fabric, woven from an impalpable thread which the fleeting night allows the first shards of sunlight to tear from its trailing cloak of mist; and as we stray among these contours polished like ivory, and dream amid this half-naked beauty ignorant of its nudity, we readily forget the two rival cocks, their quarrel and fanfare: it is surprising to see a handsome young man so occupied in encouraging a brave but intimidated fowl. The antagonist, which the gentle girl contemplates with a curious interest mingled with fear, is much more passionate; roused by its fury, it springs backwards, breathing only that relentless war of which love, it is said, is the principle in the civilization of the fowl; if this contrast is allegorical, we may readily guess that Venus Erycina will wreak her vengeance.
There is in this painting a gentleness, an elevation, an Asian *morbidezza*, and an intimate assimilation of the Greek style and sentiment, which has all the charm of a Moschus idyll and of the Sicilian muse when she sighs.
If, however, overcoming the seduction so fragrant and florid, we were to descend into the depths of truth and its dark and frozen lair, we would be obliged to add that the balance in execution of the two figures is insufficient. The modeling of the young man is much more solidly accentuated than that of the maiden; the girl, in contrast, seems to lack relief. One of the characters appears more real than the other; this character we see; the other seems to evoke the ivory gates leading to the aerial cortege of dreams.

Théophile Thoré,
***Salon de 1847*, p. 445**

We have discovered another young painter, who displays a certain distinction of style even though he does come from M. Delaroche's studio. M. Léon Gérôme is only twenty years old, apparently, the lucky artist! His *Cock Fight* has an air of Theocritus about it and the gentle poetry of the ancients. The Greek girl reclines languidly, her expression delicate, watching the two cocks goaded on by her half-naked brother, who kneels forward on the radiant sand. The illustration of the figures is correct without being cold; the color is sober, accurate, and harmonious. How did the selection jury let this first work from a nameless beginner slip through?

F. de Lagenerais,
***Revue des Deux Mondes*, 2nd qtr 1848, pp. 288–89**

M. Gérôme made his debut so successfully last year, and looked to be following in the footsteps of M. Ingres through a precise, learned style with a certain fluidity of youth and naïvety. This time, he seems to have eagerly exaggerated the qualities and, unfortunately, the flaws of his famous master; his main composition, representing Anacreon, Bacchus, and Eros contains charming details and shows intense and conscientious study. The breath of antiquity animates the whole work, which resembles a fragment of idyll purloined from the muse of André Chénier:
Come, oh divine Bacchus! Come Thyoneus ever young!
Come, as when in Naxos lone and wild
Thy voice did soothe the fears of Minos's child.[1]
...
The broad flanked tiger, furrowed with dark stains,
The fierce panther and starred lynx
That led thee with thy court to these brinks.
On wheels and axles gold shone everywhere;
The Maenads ran with loose and streaming hair,
And sang Bacchus, Evius and Thyroneus![2]

In M. Gérôme's composition we find something of the movement and color of this vivid portrayal. It is unfortunate however that the systematic dryness of execution, flattening of form, exaggerated and constant dampening of color, as well as the confines of the painter's task where abstraction is made of relief and shade, deny this highly commendable work almost all its charm. Each figure stands out as a misty or grayish brown silhouette against a crudely radiant sky, in such a way that at first glance M. Gérôme's painting resembles a cut-out stage set. The exaggerated precision in the details of certain accessories gives this composition a somewhat barren appearance, which is anything but appealing. The Greek vases for example placed near the young musician, replicas of the vases of antiquity, have a precision that is totally dissonant. Truth in painting does not only consist in rigorously reproducing each accessory, but in representing them in their exact relationships with the objects around them and the main subject—in a word, in subordinating them to the ensemble of the composition. This is one of the primary conditions of art; fail this and art returns to its infancy; it is tantamount to suppressing linear perspective. We know perfectly that, if M. Gérôme forgets this condition, it is

1. The original verse reads: "Come Bacchus, come ever young Thyoneus, Dionysus, Evius, Iacchus et Leneus;
Come as when in Naxos lone and wild
You did come to soothe the fears of Minos's child"
(Idylls, IX: Bacchus).
2. W. J. Robertson, *A Century of French Verse* (London: A. D. Innes & Co, 1895), p. 4.

deliberate, and that he willingly commits the error; but when one is gifted with superior worth, and when one possesses such fortunate qualities, and, to succeed, all one has to do is stay natural, the puerile affectations of archaism and calculated imperfections are all the more reprehensible. Should *The Virgin, the Infant Jesus, and Saint John* by the same artist be considered as a serious work or as a kind of fantasy in line with the Flemish masters of the sixteenth century or the contemporary German masters? M. Gérôme was obviously inspired by Raphael's *Belle Jardinière* when he produced the *The Virgin, the Infant Jesus, and Saint John*; but as the naïve, personal inspiration and great style of the painter from Urbino were lacking, he managed to produce a kind of complex and somewhat affected style, reminiscent in all but a few trivialities of the German imitations of Italian masterpieces. Some parts of his composition, but in particular the head of the Virgin Mary and hands, are executed with a freedom and, let us add, an offhandedness that is unusual of M. Gérôme, and which would lead us to believe that the artist soon grew tired of this unoriginal work; the eyes are neither drawn nor painted, they receive only a summary treatment as in some Chinese miniatures. The full portrait of a student of the École Polytechnique, no. 1934 of M. Gérôme's exhibits, receives much more rigorous treatment; but what a total sacrifice on the painter's part of the most appealing conditions of his art! How is it possible to abandon light, relief, and life so willingly?

Louis de Geoffroy,
"The Salon of 1850,"
Revue des Deux Mondes,
vol. 9 (1851), pp. 947–948

This young artist, running against the grain, is a rare zealot in whom we find a cult of drawing and the healthy traditions of the art. We remember M. Gérôme's début. His *Cock Fight* elevated him among the best. Today reputations of all kinds soon disappear: a speech, a stylishly written scene, or a debut painting can turn an unknown into an orator, man of State, dramatic poet, or painter overnight. Unfortunately when this early benevolence is not sustained, the turn of fortune is as sudden as the infatuation, and the artist lulled by overblown hope falls from his heights. Here, this is far from the case, and M. Gérôme's two works—*A Greek Interior* and *Drunken Bacchus and Cupid*—bear the charm and savor of novelty that made *The Cock Fight* so successful; certainly, the qualities of execution already shown by the artist have not diminished. The second of these two works represents Cupid and Bacchus after a drinking bout, arm in arm, zigzagging through paths of primroses. The small god of wine succumbs to drunkenness, his head crowned with vine leaves lolls onto his chest; his legs have lost all strength; the Etruscan cup and urn seem to slip from his grasp; his companion, in a better state, holds him up, and with his outstretched left hand, shows him—ever the corrupting influence—a copse where nymphs are dancing. The composition is gracious, poetic, and scented with the fragrant breath of the oleander of Pamisus. The Cupid and Bacchus group is perfectly constructed with an illustration that recalls the firm and chubby flesh of the two children of Raphael's *Jardinière*. Our only regret in the whole painting is the color of Cupid's hair. Without the use of such an insipid shade, M. Gérôme could, I believe, have retained the opposition he establishes between the two toddlers.

A Greek Interior—for it is indeed an interior scene—gives rise to great objections. Do artists have the right to represent any form of subject? The history of painting says yes; the morality of today says no. Leonardo and Michelangelo each produced a Leda, while Titian produced a reclining nymph (to cite only the masterpieces), which are nothing less than orthodox; I am not aware that these great men were accused of corrupting their centuries. We would even assume that their sublime impudence has been much less detrimental to moral standards than the thousands of minor infamies, scams, flops and tricks, dressed and served up on a daily basis. On the other hand, Diderot, who was no Capuchin, reprimanded Boucher for his nudes: "I like… nudities (the term is more precise) but I do not like people showing them to me." This remark is typical and well illustrates the need for decency demanded by custom even in debauchery. Hypocritical or not, this decency demands to be respected. Just as certain phrases once admired can no longer grace the lips of a well-educated man speaking in company, so we are justly shocked with the liberty taken by M. Gérôme in articulating a word that is improper at a Salon. This word is written all over his painting, if it is not in the catalogue. This image of the venal pleasures of the flesh was thus inadmissible in public. Even if M. Gérôme were to combine Michelangelo's style and Leonardo's perfection in his work, M. Gérôme would do well not to push his excursions any further in this direction, and we also permit ourselves to advise him to avoid conforming to archaism and Néo-Grec tastes, which can sometimes give the impression of a dearth of imagination.

Théophile Gautier,
"Paintings, studies and travel sketches,"
***L'Artiste*, 6th ser., vol. 3, p. 33–35.**

The lands where Islam reigns are entirely virgin from the point of view of art. The fear of idol worshipping caused the promulgator of the Koran to proscribe the representation of the human form. In this Muhammad imitated Moses; although the Bible speaks of the heads of cherubim at the corners of the Holy Ark and oxen holding up the sea of bronze, this exception only confirms the rule; the idea of the unity of God could easily have been forgotten by coarse peoples barely freed from polytheism and the worship of fetishes, always inclined to confuse the imitation with the idea it symbolized; this necessary law may have done away with sculpture, and painting—all the plastic arts, in a word—and the genius of the Orient had to seek recourse in architecture, ornamentation, arabesques, and the ingenious use of color; the living world was closed to the artist and dogma—rigorously adhered to—removed Nature from Man. When the Occident, under the kindly influence of Catholicism—we say Catholicism and not Christianity, as Luther and Calvin are as detrimental to art as Muhammad—was flourishing, producing marvelous creations and painters and sculptors by the hundred, the Orient was combining and composing mathematical lines in thousands of ways to decorate their alhambras, barely daring to introduce flowers into that labyrinth of broken lines and those long legends of Kufic script that form the heart of Arabic ornamentation. They had architects, algebraists, doctors, and poets, but no artists in the accepted meaning of the word today. However, on its sun-loved soil, the Orient has borne the finest, purest races, and the clay of humanity, less altered by civilization, seems to retain the visible imprint of the divine hand. It has conserved, in part at least, the drapery, a noble attire that plays around the form without concealing it; it has the privilege of severity and elegance that our scant clothing renders impossible. For several centuries, all this wealth has been lost, and more: beneath jealous veils and behind harem screens, mysterious beauties fade away without trace or memory, roses the fragrance of which provides the only outline and that flower only for their master, faces that Raphael could not have made more heavenly, bodies that Phidias could not have modeled more perfectly. A singular anomaly! One can only hope these lands dominated by Islamism will renounce their own peculiar civilization and embrace the ideas of our own; but what is forbidden to the faithful, the infidel may be allowed.

Until now, art, absorbed by the Greek ideal, worried little about this immense world, inhabited by unknown and unexploited races, which could revive its flagging inspiration with fresh motifs. In the age of the Crusades,

the Occident only brought back from Africa and Syria ideas of architecture and ornament; while the Saracen influence is visible in the art of the Middle Ages and mosques lent their minarets and crescents to Gothic chapels, one cannot see that the statuary and painting of these periods was modified by the encounter with, and study of, oriental types. The representations of Moors and Saracens in bas-reliefs and miniatures are purely imaginary. Later, Jean Bellin made the journey to Constantinople and reproduced, with the dry and patient fidelity so characteristic of him, figures, costumes, and monuments, the strangeness of which no doubt struck him more than their beauty, and which had no effect on art. The Orient, from a picturesque point of view, was discovered, or rather invented, by Victor Hugo around 1828; Goethe's *West-Eastern Divan* had not yet been translated; even if it had been, the French public would not have understood its mysterious and condensed poetry. But the effect of Hugo's *Orientales* was dazzling; blue skies traversed by white storks, sparkling suns, streams of gold and precious stones, pashas leaning on tigers, sultans gilded with the sun's rays, their red hair gleaming, languidly raising their kohl-lined lashes, palm trees dusted by the desert wind, towns with tin domes thrusting their ivory minarets into the azure, slender files of camels, their long ostrich necks swaying against the ruddy horizon, all this poetry as blinding as light, as intoxicating as hashish, made visitors dizzy with admiration, especially artists. Soon Decamps launched the Turkish patrol through the streets of Smyrna, Marilhat set out for Egypt, Eugène Delacroix returned from Morocco; later other artists joined the caravan dancing to the drum of Félicien David. However, it could be said that, despite a great many masterpieces, the Orient was reproduced with its strange landscapes, unusual architecture, brilliant carnival of costumes and diverse wealth of color, rather than studied in the sculptural beauty of its types. Marilhat, more of a landscape than a historical painter, only peopled his admirable canvases with episodic figures: Decamps's Turks, Zeybeks and Arnauts were little else to him than bright or dark spots against the chalk brickwork of a white wall, even if he proved by his *Punishment of the Hooks,* and his *Bazaar of Smyrna,* that he could express oriental types in all their purity. Delacroix expressed the African character with rare power, but sought out color and movement rather than line, as was his nature. Théodore Chassériau, who seemed gifted with a mysterious instinct for painting exotic races, only experienced French Africa and, better than his predecessors, he depicted those narrow oval faces, languidly parted lips, dark melancholy eyes, slender noses with expressive nostrils crested with long painted brows, the round arms with delicate hands, statuesque legs and feet, sensual poses and all the rhythm of the body swaying beneath colorful floating draperies. His *Femmes juives de Constantine* has all the wonderment of a dream: he would have explored the realms of the sun further had the shadow of death not taken him, for he lamented and longed for these beautiful countries as though they were an absent homeland. M. Gérôme, for his part, has actually made the pilgrimage of which Th. Chassériau dreamed. He has seen Cairo, that capital of the Orient, the city of the caliphs, where Saracen art shone with such brilliance while the Occident was still wallowing in harsh barbarity. He has meandered these winding streets bordered by houses with overhanging stories, with their latticework *moucharabys* shaded by striped awnings or woven mats; and from these streets here and there soaring slender palm trees fan their leaves against blue, or the minaret of a mosque surrounded by bracelets of balconies; he has followed that crowd composed of all types from the Orient: from noble-raced Arabs and stern Wahabites to the Negro with his bestial traits; from the Arnaut with his nose and eye of the eagle to the placid fellah with his face like that of an Egyptian sphinx; and the crowd which parts before the *courbach* leading the bey's horse and accompanied by his *saïs*, or that sidles back to the wall so as not to touch the noblewoman passing like a ghost beneath her taffeta *habbarah*, her face covered by a veil of black horse hair, as she scolds the Negress carrying her child in a red tarboosh and gold brocaded jacket.
The young artist, accompanied by several friends, traveled up the Nile in a cangia, both spacious and picturesque, which makes the journey to Egypt a genuine pleasure. Photography, of an only too familiar perfection today, dispenses the artist from copying monuments as it provides absolutely accurate proofs, to which a fortunate choice of moment and perspective can bring a great value of effect. So Gérôme did not focus his efforts on this aspect: his fervid studies as a painter of history; his talent as a draughtsman—refined, elegant, precise, yet stylish—a special vision, which we shall gladly call ethnographic and which shall become increasingly necessary to the artist in this age of universal and rapid locomotion where every people of the planet will be visited, in whatever faraway archipelago they are tucked away: all this made him better qualified than others to render that simple detail that the modern explorers of the Orient have neglected up to now in their landscapes, monuments and color—that is to say: mankind!
Gérôme had the kindness to let us leaf through his magnificent portfolio and study one by one his sketches dashed off by his pencil, swift notes gleaned from actual life, without preparation, without arrangement, without system, with sincere abandon and charming familiarity. What a pleasure it was to surprise talent thus in this state of undress! And to be initiated into the intentions of the artist as Nature inspired him, into his thought translated or rather materialized in shorthand script. We are verily fond of these drafts, words later turned into phrases at leisure in the picture.
Besides, the slightest of Gérôme's sketches show a stroke so pure, firm, precise and complete in their negligence, that we wonder what further work could possibly add.
The artist-voyager has made several pencil portrait-studies of different characteristic types: fellahs, Copts, Arabs, half-caste Negroes from Sermaon and Kordofan, so precisely observed that they could be used in the anthropological dissertations of M. Serres, and so masterfully drawn that they would ensure the success of any painting in which they found favor.
The fellahs and the Copts have not changed since Moses; such as you see them on the frescoes of the tombs or palaces of Amenhotep, Thutmose and Sesostris, such are they today. They still have that broad flat face with rounded cheekbones which seem to have retained, like the sphinx, the mark of the bellows of Cambyses; their slanting eyes the outer angle of whose tips is raised and accented by a touch of antimony; the slightly pug nose giving an uncouth profile; the mouth a vast cage, the sensual folds of the lips, a pout and smile combined to form an indefinable expression unknown in Europe. The chechias and burnouses that frame their strange physiognomies make them resemble mummies partially unswathed, their masks removed. Arabs are distinguished by their noses and their bird-of-prey eyes, by the Caucasian structure of their head, and by the openness of their facial angle: in their gaze, Negroes reveal a subtle animal placidity or childish frivolity, their souls as dark as their skin; their snub nostrils and thick mouths inhale the desert's flaming heat with impunity, even laden with the imperceptible dust raised by the khamsin; in addition to this collection, several women of drowsy, doleful beauty, goaded by a baksheesh, shyly lift their veils, and reveal phantom-like bearing unique to the women of the Orient.
The camel—that strange creature which seems to have survived the great forty-day deluge, with the elephant, rhinoceros, hippopotamus, giraffe and ostrich, in order to remain on earth as a specimen of the monstrous zoological furniture of the primitive world—has been studied by our traveler from all aspects, foreshortenings, attitudes when in motion or at rest, kneeling, ruminating, dreaming, licking its chops, showing its rickety teeth, stretching its long neck out to the ground, fanning its long-lashed eyes as gentle as a woman's—the only grace of this antediluvian deformity; he has carefully rendered the humps, callused hide, lolling gait, and crookedness, of this fabulous beast and the unexpected silhouettes that this deranged bundle of limbs cuts against the

white sand or blue sky. It is as though he doubts the very presence of his model and desperately tries to convince himself otherwise by capturing it from every perspective: the sketches show perfectly the difference between the heavy pack-camel and the svelte *mehari* in the foreground, which is to the former what the thoroughbred is to the carthorse. Our descriptions would be never-ending if we sought to note the infinite details contained in all these loose sheets. Great undulations of terrain, clusters of date trees, jumbles of fan palms, *saqias* the wheels of which draw successions of pots, cafés, *okkels*, staging posts, jutting pyramids, the broken profiles of sphinxes, vases of antique curves, gates to mosques, everything new and interesting that the hazards of travel present to an eye that knows how to see, and a hand that knows how to record.

We come across three sketches set to be finished for the coming exhibition. The first represents the two colossi of Medinet-Abou rising from the midst of the plain at the foot of a mountain dwarfed in comparison. Never has ancient Egypt, with its frenzied genius for enormity, been more openly defiant in the face of Time; if the shoulders of this planet were to quiver through an earthquake, by dint of shaking, it might just succeed in cracking the granite skins of the giants encumbering it, but would never turn them over. The ultimate cataclysm of the world will find them in the same place, inelegant, crumbling, crude, and disfigured but always obdurate in that eternal and impassive pose, open hands resting on stony knees, creviced heads, sculpted by thunderbolts, turned toward the infinite.

Behind these colossi or rather these mountains in human form, the emaciated chain, roasted and ground by six thousand years of sun, casts cascades of light from its sheer slopes over its blue rifts. The heavens spread their gown of indigo, numbed by a hot haze of sand.

At the foot of these stone monsters—one of which is the famous Memnon, whom the ancients heard calling for Aurora, and whose granite voice the emperor Hadrian's tampering took away—in their immense shadow, a caravan has halted, seeking shelter from the powerful rays of the sun; a man perched on a camel does not even reach as high as the toes of these tremendous statues. The effect of this painting is spellbinding; the Orient is not daubed with the deep Saturn-orange shades behind which it is usually concealed; it has that harsh light, that fervent pallor, those tones of white hot iron of the real lands of the sun.

The second painting shows recruits marching through the desert. An Arnaut, his rifle tucked behind his neck like a staff, advances at the head of the procession, composed of wretches, their wrists in stocks, chained in pairs like prisoners, manifesting the most horrifying despair; their gray feet kick up the fine dust as they stumble along, their skulls seething and streaming beneath the implacable devouring sun.

On the shifting sands, white as pulverized sandstone, the sponge-like feet of the camels have hollowed large impressions; the wind has traced, as though on water, fickle patterns, relentlessly effaced and refreshed—it is almost as sad as the Russian soldiers amusing themselves on command, so admired at the world's fair.

The third painting, the finest of all perhaps, represents Arnauts at prayer in a chamber the walls of which are decorated only with a row of rifles; a line of people stand, feet together, the palms of their hands turned upwards, as though awaiting a sacrament; on the edge of a narrow carpet, an old man with a white beard standing slightly forward recites the suras of the Koran, to which the assembled listen in religious ecstasy. In the foreground is a row of *babouches*, shoes and slippers, a profoundly oriental detail which the artist had the boldness not to omit, and which does not upset the gravity of the composition. Any imminence of a smile expires at the sight of these men, so pure, noble, and characteristic, their attitudes so beautiful in their simplicity, and this assembly of believers who does what it does so well.

We would also like to talk of a sketch of King Candaules waiting in bed for his wife Nyssia who lays her clothing on a golden frame, while Gyges peaks through the door at her unrivalled beauty; however, indiscretion is enough in itself, and one should not become proud and conceited that our own antique fashions, which have already inspired a statue from Pradier, inspire a painting by Gérôme.

Théophile Gautier,
"The Salon of 1857,"
***L'Artiste*, new ser., vol. 1, pp. 245–48**

One is sure to find a crowd before *Duel after the Ball*, by M. Gérôme. The work is the popular success of the Salon and, as the painting is not huge, one must almost wait one's turn to view it. This vogue, let us hasten to say, is not due to means that art reproves. The young master, nurtured on rigorous study and naturally gifted with a stubbornly pure taste, would scorn triumph at such a cost. The unusualness of the subject attracts the public; the merit of the execution holds the attention of the connoisseur.

It is almost trite to say that the forms and costumes of modern life lend little to painting. Artists appear more convinced than any of this truth, and they willingly look to ancient times or classical antiquity for the subjects of their compositions. Only when in dire straits, as with portraits for example, do they resign themselves to current fashions; yet they still amend them as much as possible by introducing cloaks, burnouses, shawls, scarves, and other accessories of character. In this genre they look no further than the last century, where the picturesque was sought in the Pyrenees, Brittany, Aragon, and Algeria. The number of canvases suitable as records for future ages of our interiors, costumes, furniture, types, and lifestyles is excessively restricted, and unfortunately almost always of mediocre execution. It seems that the art of today is afflicted by farsightedness and can discern objects with the distance and hindsight of centuries; it is incapable of seeing anything around it. Apart from a few portraits and official pictures, very few pictures bear their own vintage. We should therefore be grateful to M. Gérôme, the painter of Grecian grace, the archaeologist of Pompeii, for taking on a subject in our customs; he risks much in handling a reality of which everyone is or believes to be a judge, and by subjecting to the demands of art new objects, physiognomies, and adjustments. What would have happened if he had depicted a duel fought in black tail coats.

The idea of the *Duel after the Ball* is ingenious, gripping, dramatic. It impresses both mind and eye at once by the antithesis of the action and actors. The action is terrible, the actors grotesque, a duel of Pierrots and Harlequins elevated to tragic heights; no detail of the scene is spared. Young men, fired by wine no doubt, become embroiled in a quarrel on the steps of the opera or in a side room at the Maison d'Or, for an accidental elbow, some sarcastic remark that proved too biting, a pique of jealousy, or some other trifling matter. One of those busybodies always ready to show courage through the blood of others has brought swords, and the whole group, without taking the time to change costumes, has headed out to the Bois de Boulogne in two carriages, where the gray dawn has barely opened its heavy eyes amidst the morning mist through which slender skeletons of trees vaguely appear. The snow covers the ground with its white shroud, spread over night as if to receive the dead. Cold, solitude, and silence have kept watch so that nothing should disturb the combatants, and their sinister task was only too well accomplished. The trampled snow shows where the struggle took place; one of the adversaries, the Pierrot, has been wounded and could, with gallows humor, like Mercutio, say, "Ask for me tomorrow and you shall find me a grave man." The blood spreads its red stain over his paletot with its large buttons; his limbs, which life has abandoned, and which are no longer governed by will, lie inert on the snow and, within their loose garments, seem already enwrapped in their winding-sheet. Were it not for his friend, disguised as Crispin of the Comédie-Française, holding him at the chest, he would fall to the ground. The pallor of death pierces the Pierrot's patchy powdered face. His lifeless expression is already vacant, and his taut lips choke back rosy sputum through his death sigh. His right arm, sleeve rolled over the elbow for battle, offers a glimpse of the goosebumps and weak muscles of a young libertine, who still holds in his fingers, still tensed in an involuntary contraction, the blade that poorly defended its master. A character dressed in the red and green costume of a Chinese mandarin, strangely embellished with some fantastic design, casts himself to his knees to inspect the victim's bloodied breast with terrible anxiety. Behind the group, a man in a black domino raises his hands to his head as though to tear out his hair in desperation at the deplorable result of the futile quarrel.

The other group, at a distance from the first, is composed of the murderer and his second scurrying away, a Harlequin and a Mohican. For the duel Harlequin had cast his black mask and jacket to the ground; his bloodstained sword is still on the ground, and these significant accessories skillfully connect the two parts of the composition; Harlequin seems to be feverishly explaining to the savage, whose arm he clutches, that his adversary did not parry and that he alone ran himself through, and other explanations concocted in the wake of the inevitable tragedy; the other bows as though replying, "What is to be done?"

In the background, the wounded man's carriage, through the mist, assumes the lugubrious black form of a hearse; the prattling coachmen have the air of undertakers.

The work is indeed unusual and sinister, of a wild and romantic fancy, and a strange philosophical boldness! To combine the Carnival and Death, to change Harlequin's wooden saber into a sword, to transform the wine stains into blood stains, to surround the pangs of death with a circle of masks, to demand of Harlequin: "What hast thou done with thy brother, Pierrot?": it is enough to make the less intrepid waiver; M. Gérôme acquitted himself of this difficult, if not impossible task with an icy gravity, a pitiless sang-froid, and an irony superior to destiny. He has left nothing out; the rosy pits melted by drops of warm blood in the snow, the spangles glittering on the murderer's diamond costume, the bear's-claw collar of the Indian, the deformed and battered mask, or the plaster sodden by cold sweat on the dying man's face. All of this is rendered with a clean, fine, tight, steady brush that stays within its contours; with sober, neutral, wintry colors, composed of livid, quivering pallor, amidst which the clear vivid tones of the fancy dress are sinisterly discordant. Pierrot's face, sober now in death, and which from the drunken exhilaration of the masked ball slips away to the silence of the tomb, is a powerful and original creation; there is no emphasis, no melodrama, and no grimace. It is something dry, precise, and powerful as a page of Mérimée's poetry. The impression is even stronger because the narrator appears indifferent. M. Gérôme, a careful artist, does not leave the form and orientation of his frames to the gilder's fancy. To crown this one, he himself designed the masks of tragedy and comedy separated by the fool's bauble. Does Folly not dance between Joy and Agony, engendering one from the other?

Whatever the merit of the *Duel after the Ball*, we prefer *Prayer in the House of an Arnaut Chief*, which attracts fewer crowds. There is in this painting a truly admirable calm, contemplation and conviction. The stage of the scene is a chamber of oriental nudity: walls roughcast in lime around which runs a low divan, a ceiling with bare beams, and a portiere over the door. The floor is partly obscured beneath a mat of braided rushes, half-covered with a Turkish or Persian carpet. On the walls there are guns, rifles, and carbines of various forms; a panoply of axes, weapons, and *yataghans* is combined with a tall palm; from the ceiling hangs a chandelier made of glasses full of oil, as can be seen in mosques. A cedar-wood and mother-of-pearl table, of charming taste, supports a three-branched brass chandelier fitted with large candles. In the foreground is a line of *babouches,* slippers, and shoes, curious examples of the Muslim shoemaker's craft, for the followers of Muhammad remove their shoes on all occasions that Christians remove their hat. A robust old man with a venerable allure, his hands raised in a sacramental attitude, recites the suras of the Koran with an air of profound faith, facing Mecca and the tomb of Muhammad, the black stone and Zemzem well. Behind him, barefoot on the carpet, like devout soldiers at their chief's command, stands a row of eight figures, rugged fellows with vivid, picturesque physiognomies, moved for a moment by religious expression. An eager faith shines in their cruel, uncultured, swarthy faces. Each head presents a specific type and bears all the truth of portraiture. Always within the bounds of the most rigorous art, M. Gérôme has produced an ethnographical study as precise as that of M. Valério in the provinces of the Danube: the anthropologist M. Serres could, in all confidence, use these specimens in his analysis of undiscovered races. Through scrupulous fidelity, the proof of which he had already given in *Recreation in a Russian Camp* so admired at the world's fair, M. Gérôme satisfies one of the most imperious instincts of the period: the desire of peoples to encounter others, apart from in portraits produced from the imagination. He has everything required to fulfill this important mission: a quick and efficient eye, a sure and learned hand—which records every detail with the imperturbable clarity of a daguerreotype—and, above all, a sense that we shall call exotic—for want of a more precise term—which helps him to discover at once the characteristic differences between races.

We have had the chance of meeting in Constantinople most of the types M. Gérôme represents, and we recognize them perfectly. Here indeed is the Arnaut, the Armatoloi, with their noble bony frames, shaven temples, and long moustaches; the Bulgarian—who is almost Russian—with his red beard and mane; the Syrian in the chechia; the Tatar, with the short nose and prominent cheekbones: all are here, even the lovely blond child, his silken hair spilling out from his tarboosh, as handsome as a woman and as serious as a man, and reminiscent of Greek love and Victor Hugo's *Orientales*. Behind the row, a slave partakes in the prayer, rendered for a moment the equal of his masters by religion. All these characters are dressed in varied and picturesque costumes. The flared, bell-like fustanella touches the *doliman* with its straight folds; the elbow of the braided jacket touches the flowing sleeve; fezzes and turbans alternate; pommels of khanjars and pistols bristle in the belts of embroidered morocco or protrude from the folds of shawls. Everything is rendered with that delicate solidity which is the artist's signature. The almost similar attitudes avoid monotony by several differences that are not immediately striking. Among the believers some have their hands raised like the chief, others leave them hanging or resting on their hips; others have their thumbs slipped into their belts, a familiar attitude among Orientals; but all of them listen to the sacred words with an unction and faith that should put many Catholics to shame.

Before this work, the most perfect the young master has yet produced, the critic, eager not to forfeit his rights, will seek out a "but" or an "only" to qualify his well-merited praise—like the restrictive character in *Faux Bonshommes*. In order to maintain the dignity of the profession, then, let us reproach M. Gérôme for a certain drabness of color, emanating from too great a sacrifice to general harmony, and nothing need be added. He has been the first to study the Orient as a historical painter; he has sought out style where others, whom we certainly admire, only sought out color. Let us thus acknowledge, separately, the drawing of M. Gérôme and the color of Decamps. He who succeeds in uniting these qualities to an equal degree would be more than human. If Michelangelo had said: "What a pity they do not know how to draw in Venice!", Titian might have rightfully replied: "What a pity they do not know how to paint in Rome!" God alone, omniscient, is capable of capturing every facet of the world at once; it is nevertheless likely the jury would still refuse some of his works. The Institut is not always fond of Nature.

We often picture warm countries as flamboyant and torrid with heat. This is sometimes true but not always. The intense light streaming in white floods discolors the sky, earth and buildings. Fiery sand beneath a leaden sky takes on the cold appearance of snow. Impalpable dust raised on the horizon forms a kind of mist that chills and extinguishes the warmth of color. Thus the absolute truth of *Egyptian Recruits Crossing the Desert* is more surprising to the eye than convincing. We think, despite ourselves, of the deserts in operas, their brightly colored indigo and deep Saturn-orange skies, and their inevitable clusters of palm trees. Here there is nothing of the kind: sand as white as powdered stone, wind-blown lustrous ripples, broad footprints the signature of passing caravans, and impenetrable whirlwinds; the sky veiled with a haze of dust burning with the rays of the white-hot sun; before, behind, to the right and left, up and down, dreary dryness—pallid, parched, overwhelming, and oppressive, where the only drops to fall are drops of sweat, where the only breath that stirs is the suffocating khamsin. The Egyptian recruits make their way across this pleasant site leading several Arnauts. We can well imagine that, to force them to leave they had to be soundly beaten and shackled together, two by two, in wooden stocks, like galley slaves.

Leading the sad procession strides an Arnaut, his long gun slung across his shoulders and held up in his folded arms, like the batons that bears, companions of Atta Troll, clutch between their paws. He appears calm, insolent, and cruel in his handsome dust-blanched costume. The sufferings of the wretches behind who follow cumbersomely on, hindered by their fetters, do not move him in the slightest. He has for human life that quiet fatalistic contempt of the Orient. Soldiers flank the column that appears before the viewer. The first row consists of fellahs, Copts, Negroes dressed in white shirts, brown *mach'lahs*, varyingly battered white burnouses; some are barefoot, on the feet of others trail what remains of their worn-out shoes. A dull despair on their stunned faces, and they traipse along with the sluggish step of overworked beasts of burden, whom the whip no longer stings; their shackled wrists cannot even wipe their foreheads. The second row, already less distinct, appears in the gaps between their heads, and the rest of the column stretches out like a herd, in the ever thickening clouds of dust.
M. Bida has covered the same subject in illustration, a subject that never fails to upset European travelers. But he chose the moment of departure where the farewell scenes provide pathos. In M. Gérôme's work, the victims, caught between the impassiveness of nature and the impassiveness of tyranny, no longer even have the tears to shed.

Memnon and Sesostris are two mountains sculpted in the form of man, which time, tremblings of the earth or conquerors more terrible have been unable to dislodge from their base. There they stand, monstrous, shapeless, pug-nosed, their knees crushed by their colossal hands, returning slowly to rock, highlighted against the arid background of the Libyan range crumbling in the sun, pink in the light, blue in the shade. Memnon has lost his voice and, since a Roman emperor tampered with him, no longer salutes Aurora. The inscriptions on his base seem mendacious today, but the phenomenon of his melodious vibration has been confirmed by history and is undeniable. At the base of the gigantic statues, groups of men and camels provide a scale of comparison; they barely reach the baseplate. To refresh the landscape of sandstone and granite, M. Gérôme has placed patches of green grass in the foreground, which the summer will soon scorch into tawny tufts resembling a lion's mane. On this grass squat unsaddled camels, ruminating or stretching their necks over the turf. In the middle of the painting, a large camel, one foreleg bent in a shackle, seems to resist his driver's efforts to make it kneel beside a more peaceful companion. The stubborn beast raises its head, shows its gums and no doubt emits that grunting chuckle, the camel's own peculiar mode of complaint. The accessories—saddles, cushions, rugs, sticks, rags—are all treated with a conscious precision that shows the use of each item. In the background an Arab mounted on a mehari is galloping at speed; nothing is more remarkable than this ambling gait and those long legs thrashing in space like those of harvest spiders. During his travels to Egypt M. Gérôme paid particular attention to the odd profiles, in repose and in action, of the strange animal which the Arabs call the "ship of the desert"; he commands it thoroughly and reproduces all its attitudes.

The Plain of Thebes is the reverse of the picture we describe above. The foreground consists of fragments of enormous columns, in scattered blocks on one of which is carved the image of a falcon-headed god. These are the debris of an overthrown palace, probably that of Amenophis; beyond the ruins extends a floodplain, crossed by a road along which a caravan of dromedaries is passing, followed by a donkey carrying a rider on its croup after the Arab fashion. The two giants, barely reduced in size by the distance, reappear viewed from behind, their royal headdresses gathered and knotted behind their heads like a *queue à la prussienne*. Further on, the eye discovers dark lands scattered with trees and palms and, to the right, hills or mounds formed by debris, fragments of which penetrate the soil. In the background is a distant mountain range, in tones of pink and violet, the Arabian Mountains, if our sense of direction does not betray us; overhead a sky hazy with heat recedes behind the shimmering radiant atmosphere, against which a flock of migrating storks appear as microscopic specks. We describe in detail, as if we were there, these strange landscapes so foreign to Parisian ideas, which anyone but a traveler would be tempted to believe false, precisely because their representation is so true. But what can we do? The purlieus of Thebes do not resemble those of Paris. We may decide one way or another, and be content with this grand, solemn, and forlorn barrenness.

On the frame, the sacred uraeus spreads its wings and the hieroglyphic characters, so familiar to travelers, lend the painting a distinctly Egyptian expression. Before a stone trough, fed by the clay pots of a *sassaqhieh*, clusters of camels, one of which carries its driver, extend their ostrich-like necks and plunge their downy lips into the water, drinking for the thirst to come. The camels are of all kinds and coats, and M. Gérôme has been able to indulge himself in their depiction. It would be difficult to render more perfectly the character, coat, and physiognomy of the animal. Only the desire to render everything may have driven the artist on to research every tiny detail; some parts are sculpted rather than painted and the fatty envelope that dresses the muzzles is lacking in places. But how we prefer such rigor to the messy mockery of others! The palms with their fans of pointed leaves, a section of wall, and a glimpse of sky fill the background in a characteristic way.

This painting, the subject of which is far from dramatic, but which represents a scene of patriarchal life with a verisimilitude on which only the most suspicious can rely, pleases and interests us greatly. We are not of those who wish art to have a goal beyond itself, but not wanting to appear at all utilitarian, we do believe that painting is useful when,

remaining within the boundaries of beauty, it initiates us into the races, costumes, aspects, and traditions of faraway countries. Hence our praise for M. Gérôme for abandoning mythology and history and letting us journey with him.
At the corner of a street in Rome, *pifferari* stand before a Madonna sheltered in a small chapel erected on a fragment of an ancient column with a Corinthian capital. From a crossbeam affixed to the wall hangs a lamp on a level with the sacred depiction. According to the Italian custom, the *pifferari* are serenading the Holy Virgin and the Divine *Bambino*. One of them, the youngest, is playing a form of fife, the other presses beneath his arm the swollen goatskin and applies himself to some untutored finger work along the long pipes. Even in Paris one knows the picturesque rags of these wandering musicians, so beloved of artists, and who generally come from the Abruzzi. Their sharp nasal cantilena is not without charm especially when heard from afar. This time M. Gérôme has reduced his work to microscopic proportions, and his painting could be placed on the golden plate of Meissonier. It is a tiny masterpiece of finish, subtlety, and precision. Apply to the finest photographic proof a vivid, clear, charming color and add style—which is the very soul of the artist and which no instrument can give—and you will have the *Pifferari* by M. Gérôme, a miniature that has grandeur.

Charles Baudelaire, "The Salon of 1859," *La Revue française*

It is impossible not to recognize the noble qualities of M. Gérôme's work, the first of which are the search for novelty and a taste for great subjects; but his originality (if one can call it originality) is often laborious and barely visible. He brings his subjects to life frostily, with small ingredients and puerile expedients. The idea of a cock fight is naturally reminiscent of Manilla or England. M. Gérôme tries to surprise our curiosity by transposing the match into a kind of Greek pastoral. Despite great and noble efforts, *The Age of Augustus*, for example—which still proves that French tendency in M. Gérôme which goes seeking success elsewhere than in painting alone—until now he has only been, and only will be, it can only be feared, the foremost of fastidious minds. That these Roman games are represented with precision and local color is scrupulously observed, I have no doubts. On this subject I will not raise the slightest suspicion (if, however, this is the *retiarius,* where is the *mirmillo*?). But founding success on such features is maybe playing, if not a disloyal, at least a dangerous game, engendering distrust and resistance among many who will go away shaking their heads wondering if things were really like that. Supposing that such criticism is unjust (for, in M. Gérôme we generally recognize a mind curious about the past and eager for instruction), it is the deserved punishment for an artist who substitutes the entertainment provided by a page of erudition for the pleasure of pure painting. The craftsmanship of M. Gérôme, it must be said, has never been strong or original. Oscillating between Ingres and Delaroche, it has always been indecisive and weak in character. Furthermore I have a more biting criticism to make of the painting in question. Even when showing the hardening of character that accompanies crime and debauchery, and even when hinting at the secret baseness of making a hog of oneself, one does not have to join forces with caricature, and I believe that familiarity with command, especially when commanding the world, in the absence of virtue, brings a certain nobility of attitude from which this so-called Caesar, this butcher and obese vintner, is too far removed, and who at most, as his satisfied and provocative pose suggests, could aspire to the role of editor-in-chief at *Plump and Content* weekly. *King Candaules* is another snare and diversion. Many go into raptures before lugubrious and cruel Asian-style settings; but they will always provide comedy, and invariably be reminiscent of Baudouin or Biard's eighteenth-century mischievousness, where half-open doors allow pairs of gawping eyes to observe syringes teasing the overblown charms of marquises.

Julius Caesar! What splendors of setting suns the name of this man casts in the imagination. If ever a man on earth resembled the Divinity, it was Caesar. Powerful and seductive! Brave, learned, and generous! All the powers, glories, and elegances! The man, whose grandeur always surpassed the victory, grew and grew until death! The man whose breast pierced by a knife, uttered only a cry of paternal love, and who found the wound of iron less cruel than the wound of ingratitude. This time, certainly, M. Gérôme's imagination has let him down; it suffered a fit of fortune when it conceived of Caesar alone, sprawling before his toppled throne, with the corpse of this Roman pontiff, warrior, orator, historian, and master of the world filling the immense and deserted room. The way this subject is shown has been criticized; here we cannot praise it enough. The effect is truly great. All that is required is this terrible concision. We all know enough of Roman history to imagine what is implied, the disorder that went before and the turmoil that followed. We can imagine Rome beyond the walls, and hear the cries of its people, astonished and relieved, devoid of gratitude to both victim and assassin: "Let us make Brutus Caesar!" There is something inexplicable that remains to be explained in relation to the painting itself. Caesar cannot be a Maghrebi; he had very white skin; it is not naïve to recall that the dictator took as much care of himself as a dandy. Why then this muddy coloring in which the face and arms are covered? I have heard it argued that death strikes the face with a livid tone such as this. For how long, should we assume, has the living become a corpse? The proponents of this excuse must be nostalgic for putrefaction. Others simply remark that the arms and head are enveloped in shadow. But this excuse would imply that M. Gérôme is incapable of representing white flesh in twilight, which is beyond credibility. I shall therefore abandon my search for the answer to this mystery. As it is, and with all its faults, this painting is the best and undeniably the most striking that he has exhibited for a long time.

Émile Zola,
"Our painters on the Champ de Mars,"
***La Situation*, July 1, 1867**

M. Gérôme, a master of the École des Beaux-Arts, has obtained a medal of honor, no doubt for the same reasons as M. Cabanel. M. Pils, the third tutor charged with creating genius for the future, submitted a very poor work—*Fête donnée à LL. MM. l'Empereur et à l'Impératrice, à Alger*—which meant that the jury, defying logic, simply awarded him a first class medal.
M. Gérôme, a member of the Institut, is only a Knight of the Legion of Honor. He is the same age as M. Cabanel; he has traveled in Turkey and Egypt while the artist was working in Rome. Hence the difference in what they produce.
The works of M. Gérôme represent a happy medium between the tidy delicate works of M. Meissonnier and the voluptuously classic works of M. Cabanel. As a pupil of M. Paul Delaroche, this artist learned from his master not to paint and bring color to painstakingly researched and invented images.
Of course, M. Gérôme works for the Maison Goupil and therefore makes a painting so that the painting can be reproduced by photography and engraving and thus sold in thousands of copies.
Here the subject matter is everything, the painting is nothing: the reproduction is worth more than the work. The whole secret of the trade consists of finding an idea that is sad or joyous, that titillates the flesh or heart, and then to treat this idea in a banal and pretty way that makes everyone happy. There is no provincial sitting room where an engraving of *Duel after the Ball* or *Molière Breakfasting with Louis XIV* does not hang on the wall, while in bachelors' apartments you will see *Dance of the Almeh* and *Phryné before the Areopagus*, racy subjects that men can enjoy among themselves. More serious folk display *Ave Caesar* or *The Death of Caesar*. Monsieur Gérôme works to satisfy every taste. There is something sprightly in him that breathes a bit of life into these dull and dreary pictures. Furthermore, to conceal his total absence of imagination, he has set about producing antique rubbish and churns out classical interiors. This marks him out as a serious and scholarly man. Realizing perhaps that he will never be capable of assuming the mantle of painter, he tries instead to assume that of archaeologist. In this light, painting becomes a kind of cabinet making. I imagine M. Gérôme trying to create a painting, his *Phryné before the Areopagus*, for example. He starts by reconstructing the room where the hetaerae were judged, which is no mean feat: he had to consult the ancients and take advice from an architect. The room constructed, he had to arrange the subject. This is where he has to grab the public. Firstly the artist chooses a historical moment with drama, the moment when the defense for Phryné tears off her robe. This daintily posed female body would make a suitable center subject for a painting. But that is not sufficient. Instead he had to exacerbate her nudity by affording the hetaera a movement of modesty similar to that of a modern mistress caught changing into her nightdress. But that was still not sufficient; success could only be complete if the draughtsman managed to lend the judges' faces varied expressions of admiration, surprise, and concupiscence; the rows of old faces illuminated by desire will be the pepper in the sauce, the spice to titillate even the most blasé palate. Now that the work is seasoned just right it can be sold for fifty or sixty thousand francs, and the reproductions produced will flood Paris and the provinces, affording both author and publisher a nice private income.
When M. Gérôme gives the final brushstroke to a canvas, he no doubt says, *"I have created a painting!"* No, sir, you have not created a painting. What you have, if you like, is a clever picture, a subject with a certain witty treatment, a fashionable merchandise. Never does a cabinetmaker believe he has created a work of art when he has elegantly set and inlaid a small item of drawing-room furniture. You are that cabinetmaker. You know your trade inside out, and in your fingers you have tremendous dexterity. This is your talent as a worker.
I search in vain for the creator in you. You do not have spirit, character, or personality of any sort. You do not live your works; you have no experience of the fever or the all-powerful surge that drives real artists. One feels you go about your task like a laborer; you leave behind nothing that belongs to you, and you offer the public a painting as a shoemaker offers a pair of fine boots to a customer. Here is reasoning I have heard before: Delacroix draws badly, composes little, and his painting is mediocre; Delacroix is incomplete. M. Gérôme draws well, composes magnificently, and his painting is most adequate; therefore M. Gérôme is more complete than Delacroix, and is superior to him. Well? Good for him!

José-Maria de Heredia[1]
"The Prisoner,"
***L'Artiste*, February 1, 1868, pp. 253-254**

To Gérôme

Muezzins' calls have ceased. The greenish sky
Is fringed with gold and purple in the West;
The crocodile now dives to muddy rest,
And hushed to stillness is the Flood's last cry.

On crossed legs, smoker-wise, with dreamy eye,
The Chief sits mute, by hashish fumes oppressed
While on the cangia's rowing bench with zest
Their bending oars two naked Negroes ply.

Jocund and jeering, in the stern-sheets where
He scrapes harsh guzla to a savage air,
An Arnaut lolls with a brutal look and vile;

For fettered to the boat and bleeding thence
An old sheik views with grave and stupid sense
The minarets that tremble in the Nile.

1. *Sonnets of José-Maria de Heredia*, trans. E. Robeson Taylor (San Francisco: William Doxey, 1897), p. 127.

SELECT BIBLIOGRAPHY

Manuscript sources and correspondence
Except where otherwise stated, the author or the correspondent is Jean-Léon Gérôme

Los Angeles, The Getty Research Institute
- Nineteenth-century French artists' letters and other papers, 1719–1921.
- Desiré Albert Barre, letters received, ca. 1830–85.
- Adrien Beugniet, letters received, 1854–1908.
- Jean-Léon Gérôme, letters received, 1853–1904.
- Henry Lapauze, letters received, 1901–18.
- Henry François Joseph Roujon, letters received, 1892–1914.
- Albert Thiébault-Sisson, letters received, 1886–1920.

Paris, Archives Nationales – Fonds de l'École des Beaux-Arts
- Gérôme as a student at the École des Beaux-Arts, AJ 51*260.
- Reference numbers of Gérôme's students, AJ 52 234 / 236.
- Gérôme's donations and bequests, AJ 52 248.
- Mme Morot's donation (Gérôme's drawings), AJ 52 449.
- Gérôme's donation AJ 52 451.
- Gérôme's file as a member of the administration council of the École des Beaux-Arts, AJ 52 459.
- Gérôme's file as a teacher at the École des Beaux-Arts, AJ 52 461.

Paris, Bibliothèque Centrale des Musées Nationaux
- Letter to Léonce Bénédite.
- Letter to Dubufe.
- Letter to Ernest Meissonier.
- Letter to Paul Richer.

Paris, Bibliothèque de l'École des Beaux-Arts
- Letter to Charles Garnier, Ms 743.
- Letter to Machard, Ms 776.

Paris, Bibliothèque de l'Institut de France
- Fragments of Édouard Detaille's correspondence, Ms 5528.
- Collection of various autographs by members of the Institut de France, compiled by comte Henri Delaborde, Ms 2157.
- Ludovic Halévy's correspondence and papers, Ms 4485.

Paris, Bibliothèque Spoelberch-de-Lovenjoul (Institut de France)
- Émile Augier, letters received, Ms Lov. D 639 *bis*.
- Théophile Gautier, correspondence, Ms Lov. C 494, vol. IV, fols. 436–450.

Paris, Bibliothèque du Muséum National d'histoire naturelle
- Scientific correspondence between Henri Milne-Edwards and his son Alphonse Milne-Edwards, Ms 2473, 354–355.

Paris, Bibliothèque Interuniversitaire de la Sorbonne
- Letters addressed to H.-P. Nénot, architect of the Sorbonne, Ms 1791, ff. 99–100, ff. 101–102, *Marie Jean-Léon Gérôme*.

Sources: Bibliothèque Nationale de France

- Two autograph letters to Germain Bapst. Feb. 2, 1892, Apr. 26, 1892.
- Manuscript documentation concerning the painter Jean-Léon Gérôme 1847–1881 (manuscript copies of critical reception in contemporary French press), Z-47 (1-29), box 4.
- Twenty-nine original engravings and photogravures after Jean-Léon Gérôme bound together in the same album, DC 293.

GÉRÔME, Jean-Léon
- *Autobiographie de Gérôme à 50 ans* [1874], *"Notes à consulter demandées par mon ami Timbal,"* presented by G. Ackerman in *Notes autobiographiques* (Vesoul: S.A.L.S.A., 1981).
- "History of the Opéra from its foundation up to the present day," in *Le Nouvel Opéra* by Alphonse Royer (Paris, 1875).
- Prefatory letter in *Les Révélations de l'art* by Maurice Valette (Paris, 1887).
- Speech given on the occasion of Gounod's funeral, 1893.
- Speech given on the occasion of the unveiling ceremony of Raffet's monument, 1893.
- Speech given on the occasion of the unveiling ceremony of Émile Augier's monument, 1895.
- Illustrated preface to *Articles de Paris* by Miguel Zamacoïs (Paris, 1900).
- Preface to *Charles Jalabert. L'homme, l'artiste d'après sa correspondance* by Émile Reinaud (Paris, 1903).

GUILLEMIN, Victor, "Étude sur le peintre et sculpteur Jean-Léon Gérôme (1824–1904)," *Académie des sciences, belles-lettres et arts de Besançon. Procès-verbaux et mémoires. Année 1904* (Besançon: Typographie et lithographie Jacquin, 1905)

Books and articles published before 1904

ABOUT, Edmond
- *Voyage à travers l'exposition des beaux-arts* (Paris: L. Hachette, 1855), pp. 153–54.
- *Salon de 1857.*
- "Le Salon de 1868," *Revue des Deux Mondes*, vol. LXXV (June 1868), pp. 728–29.

ANONYMOUS, *Tragedy and Comedy. Opinion of the Press on Gérôme's Celebrated Picture of the Duel after the Masquerade* (London and Paris, n. d.).

ARAGO, Alfred, *Œuvres choisies de J.-L. Gérôme* (Paris, n. d.).

AUBRYET, Xavier, *Journal officiel du soir*, July 2, 1869, p. 718.

AUVRAY, Louis
- *Salon de 1863* (Paris, 1863), pp. 39–40.
- *Exposition des beaux-arts. Salon de 1864* (Paris, 1864), p. 40.
- *Exposition des beaux-arts. Salon de 1865* (Paris, 1865), pp. 21–62.
- *Salon de 1869* (Paris, 1869), pp. 27–28.

BAIGNÈRES, A., "Salon de 1866," *Revue contemporaine*, vol. 86 (1866), pp. 350–51.

BAISSAS, Jérôme, "Exposition des Beaux-Arts à Besançon. Musée de Besançon," *L'Artiste*, vol. 10 (1860), p. 83.

BARGUE, Charles, and GÉRÔME, Jean-Léon, *Cours de dessin* [1867–1870], republished by Gerald Ackerman (Courbevoie: ACR Édition, 2003).

BAUDELAIRE, Charles, *Œuvres complètes* (Paris: Gallimard Pléiade, 1961), p. 1057ff.

BERGERAT, Émile, *Journal officiel*, Mar. 28, 1877, p. 2519.

BERTALL, "Voyage de M. Perrichon au Salon de 1874," *Le Petit Moniteur*, May 16, 1874.

BLANC, Charles
- "Salon de 1866," *Gazette des Beaux-Arts*, vol. 20 (1866), pp. 516–17; vol. 21 (1866), pp. 42–44.
- "Salon de 1868," *Le Temps*, May 19, 1868, pp. 1–2.

BOUNIOL, Bathild, "L'Amateur au Salon de 1869," *Revue du monde catholique*, vol. V, p. 534.

BOYELDIEU D'AUVIGNY, L., *Salon de 1853*, p. 56.

BÜRGER, W. [THÉOPHILE THORÉ]
- *Salon de 1864*, pp. 14–15.
- "Salon de 1868," in *Salons de W. Bürger, 1861 à 1868* (Paris, 1870), vol. 2, pp. 466–69.

CALLIAS, Hector de, "Salon de 1861," *L'Artiste*, vol. XI, no. 12 (June 15, 1861), pp. 267–68.

CANINA, L., *L' Architettura antica*, 1840, vol. IX.

CANTELOUBE, Amédée, *Le Monde illustré*, vol. XXII (1868), p. 366.

CASIMIR-PÉRIER, Paul, "Salon de 1869: propos d'art," *Revue du Salon*, 1869, pp. 203–5.

CHALLEMEL-LACOUR, Paul, "Le Salon de 1864," *Revue germanique et française*, vol. 29, no. 3 (June 1, 1864), pp. 39–40.

CHENNEVIÈRES, Philippe de, *Lettres sur l'art français en 1850* (Argentan: Barbier, 1851).

CLARETIE, Jules
- "IV Gérôme," *L'Artiste*, vol. II, 1863, pp. 163–64.
- "J.-L. Gérôme," in *Grands peintres français et étrangers* (Paris: H. Launette; Goupil, 1886).

CLÉMENT DE RIS, Louis
- "Salon de 1847," *L'Artiste*, 4th ser., vol. IX (1847), p. 123.
- "Salon de 1848. Eugène Delacroix, Duveau, Diaz, Gérôme, Lehmann, Fernand Boissard," *L'Artiste*, 5th ser., vol. I (1848), pp. 59–60.
- "Salon de 1850–1851," *L'Artiste*, 5th ser., vol. VI, no. 1 (Feb. 1, 1851), p. 9.
- "Salon de 1853," *L'Artiste*, vol. XI, 1853, p. 11.

COURTOIS, "Beaux-Arts. Salon de 1850 - Peinture - Sculpture," *Le Corsaire*, Feb. 15, 1851, pp. 1–3.

DAUBAN, H., *Salon de 1863* (Paris, 1863), p. 39.

DAX, Pierre, "Chronique," *L'Artiste*, 1876, vol. I, pp. 64–65.

DELABORDE, H.
- "L'Art français au Salon de 1859," *Revue des Deux Mondes*, vol. 21 (June 1, 1859), pp. 502–5.
- "Le Salon de 1861," *Revue des Deux Mondes*, 2nd per., vol. 33 (June 15, 1861), pp. 876–78.

DELÉCLUZE, Étienne-Jean
- *Exposition des artistes vivants 1850* (Paris: Comon, 1851), pp. 116–19.
- *Salon de 1857*.

DU CAMP, Maxime
- *Souvenirs littéraires* [1892], presented by Michel Chaillou (Paris: Balland, 1984).
- *Les Beaux-Arts à l'exposition de 1855* (Paris: Librairie nouvelle, 1855), pp. 147–84.
- *Le Salon de 1859* (Paris: Librairie nouvelle, 1859), pp. 63–71.
- *Le Salon de 1861* (Paris: A. Bourdilliat & Cie, 1861), pp. 83–89.
- "Le Salon de 1863," *Revue des Deux Mondes*, 2nd per., vol. 45 (June 15, 1863), pp. 889–92.
- "Le Salon de 1866," *Revue des Deux Mondes*, 2nd per., vol. 63 (1866), pp. 701–3.

DUMESNIL, M. H., *Le Salon de 1859* (Paris, 1859), pp. 88–94.

DUMONT, Édouard, "Salon de 1881," *La Liberté*, June 3, 1881, p. 3.

FERRY, Gabriel de, *L'Ordre*, Jan. 11, 1851.

FIZELIÈRE, Albert de la, *Exposition Nationale: Salon de 1850–51* (Paris: Passard, Deflorenne, 1851).

FOURNEL, Victor
- *Salon de 1857* (Paris, 1857), p. 744.
- "L'Art et les artistes en 1861," in *L'Annuaire des artistes et des amateurs*, ed. Paul Lacroix (Paris, 1862), p. 107.

GALICHON, Émile, "M. Gérôme, peintre ethnographe," *Gazette des Beaux-Arts*, vol. 24, no. 2 (Feb. 1, 1868), pp. 147–51.

GAUTIER, Théophile
- "Beaux-Arts," *L'Artiste*, vol. 10 (July 4, 1847), p. 14.
- "Jeunes Grecs faisant battre des coqs," *L'Artiste*, 4th ser., vol. IX (1847), p. 221.
- "Salon de 1848," *La Presse*, Apr. 27, 1848, pp. 1–2.
- "Salon de 1850–1851," *La Presse*, Mar. 1, 1851, pp. 1–2.
- "Salon de 1853," *La Presse*, June 24, 1853, pp. 1–2.
- "Tableaux, études et croquis de voyage," *L'Artiste*, 6th ser., vol. III (1856), pp. 33-35.
- "Le Salon de 1857," *L'Artiste*, vol. I (July 5, 1857), pp. 245–49.
- "À travers les ateliers," *L'Artiste*, vol. IV (May 16, 1858), pp. 17–20.
- "Exposition de 1859," *Le Moniteur universel*, Apr. 18, 1859, pp. 1–2.
- "Exposition de 1859," *Le Moniteur universel*, Apr. 23, 1859.
- "Exposition de tableaux modernes au profit de la caisse de secours des artistes peintres, statuaires, architectes," *Gazette des Beaux-Arts*, vol. 5 (1860), pp. 328–30.
- *Salon de 1861* (Paris: E. Dentu, 1861), pp. 176–86.
- "Salon de 1863," *Le Moniteur universel*, June 11, 1863.
- *Le Moniteur officiel*, June 18, 1863, p. 878.
- *Le Moniteur officiel*, June 13, 1865, p. 79.
- *Le Moniteur officiel*, May 15, 1866, p. 577.
- "Salon de 1868," *Le Moniteur officiel*, no. 123 (May 2, 1868), p. 585.
- "Salon de 1869," *Journal officiel*, June 28, 1869.

GEOFFROY, Louis de, "Le Salon de 1850," *Revue des Deux Mondes*, vol. 9 (1851), pp. 947–48.

GÉRÔME, Jean-Léon
- "History of the Opéra from its foundation up to the present day," in *Le Nouvel Opéra* by Alphonse Royer (Paris, 1875).
- *Notes autobiographiques* [1874], ed. G. Ackerman (Vesoul: S.A.L.S.A., 1981).
- Preface to *Les Folies Parisiennes* by Cham (Paris, 1883).
- Prefatory letter in *Les Révolutions de l'art* by Maurice Valette (Paris, 1887).
- Speech given on the occasion of Gounod's funeral, 1893.
- Speech given on the occasion of the unveiling ceremony of Raffet's monument, 1893.
- Speech given on the occasion of the unveiling ceremony of Émile Augier's monument, 1895.
- "Le Salon et la Critique (1881-1895). L'avis des intéressés," special issue of *Grand Journal*, no. 19, Feb. 24, 1896.
- Illustrated preface to *Articles de Paris* by Miguel Zamacoïs (Paris, 1900).
- Prefatory letter in *Jean-Louis Hamon, peintre (1821-1874)* by Eugène Hoffmann (Paris, 1903).
- Preface to *Charles Jalabert. L'homme, l'artiste d'après sa correspondance* by Émile Reinaud (Paris, 1903).

GUILLEMIN, Victor, "Étude sur le peintre et sculpteur Jean-Léon Gérôme (1824–1904)," *Académie des sciences, belles-lettres et arts de Besançon. Procès-verbaux et mémoires. Année 1904* (Besançon: Typographie et lithographie Jacquin, 1905).

HALLER, Gustave [Wilhelmine Joséphine FOULD], *Nos grands peintres* (Paris: J. Boussod, Manzi, Joyant et Cie, 1899), pp. 9–32.

HAUSSARD, P., *Le National*, Apr. 18, 1847.

HEMMEL, Alexandre, "Salon de 1865," *Revue nationale et étrangère*, vol. 21, p. 139.

HÉRÉDIA, José Maria de, *Le Prisonnier*, in *Les Trophées* (Paris: Librairie Alphonse Lemerre, 1893), no. 125.

HERING, Fanny Field
- *Gérôme. The Life and Works of Jean-Léon Gérôme* (New York: Cassell, 1892).
- "Gérôme," *Century Magazine*, vol. 37 (Feb. 1889), p. 482ff.

JAHYER, *Salon de 1865* (Paris, 1865), pp. 81–84.

JAMES, Henry, "Esquisses parisiennes - Chroniques," articles sent to the *New York Tribune* (Dec. 1875–July 1876), republished as *Esquisses parisiennes* (Paris: La Différence, 2006), pp. 120–22.

LACKROY, Édouard, "Le Monde des Arts," *L'Artiste*, vol. I, 1865, pp. 83–84.

LAFENESTRE, Georges, "Le Salon de 1869," *Le Moniteur universel*, no. 178 (June 27, 1869), p. 801.

LAGENEVAIS, F. de, "Salon de 1848," *Revue des Deux Mondes*, vol. XXII, 2nd qtr. 1848, pp. 288–89.

LAGRANGE, Léon, "Le Salon de 1864," *Gazette des Beaux-Arts*, vol. 16, no. 6 (June 1, 1864), pp. 29–30.

LAVERGNE, Claudius, *Exposition universelle de 1855. Beaux-arts* (Paris: Imprimerie Bailly, Divry & Cie, 1855), pp. 78–79.

LAVERGNE, Claudius [L. VEUILLOT], "Beaux-Arts. Exposition de 1868," *L'Univers*, May 21, 1868, pp. 1–2.

LENOIR, Paul, *Le Fayoum, le Sinaï et Pétra. Expédition dans la moyenne Égypte et l'Arabie Pétrée, sous la direction de Jean-Léon Gérôme* (Paris: Henri Plon, 1872).

LESCURE, M. de, "Le Salon de 1865," *Revue contemporaine*, pp. 422–23.

MANTZ, Paul
- *Salon de 1847* (Paris, 1847), pp. 60–61.
- *L'Événement*, Jan. 30, 1851.
- "Salon de 1855," *Revue française*, vol. 2 (1855), pp. 358–60.

- "Le Salon de 1863," *Gazette des Beaux-Arts*, vol. 14, no. 6 (June 1, 1863).
- "Salon de 1865," *Gazette des Beaux-Arts*, vol. 18 (1865), p. 512.

MASSON, Frédéric
- "Jean-Léon Gérôme et son œuvre," *Les Lettres et les Arts*, May 1, 1887.
- "Jean-Léon Gérôme, peintre et sculpteur," *Figaro Salon, Les Beaux-Arts en 1900*, Apr. 1900.
- "J.-L. Gérôme, peintre de l'Orient," *Figaro illustré*, 2nd ser., no. 136 (July 1901).
- "Notes et fragments de J-L. Gérôme," *Les Arts*, no. 26 (Feb. 1904), pp. 17–32.

MÉNARD, René, "Gérôme," *The Portfolio*, 1875, pp. 82–85.

MÉRIMÉE, Prosper
- "Salon de 1853," *Le Moniteur*, 1853, p. 749.
- *Correspondance*, ser. 2, vol. 4 (Paris: Le Divan, 1941–65), pp. 311–15.

MERSON, Olivier
- *La Peinture en France: exposition de 1861* (Paris: E. Dentu, 1861), pp. 210–12.
- "Salon de 1869," *Le Monde illustré*, vol. 25, no. 639 (July 10, 1869), p. 27.

MONTIFAUD, Marc de
- "Salon de 1865," *L'Artiste*, vol. 1 (1865), p. 219.
- "Salon de 1866," *L'Artiste*, vol. 1 (1866), p. 200.
- "La peinture d'histoire au Salon de 1868," *L'Artiste*, vol. 7, June 1868, pp. 401–2.
- "Salon de 1874," *L'Artiste*, vol. 1 (1874), pp. 407–8.

MONTROSIER, Eugène, "Gérôme," *Les Artistes modernes*, 3 vols. (Paris: Launette, 1881–82), vol. 1, p. 18.

MOUY, Charles de
- "Le Salon de 1864," *Revue française*, vol. 8, no. 44 (June 1, 1864), pp. 242–44.
- "Le Salon de 1865," *Revue française*, pp. 198–99.

NETTEMENT, Alfred, *Salon de 1861* (Paris, 1861), pp. 399–400.

PALMA, É., "Salon de 1868," *Revue de Paris*, vol. XI, pp. 414–15.

PEISSE, Louis, *Le Constitutionnel*, Apr. 1, 1851, pp. 1–2.

PELLOQUET, C., "Gérôme," *La Gazette de Paris*, Feb. 13, 1859.

PELLOQUET, Théodore
- "Salon de 1861," *Le Monde illustré*, vol. 9 (1861), p. 442.
- "Salon de 1861," *Le Monde illustré*, vol. 8, no. 219 (June 22, 1861), p. 391.

PERRIN, Émile, "Salon de 1859," *Revue européenne*, vol. II, 1859, pp. 865–68.

PETROZ, Pierre
- "Salon de 1850," *Le Vote universel*, Jan. 28, 1851, pp. 1–2.
- "Exposition universelle des beaux-arts," *La Presse*, July 31, 1855, pp. 1–2.

PILLET, Fabien
- "Beaux-Arts. Salon de 1848," *Le Moniteur universel*, Apr. 11, 1848, p. 812.
- *Le Moniteur officiel*, Mar. 27, 1851, p. 891.

PLANCHE, Gustave, "Le Salon de 1847. La Peinture," *Revue des Deux Mondes*, vol. XVIII (Apr. 1, 1847), p. 363.

ROY, Elie, "Salon de 1869," *L'Artiste*, vol. III (Apr. 1, 1869), pp. 88–89.

SAINT-VICTOR, Paul de
- "Salon de 1859," *La Presse*, Apr. 30, 1859, pp. 1–2.
- "Salon de 1861," *La Presse*, June 2, 1861, pp. 1–2.
- "Salon de 1863," *La Presse*, June 14, 1863, p. 3.
- "Salon de 1864," *La Presse*, June 2, 1864, p. 3.
- "Beaux-Arts. Salon de 1868," *La Liberté*, May 13, 1868, p. 3.
- "Beaux-Arts. Salon de 1869," *La Liberté*, June 5, 1869, p. 3.

SAULT, C. de
- "Salon de 1863," *Le Temps*, no. 780 (June 14, 1863), pp. 1–2.
- "Salon de 1865," *Le Temps*, no. 1460 (May 9, 1865), p. 1.
- "Salon de 1865," *Le Temps*, no. 1504 (June 14, 1865), pp. 1–2.
- "Salon de 1866, 13e article, 3," *Le Temps*, May 26, 1866, p. 1.

SILVESTRE, Armand, "Salon de 1869," *La Revue moderne*, 12th yr., vol. 53, p. 153.

SOUBIES, Albert, *J.-L. Gérôme (1824–1904). Souvenirs et notes* (Paris: Flammarion, 1904), p. 6.

STRAHAN, Edward [Earl Shinn], *Gérôme: A Collection of the Works of J. L. Gérôme in One Hundred Photogravures* (New York: Samuel L. Hall, 1881).

TANOUARN, Alfred de, "Galerie du XIXe siècle. Gérôme," *L'Artiste*, new ser., vol. 10, no. 2 (July 15, 1860), pp. 26–27.

THIÉBAULT-SISSON, François, "Léon Gérôme," *L'Illustration*, no. 3177 (Jan. 16, 1904), p. 38.

THORÉ, Théophile (known as W. Bürger), "Salon de 1847," in *Salons de T. Thoré* (Paris, 1868), p. 445.

THORÉ, Théophile (known as W. Bürger), *Salons de T. Thoré* (Paris: Librairie Internationale, 1868), p. 851.

TIMBAL, Charles, "Gérôme," *Gazette des Beaux-Arts*, 2nd per., vol. 40, no. 3 (Sept. 1, 1876), p. 218ff, p. 344ff.

VAINES, Maurice de, *Revue nouvelle*, 1847, vol. XIV, pp. 238–39.
VÉRON, P., "Gérôme," in *Les Coulisses artistiques* (Paris, 1876), pp. 241–51.

VIGNON, Claude
- *Salon de 1850–51* (Paris, 1851), pp. 117–19.
- "Le Salon de 1863," *Le Correspondant*, vol. 23 (June 1863), pp. 382–83.

WERNER, Georges, *La Revue du XIXe siècle* [1866], pp. 290–92.

WEY, Francis, *Le Courrier français, Salon de 1847*, Apr. 13, 1847.

É. Zola, "Le Salon de 1876," in *Écrits sur l'art* (Paris: Gallimard, 1991), p. 339.

Books published after 1904

ACKERMAN, Gerald M.
- in J. Hargrove, ed., *The French Academy: Classicism and its Antagonists* (Newark: University of Delaware Press; Cranbury: Associated University Press, 1990), pp. 190–94.
- *Jean-Léon Gérôme* (Courbevoie: ACR Édition, 2000).
- *A Collector's Vision: The 1910 Bequest of Matthias Arnot* (Elmira, N.Y.: Arnot Art Gallery, 1989).

ARASSE, Daniel, *Le Détail, pour une histoire rapprochée de la peinture* (Paris: Flammarion, 1992, republished 2009).

ARGENCOURT, Louise d', and DIEDEREN, Roger, *European Paintings of the 19th Century: The Cleveland Museum of Art, Catalogue of Paintings*, 4 vols. (Cleveland: Cleveland Museum of Art, 1999), vol. 1, pp. 290–95.

BEAUFORT, Madeleine F., KLEINFIELD, Herbert L., and WELCHER, Jeanne K., eds., *The Diaries, 1871–1882, of Samuel P. Avery, Art Dealer* (New York: Arno Press, 1979).

BERCHET, Jean-Claude, ed., *Le Voyage en Orient, anthologie des voyageurs français dans le Levant au XIXe siècle* (Paris: Robert Laffont, 1985).

BLUNT, Wilfrid, *Tulipomanie* (Hardmondsworth: Penguin, 1950).

BUGNER, Ladislas, ed., *L'Image du Noir dans l'art occidental* (Paris: Bibliothèque des Arts and Fribourg: Office du livre, 1979), vol. 2, pp. 106–8, 112, 118, 163–66, 188, 229.

CHAMPFLEURY, *Le Réalisme*, texts selected and presented by Geneviève and Jean Lacambre (Paris: Hermann, 1973), p. 130.

CHAUDONNERET, Marie-Claude, *La Figure de la République. Le concours de 1848* (Paris: RMN, 1987).

CHU, Petra Ten-Doesschate, *French Realism and the Dutch Masters* (Utrecht: Haentjens Dekker & Gumbert), 1974.

CLARK, T. J., *The Absolute Bourgeois: Artists and Politics in France 1848–1851* (Greenwich, Conn.: New York Graphic Society, 1973), p. 64ff.

COMPIN, Isabelle, LACAMBRE, Geneviève, and ROQUEBERT, Anne, *Musée d'Orsay. Catalogue sommaire illustré des peintures*, vol. 1 (Paris: RMN, 1990).

CRESPELLE, Jean-Paul, *Les Maîtres de la Belle Époque* (Paris: Hachette, 1966), p. 40.

DAVIES, M., *Paintings of the French School* (London: National Gallery, 1970), p. 69.

FOUCART, Bruno, *Le Renouveau de la peinture religieuse en France (1800–1860)* (Paris: Arthena, 1987).

FOUCART, Jacques, and PRAT, Louis-Antoine, *Les Peintures de l'Opéra de Paris: de Baudry à Chagall* (new edition of *Le Nouvel Opéra de Paris*, by Charles Garnier; Paris: Arthena, 1980), no. 222.

GANGI, Sabine, and THIRIET, Jocelyne, *Musée Georges-Garret* (Vesoul: Association des Amis du Musée et de la Bibliothèque de Vesoul, 2003).

GENGE, Gabriele, *Geschichte im Négligé: geschichtsästhetische Untersuchung der Pompiermalerei* (Weimar, 2000).

GERÔME, Jean-Léon, *L'Orient* [sold at the Bon Marché department store] (Paris, 1910).

GIARD, René, *Le Peintre Victor Mottez d'après sa correspondance (1809–1897)* (Lille: Librairie René Giard, 1934), p. 172.

GRANGER, Catherine, *L'Empereur et les Arts. La liste civile de Napoléon III* (Paris: École des Chartes, 2005), pp. 142, 161, 208, 528.

HAMON, Philippe, *Imageries, littérature et image au XIXe siècle* (Paris: José Corti, 2001).

HELD, Julius S., ed, *Museo de Arte de Ponce, Catalogue I, Paintings of the European and American Schools* (Ponce, 1965), no. 73.

HERDING, Klaus, "Diogenes als Bürgerheld," *Boreas. Münstersche Beiträge zur Archäologie*, vol. 5 (1982), pp. 232–54.

JOHNSTON, W. R., *The Nineteenth Century Paintings in the Walters Art Gallery* (Baltimore: Trustees of the Walters Art Gallery, 1982).

JULER, Caroline, *Najd Collection of Orientalist Paintings* (London: Manara, 1991).

KRAFT, Eva Maria, and SCHUMANN, Karl Wolfgang, *Katalog der Meister des 19. Jahrhunderts in der Hamburger Kunsthalle*, 1969.

LAFONT-COUTURIER, Hélène, *Gérôme* (Paris: Herscher, 1998).

LANFANT, "J.-L. Gérôme, peintre officiel," unpublished thesis, Université de Paris-IV–Sorbonne, 1972.

LIMET, Charles, *À Gérôme* (Paris, 1909).

LINDSAY, Suzanne G., *Monuments for a Steel King* (Allentown, Pa.: Allentown Art Museum, 2002).

MAXON, John, ed., *The Art Institute of Chicago* (New York: H. N. Abrams, 1971), p. 264.

MACKAY, Charles, *Extraordinary Popular Delusions and the Madness of Crowds* (London, 1852).

MOREAU-VAUTHIER, Charles, *Gérôme peintre et sculpteur. L'homme et l'artiste d'après sa correspondance, ses notes, ses souvenirs, les souvenirs de ses élèves et de ses amis* (Paris: Hachette, 1906).

NERVAL, Gérard de, *Le Voyage en Orient*, 2 vols. (Paris: Garnier-Flammarion, 1980), vol. 1, p. 240.

NICOLLE, M., *Le Musée de Nantes, peintures* (Paris, 1919), no. 57.

NOCHLIN, Linda, "L'Orient imaginaire," in *Les Politiques de la vision* (Nîmes: Édition Jacqueline Chambon, 1989), pp. 76–78. English version: L. Nochlin, "The Imaginary Orient," in *The Politics of Vision: Essays on Nineteenth-Century Art and Society* (New York, 1989), pp. 33–59.

PELTRE, Christine
- *Les Arts de l'Islam, itinéraire d'une redécouverte* (Paris: Gallimard Découvertes, 2006).
- *L'Atelier du voyage : les peintres en Orient au XIXe siècle* (Paris, Le Promeneur, 1995).
- *Les Orientalistes* (Paris, Hazan, 2003).

PINGEOT, Anne, LE NORMAND-ROMAIN, Antoinette, and MARGERIE, Laure de, *Musée d'Orsay. Catalogue sommaire illustré des sculptures* (Paris: RMN, 1986).

RAMEAU, Henri, *Regards sur Jean-Léon Gérôme, peintre et sculpteur, 1824–1904* (Vesoul, 1978).

RICHIE, A. C., and NELSON, K. B., *Selected Paintings and Sculpture from the Yale University Art Gallery* (New Haven, Conn.: Yale University, 1972).

ROSENBLUM, Robert, *Les Peintures du musée d'Orsay* (Paris: Nathan, 1989), p. 41.

ROUJON, Henry
- *Gérôme* (Paris, 1911).
- *Les Peintres illustres. Gérôme* (Paris: P. Laffitte, 1912).
- *Artistes et amis des arts* (Paris: Hachette, 1912).

SANDERS, Patricia B., *The Haggin Collection* (Stockton, Calif.: Pioneer Museum and Haggin Collection, 1991), p. 84.

STERLING, C., and SALINGER, M., *French Painting: A Catalogue of the Collection of the Metropolitan Museum of Art*, (Cambridge, Mass.: Harvard University Press, 1966), vol. 2, p. 171.

VAN DYKE, John C., in *Modern French Masters*, ed. J. C. Van Dyke (London: T. Fisher Unwin, 1896), p. 33.

WEINBERG, H. Barbara
- *The American Pupils of Jean-Leon Gérôme* (Forth Worth, Tex.: Amon Carter Museum, 1984).
- *The Lure of Paris: Nineteenth-Century American Painters and their French Teachers* (New York: Abbeville Press, 1991).

Articles published after 1904

ACKERMAN, Gerald
- "Gérôme and Manet," *Gazette des Beaux-Arts*, Sept. 1967, pp. 163–76.
- "Thomas Eakins and His Parisian Masters Gérôme and Bonnat," *Gazette des Beaux-Arts*, vol. 73 (Apr. 1969), pp. 235–56.
- "A Chat by the Fireside," *The Register of the Museum of Art, University of Kansas*, vol. 4 (1971), pp. 21–33.
- *Jean-Léon Gérôme, 1824–1904: sculpteur et peintre de l'art officiel*, exh. cat. (Paris: Galerie Tanagra, 1974).
- "Drawings of a famous teacher, Charles Gleyre," *Master Drawings*, vol. 13 (1975), pp. 161–69.
- "Three Drawings by Gérôme in the Yale Collection," *Yale University Art Gallery Bulletin*, vol. 36 (Fall 1976), pp. 8–18.
- "Gérôme's Pifferari," *The Stanford Museum*, no. 8–9 (1978–79), pp. 9–13.
- "Gérôme's Sculpture: The Problems of Realist Sculpture," *Arts Magazine*, vol. 60, no. 6 (Feb. 1986), pp. 83–84.
- "Gérôme's Oriental Paintings and the Western Genre Tradition," *Arts Magazine*, vol. 60, no. 7 (Mar. 1986), pp. 75–80.
- "The Néo-Grecs. A Chink in the Wall of Neoclassicism," *The French Academy. Classicism and its Antagonists* (Newark: University of Delaware Press, 1987), pp. 168–195.

ALLEN, William, "The Abdul Hamid II Collection," *History of Photography*, vol. 8, no. 2 (Apr.–June, 1984), pp. 119–45.

ANGRAND, Pierre, "Œdipe enfant et le combat de coqs. J. F. Millet, Léon Gérôme et la critique en 1847," *Gazette des Beaux-Arts*, Nov. 1975, pp. 140–46.

"Au pays des images," in *Album de voyage des artistes en expedition au pays du Levant*, exh. cat. (Tel-Aviv: Museum of Art; also Bayonne: Musée Bonnat, and Paris: Musée Hebert, 1993), pp. 29–34.

BADEA-PAUN, Gabriel, "De l'atelier de Gérôme au cabaret du Chat Noir. Les années de formation d'Antonio de la Gandara (1861–1917)," *Le Vieux Montmartre*, special issue, no. 75 (2005), pp. 12–36.

BANN, Stephen, "Reassessing Repetition in Nineteenth-Century Academic Painting: Delaroche, Gérôme, Ingres," in E. Kahn, ed., *The Repeating Image* (Baltimore: The Walters Art Museum, 2007), pp. 26–51.

BASTIEN, Catherine, "'L'armure de gladiateur' de la collection Pourtalès conservée au Louvre," *La Revue des musées de France. Revue du Louvre*, vol. 54, no. 4 (Oct. 2004), pp. 44–52.

BLOM, Ivo, "Gérôme en *Quo vadis?* Picturale invloeden in de film," *Jong Holland* 4, XVII (2001), pp. 19–28.

BOIME, Albert
- "Jean-Léon Gérôme, Henri Rousseau's *Sleeping Gypsy* and the Academic Legacy," *The Art Quarterly*, vol. 34, no. 1 (spring 1971), pp. 3–29.
- "The Second Republic's Contest for the Figure of the Republic," *Art Bulletin*, vol. 53 (1971), pp. 68–83.
- "American Culture and the Revival of the French Academic Tradition," *Arts*, vol. 56 (1982), pp. 95–101.
- "The Second Empire's Official Realism," in *The European Realist Tradition*, ed. Gabriel P. Weisberg (Bloomington: Indiana University Press, 1982), pp. 31–123.
- "Gérôme and the Bourgeois Artist's Burden," *Arts Magazine*, vol. 57, no. 5 (Jan. 1983), pp. 64–73.
- "Le réalisme officiel du Second Empire," in *Exigences de réalisme dans la peinture française entre 1830 et 1870*, exh. cat. (Chartres: Musée des Beaux-Arts, 1983), pp. 105–11, 123.

BROWN, Jack Perry, "The Return of the Salon: Jean-Léon Gérôme in the Art Institute," *The Art Institute of Chicago Museum Studies*, vol. 15, no. 2 (1989), pp. 155–73.

COIGNARD, Jérôme, "Gérôme, le dernier des pointus," *Beaux-Arts Magazine*, no. 38 (Sept. 1986), pp. 40–49.

CORPATAUX, Jean-François, "Mise en abyme de silhouettes tournantes dans l'atelier de Jean-Léon Gérôme," *Annales d'histoire de l'art et d'archéologie* (Brussels, 2006), pp. 87–104.

CUGNIER, Gilles, "Vesoul: J.-L. Gérôme (1824–1904)," *La Revue des musées de France. Revue du Louvre*, no. 5–6 (1981), pp. 407–9.

DAGNAN-BOUVERET, Pascal, *Inauguration de la statue de Léon Gérôme à Vesoul, le 20 juillet 1913* [speech] (Paris, 1913).

DENNY, Walter B., "Quotations in and out of Context: Ottoman Turkish Art and European Orientalist Painting," *Muqarnas*, vol. 10 (1993), pp. 213–30.

ERDEGDU, Ayshe, "The Victorian Market for Ottoman Types," *History of Photography*, vol. 23, no. 3 (Fall 1999), pp. 263–73.

FLAMENG, François, *Inauguration de la statue de Léon Gérôme à Vesoul, le 20 juillet 1913* [speech] (Paris, 1913).

FONTANA, Maria Vittoria, and CURATOLA, Giovanni, "L'Oriente degli Orientalisti. Appunti sul pittore J.-L. Gérôme," in *Divàr mush dàrad, mush gush dàrad* (Naples: Arte Tipografica, 1985), pp. 29–42.

FONTSERE, Jacqueline, "Musée départemental de Moulins," *La Revue des musées de France. La Revue du Louvre*, vol. 5–6 (1980), p. 345ff.

FOUCART, Jacques, preface to *Dessins de Jean-Léon Gérôme. Acquisitions du musée de Vesoul*, exh. cat. (Vesoul: Musée Georges-Garret, 1991).

GERMER, Stefan, "Die Gestalt der Wünsche. Zur gesellschaftlichen Modellierung des Imaginären in der Salonkunst des 19. Jahrhunderts," *Imagination und Wirklichkeit. Zum Verhältnis von mentalen und realen Bildern in der Kunst der frühen Neuzeit* (Mainz, 2000), pp. 169–82.

HARENT, Sophie, "Amitiés d'artistes. Jean-Léon Gérôme, Aimé-Nicolas Morot et Émile Friant. Sur quelques œuvres des collections nancéiennes," in *Péristyles. Cahiers des Amis du musée des Beaux-Arts de Nancy*, no. 32 (Dec. 2008), pp. 32–39.

HÉRAN, Emmanuelle, "L'évolution du regard sur la sculpture polychrome," *48/14. La Revue du Musée d'Orsay*, no. 18 (Spring 2004), pp. 62–71.

HEUSINGER VON WALDEGG, J., "Jean-Léon Gérôme's Phryne vor den Richtern," *Jahrbuch der Hamburger Kunstsammlungen*, vol. 17 (1972), pp. 122–42.

HOFFMANN, H., "Hahnenkampf in Athen," *Revue archéologique*, 1974, p. 208ff.

JOHNSTON, William R., "Roman Slave Market," *The Bulletin of the Walters Art Gallery*, vol. 22, no. 6 (Mar. 1970).

KEARNS, James, "Quelle Histoire? Gautier devant l'œuvre de Gérôme au Salon de 1859," in *Le Champ Littéraire, 1860–1900*.

LAFONT-COUTURIER, Hélène, "La diffusion de l'œuvre de Gérôme par la maison Goupil en France et aux Etats-Unis," in *Thomas Eakins: peinture et masculinité* (Giverny: Musée d'Art Américain; Terra Foundation for the Arts, 2003), p. 43.

LEEMAN, Fred, "Shadows over Jean-Léon Gérôme's Career," *Van Gogh Museum Journal*, 1997–98, pp. 88–93.

LORANDI, Marco, "Le odalische francesi. Il pretesto orientalista nel nudo femminile della pittura del XIXe secolo," *L'Erasmo*, no. 7 (2002), pp. 50–65.

MATHIEU, Pierre-Louis, "Toiles à grand spectacle. Gérôme et Alma-Tadema," *Connaissance des arts*, no. 372 (Feb. 1983), pp. 70–74.

MITCHELL, Claudine, "Narrative and the Purity of History" (paper given at the Thirteenth International Congress of the History of Art, London, 2000), in *Visual Narrative Time* (Graz, 2005), pp. 101–10.

PAPET, Édouard, "Jean-Léon Gérôme. Tanagra, 1890," in *Tanagra. Mythe et archéologie*, exh. cat. (Paris: Musée du Louvre, 2003–4), pp. 43–50.

PAPET, Édouard, "Phryné au XIXe siècle: la plus jolie femme de Paris?," in *Praxitèle*, exh. cat. (Paris: Musée du Louvre, 2007), pp. 362–79.

PAPET, Édouard, "Sculpturae vitam insufflat pictura," in *Jeff Koons Versailles*, exh. cat. (Versailles: Château de Versailles, 2008–9), pp. 115–18.

PAPET, Édouard, "Autour de la *Corinthe* de Gérôme," *La Revue des musées de France. Revue du Louvre*, no. 4 (Oct. 2009), pp. 73–84.

POPRZECKA, Maria, "Le sacré au Salon," in *Saloni, gallerie, musei e loro influenza sullo sviluppo dell'arte dei secoli XIXe e XXe* (Bologna: Clueb, 1979), p. 52.

QUÉQUET, Sébastien, "Jean-Louis Hamon. Les néo-grecs et le goût pour l'antique dans les années 1850," *48/14. La Revue du Musée d'Orsay*, no. 26 (Spring 2008), pp. 16–27.

ROUJON, Henry, *Discours prononcé à l'inauguration du monument élevé à Gérôme* (Paris, 1909).

SANYAL, Sunanda K., "Allegorizing Representation. Gérôme's Final Phase," *Athanor*, no. 15 (1997), pp. 38–45.

SAURE, Wolfgang, "Jean-Léon Gérôme. Skulpturen," *Weltkunst*, no. 44 (1974), pp. 1238–39.

TRAPP, Frank, "An Aged Lion Returns. Jean-Léon Gérôme," *The Burlington Magazine*, no. 15 (1973), pp. 344–48.

VERLET, Raoul, *Discours prononcé lors de l'inauguration de la statue de Léon Gérôme à Vesoul, le 20 juillet 1913* (Paris, 1913).

WOHLMANN, Gerhard, "Die nackte Lüge. Aktdarstellungen in der französischen Orientmalerei," in *Sprachformen des Körpers in Kunst und Wissenschaft*, ed. G. Genge (Tübingen and Basel: A. Francke, 2000), pp. 230–43.

WOODWARD, Michelle L., "Between Orientalist Clichés and Images of Modernization," *History of Photography*, vol. 27, no. 4 (Feb. 2003), pp. 363–73.

Exhibition catalogues

"Le Salon imaginaire," images des grandes expositions de la seconde moitie du XIXe siècle (Berlin: Kunstverein, 1968).

Jean-Léon Gérôme (1824–1904) (Dayton: Dayton Art Institute, 1972; also Minneapolis: Minneapolis Institute of Arts, 1973, and Baltimore: The Walters Art Gallery, 1973).

Reality, Fantasy and Flesh (Lexington: University of Kansas Art Gallery, 1973).

Charles Gleyre ou les Illusions perdues (Wintertur: Kunstmuseum, 1974).

Jean-Léon Gérôme, 1824–1904: sculpteur et peintre de l'art officiel (Paris: Galerie Tanagra, 1974).

Jean-Léon Gérôme. 48 dessins (Paris: Galerie De Bayser, 1977).

D'ARGENCOURT, L. and DRUICK, D., eds., *The Other Nineteenth Century: Paintings and Sculpture in the Collection of Mr. and Mrs. Joseph M. Tanenbaum* (Ottawa: The National Gallery of Canada, 1978), p. 110.

L'Art en France sous le Second Empire (Philadelphia: Museum of Art, 1978; also Detroit: Detroit Institute of Arts, 1979, and Paris: Grand Palais, 1979).

Art Pompier (Hempstead, N.Y.: Emily Lowe Art Gallery, 1979).

FUSCO, P., and JANSON, H., *The Romantics to Rodin: French Nineteenth Century Sculpture from North American Collections* (Los Angeles: Los Angeles County Museum of Art, 1980).

J. L. Gérôme (Vesoul: Musée Georges-Garret, 1981).

Orientalism (Rochester: Memorial Art Gallery of the University of Rochester, 1982; also New York: Neuberger Museum, 1982).

French Salon Painting From Southern Collections (Atlanta: High Museum of Art, 1983).

STEVENS, Mary Anne, ed., *The Orientalists, Delacroix to Matisse: European Painters in North Africa and the Near East* (London: Royal Academy of Arts, 1984).

La Sculpture française au XIXe *siècle* (Paris: Galeries Nationales du Grand Palais, 1986).

Dessins de Jean-Gérôme. Acquisitions du Musée de Vesoul (Vesoul: Musée Georges-Garret, 1991).

ZAFRAN, Eric, *Cavaliers and Cardinals: Nineteenth-Century French Anecdotal Paintings* (Cincinnati: Taft Museum, 1992; also Washington, D.C.: Corcoran Gallery of Art, 1992, and Elmira: Arnot Art Museum, 1992–93).

Album de voyage des artistes en expédition au pays du Levant (Tel Aviv-Jaffa: Musée d'Art, 1993, also Bayonne: Musée Bonnat, 1993, and Paris: musée Hébert, 1993).

Degas beyond Impressionism (London: National Gallery, 1996; also Chicago: The Art Institute of Chicago, 1996–97).

The Colour of Sculpture 1840–1910 (Amsterdam: Vincent Van Gogh Museum, 1996; also Leeds: Henry Moore Institute, 1996–97).

Jean-Léon Gérôme and the Classical Imagination (New York: Dahesh Museum of Art, 1997).

GEORGEL, Chantal, *1848, la République et l'art vivant* (Paris: Musée d'Orsay, 1998).

1848. La République et l'art vivant (Paris: Musée d'Orsay, 1998).

Sculptures de Carpeaux à Rodin (Mont-de-Marsan: Musée Despiau-Wlerick, 2000), pp. 99–100.

Theo Van Gogh: marchand de tableaux, collectionneur, frère de Vincent (1857–1891) (Amsterdam: Van Gogh Museum, 1999; also Paris: Musée d'Orsay, 1999–2000).

LAFONT-COUTURIER, Hélène, *Gérôme and Goupil: Art and Enterprise*, trans. I. Ollivier (Bordeaux: Musée Goupil, 2000–1; also New York: Dahesh Museum of Art, 2001; and Pittsburgh: The Frick Art & Historical Center, 2001).

Voyage en Orient (Paris: Bibliothèque Nationale de France, 2002).

Dans l'atelier (Paris: Musée d'Orsay, 2005).

L'Œuvre d'art et sa reproduction photographique (Paris: Musée d'Orsay, 2006).

Purs décors ? Chefs-d'oeuvre de l'Islam aux Arts décoratifs (Paris: Musée des Arts Décoratifs, 2008).

HARENT, S. and STOULLIG, C., *Dessins de Jean-Léon Gérôme: la collection du musée des Beaux-Arts de Nancy* (Nancy: Musée des Beaux-Arts, 2009).

INDEX OF GÉRÔME'S WORKS

INDEX OF PROPER NAMES

After Jean-Léon Gérôme, *Runners of the Pasha* [1867], photograph by Goupil & Cie, "Musée Goupil & Cie" series, no. 801 (detail), 1868, albumen print, 4 ½ × 4 ¾ in., Archives, Musée d'Orsay, Paris.

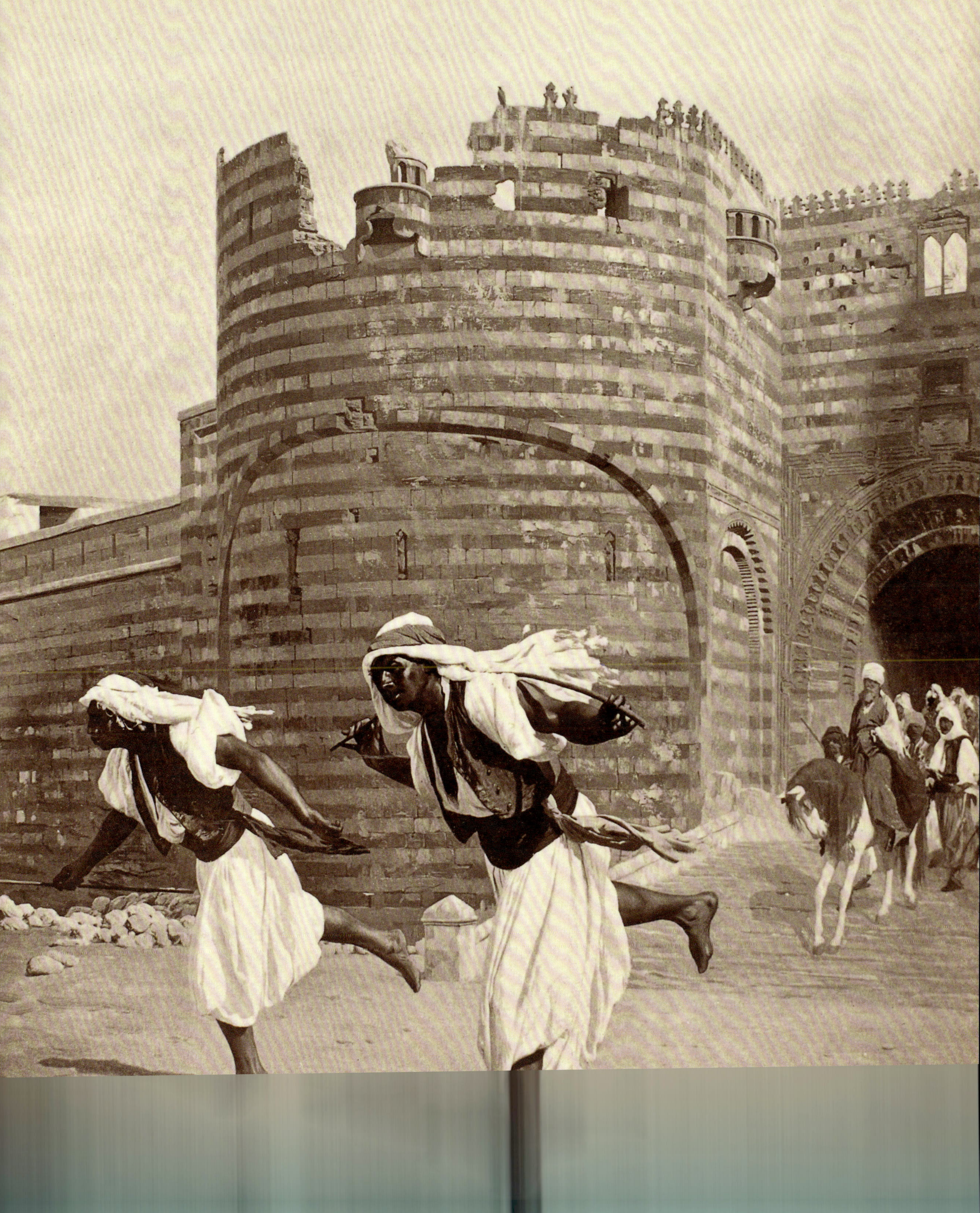

CREDITS

CATALOG

GERMANY

Hamburg
- Hamburg Kunsthalle
cat. 45 (and detail, p. 16, 88) : BPK, Berlin, Dist RMN / Elke Walford.

CANADA
Ottawa
- National Gallery of Canada
cat. 37 : Musée des Beaux-Arts du Canada, Ottawa, photo © Musée des Beaux-Arts du Canada.
Toronto
cat. 174 : Art Gallery of Ontario, Toronto, Gift from the Junior Women's Committee Fund, 1969 © 2009 AGO.

DENMARK
Copenhaguen
cat. 76 : Ny Carlsberg Glyptotek, Copenhagen / photo Ole Haupt.

USA
Baltimore
cat. 51, 67 (and detail p. 22 à 24), 80, 87, 109, 155 : Baltimore, the Walters Art Gallery Photo © The Walters Art Museum, Baltimore.
Boston
- Museum of Fine Arts
cat. 85 (and detail p. 112) : Photograph © 2010 Museum of Fine Arts, Boston, Bequest of Susan Cornelia Warren, 03.605.
cat. 166 : Photograph © 2010 Museum of Fine Arts, Boston, Gift of Robert Jordan from the collection of Eben D. Jordan, 24.217.
Chicago
cat. 36 : Photography © The Art Institute of Chicago.
Cincinnati
cat. 157 : Cincinnati Art Museum, John J. Emery Fund, 1917.368.
Cleveland
cat. 108 : The Cleveland Museum of Art, Gift of Mrs. F.W. Gehring in memory of her husband, F.W. Gehring, 1945.25.
cat. 1 : The Cleveland Museum of Art, Bequest of Noah L. Butkin, 1980.264.
Dayton
cat. 154 (and detail p. 258) : The Dayton Art Institute, Gift of Mr. Robert Badenhop, 1951.15.
Detroit
cat. 186 : Bridgeman Giraudon Detroit Institute of Arts R.H. Tannahill Foundation fund.
Elmira
cat. 163 : Collection of the Arnot Art Museum, Elmira, New York USA.
Greenwich
cat. 9 : Dahesh Museum of Art. 1999.8.
cat. 173 : Dahesh Museum of Art. 1995.104.
Lawrence
- Spencer Art Museum, University of Kansas
cat. 114 : Spencer Museum of Art, Museum purchase: State funds, 1970.0008.
Los Angeles
- The Getty Research Institute
cat. 32 : The J. Paul Getty Museum.
Malden
- Malden Public Library, Massachussets
cat. 84 : Courtesy of Malden Public Library.
Minneapolis
cat. 150 : Minneapolis Institute of Arts, The William Hood Dunwoody Fund 70.40.
New Haven
cat. 70 (and detail p. 330 à 332) : Yale University Art Gallery. Gift of Ruxton Love, Jr., B.A. 1925.
New York
cat. 46, 146, 175 : © Metropolitan Museum of Art, Dist. RMN / Image of the MMA.
cat. 147 : Courtesy of the New York Historical Society, The Robert L. Stuart Collection.
Norfolk
cat. 129 : Chrysler Museum of Art.
Omaha
- Joslyn Museum of Art
cat. 110 (and detail p. 182) : Joslyn Art Museum, Omaha, Nebraska Gift of Francis T. B. Martin (bequest).
cat. 145 : Gift of Francis T. B. Martin (bequest).
Phoenix
- Phoenix Art Museum
cat. 71 (and cover), 73, 74 : Photo by Ken Howie.
Princeton
cat. 90 : Princeton University Art Museum, Museum purchase, John Maclean Magie, Class of 1892, and Gertrude Magie Fund, y1953-78 // photo Bruce M. White.
San Francisco
- Mrs. Gordon Getty
cat. 52 : Collection of Ann and Gordon Getty.
San Mateo
- Collection Terence Garnett
cat. 31, 107, 159, 161 : Courtesy of Terence and Katrina Garnett.
San Simeon
- Hearst San Simeon State Historic Monument
cat. 92 : Photograph by Victoria Garagliano / © Hearst Castle ® / CA State Parks.
Santa Barbara
cat. 169 : Santa Barbara Museum of Art, Museum purchase, European Deaccessioning Fund.
Springfield
- The George Walter Vincent Smith Art Museum
cat. 47 : Photo David Stansbury.
Stanford
cat. 3 : Iris & B. Gerald Cantor Center for Visual Arts at Stanford University; Estate of Mrs. Frank E. Buck, 1979.67.
Stockton
- Pioneer Museum and Haggin Collection
cat. 124, 148 : The Haggin Museum, Haggin Collection, Stockton, California.
Williamstown
cat. 156, 160 (and detail p. 21) : © Sterling and Francine Clark Art Institute, Williamstown, Massachusetts, USA. Photo Michael Agee.

FRANCE
Bordeaux
cat. 26, 61 : Bordeaux Musée des Beaux-Arts, © cliché du MBA de Bordeaux/photographe Lysiane Gauthier.
cat. 39, 53 à 60, 62, 64, 66, 68, 102, 103, 105, : © Mairie de Bordeaux, photo B. Fontanel.
cat. 65, 104, 106 : © Mairie de Bordeaux, photo Coralie Guillon.
cat. 63 : © Mairie de Bordeaux, photo F. Deval.
Caen
cat. 188 : © musée des Beaux-Arts de Caen, Martine Seyve photographe
Colmar
cat. 115 à 123 : Musée Bartholdi, Colmar, reprod. C. Kempf.
Les Lilas
- Mairie
cat. 22 : © Musée d'Orsay, photo Patrice Schmidt.
Moulins
- Musée Anne-de-Beaujeu
cat. 91, 99 : © Jérôme Mondière.
Nancy
cat. 44, 48, 49, 79, 153 : Nancy, musée des beaux-arts, Lorraine, France, © Ville de Nancy – Photo P. Buren.
Nantes
cat. 8 : © Ville de Nantes – musée des Beaux-Arts – Photographie : A. Guillard
cat. 30, 127 (and detail p. 212) : © RMN / Gérard Blot.
Paris
- Bibliothèque nationale de France
cat. 21, 42, 130 à 136, 177 à 179, 184 : Bibliothèque nationale de France.
- Comédie-Française
cat. 40 : Collections de la Comédie-Française / photo Claude Angelini.
- Galerie Elstir
cat. 170 : Photo Thomas Hennocque.
- Musée du Louvre
cat. 11 : Paris, musée du Louvre, DAG (fonds Orsay) / © RMN (musée d'Orsay) / Thierry Le Mage.
- Musée d'Orsay
cat. 2, 4, 10, 14, 15, 27, 38, 78, 86 (and detail p. 117), 125, 126, 128, 192 : © Musée d'Orsay, dist. RMN / photo Patrice Schmidt.
cat. 25 : © RMN (Musée d'Orsay) / Jean Schormans.
cat. 77, 187 (and detail p. 290) : © RMN (Musée d'Orsay) / Hervé Lewandowski.
cat. 168 : © RMN (Musée d'Orsay) / René-Gabriel Ojéda.
- Société française de photographie
cat. 5, 6 : © coll. Société française de photographie. TOUS DROITS RÉSERVÉS.
Rouen
cat. 35 : Rouen, musée des Beaux-Arts, donation Henri and Suzanne Baderou, 1975 / © Musées de la Ville de Rouen, photographie C. Lancien, C. Loisel.
Tarbes
cat. 29 : Œuvre appartenant aux collections du musée Massey de la ville de Tarbes.
Toulouse
- Musée des Augustins
cat. 16 : © RMN / Philipp Bernard.
Versailles
- Musée national du château de Versailles
cat. 94 (and detail p. 116) : © RMN / droits réservés.
Vesoul
- Musée Georges Garret
cat. 12, 18, 20, 33, 82, 83, 88, 95 à 98, 100, 137 à 141, 171a, 171b, 182 : © photo studio Bernardot.

PORTO RICO
Porto Rico
- Museo de Arte
cat. 43 (and detail p. 172) : Collection Museo de Arte de Ponce, 63.0353. The Luis A. Ferré Foundation, Inc., Ponce, Puerto Rico. Photograph by John Betancourt.

QATAR
Doha
Qatar Museum Authority
cat. 158, 162 : Orientalist Museum, Doha.

UNITED KINGDOM
London
- Arcadia Art Foundation
cat. 167 : Arcadia Art Foundation. Private collection, courtesy of Libby Howie.
- National Gallery
cat. 34 : © The National Gallery, Londres, Dist. RMN / National Gallery Photographic Department.
- The Royal Collection
cat. 28 : The Royal Collection © 2010 Her Majesty Queen Elizabeth II.
Sheffield
- Museums Sheffield
cat. 93 : Sheffield Galleries and Museums Trust, UK / © Museums Sheffield / The Bridgeman Art Library.

Private collections
cat. 7, 41, 50, 72, 101, 111, 152, 165, 172 : Private collection, Dr. Edward T. Wilson, Bethesda, MD.
cat. 17 : Photo Jacqueline Hyde.
cat 19 : Private collection A. and A. Flamand.
cat. 23 : Property of Lady Micheline Connery.
cat. 24 : Suzanne Nagy.
cat. 69, 75 : © Musée d'Orsay, photo Patrice Schmidt.
cat. 81 : © Christie's Images Limited (2010).
cat. 112 (and detail p. 338-339) : © Christie's Images / Corbis.
cat. 113, 149 : Private collection.
cat. 142 : Najd Collection, Switzerland.
cat. 143, 176 : Private collection.
cat. 151 : Private collection, Courtesy of Museum of Fine Arts, Boston.
cat. 164 : Photo by Keith Petersen, courtesy of Guggenheim, Asher Associates.
cat. 180 : Ilmari Kalkkinen.
cat. 181 : © Musée d'Orsay, photo Patrice Schmidt.
cat. 185 : L'Horizon chimérique, © Alain Béguerie.
cat. 189 à 191 : © Photo George Schwartz, Professional Associate – AIC.
cat. 193 : J. Nicholson, Beverly Hills, CA.

Rights reserved
cat. 13, 89, 144.

ILLUSTRATIONS

GERMANY

Hamburg

- Hamburger Kunsthalle

ill. 114 : BPK, Berlin, Dist. RMN / Elke Walford.

Mannheim

- Städische Kunsthalle

ill. 72 : © Archives Alinari, Florence, Dist. RMN / Fratelli Alinari.

DENMARK

Copenhaguen

ill. 140 : © Ny carlsbger Glyptotek, Copenhagen, photo Ole Haupt.

USA

Appleton

ill. 124 : Appleton Museum of Art of Central Florida Community College.

Baltimore

ill. 129 : Photo © The Walters Art Museum, Baltimore.

Los Angeles

- The Getty Research Institute

ill. 88 : The J. Paul Getty Museum.

ill. 94 : Research Library, The Getty Research Institute, Los Angeles (92-S168).

ill. 111, 115 : Research Library, The Getty Research Institute, Los Angeles (2008.R.3).

ill. 177 : Research Library, The Getty Research Institute, Los Angeles (90.R.26).

New York

- Metropolitan Museum of Art

ill. 89, 92, 108, 122, 128 : © Metropolitan Museum of Art, Dist. RMN / Image of the MMA.

- The Frick Art Reference Library

ill. 90 : Courtesy of the Frick Art Reference Library.

Rochester

ill. 81 : Courtesy of George Eastman House, International Museum of Photography and Film.

Philadelphia

ill. 91 : Philadelphia Museum of Art: Gift of the Alumni Association to Jefferson Medical College in 1878 and purchased by the Pennsylvania Academy of the Fine Arts and the Philadelphia Museum of Art in 2007 with the generous support of more than 3,500 donors, 2007.

FRANCE

Aix-en-Provence

- Musée Granet

ill. 3 : © RMN / Jean Popovitch.

Alençon

- Musée des Beaux-Arts

ill. 5 : © RMN / René-Gabriel Ojéda / Thierry Le Mage.

Amboise

ill. 79 : © Ville d'Amboise.

Amiens

- Musée de Picardie

ill. 1 : © RMN / Hervé Lewandowski.

Arras

ill. 68 : © musée des Beaux-Arts d'Arras.

Bordeaux

- Musée Goupil

ill. 9, 30, 80, 83, 84: © Mairie de Bordeaux, photo B. Fontanel.

Carcassonne

- Musée des beaux-arts

ill. 20 : © RMN / Philipp Bernard.

Chantilly

- Musée Condé

ill. 50 : © RMN / Harry Bréjat.

Colmar

ill. 99 101: Musée Bartholdi, Colmar, reprod. C. Kempf.

Dijon

- Musée Magnin

ill. 6 : © RMN / René-Gabriel Ojéda.

Le Havre

- Musée des beaux-arts André Malraux

ill. 73 : © RMN / René-Gabriel Ojéda / Thierry Le Mage.

Lyon

- Musée des Beaux-Arts

ill. 35, 77 : © Lyon MBA / Photo Alain Basset

Montbrison

ill. 141 : cliché : musée d'Allard, Sandrine Montagnier – 2010.

Montpellier

ill. 46 : © Musée Fabre de Montpellier Agglomération – cliché Frédéric Jaulmes.

ill. 7 : RMN / Agence Bulloz.

Nantes

- Musée des Beaux-Arts

ill. 14, 102 : © RMN / Gérard Blot.

Paris

- Bibliothèque centrale des musées nationaux

ill. 10, 16, 17, 29, 40 : © Musée d'Orsay, photo Patrice Schmidt.

- Bibliothèque des Arts décoratifs

ill. 174 à 176, 182 : Bibliothèque des Arts décoratifs, Paris.

- Bibliothèque de l'Institut, collection. Schlumberger

ill. 112 : © RMN / Gérard Blot.

- Bibliothèque nationale de France

ill. 43, 55, 70, 105, 106, 107, 110, 116, 118, 120, 126 : Bibliothèque nationale de France.

- Comédie française

ill. 23, 37, 67 : © Collections de la Comédie-Française.

- École nationale supérieure des beaux-arts de Paris

ill. 45, 138, 147 : Beaux-Arts de Paris, l'école nationale supérieure.

- Institut national d'histoire de l'art

ill. 48, 144 : Institut national d'histoire de l'art.

- L'Illustration

ill. 75 : www. lillustration.com.

- Musée Carnavalet

ill. 69 : © Musée Carnavalet / Roger-Viollet

- Musée du Louvre

ill. 15, 71 : © RMN / Jean-Gilles Berizzi.

ill. 19, 27, 47 : © RMN / René-Gabriel Ojéda.

ill. 26, 31, 49, 52 : © Musée d'Orsay, dist. RMN / Patrice Schmidt.

ill. 59 : © RMN / René-Gabriel Ojéda / Hervé Lewandowski.

ill. 62, 74, 86, 148, 163 : © RMN / Hervé Lewandowski.

ill. 109 : © RMN / Stéphane Maréchalle.

ill. 136 : © RMN / Gérard Blot.

ill. 149 : © RMN / René-Gabriel Ojéda / Thierry Le Mage.

ill. 152 : © RMN / Gérard Blot / Christian Jean.

- Musée d'Orsay

ill. 4, 22, 133, 170, 171 : © RMN (Musée d'Orsay) / Hervé Lewandowski.

ill. 11 : © RMN (Musée d'Orsay) / Hervé Lewandowski / Stéphane Maréchalle.

ill. 12, 18, 25, 39, 51, 87, 95, 97, 100, 134, 145, 151, 153, 173, 179 : © Musée d'Orsay, dist. RMN / photo Patrice Schmidt.

ill. 28 : © RMN / Gérard Blot.

ill. 64, 172 : © Musée d'Orsay, Dist RMN / Alexis Brandt.

ill. 150, 180, 181 : © Musée d'Orsay, Dist RMN / Thierry Le Mage.

ill. 158 : © RMN (musée d'Orsay) / Droits réservés.

- Rue des Archives

ill. 167 : Rue des Archives.

Saint-Étienne

- Musée d'Art moderne

ill. 8 : © RMN / Jean Schormans.

Strasbourg

ill. 159 : Musée d'Art Moderne et Contemporain de Strasbourg. Photo Musées de la Ville de Strasbourg, A. Plisson».

Versailles

- Musée national du Château de Versailles

ill. 34 : © RMN (Château de Versailles) / Daniel Arnaudet.

ill. 488 : © RMN (Château de Versailles) / Daniel Arnaudet / Jean Schormans.

Vesoul

- Musée Georges Garret

ill. 96, 146, 157, 178, : Studio Bernardot.

ITALY

Ferrara

- Museo dell'Ottocento

ill. 168 : Ferrare Gallerie d'Arte Moderna e Contemporanea, photo Tiziano Menabò.

Milan

ill. 82 : Collection Fausta Squatriti e Massimo Angioletti, photo Walter Zerglia.

Culturali.

- Musée de Capodimonte

ill. 57 : Naples, Museo di Capodimonte. © 2010. Photo Scala, Florence – courtesy of the Ministero Beni e Att. Culturali.

- Musée national d'archéologie

ill. 24 : Naples, National Museum. © 2010. Photo Scala, Florence / Fotografica Foglia – courtesy of the Ministero Beni e Att. Culturali.

Roma

- Musée du Capitole

ill. 32 : © Archives Alinari, Florence, Dist. RMN / Anderson.

- Museo Nazionale Romano, Palazzo Massimo alle Terme

ill. 160 : © Archives Alinari, Florence, Dist. RMN / Fratelli Alinari.

Trieste

- Museo civico

ill. 132 : © 2010. DeAgostini Picture Library / Scala, Florence.

LUXEMBOURG

Luxembourg

- Musée J.-P. Pescatore

ill. 13 : © Villa Vauban – musée d'Art de la Ville de Luxembourg, inv. 92, photo : Christof Weber.

UNITED KINGDOM

London

- Collection Wallace

ill. 54, 113 : © By kind permission of the Trustees of the Wallace Collection, London.

- The Victoria and Albert Museum

ill. 104 : © V&A Images / Victoria and Albert Museum, London.

SWITZERLAND

Geneva

ill. 21 : © Musée d'art et d'histoire, ville de Genève, inv. N° 1954-8, Jean-Jacques, dit James Pradier.

Lausanne

ill. 2 : J.-C. Ducret, Musée cantonal des Beaux-Arts de Lausanne.

Private collections

ill. 38, 93 : © Christie's Images Limited 2008.

ill. 41 : © Christie's Images Limited 2000.

ill. 42 : Photograph Courtesy of Sotheby's, Inc. © 2003.

ill. 44 : Photograp Courtesy of Sotheby's, Inc. © 2009.

ill. 66, 137, 169 : © Musée d'Orsay, photo Patrice Schmidt.

ill. 121 : © Christie's Images Limited 1997.

ill. 125 : Private collection, courtesy of Libby Howie.

ill. 135 : Private collection, Courtesy of Guggenheim, Asher Associates, Inc.

ill. 155 : D. R.

Rights reserved

Images d'ouverture, p. 10 and 14 and ill. 17, 33, 53, 58, 60, 61, 63, 65, 76, 78, 85, 98, 103, 119, 123, 127, 130, 131, 142, 143, 154, 156, 161, 162, 164, 165, 166.

Others

p. 12 : © Pierre et Gilles. Courtesy Galerie Jérôme de Noirmont Paris.

p. 13 : © Jeff Koons. Courtesy Galerie Jérôme de Noirmont Paris.

p. 15 : © Paramount Publix Corporation.

ill. 56 : Photo courtesy of Gerald M. Ackerman

Musée d'Orsay

Publications manager
Annie Dufour

Editor
Juliette Sanson

Picture research
Jean-Claude Pierront

Translations from the French
Deke Dusinberre
Charles Penwarden
David Radzinowicz
Jonathan Sly

Skira Flammarion

Publications director
Sophy Thompson

Publications manager
Sophie Laporte

Editor
Mathilde Senoble,
with the assistance of Marion Lambert

Graphic design
Mateo Baronnet / Lot 49

Production
Corinne Trovarelli

Color separation
Les Artisans du Regard

Copy-editing
Sarah Kane

Proofreading
Marc Feustel and Helen Woodhall

Typesetting
Dune Lunel

June 2010
Printed in Italy by Gruppo Editoriale Zanardi Press

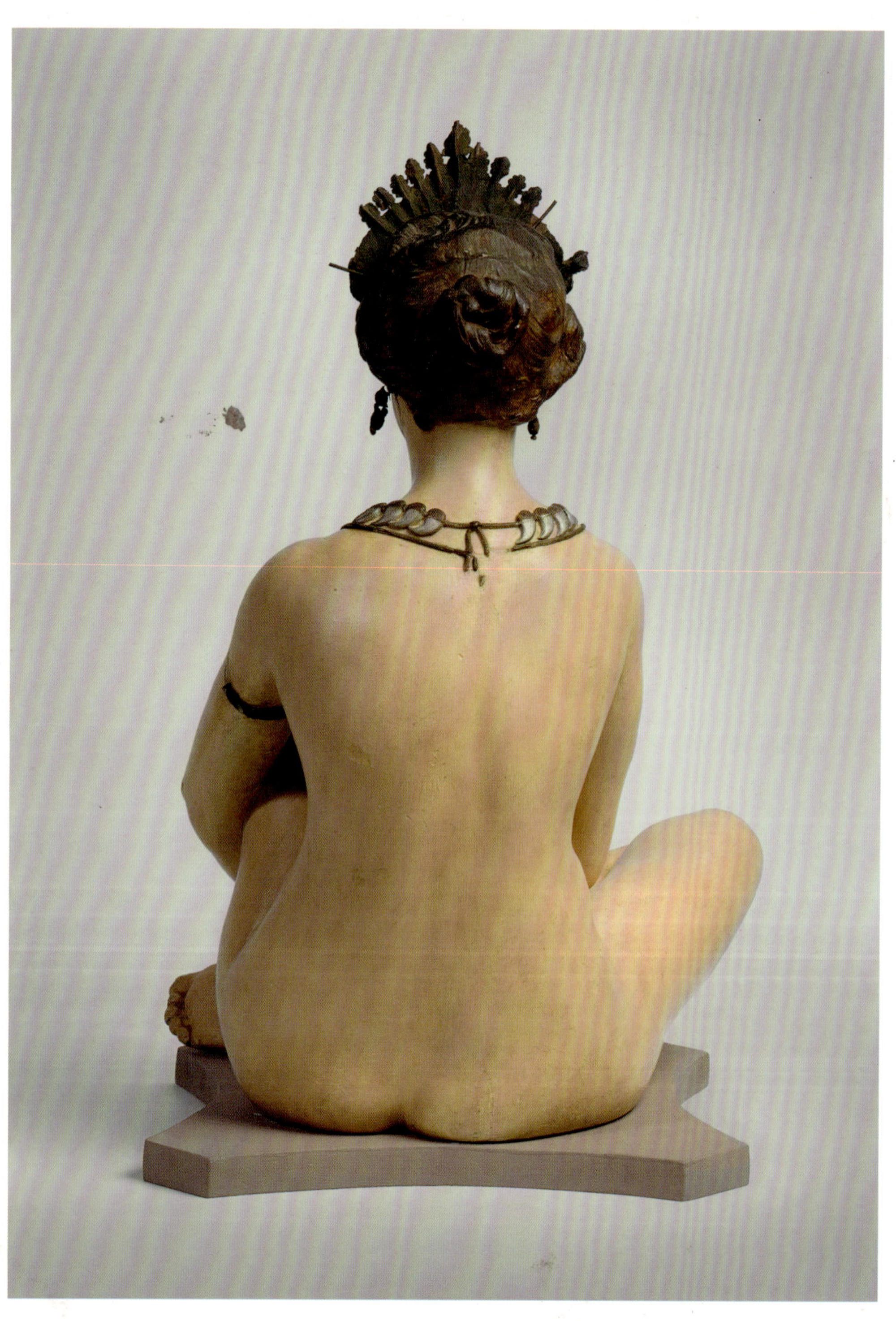